Skills in Mathematics

JEE Main & Advanced

Trigonometry

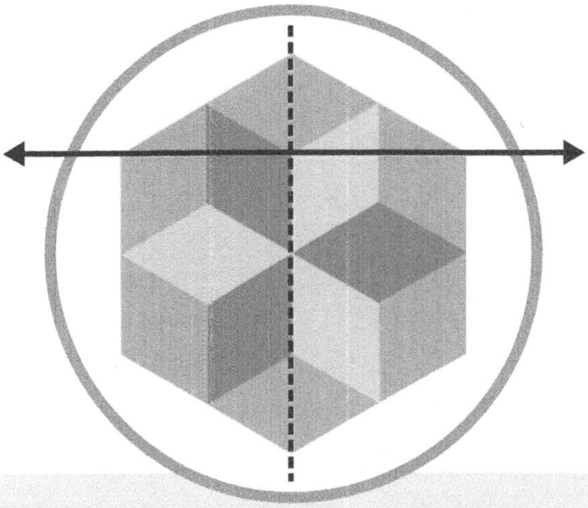

arihant
SUCCESS AND NOTHING LESS
ARIHANT PRAKASHAN (SERIES), MEERUT

Skills in Mathematics

JEE Main & Advanced

Trigonometry

Amit M Agarwal
Supported by Ankit Goel

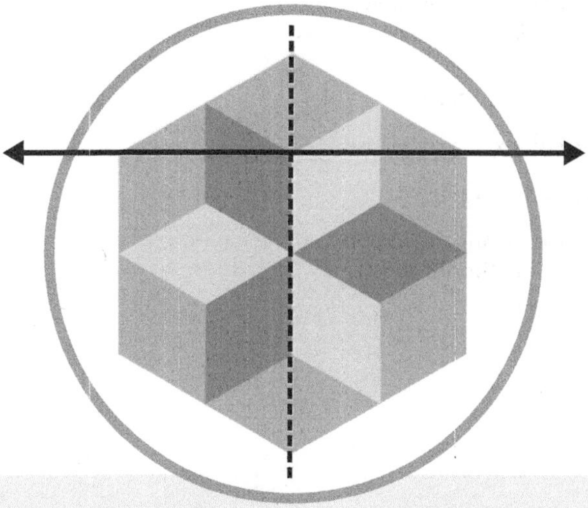

arihant
SUCCESS AND NOTHING LESS

Arihant Prakashan (Series), Meerut

Administrative & Production Offices

Regd. Office

'Ramchhaya' 4577/15, Agarwal Road, Darya Ganj, New Delhi -110002
Tele: 011- 47630600, 43518550

Head Office

Kalindi, TP Nagar, Meerut (UP) - 250002 Tel: 0121-7156203, 7156204

Sales & Support Offices

Agra, Ahmedabad, Bengaluru, Bareilly, Chennai, Delhi, Guwahati, Hyderabad, Jaipur, Jhansi, Kolkata, Lucknow, Nagpur & Pune.

PO No : TXT-XX-XXXXXXX-X-XX

Published by Arihant Publications (India) Ltd.

For further information about the books published by Arihant, log on to www.arihantbooks.com or e-mail at info@arihantbooks.com

Follow us on

Preface

It is a matter of great pride and honour for me to have received such an overwhelming response to the previous editions of this book from the readers. In a way, this has inspired me to revise this book thoroughly as per the changed pattern of JEE Main & Advanced. I have tried to make the contents more relevant as per the needs of students, many topics have been re-written, a lot of new problems of new types have been added. All possible efforts are made to remove all the printing errors that had crept in previous editions. The book is now in such a shape that the students would feel at ease while going through the problems, which will in turn clear their concepts too.

A Summary of changes that have been made in Revised & Enhanced Edition

- Theory has been completely updated so as to accommodate all the changes made in JEE Syllabus & Pattern in recent years.
- The most important point about this new edition is, now the whole text matter of each chapter has been divided into small milestones with practice exercise in each milestones. This will help reader in step by step learning
- Theory of each milestone is more precise with **JEE focus Points** and **JEE Spike**.
- **JEE Scanners** are incorporated in theory for more synced learning with JEE Main and Advanced PYQs.
- Just after completion of theory, Solved Examples of all JEE types have been given, providing the students a complete understanding of all the formats of JEE questions & the level of difficulty of questions generally asked in JEE.
- Along with exercises given with each Milestone, following three exercises have been given at the end of each chapter.
- Practice Milestone 1- JEE Main Pattern Exercises.
- Practice Milestone 2- JEE Advanced Pattern Exercises.
- Practice Milestone 3- Challenging Problems Exercises.
- Previous Years questions asked in JEE Main and Advanced have been incorporated in all the exercises.

However I have made the best efforts and put my all teaching experience in revising this book. Still I am looking forward to get the valuable suggestions and criticism from my own fraternity i.e. the fraternity of JEE teachers. I strongly believe that

"YOU CAN DO ANYTHING IF YOU SET YOUR MIND FOR IT. I ALWAYS BELIEVE THE MOST IMPORTANT FORMULA IS COURAGE + DREAMS = SUCCESS"

I would also like to motivate the students to send their suggestions or the changes that they want to be incorporated in this book. All the suggestions given by you all will be kept in prime focus at the time of next revision of the book.

Amit M Agarwal

Enhanced Features

JEE Focus Points

- θ radian is written as θ^c or can be written simply as θ. When the unit of angle is not mentioned, it must be taken as radians.
- Radian is the unit to measure angle and it does not means that π stands for $180°$, π is a real number. Where as π^c stands for $180°$.
  Remember the relation π radians = 180 degrees = 200 grade
- The relation amongst three systems of measurement of an angle is

$$\frac{D}{90°} = \frac{G}{100} = \frac{2R}{\pi}$$

Concept Inside Video

A collection of Key Points/Results prime from JEE Preparation point of View. These are further elaborated with support videos.

JEE SPIKE

In a series of sine and cosine whenever angles are in AP and power of sine and cosine is one, then we multiply each term by $2\sin\left(\frac{\text{common difference of angles}}{2}\right)$, then express each term as a difference of two terms and add.

Seggregated most valuable Pointers for JEE preparation

JEE SCANNER

Example Similar to PYQ Asked in JEE Main 2023

The value of $(3 - 4\sin^2 9°)(3 - 4\sin^2 27°)(3 - 4\sin^2 81°)(3 - 4\sin^2 243°)$ *is*

(a) 1 (b) 2 (c) 3 (d) 4

Sol. (a) $3 - 4\sin^2\theta = \frac{3\sin\theta - 4\sin^3\theta}{\sin\theta} = \frac{\sin 3\theta}{\sin\theta}$

$\therefore$ Given expression,

$(3 - 4\sin^2 9°)(3 - 4\sin^2 27°)(3 - 4\sin^2 81°)(3 - 4\sin^2 243°)$

$$= \frac{\sin(3\times 9°)}{\sin 9°} \times \frac{\sin(3\times 27°)}{\sin 27°} \times \frac{\sin(3\times 81°)}{\sin 81°} \times \frac{\sin(3\times 243°)}{\sin 243°}$$

$$= \frac{\sin 729°}{\sin 9°} = \frac{\sin(2\times 360° + 9°)}{\sin 9°}$$

$$= \frac{\sin 9°}{\sin 9°} = 1$$

Skill Builder

The value of $(4\cos^2 9° - 1)(4\cos^2 27° - 1)(4\cos^2 81° - 1)(4\cos^2 243° - 1)$ is

(a) 46 (b) 63

(c) 1 (d) 9

For Sol.

- **For more practice** See Q.8 of Milestone Practice 5.

Unmatched Concept elevation tool helpful in syncing recent JEE Main & Advanced PYQs with theory and provide additional practice through Skill Builders.

Contents

Syllabus

JEE Main

Trigonometrical identities and trigonometrical functions. Inverse trigonometrical functions and their properties.

JEE Advanced

Trigonometric functions, their periodicity and graphs, addition and subtraction formulae, formulae involving multiple and sub-multiple angles, general solution of trigonometric equations.

Inverse trigonometric functions (principal value only) and their elementary properties.

“

Without Mathematics, there’s nothing you can do. Everything around you is Mathematics. Everything around you is numbers.

–Shakuntla Devi

1

Trigonometric Ratios and Identities

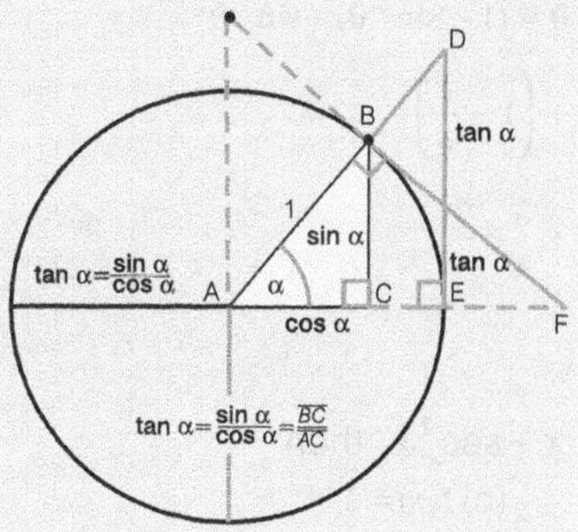

Learning Milestones

Milestone 1 Trigonometric Identities

- Introduction • Trigonometric Ratios for Acute Angles • Trigonometric Ratios for Standard Angles • Elimination of Trigonometric Ratios

Milestone 2 Measurement of Angles

- Angle • Sectorial Area • Measuring of Angle in Various Quadrants

Milestone 3 Trigonometric Functions of an Angle

- Trigonometry in Circular System • Trigonometric Ratios of Allied Angles

Milestone 4 Trigonometric Functions of Compound Angles

- Trigonometric Ratios of Compound Angles • Extended Compound Angle Formulae

Milestone 5 Trigonometric Ratios of Multiple and Submultiple of an Angle

- Trigonometric Ratios of Multiple Angles • Trigonometric Ratios of Submultiple Angle

Milestone 6 Transformation Formulae

- Expressing Product of Trigonometric Functions as Sum or Difference

Milestone 7 Trigonometric Series in which Angles are in AP

Milestone 8 Conditional Identities

Milestone 9 Graph and Properties of Trigonometric Function

- Graph and Properties of Trigonometric Function [$n \in I$]
- Some Important Graphical Deductions

Milestone 10 Range of Trigonometric Expressions

Practice Milestones

Practice Milestone 1- JEE Main Pattern

Practice Milestone 2 - JEE Advanced Pattern

Practice Milestone 3 - Challenging Problems

Milestone 1 Trigonometric Identities

- Introduction • Trigonometric Ratios for Acute Angles • Trigonometric Ratios for Standard Angles
- Elimination of Trigonometric Ratios

1.1 Introduction

The word 'Trigonometry' is derived from two Greek words.

(i) Trigonon (ii) Metron

The word trigonon means a triangle and the word metron mean a measure.

Hence, trigonometry means measuring the sides and angle of triangle. The subject was originally develop to solve geometric problems involving triangle.

1.2 Trigonometric Ratios for Acute Angles

For an acute angle θ, trigonometric Ratios (T-Ratios) can be defined using a right angled triangle with angles θ, $90° - \theta$, $90°$.

$\boxed{\sin\theta = \frac{P}{H}}$ $\boxed{\cos\theta = \frac{B}{H}}$ $\boxed{\tan\theta = \frac{P}{B}}$

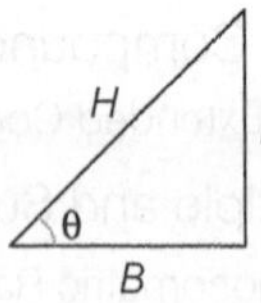

cosec θ, sec θ and cot θ are reciprocals of sin θ, cos θ and tan θ respectively.

$$\tan\theta = \frac{\sin\theta}{\cos\theta} \text{ and } \cot\theta = \frac{\cos\theta}{\sin\theta}$$

Some standards identities for above trigonometric ratios are

- $\sin^2\theta + \cos^2\theta = 1$
- $\text{cosec}^2\theta - \cot^2\theta = 1$ or $1 + \cot^2\theta = \text{cosec}^2\theta$
- $\sec^2\theta - \tan^2\theta = 1$ or $1 + \tan^2\theta = \sec^2\theta$

For acute angles, all T-ratios are positive.

Example 1. Prove that

$$\frac{\tan A + \sec A - 1}{\tan A - \sec A + 1} = \sec A + \tan A = \frac{1 + \sin A}{\cos A}.$$

Sol. $\frac{\tan A + \sec A - 1}{\tan A - \sec A + 1} = \frac{\tan A + \sec A - 1}{1 - (\sec A - \tan A)}$

$$\left[\because \sec^2\theta - \tan^2\theta = 1 \text{ or } \sec\theta - \tan\theta = \frac{1}{\sec\theta + \tan\theta}\right]$$

$$= \frac{\tan A + \sec A - 1}{1 - \left(\frac{1}{\sec A + \tan A}\right)}$$

$$= \frac{(\tan A + \sec A - 1)(\sec A + \tan A)}{(\sec A + \tan A - 1)}$$

$$= \sec A + \tan A$$

$$= \frac{1}{\cos A} + \frac{\sin A}{\cos A}$$

$$= \frac{1 + \sin A}{\cos A}$$

Example 2. If $A = \cos^2\theta + \sin^4\theta$ for all values of θ, then prove that $\frac{3}{4} \le A \le 1$.

Sol. We have, $A = \cos^2\theta + \sin^4\theta$

$$= \cos^2\theta + \sin^2\theta \sin^2\theta \le \cos^2\theta + \sin^2\theta$$

Therefore, $A \le 1$

Also, $A = \cos^2\theta + \sin^4\theta = (1 - \sin^2\theta) + \sin^4\theta$

$$A = \left(\sin^2\theta - \frac{1}{2}\right)^2 + \left(1 - \frac{1}{4}\right)$$

$$= \left(\sin^2\theta - \frac{1}{2}\right)^2 + \frac{3}{4} \ge \frac{3}{4}$$

Hence, $\frac{3}{4} \le A \le 1$.

Example 3. If $f(x) = \cos^2 x + \sec^2 x$, then

(a) $f(x) < 1$ (b) $f(x) = 1$

(c) $2 < f(x) < 1$ (d) $f(x) \ge 2$

Sol. (d) Given that $f(x)=\cos^2 x+\sec^2 x$

We know that AM≥ GM

$$\Rightarrow \frac{\cos^2 x+\sec^2 x}{2} \geq \sqrt{\cos^2 x \cdot \sec^2 x}$$

$$\Rightarrow \cos^2 x+\sec^2 x \geq 2$$

$$\Rightarrow f(x) \geq 2$$

Example 4. The value of $(5\sin\theta - 3\cos\theta)$, if $3\sin\theta + 5\cos\theta = 5$ is

(a) 2 (b) 3

(c) −2 (d) −3

Sol. (b, d) Given, $3\sin\theta+5\cos\theta=5$ ...(i)

Let $5\sin\theta-3\cos\theta=m$ ...(ii)

On squaring Eqs. (i) and (ii) and then adding, we get

$$(9\sin^2\theta+25\cos^2\theta+30\sin\theta\cos\theta) + (25\sin^2\theta+9\cos^2\theta-30\sin\theta\cos\theta)=25+m^2$$

$$\Rightarrow 9(\sin^2\theta+\cos^2\theta)+25(\sin^2\theta+\cos^2\theta)=25+m^2$$

$$\Rightarrow 34=25+m^2$$

$$\Rightarrow m^2=9 \text{ or } m=\pm 3$$

Hence, options (b) and (d) are correct.

Example 5. If $\sec x+\sec^2 x=1$, then the value of $\tan^8 x-\tan^4 x-2\tan^2 x+1$ is

(a) 1 (b) 2

(c) 3 (d) None of these

Sol. (b) We have, $\sec x+\sec^2 x=1$

$$\Rightarrow -\sec x=\sec^2 x-1$$

$$\Rightarrow -\sec x=\tan^2 x$$

On squaring both sides, we get

$$\sec^2 x=\tan^4 x$$

$$\Rightarrow 1+\tan^2 x=\tan^4 x \quad \text{...(i)}$$

Now, $\tan^8 x-\tan^4 x-2\tan^2 x+1$

$$=(1+\tan^2 x)^2-(1+\tan^2 x)-2\tan^2 x+1 \quad [\because \text{from Eq. (i)}]$$

$$=1+\tan^4 x+2\tan^2 x-1-\tan^2 x-2\tan^2 x+1$$

$$=1+\tan^4 x-\tan^2 x$$

$$=1+(1+\tan^2 x)-\tan^2 x \quad [\because \text{from Eq. (i)}]$$

$$=2$$

Example 6. If $\sec\theta+\tan\theta=p$, then $\sin\theta$ equals

(a) $\frac{1-p^2}{1+p^2}$ (b) $\frac{p^2-1}{p^2+1}$

(c) $\frac{p^2+1}{p^2-1}$ (d) $\frac{1+p^2}{1-p^2}$

Sol. (b) We have, $\sec\theta+\tan\theta=p$ ...(i)

$$\Rightarrow \sec\theta-\tan\theta=\frac{1}{p} \quad \text{...(ii)}$$

On adding Eqs. (i) and (ii), we obtain

$$2\sec\theta=p+\frac{1}{p}$$

$$\Rightarrow \sec\theta=\frac{p^2+1}{2p}$$

$$\Rightarrow \cos\theta=\frac{2p}{p^2+1}$$

On subtracting Eq. (ii) from Eq. (i), we obtain

$$2\tan\theta=p-\frac{1}{p}$$

$$\Rightarrow \tan\theta=\frac{p^2-1}{2p}$$

Now, $\sin\theta=\tan\theta\times\cos\theta$

$$\Rightarrow \sin\theta=\frac{p^2-1}{2p}\times\frac{2p}{p^2+1}$$

$$=\frac{p^2-1}{p^2+1}$$

1.3 Trigonometric Ratios of Standard Angles

In the following table is given the trigonometric ratios of standard angles.

Angles / T-ratio	0°	30°	45°	60°	90°
sin θ	0	$\frac{1}{2}$	$\frac{1}{\sqrt{2}}$	$\frac{\sqrt{3}}{2}$	1
cos θ	1	$\frac{\sqrt{3}}{2}$	$\frac{1}{\sqrt{2}}$	$\frac{1}{2}$	0
tan θ	0	$\frac{1}{\sqrt{3}}$	1	$\sqrt{3}$	ND
cot θ	ND	$\sqrt{3}$	1	$\frac{1}{\sqrt{3}}$	0
sec θ	1	$\frac{2}{\sqrt{3}}$	$\sqrt{2}$	2	ND
cosec θ	ND	2	$\sqrt{2}$	$\frac{2}{\sqrt{3}}$	1

The student is advised before proceeding any further to make himself quite familiar with the above table.

Expressing Trigonometric Ratio in Terms of Each Other

In the following table is given the result of expressing each trigonometrical ratio in terms of each of the others.

	$\sin\theta$	$\cos\theta$	$\tan\theta$	$\cot\theta$	$\sec\theta$	$\operatorname{cosec}\theta$
$\sin\theta$	$\sin\theta$	$\sqrt{1-\cos^2\theta}$	$\frac{\tan\theta}{\sqrt{1+\tan^2\theta}}$	$\frac{1}{\sqrt{1+\cot^2\theta}}$	$\frac{\sqrt{\sec^2\theta-1}}{\sec\theta}$	$\frac{1}{\operatorname{cosec}\theta}$
$\cos\theta$	$\sqrt{1-\sin^2\theta}$	$\cos\theta$	$\frac{1}{\sqrt{1+\tan^2\theta}}$	$\frac{\cot\theta}{\sqrt{1+\cot^2\theta}}$	$\frac{1}{\sec\theta}$	$\frac{\sqrt{\operatorname{cosec}^2\theta-1}}{\operatorname{cosec}\theta}$
$\tan\theta$	$\frac{\sin\theta}{\sqrt{1-\sin^2\theta}}$	$\frac{\sqrt{1-\cos^2\theta}}{\cos\theta}$	$\tan\theta$	$\frac{1}{\cot\theta}$	$\sqrt{\sec^2\theta-1}$	$\frac{1}{\sqrt{\operatorname{cosec}^2\theta-1}}$
$\cot\theta$	$\frac{\sqrt{1-\sin^2\theta}}{\sin\theta}$	$\frac{\cos\theta}{\sqrt{1-\cos^2\theta}}$	$\frac{1}{\tan\theta}$	$\cot\theta$	$\frac{1}{\sqrt{\sec^2\theta-1}}$	$\sqrt{\operatorname{cosec}^2\theta-1}$
$\sec\theta$	$\frac{1}{\sqrt{1-\sin^2\theta}}$	$\frac{1}{\cos\theta}$	$\sqrt{1+\tan^2\theta}$	$\frac{\sqrt{1+\cot^2\theta}}{\cot\theta}$	$\sec\theta$	$\frac{\operatorname{cosec}\theta}{\sqrt{\operatorname{cosec}^2\theta-1}}$
$\operatorname{cosec}\theta$	$\frac{1}{\sin\theta}$	$\frac{1}{\sqrt{1-\cos^2\theta}}$	$\frac{\sqrt{1+\tan^2\theta}}{\tan\theta}$	$\sqrt{1+\cot^2\theta}$	$\frac{\sec\theta}{\sqrt{\sec^2\theta-1}}$	$\operatorname{cosec}\theta$

Example 7. If θ is an acute angle and $\tan\theta+\cot\theta=2$, then find the value of $\tan^7\theta+\cot^7\theta$.

Sol. We have, $\tan\theta+\cot\theta=2$

$$\Rightarrow \tan\theta+\frac{1}{\tan\theta}=2$$

$$\Rightarrow \frac{\tan^2\theta+1}{\tan\theta}=2$$

$$\Rightarrow \tan^2\theta-2\tan\theta+1=0$$

$$\Rightarrow (\tan\theta-1)^2=0$$

$$\Rightarrow \tan\theta-1=0$$

$$\Rightarrow \tan\theta=1$$

$$\Rightarrow \tan\theta=\tan 45^\circ$$

$$\Rightarrow \theta=45^\circ$$

$$\therefore \tan^7\theta+\cot^7\theta=\tan^7 45^\circ+\cot^7 45^\circ=(1)^7+(1)^7=2$$

Example 8. Prove that from the equality $\frac{\sin^4\alpha}{a}+\frac{\cos^4\alpha}{b}=\frac{1}{a+b}$ follows the relation $\frac{\sin^8\alpha}{a^3}+\frac{\cos^8\alpha}{b^3}=\frac{1}{(a+b)^3}$.

Sol. $\frac{\sin^4\alpha}{a}+\frac{\cos^4\alpha}{b}=\frac{1}{a+b}$

$$\Rightarrow \left(\frac{a+b}{a}\right)\sin^4\alpha+\left(\frac{a+b}{b}\right)\cos^4\alpha=1$$

$$\Rightarrow \sin^4\alpha+\frac{b}{a}\sin^4\alpha+\frac{a}{b}\cos^4\alpha+\cos^4\alpha=1$$

$$\Rightarrow (\sin^4\alpha+\cos^4\alpha)+\frac{b}{a}\sin^4\alpha+\frac{a}{b}\cos^4\alpha=1$$

$$\Rightarrow 1-2\sin^2\alpha\cos^2\alpha+\frac{b}{a}\sin^4\alpha+\frac{a}{b}\cos^4\alpha=1$$

$$\Rightarrow \left(\sqrt{\frac{b}{a}}\sin^2\alpha-\sqrt{\frac{a}{b}}\cos^2\alpha\right)^2=0$$

$$\Rightarrow \tan^2\alpha=\frac{a}{b}$$

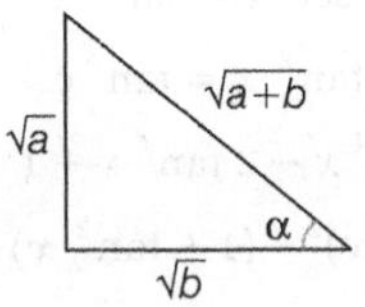

$$\text{Now, } \frac{\sin^8\alpha}{a^3}+\frac{\cos^8\alpha}{b^3}$$

$$\Rightarrow \frac{a^4}{(a+b)^4}\cdot\frac{1}{a^3}+\frac{b^4}{(a+b)^4}\cdot\frac{1}{b^3}=\frac{1}{(a+b)^3}$$

Example 9. If $\sin\theta$ and $\cos\theta$ are the roots of the equation $ax^2-bx+c=0$, then a, b and c satisfy the relation.

(a) $a^2+b^2+2ac=0$ (b) $a^2-b^2+2ac=0$

(c) $a^2+c^2+2ab=0$ (d) $a^2-b^2-2ac=c$

Sol. (b) Given that $\sin\theta$ and $\cos\theta$ are the roots of the equation $ax^2-bx+c=0$, so $\sin\theta+\cos\theta=\frac{b}{a}$ and $\sin\theta\cos\theta=\frac{c}{a}$.

Using the identity

$(\sin\theta+\cos\theta)^2=\sin^2\theta+\cos^2\theta+2\sin\theta\cos\theta$, we have

$$\frac{b^2}{a^2}=1+\frac{2c}{a} \text{ or } a^2-b^2+2ac=0$$

Example 10. If $\theta\in\left(\frac{\pi}{4},\frac{\pi}{2}\right)$ and $\sum_{n=1}^{\infty}\frac{1}{\tan^n\theta}=\sin\theta+\cos\theta$, then the value of $\tan\theta$ is

(a) $\sqrt{3}$ (b) $\sqrt{2}+1$

(c) $2+\sqrt{3}$ (d) $\sqrt{2}$

Sol. (a) $\theta\in\left(\frac{\pi}{4},\frac{\pi}{2}\right)$

$\Rightarrow \tan\theta>1\Rightarrow 0<\frac{1}{\tan\theta}<1$

$$\sum_{n=1}^{\infty}\frac{1}{\tan^n\theta}=\sin\theta+\cos\theta$$

$$\Rightarrow \frac{1}{\tan\theta}+\frac{1}{\tan^2\theta}+\frac{1}{\tan^3\theta}+\ldots=\sin\theta+\cos\theta$$

$$\Rightarrow \frac{\frac{1}{\tan\theta}}{1-\frac{1}{\tan\theta}}=\sin\theta+\cos\theta$$

$$\Rightarrow \frac{1}{\tan\theta-1}=\sin\theta+\cos\theta$$

$$\Rightarrow \frac{\cos\theta}{\sin\theta-\cos\theta}=\sin\theta+\cos\theta$$

$$\Rightarrow \cos\theta=\sin^2\theta-\cos^2\theta$$

$$\Rightarrow \cos\theta=1-2\cos^2\theta$$

$$\Rightarrow 2\cos^2\theta+\cos\theta-1=0$$

$$\Rightarrow (2\cos\theta-1)(\cos\theta+1)=0$$

$$\Rightarrow \cos\theta=\frac{1}{2} \text{ or } \cos\theta=-1 \text{ (rejected)}$$

$$\Rightarrow \cos\theta=\frac{1}{2}=\cos 60^\circ$$

$$\Rightarrow \theta=60^\circ$$

$$\Rightarrow \tan\theta=\tan 60^\circ=\sqrt{3}$$

1.4 Elimination of Trigonometric Ratios

In order to eliminate the T-Ratios from given relations, we make use of the fundamental trigonometrical identities.

Example 11. If $x=a\sin\theta+b\cos\theta$ and $y=a\cos\theta-b\sin\theta$, then prove that $x^2+y^2=a^2+b^2$.

Sol. We have, $x^2+y^2=(a\sin\theta+b\cos\theta)^2+(a\cos\theta-b\sin\theta)^2$

$$=a^2(\sin^2\theta+\cos^2\theta)+b^2(\cos^2\theta+\sin^2\theta)$$

$$=a^2+b^2$$

Hence, $x^2+y^2=a^2+b^2$

Example 12. If $a\sec\alpha-c\tan\alpha=d$ and $b\sec\alpha+d\tan\alpha=c$, then eliminate α from above equations.

Sol. Here, $a\sec\alpha-c\tan\alpha=d$ and $b\sec\alpha+d\tan\alpha=c$ could be written as

$$a=d\cos\alpha+c\sin\alpha \quad \ldots\text{(i)}$$

and $$b=c\cos\alpha-d\sin\alpha \quad \ldots\text{(ii)}$$

On squaring and adding Eqs. (i) and (ii), we get

$$a^2+b^2=(d\cos\alpha+c\sin\alpha)^2+(c\cos\alpha-d\sin\alpha)^2$$

$$\Rightarrow a^2+b^2=d^2\cos^2\alpha+c^2\sin^2\alpha+2dc\cos\alpha\sin\alpha$$
$$+c^2\cos^2\alpha+d^2\sin^2\alpha-2cd\cos\alpha\sin\alpha.$$
$$=d^2(\cos^2\alpha+\sin^2\alpha)+c^2(\sin^2\alpha+\cos^2\alpha)$$

$$\therefore a^2+b^2=c^2+d^2$$

Example 13. Eliminate θ between the equations $a\sec\theta+b\tan\theta+c=0$ and $p\sec\theta+q\tan\theta+r=0$.

Sol. Given $$a\sec\theta+b\tan\theta+c=0 \quad \ldots\text{(i)}$$

and $$p\sec\theta+q\tan\theta+r=0 \quad \ldots\text{(ii)}$$

Solving Eqs. (i) and (ii) by cross multiplication method, we get

$$\frac{\sec\theta}{br-qc}=\frac{\tan\theta}{pc-ar}=\frac{1}{aq-pb}$$
I II III

From parts I and III, we get

$$\sec\theta=\frac{br-qc}{aq-pb} \quad \ldots\text{(iii)}$$

From parts II and III, we get

$$\tan\theta=\frac{pc-ar}{aq-pb} \quad \ldots\text{(iv)}$$

$$\because \sec^2\theta-\tan^2\theta=1$$

$$\therefore \left(\frac{br-qc}{aq-pb}\right)^2-\left(\frac{pc-ar}{aq-pb}\right)^2=1$$

or $$(br-qc)^2-(pc-ar)^2=(aq-pb)^2$$

Example 14. If $0<\theta<\frac{\pi}{2}$, $x=\sum_{n=0}^{\infty}\cos^{2n}\theta$, $y=\sum_{n=0}^{\infty}\sin^{2n}\theta$ and $z=\sum_{n=0}^{\infty}\cos^{2n}\theta\cdot\sin^{2n}\theta$, then show $xyz=xy+z$.

Sol. Here, $x=\sum_{n=0}^{\infty}\cos^{2n}\theta=1+\cos^2\theta+\cos^4\theta+\cos^6\theta+\ldots\infty$

$$=\frac{1}{1-\cos^2\theta}=\frac{1}{\sin^2\theta}$$

$$\left[\text{using, } S_\infty=\frac{a}{1-r} \text{ sum of infinite GP}\right]$$

Similarly, $y = \frac{1}{1-\sin^2\theta} = \frac{1}{\cos^2\theta}$

and $z = \frac{1}{1-\sin^2\theta\cdot\cos^2\theta}$

$$\therefore \quad xyz = \frac{1}{\sin^2\theta\cos^2\theta(1-\sin^2\theta\cos^2\theta)}$$

$$= \frac{(1-\sin^2\theta\cos^2\theta)+(\sin^2\theta\cos^2\theta)}{\sin^2\theta\cos^2\theta(1-\sin^2\theta\cos^2\theta)}$$

$$= \frac{1}{\sin^2\theta\cos^2\theta} + \frac{1}{1-\sin^2\theta\cos^2\theta} = xy + z$$

Example 15. If in the given figure, $\tan(\angle BAO) = 3$, then find the ratio $BC:CA$.

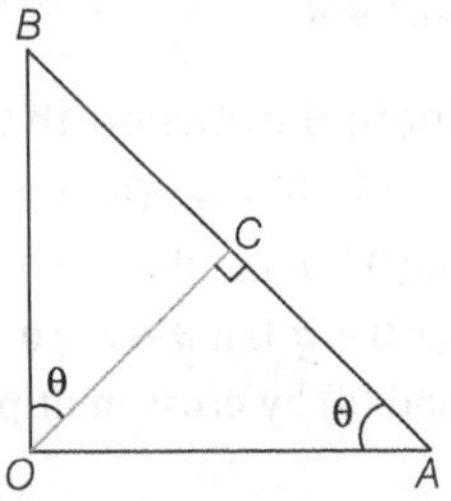

Sol. From figure, we have $\tan\theta = 3$

In ΔOCA and ΔOCB respectively, we get

$$\therefore \quad \frac{OC}{AC} = \tan\theta, \quad \frac{OC}{BC} = \cot\theta$$

On dividing, we get

$$\frac{BC}{AC} = \frac{\tan\theta}{\cot\theta} = \tan^2\theta = 9 \Rightarrow BC : AC = 9 : 1$$

Example 16. If $\angle C$ of ΔABC is $90°$, then prove that $\tan A + \tan B = \frac{c^2}{ab}$ (where a, b, c are sides opposite to angles A, B, C respectively).

Sol. Draw ΔABC with $\angle C = 90°$.

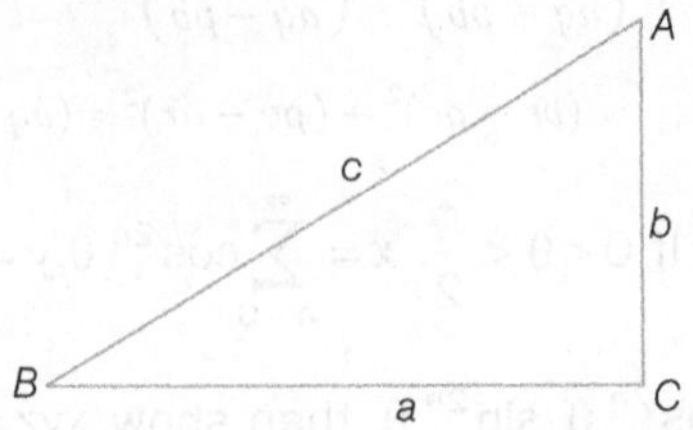

We have, $\tan A + \tan B = \frac{a}{b} + \frac{b}{a} = \frac{a^2+b^2}{ab} = \frac{c^2}{ab}$

Example 17. In ΔABC, $BC = 8$, $CA = 6$, and $AB = 10$. A line dividing the ΔABC into two regions of equal area is perpendicular to AB at point X. Find the value of $\frac{BX}{\sqrt{2}}$.

Sol.

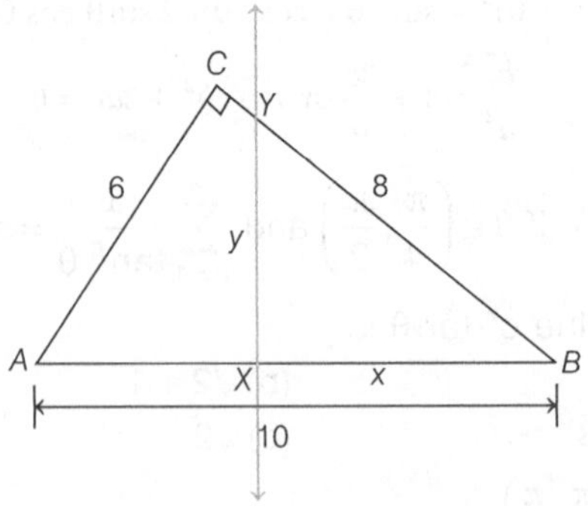

We have, area of $\Delta XYB = \frac{1}{2} \times$ Area of ΔABC

$$\therefore \quad \frac{1}{2}(XY)\cdot(XB) = \frac{1}{2} \times \frac{1}{2} \times AC \times BC$$

$$\Rightarrow \quad \frac{x \times y}{2} = \frac{8 \times 6}{4} = 12$$

$$\Rightarrow \quad x \times x\tan B = 24 \qquad [\because y = x\tan B]$$

$$\Rightarrow \quad x^2 \times \frac{3}{4} = 24 \qquad \left[\because \tan B = \frac{AC}{BC}\right]$$

$$\Rightarrow \quad x^2 = 32$$

$$\Rightarrow \quad x = 4\sqrt{2}$$

Example 18. Let PQ and RS be tangents at the extremities of the diameter PR or a circle of radius r. If PS and RQ intersect at a point X on the circumference of the circle, then prove that $2r = \sqrt{PQ \times RS}$.

Sol.

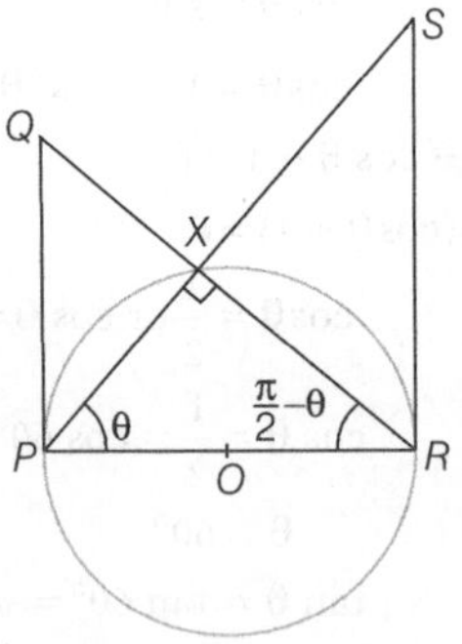

From figure, we have

$$\frac{PQ}{PR} = \tan\left(\frac{\pi}{2} - \theta\right) = \cot\theta$$

and $$\frac{RS}{PR} = \tan\theta$$

$$\therefore \quad \frac{PQ}{PR} \times \frac{RS}{PR} = 1$$

$$\Rightarrow \quad PR^2 = PQ \times RS$$

$$\Rightarrow \quad (2r)^2 = PQ \times RS \text{ or } 2r = \sqrt{PQ \times RS}$$

Milestone Practice 1.1

1. Using the identity $\text{cosec}^2\theta = 1+\cot^2\theta$, prove that $\frac{\cot\theta+\text{cosec}\,\theta-1}{\cot\theta-\text{cosec}\,\theta+1}=\frac{1+\cos\theta}{\sin\theta}$.

2. If $f(x)=\sec^2 x\,\text{cosec}^2 x$, then
(a) $f(x)<4$ (b) $f(x)=4$ (c) $f(x)\geq 4$ (d) $f(x)\leq 4$

3. If $13\sec\theta - 5\tan\theta = 13$, then the sum of possible values of $13\tan\theta - 5\sec\theta$ is
(a) -5 (b) 0 (c) 5 (d) 10

4. If $\sin^2 x+\sin x = 1$, then the value of $\cos^{12}x+3\cos^{10}x+3\cos^8 x+\cos^6 x$ is
(a) 1 (b) 2
(c) 3 (d) None of these

5. The value of $\sin^6\theta+\cos^6\theta+3\sin^2\theta\cos^2\theta$ equals to
(a) -1 (b) 0 (c) 1 (d) 3

6. If $\sec\theta+\tan\theta = e^x$, then $\cos\theta$ equals to
(a) $\frac{(e^x+e^{-x})}{2}$ (b) $\frac{2}{e^x+e^{-x}}$
(c) $\frac{e^x-e^{-x}}{2}$ (d) $\frac{e^x-e^{-x}}{e^x+e^{-x}}$

7. If $\tan A=\sqrt{2}-1$, then show that $\sin A\cos A=\frac{1}{2\sqrt{2}}$.

8. Find an acute angle θ when $\frac{\cos\theta-\sin\theta}{\cos\theta+\sin\theta}=\frac{1-\sqrt{3}}{1+\sqrt{3}}$.

9. If $\sec\theta = x+\frac{1}{4x}$, then prove that $\sec\theta+\tan 2\theta = 2x$ or $\frac{1}{2x}$.

10. If $\frac{\sin^2 x-2\cos^2 x+1}{\sin^2 x+2\cos^2 x-1}=4$, then the value of $2\tan^2 x$ is
(a) 3 (b) 4 (c) 5 (d) 6

11. If $\sin x+\cos x=\frac{5}{4}$, then find the value of $\tan x+\cot x+\sec x+\text{cosec} x$.

12. If $\tan\theta+\sin\theta = m$ and $\tan\theta-\sin\theta = n$, then prove that $(m^2-n^2)=4\sqrt{mn}$.

13. If $P=\frac{2\sin\theta}{1+\sin\theta+\cos\theta}$ and $Q=\frac{\cos\theta}{1+\sin\theta}$, then
(a) $PQ=1$ (b) $\frac{Q}{P}=1$
(c) $Q-P=1$ (d) $Q+P=1$

14. If $x=\sec\theta-\tan\theta$ and $y=\text{cosec}\,\theta+\cot\theta$, then the value of $xy+x-y$ is
(a) 1 (b) 0
(c) -1 (d) None of these

15. If $x=r\sin\theta\cos\phi$, $y=r\sin\theta\sin\phi$ and $z=r\cos\theta$, then the value of $x^2+y^2+z^2$ is
(a) 1 (b) r^2 (c) $2r^2$ (d) $3r^2$

16. If $\tan\theta-\cot\theta = a$ and $\sin\theta+\cos\theta = b$, then $(b^2-1)^2(a^2+4)$ is equal to
(a) 2 (b) -4 (c) ± 4 (d) 4

17. A rhombus of side 20 cm has two angles of 60° each. Find the length of the diagonals.

18. An equilateral triangle is inscribed in a circle of radius 6 cm. Find its side.

19. The radii of two circles 4 cm and 1 cm touch each other externally and θ is the angle contained by their direct common tangents. Find the value of $\sin\frac{\theta}{2}+\cos\frac{\theta}{2}$.

20. The value of $(\text{cosec}\,\theta-\sin\theta)(\sec\theta-\cos\theta)(\tan\theta+\cot\theta)$ is
(a) 0 (b) 1 (c) 2 (d) 3

21. If $\sin^6\theta+\cos^6\theta-1=\lambda\sin^2\theta\cos^2\theta$, then the value of λ is
(a) -3 (b) 3 (c) 1 (d) 2

22. If $\sin\theta+2\,\text{cosec}\,\theta=3$, then the value of $\sin^{20}\theta+\text{cosec}^{20}\theta$ is
(a) 0 (b) 1
(c) 2 (d) None of these

23. Let $f_k(x)=\frac{1}{k}(\sin^k x+\cos^k x)$, where $x\in R$ and $k\geq 1$, then the value of $f_4(x)-f_6(x)$ is
(a) $\frac{1}{5}$ (b) $\frac{1}{12}$ (c) $\frac{1}{10}$ (d) $\frac{1}{3}$

24. If $\sin\theta$, $\tan\theta$ and $\cos\theta$ are in GP, then $4\sin^2\theta-3\sin^4\theta+\sin^6\theta=$
(a) -1 (b) 2
(c) 1 (d) None of these

25. If $\frac{\sin^4 x}{2}+\frac{\cos^4 x}{3}=\frac{1}{5}$, then the value of $\frac{\sin^8 x}{8}+\frac{\cos^8 x}{27}$ is
(a) $\frac{1}{5}$ (b) $\frac{1}{10}$ (c) $\frac{1}{25}$ (d) $\frac{1}{125}$

26. If $A = \sin^8\theta + \cos^{14}\theta$, then for all values of θ,

(a) $A \geq 1$ (b) $0 < A < 1$
(c) $1 < 2A < 3$ (d) None of these

27. If $\sum_{i=1}^{n} \cos\theta_i = n$, then $\sum_{i=1}^{n} \sin\theta_i$ is equal to

(a) $n-1$ (b) 0
(c) n (d) $n+1$

28. If $a\sin^2 x + b\cos^2 x = c$, $b\sin^2 y + a\cos^2 y = d$ and $a\tan x = b\tan y$, then $\frac{a^2}{b^2}$ is equal to

(a) $\frac{(b-c)(d-b)}{(a-d)(d-b)}$ (b) $\frac{(a-d)(c-a)}{(b-c)(d-b)}$
(c) $\frac{(d-a)(c-a)}{(b-c)(d-b)}$ (d) $\frac{(b-c)(b-d)}{(a-c)(a-d)}$

29. If $a\sin^2\theta + b\cos^2\theta = m$, $b\sin^2\phi + a\cos^2\phi = n$ and $a\tan\theta = b\tan\phi$, then $\frac{1}{m} + \frac{1}{n}$ is equal to

(a) $\frac{1}{a} - \frac{1}{b}$ (b) $\frac{1}{a} + \frac{1}{b}$ (c) $\frac{1}{a}$ (d) $\frac{1}{b}$

30. If $\sin x + \operatorname{cosec} x = 2$, then $\sin^n x + \operatorname{cosec}^n x$ is equal to

(a) 2^{n-2} (b) 2^{n-1} (c) 2^n (d) 2

31. If $x = \frac{2\sin\theta}{1+\cos\theta+\sin\theta}$, then $\frac{1-\cos\theta+\sin\theta}{1+\sin\theta}$ is equal to

(a) $1+x$ (b) $1-x$
(c) x (d) $\frac{1}{x}$

32. If $\sec\alpha$ and $\operatorname{cosec}\alpha$ are the roots of $x^2 - px + q = 0$, then

(a) $p^2 = q(q-2)$ (b) $p^2 = q(q+2)$
(c) $p^2 + q^2 = 2q$ (d) None of these

33. Which of the following is not the quadratic equation whose roots are $\operatorname{cosec}^2\theta$ and $\sec^2\theta$?

(a) $x^2 - 6x + 6 = 0$ (b) $x^2 - 7x + 7 = 0$
(c) $x^2 - 4x + 4 = 0$ (d) None of these

34. $(1 + \tan\alpha\tan\beta)^2 + (\tan\alpha - \tan\beta)^2$ is equal to

(a) $\tan^2\alpha\tan^2\beta$ (b) $\sec^2\alpha\sec^2\beta$
(c) $\tan^2\alpha\cot^2\beta$ (d) $\sec^2\alpha\cos^2\beta$

35. A right angled triangle has perimeter of length 7 units and hypotenuse of length 3 units. If θ is the larger non-right angle in the triangle, then the value of $\cos\theta$ equals

(a) $\frac{\sqrt{6}-\sqrt{2}}{4}$ (b) $\frac{4+\sqrt{2}}{3}$
(c) $\frac{4-\sqrt{2}}{3}$ (d) $\frac{4-\sqrt{2}}{6}$

36. If $x\sin^3\theta + y\cos^3\theta = \sin\theta\cos\theta$ and $x\sin\theta - y\cos\theta = 0$, then (x, y) lie on

(a) a circle (b) a parabola
(c) an ellipse (d) a hyperbola

37. If $\frac{x}{a\cos\theta} = \frac{y}{b\sin\theta}$ and $\frac{ax}{\cos\theta} - \frac{by}{\sin\theta} = a^2 - b^2$, then (x, y) lie on

(a) a circle (b) a parabola
(c) an ellipse (d) a hyperbola

38. If $\sin\theta + \cos\theta = a$ and $\sin^3\theta + \cos^3\theta = b$, then we get $\lambda a^3 + \mu b + \gamma a = 0$ when λ, μ, γ are independent of θ, then the value of $\lambda^3 + \mu^3 + \gamma^3$ is

(a) -6 (b) -18 (c) -36 (d) -98

39. Let $P = \{\theta : \sin\theta - \cos\theta = \sqrt{2}\cos\theta\}$ and $Q = \{\theta : \sin\theta + \cos\theta = \sqrt{2}\sin\theta\}$ be two sets. Then,

(a) $P \subset Q$ and $Q - P \neq \phi$ (b) $Q \not\subset P$
(c) $P \not\subset Q$ (d) $P = Q$

Answer Key

2. (c)	3. (b)	4. (a)	5. (c)	6. (b)	8. 60°
10. (c)	11. 8	13. (d)	14. (c)	15. (b)	16. (d)
17. $20\sqrt{3}$ cm and 20 cm	18. $6\sqrt{3}$ cm	19. 7/5	20. (b)	21. (a)	22. (c)
23. (b)	24. (c)	25. (d)	26. (d)	27. (b)	28. (b)
29. (b)	30. (d)	31. (c)	32. (b)	33. (d)	34. (b)
35. (d)	36. (a)	37. (c)	38. (b)	39. (d)	

For Detailed Solution

Milestone 2 Measurement of Angles

• Angle • Sectorial Area • Measuring of Angle in Various Quadrants

1.5 Angle

An angle is the amount of rotation of revolving line with respect to a fixed line.

There are three systems of measuring an angle

(i) Sexagecimal system or English system (degree)

(ii) Centesimal or french system (grade)

(iii) Circular system (radian)

Sexagecimal System Or Degree Measures

In this system a right angle is divided into 90 equal parts, called degrees. The symbol 1° is used to denote one degree. Thus, one degree is one-ninetieth part of right angle. Each degree is divided into 60 equal parts, called minutes and one minute is divided into 60 equal parts, called second. The symbol $1'$ and $1''$ are used to denoted one minute and one second, respectively.

Thus, 1 right angle = 90 degrees (= 90°)

$$1^\circ = 60 \text{ minutes } (= 60')$$
$$1' = 60 \text{ seconds } (= 60'')$$

Example 19. Express 90′ in degrees.

Sol. $60' = 1$ degree

$$1' = \frac{1}{60} \text{ degree}$$
$$90' = \frac{90}{60} \text{ degree}$$
$$90' = 1.5^\circ$$

Example 20. Express 30.54° in degrees, minutes and seconds.

Sol. $30^\circ + (0.54 \times 60)' = 30^\circ + (32.4)'$
$$= 30^\circ + 32' + (0.4 \times 60)''$$
$$= 30^\circ + 32' + 24'' = 30^\circ 32' 24''$$

Example 21. The angle between the minute and hour hand at 07:20 pm is

(a) 90° (b) 95°

(c) 100° (d) 115°

Sol. (c) 12 Division = 360°

1 Division = 30°

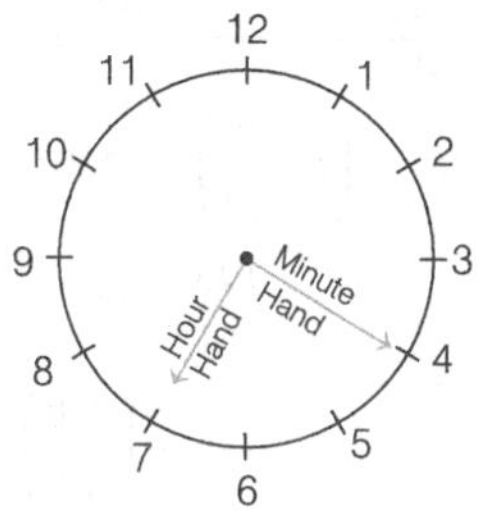

Angle when hour hand is at 7 and minute hand is at 4
$$= 3 \times 30^\circ = 90^\circ$$

At 07:00 pm, hour hand at 7 and minute hand at 12.

At 07:20 pm, minute hand at 4 and hour hand between 7 and 8.

Hour hand will rotate 30° in 60 min.

Hour hand will rotate 1° in 2 min.

Hour hand will rotate 10° in 20 min.

Hence, angle between the minute and hour hand at 07:20 pm = 90°+10° = 100°

Centesimal System

In this system, a right angle is divided into 100 equal parts, called grades; each grade is subdivided into 100 min each minute is divided into 100 sec.

The symbol 1^g, $1'$ and $1''$ are used to denote a grade, a minute and a second respectively.

Thus, 1 right angle = 100 grades $(= 100^g)$

$$1 \text{ grade} = 100 \text{ min } (= 100')$$
$$1 \text{ min} = 100 \text{ sec } (= 100'')$$

Inter Conversion of Degree and Grade

$$1 \text{ right angle} = 90^\circ = 100^g$$

$$1^\circ = \left(\frac{100}{90}\right)^g = \left(\frac{10}{9}\right)^g \Rightarrow x^\circ = \left(x \cdot \frac{10}{9}\right)^g$$

$$1^g = \left(\frac{90}{100}\right)^\circ = \left(\frac{9}{10}\right)^\circ \Rightarrow y^g = \left(y \cdot \frac{9}{10}\right)^\circ$$

Example 22. Express 81° in grade measure.

Sol. $81° = \left(81 \times \frac{10}{9}\right)^g = 90^g$

Example 23. In right angle ΔABC, right angled at B, angle A in degrees and angle C in grades are numerically equal. Find angle A.

Sol.

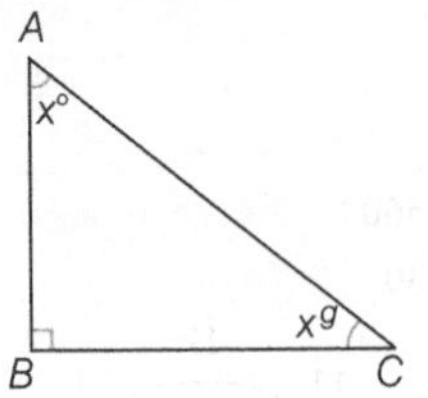

In ΔABC, $x° + 90° + \left(x \cdot \frac{9}{10}\right)^° = 180°$

$$\Rightarrow \quad \frac{19x}{10} = 90°$$

$$\Rightarrow \quad x = \left(\frac{900}{19}\right)^°$$

Circular System

In this system the unit of measurement is radian as defined below.

Radians

One radian, written as 1^c, is the measure of an angle subtended at the centre of circle by an arc of length equal to radius of the circle.

Consider an arc AB of a circle of radius r subtended an angle θ at its centre. The ratio between length of arc AB the radius of circle represent the measure of angle θ in the radians.

i.e. $$\theta \text{ (in radians)} = \frac{\text{arc } AB}{r}$$

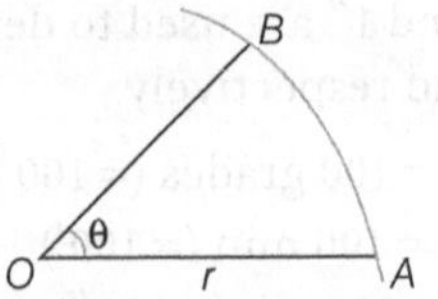

One radian is the angle subtended at the centre of a circle by an arc whose length is equal to the radius of circle.

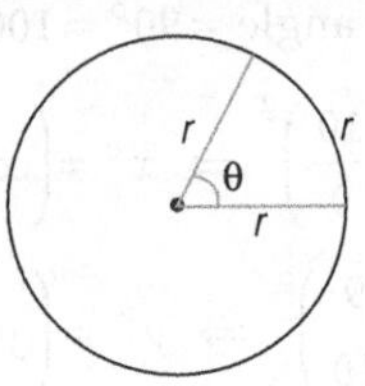

Relation between Degree and Radians

Let θ be the angle subtended at centre by a semi-circle be 180°.

From figure, $\theta = 180°$

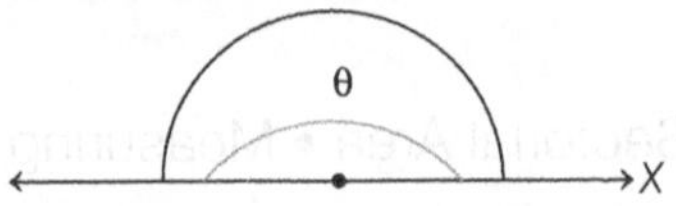

In radians, $$\theta = \frac{\text{arc}}{\text{radius}} = \frac{\pi r}{r} = \pi$$

$\Rightarrow$ 180° degree = π radian

Radian is an important unit for measuring angles. So, the following conversions must be remembered.

Degree	Radian
0°	0
30°	$\frac{\pi}{6}$
45°	$\frac{\pi}{4}$
60°	$\frac{\pi}{3}$
90°	$\frac{\pi}{2}$
120°	$\frac{2\pi}{3}$
135°	$\frac{3\pi}{4}$
150°	$\frac{5\pi}{6}$
180°	π
270°	$\frac{3\pi}{2}$

JEE Focus Points

Concept Inside Video

- θ radian is written as θ^c or can be written simply as θ. When the unit of angle is not mentioned, it must be taken as radians.
- Radian is the unit to measure angle and it does not means that π stands for 180°, π is a real number. Where as π^c stands for 180°.
  Remember the relation π radians = 180 degrees = 200 grade
- The relation amongst three systems of measurement of an angle is

$$\frac{D}{90°} = \frac{G}{100} = \frac{2R}{\pi}$$

Relation between an Arc and an Angle

It l is the length of an arc of a circle of radius r, then the angle θ (in radians) subtended by this arc at the centre of the circle is given by

$$\theta = \frac{l}{r} \quad \text{or} \quad l = r\theta$$

i.e. Arc = Radius × Angle in radians

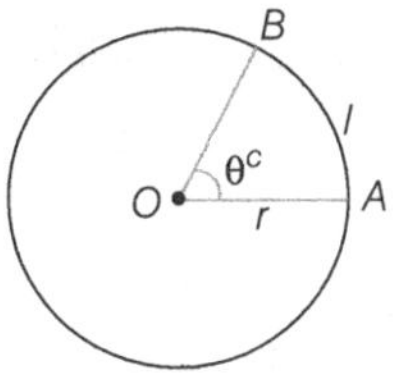

Example 24. In the circle of 5 cm radius, what is the length of the arc which subtends an angle of 33°15′ at the centre.

Sol. Here, $r = 5$ cm, $15' = \frac{15}{60} = \left(\frac{1}{4}\right)^{\circ}$

$$\therefore \quad \theta = 33^{\circ}15' = 33 + \frac{1}{4} = \frac{133}{4} \text{ degrees}$$

$$= \frac{133}{4} \times \frac{\pi}{180} = \frac{133}{4} \times \frac{22}{7 \times 180}$$

$$= \frac{1463}{2520} \text{ radians}$$

Now, $\theta = \frac{l}{r}$

$$\therefore \quad l = \theta r = \frac{1463}{2520} \times 5$$

$$= 2\frac{65}{72} \text{ cm (approx.)}$$

1.6 Sectorial Area

Let OAB be a sector having central angle θ^c and radius r. Then, the area of the sector OAB is given by $\frac{1}{2}r^2\theta$.

Example 25. The minute hand of a watch is 35 cm long. How far does its tip move in 18 min? Also, find the area covered by minute hand. $\left(\text{use } \pi = \frac{22}{7}\right)$

Sol. The minute hand of a watch completes one revolution in 60 min. Therefore, the angle traced by a minute hand in 60 min = 360° = 2π radians.

∴ Angle traced by the minute hand in 18 min

$$= 2\pi \times \frac{18}{60} \text{ radians}$$

$$= \frac{3\pi}{5} \text{ radians}$$

Let the distance moved by the tip in 18 min be l, then $l = r\theta$, where θ is in radians

$$= 35 \times \frac{3\pi}{5} = 21\pi = 21 \times \frac{22}{7} = 66 \text{ cm}$$

Area covered by minute hand

$$= \frac{1}{2}r^2\theta = \frac{1}{2} \times 35 \times 35 \times \frac{3\pi}{5} = \frac{35 \times 35}{2} \times \frac{3}{5} \times \frac{22}{7} = 1155 \text{ cm}^2$$

1.7 Measuring of Angle in Various Quadrants

The perpendicular lines XOX' and YOY' divide the plane in four parts.

Q I. First Quadrant (all points have $+X$ and $+Y$)

Q II. Second Quadrant (all points have $-X$ and $+Y$)

Q III. Third Quadrant (all points $-X$ and $-Y$)

Q IV. Fourth Quadrant (all points have $+X$ and $-Y$)

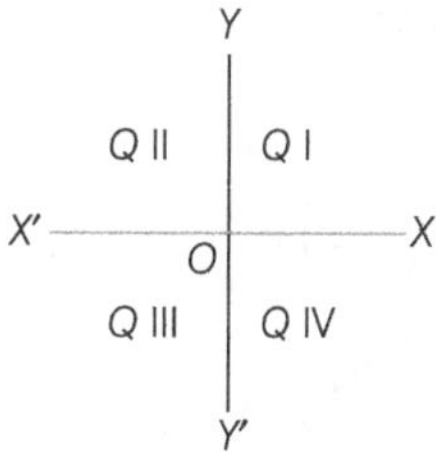

- The angles in trigonometry can be positive or negative and can have any magnitude. Every angle is represented by one position of a revolving ray OP of length r. The starting position for ray OP is taken along $+X$-axis.

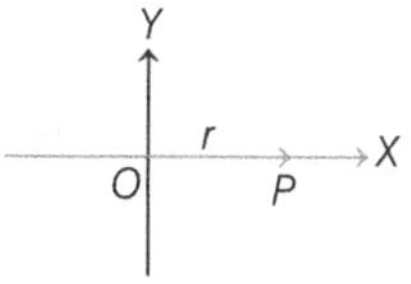

- If an angle α (alpha) is positive, OP rotates through angle α in anticlockwise direction.

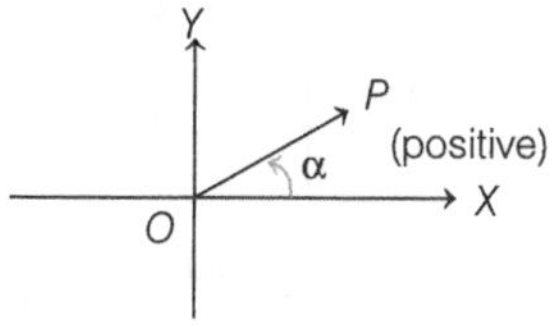

- If an angle α is negative, OP rotates through angle α in clockwise direction.

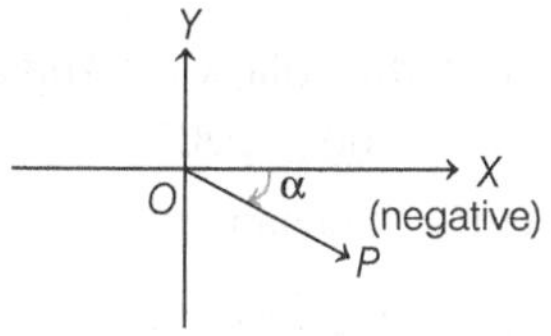

- An angle can lie in any of four quadrants according to the position of revolving ray for the angle.

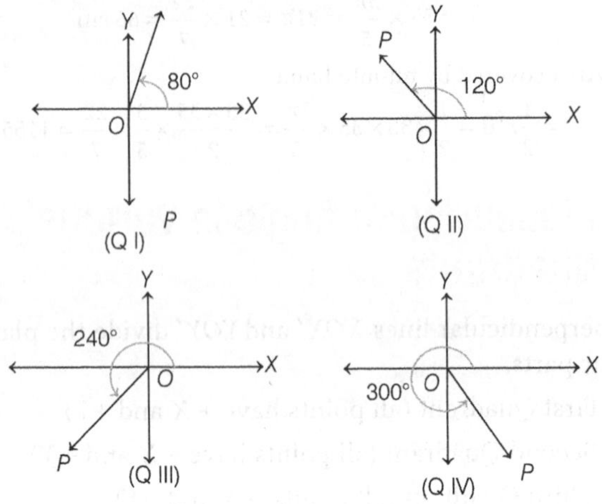

- Two or more angles may correspond to same position of revolving ray *OP*.

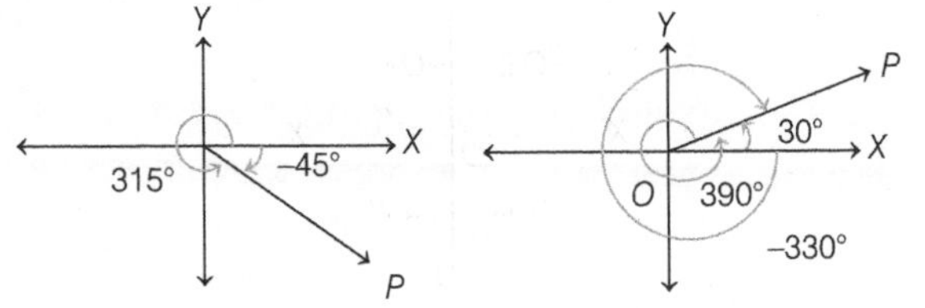

This position of *OP* represents – 45° and +315°

This position of *OP* represents +30°, +390° and – 330°

- The position of revolving ray for angles 0°, 30°, 45°, 60°, 90°, 120°, 135°, 180°, 270°, 360° must be remembered.

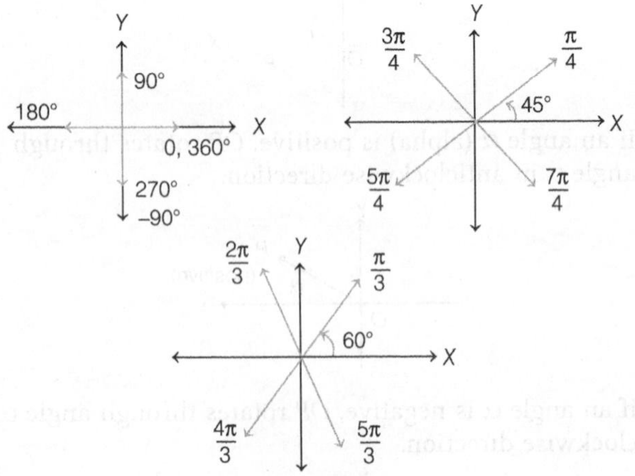

Example 26. Express the following angles in radians.

(i) 120° (ii) – 600° (iii) – 144°

Sol. We know that 180° = π radian

(i) $120° = \left(120 \times \dfrac{\pi}{180}\right)^c = \left(\dfrac{2\pi}{3}\right)^c$

(ii) $-600° = -\left(600 \times \dfrac{\pi}{180}\right)^c = -\left(\dfrac{10\pi}{3}\right)^c$

(iii) $-144° = -\left(144 \times \dfrac{\pi}{180}\right)^c = -\left(\dfrac{4\pi}{5}\right)^c$

Example 27. Convert 45°20′10″ in radian measure (π = 3.1415).

Sol. $10'' = \dfrac{10}{60}\text{ min} = \left(\dfrac{10}{60 \times 60}\right)^\circ = \left(\dfrac{1}{360}\right)^\circ$

$20' = \left(\dfrac{20}{60}\right)^\circ = \left(\dfrac{1}{3}\right)^\circ$

$\therefore\ 45°20'10'' = \left(45 + \dfrac{1}{360} + \dfrac{1}{3}\right)^\circ$

$= \left(\dfrac{16200 + 1 + 120}{360}\right)^\circ = \left(\dfrac{16321}{360}\right)^\circ$

Now, $\left(\dfrac{16321}{360}\right)^\circ = \dfrac{16321}{360} \times \dfrac{\pi}{180}\text{ rad}$

$= \dfrac{16321}{360} \times \dfrac{3.1416}{180} = \dfrac{51274.054}{64800} = 0.79\text{ radian}$

$45°20'10'' = 0.79\text{ radian}$

Example 28. Express the following angle in degrees, minutes and seconds form

(i) (245.33)° (ii) $\left(\dfrac{1}{5}\right)^c$

Sol. (i) $(245.33)° = 245° + (0.33)°$

$= 245° + (0.33 \times 60)'$ $[\because 1° = 60']$

$= 245° + (19.8)' = 245° + 19' + 0.8'$

$= 245° + 19' + (0.8 \times 60)''$ $[\because 1' = 60'']$

$= 245° + 19' + 48''$

Hence, $(245.33)° = 245°19'48''$

(ii) $\left(\dfrac{1}{5}\right)^c = \left(\dfrac{1}{5} \times \dfrac{180}{\pi}\right)^\circ$ $\left[\because 1^c = \dfrac{180°}{\pi}\right]$

$= \left(\dfrac{36}{\pi}\right)^\circ = \left(\dfrac{36}{3.14}\right)^\circ$ $[\because \pi = 3.14]$

$= (11.46)° = 11° + (0.46)°$

$= 11° + (0.46 \times 60)'$ $[\because 1° = 60']$

$= 11° + (27.6)' = 11° + 27' + 0.6'$

$= 11° + 27' + (0.6 \times 60)''$ $[\because 1' = 60'']$

$= 11° + 27' + 36''$

Hence, $\left(\dfrac{1}{5}\right)^c = 11°27'36''$

Example 29. Express the following angle in degrees.

(i) $\left(\dfrac{5\pi}{12}\right)^c$ (ii) $-\left(\dfrac{7\pi}{12}\right)^c$ (iii) $-\left(\dfrac{2\pi}{9}\right)^c$

Sol. (i) $\left(\frac{5\pi}{12}\right)^c = \left(\frac{5\pi}{12} \times \frac{180}{\pi}\right)^\circ = (5 \times 15)^\circ = 75^\circ$

(ii) $-\left(\frac{7\pi}{12}\right)^c = -\left(\frac{7\pi}{12} \times \frac{180}{\pi}\right)^\circ = -(7 \times 15)^\circ = -105^\circ$

(iii) $-\left(\frac{2\pi}{9}\right)^c = -\left(\frac{2\pi}{9} \times \frac{180}{\pi}\right)^\circ = -(2 \times 20)^\circ = -40^\circ$

Example 30. The wheel of a railway carriage is 40 cm in diameter and makes 6 revolutions in a second, then how fast is the train going?

Sol. Diameter of the wheel = 40 cm

∴ Radius of the wheel = 20 cm

Circumference of the wheel $= 2\pi r = 2\pi \times 20 = 40\pi$ cm

Number of revolutions made in 1 s = 6

∴ Distance covered in 1 s $= 40\pi \times 6 = 240\pi$ cm

∴ Speed of the train $= 240\pi$ cm/s

Example 31. Assuming that a person of normal sight can read print at such a distance that the letters subtend an angle of 5′ at his eye. Find the height of the letters that he can read at a distance of 12 m.

Sol. Let the height of the letters be h metres.

Now, h may be considered as the arc of a circle of radius 12 m, which subtends an angle of 5′ at its centre.

∴ $\theta = 5' = \left(\frac{5}{60} \times \frac{\pi}{180}\right)$ radians $= \left(\frac{\pi}{12 \times 180}\right)$ radian

and $r = 12$ m

∴ $h = r\theta = 12 \times \frac{\pi}{12 \times 180} = \left(\frac{\pi}{180}\right)$ m ≈ 1.7 cm

Example 32. The difference between two acute angles of a right angled triangle is $\frac{22}{35}$ radians. Find these angles in degrees.

Sol. Let x and y be two acute angles.

Then, $x - y = \frac{22}{35}$ radian $= \frac{22}{35} \times \frac{180}{\pi}$ degrees

or $x - y = \frac{180}{5} = 36^\circ$ ...(i)

Also, $x + y = 90^\circ$ ...(ii)

$\Rightarrow$ $x = 63^\circ$ and $y = 27^\circ$

Example 33. If the arcs of the same lengths in two circles subtend angles 65° and 110° at the centre, find the ratio of their radii.

Sol. Let r_1 and r_2 be the radii of the two circles.

Given that $\theta_1 = 65^\circ = \frac{\pi}{180} \times 65 = \frac{13\pi}{36}$ radian

and $\theta_2 = 110^\circ = \frac{\pi}{180} \times 110 = \frac{22\pi}{36}$ radian

Let l be the length of each of the arc.

Then, $l = r_1\theta_1 = r_2\theta_2$,

which gives $\frac{13\pi}{36} \times r_1 = \frac{22\pi}{36} \times r_2$, i.e. $\frac{r_1}{r_2} = \frac{22}{13}$

Hence, $r_1 : r_2 = 22 : 13$

Example 34. The angles of a quadrilateral are in AP and the greatest angle is 120°, the angles in radians are

(a) $\frac{\pi}{3}, \frac{4\pi}{9}, \frac{5\pi}{9}, \frac{2\pi}{3}$
(b) $\frac{\pi}{3}, \frac{\pi}{2}, \frac{2\pi}{3}, \frac{3\pi}{3}$
(c) $\frac{5\pi}{18}, \frac{8\pi}{18}, \frac{11\pi}{18}, \frac{12\pi}{18}$
(d) None of these

Sol. (a) Let the angles in degrees be $a - 3d, a - d, a + d, a + 3d$.

Sum of angles $= 4a = 360^\circ$, therefore $a = 90^\circ$

Also, greatest angle $= a + 3d = 120^\circ$,

Hence, $3d = 120^\circ - a = 120^\circ - 90^\circ = 30^\circ$.

Therefore, $d = 10^\circ$

Hence, the angles are $90^\circ - 30^\circ, 90^\circ - 10^\circ, 90^\circ + 10^\circ, 90^\circ + 30^\circ$.

i.e. The angles in degrees are 60°, 80°, 100° and 120°.

Therefore, in terms of radians the angles are

$60^\circ \times \frac{\pi}{180}, 80^\circ \times \frac{\pi}{180}, 100^\circ \times \frac{\pi}{180}$ and $120^\circ \times \frac{\pi}{180}$

i.e. $\frac{\pi}{3}, \frac{4\pi}{9}, \frac{5\pi}{9}$ and $\frac{2\pi}{3}$.

Example 35. Assuming the distance of the earth from the moon to be 384400 km and the angle subtended by the moon at the eye of a person on the earth to be 31′. Find the diameter of the moon.

Sol. Let AB be the diameter of the moon and O be the observer.

Given, $\angle AOB = 31' = \frac{31}{60} \times \frac{\pi}{180}$ rad

Since, the angle subtended by the moon is very small, its diameter will be approximately equal to the small arc of a circle whose centre is the eye of the observer and the radius is the distance of the earth from the moon.

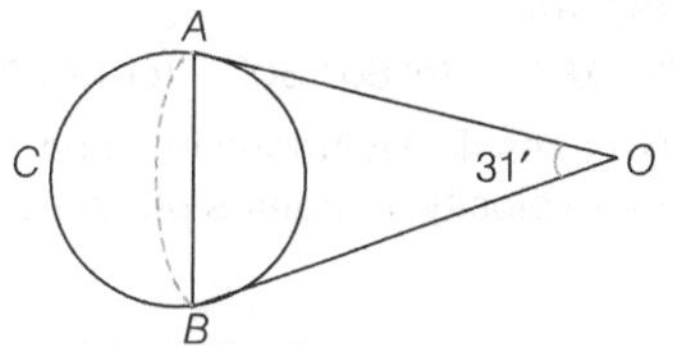

Also, the moon subtends an angle of 31′ at the center of this circle.

Thus, $\theta = \frac{l}{r}$

∴ $\frac{31}{60} \times \frac{\pi}{180} = \frac{AB}{384400}$

$\Rightarrow$ $AB = \frac{31}{60} \times \frac{22}{7 \times 180} \times 384400 = 3467.74$ km

$\Rightarrow$ $AB = 3467.74$ km

Milestone Practice 1.2

1. Find the angle between the hour hand and the minute hand in circular measure at half past 4.

2. The angle between the minute hand and hour hand of a clock, when the time is 7 : 30 pm, is
   (a) 45° (b) 30°
   (c) 60° (d) None of these

3. Find the radian measure corresponding to the following degree measures:
   (i) – 56° (ii) 135° (iii) – 300°
   (iv) 125°30′ (v) – 47°30′

4. Find the degree measure corresponding to the following radian measures. $\left(\text{use } \pi = \frac{22}{7}\right)$
   (i) $\left(\frac{9\pi}{5}\right)^c$ (ii) $\left(\frac{-5\pi}{6}\right)^c$ (iii) $\left(\frac{18\pi}{5}\right)^c$
   (iv) $(-3)^c$ (v) 1^c

5. One angle of a triangle is $\frac{2}{3}x$ grades and another is $\frac{3}{2}x$ degrees while the third is $\frac{\pi x}{75}$ radians. Express all the angles in degrees.

6. Express in radians the fourth angle of a quadrilateral which has three angles 60°, 55° and 100°.

7. The angles of a triangle are $3x°$, $\left(\frac{4x}{3}\right)^g$ and $\frac{2\pi x}{75}$ radians. Find all the angles.

8. The difference between two acute angles of a right angled triangle is $\frac{3\pi}{10}$ rad. Then, the angles in degree, are
   (a) 72°, 18° (b) 60°, 30° (c) 42°, 48° (d) 12°, 78°

9. If OQ makes 4 revolutions in 1 sec, then the angular velocity in radians per second, is
   (a) 4π (b) 6π
   (c) 7π (d) 8π

10. A horse is tied to post by a rope. If the horse moves along circular path always keeping the tight and describes 88 m, when it has traces out 72° at centre, find the length of rope.

11. Find the distance from the eye at which a coin of 2.2 cm diameter should be held so as to conceal the full moon with angular diameter 30′.

12. If a train is moving on the circular path of 1500 m radius at the rate of 66 km/h, Find the angle in radian, if it has in 10 sec.

13. The wheel of a railway carriage is 40 cm in diameter and makes 7 revolutions in a second. Find the speed of train.

14. There is an equilateral triangle with each side 4 unit and a circle with the center on one of the vertex of that triangle. The arc of that circle divides the triangle into two parts of equal area. How long is the radius of the circle?

15. The interior angles of a polygon are in AP.The smallest angle is 120° and the common difference is 5°. Find the number of sides of the polygon.

16. An equilateral triangle has side length 8. The area of the region containing all points outside the triangle but not more than 3 units from a point on the triangle is
    (a) $9(8+\pi)$ (b) $8(9+\pi)$
    (c) $9\left(8+\frac{\pi}{2}\right)$ (d) $8\left(9+\frac{\pi}{2}\right)$

17. The perimeter of a certain sector of a circle is equal to half that the circle of which it is a sector. The circular measure of one angle of the sector is
    (a) $(\pi - 2)$ radian (b) $(\pi + 2)$ radian
    (c) π radian (d) $(\pi - 3)$ radian

Answer Key

1. 45° 2. (a) 3. (i) $-\frac{14\pi}{45}$ (ii) $\frac{9\pi}{12}$ (iii) $-\frac{5\pi}{3}$ (iv) $\frac{251\pi}{360}$ (v) $-\frac{19\pi}{72}$
4. (i) 324° (ii) –150° (iii) 648° (iv) –171°49′5″ (v) 57°16′21″ 5. 24°, 60°, 96° 6. $\frac{29\pi}{36}$ rad
7. 60°, 24°, 96° 8. (a) 9. (d) 10. 70 m 11. 252 cm
12. $\frac{11}{90}$ rad 13. 280π cm/sec 14. $\sqrt{\frac{12\sqrt{3}}{\pi}}$ 15. 9 16. (a) 17. (a)

For Detailed Solution

Milestone 3 Trigonometric Ratios of an Angle

• Trigonometric Ratio in Circular System • Trigonometric Ratios of Allied Angles

1.8 Trigonometric Ratio in Circular System

Let θ be a given angle with specified initial ray. We introduced a rectangular coordinate system in the plane with the vertex of angle θ as the origin and the initial ray of angle θ as the positive ray of the X-axis.

We choose any point P on the circle on the terminal ray of angle θ.

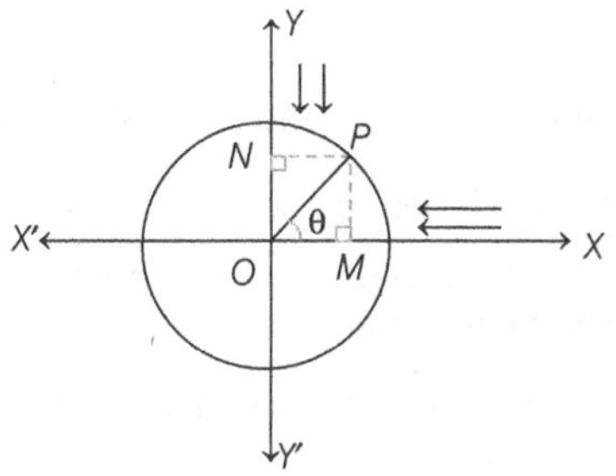

In ΔOPM, $\sin\theta = \dfrac{PM}{OP} = \dfrac{ON}{OP}$

$$= \frac{\text{Projection of } OP \text{ on } Y\text{- axis}}{\text{Length of radius}}$$

$$\cos\theta = \frac{OM}{OP} = \frac{\text{Projection of } OP \text{ on } X\text{- axis}}{\text{Length of radius}}$$

$$\tan\theta = \frac{PM}{OM} = \frac{ON}{OM}$$

$$= \frac{\text{Projection of } OP \text{ on } Y \text{ - axis}}{\text{Projection of } OP \text{ on } X \text{ - axis}}$$

T-Ratios of 0° and 90°

(i) $\sin\theta = \sin 0° = \dfrac{0}{r} = 0$

(ii) $\cos\theta = \cos 0° = \dfrac{r}{r} = 1$

(iii) $\tan\theta = \tan 0° = \dfrac{0}{r} = 0$

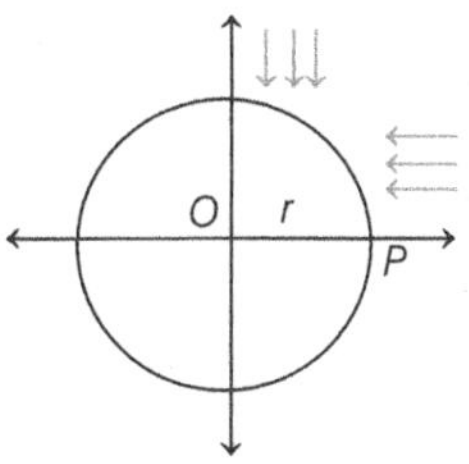

(i) $\sin\theta = \sin 90° = \dfrac{r}{r} = 1$

(ii) $\cos\theta = \cos 90° = \dfrac{0}{r} = 0$

(iii) $\tan\theta = \tan 90° = \dfrac{r}{0} = \text{undefined}$

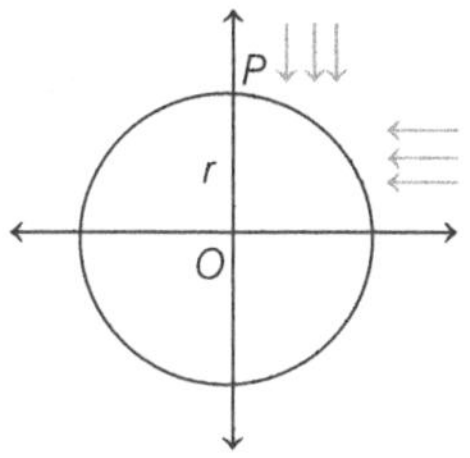

- Projection on positive X-axis and positive Y-axis is considered with a positive sign.
- Projection on negative X-axis and negative Y-axis is considered with a negative sign.

$$\cos\theta = \frac{\text{Projection of radius on } X \text{ - axis}}{\text{Length of radius}}$$

$$\cos\theta = -\frac{OM}{OP}$$

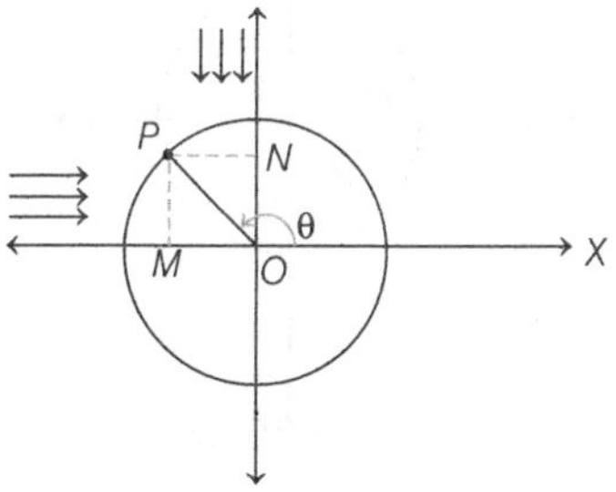

Signs of T-Ratios in Four Quadrants

I Quadrant $0° < \theta < 90°$

$\sin\theta : (+)$ ve

$\cos\theta : (+)$ ve

$\tan\theta : (+)$ ve

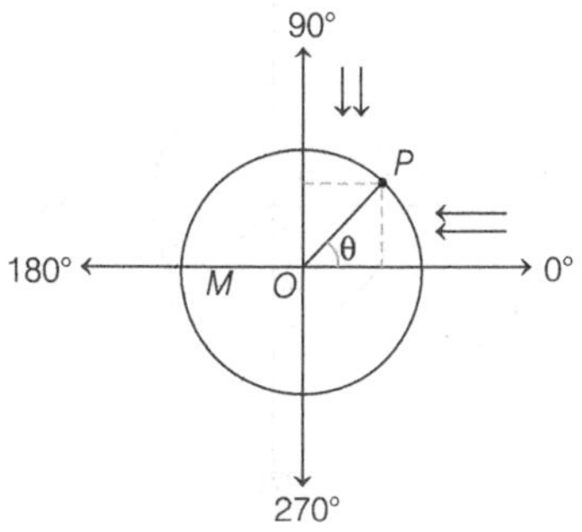

II Quadrant : $90° < \theta < 180°$

$\sin\theta : (+)$ ve

$\cos\theta : (-)$ ve

$\tan\theta : (-)$ ve

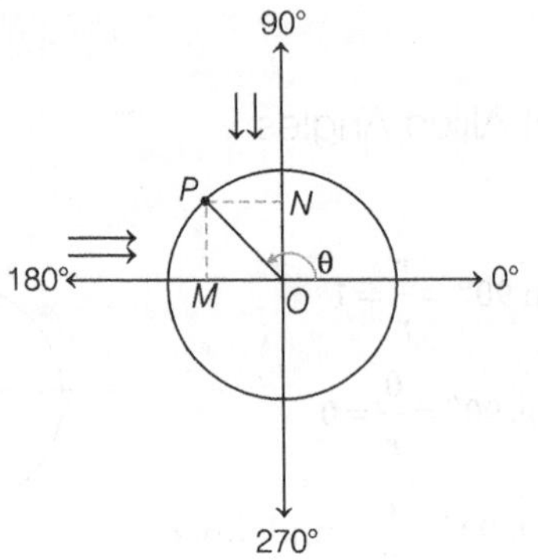

III Quadrant : $180° < \theta < 270°$

$\sin\theta : (-)$ ve

$\cos\theta : (-)$ ve

$\tan\theta : (+)$ ve

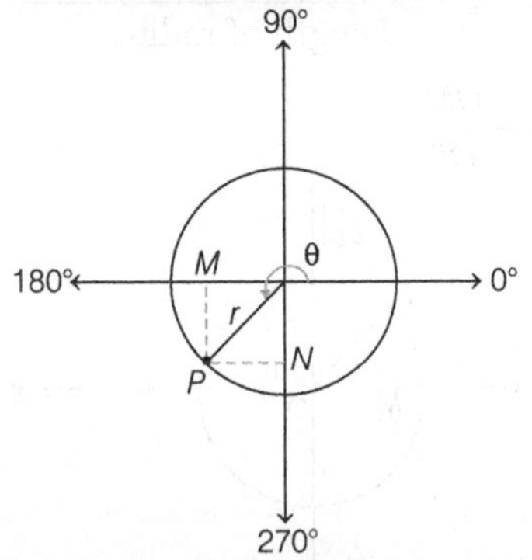

IV Quadrant : $270° < \theta < 360°$

$\sin\theta : (-)$ ve

$\cos\theta : (+)$ ve

$\tan\theta : (-)$ ve

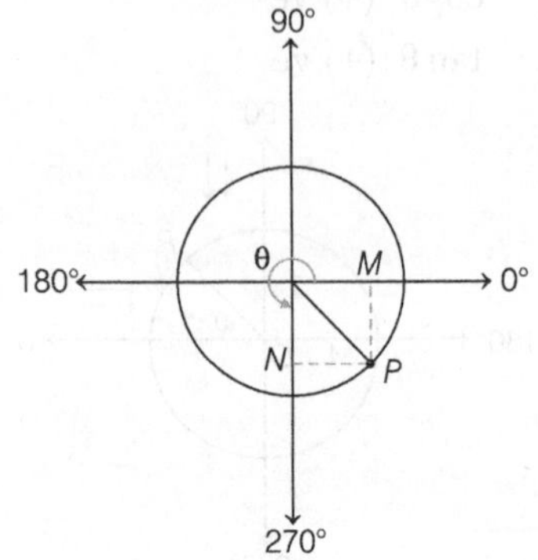

Summary

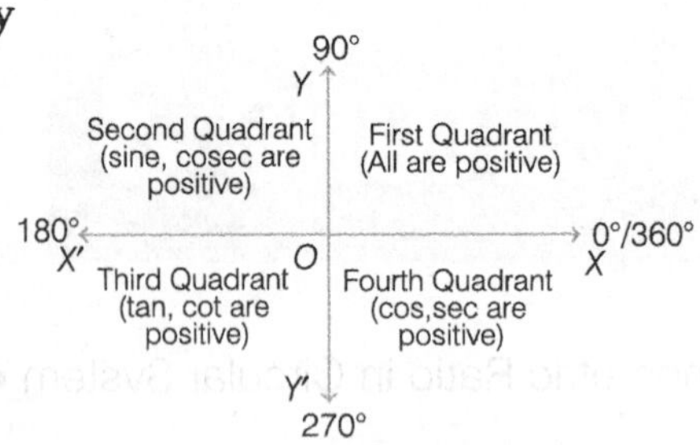

Quadrants →	I	II	III	IV
$\sin\theta$	+	+	−	−
$\cos\theta$	+	−	−	+
$\tan\theta$	+	−	+	−
$\text{cosec}\,\theta$	+	+	−	−
$\sec\theta$	+	−	−	+
$\cot\theta$	+	−	+	−

Example 36. If $\cos x = -\dfrac{1}{2}$ and $\pi < x < \dfrac{3\pi}{2}$, find the value of $4\tan^2 x - 3\,\text{cosec}^2\, x$.

Sol. It is given that x lies in the third quadrant. Therefore, $\sin x$ is negative and $\tan x$ is positive.

Thus, $\sin x = \pm\sqrt{1-\cos^2 x} \Rightarrow \sin x = -\sqrt{1-\dfrac{1}{4}} = -\dfrac{\sqrt{3}}{2}$

$\Rightarrow \text{cosec}\, x = -\dfrac{2}{\sqrt{3}}$

And $\tan x = \dfrac{\sin x}{\cos x} = \dfrac{-\dfrac{\sqrt{3}}{2}}{-\dfrac{1}{2}} = \sqrt{3}$

Hence, $4\tan^2 x - 3\,\text{cosec}^2\, x = 4\times 3 - 3\times\dfrac{4}{3} = 8.$

Example 37. Prove that

$$\sqrt{\frac{1-\sin x}{1+\sin x}} = \begin{cases} \sec x - \tan x, & \text{if } -\dfrac{\pi}{2} < x < \dfrac{\pi}{2} \\ -\sec x + \tan x, & \text{if } \dfrac{\pi}{2} < x < \dfrac{3\pi}{2} \end{cases}.$$

Sol. We have, $\sqrt{\dfrac{1-\sin x}{1+\sin x}} = \sqrt{\dfrac{(1-\sin x)^2}{1-\sin^2 x}} = \dfrac{1-\sin x}{\sqrt{\cos^2 x}} = \dfrac{1-\sin x}{|\cos x|}$

$$= \begin{cases} \dfrac{1-\sin x}{\cos x}, & \text{if } -\dfrac{\pi}{2} < x < \dfrac{\pi}{2} \\ \dfrac{1-\sin x}{-\cos x}, & \text{if } \dfrac{\pi}{2} < x < \dfrac{3\pi}{2} \end{cases}$$

$$= \begin{cases} \sec x - \tan x, & \text{if } -\dfrac{\pi}{2} < x < \dfrac{\pi}{2} \\ -\sec x + \tan x, & \text{if } \dfrac{\pi}{2} < x < \dfrac{3\pi}{2} \end{cases}$$

Example 38. How much is sin 120°?

Sol.
$$\sin 120^\circ = \frac{ON}{OP} \quad ...(i)$$
$$\Delta ONP \cong \Delta OM_1P_1$$
$$\frac{ON}{OP} = \frac{OM_1}{OP_1} \quad ...(ii)$$
$$\sin 120^\circ = \frac{ON}{OP} = \frac{OM_1}{OP_1}$$

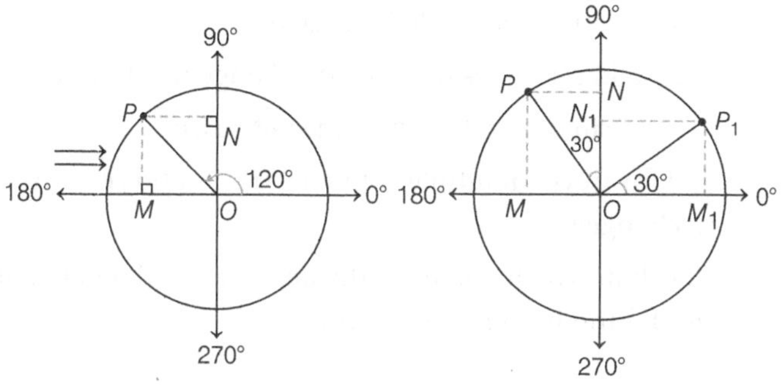

In ΔOM_1P_1, $\cos 30^\circ = \frac{OM_1}{OP_1}$, $\sin 120^\circ = \frac{OM_1}{OP_1} = \cos 30^\circ = \frac{\sqrt{3}}{2}$

$\therefore \quad \sin 120^\circ = \frac{\sqrt{3}}{2}$

Example 39. How much is cos 225°?

Sol.

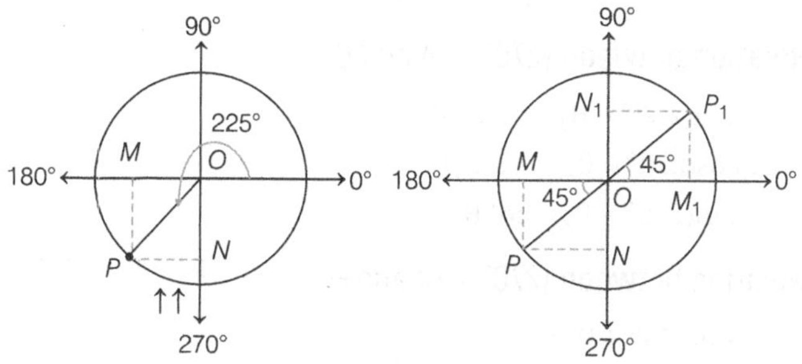

$$\cos 225^\circ = -\frac{OM}{OP}$$

In ΔOP_1M_1, $\cos 45^\circ = \frac{OM_1}{OP_1}$

ΔOPM and ΔOM_1P_1 are congruent.

i.e. $\quad \Delta OPM \cong \Delta OM_1P_1$
$$\frac{OM}{OP} = \frac{OM_1}{OP_1}$$
$$\cos 225^\circ = -\frac{OM}{OP} = -\frac{OM_1}{OP_1}$$
$$= -\cos 45^\circ = -\frac{1}{\sqrt{2}}$$
$$\cos 225^\circ = -\frac{1}{\sqrt{2}}$$

1.9 Trigonometric Ratios of Allied Angles

Allied Angles

If two angles are such that their sum or difference is zero or multiple of 90°, then they are called allied angles.

$$(60^\circ, 30^\circ) \xrightarrow{\text{Sum}} 90^\circ$$
$$(120^\circ, 60^\circ) \xrightarrow{\text{Sum}} 180^\circ$$
$$(120^\circ, 30^\circ) \xrightarrow{\text{Difference}} 90^\circ$$

Relation between $(90^\circ - \theta)$ and θ

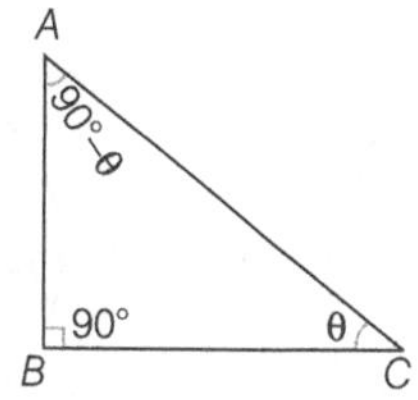

In right angled ΔABC,
$$\sin(90^\circ - \theta) = \frac{BC}{AC} \quad ...(i)$$
$$\cos\theta = \frac{BC}{AC} \quad ...(ii)$$

From Eqs. (i) and (ii), we get
$$\sin(90^\circ - \theta) = \cos\theta$$

Similarly,
$$\cos(90^\circ - \theta) = \frac{AB}{AC} = \sin\theta$$
$\Rightarrow \quad \mathbf{\cos(90^\circ - \theta) = \sin\theta}$

and $\quad \tan(90^\circ - \theta) = \frac{BC}{AB} = \cot\theta$

$\Rightarrow \quad \mathbf{\tan(90^\circ - \theta) = \cot\theta}$

Relation between $(90^\circ + \theta)$ and θ

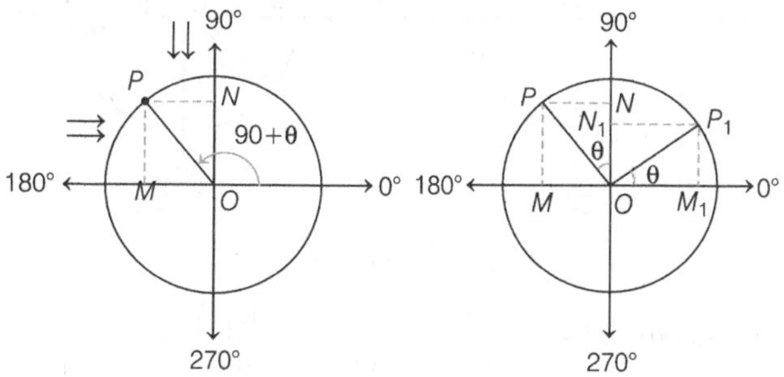

1. $\sin(90° + \theta) = \dfrac{ON}{OP}$

$\Delta OPN \cong \Delta OP_1M_1$

$\sin(90° + \theta) = \dfrac{ON}{OP} = \dfrac{OM_1}{OP_1} = \cos\theta$

$\Rightarrow$ $\mathbf{\sin(90° + \theta) = \cos\theta}$

2. $\cos(90° + \theta) = \dfrac{-OM}{OP} = \dfrac{-NP}{OP} = \dfrac{-M_1P_1}{OP_1} = -\sin\theta$

$\Rightarrow$ $\mathbf{\cos(90° + \theta) = -\sin\theta}$

3. $\mathbf{\tan(90° + \theta) = -\cot\theta}$

Relation between (180° – θ) and θ

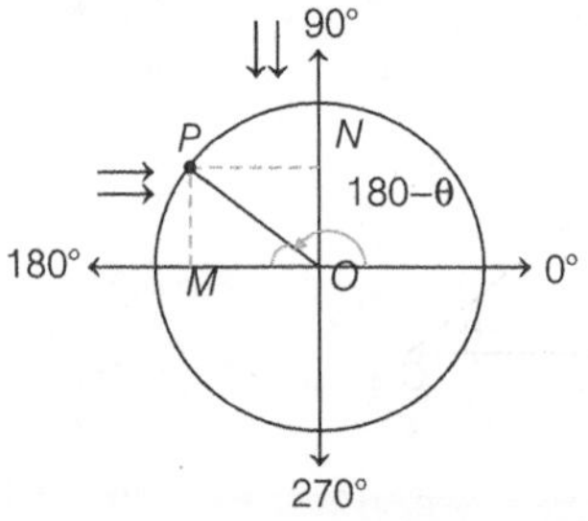

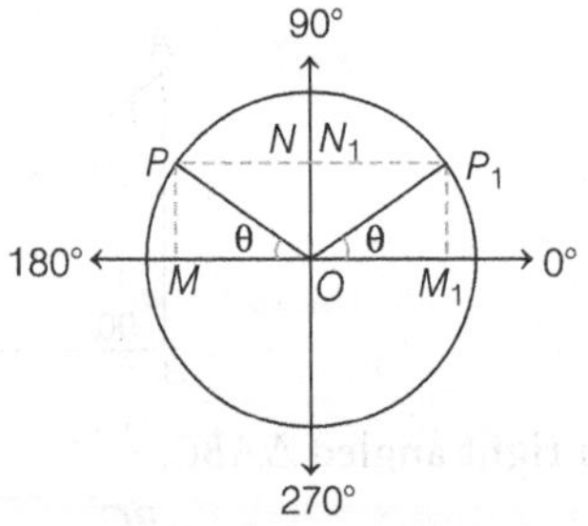

$\Delta OPM \cong \Delta OP_1M_1$

1. $\sin(180° - \theta) = \dfrac{ON}{OP} = \dfrac{MP}{OP} = \dfrac{M_1P_1}{OP_1} = \sin\theta$

$\Rightarrow$ $\mathbf{\sin(180° - \theta) = \sin\theta}$

2. $\cos(180° - \theta) = -\dfrac{OM}{OP} = -\dfrac{OM_1}{OP_1} = -\cos\theta$

$\Rightarrow$ $\mathbf{\cos(180° - \theta) = -\cos\theta}$

3. $\mathbf{\tan(180° - \theta) = -\tan\theta}$

Relation between (180° + θ) and θ

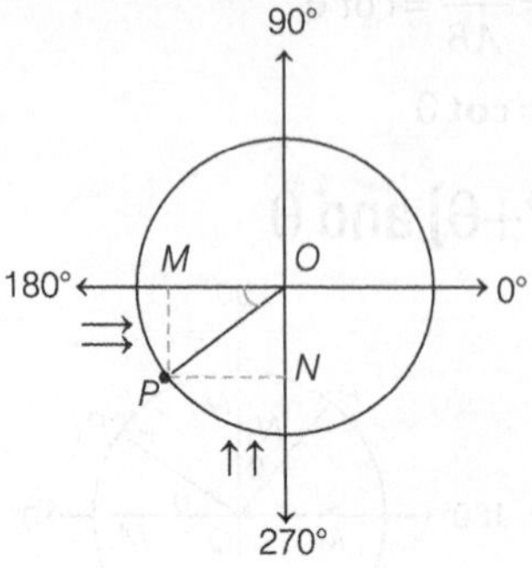

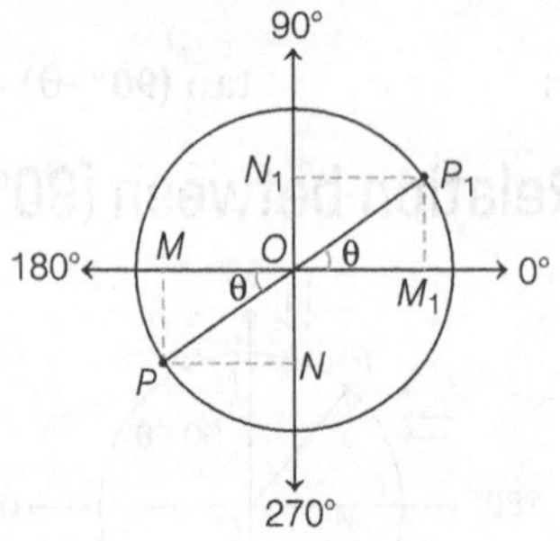

$\Delta OPM \cong \Delta OP_1M_1$

1. $\sin(180° + \theta) = -\dfrac{ON}{OP} = -\dfrac{MP}{OP} = \dfrac{-M_1P_1}{OP_1} = -\sin\theta$

$\Rightarrow$ $\mathbf{\sin(180° + \theta) = -\sin\theta}$

2. $\cos(180° + \theta) = -\dfrac{OM}{OP} = -\dfrac{OM_1}{OP_1} = -\cos\theta$

$\Rightarrow$ $\mathbf{\cos(180° + \theta) = -\cos\theta}$

3. $\mathbf{\tan(180° + \theta) = \tan\theta}$

How to Use in Questions ?

1. Check how allied angle is created?

   For [(odd multiples of 90°) ± θ], change the T-ratio

   sin ⇄ cos; tan ⇄ cot; sec ⇄ cosec

   and for [(even multiples of 90°) ± θ], T-ratio remains unchanged.

2. Check in which quadrant the angle lies and what sign the T-ratio has in that quadrant.

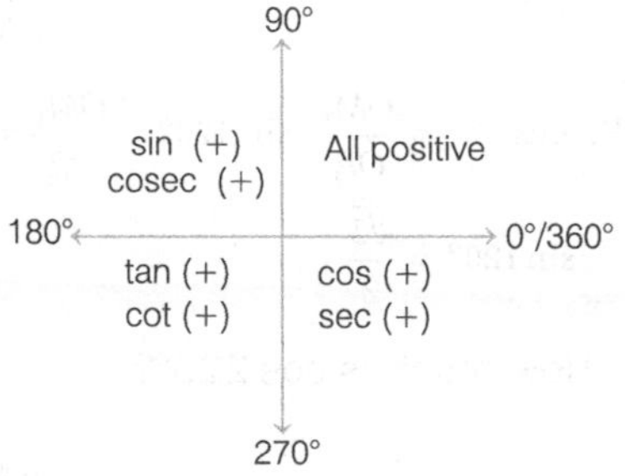

Relation between (270° – θ) and θ

1. $\sin(270° - \theta) = -\cos\theta$
2. $\cos(270° - \theta) = -\sin\theta$
3. $\tan(270° - \theta) = \cot\theta$

Relation between (270° + θ) and θ

1. $\sin(270° + \theta) = -\cos\theta$
2. $\cos(270° + \theta) = \sin\theta$
3. $\tan(270° + \theta) = -\cot\theta$

Relation between (360° – θ) and θ

1. $\sin(360° - \theta) = -\sin\theta$
2. $\cos(360° - \theta) = \cos\theta$
3. $\tan(360° - \theta) = -\tan\theta$

Relation between (360° + θ) and θ

1. $\sin(360° + \theta) = \sin\theta$
2. $\cos(360° + \theta) = \cos\theta$
3. $\tan(360° + \theta) = \tan\theta$

JEE Focus Points

- $\cos(n\pi \pm \theta) = (-1)^n \cos\theta$
- $\sin(n\pi + \theta) = (-1)^n \sin\theta$
- $\sin(n\pi - \theta) = (-1)^{n-1} \sin\theta$
- $(-\theta, \theta)$: **Allied Angles**
  - (i) $\sin(-\theta) = -\sin\theta$
  - (ii) $\cos(-\theta) = \cos\theta$
  - (iii) $\tan(-\theta) = -\tan\theta$

Concept Inside Video

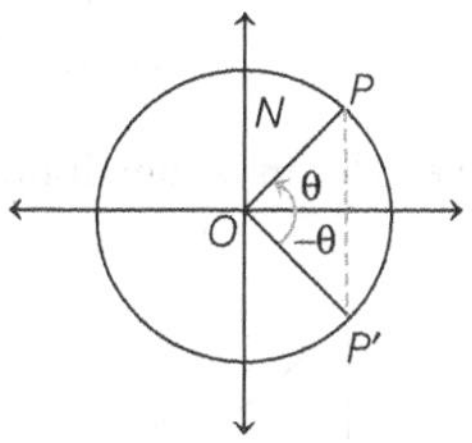

- Adding or subtracting multiple of 360° or $(2\pi)^c$ does not change the value of trigonometric ratio.
  $\sin(720° + \theta) = \sin(2 \times 360° + \theta) = \sin\theta$

Example 40. Find the value of

(i) $\sin(1050°)$ (ii) $\sin(120°)$

(iii) $\cos(120°)$ (iv) $\tan(120°)$

(v) $\sin(135°)$ (vi) $\sin\left(\frac{9\pi}{4}\right)$

(vii) $\sin\left(\frac{11\pi}{3}\right)$ (viii) $\cos\left(\frac{31\pi}{6}\right)$

(ix) $\tan\left(\frac{41\pi}{6}\right)$

Sol. (i) $\sin(1050°) = \sin(1080° - 30°) = \sin\left(6\pi - \frac{\pi}{6}\right) = \sin\left(-\frac{\pi}{6}\right)$

$= -\sin\frac{\pi}{6} = -\frac{1}{2}$

(ii) $\sin(120°) = \sin\left(\frac{2\pi}{3}\right) = \sin\left(\pi - \frac{\pi}{3}\right) = \sin\frac{\pi}{3} = \frac{\sqrt{3}}{2}$

(iii) $\cos(120°) = \cos\left(\frac{2\pi}{3}\right) = \cos\left(\pi - \frac{\pi}{3}\right) = -\cos\frac{\pi}{3} = -\frac{1}{2}$

(iv) $\tan(120°) = \tan\left(\frac{2\pi}{3}\right) = \tan\left(\pi - \frac{\pi}{3}\right) = -\tan\frac{\pi}{3} = -\sqrt{3}$

(v) $\sin(135°) = \sin\left(\frac{3\pi}{4}\right) = \sin\left(\pi - \frac{\pi}{4}\right) = \sin\left(\frac{\pi}{4}\right) = \frac{1}{\sqrt{2}}$

(vi) $\sin\left(\frac{9\pi}{4}\right) = \sin\left(2\pi + \frac{\pi}{4}\right) = \sin\left(\frac{\pi}{4}\right) = \frac{1}{\sqrt{2}}$

(vii) $\sin\left(\frac{11\pi}{3}\right) = \sin\left(4\pi - \frac{\pi}{3}\right) = -\sin\frac{\pi}{3} = -\frac{\sqrt{3}}{2}$

(viii) $\cos\left(\frac{31\pi}{6}\right) = \cos\left(5\pi + \frac{\pi}{6}\right) = \cos\left(\pi + \frac{\pi}{6}\right)$

$= -\cos\left(\frac{\pi}{6}\right) = -\frac{\sqrt{3}}{2}$

(ix) $\tan\left(\frac{41\pi}{6}\right) = \tan\left(7\pi - \frac{\pi}{6}\right)$

$= \tan\left(\pi - \frac{\pi}{6}\right) = -\tan\left(\frac{\pi}{6}\right) = -\frac{1}{\sqrt{3}}$

Example 41. Show that $\tan 1° \tan 2° \ldots \tan 89° = 1$

Sol. LHS $= (\tan 1° \tan 89°)(\tan 2° \cdot \tan 88°) \ldots$

$= [\tan 1° \tan(90° - 1°)] \cdot [\tan 2° \tan(90° - 2°)]$

$\ldots [\tan 44° \tan(90° - 44°)] \tan 45°$

$= (\tan 1° \cdot \cot 1°)(\tan 2° \cdot \cot 2°)$

$\ldots (\tan 44° \cdot \cot 44°) \tan 45°$

$= 1 =$ RHS $\quad [\because \tan\theta \cot\theta = 1 \text{ and } \tan 45° = 1]$

Example 42. Show that

$$\sin^2 5° + \sin^2 10° + \sin^2 15° + \ldots + \sin^2 90° = 9\frac{1}{2}$$

Sol. LHS $= (\sin^2 5° + \sin^2 85°) + (\sin^2 10° + \sin^2 80°)$

$+ \ldots + (\sin^2 40° + \sin^2 50°) + \sin^2 45° + \sin^2 90°$

$= (\sin^2 5° + \cos^2 5°) + (\sin^2 10 + \cos^2 10°)$

$+ \ldots + (\sin^2 40° + \cos^2 40°) + \sin^2 45° + \sin^2 90°$

$= (1 + 1 + 1 + 1 + 1 + 1 + 1 + 1) + \left(\frac{1}{\sqrt{2}}\right)^2 + 1$

$= 9\frac{1}{2} =$ RHS

Example 43. Find the value of

$$\cos^2\frac{\pi}{16} + \cos^2\frac{3\pi}{16} + \cos^2\frac{5\pi}{16} + \cos^2\frac{7\pi}{16}$$

Sol. $\cos^2\frac{\pi}{16} + \cos^2\frac{3\pi}{16} + \cos^2\left(\frac{\pi}{2} - \frac{3\pi}{16}\right) + \cos^2\left(\frac{\pi}{2} - \frac{\pi}{16}\right)$

$= \cos^2\frac{\pi}{16} + \cos^2\frac{3\pi}{16} + \sin^2\frac{3\pi}{16} + \sin^2\frac{\pi}{16}$

$= \left(\cos^2\frac{\pi}{16} + \sin^2\frac{\pi}{16}\right) + \left(\cos^2\frac{3\pi}{16} + \sin^2\frac{3\pi}{16}\right)$

$= 1 + 1 = 2$

Example 44. Find the value of

$$\sin(-420°)\cos(390°) + \cos(-660°)\sin(330°).$$

Sol. $\sin(-420°)\cos(390°) + \cos(-660°)\sin(330°)$

$= -\sin(420°)\cos(390°) + \cos(660°)\sin(330°)$

$= -\sin(90° \times 4 + 60°)\cos(90° \times 4 + 30°)$

$+ \cos(90° \times 7 + 30°)\sin(90° \times 3 + 60°)$

$= -(\sin 60°)(\cos 30°) + \sin(30°)(-\cos 60°)$

$= -\frac{\sqrt{3}}{2} \times \frac{\sqrt{3}}{2} + \frac{1}{2} \times \left(-\frac{1}{2}\right)$

$= -\frac{3}{4} - \frac{1}{4} = -1$

Example 45. If $\sin(140° - \alpha) = \sin(140° - \beta)$, $0° < \alpha, \beta < 180°$, then find the relation between α and β.

Sol. If $\sin A = \sin B$,

where $A = 140° - \alpha$ and $B = 140° - \beta$,

then $A = B$ or $A = \pi - B$ i.e. $A + B = \pi$

$\Rightarrow 140° - \alpha = 140° - \beta$ or $140° - \alpha + 140° - \beta = 180°$

$\Rightarrow \quad \alpha = \beta$ or $\alpha + \beta = 100°$

Example 46. Find the sign of the values of $\tan 114° - \cos 106° = a$ and $\cot 106° + \sin 107° = b$.

Sol. $a = \tan 114° - \cos 106°$

$= \cos 74° - \tan 66° < \cos 74° - \tan 45° < 0$

$\therefore$ Sign of a is negative.

$b = \cot 106° + \sin 107°$

$= \sin 73° - \cot 74° > \sin 73° - \cot 90° = \sin 73° > 0$

$\therefore$ Sign of b is positive.

Example 47. Find the value of $\sec(270° - A)\sec(90° - A) - \tan(270° - A)\tan(90° + A)$

(a) 1 (b) −1

(c) 0 (d) None of these

Sol. (b) $\sec(270° - A)\sec(90° - A) - \tan(270° - A)\tan(90° + A)$

$= (-\operatorname{cosec} A)(\operatorname{cosec} A) - (\cot A)(-\cot A)$

$= -\operatorname{cosec}^2 A + \cot^2 A$

$= -[\operatorname{cosec}^2 A - \cot^2 A] = -1$

Example 48. Find the value of $\tan 225° \cot 405° + \tan 765° \cot 675°$.

(a) 1 (b) −1

(c) 0 (d) None of these

Sol. (c) $\tan 225° \cot 405° + \tan 765° \cot 675°$

$= \tan(180° + 45°)\cot(360° + 45°) + \tan(2 \times 360° + 45°)\cot(2 \times 360° - 45°)$

$= (\tan 45°)(\cot 45°) + (\tan 45°)(-\cot 45°)$

$= 1 \times 1 + 1 \times (-1)$

$= 1 - 1 = 0$

Example 49. Find the value of $\sin\left(\frac{3\pi}{5}\right) + \sin\left(\frac{4\pi}{5}\right) + \sin\left(\frac{6\pi}{5}\right) + \sin\left(\frac{7\pi}{5}\right)$.

Sol. $\sin\left(\frac{3\pi}{5}\right) + \sin\left(\frac{4\pi}{5}\right) + \sin\left(\frac{6\pi}{5}\right) + \sin\left(\frac{7\pi}{5}\right)$

$= \sin\left(\frac{3\pi}{5}\right) + \sin\left(\frac{4\pi}{5}\right) + \sin\left(2\pi - \frac{4\pi}{5}\right) + \sin\left(2\pi - \frac{3\pi}{5}\right)$

$= \sin\left(\frac{3\pi}{5}\right) + \sin\left(\frac{4\pi}{5}\right) - \sin\left(\frac{4\pi}{5}\right) - \sin\left(\frac{3\pi}{5}\right)$

$= 0$

Example 50. If $\tan\theta = \frac{3}{4}$ and θ is not in the Ist quadrant, then the find the value of $\frac{\sin(90° + \theta) - \cot(180° - \theta)}{\tan(270° - \theta) - \cos(270° + \theta)}$.

Sol. $\frac{\sin(90° + \theta) - \cot(180° - \theta)}{\tan(270° - \theta) - \cos(270° + \theta)} = \frac{\cos\theta - (-\cot\theta)}{\cot\theta - \sin\theta}$

$= \frac{\cos\theta + \cot\theta}{\cot\theta - \sin\theta}$

$\tan\theta = \frac{3}{4} = (+)$ ve : Not in Ist quadrant hence θ will be in IIIrd Quadrant.

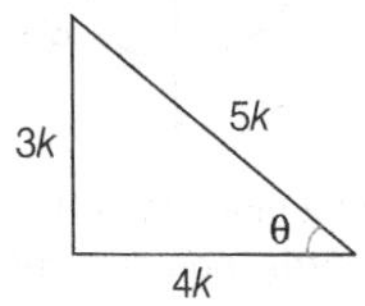

In IIIrd Quadrant,

$\sin\theta = -\frac{3}{5}$, $\cos\theta = -\frac{4}{5}$ and $\cot\theta = \frac{4}{3}$

$= \frac{\cos\theta + \cot\theta}{\cot\theta - \sin\theta} = \frac{-\frac{4}{5} + \frac{4}{3}}{\frac{4}{3} + \frac{3}{5}} = \frac{\frac{-12 + 20}{15}}{\frac{20 + 9}{15}} = \frac{8}{29}$

Example 51. If A, B, C, D are angles of a cyclic quadrilateral, then prove that $\cos A + \cos B + \cos C + \cos D = 0$.

Sol. We know that the opposite angles of a cyclic quadrilateral are supplementary

i.e. $A + C = \pi$ and $B + D = \pi$.

Therefore, $A = \pi - C$ and $B = \pi - D$

$\Rightarrow \quad \cos A = \cos(\pi - C) = -\cos C$

and $\quad \cos B = \cos(\pi - D) = -\cos D$

$\therefore \cos A + \cos B + \cos C + \cos D$

$= -\cos C - \cos D + \cos C + \cos D = 0$

Example 52. If $\theta = \frac{\pi}{4n}$, then find the value of $\tan\theta \tan 2\theta \ldots \tan[(2n-2)\theta]\tan[(2n-1)\theta]$.

Sol. We have, $\theta = \frac{\pi}{4n}$ or $2n\theta = \frac{\pi}{2}$

$\therefore \quad \theta, (2n-1)\theta = \left(\frac{\pi}{2}\right) - \theta \Rightarrow 2\theta, (2n-2)\theta = \left(\frac{\pi}{2}\right) - 2\theta, \ldots$

They form complementary angles A and B so that $\tan A \tan B = \tan A \cot A = 1$ for each pair.

Also, $\tan(n\theta) = \tan\frac{\pi}{4} = 1$.

Hence, the value of product is 1.

Milestone Practice 1.3

1. Find the values of cos x and tan x, if $\sin x = -\frac{3}{5}$ and $\pi < x < \frac{3\pi}{2}$.

2. Find all other trigonometric ratios, if $\sin x = \frac{-2\sqrt{6}}{5}$ and x lies in quadrant III.

3. If $\sin\theta = \frac{21}{29}$ and 'θ' lies in the second quadrant, show that $\sec\theta + \tan\theta = -\frac{5}{2}$.

4. If $\sec x = \sqrt{2}$ and $\frac{3\pi}{2} < x < 2\pi$, find the value of $\frac{1 + \tan x + \operatorname{cosec} x}{1 + \cot x - \operatorname{cosec} x}$.

5. Prove that

$$\sqrt{\frac{1-\sin x}{1+\sin x}} + \sqrt{\frac{1+\sin x}{1-\sin x}} = \begin{cases} \frac{2}{\cos x}, & \text{if } 0 \le x < \frac{\pi}{2} \\ \frac{-2}{\cos x}, & \text{if } \frac{\pi}{2} < x \le \frac{3\pi}{2} \end{cases}$$

6. Evaluate the following.
   (i) $\sin\left(\frac{7\pi}{4}\right)$ (ii) $\cos\frac{7\pi}{6}$
   (iii) $\cos\left(\frac{-8\pi}{6}\right)$ (iv) $\sin\left(\frac{-25\pi}{4}\right)$

7. Evaluate the following.
   (i) cosec 390° (ii) cot 570°
   (iii) tan 480° (iv) cos 270°
   (v) $\tan\frac{19\pi}{3}$ (vi) $\sin\left(-\frac{11\pi}{3}\right)$
   (vii) $\cot\left(-\frac{15\pi}{4}\right)$

8. Find the value of expression

$$3\left\{\sin^4\left(\frac{3\pi}{2} - x\right) + \sin^4(3\pi + x)\right\} - 2\left\{\sin^6\left(\frac{\pi}{2} + x\right) + \sin^6(5\pi - x)\right\}.$$

9. Prove that
   (i) $\cos 24^\circ + \cos 55^\circ + \cos 125^\circ + \cos 204^\circ + \cos 300^\circ = \frac{1}{2}$
   (ii) $\cos 570^\circ \sin 510^\circ + \sin(-330^\circ)\cos(-390^\circ) = 0$
   (iii) $\sin\frac{8\pi}{3}\cos\frac{23\pi}{6} + \cos\frac{13\pi}{3}\sin\frac{35\pi}{6} = \frac{1}{2}$
   (iv) $\tan\frac{11\pi}{3} - 2\sin\frac{4\pi}{6} - \frac{3}{4}\operatorname{cosec}^2\frac{\pi}{4} + 4\cos^2\frac{17\pi}{6} = \frac{3-4\sqrt{3}}{2}$

10. If $\alpha = \frac{\pi}{3}$, prove that $\cos\alpha\cos 2\alpha\cos 3\alpha\cos 4\alpha\cos 5\alpha\cos 6\alpha = -\frac{1}{16}$.

11. Find the value of $\tan\frac{\pi}{20}\tan\frac{3\pi}{20}\tan\frac{5\pi}{20}\tan\frac{7\pi}{20}\tan\frac{9\pi}{20}$.

12. In ΔPQR, show that
   (i) $\sin\left(\frac{P+Q}{2}\right) = \cos\frac{R}{2}$
   (ii) $\cos Q = -\cos(P+R)$
   (iii) $\sin P = \sin(Q+R)$

13. In any quadrilateral $PQRS$, prove that $\cos(P+Q) = \cos(R+S)$.

14. Find the value of $\sum_{r=1}^{9}\sin^2\left(\frac{r\pi}{18}\right)$.

15. The value of $\frac{\cot 54^\circ}{\tan 36^\circ} + \frac{\tan 20^\circ}{\cot 70^\circ}$ is
   (a) 1 (b) 0 (c) -1 (d) 2

16. If θ lies in the second quadrant, then the value of $\sqrt{\frac{1-\sin\theta}{1+\sin\theta}} + \sqrt{\frac{1+\sin\theta}{1-\sin\theta}}$.
   (a) $2\sec\theta$ (b) $-2\sec\theta$
   (c) $2\cos\theta$ (d) $-2\cos\theta$

17. The value of x from the equation $\operatorname{cosec}(90^\circ + \theta) + x\cos\theta\cot(90^\circ + \theta) = \sin(90^\circ + \theta)$ is
   (a) $\sin\theta$ (b) $\cos\theta$ (c) $\tan\theta$ (d) $\sec\theta$

18. If $\tan\theta = \frac{x\sin\phi}{1 - x\cos\phi}$ and $\tan\phi = \frac{y\sin\theta}{1 - y\cos\theta}$, then $\frac{x}{y}$ equals to
   (a) $\frac{\sin\phi}{\sin\theta}$ (b) $\frac{\sin\theta}{\sin\phi}$
   (c) $\frac{\sin\phi}{1-\cos\theta}$ (d) $\frac{\sin\theta}{1-\cos\phi}$

19. The value of

$e^{\log_{10} \tan 1° + \log_{10} \tan 2° + \log_{10} \tan 3° + \dots + \log_{10} \tan 89°}$ is

(a) 0 (b) e

(c) $\frac{1}{e}$ (d) None of these

20. Find set of all possible values of α in $[-\pi, \pi]$. Such that $\sqrt{\frac{1-\sin\alpha}{1+\sin\alpha}}$ is equal to $(\sec\alpha - \tan\alpha)$.

(a) $0 < \alpha < \frac{\pi}{3}$ (b) $-\pi < \alpha < \frac{\pi}{4}$

(c) $-\frac{\pi}{2} < \alpha < \frac{\pi}{2}$ (d) $-\pi < \alpha < \pi$

21. The value of $\cos 1° + \cos 2° + \cos 3° + \dots + \cos 180°$ is

(a) 1 (b) -1

(c) 0 (d) None of these

22. The value of $\sin 1 \cdot \cos 2 \cdot \tan 3 \cdot \cot 4 \cdot \sec 5 \cdot \operatorname{cosec} 6$ is

(a) positive

(b) negative

(c) zero

(d) May be positive and negative

23. The value of the expression $\log_{10}(\tan 6°) + \log_{10}(\tan 12°) + \log_{10}(\tan 18°) + \dots + \log_{10}(\tan 84°)$ is

(a) -1

(b) 0

(c) 1

(d) 2

24. Let $f(\theta) = \frac{1}{1+(\cot\theta)^2}$ and $S = \sum_{\theta=1°}^{89°} f(\theta)$, then find the value of S.

Answer Key

1. $\cos x = -\frac{4}{5}$ and $\tan x = \frac{3}{4}$
2. $\cos x = -\frac{1}{5}$, $\tan x = 2\sqrt{6}$, $\operatorname{cosec} x = -\frac{5}{2\sqrt{6}}$, $\sec x = -5$, $\cot x = \frac{1}{2\sqrt{6}}$
4. -1
6. (i) $-\frac{1}{\sqrt{2}}$ (ii) $-\frac{\sqrt{3}}{2}$ (iii) $-\frac{1}{2}$ (iv) $-\frac{1}{\sqrt{2}}$
7. (i) 2 (ii) $\sqrt{3}$ (iii) $-\sqrt{3}$ (iv) 0 (v) $\sqrt{3}$ (vi) $\frac{\sqrt{3}}{2}$ (vii) 1
8. 1

11. 1	14. 5	15. (d)	16. (b)	
17. (c)	18. (b)	19. (d)	20. (c)	
21. (b)	22. (b)	23. (b)	24. 44.5	

For Detailed Solution

Milestone 4 Trigonometric Functions of Compound Angles

- Trigonometric Ratios of Compound Angles • Extended Compound Angle Formulae

1.10 Trigonometric Ratios of Compounds Angles

Algebraic sum of two or more angles is called a compound angle such as $A+B$, $A-B$, $A+B+C$, $A+B-C$, etc.

Formulae for the Trigonometric Ratio of Sum and Difference of Two Angles

1. $\sin(A+B)=\sin A\cos B+\cos A\sin B$
2. $\sin(A-B)=\sin A\cos B-\cos A\sin B$
3. $\cos(A+B)=\cos A\cos B-\sin A\sin B$
4. $\cos(A-B)=\cos A\cos B+\sin A\sin B$
5. $\tan(A+B)=\dfrac{\tan A+\tan B}{1-\tan A\tan B}$,

   where $A\neq n\pi+\dfrac{\pi}{2}$, $B\neq n\pi+\dfrac{\pi}{2}$ and $A\pm B\neq m\pi+\dfrac{\pi}{2}$
6. $\tan(A-B)=\dfrac{\tan A-\tan B}{1+\tan A\tan B}$,

   where $A\neq n\pi+\dfrac{\pi}{2}$, $B\neq n\pi+\dfrac{\pi}{2}$ and $A\pm B\neq m\pi+\dfrac{\pi}{2}$
7. $\cot(A+B)=\dfrac{\cot A\cot B-1}{\cot A+\cot B}$,

   where $A\neq n\pi$, $B\neq n\pi$ and $A\pm B\neq m\pi$
8. $\cot(A-B)=\dfrac{\cot A\cot B+1}{\cot B-\cot A}$,

   where $A\neq n\pi$, $B\neq n\pi$ and $A\pm B\neq m\pi$

JEE Focus Points

- $\sin(A+B)\cdot\sin(A-B)=\sin^2 A-\sin^2 B$
  $=\cos^2 B-\cos^2 A$
- $\cos(A+B)\cdot\cos(A-B)=\cos^2 A-\sin^2 B$
  $=\cos^2 B-\sin^2 A$

Example 53. Prove that

$$\sin(\alpha+\beta)\cos(\alpha-\beta)+\cos(\alpha+\beta)\sin(\alpha-\beta)=\sin 2\alpha.$$

Sol. Let $\alpha+\beta=A$ and $\alpha-\beta=B$

$$\text{LHS}=\sin A\cos B+\cos A\sin B=\sin(A+B)$$
$$=\sin(\alpha+\beta+\alpha-\beta)=\sin 2\alpha=\text{RHS}$$

Example 54. Simplify $\dfrac{\cos\theta+\sin\theta}{\cos\theta-\sin\theta}$.

Sol. Given expression,

$$\frac{\cos\theta+\sin\theta}{\cos\theta-\sin\theta}=\frac{1+\tan\theta}{1-\tan\theta}=\frac{\tan\frac{\pi}{4}+\tan\theta}{1-\tan\frac{\pi}{4}\tan\theta}=\tan\left(\frac{\pi}{4}+\theta\right)$$

Example 55. If $\tan A+\tan B=p$ and $\cot A+\cot B=q$, then $\cot(A+B)$ is

(a) $\dfrac{p-q}{pq}$ (b) $\dfrac{p+q}{pq}$

(c) $\dfrac{q-p}{pq}$ (d) None of these

Sol. (c) $\cot(A+B)=\dfrac{1}{\tan(A+B)}=\dfrac{1-\tan A\tan B}{\tan A+\tan B}$

$\tan A+\tan B=p$ and $\cot A+\cot B=q$

$$\Rightarrow \frac{1}{\tan A}+\frac{1}{\tan B}=q$$

$$\Rightarrow \frac{\tan A+\tan B}{\tan A\tan B}=q\Rightarrow \tan A\tan B=\frac{p}{q}$$

$$\Rightarrow \cot(A+B)=\frac{\cot A\cot B-1}{\cot A+\cot B}=\frac{\frac{q}{p}-1}{q}=\frac{q-p}{pq}$$

Example 56. If $\tan 70^\circ=\tan 20^\circ+k\tan 50^\circ$, then k is equal to

(a) 1 (b) 2

(c) 3 (d) None of these

Sol. (b) $\tan 70^\circ=\tan(50^\circ+20^\circ)=\dfrac{\tan 50^\circ+\tan 20^\circ}{1-\tan 50^\circ\tan 20^\circ}$

$$\Rightarrow \tan 70^\circ-\tan 20^\circ\tan 50^\circ\tan 70^\circ=\tan 20^\circ+\tan 50^\circ$$
$$\Rightarrow \tan 70^\circ-\tan(90^\circ-70^\circ)\tan 50^\circ\tan 70^\circ=\tan 20^\circ+\tan 50^\circ$$
$$\Rightarrow \tan 70^\circ-\cot 70^\circ\tan 50^\circ\tan 70^\circ=\tan 20^\circ+\tan 50^\circ$$
$$\Rightarrow \tan 70^\circ-\tan 50^\circ=\tan 20^\circ+\tan 50^\circ$$
$$\Rightarrow \tan 70^\circ=\tan 20^\circ+2\tan 50^\circ$$

Hence, $k=2$

Example 57. If $\sin\alpha\sin\beta-\cos\alpha\cos\beta+1=0$, then prove that $1+\cot\alpha\tan\beta=0$

Sol. Given, $\sin\alpha\sin\beta-\cos\alpha\cos\beta+1=0$

$$\Rightarrow \quad \cos\alpha\cos\beta-\sin\alpha\sin\beta=1$$

$$\Rightarrow \quad \cos(\alpha+\beta)=1 \quad \text{...(i)}$$

Now, $1+\cot\alpha\tan\beta=1+\dfrac{\cos\alpha}{\sin\alpha}\cdot\dfrac{\sin\beta}{\cos\beta}$

$$=\frac{\sin\alpha\cos\beta+\cos\alpha\sin\beta}{\sin\alpha\cos\beta}$$

$$=\frac{\sin(\alpha+\beta)}{\sin\alpha\cos\beta}=\frac{0}{\sin\alpha\cos\beta}=0$$

$$[\because \sin^2(\alpha+\beta)=1-\cos^2(\alpha+\beta)=1-1=0]$$

Example 58. If $\tan\beta=\dfrac{n\sin\alpha\cos\alpha}{1-n\sin^2\alpha}$, then prove that $\tan(\alpha-\beta)=(1-n)\tan\alpha$.

Sol. $\tan\beta=\dfrac{n\sin\alpha\cos\beta}{1-n\sin^2\alpha}=\dfrac{\dfrac{n\sin\alpha\cos\alpha}{\cos^2\alpha}}{\dfrac{1}{\cos^2\alpha}-\dfrac{n\sin^2\alpha}{\cos^2\alpha}}$

[dividing numerator and denominator by $\cos^2\alpha$]

$$=\frac{n\tan\alpha}{\sec^2\alpha-n\tan^2\alpha}=\frac{n\tan\alpha}{1+\tan^2\alpha-n\tan^2\alpha}$$

$$=\frac{n\tan\alpha}{1+(1-n)\tan^2\alpha} \quad \text{...(i)}$$

Now, LHS $=\tan(\alpha-\beta)=\dfrac{\tan\alpha-\tan\beta}{1+\tan\alpha\tan\beta}$

$$=\frac{\tan\alpha-\dfrac{n\tan\alpha}{1+(1-n)\tan^2\alpha}}{1+\tan\alpha\dfrac{n\tan\alpha}{1+(1-n)\tan^2\alpha}} \quad \text{[from Eqs. (i)]}$$

$$=\frac{\tan\alpha+(1-n)\tan^3\alpha-n\tan\alpha}{1+(1-n)\tan^2\alpha+n\tan^2\alpha}$$

$$=\frac{(1-n)\tan\alpha+(1-n)\tan^3\alpha}{1+\tan^2\alpha}$$

$$=\frac{(1-n)\tan\alpha(1+\tan^2\alpha)}{1+\tan^2\alpha}=(1-n)\tan\alpha$$

Example 59. In a ΔABC, angle A is an obtuse angle such that $\sin A=\dfrac{3}{5}$ and $\sin B=\dfrac{5}{13}$, then find the value of $\sin C$.

Sol. In ΔABC, $A+B+C=\pi$ or $A+B=\pi-C$

$$\sin(A+B)=\sin(\pi-C)=\sin C$$

$$\sin C=\sin(A+B)$$

$$\sin C=\sin A\cos B+\cos A\sin B$$

$$\sin A=\frac{3}{5}$$

$$\cos^2 A=1-\sin^2 A=1-\frac{9}{25}=\frac{16}{25}$$

$$\cos A=\pm\frac{4}{5}$$

Since, A is obtuse.

$$\cos A=-\frac{4}{5}$$

$$\sin B=\frac{5}{13}$$

$$\cos^2 B=1-\sin^2 B=1-\frac{25}{169}=\frac{12}{13}$$

$$\cos B=\pm\frac{12}{13}$$

Since, B is acute.

$$\cos B=\frac{12}{13}$$

$$\sin C=\sin A\cos B+\cos A\sin B$$

$$\sin C=\frac{3}{5}\times\frac{12}{13}+\left(-\frac{4}{5}\right)\times\frac{5}{13}$$

$$\sin C=\frac{36-20}{65}=\frac{16}{65}$$

Example 60. Let A, B, C be the three angles such that $A+B+C=\pi$. If $\tan A\cdot\tan B=2$, then find the value of $\dfrac{\cos A\cos B}{\cos C}$.

Sol. Given, $\tan A\cdot\tan B=2$

Let $\quad y=\dfrac{\cos A\cos B}{\cos C}=-\dfrac{\cos A\cdot\cos B}{\cos(A+B)}$

$$[\because \cos C=\cos(\pi-(A+B)=-\cos(A+B)]$$

$$=\frac{\cos A\cdot\cos B}{\sin A\sin B-\cos A\cos B}$$

$$=\frac{1}{\tan A\tan B-1}=\frac{1}{2-1}=1$$

Example 61. If $\sin(A-B)=\dfrac{1}{\sqrt{10}}$, $\cos(A+B)=\dfrac{2}{\sqrt{29}}$, find the value of $\tan 2A$ where A and B lie between 0 and $\dfrac{\pi}{4}$.

Sol. $\tan 2A=\tan[(A+B)+(A-B)]$

$$=\frac{\tan(A+B)+\tan(A-B)}{1-\tan(A+B)\tan(A-B)} \quad \text{...(i)}$$

Given that, $0<A<\dfrac{\pi}{4}$ and $0<B<\dfrac{\pi}{4}$.

Therefore, $\quad 0<A+B<\dfrac{\pi}{2}$

Also, $-\frac{\pi}{4} < A - B < \frac{\pi}{4}$ and $\sin(A - B) = \frac{1}{\sqrt{10}}$

$\therefore \quad 0 < A - B < \frac{\pi}{4}$

Now, $\sin(A - B) = \frac{1}{\sqrt{10}} \Rightarrow \tan(A - B) = \frac{1}{3}$ ...(ii)

$$\cos(A + B) = \frac{2}{\sqrt{29}}$$

$\Rightarrow \quad \tan(A + B) = \frac{5}{2}$ ...(iii)

From Eqs. (i), (ii) and (iii), we get

$$\tan 2A = \frac{\frac{5}{2} + \frac{1}{3}}{1 - \frac{5}{2} \times \frac{1}{3}} = \frac{17}{6} \times \frac{6}{1} = 17$$

Example 62. Prove that

$$(1 + \tan 1^\circ)(1 + \tan 2^\circ) \ldots (1 + \tan 45^\circ) = 2^{23}.$$

Sol. $(1 + \tan x)(1 + \tan(45^\circ - x))$

$$= (1 + \tan x)\left(1 + \frac{1 - \tan x}{1 + \tan x}\right) = 2$$

$\therefore \ (1 + \tan 1^\circ)(1 + \tan 44^\circ)$

$= (1 + \tan 2^\circ)(1 + \tan 43^\circ)$

$= (1 + \tan 3^\circ)(1 + \tan 42^\circ)$

...

...

$= (1 + \tan 22^\circ)(1 + \tan 23^\circ) = 2$

$(1 + \tan 1^\circ)(1 + \tan 2^\circ) \ldots (1 + \tan 45^\circ) = 2^{23}$

[as $1 + \tan 45^\circ = 2$]

Example 63. If $\cos(\beta - \gamma) + \cos(\gamma - \alpha) + \cos(\alpha - \beta) = -\frac{3}{2}$, then prove that

$\cos \alpha + \cos \beta + \cos \gamma = \sin \alpha + \sin \beta + \sin \gamma = 0$.

Sol. Given, $\cos(\beta - \gamma) + \cos(\gamma - \alpha) + \cos(\alpha - \beta) = -\frac{3}{2}$

$\Rightarrow 3 + 2\cos(\beta - \gamma) + 2\cos(\gamma - \alpha) + 2\cos(\alpha - \beta) = 0$

$\Rightarrow 3 + 2(\cos \beta \cos \gamma + \sin \beta \sin \gamma)$

$+ 2(\cos \gamma \cos \alpha + \sin \gamma \sin \alpha)$

$+ 2(\cos \alpha \cos \beta + \sin \alpha \sin \beta) = 0$

$\Rightarrow (\cos^2 \alpha + \sin^2 \alpha) + (\cos^2 \beta + \sin^2 \beta) + (\cos^2 \gamma + \sin^2 \gamma)$

$+ 2(\cos \beta \cos \gamma + \sin \beta \sin \gamma) + 2(\cos \gamma \cos \alpha + \sin \gamma \sin \alpha)$

$+ 2(\cos \alpha \cos \beta + \sin \alpha \sin \beta) = 0$

$\Rightarrow (\cos^2 \alpha + \cos^2 \beta + \cos^2 \gamma + 2\cos \alpha \cos \beta + 2\cos \beta \cos \gamma$

$+ 2\cos \gamma \cos \alpha) + (\sin^2 \alpha + \sin^2 \beta + \sin^2 \gamma$

$+ 2\sin \alpha \sin \beta + 2\sin \beta \sin \gamma + 2\sin \gamma \sin \alpha) = 0$

$\Rightarrow (\cos \alpha + \cos \beta + \cos \gamma)^2 + (\sin \alpha + \sin \beta + \sin \gamma)^2 = 0$

which is possible only when

$\cos \alpha + \cos \beta + \cos \gamma = 0$ and $\sin \alpha + \sin \beta + \sin \gamma = 0$

Example 64. If $\tan x \tan y = a$ and $x + y = \frac{\pi}{6}$, then $\tan x$ and $\tan y$ satisfy the equation

(a) $t^2 - \sqrt{3}(1 - a)t + a = 0$

(b) $\sqrt{3}t^2 - (1 - a)t + a\sqrt{3} = 0$

(c) $t^2 + \sqrt{3}(1 + a)t - a = 0$

(d) $\sqrt{3}t^2 - (1 + a)t - a\sqrt{3} = 0$

Sol. (b) $\tan x \tan y = a$ and $x + y = \frac{\pi}{6}$

$$\tan(x + y) = \tan \frac{\pi}{6}$$

$\Rightarrow \quad \frac{\tan x + \tan y}{1 - \tan x \tan y} = \frac{1}{\sqrt{3}} \Rightarrow \tan x + \tan y = \frac{1 - a}{\sqrt{3}}$

If $\tan x$ and $\tan y$ are the roots of quadratic equation,

$$t^2 - (\tan x + \tan y)t + \tan x \tan y = 0$$

$\Rightarrow \quad t^2 - \left(\frac{1 - a}{\sqrt{3}}\right)t + a = 0$

$\Rightarrow \quad \sqrt{3}t^2 - (1 - a)t + a\sqrt{3} = 0$

T-Ratios for 75°

1. $\sin 75^\circ = \sin(45^\circ + 30^\circ)$

$= \sin 45^\circ \cos 30^\circ + \cos 45^\circ \sin 30^\circ$

$$\sin 75^\circ = \frac{1}{\sqrt{2}} \times \frac{\sqrt{3}}{2} + \frac{1}{\sqrt{2}} \times \frac{1}{2} = \frac{\sqrt{3} + 1}{2\sqrt{2}}$$

2. $\cos 75^\circ = \cos(45^\circ + 30^\circ)$

$= \cos 45^\circ \cos 30^\circ - \sin 45^\circ \sin 30^\circ$

$$\cos 75^\circ = \frac{1}{\sqrt{2}} \times \frac{\sqrt{3}}{2} - \frac{1}{\sqrt{2}} \times \frac{1}{2} = \frac{\sqrt{3} - 1}{2\sqrt{2}}$$

3. $\tan 75^\circ = \frac{\sin 75^\circ}{\cos 75^\circ} = \frac{\sqrt{3} + 1}{\sqrt{3} - 1}$

T-Ratios for 15°

1. $\sin 15^\circ = \sin(45^\circ - 30^\circ)$

$= \sin 45^\circ \cos 30^\circ - \cos 45^\circ \sin 30^\circ$

$$\sin 15^\circ = \frac{1}{\sqrt{2}} \cdot \frac{\sqrt{3}}{2} - \frac{1}{\sqrt{2}} \cdot \frac{1}{2} = \frac{\sqrt{3} - 1}{2\sqrt{2}}$$

Or

$$\sin 15^\circ = \sin(90^\circ - 75^\circ) = \cos 75^\circ = \frac{\sqrt{3} - 1}{2\sqrt{2}}$$

$$\mathbf{\sin 15^\circ = \cos 75^\circ = \frac{\sqrt{3} - 1}{2\sqrt{2}}}$$

2. $\cos 15^\circ = \cos(90^\circ - 75^\circ) = \sin 75^\circ = \frac{\sqrt{3} + 1}{2\sqrt{2}}$

$$\mathbf{\cos 15^\circ = \sin 75^\circ = \frac{\sqrt{3} + 1}{2\sqrt{2}}}$$

3. $\tan 15^\circ = \dfrac{\sin 15^\circ}{\cos 15^\circ} = \dfrac{\sqrt{3}-1}{\sqrt{3}+1}$

$$\tan 15^\circ = \frac{\sqrt{3}-1}{\sqrt{3}+1}$$

Example 65. For $0<\theta<\dfrac{\pi}{2}$, then solution(s) of $\sum_{m=1}^{6} \operatorname{cosec}\left[\theta+\dfrac{(m-1)\pi}{4}\right]\operatorname{cosec}\left(\theta+\dfrac{m\pi}{4}\right)=4\sqrt{2}$ is (are)

(a) $\dfrac{\pi}{4}$ (b) $\dfrac{\pi}{6}$ (c) $\dfrac{\pi}{12}$ (d) $\dfrac{5\pi}{12}$

Sol. (c) Let $\alpha = \theta + \dfrac{(m-1)\pi}{4} = \theta + \dfrac{m\pi}{4} - \dfrac{\pi}{4}$ or $\alpha + \dfrac{\pi}{4} = \theta + \dfrac{m\pi}{4}$

$$\sum_{m=1}^{6} \frac{1}{\sin\alpha \sin\left(\alpha+\frac{\pi}{4}\right)} = 4\sqrt{2}$$

$$\Rightarrow \sum_{m=1}^{6} \frac{\frac{1}{\sqrt{2}}}{\sin\alpha \sin\left(\alpha+\frac{\pi}{4}\right)} = 4$$

$$\Rightarrow \sum_{m=1}^{6} \frac{\sin\left(\frac{\pi}{4}\right)}{\sin\alpha \sin\left(\alpha+\frac{\pi}{4}\right)} = 4$$

$$\Rightarrow \sum_{m=1}^{6} \frac{\sin\left[\left(\alpha+\frac{\pi}{4}\right)-\alpha\right]}{\sin\alpha \sin\left(\alpha+\frac{\pi}{4}\right)} = 4$$

$$\Rightarrow \sum_{m=1}^{6} \frac{\sin\left(\alpha+\frac{\pi}{4}\right)\cos\alpha - \cos\left(\alpha+\frac{\pi}{4}\right)\sin\alpha}{\sin\alpha \sin\left(\alpha+\frac{\pi}{4}\right)} = 4$$

$$\Rightarrow \sum_{m=1}^{6} \left(\frac{\cos\alpha}{\sin\alpha} - \frac{\cos\left(\alpha+\frac{\pi}{4}\right)}{\sin\left(\alpha+\frac{\pi}{4}\right)}\right) = 4$$

$$\Rightarrow \sum_{m=1}^{6} \left(\cot\alpha - \cot\left(\alpha+\frac{\pi}{4}\right)\right) = 4$$

$$\Rightarrow \sum_{m=1}^{6} \left[\cot\left(\theta+\frac{m\pi}{4}-\frac{\pi}{4}\right) - \cot\left(\theta+\frac{m\pi}{4}\right)\right] = 4$$

$$\Rightarrow \sum_{m=1}^{6} \left[\cot\left[\theta+\frac{(m-1)\pi}{4}\right] - \cot\left[\theta+\frac{m\pi}{4}\right]\right] = 4$$

$$\Rightarrow \cot\theta - \cot\left(\theta+\frac{\pi}{4}\right) + \cot\left(\theta+\frac{\pi}{4}\right) - \cot\left(\theta+\frac{2\pi}{4}\right) + \cot\left(\theta+\frac{2\pi}{4}\right) + \ldots = 4$$

$$\Rightarrow \cot\theta - \cot\left(\theta+\frac{6\pi}{4}\right) = 4$$

$$\Rightarrow \cot\theta - \cot\left(\theta+\frac{3\pi}{2}\right) = 4$$

$$\Rightarrow \cot\theta + \tan\theta = 4$$

$$\Rightarrow \tan^2\theta + 1 = 4\tan\theta$$

$$\Rightarrow \tan^2\theta - 4\tan\theta + 1 = 0$$

$$\Rightarrow \tan\theta = \frac{4\pm\sqrt{16-4}}{2} = 2\pm\sqrt{3}$$

$$\Rightarrow \tan\theta = 2+\sqrt{3} \text{ and } \tan\theta = 2-\sqrt{3}$$

$$\Rightarrow \tan\theta = 2+\sqrt{3} = \tan 75^\circ = \tan(45^\circ+30^\circ)$$

$$\Rightarrow \theta = 75^\circ \text{ or } \frac{5\pi}{12}$$

and $\tan\theta = 2-\sqrt{3} = \tan 15^\circ = \tan(45^\circ - 30^\circ)$

$$\theta = 15^\circ \text{ or } \frac{\pi}{12}$$

Example 66. Prove that

$$\sum_{k=1}^{100} \sin(kx)\cos(101-k)x = 50\sin(101x).$$

Sol. Let $S = \sum_{k=1}^{100} \sin(kx)\cos(101-k)x$

$\Rightarrow S = \sin x \cos 100x + \sin 2x \cos 99x + \ldots + \sin 100x \cos x$ ...(i)

$S = \cos x \sin 100x + \cos 2x \sin 99x + \ldots + \sin x \cos 100x$ ...(ii)

(on writing in reverse order)

On adding Eqs. (i) and (ii), we get

$2S = (\sin x \cos 100x + \cos x \sin 100x) + (\sin 2x \cos 99x + \cos 2x \sin 99x)$

...

...

$+ (\sin 100x \cos x + \sin x \cos 100x)$

$= \sin 101x + \sin 101x + \ldots + \sin 101x$ (100 times)

Hence, $S = 50\sin(101x)$

Example 67. Prove that $\sin\theta\cdot\sec 3\theta + \sin 3\theta\cdot\sec 3^2\theta + \sin 3^2\theta\cdot\sec 3^3\theta + \ldots$ upto n terms $= \dfrac{1}{2}[\tan 3^n\theta - \tan\theta]$.

Sol. $\sin\theta\cdot\sec 3\theta + \sin 3\theta\cdot\sec 3^2\theta + \sin 3^2\theta\cdot\sec 3^3\theta + \ldots$ upto n terms

$$= \sum_{r=1}^{n} \sin 3^{r-1}\theta\cdot\sec 3^r\theta = \sum_{r=1}^{n} \frac{2\cos 3^{r-1}\theta \sin 3^{r-1}\theta}{2\cos 3^{r-1}\theta\cdot\cos 3^r\theta}$$

$$= \frac{1}{2}\sum_{r=1}^{n} \frac{\sin(3^{r-1}\theta + 3^{r-1}\theta)}{\cos 3^{r-1}\theta\cdot\cos 3^r\theta} = \frac{1}{2}\sum_{r=1}^{n} \frac{\sin(3^r\theta - 3^{r-1}\theta)}{\cos 3^{r-1}\theta\cdot\cos 3^r\theta}$$

$$= \frac{1}{2}\sum_{r=1}^{n} \frac{\sin 3^r\theta\cdot\cos 3^{r-1}\theta - \cos 3^r\theta\cdot\sin 3^{r-1}\theta}{\cos 3^{r-1}\theta\cdot\cos 3^r\theta}$$

$$= \frac{1}{2}\sum_{r=1}^{n} (\tan 3^r\theta - \tan 3^{r-1}\theta) = \frac{1}{2}[\tan 3^n\theta - \tan\theta]$$

Example 68. In a ΔABC, if $\sin A \sin(B-C) = \sin C \sin(A-B)$, then prove that $\cot A$, $\cot B$, $\cot C$ are in AP.

Sol. $\sin A \sin(B-C) = \sin C \sin(A-B)$

$$\Rightarrow \frac{\sin(B-C)}{\sin C \sin B} = \frac{\sin(A-B)}{\sin A \sin B}$$

$$\Rightarrow \frac{\sin B \cos C - \sin C \cos B}{\sin C \sin B} = \frac{\sin A \cos B - \sin B \cos A}{\sin A \sin B}$$

$$\Rightarrow \cot C - \cot B = \cot B - \cot A$$

$$\Rightarrow 2\cot B = \cot A + \cot C$$

$\therefore$ $\cot A$, $\cot B$, $\cot C$ are in AP.

Example 69. If $\cos\alpha = \frac{1}{2}\left(x + \frac{1}{x}\right)$, $\cos\beta = \frac{1}{2}\left(y + \frac{1}{y}\right)$, then evaluate $\cos(\alpha - \beta)$.

Sol. $\cos\alpha = \frac{1}{2}\left(x + \frac{1}{x}\right)$

$$\Rightarrow x^2 - 2x\cos\alpha + 1 = 0$$

$$\Rightarrow x = \frac{2\cos\alpha \pm \sqrt{4\cos^2\alpha - 4}}{2} \Rightarrow x = \frac{2\cos\alpha \pm 2i\sin\alpha}{2}$$

[as $\sqrt{-1} = i$]

$\therefore$ $x = \cos\alpha \pm i\sin\alpha$

Similarly, $y = \cos\beta \pm i\sin\beta$

$$\therefore \frac{x}{y} = \frac{\cos\alpha \pm i\sin\alpha}{\cos\beta \pm i\sin\beta}$$

$$= \cos(\alpha-\beta) \pm i\sin(\alpha-\beta) \quad \text{...(i)}$$

and $$\frac{y}{x} = \frac{\cos\beta \pm i\sin\beta}{\cos\alpha \pm i\sin\alpha}$$

$$= \cos(\alpha-\beta) \mp i\sin(\alpha-\beta) \quad \text{...(ii)}$$

On adding Eqs. (i) and (ii), we get

$$\frac{x}{y} + \frac{y}{x} = 2\cos(\alpha-\beta)$$

i.e. $$\cos(\alpha-\beta) = \frac{1}{2}\left(\frac{x}{y} + \frac{y}{x}\right).$$

Example 70. The value of $\dfrac{\sin\theta}{\sin^2\left(\frac{\theta}{2} + \frac{\pi}{12}\right) - \sin^2\left(\frac{\theta}{2} - \frac{\pi}{12}\right)}$ is

(a) $\frac{1}{2}$ (b) -2 (c) 2 (d) $-\frac{1}{2}$

Sol. (c) Given, $$\frac{\sin\theta}{\sin^2\left(\frac{\theta}{2} + \frac{\pi}{12}\right) - \sin^2\left(\frac{\theta}{2} - \frac{\pi}{12}\right)} = \frac{\sin\theta}{\sin\theta \sin\left(\frac{\pi}{6}\right)}$$

$$= \frac{1}{\sin\frac{\pi}{6}} = \frac{1}{\left(\frac{1}{2}\right)} = 2$$

Example 71. If $A + B = \frac{\pi}{3}$, then the value of $\cos^2 A + \cos^2 B - \cos A \cos B$ is

(a) $\frac{1}{2}$ (b) $\frac{3}{2}$ (c) $\frac{3}{4}$ (d) 1

Sol. (c) $\cos^2 A + \cos^2 B - \cos A \cos B$

$$= (1 - \sin^2 A) + \cos^2 B - \cos A \cos B$$

$$= 1 + \cos^2 B - \sin^2 A - \cos A \cos B$$

$$= 1 + \cos(A+B)\cos(A-B) - \cos A \cos B$$

$$= 1 + \cos\left(\frac{\pi}{3}\right)\cos(A-B) - \cos A \cos B$$

$$= 1 + \frac{1}{2}(\cos A \cos B + \sin A \sin B) - \cos A \cos B$$

$$= 1 + \left(\frac{\cos A \cos B + \sin A \sin B - 2\cos A \cos B}{2}\right)$$

$$= \frac{2 - (\cos A \cos B - \sin A \sin B)}{2} = 1 - \frac{\cos(A+B)}{2}$$

$$= 1 - \frac{1}{4} = \frac{3}{4}$$

Time Saving Technique

$A + B = \frac{\pi}{3}$, Let $A = B = \frac{\pi}{6}$

$$\Rightarrow \cos^2\frac{\pi}{6} + \cos^2\frac{\pi}{6} - \cos\frac{\pi}{6}\cos\frac{\pi}{6} = \cos^2\frac{\pi}{6} = \left(\frac{\sqrt{3}}{2}\right)^2 = \frac{3}{4}$$

Example 72. Show that $\cot\left(\frac{\pi}{4} + x\right)\cot\left(\frac{\pi}{4} - x\right) = 1$

Sol. $$\text{LHS} = \frac{\cos\left(\frac{\pi}{4} + x\right)\cos\left(\frac{\pi}{4} - x\right)}{\sin\left(\frac{\pi}{4} + x\right)\sin\left(\frac{\pi}{4} - x\right)}$$

$$= \frac{\cos^2\frac{\pi}{4} - \sin^2 x}{\sin^2\frac{\pi}{4} - \sin^2 x} = \frac{\frac{1}{2} - \sin^2 x}{\frac{1}{2} - \sin^2 x} = 1 = \text{RHS}$$

Example 73. Show that $\cos^2\theta + \cos^2(\alpha+\theta) - 2\cos\alpha\cos\theta\cos(\alpha+\theta)$ is independent of θ.

Sol. $\cos^2\theta + \cos^2(\alpha+\theta) - 2\cos\alpha\cos\theta\cos(\alpha+\theta)$

$$= \cos^2\theta + \cos(\alpha+\theta)[\cos(\alpha+\theta) - 2\cos\alpha\cos\theta]$$

$$= \cos^2\theta + \cos(\alpha+\theta)[\cos\alpha\cos\theta - \sin\alpha\sin\theta - 2\cos\alpha\cos\theta]$$

$$= \cos^2\theta - \cos(\alpha+\theta)[\cos\alpha\cos\theta + \sin\alpha\sin\theta]$$

$$= \cos^2\theta - \cos(\alpha+\theta)\cos(\alpha-\theta)$$

$$= \cos^2\theta - [\cos^2\alpha - \sin^2\theta]$$

$$= \cos^2\theta + \sin^2\theta - \cos^2\alpha = 1 - \cos^2\alpha,$$

which is independent of θ.

1.11 Extended Compound Angle Formulae

1. $\sin(A+B+C) = \sin A\cos B\cos C + \cos A\sin B\cos C + \cos A\cos B\sin C - \sin A\sin B\sin C$

Or

$\sin(A+B+C) = \cos A\cos B\cos C(\tan A + \tan B + \tan C - \tan A\tan B\tan C)$

2. $\cos(A+B+C) = \cos A\cos B\cos C - \cos A\sin B\sin C - \sin A\cos B\sin C - \sin A\sin B\cos C$

Or

$\cos(A+B+C) = \cos A\cos B\cos C(1 - \tan B\tan C - \tan A\tan C - \tan A\tan B)$

3. $\tan(A+B+C) = \dfrac{\sin(A+B+C)}{\cos(A+B+C)}$

$$\tan(A+B+C) = \frac{\tan A + \tan B + \tan C - \tan A\tan B\tan C}{1 - \tan A\tan B - \tan B\tan C - \tan C\tan A}$$

$$\tan(A+B+C) = \frac{\Sigma\tan A - \tan A\tan B\tan C}{1 - \Sigma\tan A\tan B}$$

4. $\sin(A_1 + A_2 + \ldots + A_n) = \cos A_1\cos A_2\ldots\cos A_n(S_1 - S_3 + S_5 - S_7 + \ldots)$

5. $\cos(A_1 + A_2 + A_3 + \ldots + A_n) = \cos A_1\cos A_2\ldots\cos A_n(1 - S_2 + S_4 - S_6 + \ldots)$

6. $\tan(A_1 + A_2 + \ldots + A_n) = \dfrac{S_1 - S_3 + S_5 - S_7 + \ldots}{1 - S_2 + S_4 - S_6 + \ldots}$,

where $S_1 = \tan A_1 + \tan A_2 + \ldots + \tan A_n$

= the sum of the tangents of the separate angles

$S_2 = \tan A_1\tan A_2 + \tan A_2\tan A_3 + \ldots$

= the sum of the tangents taken two at a time,

$S_3 = \tan A_1\tan A_2\tan A_3 + \tan A_2\tan A_3\tan A_4 + \ldots$

= the sum of the tangent taken three at a time

and so on.

If $A_1 = A_2 = \ldots = A_n = A$, then

$S_1 = n\tan A$

$S_2 = {}^nC_2\tan^2 A$

$S_3 = {}^nC_3\tan^3 A, \ldots$

7. $\sin nA = \cos^n A({}^nC_1\tan A - {}^nC_3\tan^3 A + {}^nC_5\tan^5 A\ldots)$

8. $\cos nA = \cos^n A(1 - {}^nC_2\tan^2 A + {}^nC_4\tan^4 A - \ldots)$

9. $\tan nA = \dfrac{{}^nC_1\tan A - {}^nC_3\tan^3 A + {}^nC_5\tan^5 A\ldots}{1 - {}^nC_2\tan^2 A + {}^nC_4\tan^4 A - {}^nC_6\tan^6 A + \ldots}$

10. $\sin nA + \cos nA = \cos^n A(1 + {}^nC_1\tan A - {}^nC_2\tan^2 A - {}^nC_3\tan^3 A + {}^nC_4\tan^4 A + {}^nC_5\tan^5 A - {}^nC_6\tan^6 A\ldots)$

11. $\sin nA - \cos nA = \cos^n A(-1 + {}^nC_1\tan A + {}^nC_2\tan^2 A - {}^nC_3\tan^3 A - {}^nC_4\tan^4 A + {}^nC_5\tan^5 A + {}^nC_6\tan^6 A\ldots)$

Example 74. In a ΔABC, if $\cos A\cos B\cos C = \dfrac{1}{3}$, then the value of $\Sigma\tan A\tan B$ is

(a) 1 (b) 2 (c) 3 (d) 4

Sol. (d) In ΔABC, $A + B + C = \pi$

$\Rightarrow \cos(A+B+C) = \cos\pi = -1$

$\Rightarrow \cos A\cos B\cos C(1 - \tan A\tan B - \tan B\tan C - \tan C\tan A) = -1$

$\Rightarrow \cos A\cos B\cos C(1 - \Sigma\tan A\tan B) = -1$

$\Rightarrow \frac{1}{3}(1 - \Sigma\tan A\tan B) = -1$

$\Rightarrow 1 - \Sigma\tan A\tan B = -3$

$\Rightarrow \Sigma\tan A\tan B = 4$

Milestone Practice 1.4

1. If $3\tan A\tan B = 1$, then the value of $\dfrac{\cos(A-B)}{\cos(A+B)}$ is equal to

(a) 1 (b) 2

(c) 3 (d) None of these

2. If $\tan\alpha = \dfrac{m}{m+1}$ and $\tan\beta = \dfrac{1}{2m+1}$, then the value of $\alpha + \beta$ is

(a) $\dfrac{\pi}{3}$ (b) $\dfrac{\pi}{6}$ (c) $\dfrac{\pi}{2}$ (d) $\dfrac{\pi}{4}$

3. If $\cos(\theta - \alpha) = a$ and $\cos(\theta - \beta) = b$, then the value of $\sin^2(\alpha - \beta) + 2ab\cos(\alpha - \beta)$ is

(a) $a^2 + b^2$ (b) $a^2 - b^2$ (c) $a + b$ (d) $a - b$

4. The value of $\cos^2 10° - \cos 10°\cos 50° + \cos^2 50°$ is

(a) $\dfrac{3}{4} + \cos 20°$ (b) $\dfrac{3}{4}$

(c) $\dfrac{3}{2}(1 + \cos 20°)$ (d) $\dfrac{3}{2}$

5. If $0<\beta<\alpha<\dfrac{\pi}{4}$, $\cos(\alpha+\beta)=\dfrac{3}{5}$ and $\cos(\alpha-\beta)=\dfrac{4}{5}$, then evaluate $\sin 2\alpha$.

6. If $y=(1+\tan A)(1-\tan B)$, where $A-B=\dfrac{\pi}{4}$, then the value of $(y+1)^{y+1}$ is
(a) 9 (b) 4 (c) 64 (d) 27

7. The value of $\dfrac{\sin 22^\circ \cos 8^\circ + \cos 158^\circ \cos 98^\circ}{\sin 23^\circ \cos 7^\circ + \cos 157^\circ \cos 97^\circ}$ is
(a) 2 (b) $\dfrac{1}{2}$ (c) 1 (d) 2

8. The expression $\dfrac{\sin(A-\theta)-\sin(A+\theta)}{\cos(B-\theta)-\cos(B+\theta)}$ is
(a) independent of A only
(b) independent of B only
(c) independent of θ
(d) independent of both A and B

9. If $\cos(\alpha-\beta)+\cos(\beta-\gamma)+\cos(\gamma-\alpha)=-\dfrac{3}{2}$ and $\cos\alpha+\cos\beta+\cos\gamma=p$ and $\sin\alpha+\sin\beta+\sin\gamma=q$, then find the value of p^2+q^2 is
(a) 0 (b) 4 (c) 9 (d) 16

10. Let's consider two statements.
$S_1: 3\cos x-4\sin x=5\sin(\theta-x)$, where $\tan\theta=\dfrac{4}{3}$
$S_2: 3\cos x-4\sin x=5\cos(\theta+x)$, where $\tan\theta=\dfrac{3}{4}$
(a) Only S_1 is true
(b) Only S_2 is true
(c) Both S_1 and S_2 are true
(d) Both S_1 and S_2 are false

11. If $A+B=\dfrac{7\pi}{6}$, then find the value of $(\sqrt{3}+\tan A)(\sqrt{3}+\tan B)$.

12. If $2\cos A=x+\dfrac{1}{x}$, $2\cos B=y+\dfrac{1}{y}$, then show that $2\cos(A-B)=\dfrac{x}{y}+\dfrac{y}{x}$

13. If $\tan^3 A+\tan^3 B+\tan^3 C=3\tan A\tan B\tan C$, then find the value of $A+B+C$.

14. Given, $a_1\cos\alpha_1+a_2\cos\alpha_2+\ldots+a_n\cos\alpha_n=0$ and $a_1\cos(\alpha_1+\theta)+a_2\cos(\alpha_2+\theta)+\ldots+a_n\cos(\alpha_n+\theta)=0\ (\theta\neq k\pi)$.
Now, consider the following two statements
$S_1: a_1\cos(\alpha_1+\lambda)+a_2\cos(\alpha_2+\lambda)+\ldots+a_n\cos(\alpha_n+\lambda)=0$
$S_2: a_1\sin\alpha_1+a_2\sin\alpha_2+\ldots+a_n\sin\alpha_n=0$
(a) Only S_1 is true
(b) Only S_2 is true
(c) Both S_1 and S_2 are true
(d) Both S_1 and S_2 are false

15. In a ΔABC, $\tan A+\tan B+\tan C$ has the value 6, then the value of $6\cot A\cot B\cot C$ is ....

16. If $\cos(\alpha-\beta)+\cos(\beta-\gamma)+\cos(\gamma-\alpha)=-\dfrac{3}{2}$, $\cos\alpha+\cos\beta+\cos\gamma=p$ and $\sin\alpha+\sin\beta+\sin\gamma=q$, then the value of $3p+4q$ is ....

17. Find the value of
$$\frac{\cot 25^\circ+\cot 55^\circ}{\tan 25^\circ+\tan 55^\circ}+\frac{\cot 55^\circ+\cot 100^\circ}{\tan 55^\circ+\tan 100^\circ}+\frac{\cot 100^\circ+\cot 25^\circ}{\tan 100^\circ+\tan 25^\circ}.$$

18. Find the value of
$$\frac{(\cos 1^\circ+\sin 1^\circ)(\cos 2^\circ+\sin 2^\circ)(\cos 3^\circ+\sin 3^\circ)\ldots(\cos 45^\circ+\sin 45^\circ)}{\cos 1^\circ\cos 2^\circ\cos 3^\circ\ldots\cos 45^\circ}.$$

19. If α,β are two different values of x lying between 0 and 2π which satisfy the equation $6\cos x+8\sin x=9$, then find the value of $\sin(\alpha+\beta)$.

20. If α and β are two solutions of the equation $a\tan x+b\sec x=c$, then find the values of $\sin(\alpha+\beta)$ and $\cos(\alpha+\beta)$.

21. If $\alpha+\beta=90^\circ$ and $\beta+\gamma=\alpha$, then prove that $\tan\alpha=\tan\beta+2\tan\gamma$.

22. If $\sin\left(x+\dfrac{4\pi}{9}\right)=a$; $\dfrac{\pi}{9}<x<\dfrac{\pi}{3}$, then $\cos\left(x+\dfrac{7\pi}{9}\right)$ equals
(a) $\dfrac{\sqrt{(1-a^2)}-a\sqrt{3}}{2}$ (b) $\dfrac{1-a^2+a\sqrt{3}}{2}$
(c) $\dfrac{a\sqrt{3}-\sqrt{(1-a^2)}}{2}$ (d) $\dfrac{-\sqrt{(1-a^2)}-a\sqrt{3}}{2}$

Answer Key

1. (b)	2. (d)	3. (a)	4. (b)	5. (1)	6. (d)
7. (c)	8. (c)	9. (a)	10. (d)	11. (4)	
13. (π)	14. (c)	15. (1)	16. (0)	17. (1)	
18. (2^{23})	19. $\left(\dfrac{24}{25}\right)$	20. $\sin(\alpha+\beta)=\dfrac{2ac}{a^2+c^2}$, $\cos(\alpha+\beta)=\dfrac{a^2-c^2}{a^2+c^2}$		22. (d)	

For Detailed Solution

Milestone 5 Trigonometric Ratios of Multiple and Submultiple of an Angle

• Trigonometric Ratios of Multiple Angles • Trigonometric Ratios of Submultiple of an Angle

1.12 Trigonometric Ratios of Multiple Angles

An angle of the form nA, where n is an integer is called multiple angle.

(i) $\sin 2A = 2\sin A \cos A$

Example 75. Prove that $\cot\theta + \tan\theta = 2\operatorname{cosec} 2\theta$.

Sol. LHS $= \cot\theta + \tan\theta = \dfrac{\cos\theta}{\sin\theta} + \dfrac{\sin\theta}{\cos\theta} = \dfrac{\cos^2\theta + \sin^2\theta}{\sin\theta\cos\theta}$

$$= \frac{1}{\sin\theta\cos\theta} = \frac{2}{2\sin\theta\cos\theta}$$

$$= \frac{2}{\sin 2\theta} = 2\operatorname{cosec} 2\theta = \text{RHS}$$

(ii) $\cos 2A = \cos^2 A - \sin^2 A$

(iii) $\cos 2A = 2\cos^2 A - 1$ or $1 + \cos 2A = 2\cos^2 A$

(iv) $\cos 2A = 1 - 2\sin^2 A$ or $1 - \cos 2A = 2\sin^2 A$

Example 76. Prove that $\dfrac{\sin\theta + \sin 2\theta}{1 + \cos\theta + \cos 2\theta} = \tan\theta$.

Sol. LHS $= \dfrac{\sin\theta + \sin 2\theta}{1 + \cos\theta + \cos 2\theta} = \dfrac{\sin\theta + 2\sin\theta\cos\theta}{1 + \cos\theta + 2\cos^2\theta - 1}$

$$= \frac{\sin\theta(1 + 2\cos\theta)}{\cos\theta(1 + 2\cos\theta)} = \tan\theta$$

(v) $\tan 2A = \dfrac{2\tan A}{1 - \tan^2 A}$

Example 77. If $\sin A = \dfrac{3}{5}$, where $0° < A < 90°$, then find the values of $\sin 2A$, $\cos 2A$, $\tan 2A$ and $\sin 4A$.

Sol. We have, $\sin A = \dfrac{3}{5}$, where $0° < A < 90°$

$\therefore \quad \cos^2 A = 1 - \sin^2 A$

$\Rightarrow \quad \cos A = +\sqrt{1 - \sin^2 A} = \sqrt{1 - \dfrac{9}{25}} = \dfrac{4}{5}$

$\therefore \quad \tan A = \dfrac{\sin A}{\cos A} = \dfrac{3}{4}$

$$\sin 2A = 2\sin A\cos A = 2 \times \frac{3}{5} \times \frac{4}{5} = \frac{24}{25}$$

$$\cos 2A = 1 - 2\sin^2 A = 1 - 2 \times \left(\frac{3}{5}\right)^2 = \frac{7}{25}$$

$$\tan 2A = \frac{2\tan A}{1 - \tan^2 A} = \frac{2 \times \frac{3}{4}}{1 - \left(\frac{3}{4}\right)^2} = \frac{\frac{6}{4}}{1 - \frac{9}{16}} = \frac{24}{7}$$

$$\left[\because \tan A = \frac{3}{4}\right]$$

$$\sin 4A = \sin 2A\cos 2A = 2 \times \frac{24}{25} \times \frac{7}{25} = \frac{336}{625}$$

$$\left[\because \sin 2A = \frac{24}{25} \text{ and } \cos 2A = \frac{7}{25}\right]$$

Example 78. Prove that $\dfrac{1 + \sin 2\theta}{1 - \sin 2\theta} = \left(\dfrac{1 + \tan\theta}{1 - \tan\theta}\right)^2$.

Sol. LHS $= \dfrac{1 + \sin 2\theta}{1 - \sin 2\theta} = \dfrac{\sin^2\theta + \cos^2\theta + 2\sin\theta\cos\theta}{\sin^2\theta + \cos^2\theta - 2\sin\theta\cos\theta}$

$$= \left(\frac{\sin\theta + \cos\theta}{\sin\theta - \cos\theta}\right)^2 = \left(\frac{1 + \tan\theta}{1 - \tan\theta}\right)^2$$

[dividing numerator and denominator by $\cos\theta$]

Example 79. Prove that $\dfrac{\sec 8\theta - 1}{\sec 4\theta - 1} = \dfrac{\tan 8\theta}{\tan 2\theta}$.

Sol. We have, LHS $= \dfrac{\sec 8\theta - 1}{\sec 4\theta - 1} = \dfrac{\dfrac{1}{\cos 8\theta} - 1}{\dfrac{1}{\cos 4\theta} - 1}$

$$= \frac{1 - \cos 8\theta}{\cos 8\theta} \cdot \frac{\cos 4\theta}{1 - \cos 4\theta} = \frac{2\sin^2 4\theta}{\cos 8\theta} \cdot \frac{\cos 4\theta}{2\sin^2 2\theta}$$

$$\left[\begin{aligned} &\because 1 - \cos 8\theta = 2\sin^2\frac{8\theta}{2} = 2\sin^2 4\theta \\ &\text{and, } 1 - \cos 4\theta = 2\sin^2\frac{4\theta}{2} = 2\sin^2 2\theta \end{aligned}\right]$$

$$= \frac{(2\sin 4\theta \cos 4\theta)}{\cos 8\theta} \times \frac{\sin 4\theta}{2\sin^2 2\theta}$$

$$= \left(\frac{2\sin 4\theta \cos 4\theta}{\cos 8\theta}\right) \times \left(\frac{2\sin 2\theta \cos 2\theta}{2\sin^2 2\theta}\right)$$

$$= \left(\frac{\sin 2(4\theta)}{\cos 8\theta}\right) \times \left(\frac{\cos 2\theta}{\sin 2\theta}\right)$$

$$= \left(\frac{\sin 8\theta}{\cos 8\theta}\right) \times \left(\frac{\cos 2\theta}{\sin 2\theta}\right)$$

$$= \tan 8\theta \cot 2\theta$$

$$= \frac{\tan 8\theta}{\tan 2\theta} = \text{RHS}$$

(vi) $\sin 2A = \dfrac{2\tan A}{1+\tan^2 A}$

(vii) $\cos 2A = \dfrac{1-\tan^2 A}{1+\tan^2 A}$

(viii) $\sin 3A = 3\sin A - 4\sin^3 A$

(ix) $\cos 3A = 4\cos^3 A - 3\cos A$

(x) $\tan 3A = \dfrac{3\tan A - \tan^3 A}{1-3\tan^2 A}$

Example 80. Prove that $\dfrac{\sin^3\theta + \sin 3\theta}{\cos^3\theta - \cos 3\theta} = \cot\theta$.

Sol. LHS $= \dfrac{\sin^3\theta + \sin 3\theta}{\cos^3\theta - \cos 3\theta}$

$$= \frac{\sin^3\theta + 3\sin\theta - 4\sin^3\theta}{\cos^3\theta - (4\cos^3\theta - 3\cos\theta)}$$

$$= \frac{3\sin\theta - 3\sin^3\theta}{3\cos\theta - 3\cos^3\theta}$$

$$= \frac{3\sin\theta(1-\sin^2\theta)}{3\cos\theta(1-\cos^2\theta)}$$

$$= \frac{\sin\theta \cdot \cos^2\theta}{\cos\theta \sin^2\theta}$$

$$= \frac{\cos\theta}{\sin\theta}$$

$$= \cot\theta$$

JEE SCANNER

Example Similar to PYQ Asked in JEE Main 2023

The value of $(3-4\sin^2 9°)(3-4\sin^2 27°)(3-4\sin^2 81°)(3-4\sin^2 243°)$ *is*

(a) 1 (b) 2 (c) 3 (d) 4

Sol. (a) $3 - 4\sin^2\theta = \dfrac{3\sin\theta - 4\sin^3\theta}{\sin\theta} = \dfrac{\sin 3\theta}{\sin\theta}$

$\therefore$ Given expression,

$(3-4\sin^2 9°)(3-4\sin^2 27°)(3-4\sin^2 81°)$
$(3-4\sin^2 243°)$

$$= \frac{\sin(3\times 9°)}{\sin 9°} \times \frac{\sin(3\times 27°)}{\sin 27°} \times \frac{\sin(3\times 81°)}{\sin 81°} \times \frac{\sin(3\times 243°)}{\sin 243°}$$

$$= \frac{\sin 729°}{\sin 9°} = \frac{\sin(2\times 360° + 9°)}{\sin 9°}$$

$$= \frac{\sin 9°}{\sin 9°} = 1$$

Skill Builder

The value of $(4\cos^2 9° - 1)(4\cos^2 27° - 1)(4\cos^2 81° - 1)(4\cos^2 243° - 1)$ is

(a) 46 (b) 63
(c) 1 (d) 9

For Sol.

- **For more practice** See Q.8 of Milestone Practice 5.

Example 81. Show that
$\tan\theta + \tan(60° + \theta) + \tan(120° + \theta) = 3\tan 3\theta$.

Sol. LHS $= \tan\theta + \tan(60° + \theta) + \tan(120° + \theta)$

$$= \tan\theta + \frac{\tan 60° + \tan\theta}{1 - \tan 60°\tan\theta} + \frac{\tan 120° + \tan\theta}{1 - \tan 120°\tan\theta}$$

$$= \tan\theta + \frac{\sqrt{3} + \tan\theta}{1 - \sqrt{3}\tan\theta} + \left(\frac{-\sqrt{3} + \tan\theta}{1 + \sqrt{3}\tan\theta}\right)$$

$$= \frac{\tan\theta - 3\tan^3\theta + \sqrt{3} + 3\tan\theta + \tan\theta + \sqrt{3}\tan^2\theta - \sqrt{3} + 3\tan\theta + \tan\theta - \sqrt{3}\tan^2\theta}{1 - 3\tan^2\theta}$$

$$= \frac{9\tan\theta - 3\tan^3\theta}{1 - 3\tan^2\theta} = 3\left(\frac{3\tan\theta - \tan^3\theta}{1 - 3\tan^2\theta}\right)$$

$$= 3\tan 3\theta = \text{RHS}$$

Example 82. Show that $\sqrt{3}\operatorname{cosec} 20° - \sec 20° = 4$

Sol. We have, LHS $= \sqrt{3}\operatorname{cosec} 20° - \sec 20°$

$$= \frac{\sqrt{3}}{\sin 20°} - \frac{1}{\cos 20°} = \frac{\sqrt{3}\cos 20° - \sin 20°}{\sin 20° \cos 20°}$$

$$= \frac{2\left\{\frac{\sqrt{3}}{2}\cos 20^\circ - \frac{1}{2}\sin 20^\circ\right\}}{\sin 20^\circ \cos 20^\circ}$$
$$= \frac{2(\sin 60^\circ \cos 20^\circ - \cos 60^\circ \sin 20^\circ)}{\sin 20^\circ \cos 20^\circ}$$
$$= \frac{2\sin(60^\circ - 20^\circ)}{\sin 20^\circ \cos 20^\circ} = \frac{2\sin 40^\circ}{\sin 20^\circ \cos 20^\circ}$$
$$= \frac{4\sin 40^\circ}{2\sin 20^\circ \cos 20^\circ} = \frac{4\sin 40^\circ}{\sin 40^\circ} = 4 = \text{RHS}$$

Example 83. Prove that $\left(1+\cos\frac{\pi}{8}\right)\left(1+\cos\frac{3\pi}{8}\right)\left(1+\cos\frac{5\pi}{8}\right)\left(1+\cos\frac{7\pi}{8}\right) = \frac{1}{8}$.

Sol. We have, $\cos\frac{7\pi}{8} = \cos\left(\pi - \frac{\pi}{8}\right) = -\cos\frac{\pi}{8}$

and $\cos\frac{5\pi}{8} = \cos\left(\pi - \frac{3\pi}{8}\right) = -\cos\frac{3\pi}{8}$

$$\therefore \text{LHS} = \left(1+\cos\frac{\pi}{8}\right)\left(1+\cos\frac{3\pi}{8}\right)\left(1-\cos\frac{3\pi}{8}\right)\left(1-\cos\frac{\pi}{8}\right)$$
$$= \left(1-\cos^2\frac{\pi}{8}\right)\left(1-\cos^2\frac{3\pi}{8}\right) = \sin^2\frac{\pi}{8}\sin^2\frac{3\pi}{8}$$
$$= \frac{1}{4}\left(2\sin^2\frac{\pi}{8}\right)\left(2\sin^2\frac{3\pi}{8}\right)$$
$$= \frac{1}{4}\left[\left(1-\cos\frac{\pi}{4}\right)\left(1-\cos\frac{3\pi}{4}\right)\right]$$
$$\left[\because 1-\cos\theta = 2\sin^2\frac{\theta}{2}\right]$$
$$= \frac{1}{4}\left[\left(1-\frac{1}{\sqrt{2}}\right)\left(1+\frac{1}{\sqrt{2}}\right)\right] = \frac{1}{4}\left(1-\frac{1}{2}\right) = \frac{1}{8} = \text{RHS}$$

Example 84. Determine the smallest positive value of x (in degrees) for which $\tan(x+100^\circ) = \tan(x+50^\circ)\tan x \tan(x-50^\circ)$

Sol. We have, $\tan(x+100^\circ) = \tan(x+50^\circ)\tan x\tan(x-50^\circ)$

$$\Rightarrow \frac{\tan(x+100^\circ)}{\tan(x-50^\circ)} = \tan(x+50^\circ)\tan x$$
$$\Rightarrow \frac{\sin(x+100^\circ)\cos(x-50^\circ)}{\cos(x+100^\circ)\sin(x-50^\circ)} = \frac{\sin(x+50^\circ)\sin x}{\cos(x+50^\circ)\cos x}$$
$$\Rightarrow \frac{\sin(x+100^\circ)\cos(x-50^\circ)+\cos(x+100^\circ)\sin(x-50^\circ)}{\sin(x+100^\circ)\cos(x-50^\circ)-\cos(x+100^\circ)\sin(x-50^\circ)}$$
$$= \frac{\sin(x+50^\circ)\sin x + \cos(x+50^\circ)\cos x}{\sin(x+50^\circ)\sin x - \cos(x+50^\circ)\cos x}$$
$$\Rightarrow \frac{\sin(x+100^\circ+x-50^\circ)}{\sin(x+100^\circ-x+50^\circ)} = \frac{\cos(x+50^\circ-x)}{-\cos(x+50^\circ+x)}$$
$$\Rightarrow \frac{\sin(2x+50^\circ)}{\sin 150^\circ} = \frac{\cos 50^\circ}{-\cos(2x+50^\circ)}$$
$$\Rightarrow \sin(2x+50^\circ)\cos(2x+50^\circ) = -\sin 150^\circ \cos 50^\circ$$
$$\Rightarrow 2\sin(2x+50^\circ)\cos(2x+50^\circ) = -2\cos 60^\circ\cos 50^\circ$$
$$[\because \sin 150^\circ = \cos 60^\circ]$$
$$\Rightarrow \sin(4x+100^\circ) = \sin(270^\circ - 50^\circ)$$
$$\Rightarrow \sin(4x+100^\circ) = \sin 220^\circ$$
$$\Rightarrow 4x + 100^\circ = 220^\circ \Rightarrow x = 30^\circ$$

Example 85. The value of expression $\tan A + 2\tan 2A + 4\tan 4A + 8\cot 8A$ is

(a) $\tan A$ (b) $\cot A$
(c) $\tan\frac{A}{2}$ (d) $\cot\frac{A}{2}$

Sol. (b) $\tan A + 2\tan 2A + 4\tan 4A + 8\left(\frac{1-\tan^2 4A}{2\tan 4A}\right)$

$$\left[\text{by using } \cot 2\theta = \frac{1}{\tan 2\theta} = \frac{1-\tan^2\theta}{2\tan\theta}\right]$$
$$= \tan A + 2\tan 2A + \left(\frac{4\tan^2 4A + 4 - 4\tan^2 4A}{\tan 4A}\right)$$
$$= \tan A + 2\tan 2A + 4\cot 4A$$
$$= \tan A + 2\tan 2A + 4\left(\frac{1-\tan^2 2A}{2\tan 2A}\right)$$
$$\left[\text{by using } \cot 2\theta = \left(\frac{1-\tan^2\theta}{2\tan\theta}\right)\right]$$
$$= \tan A + \left[\frac{2\tan^2 2A + 2 - 2\tan^2 2A}{\tan 2A}\right] = \tan A + 2\cot 2A$$
$$= \tan A + 2\left(\frac{1-\tan^2 A}{2\tan A}\right)$$
$$= \frac{\tan^2 A + 1 - \tan^2 A}{\tan A} = \cot A$$

Note Students are advised to learn above result as formula. i.e. $\tan A + 2\cot 2A = \cot A$

1.13 Trigonometric Ratios of Submultiple of an Angle

An angle of the form $\frac{A}{n}$, where n is an integer is called a submultiple angle of A.

Trigonometric Ratios of *A* in Terms of Trigonometric Ratios of $\frac{A}{2}$

(i) $\sin A = 2\sin\frac{A}{2}\cos\frac{A}{2} = \frac{2\tan\frac{A}{2}}{1+\tan^2\frac{A}{2}}$

(ii) $\cos A = \cos^2 \frac{A}{2} - \sin^2 \frac{A}{2}$

$$= 2\cos^2 \frac{A}{2} - 1 = 1 - 2\sin^2 \frac{A}{2} = \frac{1 - \tan^2 \frac{A}{2}}{1 + \tan^2 \frac{A}{2}}$$

(iii) $\tan A = \dfrac{2 \tan \frac{A}{2}}{1 - \tan^2 \frac{A}{2}}$

(iv) $\cot A = \dfrac{\cot^2 \frac{A}{2} - 1}{2 \cot \frac{A}{2}}$

Trigonometric Ratios of A in Terms of Trigonometric Ratios of $\frac{A}{3}$

(i) $\sin A = 3 \sin \frac{A}{3} - 4 \sin^3 \frac{A}{3}$

(ii) $\cos A = 4 \cos^3 \frac{A}{3} - 3 \cos \frac{A}{3}$

(iii) $\tan A = \dfrac{3 \tan \frac{A}{3} - \tan^3 \frac{A}{3}}{1 - 3 \tan^2 \frac{A}{3}}$

(iv) $\cot A = \dfrac{\cot^3 \frac{A}{3} - 3 \cot \frac{A}{3}}{3 \cot^2 \frac{A}{3} - 1}$

Values of $\cos \frac{A}{2}$, $\sin \frac{A}{2}$ and $\tan \frac{A}{2}$ in Terms of $\cos A$

(i) $\cos^2 \frac{A}{2} = \frac{1 + \cos A}{2} \quad \therefore \cos \frac{A}{2} = \pm \sqrt{\frac{1 + \cos A}{2}}$

(ii) $\sin^2 \frac{A}{2} = \frac{1 - \cos A}{2} \quad \therefore \sin \frac{A}{2} = \pm \sqrt{\frac{1 - \cos A}{2}}$

(iii) $\tan^2 \frac{A}{2} = \frac{1 - \cos A}{1 + \cos A} \quad \therefore \tan \frac{A}{2} = \pm \sqrt{\frac{1 - \cos A}{1 + \cos A}}$

Values of $\sin \frac{A}{2}$ and $\cos \frac{A}{2}$ in Terms of $\sin A$

$$\left(\cos \frac{A}{2} + \sin \frac{A}{2}\right)^2 = \cos^2 \frac{A}{2} + \sin^2 \frac{A}{2} + 2 \cos \frac{A}{2} \sin \frac{A}{2}$$

$$= 1 + \sin A$$

$$\therefore \quad \cos \frac{A}{2} + \sin \frac{A}{2} = \pm \sqrt{1 + \sin A} \quad \text{...(i)}$$

Similarly, $\cos \frac{A}{2} - \sin \frac{A}{2} = \pm \sqrt{1 - \sin A}$ ...(ii)

Adding Eqs. (i) and (ii), we get

$$\cos \frac{A}{2} = \pm \frac{1}{2} \sqrt{1 + \sin A} \pm \frac{1}{2} \sqrt{1 - \sin A} \quad \text{...(iii)}$$

Subtracting Eq. (ii) from Eq. (i), we get

$$\sin \frac{A}{2} = \pm \frac{1}{2} \sqrt{1 + \sin A} \mp \frac{1}{2} \sqrt{1 - \sin A} \quad \text{...(iv)}$$

JEE SPIKE

If $\sin A$ is given, then there will be 4 values of $\sin \frac{A}{2}$ and $\cos \frac{A}{2}$ but if A is given. There will be one and only one value of $\cos \frac{A}{2}$ and $\sin \frac{A}{2}$ because + or – sign can be fixed before the radical sign in the following way

Concept Inside Video

$$\cos \frac{A}{2} + \sin \frac{A}{2} = \sqrt{2} \left(\frac{1}{\sqrt{2}} \cos \frac{A}{2} + \frac{1}{\sqrt{2}} \sin \frac{A}{2} \right)$$

$$= \sqrt{2} \left(\sin \frac{\pi}{4} \cos \frac{A}{2} + \cos \frac{\pi}{4} \sin \frac{A}{2} \right) = \sqrt{2} \sin \left(\frac{\pi}{4} + \frac{A}{2} \right)$$

Similarly, $\cos \frac{A}{2} - \sin \frac{A}{2} = \sqrt{2} \cos \left(\frac{\pi}{4} + \frac{A}{2} \right)$

Thus, the sign of $\cos \frac{A}{2} + \sin \frac{A}{2}$ and $\cos \frac{A}{2} - \sin \frac{A}{2}$ can be fixed by knowing the quadrant in which $\frac{\pi}{4} + \frac{A}{2}$ lies.

Values of Trigonometric Ratios of Some Particular Angles

I. (i) Value of sin 18°

Let $\theta = 18°$, then $5\theta = 90° \therefore 2\theta + 3\theta = 90°$

or $2\theta = 90° - 3\theta \therefore \sin 2\theta = \sin(90° - 3\theta)$

or $\sin 2\theta = \cos 3\theta$ or $2 \sin \theta \cos \theta = 4 \cos^3 \theta - 3 \cos \theta$

or $2 \sin \theta = 4 \cos^2 \theta - 3$ [dividing by $\cos \theta$]

or $2 \sin \theta = 4(1 - \sin^2 \theta) - 3 = 1 - 4 \sin^2 \theta$

or $4 \sin^2 \theta + 2 \sin \theta - 1 = 0$

$$\therefore \sin \theta = \frac{-2 \pm \sqrt{4 + 16}}{8} = \frac{-2 \pm 2\sqrt{5}}{8} = \frac{-1 \pm \sqrt{5}}{4}$$

Thus, $\sin \theta = \frac{-1 + \sqrt{5}}{4}, \frac{-1 - \sqrt{5}}{4}$

$\because \quad \theta = 18°$

$\therefore \sin \theta = \sin 18° > 0$, for 18° lies in the 1st quadrant

$$\therefore \sin \theta \text{ i.e. } \sin 18° = \frac{\sqrt{5} - 1}{4}$$

(ii) Value of cos 18°

$$\cos^2 18^\circ = 1 - \sin^2 18^\circ = 1 - \left(\frac{\sqrt{5}-1}{4}\right)^2$$

$$= 1 - \frac{5+1-2\sqrt{5}}{16} = 1 - \frac{6-2\sqrt{5}}{16}$$

$$= \frac{10+2\sqrt{5}}{16}$$

$$\therefore \cos 18^\circ = \frac{1}{4}\sqrt{10+2\sqrt{5}} \qquad [\because \cos 18^\circ > 0]$$

(iii) Value of tan 18°

$$\tan 18^\circ = \frac{\sin 18^\circ}{\cos 18^\circ} = \frac{\sqrt{5}-1}{4} \div \frac{\sqrt{10+2\sqrt{5}}}{4}$$

$$= \frac{\sqrt{5}-1}{\sqrt{10+2\sqrt{5}}} = \sqrt{1-\frac{2}{\sqrt{5}}}$$

(iv) Value of cot 18°

$$\cot 18^\circ = \frac{1}{\tan 18^\circ} = \frac{1}{\sqrt{1-\frac{2}{\sqrt{5}}}}$$

$$= \sqrt{5+2\sqrt{5}}$$

II. (i) Value of cos 36°

$$\cos 36^\circ = 1 - 2\sin^2 18^\circ = 1 - 2 \times \left(\frac{\sqrt{5}-1}{4}\right)^2$$

$$= 1 - 2 \times \frac{5+1-2\sqrt{5}}{16}$$

$$= 1 - \frac{3-\sqrt{5}}{4}$$

$$= \frac{4-3+\sqrt{5}}{4} = \frac{\sqrt{5}+1}{4}$$

Thus, $\cos 36^\circ = \dfrac{\sqrt{5}+1}{4}$

(ii) Value of sin 36°

$$\sin^2 36^\circ = 1 - \cos^2 36^\circ = 1 - \left(\frac{\sqrt{5}+1}{4}\right)^2$$

$$= 1 - \frac{6+2\sqrt{5}}{16}$$

$$= \frac{16-6-2\sqrt{5}}{16}$$

$$= \frac{10-2\sqrt{5}}{16}$$

$$\therefore \sin 36^\circ = \frac{1}{4}\sqrt{10-2\sqrt{5}} \qquad [\because \sin 36^\circ > 0]$$

(iii) Value of tan 36°

$$\tan 36^\circ = \frac{\sin 36^\circ}{\cos 36^\circ} = \frac{\frac{1}{4}\sqrt{10-2\sqrt{5}}}{\frac{\sqrt{5}+1}{4}}$$

$$= \sqrt{5-2\sqrt{5}}$$

(iv) Value of cot 36°

$$\cot 36^\circ = \frac{1}{\tan 36^\circ} = \frac{1}{\sqrt{5-2\sqrt{5}}} = \sqrt{1+\frac{2}{\sqrt{5}}}$$

III. (i) Value of tan $7\frac{1}{2}^\circ$

Let $\theta = 7\frac{1}{2}^\circ$, then $2\theta = 15^\circ$

Now, $\tan\theta = \dfrac{1-\cos 2\theta}{\sin 2\theta}$

$$[\because 1-\cos 2\theta = 2\sin^2\theta \text{ and } \sin 2\theta = 2\sin\theta\cos\theta]$$

$$= \frac{1-\cos 15^\circ}{\sin 15^\circ} = \frac{1-\frac{\sqrt{3}+1}{2\sqrt{2}}}{\frac{\sqrt{3}-1}{2\sqrt{2}}}$$

$$= \frac{2\sqrt{2}-\sqrt{3}-1}{\sqrt{3}-1} = \frac{(2\sqrt{2}-\sqrt{3}-1)(\sqrt{3}+1)}{(\sqrt{3}-1)(\sqrt{3}+1)}$$

$$= \frac{2\sqrt{6}-3-\sqrt{3}+2\sqrt{2}-\sqrt{3}-1}{3-1}$$

$$= \frac{2\sqrt{6}-2\sqrt{3}-4+2\sqrt{2}}{2}$$

$$= \sqrt{6}-\sqrt{3}-2+\sqrt{2}$$

$$= \sqrt{3}(\sqrt{2}-1)-\sqrt{2}(\sqrt{2}-1)$$

$$= (\sqrt{3}-\sqrt{2})(\sqrt{2}-1)$$

(ii) Value of cot $7\frac{1}{2}^\circ$

Let $\theta = 7\frac{1}{2}^\circ$

Now, $\cot\theta = \dfrac{1}{\tan\theta} = \dfrac{1}{\tan 7\frac{1}{2}^\circ}$

$$= \frac{1}{(\sqrt{3}-\sqrt{2})(\sqrt{2}-1)}$$

$$= (\sqrt{3}+\sqrt{2})(\sqrt{2}+1)$$

$$\therefore \quad \cot 7\frac{1}{2}^\circ = (\sqrt{3}+\sqrt{2})(\sqrt{2}+1)$$

(iii) **Value of sin 7.5°**

$$\sin 7.5^\circ = \sqrt{\frac{1-\cos(2\times 7.5^\circ)}{2}} \qquad [\because \cos 2\theta = 1 - 2\sin^2\theta]$$

$$= \sqrt{\frac{1-\cos 15^\circ}{2}} = \sqrt{\frac{1-\frac{\sqrt{3}+1}{2\sqrt{2}}}{2}} = \frac{\sqrt{8-2\sqrt{6}-2\sqrt{2}}}{4}$$

(iv) **Value of cos 7.5°**

$$\cos 7.5^\circ = \sqrt{\frac{1+\cos(2\times 7.5^\circ)}{2}} \qquad [\because \cos 2\theta = 2\cos^2\theta - 1]$$

$$= \sqrt{\frac{1+\cos 15^\circ}{2}} = \sqrt{\frac{1+\frac{\sqrt{3}+1}{2\sqrt{2}}}{2}} = \frac{\sqrt{8+2\sqrt{6}+2\sqrt{2}}}{4}$$

IV. (i) **Value of $\cos 22\frac{1^\circ}{2}$**

Let $\theta = 22\frac{1^\circ}{2}$, then $2\theta = 45^\circ$

$$\text{Now, } \cos^2 22\frac{1^\circ}{2} = \frac{1+\cos 45^\circ}{2} = \frac{1+\frac{1}{\sqrt{2}}}{2}$$

$$= \frac{\sqrt{2}+1}{2\sqrt{2}} = \frac{2+\sqrt{2}}{4}$$

$$\therefore \cos 22\frac{1^\circ}{2} = \frac{1}{2}\sqrt{2+\sqrt{2}} \qquad \left[\because \cos 22\frac{1^\circ}{2} > 0\right]$$

(ii) **Value of $\sin 22\frac{1^\circ}{2}$**

$$\sin^2 22\frac{1^\circ}{2} = \frac{1-\cos 45^\circ}{2} = \frac{1-\frac{1}{\sqrt{2}}}{2} = \frac{\sqrt{2}-1}{2\sqrt{2}} = \frac{2-\sqrt{2}}{4}$$

$$\therefore \sin 22\frac{1^\circ}{2} = \frac{1}{2}\sqrt{2-\sqrt{2}} \qquad \left[\because \sin 22\frac{1^\circ}{2} > 0\right]$$

(iii) **Value of $\tan 22\frac{1^\circ}{2}$**

$$\tan 22\frac{1^\circ}{2} = \frac{\sin 22\frac{1^\circ}{2}}{\cos 22\frac{1^\circ}{2}} = \sqrt{2}-1$$

(iv) **Value of $\cot 22\frac{1^\circ}{2}$**

$$\cot 22\frac{1^\circ}{2} = \frac{1}{\tan 22\frac{1^\circ}{2}} = \frac{1}{\sqrt{2}-1} = \sqrt{2}+1$$

V. **Value of $\cos 67\frac{1^\circ}{2}$, $\sin 67\frac{1^\circ}{2}$, $\tan 67\frac{1^\circ}{2}$ and $\cot 67\frac{1^\circ}{2}$**

$$\cos 67\frac{1^\circ}{2} = \sin 22\frac{1^\circ}{2} = \frac{1}{2}\sqrt{2-\sqrt{2}}$$

$$\sin 67\frac{1^\circ}{2} = \cos 22\frac{1^\circ}{2} = \frac{1}{2}\sqrt{2+\sqrt{2}}$$

$$\tan 67\frac{1^\circ}{2} = \frac{\sin 22\frac{1^\circ}{2}}{\cos 22\frac{1^\circ}{2}} = \frac{\frac{1}{2}\sqrt{2+\sqrt{2}}}{\frac{1}{2}\sqrt{2-\sqrt{2}}}$$

$$= \sqrt{2}+1$$

$$\cot 67\frac{1^\circ}{2} = \frac{1}{\tan 67\frac{1^\circ}{2}} = \frac{1}{\sqrt{2}+1} = \sqrt{2}-1$$

All these values are tabulated as follows:

	7.5°	15°	18°	22.5°	36°	67.5°	75°
sin	$\frac{\sqrt{8-2\sqrt{6}-2\sqrt{5}}}{4}$	$\frac{\sqrt{3}-1}{2\sqrt{2}}$	$\frac{\sqrt{5}-1}{4}$	$\frac{\sqrt{2-\sqrt{2}}}{2}$	$\frac{\sqrt{10-2\sqrt{5}}}{4}$	$\frac{\sqrt{2+\sqrt{2}}}{2}$	$\frac{\sqrt{3}+1}{2\sqrt{2}}$
cos	$\frac{\sqrt{8+2\sqrt{6}+2\sqrt{5}}}{4}$	$\frac{\sqrt{3}+1}{2\sqrt{2}}$	$\frac{\sqrt{10+2\sqrt{5}}}{4}$	$\frac{\sqrt{2+\sqrt{2}}}{2}$	$\frac{\sqrt{5}+1}{4}$	$\frac{\sqrt{2-\sqrt{2}}}{2}$	$\frac{\sqrt{3}-1}{2\sqrt{2}}$
tan	$\frac{(\sqrt{3}-\sqrt{2})}{(\sqrt{2}-1)}$	$2-\sqrt{3}$	$\sqrt{1-\frac{2}{\sqrt{5}}}$	$\sqrt{2}-1$	$\sqrt{5-2\sqrt{5}}$	$\sqrt{2}+1$	$2+\sqrt{3}$
cot	$\frac{(\sqrt{3}+\sqrt{2})}{(\sqrt{2}+1)}$	$2+\sqrt{3}$	$\sqrt{5+2\sqrt{5}}$	$\sqrt{2}+1$	$\sqrt{1+\frac{2}{\sqrt{5}}}$	$\sqrt{2}-1$	$2-\sqrt{3}$

JEE SCANNER

Example Similar to PYQ Asked in JEE Main 2022

$\alpha = \cos 36°$ is a root of which of the following equation :

(a) $16x^4 + 12x^2 - 1 = 0$ (b) $16x^4 - 12x^2 + 1 = 0$

(c) $16x^4 + 12x^2 + 1 = 0$ (d) $16x^4 - 12x^2 - 1 = 0$

Sol. (b) Take $\cos 72° = \dfrac{\sqrt{5}-1}{4}$

Let $\cos 36° = \alpha$

Now, $2\cos^2 36° - 1 = \cos 72°$

$$\Rightarrow \quad 2\cos^2 36° - 1 = \frac{\sqrt{5}-1}{4}$$

$$\Rightarrow \quad 8\alpha^2 - 4 = \sqrt{5} - 1 \Rightarrow 8\alpha^2 - 3 = \sqrt{5}$$

Take square on both sides,

$$(8\alpha^2 - 3)^2 = 5$$

$$\Rightarrow \quad 64\alpha^4 + 9 - 48\alpha^2 = 5$$

$$\Rightarrow \quad 64\alpha^4 - 48\alpha^2 + 4 = 0 \Rightarrow 16\alpha^4 - 12\alpha^2 + 1 = 0$$

So, $\alpha = \cos 36°$ is a roots of $16x^4 - 12x^2 + 1 = 0$

Skill Builder

$\alpha = \sin 36°$ is a root of which of the following equation:

(a) $16x^4 + 20x^2 - 5 = 0$

(b) $16^4 + 20x^2 + 5 = 0$

(c) $-16x^4 - 20x^2 = 5 = 0$

(d) $16x^4 - 20x^2 + 5 = 0$

For Sol.

- **For more practice** See Q.15 of Milestone Practice 5.

Example 86. Find an angle θ such that $\sec\theta = \cot\theta$.

Sol. Given, $\sec\theta = \cot\theta$

$$\Rightarrow \quad \frac{1}{\cos\theta} = \frac{\cos\theta}{\sin\theta} \Rightarrow \sin\theta = \cos^2\theta$$

$$\Rightarrow \quad \sin\theta = 1 - \sin^2\theta \Rightarrow \sin^2\theta + \sin\theta - 1 = 0$$

$$\Rightarrow \quad \sin\theta = \frac{-1 \pm \sqrt{(-1)^2 - 4(1)(-1)}}{2(1)}$$

$$\Rightarrow \quad \sin\theta = \frac{-1 \pm \sqrt{5}}{2} \Rightarrow \sin\theta = \frac{-1+\sqrt{5}}{2} \quad [\because \sin\theta \le 1]$$

$$\Rightarrow \quad \sin\theta = 2 \times \frac{\sqrt{5}-1}{4}$$

$$\Rightarrow \quad \sin\theta = 2\sin 18°$$

$$\Rightarrow \quad \theta = \sin^{-1}(2\sin 18°)$$

Example 87. Prove that

$$\cos^4\frac{\pi}{8} + \cos^4\frac{3\pi}{8} + \cos^4\frac{5\pi}{8} + \cos^4\frac{7\pi}{8} = \frac{3}{2}.$$

Sol. $\text{LHS} = \left(\cos^4\frac{\pi}{8} + \cos^4\frac{7\pi}{8}\right) + \left(\cos^4\frac{3\pi}{8} + \cos^4\frac{5\pi}{8}\right)$

$$= \left[\cos^4\frac{\pi}{8} + \cos^4\left(\pi - \frac{\pi}{8}\right)\right] + \left[\cos^4\frac{3\pi}{8} + \cos^4\left(\pi - \frac{3\pi}{8}\right)\right]$$

$$= 2\cos^4\frac{\pi}{8} + 2\cos^4\frac{3\pi}{8} \quad [\because \cos(\pi - \theta) = -\cos\theta]$$

$$= 2\left[\left(\cos^2\frac{\pi}{8}\right)^2 + \left(\cos^2\frac{3\pi}{8}\right)^2\right]$$

$$= 2\left[\left(\frac{1+\cos\frac{\pi}{4}}{2}\right)^2 + \left(\frac{1+\cos\frac{3\pi}{4}}{2}\right)^2\right]$$

$$= \frac{1}{2}\left[\left(1+\frac{1}{\sqrt{2}}\right)^2 + \left(1-\frac{1}{\sqrt{2}}\right)^2\right]$$

$$= \frac{1}{2}\left[1 + \frac{1}{2} + 2\cdot\frac{1}{\sqrt{2}} + 1 + \frac{1}{2} - 2\cdot\frac{1}{\sqrt{2}}\right] = \frac{3}{2} = \text{RHS}$$

Example 88. Show that

$$4\sin 27° = \sqrt{5+\sqrt{5}} - \sqrt{3-\sqrt{5}}.$$

Sol. LHS $= 4\sin 27°$

$$= \sqrt{16\sin^2 27°} \quad [\because \sin 27° > 0]$$

$$= \sqrt{16\left(\frac{1-\cos(2\times 27°)}{2}\right)} \quad [\because \cos 2\theta = 1 - 2\sin^2\theta]$$

$$= \sqrt{8(1-\cos 54°)}$$

$$= \sqrt{8(1-\sin 36°)} \quad [\because \cos(90° - \theta) = \sin\theta]$$

$$= \sqrt{8\left(1 - \frac{\sqrt{10-2\sqrt{5}}}{4}\right)}$$

$$= \sqrt{2(4 - \sqrt{10-2\sqrt{5}})} = \sqrt{8 - 2\sqrt{10-2\sqrt{5}}}$$

$$= \sqrt{(5+\sqrt{5}) + (3-\sqrt{5}) - 2\sqrt{(5+\sqrt{5})(3-\sqrt{5})}}$$

$$= \sqrt{(\sqrt{5+\sqrt{5}})^2 + (\sqrt{3-\sqrt{5}})^2 - 2\sqrt{(5+\sqrt{5})(3-\sqrt{5})}}$$

$$= \sqrt{(\sqrt{5+\sqrt{5}} - \sqrt{3-\sqrt{5}})^2}$$

$$= \sqrt{5+\sqrt{5}} - \sqrt{3-\sqrt{5}}$$

Example 89. If $\tan x = -\dfrac{4}{3}, \dfrac{\pi}{2} < x < \pi$, then find the value of $\sin\dfrac{x}{2}, \cos\dfrac{x}{2}$ and $\tan\dfrac{x}{2}$.

Sol. Here, $\dfrac{\pi}{2} < x < \pi$

$$\therefore \quad \frac{\pi}{4} < \frac{x}{2} < \frac{\pi}{2}$$

Hence, $\sin\frac{x}{2}, \cos\frac{x}{2}, \tan\frac{x}{2}$ will be all positive.

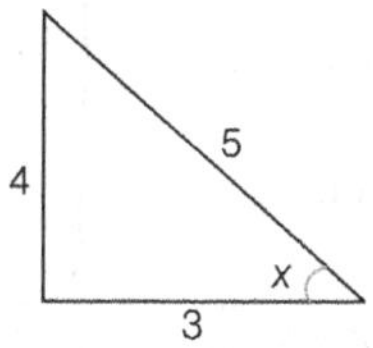

Given, $\tan x = -\frac{4}{3}$ and $\frac{\pi}{2} < x < \pi$

$\therefore \quad \cos x = -\frac{3}{5}$

Now, $\sin\frac{x}{2} = \sqrt{\frac{1-\cos x}{2}}$ $\left[\because \sin\frac{x}{2} > 0\right]$

$= \sqrt{\frac{1+\frac{3}{5}}{2}} = \frac{2}{\sqrt{5}} = \frac{2\sqrt{5}}{5}$

$\cos\frac{x}{2} = \sqrt{\frac{1+\cos x}{2}}$ $\left[\because \cos\frac{x}{2} > 0\right]$

$= \sqrt{\frac{1-\frac{3}{5}}{2}} = \frac{1}{\sqrt{5}} = \frac{\sqrt{5}}{5}$

and $\tan\frac{x}{2} = \frac{\sin\frac{x}{2}}{\cos\frac{x}{2}} = 2$

Example 90. Find the value of $\sin\frac{23\pi}{24}$.

Sol. $\sin\frac{23\pi}{24} = \sin\left(\pi - \frac{\pi}{24}\right) = \sin\frac{\pi}{24} = \sin 7\frac{1^\circ}{2}$

Let $\theta = 7\frac{1^\circ}{2}$, then $2\theta = 15^\circ$

Now, $\sin^2\theta = \frac{1-\cos 2\theta}{2} = \frac{1}{2}(1-\cos 15^\circ)$

$= \frac{1}{2}\left(1 - \frac{\sqrt{3}+1}{2\sqrt{2}}\right) = \frac{1}{2}\left(\frac{2\sqrt{2}-\sqrt{3}-1}{2\sqrt{2}}\right)$

$= \frac{2\sqrt{2}-\sqrt{3}-1}{4\sqrt{2}}$

$\therefore \quad \sin\theta = \sin 7\frac{1^\circ}{2} > 0$

$\therefore \quad \sin 7\frac{1^\circ}{2} = \sqrt{\frac{2\sqrt{2}-\sqrt{3}-1}{4\sqrt{2}}} = \frac{1}{4}\sqrt{8-2\sqrt{6}-2\sqrt{2}}$

Example 91. If $\alpha = 112°30'$, then find the value of $\sin\alpha$ and $\cos\alpha$.

Sol. Given, $\alpha = 112°30'$

$\therefore \quad 2\alpha = 225^\circ$

or $\cos 2\alpha = \cos 225^\circ = \cos(180^\circ + 45^\circ) = -\cos 45^\circ = -\frac{1}{\sqrt{2}}$

Now, $\sin^2\alpha = \frac{1-\cos 2\alpha}{2}$

Since, α lies in the 2nd quadrant.

$\therefore$ $\sin\alpha$ is positive.

$\therefore \quad \sin\alpha = \sqrt{\frac{1-\cos 2\alpha}{2}} = \sqrt{\frac{1-\left(-\frac{1}{\sqrt{2}}\right)}{2}}$

$= \sqrt{\frac{\sqrt{2}+1}{2\sqrt{2}}} = \frac{\sqrt{2+\sqrt{2}}}{2}$

Hence, $\sin\alpha = \frac{\sqrt{2+\sqrt{2}}}{2}$

But $\cos\alpha$ is negative in 2nd quadrant.

$\therefore \quad \cos\alpha = -\sqrt{\frac{1+\cos 2\alpha}{2}} = -\sqrt{\frac{1-\frac{1}{\sqrt{2}}}{2}} = -\frac{\sqrt{2-\sqrt{2}}}{2}$

Example 92. If $\tan\frac{\theta}{2} = \sqrt{\frac{a-b}{a+b}}\tan\frac{\phi}{2}$, then prove that $\cos\theta = \frac{a\cos\phi + b}{a + b\cos\phi}$.

Sol. Given, $\tan\frac{\theta}{2} = \sqrt{\frac{a-b}{a+b}}\tan\frac{\phi}{2}$

Now, $\cos\theta = \frac{1-\tan^2\frac{\theta}{2}}{1+\tan^2\frac{\theta}{2}} = \frac{1-\frac{a-b}{a+b}\tan^2\frac{\phi}{2}}{1+\frac{a-b}{a+b}\tan^2\frac{\phi}{2}}$

$= \frac{1-\frac{a-b}{a+b}\cdot\frac{\sin^2\frac{\phi}{2}}{\cos^2\frac{\phi}{2}}}{1+\frac{a-b}{a+b}\cdot\frac{\sin^2\frac{\phi}{2}}{\cos^2\frac{\phi}{2}}}$

$= \frac{(a+b)\cos^2\frac{\phi}{2} - (a-b)\sin^2\frac{\phi}{2}}{(a+b)\cos^2\frac{\phi}{2} + (a-b)\sin^2\frac{\phi}{2}}$

$= \frac{a\left(\cos^2\frac{\phi}{2} - \sin^2\frac{\phi}{2}\right) + b\left(\cos^2\frac{\phi}{2} + \sin^2\frac{\phi}{2}\right)}{a\left(\cos^2\frac{\phi}{2} + \sin^2\frac{\phi}{2}\right) + b\left(\cos^2\frac{\phi}{2} - \sin^2\frac{\phi}{2}\right)}$

$= \frac{a\cos\phi + b}{a + b\cos\phi}$

Example 93. If $\cos\theta = \frac{\cos\alpha - \cos\beta}{1 - \cos\alpha\cos\beta}$, then prove that one of the values of $\tan\frac{\theta}{2}$ is $\tan\frac{\alpha}{2}\cot\frac{\beta}{2}$.

Sol. $\tan^2\frac{\theta}{2}=\frac{1-\cos\theta}{1+\cos\theta}=\frac{1-\frac{\cos\alpha-\cos\beta}{1-\cos\alpha\cos\beta}}{1+\frac{\cos\alpha-\cos\beta}{1-\cos\alpha\cos\beta}}$

$$=\frac{1-\cos\alpha\cos\beta-\cos\alpha+\cos\beta}{1-\cos\alpha\cos\beta+\cos\alpha-\cos\beta}$$

$$=\frac{(1-\cos\alpha)+\cos\beta(1-\cos\alpha)}{(1+\cos\alpha)-\cos\beta(1+\cos\alpha)}$$

$$=\frac{(1-\cos\alpha)(1+\cos\beta)}{(1+\cos\alpha)(1-\cos\beta)}=\tan^2\frac{\alpha}{2}\cot^2\frac{\beta}{2}$$

$\therefore\ \tan\frac{\theta}{2}=\pm\tan\frac{\alpha}{2}\cot\frac{\beta}{2}$

Hence, one of the values of $\tan\frac{\theta}{2}$ is $\tan\frac{\alpha}{2}\cot\frac{\beta}{2}$.

Example 94. Prove that

$$\sin\frac{\pi}{5}\sin\frac{2\pi}{5}\sin\frac{3\pi}{5}\sin\frac{4\pi}{5}=\frac{5}{16}.$$

Sol. We have, LHS $=\sin\frac{\pi}{5}\sin\frac{2\pi}{5}\sin\frac{3\pi}{5}\sin\frac{4\pi}{5}$

$$=\sin\frac{\pi}{5}\sin\frac{2\pi}{5}\sin\left(\pi-\frac{2\pi}{5}\right)\sin\left(\pi-\frac{\pi}{5}\right)$$

$$=\sin^2\frac{\pi}{5}\sin^2\frac{2\pi}{5}\qquad[\because \sin(\pi-\theta)=\sin\theta]$$

$$=(\sin 36^\circ)^2\times(\sin 72^\circ)^2$$

$$=(\sin 36^\circ)^2\times(\cos 18^\circ)^2$$

$$[\because \sin 72^\circ=\sin(90^\circ-18^\circ)=\cos 18^\circ]$$

$$=\frac{(10-2\sqrt{5})}{16}\times\frac{(10+2\sqrt{5})}{16}=\frac{(100-20)}{(16\times16)}$$

$$\left[\because \sin 36^\circ=\frac{\sqrt{10-2\sqrt{5}}}{4}\text{ and }\cos 18^\circ=\frac{\sqrt{10+2\sqrt{5}}}{4}\right]$$

$$=\frac{80}{(16\times16)}=\frac{5}{16}$$

= RHS

Example 95. If $0<x<\pi$ and $\cos x+\sin x=\frac{1}{2}$, then find the value of $\tan x$.

Sol. Given, $\cos x+\sin x=\frac{1}{2}\Rightarrow\frac{1-\tan^2\frac{x}{2}}{1+\tan^2\frac{x}{2}}+\frac{2\tan\frac{x}{2}}{1+\tan^2\frac{x}{2}}=\frac{1}{2}$

Let $\tan\frac{x}{2}=t$, then $\frac{1-t^2}{1+t^2}+\frac{2t}{1+t^2}=\frac{1}{2}$

$\Rightarrow\ 3t^2-4t-1=0\Rightarrow t=\frac{2\pm\sqrt{7}}{3}$

$\Rightarrow\quad t=\tan\frac{x}{2}=\frac{2+\sqrt{7}}{3}\qquad\left[\because 0<\frac{x}{2}<\frac{\pi}{2},\ \tan\frac{x}{2}>0\right]$

Now, $\tan x=\frac{2\tan\frac{x}{2}}{1-\tan^2\frac{x}{2}}=\frac{2\left(\frac{2+\sqrt{7}}{3}\right)}{1-\left(\frac{2+\sqrt{7}}{3}\right)^2}$

$$=-\frac{3(2+\sqrt{7})}{1+2\sqrt{7}}\times\frac{1-2\sqrt{7}}{1-2\sqrt{7}}$$

$\therefore\quad \tan x=-\left(\frac{4+\sqrt{7}}{3}\right)$

Example 96. The value of $\tan 9^\circ-\tan 27^\circ-\tan 63^\circ+\tan 81^\circ$ is

(a) 2 (b) 4

(c) 8 (d) 0

Sol. (b) $(\tan 9^\circ+\tan 81^\circ)-(\tan 27^\circ+\tan 63^\circ)$

$$=(\tan 9^\circ+\tan(90^\circ-9^\circ))-(\tan 27^\circ+\tan(90^\circ-27^\circ))$$

$$=(\tan 9^\circ+\cot 9^\circ)-(\tan 27^\circ+\cot 27^\circ)$$

$$=\left(\tan 9^\circ+\frac{1}{\tan 9^\circ}\right)-\left(\tan 27^\circ+\frac{1}{\tan 27^\circ}\right)$$

$$=\left(\frac{\sin 9^\circ}{\cos 9^\circ}+\frac{\cos 9^\circ}{\sin 9^\circ}\right)-\left(\frac{\sin 27^\circ}{\cos 27^\circ}+\frac{\cos 27^\circ}{\sin 27^\circ}\right)$$

$$=\left(\frac{\sin^2 9^\circ+\cos^2 9^\circ}{\sin 9^\circ\cos 9^\circ}\right)-\left(\frac{\sin^2 27^\circ+\cos^2 27^\circ}{\sin 27^\circ\cos 27^\circ}\right)$$

$$=\frac{2}{2\sin 9^\circ\cos 9^\circ}-\frac{2}{2\sin 27^\circ\cos 27^\circ}=\frac{2}{\sin 18^\circ}-\frac{2}{\sin 54^\circ}$$

$$=2\left[\frac{1}{\left(\frac{\sqrt{5}-1}{4}\right)}-\frac{1}{\left(\frac{\sqrt{5}+1}{4}\right)}\right]$$

$$=2\left[\frac{4}{\sqrt{5}-1}-\frac{4}{\sqrt{5}+1}\right]=8\left[\frac{1}{\sqrt{5}-1}-\frac{1}{\sqrt{5}+1}\right]$$

$$=8\left[\frac{\sqrt{5}+1-\sqrt{5}+1}{(\sqrt{5}-1)(\sqrt{5}+1)}\right]=\frac{8\times2}{(\sqrt{5})^2-1}=\frac{16}{4}=4$$

Some Important Results

1. $\mathbf{\sin\theta\cdot\sin(60^\circ-\theta)\cdot\sin(60^\circ+\theta)=\frac{1}{4}\sin 3\theta}$

Proof LHS $=\sin\theta\sin(60^\circ-\theta)\sin(60^\circ+\theta)$

$$=\sin\theta[\sin 60^\circ\cos\theta-\cos 60^\circ\sin\theta]$$

$$[\sin 60^\circ\cos\theta+\cos 60^\circ\sin\theta]$$

$$=\sin\theta\left[\frac{\sqrt{3}}{2}\cos\theta-\frac{1}{2}\sin\theta\right]\left[\frac{\sqrt{3}}{2}\cos\theta+\frac{1}{2}\sin\theta\right]$$

$$= \sin\theta\left[\frac{3}{4}\cos^2\theta - \frac{1}{4}\sin^2\theta\right]$$

$$= \frac{\sin\theta}{4}[3\cos^2\theta - \sin^2\theta]$$

$$= \frac{\sin\theta}{4}[3(1-\sin^2\theta) - \sin^2\theta] = \frac{\sin\theta}{4}[3 - 4\sin^2\theta]$$

$$= \frac{1}{4}[3\sin\theta - 4\sin^3\theta] = \frac{\sin 3\theta}{4}$$

2. $\cos\theta \cdot \cos(60° - \theta)\cos(60° + \theta) = \frac{1}{4}\cos 3\theta$
3. $\tan\theta \cdot \tan(60° - \theta)\tan(60° + \theta) = \tan 3\theta$
4. $\cot\theta \cdot \cot(60° - \theta)\cot(60° + \theta) = \cot 3\theta$

JEE SCANNER

Example Similar to PYQ Asked in JEE Main 2022

The value of $4\cos 15° \cos 45° \cos 75°$ *is equal to*

(a) $\frac{1}{2}$ (b) $\frac{1}{\sqrt{2}}$ (c) $\frac{\sqrt{3}}{2}$ (d) 1

Sol. (b) Given trigonometric equation is

$$4\cos 15° \cos 45° \cos 75°$$

$$= 4\cos 15° \cos(60° - 15°)\cos(60° + 15°)$$

$$\left[\because \frac{1}{4}\cos 3\theta = \cos\theta\cos(60° - \theta)\cos(60° + \theta)\right]$$

$$= 4 \times \frac{1}{4}\cos(3 \times 15°) = \frac{1}{\sqrt{2}}$$

Skill Builder

The value of $\cos 15° \cos 45° \times 2\operatorname{cosec} 75°$ is

(a) $\frac{1}{\sqrt{2}}$ (b) $\sqrt{2}$

(c) $2\sqrt{2}$ (d) $\frac{3}{\sqrt{2}}$

For Sol.

- **For more practice** See Q.17 of Milestone Practice 5.

Example 97. Find the value of $\dfrac{\cos 20° + 8\sin 10° \sin 50° \sin 70°}{\sin^2 80°}$.

Sol. $\dfrac{\cos 20° + 8\sin 10° \sin 50° \sin 70°}{\sin^2 80°}$

$$= \frac{\cos 20° + 8\sin 10° \sin(60° - 10°)\sin(60° + 10°)}{\sin^2 80°}$$

$$= \frac{\cos 20° + 8\left(\frac{1}{4}\sin 3 \times 10°\right)}{\sin^2 80°}$$

$$= \frac{\cos 20° + 2\sin 30°}{\sin^2 80°} = \frac{\cos 20° + 2 \times \frac{1}{2}}{\sin^2 80°}$$

$$= \frac{1 + \cos 20°}{\sin^2(90° - 10°)} = \frac{1 + (2\cos^2 10° - 1)}{\cos^2 10°} = \frac{2\cos^2 10°}{\cos^2 10°} = 2$$

Example 98. The value of the expression $2\tan 2A + 4\tan 4A + 8\cot 8A$ is

(a) $\cot\frac{A}{2} - \tan\frac{A}{2}$ (b) $\cot A + \tan A$

(c) $\cot A - \tan A$ (d) $\tan\frac{A}{2} + \cot\frac{A}{2}$

Sol. (c) $2\tan 2A + 4\tan 4A + 8\cot 8A$

$$= 2\tan 2A + 4\tan 4A + 8\left(\frac{1 - \tan^2 4A}{2\tan 4A}\right)$$

$$\left[\text{by using } \cot 2\theta = \left(\frac{1 - \tan^2\theta}{2\tan\theta}\right)\right]$$

$$= 2\tan 2A + \left(\frac{4\tan^2 4A + 4 - 4\tan^2 4A}{\tan 4A}\right)$$

$$= 2\tan 2A + 4\cot 4A$$

$$= 2\tan 2A + 4\left(\frac{1 - \tan^2 2A}{2\tan 2A}\right)$$

$$\left[\text{by using } \cot 2\theta = \frac{1 - \tan^2\theta}{2\tan\theta}\right]$$

$$= \frac{2\tan^2 2A + 2 - 2\tan^2 2A}{\tan 2A} = 2\cot 2A$$

$$= 2\left(\frac{1 - \tan^2 A}{2\tan A}\right) = \frac{1 - \tan^2 A}{\tan A} = \cot A - \tan A$$

Note Students are advised to learn above result as formula.

i.e. $\tan A + 2\cot 2A = \cot A$

Example 99. If $\sin\theta + \cos\theta = \frac{1}{2}$, then $[\sin(2\theta) + \sin(6\theta)]$ is equal to

(a) $\frac{21}{16}$ (b) $\frac{23}{16}$ (c) $-\frac{21}{16}$ (d) $-\frac{23}{16}$

Sol. (c) $\sin\theta + \cos\theta = \frac{1}{2} \Rightarrow \sin^2\theta + \cos^2\theta + 2\sin\theta\cos\theta = \frac{1}{4}$

$$\Rightarrow \quad \sin 2\theta = \frac{1}{4} - 1 = -\frac{3}{4}$$

$$\therefore \cos 2\theta = \sqrt{1 - \sin^2(2\theta)} = \sqrt{1 - \frac{9}{16}} = \pm\frac{\sqrt{7}}{4}$$

$$\therefore \sin 2\theta + \sin 6\theta = 2\sin 4\theta\cos 2\theta = 4\sin 2\theta\cos^2 2\theta$$

$$= 4\left(-\frac{3}{4}\right)\left(\frac{7}{16}\right) = -\frac{21}{16}$$

Milestone Practice 1.5

1. If $A+B=\frac{\pi}{2}$, then maximum value of $\sin A \sin B$ is

(a) 2 (b) 0
(c) $\frac{1}{2}$ (d) Not defined

2. The value of $\tan 15^\circ \tan 45^\circ \tan 105^\circ$ is

(a) -1 (b) 1
(c) $-\sqrt{3}$ (d) None of these

3. The value of $\cos 4A$ is

(a) $\cos^4 A + 6\cos^2 A \sin^2 A + \sin^4 A$
(b) $\sin^4 A - 6\sin^2 A \cos^2 A + \cos^4 A$
(c) $\cos^4 A - 4\cos^2 A \sin^2 A + \sin^4 A$
(d) $\sin^4 A + 4\sin^2 A \cos^2 A + \cos^4 A$

4. The value of $\sin 5A$ is

(a) $5\cos^4 A \sin A - 10\cos^2 A \sin^3 A + \sin^5 A$
(b) $5\cos^4 A \sin A + 10\cos^2 A \sin^3 A + \sin^5 A$
(c) $5\sin^4 A \cos A - 10\sin^2 A \cos^3 A + \sin^5 A$
(d) $5\sin^4 A \cos A + 10\sin^2 A \cos^3 A + \sin^5 A$

5. If $\sqrt{2+\sqrt{2+\sqrt{2+\sqrt{2+2\cos 16\theta}}}} = k\cos\theta$, then value of k is

(a) $2^{\frac{1}{4}}$ (b) 2^4
(c) 2^0 (d) 2^1

6. If A and B are two different roots of equation $a\cos\theta + b\sin\theta = c$, then show that

(i) $\tan(A+B) = \frac{2ab}{a^2-b^2}$

(ii) $\cos(A+B) = \frac{a^2-b^2}{a^2+b^2}$

7. If $\pi < \theta < \frac{3\pi}{2}$, then find the value of $\sqrt{\frac{1-\cos 2\theta}{1+\cos 2\theta}}$.

8. The value of $\sin^4\frac{\pi}{8} + \sin^4\frac{3\pi}{8} + \sin^4\frac{5\pi}{8} + \sin^4\frac{7\pi}{8}$ is equal to

(a) 1 (b) 2 (c) $\frac{3}{2}$ (d) $\frac{1}{2}$

9. If $A = 2\sin^2\theta - \cos 2\theta$ and $A \in [\alpha, \beta]$, then find the values of α and β.

10. If $\sin x + \cos x = \frac{1}{5}$, then find the value of $\tan 2x$.

11. If $\tan A + 2\tan 2A + 4\tan 4A + 8\cot 8A = k\cot A$, then find the value of k.

12. If $m^2 \cos\frac{2\pi}{15}\cos\frac{4\pi}{15}\cos\frac{8\pi}{15}\cos\frac{14\pi}{15} = n^2$, then find the value of $\frac{m^2-n^2}{n^2}$.

13. If $(2^n+1)\theta = \pi$, then find the value of $2^n \cos\theta \cos 2\theta \cos 2^2\theta \ldots \cos 2^{n-1}\theta$.

14. If $\tan\theta \tan\phi = \sqrt{\frac{a-b}{a+b}}$, then show that $(a - b\cos 2\theta)(a - b\cos 2\phi)$ is independent of θ and ϕ.

15. The equation whose roots are $\tan\left(\frac{\pi}{8}\right)$ and $\tan\left(\frac{5\pi}{8}\right)$ is

(a) $x^2-2x+1=0$ (b) $x^2-2x-1=0$
(c) $x^2+2x+1=0$ (d) $x^2+2x-1=0$

16. If $\tan\left(\frac{x}{2}\right) = \operatorname{cosec} x - \sin x$, then the value of $\tan^2\left(\frac{x}{2}\right)$ is

(a) $\sqrt{5}-2$ (b) $\sqrt{5}+2$
(c) $2\sqrt{5}+2$ (d) $2\sqrt{5}-2$

17. The value of $\sin 12^\circ \sin 48^\circ \sin 54^\circ$ is

(a) $\frac{1}{4}$ (b) 1 (c) $\frac{1}{8}$ (d) $\frac{1}{2}$

18. The value of expression $\frac{1}{\cos 290^\circ} + \frac{1}{\sqrt{3}\sin 250^\circ}$ is

(a) $\frac{\sqrt{3}}{4}$ (b) $\frac{4}{\sqrt{3}}$
(c) $\frac{2}{\sqrt{3}}$ (d) $\frac{\sqrt{3}}{2}$

19. If $x + \frac{1}{x} = 2\cos\theta$, then find the value of $x^n + \frac{1}{x^n}$.

20. Show that $\sin 47^\circ + \sin 61^\circ - \sin 11^\circ - \sin 25^\circ = \cos 7^\circ$.

21. If α and β be two different roots of equation $a\cos\theta + b\sin\theta = c$, then show that $\sin(\alpha+\beta) = \frac{2ab}{a^2+b^2}$.

22. If $\sin\alpha + \sin\beta = a$ and $\cos\alpha + \cos\beta = b$, then show that $\tan\left(\frac{\alpha-\beta}{2}\right) = \pm\sqrt{\frac{4-a^2-b^2}{a^2+b^2}}$.

23. Show that $\cot 142\frac{1}{2}^\circ = \sqrt{2} + \sqrt{3} - 2 - \sqrt{6}$.

24. Find the value $\tan\frac{\pi}{5} + 2\tan\frac{2\pi}{5} + 4\cot\frac{4\pi}{5}$.

25. Show that $\cos\frac{\pi}{15}\cos\frac{2\pi}{15}\cos\frac{3\pi}{15}\cos\frac{4\pi}{15}\cos\frac{5\pi}{15}\cos\frac{6\pi}{15}\cos\frac{7\pi}{15} = \frac{1}{2^7}$.

26. If $\sin\alpha + \sin\beta = a$ and $\cos\alpha + \cos\beta = b$, then show that

(i) $\sin(\alpha + \beta) = \frac{2ab}{a^2 + b^2}$

(ii) $\cos(\alpha - \beta) = \frac{1}{2}(a^2 + b^2 - 2)$

27. Find the values of $\sin 67\frac{1}{2}^\circ$ and $\cos 67\frac{1}{2}^\circ$.

28. If $\tan x = \frac{b}{a}$, then $\sqrt{\frac{a+b}{a-b}} + \sqrt{\frac{a-b}{a+b}}$ is equal to

(a) $\frac{2\sin x}{\sqrt{\sin 2x}}$ (b) $\frac{2\cos x}{\sqrt{\cos 2x}}$

(c) $\frac{2\cos x}{\sqrt{\sin 2x}}$ (d) $\frac{2\sin x}{\sqrt{\cos 2x}}$

29. $\frac{\sqrt{1+\sin x} + \sqrt{1-\sin x}}{\sqrt{1+\sin x} - \sqrt{1-\sin x}}$ is equal to (when x lies in IInd quadrant).

(a) $\sin\frac{x}{2}$ (b) $\tan\frac{x}{2}$

(c) $\sec\frac{x}{2}$ (d) $\operatorname{cosec}\frac{x}{2}$

30. If $\sin^2(10^\circ)\sin(20^\circ)\sin(40^\circ)\sin(50^\circ)\sin(70^\circ) = \alpha - \frac{1}{16}\sin 10^\circ$, then $16 + \alpha^{-1}$ is equal to ....

Answer Key

1. (c)	2. (a)	3. (b)	4. (a)
5. (d)	7. $(\tan\theta)$	8. (c)	9. $(\alpha = -1, \beta = 3)$
10. $\left(\frac{24}{7}\right)$	11. (1)	12. (15)	13. (1)
15. (d)	16. (a)	17. (c)	18. (b)
19. $(2\cos n\theta)$	24. $\left(\cot\frac{\pi}{5}\right)$	27. $\left(\sin 67\frac{1}{2}^\circ = \frac{\sqrt{2+\sqrt{2}}}{2} \text{ and } \cos 67\frac{1}{2}^\circ = \frac{\sqrt{2-\sqrt{2}}}{2}\right)$	
28. (b)	29. (b)	30. 80	

For Detailed Solution

Milestone 6 Transformation Formulae

- Expressing Product of Trigonometric Functions as Sum or Difference

1.14 Expressing Product of Trigonometric Functions as Sum or Difference

(i) $2\sin A\cos B = \sin(A+B)+\sin(A-B)$

(ii) $2\cos A\sin B = \sin(A+B)-\sin(A-B)$

(iii) $2\cos A\cos B = \cos(A+B)+\cos(A-B)$

(iv) $2\sin A\sin B = \cos(A-B)-\cos(A+B)$

The above four formula can be obtained by expanding the right hand side and simplifying.

Example 100. The value of

$\sin 21°\cos 9° - \cos 84°\cos 6°$ is equal to

(a) 1 (b) $\frac{3}{2}$ (c) $\frac{1}{4}$ (d) $\frac{1}{2}$

Sol. (c) $\sin 21°\cos 9° - \cos 84°\cos 6°$

$$= \frac{1}{2}[2\sin 21°\cos 9° - 2\cos 84°\cos 6°]$$

$$= \frac{1}{2}[\sin(21°+9°)+\sin(21°-9°)] - \frac{1}{2}[\cos(84°+6°)+\cos(84°-6°)]$$

$$= \frac{1}{2}[\sin 30° + \sin 12°] - \frac{1}{2}[\cos 90° + \cos 78°]$$

$$= \frac{1}{2}\times\frac{1}{2}+\frac{1}{2}\sin 12° - \frac{1}{2}\times 0 - \frac{1}{2}\cos(90°-12°)$$

$$= \frac{1}{4}+\frac{1}{2}\sin 12° - \frac{1}{2}\sin 12° = \frac{1}{4}$$

Example 101. Prove that $\sin 20°\sin 40°\sin 80° = \frac{\sqrt{3}}{8}$.

Sol. LHS $= \sin 20°\sin 40°\sin 80° = \frac{1}{2}(2\sin 80°\sin 40°)\sin 20°$

$$= \frac{1}{2}[\cos(80°-40°)-\cos(80°+40°)]\sin 20°$$

$$= \frac{1}{2}[\cos 40° - \cos 120°]\sin 20°$$

$$= \frac{1}{4}(2\cos 40°\sin 20° - 2\cos 120°\sin 20°)$$

$$= \frac{1}{4}\left[\sin(40°+20°)-\sin(40°-20°)-2\left(-\frac{1}{2}\right)\sin 20°\right]$$

$$= \frac{1}{4}[\sin 60° - \sin 20° + \sin 20°]$$

$$= \frac{1}{4}\sin 60° = \frac{1}{4}\cdot\frac{\sqrt{3}}{2} = \frac{\sqrt{3}}{8} = \text{RHS}$$

JEE SCANNER

Example Similar to PYQ Asked in JEE Main 2024

Let $0<\alpha,\beta<\frac{\pi}{2}$ satisfying the equation $3\sin^2\alpha+2\sin^2\beta=1$ and $3\sin 2\alpha-2\sin 2\beta=0$, and a real number k be such that $\sin(\alpha+2\beta)=k-4$. Then, the value of k is equal to

(a) 5 (b) $\frac{\pi}{2}$ (c) $\frac{\pi}{4}$ (d) 4

Sol. (a) Given, $3\sin 2\alpha - 2\sin 2\beta = 0 \Rightarrow \sin 2\beta = \frac{3}{2}\sin 2\alpha$ ...(i)

and $3\sin^2\alpha + 2\sin^2\beta = 1$

$\Rightarrow$ $3\sin^2\alpha = 1-2\sin^2\beta \Rightarrow 3\sin^2\alpha = \cos 2\beta$ ...(ii)

Now, $\cos(\alpha+2\beta) = \cos\alpha\cos 2\beta - \sin\alpha\sin 2\beta$

$$= \cos\alpha(3\sin^2\alpha) - \sin\alpha\left(\frac{3}{2}\sin 2\alpha\right)$$

[from Eqs. (i) and (ii)]

$$= 3\cos\alpha\sin^2\alpha - \frac{3}{2}\sin\alpha\sin 2\alpha$$

$$= 3\cos\alpha\sin^2\alpha - \frac{3}{2}\sin\alpha(2\sin\alpha\cos\alpha)$$

$$= 3\cos\alpha\sin^2\alpha - 3\sin^2\alpha\cos\alpha = 0$$

$\Rightarrow$ $(\alpha+2\beta) = \cos^{-1}(0) = \frac{\pi}{2}$

$\therefore$ $\alpha+2\beta = \frac{\pi}{2}$ $\left[\because 0<\alpha+2\beta<\frac{3\pi}{2}\right]$

Now, $\sin(\alpha+2\beta) = \sin\left(\frac{\pi}{2}\right) = 1 = k-4$ [given]

$\Rightarrow$ $k = 1+4 = 5 \Rightarrow k = 5$

Skill Builder

If $3\sin\beta = \sin(2\alpha+\beta)$ and $\tan(\alpha+\beta) = \frac{k}{2}\tan\alpha$, then the value of k is

(a) 2 (b) 3

(c) 4 (d) 6

For Sol.

■ **For more practice** See Q.10 of Milestone Practice 6.

Expressing Sum or Difference of Two Sines or Two Cosines as a Product

(i) $\sin C + \sin D = 2\sin\frac{C+D}{2}\cdot\cos\frac{C-D}{2}$

(ii) $\sin C - \sin D = 2\sin\frac{C-D}{2}\cdot\cos\frac{C+D}{2}$

(iii) $\cos C + \cos D = 2\cos\frac{C+D}{2}\cdot\cos\frac{C-D}{2}$

(iv) $\cos C - \cos D = -2\sin\frac{C+D}{2}\cdot\sin\frac{C-D}{2}$

or $2\sin\frac{C+D}{2}\cdot\sin\frac{D-C}{2}$

Some Other Useful Results

(i) $\tan A \pm \tan B = \frac{\sin(A\pm B)}{\cos A\cos B}$,

where $A, B \neq n\pi + \frac{\pi}{2}, n\in Z$

(ii) $\cot A \pm \cot B = \frac{\sin(B\pm A)}{\sin A\sin B}$,

where $A, B \neq n\pi, n\in Z$

(iii) $1 \pm \tan A\tan B = \frac{\cos(A\mp B)}{\cos A\cos B}$,

where $A, B \neq n\pi + \frac{\pi}{2}, n\in Z$

(iv) $1 \pm \cot A\cot B = \pm\frac{\cos(A\mp B)}{\sin A\sin B}$,

where $A, B \neq n\pi, n\in Z$

Example 102. The value of $\frac{\sin 70° + \cos 40°}{\cos 70° + \sin 40°}$ is

(a) $\frac{1}{2}$ (b) $\frac{1}{\sqrt{3}}$ (c) $\sqrt{3}$ (d) 2

Sol. (c) $\frac{\sin 70° + \cos 40°}{\cos 70° + \sin 40°} = \frac{\sin 70° + \cos(90° - 50°)}{\cos 70° + \sin(90° - 50°)}$

$$= \frac{\sin 70° + \sin 50°}{\cos 70° + \cos 50°}$$

$$= \frac{2\sin\frac{70° + 50°}{2}\cos\frac{70° - 50°}{2}}{2\cos\frac{70° + 50°}{2}\cos\frac{70° - 50°}{2}}$$

$$= \frac{2\sin 60°\cos 10°}{2\cos 60°\cos 10°}$$

$$= \frac{\sin 60°}{\cos 60°} = \tan 60° = \sqrt{3}$$

Example 103. Prove that

$$\cos 55° + \cos 65° + \cos 175° = 0.$$

Sol. LHS $= \cos 55° + \cos 65° + \cos 175°$

$$= 2\cos\frac{55° + 65°}{2}\cos\frac{55° - 65°}{2} + \cos 175°$$

$$= 2\cos 60°\cos(-5°) + \cos 175°$$

$$= 2\times\frac{1}{2}\cos 5° + \cos(180° - 5°)$$

$$= \cos 5° - \cos 5° = 0 = \text{RHS}$$

Example 104. Prove that

$$\frac{\sin A + \sin 2A + \sin 4A + \sin 5A}{\cos A + \cos 2A + \cos 4A + \cos 5A} = \tan 3A.$$

Sol. LHS $= \frac{\sin A + \sin 2A + \sin 4A + \sin 5A}{\cos A + \cos 2A + \cos 4A + \cos 5A}$

$$= \frac{(\sin 5A + \sin A) + (\sin 4A + \sin 2A)}{(\cos 5A + \cos A) + (\cos 4A + \cos 2A)}$$

$$= \frac{2\sin 3A\cos 2A + 2\sin 3A\cos A}{2\cos 3A\cos 2A + 2\cos 3A\cos A}$$

$$= \frac{2\sin 3A(\cos 2A + \cos A)}{2\cos 3A(\cos 2A + \cos A)} = \tan 3A = \text{RHS}$$

Example 105. If $\sin A = \sin B$ and $\cos A = \cos B$, then prove that $\sin\frac{A-B}{2} = 0$.

Sol. We have, $\sin A = \sin B$ and $\cos A = \cos B$

or $\sin A - \sin B = 0$ and $\cos A - \cos B = 0$

or $2\sin\left(\frac{A-B}{2}\right)\cos\left(\frac{A+B}{2}\right) = 0$

and $-2\sin\left(\frac{A-B}{2}\right)\sin\left(\frac{A+B}{2}\right) = 0$ or $\sin\frac{A-B}{2} = 0$

which is common for both the equations.

Example 106. If $\sin A = n\sin B$, then find the value of $\frac{\tan\frac{A+B}{2}}{\tan\frac{A-B}{2}}$ in terms of n.

Sol. We have, $\sin A = n\sin B$

$$n = \frac{\sin A}{\sin B} \Rightarrow \frac{n+1}{n-1} = \frac{\sin A + \sin B}{\sin A - \sin B}$$

$$\Rightarrow \frac{n+1}{n-1} = \frac{2\sin\left(\frac{A+B}{2}\right)\cos\left(\frac{A-B}{2}\right)}{2\cos\left(\frac{A+B}{2}\right)\sin\left(\frac{A-B}{2}\right)}$$

$$\Rightarrow \frac{\tan\left(\frac{A+B}{2}\right)}{\tan\left(\frac{A-B}{2}\right)} = \frac{n+1}{n-1}$$

JEE SCANNER

Example Similar to PYQ Asked in JEE Main 2022

The value of $\cos\frac{\pi}{7}+\cos\frac{2\pi}{7}+\cos\frac{3\pi}{7}+\cos\frac{4\pi}{7}+\cos\frac{5\pi}{7}+\cos\frac{6\pi}{7}$ *is equal to*

(a) 1 (b) $-\frac{1}{2}$

(c) 0 (d) $\frac{\sqrt{3}}{2}$

Sol. (c) We have, $\cos\frac{\pi}{7}+\cos\frac{2\pi}{7}+\cos\frac{3\pi}{7}+\cos\frac{4\pi}{7}+\cos\frac{5\pi}{7}+\cos\frac{6\pi}{7}$

$$=\left(\cos\frac{\pi}{7}+\cos\frac{6\pi}{7}\right)+\left(\cos\frac{2\pi}{7}+\cos\frac{5\pi}{7}\right)+\left(\cos\frac{3\pi}{7}+\cos\frac{4\pi}{7}\right)$$

$$=2\cos\left[\frac{1}{2}\left(\frac{\pi}{7}+\frac{6\pi}{7}\right)\right]\cdot\cos\left[\frac{1}{2}\left(\frac{\pi}{7}-\frac{6\pi}{7}\right)\right]+2\cos\left[\frac{1}{2}\left(\frac{2\pi}{7}+\frac{5\pi}{7}\right)\right]\cdot\cos\left[\frac{1}{2}\left(\frac{2\pi}{7}-\frac{5\pi}{7}\right)\right]+2\cos\left[\frac{1}{2}\left(\frac{3\pi}{7}+\frac{4\pi}{7}\right)\right]\cdot\cos\left[\frac{1}{2}\left(\frac{3\pi}{7}-\frac{4\pi}{7}\right)\right]$$

$$=2\cos\frac{\pi}{2}\cdot\cos\frac{\pi}{14}+2\cos\frac{\pi}{2}\cdot\cos\frac{3\pi}{14}+2\cos\frac{\pi}{2}\cdot\cos\frac{\pi}{14}$$

$$=0 \qquad \left[\because \cos\frac{\pi}{2}=0\right]$$

Skill Builder

The value of $\cos\left(\frac{\pi}{7}\right)+\cos\left(\frac{2\pi}{7}\right)+\cos\left(\frac{3\pi}{7}\right)+\cos\left(\frac{4\pi}{7}\right)+\cos\left(\frac{5\pi}{7}\right)+\cos\left(\frac{6\pi}{7}\right)+\cos\left(\frac{7\pi}{7}\right)=\frac{1}{a}$. Then, the value of a is

(a) 1 (b) −1

(c) 2 (d) −2

For Sol.

- **For more practice** See Q.3 of Milestone Practice 6.

Example 107. If $\sin\alpha+\sin\beta=\frac{1}{3}$ and $\cos\alpha+\cos\beta=\frac{1}{4}$, then the value of $\sin(\alpha+\beta)$ is

(a) $\frac{24}{25}$ (b) $\frac{13}{25}$ (c) $\frac{12}{13}$ (d) None of these

Sol. (a) $\sin\alpha+\sin\beta=\frac{1}{3}$

$$\Rightarrow 2\sin\left(\frac{\alpha+\beta}{2}\right)\cos\left(\frac{\alpha-\beta}{2}\right)=\frac{1}{3} \qquad \text{...(i)}$$

$$\cos\alpha+\cos\beta=\frac{1}{4}$$

$$\Rightarrow 2\cos\left(\frac{\alpha+\beta}{2}\right)\cos\left(\frac{\alpha-\beta}{2}\right)=\frac{1}{4} \qquad \text{...(ii)}$$

$$\Rightarrow \tan\left(\frac{\alpha+\beta}{2}\right)=\frac{4}{3}$$

[dividing Eq. (i) by Eq. (ii)]

$$\Rightarrow \sin(\alpha+\beta)=\frac{2\tan\left(\frac{\alpha+\beta}{2}\right)}{1+\tan^2\left(\frac{\alpha+\beta}{2}\right)}$$

$$\Rightarrow \sin(\alpha+\beta)=\frac{2\times\frac{4}{3}}{1+\frac{16}{9}}=\frac{\frac{8}{3}}{\frac{25}{9}}=\frac{24}{25}$$

Example 108. If $\sin 2\theta+\sin 2\phi=\frac{1}{2}$ and $\cos 2\theta+\cos 2\phi=\frac{3}{2}$, then $\cos^2(\theta-\phi)$ is equal to

(a) $\frac{3}{8}$ (b) $\frac{5}{8}$ (c) $\frac{3}{4}$ (d) $\frac{5}{4}$

Sol. (b) $\sin 2\theta+\sin 2\phi=\frac{1}{2}$

On squaring both sides, we get

$$(\sin 2\theta+\sin 2\phi)^2=\frac{1}{4}$$

$$\Rightarrow \sin^2 2\theta+\sin^2 2\phi+2\sin 2\theta\sin 2\phi=\frac{1}{4} \qquad \text{...(i)}$$

$$\cos 2\theta+\cos 2\phi=\frac{3}{2}$$

$$\Rightarrow (\cos 2\theta+\cos 2\phi)^2=\frac{9}{4}$$

$$\Rightarrow \cos^2 2\theta+\cos^2 2\phi+2\cos 2\theta\cos 2\phi=\frac{9}{4} \qquad \text{...(ii)}$$

On adding Eqs. (i) and (ii), we get

$$(\sin^2 2\theta+\cos^2 2\theta)+(\sin^2 2\phi+\cos^2 2\phi)+2(\sin 2\theta\sin 2\phi+\cos 2\theta\cos 2\phi)=\frac{10}{4}$$

$$\Rightarrow 1+1+2\cos(2\theta-2\phi)=\frac{5}{2}$$

$$\Rightarrow 2\cos(2\theta-2\phi)=\frac{5}{2}-2=\frac{1}{2}$$

$$\Rightarrow \cos(2\theta-2\phi)=\frac{1}{4}$$

$$\Rightarrow 2\cos^2(\theta-\phi)-1=\frac{1}{4}$$

$$\Rightarrow \quad 2\cos^2(\theta-\phi)=\frac{5}{4}$$

$$\Rightarrow \quad \cos^2(\theta-\phi)=\frac{5}{8}$$

Example 109. If $\cos^3 x \sin 2x = \sum_{r=0}^{n} a_r \sin(rx),\ \forall\, x \in R$, then find the value of $\frac{a_3}{a_1}$?

Sol. $\cos^3 x \sin 2x = \sum_{r=0}^{n} a_r \sin(rx)$

$$\Rightarrow \cos^3 x \sin 2x = a_0 \sin 0 + a_1 \sin x + a_2 \sin 2x + a_3 \sin 3x + a_4 \sin 4x + a_5 \sin 5x + \dots + a_n \sin nx$$

$$\because \quad \cos 3\theta = 4\cos^3\theta - 3\cos\theta$$

$$\Rightarrow \quad \cos^3\theta = \frac{\cos 3\theta + 3\cos\theta}{4}$$

$$\text{LHS} = \left(\frac{\cos 3x + 3\cos x}{4}\right)\sin 2x$$

$$= \frac{1}{4}(\cos 3x + 3\cos x)\sin 2x$$

$$= \frac{1}{4}(\cos 3x \sin 2x + 3\sin 2x \cos x)$$

$$= \frac{1}{8}[2\sin 2x \cos 3x + 6\sin 2x \cos x]$$

$$= \frac{1}{8}[(\sin(5x) + \sin(-x)) + 3(\sin 3x + \sin x)]$$

$$= \frac{1}{8}[\sin 5x - \sin x + 3\sin 3x + 3\sin x]$$

$$= \frac{1}{8}[\sin 5x + 2\sin x + 3\sin 3x]$$

$$= \frac{1}{8}\sin 5x + \frac{1}{4}\sin x + \frac{3}{8}\sin 3x$$

$$\text{RHS} = a_0 \sin 0 + a_1 \sin x + a_2 \sin 2x + a_3 \sin 3x + \dots + a_n \sin nx$$

On comparing LHS and RHS, we get

$$a_1 = \frac{1}{4},\ a_3 = \frac{3}{8},\ a_5 = \frac{1}{8}$$

$$\frac{a_3}{a_1} = \frac{\frac{3}{8}}{\frac{1}{4}} = \frac{3}{2} \Rightarrow \frac{a_3}{a_1} = \frac{3}{2}$$

Example 110. $\left(\frac{\sin 3\theta}{\sin\theta}\right)^2 - \left(\frac{\cos 3\theta}{\cos\theta}\right)^2 = a\cos 2\theta$, whenever it is defined. Then, the value of a is

(a) 1 (b) 0

(c) 2 (d) 8

Sol. (d) We have, $\left(\frac{\sin 3\theta}{\sin\theta}\right)^2 - \left(\frac{\cos 3\theta}{\cos\theta}\right)^2 = a\cos 2\theta$

$$\Rightarrow \left(\frac{3\sin\theta - 4\sin^3\theta}{\sin\theta}\right)^2 - \left(\frac{4\cos^3\theta - 3\cos\theta}{\cos\theta}\right)^2 = a\cos 2\theta$$

$$\Rightarrow \quad (3-4\sin^2\theta)^2 - (4\cos^2\theta - 3)^2 = a\cos 2\theta$$

$$\Rightarrow (9 + 16\sin^4\theta - 24\sin^2\theta) - (16\cos^4\theta + 9 - 24\cos^2\theta) = a\cos 2\theta$$

$$\Rightarrow \quad 16(\sin^4\theta - \cos^4\theta) - 24(\sin^2\theta - \cos^2\theta) = a\cos 2\theta$$

$$\Rightarrow 16(\sin^2\theta - \cos^2\theta)(\sin^2\theta + \cos^2\theta) - 24(\sin^2\theta - \cos^2\theta) = a\cos 2\theta$$

$$\Rightarrow \quad -16(\cos^2\theta - \sin^2\theta) + 24(\cos^2\theta - \sin^2\theta) = a\cos 2\theta$$

$$\Rightarrow \quad -16\cos 2\theta + 24\cos 2\theta = a\cos 2\theta$$

$$\Rightarrow \quad 8\cos 2\theta = a\cos 2\theta$$

$$\Rightarrow \quad a = 8$$

Milestone Practice 1.6

1. The value of $\frac{2\sin 40^\circ \cdot \sin 50^\circ \cdot \tan 10^\circ}{\cos 80^\circ}$ is

(a) $\frac{1}{2}$ (b) 1

(c) 2 (d) None of these

2. The value of $(\cos 65^\circ \cos 55^\circ \cos 5^\circ)$ is

(a) $\frac{\sqrt{3}+1}{8\sqrt{2}}$ (b) $\frac{\sqrt{3}-1}{8\sqrt{2}}$

(c) $\frac{\sqrt{3}+1}{4\sqrt{2}}$ (d) $\frac{\sqrt{3}-1}{4\sqrt{2}}$

3. The value of $\left(\sin\frac{2\pi}{7}\cdot\sin\frac{4\pi}{7} + \sin\frac{4\pi}{7}\sin\frac{8\pi}{7} + \sin\frac{8\pi}{7}\sin\frac{2\pi}{7}\right)$ equals

(a) 0 (b) $\frac{1}{2}$ (c) $-\frac{1}{2}$ (d) 1

4. The value of

$$\frac{\cos 5^\circ \cos 20^\circ + \cos 35^\circ \cos 50^\circ - \sin 5^\circ \sin 20^\circ - \sin 35^\circ \sin 50^\circ}{\sin 5^\circ \cos 20^\circ - \sin 35^\circ \cos 50^\circ + \cos 5^\circ \sin 20^\circ - \cos 35^\circ \sin 50^\circ}$$ is

(a) $-\frac{1}{\sqrt{3}}$ (b) $\frac{1}{\sqrt{3}}$ (c) $-\sqrt{3}$ (d) $\sqrt{3}$

5. The value of $\dfrac{\cos^2 33^\circ - \cos^2 57^\circ}{\sin 21^\circ - \cos 21^\circ}$ is equal to

(a) $\dfrac{1}{\sqrt{2}}$ (b) $-\dfrac{1}{\sqrt{2}}$

(c) $\dfrac{\sqrt{3}}{2}$ (d) $-\dfrac{\sqrt{3}}{2}$

6. If $\sin 65^\circ + \cos 65^\circ = k \cos 20^\circ$, then the value of k is

(a) 2 (b) $\sqrt{2}$

(c) 3 (d) $\sqrt{3}$

7. The value of expression $2\cos\dfrac{\pi}{13}\cos\dfrac{9\pi}{13} + \cos\dfrac{3\pi}{13} + \cos\dfrac{5\pi}{13}$ is

(a) 0 (b) 1

(c) 2 (d) None of these

8. In ΔABC, if $\sin C + \cos C + \sin(2B + C) - \cos(2B + C) = 2\sqrt{2}$, then ΔABC is a/an

(a) scalene triangle

(b) isosceles triangle

(c) equilateral triangle

(d) right angled isosceles triangle

9. In quadrilateral $PQRS$, if $\sin\left(\dfrac{P+Q}{2}\right)\cos\left(\dfrac{P-Q}{2}\right) + \sin\left(\dfrac{R+S}{2}\right)\cos\left(\dfrac{R-S}{2}\right) = 2$, then quadrilateral $PQRS$ is a

(a) rectangle (b) parallelogram

(c) rhombus (d) trapezium

10. If $\sin\alpha - \sin\beta = \dfrac{1}{3}$ and $\cos\beta - \cos\alpha = \dfrac{1}{2}$, then the value of $\cot\left(\dfrac{\alpha+\beta}{2}\right)$ is

(a) 1 (b) 0

(c) $\dfrac{1}{3}$ (d) $\dfrac{2}{3}$

11. The value of $\dfrac{\sin 35^\circ \cos 125^\circ}{\sin 20^\circ - 1}$ is

(a) 1 (b) 0 (c) -1 (d) $\dfrac{1}{2}$

12. Show that $\sin A \cdot \sin(B - C) + \sin B \cdot \sin(C - A) + \sin C \cdot \sin(A - B) = 0$.

13. Show that $\cos\alpha + \cos\beta + \cos\gamma + \cos(\alpha+\beta+\gamma) = 4\cos\dfrac{\alpha+\beta}{2}\cdot\cos\dfrac{\beta+\gamma}{2}\cdot\cos\dfrac{\gamma+\alpha}{2}$.

14. If x and y are acute angles, such that $\cos x + \cos y = \dfrac{3}{2}$ and $\sin x + \sin y = \dfrac{3}{4}$, then find the value of $\sin(x + y)$.

15. Find the value of $\left(\dfrac{\cos A + \cos B}{\sin A - \sin B}\right)^n + \left(\dfrac{\sin A + \sin B}{\cos A - \cos B}\right)^n$ (where, n is an even)

16. In a ΔABC, $\cos 3A + \cos 3B + \cos 3C = 1$, then find any one angle.

17. If α, β and γ are in AP, then show that $\cot\beta = \dfrac{\sin\alpha - \sin\gamma}{\cos\gamma - \cos\alpha}$.

18. Show that $\sin 12^\circ \cdot \sin 48^\circ \cdot \sin 54^\circ = \dfrac{1}{8}$.

19. If $\cos A = m\cos B$, then prove that $\cot\dfrac{A+B}{2} = \dfrac{m+1}{m-1}\tan\dfrac{B-A}{2}$.

20. If $\dfrac{\tan(\alpha+\beta-\gamma)}{\tan(\alpha-\beta+\gamma)} = \dfrac{\tan\gamma}{\tan\beta}$, prove that $\sin 2\alpha + \sin 2\beta + \sin 2\gamma = 0$

21. If $\dfrac{\cos 6x + 6\cos 4x + 15\cos 2x + 10}{\cos 5x + 5\cos 3x + 10\cos x} = 1$, then find the smallest positive value of x.

Answer Key

1. (b)	2. (a)	3. (a)	4. (c)	5. (b)	
6. (b)	7. (a)	8. (d)	9. (a)	10. (d)	
11. (d)	14. $\dfrac{4}{5}$	15. $2\cot^n\left(\dfrac{A-B}{2}\right)$	16. $C = 120^\circ$	21. 60°	For Detailed Solution

Milestone 7 Trigonometric Series in which Angles are in AP

TYPE 1

Problems based on finding the sum of series of sines or cosines whose angles are in AP.

Following two results are very useful in solving such problems.

Result I

$\sin\alpha + \sin(\alpha+\beta) + \sin(\alpha+2\beta) + \ldots + \sin(\alpha+(n-1)\beta)$

$$= \frac{\sin\frac{n\beta}{2}}{\sin\frac{\beta}{2}} \cdot \sin\left[\alpha + (n-1)\frac{\beta}{2}\right]$$

Result II

$\cos\alpha + \cos(\alpha+\beta) + \cos(\alpha+2\beta) + \ldots + \cos(\alpha+(n-1)\beta)$

$$= \frac{\sin\frac{n\beta}{2}}{\sin\frac{\beta}{2}} \cdot \cos\left[\alpha + (n-1)\frac{\beta}{2}\right]$$

Proof for Result I

Let $S = \sin\alpha + \sin(\alpha+\beta) + \sin(\alpha+2\beta) + \ldots + \sin(\alpha+(n-1)\beta)$

Here, angles are in AP and common difference of angles $= \beta$

Multiplying and dividing by $2\sin\frac{\beta}{2}$, we get

$$= \frac{1}{2\sin\left(\frac{\beta}{2}\right)}\left\{2\sin\alpha\sin\left(\frac{\beta}{2}\right) + 2\sin(\alpha+\beta)\sin\left(\frac{\beta}{2}\right) + \ldots + 2\sin(\alpha+(n-1)\beta)\sin\left(\frac{\beta}{2}\right)\right\}$$

$$= \frac{1}{2\sin\left(\frac{\beta}{2}\right)}\left\{\left(\cos\left(\alpha-\frac{\beta}{2}\right) - \cos\left(\alpha+\frac{\beta}{2}\right)\right) + \left(\cos\left(\alpha+\frac{\beta}{2}\right) - \cos\left(\alpha+\frac{3\beta}{2}\right)\right) + \ldots + \left(\cos\left(\alpha+\left(n-\frac{3}{2}\right)\beta\right) - \cos\left[\left(\alpha+\left(n-\frac{1}{2}\right)\beta\right]\right.\right.$$

$$= \frac{1}{2\sin\left(\frac{\beta}{2}\right)}\left\{\cos\left(\alpha-\frac{\beta}{2}\right) - \cos\left(\alpha+\left(n-\frac{1}{2}\right)\beta\right)\right\}$$

$$= \frac{2\sin\left(\alpha+\left(\frac{n-1}{2}\right)\beta\right)\sin\left(n\frac{\beta}{2}\right)}{2\sin\frac{\beta}{2}}$$

$\therefore \sin\alpha + \sin(\alpha+\beta) + \sin(\alpha+2\beta) + \ldots + \sin[(\alpha+(n-1)\beta)]$

$$= \frac{\sin\left(n\frac{\beta}{2}\right)\sin\left[\alpha+(n-1)\frac{\beta}{2}\right]}{\sin\left(\frac{\beta}{2}\right)}$$

JEE SPIKE

In a series of sine and cosine whenever angles are in AP and power of sine and cosine is one, then we multiply each term by $2\sin\left(\frac{\text{common difference of angles}}{2}\right)$, then express each term as a difference of two terms and add.

Proof for Result II

Let $S = \cos(\alpha) + \cos(\alpha+\beta) + \cos(\alpha+2\beta) + \ldots + \cos[\alpha+(n-1)\beta]$

Multiplying and dividing by $2\sin\left(\frac{\beta}{2}\right)$, we get

$$S = \frac{1}{2\sin\left(\frac{\beta}{2}\right)}\left\{2\sin\left(\frac{\beta}{2}\right)\cos(\alpha) + 2\sin\left(\frac{\beta}{2}\right)\cos(\alpha+\beta) + 2\sin\left(\frac{\beta}{2}\right)\cos(\alpha+2\beta) + \ldots + 2\sin\left(\frac{\beta}{2}\right)\cos(\alpha+(n+1)\beta\right\}$$

$$= \frac{1}{2\sin\left(\frac{\beta}{2}\right)}\left[\sin\left(\alpha+\frac{\beta}{2}\right)-\sin\left(\alpha-\frac{\beta}{2}\right)\right]$$
$$+\left[\sin\left(\alpha+\frac{3\beta}{2}\right)-\sin\left(\alpha+\frac{\beta}{2}\right)\right]$$
$$+\ldots+\left[\sin\left[\alpha+\left(n-\frac{3}{2}\right)\beta\right]-\sin\left[\alpha+\left(n-\frac{5}{2}\right)\beta\right]\right]$$
$$= \frac{1}{2\sin\left(\frac{\beta}{2}\right)}\left[\sin\left(\alpha+\left(n-\frac{1}{2}\right)\beta\right)-\sin\left(\alpha-\frac{\beta}{2}\right)\right]$$
$$= \frac{\cos\left(\alpha+(n-1)\left(\frac{\beta}{2}\right)\right)\sin\left(n\frac{\beta}{2}\right)}{\sin\left(\frac{\beta}{2}\right)}$$

$\therefore \cos(\alpha)+\cos(\alpha+\beta)+\ldots+\cos(\alpha+(n-1)\beta)$
$$= \frac{\sin\left(n\frac{\beta}{2}\right)}{\sin\left(\frac{\beta}{2}\right)}\left\{\cos\left(\alpha+(n-1)\left(\frac{\beta}{2}\right)\right)\right\}$$

Example 111. Show that
$$\sin\theta+\sin 3\theta+\sin 5\theta+\ldots+\sin(2n-1)\theta=\frac{\sin^2 n\theta}{\sin\theta}.$$

Sol. LHS $= \sin\theta+\sin 3\theta+\sin 5\theta+\ldots+\sin(2n-1)\theta$
$= \sin\theta+\sin(\theta+2\theta)+\sin(\theta+2\times 2\theta)$
$+\ldots+\sin(\theta+(n-1)2\theta)$
$$= \frac{\sin\left(n\times\frac{2\theta}{2}\right)}{\sin\frac{2\theta}{2}}\sin\left[\theta+\frac{(n-1)2\theta}{2}\right]$$
$$= \frac{\sin n\theta}{\sin\theta}\times\sin n\theta$$
$$= \frac{\sin^2 n\theta}{\sin\theta} = \text{RHS}$$

Example 112. The value of expression
$\cos\frac{2\pi}{7}+\cos\frac{4\pi}{7}+\cos\frac{6\pi}{7}$ is

(a) $\frac{1}{2}$ (b) $-\frac{1}{2}$

(c) 0 (d) 1

Sol. (b) $\dfrac{2\sin\frac{\pi}{7}\left(\cos\frac{2\pi}{7}+\cos\frac{4\pi}{7}+\cos\frac{6\pi}{7}\right)}{2\sin\frac{\pi}{7}}$

$$= \frac{1}{2\sin\frac{\pi}{7}}\left[\left(\sin\frac{3\pi}{7}-\sin\frac{\pi}{7}\right)+\left(\sin\frac{5\pi}{7}-\sin\frac{3\pi}{7}\right)+\left(\sin\frac{7\pi}{7}-\sin\frac{5\pi}{7}\right)\right]$$
$$= \frac{\sin\pi-\sin\frac{\pi}{7}}{2\sin\frac{\pi}{7}} = -\frac{1}{2}$$

Alternate Solution

We can also use the relation
$\cos a+\cos(a+d)+\ldots+\cos(a+(n-1)d)$
$$= \frac{\sin\frac{nd}{2}}{\sin\frac{d}{2}}\cos\left(\frac{2a+(n-1)d}{2}\right)$$
[where d is common difference of AP]
$$= \frac{\sin\left[3\left(\frac{\frac{2\pi}{7}}{2}\right)\right]}{\sin\frac{\frac{2\pi}{7}}{2}}\cos\left[\frac{\frac{4\pi}{7}+2\left(\frac{2\pi}{7}\right)}{2}\right]$$
$$= \frac{\sin\frac{3\pi}{7}\cdot\cos\frac{4\pi}{7}}{\sin\frac{\pi}{7}}$$
$$= \frac{\cos\left(\frac{\pi}{2}-\frac{3\pi}{7}\right)\sin\left(\frac{\pi}{2}-\frac{4\pi}{7}\right)}{\sin\frac{\pi}{7}}$$
$$= \frac{\cos\frac{\pi}{14}\cdot\sin\left(-\frac{\pi}{14}\right)}{\sin\frac{\pi}{7}}$$
$$= -\frac{1}{2}\frac{\sin\left(\frac{\pi}{7}\right)}{\sin\left(\frac{\pi}{7}\right)} = -\frac{1}{2}$$

TYPE 2

If angles are in AP and sum of the first and the last angles is π or $\frac{\pi}{2}$, then we will use the following working rule and power of sine and cosine may or may not be one.

Working Rule

If angles are in AP and sum of the first and last angles is $\frac{\pi}{2}$ or π etc. then the group equidistant terms from both ends, express last angle in terms of the first in each group and simplify.

Example 113. The value of expression

$\cos^4 \frac{\pi}{8} + \cos^4 \frac{3\pi}{8} + \cos^4 \frac{5\pi}{8} + \cos^4 \frac{7\pi}{8}$ is

(a) $\frac{1}{2}$ (b) $\frac{3}{2}$ (c) $\frac{1}{4}$ (d) $\frac{3}{4}$

Sol. (b) $\left(\cos^4 \frac{\pi}{8} + \cos^4 \frac{7\pi}{8}\right) + \left(\cos^4 \frac{3\pi}{8} + \cos^4 \frac{5\pi}{8}\right)$

$$= \left[\cos^4 \frac{\pi}{8} + \cos^4\left(\pi - \frac{\pi}{8}\right)\right] + \left[\cos^4 \frac{3\pi}{8} + \cos^4\left(\pi - \frac{3\pi}{8}\right)\right]$$

$$= 2\cos^4 \frac{\pi}{8} + 2\cos^4 \frac{3\pi}{8} \qquad [\text{as } \cos(\pi - \theta) = -\cos\theta]$$

$$= 2\left[\left(\cos^2 \frac{\pi}{8}\right)^2 + \left(\cos^2 \frac{3\pi}{8}\right)^2\right]$$

$$= 2\left[\left(\frac{1 + \cos\frac{\pi}{4}}{2}\right)^2 + \left(\frac{1 + \cos\frac{3\pi}{4}}{2}\right)^2\right]$$

$$= \frac{2}{4}\left[\left(1 + \frac{1}{\sqrt{2}}\right)^2 + \left(1 - \frac{1}{\sqrt{2}}\right)^2\right] = \frac{1}{2}\left[1 + \frac{1}{2} + 1 + \frac{1}{2}\right] = \frac{3}{2}$$

TYPE 3

If angles are in GP having common ratio 2 or $\frac{1}{2}$, terms of sine or cosine are in power one and in product.

Product of series containing cosines of angles

Forming a GP with common ratio $r = 2$

$$\cos A \cos 2A \cos 2^2 A \cos 2^3 A \ldots \cos 2^{n-1} A = \frac{\sin 2^n A}{2^n \sin A}$$

Proof

$$\text{LHS} = \cos A \cos 2A \cos 2^2 A \ldots \cos 2^{n-1} A$$

$$= \frac{1}{2\sin A}[(2\sin A \cos A)\cos 2A \cos 2^2 A \ldots \cos 2^{n-1} A]$$

$$= \frac{1}{2\sin A}[\sin 2A \cos 2A \cos 2^2 A \ldots \cos 2^{n-1} A]$$

$$= \frac{1}{2^2 \sin A}[(2\sin 2A \cos 2A)\cos 2^2 A \cos 2^3 A \ldots \cos 2^{n-1} A]$$

$$= \frac{1}{2^2 \sin A}[\sin 2^2 A \cos 2^2 A \cos 2^3 A \ldots \cos 2^{n-1} A]$$

$$\vdots$$

$$= \frac{1}{2^{n-1}\sin A}[\sin 2^{n-1} A \cos 2^{n-1} A]$$

$$= \frac{1}{2^n \sin A}[2\sin 2^{n-1} A \cos 2^{n-1} A]$$

$$= \frac{\sin 2^n A}{2^n \sin A} = \text{RHS}$$

JEE SCANNER

Example Similar to PYQ Asked in JEE Main 2023, 22 & 19

The value of expression $\cos 20° \cos 40° \cos 60° \cos 80°$ *is*

(a) $\frac{1}{16}$ (b) $\frac{3}{16}$ (c) $\frac{1}{8}$ $\frac{2}{9}$

Sol. (a) In given expression : $\cos 60° = \frac{1}{2}$

$$A = \cos 20° \cos 40° \cdot \frac{1}{2} \cdot \cos 80°$$

$$\Rightarrow 2A \sin 20° = \frac{1}{2}(2\sin 20° \cos 20°)\cos 40° \cos 80°$$

$$\Rightarrow 2A \sin 20° = \frac{1}{2}\sin 40° \cos 40° \cos 80°$$

$$\Rightarrow 4A \sin 20° = \frac{1}{2}\sin 80° \cos 80° \Rightarrow 8A \sin 20° = \frac{1}{2}\sin 160°$$

$$\Rightarrow \quad A = \frac{\sin 160°}{16\sin 20°} = \frac{\sin 20°}{16 \sin 20°} = \frac{1}{16} \Rightarrow A = \frac{1}{16}$$

Skill Builder

The value of expression $\sin 20° \sin 40° \sin 60° \sin 80°$ is

(a) $\frac{2}{9}$ (b) $\frac{3}{7}$ (c) $\frac{3}{16}$ $\frac{1}{16}$

For Sol.

■ **For more practice** See Q.4 of Milestone Practice 7.

Example 114. The value of expression $\sin 10° \sin 30° \sin 50° \sin 70°$ is

(a) $\frac{1}{8}$ (b) $\frac{1}{16}$ (c) $\frac{1}{4}$ (d) $\frac{3}{4}$

Sol. (b) By complementary rule,

$$\sin\theta = \cos(90° - \theta)$$

The given expression reduces to

$$\cos 20° \cos 40° \cos 60° \cos 80°$$

Let $\quad A = \cos 20° \cos 40° \cos 60° \cos 80°$

$$\Rightarrow \quad A = \cos 20° \cos 40° \frac{1}{2}\cos 80° \qquad \left[\because \cos 60° = \frac{1}{2}\right]$$

$$\Rightarrow 2A \sin 20° = \frac{1}{2}(2\sin 20° \cos 20°)\cos 40° \cos 80°$$

$$\Rightarrow 2A\sin 20° = \frac{1}{2}\sin 40° \cos 40° \cos 80°$$

$$\Rightarrow 4A\sin 20° = \frac{1}{2}\sin 80° \cos 80°$$

$$\Rightarrow 8A\sin 20° = \frac{1}{2}\sin 160°$$

$$\Rightarrow A = \frac{\sin 160°}{16\sin 20°} = \frac{\sin 20°}{16\sin 20°} = \frac{1}{16}$$

$$\Rightarrow A = \frac{1}{16}$$

TYPE 4

If angle are in AP, terms in sine or cosine having power one, and in product and sum of the first and last angles is not $\frac{\pi}{2}$ or π etc.

Working Rule

(i) Change the last angle using formula for $\pi - \theta$ etc.

(ii) Rearrange the terms in ascending order of angles.

(iii) Group the terms in two parts: one part consisting of terms having angles in GP and the other part consisting of remaining terms.

(iv) Simplify

Example 115. The value of expression $\cos\frac{2\pi}{7}\cdot\cos\frac{4\pi}{7}\cdot\cos\frac{6\pi}{7}$ is

(a) 1 (b) $\frac{1}{2}$ (c) $\frac{1}{8}$ (d) $\frac{1}{16}$

Sol. (c) Let $y = \cos\frac{2\pi}{7}\cdot\cos\frac{4\pi}{7}\cdot\cos\frac{6\pi}{7}$

$$y = \cos\frac{2\pi}{7}\cdot\cos\frac{4\pi}{7}\cdot\cos\left(\pi - \frac{\pi}{7}\right)$$

$$y = -\cos\frac{\pi}{7}\cdot\cos\frac{2\pi}{7}\cdot\cos\frac{4\pi}{7}$$

[here, there is only one group consisting of terms having angles in GP, so we multiply both sides by $2\sin\frac{\pi}{7}$ and simplify]

$$\therefore\ 2y\sin\frac{\pi}{7} = -\left(2\sin\frac{\pi}{7}\cos\frac{\pi}{7}\right)\cos\frac{2\pi}{7}\cos\frac{4\pi}{7}$$

$$\Rightarrow 2y\sin\frac{\pi}{7} = -\sin\frac{2\pi}{7}\cos\frac{2\pi}{7}\cos\frac{4\pi}{7}$$

$$\Rightarrow 4y\sin\frac{\pi}{7} = -\left(2\sin\frac{2\pi}{7}\cos\frac{2\pi}{7}\right)\cdot\cos\frac{4\pi}{7}$$

[multiplying both sides by 2]

$$\Rightarrow 4y\sin\frac{\pi}{7} = -\sin\frac{4\pi}{7}\cos\frac{4\pi}{7}$$

$$\Rightarrow 8y\sin\frac{\pi}{7} = -2\sin\frac{4\pi}{7}\cos\frac{4\pi}{7}$$

[multiplying both sides by 2]

$$\Rightarrow 8y\sin\frac{\pi}{7} = -\sin\frac{8\pi}{7} = -\sin\left(\pi + \frac{\pi}{7}\right)$$

$$\Rightarrow 8y\sin\frac{\pi}{7} = \sin\frac{\pi}{7} \Rightarrow y = \frac{1}{8}$$

Example 116. Show that

$$\cos\frac{2\pi}{15}\cos\frac{4\pi}{15}\cos\frac{8\pi}{15}\cos\frac{14\pi}{15} = \frac{1}{16}.$$

Sol. LHS $= \cos\frac{2\pi}{15}\cos\frac{4\pi}{15}\cos\frac{8\pi}{15}\cos\frac{14\pi}{15}$

$$= \cos\left(\frac{2\pi}{15}\right)\cos\left(\frac{4\pi}{15}\right)\cos\left(\frac{8\pi}{15}\right)\cos\left(\pi - \frac{\pi}{15}\right)$$

$$= -\cos\frac{\pi}{15}\cos\frac{2\pi}{15}\cos\frac{4\pi}{15}\cos\frac{8\pi}{15}$$

$$= -\frac{\sin\left(2^4 \times \frac{\pi}{15}\right)}{2^4\sin\frac{\pi}{15}} = -\frac{\sin\left(\frac{16\pi}{15}\right)}{16\sin\left(\frac{\pi}{15}\right)}$$

$$= -\frac{\sin\left(\pi + \frac{\pi}{15}\right)}{16\sin\left(\frac{\pi}{15}\right)} = -\frac{\left(-\sin\frac{\pi}{15}\right)}{16\sin\frac{\pi}{15}} = \frac{1}{16} = \text{RHS}$$

Example 117. The value of expression is $\sin^2 12° + \sin^2 21° + \sin^2 39° + \sin^2 48° - \sin^2 9° - \sin^2 18°$ is

(a) 1 (b) 0

(c) -1 (d) None of these

Sol. (a) $\sin^2 12° + \sin^2 21° + \sin^2 39° + \sin^2 48° - \sin^2 9° - \sin^2 18°$

$$= \sin^2 12° + \sin^2 21° + (\sin^2 39° - \sin^2 9°) + (\sin^2 48° - \sin^2 18°)$$

Multiplying and dividing by 2, we get

$$= \frac{1}{2}[2\sin^2 12° + 2\sin^2 21° + 2(\sin^2 39° - \sin^2 9°) + 2(\sin^2 48° - \sin^2 18°)]$$

[by using $2\sin^2\theta = 1 - \cos 2\theta$ and $\sin^2\theta - \sin^2\phi = \sin(\theta+\phi)\cdot\sin(\theta-\phi)$]

$$= 1$$

As, $\sin 30° = \frac{1}{2}$ and by complementary rule $\sin 66° = \cos 24°$; $\sin 48° = \cos 42°$

Example 118. Show that

$$\sin 6° \sin 42° \sin 66° \sin 78° = \frac{1}{16}.$$

Sol. LHS $= \sin 6° \sin 42° \sin 66° \sin 78°$

$$= \sin 6° \cos 48° \cos 24° \cos 12°$$

$$= (\sin 6^\circ)\left[\frac{\sin(2^3 \times 12^\circ)}{2^3 \sin 12^\circ}\right] = \frac{1}{2^3}\left(\frac{\sin 6^\circ \sin 96^\circ}{\sin 12^\circ}\right)$$

$$= \frac{1}{8 \times 2}\left(\frac{2 \sin 6^\circ \cos 6^\circ}{\sin 12^\circ}\right)$$

$$= \frac{1}{16}\frac{\sin(2 \times 6^\circ)}{\sin 12^\circ}$$

$$= \frac{1}{16} = \text{RHS}$$

Example 119. The value of expression: $\sin 20^\circ \sin 40^\circ \sin 80^\circ$ is

(a) $\frac{1}{8}$ (b) $\frac{1}{4}$ (c) $\frac{1}{16}$ (d) $\frac{\sqrt{3}}{8}$

Sol. (d) Consider $\sin 20^\circ \sin 40^\circ \sin 80^\circ$

$$= \sin 20^\circ \sin(60^\circ - 20^\circ)\sin(60^\circ + 20^\circ)$$

$$= \frac{1}{4}\sin 3(20^\circ) = \frac{1}{4}\sin 60^\circ = \frac{\sqrt{3}}{8}$$

Example 120. The value of expression:

$\sin\frac{\pi}{14}\sin\frac{3\pi}{14}\sin\frac{5\pi}{14}\sin\frac{7\pi}{14}$ is

(a) $\frac{1}{8}$ (b) $\frac{1}{4}$ (c) $\frac{1}{2}$ (d) $\frac{1}{16}$

Sol. (a) (i) $\sin\frac{\pi}{14} = \sin\left(\frac{\pi}{2} - \frac{6\pi}{14}\right) = \cos\frac{6\pi}{14} = \cos\left(\pi - \frac{8\pi}{14}\right)$

$$= -\cos\frac{8\pi}{14}$$

$$\sin\frac{3\pi}{14} = \sin\left(\frac{\pi}{2} - \frac{4\pi}{14}\right) = \cos\frac{4\pi}{14}$$

$$\sin\frac{5\pi}{14} = \sin\left(\frac{\pi}{2} - \frac{2\pi}{14}\right) = \cos\frac{2\pi}{14}$$

$$\therefore \quad \text{LHS} = -\cos\frac{2\pi}{14}\cos\frac{4\pi}{14}\cos\frac{8\pi}{14}$$

$$= -\frac{1}{2^3 \sin A}\cdot\sin(2^3 A) \qquad \left[\text{where } A = \frac{2\pi}{14}\right]$$

$$= -\frac{1}{8\sin\frac{\pi}{7}}\cdot\sin\frac{8\pi}{7} = -\frac{1}{8\sin\frac{\pi}{7}}\sin\left(\pi + \frac{\pi}{7}\right)$$

$$= -\frac{1}{8}(-1) = \frac{1}{8}\,[\sin(\pi + \theta) = -\sin\theta]$$

Example 121. For a positive integer n, let

$f_n(\theta) = \left(\tan\frac{\theta}{2}\right)(1 + \sec\theta)(1 + \sec 2\theta)(1 + \sec 4\theta) \dots (1 + \sec 2^n\theta)$. Then,

(a) $f_2\left(\frac{\pi}{16}\right) = 1$ (b) $f_3\left(\frac{\pi}{32}\right) = 1$

(c) $f_4\left(\frac{\pi}{64}\right) = 1$ (d) $f_5\left(\frac{\pi}{128}\right) = 1$

Sol. (a,b,c,d) We have,

$$\left(\tan\frac{\theta}{2}\right)(1 + \sec\theta) = \frac{\sin\left(\frac{\theta}{2}\right)}{\cos\left(\frac{\theta}{2}\right)}\left[1 + \frac{1}{\cos\theta}\right]$$

$$= \frac{\sin\left(\frac{\theta}{2}\right)}{\cos\left(\frac{\theta}{2}\right)}\cdot\frac{2\cos^2\left(\frac{\theta}{2}\right)}{\cos\theta}$$

$$= \frac{2\sin\left(\frac{\theta}{2}\right)\cos\left(\frac{\theta}{2}\right)}{\cos\theta} = \frac{\sin\theta}{\cos\theta}$$

$$= \tan\theta$$

Thus, $f_n(\theta) = \left(\tan\frac{\theta}{2}\right)(1 + \sec\theta)(1 + \sec 2\theta)(1 + \sec 4\theta)\dots(1 + \sec 2^n\theta)$

$$f_n(\theta) = (\tan\theta)(1 + \sec 2\theta)(1 + \sec 4\theta)\dots(1 + \sec 2^n\theta)$$

$$f_n(\theta) = (\tan 2\theta)(1 + \sec 4\theta)\dots(1 + \sec 2^n\theta)$$

$$f_n(\theta) = (\tan 4\theta)(1 + \sec 8\theta)\dots(1 + \sec 2^n\theta)$$

$$f_n(\theta) = \dots$$

$$f_n(\theta) = \tan(2^n\theta)$$

Now, $f_2\left(\frac{\pi}{16}\right) = \tan\left(2^2\frac{\pi}{16}\right) = \tan\left(\frac{\pi}{4}\right) = 1$

$$f_3\left(\frac{\pi}{32}\right) = \tan\left(2^3\frac{\pi}{32}\right) = \tan\left(\frac{\pi}{4}\right) = 1$$

$$f_4\left(\frac{\pi}{64}\right) = \tan\left(2^4\frac{\pi}{64}\right) = \tan\left(\frac{\pi}{4}\right) = 1$$

and $f_5\left(\frac{\pi}{128}\right) = \tan\left(2^5\frac{\pi}{128}\right) = \tan\left(\frac{\pi}{4}\right) = 1$

Example 122. Evaluate $\sum_{r=1}^{n-1}\cos^2\left(\frac{r\pi}{n}\right)$.

Sol. Sum $= \frac{1}{2}\sum_{r=1}^{n-1}\left(1 + \cos\frac{2r\pi}{n}\right)$

$$= \frac{1}{2}(n-1) + \frac{1}{2}\left\{\cos\frac{2\pi}{n} + \cos\frac{4\pi}{n} + \dots + \cos\frac{(2n-2)\pi}{n}\right\}$$

$$= \frac{1}{2}(n-1) + \frac{1}{2}\left\{\frac{\sin(n-1)\frac{2\pi}{2n}}{\sin\frac{2\pi}{n.2}}\cdot\cos\left\{\frac{2\left(\frac{2\pi}{n}\right) + (n-2)\frac{2\pi}{n}}{2}\right\}\right\}$$

Using $\cos\alpha + \cos(\alpha + \beta) + \cos(\alpha + 2\beta) + \dots + \cos[\alpha + (n-1)\beta]$

$$= \frac{\sin\frac{n\beta}{2}}{\sin\frac{\beta}{2}}\cdot\cos\left\{\frac{2\alpha + (n-1)\beta}{2}\right\}$$

$$= \frac{1}{2}(n-1) + \frac{1}{2}\left\{\frac{\sin\frac{(n-1)\pi}{n}\cdot\cos\pi}{\sin(\pi/n)}\right\}$$

$$= \frac{1}{2}(n-1) + \frac{1}{2}\left\{\frac{\left(\sin\frac{\pi}{n}\right)(-1)}{\sin(\pi/n)}\right\} = \frac{1}{2}(n-1) - \frac{1}{2} = \frac{n}{2} - 1$$

$$\therefore \quad \sum_{r=1}^{n-1}\cos^2\left(\frac{r\pi}{n}\right) = \frac{n}{2} - 1$$

Example 123. Evaluate $\sin\frac{\pi}{n} + \sin\frac{3\pi}{n} + \sin\frac{5\pi}{n} + \ldots$ upto n terms.

Sol. $\sin\frac{\pi}{n} + \sin\frac{3\pi}{n} + \sin\frac{5\pi}{n} + \ldots +$ upto n terms

$$= \frac{\sin n\cdot\frac{2\pi}{2\cdot n}}{\sin\frac{2\pi}{2\cdot n}}\cdot\sin\left\{\frac{2\cdot\frac{\pi}{n} + (n-1)\cdot\frac{2\pi}{n}}{2}\right\}$$

Using $\sin\alpha + \sin(\alpha+\beta) + \ldots + \sin[\alpha + (n-1)\beta]$

$$= \frac{\sin n\beta/2}{\sin\beta/2}\cdot\sin\left\{\frac{2\alpha + (n-1)\beta}{2}\right\}$$

$$= \frac{\sin\pi}{\sin\pi/n}\sin\left\{\frac{2\pi + 2n\pi - 2\pi}{2n}\right\} = \frac{\sin^2\pi}{\sin\pi/n} = 0$$

$$\therefore \quad \sin\frac{\pi}{n} + \sin\frac{3\pi}{n} + \sin\frac{5\pi}{n} + \ldots + \text{upto } n \text{ terms} = 0$$

Milestone Practice 1.7

1. The value of $\tan\frac{\pi}{7}\tan\frac{2\pi}{7}\tan\frac{3\pi}{7}$ is
   (a) $\frac{\sqrt{7}}{3}$ (b) $\sqrt{7}$ (c) $3\sqrt{7}$ (d) $\frac{\sqrt{7}}{2}$
2. $\tan\frac{\pi}{10}$ is a root of polynomial equation
   (a) $5x^4 - 10x^2 + 1 = 0$ (b) $5x^4 + 10x^2 - 1 = 0$
   (c) $5x^4 - 10x^2 - 1 = 0$ (d) $5x^2 + 10x^2 + 1 = 0$
3. The value of $\cos\frac{\pi}{11} + \cos\frac{3\pi}{11} + \cos\frac{5\pi}{11} + \cos\frac{7\pi}{11} + \cos\frac{9\pi}{11}$ is
   (a) $\frac{1}{4}$ (b) $\frac{1}{16}$ (c) $\frac{1}{32}$ (d) $\frac{1}{2}$
4. The value of $\cos\frac{2\pi}{15}\cos\frac{4\pi}{15}\cos\frac{8\pi}{15}\cos\frac{14\pi}{15}$ is
   (a) $\frac{1}{16}$ (b) $\frac{1}{8}$ (c) $\frac{1}{4}$ (d) $\frac{1}{2}$
5. Find the value of $\left(\tan^2\frac{\pi}{7} + \tan^2\frac{2\pi}{7} + \tan^2\frac{3\pi}{7}\right)\cdot\left(\cot^2\frac{\pi}{7} + \cot^2\frac{2\pi}{7} + \cot^2\frac{3\pi}{7}\right)$.
6. Find the average value of $\sin 2°, \sin 4°, \sin 6°, \ldots, \sin 180°$.
7. Sum of series: $\sqrt{1+\cos\alpha} + \sqrt{1+\cos 2\alpha} + \sqrt{1+\cos 3\alpha} + \ldots +$ upto n terms, where $0 < \alpha < \pi$.
8. Find the value of $(\cos^4 1° + \cos^4 2° + \cos^4 3° + \ldots + \cos^4 179°) - (\sin^4 1° + \sin^4 2° + \sin^4 3° + \ldots + \sin^4 179°)$.
9. Show that $\sin 12°\sin 18°\sin 42°\sin 48°\sin 72°\sin 78° = \frac{\cos 18°}{32}$.
10. Find the value of $\sin\frac{\pi}{14}\sin\frac{3\pi}{14}\sin\frac{5\pi}{14}\sin\frac{7\pi}{14}\sin\frac{9\pi}{14}\sin\frac{11\pi}{14}\sin\frac{13\pi}{14}$.
11. If $2\sin 2° + 4\sin 4° + 6\sin 6° + \ldots + 180\sin 180° = k\cot 1°$, then find the value of k.
12. If $\cos\theta\cos 2\theta\cos 2^2\theta \ldots \cos 2^{n-1}\theta = \frac{1}{2^n}$, then find θ.

Answer Key

1. (b) 2. (a) 3. (d) 4. (a) 5. 105 6. $\frac{1}{90}(\cot 1°)$

7. $\sqrt{2}\,\frac{\sin\frac{n\alpha}{4}}{\sin\frac{\alpha}{4}}\cos\left[(n+1)\frac{\alpha}{4}\right]$ 8. -1 10. $\frac{1}{64}$ 11. 90 12. $\theta = \frac{\pi}{2^n + 1}$

For Detailed Solution

Milestone 8 Conditional Identities

TYPE 1

Problems based on transformation of the plus form of sine or cosine into product form.

Working Method

(i) Simplify the terms containing A and B using the formula of $\sin C \pm \sin D$ and $\cos C \pm \cos D$ whichever is applicable.

(ii) Simplify the term containing C by using $\sin 2\theta = 2\sin\theta\cos\theta$ or $\cos 2\theta = 2\cos^2\theta - 1$ or $\cos 2\theta = 1 - 2\sin^2\theta$ and write $A + B$ in terms of C and then take out the common factor (which will be a term containing C).

(iii) Then, transform C is $A + B$ (not in the factor which has been taken common).

(iv) Then, simplify to get the desired result.

Example 124. If $A + B + C = \pi$, then show that

(i) $\sin 2A + \sin 2B + \sin 2C = 4\sin A \sin B \cos C$

(ii) $\cos 2A + \cos 2B + \cos 2C = -1 - 4\cos A \cos B \cos C$

(iii) $\cos A + \cos B + \cos C = 1 + 4\sin\frac{A}{2}\sin\frac{B}{2}\sin\frac{C}{2}$

(iv) $\sin A + \sin B + \sin C = 4\cos\frac{A}{2}\cos\frac{B}{2}\cos\frac{C}{2}$

Sol. (i) LHS $= \sin 2A + \sin 2B + \sin 2C$

$= 2\sin(A + B)\cos(A - B) + \sin 2C$

$= 2\sin(\pi - C)\cos(A - B) + \sin 2C$ [convert $A + B$ to $\pi - C$]

$= 2\sin C\cos(A - B) + 2\sin C\cos C$

$= 2\sin C[\cos(A - B) + \cos C]$ [take the term involving C as factor]

Convert the expression with-in-brackets in A and B only.

$= 2\sin C[\cos(A - B) + \cos(\pi - (A - B))]$

$= 2\sin C[\cos(A - B) - \cos(A + B)]$

$= 2\sin C(2\sin A\sin B)$

$= 4\sin A\sin B\sin C =$ RHS

(ii) LHS $= \cos 2A + \cos 2B + \cos 2C$

$= 2\cos(A + B)\cos(A - B) + \cos 2C$

$= -2\cos C\cos(A - B) + 2\cos^2 C - 1$

$= -2\cos C[\cos(A - B) - \cos C] - 1$

$= -2\cos C[\cos(A - B) + \cos(A + B)] - 1$

$= -2\cos C[2\cos A\cos B] - 1$

$= -1 - 4\cos A\cos B\cos C =$ RHS

(iii) LHS $= \cos A + \cos B + \cos C$

$= 2\cos\frac{A+B}{2}\cos\frac{A-B}{2} + \cos C$

$= 2\cos\left(\frac{\pi}{2} - \frac{C}{2}\right)\cos\frac{A-B}{2} + \cos C$

$= 2\sin\frac{C}{2}\cos\frac{A-B}{2} + 1 - 2\sin^2\frac{C}{2}$

[express $\cos C$ in terms of $\sin\frac{C}{2}$]

$= 2\sin\frac{C}{2}\left[\cos\frac{A-B}{2} - \sin\frac{C}{2}\right] + 1$

$= 2\sin\frac{C}{2}\left[\cos\frac{A-B}{2} - \cos\frac{A+B}{2}\right] + 1$

$= 2\sin\frac{C}{2}\left[2\sin\frac{A}{2}\sin\frac{B}{2}\right] + 1$

$= 1 - 4\sin\frac{A}{2}\sin\frac{B}{2}\sin\frac{C}{2} =$ RHS

(iv) Try on the same pattern as in Part (iii) above.

TYPE 2

Problems involving squares of sines or cosines of angles.

Working Method

(i) First, rearrange the terms in LHS. So that either $\sin^2 A - \sin^2 B = \sin(A + B)\sin(A - B)$ or $\cos^2 A - \sin^2 B = \cos(A + B)\cos(A - B)$ can be applied.

(ii) Simplify the term containing C and then take out the common factors (which will be a term containing C).

(iii) Then, transform C in $A + B$ (not in the factor which has been taken common).

(iv) Then, simplify to get the desired result.

Example 125. If $A+B+C=\pi$, then show that

(i) $\sin^2 A+\sin^2 B-\sin^2 C=2\sin A\sin B\cos C$

(ii) $\cos^2\frac{A}{2}+\cos^2\frac{B}{2}+\cos^2\frac{C}{2}=2+2\sin\frac{A}{2}\sin\frac{B}{2}\sin\frac{C}{2}$

(iii) $\sin^2 A+\sin^2 B+\sin^2 C=2+2\cos A\cos B\cos C$

Sol. (i) Starting from LHS

$$= \sin^2 A+\sin^2 B-\sin^2 C$$
$$= \sin^2 A+\sin(B+C)\sin(B-C)$$
$$= \sin^2 A+\sin(\pi-A)\sin(B-C)$$
$$= \sin A\,[\sin A+\sin(B-C)]$$
$$= \sin A\,[\sin(\pi-(B+C))+\sin(B-C)]$$
$$= \sin A\,[\sin(B+C)+\sin(B-C)]$$
$$= \sin A\,[2\sin B\cos C]=2\sin A\sin B\cos C$$

(ii) $\text{LHS}=\cos^2\frac{A}{2}+\cos^2\frac{B}{2}+\cos^2\frac{C}{2}$

$$=\cos^2\frac{A}{2}+\left(1-\sin^2\frac{B}{2}\right)+\cos^2\frac{C}{2}$$
$$=1+\left(\cos^2\frac{A}{2}-\sin^2\frac{B}{2}\right)+\cos^2\frac{C}{2}$$
$$=1+\cos\frac{(A+B)}{2}\cos\frac{(A-B)}{2}+\cos^2\frac{C}{2}$$
$$=1+\sin\frac{C}{2}\cos\frac{(A-B)}{2}+1-\sin^2\frac{C}{2}$$
$$=2+\sin\frac{C}{2}\left[\cos\frac{(A-B)}{2}-\sin\frac{C}{2}\right]$$
$$=2+\sin\frac{C}{2}\left[\cos\frac{(A-B)}{2}-\cos\frac{(A+B)}{2}\right]$$
$$=2+2\sin\frac{C}{2}\sin\frac{A}{2}\cos\frac{B}{2}$$

(iii) $\text{LHS}=\sin^2 A+\sin^2 B+\sin^2 C$

$$=1-\cos^2 A+\sin^2 B+\sin^2 C$$
$$=1-(\cos^2 A-\sin^2 B)+\sin^2 C$$
$$=1-\cos(A+B)\cos(A-B)+\sin^2 C$$
$$=1+\cos C\cos(A-B)+1-\cos^2 C$$
$$=2+\cos C[\cos(A-B)-\cos C]$$
$$=2+\cos C[\cos(A-B)+\cos(A+B)]$$
$$=2+2\cos C\cos A\cos B$$

TYPE 3

Problems involving only tangents or cotangents of angles.

Working Method

(i) Write the given relation between angles keeping two angles on one side and remaining on the other side.

(ii) Take tangent or cotangent of both sides and simplify to get the desired result.

Example 126.

(i) In a ΔABC, prove that

$$\tan A+\tan B+\tan C=\tan A\tan B\tan C.$$

(ii) If $A+B+C=\pi$, then prove that

$$\tan\frac{A}{2}\tan\frac{B}{2}+\tan\frac{B}{2}\tan\frac{C}{2}+\tan\frac{C}{2}\tan\frac{A}{2}=1.$$

(iii) If $A+B+C=\pi$, then prove that

$$\cot B\cot C+\cot C\cot A+\cot A\cot B=1.$$

Sol. (i) In ΔABC,

$\because\ A+B+C=\pi$

$\therefore\ A+B=\pi-C \Rightarrow \tan(A+B)=\tan(\pi-C)$ [by taking tan on both sides]

$\Rightarrow \dfrac{\tan A+\tan B}{1-\tan A\tan B}=-\tan C\quad [\because \tan(\pi-C)=-\tan C]$

$\Rightarrow \tan A+\tan B=-\tan C+\tan A\tan B\tan C$

$\Rightarrow \tan A+\tan B+\tan C=\tan A\tan B\tan C$

(ii) $\because A+B+C=\pi$

$\therefore \frac{A}{2}+\frac{B}{2}+\frac{C}{2}=\frac{\pi}{2}$ or $\frac{A}{2}+\frac{B}{2}=\frac{\pi}{2}-\frac{C}{2}$

$\therefore \tan\left(\frac{A}{2}+\frac{B}{2}\right)=\tan\left(\frac{\pi}{2}-\frac{C}{2}\right)=\cot\frac{C}{2}$

$\Rightarrow \dfrac{\tan\frac{A}{2}+\tan\frac{B}{2}}{1-\tan\frac{A}{2}\tan\frac{B}{2}}=\dfrac{1}{\tan\frac{C}{2}}$

$\Rightarrow \tan\frac{A}{2}\tan\frac{C}{2}+\tan\frac{B}{2}\tan\frac{C}{2}=1-\tan\frac{A}{2}\tan\frac{B}{2}$

$\Rightarrow \tan\frac{A}{2}\tan\frac{C}{2}+\tan\frac{B}{2}\tan\frac{C}{2}+\tan\frac{A}{2}\tan\frac{B}{2}=1$

(iii) $\because\ A+B+C=\pi$

$\therefore\ A+B=\pi-C\Rightarrow\cot(A+B)=\cot(\pi-C)$ [by taking cot on both sides]

$\Rightarrow \dfrac{\cos A\cot B-1}{\cot B+\cot A}=-\cot C$

$\Rightarrow \cot A\cot B-1=-\cot B\cot C-\cot C\cot A$

$\Rightarrow \cot A\cot B+\cot B\cot C+\cot C\cot A=1$

TYPE 4

Problems which can be solved by transforming the given problem in trigonometrical form.

Working Method

(i) If it is given that $x+y+z=xyz$ or $xy+yz+zx=1$, then put $x=\tan A$, $y=\tan B$ and $z=\tan C$ in it and simplify it to find the value of $A+B+C$.

(ii) Then, put $\tan A$, $\tan B$ and $\tan C$ in place of x, y and z respectively, in the LHS and simplify it to get the desired identity using the value of $A+B+C$.

Example 127. If $xy+yz+zx=1$, prove that

$$\frac{x}{1-x^2}+\frac{y}{1-y^2}+\frac{z}{1-z^2}=\frac{4xyz}{(1-x^2)(1-y^2)(1-z^2)}.$$

Sol. Let $x=\tan A$, $y=\tan B$, $z=\tan C$

Given, $xy+yz+zx=1$

$\therefore\ \tan A\tan B+\tan B\tan C+\tan C\tan A=1$

$\Rightarrow\quad \tan C(\tan A+\tan B)=1-\tan A\tan B$

$\Rightarrow\ \dfrac{\tan A+\tan B}{1-\tan A\tan B}=\dfrac{1}{\tan C}=\cot C=\tan\left(\dfrac{\pi}{2}-C\right)$

$\Rightarrow\quad \tan(A+B)=\tan\left(\dfrac{\pi}{2}-C\right)$

$\therefore\quad A+B=\dfrac{\pi}{2}-C$ [taking principal value]

$\Rightarrow\quad A+B+C=\dfrac{\pi}{2}$ ...(i)

Now, LHS $=\dfrac{x}{1-x^2}+\dfrac{y}{1-y^2}+\dfrac{z}{1-z^2}$

$=\dfrac{\tan A}{1-\tan^2 A}+\dfrac{\tan B}{1-\tan^2 B}+\dfrac{\tan C}{1-\tan^2 C}$

$=\dfrac{1}{2}\left[\dfrac{2\tan A}{1-\tan^2 A}+\dfrac{2\tan B}{1-\tan^2 B}+\dfrac{2\tan C}{1-\tan^2 C}\right]$

$=\dfrac{1}{2}(\tan 2A+\tan 2B+\tan 2C)$ ...(ii)

Now, from Eq. (i), $A+B+C=\dfrac{\pi}{2}$

$\Rightarrow\quad 2A+2B+2C=\pi$

$\Rightarrow\quad 2A+2B=\pi-2C$

$\Rightarrow\quad \tan(2A+2B)=\tan(\pi-2C)$

$\Rightarrow\quad \dfrac{\tan 2A+\tan 2B}{1-\tan 2A\tan 2B}=-\tan 2C$

$\Rightarrow\quad \tan 2A+\tan 2B=-\tan 2C+\tan 2A\tan 2B\tan 2C$ ...(iii)

From Eq. (ii),

LHS $=\dfrac{1}{2}(\tan 2A+\tan 2B+\tan 2C)$

$=\dfrac{1}{2}(\tan 2A\cdot\tan 2B\cdot\tan 2C)$ [from Eq. (iii)]

$=\dfrac{1}{2}\left(\dfrac{2\tan A}{1-\tan^2 A}\right)\left(\dfrac{2\tan B}{1-\tan^2 B}\right)\left(\dfrac{2\tan C}{1-\tan^2 C}\right)$

$=\dfrac{1}{2}\left(\dfrac{2x}{1-x^2}\right)\left(\dfrac{2y}{1-y^2}\right)\left(\dfrac{2z}{1-z^2}\right)$

$=\dfrac{4xyz}{(1-x)^2(1-y^2)(1-z^2)}$

JEE SCANNER

Example Similar to PYQ Asked in JEE Main 2024

If $A+B+C=\dfrac{\pi}{2}$, then the value of $2(\tan A\cdot\tan B+\tan B\cdot\tan C+\tan C\cdot\tan A)^2$ is equal to

(a) 0 (b) 1

(c) 2 (d) 4

Sol. (c) Given, $A+B+C=\dfrac{\pi}{2}\Rightarrow A+B=\dfrac{\pi}{2}-C$

$\therefore\quad \tan(A+B)=\tan\left(\dfrac{\pi}{2}-C\right)$

$\Rightarrow\quad \dfrac{\tan A+\tan B}{1-\tan A\tan B}=\cot(C)$

$\Rightarrow\quad \dfrac{\tan A+\tan B}{1-\tan A\tan B}=\dfrac{1}{\tan C}$

$\Rightarrow\quad \tan A\cdot\tan C+\tan B\cdot\tan C=1-\tan A\cdot\tan B$

$\Rightarrow\quad \tan A\tan B+\tan A\cdot\tan C+\tan B\cdot\tan C=1$

$\therefore\quad 2(\tan A\tan B+\tan A\cdot\tan C+\tan B\cdot\tan C)^2=2(1)^2=2$

Skill Builder

If $\cos 2B=\dfrac{\cos(A+C)}{\cos(A-C)}$, then $\tan A$, $\tan B$, $\tan C$ are in

(a) AP (b) GP

(c) HP (d) None of these

For Sol.

▪ **For more practice** See Q.19 of Milestone Practice 8.

Example 128. In ΔABC, show that

$$\frac{\tan A}{\tan B\tan C}+\frac{\tan B}{\tan A\tan C}+\frac{\tan C}{\tan A\tan B}=\tan A+\tan B+\tan C-2\cot A-2\cot B-2\cot C.$$

Sol. LHS $=\dfrac{\tan A}{\tan B\tan C}+\dfrac{\tan B}{\tan A\tan C}+\dfrac{\tan C}{\tan A\tan B}$

$=\dfrac{\tan^2 A+\tan^2 B+\tan^2 C}{\tan A\tan B\tan C}$

$=\dfrac{(\tan A+\tan B+\tan C)^2-2(\tan A\tan B+\tan B\tan C+\tan C\tan A)}{\tan A\tan B\tan C}$

$=\dfrac{(\tan A+\tan B+\tan C)^2}{\tan A+\tan B+\tan C}-\dfrac{2(\tan A\tan B+\tan B\tan C+\tan C\tan A)}{\tan A\tan B\tan C}$

[$\because$ In ΔABC, $\tan A+\tan B+\tan C=\tan A\tan B\tan C$]

$=\tan A+\tan B+\tan C-2\cot A-2\cot B-2\cot C=$ RHS

Milestone Practice 1.8

1. If $A+B+C=180°$ and $\cos 2A+\cos 2B+\cos 2C = a+b\cos A\cos B\cos C$, then (a, b) is
(a) (1, 4) (b) (– 1, – 4) (c) (1, – 4) (d) (– 1, 4)

2. If $A+B+C=180°$ and $\sin^2\frac{A}{2}+\sin^2\frac{B}{2}-\sin^2\frac{C}{2} = a+b\cos\frac{A}{2}\cos\frac{B}{2}\sin\frac{C}{2}$, then (a,b) is
(a) (1, 2) (b) (– 1, 2) (c) (– 1, – 2) (d) (1, – 2)

3. If $A+B+C=180°$, $\cot A\cot C=\frac{1}{2}$ and $\cot B\cot C=\frac{1}{18}$, then the value of $\tan C$ is
(a) 4 (b) 1 (c) 2 (d) 0

4. If $x+y+z=90°$, then the value of
$$\begin{vmatrix} \sin x & \sin y & \sin z \\ \cos x & \cos y & \cos z \\ \cos^3 x & \cos^3 y & \cos^3 z \end{vmatrix}$$ is
(a) 1 (b) 2 (c) 0 (d) 4

5. If $A+B+C=180°$, then prove that $\tan^2\frac{\theta}{2}=\tan\frac{B}{2}\tan\frac{C}{2}$ when $\cos\theta(\sin B+\sin C)=\sin A$.

6. If in a ΔABC, $\frac{\sin A+\sin B+\sin C}{\sin A+\sin B-\sin C}=2\lambda\cot\frac{A}{2}\cot\frac{B}{2}$, then find the value of λ.

7. If $A+B+C=180°$, then find the value of $\frac{\cos A}{\sin B\sin C}+\frac{\cos B}{\sin C\sin A}+\frac{\cos C}{\sin A\sin B}$.

8. In ΔABC, show that $\frac{1-\cos A+\cos B+\cos C}{1-\cos C+\cos A+\cos B}=\tan\frac{A}{2}\cot\frac{C}{2}$.

9. In a ΔABC, if $\tan\left(\frac{B+C-A}{4}\right)\tan\left(\frac{C+A-B}{4}\right)\tan\left(\frac{A+B-C}{4}\right)=1$, then find the value of $\cos A+\cos B+\cos C$.

10. If in a ΔABC, $\cot\frac{A}{2}+\cot\frac{B}{2}+\cot\frac{C}{2}=\lambda\cot\frac{A}{2}\cot\frac{B}{2}\cot\frac{C}{2}$, then find the value of λ.

11. If in a ΔABC, $\sin^2 A+\sin^2 B+\sin^2 C=2$, then the triangle is always
(a) isosceles triangle (b) right angled
(c) acute angled (d) obtuse angled

12. If A, B, C are acute positive angles such that $A+B+C=\pi$ and $\cot A\cot B\cot C=k$, then
(a) $k\le\frac{1}{3\sqrt{3}}$ (b) $k\ge\frac{1}{3\sqrt{3}}$
(c) $k<\frac{1}{9}$ (d) $k>\frac{1}{3}$

13. In ΔABC, prove that $\sin(B+C-A)+\sin(C+A-B)+\sin(A+B-C)=4\sin A\sin B\sin C$.

14. If $A+B+C=\pi$, prove that $\cot A+\cot B+\cot C-\text{cosec}A\cdot\text{cosec}B\cdot\text{cosec}C=\cot A\cdot\cot B\cdot\cot C$.

15. If $\cos(A+B+C)=\cos A\cos B\cos C$, then find the value of $\frac{8\sin(B+C)\sin(C+A)\sin(A+B)}{\sin 2A\sin 2B\sin 2C}$.

16. The product of the sines of the angles of a triangle is p and the product of their cosines is q. Show that the tangents of the angles are the roots of the equation $qx^3-px^2+(1+q)x-p=0$.

17. Prove that $\cos^2(\beta-\gamma)+\cos^2(\gamma-\alpha)+\cos^2(\alpha-\beta)=1+2\cos(\beta-\alpha)\cos(\gamma-\alpha)\cos(\alpha-\beta)$.

18. In ΔABC, if $2\sin^2 C=2+\cos 2A+\cos 2B$, then prove that triangle is right angled.

19. If $A+B+C=\pi$, then prove that $\tan 3A+\tan 3B+\tan 3C=\tan 3A\tan 3B\tan 3C$.

Answer Key

1. (b) 2. (d) 3. (a) 4. (c) 6. $\left(\frac{1}{2}\right)$ 7. (2) 9. (– 1) 10. (1)
11. (b) 12. (b) 15. (–1)

For Detailed Solution

Milestone 9 Graph and Properties of Trigonometric Functions

• Graph and Properties of Trigonometric Function [$n \in I$] • Some Important Graphical Deductions

1.15 Graph and Properties of Trigonometric Functions [$n \in I$]

1. $y = \sin\theta$ or $\sin x$

As we have explained all trigonometric ratios are functions (i.e. relations between angle and ratio) which implies that each trigonometric function must possess pictorial representation i.e. graph.

Now, for graph of trigonometry $y = \sin x$, we have to observe nature of $y = \sin x$ in different quadrants.

- **In 1st quadrant** As x varies from 0 to $\frac{\pi}{2}$, then corresponding ratio of $y = \sin x$ is positive and increases from 0 to 1.
- **In 2nd quadrant** As x varies from $\frac{\pi}{2}$ to π, then corresponding ratio of $y = \sin x$ is positive and decreases from 1 to 0.
- **In 3rd quadrant** As x varies from π to $\frac{3\pi}{2}$, then corresponding ratio of $y = \sin x$ is negative and decreases from 0 to −1.
- **In 4th quadrant** As θ varies from $\frac{3\pi}{2}$ to 2π, then corresponding ratio of $y = \sin x$ is negative and increases from −1 to 0.

  Now, from the above discussion, we have the graph of $y = \sin x$ in 0 to 2π as

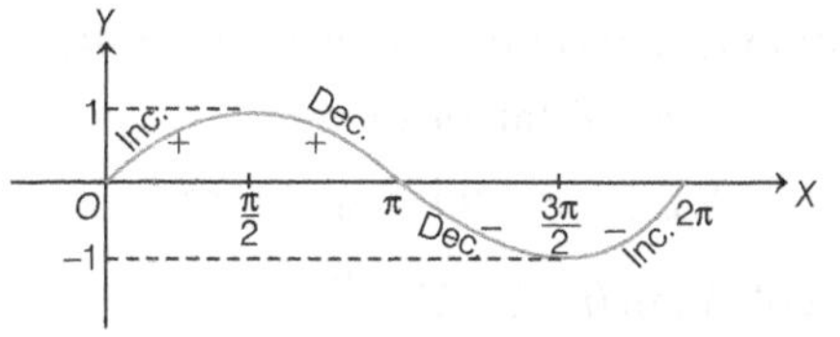

If angle is increased further from 2π, then we observe that its ratio i.e. output starts repeating.

Which implies $y = \sin x$ is periodic function with fundamental period $= 2\pi$.

Properties of $y = \sin x$

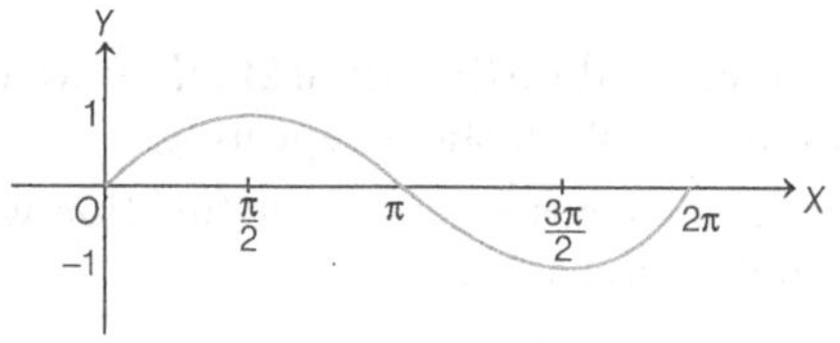

(i) Domain of $y = \sin x$ is $x \in R$

(ii) Range of $y = \sin x$ is $y \in [-1, 1]$

(iii) It is periodic function with fundamental period of 2π.

(iv) Variation of $y = \sin x$ is

$$y \in [-1, 1] \Rightarrow -1 \le \sin x \le 1$$

$$\Rightarrow \quad y_{\max} = 1 \text{ and } y_{\min} = -1$$

(v) Variation of $y = A\sin(mx)$

$$y \in [-A, A]$$

$$\Rightarrow \quad -A \le A\sin(mx) \le A$$

$\Rightarrow A\sin(mx)$ can never be greater than A or less than $-A$

$\Rightarrow y_{\max} = A$ and $y_{\min} = -A$

(vi) Period of $A\sin mx$ is $T = \frac{2\pi}{m}$

2. $y = \cos\theta$ or $\cos x$

- **In 1st quadrant** As x varies from 0 to $\frac{\pi}{2}$, then corresponding ratio of $y = \cos x$ is positive and decreases from 1 to 0.
- **In 2nd quadrant** As x varies from $\frac{\pi}{2}$ to π, then corresponding ratio of $y = \cos x$ is negative and decreases from 0 to −1.
- **In 3rd quadrant** As x varies from π to $\frac{3\pi}{2}$, then corresponding ratio of $y = \cos x$ is negative and increases from −1 to 0.

- **In 4th quadrant** As x varies from $\frac{3\pi}{2}$ to 2π, then corresponding ratio of $y = \cos x$ is positive and increases from 0 to 1.

Now, from the above discussion, we have the graph of $y = \cos x$ in 0 to 2π as

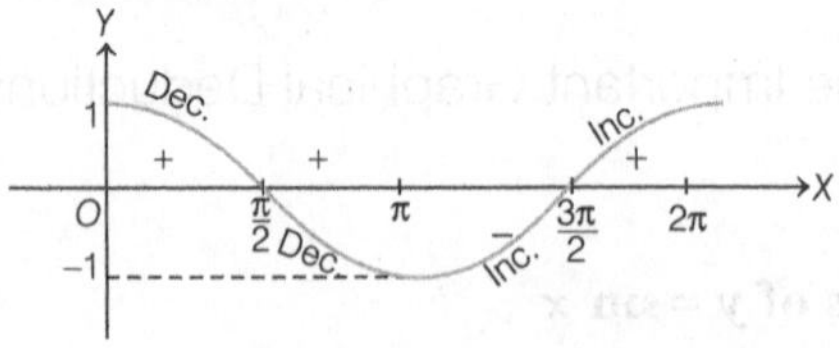

If angle is increased further from 2π, then we observe that its ratio i.e. output starts repeating.

Which implies $y = \cos x$ is periodic function with fundamental period $= 2\pi$.

Properties of $y = \cos x$

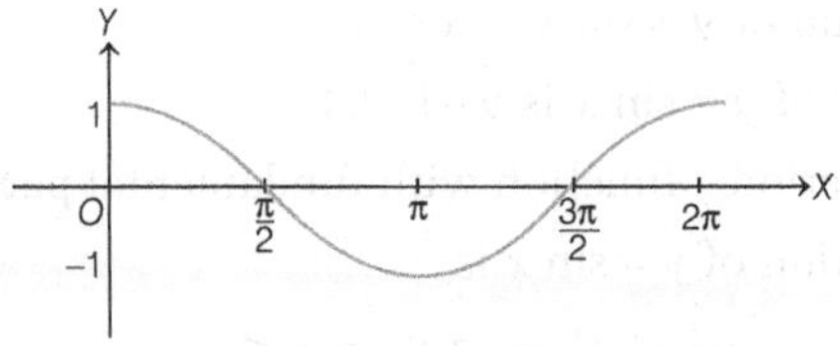

(i) Domain of $y = \cos x$ is $x \in R$

(ii) Range of $y = \cos x$ is $y \in [-1, 1]$

(iii) It is periodic function with fundamental period of 2π.

(iv) Variation of $y = \cos x$

$$y \in [-1, 1] \Rightarrow -1 \le \cos x \le 1$$

$$\Rightarrow \quad y_{\max} = 1 \text{ and } y_{\min} = -1$$

(v) Variation of $y = A\cos(mx)$ is

$$y \in [-A, A] \Rightarrow -A \le A\cos(mx) \le A$$

$\Rightarrow A\cos(mx)$ can never be greater than A or less than $-A$

$\Rightarrow y_{\max} = A$ and $y_{\min} = -A$

(vi) Period of $A\cos mx$ is $T = \frac{2\pi}{m}$

3. $y = \tan\theta$ or $\tan x$

- **In 1st quadrant** As x varies from 0 to $\frac{\pi}{2}$, then corresponding ratio of $y = \tan x$ is positive and increases from 0 to ∞ and at $x = \frac{\pi}{2}$, $y = \tan x$ is not defined.

- **In 2nd quadrant** As x varies from $\frac{\pi}{2}$ to π, then corresponding ratio of $y = \tan x$ is negative and increases from $-\infty$ to 0.

Now, from the above discussion, we have the graph of $y = \tan x$ in 0 to π as

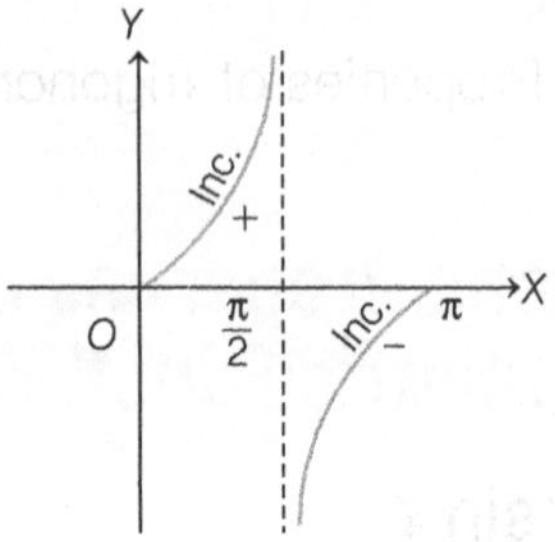

If angle is increased further from π, then we observe that its ratio i.e. output starts repeating.

Which implies $y = \tan x$ is periodic function with fundamental period $= \pi$.

Properties of $y = \tan x$

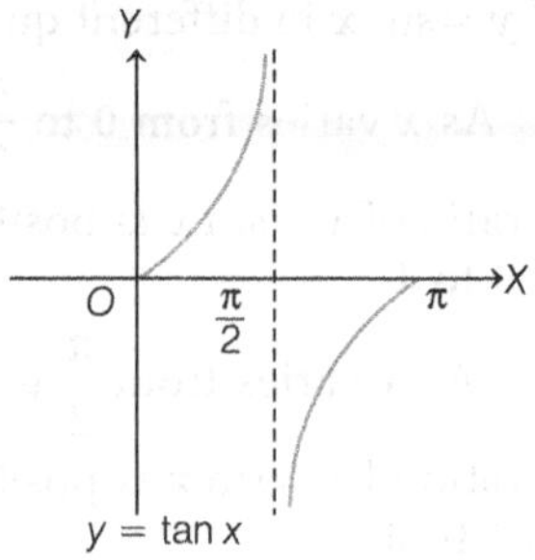

(i) Domain of $y = \tan x$ is

$$x \in R - \left\{(2n+1)\frac{\pi}{2} : n \in I\right\}$$

(ii) Range of $y = \tan x$ is $y \in (-\infty, \infty)$

(iii) It is periodic function with fundamental period of π.

(iv) Variation of $y = \tan x$

$$y \in (-\infty, \infty) \Rightarrow -\infty < \tan(x) < \infty$$

$$\Rightarrow \quad y_{\max} = \infty \text{ and } y_{\min} = -\infty$$

(v) Variation of $y = A\tan(mx)$ is $y \in (-\infty, \infty)$

$$\Rightarrow \quad -\infty < A\tan(mx) < \infty$$

$$\Rightarrow \quad y_{\max} = \infty \text{ and } y_{\min} = -\infty$$

(vi) Period of $A\tan(mx)$ is $T = \frac{\pi}{m}$

$$A\tan(mx) \text{ is } T = \frac{\pi}{m}$$

4. $y = \cot x$

Properties of $y = \cot x$

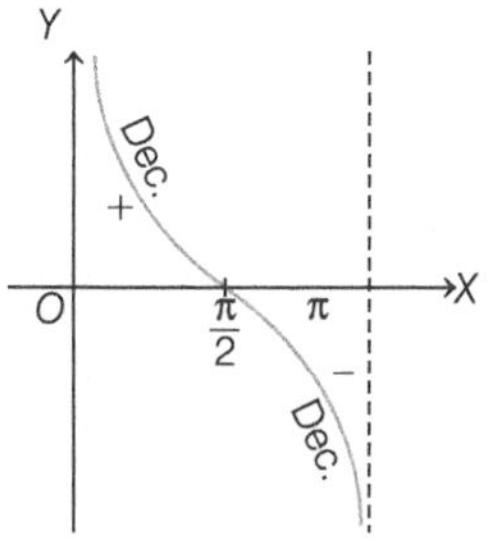

(i) Domain of the $y = \cot x$ is $x \in R - \{n\pi : n \in I\}$.

(ii) Range of the $y = \cot x$ is $y \in (-\infty, \infty)$

(iii) It is a periodic function with period of π.

(iv) Variation of $y = \tan x$

$$y \in (-\infty, \infty) \Rightarrow -\infty < \cot(mx) < \infty$$

$$\Rightarrow \quad y_{\max} = \infty \text{ and } y_{\min} = -\infty$$

(v) Variation of $y = A\cot(mx)$

As, $y \in (-\infty, \infty) \Rightarrow -\infty < A\cot(mx) < \infty$

$\Rightarrow y_{\max} = \infty$ and $y_{\min} = -\infty$

(vi) Period of $A\cot(mx)$ is $T = \dfrac{\pi}{m}$

5. $y = \operatorname{cosec} x$

Properties of $y = \operatorname{cosec} x$

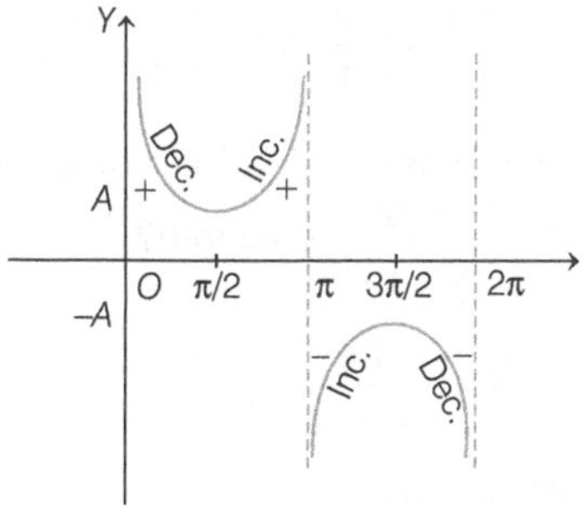

(i) Domain of the $y = \operatorname{cosec} x$ is $x \in R - \{n\pi : n \in I\}$.

(ii) Range of the $y = \operatorname{cosec} x$ is $y \in (-\infty, -1] \cup [1, \infty)$.

(iii) It is a periodic function with period of 2π.

(iv) Variation of $y = \operatorname{cosec} x$

$$y \in (-\infty, -1] \cup [1, \infty) \Rightarrow y_{\max} = \infty \text{ and } y_{\min} = -\infty$$

(v) Variation of $y = A\operatorname{cosec}(mx)$ as

$$y \in (-\infty, -A] \cup [A, \infty)$$

$\Rightarrow A\operatorname{cosec}(mx)$ can be greater than A or less than $-A$

$\Rightarrow y_{\max} = \infty$ and $y_{\min} = -\infty$

(vi) Period of $A\operatorname{cosec}(mx)$ is $T = \dfrac{2\pi}{m}$

6. $y = \sec x$

Properties of $y = \sec x$

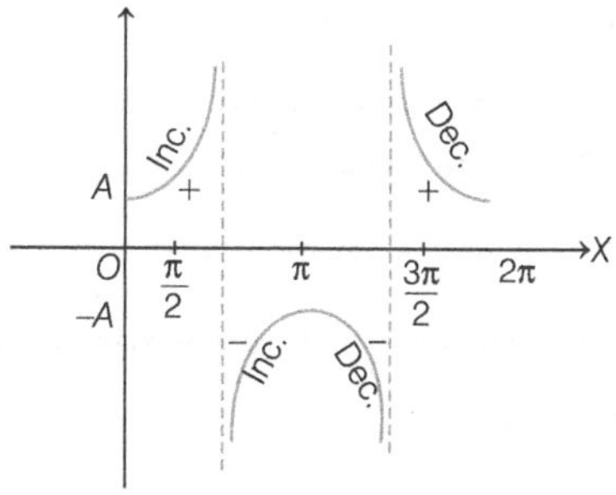

(i) Domain of the $y = \sec x$ is $x \in R - \left\{(2n+1)\dfrac{\pi}{2} : n \in I\right\}$

(ii) Range of the $y = \sec x$ is $y \in (-\infty, -1] \cup [1, \infty)$.

(iii) It is periodic function with period of 2π.

(iv) Variation of $y = \sec x$

$$y \in (-\infty, 1] \cup [1, \infty)$$

$$\Rightarrow \quad y_{\max} = \infty \text{ and } y_{\min} = -\infty$$

(v) Variation of $y = A\sec(mx)$ as

$$y \in (-\infty, -A] \cup [A, \infty)$$

$\Rightarrow A\sec(mx)$ can be greater than A or less than $-A$

$\Rightarrow y_{\max} = \infty$ and $y_{\min} = -\infty$

(vi) Period of $A\sec(mx)$ is $T = \dfrac{2\pi}{m}$

Summary

Function	1st quadrant	2nd quadrant	3rd quadrant	4th quadrant
$\sin\theta$	↑ from 0 to 1	↓ from 1 to 0	↓ from 0 to −1	↑ from −1 to 0
$\cos\theta$	↓ from 1 to 0	↓ from 0 to −1	↑ from −1 to 0	↑ from 0 to 1
$\tan\theta$	↑ from 0 to ∞	↑ from −∞ to 0	↑ from 0 to ∞	↑ from −∞ to 0
$\cot\theta$	↓ from ∞ to 0	↓ from 0 to −∞	↓ from ∞ to 0	↓ from 0 to −∞
$\sec\theta$	↑ from 1 to ∞	↑ from −∞ to −1	↓ from −1 to −∞	↓ from ∞ to 1
$\operatorname{cosec}\theta$	↓ from ∞ to 1	↑ from 1 to ∞	↑ from −∞ to −1	↓ from −1 to −∞

JEE SPIKE

$+\infty$ and $-\infty$ are two symbols. These are not real numbers. When we say that $\tan\theta$ increases from 0 to ∞ as θ varies from 0 to $\frac{\pi}{2}$, it means that $\tan\theta$ increases in the interval $\left(0, \frac{\pi}{2}\right)$ and it attains arbitrarily large positive values as θ tends to $\frac{\pi}{2}$. This rule applies to other trigonometric functions also.

Concept Inside Video

Example 129. Which of the following is the least?

(a) $\sin 3$ (b) $\sin 2$

(c) $\sin 1$ (d) $\sin 7$

Sol. (a) $\sin 3 = \sin[\pi - (\pi - 3)] = \sin(\pi - 3) = \sin(0.14)$

$\sin 2 = \sin[\pi - (\pi - 2)]$

$= \sin(\pi - 2) = \sin(1.14)$

$\sin 7 = \sin[2\pi + (7 - 2\pi)]$

$= \sin(7 - 2\pi) = \sin(0.72)$

Now, $1.14 > 1 > 0.72 > 0.14$

$\Rightarrow \quad \sin(1.14) > \sin 1 > \sin(0.72) > \sin(0.14)$

[as 1.14, 0.72, 0.14 lie in the first quadrant and sine functions increase in the first quadrant]

Hence, among the given values, $\sin 3$ is the least.

Alternate Solution

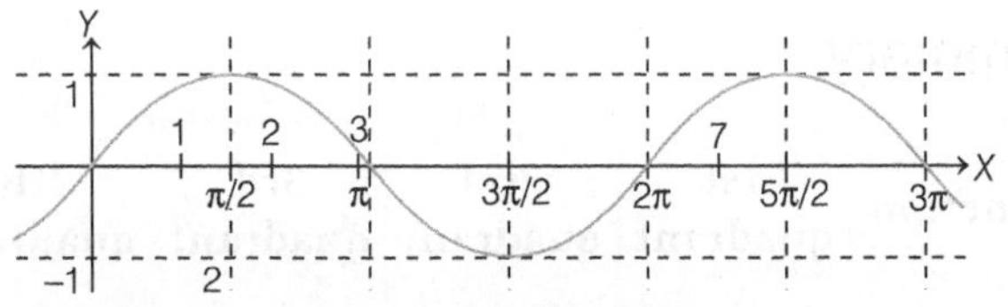

From the graph, obviously $\sin 3$ is the least.

Example 130. Find the value of x for which $f(x) = \sqrt{\sin x - \cos x}$ is defined, $x \in [0, 2\pi]$.

Sol. $f(x) = \sqrt{\sin x - \cos x}$ is defined, if $\sin x \geq \cos x$

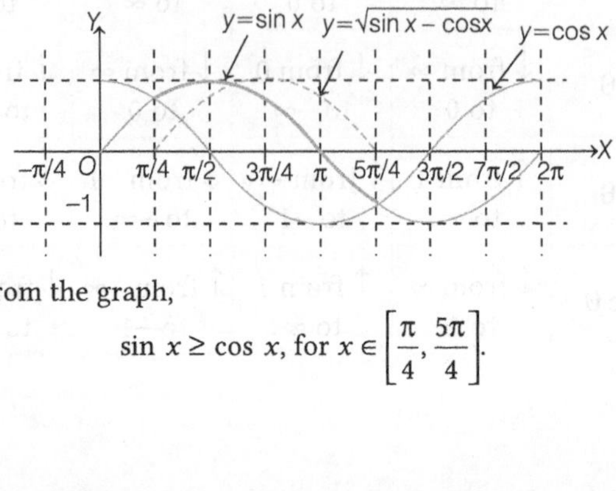

From the graph,

$$\sin x \geq \cos x, \text{ for } x \in \left[\frac{\pi}{4}, \frac{5\pi}{4}\right].$$

Example 131. Solve $\tan x > \cot x$, where $x \in [0, 2\pi]$.

Sol.

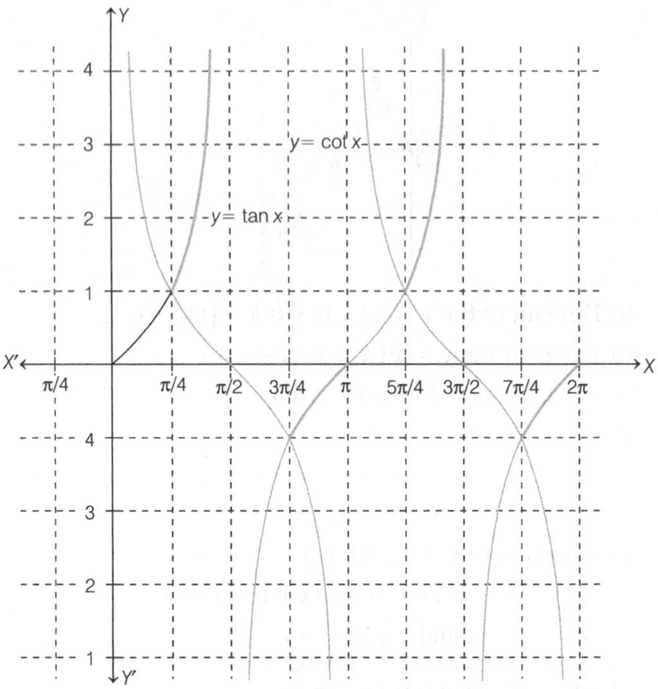

We find that $\tan x > \cot x$. Therefore, the values of $\tan x$ are more than the value of $\cot x$. That is, the value of x for which graph of $y = \tan x$ is above the graph of $y = \cot x$.

From the graph, it is clear that

$$x \in \left(\frac{\pi}{4}, \frac{\pi}{2}\right) \cup \left(\frac{3\pi}{4}, \pi\right) \cup \left(\frac{5\pi}{4}, \frac{3\pi}{2}\right) \cup \left(\frac{7\pi}{4}, 2\pi\right).$$

Example 132. For what real values of x and y is the equation $\sec^2\theta = \dfrac{4xy}{(x+y)^2}$ possible?

Sol. Here, $\quad \sec^2\theta = \dfrac{4xy}{(x+y)^2}$

We know that $\sec^2\theta \geq 1$

and $\quad \dfrac{4xy}{(x+y)^2} \leq 1 \quad$ [as AM $\geq$ GM]

$\Rightarrow \quad \sec^2\theta = \dfrac{4xy}{(x+y)^2}$ is only possible, if $\sec^2\theta = 1$

i.e. $\quad \dfrac{4xy}{(x+y)^2} = 1, \forall\, x, y \in R^+$

or $\quad 4xy = (x+y)^2, \forall\, x, y \in R^+$

$\Rightarrow \quad x^2 + y^2 - 2xy = 0, \forall\, x, y \in R^+$

$\Rightarrow \quad (x-y)^2 = 0, \forall\, x, y \in R^+$

or $\quad x = y, \forall\, x, y \in R^+$

Example 133. Show that the equation $\sin\theta = x + \frac{1}{x}$ is impossible, if x is real.

Sol. Given, $\sin\theta = x + \frac{1}{x}$

$$\therefore \quad \sin^2\theta = x^2 + \frac{1}{x} + 2x\cdot\frac{1}{x} = x^2 + \frac{1}{x^2} + 2 \geq 2$$

which is not possible since, $\sin^2\theta \leq 1$.

Example 134. Find the values of x for which $3\cos\theta = x^2 - 8x + 19$ holds good.

Sol. $3\cos\theta = x^2 - 8x + 19 = (x-4)^2 + 3$

Now, LHS $\Rightarrow 3\cos\theta \leq 3$

or LHS has greatest value 3.

but RHS $\Rightarrow (x-4)^2 + 3 \geq 3$

or RHS has least value 3.

Hence, LHS = RHS

when $3\cos\theta = (x-4)^2 + 3 = 3$

$\Rightarrow \quad \cos\theta = 1$ and $x - 4 = 0$ or $x = 4$

Example 135. If $\sin x_1 + \sin x_2 + \sin x_3 + \ldots + \sin x_{2008} = 2008$, then find the value of $\sin^{2008} x_1 + \sin^{2008} x_2 + \sin^{2008} x_3 + \ldots + \sin^{2008} x_{2008}$ and $\cos^{2009} x_1 + \cos^{2009} x_2 + \cos^{2009} x_3 + \ldots + \cos^{2009} x_{2008}$.

Sol. We know that $\sin x_i \leq 1, \forall\, i$

$\Rightarrow \sin x_1 + \sin x_2 + \sin x_3 + \ldots + \sin x_{2008} \leq 2008$

Thus, equality holds only when each of the term is 1.

i.e. $\sin x_i = 1, \forall\, i = 1, 2, 3, \ldots, 2008$

and consequently $\cos x_i = 0, \forall\, i = 1, 2, 3, \ldots, 2008$

Now, $\sin^{2008} x_1 + \sin^{2008} x_2 + \sin^{2008} x_3 + \ldots + \sin^{2008} x_{2008}$
$= 1 + 1 + 1 + \ldots + 1 = 2008$

and $\cos^{2009} x_1 + \cos^{2009} x_2 + \cos^{2009} x_3 + \ldots + \cos^{2009} x_{2008}$
$= 0 + 0 + 0 + \ldots + 0 = 0$

Trigonometric Ratios of Some Standard Acute Angles

The values or trigonometric ratios of standard acute angles are put in the following tabular form for ready reference.

Trigonometric Ratios of Standard Angles

Degree	0	30	45	60	90	120	135	150	180	270
Radian	0	$\frac{\pi}{6}$	$\frac{\pi}{4}$	$\frac{\pi}{3}$	$\frac{\pi}{2}$	$\frac{2\pi}{3}$	$\frac{3\pi}{4}$	$\frac{5\pi}{6}$	π	$\frac{3\pi}{2}$
sin θ	0	$\frac{1}{2}$	$\frac{1}{\sqrt{2}}$	$\frac{\sqrt{3}}{2}$	1	$\frac{\sqrt{3}}{2}$	$\frac{1}{\sqrt{2}}$	$\frac{1}{2}$	0	−1
cos θ	1	$\frac{\sqrt{3}}{2}$	$\frac{1}{\sqrt{2}}$	$\frac{1}{2}$	0	$-\frac{1}{2}$	$-\frac{1}{\sqrt{2}}$	$-\frac{\sqrt{3}}{2}$	−1	0
tan θ	0	$\frac{1}{\sqrt{3}}$	1	$\sqrt{3}$	∞	$-\sqrt{3}$	−1	$-\frac{1}{\sqrt{3}}$	0	∞

Transformation of the Graphs of Trigonometric Functions

1. To draw the graph of $y = f(x+a)$; $(a > 0)$ from the graph of $y = f(x)$, shift the graph of $y = f(x)$ by a units left along the X-axis.

   Let's consider the function $y = \sin(x+1)$

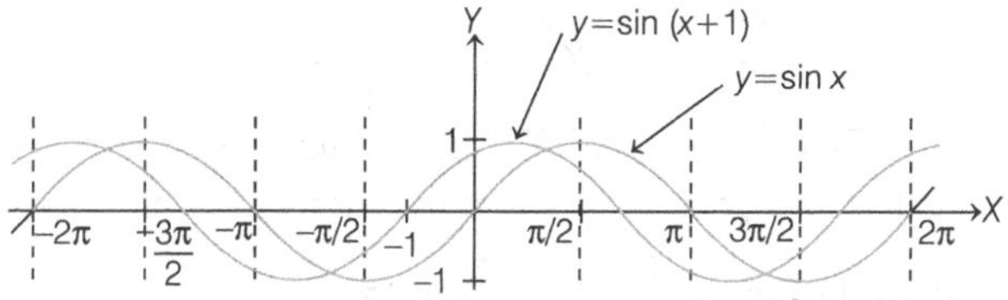

   To draw the graph of $y = f(x-a)$; $(a > 0)$ from the graph of $y = f(x)$, shift the graph of $y = f(x)$ by a units right along the X-axis.

   Let's consider the following function $y = \cos(x-2)$.

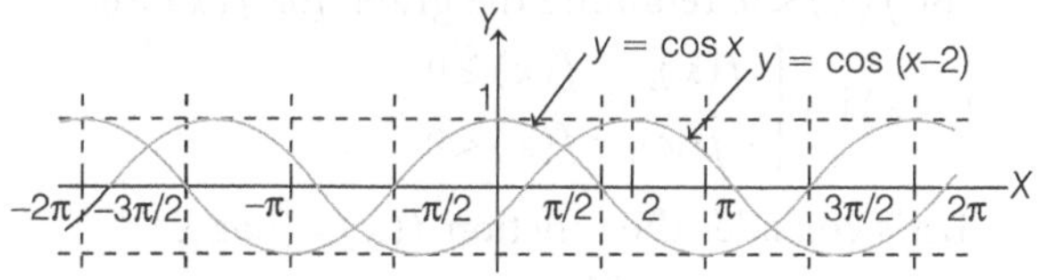

   As the shape of the transformed graph remains same, so the period does not change.

2. To draw the graph of $y = f(x) + a$; $(a > 0)$ from the graph of $y = f(x)$, shift the graph of $y = f(x)$ by a units upwards along the Y-axis.

   To draw the graph of $y = f(x) - a$; $(a > 0)$ from the graph of $y = f(x)$, shift the graph of $y = f(x)$ by a units downward along the Y-axis.

   Let's consider the function $y = \cos x + 1$ and $y = \cos x - 2$.

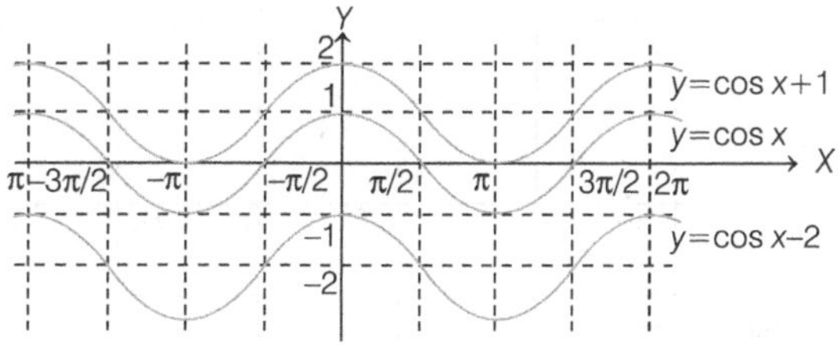

   As the shape of the transformed graph remains same, so the period does not change.

3. If $y = f(x)$ has period T, then period of $y = f(ax)$ is $\frac{T}{|a|}$.

Range remains same.

Let's consider the function $y = \sin 2x$.

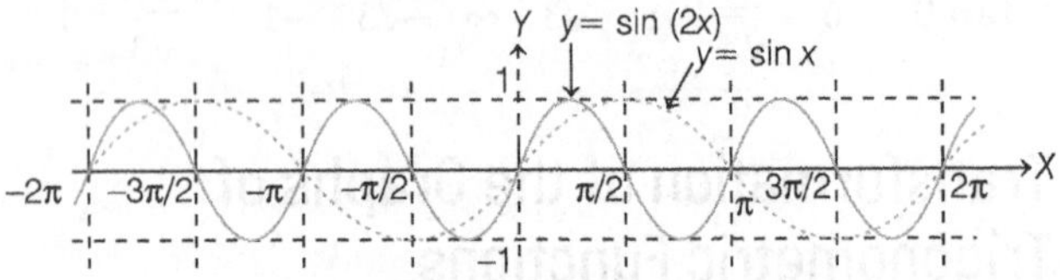

Period of $y = \sin(2x)$ is $\frac{2\pi}{2} = \pi$

Let's consider another function $y = \sin\left(\frac{x}{2}\right)$

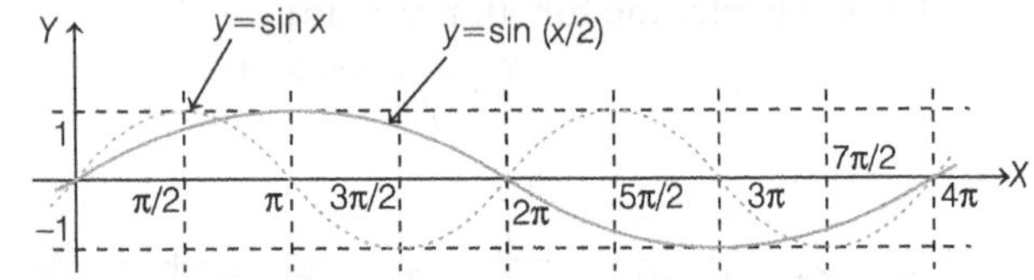

Period of $y = \sin\left(\frac{x}{2}\right)$ is $\frac{2\pi}{\left(\frac{1}{2}\right)} = 4\pi$

4. Since, $y = |f(x)| \geq 0$, to draw the graph of $y = |f(x)|$, take the mirror of the graph of $y = f(x)$ in the X-axis for $f(x) < 0$, retaining the graph for $f(x) > 0$.

$$|f(x)| = \begin{cases} f(x), & f(x) \geq 0 \\ -f(x), & f(x) < 0 \end{cases}$$

Let's consider the function $f(x) = |\cos x|$

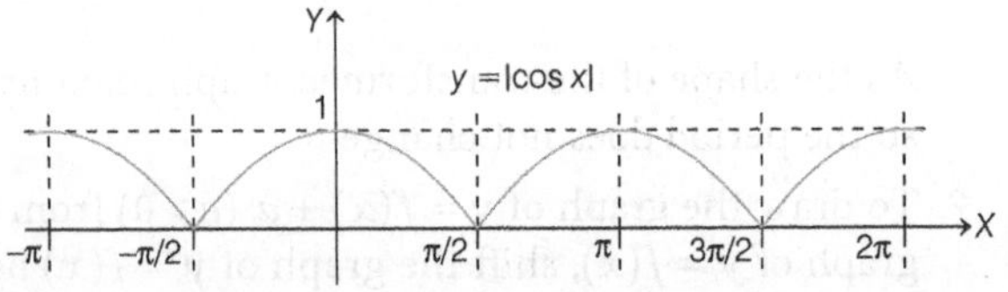

Here, the period of $f(x) = |\cos x|$ is π.

Let's consider another function $f(x) = |\tan x|$

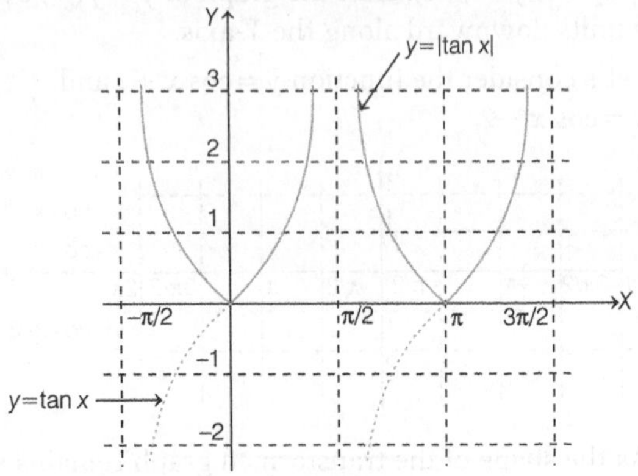

Here, the period of $f(x) = |\tan x|$ is π.

5. Graph of $y = af(x)$ from the graph of $y = f(x)$

To draw the graph of $y = af(x)$,

(i) Stretch vertically the graph of $y = f(x)$, if $a > 1$.

(ii) Compress vertically the graph of $y = f(x)$, if $0 < a < 1$.

(iii) Stretch and flip the graph of $y = f(x)$, about X-axis, if $a < -1$.

(iv) Compress and flip the graph of $y = f(x)$, about X-axis, if $-1 < a < 0$.

(v) Flip the graph of $y = f(x)$, about X-axis, if $a = -1$.

Let us consider some functions i.e. $y = 2 \sin x$, $y = 0.5 \sin x$, $y = -0.5 \sin x$ and $y = -3 \sin x$.

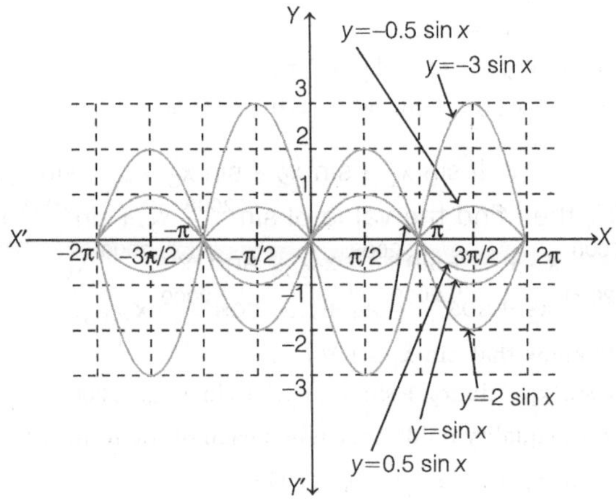

6. Graph of $y = f(-x)$ from the graph of $y = f(x)$

To draw the graph of $y = f(-x)$, flip the graph of $y = f(x)$ about Y-axis.

Let us consider the function $f(x) = \sin(-x)$

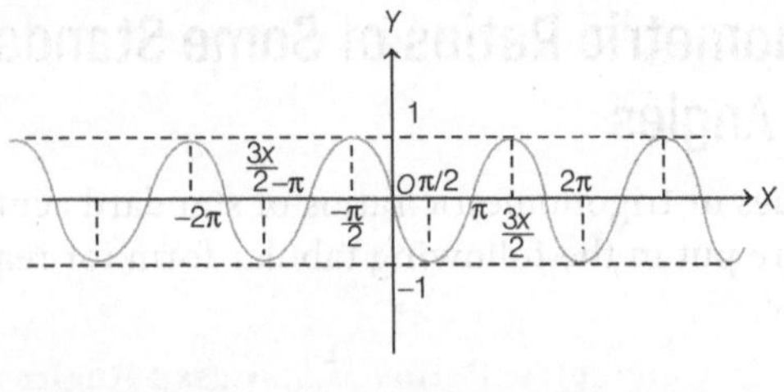

7. Graph of $y = f(|x|)$ from the graph of $y = f(x)$

To draw the graph of $y = f(|x|)$, keep only the portion right of Y-axis, and the reflect it about Y-axis, keeping original portion infact.

$$y = \begin{cases} f(x); & x > 0 \\ f(-x); & x < 0 \end{cases}$$

Let's consider the function $f(x) = \sin|x|$

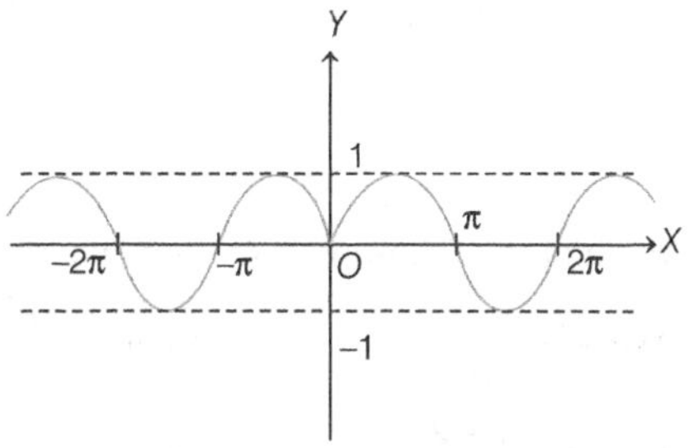

1.16 Some Important Graphical Deductions

To find relation between $\sin x$, x and $\tan x$

(i)

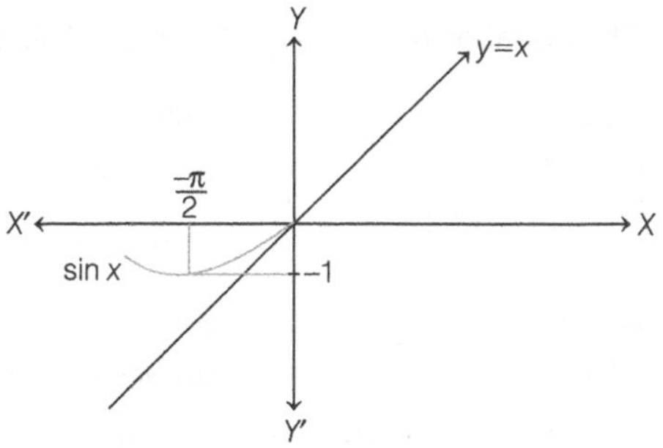

$\therefore$ $\sin x > x$ when $-\infty < x < 0$

(ii)

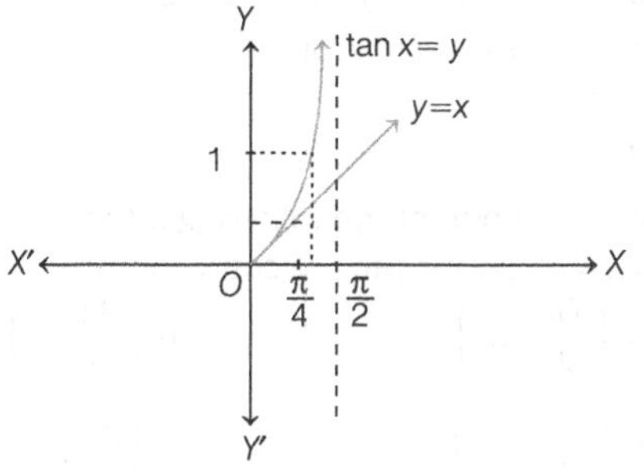

$\therefore$ $\tan x > x$ when $0 < x < \frac{\pi}{2}$

(iii) In general,

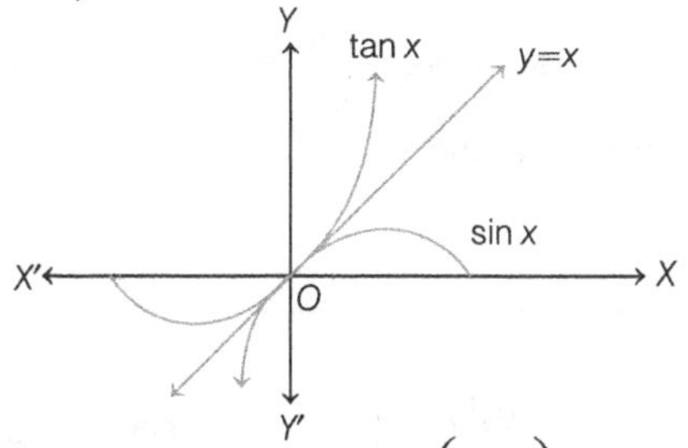

Thus, $\tan x > x > \sin x, \forall\, x \in \left(0, \frac{\pi}{2}\right)$

and $\sin x > x > \tan x, \forall\, x \in \left(-\frac{\pi}{2}, 0\right)$

Example 136. Draw the graph of $y = 3\sin 2x$.

Sol. $\sin x$ is a periodic function with period 2π, therefore, $\sin 2x$ will be a periodic function of period $\frac{2\pi}{|2|} = \pi$.

Also, $\quad -1 \le \sin 2x \le 1$

$\therefore \quad -3 \le 3\sin 2x \le 3$

In order to draw the graph of $y = 3\sin 2x$, draw the graph of $y = \sin x$ and on X-axis change k to $\frac{k}{2}$, i.e. write $\frac{k}{2}$ wherever it is k.

e.g. write 15° in place of 30°, 45° in place of 90° etc.

On Y-axis change k to $3k$ i.e. write $3k$ wherever it is k

e.g. write 3 in place of 1, − 3 in place of − 1, 1.5 in place of 0.5 etc.

The graph of $y = 3\sin 2x$ will be as given in the figure.

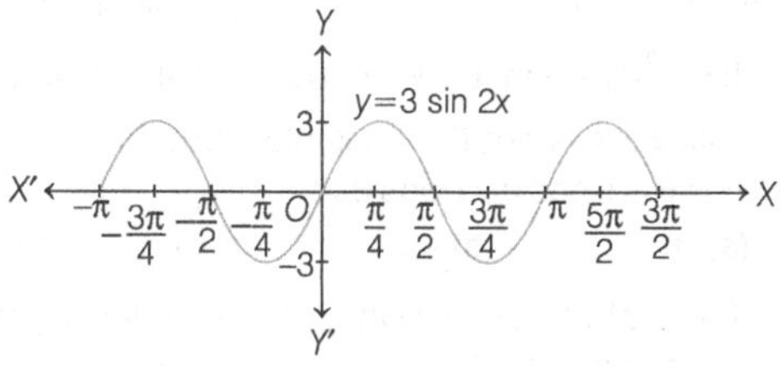

Example 137. Draw the graph of $y = \cos\left(x - \frac{\pi}{4}\right)$

Sol. Given function is $y = \cos\left(x - \frac{\pi}{4}\right)$ ...(i)

Given function is $Y = \cos X$, where

$$X = x - \frac{\pi}{4} \text{ and } Y = y$$

or $\quad Y = 0 \Rightarrow y = 0$

and $X = 0 \Rightarrow x - \frac{\pi}{4} = 0 \Rightarrow \quad x = \frac{\pi}{4}$

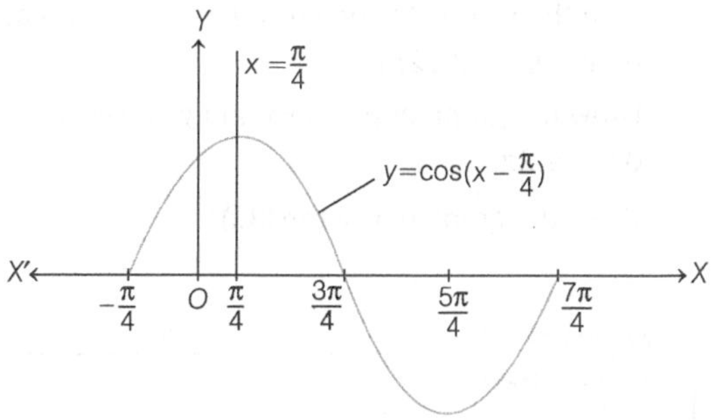

In order to draw the graph of $y = \cos\left(x - \frac{\pi}{4}\right)$, we draw the graph of $y = \cos x$ and shift it on the right side through a distance of $\frac{\pi}{4}$ units.

Milestone Practice 1.9

1. The maximum value of $\sin x_1 + 2\sin x_2 + 3\sin x_3$ is
   (a) 5 (b) 6 (c) 7 (d) 8
2. Domain of $\sin 8x$ is
   (a) $[-8, 8]$ (b) $\left[-\frac{1}{8}, \frac{1}{8}\right]$ (c) $[-1, 1]$ (d) R
3. Range of $\cos 4x$ is
   (a) $[-4, 4]$ (b) $[-1, 1]$
   (c) All positive integer (d) $(0, \infty)$
4. Which of the following is the greatest?
   (a) cosec 1 (b) cosec 2
   (c) cosec 4 (d) cosec (–6)
5. If $\sin^2\theta_1 + \sin^2\theta_2 + \sin^2\theta_3 = 0$, then which of the following is not the possible value of $\cos\theta_1 + \cos\theta_2 + \cos\theta_3$?
   (a) 3 (b) –3 (c) –1 (d) –2
6. For real values of θ which of the following is/are always positive?
   (a) $\cos(\cos\theta)$ (b) $\cos(\sin\theta)$
   (c) $\sin(\cos\theta)$ (d) $\sin(\sin\theta)$
7. Show that $\cos\theta = p + \frac{1}{p}$ is impossible, if p is real.
8. Draw the graph of $y = \sin x$ and $y = \sin\frac{x}{2}$.
9. Draw the graph of $y = \sec^2 x - \tan^2 x$. Is $f(x)$ periodic? If yes, what is its fundamental period?
10. Prove that $\sin\theta < \theta < \tan\theta$ for $\theta \in \left(0, \frac{\pi}{2}\right)$.
11. Find the value of x for which $f(x) = \sqrt{\sin x - \cos x}$ is defined, $x \in [0, 2\pi]$.
12. Draw the graph of $y = \sin x$ and $y = \cos x$, $0 \le x \le 2\pi$.
13. Draw the graph of $y = \tan(3x)$.
14. Which of the following is correct (where $n \in N$)?
    (a) $\sin\theta = \frac{n+1}{n}$ (b) $\sin\theta = \frac{n^2+1}{n+1}$
    (c) $\sec\theta = \frac{n+2}{n-1}$ (d) $\sec\theta = \frac{n}{\sqrt{n^2+1}}$
15. If $a, b, c \in R$, then prove that $\sec^2\theta = \frac{bc+ca+ab}{a^2+b^2+c^2}$ only if $a = b = c$.
16. The equation $\sin^2\theta = \frac{x^2+y^2}{2xy}$, $x, y \ne 0$ is possible if
    (a) $x = y$ (b) $x = -y$
    (c) $2x = y$ (d) None of these
17. If $\sin^2\theta = \frac{x^2+y^2+1}{2x}$, then x must be
    (a) –3 (b) –2
    (c) 1 (d) None of these
18. If $\sin x + \sin y + \sin z + \sin w = -4$, then the value of $\sin^{400}x + \sin^{300}y + \sin^{200}z + \sin^{100}w$ is
    (a) $\sin^{400}x \cdot \sin^{300}y \cdot \sin^{200}z + \sin^{100}w$
    (b) $\sin x \cdot \sin y \cdot \sin z \cdot \sin w$
    (c) 4
    (d) 3
19. In which one of the following intervals the inequality $\sin x < \cos x < \tan x < \cot x$ can hold good?
    (a) $\left(\frac{7\pi}{4}, 2\pi\right)$ (b) $\left(\frac{3\pi}{4}, \pi\right)$
    (c) $\left(\frac{5\pi}{4}, \frac{3\pi}{2}\right)$ (d) $\left(0, \frac{\pi}{4}\right)$
20. If $\cos^2 x + \cos x = a + 2$, then find the values of a for which equation has solution.
21. If $a^2 + 2a + \text{cosec}^2\left(\frac{\pi}{2}(a+x)\right) = 0$, then find the values of a and x.

Answer Key

1. (b)	2. (d)	3. (b)	4. (d)	5. (d)	6. (a,b)
11. $\left[\frac{\pi}{4}, \frac{5\pi}{4}\right]$	14. (c)	16. (a)	17. (c)	18. (c)	19. (d)
20. $\left[-\frac{9}{4}, 0\right]$	21. $a = -1$ and $x = 2n, n \in Z$				

For Detailed Solution

Milestone 10 Range of Trigonometric Expressions

In this section, we shall discuss problems on finding the maximum and minimum values of various trigonometrical expressions.

As discussed that $-1 \le \sin x \le 1$, $-1 \le \cos x \le 1$,

$$-\infty < \tan x < \infty, |\sec x| \ge 1, \text{ and } |\operatorname{cosec} x| \ge 1.$$

TYPE 1

Problems based on Simple Trigonometric Expressions

Example 138. Find the range of following trigonometric expressions.

(i) $f(x) = 2\sin x$ (ii) $f(x) = 3\sin\left(x + \frac{\pi}{6}\right)$

(iii) $f(x) = 2\sin(5x) - 3$ (iv) $f(x) = \sin^2 x$

Sol. (i) Given, $f(x) = 2\sin x$

$$-1 \le \sin x \le 1$$

$$-2 \le 2\sin x \le 2$$

Range : $x \in [-2, 2]$

(ii) Given, $f(x) = 3\sin\left(x + \frac{\pi}{6}\right)$

$$-1 \le \sin x \le 1$$

$$-1 \le \sin\left(x + \frac{\pi}{6}\right) \le 1$$

$$-3 \le 3\sin\left(x + \frac{\pi}{6}\right) \le 3$$

$$-3 \le f(x) \le 3$$

Range : $x \in [-3, 3]$

(iii) Given, $f(x) = 2\sin(5x) - 3$

$$-1 \le \sin x \le 1$$

$$-2 \le 2\sin(5x) \le 2$$

$$-2 - 3 \le 2\sin(5x) - 3 \le 2 - 3$$

$$-5 \le 2\sin(5x) - 3 \le -1$$

$$-5 \le f(x) \le -1$$

Range : $x \in [-5, -1]$

(iv) Given, $f(x) = \sin^2 x$

$$\sin^2 x = \frac{1 - \cos 2x}{2} = \frac{1}{2} - \frac{1}{2}\cos 2x$$

[by using $\cos 2\theta = 1 - 2\sin^2\theta$]

$$-1 \le \cos x \le 1$$

$$-\frac{1}{2} \le -\frac{1}{2}\cos 2x \le \frac{1}{2}$$

$$\frac{1}{2} - \frac{1}{2} \le \frac{1}{2} - \frac{1}{2}\cos 2x \le \frac{1}{2} + \frac{1}{2}$$

$$0 \le f(x) \le 1$$

Range : $x \in [0, 1]$

Example 139. Find the maximum and minimum values of $\sin^6 x + \cos^6 x$.

Sol. We have, $f(x) = \sin^6 x + \cos^6 x$

$$\Rightarrow (\sin^2 x + \cos^2 x)^3 = \sin^6 x + \cos^6 x + 3\sin^2 x\cos^2 x(\sin^2 x + \cos^2 x)$$

$$\Rightarrow 1 = \sin^6 x + \cos^6 x + 3\sin^2 x\cos^2 x$$

$$\Rightarrow \sin^6 x + \cos^6 x = 1 - 3\sin^2 x\cos^2 x$$

$$\Rightarrow \sin^6 x + \cos^6 x = 1 - \frac{3}{4}\sin^2 2x = f(x)$$

$$\Rightarrow -1 \le \sin 2x \le 1 \Rightarrow 0 \le \sin^2 2x \le 1$$

$$\Rightarrow 0 \le \frac{3}{4}\sin^2 2x \le \frac{3}{4} \Rightarrow -\frac{3}{4} \le -\frac{3}{4}\sin^2 2x \le 0$$

$$\Rightarrow 1 - \frac{3}{4} \le 1 - \frac{3}{4}\sin^2 2x \le 1 \Rightarrow \frac{1}{4} \le f(x) \le 1$$

Hence, the maximum value is 1 and minimum value is $\frac{1}{4}$.

Example 140. If in ΔABC, $\angle C = 45°$, then find the range of the values of $\sin^2 A + \sin^2 B$.

Sol. $E = \sin^2 A + \sin^2 B$

$$\Rightarrow E = \sin^2 A + \sin^2(135° - A)$$

$$\Rightarrow E = \sin^2 A + \cos^2(45° - A)$$

$$\Rightarrow E = 1 + \sin^2 A - \sin^2(45° - A)$$

$$\Rightarrow E = 1 + \sin(2A - 45°)\sin 45°$$

$$\Rightarrow E = 1 + \frac{1}{\sqrt{2}}\sin(2A - 45°)$$

Now, $0 < A < 135° \Rightarrow 0 < 2A < 270°$

$$\Rightarrow -45° < 2A - 45° < 225° \Rightarrow -\frac{1}{\sqrt{2}} < \sin(2A - 45°) \le 1$$

$$\Rightarrow -\frac{1}{2} < \frac{1}{\sqrt{2}}\sin(2A - 45°) \le \frac{1}{\sqrt{2}}$$

$$\Rightarrow \frac{1}{2} < 1 + \frac{1}{\sqrt{2}}\sin(2A - 45°) \le 1 + \frac{1}{\sqrt{2}}$$

Example 141. If $\theta \in R$, the expression $a\sin^2\theta + b\sin\theta\cos\theta + c\cos^2\theta$ lies between

(a) $-\frac{1}{2}\sqrt{b^2+(a-c)^2}$ and $\frac{1}{2}\sqrt{b^2+(a-c)^2}$

(b) $\frac{a+c}{2}$ and $\frac{a-c}{2}$

(c) $\frac{a+c}{2}-\frac{1}{2}\sqrt{b^2+(a-c)^2}$ and $\frac{a+c}{2}+\frac{1}{2}\sqrt{b^2+(a-c)^2}$

(d) None of the above

Sol. (c) Let $f(\theta) = a\sin^2\theta + b\sin\theta\cos\theta + c\cos^2\theta$

$$f(\theta) = \frac{a(1-\cos 2\theta)}{2} + \frac{b}{2}\sin 2\theta + \frac{c(1+\cos 2\theta)}{2}$$

$$f(\theta) = \left(\frac{c}{2}-\frac{a}{2}\right)\cos 2\theta + \frac{b}{2}\sin 2\theta + \frac{a}{2}+\frac{c}{2}$$

$$f(\theta) = \frac{1}{2}(a+c) + [\sqrt{b^2+(a-c)^2}]$$

$$(\sin 2\theta\cos\alpha - \cos 2\theta\sin\alpha)$$

$$f(\theta) = \frac{1}{2}(a+c) + \frac{\sqrt{b^2+(a-c)^2}}{2}\sin(2\theta-\alpha)$$

As, $-1 \le \sin(2\theta-\alpha) \le 1$

$$\therefore \quad \left\{\frac{a+c}{2}\right\} - \frac{\sqrt{b^2+(a-c)^2}}{2} \le f(\theta)$$

$$\le \left\{\frac{a+c}{2}\right\} + \frac{\sqrt{b^2+(a-c)^2}}{2}$$

TYPE 2

Problems based on trigonometric expressions of quadratic form.

Working rules

1. If quadratic equation is given and we have to find the roots of equation, then first convert the given equation in the form of $ax^2+bx+c=0$,

   whose Sum of roots $= -\frac{b}{a}$, Product of roots $= \frac{c}{a}$

   and if α and β are the roots of the given equation,

   then (α, β) roots $= \frac{-b \pm \sqrt{b^2-4ac}}{2a}$

2. If we want to form quadrantic equation whose roots are given then first find the sum and product of roots and then apply

   $$x^2 - (\text{Sum of roots})\,x + (\text{Product of roots}) = 0$$

As above mentioned results are basics for quadrantic equations, we discuss certain application on trigonometry.

Example 142. Find the range of the expression $\sin^2 x - \sin x + 2$.

Sol. $f(x) = \sin^2 x - \sin x + 2$

$$\Rightarrow f(x) = \sin^2 x - \sin x + \left(\frac{1}{2}\right)^2 - \left(\frac{1}{2}\right)^2 + 2$$

$$\Rightarrow f(x) = \left(\sin x - \frac{1}{2}\right)^2 + \frac{7}{4}$$

Minimum value of $f(x) = 0 + \frac{7}{4} = \frac{7}{4}$ and

Maximum value of $f(x) = \left(-1-\frac{1}{2}\right)^2 + \frac{7}{4} = \frac{9}{4}+\frac{7}{4} = 4$

Hence, the range $= \left[\frac{7}{4}, 4\right]$

Example 143. Find $\cos(\alpha+\beta)$, if $\tan\frac{\alpha}{2}$ and $\tan\frac{\beta}{2}$ are roots of the equations $8x^2 - 26x + 15 = 0$.

Sol. It is given $\tan\frac{\alpha}{2}$ and $\tan\frac{\beta}{2}$ are roots of $8x^2 - 26x + 15 = 0$.

$$\Rightarrow \quad \tan\frac{\alpha}{2} + \tan\frac{\beta}{2} = \frac{13}{4} \text{ and } \tan\frac{\alpha}{2}.\tan\frac{\beta}{2} = \frac{15}{8}$$

$$\therefore \quad \cos(\alpha+\beta) = \frac{1-\tan^2\left(\frac{\alpha+\beta}{2}\right)}{1+\tan^2\left(\frac{\alpha+\beta}{2}\right)},$$

$$\text{where } \tan\left(\frac{\alpha+\beta}{2}\right) = \frac{\tan\frac{\alpha}{2}+\tan\frac{\beta}{2}}{1-\tan\frac{\alpha}{2}\tan\frac{\beta}{2}}$$

$$\text{or} \quad \tan\left(\frac{\alpha+\beta}{2}\right) = \frac{\frac{13}{4}}{1-\frac{15}{8}} = \frac{-26}{7}$$

$$\Rightarrow \quad \cos(\alpha+\beta) = \frac{1-\left(\frac{676}{49}\right)}{1+\left(\frac{676}{49}\right)} = \frac{-627}{725}$$

$$\Rightarrow \quad \cos(\alpha+\beta) = \frac{-627}{725}$$

Example 144. If the solutions for θ from the equation $\sin^2\theta - 2\sin\theta + \lambda = 0$ lie in $\bigcup_{n\in z}\left(2n\pi - \frac{\pi}{6}, (2n+1)\pi + \frac{\pi}{6}\right)$, then find the possible set values of λ.

Sol. $\sin^2\theta - 2\sin\theta + \lambda = 0 \Rightarrow \sin\theta = \frac{2\pm\sqrt{4-4\lambda}}{2} = 1 \pm \sqrt{1-\lambda}$.

For real values, $1-\lambda \ge 0$ i.e. $\lambda \le 1$.

As $-1 \le \sin\theta \le 1$, $\sin\theta = 1 - \sqrt{1-\lambda}$ (neglecting $1+\sqrt{1-\lambda}$)

From question, $\sin\theta > -\frac{1}{2}$

Thus, $-\frac{1}{2} < 1 - \sqrt{1-\lambda} \le 1$

or $-\frac{3}{2} < -\sqrt{1-\lambda} \le 0 \Rightarrow \sqrt{1-\lambda} < \frac{3}{2}$

$\Rightarrow \quad 1-\lambda < \frac{9}{4} \Rightarrow \lambda > -\frac{5}{4}$

Example 145. $0 \le a \le 3$, $0 \le b \le 3$ and the equation, $x^2 + 4 + 3\cos(ax+b) = 2x$ has atleast one solution, then find the value of $(a+b)$.

Sol. $x^2 - 2x + 4 = -3\cos(ax+b)$

$\Rightarrow (x-1)^2 + 3 = -3\cos(ax+b)$ ...(i)

As $-1 \le \cos(ax+b) \le 1$ and $(x-1)^2 \ge 0$

$\therefore$ Eq. (i) is only possible, if

$\cos(ax+b) = -1$ and $(x-1) = 0$.

So, $a+b = \pi, 3\pi, 5\pi, \ldots$ and $3\pi > 6$

where $a+b \le 6 \Rightarrow a+b = \pi$

Example 146. Find the set of values of $\lambda \in R$ such that $\tan^2\theta + \sec\theta = \lambda$ holds for some θ.

Sol. $\tan^2\theta + \sec\theta = \lambda \Rightarrow \sec^2\theta + \sec\theta - (\lambda+1) = 0$

$\therefore \quad \sec\theta = \dfrac{-1 \pm \sqrt{1+4(\lambda+1)}}{2} = \dfrac{-1 \pm \sqrt{4\lambda+5}}{2}$

For real $\sec\theta$, $4\lambda + 5 \ge 0$ i.e. $\lambda \ge -\frac{5}{4}$ ...(i)

Also, $\sec\theta \ge 1$ or $\sec\theta \le -1$

$\therefore \quad \dfrac{-1 \pm \sqrt{4\lambda+5}}{2} \ge 1$ or $\dfrac{-1 \pm \sqrt{4\lambda+5}}{2} \le -1$

$\Rightarrow \quad -1 \pm \sqrt{4\lambda+5} \ge 2$ or $-1 \pm \sqrt{4\lambda+5} \le -2$

$\Rightarrow \quad 4\lambda + 5 \ge 9$ or $4\lambda + 5 \ge 1$

$\Rightarrow \quad \lambda \ge 1$ or $\lambda \ge -1$ ...(ii)

From Eqs. (i) and (ii),

$\therefore \quad \lambda \ge -\frac{5}{4}$ and $\lambda \ge 1$ or $\lambda \ge -\frac{5}{4}$ and $\lambda \ge -1$

$\therefore \quad \lambda \ge 1$ or $\lambda \ge -1$

$\therefore \quad \lambda \in [1, \infty)$.

TYPE 3

Problems based on trigonometric expression of type $a\cos x + b\sin x$.

We have expression, $f(x) = a\cos x + b\sin x$

$$\therefore f(x) = \sqrt{a^2+b^2}\left[\frac{a}{\sqrt{a^2+b^2}}\cos x + \frac{b}{\sqrt{a^2+b^2}}\sin x\right] \quad \text{...(i)}$$

Let $\dfrac{a}{\sqrt{a^2+b^2}} = \sin\alpha \Rightarrow \dfrac{b}{\sqrt{a^2+b^2}} = \cos\alpha$

$$\therefore \quad f(x) = \sqrt{a^2+b^2}\,(\sin\alpha\cos x + \cos\alpha\sin x)$$
$$= \sqrt{a^2+b^2}\,\sin(x+\alpha)$$

Since, $-1 \le \sin(x+\alpha) \le 1$, we have

$$-\sqrt{a^2+b^2} \le \sqrt{a^2+b^2}\,\sin(x+\alpha) \le \sqrt{a^2+b^2}$$

$$\therefore \quad a\cos x + b\sin x \in [-\sqrt{a^2+b^2}, \sqrt{a^2+b^2}]$$

In Eq. (i), if we let $\dfrac{a}{\sqrt{a^2+b^2}} = \cos\alpha \Rightarrow \dfrac{b}{\sqrt{a^2+b^2}} = \sin\alpha$,

then $f(x) = \sqrt{a^2+b^2}\,(\cos\alpha\cos x + \sin\alpha\sin x)$

$$= \sqrt{a^2+b^2}\,\cos(x-\alpha)$$

Also, $-\sqrt{a^2+b^2} \le \sqrt{a^2+b^2}\,\cos(x-\alpha) \le \sqrt{a^2+b^2}$

JEE SPIKE

$|a\cos x + b\sin x| \le \sqrt{a^2+b^2}$

Also, $\cos x \pm \sin x = \sqrt{2}\sin\left(\frac{\pi}{4} \pm x\right)$

$= \sqrt{2}\cos\left(x \pm \frac{\pi}{4}\right)$

Concept Inside Video

Example 147. Prove that $-4 \le 5\cos\theta + 3\cos\left(\theta + \frac{\pi}{3}\right) + 3 \le 10$, for all values of θ.

Sol. We have, $5\cos\theta + 3\cos\left(\theta + \frac{\pi}{3}\right)$

$\Rightarrow \quad 5\cos\theta + 3\cos\theta\cos\frac{\pi}{3} - 3\sin\theta\sin\frac{\pi}{3}$

$\Rightarrow \quad \frac{13}{2}\cos\theta - \frac{3\sqrt{3}}{2}\sin\theta \Rightarrow -7 \le \frac{13}{2}\cos\theta - \frac{3\sqrt{3}}{2}\sin\theta \le 7$

$\Rightarrow \quad -7 \le 5\cos\theta + 3\cos(\theta + \pi/3) \le 7$, for all θ.

$\Rightarrow \quad -7 + 3 \le 5\cos\theta + 3\cos(\theta + \pi/3) + 3 \le 7 + 3$, for all θ.

$\Rightarrow \quad -4 \le 5\cos\theta + 3\cos(\theta + \pi/3) + 3 \le 10$, for all θ.

Hence proved.

Example 148. Find the maximum and minimum value of $\cos^2\theta - 6\sin\theta\cos\theta + 3\sin^2\theta + 2$.

Sol. We have, $\cos^2\theta - 6\sin\theta\cos\theta + 3\sin^2\theta + 2$

$= (1 - \sin^2\theta) - 3\sin 2\theta + 3\sin^2\theta + 2$

$= 2\sin^2\theta - 3\sin 2\theta + 3 = (1 - \cos 2\theta) - 3\sin 2\theta + 3$

$= 4 - (\cos 2\theta + 3\sin 2\theta)$ ...(i)

As we have, $-\sqrt{10} \le \cos 2\theta + 3\sin 2\theta \le \sqrt{10}$

$\therefore \quad -\sqrt{10} \le -(\cos 2\theta + 3\sin 2\theta) \le \sqrt{10}$

or $\quad 4 - \sqrt{10} \le 4 - (\cos 2\theta + 3\sin 2\theta) \le 4 + \sqrt{10}$ ...(ii)

$\therefore$ From Eqs. (i) and (ii), we get

$4 - \sqrt{10} \le \cos^2\theta - 6\sin\theta\cos\theta + 3\sin^2\theta + 2 \le 4 + \sqrt{10}$

JEE SCANNER

Example Similar to PYQ Asked in JEE Main 2019

The maximum value of $\frac{3}{4}\sin\theta+\sqrt{2}\cos\left(\theta-\frac{\pi}{4}\right)$ *for any real value of* θ *is*

(a) $\frac{\sqrt{65}}{4}$ (b) $\sqrt{\frac{65}{16}}$ (c) $\frac{\sqrt{65}}{16}$ (d) $\frac{65}{16}$

Sol. (a) Let $y=\frac{3}{4}\sin\theta+\sqrt{2}\cos\left(\theta-\frac{\pi}{4}\right)$

$$\therefore \quad y=\frac{3}{4}\sin\theta+\sqrt{2}\cos\left(\theta-\frac{\pi}{4}\right)$$

$$=\frac{3}{4}\sin\theta+\sqrt{2}\left[\cos\theta\cos\frac{\pi}{4}+\sin\theta\sin\frac{\pi}{4}\right]$$

$$=\frac{3}{4}\sin\theta+\sqrt{2}\left[\cos\theta\frac{1}{\sqrt{2}}+\sin\theta\cdot\frac{1}{\sqrt{2}}\right]$$

$$=\frac{3}{4}\sin\theta+\frac{\sqrt{2}}{\sqrt{2}}[\cos\theta+\sin\theta]$$

$$=\frac{3}{4}\sin\theta+\cos\theta+\sin\theta=\frac{7}{4}\sin\theta+\cos\theta$$

Now $y_{\max}=\sqrt{\left(\frac{7}{4}\right)^2+(1)^2}=\sqrt{\frac{49}{16}+1}=\sqrt{\frac{65}{16}}=\frac{\sqrt{65}}{4}$

Skill Builder

The minimum value of $\cos 2\theta+\cos\theta$ for all real values of θ is

(a) $-\frac{9}{8}$ (b) $\frac{9}{8}$ (c) $\frac{8}{9}$ (d) $-\frac{8}{9}$

For Sol.

- **For more practice** See Q.2 of Milestone Practice 10.

Example 149. If $f(x)=\frac{\sin 3x}{\sin x}$, $x\neq n\pi$, then find the range of $f(x)$.

Sol. $f(x)=\frac{\sin 3x}{\sin x}=\frac{3\sin x-4\sin^3 x}{\sin x}\Rightarrow f(x)=3-4\sin^2 x$ ...(i)

We know that $0<\sin^2 x\le 1(\sin x\neq 0 \text{ as } x\neq n\pi)$

or $\quad -1\le -\sin^2 x<0$

or $\quad -4\le -4\sin^2 x<0$ or $3-4\le 3-4\sin^2 x<3$

or $\quad -1\le 3-4\sin^2 x<3\Rightarrow -1\le f(x)<3$

Hence, the range of $f(x)\in[-1,3)$.

Example 150. Find the range of $f(x)=\frac{1}{\sin^2 x+3\sin x\cos x+5\cos^2 x}$.

Sol. $f(x)=\frac{1}{\sin^2 x+\cos^2 x+2\sin x\cos x+\sin x\cos x+4\cos^2 x}$

$$f(x)=\frac{1}{1+\frac{3}{2}\sin 2x+2(1+\cos 2x)}$$

$$f(x)=\frac{1}{3+\frac{3}{2}\sin 2x+2\cos 2x}$$

Now, $\frac{3}{2}\sin 2x+2\cos 2x\in\left[-\sqrt{\frac{9}{4}+4},\sqrt{\frac{9}{4}+4}\right]$

$$\Rightarrow \frac{3}{2}\sin 2x+2\cos 2x\in\left[-\frac{5}{2},\frac{5}{2}\right]$$

$$\Rightarrow 3+\frac{3}{2}\sin 2x+2\cos 2x\in\left[\frac{1}{2},\frac{11}{2}\right]$$

$$\Rightarrow \frac{2}{11}\le\frac{1}{3+\frac{3}{2}\sin 2x+2\cos 2x}\le 2$$

Hence, the range of $f(x)$ is $\left[\frac{2}{11},2\right]$.

Example 151. If $u=\sqrt{a^2\cos^2\theta+b^2\sin^2\theta}+\sqrt{a^2\sin^2\theta+b^2\cos^2\theta}$, then the difference between the maximum and minimum value of u^2 is given by

(a) $(a-b)^2$

(b) $2\sqrt{a^2+b^2}$

(c) $(a+b)^2$

(d) $2(a^2+b^2)$

Sol. (a) $u^2=(a^2+b^2)+2\sqrt{(a^2\cos^2\theta+b^2\sin^2\theta)(a^2\sin^2\theta+b^2\cos^2\theta)}$

$$u^2=(a^2+b^2)+2\sqrt{(a^4+b^4)\sin^2\theta\cos^2\theta+a^2b^2(\sin^4\theta+\cos^4\theta)}$$

$$u^2=(a^2+b^2)+2\sqrt{(a^4+b^4)\sin^2\theta\cos^2\theta+a^2b^2[(\sin^2\theta+\cos^2\theta)^2-2\sin^2\theta\cos^2\theta]}$$

$$u^2=(a^2+b^2)+2\sqrt{[(a^2-b^2)\sin\theta\cos\theta]^2+a^2b^2}$$

$$u^2=(a^2+b^2)+2\sqrt{a^2b^2+\frac{1}{4}\sin^2 2\theta(a^2-b^2)^2}$$

$$(u^2)_{\max}=(a^2+b^2)+2\sqrt{a^2b^2+\frac{1}{4}(a^2-b^2)^2}$$

$$=(a^2+b^2)+\sqrt{(a^2+b^2)^2}$$

$$(u^2)_{\max}=2(a^2+b^2)$$

For $(u^2)_{\min}$, put $\sin 2\theta=0$

$$(u^2)_{\min}=a^2+b^2+2ab=(a+b)^2$$

$$\Rightarrow (u^2)_{\max}-(u^2)_{\min}=2a^2+2b^2-(a^2+b^2+2ab)$$

$$\Rightarrow (u^2)_{\max}-(u^2)_{\min}=a^2+b^2-2ab$$

$$\Rightarrow (u^2)_{\max}-(u^2)_{\min}=(a-b)^2$$

TYPE 4

Problems based on using trigonometric substitution to find the range of expression.

Range of different trigonometric functions helps us to use these functions as substitutions in many algebraic expressions. This simplifies the given expression to another expression, the range of which can be easily determined.

Example 152. If $x^2 + y^2 = x^2y^2$, then find the range of $\dfrac{5x+12y+13xy}{xy}$.

Sol. We have, $x^2 + y^2 = x^2y^2$ or $\left(\frac{1}{x}\right)^2 + \left(\frac{1}{y}\right)^2 = 1$

Let $x = \sec\theta$ and $y = \operatorname{cosec}\theta$

$\therefore \dfrac{5x + 12y + 13xy}{xy} = \dfrac{5}{y} + \dfrac{12}{x} + 13 = 5\sin\theta + 12\cos\theta + 13$

$\because \quad a\sin\theta + b\cos\theta \in [-\sqrt{a^2+b^2}, \sqrt{a^2+b^2}]$

$\therefore \quad 5\sin\theta + 12\cos\theta \in [-\sqrt{5^2+12^2}, \sqrt{5^2+12^2}]$

$\Rightarrow \quad 5\sin\theta + 12\cos\theta \in [-13, 13]$

$\Rightarrow 5\sin\theta + 12\cos\theta + 13 \in [0, 26]$

Hence, the required range is [0, 26].

TYPE 5

Problems based on Jensen's inequality

(i) Suppose that 'f' is a convex function on $[a, b] \in R$, for all $x_1, x_2, x_3 \ldots, x_n \in [a, b]$, we have

$$f(x_1) + f(x_2) + \ldots + f(x_n) \ge n \cdot f\left(\frac{x_1 + x_2 + \ldots + x_n}{n}\right)$$

Proof If $f(x)$ is concave up,

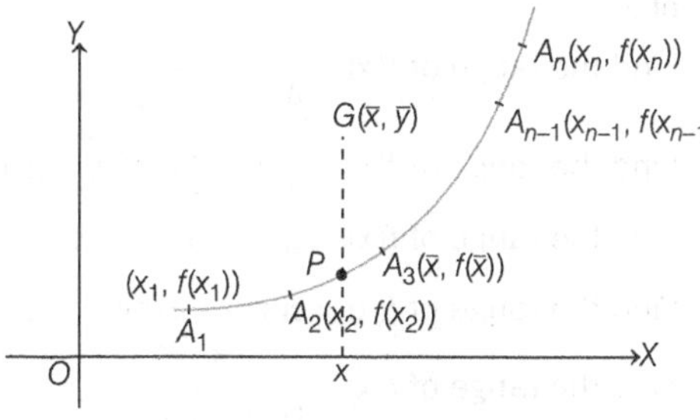

Here, $G\left(\dfrac{x_1 + x_2 + \ldots + x_n}{n}, \dfrac{f(x_1) + f(x_2) + \ldots + f(x_n)}{n}\right)$

and $P\left(\dfrac{x_1 + x_2 + \ldots + x_n}{n}, f\left(\dfrac{x_1 + x_2 + \ldots + x_n}{n}\right)\right)$

From figure, ordinate of $G \ge$ ordinate of P.

$$\frac{f(x_1) + f(x_2) + \ldots + f(x_n)}{n} \ge f\left(\frac{x_1 + x_2 + \ldots + x_n}{n}\right)$$

$$\therefore f(x_1) + f(x_2) + \ldots + f(x_n) \ge n \cdot f\left(\frac{x_1 + x_2 + \ldots + x_n}{n}\right)$$

(ii) Similarly, suppose that f is concave function on $[a, b] \in R$, for all $x_1, x_2, x_3, \ldots, x_n \in [a, b]$, we have

$$f(x_1) + f(x_2) + \ldots + f(x_n) \le n \cdot f\left(\frac{x_1 + x_2 + \ldots + x_n}{n}\right).$$

Example 153. In acute angled ΔABC, show that $\tan A + \tan B + \tan C \ge 3\sqrt{3}$.

Sol. Since, for a function which is concave upwards

$$f(x_1) + f(x_2) + f(x_3) \ge 3 \cdot f\left(\frac{x_1 + x_2 + x_3}{3}\right)$$

and we know that the graph of $y = \tan x$ is concave upwards for all $x \in \left(0, \frac{\pi}{2}\right)$.

$\therefore \tan A + \tan B + \tan C \ge 3 \cdot \tan\left(\dfrac{A + B + C}{3}\right)$

$\left[\because A, B, C \in \left(0, \frac{\pi}{2}\right) \text{ as } \Delta ABC \text{ is acute}\right]$

$\Rightarrow \tan A + \tan B + \tan C \ge 3 \cdot \tan\left(\frac{\pi}{3}\right) = 3 \cdot \sqrt{3} = 3\sqrt{3}$

$\Rightarrow \tan A + \tan B + \tan C \ge 3\sqrt{3}$

Alternate Solution

In ΔABC, we know that

$\tan A + \tan B + \tan C = \tan A \tan B \tan C$

$\tan A, \tan B, \tan C > 0$ as $A, B, C \in \left(0, \frac{\pi}{2}\right)$

So, using AM $\ge$ GM, we get

$\dfrac{\tan A + \tan B + \tan C}{3} \ge \sqrt[3]{\tan A \tan B \tan C}$

$\Rightarrow \quad \tan A \tan B \tan C \ge 3 (\tan A \tan B \tan C)^{1/3}$

$\Rightarrow \tan^3 A \tan^3 B \tan^3 C \ge 27 \tan A \tan B \tan C$

$\Rightarrow \tan^2 A \tan^2 B \tan^2 C \ge 27 \Rightarrow \tan A \tan B \tan C \ge 3\sqrt{3}$

$\Rightarrow \tan A + \tan B + \tan C \ge 3\sqrt{3}$

Example 154. Find the range of the expression $27^{\cos 2x} 81^{\sin 2x}$.

Sol. Let $f(x) = 27^{\cos 2x} \times 81^{\sin 2x}$

$= 3^{3\cos 2x} \times 3^{4\sin 2x} = 3^{3\cos 2x + 4\sin 2x}$

Now, $-\sqrt{3^2 + 4^2} \le 3\cos 2x + 4\sin 2x \le \sqrt{3^2 + 4^2}$

$\therefore \quad -5 \le 3\cos 2x + 4\sin 2x \le 5$

$\Rightarrow \quad 3^{-5} \le 3^{3\cos 2x + 4\sin 2x} \le 3^5$

Example 155. If $\sin^2(\theta - \alpha)\cos\alpha = \cos^2(\theta - \alpha)\sin\alpha = m\sin\alpha\cos\alpha$, then prove that $|m| \ge \dfrac{1}{\sqrt{2}}$.

Sol. $\sin^2(\theta - \alpha)\cos\alpha = \cos^2(\theta - \alpha)\sin\alpha = m\sin\alpha\cos\alpha$

or $\quad \sin^2(\theta - \alpha) = m\sin\alpha$

$\cos^2(\theta - \alpha) = m\cos\alpha$

On adding, we get $1 = m(\sin\alpha + \cos\alpha)$

or $\sin\alpha + \cos\alpha = \frac{1}{m}$ or $\sin\left(\alpha + \frac{\pi}{4}\right) = \frac{1}{\sqrt{2}m}$

Since, $\left|\sin\left(\alpha + \frac{\pi}{4}\right)\right| \le 1 \Rightarrow \left|\frac{1}{m\sqrt{2}}\right| \le 1$ or $|m| \ge \frac{1}{\sqrt{2}}$

Example 156. In ΔABC, if $\sqrt{3}\sin C = 2\sec A - \tan A$, then prove that triangle is right angled.

Sol. We have, $\sqrt{3}\sin C = 2\sec A - \tan A$

$\therefore \quad (\sqrt{3}\sin C)\cos A + \sin A = 2$

Now, $(\sqrt{3}\sin C)\cos A + \sin A \le \sqrt{(\sqrt{3}\sin C)^2 + 1}$

$\Rightarrow \quad 2 \le \sqrt{3\sin^2 C + 1}$

$\Rightarrow \quad \sin^2 C \ge 1 \Rightarrow \sin C = 1 \Rightarrow \angle C = \frac{\pi}{2}$

Milestone Practice 1.10

1. The greatest and least value of $\sin x \cos x$ are
   (a) 1, −1 (b) $\frac{1}{2}, -\frac{1}{2}$ (c) $\frac{1}{4}, -\frac{1}{4}$ (d) 2, −2
2. The maximum value of $\sin^2 x + 3\cos^2 x$ is
   (a) 3 (b) 4 (c) 5 (d) 7
3. If $\sin\theta_1 + \sin\theta_2 + \sin\theta_3 = 3$, then the value of $\cos\theta_1 + \cos\theta_2 + \cos\theta_3$ is
   (a) 1 (b) 0
   (c) 3 (d) cannot say anything
4. α, β and γ are real numbers satisfying $\alpha + \beta + \gamma = \pi$. Then, the minimum value of expression $\sin\alpha + \sin\beta + \sin\gamma$ must be a negative number. (True/False)
5. Find the least value of $2\sin^3\theta + 3\cos^2\theta$.
6. If $A = \sin^2\theta + \cos^4\theta$, then find all real values of A.
7. Find the minimum value of $\sec^2\theta + \text{cosec}^2\theta - 4$.
8. The minimum value of $3\cos x + 4\sin x + 5$ is
   (a) 0 (b) 1 (c) 5 (d) 10
9. If $f(x) = |\sin x| + |\cos x|$, $x \in R$, then
   (a) $f(x) \in [0, 2]$ (b) $f(x) \in [0, \sqrt{2}]$
   (c) $f(x) \in [0, 1]$ (d) $f(x) \in [1, \sqrt{2}]$
10. Find the range of $f(x) = \frac{1}{(\cos x - 3)^2 + (\sin x + 4)^2}$.
11. Find the range of $f(x) = \frac{1}{5\cos x + 12\sin x}$.
12. If $P = \cos(\cos x) + \sin(\cos x)$, then find the least and greatest value of P.
13. If $\sec\alpha$ and $\text{cosec}\,\alpha$ are roots of $x^2 - px + q = 0$, then show that $p^2 = q(q+2)$.
14. Find the ratio of greatest value of $2 - \cos x + \sin^2 x$ to its least value.
15. If $x^2 + y^2 = 9$, then the minimum value of $\frac{x^3 + y^3}{x + y}$ is
    (a) 11 (b) 9 (c) 9/2 (d) 27
16. If $\frac{x^2}{4} + \frac{y^2}{9} = 1$, then the maximum value of $2x + y$ is
    (a) 13 (b) 7 (c) 3 (d) 5
17. If $x^2 + y^2 + xy = 1$, then find the minimum value of $x^3y + xy^3 + 4$.
18. If $ABCD$ is a convex quadrilateral such that $4\sec A + 5 = 0$, then find the quadratic equation whose roots are $\tan A$ and $\text{cosec}\,A$.
19. In acute angled ΔABC, show that $\sec A + \sec B + \sec C \ge 6$.
20. Show that $2^{\sin x} + 2^{\cos x} \ge 2^{1 - \frac{1}{\sqrt{2}}}$ for all real values of x.
21. Find the range of $f(x) = \frac{1}{4\sin x - 3}$.
22. Find the range of $f(x) = \sqrt{\sin^2 x - 10\sin x + 25} + 4$.
23. Find the range of $f(x) = \tan^2 x + \cot^2 x$.
24. Find the range of $f(x) = \sin^2 x - 5\sin x + 2$.
25. Find the range of $f(x) = \frac{1}{|\cos x| - 3}$.

Answer Key

1. (b) 2. (a) 3. (b) 4. False 5. 2 6. $\left[\frac{3}{4}, 1\right]$ 7. 0 8. (a)
9. (d) 10. $\left[\frac{1}{36}, \frac{1}{16}\right]$ 11. $\left[\frac{1}{13}, -\frac{1}{13}\right]$ 12. $(-\sqrt{2}, \sqrt{2})$ 14. 13: 4 15. (c) 16. (d) 17. $\frac{17}{4}$
18. $12x^2 - 11x - 15 = 0$ 21. $\left(-\infty, -\frac{1}{7}\right] \cup [1, \infty)$ 22. [8, 10] 23. $[2, \infty)$ 24. $\left[\frac{5-\sqrt{17}}{2}, \frac{5+\sqrt{17}}{2}\right]$ 25. $\left[-\frac{1}{2}, -\frac{1}{4}\right]$

For Detailed Solution

JEE Pattern
EXAMPLES

Single Option Correct Type Questions

Example 1 *In the inequality below, the value of the angle is expressed in radian measure. Which one of the inequalities below is true?*

(a) $\sin 1 < \sin 2 < \sin 3$ (b) $\sin 3 < \sin 2 < \sin 1$
(c) $\sin 2 < \sin 1 < \sin 3$ (d) $\sin 3 < \sin 1 < \sin 2$

Sol. (d) We have, $\sin 1 - \sin 2 = -2\cos\frac{3}{2}\cdot\sin\frac{1}{2} < 0$

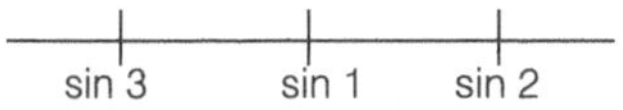

$\therefore$ $\sin 1 < \sin 2$ ...(i)

Similarly, $\sin 1 - \sin 3 = -2\cos 2 \sin 1 > 0$

$\Rightarrow$ $\sin 1 > \sin 3$ ...(ii)

From Eqs. (i) and (ii), we get

$\sin 3 < \sin 1 < \sin 2$

Example 2 *In a ΔABC, $\angle B < \angle C$ and the values of B and C satisfy the equation $2\tan x - k(1+\tan^2 x) = 0$, where $(0 < k < 1)$. Then, the measure of $\angle A$ is*

(a) $\frac{\pi}{3}$ (b) $\frac{2\pi}{3}$ (c) $\frac{\pi}{2}$ (d) $\frac{3\pi}{4}$

Sol. (c) $\because k = \frac{2\tan x}{1+\tan^2 x} = \sin 2x \Rightarrow \sin 2C = \sin 2B$

But $\angle C > \angle B \Rightarrow 2C = \pi - 2B \Rightarrow B + C = \frac{\pi}{2}$

$\therefore$ $\angle A = \frac{\pi}{2}$

Example 3 *For $0 < A < \frac{\pi}{2}$, the value of*

$\log_{\frac{1}{2}}\left(\frac{1}{1+2\cos^2 A} + \frac{2}{\sec^2 A + 2}\right)$ *is equal to*

(a) 1 (b) -1 (c) 2 (d) 0

Sol. (d) As, $\left(\frac{1}{1+2\cos^2 A} + \frac{2}{\sec^2 A + 2}\right)$

$$= \left(\frac{1}{1+2\cos^2 A} + \frac{2\cos^2 A}{1+2\cos^2 A}\right) = \frac{(1+2\cos^2 A)}{(1+2\cos^2 A)} = 1$$

Hence, $\log_{\frac{1}{2}}(1) = 0$.

JEE SCANNER

Example 4 Similar to PYQ Asked in JEE Main 2023

The value of

$\cos\frac{\pi}{65}\cos\frac{2\pi}{65}\cos\frac{4\pi}{65}\cos\frac{8\pi}{65}\cos\frac{16\pi}{65}\cos\frac{32\pi}{65}$ *is equal to*

(a) $\frac{1}{8}$ (b) $\frac{1}{32}$ (c) $\frac{1}{28}$ (d) $\frac{1}{64}$

Sol. (d) Given, $\cos\frac{\pi}{65}\cos\frac{2\pi}{65}\cos\frac{4\pi}{65}\cos\frac{8\pi}{65}\cos\frac{16\pi}{65}\cos\frac{32\pi}{65}$

$$= \frac{\left(2^6\sin\frac{\pi}{65}\cos\frac{\pi}{65}\right)\cos\frac{2\pi}{65}\cos\frac{4\pi}{65}\cos\frac{8\pi}{65}\cos\frac{16\pi}{65}\cos\frac{32\pi}{65}}{2^6\sin\frac{\pi}{65}}$$

[divide and multiply by $2^6\sin\frac{\pi}{65}$]

$$= \frac{2^5\sin\frac{2\pi}{65}\cos\frac{2\pi}{65}\cos\frac{4\pi}{65}\cos\frac{8\pi}{65}\cos\frac{16\pi}{65}\cos\frac{32\pi}{65}}{2^6\sin\frac{\pi}{65}}$$

$$= \frac{2^4\sin\frac{4\pi}{65}\cos\frac{4\pi}{65}\cos\frac{8\pi}{65}\cos\frac{16\pi}{65}\cos\frac{32\pi}{65}}{2^6\sin\frac{\pi}{65}}$$

$$= \frac{2^3\sin\frac{8\pi}{65}\cos\frac{8\pi}{65}\cos\frac{16\pi}{65}\cos\frac{32\pi}{65}}{2^6\sin\frac{\pi}{65}}$$

$$= \frac{2^2\sin\frac{16\pi}{65}\cos\frac{16\pi}{65}\cos\frac{32\pi}{65}}{2^6\sin\frac{\pi}{65}} = \frac{2\sin\frac{32\pi}{65}\cos\frac{32\pi}{65}}{2^6\sin\frac{\pi}{65}}$$

$$= \frac{\sin\frac{64\pi}{65}}{2^6\sin\frac{\pi}{65}} = \frac{\sin\left(\pi - \frac{\pi}{65}\right)}{2^6\sin\frac{\pi}{65}} = \frac{1}{2^6}\frac{\sin\left(\frac{\pi}{65}\right)}{\sin\left(\frac{\pi}{65}\right)} = \frac{1}{2^6} = \frac{1}{64}$$

Skill Builder

The value of $\sin\frac{\pi}{16}\sin\frac{3\pi}{16}\sin\frac{5\pi}{16}\sin\frac{7\pi}{16}$ is

(a) $\frac{\sqrt{2}}{16}$ (b) $\frac{1}{8}$ (c) $\frac{1}{6}$ (d) $\frac{\sqrt{2}}{32}$

For Sol.

Example 5 *If M and m are maximum and minimum value of the function* $f(x)=\dfrac{\tan^2 x+4\tan x+9}{1+\tan^2 x}$, *then* $(M+m)$ *equals*

(a) 20 (b) 14

(c) 10 (d) 8

Sol. (c) Given, $f(x)=\dfrac{\tan^2 x+4\tan x+9}{1+\tan^2 x}$

$$=\frac{2(2\tan x)}{1+\tan^2 x}+4\left(\frac{1-\tan^2 A}{1+\tan^2 A}\right)+5$$

$$=2\sin 2x+4\cos 2x+5$$

$$\therefore \quad R_f=[5-\sqrt{20},5+\sqrt{20}]$$

Hence, $(M+m)=10$.

Alternate Solution

$$f(x)=\frac{\tan^2 x}{1+\tan^2 x}+\frac{4\tan x}{1+\tan^2 x}+\frac{9}{1+\tan^2 x}$$

$$=\sin^2 x+2\sin 2x+9\cos^2 x$$

$$=1+4(1+\cos 2x)+2\sin 2x$$

$$=5+2\sin 2x+4\cos 2x$$

$$\therefore \quad R_f=[5-\sqrt{20},5+\sqrt{20}]$$

Example 6 *The sum* $\dfrac{1}{\sin 45^\circ \sin 46^\circ}+\dfrac{1}{\sin 47^\circ \sin 48^\circ}+\dfrac{1}{\sin 49^\circ \sin 50^\circ}+\ldots+\dfrac{1}{\sin 133^\circ \sin 134^\circ}$ is equal to

(a) $\sec(1^\circ)$ (b) $\operatorname{cosec}(1^\circ)$

(c) $\cot(1^\circ)$ (d) None of these

Sol. (b) $T_1=\dfrac{1}{\sin 1^\circ}\left[\dfrac{\sin(46^\circ-45^\circ)}{\sin 45^\circ \sin 46^\circ}\right]$

$$=\frac{1}{\sin 1^\circ}[\cot 45^\circ-\cot 46^\circ]$$

$$T_2=\frac{1}{\sin 1^\circ}\left[\frac{\sin(48^\circ-47^\circ)}{\sin 48^\circ \sin 47^\circ}\right]$$

$$=\frac{1}{\sin 1^\circ}[\cot 47^\circ-\cot 48^\circ]$$

$$T_l=\frac{1}{\sin 1^\circ}\left[\frac{\sin(133^\circ-134^\circ)}{\sin 133^\circ \sin 134^\circ}\right]$$

$$=\frac{1}{\sin 1^\circ}[\cot 133^\circ-\cot 134^\circ]$$

On adding

$$\sum_{r=1} T_r=\frac{1}{\sin 1^\circ}[\{\cot 45^\circ+\cot 47^\circ+\cot 49^\circ+\ldots+\cot 133^\circ\}$$

$$-\{\cot 46^\circ+\cot 48^\circ+\cot 50^\circ+\ldots+\cot 134^\circ\}]$$

$=\operatorname{cosec} 1^\circ$ [all terms cancelled except $\cot 45^\circ$ remains]

JEE SCANNER

Example 7 Similar to PYQ Asked in JEE Main 2022

If $\sin\theta=\dfrac{3}{5}$, $\tan\phi=\dfrac{1}{2}$, *where* $\dfrac{\pi}{2}<\theta<\pi<\phi<\dfrac{3\pi}{2}$, *then the value of* $8\tan\theta-\sqrt{5}\sec\phi$ *is*

(a) $\dfrac{7}{2}$ (b) $\dfrac{5}{2}$ (c) $-\dfrac{7}{2}$ (d) $-\dfrac{5}{2}$

Sol. (c) Given, $\sin\theta=\dfrac{3}{5}$

$\because \quad AB=\sqrt{CA^2-BC^2}=\sqrt{5^2-3^2}=\sqrt{16}=4$

Here, θ lies in second quadrant. $\left[\because \dfrac{\pi}{2}<\theta<\pi\right]$

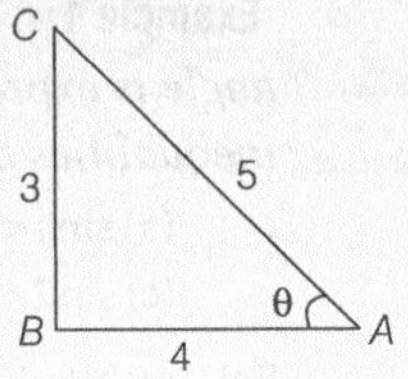

$\because$ $\tan\theta$ is negative.

$\therefore \quad \tan\theta=-\dfrac{3}{4}$

Also, $\tan\phi=\dfrac{1}{2}$

$\therefore PR=\sqrt{PQ^2+QR^2}=\sqrt{4+1}=\sqrt{5}$

Here, ϕ lies in third quadrant. $\left[\because \pi<\phi<\dfrac{3\pi}{2}\right]$

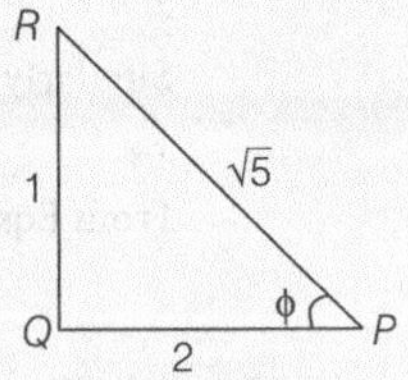

$\therefore$ $\sec\phi$ is negative.

$\therefore \quad \sec\phi=\dfrac{1}{\cos\phi}=-\dfrac{1}{2/\sqrt{5}}=-\dfrac{\sqrt{5}}{2}$

Now, $8\tan\theta-\sqrt{5}\sec\phi=8\left(-\dfrac{3}{4}\right)-\sqrt{5}\left(-\dfrac{\sqrt{5}}{2}\right)$

$$=-6+\frac{5}{2}=\frac{-12+5}{2}=-\frac{7}{2}$$

Skill Builder

If $\sin A=\dfrac{3}{5}, 0<A<\dfrac{\pi}{2}$ and $\cos B=-\dfrac{12}{13}$, $\pi<B<\dfrac{3\pi}{2}$. Then, the value of $\cos(A+B)$ is

(a) $-\dfrac{33}{65}$ (b) $-\dfrac{28}{65}$

(c) $\dfrac{-32}{65}$ (d) $-\dfrac{31}{65}$

For Sol.

Example 8 *If* $f(\theta)=\dfrac{1-\sin 2\theta+\cos 2\theta}{2\cos 2\theta}$, *then value of* $f(11^\circ)\cdot f(34^\circ)$ *equals*

(a) $\dfrac{1}{2}$ (b) $\dfrac{3}{4}$

(c) $\dfrac{1}{4}$ (d) 1

Sol. (a) $f(\theta) = \dfrac{1 - \sin 2\theta + \cos 2\theta}{2\cos 2\theta}$

$$= \frac{(\cos\theta - \sin\theta)^2 + (\cos^2\theta - \sin^2\theta)}{2(\cos\theta - \sin\theta)(\cos\theta + \sin\theta)}$$

$$= \frac{(\cos\theta - \sin\theta) + (\cos\theta + \sin\theta)}{2(\cos\theta + \sin\theta)}$$

$$= \frac{2\cos\theta}{2(\cos\theta + \sin\theta)} = \frac{1}{1 + \tan\theta}$$

$$f(11^\circ)\cdot f(34^\circ) = \frac{1}{(1 + \tan 11^\circ)}\cdot\frac{1}{(1 + \tan 34^\circ)}$$

$$= \frac{1}{(1 + \tan 11^\circ)}\cdot\frac{1}{(1 + \tan(45^\circ - 11^\circ))}$$

$$= \frac{1}{(1 + \tan 11^\circ)}\cdot\frac{1}{1 + \dfrac{1 - \tan 11^\circ}{1 + \tan 11^\circ}}$$

$$= \frac{1}{(1 + \tan 11^\circ)}\cdot\frac{1 + \tan 11^\circ}{2} = \frac{1}{2}$$

Example 9 *The variable 'x' satisfying the equation* $|\sin x \cos x| + \sqrt{2 + \tan^2 x + \cot^2 x} = \sqrt{3}$, belongs to the interval

(a) $\left[0, \dfrac{\pi}{3}\right]$ (b) $\left[\dfrac{\pi}{3}, \dfrac{\pi}{2}\right]$

(c) $\left[\dfrac{3\pi}{4}, \pi\right]$ (d) Non-existent

Sol. (d) $|\sin x \cos x| + |\tan x + \cot x| = \sqrt{3}$

$$\Rightarrow \quad |\sin x \cos x| + \frac{1}{|\sin x \cos x|} = \sqrt{3}$$

but $|\sin x \cos x| + \dfrac{1}{|\sin x \cos x|} \geq 2$

Hence, no solution.

Example 10 *Let α be a real number such that $0 \leq \alpha \leq \pi$. If $f(x) = \cos x + \cos(x + \alpha) + \cos(x + 2\alpha)$ takes some constant number c for any $x \in R$, then the value of $[c + \alpha]$ is equal to*

Note $[y]$ denotes greatest integer less than or equal to y.

(a) 0 (b) 1

(c) −1 (d) 2

Sol. (d) $f(x) = \cos x + \cos(x + 2\alpha) + \cos(x + \alpha)$

$$= 2\cos(x + \alpha)\cos\alpha + \cos(x + \alpha)$$

$$= (2\cos\alpha + 1)\cos(x + \alpha)$$

As $\cos(x + \alpha)$ can take any real value from − 1 to 1, $\forall x \in R$

$\therefore$ $f(x)$ is constant, so $(2\cos\alpha + 1) = 0$ must hold.

$$\Rightarrow \quad \alpha = \frac{2\pi}{3} \text{ and } c = 0$$

Hence, $[c + \alpha] = \left[0 + \dfrac{2\pi}{3}\right] = 2$

Example 11 *In a ΔABC, if $4\cos A \cos B + \sin 2A + \sin 2B + \sin 2C = 4$, then ΔABC is*

(a) right angle but not isosceles

(b) isosceles but not right angled

(c) right angle isosceles

(d) obtuse angled

Sol. (c) We have, $4\cos A \cos B + 4\sin A \sin B \sin C = 4$

$$\Rightarrow \quad \sin C = \frac{1 - \cos A \cos B}{\sin A \cos B} \leq 1$$

$$\Rightarrow \quad 1 \leq \sin A \sin B + \cos A \cos B \Rightarrow \cos(A - B) \geq 1$$

$$\Rightarrow \quad A = B \text{ and } \sin C = \frac{1 - \cos^2 A}{\sin^2 A} = 1$$

$$\therefore \quad C = 90^\circ \text{ and } A = B = \frac{\pi}{4} \text{ (each).}$$

JEE SCANNER

Example 12 Similar to PYQ Asked in JEE Main 2021

If $\cos\alpha + \cos\beta = \dfrac{3}{2}$ and $\sin\alpha + \sin\beta = \dfrac{1}{2}$ and θ is an arithmetic mean of α and β, then $\sin 2\theta + \cos 2\theta$ is equal to

(a) $\dfrac{5}{7}$ (b) $\dfrac{3}{7}$ (c) $\dfrac{4}{8}$ (d) $\dfrac{7}{5}$

Sol. (d) Since, θ is an arithmetic mean of α and β.

$$\therefore \quad \theta = \frac{\alpha + \beta}{2}$$

Also, $\cos\alpha + \cos\beta = \dfrac{3}{2} \Rightarrow 2\cos\left(\dfrac{\alpha + \beta}{2}\right)\cos\left(\dfrac{\alpha - \beta}{2}\right) = \dfrac{3}{2}$

$$\Rightarrow 2\cos\theta\cos\left(\frac{\alpha - \beta}{2}\right) = \frac{3}{2} \quad \text{...(i)}$$

$$\sin\alpha + \sin\beta = \frac{1}{2} \Rightarrow 2\sin\left(\frac{\alpha + \beta}{2}\right)\cos\left(\frac{\alpha - \beta}{2}\right) = \frac{1}{2}$$

$$\Rightarrow 2\sin\theta\cos\left(\frac{\alpha - \beta}{2}\right) = \frac{1}{2} \quad \text{...(ii)}$$

On dividing Eq. (i) by Eq. (ii), we get

$\cot\theta = 3$

$$\therefore \quad \cos\theta = \frac{3}{\sqrt{10}} \text{ and } \sin\theta = \frac{1}{\sqrt{10}}$$

Now, $\sin 2\theta + \cos 2\theta = 2\sin\theta\cos\theta + 1 - 2\sin^2\theta$

$$= 2 \times \frac{1}{\sqrt{10}} \times \frac{3}{\sqrt{10}} + 1 - 2 \times \frac{1}{10} = \frac{6}{10} - \frac{2}{10} + 1$$

$$= \frac{4}{10} + 1 = \frac{7}{5}$$

Skill Builder

If $\tan\theta + \cot\theta = 2$ and $0^\circ < \theta < 90^\circ$, then $\tan^{10}\theta + \cot^{10}\theta$ is equal to

(a) 0 (b) 1

(c) 2 (d) 3

For Sol.

Example 13 *For* $\theta_1, \theta_2, \ldots, \theta_n \in \left(0, \frac{\pi}{2}\right)$, *if* $ln(\sec\theta_1 - \tan\theta_1) + ln(\sec\theta_2 - \tan\theta_2) + \ldots +$ $ln(\sec\theta_n - \tan\theta_n) + ln\,\pi = 0$, *then the value of* $\cos((\sec\theta_1 + \tan\theta_1)(\sec\theta_2 + \tan\theta_2)\ldots\ldots(\sec\theta_n + \tan\theta_n))$ *is equal to*

(a) $\cos\left(\frac{1}{\pi}\right)$ (b) -1

(c) 1 (d) 0

Sol. (b) $\ln\{(\sec\theta_1 - \tan\theta_1)(\sec\theta_2 - \tan\theta_2)\ldots(\sec\theta_n - \tan\theta_n)\}$

$$= \ln\left\{\frac{1}{\pi}\right\}$$

[**Note** If $0 < x < \frac{\pi}{2}$, $\sec x - \tan x = \frac{1 - \sin x}{\cos x} > 0$]

$\therefore (\sec\theta_1 - \tan\theta_1)(\sec\theta_2 - \tan\theta_2)\ldots(\sec\theta_n - \tan\theta_n) = \frac{1}{\pi}$ ...(i)

Let $(\sec\theta_1 + \tan\theta_1)(\sec\theta_2 + \tan\theta_2)\ldots(\sec\theta_n + \tan\theta_n) = x$ ...(ii)

On multiplying Eqs. (i) and (ii), we get

$$1 = \frac{x}{\pi}$$

$\therefore$ $x = \pi$

$\therefore \cos((\sec\theta_1 + \tan\theta_1)(\sec\theta_2 + \tan\theta_2)\ldots(\sec\theta_n + \tan\theta_n))$

$$= \cos\pi = -1$$

Example 14 *If* $\operatorname{cosec}\frac{\pi}{32} + \operatorname{cosec}\frac{\pi}{16} + \operatorname{cosec}\frac{\pi}{8} + \operatorname{cosec}\frac{\pi}{4} + \operatorname{cosec}\frac{\pi}{2} = \cot\frac{\pi}{k}$, *then the value of k is*

(a) 64 (b) 96

(c) 48 (d) 32

Sol. (a) $T_1 = \operatorname{cosec}\theta = \dfrac{\sin\left(\theta - \frac{\theta}{2}\right)}{\sin\frac{\theta}{2}\sin\theta}$; $\theta = \frac{\pi}{32}$

$T_1 = \cot\frac{\theta}{2} - \cot\theta$

$T_2 = \cot\theta - \cot 2\theta$

$T_3 = \cot 2\theta - \cos 2^2\theta$

$T_4 = \cot 2^2\theta - \cos 2^3\theta$

$T_5 = 1$

sum $= 1 + \cot\frac{\theta}{2} - \cot 8\theta$

$$\text{Sum} = 1 + \cot\frac{\theta}{2} - \cot 8\theta$$

$$= 1 + \cot\frac{\pi}{64} - \cot\frac{\pi}{4}$$

$$= \cot\frac{\pi}{64}$$

$$= \cot\frac{\pi}{k}$$

$\therefore$ $k = 64$

Example 15 *Let* $S = \sum_{r=1}^{5} \cos(2r-1)\frac{\pi}{11}$ *and* $P = \prod_{r=1}^{4} \cos\left(2^r \frac{\pi}{15}\right)$, *then*

(a) $\log_S P = -4$ (b) $P = 3S$

(c) $\operatorname{cosec} S > \operatorname{cosec} P$ (d) $\tan^{-1} P < \tan^{-1} S$

Sol. (d) We have, $\sum_{r=1}^{5} \cos(2r-1)\frac{\pi}{11}$

$$= \underbrace{\cos\frac{\pi}{11} + \cos\frac{3\pi}{11} + \cos\frac{5\pi}{11} + \cos\frac{7\pi}{11} + \cos\frac{9\pi}{11}}_{\text{cosine series}}$$

$$= \frac{2\cos\left(\frac{5\pi}{11}\right)\sin\left(\frac{5\pi}{11}\right)}{2\sin\frac{\pi}{11}} = \frac{\sin\left(\frac{10\pi}{11}\right)}{2\sin\left(\frac{\pi}{11}\right)} = \frac{1}{2}$$

Also, $\prod_{r=1}^{4} \cos\left(2^r \frac{\pi}{15}\right) = \cos\frac{2\pi}{15}\cos\frac{4\pi}{15}\cos\frac{8\pi}{15}\cos\frac{16\pi}{15}$

$$= \frac{\sin\left(\frac{32\pi}{15}\right)}{2^4\sin\left(\frac{2\pi}{15}\right)} = \frac{\sin\left(2\pi + \frac{2\pi}{15}\right)}{16\sin\left(\frac{2\pi}{15}\right)}$$

$$= \frac{\sin\left(\frac{2\pi}{15}\right)}{16\cdot\sin\left(\frac{2\pi}{15}\right)} = \frac{1}{16}$$

Therefore, $\tan^{-1} P < \tan^{-1} S$.

Example 16 *Set of values of x lying in* $[0, 2\pi]$ *satisfying the inequality* $|\sin x| > 2\sin^2 x$ *contains*

(a) $\left(0, \frac{\pi}{6}\right) \cup \left(\pi, \frac{7\pi}{6}\right)$ (b) $\left(0, \frac{7\pi}{6}\right)$

(c) $\frac{\pi}{6}$ (d) None of these

Sol. (a) $|\sin x| > 2\sin^2 x$

$\Rightarrow |\sin x|(2|\sin x| - 1) < 0$

$\Rightarrow 0 < |\sin x| < \frac{1}{2}$

$\Rightarrow x \in \left(0, \frac{\pi}{6}\right) \cup \left(\frac{5\pi}{6}, \pi\right) \cup \left(\pi, \frac{7\pi}{6}\right) \cup \left(\frac{11\pi}{6}, 2\pi\right)$

Example 17 *The least values of* $\operatorname{cosec}^2 x + 25\sec^2 x$ *is*

(a) 0 (b) 26

(c) 28 (d) 36

Sol. (*d*) $\operatorname{cosec}^2 x + 25\sec^2 x = 26 + \cot^2 x + 25\tan^2 x$

$$= 26 + 10 + (\cot x - 5\tan x)^2 \geq 36$$

JEE SCANNER

Example 18 Similar to PYQ Asked in JEE Main 2019

If $y = \dfrac{2}{\sin\theta + \sqrt{3}\cos\theta}$, *then the minimum value of* y, *where* $\theta \in \left[0, \dfrac{\pi}{2}\right]$ *is*

(a) 1 (b) 2 (c) 3 (d) 4

Sol. (a) $y = \dfrac{2}{\sin\theta + \sqrt{3}\cos\theta}$

y is minimum when $\sin\theta + \sqrt{3}\cos\theta$ is maximum

$$G(\theta) = \sin\theta + \sqrt{3}\cos\theta$$

Differentiate w.r.t. θ, we get

$$G'(\theta) = \cos\theta - \sqrt{3}\sin\theta$$

Put $G'(\theta) = 0$

$\Rightarrow \quad \cos\theta - \sqrt{3}\sin\theta = 0$

$\Rightarrow \quad \cos\theta = \sqrt{3}\sin\theta$

$\Rightarrow \quad \tan\theta = \dfrac{1}{\sqrt{3}}$

$\Rightarrow \quad \theta = \tan^{-1}\left(\dfrac{1}{\sqrt{3}}\right) = 30°$

$\Rightarrow \quad G(30°) = \sin(30°) + \sqrt{3}\cos(30°)$

$$= \frac{1}{2} + \sqrt{3} \times \frac{\sqrt{3}}{2} = \frac{4}{2} = 2$$

$\therefore \quad y_{\min} = \dfrac{2}{G(30°)} = \dfrac{2}{2} = 1$

Skill Builder

The maximum value of $3\cos\theta + 4\sin\theta$ is

(a) 4 (b) 5

(c) 6 (d) 7

For Sol.

Example 19 *If* $x\sin a + y\sin 2a + z\sin 3a = \sin 4a$

$$x\sin b + y\sin 2b + z\sin 3b = \sin 4b$$

$$x\sin c + y\sin 2c + z\sin 3c = \sin 4c$$

Then, the roots of the equation

$t^3 - \left(\dfrac{z}{2}\right)t^2 - \left(\dfrac{y+2}{4}\right)t + \left(\dfrac{z-x}{8}\right) = 0$, $a, b, c \neq n\pi$, *are*

(a) $\sin a, \sin b, \sin c$ (b) $\cos a, \cos b, \cos c$

(c) $\sin 2a, \sin 2b, \sin 2c$ (d) $\cos 2a, \cos 2b, \cos 2c$

Sol. (b) Equation first can be written as

$x\sin a + y \times 2\sin a\cos a + z \times \sin a(3 - 4\sin^2 a)$

$$= 2 \times 2\sin a\cos a\cos 2a$$

$\Rightarrow x + 2y\cos a + z(3 + 4\cos^2 a - 4)$

$$= 4\cos a(2\cos^2 a - 1) \text{ as } \sin a \neq 0$$

$\Rightarrow \quad 8\cos^3 a - 4z\cos^2 a - (2y + 4)\cos a + (z - x) = 0$

$\Rightarrow \quad \cos^3 a - \left(\dfrac{z}{2}\right)\cos^2 a - \left(\dfrac{y+2}{4}\right)\cos a + \left(\dfrac{z-x}{8}\right) = 0$

which shows that $\cos a$ is a root of the equation

$$t^3 - \left(\frac{z}{2}\right)t^2 - \left(\frac{y+z}{4}\right)t + \left(\frac{z-x}{8}\right) = 0$$

Similarly, from second and third equation we can verify that $\cos b$ and $\cos c$ are the roots of the given equation.

Example 20 *Let* α *and* β *be any two positive values of* x *for which* $2\cos x, |\cos x|$ *and* $1 - 3\cos^2 x$ *are in GP. The minium value of* $|\alpha - \beta|$ *is*

(a) $\dfrac{\pi}{3}$ (b) $\dfrac{\pi}{4}$

(c) $\dfrac{\pi}{2}$ (d) None of these

Sol. (d) $\because$ $2\cos x, |\cos x|, 1 - 3\cos^2 x$ are in GP.

$\therefore \quad \cos^2 x = 2\cos x \cdot (1 - 3\cos^2 x)$

$\Rightarrow 6\cos^3 x + \cos^2 x - 2\cos x = 0$

$\therefore \quad \cos x = 0, \dfrac{1}{2}, -\dfrac{2}{3}$

$\therefore \quad x = \dfrac{\pi}{2}, \dfrac{\pi}{3}, \cos^{-1}\left(-\dfrac{2}{3}\right)$ [$\because \alpha, \beta$ are positive]

If $\quad \alpha = \dfrac{\pi}{2}, \beta = \dfrac{\pi}{3}$

Then, $|\alpha - \beta| = \dfrac{\pi}{6}$

Example 21 *Let* n *be an odd integer. If* $\sin n\theta = \sum_{r=0}^{n} b_r \sin^r \theta$ *for all real* θ, *then*

(a) $b_0 = 1, b_1 = 3$ (b) $b_0 = 0, b_1 = n$

(c) $b_0 = -1, b_1 = n$ (d) $b_0 = 0, b_1 = n^2 - 3n - 3$

Sol. (b) Given, $\sin n\theta = \sum_{r=0}^{n} b_r \sin^r \theta = b_0 + b_1 \sin\theta + b_2 \sin^2\theta + \dots + b_n \sin^n \theta$ ...(i)

On putting $\theta = 0$ in Eq. (i), we get $0 = b_0$

Again, Eq. (i) can be written as $\sin n\theta = \sum_{r=0}^{n} b_r \sin^r \theta$

$$\frac{\sin n\theta}{\sin\theta} = \sum_{r=0}^{n} b_r \sin^{r-1}\theta$$

On taking limit as $\theta \to 0$, we get

$$\lim_{\theta \to 0} \frac{\sin n\theta}{\sin\theta} = b_1$$

$\Rightarrow \quad \lim_{\theta \to 0} n\left(\dfrac{\sin n\theta}{n\theta}\right)\left(\dfrac{\theta}{\sin\theta}\right) = b_1$

$\Rightarrow \quad n = b_1$

Hence, $b_0 = 0; b_1 = n$

Example 22 *The minimum and maximum values of $ab\sin x + b\sqrt{(1-a^2)}\cos x + c$ ($|a|<1, b>0$) respectively are*

(a) $\{b-c, b+c\}$ (b) $\{b+c, b-c\}$
(c) $\{c-b, b+c\}$ (d) None of these

Decoding the Question

If any expression in the form of $a\sin x \pm b\cos x$, then maximum value of expression is given by $\sqrt{a^2+b^2}$ and minimum value of expression is given by $-\sqrt{a^2+b^2}$, use this fact to solve the question.

Sol. (c) $ab\sin x + b\sqrt{(1-a^2)}\cos x$

$$\text{Now, } \sqrt{(ab)^2+(b\sqrt{(1-a^2)})^2} = \sqrt{a^2b^2+b^2(1-a^2)}$$
$$= b\sqrt{(a^2+1-a^2)} = b$$
$$= b\{(a\sin x + \sqrt{(1-a^2)}\cos x)\}$$

Let $a = \cos\alpha$

$\therefore \quad \sqrt{(1-a^2)} = \sin\alpha$

$\Rightarrow \quad b\sin(x+\alpha)$

$\because \quad -1 \le \sin(x+\alpha) \le 1$

$\therefore \quad c-b \le b\sin(x+\alpha)+c \le b+c$

$\therefore \quad b\sin(x+\alpha)+c \in [c-b, c+b]$

Example 23 *If* $\dfrac{\sin^3\theta-\cos^3\theta}{\sin\theta-\cos\theta} - \dfrac{\cos\theta}{\sqrt{(1+\cot^2\theta)}}$ $-2\tan\theta\cot\theta = -1, \theta\in[0,2\pi]$, *then*

(a) $\theta\in\left(0,\frac{\pi}{2}\right)-\left\{\frac{\pi}{4}\right\}$ (b) $\theta\in\left(\frac{\pi}{2},\pi\right)-\left\{\frac{3\pi}{4}\right\}$
(c) $\theta\in\left(\pi,\frac{3\pi}{2}\right)-\left\{\frac{5\pi}{4}\right\}$ (d) $\theta\in(0,\pi)-\left\{\frac{\pi}{4},\frac{\pi}{2}\right\}$

Sol. (d) $\dfrac{\sin^3\theta-\cos^3\theta}{\sin\theta-\cos\theta} = \sin^2\theta+\cos^2\theta+\sin\theta\cos\theta, \theta\ne\dfrac{\pi}{4},\dfrac{5\pi}{4}$

$$= 1+\sin\theta\cos\theta$$

and $\dfrac{\cos\theta}{\sqrt{(1+\cot^2\theta)}} = \dfrac{\cos\theta}{|\operatorname{cosec}\theta|}$

$$= \sin\theta\cos\theta \ \forall\ \theta\in(0,\pi)$$

and $-2\tan\theta\cot\theta = -2, \theta\ne\dfrac{\pi}{2}$

Hence, LHS = RHS

But $\theta\ne\dfrac{\pi}{4},\dfrac{5\pi}{4},\dfrac{\pi}{2}$

Hence, $\theta\in(0,\pi)\sim\left\{\dfrac{\pi}{4},\dfrac{\pi}{2}\right\}$

Example 24 *If* $\cos x+\sin x = a\left(-\dfrac{\pi}{2}<x<-\dfrac{\pi}{4}\right)$, *then* $\cos 2x$ *is equal to*

(a) a^2 (b) $a\sqrt{(2-a)}$
(b) $a\sqrt{(2+a)}$ (d) $a\sqrt{(2-a^2)}$

Sol. (d) $\because -\dfrac{\pi}{2}<x<-\dfrac{\pi}{4}\left(-\pi<2x<-\dfrac{\pi}{2}, \text{ i.e. in III quadrant}\right)$

$\Rightarrow \quad \cos x+\sin x = a$

On squaring both sides $\cos^2 x+\sin^2 x+2\cos x\sin x = a^2$

$\Rightarrow \quad \sin 2x = (a^2-1)$

$$\cos 2x = \sqrt{1-(a^2-1)^2}$$
$$= \sqrt{a^2(2-a^2)}$$
$$= a\sqrt{(2-a^2)}$$

Example 25 *If* $S = \cos^2\dfrac{\pi}{2}+\cos^2\dfrac{2\pi}{n}+\ldots+\cos^2\dfrac{(n-1)\pi}{n}$, *then S equals*

(a) $\dfrac{n}{2(n+1)}$ (b) $\dfrac{1}{2(n-1)}$
(c) $\dfrac{1}{2}(n-2)$ (d) $\dfrac{n}{2}$

Sol. (c) $S = \cos^2\dfrac{\pi}{n}+\cos^2\dfrac{2\pi}{n}+\ldots+\cos^2(n-1)\dfrac{\pi}{n}$

$$\frac{1}{2}\left[\begin{array}{l}1+\cos\frac{2\pi}{n}+1+\cos\frac{4\pi}{n}+1+\cos\frac{6\pi}{n}\\+\ldots+1+\cos 2(n-1)\frac{\pi}{n}\end{array}\right]$$

$$= \frac{1}{2}\left[n-1+\sum_{k=1}^{n-1}\cos\frac{2k\pi}{n}\right] = \frac{1}{2}[n-1-1] = \frac{1}{2}(n-2)$$

Example 26 *If* $\cos 5\theta = a\cos\theta+b\cos^3\theta+c\cos^5\theta+d$, *then*

(a) $a=20$ (b) $b=-30$
(c) $a+b+c=2$ (d) $a+b+c+d=1$

Sol. (*d*) Put $\theta=\dfrac{\pi}{2}$ in the given inequality, we get $d=0$

Put $\theta=0$ in the given inequality, we get

$$a+b+c+d=1 \quad \text{...(i)}$$

So, (d) is correct and (c) is not correct.

Now, differentiate both sides with respect to θ, we get

$$-5\sin 5\theta = -a\sin\theta-3b\cos^2\theta\sin\theta -5c\cos^4\theta\sin\theta \quad \text{...(ii)}$$

Put $\quad \theta=\dfrac{\pi}{2}$, then $a=5$ ...(iii)

Again, putting $\theta = \frac{\pi}{4}$ in the given expression or in Eq. (ii), we get

$$4a + 2b + c = -4 \quad \text{...(iv)}$$

From Eqs. (i), (iii) and (iv), we have

$$b = -20 \text{ and } c = 16$$

[**Note** We have found correct answer at the second step only however the complete solution is desired for better understanding of the solution.]

Alternate Solution

$$\cos 5\theta = \cos(2\theta + 3\theta) = \cos 2\theta \cos 3\theta - \sin 2\theta \sin 3\theta$$
$$= (2\cos^2\theta - 1)(4\cos^3\theta - 3\cos\theta) - (2\sin\theta\cos\theta)(3\sin\theta - 4\sin^3\theta)$$
$$= 8\cos^5\theta - 10\cos^3\theta + 3\cos\theta - 2(1-\cos^2\theta)\cos\theta\{3 - 4(1-\cos^2\theta)\}$$
$$= 8\cos^5\theta - 10\cos^3\theta + 3\cos\theta - 2(\cos\theta - \cos^3\theta)(4\cos^2\theta - 1)$$
$$= 16\cos^5\theta - 20\cos^3\theta + 5\cos\theta$$

Example 27 *If A and B are acute positive angles satisfying the equations* $3\sin^2 A + 2\sin^2 B = 1$ *and* $3\sin 2A - 2\sin 3B = 0$, *then* $A + 2B$ *is equal to*

(a) $\frac{\pi}{4}$ (b) $\frac{\pi}{2}$ (c) $\frac{3\pi}{4}$ (d) $\frac{2\pi}{3}$

Sol. (b) From the given relations, we have

$$\sin 2B = \left(\frac{3}{2}\right)\sin 2A$$

and $3\sin^2 A = 1 - 2\sin^2 B = \cos 2B$

so that

$$\cos(A + 2B) = \cos A \cos 2B - \sin A \sin 2B$$
$$= \cos A \cdot 3\sin^2 A - \left(\frac{3}{2}\right)\sin A \sin 2A$$
$$= 3\cos A \sin^2 A - 3\sin^2 A \cos A = 0$$
$$A + 2B = \frac{\pi}{2}$$

Example 28 *If* $A = \begin{bmatrix} \cos^2\alpha & \cos\alpha\sin\alpha \\ \cos\alpha\sin\alpha & \sin^2\alpha \end{bmatrix}$ *and* $B = \begin{bmatrix} \cos^2\beta & \cos\beta\sin\beta \\ \cos\beta\sin\beta & \sin^2\beta \end{bmatrix}$ *are two matrices such that AB is the null matrix, then*

(a) $\alpha = \beta$ (b) $\cos(\alpha - \beta) = 0$
(c) $\sin(\alpha - \beta) = 0$ (d) None of these

Decoding the Question

We know that a null matrix or zero matrix is a matrix all of whose entries are zero.

Sol. (b) $AB = 0$

$$\Rightarrow \begin{bmatrix} \cos^2\alpha & \cos\alpha\sin\alpha \\ \cos\alpha\sin\alpha & \sin^2\alpha \end{bmatrix}\begin{bmatrix} \cos^2\beta & \cos\beta\sin\beta \\ \cos\beta\sin\beta & \sin^2\beta \end{bmatrix} = \begin{bmatrix} 0 & 0 \\ 0 & 0 \end{bmatrix}$$

$$\Rightarrow \begin{bmatrix} \cos\alpha\cos\beta\cos(\alpha-\beta) & \cos\alpha\sin\beta\cos(\alpha-\beta) \\ \cos\beta\sin\alpha\cos(\alpha-\beta) & \sin\alpha\sin\beta\cos(\alpha-\beta) \end{bmatrix} = \begin{bmatrix} 0 & 0 \\ 0 & 0 \end{bmatrix}$$

$$\Rightarrow \cos(\alpha - \beta) = 0$$

Example 29 *If* $k_1 = \tan 27\theta - \tan\theta$ *and* $k_2 = \frac{\sin\theta}{\cos 3\theta} + \frac{\sin 3\theta}{\cos 9\theta} + \frac{\sin 9\theta}{\cos 27\theta}$, *then*

(a) $k_1 = k_2$ (b) $k_1 = 2k_2$
(c) $k_1 + k_2 = 2$ (d) $k_2 = 2k_1$

Sol. (b) We can write

$$k_1 = \tan 27\theta - \tan 9\theta + \tan 9\theta - \tan 3\theta + \tan 3\theta - \tan\theta$$

But $\tan 3\theta - \tan\theta = \frac{\sin 3\theta\cos\theta - \cos 3\theta\sin\theta}{\cos 3\theta\cos\theta}$

$$= \frac{\sin 2\theta}{\cos 3\theta\cos\theta} = \frac{2\sin\theta}{\cos 3\theta}$$

$$\therefore k_1 = 2\left[\frac{\sin 9\theta}{\cos 27\theta} + \frac{\sin 3\theta}{\cos 9\theta} + \frac{\sin\theta}{\cos 3\theta}\right] = 2k_2$$

Example 30 *If* $a^2 - 2a\cos x + 1 = 674$ *and* $\tan\left(\frac{x}{2}\right) = 7$, *then the integral value of a is*

(a) 25 (b) 49 (c) 67 (d) 74

Sol. (a) $674 = a^2 - 2a\dfrac{1 - \tan^2\left(\frac{x}{2}\right)}{1 + \tan^2\left(\frac{x}{2}\right)} + 1$

$$= a^2 - 2a \times \frac{1 - 49}{1 + 49} + 1$$
$$= a^2 + 2a \times \frac{48}{50} + 1$$
$$\Rightarrow 25a^2 + 48a - 673 \times 25 = 0$$
$$\Rightarrow (a - 25)(25a + 673) = 0$$
$$\Rightarrow a = 25 \quad \text{[taking the integral value of } a]$$

Example 31 *The maximum value of* $(\cos\alpha_1)(\cos\alpha_2)\ldots(\cos\alpha_n)$ *under the restriction* $0 \le \alpha_1, \alpha_2, \ldots, \alpha_n \le \frac{\pi}{2}$ *and* $(\cot\alpha_1)(\cot\alpha_2)\ldots(\cot\alpha_n) = 1$ *is*

(a) $\frac{1}{2^{\frac{n}{2}}}$ (b) $\frac{1}{2^n}$ (c) $\frac{1}{2n}$ (d) 1

Sol. (a) From the given relations, we have

$$\prod_{i=1}^{n}(\cos\alpha_i)=\prod_{i=1}^{n}(\sin\alpha_i)$$

$$\Rightarrow \prod_{i=1}^{n}(\cos^2\alpha_i)=\prod_{i=1}^{n}(\cos\alpha_i\sin\alpha_i)=\prod_{i=1}^{n}\left(\frac{\sin 2\alpha_i}{2}\right)$$

Since, $0\le\alpha_i\le\frac{\pi}{2} \Rightarrow 0\le 2\alpha_i\le\pi$

$\therefore \prod_{i=1}^{n}(\cos^2\alpha_i)\le\frac{1}{2^n}$ as max. value of $\sin 2\alpha_i$ is 1 for all i.

$$\Rightarrow \prod_{i=1}^{n}(\cos\alpha_i)\le\frac{1}{2^{\frac{n}{2}}}$$

So, the maximum value of the given expression is $\frac{1}{2^{\frac{n}{2}}}$.

Example 32 *The value of expression* $\frac{\sin^3 x}{1+\cos x}+\frac{\cos^3 x}{1-\sin x}$ *is/are*

(a) $\sqrt{2}\cos\left[\frac{\pi}{4}-x\right]$ (b) $\sqrt{2}\cos\left[\frac{\pi}{4}+x\right]$

(c) $\sqrt{2}\sin\left[\frac{\pi}{4}-x\right]$ (d) None of these

Sol. (a) Let $\frac{\sin^3 x}{1+\cos x}+\frac{\cos^3 x}{1-\sin x}=A$, then

$$A=\frac{(\sin^3 x+\cos^3 x)+(\cos^4 x-\sin^4 x)}{(1+\cos x)(1-\sin x)}$$

or $A=\frac{\{(\sin^3 x+\cos^3 x)\}+\{(\cos x+\sin x)(\cos x-\sin x)(\cos^2 x+\sin^2 x)\}}{(1+\cos x)(1-\sin x)}$

or $A=\frac{(\sin x+\cos x)\{(1-\sin x\cos x)+(\cos x-\sin x)\}}{1+\cos x-\sin x-\sin x\cos x}$

or $A=\sin x+\cos x$

or $A=\sqrt{2}\left[\frac{1}{\sqrt{2}}\sin x+\frac{1}{\sqrt{2}}\cos x\right]$ ...(i)

or $A=\sqrt{2}\left[\cos\frac{\pi}{4}\sin x+\sin\frac{\pi}{4}\cos x\right]=\sqrt{2}\sin\left[\frac{\pi}{4}+x\right]$

Again, by Eq. (i),

$$A=\sqrt{2}\left[\sin\frac{\pi}{4}\sin x+\cos\frac{\pi}{4}\cos x\right]=\sqrt{2}\cos\left[\frac{\pi}{4}-x\right]$$

Example 33 *Let* $0\le\theta\le\frac{\pi}{2}$ *and* $x=X\cos\theta+Y\sin\theta$, $y=X\sin\theta-Y\cos\theta$ *such that* $x^2+2xy+y^2=aX^2+bY^2$, *where a and b are constant, then*

(a) $a=-1, b=-3$ (b) $\theta=\frac{\pi}{2}$

(c) $a=3, b=-1$ (d) $\theta=\frac{\pi}{3}$

Sol. (c) $x^2+y^2=X^2+Y^2$,

$$xy=(X^2-Y^2)\sin\theta\cdot\cos\theta-XY(\cos^2\theta-\sin^2\theta)$$

$$x^2+4xy+y^2=X^2+Y^2+2(X^2-Y^2)\sin 2\theta-2XY\cos 2\theta$$

$$=(1+2\sin 2\theta)X^2+(1-2\sin 2\theta)Y^2-2\cos 2\theta\cdot XY$$

From the question,

$a=1+2\sin 2\theta$, $b=1-2\sin 2\theta$, $\cos 2\theta=0$

$\cos 2\theta=0 \Rightarrow \theta=\frac{\pi}{4}$, then

$a=1+2\sin\frac{\pi}{2}$, $b=1-2\sin\frac{\pi}{2}$

$\therefore a=3, b=-1$

Example 34 *If* $0<x<\frac{\pi}{2}$ *and* $\sin^n x+\cos^n x\ge 1$, *then*

(a) $n\in[2,\infty)$ (b) $n\in(-\infty, 2]$

(c) $n\in[-1, 1]$ (d) None of these

Sol. (b) Since, $0<x<\frac{\pi}{2}$

$\therefore$ $0<\sin x<1$ and $0<\cos x<1$

when $n=2$, $\sin^n x+\cos^n x=1$

when $n>2$, both $\sin^n x$ and $\cos^n x$ will decreases and hence $\sin^n x+\cos^n x<1$.

when $n<2$, both $\sin^n x$ and $\cos^n x$ will increase and hence $\sin^n x+\cos^n x>1$.

Thus, $\sin^n x+\cos^n x\ge 1$ for $n\le 2$.

Example 35 *If* $a=\sin\frac{\pi}{18}\sin\frac{5\pi}{18}\sin\frac{7\pi}{18}$, *and x is the solution the equation* $y=2[x]+2$ *and* $y=3[x-2]$, *where* $[x]$ *denotes the integral part of x, then a is equal to*

(a) $[x]$ (b) $\frac{1}{[x]}$ (c) $2[x]$ (d) $[x]^2$

Sol. (b) $a=\sin\frac{\pi}{18}\sin\frac{5\pi}{18}\sin\frac{7\pi}{18}$

$=\sin 10^\circ\sin 50^\circ\sin 70^\circ$

$=\frac{1}{2}[2\sin 70^\circ\sin 10^\circ]\sin 50^\circ$

$=\frac{1}{2}[\cos 60^\circ-\cos 80^\circ]\sin 50^\circ$

$=\frac{1}{4}\sin 50^\circ-\frac{1}{4}(2\cos 80^\circ\sin 50^\circ)$

$=\frac{1}{4}\sin 50^\circ-\frac{1}{4}(\sin 130^\circ-\sin 30^\circ)$

$=\frac{1}{4}\sin 50^\circ-\frac{1}{4}\sin 50^\circ+\frac{1}{4}\cdot\frac{1}{2}=\frac{1}{8}$

$y=2[x]+2$ and $y=3[x-2]$

$\Rightarrow 2[x]+2=3[x-2]=3[x]+3[-2] \Rightarrow [x]=8$

$\therefore a=\frac{1}{[x]}$

Example 36 *If the mapping $f(x) = ax + b, a < 0$ and maps $[-1, 1]$ onto $[0, 2]$, then for all values of θ, $A = \cos^2\theta + \sin^4\theta$ is such that*

(a) $f\left(\frac{1}{4}\right) \le A \le f(0)$ (b) $f(0) \le A \le f(-2)$

(c) $f\left(\frac{1}{3}\right) \le A \le f(0)$ (d) $f(-1) < A \le f(-2)$

Sol. (a) Given, $f(x) = ax + b$

$\therefore \quad f'(x) = a$

Since, $a < 0$, $f(x)$ is a decreasing function

$\therefore \quad f(-1) = 2$ and $f(1) = 0$

$\Rightarrow \quad -a + b = 2$ and $a + b = 0$

$\therefore \quad a = -1$ and $b = 1$

Thus, $\quad f(x) = -x + 1$

Clearly, $f(0) = 1, f\left(\frac{1}{4}\right) = \frac{3}{4}, f(-2) = 3,$

$f\left(\frac{1}{3}\right) = \frac{2}{3}, f(-1) = 2$

Also, $\quad A = \frac{1 + \cos 2\theta}{2} + \left(\frac{1 - \cos 2\theta}{2}\right)^2$

$= \frac{1}{2} + \frac{1}{2}\cos 2\theta + \frac{1}{4} - \frac{1}{2}\cos 2\theta + \frac{1}{4}\cos^2 2\theta$

$= \frac{3}{4} + \frac{1}{4}\left(\frac{1 + \cos 4\theta}{2}\right) = \frac{7}{8} + \frac{1}{8}\cos 4\theta$

$\therefore \quad \frac{3}{4} \le A \le 1 \Rightarrow f\left(\frac{1}{4}\right) \le A \le f(0)$

Example 37 *The value of* $\cos\frac{2\pi}{7} + \cos\frac{4\pi}{7} + \cos\frac{6\pi}{7}$ *is equal to*

(a) 1 (b) -1 (c) $\frac{1}{2}$ (d) $-\frac{1}{2}$

Sol. (*d*) $\cos\left(\frac{2\pi}{7}\right) + \cos\left(\frac{4\pi}{7}\right) + \cos\left(\frac{6\pi}{7}\right)$

$= \text{Re}\left\{e^{\frac{2\pi i}{7}} + e^{\frac{4\pi i}{7}} + e^{\frac{6\pi i}{7}}\right\}$

$= \frac{e^{\frac{2\pi i}{7}} + e^{\frac{4\pi i}{7}} + e^{\frac{6\pi i}{7}} + e^{\frac{-2\pi i}{7}} + e^{\frac{-4\pi i}{7}} + e^{\frac{-6\pi i}{7}}}{2}$

$= \frac{-1 + \left(1 + e^{\frac{2\pi i}{7}} + e^{\frac{4\pi i}{7}} + e^{\frac{6\pi i}{7}} + e^{\frac{-2\pi i}{7}} + e^{\frac{-4\pi i}{7}} + e^{\frac{-6\pi i}{7}}\right)}{2}$

$= \frac{-1 + (\text{Sum of seven roots of unity})}{2}$

$= \frac{-1 + 0}{2} = -\frac{1}{2}$

Example 38 *The number of integral value of k for which the equation* $7\cos x + 5\sin x = 2k + 1$ *has a solution is*

(a) 4 (b) 8 (c) 10 (d) 12

Sol. (b) Since, $-\sqrt{a^2 + b^2} \le a\sin x + b\cos x \le \sqrt{a^2 + b^2}$

$\therefore \quad -\sqrt{74} \le 7\cos x + 5\sin x \le \sqrt{74}$

So, $-\sqrt{74} < 2k + 1 < \sqrt{74}$

Therefore, $\quad 2k + 1 = \pm 8, \pm 7, \pm 6, \ldots, \pm 1, 0$

So, $\quad k = -4, \pm 3, \pm 2, \pm 1, 0$, so, 8 values of k.

Example 39 *If* $y = \frac{\sin^4 x - \cos^4 x + \sin^2 x \cos^2 x}{\sin^4 x + \cos^4 x + \sin^2 x \cos^2 x}$, $x \in \left(0, \frac{\pi}{2}\right)$, *then*

(a) $-\frac{3}{2} \le y \le \frac{1}{2}$ (b) $1 \le y \le \frac{1}{2}$

(c) $-\frac{5}{3} \le y \le 1$ (d) None of these

Sol. (d) $y = \frac{\sin^4 x - \cos^4 x + \sin^2 x \cos^2 x}{\sin^4 x + \cos^4 x + \sin^2 x \cos^2 x}$

$= \frac{(\sin^2 x - \cos^2 x)(\sin^2 x + \cos^2 x) + \sin^2 x \cos^2 x}{(\sin^2 x + \cos^2 x)^2 - \sin^2 x \cos^2 x}$

$= \frac{-\cos 2x + \frac{1}{4}\sin^2 2x}{1 - \frac{1}{4}\sin^2 2x}$

$= \frac{-4\cos 2x + 1 - \cos^2 2x}{4 - 1 + \cos^2 2x} = \frac{1 - 4\cos 2x - \cos^2 2x}{3 + \cos^2 2x}$

$\Rightarrow \quad (1 + y)\cos^2 2x + 4\cos 2x + 3y - 1 = 0$

Since, $\cos 2x$ is real, we have

$16 - 4(3y - 1)(1 + y) > 0$

or $\quad 3y^2 + 2y - 5 \le 0$

or $\quad (3y + 5)(y - 1) \le 0 \Rightarrow -\frac{5}{3} \le y \le 1$

But $y = 1$ implies $\cos 2x = -1$ i.e. $x = \frac{\pi}{2}$ which is not permissible.

Example 40 *The distance between the two parallel lines is 1 unit. A point 'A' is chosen to lie between the lines at a distance 'd' from one of them. Triangle ABC is equilateral with B on one line and C on the other parallel line. The length of the side of the equilateral triangle is*

(a) $\frac{2}{3}\sqrt{d^2 + d + 1}$ (b) $2\sqrt{\frac{d^2 - d + 1}{3}}$

(c) $2\sqrt{d^2 - d + 1}$ (d) $\sqrt{d^2 - d + 1}$

Sol. (b) From, figure

$$x\cos(\theta + 30°) = d \quad \text{...(i)}$$

and

$$x\sin\theta = 1 - d \quad \text{...(ii)}$$

Dividing Eq. (i) by Eq. (ii), we get

$$\sqrt{3}\cot\theta = \frac{1+d}{1-d}$$

Squaring Eq. (ii) and putting the value of $\cot\theta$, we get

$$x^2\sin^2\theta = (1-d)^2$$

$$\Rightarrow \quad x^2 = (1-d)^2\operatorname{cosec}^2\theta = (1-d)^2(1+\cot^2\theta)$$

$$\Rightarrow \quad x^2 = \frac{1}{3}(4d^2 - 4d + 4)$$

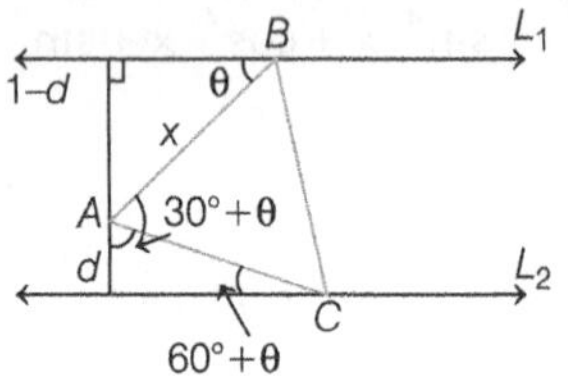

$$\Rightarrow x^2 = \frac{4}{3}(d^2 - d + 1) \Rightarrow x = 2\sqrt{\frac{d^2 - d + 1}{3}}$$

Example 41 *If $a\sin x + b\cos(x+\theta) + b\cos(x-\theta) = d$, then the minimum value of $|\cos\theta|$ is equal to*

(a) $\frac{1}{2|b|}\sqrt{d^2 - a^2}$ (b) $\frac{1}{2|a|}\sqrt{d^2 - a^2}$

(c) $\frac{1}{2|d|}\sqrt{d^2 - a^2}$ (d) None of these

Sol. (a) $a\sin x + b\cos(x+\theta) + b\cos(x-\theta) = d$

$$\Rightarrow \quad a\sin x + 2b\cdot\cos x\cdot\cos\theta = d$$

$$\Rightarrow \quad |d| \le \sqrt{a^2 + 4b^2\cdot\cos^2\theta}$$

$$\Rightarrow \quad \frac{d^2 - a^2}{4b^2} \le \cos^2\theta \Rightarrow |\cos\theta| \ge \frac{\sqrt{d^2 - a^2}}{2|b|}$$

Example 42 *The set of values of $\lambda \in R$ such that $\tan^2\theta + \sec\theta = \lambda$ holds for some θ is*

(a) $(-\infty, 1]$ (b) $(-\infty, -1]$

(c) ϕ (d) $[1, \infty)$

Sol. (d) $\because \tan^2\theta + \sec\theta = \lambda$

$$\Rightarrow \quad \sec^2\theta + \sec\theta - 1 - \lambda = 0$$

$$\therefore \quad \sec\theta = \frac{-1 \pm \sqrt{(4\lambda + 5)}}{2}$$

for real $\sec\theta$, $4\lambda + 5 \ge 0$ i.e. $\lambda \ge -\frac{5}{4}$

But we know that

$$\sec\theta \le -1 \text{ and } \sec\theta \ge 1$$

$$\therefore \quad \frac{-1 \pm \sqrt{(4\lambda+5)}}{2} \le -1 \text{ and } \frac{-1 \pm \sqrt{(4\lambda+5)}}{2} \ge 1$$

$$\Rightarrow \quad -1 - \sqrt{(4\lambda+5)} \le -2 \text{ and } -1 + \sqrt{(4\lambda+5)} \ge 2$$

$$\Rightarrow \quad \sqrt{(4\lambda+5)} \ge 1 \text{ and } \sqrt{(4\lambda+5)} \ge 3$$

$$\Rightarrow \quad \sqrt{4\lambda+5} \ge 3 \text{ or } 4\lambda + 5 \ge 9 \text{ or } \lambda \ge 1$$

$$\therefore \quad \lambda \in [1, \infty)$$

Example 43 *For $0 < \phi, \frac{\pi}{2}$, if $x = \sum_{n=0}^{\infty}\cos^{2n}\phi$, $y = \sum_{n=0}^{\infty}\sin^{2n}\phi$ and $z = \sum_{n=0}^{\infty}\cos^{2n}\phi\sin^{2n}\phi$, then*

(a) $xyz = xz + y$ (b) $xyz = xy + z$

(c) $xyz = x + y + z$ (d) $xyz = yz + x$

Sol. (b) We have, $x = \sum_{n=0}^{\infty}\cos^{2n}\phi = 1 + \cos^2\phi + \cos^4\phi + \dots$

$$= \frac{1}{1-\cos^2\phi} = \frac{1}{\sin^2\phi}$$

Similarly, $y = \frac{1}{1-\sin^2\phi} = \frac{1}{\cos^2\phi}$ and $z = \frac{1}{1-\sin^2\phi\cos^2\phi}$

$$\therefore \quad z = \frac{1}{1 - \frac{1}{x}\cdot\frac{1}{y}} = \frac{xy}{xy-1}$$

$$\Rightarrow \quad xyz = xy + z$$

Example 44 *If $\frac{x}{a}\cos\alpha + \frac{y}{b}\sin\alpha = 1$, $\frac{x}{a}\cos\beta + \frac{y}{b}\sin\beta = 1$ and $\frac{\cos\alpha\cos\beta}{a^2} + \frac{\sin\alpha\sin\beta}{b^2} = 0$, then*

(a) $\tan\alpha\tan\beta = \frac{b^2(x^2+a^2)}{a^2(y^2+b^2)}$

(b) $x^2 + y^2 = a^2 + b^2$

(c) $\tan\alpha\tan\beta = \frac{a^2}{b^2}$

(c) None of the above

Sol. (b) $\frac{x}{a}\cos\alpha + \frac{y}{b}\sin\alpha = 1$ ...(i)

$$\frac{x}{a}\cos\beta + \frac{y}{b}\sin\beta = 1 \quad \text{...(ii)}$$

$$\frac{\cos\alpha\cdot\cos\beta}{a^2} + \frac{\sin\alpha\cdot\sin\beta}{b^2} = 0 \quad \text{...(iii)}$$

From Eqs. (i) and (ii), we get

$$x = a\frac{\sin\alpha - \sin\beta}{\sin(\alpha - \beta)} \text{ and } y = b\frac{\cos\beta - \cos\alpha}{\sin(\alpha-\beta)}$$

Now, $x^2 + y^2 = \frac{a^2(\sin\alpha - \sin\beta)^2 + b^2(\cos\beta - \cos\alpha)^2}{\sin^2(\alpha-\beta)}$

$$= \frac{a^2(\sin^2\alpha + \sin^2\beta) + b^2(\cos^2\alpha + \cos^2\beta) - 2(a^2\sin\alpha\sin\beta + b^2\cos\alpha\cos\beta)}{\sin^2(\alpha-\beta)}$$

$$= \frac{a^2(\sin^2\alpha + \sin^2\beta) + b^2(\cos^2\alpha + \cos^2\beta)}{\sin^2(\alpha - \beta)} \quad \text{[from Eq. (iii)]}$$

$$= a^2 + b^2 + \frac{a^2\{\sin^2\alpha + \sin^2\beta - \sin^2(\alpha - \beta)\} + b^2\{\cos^2\alpha + \cos^2\beta - \sin^2(\alpha - \beta)\}}{\sin^2(\alpha - \beta)}$$

$$= a^2 + b^2 + \frac{1}{\sin^2(\alpha - \beta)}\left[a^2\left(\begin{matrix}\sin^2\alpha + \sin^2\beta - \sin^2\alpha\cos^2\beta \\ -\cos^2\alpha\sin^2\beta + 2\sin\alpha\sin\beta \\ \cos\alpha\cos\beta\end{matrix}\right) + b^2\left\{\begin{matrix}\cos^2\alpha(1 - \sin^2\beta) \\ +\cos^2\beta(1 - \sin^2\alpha) \\ +2\sin\alpha\sin\beta\sin\alpha \\ \sin\beta\cos\alpha\cos\beta\end{matrix}\right\}\right]$$

$$= a^2 + b^2 + \frac{2a^2\sin\alpha\sin\beta\cos(\alpha - \beta) + 2b^2\cos\alpha\cos\beta\cos(\alpha - \beta)}{\sin^2(\alpha - \beta)}$$

$$= a^2 + b^2 + \frac{2a^2b^2\cos(\alpha - \beta)}{\sin^2(\alpha - \beta)}\left[\frac{\sin\alpha\sin\beta}{b^2} + \frac{\cos\alpha\cos\beta}{a^2}\right] \quad \text{[from Eq. (iii)]}$$

$$= a^2 + b^2 + 0 = a^2 + b^2$$

Thus, $x^2 + y^2 = a^2 + b^2$

Now, $x^2 + y^2 = a^2 + b^2$

$\Rightarrow \quad x^2 - a^2 = -(y^2 - b^2)$

$\Rightarrow \quad \dfrac{x^2 - a^2}{y^2 - b^2} = -1$

$\Rightarrow \quad \dfrac{b^2(x^2 - a^2)}{a^2(y^2 - b^2)} = -\dfrac{b^2}{a^2} = \tan\alpha\tan\beta$ [from Eq. (iii)]

Example 45 If α, β, γ are acute angles and $\cos\theta = \sin\beta/\sin\alpha$, $\cos\phi = \sin\gamma/\sin\alpha$ and $\cos(\theta - \phi) = \sin\beta\sin\gamma$, then the value of $\tan^2\alpha - \tan^2\beta - \tan^2\gamma$ is equal to

(a) -1 (b) 0 (c) 1 (d) 2

Sol. (b) From the third relation we get

$$\cos\theta\cos\phi + \sin\theta\sin\phi = \sin\beta\sin\gamma$$

$\Rightarrow \quad \sin^2\theta\sin^2\phi = (\cos\theta\cos\phi - \sin\beta\sin\gamma)^2$

$\Rightarrow \quad \left(1 - \dfrac{\sin^2\beta}{\sin^2\alpha}\right)\left(1 - \dfrac{\sin^2\gamma}{\sin^2\alpha}\right) = \left(\dfrac{\sin\beta\sin\gamma}{\sin^2\alpha} - \sin\beta\sin\gamma\right)^2$

$\Rightarrow \quad (\sin^2\alpha - \sin^2\beta)(\sin^2\alpha - \sin^2\gamma) = \sin^2\beta\sin^2\gamma(1 - \sin^2\alpha)^2$

$\Rightarrow \quad \sin^4\alpha(1 - \sin^2\beta\sin^2\gamma) - \sin^2\alpha(\sin^2\beta + \sin^2\gamma - 2\sin^2\beta\sin^2\gamma) = 0$

$\therefore \quad \sin^2\alpha = \dfrac{\sin^2\beta + \sin^2\gamma - 2\sin^2\beta\sin^2\gamma}{1 - \sin^2\beta\sin^2\gamma}$

and $\quad \cos^2\alpha = \dfrac{1 - \sin^2\beta - \sin^2\gamma + \sin^2\beta\sin^2\gamma}{1 - \sin^2\beta\sin^2\gamma}$

$\Rightarrow \quad \tan^2\alpha = \dfrac{\sin^2\beta - \sin^2\beta\sin^2\gamma + \sin^2\gamma - \sin^2\beta\sin^2\gamma}{\cos^2\beta - \sin^2\gamma(1 - \sin^2\beta)}$

$$= \frac{\sin^2\beta\cos^2\gamma + \cos^2\beta\sin^2\gamma}{\cos^2\beta\cos^2\gamma}$$

$$= \tan^2\beta + \tan^2\gamma$$

$\Rightarrow \quad \tan^2\alpha - \tan^2\beta - \tan^2\gamma = 0$

Example 46 *If* $\sqrt{2}\cos A = \cos B + \cos^3 B$, *and* $\sqrt{2}\sin A = \sin B - \sin^3 B$, *then* $\sin(A - B)$ *is equal to*

(a) ± 1 (b) $\pm\dfrac{1}{2}$ (c) $\pm\dfrac{1}{3}$ (d) $\pm\dfrac{1}{4}$

Sol. (c) $\sqrt{2}\cos A = \cos B + \cos^3 B$ ...(i)

and $\sqrt{2}\sin A = \sin B - \sin^3 B$ ...(ii)

$\Rightarrow \quad \sqrt{2}\sin A\cos B - \sqrt{2}\cos A\sin B$

$$= (\sin B - \sin^3 B)\cos B - (\cos B + \cos^3 B)\sin B$$

$$= -\sin B\cos B$$

$\Rightarrow \quad \sin(A - B) = \dfrac{-1}{2\sqrt{2}}\sin 2B$

Now, on squaring and adding Eqs. (i) and (ii), we get

$$2 = \cos^2 B + \sin^2 B + \cos^6 B + \sin^6 B + 2(\cos^4 B - \sin^4 B)$$

$\Rightarrow \quad 1 = (\cos^2 B + \sin^2 B)^3 - 3\cos^2 B\sin^2 B(\cos^2 B + \sin^2 B) + 2\cos 2B$

$\Rightarrow \quad 1 = 1 - \left(\dfrac{3}{4}\right)\sin^2 2B + 2\cos 2B$

$\Rightarrow \quad -3\sin^2 2B + 8\cos 2B = 0$

$\Rightarrow \quad 3\cos^2 2B + 8\cos 2B - 3 = 0$

$\Rightarrow \quad \cos 2B = \dfrac{1}{3}$

$\Rightarrow \quad \sin 2B = \pm\dfrac{2\sqrt{2}}{3}$

$\therefore \quad \sin(A - B) = \pm\dfrac{1}{3}$

Example 47 *If* x_1 *and* x_2 *are two distinct roots of the equation* $a\cos x + b\sin x = c$, *then* $\tan\dfrac{x_1 + x_2}{2}$ *is equal to*

(a) $\dfrac{a}{b}$ (b) $\dfrac{b}{a}$ (c) $\dfrac{c}{a}$ (d) $\dfrac{a}{c}$

Sol. (b) $a\cos x + b\sin x = c$

$\Rightarrow \quad \dfrac{a\left(1 - \tan^2\dfrac{x}{2}\right)}{1 + \tan^2\dfrac{x}{2}} + \dfrac{2b\tan\dfrac{x}{2}}{1 + \tan^2\dfrac{x}{2}} = c$

$\Rightarrow \quad (c + a)\tan^2\dfrac{x}{2} - 2b\tan\dfrac{x}{2} + c - a = 0$

$$\Rightarrow \quad \tan\frac{x_1}{2} + \tan\frac{x_2}{2} = \frac{2b}{c+a},$$

$$\tan\frac{x_1}{2}\cdot\tan\frac{x_2}{2} = \frac{c-a}{c+a}$$

Thus, $$\tan\left(\frac{x_1+x_2}{2}\right) = \frac{\tan\frac{x_1}{2}+\tan\frac{x_2}{2}}{1-\tan\frac{x_1}{2}\tan\frac{x_2}{2}}$$

$$= \frac{\frac{2b}{c+a}}{1-\left(\frac{c-a}{c+a}\right)} = \frac{b}{a}$$

Example 48 *The minimum value of the function*

$$f(x) = \frac{\sin x}{\sqrt{1-\cos^2 x}} + \frac{\cos x}{\sqrt{1-\sec^2 x}} + \frac{\tan x}{\sqrt{\sec^2 x - 1}} + \frac{\cot x}{\sqrt{\operatorname{cosec}^2 x - 1}}$$ *whenever it is defined is*

(a) 4 (b) − 2 (c) 0 (d) 2

Sol. (b) $$f(x) = \frac{\sin x}{\sqrt{1-\cos^2 x}} + \frac{\cos x}{\sqrt{1-\sin^2 x}} + \frac{\tan x}{\sqrt{\sec^2 x - 1}} + \frac{\cot x}{\sqrt{\operatorname{cosec}^2 x - 1}}$$

$$= \frac{\sin x}{|\sin x|} + \frac{\cos x}{|\cos x|} + \frac{\tan x}{|\tan x|} + \frac{\cot x}{|\cot x|}$$

$$= \begin{cases} 4, & x \in \text{1st quadrant} \\ -2, & x \in \text{2nd quadrant} \\ 0, & x \in \text{3rd quadrant} \\ -2, & x \in \text{4th quadrant} \end{cases}$$

$$f(x)_{\text{min.}} = -2$$

Example 49 *If* $0 < \alpha < \frac{\pi}{6}$, *then* $\alpha(\operatorname{cosec}\alpha)$ *is*

(a) less than $\frac{\pi}{6}$ (b) greater than $\frac{\pi}{6}$

(c) less than $\frac{\pi}{3}$ (d) greater than $\frac{\pi}{3}$

Sol. (c) In the graph of $y = \sin x$. Let

$$A \equiv (\alpha, \sin\alpha),\ B = \left(\frac{\pi}{6}, \sin\frac{\pi}{6}\right)$$

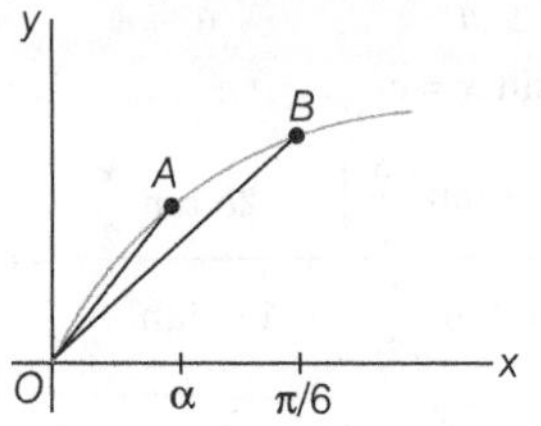

Clearly, slope of $OA >$ slope of OB, so

$$\frac{\sin\alpha}{\alpha} > \frac{\sin\frac{\pi}{6}}{\frac{\pi}{6}} = \frac{3}{\pi} \Rightarrow \frac{\alpha}{\sin\alpha} < \frac{\pi}{3}.$$

Example 50 *In which one of the following intervals the inequality* $\sin x < \cos x < \tan x < \cot x$ *can hold good?*

(a) $\left(\frac{7\pi}{4}, 2\pi\right)$ (b) $\left(\frac{3\pi}{4}, \pi\right)$

(c) $\left(\frac{5\pi}{4}, \frac{3\pi}{2}\right)$ (d) $\left(0, \frac{\pi}{4}\right)$

Sol. (d) In the second quadrant, $\sin x < \cos x$ is false, as $\sin x$ is positive and $\cos x$ is negative.

In the fourth quadrant, $\cos x < \tan x$ is false, as $\cos x$ is positive and $\tan x$ is negative.

In the third quadrant i.e. $\left(\frac{5\pi}{4}, \frac{3\pi}{2}\right)$ if $\tan x < \cot x$ then $\tan^2 x < 1$, which is false.

Now, $\sin x < \cos x$ is true in $\left(0, \frac{\pi}{4}\right)$ and $\tan x < \cot x$ is also true.

Further, $\cos x < \tan x$, as $\tan x = \frac{(\sin x)}{(\cos x)}$ and $\cos x < 1$.

Example 51 *Let A and B be such that* $\pi < A - B < 3\pi$. *If* $\sin A + \sin B = -\frac{21}{65}$ *and* $\cos A + \cos B = -\frac{27}{65}$, *then the value of* $\frac{1}{3}\cos\frac{A-B}{2}$ *is*

(a) $-\frac{1}{\sqrt{130}}$ (b) $\frac{1}{\sqrt{130}}$

(c) $\frac{2}{65}$ (d) $-\frac{2}{65}$

Sol. (a) We have, $$\sin A + \sin B = -\frac{21}{65} \quad \text{...(i)}$$

and $$\cos A + \cos B = -\frac{27}{65} \quad \text{...(ii)}$$

On squaring Eq. (i), we get

$$\sin^2 A + \sin^2 B + 2\sin A\sin B = \left(-\frac{21}{65}\right)^2 \quad \text{...(iii)}$$

On squaring Eq. (ii), we get

$$\cos^2 A + \cos^2 B + 2\cos A\cos B = \left(-\frac{27}{65}\right)^2 \quad \text{...(iv)}$$

On adding Eqs. (iii) and (iv), we get

$$2 + 2\cos(A-B) = \frac{1}{(65)^2}[(-27)^2 + (-21)^2]$$

$$= \frac{1}{(65)^2}(729 + 441) = \frac{1}{(65)^2}(1170) = \frac{18}{65}$$

$$\Rightarrow \quad 1+\cos(A-B)=\frac{9}{65} \Rightarrow 2\cos^2\left(\frac{A-B}{2}\right)=\frac{9}{65}$$

$$\Rightarrow \quad \frac{1}{3}\cos\frac{A-B}{2}=-\frac{1}{\sqrt{130}}$$

$$\left[\because \pi < A-B < 3\pi \Rightarrow \frac{\pi}{2}<\frac{A-B}{2}<\frac{3\pi}{2} \Rightarrow \cos\left(\frac{A-B}{2}\right)<0\right]$$

Example 52 *The value of* $\sum_{n=1}^{\infty}\frac{\tan\left(\frac{\theta}{2^n}\right)}{2^{n-1}\cos\frac{\theta}{2^{n-1}}}$ *is*

(a) $\frac{2}{\sin 2\theta}-\frac{1}{\theta}$ (b) $\frac{2}{\sin 2\theta}+\frac{1}{\theta}$

(c) $\frac{1}{\sin 2\theta}-\frac{1}{\theta}$ (d) $\frac{1}{\sin \theta}-\frac{1}{\theta}$

Sol. (a) $S_n=\sum_{r=1}^{n}\frac{\tan\left(\frac{\theta}{2^r}\right)}{2^{r-1}\cos\left(\frac{\theta}{2^{r-1}}\right)}=\sum_{r=1}^{n}\frac{\sin\left(\frac{\theta}{2^r}\right)}{2^{r-1}\cos\left(\frac{\theta}{2^r}\right)\cos\left(\frac{\theta}{2^{r-1}}\right)}$

$$=\sum_{r=1}^{n}\frac{2\sin^2\left(\frac{\theta}{2^r}\right)}{2^{r-1}\left\{2\sin\left(\frac{\theta}{2^r}\right)\cos\left(\frac{\theta}{2^r}\right)\right\}\cos\left(\frac{\theta}{2^{r-1}}\right)}$$

$$=\sum_{r=1}^{n}\frac{1-\cos\left(\frac{\theta}{2^{r-1}}\right)}{2^{r-1}\sin\left(\frac{\theta}{2^{r-1}}\right)\cos\left(\frac{\theta}{2^{r-1}}\right)}$$

$$=\sum_{r=1}^{n}\left(\frac{1}{2^{r-2}\sin\left(\frac{\theta}{2^{r-2}}\right)}-\frac{1}{2^{r-1}\sin\left(\frac{\theta}{2^{r-1}}\right)}\right)$$

$$=\frac{2}{\sin 2\theta}-\frac{1}{2^{n-1}\sin\left(\frac{\theta}{2^{n-1}}\right)}$$

$$\therefore S_\infty=\frac{2}{\sin 2\theta}-\lim_{n\to\infty}\frac{\frac{\theta}{2^{n-1}}\cdot\frac{1}{\theta}}{\sin\left(\frac{\theta}{2^{n-1}}\right)}=\frac{2}{\sin 2\theta}-\frac{1}{\theta}$$

More than One Correct Option Type Questions

Example 53 *If* $x\in(0,\pi)$ *and* $\cos x+\sin x=\frac{1}{2}$, *then* $\tan x$ *is equal to*

(a) $\frac{4-\sqrt{7}}{3}$ (b) $\frac{4+\sqrt{7}}{3}$

(c) $\frac{-(4+\sqrt{7})}{3}$ (d) $\frac{-4+\sqrt{7}}{3}$

Sol. (c,d) Given, $\cos x+\sin x=\frac{1}{2}$

$$\Rightarrow \quad 1+\sin 2x=\frac{1}{4}$$

$$\sin 2x=-\frac{3}{4} \quad \Rightarrow \quad 2x\in(\pi, 2\pi)$$

$$\Rightarrow \quad x\in\left(\frac{\pi}{2},\pi\right) \quad \Rightarrow \quad \tan x<0$$

$$\frac{2t}{1+t^2}=-\frac{3}{4} \quad \Rightarrow \quad 8t=-3-3t^2$$

$\Rightarrow 3t^2+8t+3=0,$

where $t=\tan x$

$$t=\frac{-8\pm\sqrt{64-36}}{2\cdot 3};$$

$$t=\frac{-8\pm\sqrt{28}}{2\cdot 3};$$

$$t=\frac{-(4+\sqrt{7})}{3}, \frac{-4+\sqrt{7}}{3}$$

Example 54 *The value of the expression* $\tan\frac{\pi}{7}+2\tan\frac{2\pi}{7}+4\tan\frac{4\pi}{7}+8\cot\frac{8\pi}{7}$ *is equal to*

(a) $\operatorname{cosec}\frac{2\pi}{7}+\cot\frac{2\pi}{7}$ (b) $\tan\frac{\pi}{14}-\cot\frac{\pi}{14}$

(c) $\frac{\sin\frac{2\pi}{7}}{1-\cos\frac{2\pi}{7}}$ (d) $\frac{1+\cos\frac{\pi}{7}+\cos\frac{2\pi}{7}}{\sin\frac{\pi}{7}+\sin\frac{2\pi}{7}}$

Sol. (a,c,d) $\tan\frac{\pi}{7}+2\tan\frac{2\pi}{7}+4\tan\frac{4\pi}{7}+8\cot\frac{8\pi}{7}=\cot\frac{\pi}{7}$

$$\left[\tan\theta+2\tan 2\theta+4\tan 4\theta+8\cot 8\theta=\cot\theta \text{ when } \theta=\frac{\pi}{7}\right]$$

(a) $\operatorname{cosec} 2\theta+\cot 2\theta=\frac{1+\cot 2\theta}{\sin 2\theta}=\cot\theta=\cot\frac{\pi}{7}$

$$\left[\text{where, } \theta=\frac{\pi}{7}\right]$$

(b) $\tan\frac{\pi}{14}-\cot\frac{\pi}{14}=-2\cot\frac{\pi}{7}$

(c) $\frac{\sin\frac{2\pi}{7}}{1-\cos\frac{2\pi}{7}}=\frac{2\sin\frac{\pi}{7}\cos\frac{\pi}{7}}{2\sin^2\frac{\pi}{7}}=\cot\frac{\pi}{7}$

(d) $\frac{\left(1+\cos\frac{2\pi}{7}\right)+\cos\frac{\pi}{7}}{2\sin\frac{\pi}{7}\cos\frac{\pi}{7}+\sin\frac{\pi}{7}}=\frac{2\cos^2\frac{\pi}{7}+\cos\frac{\pi}{7}}{2\sin\frac{\pi}{7}\left(\cos\frac{\pi}{7}+1\right)}$

$$=\cot\frac{\pi}{7}$$

Example 55 *Two parallel chords are drawn on the same side of the centre of a circle of radius R. It is found that they subtend and angle of θ and 2θ at the centre of the circle. The perpendicular distance between the chords is*

(a) $2R \sin\frac{3\theta}{2} \sin\frac{\theta}{2}$

(b) $\left(1-\cos\frac{\theta}{2}\right)\left(1+2\cos\frac{\theta}{2}\right)R$

(c) $\left(1+\cos\frac{\theta}{2}\right)\left(1-2\cos\frac{\theta}{2}\right)R$

(d) $2R\sin\frac{3\theta}{4} \sin\frac{\theta}{4}$

Sol. (b,d) $OM = p_1 = R\cos\frac{\theta}{2}$

$$ON = p_2 = R\cos\theta$$

$$MN = p_1 - p_2 = R\left(\cos\frac{\theta}{2} - \cos\theta\right)$$

$$= R\, 2\sin\frac{3\theta}{4} \sin\frac{\theta}{4}$$

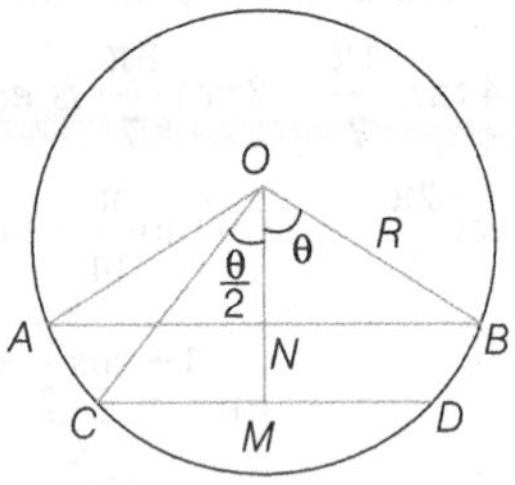

Again, convert $\cos\theta = 2\cos^2\frac{\theta}{2} - 1$ and factorise, we get

$$= R(1-\cos\theta/2)^2(1+2\cos\theta/2)$$

Example 56 *If 2x and 2y are complementary angles and* $\tan(x+2y) = 2$, *then which of the following is(are) correct ?*

(a) $\sin(x+y) = \frac{1}{2}$ (b) $\tan(x-y) = \frac{1}{7}$

(c) $\cot x + \cot y = 5$ (d) $\tan x \tan y = 6$

Sol. (b,c) We have, $2x + 2y = \frac{\pi}{2}$

$$\Rightarrow \quad x + y = \frac{\pi}{4}$$

$$\Rightarrow \quad \sin(x+y) = \frac{1}{\sqrt{2}}$$

Also, $y = \left(\frac{\pi}{4} - x\right)$,

So, $\tan(x+2y) = \tan\left(x + \frac{\pi}{2} - 2x\right)$

$$= \tan\left(\frac{\pi}{2} - x\right) = \cot x$$

$$\therefore \quad 2 = \cot x \Rightarrow \tan x = \frac{1}{2}$$

Similarly, $x = \left(\frac{\pi}{4} - y\right)$

So, $\tan(x+2y) = \tan\left(\frac{\pi}{4} + y\right) = \frac{1+\tan y}{1-\tan y}$

$$\Rightarrow \quad 2 = \frac{1+\tan y}{1-\tan y} \Rightarrow \tan y = \frac{1}{3}$$

$$\cot y = 3$$

Also, $\tan(x-y) = \frac{\tan x - \tan y}{1+\tan x \tan y} = \frac{\frac{1}{2}-\frac{1}{3}}{1+\left(\frac{1}{2}\right)\left(\frac{1}{3}\right)} = \left(\frac{1}{6}\right)\left(\frac{6}{7}\right) = \frac{1}{7}$

Now, $\cot x + \cot y = 2 + 3 = 5$

and $\tan x \tan y = \frac{1}{2}\cdot\frac{1}{3} = \frac{1}{6}$

Example 57 *If* $2\cos\theta + 2\sqrt{2} = 3\sec\theta$, *where* $\theta \in (0, 2\pi)$, *then which of the following can be correct?*

(a) $\cos\theta = \frac{1}{\sqrt{2}}$ (b) $\tan\theta = 1$

(c) $\sin\theta = -\frac{1}{\sqrt{2}}$ (d) $\cot\theta = -1$

Sol. (a,b,c,d) $2\cos\theta + 2\sqrt{2} = 3\sec\theta$

$$\therefore \quad 2\cos^2\theta + 2\sqrt{2}\cos\theta - 3 = 0$$

$$\cos\theta = \frac{-2\sqrt{2} \pm \sqrt{32}}{4} = \frac{-2\sqrt{2} \pm 4\sqrt{2}}{4}$$

$$\therefore \quad \cos\theta = \frac{1}{\sqrt{2}} \text{ or } \cos\theta = -\frac{3}{\sqrt{2}} \text{ (rejected)}$$

$$\therefore \quad \theta = \frac{\pi}{4} \text{ or } \frac{7\pi}{4}$$

$$\Rightarrow \quad \sin\theta = -\frac{1}{\sqrt{2}};\ \cot\theta = -1;\ \tan\theta = 1$$

Example 58 *The value of x in* $(0, \pi/2)$ *satisfying the equation,* $\frac{\sqrt{3}-1}{\sin x} + \frac{\sqrt{3}+1}{\cos x} = 4\sqrt{2}$ *is*

(a) $\frac{\pi}{12}$ (b) $\frac{5\pi}{12}$ (c) $\frac{7\pi}{24}$ (d) $\frac{11\pi}{36}$

Sol. (a,d) $\frac{\sqrt{3}-1}{2\sqrt{2}\sin x} + \frac{\sqrt{3}+1}{2\sqrt{2}\cos x} = 2$

$$\sin\frac{\pi}{12}\cos x + \cos\frac{\pi}{12}\sin x = \sin 2x$$

$$\sin 2x = \sin\left(x + \frac{\pi}{12}\right)$$

$$\therefore \quad 2x = x + \frac{\pi}{12} \text{ or } 2x = \pi - x - \frac{\pi}{12}$$

$$x = \frac{\pi}{12} \text{ or } 3x = \frac{11\pi}{12}$$

$$\therefore \quad x = \frac{\pi}{12} \text{ or } \frac{11\pi}{36}$$

Example 59 *Let in* ΔABC, $\cos A = \frac{3}{\sqrt{10}}$ *and* $\cos B = \frac{6}{\sqrt{61}}$, *then*

(a) ΔABC is an acute angled triangle.

(b) ΔABC is an obtuse angled triangle.

(c) $\tan A + \tan B + \tan C > 2$

(d) $\tan A + \tan B + \tan C < 1$

Sol. (b, d) $\cos A = \frac{3}{\sqrt{10}} \Rightarrow \tan A = \frac{1}{3}$

$$\cos B = \frac{6}{\sqrt{61}} \Rightarrow \tan B = \frac{5}{6}$$

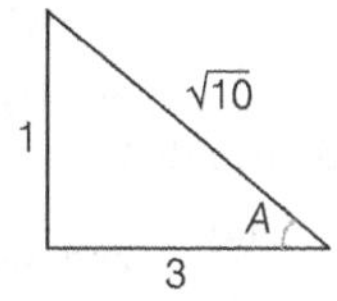

$$\tan A + \tan B + \tan C = \tan A \tan B \tan C$$

$$\frac{1}{3} + \frac{5}{6} + \tan C = \frac{1}{3} \times \frac{5}{6} \tan C$$

$$\frac{7}{6} + \tan C = \frac{5}{18} \tan C$$

$$\tan C \left[\frac{5}{18} - 1\right] = \frac{7}{6}$$

$$\tan C \left[-\frac{13}{18}\right] = \frac{7}{6}$$

$$\tan C = -\frac{21}{13}$$

Hence, ΔABC is an obtuse angled triangle and

$$\tan A \tan B \tan C = \frac{1}{3} \times \frac{5}{6} \times \left(-\frac{21}{13}\right) = (-) \text{ ve}$$

Example 60 *If* $\cos(x - y) = 1$ *and* $\cos(x + y) = \frac{1}{3}$, *where* $x, y \in [-\pi, \pi]$, *then*

(a) $\frac{\tan(x + y)}{\tan x + \tan y} = 2$ (b) $\frac{\tan(x + y)}{\tan x + \tan y} = \frac{1}{2}$

(c) $\cos 2x = \frac{1}{3}$ (d) $\cos 2x = \frac{2}{3}$

Sol. (a, c) $\cos x \cos y + \sin x \sin y = 1$

$$\cos x \cos y - \sin x \sin y = \frac{1}{3}$$

$$2 \cos x \cos y = \frac{4}{3}$$

$$\Rightarrow \quad \cos x \cos y = \frac{2}{3}$$

$$\text{and} \quad 2 \sin x \sin y = \frac{2}{3}$$

$$\sin x \sin y = \frac{1}{3}$$

$$\tan x \tan y = \frac{\sin x \sin y}{\cos x \cos y} = \frac{1}{2}$$

$$\tan x \tan y = \frac{1}{2}$$

$$\tan(x + y) = \frac{\tan x + \tan y}{1 - \tan x \tan y}$$

$$\frac{\tan(x + y)}{\tan x + \tan y} = \frac{1}{1 - \tan x \tan y} = \frac{1}{1 - \frac{1}{2}} = 2$$

$$\cos 2x = \cos(x + x) = \cos[(x + y) + (x - y)]$$
$$= \cos(x + y)\cos(x - y) - \sin(x + y)\sin(x - y)$$
$$= 1 \times \frac{1}{3} - 0 = \frac{1}{3}$$

Example 61 *If maximum value of* $f(x) = a \sin x + 2\sqrt{2}\, a \cos x$ *is 9, then*

(a) sum of all possible values of a is 3

(b) sum of all possible values of a is 0

(c) number of possible values of a is 2

(d) number of possible values of a is 1

> **Decoding the Question**
>
> We know that maximum and minimum value of $a\sin\theta + b\cos\theta$ is $\pm\sqrt{a^2 + b^2}$ respectively.

Sol. (b, c) $f(x) = a \sin x + 2\sqrt{2}\, a \cos x$

$$\max[f(x)] = \sqrt{a^2 + 8a^2} = \sqrt{9a^2} = 3|a| = 9$$

$$|a| = 3 \Rightarrow a = \pm 3$$

Example 62 *Which of the following statements are always correct? (where, Q denotes the set of rationals)*

(a) $\cos 2\theta \in Q$ and $\sin 2\theta \in Q \Rightarrow \tan\theta \in Q$ (if defined)

(b) $\tan\theta \in Q \Rightarrow \sin 2\theta, \cos 2\theta$ and $\tan 2\theta \in Q$ (if defined)

(c) If $\sin\theta \in Q$ and $\cos\theta \in Q \Rightarrow \tan 3\theta \in Q$ (if defined)

(d) If $\sin\theta \in Q \Rightarrow \cos 3\theta \in Q$

Sol. (a,b,c)

(a) $\tan\theta = \frac{1 - \cos 2\theta}{\sin 2\theta} \Rightarrow$ (a) is correct

(b) $\sin 2\theta = \frac{2\tan\theta}{1 + \tan^2\theta}$; $\cos 2\theta = \frac{1 - \tan^2\theta}{1 + \tan^2\theta}$;

$\tan 2\theta = \frac{2\tan\theta}{1 - \tan^2\theta} \Rightarrow$ (b) is correct

(c) $\tan 3\theta = \frac{\sin 3\theta}{\cos 3\theta} \Rightarrow$ (c) is correct

(d) $\sin\theta = \frac{1}{3}$ which is rational but $\cos 3\theta = \cos\theta(4\cos^2\theta - 3)$ which is irrational $\Rightarrow$ (d) is incorrect.

Example 63 *In ΔABC, $\tan B + \tan C = 5$ and $\tan A \tan C = 3$, then*

(a) ΔABC is an acute angled triangle
(b) ΔABC is an obtuse angled triangle
(c) sum of all possible values of $\tan A$ is 10
(d) sum of all possible values of $\tan A$ is 9

Sol. (a, c) $\tan A + \tan B + \tan C = \tan A \tan B \tan C$

$\Rightarrow \quad \tan A + 5 = 3 \tan B$

$\Rightarrow \quad 5 + \tan A = 3(5 - \tan C)$

$\Rightarrow \quad 5 + \tan A = 15 - \dfrac{9}{\tan A}$

$\Rightarrow \quad \tan^2 A - 10 \tan A + 9 = 0$

$\Rightarrow \quad \tan A = 1$ or $\tan A = 9$

$\Rightarrow \tan B$ and $\tan C$ are 2, 3 or $\dfrac{14}{3}, \dfrac{1}{3}$, respectively.

$\Rightarrow \Delta ABC$ is always on acute angled triangle and sum of all possible values of $\tan A$ is 10.

Example 64 *$(m+2)\sin\theta + (2m-1)\cos\theta = 2m+1$, if*

(a) $\tan\theta = \dfrac{3}{4}$ (b) $\tan\theta = \dfrac{4}{3}$

(c) $\tan\theta = \dfrac{2m}{(m^2-1)}$ (d) $\tan\theta = \dfrac{2m}{(m^2+1)}$

Sol. (b, c) The given relation can be written as

$(m+2)\tan\theta + (2m-1) = (2m+1)\sec\theta$

$\Rightarrow (m+2)^2 \tan^2\theta + 2(m+2)(2m-1)\tan\theta + (2m-1)^2$
$= (2m+1)^2 (1 + \tan^2\theta)$

$\Rightarrow [(m+2^2) - (2m+1)^2]\tan^2\theta + 2(m+2)\tan\theta + (2m-1)^2 - (2m+1)^2 = 0$

$\Rightarrow 3(1-m^2)\tan^2\theta + (4m^2+6m-4)\tan\theta - 8m = 0$

$\Rightarrow \quad (3\tan\theta - 4)[(1-m)^2 \tan\theta + 2m] = 0$

which is true if $\tan\theta = \dfrac{4}{3}$ or $\tan\theta = \dfrac{2m}{(m^2-1)}$.

Example 65 *If $x\cos\alpha + y\sin\alpha = x\cos\beta + y\sin\beta = 2a \left(0 < \alpha, \beta < \dfrac{\pi}{2}\right)$, then*

(a) $\cos\alpha + \cos\beta = \dfrac{4ax}{x^2+y^2}$

(b) $\cos\alpha \cos\beta = \dfrac{4a^2-y^2}{x^2+y^2}$

(c) $\sin\alpha + \sin\beta = \dfrac{4ay}{x^2+y^2}$

(d) $\sin\alpha \sin\beta = \dfrac{4a^2-x^2}{x^2+y^2}$

Sol. (a, b, c, d) We find out the given relations that α and β are the roots of the equation

$x\cos\theta + y\sin\theta = 2a$

$\Rightarrow \quad (x\cos\theta - 2a)^2 = (-y\sin\theta)^2$

$\Rightarrow x^2\cos^2\theta - 4ax\cos\theta + 4a^2 = y^2\sin^2\theta = y^2(1-\cos^2\theta)$

$\Rightarrow (x^2+y^2)\cos^2\theta - 4ax\cos\theta + 4a^2 - y^2 = 0 \quad \text{...(i)}$

which being quadratic in $\cos\theta$, has two roots $\cos\alpha$ and $\cos\beta$, such that

$$\cos\alpha + \cos\beta = \frac{4ax}{x^2+y^2}$$

and $$\cos\alpha\cos\beta = \frac{4a^2-y^2}{x^2+y^2}$$

Similarly, we can write (i) as a quadratic in $\sin\theta$, giving two values $\sin\alpha$ and $\sin\beta$, such that

$$\sin\alpha + \sin\beta = \frac{4ay}{x^2+y^2} \text{ and } \sin\alpha\sin\beta = \frac{4a^2-x^2}{x^2+y^2}.$$

Example 66 *Let $y = \sin^2 x + \cos^4 x$. Then, for all real x*

(a) the maximum value of y is 2
(b) the minimum value of y is $\dfrac{3}{4}$
(c) $y \le 1$
(d) $y \ge \dfrac{1}{4}$

Sol. (b, c) $y = \cos^4 x - \cos^2 x + 1 = \left(\cos^2 x - \dfrac{1}{2}\right)^2 + \dfrac{3}{4}$

$\therefore y_{\min} = \dfrac{3}{4}$ and y is maximum when $\left(\cos^2 x - \dfrac{1}{2}\right)^2$ is then maximum.

$\therefore \quad y_{\max} = \dfrac{1}{4} + \dfrac{3}{4} = 1$

Example 67 *Value of $(\tan 11° + \tan 13° + \tan 11° \tan 34° + \tan 32° + \tan 34° + \tan 32° \tan 13°)$ is*

(a) prime number (b) composite number
(c) even number (d) odd number

Sol. (a, c) $11° + 34° = 45°$ and $13° + 32° = 45°$

If $A + B = 45° \Rightarrow (1 + \tan A)(1 + \tan B) = 2$

$\Rightarrow \quad 1 + \tan A + \tan B + \tan A \tan B = 2$

$\Rightarrow \quad \tan A + \tan B + \tan A \tan B = 1$

$\Rightarrow \quad \tan 11° + \tan 34° + \tan 11° \tan 34° = 1$

$\Rightarrow \quad \tan 13° + \tan 32° + \tan 13° \tan 32° = 1$

Hence, value of given expression is 2.

Example 68 *If $\sin^3 A + \cos^3 A = 8k^3 - 3k \sin 2A$, then k can be*

(a) 0 (b) 1 (c) $-\dfrac{1}{\sqrt{2}}$ (d) $\dfrac{1}{2}$

Sol. (c, d) $(\sin A)^3 + (\cos A)^3 + (-2k)^3 = 3 \sin A \cos A (-2k)$

$\Rightarrow \quad a^3 + b^3 + c^3 = 3abc$

$\Rightarrow \quad \sin A + \cos A - 2k = 0$

or $\quad \sin A = \cos A = -2k$

$\Rightarrow \quad \sin A + \cos A = 2k$

$\Rightarrow \quad 2k \in [-\sqrt{2}, \sqrt{2}]$

$\Rightarrow \quad k \in \left[-\frac{1}{\sqrt{2}}, \frac{1}{\sqrt{2}}\right]$

or $\quad \sin A = \cos A = -2k$

Hence, possible values of k can be 0, $-\frac{1}{\sqrt{2}}$ and $\frac{1}{2}$.

Example 69 *Which of the following is/are incorrect.*

(a) $\tan\left(\frac{2015\pi}{2} - \frac{\pi}{4}\right) = 1$ (b) $\sin(2014\pi) = 0$

(c) $|\cos 125°| > |\sin 125°|$ (d) $\cos\left(\frac{2013\pi}{2} + \frac{\pi}{6}\right) = \frac{1}{2}$

Sol. (c, d) $\tan\left(\frac{2015\pi}{2} - \frac{\pi}{4}\right) = \tan\left(1007\pi + \frac{\pi}{2} - \frac{\pi}{4}\right)$

$= \tan\left(\frac{\pi}{2} - \frac{\pi}{4}\right) = 1$

$\Rightarrow \quad \sin(2014\pi) = 0$

$\Rightarrow \quad |\cos 125°| = |\sin 35°|$

$\Rightarrow \quad |\sin 125°| = |\cos 35°|$

$\Rightarrow \quad 0 < \theta < \frac{\pi}{4} \Rightarrow |\cos\theta| > |\sin\theta|$

$\Rightarrow \quad |\cos 35°| > |\sin 35°|$

$\Rightarrow \quad |\sin 125°| > |\cos 125°|$

Hence, option (c) is incorrect.

$$\cos\left(\frac{2013\pi}{2} + \frac{\pi}{6}\right) = \cos\left(1006\pi + \frac{\pi}{2} + \frac{\pi}{6}\right)$$

$$= -\sin\frac{\pi}{6} = -\frac{1}{2}$$

Hence, option (d) is also incorrect.

Example 70 *If $A = \sin 44° + \cos 44°$, $B = \sin 45° + \cos 45°$ and $C = \sin 46° + \cos 46°$, then correct option(s) is/are*

(a) $A < B < C$ (b) $C < B < A$

(c) $B > A$ (d) $A = C$

Sol. (c, d) $A = \sqrt{2}\left(\frac{1}{\sqrt{2}}\sin 44° + \frac{1}{\sqrt{2}}\cos 44°\right)$

$A = \sqrt{2}(\cos 45° \sin 44° + \sin 45° \cos 44°)$

$A = \sqrt{2} \sin 89° < \sqrt{2}$

$B = \frac{1}{\sqrt{2}} + \frac{1}{\sqrt{2}} = \sqrt{2}$

$A < B \Rightarrow$ Option (c) is correct.

$C = \sin(90° - 44°) + \cos(90° - 44°)$

$C = \cos 44° + \sin 44°$

$C = \sin 44° + \cos 44° = A$

$A = C \Rightarrow$ Option (d) is also correct.

Example 71 *If in ΔABC, $\tan A + \tan B + \tan C = 6$ and $\tan A \tan B = 2$, then $\sin^2 A : \sin^2 B : \sin^2 C$ is*

(a) 8 : 9 : 5 (b) 8 : 5 : 9

(c) 5 : 8 : 9 (d) 5 : 8 : 5

Sol. (b, c) $\tan A + \tan B + \tan C = 6$ ...(i)

$\Rightarrow \quad \tan A \tan B \tan C = 6$

$2 \tan C = 6$

$\therefore \quad \tan C = 3$

$\therefore \quad \sin^2 C = \frac{\tan^2 C}{1 + \tan^2 C} = \frac{9}{1+9} = \frac{9}{10}$

From Eq. (i), $\tan A + \tan B = 3$ and $\tan A \tan B = 2$

$\tan A - \tan B = \pm\sqrt{\{(\tan A + \tan B)^2 - 4\tan A \tan B)\}} = \pm 1$

we get, $\tan A = 2, 1$ and $\tan B = 1, 2$

$\therefore \quad \sin^2 A = \frac{4}{1+4}, \frac{1}{1+1}$ and $\sin^2 B = \frac{1}{1+1}, \frac{4}{1+4}$

$\Rightarrow \quad \sin^2 A = \frac{8}{10}, \frac{5}{10}$ and $\sin^2 B = \frac{5}{10}, \frac{8}{10}$

$\therefore \quad \sin^2 A : \sin^2 B : \sin^2 C = 8 : 5 : 9$ or $5 : 8 : 9$

Example 72 *If $0 \le x, y \le 180°$ and $\sin(x - y) = \cos(x + y) = \frac{1}{2}$, then the values of x and y are given by*

(a) $x = 45°, y = 15°$ (b) $x = 45°, y = 135°$

(c) $x = 165°, y = 15°$ (d) $x = 165°, y = 135°$

Sol. (a, d) $\sin(x - y) = \frac{1}{2} \Rightarrow x - y = 30°$ or $150°$ (1)

and $\cos(x + y) = \frac{1}{2} \Rightarrow x + y = 60°$ or $300°$ (2)

Since, x and y lie between 0° and 180°, (1) and (2) are simultaneously true when $x = 45°, y = 15°$, or $x = 165°$, $y = 135°$. But, for the values given by (b) or (c), (1) and (2) do not hold simultaneously.

Example 73 *If $\sin\alpha + \sin\beta = l$, $\cos\alpha + \cos\beta = m$ and $\tan\left(\frac{\alpha}{2}\right)\tan\left(\frac{\beta}{2}\right) = n (\ne 1)$, then*

(a) $\cos(\alpha - \beta) = \frac{l^2 + m^2 - 2}{2}$

(b) $\cos(\alpha + \beta) = \frac{m^2 - l^2}{m^2 + l^2}$

(c) $\frac{1+n}{1-n} = \frac{l^2 + m^2}{2n}$

(d) $\alpha + \beta = \frac{\pi}{2}$ if $l = m$

Sol. (a, b, d) Now, $l^2 = \sin^2\alpha + \sin^2\beta + 2\sin\alpha\sin\beta$ and
$m^2 = \cos^2\alpha + \cos^2\beta + 2\cos\alpha\cos\beta$

$$2\cos(\alpha-\beta) = l^2 + m^2 - 2 \quad \text{[by adding]}$$

$$\Rightarrow \cos 2\alpha + \cos 2\beta + 2\cos(\alpha+\beta) = m^2 - l^2 \quad \text{[by subtracting]}$$

$$\Rightarrow 2\cos(\alpha+\beta)\cos(\alpha-\beta) + 2\cos(\alpha+\beta) = m^2 - l^2$$

$$\Rightarrow \cos(\alpha+\beta) = \frac{m^2 - l^2}{m^2 + l^2}$$

Now, $\dfrac{1+n}{1-n} = \dfrac{1+\tan\alpha\tan\beta}{1-\tan\alpha\tan\beta} = \dfrac{\cos\alpha\cos\beta + \sin\alpha\sin\beta}{\cos\alpha\cos\beta - \sin\alpha\sin\beta}$

$$= \frac{\cos(\alpha-\beta)}{\cos(\alpha+\beta)} = \frac{(l^2+m^2-2)(m^2+l^2)}{m^2-l^2}$$

If $l = m$, $\cos(\alpha+\beta) = 0 \Rightarrow \alpha+\beta = \dfrac{\pi}{2}$

Example 74 *Let $f(x) = ab\sin x + b\sqrt{1-a^2}\cos x + c$, where $|a| < 1, b > 0$ then*

(a) maximum value of $f(x)$ is b, if $c = 0$
(b) difference of maximum and minimum values of $f(x)$ is $2b$
(c) $f(x) = c$, if $x = -\cos^{-1}\alpha$
(d) $f(x) = c$, if $x = \cos^{-1}\alpha$

Sol. (a, b, c) $f(x) = ab\sin x + b\sqrt{1-a^2}\cos x + c$,

where $|a| < 1$, $b > 0$

$$f(x) = \sqrt{a^2b^2 + b^2 - b^2a^2}\sin(x+\alpha) + c$$

$$= b\sin(x+\alpha) + c, \text{ where } \tan\alpha = \frac{b\sqrt{1-a^2}}{ab} = \frac{\sqrt{1-a^2}}{a}$$

$$= b\cos(x-\alpha) + c, \text{ where } \tan\alpha = \frac{ab}{b\sqrt{1-a^2}} = \frac{a}{\sqrt{1-a^2}}$$

$$f(x)_{\max} - f(x)_{\min} = c + b - (c - b) = 2b$$

$$f(x) = c \text{ if } x + \alpha = 0$$

or $\quad x = -\alpha$ or $x = -\cos^{-1}\alpha$

Example 75 *If $(x-a)\cos\theta + y\sin\theta = (x-a)\cos\phi + y\sin\phi = a$ and $\tan\left(\frac{\theta}{2}\right) - \tan\left(\frac{\phi}{2}\right) = 2b$, then*

(a) $y^2 = 2ax - (1-b^2)x^2$ (b) $\tan\dfrac{\theta}{2} = \dfrac{1}{x}(y+bx)$

(c) $y^2 = 2bx - (1-a^2)x^2$ (d) $\tan\dfrac{\phi}{2} = \dfrac{1}{x}(y-bx)$

Sol. (a, b, d) Let $\tan\left(\dfrac{\theta}{2}\right) = \alpha$ and $\tan\left(\dfrac{\phi}{2}\right) = \beta$,

so that $\alpha - \beta = 2b$.

Also, $$\cos\theta = \frac{1-\tan^2\left(\frac{\theta}{2}\right)}{1+\tan^2\left(\frac{\theta}{2}\right)} = \frac{1-\alpha^2}{1+\alpha^2}$$

And $$\sin\theta = \frac{2\tan\left(\frac{\theta}{2}\right)}{1+\tan^2\left(\frac{\theta}{2}\right)} = \frac{2\alpha}{1+\alpha^2}$$

Similarly, $\cos\phi = \dfrac{1-\beta^2}{1+\beta^2}$ and $\sin\phi = \dfrac{2\beta}{1+\beta^2}$

Therefore, we have from the given relations

$$(x-a)\frac{1-\alpha^2}{1+\alpha^2} + y\left(\frac{2\alpha}{1+\alpha^2}\right) = a$$

$$\Rightarrow x\alpha^2 - 2y\alpha + 2a - x = 0$$

Similarly, $$x\beta^2 - 2y\beta + 2a = 0$$

We see that α and β are roots of the equation

$$xz^2 - 2yz + 2a - x = 0,$$

So that $\alpha + \beta = \dfrac{2y}{x}$ and $\alpha\beta = \dfrac{(2a-x)}{x}$.

Now, from $(\alpha+\beta)^2 = (\alpha-\beta)^2 + 4\alpha\beta$, we get

$$\Rightarrow \left(\frac{2y}{x}\right)^2 = (2b)^2 + \frac{4(2a-x)}{x}$$

$$\Rightarrow y^2 = 2ax - (1-b^2)x^2$$

Also, from $\alpha + \beta = \dfrac{2y}{x}$ and $\alpha - \beta = 2b$, we get

$$\alpha = \frac{y}{x} + b \text{ and } \beta = \frac{y}{x} - b$$

$$\Rightarrow \tan\frac{\theta}{2} = \frac{1}{x}(y+bx) \text{ and } \tan\frac{\phi}{2} = \frac{1}{x}(y-bx)$$

Example 76 *If $\cos(\beta-\gamma) + \cos(\gamma-\alpha) + \cos(\alpha-\beta) = -\dfrac{3}{2}$ then*

(a) $\Sigma\cos\alpha = 0$ (b) $\Sigma\sin\alpha = 0$
(c) $\Sigma\cos\alpha\sin\alpha = 0$ (d) $\Sigma(\cos\alpha + \sin\alpha) = 0$

Sol. (a, b, d) The given expression can be written as

$$2[\cos\beta\cos\gamma + \cos\gamma\cos\alpha + \cos\alpha\cos\beta] + 2[\sin\beta\sin\gamma + \sin\gamma\sin\alpha + \sin\alpha\sin\beta] + (\sin^2\alpha + \cos^2\alpha) + (\sin^2\beta + \cos^2\beta) + (\sin^2\gamma + \cos^2\gamma) = 0$$

$$\Rightarrow (\cos\alpha + \cos\beta + \cos\gamma)^2 + (\sin\alpha + \sin\beta + \sin\gamma)^2 = 0$$

$$\Rightarrow \Sigma\cos\alpha = 0 \text{ and } \Sigma\sin\alpha = 0$$

$$\Rightarrow \Sigma(\cos\alpha + \sin\alpha) = 0$$

Passage Based Questions

Passage I

(Ex. Nos. 77 to 79)

Let $\sin A + \sin B = \dfrac{\sqrt{3}}{4}$ and $\cos A + \cos B = \dfrac{1}{2}$

Example 77 *The value of $\cos(A+B)$ is*

(a) $\dfrac{2}{3}$ (b) $\dfrac{1}{7}$ (c) $-\dfrac{1}{2}$ (d) $-\dfrac{2}{3}$

Sol. (b) $\sin A + \sin B = \frac{\sqrt{3}}{4}$

$$\Rightarrow \quad 2\sin\left(\frac{A+B}{2}\right)\cos\left(\frac{A-B}{2}\right) = \frac{\sqrt{3}}{4} \qquad \text{...(i)}$$

$$\cos A + \cos B = \frac{1}{2}$$

$$\Rightarrow \quad 2\cos\left(\frac{A+B}{2}\right)\cos\left(\frac{A-B}{2}\right) = \frac{1}{2} \qquad \text{...(ii)}$$

From Eqs. (i) and (ii), we get

$$\tan\left(\frac{A+B}{2}\right) = \frac{\sqrt{3}}{2}$$

$$\Rightarrow \quad \cos(A+B) = \frac{1-\tan^2\left(\frac{A+B}{2}\right)}{1+\tan^2\left(\frac{A+B}{2}\right)} = \frac{1-\frac{3}{4}}{1+\frac{3}{4}} = \frac{1/4}{7/4} = \frac{1}{7}$$

Example 78 *The value of* $\cos(A-B)$ *is*

(a) $-\frac{25}{32}$ (b) $\frac{24}{33}$ (c) $\frac{18}{25}$ (d) $\frac{13}{24}$

Sol. (a) $(\sin A + \sin B)^2 = \frac{3}{16}$

and $(\cos A + \cos B)^2 = \frac{1}{4}$

$$\sin^2 A + \sin^2 B + 2\sin A\sin B + \cos^2 A + \cos^2 B + 2\cos A\cos B = \frac{1}{4} + \frac{3}{16}$$

$$\Rightarrow \quad 1 + 1 + 2(\cos A\cos B + \sin A\sin B) = \frac{7}{16}$$

$$\Rightarrow \quad 2\cos(A-B) = \frac{7}{16} - 2 = \frac{7-32}{16} = -\frac{25}{16}$$

$$\Rightarrow \quad \cos(A-B) = -\frac{25}{32}$$

Example 79 *The value of* $[\sin 2A + \sin 2B + 2\sin(A+B)]$ *is*

(a) $-\frac{1}{2}$ (b) $\frac{1}{2}$

(c) $\frac{\sqrt{3}}{2}$ (d) $\frac{\sqrt{3}}{4}$

Sol. (d) $(\sin A + \sin B)(\cos A + \cos B) = \frac{1}{2} \times \frac{\sqrt{3}}{4}$

$$\Rightarrow \sin A\cos A + \sin A\cos B + \sin B\cos A + \sin B\cos B = \frac{\sqrt{3}}{8}$$

$$\Rightarrow \frac{1}{2}[2\sin A\cos A + 2(\sin A\cos B + \cos A\sin B) + 2\sin B\cos B] = \frac{\sqrt{3}}{8}$$

$$\Rightarrow \quad \sin 2A + \sin 2B + 2\sin(A+B) = \frac{\sqrt{3}}{4}$$

Passage II

(Ex. Nos. 80 to 82)

Consider, $f(x) = (x+2a)(x+a-4)\ (a \in R)$,

$g(x) = k(x^2+x) + 3k + x\ (k \in R)$ and

$h(x) = (1-\sin\theta)x^2 + 2(1-\sin\theta)x - 3\sin\theta$

$\left(\theta \in R - (4n+1)\frac{\pi}{2}, n \in I\right)$

Example 80 *If* $f(x) < 0$ *for* $-1 \le x \le 1$*, then 'a' satisfies*

(a) $\frac{1}{2} < a < 3$ (b) $-\frac{1}{2} < a < \frac{1}{2}$

(c) $-3 < a < -\frac{1}{2}$ (d) $-3 < a < \frac{1}{2}$

Sol. (a) Given, $f(x) = (x+2a)(x+a-4)$

$$= x^2 + (3a-4)x + 2a(a-4)$$

Now, $\left.\begin{matrix} f(-1) < 0 \\ f(1) < 0 \end{matrix}\right\} n$

$f(-1) = 2a^2 - 11a + 5 < 0$

$f(1) = 2a^2 - 5a - 3 < 0$

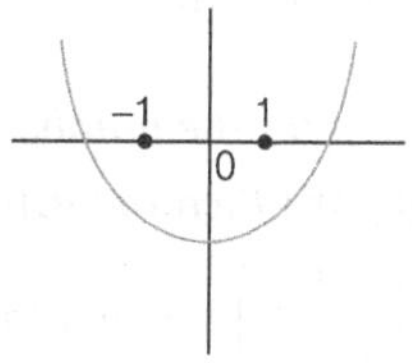

On solving, we get $\frac{1}{2} < a < 3$.

Example 81 *If* $g(x) > -3$ *for all real x, then the values of k are given by*

(a) $-1 < k < \frac{1}{11}$ (b) $-1 < k < 0$

(c) $0 < k < \frac{1}{11}$ (d) $k > \frac{1}{11}$

Sol. (d) $g(x) = k(x^2+x) + 3k + x > -3,\ \forall\ x$

$$\Rightarrow \quad k(x^2+x) + 3k + x + 3 > 0,\ \forall\ x$$

or $\quad kx^2 + (k+1)x + (3k+3) > 0,\ \forall\ x$

$$\left.\begin{matrix} k > 0 \\ D < 0 \end{matrix}\right\} n$$

Here, $D = (k+1)^2 - 4k \cdot 3(k+1) < 0$

$$\Rightarrow \quad k^2 + 2k + 1 - 12k^2 - 12k < 0$$

$$\Rightarrow \quad 11k^2 + 10k - 1 > 0$$

$$\Rightarrow \quad (k+1)(11k-1) > 0$$

$$\Rightarrow \quad k < -1 \text{ or } k > \frac{1}{11}$$

$$\Rightarrow \quad k > \frac{1}{11} \qquad [\because k > 0]$$

Example 82 *If the quadratic equation $h(x) = 0$ has both roots complex, then θ belongs to*

(a) $\left(-\frac{\pi}{2}, \frac{\pi}{2}\right)$ (b) $\left(0, \frac{3\pi}{2}\right)$

(c) $\left(\frac{\pi}{6}, \frac{7\pi}{6}\right)$ (d) $\left(\frac{7\pi}{6}, \frac{11\pi}{6}\right)$

Sol. (d) Given, $(1-\sin\theta)x^2 + 2(1-\sin\theta)x - 3\sin\theta = 0$ has both roots complex, then $D < 0$

$$(1-\sin\theta)(1+2\sin\theta) < 0$$

$$\underbrace{(\sin\theta - 1)}_{(-)\text{ ve number}}(2\sin\theta + 1) > 0$$

$$\Rightarrow \quad 2\sin\theta + 1 < 0 \Rightarrow \sin\theta < -\frac{1}{2}$$

$$\Rightarrow \quad \theta \in \left(\frac{7\pi}{6}, \frac{11\pi}{6}\right)$$

Passage III

(Ex. Nos. 83 to 85)

Let $f(\theta) = \sin\theta - \cos^2\theta - 1$,

where $\theta \in R$ and $m \le f(\theta) \le M$.

Example 83 *Let N denotes the number of solution of the equation $f(\theta) = 0$ in $[0, 4\pi]$ then the value of*

$\log_{\sqrt{m^2}}(N) + \log_{\sqrt{m^2}}\left(\frac{1}{N+1}\right)$ *is equal to*

(a) $\frac{1}{2}$ (b) 1 (c) $\frac{-1}{2}$ (d) -1

Sol. (c) $f(\theta) = \sin\theta - (1-\sin^2\theta) - 1$

$$= \sin^2\theta + \sin\theta - 2$$

$$= \left(\sin\theta + \frac{1}{2}\right)^2 - 2 - \frac{1}{4}$$

$$= \left(\sin\theta + \frac{1}{2}\right)^2 - \frac{9}{4}$$

$$\therefore \quad f(\theta)_{\min} = 0 - \frac{9}{4} = \frac{-9}{4}$$

$$\Rightarrow \quad m = \frac{-9}{4}$$

$$f(\theta)_{\max} = \left(1 + \frac{1}{2}\right)^2 - \frac{9}{4} = \frac{9}{4} - \frac{9}{4} = 0$$

$$\Rightarrow \quad M = 0$$

Hence, $m = \frac{-9}{4}$, $M = 0$

Now, $f(\theta) = 0$

$$\Rightarrow \quad (\sin\theta + 2)(\sin\theta - 1) = 0 \Rightarrow \sin\theta = 1$$

$$\Rightarrow \quad \theta = \frac{\pi}{2} \text{ and } \frac{5\pi}{2}$$

Hence, $N = 2$ i.e. number of solutions of $\sin\theta = 1$ in $[0, 4\pi]$.

$$\therefore \quad \log_{\sqrt{m^2}}(N) + \log_{\sqrt{m^2}}\left(\frac{1}{N+1}\right)$$

$$= \log_{|m|}\left(\frac{N}{N+1}\right) = \log_{|m|}\left(\frac{2}{3}\right)$$

$$= \log_{\frac{9}{4}}\left(\frac{2}{3}\right) = \frac{-1}{2}.$$

Example 84 *The value of $(4m + 13)$ is equal to*

(a) 0 (b) 4 (c) 5 (d) 6

Sol. (b) As $m = \frac{-9}{4}$, so $(4m + 13) = 4$

Example 85 *Sum of all values of x satisfying the equation*

$x = \sqrt{\frac{1}{|m|} + \sqrt{\frac{1}{|m|} + \sqrt{\frac{1}{|m|} + \ldots\ldots\ldots\ldots \infty}}}$, *is*

(a) $\frac{1}{3}$ (b) $\frac{2}{3}$

(c) $\frac{3}{3}$ (d) $\frac{4}{3}$

Sol. (d) $x = \sqrt{\frac{4}{9} + \sqrt{\frac{4}{9} + \sqrt{\frac{4}{9} + \ldots\ldots\ldots\ldots \infty}}}$

$$\Rightarrow \quad x = \sqrt{\frac{4}{9} + x}$$

$$\Rightarrow \quad x^2 = \frac{4}{9} + x \Rightarrow 9x^2 = 4 + 9x$$

$$\Rightarrow \quad 9x^2 - 9x - 4 = 0$$

$$\Rightarrow \quad 9x^2 - 12x + 3x - 4 = 0$$

$$\Rightarrow \quad (3x-4)(3x+1) = 0$$

$$\therefore \quad x = \frac{4}{3} \text{ and } x = \frac{-1}{3} \text{ (rejected)}$$

Passage IV

(Ex. Nos. 86 to 87)

The method of eliminating 'θ' from two given equations involving trigonometrical functions of 'θ'. By using given equations involving 'θ' and trigonometrical identities, we shall obtain an equation not involving 'θ'.

On the basis of above information answer the following questions.

Example 86 *If $x\sin^3\theta + y\cos^3\theta = \sin\theta\cos\theta$ and $x\sin\theta - y\cos\theta = 0$ then (x, y) lie one*

(a) a circle (b) a parabola

(c) an ellipse (d) a hyperbola

Sol. (a) We have, $x\sin^3\theta + y\cos^3\theta = \sin\theta\cos\theta$ ...(i)

and $x\sin\theta - y\cos\theta = 0$ ...(ii)

From Eq. (ii), $\tan\theta = \frac{y}{x}$

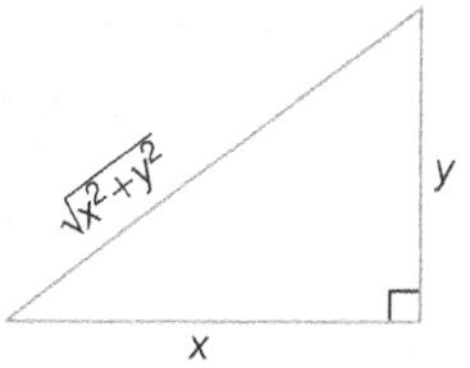

$\therefore \quad \sin\theta = \frac{y}{\sqrt{(x^2+y^2)}}$ and $\cos\theta = \frac{x}{\sqrt{(x^2+y^2)}}$

From Eq. (i), $x \times \frac{y^3}{(x^2+y^2)^{\frac{3}{2}}} + y \times \frac{x^3}{(x^2+y^2)^{\frac{3}{2}}} = \frac{xy}{(x^2+y^2)}$

or $\quad \frac{(x^2+y^2)}{(x^2+y^2)^{\frac{3}{2}}} = \frac{1}{(x^2+y^2)} \Rightarrow (x^2+y^2)^{\frac{1}{2}} = 1$

or $\quad x^2+y^2 = 1$, which is a circle

Example 87 *If* $\tan\theta + \sin\theta = m$ *and* $\tan\theta - \sin\theta = n$, *then* $(m^2-n^2)^2$ *is*

(a) $4\sqrt{mn}$ (b) $4mn$

(c) $16\sqrt{mn}$ (d) $16mn$

Sol. (*d*) $\because m+n = 2\tan\theta,\ m-n = 2\sin\theta$ ...(i)

and $\quad mn = \tan^2\theta - \sin^2\theta = \sin^2\theta(\sec^2\theta - 1)$

$= \sin^2\theta\tan^2\theta$

$= \left(\frac{m-n}{2}\right)^2\left(\frac{m+n}{2}\right)^2$ [from Eq. (i)]

$\therefore (m^2-n^2)^2 = 16\,mn$

Passage V

(Ex. Nos. 88 to 89)

Let $f(\theta) = 9\sin\theta - 12\cos\theta - 12\sin^3\theta + 16\cos^3\theta$, where $\theta \in R$.

Example 88 *Number of possible integral values of $f(\theta)$ is*

(a) 7 (b) 9

(c) 11 (d) 13

Sol. (c) $f(\theta) = 3[3\sin\theta - 4\sin^3\theta] + 4[4\cos^3\theta - 3\cos\theta]$

$f(\theta) = 3\sin 3\theta + 4\cos 3\theta$

Range $= [-5, 5]$

Hence, number of possible integral values of $f(\theta)$ is 11.

Example 89 $\left[f\left(\frac{\pi}{9}\right) - f\left(\frac{\pi}{18}\right)\right]\left[f\left(\frac{\pi}{9}\right) + f\left(\frac{\pi}{18}\right)\right]$ *is equal to*

(a) $\frac{7}{2}$ (b) $\frac{15}{2}$ (c) $\frac{21}{2}$ (d) $-\frac{7}{2}$

Sol. (d) $f(\theta) = 3\sin 3\theta + 4\cos 3\theta$

$$f\left(\frac{\pi}{9}\right) = 3\sin\frac{\pi}{3} + 4\cos\frac{\pi}{3} = 3\times\frac{\sqrt{3}}{2} + 4\times\frac{1}{2} = \frac{3\sqrt{3}}{2} + 2$$

$$f\left(\frac{\pi}{18}\right) = 3\sin\frac{\pi}{6} + 4\cos\frac{\pi}{6} = 3\times\frac{1}{2} + 4\times\frac{\sqrt{3}}{2} = \frac{3}{2} + 2\sqrt{3}$$

$$\left[f\left(\frac{\pi}{9}\right) - f\left(\frac{\pi}{18}\right)\right]\left[f\left(\frac{\pi}{9}\right) + f\left(\frac{\pi}{18}\right)\right] = \left(\frac{1-\sqrt{3}}{2}\right)\left(\frac{7\sqrt{3}}{2} + \frac{7}{2}\right)$$

$$= -\frac{7}{2}\times\frac{1}{2}(\sqrt{3}+1)(\sqrt{3}-1)$$

$$= -\frac{7}{4}\times 2$$

$$= -\frac{7}{2}$$

Stem Based Questions

Stem I

(Ex. Nos. 90 to 91)

Consider,

$$f_n(\theta) = \left(\tan\frac{\theta}{2}\right)(1+\sec\theta)(1+\sec 2\theta)\ ...(1+\sec 2^n\theta),$$

where n is a positive integer.

Example 90 *The value of* $f_4\left(\frac{\pi}{16}\right)$ *is ....*

Example 91 *The value of* $f_8\left(\frac{\pi}{1024}\right)$ *is ....*

Sol. (Ex. Nos. 90-91)

90. $\because \left(\tan\frac{\theta}{2}\right)(1+\sec\theta) = \left(\tan\frac{\theta}{2}\right)\left(\frac{1+\cos\theta}{\cos\theta}\right)$

$$= \frac{\sin\frac{\theta}{2}}{\cos\frac{\theta}{2}}\cdot\frac{2\cos^2\frac{\theta}{2}}{\cos\theta}$$

$$= \frac{2\sin\frac{\theta}{2}\cos\frac{\theta}{2}}{\cos\theta}$$

$$= \frac{\sin\theta}{\cos\theta} = \tan\theta \quad ...(i)$$

$\therefore$ By repeated use of Eq. (i), we have

$f_n(\theta) = (\tan\theta)(1+\sec 2\theta)(1+\sec 4\theta)(1+\sec 6\theta)$ ... $(1+\sec 2^n\theta)$

$= (\tan 2\theta)(1+\sec 4\theta)(1+\sec 6\theta)\ ...\ (1+\sec 2^n\theta)$

$= (\tan 4\theta)(1+\sec 6\theta)\ ...(1+\sec 2^n\theta)$

$= \ldots = (\tan 2^{n-1}\theta)(1+\sec 2^n\theta) = \tan 2^n\theta$

$\therefore \quad f_4\left(\frac{\pi}{16}\right) = \tan\left(2^4\cdot\frac{\pi}{16}\right) = \tan(\pi) = 0$

91. We know that $f_n(\theta) = \tan 2^n\theta$.

$$\therefore \quad f_8\left(\frac{\pi}{1024}\right) = \tan\left(2^8 \cdot \frac{\pi}{1024}\right)$$

$$= \tan\left(\frac{\pi}{4}\right) = 1$$

Ans. 90. 0   **91.** 1

Stem II

(Ex. Nos. 92 to 93)

Consider $\sin\alpha + \sin\beta = \frac{1}{4}$ and $\cos\alpha + \cos\beta = \frac{1}{3}$.

Example 92 *The value of* $25\sin(\alpha+\beta)$ *is ....*

Example 93 *The value of* $25\cos(\alpha+\beta)$ *is ....*

Sol. (Ex. Nos. 92-93)

92. Given, $\sin\alpha + \sin\beta = \frac{1}{4}$ ...(i)

and $\cos\alpha + \cos\beta = \frac{1}{3}$ ...(ii)

So, $2\sin\left(\frac{\alpha+\beta}{2}\right)\cos\left(\frac{\alpha-\beta}{2}\right) = \frac{1}{4}$ ...(iii)

and $2\cos\left(\frac{\alpha+\beta}{2}\right)\cos\left(\frac{\alpha-\beta}{2}\right) = \frac{1}{3}$ ...(iv)

On dividing Eq.(iii) by Eq. (iv), we get

$$\tan\left(\frac{\alpha+\beta}{2}\right) = \frac{3}{4}$$

$$\because \quad \sin(\alpha+\beta) = \frac{2\tan\left(\frac{\alpha+\beta}{2}\right)}{1+\tan^2\left(\frac{\alpha+\beta}{2}\right)}$$

$$\therefore \quad \sin(\alpha+\beta) = \frac{2\times\frac{3}{4}}{1+\left(\frac{3}{4}\right)^2} = \frac{24}{25}$$

$\therefore 25\sin(\alpha+\beta) = 24$

93. We know that $\tan\left(\frac{\alpha+\beta}{2}\right) = \frac{3}{4}$

$$\because \quad \cos(\alpha+\beta) = \frac{1-\tan^2\left(\frac{\alpha+\beta}{2}\right)}{1+\tan^2\left(\frac{\alpha+\beta}{2}\right)}$$

$$\therefore \quad \cos(\alpha+\beta) = \frac{1-\left(\frac{3}{4}\right)^2}{1+\left(\frac{3}{4}\right)^2}$$

$$= \frac{16-9}{16+9} = \frac{7}{25}$$

$\therefore 25\cos(\alpha+\beta) = 7$

Single Integer Answer Type Questions

Example 94 *Given that a, b, c are the sides of a ΔABC which is right angled at B, then the minimum value of* $\left(\frac{b}{a}+\frac{b}{c}\right)^2$ *is ....*

Sol. (8) Let the ΔABC be

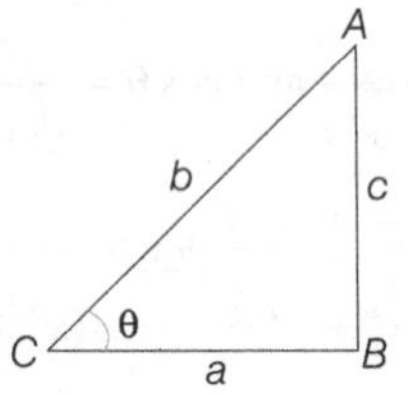

Now, $a = b\cos\theta$ and $c = b\sin\theta$,

where $\theta \in \left(0, \frac{\pi}{2}\right)$

$$\therefore \quad \left(\frac{b}{a}+\frac{b}{c}\right)^2 = \left(\frac{b}{b\cos\theta}+\frac{b}{b\sin\theta}\right)^2$$

$$= \left(\frac{1}{\cos\theta}+\frac{1}{\sin\theta}\right)^2$$

$$= \frac{\sin^2\theta+\cos^2\theta+2\sin\theta\cos\theta}{(\sin\theta\cos\theta)^2}$$

$$= \frac{4(1+\sin 2\theta)}{\sin^2 2\theta} = 4\left(\frac{1}{\sin^2 2\theta}+\frac{1}{\sin 2\theta}\right)$$

The minimum value of $\frac{1}{\sin^2 2\theta}+\frac{1}{\sin 2\theta}$ occurs at $\theta = \frac{\pi}{4}$.

$$\therefore \quad \left(\frac{b}{a}+\frac{b}{c}\right)^2_{\min} = 4\left(\frac{1}{\sin^2\frac{\pi}{2}}+\frac{1}{\sin\frac{\pi}{2}}\right) = 4(1+1) = 8$$

Example 95 $\tan 46°\tan 14° - \tan 74°\tan 14° + \tan 74°\tan 46°$ *is equal to*

Sol. (3) $\frac{\tan 46° + \tan 14°}{1-\tan 46°\tan 14°} = \tan(46°+14°) = \sqrt{3}$ ...(i)

$\frac{\tan 74° - \tan 14°}{1+\tan 74°\tan 14°} = \tan(74°-14°) = \sqrt{3}$ ...(ii)

$\frac{\tan 74° + \tan 46°}{1-\tan 74°\tan 46°} = \tan(74°+46°) = -\sqrt{3}$ ...(iii)

From Eqs. (i), (ii) and (iii), we get

$$\tan 46°\tan 14° = 1 - \frac{\tan 46° + \tan 14°}{\sqrt{3}}$$

$$\tan 74°\tan 14° = \frac{\tan 74° - \tan 14°}{\sqrt{3}} - 1$$

$$\tan 74°\tan 46° = 1 - \frac{\tan 74° + \tan 46°}{-\sqrt{3}}$$

$\therefore \tan 46°\tan 14° - \tan 74°\tan 14° + \tan 74°\tan 46° = 3$

Example 96 *Let* $f(x)=\dfrac{\sin^3 x}{1-\cos x}+\dfrac{\cos^3 x}{1+\sin x}, x\in\left(0,\dfrac{\pi}{2}\right)$. *If maximum value of* $f(x)$ *is* k, *then value of* k^2 *is*

Sol. (2) $f(x)=\dfrac{\sin x(1-\cos^2 x)}{1-\cos x}+\dfrac{\cos x(1-\sin^2 x)}{1+\sin x}$

$$f(x)=\sin x(1+\cos x)+\cos x(1-\sin x)$$
$$f(x)=\sin x+\cos x$$

Maximum value $k=\sqrt{2}$

Hence, $k^2=2$

Example 97 *Maximum value of the expression* $\log_3(9-2\cos^2\theta-4\sec^2\theta)$ *is equal to*

Sol. (1) $\log_3(9-2\cos^2\theta-4\sec^2\theta)$

$$=\log_3[9-2(\cos^2\theta+2\sec^2\theta)]$$

To get the maximum value of expression $\cos^2\theta+2\sec^2\theta$ should be minimum.

$$\cos^2\theta+2\sec^2\theta=\cos^2\theta+\sec^2\theta+\sec^2\theta$$
$$\cos^2\theta+\sec^2\theta\geq 2 \text{ and } \sec^2\theta\geq 1$$

So, $(\cos^2\theta+2\sec^2\theta)_{\min}=2+1=3$

$\log_3(9-2\times 3)=\log_3 3=1$

Hence, maximum value of expression is 1.

Example 98 *Let* $x\in\left(0,\dfrac{\pi}{2}\right)$ *and* $\log_{24\sin x}(24\cos x)=\dfrac{3}{2}$, *then find the value of* $\operatorname{cosec}^2 x$.

Sol. (9) $(24\sin x)^{3/2}=24\cos x$

$$\Rightarrow \sqrt{24}(\sin x)^{3/2}=\cos x$$
$$\Rightarrow 24\sin^3 x=\cos^2 x=1-\sin^2 x$$

Put $\sin x=t$, we get

$$24t^3+t^2-1=0$$
$$\Rightarrow (3t-1)\underbrace{(8t^2+3t+1)}_{>0}=0$$
$$\Rightarrow t=\frac{1}{3}$$
$$\therefore t=\frac{1}{3} \text{ i.e. } \sin x=\frac{1}{3}$$
$$\Rightarrow \operatorname{cosec} x=3$$
$$\Rightarrow \operatorname{cosec}^2 x=9$$

Example 99 *If* x *and* y *are non-zero real numbers satisfying* $xy(x^2-y^2)=x^2+y^2$, *then find the minimum value of* x^2+y^2.

Sol. (4) Put $x=r\cos\theta$ and $y=r\sin\theta$

Hence, we have to minimise r^2?

Now, $r^2\cos\theta\sin\theta r^2(\cos^2\theta-\sin^2\theta)=r^2$

$$r^2\sin 2\theta\cos 2\theta=2$$
$$\Rightarrow r^2\frac{\sin 4\theta}{4}=1$$
$$\Rightarrow r^2=\frac{4}{\sin 4\theta}$$
$$\Rightarrow r^2=4\operatorname{cosec}^2 4\theta$$
$$\therefore r^2_{\min}=4$$

Example 100 *Using the identity* $\sin^4 x=\dfrac{3}{8}-\dfrac{1}{2}\cos 2x+\dfrac{1}{8}\cos 4x$ *or otherwise, if the value of* $\sin^4\left(\dfrac{\pi}{7}\right)+\sin^4\left(\dfrac{3\pi}{7}\right)+\sin^4\left(\dfrac{5\pi}{7}\right)=\dfrac{a}{b}$, *where* a *and* b *are coprime, find the value of* $(a-b)$.

Sol. (5) $\sin^4\left(\dfrac{\pi}{7}\right)=\dfrac{3}{8}-\dfrac{1}{2}\cos\left(\dfrac{2\pi}{7}\right)+\dfrac{1}{8}\cos\left(\dfrac{4\pi}{7}\right)$ ...(i)

and $\sin^4\left(\dfrac{3\pi}{7}\right)=\dfrac{3}{8}-\dfrac{1}{2}\cos\left(\dfrac{6\pi}{7}\right)+\dfrac{1}{8}\cos\left(\dfrac{12\pi}{7}\right)$

or $\sin^4\left(\dfrac{3\pi}{7}\right)=\dfrac{3}{8}+\dfrac{1}{2}\cos\left(\dfrac{\pi}{7}\right)-\dfrac{1}{8}\cos\left(\dfrac{5\pi}{7}\right)$ ...(ii)

Similarly, $\sin^4\left(\dfrac{5\pi}{7}\right)=\dfrac{3}{8}-\dfrac{1}{2}\cos\left(\dfrac{10\pi}{7}\right)+\dfrac{1}{8}\cos\left(\dfrac{20\pi}{7}\right)$

or $\sin^4\left(\dfrac{5\pi}{7}\right)=\dfrac{3}{8}+\dfrac{1}{2}\cos\left(\dfrac{3\pi}{7}\right)-\dfrac{1}{8}\cos\left(\dfrac{\pi}{7}\right)$ ...(iii)

On adding Eqs. (i), (ii) and (iii), we get

$$\sin^4\left(\frac{\pi}{7}\right)+\sin^4\left(\frac{3\pi}{7}\right)+\sin^4\left(\frac{5\pi}{7}\right)$$
$$=\frac{9}{8}+\frac{1}{2}\cos\left(\frac{5\pi}{7}\right)-\frac{1}{8}\cos\left(\frac{3\pi}{7}\right)+\frac{1}{2}\cos\left(\frac{\pi}{7}\right)-\frac{1}{8}\cos\left(\frac{5\pi}{7}\right)+\frac{1}{2}\cos\left(\frac{3\pi}{7}\right)-\frac{1}{8}\cos\left(\frac{\pi}{7}\right)$$
$$=\frac{9}{8}+\frac{3}{8}\underbrace{\left[\cos\left(\frac{\pi}{7}\right)+\cos\left(\frac{3\pi}{7}\right)+\cos\left(\frac{5\pi}{7}\right)\right]}_{\frac{1}{2}\left(\text{use } S=\frac{\sin\frac{n\alpha}{2}}{\sin\frac{\alpha}{2}}\cos\left(\frac{\theta_1+\theta_2}{2}\right)\right)}$$
$$=\frac{9}{8}+\frac{3}{16}$$
$$=\frac{21}{16}$$

$\therefore\ a-b=21-16=5.$

Example 101 *In any triangle, if* $(\sin A+\sin B+\sin C)(\sin A+\sin B-\sin C)=3\sin A\sin B$, *then the angle* $\frac{C}{10}$ *(in degree).*

Sol. (6) We have, $(\sin A+\sin B)^2-\sin^2 C=3\sin A\sin B$

$$\sin^2 A-\sin^2 C+\sin^2 B=\sin A\sin B$$
$$\sin(A+C)\sin(A-C)+\sin^2 B=\sin A\sin B$$
$$\sin B[\sin(A-C)+\sin(A+C)]=\sin A\sin B$$
[using $\sin(A+C)=\sin B$]
$$2\sin A\cos C=\sin A \quad [\sin B\neq 0]$$
$$\cos C=\frac{1}{2}\Rightarrow \frac{C}{10}=\frac{60^\circ}{10}=6^\circ$$

Example 102 *Find the exact value of the expression*

$$T=\frac{\sin 40^\circ}{\sin 80^\circ}+\frac{\sin 80^\circ}{\sin 20^\circ}-\frac{\sin 20^\circ}{\sin 40^\circ}$$

Sol. (3) We have, $\frac{1}{2\cos 40^\circ}+4\cos 40^\circ\cdot\cos 20^\circ-\frac{1}{2\cos 20^\circ}$

$$=\frac{1}{2}\left[\frac{1}{\cos 40^\circ}-\frac{1}{\cos 20^\circ}\right]+2(\cos 60^\circ+\cos 20^\circ)$$
$$=\frac{1}{2}\left[\frac{\cos 20^\circ-\cos 40^\circ}{\cos 40^\circ\cos 20^\circ}\right]+1+2\cos 20^\circ$$
$$=\frac{2\sin 30^\circ\sin 10^\circ}{2\cos 40^\circ\cos 20^\circ}+1+2\cos 20^\circ$$
$$=\frac{2\sin 10^\circ\sin 20^\circ}{\sin 80^\circ}+1+2\cos 20^\circ$$
$$=\frac{2\sin 10^\circ\, 2\sin 10^\circ\cos 10^\circ}{\cos 10^\circ}+2\cos 20^\circ+1$$
$$=2(1-\cos 20^\circ)+2\cos 20^\circ+1=3$$

Alternate Solution

$$T_1=\frac{2\sin 20^\circ\cos 20^\circ}{\cos 10^\circ}=2\cdot 2\cdot\sin 10^\circ\cdot\cos 20^\circ$$
$$=2(\sin 30^\circ-\sin 10^\circ)$$
$$T_1=1-2\sin 10^\circ$$
$$T_2=\frac{\sin 80^\circ}{\sin 20^\circ}=\frac{2\sin 40^\circ\cos 40^\circ}{\sin 20^\circ}=4\cos 20^\circ\cdot\cos 40^\circ$$
$$T_2=2[\cos 60^\circ+\cos 20^\circ]=1+2\cos 20^\circ$$
$$T_2=\frac{\sin 20^\circ}{\sin 40^\circ}=\frac{1}{2\cos 20^\circ}$$
$$\therefore\quad T=T_1+T_2+T_3$$
$$=(1-2\sin 10^\circ)+(1+2\cos 20^\circ)-\frac{1}{2\cos 20^\circ}$$
$$=2+2(\cos 20^\circ-\sin 10^\circ)-\frac{1}{2\cos 20^\circ}$$
$$=2+2(\cos 20^\circ-\cos 80^\circ)-\frac{1}{2\cos 20^\circ}$$
$$=2+2\cdot 2\sin 50^\circ\cdot\sin 30^\circ-\frac{1}{2\cos 20^\circ}$$
$$=2+2\sin 50^\circ-\frac{1}{2\cos 20^\circ}$$
$$T=2+\frac{4\sin 50^\circ\cos 20^\circ-1}{2\cos 20^\circ}=2+\frac{2[\sin 70^\circ+\sin 30^\circ]-1}{2\cos 20^\circ}$$
$$=2+\frac{2\sin 70^\circ}{2\cos 20^\circ}=2+1=3$$

Example 103 *If* $\cot(\theta-\alpha), 3\cot\theta, \cot(\theta+\alpha)$ *are in* AP *(where,* $\theta\neq\frac{n\pi}{2}, \alpha\neq k\pi, n, k\in I$*), then* $\frac{2\sin^2\theta}{\sin^2\alpha}$ *is equal to*

Sol. (3) We have, $6\cot\theta=\cot(\theta-\alpha)+\cot(\theta+\alpha)$

$$\Rightarrow\quad \frac{6\cos\theta}{\sin\theta}=\frac{\sin 2\theta}{\sin(\theta-\alpha)\sin(\theta+\alpha)}$$
$$\Rightarrow\quad \frac{6\cos\theta}{\sin\theta}=\frac{2\sin\theta\cos\theta}{\sin^2\theta-\sin^2\alpha}$$
$$\Rightarrow\quad 3(\sin^2\theta-\sin^2\alpha)=\sin^2\theta$$
$$\text{or}\quad 2\sin^2\theta=3\sin^2\alpha$$
$$\Rightarrow\quad \frac{2\sin^2\theta}{\sin^2\alpha}=3$$

Example 104 *If* $4\sin^2 x+\operatorname{cosec}^2 x, a, \sin^2 y+4\operatorname{cosec}^2 y$ *are in* AP, *then minimum value of* $(2a)$ *is*

Sol. (9) $2a=4\sin^2 x+\operatorname{cosec}^2 x+\sin^2 y+4\operatorname{cosec}^2 y$

$$=(2\sin x-\operatorname{cosec} x)^2+4+(\sin y-\operatorname{cosec} y)^2+3\operatorname{cosec}^2 y+2$$
$$=6+(2\sin x-\operatorname{cosec} x)^2+(\sin y-\operatorname{cosec} y)^2+3\operatorname{cosec}^2 y$$

$\therefore$ Minimum value of $2a=6+3=9$,

when $2\sin x=\operatorname{cosec} x$ and $\sin y=\operatorname{cosec} y$

Example 105 *If* $\sin\alpha, \sin\beta, \sin\gamma$ *are in* AP *and* $\cos\alpha, \cos\beta, \cos\gamma$ *are in* GP, *then the value of*

$$\frac{\cos^2\alpha+\cos^2\gamma+4\cos\alpha\cos\gamma-2\sin\alpha\sin\gamma-2}{1-2\sin^2\beta},$$

where $\beta\neq\frac{\pi}{4}$, *is equal to ....*

Decoding the Question

We know that if three numbers a, b and c are in AP, then $2b=a+c$ and if a, b and c are in GP, then $b^2=ac$.

Sol. (4) Now, $\sin\alpha+\sin\gamma=2\sin\beta$ and $\cos^2\beta=\cos\alpha.\cos\gamma$

$$=\frac{\cos^2\alpha+\cos^2\gamma+4\cos\alpha\cos\gamma-2-2\sin\alpha\sin\gamma}{1-2\sin^2\beta}$$
$$=\frac{-\sin^2\alpha-\sin^2\gamma-2\sin\alpha\sin\gamma+4\cos\alpha\cos\gamma}{1-2\sin^2\beta}$$
$$=\frac{-(\sin\alpha+\sin\gamma)^2+4\cos\alpha\cos\gamma}{1-2\sin^2\beta}=\frac{-4\sin^2\beta+4\cos^2\beta}{\cos 2\beta}=4$$

Example 106 *Let*

$$\prod_{r=1}^{51}\tan\left(\frac{\pi}{3}\left(1+\frac{3^r}{3^{50}-1}\right)\right)=k\prod_{r=1}^{51}\cot\left[\frac{\pi}{3}\left(1-\frac{3^r}{3^{50}-1}\right)\right]$$

On solving equation, we get, $1-3\tan^2\left(\frac{\pi}{3^{50}-1}\right)=\frac{a}{bk-1}$, *(a, b* $\in I$*), then value of* $(a-b)$ *is equal to ....*

Sol. (5) We have,

$$\prod_{r=1}^{51} \tan\left(\frac{\pi}{3}\left(1+\frac{3^r}{3^{50}-1}\right)\right) = \prod_{r=1}^{51} \cot\left[\frac{\pi}{3}\left(1-\frac{3^r}{3^{50}-1}\right)\right]$$

Let $\frac{3^{r-1}\pi}{3^{50}-1} = \theta_r$

$$\prod_{r=1}^{51} \tan\left(\frac{\pi}{3}+\theta_r\right)\tan\left(\frac{\pi}{3}+\theta_r\right) = k$$

$$\prod_{r=1}^{51} \frac{\tan 3\theta_r}{\tan\theta^r} = k$$

$$k = \frac{\tan\theta_2}{\tan\theta_1} \times \frac{\tan\theta_3}{\tan\theta_2} \times \ldots \times \frac{\tan\theta_{52}}{\tan\theta_{51}} = \frac{\tan\theta_{52}}{\tan\theta} = \frac{\tan\left(\frac{3^{51}\pi}{3^{50}-1}\right)}{\tan\left(\frac{\pi}{3^{50}-1}\right)}$$

$$= \frac{\tan\left(3\pi + \frac{3\pi}{3^{50}-1}\right)}{\tan\left(\frac{\pi}{3^{50}-1}\right)} = \frac{\tan\left(\frac{3\pi}{3^{50}-1}\right)}{\tan\left(\frac{\pi}{3^{50}-1}\right)}$$

Let $\alpha = \frac{\pi}{3^{50}-1}$; $k = \frac{\tan 3\alpha}{\tan\alpha}$;

$$1 - 3\tan^2\alpha = \frac{8}{3k-1}$$

So, $a = 8$, $b = 3$ and $a - b = 5$

Numerical Value Type Questions

Example 107 *If* $\sec A \tan B + \tan A \sec B = 91$*, then the value of* $(\sec A \sec B + \tan A \tan B)^2$ *is equal to*

Sol. (8282) $(\sec A \sec B + \tan A \tan B)^2 - (\sec A \tan B + \tan A \sec B)^2$

$$= \left[\frac{1+\sin A \sin B}{\cos A \cos B}\right]^2 - \left[\frac{\sin B + \sin A}{\cos A \cos B}\right]^2$$

$$= \frac{1 + \sin^2 A \sin^2 B - \sin^2 B - \sin^2 A}{\cos^2 A \cos^2 B}$$

$$= \frac{1 - \sin^2 B \cos^2 A - \sin^2 A}{\cos^2 A \cos^2 B} = \frac{\cos^2 A \cos^2 B}{\cos^2 A \cos^2 B}$$

$$= 1$$

$\Rightarrow (\sec A \sec B + \tan A \tan B)^2 = (91)^2 + 1 = 8282$

Example 108 *If* $(25)^2 + a^2 + 50a\cos\theta = (31)^2 + b^2 + 62b\cos\theta = 1$ *and* $775 + ab + (31a + 25b)\cos\theta = 0$*, then the value of* $\text{cosec}^2\theta$ *is ....*

Sol. (1586) We can write $(a + 25\cos\theta)^2 + (25)^2 - (25\cos\theta)^2 = 1$

$\Rightarrow \quad (a + 25\cos\theta)^2 = 1 - (25\sin\theta)^2$

Similarly $\quad (b + 31\cos\theta)^2 = 1 - (31\sin\theta)^2$

On multiplying, we get

$[(a + 25\cos\theta)(b + 31\cos\theta)]^2 = [1 - (25\sin\theta)^2][1 - (31\sin\theta)^2]$

$\Rightarrow [ab + (31a + 25b)\cos\theta + 775\cos^2\theta]^2$

$= 1 - (625 + 961)\sin^2\theta + (775\sin^2\theta)^2$

$\Rightarrow (-775 + 775\cos^2\theta)^2 = 1 - 1586\sin^2\theta + (775\sin^2\theta)^2$

$\Rightarrow \quad \text{cosec}^2\theta = 1586$

Example 109 *If* $\sin x_1 + \sin x_2 + \sin x_3 + \ldots + \sin x_{2024} = 2024$*, then find the value of* $\sin^{2024} x_1 + \sin^{2024} x_2 + \sin^{2024} x_3 + \ldots + \sin^{2024} x_{2024}$.

Sol. (2024) We know that $\sin x_i \le 1 \ \forall\ i$

$\Rightarrow \sin x_1 + \sin x_2 + \sin x_3 + \ldots + \sin x_{2024} \le 2024$

Thus, equality holds only when each of the terms is 1

i.e. $\sin x_i = 1 \ \forall\ i = 1, 2, 3, \ldots, 2024$.

and consequently

$$\cos x_i = 0, \forall i = 1,2,3, \ldots, 2024$$

Now, $\sin^{2024} x_1 + \sin^{2024} x_2 + \sin^{2024} x_3 + \ldots \sin^{2024} x_{2024}$

$= 1 + 1 + 1 + \ldots + 1$

$= 2024$

Example 110 *If* $4\sin 27° = \sqrt{\alpha} + \sqrt{\beta}$*, then the value of* $(\alpha + \beta - \alpha\beta + 2)^4$ *must be ....*

Sol. (400), We know $(\cos 27° + \sin 27°)^2 = 1 + \sin 54° = 1 + \cos 36°$

$\Rightarrow \quad \cos 27° + \sin 27° = \sqrt{(1 + \cos 36°)} \quad [\because \text{LHS} > 0]$

Also, $\quad \cos 27° - \sin 27° = \sqrt{(1 - \cos 36°)}$

$[\because \cos 27° > \sin 27°]$

$\therefore \quad 2\sin 27° = \sqrt{(1 + \cos 36°)} - \sqrt{(1 - \cos 36°)}$

$$= \sqrt{\left(1 + \left(\frac{\sqrt{5}+1}{4}\right)\right)} - \sqrt{\left(1 - \left(\frac{\sqrt{5}+1}{4}\right)\right)}$$

$\therefore \quad 4\sin 27° = \sqrt{(5 + \sqrt{5})} - \sqrt{(3 - \sqrt{5})}$

On comparing, we get

$$\alpha = 5 + \sqrt{5}, \beta = 3 - \sqrt{5}$$

$\therefore \quad \alpha + \beta = 8, \alpha\beta = 10 - 2\sqrt{5}$

$\alpha + \beta - \alpha\beta + 2 = 2\sqrt{5}$

$\therefore (\alpha + \beta - \alpha\beta + 2)^4 = 400$

Example 111 *If* $0 < A < \frac{\pi}{2}$ *and* $\sin A + \cos A + \tan A + \cot A + \sec A + \text{cosec}\, A = 7$ *and* $\sin A$ *and* $\cos A$ *are the roots of the equation* $4x^2 - 3x + a = 0$*, then the value of* $25a$ *must be ....*

Sol. (28) $\sin A$ and $\cos A$ are the roots of the equation $4x^2 - 3x + a = 0$, then

$$\sin A + \cos A = \frac{3}{4}, \sin A \cos A = \frac{a}{4} \quad \ldots(i)$$

Also, $\sin A + \cos A + \tan A + \cot A + \sec A + \operatorname{cosec} A = 7$

$$\Rightarrow (\sin A + \cos A) + \left(\frac{\sin A}{\cos A} + \frac{\cos A}{\sin A}\right) + \left(\frac{1}{\cos A} + \frac{1}{\sin A}\right) = 7$$

$$\Rightarrow \quad (\sin A + \cos A) + \frac{1}{\sin A \cos A} + \frac{(\sin A + \cos A)}{\sin A \cos A} = 7$$

$$\Rightarrow \quad \frac{3}{4} + \frac{4}{a} + \frac{3}{a} = 7$$

$$\Rightarrow \quad \frac{3}{4} + \frac{7}{a} = 7$$

$$\Rightarrow \quad \frac{7}{a} = 7 - \frac{3}{4} = \frac{25}{4}$$

$$\therefore \quad 25a = 28$$

Example 112 *If the value of* $(\sin^2 65° - \sin^2 25°)$ $(\cos^2 35° - \sin^2 35°)(\cos^2 5° - \cos^2 85°)$ *is of the form* $\frac{\sqrt{p}}{q}$, *where p and q are coprime numbers. Then, the value of* $p + q$ *is*

Sol. (11) $\sin(65° + 25°)\sin(65° - 25°)\cos(35° + 35°)\cos(35° - 35°)$ $\sin(5° + 85°)\sin(5° - 85°)$

$$= \sin 90° \sin 40° \cos 70° \sin 90° \sin 80°$$

$$= \sin 40° \cos 70° \sin 80°$$

$$= \sin(60° - 20°)\sin(60° + 20°)\sin 20°$$

$$= \frac{1}{4}\sin 60° = \frac{\sqrt{3}}{8} = \frac{\sqrt{p}}{q}$$

So, $\quad p = 3, q = 8$

$\Rightarrow p + q = 3 + 8 = 11$

Example 113 *Given that* $f(n\theta) = \frac{2\sin 2\theta}{\cos 2\theta - \cos 4n\theta}$ *and* $f(\theta) + f(2\theta) + f(3\theta) + \ldots + f(n\theta) = \frac{\sin \lambda\theta}{\sin\theta \sin\mu\theta}$, *then the value of* $100(\mu - \lambda)$ *is*

Sol. (100) $\quad f(n\theta) = \frac{2\sin 2\theta}{\cos 2\theta - \cos 4n\theta}$

$$= \frac{2\sin 2\theta}{2\sin(2n+1)\theta \sin(2n-1)\theta}$$

$$= \frac{\sin((2n+1)\theta - (2n-1)\theta)}{\sin(2n+1)\theta \sin(2n-1)\theta}$$

$$= \frac{\sin(2n+1)\theta\cos(2n-1)\theta - \cos(2n+1)\theta\sin(2n-1)\theta}{\sin(2n+1)\theta\sin(2n-1)\theta}$$

$$= \cot(2n-1)\theta - \cot(2n+1)\theta$$

$\therefore f(\theta) + f(2\theta) + f(3\theta) + \ldots + f(n\theta)$

$$= \cot\theta - \cot(2n+1)\theta$$

$$= \frac{\sin(2n+1)\theta\cos\theta - \cos(2n+1)\theta\sin\theta}{\sin(2n+1)\theta\sin\theta}$$

$$= \frac{\sin 2n\theta}{\sin(2n+1)\theta\sin\theta}$$

$\therefore \quad \lambda = 2n$ and $\mu = 2n + 1$

Hence, $100(\mu - \lambda) = 100(2n + 1 - 2n)$

$= 100$

Example 114 *If* $\frac{1}{\cos 290°} + \frac{1}{\sqrt{3}\sin 250°} = \lambda$, *then the value of* $9\lambda^4 + 81\lambda^2 + 97$ *must be*

Sol. (785) Here, $\cos 290° = \cos(270° + 20°) = \sin 20°$ and $\sin 250° = \sin(270° - 20°) = -\cos 20°$

$\therefore$ The given expression $= \frac{1}{\sin 20°} - \frac{1}{\sqrt{3}\cos 120°} = \lambda$

$$\Rightarrow \quad \frac{1}{\sin 20°} - \frac{\cos 60°}{\sin 60° \cos 20°} = \lambda$$

$$\Rightarrow \quad \frac{\sin 60°\cos 20° - \cos 60°\sin 20°}{\sin 20°\cos 20°\sin 60°} = \lambda$$

$$\Rightarrow \quad \frac{\sin(60° - 20°)}{\frac{\sin 40°}{2} \times \frac{\sqrt{3}}{2}} = \lambda$$

$$\therefore \quad \lambda = \frac{4}{\sqrt{3}}$$

$$\Rightarrow \quad \lambda^2 = \frac{16}{3}$$

Then, $9\lambda^4 + 81\lambda^2 + 97 = 9 \times \frac{256}{9} + 81 \times \frac{16}{3} + 97$

$$= 256 + 432 + 97 = 785$$

Example 115 *If* $\log_{10}\sin x + \log_{10}\cos x = -1$ *and* $\log_{10}(\sin x + \cos x) = \frac{(\log_{10} n) - 1}{2}$, *then the value of n is ....*

Sol. (12) Given, $\log_{10}\left(\frac{\sin 2x}{2}\right) = -1$

$$\Rightarrow \quad \frac{\sin 2x}{2} = \frac{1}{10}$$

$$\Rightarrow \quad \sin 2x = \frac{1}{5}$$

Also, $\log_{10}(\sin x + \cos x) = \frac{\log_{10}\left(\frac{n}{10}\right)}{2}$

$$\Rightarrow \quad \log_{10}(\sin x + \cos x)^2 = \log_{10}\left(\frac{n}{10}\right)$$

$$\Rightarrow \quad 1 + \sin 2x = \frac{n}{10}$$

$$\Rightarrow \quad 1 + \frac{1}{5} = \frac{n}{10}$$

$$\Rightarrow \quad \frac{6}{5} = \frac{n}{10} \Rightarrow n = 12$$

Example 116 *If* $498[16\cos x + 12\sin x] = 2k + 60$, *then the maximum value of k is*

Sol. (4950) $16\cos x + 12\sin x = \sqrt{16^2 + 12^2}\cos(x - \alpha)$,

$$\alpha = \tan^{-1}\left(\frac{3}{4}\right)$$

$$\Rightarrow |2k + 60| \le 498 \times 20 \text{ as } |\cos(x - \alpha)| \le 1 \Rightarrow k \le 4950$$

Example 117 *If* $a\tan\alpha + \sqrt{(a^2 - 1)}\tan\beta + \sqrt{(a^2 + 1)}\tan\gamma = 2a$, *where 'a' is constant and* α, β, γ *are variable angles, then the least value of* $2727(\tan^2\alpha + \tan^2\beta + \tan^2\gamma)$ *must be*

Sol. (3636) We have,

$$(a\tan\beta - \sqrt{(a^2-1)}\tan\alpha)^2 + (\sqrt{(a^2-1)}\tan\gamma - \sqrt{(a^2+1)}\tan\beta)^2 + (\sqrt{(a^2+1)}\tan\alpha - a\tan\gamma)^2 \ge 0$$

$$\Rightarrow (a^2 + a^2 - 1 + a^2 + 1)(\tan^2\alpha + \tan^2\beta + \tan^2\gamma) - \{a\tan\alpha + \sqrt{(a^2-1)}\tan\beta + \sqrt{(a^2+1)}\tan\gamma\}^2 \ge 0$$

(using Lagrange's identity)

$$\Rightarrow 3a^2(\tan^2\alpha + \tan^2\beta + \tan^2\gamma) - (2a)^2 \ge 0$$

$$\therefore \quad 3(\tan^2\alpha + \tan^2\beta + \tan^2\gamma) \ge 4$$

Hence, $2727(\tan^2\alpha + \tan^2\beta + \tan^2\gamma) \ge 3636$

$\therefore$ Least value is 3636.

Example 118 *If* $\log_2(\cos x) = \log_4(\sin x)$, *then the value of* $(50\cos^2 x + 100\cos^4 x + 100\cos^6 x + 50\cos^8 x)$ *is*

Sol. (100) $\log_2 \cos x + \log_{2^2}(\sin x) = \frac{1}{2}\log_2 \sin x$

$$\Rightarrow \quad 2\log_2 \cos x = \log_2 \sin x$$

$$\Rightarrow \quad \log_2 \cos^2 x = \log_2 \sin x$$

$$\Rightarrow \quad \cos^2 x = \sin x$$

$$\Rightarrow \quad \cos^4 x = \sin^2 x = 1 - \cos^2 x$$

$$\Rightarrow \quad \cos^4 x + \cos^2 x = 1$$

$$= 50\cos^2 x + 50\cos^4 x + 50\cos^4 x + 50\cos^6 x + 50\cos^6 x + 50\cos^8 x$$

$$= 50[(\cos^2 x + \cos^4 x) + \cos^2 x(\cos^2 x + \cos^4 x) + \cos^4 x(\cos^2 x + \cos^4 x)]$$

$$= 50[1 + \cos^2 x + \cos^4 x] = 50[1 + 1] = 100$$

Example 119 *The value of* $4\cos 15^\circ \cos 45^\circ \cos 75^\circ$ *is equal to*

Sol. (0.707) $4\cos 15^\circ \cos 45^\circ \cos 75^\circ$

$$= 4\cos 15^\circ \cos(60^\circ - 15^\circ)\cos(60^\circ + 15^\circ)$$

$$= 4 \times \frac{1}{4}\cos 45^\circ = \frac{1}{\sqrt{2}} = 0.707$$

Example 120 *If* $\frac{\tan x}{2} = \frac{\tan y}{3} = \frac{\tan z}{5}$, $x + y + z = \pi$ *and* $\tan^2 x + \tan^2 y + \tan^2 z = \frac{76}{K}$, *then* $K = \ldots$

Sol. (6) $\tan x = 2t$, $\tan y = 3t$, $\tan z = 5t$

Also, $\quad x + y + z = \pi$

$\therefore \tan x + \tan y + \tan z = \tan x \tan y \tan z$

$$\Rightarrow \quad t^2 = \frac{1}{3}$$

$$\Rightarrow \tan^2 x + \tan^2 y + \tan^2 z = t^2(4 + 9 + 25) = 38t^2,$$

$$\therefore \quad K = 6$$

Example 121 *If* $\tan\left(\frac{3\pi}{11}\right) + 4\sin\left(\frac{2\pi}{11}\right) = \lambda$, *then the value of* $1 + \lambda^2 + \lambda^4 + \lambda^6$ *must be*

Sol. (1464) Let $\lambda = \tan\left(\frac{3\pi}{11}\right) + 4\sin\left(\frac{2\pi}{11}\right)$

$$= \frac{1}{\cos\left(\frac{3\pi}{11}\right)}\left\{\sin\left(\frac{3\pi}{11}\right) + 4\sin\left(\frac{2\pi}{11}\right)\cos\left(\frac{3\pi}{11}\right)\right\}$$

$$\lambda\cos\left(\frac{3\pi}{11}\right) = \sin\left(\frac{3\pi}{11}\right) + 4\sin\left(\frac{2\pi}{11}\right)\cos\left(\frac{3\pi}{11}\right)$$

$$\lambda^2\cos^2\left(\frac{3\pi}{11}\right) = \sin^2\left(\frac{3\pi}{11}\right) + 16\sin^2\left(\frac{2\pi}{11}\right)\cos^2\left(\frac{3\pi}{11}\right) + 8\sin\left(\frac{2\pi}{11}\right)\sin\left(\frac{3\pi}{11}\right)\cos\left(\frac{3\pi}{11}\right)$$

$$\lambda^2\left(2\cos^2\left(\frac{3\pi}{11}\right)\right) = 2\sin^2\left(\frac{3\pi}{11}\right) + 32\sin^2\left(\frac{2\pi}{11}\right)\cos^2\left(\frac{3\pi}{11}\right) + 8\sin\left(\frac{2\pi}{11}\right)\sin\left(\frac{6\pi}{11}\right)$$

$$= \left(1 - \cos\left(\frac{6\pi}{11}\right)\right) + 8\left(1 - \cos\frac{4\pi}{11}\right)\left(1 + \cos\frac{6\pi}{11}\right) + 4\left(\cos\frac{4\pi}{11} - \cos\frac{8\pi}{11}\right)$$

$$= 9 + 7\cos\left(\frac{6\pi}{11}\right) - 4\cos\left(\frac{4\pi}{11}\right) - 8\cos\left(\frac{4\pi}{11}\right)\cos\left(\frac{6\pi}{11}\right) - 4\cos\left(\frac{8\pi}{11}\right)$$

$$= 9 + 7\cos\left(\frac{6\pi}{11}\right) - 4\cos\left(\frac{4\pi}{11}\right) - 4\left(\cos\left(\frac{10x}{11}\right) + \cos\left(\frac{2\pi}{11}\right)\right) - 4\cos\left(\frac{8\pi}{11}\right)$$

$$= 9 + 11\cos\left(\frac{6\pi}{11}\right) - 4\left\{\cos\left(\frac{2\pi}{11}\right) + \cos\left(\frac{4\pi}{11}\right) + \cos\left(\frac{6\pi}{11}\right) + \cos\left(\frac{8\pi}{11}\right) + \cos\left(\frac{10\pi}{11}\right)\right\}$$

$$= 9 + 11\cos\left(\frac{6\pi}{11}\right) - \frac{4\cdot\cos\left(\frac{6\pi}{11}\right)\sin\left(\frac{5\pi}{11}\right)}{\sin\left(\frac{\pi}{11}\right)}$$

$$= 9 + 11\cos\left(\frac{6\pi}{11}\right) - \frac{2\left\{\sin\pi - \sin\left(\frac{\pi}{11}\right)\right\}}{\sin\left(\frac{\pi}{11}\right)}$$

$$= 9 + 11\cos\left(\frac{6\pi}{11}\right) + 2$$

$$= 11\left(1 + \cos\left(\frac{6\pi}{11}\right)\right) = 11\left(2\cos^2\left(\frac{3\pi}{11}\right)\right)$$

$\therefore \quad \lambda^2 = 11$

Then, $1 + \lambda^2 + \lambda^4 + \lambda^6 = 1 + 11 + 121 + 1331 = 1464$

Matching Type Questions

Example 122 *Match the statement of Column I with values of Column II.*

Column I	Column II
(A) The number of real roots of the equation $\cos^7 x + \sin^4 x = 1$ in $(-\pi, \pi)$ is	(p) 1
(B) The value of $\sqrt{3}$ cosec $20° - \sec 20°$ is	(q) 4
(C) $4\cos 36° - 4\cos 72° + 4\sin 18°$ $\cos 36°$ equals	(r) 3
(D) The number of values of x where $x \in [-2\pi, 2\pi]$, which satisfy cosec $x = 1 + \cot x$	(s) 2

Sol. (A) → (r), (B) → (q), (C) → (r), (D) → (s)

(A) $\cos^7 x + \sin^4 x = 1$

$$\cos^7 x = (1 + \sin^2 x)\cos^2 x$$

$\Rightarrow \quad \cos x = 0$ or $\cos^5 x = 1 + \sin^2 x$

$$\cos x = 0 \Rightarrow x - \frac{\pi}{2}, \frac{\pi}{2}; \cos^5 x = 1 + \sin^2 x$$

$\Rightarrow \quad x = 0 \quad$ [$\because$ LHS ≤ 1 and RHS ≥ 1]

$\therefore \quad x = -\frac{\pi}{2}, 0, \frac{\pi}{2}$

(B) $\sqrt{3}$ cosec $20° - \sec 20°$

$$= \frac{\sqrt{3}}{\sin 20°} - \frac{1}{\cos 20°} = \frac{\sqrt{3}\cos 20° - \sin 20°}{\sin 20° \cos 20°}$$

$$= \frac{2\left(\frac{\sqrt{3}}{2}\cos 20° - \frac{1}{2}\sin 20°\right)}{\sin 20° \cos 20°} = \frac{4\sin 40°}{\sin 40°} = 4$$

(C) $4\cos 36° - 4\cos 72° + 4\sin 18° \cdot \cos 36°$

$$= 4\left(\frac{\sqrt{5}+1}{4}\right) - 4\left(\frac{\sqrt{5}-1}{4}\right) + 4\left(\frac{\sqrt{5}-1}{4}\right)\left(\frac{\sqrt{5}+1}{4}\right)$$

$$= \sqrt{5} + 1 - \sqrt{5} + 1 + 1 = 3$$

(D) cosec $x = 1 + \cot x$; $\frac{1}{\sin x} = \frac{\sin x + \cos x}{\sin x}$

$\Rightarrow \sin x + \cos x = 1$ and $\sin x \ne 0$

$$\cos\left(x - \frac{\pi}{4}\right) = \frac{1}{\sqrt{2}}$$

$\Rightarrow \quad x - \frac{\pi}{4} = -2\pi + \frac{\pi}{4}, \frac{\pi}{4}$

$$\left[\because x - \frac{\pi}{4} \in \left[-2\pi - \frac{\pi}{4}, 2\pi - \frac{\pi}{4}\right]\right]$$

$\Rightarrow \quad x = -\frac{3\pi}{2}, \frac{\pi}{2}$

Example 123 *Match the statement of Column I with values of Column II.*

Column I	Column II
(A) The tangents of two acute angles are 3 and 2. The sine of twice their difference is	(p) 1
(B) If $n = \frac{\pi}{4\alpha}$, then $\tan\alpha \tan 2\alpha \tan 3\alpha$ ... $\tan(2n-1)\alpha$ is equal to	(q) 0
(C) If $x = y\cos\frac{2\pi}{3} = z\cos\frac{4\pi}{3}$, then $xy + yz + zx =$	(r) $\frac{7}{25}$
(D) The ratio of the greatest value of $2 - \cos x + \sin^2 x$ to its least value is	(s) $\frac{13}{4}$

Sol. (A) → (r), (B) → (p), (C) → (q), (D) → (s)

(A) Given, $\tan\alpha = 3$

and $\quad \tan\beta = 2$

$$\therefore \quad \tan(\alpha - \beta) = \frac{\tan\alpha - \tan\beta}{1 - \tan\alpha\tan\beta}$$

$$= \frac{3-2}{1 + 3\times 2} = \frac{1}{7}$$

$\Rightarrow \quad \sin(\alpha - \beta) = \frac{1}{\sqrt{50}}$ and $\cos(\alpha - \beta) = \frac{7}{\sqrt{50}}$

$\therefore \quad \sin 2(\alpha - \beta) = 2\sin(\alpha - \beta)\cos(\alpha - \beta)$

$$= 2 \times \frac{1}{\sqrt{50}} \times \frac{7}{\sqrt{50}}$$

$$= \frac{7}{25}$$

(B) We have, $\tan\alpha \cdot \tan(2n-1)\alpha = \tan\alpha \cdot \tan\left(\frac{\pi}{2\alpha} - 1\right)\alpha$

$$= \tan\alpha \cdot \tan\left(\frac{\pi}{2} - \alpha\right)$$

$$= \tan\alpha \cot\alpha = 1$$

$\therefore$ The given expression = 1.

(C) We have, $x = y\cos\frac{2\pi}{2} = z\cos\frac{4\pi}{3} = k$ (say)

$$\Rightarrow \quad \frac{1}{x} = \frac{1}{k}, \frac{1}{y} = \frac{\cos\frac{2\pi}{3}}{k}, \frac{1}{z} = \frac{\cos\frac{4\pi}{3}}{k}$$

$$\therefore \quad \frac{1}{x} + \frac{1}{y} + \frac{1}{z} = \frac{1}{k}\left(1 + \cos\frac{2\pi}{3} + \cos\frac{4\pi}{3}\right)$$

$$= \frac{1}{k}\left(1 - \frac{1}{2} - \frac{1}{2}\right) = 0$$

$\Rightarrow xy + xz + yz = 0$

(D) We have, $2 - \cos x + \sin^2 x = 2 - \cos x + 1 - \cos^2 x$

$$= -(\cos^2 x + \cos x) + 3$$

$$= -\left[\left(\cos x + \frac{1}{2}\right)^2 - \frac{1}{4}\right] + 3$$

$$= \frac{13}{4} - \left(\cos x + \frac{1}{2}\right)^2$$

$\therefore$ Maximum value occurs at $\cos x = -\frac{1}{2}$ and it is $\frac{13}{4}$ and minimum value occurs at $\cos x = 1$ and it is 1.

$\therefore$ The required ratio is $\frac{13}{4}$.

Example 124 *Match the statement of Column I with values of Column II.*

	Column I		Column II
(A)	If α, β, γ and δ are four solutions of the equation $\tan\left(\theta + \frac{\pi}{4}\right) = 3\tan 3\theta$, no two of which have equal tangents, then the value of $\tan\alpha + \tan\beta + \tan\gamma + \tan\delta$ is	(p)	$\sqrt{2}$
(B)	If $\frac{\cos(\theta_1 - \theta_2)}{\cos(\theta_1 + \theta_2)} + \frac{\cos(\theta_3 + \theta_4)}{\cos(\theta_3 - \theta_4)} = 0$ then $\tan\theta_1 \tan\theta_2 \tan\theta_3 \tan\theta_4 =$	(q)	$\sqrt{3}$
(C)	If $\sec(\alpha - \beta)$, $\sec\alpha$ and $\sec(\alpha + \beta)$ are in A.P. (with $\beta \neq 0$), then $\cos\alpha \sec\frac{\beta}{2} =$	(r)	-1
(D)	If $\cos\alpha = \frac{2\cos\beta - 1}{2 - \cos\beta}$ $(0 < \alpha < \beta < \pi)$, then $\frac{\tan\frac{\alpha}{2}}{\tan\frac{\beta}{2}}$ is equal to	(s)	0

Sol. (A) $\to$ (s), (B) $\to$ (r), (C) $\to$ (p), (D) $\to$ (q)

(A) Using $\tan\left(\theta + \frac{\pi}{4}\right) = \frac{1 + \tan\theta}{1 - \tan\theta}$

and $\quad 3\tan 3\theta = \frac{3(3\tan\theta - \tan^3\theta)}{1 - 3\tan^2\theta}$

the given equation becomes

$$3\tan^4\theta - 6\tan^2\theta + 8\tan\theta - 1 = 0$$

If $\tan\alpha$, $\tan\beta$, $\tan\gamma$ and $\tan\delta$ are the roots of this equation, then the sum of these roots, $\tan\alpha + \tan\beta + \tan\gamma + \tan\delta$ equals zero, since the coefficient of $\tan^3\theta$ is zero.

(B) The given equation can be written as

$$\Rightarrow \frac{\cos\theta_1\cos\theta_2 + \sin\theta_1\sin\theta_2}{\cos\theta_1\cos\theta_2 - \sin\theta_1\sin\theta_2} + \frac{\cos\theta_3\cos\theta_4 - \sin\theta_3\sin\theta_4}{\cos\theta_3\cos\theta_4 + \sin\theta_3\sin\theta_4}$$

$$\Rightarrow \frac{1 + \tan\theta_1\tan\theta_2}{1 - \tan\theta_1\tan\theta_2} + \frac{1 - \tan\theta_3\tan\theta_4}{1 + \tan\theta_3\tan\theta_4} = 0$$

$$\Rightarrow \frac{2 + 2\tan\theta_1\tan\theta_2\tan\theta_3\tan\theta_4}{(1 - \tan\theta_1\tan\theta_2)(1 + \tan\theta_3\tan\theta_4)} = 0$$

Showing that $\tan\theta_1\tan\theta_2\tan\theta_3\tan\theta_4 = -1$.

(C) For the given AP, we have

$2\sec\alpha = \sec(\alpha - \beta) + \sec(\alpha + \beta)$, which gives

$$\frac{2}{\cos\alpha} = \frac{1}{\cos(\alpha - \beta)} + \frac{1}{\cos(\alpha + \beta)} = \frac{2\cos\alpha\cos\beta}{\cos^2\alpha - \sin^2\beta}$$

$$\Rightarrow \quad \cos^2\alpha - \sin^2\beta = \cos^2\alpha\cos\beta$$

$$\Rightarrow \cos^2\alpha(1 - \cos\beta) = \sin^2\beta$$

$$\Rightarrow \cos^2\alpha\left(2\sin^2\frac{\beta}{2}\right) = 4\sin^2\frac{\beta}{2}\cos^2\frac{\beta}{2}$$

$$\Rightarrow \quad \cos^2\alpha\sec^2\frac{\beta}{2} = 2$$

(D) $1 + \cos\alpha = 1 + \frac{2\cos\beta - 1}{2 - \cos\beta}$

$$= \frac{2 - \cos\beta + 2\cos\beta - 1}{2 - \cos\beta}$$

$$= \frac{1 + \cos\beta}{2 - \cos\beta}$$

$$\Rightarrow \quad \cos^2\frac{\alpha}{2} = \frac{\cos^2\frac{\beta}{2}}{1 + 2\sin^2\frac{\beta}{2}} \quad \text{...(i)}$$

$$\Rightarrow 1 - \cos^2\frac{\alpha}{2} = 1 - \frac{\cos^2\frac{\beta}{2}}{1 + 2\sin^2\frac{\beta}{2}}$$

$$= \frac{1 + 2\sin^2\frac{\beta}{2} - \cos^2\frac{\beta}{2}}{1 + 2\sin^2\frac{\beta}{2}}$$

$$= \frac{1 + 2\sin^2\frac{\beta}{2} - \left[1 - \sin^2\frac{\beta}{2}\right]}{1 + 2\sin^2\frac{\beta}{2}}$$

$$\Rightarrow \quad \sin^2 \frac{\alpha}{2} = \frac{3 \sin^2 \frac{\beta}{2}}{1 + 2 \sin^2 \frac{\beta}{2}} \quad \text{...(ii)}$$

Dividing Eq. (ii) by Eq. (i), we get

$$\tan^2 \frac{\alpha}{2} = 3 \tan^2 \frac{\beta}{2}$$

$$\Rightarrow \quad \frac{\tan \frac{\alpha}{2}}{\tan \frac{\beta}{2}} = \sqrt{3}$$

Example 125 *Match the statement of column I with types of quadrant of column II.*

	Column I		Column II
(A)	Suppose ABC is a triangle with three acute angles $\angle A$, $\angle B$ and $\angle C$. The point whose coordinates are $(\cos B - \sin A, \sin B - \sin A)$ can be in the	(p)	1st quadrant
(B)	If $2^{\sin \theta} > 1$ and $3^{\cos \theta} < 1$, then $\theta \in$	(q)	2nd quadrant
(C)	For $\lvert \cos x + \sin x \rvert = \lvert \sin x \rvert + \lvert \cos x \rvert$, x belongs to	(r)	3rd quadrant
(D)	If $\sqrt{\frac{1 - \sin A}{1 + \sin A}} + \frac{\sin A}{\cos A} = \frac{1}{\cos A}$, for all permissible values of A, then A can belongs to	(s)	4th quadrant

Sol. (A) → (q); (B) → (q); (C) → (p), (r); (D) → (p), (s)

(A) Since, $\angle A$, $\angle B$ and $\angle C$ are acute angles, we have

$$A + B > \frac{\pi}{2}$$

$$\Rightarrow \quad A > \frac{\pi}{2} - B$$

$$\Rightarrow \quad \sin A - \cos B > 0$$

$$\Rightarrow \quad \cos B - \sin A < 0 \quad \text{...(i)}$$

Again, $\quad B > \frac{\pi}{2} - A$

$$\Rightarrow \quad \sin B > \cos A$$

$$\Rightarrow \quad \sin B - \cos A > 0 \quad \text{...(ii)}$$

From Eqs. (i) and (ii), we get that x-coordinate is – ve and y-coordinate is + ve.

Therefore, point is in 2nd quadrant only.

(B) $2^{\sin \theta} > 1 \Rightarrow \sin \theta > 0$

$\Rightarrow \theta \in$ 1st or 2nd quadrant.

$3^{\cos \theta} < 1 \Rightarrow \cos\theta < 0$

$\Rightarrow \theta \in$ 2nd or 3rd quadrant.

Hence, $\theta \in$ 2nd quadrant.

(C) $\lvert \cos x + \sin x \rvert = \lvert \sin x \rvert + \lvert \cos x \rvert$

Thus, $\cos x$ and $\sin x$ must have same sign or atleast one is zero.

So, $x \in$ 1st or 3rd quadrant.

(D) LHS $= \frac{1 - \sin A}{\lvert \cos A \rvert} + \frac{\sin A}{\cos A} = \frac{1}{\cos A}$,

which is true only if $\lvert \cos A \rvert = \cos A$.

EXERCISE 1

JEE Main Pattern

Single Option Correct Type Questions

1. The value of $\sum_{n=1}^{10}\left(\sin\frac{2n\pi}{11}-\cos\frac{2n\pi}{11}\right)$ is equal to

(a) 2 (b) 1 (c) 0 (d) -1

2. Given, $a^2+2a+\text{cosec}^2\left(\frac{\pi}{2}(a+x)\right)=0$, then which of the following holds good?

(a) $a=1; \frac{x}{2}\in 1$

(b) $a=-1; \frac{x}{2}\in I$

(c) $a\in R; x\in\phi$

(d) a, x are finite but not possible to find

3. The minimum value of the function $f(x)=(3\sin x-4\cos x-10)(3\sin x+4\cos x-10)$, is

(a) 49 (b) $\frac{195-60\sqrt{2}}{2}$

(c) 84 (d) 48

4. The value of expression $\sum_{\theta=0}^{8}\frac{1}{1+\tan^3(10\theta)^\circ}$ is equal to

(a) 5 (b) $\frac{21}{4}$ (c) $\frac{14}{3}$ (d) $\frac{9}{2}$

5. The value of $\sqrt{1-\sin^2 110^\circ}\cdot\sec 110^\circ$ is equal to

(a) 2 (b) -1 (c) -2 (d) 1

6. If $\tan\alpha$, $\tan\beta$ are the roots of the equation $x^2+px+q=0$, then the value of

$\sin^2(\alpha+\beta)+p\sin(\alpha+\beta)\cos(\alpha+\beta)+q\cos^2(\alpha+\beta)$ is

(a) independent of p but dependent on q

(b) independent of q but dependent on p

(c) independent of both p and q

(d) dependent on both p and q

7. The value of the product

$\sin\left(\frac{\pi}{2^{2009}}\right)\cos\left(\frac{\pi}{2^{2009}}\right)\cos\left(\frac{\pi}{2^{2008}}\right)$

$\cos\left(\frac{\pi}{2^{2007}}\right)\cos\left(\frac{\pi}{2^{2006}}\right)\ldots\cos\left(\frac{\pi}{2^3}\right)\cos\left(\frac{\pi}{2^2}\right)$, is

(a) $\frac{1}{2^{2007}}$ (b) $\frac{1}{2^{2008}}$ (c) $\frac{1}{2^{2009}}$ (d) $\frac{1}{2^{2010}}$

8. If $\tan B=\frac{n\sin A\cos A}{1-n\cos^2 A}$, then $\tan(A+B)$ equals to

(a) $\frac{\sin A}{(1-n)\cos A}$ (b) $\frac{(n-1)\cos A}{\sin A}$

(c) $\frac{\sin A}{(n-1)\cos A}$ (d) $\frac{\sin A}{(n+1)\cos A}$

9. The value of

$(\cos^4 1^\circ+\cos^4 2^\circ+\cos^4 3^\circ+\ldots+\cos^4 179^\circ)$

$-(\sin^4 1^\circ+\sin^4 2^\circ+\sin^4 3^\circ+\ldots+\sin^4 179^\circ)$ equals to

(a) $2\cos 1^\circ$ (b) -1

(c) $2\sin 1^\circ$ (d) 0

10. Suppose that 'a' is a non-zero real number for which $\sin x+\sin y=a$ and $\cos x+\cos y=2a$. The value of $\cos(x-y)$, is

(a) $\frac{3a^2-2}{2}$ (b) $\frac{7a^2-2}{2}$

(c) $\frac{9a^2-2}{2}$ (d) $\frac{5a^2-2}{2}$

11. Let $P(x)=$

$\sqrt{(\cos x+\cos 2x+\cos 3x)^2+(\sin x+\sin 2x+\sin 3x)^2}$,

then $P(x)$ is equal to

(a) $1+2\cos x$ (b) $1+\sin 2x$

(c) $1-2\cos x$ (d) None of these

12. If $\cos 2B=\frac{\cos(A+C)}{\cos(A-C)}$, then $\cot A$, $\cot B$, $\cot C$ are in

(a) AP (b) GP

(c) HP (d) None of these

13. In a ΔABC, the minimum value of $\sec^2\frac{A}{2}+\sec^2\frac{B}{2}+\sec^2\frac{C}{2}$ is equal to

(a) 3 (b) 4 (c) 5 (d) 6

14. The number of ordered pairs (x, y) of real numbers satisfying $4x^2-4x+2=\sin^2 y$ and $x^2+y^2\leq 3$, is equal to

(a) 0 (b) 2 (c) 4 (d) 8

15. In a ΔABC, $3\sin A+4\cos B=6$ and $3\cos A+4\sin B=1$, then $\angle C$ can be

(a) 30° (b) 60°

(c) 90° (d) 150°

16. An equilateral triangle has side length 8 units. The area of the region containing all points outside the triangle but not more than 3 units from a point on the triangle is
(a) $9(8+\pi)$ (b) $8(9+\pi)$
(c) $9\left(8+\frac{\pi}{2}\right)$ (d) $8\left(9+\frac{\pi}{2}\right)$

17. If $a\cos^3\alpha + 3a\cos\alpha\sin^2\alpha = m$ and $a\sin^3\alpha + 3a\cos^2\alpha\sin\alpha = n$, then $(m+n)^{2/3} + (m-n)^{2/3}$ is equal to
(a) $2a^2$ (b) $2a^{1/3}$
(c) $2a^{2/3}$ (d) $2a^3$

18. If $\theta_i > 0$ for $1 \le i \le n$ and $\theta_1 + \theta_2 + \theta_3 + \ldots + \theta_n = \pi$, then the greatest value of sum $\sin\theta_1 + \sin\theta_2 + \sin\theta_3 + \ldots + \sin\theta_n$ is equal to
(a) n (b) $n\sin\left(\frac{\pi}{n}\right)$
(c) π (d) None of these

19. The value of $\sum_{r=1}^{18} \cos^2(5r)^\circ$, where x° denotes the x degrees, is equal to
(a) 0 (b) $\frac{7}{2}$ (c) $\frac{17}{2}$ (d) $\frac{25}{2}$

20. Minimum value of $4x^2 - 4x|\sin x| - \cos^2\theta$ is equal to
(a) -2 (b) -1 (c) $-\frac{1}{2}$ (d) 0

21. If in a ΔABC, $\cos 3A + \cos 3B + \cos 3C = 1$, then one angle must be exactly equal to
(a) $\frac{\pi}{3}$ (b) $\frac{2\pi}{3}$ (c) π (d) $\frac{4\pi}{3}$

22. If $|\tan A| < 1$ and $|A|$ is acute, then $\frac{\sqrt{(1+\sin 2A)} + \sqrt{(1-\sin 2A)}}{\sqrt{(1+\sin 2A)} - \sqrt{(1-\sin 2A)}}$ is equal to
(a) $\tan A$ (b) $-\tan A$
(c) $\cot A$ (d) $-\cot A$

23. For any real θ, the maximum value of $\cos^2(\cos\theta) + \sin^2(\sin\theta)$ is
(a) 1 (b) $1+\sin^2 1$
(c) $1+\cos^2 1$ (d) does not exist

24. Minimum value of $27^{\cos 2x} \cdot 81^{\sin 2x}$ is
(a) -5 (b) $\frac{1}{5}$ (c) $\frac{1}{243}$ (d) $\frac{1}{27}$

25. If $4n\alpha = \pi$, then $\cot\alpha\cot 2\alpha\cot 3\alpha \ldots \cot(2n-1)\alpha$ is equal to
(a) 0 (b) 1
(c) n (d) None of these

26. If in a $\Delta ABC(\sin A + \sin B + \sin C)(\sin A + \sin B - \sin C) = 3\sin A\sin B$, then $\angle C$ is equal to
(a) 30° (b) 45° (c) 60° (d) 75°

27. If α, β and γ are acute angles and $\cos\theta = \frac{\sin\beta}{\sin\alpha}$, $\cos\phi = \frac{\sin\gamma}{\sin\alpha}$ and $\cos(\theta-\phi) = \sin\beta\sin\gamma$, then $\tan^2\alpha - \tan^2\beta - \tan^2\gamma$ is equal to
(a) -1 (b) 0
(c) 1 (d) None of these

28. If $\tan\beta = \frac{n\sin\alpha\cos\alpha}{1-n\sin^2\alpha}$, then $\tan(\alpha-\beta)$ is equal to
(a) $n\tan\alpha$ (b) $(1-n)\tan\alpha$
(c) $(1+n)\tan\alpha$ (d) None of these

29. If $\frac{\cos\theta}{a} = \frac{\sin\theta}{b}$, then $\frac{a}{\sec 2\theta} + \frac{b}{\operatorname{cosec} 2\theta}$ is equal to
(a) a (b) b (c) $\frac{a}{b}$ (d) $a+b$

30. $f(\theta) = |\sin\theta| + |\cos\theta|, \theta \in R$, then
(a) $f(\theta) \in [0, 2]$ (b) $f(\theta) \in [0, \sqrt{2}]$
(c) $f(\theta) \in [0, 1]$ (d) $f(\theta) \in [1, \sqrt{2}]$

31. If $A = \cos(\cos x) + \sin(\cos x)$, then the least and greatest value of A are
(a) 0 and 2 (b) -1 and 1
(c) $-\sqrt{2}$ and $\sqrt{2}$ (d) 0 and $\sqrt{2}$

32. If $U_n = \sin n\theta\sec^n\theta$, $V_n = \cos n\theta\sec^n\theta$, then $\frac{V_n - V_{n-1}}{U_{n-1}} + \frac{1}{n}\frac{U_n}{V_n}$ is equal to
(a) 0 (b) $\tan\theta$
(c) $-\tan\theta + \frac{\tan n\theta}{n}$ (d) $\tan\theta + \frac{\tan n\theta}{n}$

33. The expression $3\left\{\sin^4\left(\frac{3\pi}{2}-\alpha\right) + \sin^4(3\pi+\alpha)\right\} - 2\left\{\sin^6\left(\frac{\pi}{2}+\alpha\right) + \sin^6(5\pi-\alpha)\right\}$ is equal to
(a) 0 (b) -1 (c) 1 (d) 3

34. The maximum value of $\sin\left(x+\frac{\pi}{6}\right) + \cos\left(x+\frac{\pi}{6}\right)$ in the interval $\left(0, \frac{\pi}{2}\right)$ is attained at
(a) $\frac{\pi}{12}$ (b) $\frac{\pi}{6}$ (c) $\frac{\pi}{3}$ (d) $\frac{\pi}{2}$

35. If $\cos x - \sin\alpha\cot\beta\sin x = \cos\alpha$, then $\tan\frac{x}{2}$ is equal to
(a) $\cot\frac{\alpha}{2}\tan\frac{\beta}{2}$ (b) $\cot\frac{\beta}{2}\tan\frac{\alpha}{2}$
(c) $\tan\frac{\alpha}{2}\tan\frac{\beta}{2}$ (d) None of these

36. If $1+\sin x+\sin^2 x+\sin^3 x+\ldots=4+2\sqrt{3}, 0<x<\pi$, then x is equal to

(a) $\frac{\pi}{6}$ (b) $\frac{\pi}{4}$

(c) $\frac{\pi}{3}$ or $\frac{2\pi}{3}$ (d) $\frac{\pi}{4}$ or $\frac{2\pi}{3}$

37. If $y=(\sin x+\cos x)+(\sin 4x+\cos 4x)^2$, then

(a) $y>0, \forall x \in R$ (b) $y \geq 0, \forall x \in R$

(c) $y<2+\sqrt{2}, \forall x \in R$ (d) $y=2+\sqrt{2}$ for some $x \in R$

38. In the figure, $l(\text{Arc } AB)=1$, $l(OA)=l(BC)=l(DE)=l(OB)=1, l(OD)=2, l(OF)=3$, $m\angle OEF=2^c$. If $l(\text{Arc } CD)+l(\text{Arc } EF)=N$, then N is equal to (O is the centre of all the arcs)

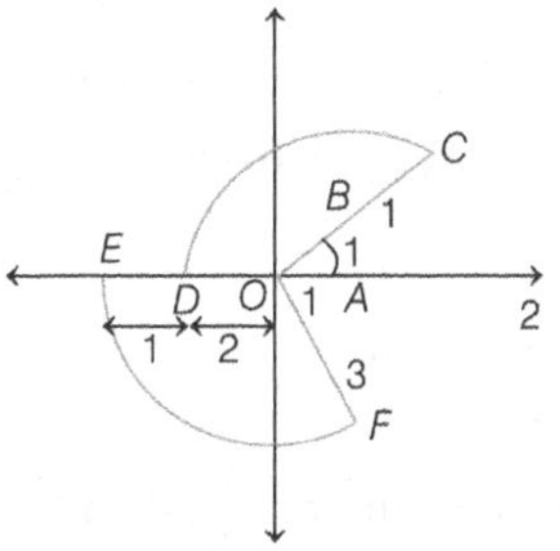

(a) 2π (b) $2\pi-4$

(c) $2\pi-2$ (d) $2\pi+4$

39. Let $f(\theta)=16\cos^3 2\theta-32\sin^3\theta-12\cos 2\theta+24\sin\theta$. If $f\left(\frac{\pi}{30}\right)=3\sqrt{a}-b, a, b \in N$, then the value of $(a+b)$ is

(a) 4 (b) 5 (c) 6 (d) 7

40. If $\frac{\sin 2A}{\cos 3A}>0$, then A can attain any value in the interval

(a) $\left(0, \frac{\pi}{4}\right)$ (b) $\left(\frac{\pi}{4}, \frac{\pi}{3}\right)$ (c) $\left(\frac{\pi}{3}, \frac{\pi}{2}\right)$ (d) $\left(0, \frac{\pi}{6}\right)$

41. If $x=\sin(\alpha-\beta)\cdot\sin(\gamma-\delta)$; $y=\sin(\beta-\gamma)\cdot\sin(\alpha-\delta)$; and $z=\sin(\gamma-\alpha)\cdot\sin(\beta-\delta)$, then

(a) $x+y+z=0$ (b) $x+y-z=0$

(c) $y+z-x=0$ (d) None of these

42. If $\tan(2\alpha+\beta)=x$ and $\tan(\alpha+2\beta)=y$, then $[\tan 3(\alpha+\beta)]\cdot[\tan(\alpha-\beta)]$ is equal to (wherever defined)

(a) $\frac{x^2+y^2}{1-x^2y^2}$ (b) $\frac{x^2-y^2}{1+x^2y^2}$

(c) $\frac{x^2+y^2}{1+x^2y^2}$ (d) $\frac{x^2-y^2}{1-x^2y^2}$

43. The value of $\frac{\sin\frac{2\pi}{9}-\sin\frac{\pi}{36}}{\cos\frac{2\pi}{9}-\cos\frac{\pi}{36}}$ is

(a) $\sqrt{2}-1$ (b) $1-\sqrt{2}$ (c) $-(\sqrt{2}+1)$ (d) $(\sqrt{2}+1)$

44. Consider angles $\alpha=\left(2n+\frac{1}{2}\right)\pi \pm A$ and $\beta=m\pi+(-1)^m\left(\frac{\pi}{2}-A\right)$ where $n, m \in I$. Which of the following is not true?

(a) α and β are always the same angles

(b) $\sin\alpha=\sin\beta$ and $\cos\alpha=\cos\beta$

(c) $\sin\alpha=\sin\beta$ but $\cos\alpha\neq\cos\beta$

(d) None of the above

45. Let $y=(\sin x+\operatorname{cosec} x)^2+(\cos x+\sec x)^2$, then the minimum value of $y, \forall x \in R$ is

(a) 7 (b) 3 (c) 9 (d) 0

46. Sum of squares of minimum and maximum values of $\sqrt{4-|2-3\sqrt{\sin^2 x}|}$ is

(a) 0 (b) 6 (c) 8 (d) 10

47. Number of values of x for which $\sin y=x^2-2x$ is possible.

(a) 0 (b) 1

(c) infinite (d) None of these

48. In ΔABC, the value of $\sum\frac{\sec A\cdot\sec B}{\tan A\tan B\sec C}$ is

(a) 1 (b) 2 (c) 3 (d) 4

49. In ΔABC, internal angle bisector of $\angle A$ makes an angle θ with side BC. Value of $\sin\theta$ is equal to

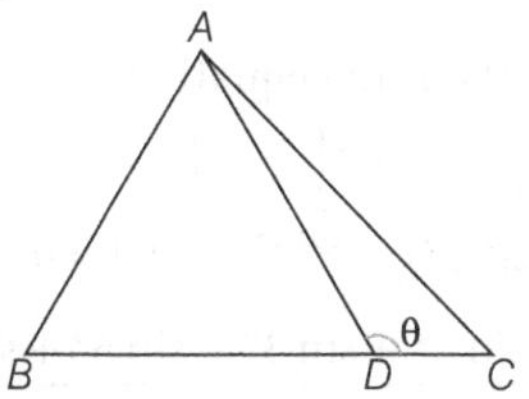

(a) $\left|\sin\left(\frac{B-C}{2}\right)\right|$ (b) $\left|\sin\left(\frac{B}{2}-C\right)\right|$

(c) $\cos\left(\frac{B-C}{2}\right)$ (d) $\cos\left(\frac{B}{2}-C\right)$

50. Consider the following two statements

S_1 : If $\sin^2\theta_1+\sin^2\theta_2+\ldots+\sin^2\theta_n=0$, then number of different sets $(\theta_1, \theta_2, \ldots, \theta_n)$ for which $\cos\theta_1+\cos\theta_2+\ldots+\cos\theta_n=n-2$ is n.

S_2 : Let f be any one of the six trigonometric functions satisfying $f(2A)=f(2B)$, $A, B \in R$, then $A-B=n\pi, n \in Z$.

(a) Only S_1 is true (b) Only S_2 is true

(c) Both S_1 and S_2 are false (d) Both S_1 and S_2 are true

51. If $\sin(x+3\alpha)=3\sin(\alpha-x)$, then

(a) $\tan x=\tan\alpha$ (b) $\tan x=\tan^2\alpha$

(c) $\tan x=\tan^3\alpha$ (d) $\tan x=3\tan\alpha$

52. If the median of ΔABC through A is perpendicular to AB, then

(a) $\tan A + \tan B = 0$ (b) $2\tan A + \tan B = 0$
(c) $\tan A + 2\tan B = 0$ (d) None of these

53. The expression $\dfrac{1+\sin 2\alpha}{\cos(2\alpha - 2\pi)\cdot\tan\left(\alpha - \dfrac{3\pi}{4}\right)} - \dfrac{1}{4}\sin 2\alpha\left[\cot\dfrac{\alpha}{2} + \cot\left(\dfrac{3\pi}{2} + \dfrac{\alpha}{2}\right)\right]$

is equal to

(a) 1 (b) 0 (c) $\sin^2\left(\dfrac{\alpha}{2}\right)$ (d) $\sin^2\alpha$

54. If A and B are positive acute angles satisfying the equalities $3\cos^2 A + 2\cos^2 B = 4$ and $\dfrac{3\sin A}{\sin B} = \dfrac{2\cos B}{\cos A}$, then $A + 2B$ is equal to

(a) $\dfrac{\pi}{4}$ (b) $\dfrac{\pi}{3}$ (c) $\dfrac{\pi}{6}$ (d) $\dfrac{\pi}{2}$

Numerical Value Type Questions

55. If $f(\theta) = \dfrac{1-\sin 2\theta + \cos 2\theta}{2\cos 2\theta}$, then value of $8f(11^\circ)\cdot f(34^\circ)$ is ....

56. If $f(x) = 2(7\cos x + 24\sin x)(7\sin x - 24\cos x)$, for every $x \in R$, then maximum value of $\{f(x)\}^{1/4}$ is ....

57. Number of roots of the equation

$$2^{\tan\left(x-\frac{\pi}{4}\right)} - 2(0.25)^{\frac{\sin^2\left(x-\frac{\pi}{4}\right)}{\cos 2x}} + 1 = 0$$ is ....

58. The value of $\dfrac{\sin 1^\circ + \sin 3^\circ + \sin 5^\circ + \sin 7^\circ}{\cos 1^\circ\cdot\cos 2^\circ\cdot\sin 4^\circ}$ is ....

59. If $\sin^4\alpha + \cos^4\beta + 2 = 4\sin\alpha\cos\beta,\ 0 \le \alpha, \beta \le \dfrac{\pi}{2}$, then $(\sin\alpha + \cos\beta)$ is equal to ....

60. Let $0 \le a, b, c, d \le \pi$, where b and c are not complementary, such that

$$2\cos a + 6\cos b + 7\cos c + 9\cos d = 0$$

and $2\sin a - 6\sin b + 7\sin c - 9\sin d = 0$, then the value of $3\dfrac{\cos(a+d)}{\cos(b+c)}$ is ....

61. The value of $\dfrac{2\sin x}{\sin 3x} + \dfrac{\tan x}{\tan 3x}$ is ....

62. If $\tan^2\alpha\tan^2\beta + \tan^2\beta\tan^2\gamma + \tan^2\gamma\tan^2\alpha + 2\tan^2\alpha\tan^2\beta\tan^2\gamma = 1$, then the value of $\sin^2\alpha + \sin^2\beta + \sin^2\gamma$ is ....

63. α and β are the positive acute angles and satisfying equations $5\sin 2\beta = 3\sin 2\alpha$ and $\tan\beta = 3\tan\alpha$ simultaneously. Then, the value of $\tan\alpha + \tan\beta$ is ....

64. The value of $\sin^2 12^\circ + \sin^2 21^\circ + \sin^2 39^\circ + \sin^2 48^\circ - \sin^2 9^\circ - \sin^2 18^\circ$ is ....

65. The greatest integer less than or equal to $\dfrac{1}{\cos 290^\circ} + \dfrac{1}{\sqrt{3}\sin 250^\circ}$ is ....

66. If $p\,\mathrm{cosec}\,\theta + q\cot\theta = 2$ and $p^2\,\mathrm{cosec}^2\theta - q^2\cot^2\theta = 5$, then the value of $81p^{-2} - q^{-2}$ is ....

67. The value of $\left[\left(\sin\dfrac{\pi}{9}\right)\left(4 + \sec\dfrac{\pi}{9}\right)\right]^2$ is ....

68. If $\log_{10}\sin x + \log_{10}\cos x = -1$ and $\log_{10}(\sin x + \cos x) = \dfrac{(\log_{10} n) - 1}{2}$, then the value of n is ....

69. If $\dfrac{\tan x}{2} = \dfrac{\tan y}{3} = \dfrac{\tan z}{5}$, $x + y + z = \pi$ and $\tan^2 x + \tan^2 y + \tan^2 z = \dfrac{38}{k}$, then k is equal to ....

70. The reciprocal of the value of the product $\sin\left(\dfrac{5\pi}{2^{11}}\right)\cos\left(\dfrac{5\pi}{2^{11}}\right)\cos\left(\dfrac{5\pi}{2^{10}}\right)\cos\left(\dfrac{5\pi}{2^{9}}\right)\cdots\cos\left(\dfrac{5\pi}{2^{3}}\right)\cos\left(\dfrac{5\pi}{2^{2}}\right)$ is ....

71. If $\cot(\theta - \alpha)$, $3\cot\theta$, $\cot(\theta + \alpha)$ are in AP and θ is not an integral multiple of $\dfrac{\pi}{2}$, then the value of $\dfrac{4\sin^2\theta}{3\sin^2\alpha}$ is equal to ....

Previous Year Questions

72. If $\tan A = \dfrac{1}{\sqrt{x(x^2+x+1)}}$, $\tan B = \dfrac{\sqrt{x}}{\sqrt{x^2+x+1}}$ and $\tan C = (x^{-3} + x^{-2} + x^{-1})^{1/2}$, $0 < A, B, C < \dfrac{\pi}{2}$, then $A + B$ is equal to **[Single Correct Type, 2024 Main]**

(a) $\dfrac{\pi}{2} - C$ (b) C (c) $\pi - C$ (d) $2\pi - C$

73. For $\alpha, \beta \in \left(0, \dfrac{\pi}{2}\right)$, let $3\sin(\alpha+\beta) = 2\sin(\alpha-\beta)$ and a real number k be such that $\tan\alpha = k\tan\beta$. Then, the value of k is equal to **[Single Correct Type, 2024 Main]**

(a) $-\dfrac{2}{3}$ (b) -5 (c) $\dfrac{2}{3}$ (d) 5

74. Let the set of all $a \in R$ such that the equation $\cos 2x + a \sin x = 2a - 7$ has a solution be $[p, q]$ and $r = \tan 9° - \tan 27° - \dfrac{1}{\cot 63°} + \tan 81°$, then pqr is equal to .... **[Numerical Value Type, 2024 Main]**

75. Let $S = \left\{x \in \left(-\frac{\pi}{2}, \frac{\pi}{2}\right) : 9^{1-\tan^2 x} + 9^{\tan^2 x} = 10\right\}$ and $\beta = \sum_{x \in S} \tan^2\left(\frac{x}{3}\right)$, then $\frac{1}{6}(\beta - 14)^2$ is equal to

[Single Correct Type, 2023 Main]

(a) 8 (b) 16 (c) 64 (d) 32

76. $96 \cos\frac{\pi}{33} \cos\frac{2\pi}{33} \cos\frac{4\pi}{33} \cos\frac{8\pi}{33} \cos\frac{16\pi}{33}$ is equal to

[Single Correct Type, 2023 Main]

(a) 4 (b) 3 (c) 2 (d) 1

77. The value of $36(4\cos^2 9° - 1)(4\cos^2 27° - 1)(4\cos^2 81° - 1)(4\cos^2 243° - 1)$ is

[Single Correct Type, 2023 Main]

(a) 27 (b) 36 (c) 18 (d) 54

78. The value of $\tan 9° - \tan 27° - \tan 63° + \tan 81°$ is ....

[Numerical Value Type, 2023 Main]

79. $2 \sin\left(\frac{\pi}{22}\right) \sin\left(\frac{3\pi}{22}\right) \sin\left(\frac{5\pi}{22}\right) \sin\left(\frac{7\pi}{22}\right) \sin\left(\frac{9\pi}{22}\right)$ is equal to

[Single Correct Type, 2022 Main]

(a) 3/16 (b) 1/16 (c) 1/32 (d) 9/32

80. If $\cot \alpha = 1$ and $\sec \beta = -\frac{5}{3}$, where $\pi < \alpha < \frac{3\pi}{2}$ and $\frac{\pi}{2} < \beta < \pi$, then the value of $\tan(\alpha + \beta)$ and the quadrant in which $\alpha + \beta$ lies, respectively are

[Single Correct Type, 2022 Main]

(a) $-\frac{1}{7}$ and IVth quadrant (b) 7 and Ist quadrant

(c) -7 and IVth quadrant (d) 1/7 and Ist quadrant

81. $\alpha = \sin 36°$ is a root of which of the following equation

[Single Correct Type, 2022 Main]

(a) $10x^4 - 10x^2 - 5 = 0$ (b) $16x^4 + 20x^2 - 5 = 0$

(c) $16x^4 - 20x^2 + 5 = 0$ (d) $16x^4 - 10x^2 + 5 = 0$

82. The value of $\cos\left(\frac{2\pi}{7}\right) + \cos\left(\frac{4\pi}{7}\right) + \cos\left(\frac{6\pi}{7}\right)$ is equal to

[Single Correct Type, 2022 Main]

(a) -1 (b) $-\frac{1}{2}$ (c) $-\frac{1}{3}$ (d) $-\frac{1}{4}$

83. $16 \sin(20°) \sin(40°) \sin(80°)$ is equal to

[Single Correct Type, 2022 Main]

(a) $\sqrt{3}$ (b) $2\sqrt{3}$

(c) 3 (d) $4\sqrt{3}$

84. The value of $2\sin(12°) - \sin(72°)$ is

[Single Correct Type, 2022 Main]

(a) $\frac{\sqrt{5}(1-\sqrt{3})}{4}$ (b) $\frac{1-\sqrt{5}}{8}$

(c) $\frac{\sqrt{3}(1-\sqrt{5})}{2}$ (d) $\frac{\sqrt{3}(1-\sqrt{5})}{4}$

85. If $\sin^2(10°)\sin(20°)\sin(40°)\sin(50°)\sin(70°) = \alpha - \frac{1}{16}\sin(10°)$, then $16 + \alpha^{-1}$ is equal to ....

[Numerical Value Type, 2022 Main]

86. The value of $2\sin\left(\frac{\pi}{8}\right)\sin\left(\frac{2\pi}{8}\right)\sin\left(\frac{3\pi}{8}\right)\sin\left(\frac{5\pi}{8}\right)\sin\left(\frac{6\pi}{8}\right)\sin\left(\frac{7\pi}{8}\right)$ **[Single Correct Type, 2021 Main]**

(a) $\frac{1}{4\sqrt{2}}$ (b) $\frac{1}{4}$ (c) $\frac{1}{8}$ (d) $\frac{1}{8\sqrt{2}}$

87. If $\sin\theta + \cos\theta = \frac{1}{2}$, then $16[\sin(2\theta) + \cos(4\theta) + \sin(6\theta)]$ is equal to

[Single Correct Type, 2021 Main]

(a) 23 (b) -27 (c) -23 (d) 27

88. The value of $\cot\frac{\pi}{24}$ is **[Single Correct Type, 2021 Main]**

(a) $\sqrt{2} + \sqrt{3} + 2 - \sqrt{6}$ (b) $\sqrt{2} + \sqrt{3} + 2 + \sqrt{6}$

(c) $\sqrt{2} - \sqrt{3} - 2 + \sqrt{6}$ (d) $3\sqrt{2} - \sqrt{3} - \sqrt{6}$

89. If $0 < x, y < \pi$ and $\cos x + \cos y - \cos(x+y) = \frac{3}{2}$, then $\sin x + \cos y$ is equal to **[Single Correct Type, 2021 Main]**

(a) $\frac{1}{2}$ (b) $\frac{\sqrt{3}}{2}$

(c) $\frac{1-\sqrt{3}}{2}$ (d) $\frac{1+\sqrt{3}}{2}$

90. The value of $\cos^3\left(\frac{\pi}{8}\right)\cdot\cos\left(\frac{3\pi}{8}\right) + \sin^3\left(\frac{\pi}{8}\right)\cdot\sin\left(\frac{3\pi}{8}\right)$ is

[Single Correct Type, 2020 Main]

(a) $\frac{1}{4}$ (b) $\frac{1}{2\sqrt{2}}$ (c) $\frac{1}{2}$ (d) $\frac{1}{\sqrt{2}}$

91. If $\frac{\sqrt{2}\sin\alpha}{\sqrt{1+\cos 2\alpha}} = \frac{1}{7}$ and $\sqrt{\frac{1-\cos 2\beta}{2}} = \frac{1}{\sqrt{10}}$, $\alpha, \beta \in \left(0, \frac{\pi}{2}\right)$, then $\tan(\alpha + 2\beta)$ is equal to ....

[Numerical Value Type, 2020 Main]

92. The maximum value of $3\cos\theta + 5\sin\left(\theta - \frac{\pi}{6}\right)$ for any real value of θ is **[Single Correct Type, 2019 Main]**

(a) $\frac{\sqrt{79}}{2}$ (b) $\sqrt{34}$

(c) $\sqrt{31}$ (d) $\sqrt{19}$

EXERCISE 2

JEE Advanced Pattern

Single Option Correct Type Questions

1. Let $S = \{a \in N, a \le 100\}$. If the equation $[\tan^2 x] - \tan x - a = 0$ has real roots, then number of elements in S is (where $[\cdot]$ is step function).
(a) 10 (b) 8 (c) 9 (d) 0

2. If $\tan\left(\frac{\pi}{4} + \frac{y}{2}\right) = \tan^3\left(\frac{\pi}{4} + \frac{x}{2}\right)$, then $\sin x \left(\frac{3 + \sin^2 x}{1 + 3\sin^2 x}\right)$ equals
(a) $\cos y$ (b) $\sin y$ (c) $\sin 2y$ (d) 0

3. If $P = (\tan(3^{n+1}\theta) - \tan\theta)$ and $Q = \sum_{r=0}^{n} \frac{\sin(3^r \theta)}{\cos(3^{r+1}\theta)}$, then
(a) $P = 2Q$ (b) $P = 3Q$
(c) $2P = Q$ (d) $3P = Q$

4. If the maximum value of the expression $\frac{1}{5\sec^2\theta - \tan^2\theta + 4\,\text{cosec}^2\theta}$ is equal to $\frac{p}{q}$ (where, p and q are coprime), then the value of $(p + q)$ is
(a) 14 (b) 15 (c) 16 (d) 18

5. Let $f_n(a) = \frac{\sin\alpha + \sin 3\alpha + \sin 5\alpha + \ldots + \sin(2n-1)\alpha}{\cos\alpha + \cos 3\alpha + \cos 5\alpha + \ldots + \cos(2n-1)\alpha}$.
Then, the value of $f_4\left(\frac{\pi}{32}\right)$ is equal to
(a) $\sqrt{2} + 1$ (b) $\sqrt{2} - 1$
(c) $2 + \sqrt{3}$ (d) $2 - \sqrt{3}$

6. As shown in the figure, AD is the altitude on BC and AD produced meets the circumcircle of ΔABC at P where $DP = x$. Similarly, $EQ = y$ and $FR = z$. If a, b, c respectively denotes the sides BC, CA and AB, then $\frac{a}{2x} + \frac{b}{2y} + \frac{c}{2z}$ has the value equal to

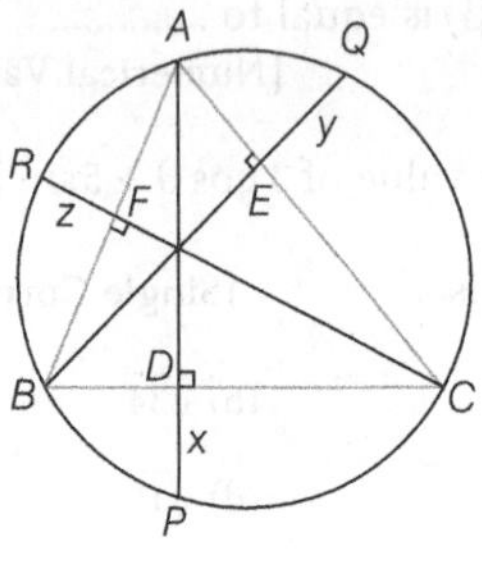

(a) $\tan A + \tan B + \tan C$
(b) $\cot A + \cos B + \cot C$
(c) $\cos A + \cos B + \cos C$
(d) $\text{cosec}\, A + \text{cosec}\, B + \text{cosec}\, C$

7. The minimum value of $\left|\sin x + \cos x + \frac{\cos x + \sin x}{\cos^4 x - \sin^4 x}\right|$ is
(a) 2 (b) $\frac{3}{2}$ (c) $\sqrt{2}$ (d) 1

8. One side of a rectangular piece of paper is 6 cm, the adjacent sides being longer than 6 cm. One corner of the paper is folded so that is sets on the opposite longer side. If the length of the crease is l cm and it makes an angle θ with the long side as shown, then l is

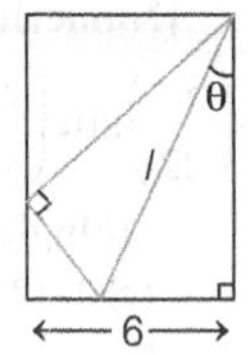

(a) $\frac{3}{\sin\theta\cos^2\theta}$ (b) $\frac{6}{\sin^2\theta\cos\theta}$
(c) $\frac{3}{\sin\theta\cos\theta}$ (d) $\frac{3}{\sin^2\theta}$

9. A circle is inscribed inside a regular pentagon and another circle is circumscribed about this pentagon. Similarly, a circle is inscribed in a regular heptagon and another circumscribed about the heptagon. The area of the regions between the two circles in two cases are A_1 and A_2, respectively. If each polygon has a side length of 2 units, then which one of the following is true ?
(a) $A_1 = \frac{5}{7}A_2$ (b) $A_1 = \frac{25}{49}A_2$
(c) $A_1 = \frac{49}{25}A_2$ (d) $A_1 = A_2$

10. $ABCD$ is a trapezium, such that AB and CD are parallel $BC \perp CD$. If $\angle ADB = \theta$, $BC = p$ and $CD = q$, then AB is equal to
(a) $\frac{(p^2 + q^2)\sin\theta}{p\cos\theta + q\sin\theta}$ (b) $\frac{p^2 + q^2\cos\theta}{p\cos\theta + q\sin\theta}$
(c) $\frac{p^2 + q^2}{p^2\cos\theta + q^2\sin\theta}$ (d) $\frac{(p^2 + q^2)\sin\theta}{(p\cos\theta + q\sin\theta)^2}$

11. The graph of the function $\cos x \cos(x+2) - \cos^2(x+1)$ is
(a) a straight line passing through $(0, -\sin^2 \theta)$ with slope 2.
(b) a straight line passing through (0, 0).
(c) a parabola with vertex $(1, -\sin^2 1)$.
(d) a straight line passing through the point $\left(\frac{\pi}{2}, -\sin^2 1\right)$ and parallel to the X-axis.

12. If $0 \le x \le \frac{\pi}{3}$, then range of $f(x) = \sec\left(\frac{\pi}{6} - x\right) + \sec\left(\frac{\pi}{6} + x\right)$ is
(a) $\left(\frac{4}{\sqrt{3}}, \infty\right)$ (b) $\left[\frac{4}{\sqrt{3}}, \infty\right)$ (c) $\left(0, \frac{4}{\sqrt{3}}\right]$ (d) $\left(0, \frac{4}{\sqrt{3}}\right)$

13. If $A = \sin^8 \theta + \cos^{14} \theta$, then for all values of θ,
(a) $A \ge 1$ (b) $0 < A \le 1$
(c) $1 < 2a \le 3$ (d) None of these

14. If $\cot^2 x = \cot(x-y) \cdot \cot(x-z)$, then $\cot 2x$ is equal to $\left(x \ne \pm \frac{\pi}{4}\right)$
(a) $\frac{1}{2}(\tan y + \tan z)$ (b) $\frac{1}{2}(\cot y + \cot z)$
(c) $\frac{1}{2}(\sin y + \sin z)$ (d) None of these

15. The minimum value of the expression $\sin \alpha + \sin \beta + \sin \gamma$, where α, β, γ are real numbers satisfying $\alpha + \beta + \gamma = \pi$, is
(a) positive (b) zero
(c) negative (d) None of these

16. If $\cos^4 \theta \sec^2 \alpha, \frac{1}{2}$ and $\sin^4 \theta \operatorname{cosec}^2 \alpha$ are in AP, then $\cos^8 \theta \sec^6 \alpha, \frac{1}{2}$ and $\sin^8 \theta \cdot \operatorname{cosec}^6 \alpha$ are in
(a) AP (b) GP
(c) HP (d) None of these

17. The maximum value of $\cos \alpha_1 \cdot \cos \alpha_2 \cdot \cos \alpha_3 \cdot \ldots \cdot \cos \alpha_n$ under the restriction $0 \le \alpha_1, \alpha_2, \ldots, \alpha_n \le \frac{\pi}{2}$ and $\cot \alpha_1 \cdot \cot \alpha_2 \cdot \ldots \cdot \cot \alpha_n = 1$ is
(a) $\frac{1}{2^{\frac{n}{2}}}$ (b) $\frac{1}{2^n}$ (c) $\frac{-1}{2^n}$ (d) 1

18. If $x \in (0, \pi)$ and $\sin x \cdot \cos^3 x > \cos x \cdot \sin^3 x$, then complete set of values of x is
(a) $x \in \left(0, \frac{\pi}{4}\right) \cup \left(\frac{\pi}{2}, \frac{3\pi}{4}\right)$ (b) $x \in \left(\frac{\pi}{4}, \frac{\pi}{2}\right) \cup \left(\frac{3\pi}{4}, \pi\right)$
(c) $x \in \left(\frac{\pi}{4}, \frac{\pi}{2}\right)$ (d) None of these

19. If $u = \sqrt{a^2 \cos^2 \theta + b^2 \sin^2 \theta} + \sqrt{a^2 \sin^2 \theta + b^2 \cos^2 \theta}$, then the difference between the maximum and minimum values of u^2 is given by
(a) $2(a^2 + b^2)$ (b) $2\sqrt{a^2 + b^2}$
(c) $(a+b)^2$ (d) $(a-b)^2$

More than One Correct Option Type Questions

20. Suppose $\cos x = 0$ and $\cos(x+z) = \frac{1}{2}$. Then, the possible value(s) of z is (are)
(a) $\frac{\pi}{6}$ (b) $\frac{5\pi}{6}$ (c) $\frac{7\pi}{6}$ (d) $\frac{11\pi}{6}$

21. Let $f_n(\theta) = 2\sin\frac{\theta}{2}\sin\frac{3\theta}{2} + 2\sin\frac{\theta}{2}\sin\frac{5\theta}{2} + 2\sin\frac{\theta}{2}\sin\frac{7\theta}{2} + \ldots + 2\sin\frac{\theta}{2}\sin(2n+1)\frac{\theta}{2}, n \in N$, then which of the following is/are correct?
(a) $f_9\left(\frac{\pi}{4}\right) = \frac{1}{\sqrt{2}}$
(b) $f_n\left(\frac{2\pi}{n}\right) = 0, n \in N$
(c) $f_5\left(\frac{2\pi}{7}\right) = 0$
(d) $f_9\left(\frac{\pi}{4}\right) = -\frac{1}{\sqrt{2}}$

22. Let $P = \sin 25° \sin 35° \sin 60° \sin 85°$ and $Q = \sin 20° \sin 40° \sin 75° \sin 80°$. Which of the following relation(s) is (are) correct ?
(a) $P + Q = 0$ (b) $P - Q = 0$
(c) $P^2 + Q^2 = 1$ (d) $P^2 - Q^2 = 0$

23. For $0 < \theta < \frac{\pi}{2}$, if $x = \sum_{n=0}^{\infty} \cos^{2n} \theta$, $y = \sum_{n=0}^{\infty} \sin^{2n} \theta$, $z = \sum_{n=0}^{\infty} \cos^{2n} \theta \sin^{2n} \theta$, then
(a) $xyz = xz + y$ (b) $xyz = xy + z$
(c) $xyz = x + y + z$ (d) $xyz = yz + x$

24. Let $P(x) = \cot^2 x \left(\frac{1 + \tan x + \tan^2 x}{1 + \cot x + \cot^2 x}\right) + \left(\frac{\cos x - \cos 3x + \sin 3x - \sin x}{2(\sin 2x + \cos 2x)}\right)^2$. Then, which of the following is (are) correct?
(a) The value of $P(18°) + P(72°)$ is 2.
(b) The value of $P(18°) + P(72°)$ is 3.
(c) The value of $P\left(\frac{4\pi}{3}\right) + P\left(\frac{7\pi}{6}\right)$ is 3.
(d) The value of $P\left(\frac{4\pi}{3}\right) + P\left(\frac{7\pi}{6}\right)$ is 2.

25. It is known that $\sin\beta = \frac{4}{5}$ and $0 < \beta < \pi$, then these value of $\dfrac{\sqrt{3}\sin(\alpha+\beta) - \dfrac{2}{\cos\dfrac{11\pi}{6}}\cos(\alpha+\beta)}{\sin\alpha}$ is

(a) independent of α for all β in $(0, \pi)$.

(b) $\frac{5}{\sqrt{3}}$ for $\tan\beta > 0$

(c) $\frac{\sqrt{3}(7 + 24\cot\alpha)}{15}$ for $\tan\beta < 0$

(d) zero for $\tan\beta > 0$

26. In cyclic quadrilateral $ABCD$, if $\cot A = \frac{3}{4}$ and $\tan B = \frac{-12}{5}$, then which of the following is (are) correct?

(a) $\sin D = \frac{12}{13}$ (b) $\sin(A + B) = \frac{16}{65}$

(c) $\cos D = \frac{-15}{13}$ (d) $\sin(C + D) = \frac{-16}{65}$

27. If the equation $2\cos^2 x + \cos x - a = 0$ has solutions, then a can be

(a) $\frac{-1}{4}$ (b) $\frac{-1}{8}$ (c) 2 (d) 5

28. If $A = \sin 44^\circ + \cos 44^\circ$, $B = \sin 45^\circ + \cos 45^\circ$ and $C = \sin 46^\circ + \cos 46^\circ$. Then, correct option(s) is/are

(a) $A < B < C$ (b) $C < B < A$

(c) $B > A$ (d) $A = C$

29. If $x = \sec\phi - \tan\phi$ and $y = \operatorname{cosec}\phi + \cot\phi$, then

(a) $x = \frac{y+1}{y-1}$ (b) $x = \frac{y-1}{y+1}$

(c) $y = \frac{1+x}{1-x}$ (d) $xy + x - y + 1 = 0$

30. If $\tan\left(\frac{x}{2}\right) = \operatorname{cosec} x - \sin x$, then $\tan^2\left(\frac{x}{2}\right)$ is equal to

(a) $2 - \sqrt{5}$ (b) $\sqrt{5} - 2$

(c) $(9 - 4\sqrt{5})(2 + \sqrt{5})$ (d) $(9 + 4\sqrt{5})(2 - \sqrt{5})$

31. If $y = \frac{\sqrt{1 - \sin 4A} + 1}{\sqrt{1 + \sin 4A} - 1}$, then one of the value of y is

(a) $-\tan A$ (b) $\cot A$

(c) $\tan\left(\frac{\pi}{4} + A\right)$ (d) $-\cot\left(\frac{\pi}{4} + A\right)$

32. If $3\sin\beta = \sin(2\alpha + \beta)$, then

(a) $[\cot\alpha + \cot(\alpha + \beta)][\cot\beta - 3\cot(2\alpha + \beta)] = 6$

(b) $\sin\beta = \cos(\alpha + \beta)\sin\alpha$

(c) $2\sin\beta = \sin(\alpha + \beta)\cos\alpha$

(d) $\tan(\alpha + \beta) = 2\tan\alpha$

33. Let $P_n(u)$ be a polynomial is u of degree n. Then, for every positive integer n, $\sin 2nx$ is expressible is

(a) $P_{2n}(\sin x)$

(b) $P_{2n}(\cos x)$

(c) $\cos x\, P_{2n-1}(\sin x)$

(d) $\sin x\, P_{2n-1}(\cos x)$

34. If $\tan\theta = \frac{\sin\alpha - \cos\alpha}{\sin\alpha + \cos\alpha}$, then

(a) $\sin\alpha - \cos\alpha = \pm\sqrt{2}\sin\theta$

(b) $\sin\alpha + \cos\alpha = \pm\sqrt{2}\cos\theta$

(c) $\cos 2\theta = \sin 2\alpha$

(d) $\sin 2\theta + \cos 2\alpha = 0$

35. If $\cos 5\theta = a\cos\theta + b\cos^3\theta + c\cos^5\theta + d$, then

(a) $a = 20$ (b) $b = -20$

(c) $c = 16$ (d) $d = 5$

36. $x = \sqrt{a^2\cos^2\alpha + b^2\sin^2\alpha} + \sqrt{a^2\sin^2\alpha + b^2\cos^2\alpha}$, then $x^2 = a^2 + b^2 + 2\sqrt{p(a^2 + b^2) - p^2}$, where p is equal to

(a) $a^2\cos^2\alpha + b^2\sin^2\alpha$

(b) $a^2\sin^2\alpha + b^2\cos^2\alpha$

(c) $\frac{1}{2}[a^2 + b^2 + (a^2 - b^2)\cos 2\alpha]$

(d) $\frac{1}{2}[a^2 + b^2 - (a^2 - b^2)\cos 2\alpha]$

37. $\left(\frac{\cos A + \cos B}{\sin A - \sin B}\right)^n + \left(\frac{\sin A + \sin B}{\cos A - \cos B}\right)^n$ (n, even or odd) is equal to

(a) $2\tan^n\left(\frac{A-B}{2}\right)$ (b) $2\cot^n\left(\frac{A-B}{2}\right)$

(c) 0 (d) None of these

38. Let $P(k) = \left(1 + \cos\frac{\pi}{4k}\right)\left(1 + \cos\frac{(2k-1)\pi}{4k}\right)\left(1 + \cos\frac{(2k+1)\pi}{4k}\right)\left(1 + \cos\frac{(4k-1)\pi}{4k}\right)$. Then,

(a) $P(3) = \frac{1}{16}$ (b) $P(4) = \frac{2 - \sqrt{2}}{16}$

(c) $P(5) = \frac{3 - \sqrt{5}}{32}$ (d) $P(6) = \frac{2 - \sqrt{3}}{16}$

39. If $x = a\cos^3\theta\sin^2\theta$, $y = a\sin^3\theta\cos^2\theta$ and $\frac{(x^2 + y^2)^p}{(xy)^q}$ $(p, q \in N)$ is independent of θ, then

(a) $p = 4$ (b) $p = 5$

(c) $q = 4$ (d) $q = 5$

Passage Based Questions

Passage I

(Q. Nos. 40 and 41)

- If a, b, c are the sides of ΔABC such that $3^{2a^2} - 2\cdot 3^{a^2+b^2+c^2} + 3^{2b^2+2c^2} = 0$, then

40. ΔABC is

(a) equilateral (b) right angled
(c) isosceles right angled (d) obtuse angled

41. If sides of ΔPQR are a, $b \sec C$, $c \operatorname{cosec} C$, then area of ΔPQR is

(a) $\frac{\sqrt{3}}{4}a^2$ (b) $\frac{\sqrt{3}}{4}b^2$ (c) $\frac{\sqrt{3}}{4}c^2$ (d) $\frac{1}{2}abc$

Passage II

(Q. Nos. 42 to 43)

- For $0 < x < \frac{\pi}{2}$, let

$P_{mn}(x) = m\log_{\cos x}(\sin x) + n\log_{\cos x}(\cot x)$;
where $m, n \in \{1, 2, \ldots, 9\}$
[For example :
$P_{29}(x) = 2\log_{\cos x}(\sin x) + 9\log_{\cos x}(\cot x)$ and
$P_{77}(x) = 7\log_{\cos x}(\sin x) + 7\log_{\cos x}(\cot x)$]
On the basis of above information, answer the following questions.

42. Which of the following is always correct?

(a) $P_{mn}(x) \ge m, \forall\, m \ge n$ (b) $P_{mn}(x) \ge n, \forall\, m \ge n$
(c) $2P_{mn}(x) \le n, \forall\, m \le n$ (d) $2P_{mn}(x) \le m, \forall\, m \le n$

43. The mean proportional of numbers $P_{49}\left(\frac{\pi}{4}\right)$ and $P_{94}\left(\frac{\pi}{4}\right)$ is equal to

(a) 4 (b) 6 (c) 9 (d) 10

Passage III

(Q. Nos. 44 to 45)

- If $7\theta = (2n+1)\pi$, where $n = 0, 1, 2, 3, 4, 5, 6$, then answer the following questions.

44. The equations whose roots are $\cos\frac{\pi}{7}, \cos\frac{3\pi}{7}, \cos\frac{5\pi}{7}$ is

(a) $8x^3 + 4x^2 + 4x + 1 = 0$ (b) $8x^3 - 4x^2 - 4x - 1 = 0$
(c) $8x^3 - 4x^2 - 4x - 1 = 0$ (d) $8x^3 + 4x^2 + 4x - 1 = 0$

45. The value of $\sec\frac{\pi}{7} + \sec\frac{3\pi}{7} + \sec\frac{5\pi}{7}$ is

(a) 4 (b) -4
(c) 3 (d) -3

Passage IV

(Q. Nos. 46 to 47)

- If $1 + 2\sin x + 3\sin^2 x + 4\sin^3 x + \ldots$ upto infinite terms $= 4$ and number of solutions of the equation in $\left[\frac{-3\pi}{2}, 4\pi\right]$ is k.

46. The value of k is equal to

(a) 4 (b) 5
(c) 6 (d) 7

47. The value of $\left|\frac{\cos 2x - 1}{\sin 2x}\right|$ is equal to

(a) 1 (b) $\sqrt{3}$
(c) $2 - \sqrt{3}$ (d) $\frac{1}{\sqrt{3}}$

Passage V

(Q. Nos. 48 to 49)

- Let α be a root of the equation $(2\sin x - \cos x)(1 + \cos x) = \sin^2 x$, β is a root of the equation $3\cos^2 x - 10\cos x + 3 = 0$ and γ is a root of the equation $1 - \sin 2x = \cos x - \sin x$, $0 \le \alpha, \beta, \gamma \le \frac{\pi}{2}$.

48. $\cos\alpha + \cos\beta + \cos\gamma$ can be equal to

(a) $\frac{3\sqrt{6} + 2\sqrt{2} + 6}{6\sqrt{2}}$ (b) $\frac{3\sqrt{3} + 8}{6}$
(c) $\frac{3\sqrt{3} + 2}{6}$ (d) None of these

49. $\sin(\alpha - \beta)$ is equal to

(a) 1 (b) 0
(c) $\frac{1 - 2\sqrt{6}}{6}$ (d) $\frac{\sqrt{3} - 2\sqrt{2}}{6}$

Stem Based Questions

Stem I

(Q. Nos. 50 to 51)

- Let consider the function

$$f_n(\theta) = \frac{\cos\frac{\theta}{2} + \cos 2\theta + \cos\frac{7\theta}{2} + \ldots + \cos(3n-2)\frac{\theta}{2}}{\sin\frac{\theta}{2} + \sin 2\theta + \sin\frac{7\theta}{2} + \ldots + \sin(3n-2)\frac{\theta}{2}},$$ then

50. If the value of $f_3\left(\frac{3\pi}{16}\right)$ is $\sqrt{k} - 1$, then k is .....

51. If the value of $f_5\left(\frac{\pi}{28}\right)$ is $\sqrt{k} + 1$, then k is .....

Stem II

(Q. Nos. 52 to 53)

- Let $\alpha, \beta, \gamma, \delta$ are the solutions of the equation $\tan\left(\theta + \frac{\pi}{4}\right) = 3\tan 3\theta$, no two of which have equal tangents.

52. The value of $3(\tan\alpha + \tan\beta + \tan\gamma + \tan\delta)$ is .....

53. The value of $-3\tan\alpha\tan\beta\tan\gamma\tan\delta$ is ....

Single Integer Type Questions

54. If $\sec x + \sec^2 x = 1$, then the value of $\tan^8 x - \tan^4 x - 2\tan^2 x$ is ....

55. In a ΔABC, $\dfrac{1}{1+\tan^2\frac{A}{2}} + \dfrac{1}{1+\tan^2\frac{B}{2}} + \dfrac{1}{1+\tan^2\frac{C}{2}} = k\left(1 + \sin\frac{A}{2}\sin\frac{B}{2}\sin\frac{C}{2}\right)$, then the value of k is ....

56. If $\dfrac{\sin\alpha}{\sin\beta} = \dfrac{\cos\gamma}{\cos\delta}$, then $\dfrac{\sin\left(\frac{\alpha-\beta}{2}\right)\cdot\cos\left(\frac{\alpha+\beta}{2}\right)\cdot\cos\delta}{\sin\left(\frac{\delta-\gamma}{2}\right)\cdot\sin\left(\frac{\delta+\gamma}{2}\right)\cdot\sin\beta}$ is equal to ....

57. Find the exact value of the expression $\tan\frac{\pi}{20} - \tan\frac{3\pi}{20} + \tan\frac{5\pi}{20} - \tan\frac{7\pi}{20} + \tan\frac{9\pi}{20}$.

58. Let $x = \dfrac{\sum_{n=1}^{44}\cos n^\circ}{\sum_{n=1}^{44}\sin n^\circ}$, find the greatest integer that does not exceed.

59. Find θ (in degree) satisfying the equation, $\tan 15^\circ\cdot\tan 25^\circ\cdot\tan 35^\circ = \tan\theta$, where $\theta \in (0, 45^\circ)$

60. Find the exact value of $\operatorname{cosec} 10^\circ + \operatorname{cosec} 50^\circ - \operatorname{cosec} 70^\circ$.

61. If $\cos 5\alpha = \cos^5\alpha$, where $\alpha \in \left(0, \frac{\pi}{2}\right)$, then find the possible values of $(\sec^2\alpha + \operatorname{cosec}^2\alpha + \cot^2\alpha)$.

62. If $k = \tan^2\frac{\pi}{16} + \tan^2\frac{2\pi}{16} + \tan^2\frac{3\pi}{16} + \ldots + \tan^2\frac{7\pi}{16}$, then find the value of $\frac{k}{7}$.

63. Compute the square of the value of the expression $\dfrac{4+\sec 20^\circ}{\operatorname{cosec} 20^\circ}$

64. In ΔABC, if $\dfrac{\sin A}{3} = \dfrac{\cos B}{3} = \dfrac{\tan C}{2}$, then the value of $\left(\dfrac{\sin A}{\cot 2A} + \dfrac{\cos B}{\cot 2B} + \dfrac{\tan C}{\cot 2C}\right)$ is ....

65. Let f and g be function defined by $f(\theta) = \cos^2\theta$ and $g(\theta) = \tan^2\theta$, suppose α and β satisfy $2f(\alpha) - g(\beta) = 1$, then value of $2f(\beta) - g(\alpha)$ is ....

66. If sum of the series $1 + x\log_{\left|\frac{1-\sin x}{\cos x}\right|}\left(\dfrac{1+\sin x}{\cos x}\right)^{1/2} + x^2\log_{\left|\frac{1-\sin x}{\cos x}\right|}\left(\dfrac{1+\sin x}{\cos x}\right)^{1/4} + \ldots\infty$ (wherever defined) is equal to $\dfrac{k(1-x)}{(2-x)}$, then k is equal to ....

Numerical Value Type Questions

67. If $\dfrac{9x}{\cos\theta} + \dfrac{5y}{\sin\theta} = 56$ and $\dfrac{9x\sin\theta}{\cos^2\theta} - \dfrac{5y\cos\theta}{\sin^2\theta} = 0$, then the value of $\left[(9x)^{\frac{2}{3}} + (5y)^{\frac{2}{3}}\right]^3$ is ....

68. The $\angle A$ of the ΔABC is obtuse. $x = 2635 - \tan B\tan C$, if $[x]$ denotes the greatest integer function, the value of $[x]$ is ....

69. If $4\cos 36^\circ + \cot\left(7\frac{1}{2}^\circ\right) = \sqrt{n_1} + \sqrt{n_2} + \sqrt{n_3} + \sqrt{n_4} + \sqrt{n_5} + \sqrt{n_6}$, then the value of $\sum_{i=1}^{6} n_i^2$ must be ....

70. If $\sin^2 A = x$ and $\prod_{r=1}^{4}\sin(rA) = ax^2 + bx^3 + cx^4 + dx^5$, then the value of $10a - 7b + 15c - 5d$ must be ....

71. If $x, y \in R$ satisfies $(x+5)^2 + (y-12)^2 = (14)^2$, then the minimum value of $10\sqrt{x^2+y^2}$ is ....

72. If the least degree of a polynomial with integer coefficient whose one of the roots may be $\cos 12^\circ$ is k, then the value of $11k$ is ....

73. If $A+B+C=180°$, $\dfrac{\sin 2A+\sin 2B+\sin 2C}{\sin A+\sin B+\sin C}=k\sin\dfrac{A}{2}$ $\sin\dfrac{B}{2}\sin\dfrac{C}{2}$, then the value of $3k^3+2k^2+k+1$ is equal to ....

74. The value of $(x)=x^4+4x^3+2x^2-4x+17$, when $x=\cot\dfrac{11\pi}{8}$ is ....

75. In any ΔABC, then minimum value of $2020\sum\dfrac{\sqrt{(\sin A)}}{(\sqrt{(\sin B)}+\sqrt{(\sin C)}-\sqrt{(\sin A)}}$ must be ....

76. If $\sin\theta+\sin^2\theta+\sin^3\theta=1$, then the value of $10+\cos^6\theta-4\cos^4\theta+8\cos^2\theta$ must be ....

77. $80\left(\cos\theta-\cos\dfrac{\pi}{8}\right)\left(\cos\theta-\cos\dfrac{3\pi}{8}\right)\left(\cos\theta-\cos\dfrac{5\pi}{8}\right)$ $\left(\cos\theta-\cos\dfrac{7\pi}{8}\right)=\lambda\cos 4\theta$, then the value of λ is ....

78. If $\dfrac{1}{\sin 20°}+\dfrac{1}{\sqrt{3}\cos 20°}=2k\cos 40°$, then $18k^4+162k^2+369$ is equal to ....

Matching Type Questions

79. Match the statement of Column I with values of Column II.

Column I		Column II
(A) If $\theta+\phi=\dfrac{\pi}{2}$, where θ and ϕ are positive, then $(\sin\theta+\sin\phi)\sin\left(\dfrac{\pi}{4}\right)$ is always less than	(p)	1
(B) If $\sin\theta-\sin\phi=a$ and $\cos\theta+\cos\phi=b$, then a^2+b^2 cannot exceed	(q)	2
(C) If $3\sin\theta+5\cos\theta=5$, $(\theta\neq 0)$, then the value of $5\sin\theta-3\cos\theta$ is	(r)	3
(D) Maximum value of $4\sin\theta-3\cos\theta$ is	(s)	4
	(t)	5

80. Match the statement of Column I with values of Column II.

Column I		Column II
(A) If maximum and minimum values of $\dfrac{7+6\tan\theta-\tan^2\theta}{(1+\tan^2\theta)}$ for all real values of $\theta\neq(2n+1)\dfrac{\pi}{2}$ are λ and μ respectively, then	(p)	$\lambda+\mu=2$
(B) If maximum and minimum values of $5\cos\theta+3\cos\left(\theta+\dfrac{\pi}{3}\right)+3$ for all real values of θ are λ and μ respectively, then	(q)	$\lambda-\mu=6$
(C) If maximum and minimum values of $1+\sin\left(\dfrac{\pi}{4}+\theta\right)+2\cos\left(\dfrac{\pi}{4}-\theta\right)$ for all real values of θ are λ and μ respectively, then	(r)	$\lambda+\mu=6$
(D) If maximum and minimum values of $3+\sin\left(\dfrac{\pi}{4}+\theta\right)+2\cos\left(\dfrac{\pi}{4}+\theta\right)$ for all real values of θ are λ and μ respectively, then	(s)	$\lambda-\mu=10$
	(t)	$\lambda-\mu=14$

81. Match the statement of Column I with values of Column II.

Column I		Column II
(A) The number of solutions of the equation $\lvert\cot x\rvert=\cot x+\dfrac{1}{\sin x}(0<x<\pi)$ is	(p)	0
(B) If $\sin\theta+\sin\phi=\dfrac{1}{2}$ and $\cos\theta+\cos\phi=2$, then value of $\cot\left(\dfrac{\theta+\phi}{2}\right)$ is	(q)	$\dfrac{1}{3}$
(C) The value of $\sin^2\alpha+\sin\left(\dfrac{\pi}{3}-\alpha\right)$ $\sin\left(\dfrac{\pi}{3}+\alpha\right)$ is	(r)	1
(D) If $\tan\theta=3\tan\phi$, then maximum value of $\tan^2(\theta-\phi)$ is	(s)	$\dfrac{3}{4}$
	(t)	4

82. Match the statement of Column I with values of Column II.

Column I	Column II
(A) In a ΔABC, $\sin\left(\frac{A}{2}\right) + \sin\left(\frac{B}{2}\right) + \sin\left(\frac{C}{2}\right) =$	(p) $-1 + 4\sin\left(\frac{\pi + A}{4}\right)\sin\left(\frac{\pi + B}{4}\right)\cos\left(\frac{\pi + C}{4}\right)$
(B) In a ΔABC, $\sin\left(\frac{A}{2}\right) + \sin\left(\frac{B}{2}\right) - \sin\left(\frac{C}{2}\right) =$	(q) $4\cos\left(\frac{\pi + A}{4}\right)\cos\left(\frac{\pi + B}{4}\right)\cos\left(\frac{\pi - C}{4}\right)$
(C) In a ΔABC, $\cos\left(\frac{A}{2}\right) + \cos\left(\frac{B}{2}\right) - \cos\left(\frac{C}{2}\right)$	(r) $1 + 4\sin\left(\frac{\pi - A}{4}\right)\sin\left(\frac{\pi - B}{4}\right)\sin\left(\frac{\pi - C}{4}\right)$
(D) In a ΔABC, $\cos\left(\frac{A}{2}\right) + \cos\left(\frac{B}{2}\right) + \cos\left(\frac{C}{2}\right)$	(s) $-1 + 4\cos\left(\frac{\pi - A}{4}\right)\cos\left(\frac{\pi - B}{4}\right)\sin\left(\frac{\pi - C}{4}\right)$
	(t) $4\cos\left(\frac{\pi - A}{4}\right)\cos\left(\frac{\pi - B}{4}\right)\cos\left(\frac{\pi - C}{4}\right)$

83. Match the statement of column I with types of triangles of column II.

Column I	Column II
(A) In ΔABC, if $\cos 2A + \cos 2B + \cos 2C = -1$, then we can conclude that triangle is	(p) Equilateral triangle
(B) In ΔABC, if $\tan A > 0$, $\tan B > 0$ and $\tan A \tan B < 1$, then triangle is	(q) Right angled triangle
(C) In ΔABC, if $\cos^3 A + \cos^3 B + \cos^3 C = 3\cos A \cos B \cos C$, then triangle is	(r) Acute angled triangle
(D) In ΔABC, if $\cot A > 0$, $\cot B > 0$ and $\cot A \cot B < 1$, then triangle is	(s) Obtuse angled triangle

Previous Years Questions

84. Let α and β be real numbers such that $-\frac{\pi}{4} < \beta < 0 < \alpha < \frac{\pi}{4}$. If $\sin(\alpha + \beta) = \frac{1}{3}$ and $\cos(\alpha - \beta) = \frac{2}{3}$, then the greatest integer less than or equal to $\left(\frac{\sin\alpha}{\cos\beta} + \frac{\cos\beta}{\sin\alpha} + \frac{\cos\alpha}{\sin\beta} + \frac{\sin\beta}{\cos\alpha}\right)^2$ is ....

[Numerical Value Type, 2022 Adv.]

85. Let α and β be non-zero real numbers such that $2(\cos\beta - \cos\alpha) + \cos\alpha\cos\beta = 1$. Then which of the following is/are true?

[More Than One Correct, 2017 Adv.]

(a) $\sqrt{3}\tan\left(\frac{\alpha}{2}\right) - \tan\left(\frac{\beta}{2}\right) = 0$

(b) $\tan\left(\frac{\alpha}{2}\right) - \sqrt{3}\tan\left(\frac{\beta}{2}\right) = 0$

(c) $\tan\left(\frac{\alpha}{2}\right) + \sqrt{3}\tan\left(\frac{\beta}{2}\right) = 0$

(d) $\sqrt{3}\tan\left(\frac{\alpha}{2}\right) + \tan\left(\frac{\beta}{2}\right) = 0$

86. Let $-\frac{\pi}{6} < \theta < -\frac{\pi}{12}$. Suppose α_1 and β_1 are the roots of the equation $x^2 - 2x\sec\theta + 1 = 0$, and α_2 and β_2 are the roots of the equation $x^2 + 2x\tan\theta - 1 = 0$. If $\alpha_1 > \beta_1$ and $\alpha_2 > \beta_2$, then $\alpha_1 + \beta_2$ equals to

[Single Correct Type, 2016 Adv.]

(a) $2(\sec\theta - \tan\theta)$ (b) $2\sec\theta$
(c) $-2\tan\theta$ (d) 0

87. The value of

$$\sum_{k=1}^{13} \frac{1}{\sin\left(\frac{\pi}{4} + \frac{(k-1)\pi}{6}\right)\sin\left(\frac{\pi}{4} + \frac{k\pi}{6}\right)}$$ is equal to

[Single Correct Type, 2016 Adv.]

(a) $3 - \sqrt{3}$ (b) $2(3 - \sqrt{3})$
(c) $2(\sqrt{3} - 1)$ (d) $2(2 + \sqrt{3})$

EXERCISE 3

Challenging Problems

1. For all θ in $[0, \pi/2]$, show that $\cos(\sin\theta) > \sin(\cos\theta)$.

2. Show that $2^{\sin x} + 2^{\cos x} \geq 2^{1-\frac{1}{\sqrt{2}}}$ for all real x.

3. If $\dfrac{\tan 3A}{\tan A} = k$, show that $\dfrac{\sin 3A}{\sin A} = \dfrac{2k}{k-1}$ and hence or otherwise prove that either $k > 3$ or $k < \dfrac{1}{3}$.

4. If ABC is a triangle and $\tan\dfrac{A}{2}, \tan\dfrac{B}{2}, \tan\dfrac{C}{2}$ are in HP, then find minimum value of $\cot\dfrac{B}{2}$.

5. (i) If $\tan A - \tan B = x$ and $\cot B - \cot A = y$.

   Prove that $\cot(A - B) = \dfrac{1}{x} + \dfrac{1}{y}$.

   (ii) If $2\cos A = x + \dfrac{1}{x}$, $2\cos B = y + \dfrac{1}{y}$, then show that

   $2\cos(A - B) = \dfrac{x}{y} + \dfrac{y}{x}$.

6. Find the roots of the following cubic equations $2x^3 - 3x^2\cos(A - B) - 2x\cos^2(A + B) + \sin 2A \sin 2B \cos(A - B) = 0$.

7. If $m^2 + m'^2 + 2mm'\cos\theta = 1$, $n^2 + n'^2 + 2nn'\cos\theta = 1$ and $mn + m'n' + (mn' + m'n)\cos\theta = 0$, then prove that $m^2 + n^2 = \text{cosec}^2\theta$.

8. Prove that from the equality $\dfrac{\sin^4\alpha}{a} + \dfrac{\cos^4\alpha}{b} = \dfrac{1}{a+b}$ follows the relation,

$$\frac{\sin^8\alpha}{a^3} + \frac{\cos^8\alpha}{b^3} = \frac{1}{(a+b)^3}$$

and $$\frac{\sin^{4n} x}{a^{2n-1}} + \frac{\cos^{4n} x}{b^{2n-1}} = \frac{1}{(a+b)^{2n-1}}.$$

9. Evaluate $\sum_{r=2}^{n} \sin r\alpha$, where $(n+2)\alpha = 2\pi$ (without using formula.)

10. Sum the series $\sqrt{1 + \cos\alpha} + \sqrt{1 + \cos 2\alpha} + \sqrt{1 + \cos 3\alpha} + \ldots$ to n terms.

11. If $A + B + C = \pi$, then show that $\cot A + \cot B + \cot C - \text{cosec}\, A \cdot \text{cosec}\, B \cdot \text{cosec}\, C = \cot A \cdot \cot B \cdot \cot C$

12. In ΔABC, if $\cot\theta = \cot A + \cot B + \cot C$, prove that $\sin^3\theta = \sin(A - \theta)\sin(B - \theta)\sin(C - \theta)$.

13. If α, β are two different values of θ which satisfy is $bc\cos\theta\cos\phi + ac\sin\theta\sin\phi = ab$, then prove that $(b^2 + c^2 - a^2)\cos\alpha\cos\beta + ac\sin\alpha\sin\beta = a^2 + b^2 - c^2$.

14. Find all number pairs x, y that satisfy the equation;

$$\tan^4 x + \tan^4 y + 2\cot^2 x \cot^2 y = 3 + \sin^2(x + y); \quad \forall x, y \in \left[0, \frac{\pi}{2}\right]$$

15. Prove that $\tan\dfrac{3\pi}{11} + 4\sin\dfrac{2\pi}{11} = \sqrt{11}$.

16. In a ΔABC, $\tan A + \tan B + \tan C = k$, then find the interval in which k should lie so that

   (A) there exists exactly one isosceles ΔABC

   (B) there exists exactly two isosceles ΔABC

   (C) can there exist three non-similar isosceles triangles for any real value of k.

Answer Key

Exercise 1

1. (b)	2. (b)	3. (a)	4. (a)	5. (b)	6. (a)	7. (b)	8. (a)	9. (b)	10. (d)
11. (a)	12. (b)	13. (b)	14. (b)	15. (a)	16. (a)	17. (c)	18. (b)	19. (c)	20. (b)
21. (b)	22. (c)	23. (b)	24. (c)	25. (b)	26. (c)	27. (b)	28. (b)	29. (a)	30. (d)
31. (c)	32. (c)	33. (c)	34. (a)	35. (c)	36. (c)	37. (c)	38. (d)	39. (c)	40. (d)
41. (a)	42. (d)	43. (c)	44. (c)	45. (c)	46. (b)	47. (c)	48. (b)	49. (c)	50. (d)
51. (c)	52. (c)	53. (d)	54. (d)	55. (4)	56. (5)	57. (0)	58. (4)	59. (2)	60. (7)
61. (1)	62. (1)	63. (4)	64. (1)	65. (2)	66. (16)	67. (3)	68. (12)	69. (3)	70. (1024)
71. (2)	72. (b)	73. (b)	74. (48)	75. (d)	76. (b)	77. (b)	78. (4)	79. (b)	80. (a)
81. (c)	82. (b)	83. (b)	84. (d)	85. (80)	86. (c)	87. (c)	88. (b)	89. (d)	90. (b)
91. (1)	92. (d)								

Exercise 2

1. (c)	2. (b)	3. (a)	4. (d)	5. (b)	6. (a)	7. (a)	8. (a)	9. (d)	10. (a)
11. (d)	12. (b)	13. (b)	14. (b)	15. (c)	16. (a)	17. (a)	18. (a)	19. (d)	20. (a,b,c,d)
21. (a,b,c)	22. (b,d)	23. (b,c)	24. (b,c)	25. (b,c)	26. (a,b,d)	27. (b,c)	28. (c,d)	29. (b,c,d)	30. (b,c)
31. (a,b,c,d)	32. (a,b,c,d)	33. (c,d)	34. (a,b,c,d)	35. (b,c)	36. (a,b,c,d)	37. (b,c)	38. (a,b,c,d)	39. (b,c)	40. (b)
41. (a)	42. (b)	43. (b)	44. (b)	45. (a)	46. (b)	47. (d)	48. (b)	49. (c)	50. (2)
51. (2)	52. (0)	53. (1)	54. (1)	55. (2)	56. (1)	57. (5)	58. (2)	59. (5)	60. (6)
61. (5)	62. (5)	63. (3)	64. (4)	65. (1)	66. (2)	67. (3136)	68. (2634)	69. (91)	70. (3448)
71. (10)	72. (44)	73. (1673)	74. (16)	75. (6060)	76. (14)	77. (10)	78. (1521)		

79. A—(p, q, r, s, t); B—(s, t); C—(r); D—(t)
80. A—(r, s); B—(r, t); C—(p, q); D—(r)
81. A—(r); B—(p); C—(s); D—(q)
82. A—(r); B—(p, s); C—(q); D—(t)
83. A—(q); B—(s); C—(p); D—(r)
84. (1) 85. (b,c) 86. (c) 87. (c)

Solutions

Exercise 1 - JEE Main Pattern

1. Given series $= \left(\sin\frac{2\pi}{11} - \cos\frac{2\pi}{11}\right) + \left(\sin\frac{4\pi}{11} - \cos\frac{4\pi}{11}\right)$

$$+ \left(\sin\frac{6\pi}{11} - \cos\frac{6\pi}{11}\right) + \ldots + \left(\sin\frac{20\pi}{11} - \cos\frac{20\pi}{11}\right)$$

$$= \left(\sin\frac{2\pi}{11} + \sin\frac{4\pi}{11} + \ldots + \sin\frac{20\pi}{11}\right)$$

$$-\left(\cos\frac{2\pi}{11} + \cos\frac{4\pi}{11} + \ldots + \cos\frac{20\pi}{11}\right)$$

$$= \frac{\sin\pi\cdot\sin\frac{10\pi}{11}}{\sin\frac{\pi}{11}} - \frac{\cos\pi\cdot\sin\frac{10\pi}{11}}{\sin\frac{\pi}{11}}$$

$$= 0 + \frac{\sin\left(\pi - \frac{\pi}{11}\right)}{\sin\frac{\pi}{11}} = 1$$

2. $(a+1)^2 + \text{cosec}^2\left(\frac{\pi a}{2} + \frac{\pi x}{2}\right) - 1 = 0$

or $\quad (a+1)^2 + \cot^2\left(\frac{\pi a}{2} + \frac{\pi x}{2}\right) = 0$

From option (b), if $a = -1$ and $\cot^2\left(\frac{-\pi}{2} + \frac{\pi x}{2}\right) = 0$

$\Rightarrow \quad \tan^2\left(\frac{\pi x}{2}\right) = 0$

$\Rightarrow \quad \frac{x}{2} = I$

3. $f(x) = 9\sin^2 x - 16\cos^2 x - 10(3\sin x - 4\cos x)$

$$-10(3\sin x + 4\cos x) + 100$$

$$= 25\sin^2 x - 60\sin x + 84 = (5\sin x - 6)^2 + 48$$

$\therefore f(x)_{\min}$ occurs when $\sin x = 1$

Minimum value = 49

4. $S = \frac{1}{1+\tan^3 0°} + \frac{1}{1+\tan^3 10°} + \ldots + \frac{1}{1+\tan^3 80°}$

Now, $\frac{1}{1+\tan^3\theta} + \frac{1}{1+\tan^3(90° - \theta)}$

$$= \frac{1}{1+\tan^3\theta} + \frac{1}{1+\cot^3\theta}$$

$$= \frac{1}{1+\tan^3\theta} + \frac{\tan^3\theta}{1+\tan^3\theta}$$

$$= \frac{1+\tan^3\theta}{1+\tan^3\theta} = 1$$

Hence, $S = 1 + (1+1+1+1) = 5$

5. Clearly, $\sqrt{1-\sin^2 110°}\cdot\sec 110°$

$$= |\cos 110°|\sec 110°$$

$$= -\cos 110°\sec 110°$$

$$= -1$$

6. $\tan\alpha + \tan\beta = -p$

$\tan\alpha\tan\beta = q$

$\tan(\alpha+\beta) = \frac{-p}{1-q} = \frac{p}{q-1}$

$$\frac{1}{1+\tan^2(\alpha+\beta)}[\tan^2(\alpha+\beta) + p\tan(\alpha+\beta) + q]$$

$$= \frac{1}{1+\frac{p^2}{(q-1)^2}}\left[\frac{p^2}{(q-1)^2} + \frac{p^2}{(q-1)} + q\right]$$

$$= \frac{1}{(q-1)^2 + p^2}[p^2 + p^2(q-1) + q(q-1)^2]$$

$$= \frac{1}{p^2 + (q-1)^2}[p^2 q + q(q-1)^2]$$

$$= q\left[\frac{p^2 + (q-1)^2}{p^2 + (q-1)^2}\right] = q$$

7. $\sin\left(\frac{\pi}{2^{2009}}\right)\cos\left(\frac{\pi}{2^{2009}}\right) = \frac{1}{2}\sin\left(\frac{\pi}{2^{2008}}\right)$

$$= \frac{1}{2^2}2\sin\left(\frac{\pi}{2^{2008}}\right)\cos\left(\frac{\pi}{2^{2008}}\right)$$

$$= \frac{1}{2^2}\sin\left(\frac{\pi}{2^{2007}}\right)$$

Similarly, continued product upto,

$$\cos\left(\frac{\pi}{2^2}\right) = \frac{1}{2^{2008}}\sin\left(\frac{\pi}{2}\right) = \frac{1}{2^{2008}}$$

8. $\tan(A+B) = \frac{\tan A + \tan B}{1 - \tan A\tan B}$

$$= \frac{\tan A + \frac{n\sin A\cos A}{1 - n\cos^2 A}}{1 - \tan A\cdot\frac{n\sin A\cos A}{1 - n\cos^2 A}}$$

$$= \frac{\sin A(1 - n\cos^2 A) + n\sin A\cos^2 A}{\cos A(1 - n\cos^2 A) - n\sin^2 A\cos A}$$

$$= \frac{\sin A - 0}{\cos A(1 - n\cos^2 A - n\sin^2 A)}$$

$$= \frac{\sin A}{(1-n)\cos A}$$

9. Expression $(\cos^4 1^\circ + \cos^4 2^\circ + \cos^4 3^\circ + \ldots + \cos^4 179^\circ)$

$$- (\sin^4 1^\circ + \sin^4 2^\circ + \sin^4 3^\circ + \ldots + \sin^4 179^\circ)$$

$$= \cos 2^\circ + \cos 4^\circ + \cos 6^\circ + \ldots + \cos(358^\circ)$$

$$= \frac{\cos\left(\frac{2^\circ + 358^\circ}{2}\right) \cdot \sin(179 \times 1^\circ)}{\sin 1^\circ} = \cos(180^\circ) = -1$$

10. $\sin x + \sin y = a$ ...(i)

$\cos x + \cos y = 2a$ ...(ii)

On squaring and adding Eqs. (i) and (ii), we get

$$2 + 2\cos(x - y) = 5a^2 \Rightarrow \cos(x - y) = \frac{5a^2 - 2}{2}$$

11. $P(x) = \sqrt{3 + 2(\cos x + \cos x + \cos 2x)}$

$$= \sqrt{3 + 2(2\cos x + 2\cos^2 x) - 2}$$

$$= \sqrt{4\cos^2 x + 4\cos x + 1} = |2\cos x + 1|$$

12. Given, $\dfrac{\cos 2B}{1} = \dfrac{\cos(A + C)}{\cos(A - C)}$

On applying componendo and dividendo, we get

$$\frac{1 + \cos 2B}{1 - \cos 2B} = \frac{\cos(A - C) + \cos(A + C)}{\cos(A - C) - \cos(A + C)}$$

$$\Rightarrow \quad \frac{2\cos^2 B}{2\sin^2 B} = \frac{2\cos A \cos C}{2\sin A \sin C}$$

$$\Rightarrow \quad \cot^2 B = \cot A \cot C$$

Thus, $\cot A, \cot B, \cot C$ are in GP.

13. In ΔABC, $\quad \sum \tan\frac{A}{2} \cdot \tan\frac{B}{2} = 1$

$$\therefore \quad \sum \tan^2\frac{A}{2} \ge \sum \tan\frac{A}{2} \tan\frac{B}{2} = 1$$

$$[\because a^2 + b^2 + c^2 - ab - bc - ca \ge 0, \forall a, b, c \in R]$$

$$\therefore \quad 3 + \sum \tan^2\frac{A}{2} \ge 4$$

$$\Rightarrow \quad 3 + \tan^2\frac{A}{2} + \tan^2\frac{B}{2} + \tan^2\frac{C}{2} \ge 1 + 3$$

$$\Rightarrow \quad \sec^2\frac{A}{2} + \sec^2\frac{B}{2} + \sec^2\frac{C}{2} \ge 4$$

14. The given equation can be rewritten as $(2x - 1)^2 + 1 = \sin^2 y$ which is possible only when

$$x = \frac{1}{2}, \sin^2 y = 1 \Rightarrow y = \frac{-\pi}{2}, \frac{\pi}{2} \quad [\text{as } x^2 + y^2 \le 3]$$

Thus, there are only two pairs (x, y) satisfying the given equation. They are $\left(\frac{1}{2}, \frac{-\pi}{2}\right)$ and $\left(\frac{1}{2}, \frac{\pi}{2}\right)$.

15. Given, $3\sin A + 4\cos B = 6$ ...(i)

$3\cos A + 4\sin B = 1$ ...(ii)

On squaring and adding Eqs. (i) and (ii), we get

$$9 + 16 + 24\sin(A + B) = 37$$

$$\Rightarrow \quad 24\sin(A + B) = 12$$

$$\Rightarrow \quad \sin(A + B) = \frac{1}{2} \Rightarrow \sin C = \frac{1}{2}$$

$$\Rightarrow \quad C = 30^\circ \text{ or } 150^\circ$$

If $C = 150^\circ$, then even of $B = 0$ and $A = 30^\circ$.

The quantity $3\sin A + 4\cos B$

$$3 \cdot \frac{1}{2} + 4 = 5\frac{1}{2} < 6$$

Hence, $C = 150^\circ$ is not possible

$$\Rightarrow \quad \angle C = 30^\circ \text{ only}$$

16. **Decoding the Question**

We use the fact that area of sector of a circle, if θ in radians is $\frac{1}{2}r^2\theta$.

$$\text{Area} = 3 \cdot (8 \cdot 3) + 3 \cdot \frac{1}{2}r^2\theta$$

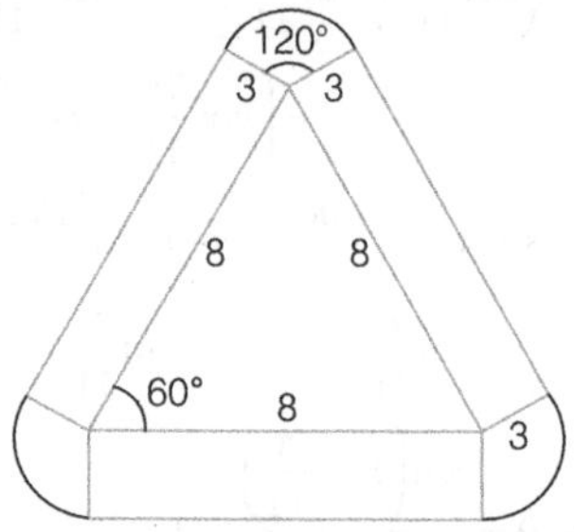

$$= 72 + \frac{3}{2} \cdot 9 \cdot \frac{2\pi}{3} = 72 + 9\pi = 9(8 + \pi)$$

17. $m + n = a\{(\cos^3\alpha + \sin^3\alpha) + 3\cos\alpha \sin\alpha(\cos\alpha + \sin\alpha)\}$

$m + n = a\{\cos\alpha + \sin\alpha\}^3$

Similarly, $\quad m - n = a\{\cos\alpha - \sin\alpha\}^3$

$(m + n)^{2/3} = a^{2/3}(\cos\alpha + \sin\alpha)^2$ ...(i)

Similarly, $(m - n)^{2/3} = a^{2/3}(\cos\alpha - \sin\alpha)^2$ ...(ii)

On adding Eqs. (i) and (ii), we get

$$(m + n)^{2/3} + (m - n)^{2/3} = a^{2/3}(2) = 2a^{2/3}$$

18. We have, $0 < \theta_i < \pi$ for $1 \le i \le n$

$\therefore \sin\theta_i > 0, i = 1, 2, 3, \ldots, n$

Now, $\dfrac{\sin\theta_1 + \sin\theta_2 + \sin\theta_3 + \ldots + \sin\theta_n}{n}$

$$\le \sin\left(\frac{\theta_1 + \theta_2 + \theta_3 + \ldots + \theta_n}{n}\right)$$

$$\Rightarrow \frac{\sin\theta_1 + \sin\theta_2 + \sin\theta_3 + \ldots + \sin\theta_n}{n} \le \sin\left(\frac{\pi}{n}\right)$$

$$\therefore \quad \sin\theta_1 + \sin\theta_2 + \sin\theta_3 + \ldots + \sin\theta_n \le n\sin\left(\frac{\pi}{n}\right)$$

19. $\displaystyle\sum_{r=1}^{18} \cos^2(5r)^\circ = \cos^2 5^\circ + \cos^2 10^\circ$

$$+ \cos^2 15^\circ + \ldots + \cos^2 85^\circ + \cos^2 90^\circ$$

$$= (\cos^2 5^\circ + \cos^2 85^\circ) + (\cos^2 10^\circ + \cos^2 80^\circ)$$

$$+ (\cos^2 15^\circ + \cos^2 75^\circ) + \ldots + (\cos^2 40^\circ + \cos^2 50^\circ) + \cos^2 45^\circ$$

$$= (\cos^2 5^\circ + \sin^2 5^\circ) + (\cos^2 10^\circ + \sin^2 10^\circ)$$

$$+ (\cos^2 15^\circ + \sin^2 15^\circ) + \ldots + (\cos^2 40^\circ + \sin^2 40^\circ) + \cos^2 45^\circ$$

$$= 1 + 1 + 1 + \ldots + 1 + \frac{1}{2} = 8 + \frac{1}{2} = \frac{17}{2}$$

20. $4x^2 - 4x|\sin\theta| - (1-\sin^2\theta) = -1 + (2x - |\sin\theta|)^2$

$\therefore$ Minimum value $= -1$

21. $\because \cos 3A + \cos 3B + \cos 3C = 1$

$$\Rightarrow \cos 3A + \cos 3B + \cos 3C - 1 = 0$$

$$\Rightarrow \cos 3A + \cos 3B + \cos 3C + \cos 3\pi = 0$$

$$\Rightarrow 2\cos\left(\frac{3A+3B}{2}\right)\cos\left(\frac{3A-3B}{2}\right) + 2\cos\left(\frac{3\pi+3C}{2}\right)\cos\left(\frac{3\pi-3C}{2}\right) = 0$$

$$\Rightarrow 2\cos\left(\frac{3\pi-3C}{2}\right)\left\{\cos\left(\frac{3A-3B}{2}\right) + \cos\left(\frac{3\pi+3C}{2}\right)\right\} = 0$$

$$\Rightarrow 2\cos\left(\frac{3\pi}{2} - \frac{3C}{2}\right)\cdot 2\cos\left(\frac{3\pi+3C+3A-3B}{4}\right)\cdot\cos\left(\frac{3\pi+3C-3A+3B}{4}\right) = 0$$

$$\Rightarrow 2\cos\left(\frac{3\pi}{2} - \frac{3C}{2}\right)\cdot 2\cos\left(\frac{3\pi}{2} - \frac{3B}{2}\right)\cdot\cos\left(\frac{3\pi}{2} - \frac{3A}{2}\right) = 0$$

$$\Rightarrow -4\sin\left(\frac{3A}{2}\right)\sin\left(\frac{3B}{2}\right)\sin\left(\frac{3C}{2}\right) = 0$$

$$\Rightarrow \sin\left(\frac{3A}{2}\right)\sin\left(\frac{3B}{2}\right)\sin\left(\frac{3C}{2}\right) = 0$$

$$\therefore \frac{3A}{2} = \pi \text{ or } \frac{3B}{2} = \pi \text{ or } \frac{3C}{2} = \pi$$

$$\therefore A = \frac{2\pi}{3} \text{ or } B = \frac{2\pi}{3} \text{ or } C = \frac{2\pi}{3}$$

22. $\because |\tan A| < 1$

$$\Rightarrow -1 < \tan A < 1 \text{ and } 0 \le |A| < \frac{\pi}{2}$$

$$\Rightarrow -\frac{\pi}{2} < A < \frac{\pi}{2}$$

$$\because \sqrt{(1+\sin 2A)} = \sqrt{1 + \frac{2\tan A}{1+\tan^2 A}} = \frac{|1+\tan A|}{\sqrt{(1+\tan^2 A)}} = \frac{(1+\tan A)}{\sqrt{(1+\tan^2 A)}}$$

$$\text{and } \sqrt{(1-\sin 2A)} = \sqrt{1 - \left(\frac{2\tan A}{1+\tan^2 A}\right)} = \frac{|1-\tan A|}{\sqrt{(1+\tan^2 A)}} = \frac{(1-\tan A)}{\sqrt{(1-\tan^2 A)}}$$

$$\therefore \frac{\sqrt{(1+\sin 2A)} + \sqrt{(1-\sin 2A)}}{\sqrt{(1+\sin 2A)} - \sqrt{(1-\sin 2A)}} = \frac{2}{2\tan A} = \cot A$$

23. Let $f(\theta) = \cos^2(\cos\theta) + \sin^2(\sin\theta)$

$\because \quad -1 \le \cos\theta \le 1$ and $-1 \le \sin\theta \le 1$

$\therefore \quad \cos 1 \le \cos(\cos\theta) \le 1$ and $-\sin 1 \le \sin(\sin\theta) \le \sin 1$

$\therefore \quad \cos^2 1 \le \cos^2(\cos\theta) \le 1$ and $0 \le \sin^2(\sin\theta) \le \sin^2 1$

$\therefore$ Maximum value of $f(\theta) = 1 + \sin^2 1$

24. Let $f(x) = 27^{\cos 2x}\, 81^{\sin 2x} = 3^{3\cos 2x + 4\sin 2x}$

$$= 3^{5\left(\frac{3}{5}\cos 2x + \frac{4}{5}\sin 2x\right)}$$

Let $\frac{3}{5} = \sin\phi$ and $\frac{4}{5} = \cos\phi$

Thus, $\quad f(x) = 3^{5(\sin\phi\cos 2x + \cos\phi\sin 2x)} = 3^{5[(\sin(\phi+2x))]}$

For minimum value of given function, $\sin(\phi + 2x)$ will be minimum.

i.e. $\quad \sin(\phi + 2x) = -1$

$$\therefore \quad f(x) = 3^{5(-1)} = \frac{1}{243}$$

Alternate Solution

Let $\quad f(x) = 27^{\cos 2x}\, 81^{\sin 2x} = 3^{4\sin 2x} = 3^{3\cos 2x + 4\sin 2x}$

For minimum value of given function, $3\cos 2x + 4\sin 2x$ will be minimum.

$$\therefore \quad -\sqrt{3^2+4^2} \le 3\cos 2x + 4\sin 2x \le \sqrt{3^2+4^2}$$

$$\Rightarrow \quad -5 \le 3\cos 2x + 4\sin 2x \le 5$$

$\therefore$ Minimum of $3\cos 2x + 4\sin 2x = -5$

So, min $f(x) = 3^{-5} = \frac{1}{243}$

25. Given $4n\alpha = \pi \Rightarrow 2n\alpha = \frac{\pi}{2}$

Now, $\cot\alpha\cdot\cot(2n-1)\alpha = \cot\alpha\cot\left(\frac{\pi}{2} - \alpha\right)$

$$= \cot\alpha\cdot\tan\alpha = 1$$

Similarly, $\cot 2\alpha \cos(2n-2)\alpha = 1$,

$\cot 3\alpha\cdot\cot(2n-3)\alpha = 1, \ldots, \cot(n-1)\alpha\cot(n+1)\alpha = 1$

Thus, $\cot\alpha\cot 2\alpha\cot 3\alpha \ldots \cot(2n-1)\alpha$

$= \{\cot\alpha\cot(2n-1)\alpha\}\{\cot 2\alpha\cot(2n-2)\alpha\}$

$\ldots\{\cot(n-1)\alpha\cot(n+1)\alpha\}\cdot\cot n\alpha$

$= 1\cdot 1\cdot 1\ldots 1\cdot 1 \quad \left[\because \cot n\alpha = \cot\frac{\pi}{4} = 1\right]$

$= 1$

26. We have, $(\sin A + \sin B + \sin C)(\sin A + \sin B - \sin C) = 3\sin A\sin B$

$$\Rightarrow (\sin A + \sin B)^2 - \sin^2 C = 3\sin A\sin B$$

$$\Rightarrow \sin^2 A + \sin^2 B - \sin^2 C = \sin A\sin B$$

$$\Rightarrow \sin^2 A + \sin(B+C)\sin(B-C) = \sin A\sin B$$

$$\Rightarrow \sin A[\sin(B+C) + \sin(B-C)] = \sin A\sin B$$

$[\because A + B + C = \pi]$

$$\Rightarrow \sin A(2\sin B\cos C) = \sin A\sin B$$

$$\therefore \cos C = \frac{1}{2} \Rightarrow C = 60^\circ$$

27. From the third relation we get

$$\cos\theta\cos\phi + \sin\theta\sin\phi = \sin\beta\sin\gamma$$

$$\Rightarrow \sin^2\theta\sin^2\phi = (\cos\theta\cos\phi - \sin\beta\sin\gamma)^2$$

$$\Rightarrow \left(1 - \frac{\sin^2\beta}{\sin^2\alpha}\right)\left(1 - \frac{\sin^2\gamma}{\sin^2\alpha}\right) = \left(\frac{\sin\beta\sin\gamma}{\sin^2\alpha} - \sin\beta\sin\gamma\right)^2$$

[from the first and second relations]

$\Rightarrow (\sin^2 \alpha - \sin^2 \beta)(\sin^2 \alpha - \sin^2 \gamma) = \sin^2 \beta \sin^2 \gamma (1 - \sin^2 \alpha)^2$

$\Rightarrow \sin^4 \alpha(1 - \sin^2 \beta \sin^2 \gamma)$

$- \sin^2 \alpha(\sin^2 \beta + \sin^2 \gamma - 2\sin^2 \beta \sin^2 \gamma) = 0$

$\therefore \quad \sin^2 \alpha = \dfrac{\sin^2 \beta - \sin^2 \gamma - 2\sin^2 \beta \sin^2 \gamma}{1 - \sin^2 \beta \sin^2 \gamma} \quad [\because \sin \alpha \neq 0]$

and $\cos^2 \alpha = \dfrac{1 - \sin^2 \beta - \sin^2 \gamma + \sin^2 \beta \sin^2 \gamma}{1 - \sin^2 \beta \sin^2 \gamma}$

$\Rightarrow \tan^2 \alpha = \dfrac{\sin^2 \beta - \sin^2 \beta - \sin^2 \gamma + \sin^2 \gamma - \sin^2 \beta \sin^2 \gamma}{\cos^2 \beta - \sin^2 \gamma (1 - \sin^2 \beta)}$

$= \dfrac{\sin^2 \beta \cos^2 \gamma + \cos^2 \beta \sin^2 \gamma}{\cos^2 \beta \cos^2 \gamma}$

$= \tan^2 \beta + \tan^2 \gamma$

$\Rightarrow \tan^2 \alpha - \tan^2 \beta - \tan^2 \gamma = 0$

28. $\tan \beta = \dfrac{n \tan \alpha}{1 + \tan^2 \alpha - n \tan^2 \alpha} = \dfrac{n \tan \alpha}{1 + (1-n)\tan^2 \alpha}$

$\Rightarrow \tan(\alpha - \beta) = \dfrac{\tan \alpha - \dfrac{n \tan \alpha}{1 + (1-n)\tan^2 \alpha}}{1 + \dfrac{\tan \alpha \cdot n \tan \alpha}{1 + (1-n)\tan^2 \alpha}}$

$= \dfrac{\tan \alpha + (1-n)\tan^3 \alpha - n \tan \alpha}{1 + (1-n)\tan^2 \alpha + n \tan^2 \alpha}$

$= \dfrac{(1-n)\tan \alpha (1 + \tan^2 \alpha)}{1 + \tan^2 \alpha} = (1-n)\tan \alpha$

29. Let $\dfrac{(\cos \theta)}{a} = \dfrac{(\sin \theta)}{b} = k$, so that $\cos \theta = ak$ and $\sin \theta = bk$. Then

$a \cos 2\theta + b \sin 2\theta = a(1 - 2\sin^2 \theta) + 2b \sin \theta \cos \theta$

$= a - 2ab^2k^2 + 2b \cdot bk \cdot ak$

$= a - 2ab^2k^2 + 2ab^2k^2 = a$

30. $f(\theta) = |\sin \theta| + |\cos \theta|, \forall \theta \in R$ Clearly, $f(\theta) > 0$.

Also, $f^2(\theta) = \sin^2 \theta + \cos^2 \theta + |2 \sin \theta \cdot \cos \theta|$

$= 1 + |\sin 2\theta|$

$0 \leq |\sin 2\theta| \leq 1$

$\Rightarrow \quad 1 \leq f^2(\theta) \leq 2 \Rightarrow 1 \leq f(\theta) \leq \sqrt{2}$

31. $A = \cos(\cos x) + \sin(\cos x)$

$= \sqrt{2}\left\{\cos(\cos x)\cos\dfrac{\pi}{4} + \sin(\cos x)\sin\dfrac{\pi}{4}\right\}$

$= \sqrt{2}\left\{\cos\left(\cos x - \dfrac{\pi}{4}\right)\right\}$

$\because \quad -1 \leq \cos\left(\cos x - \dfrac{\pi}{4}\right) \leq 1$

$\therefore \quad -\sqrt{2} \leq A \leq \sqrt{2}$

32. We have, $\dfrac{U_n}{V_n} = \tan n\theta$

and $\dfrac{V_n - V_{n-1}}{U_{n-1}} = \dfrac{\cos n\theta \sec^n \theta - \cos(n-1)\theta \sec^{n-1}\theta}{\sin(n-1)\theta \sec^{n-1}\theta}$

$= \dfrac{\cos n\theta \sec \theta - \cos(n-1)\theta}{\sin(n-1)\theta}$

$= \dfrac{\cos n\theta - \cos(n-1)\theta \cos \theta}{\cos \theta \sin(n-1)\theta}$

$= \dfrac{\cos(n-1)\theta \cos \theta - \sin(n-1)\theta \sin \theta - \cos(n-1)\theta \cos \theta}{\cos \theta \sin(n-1)\theta}$

$= -\tan \theta$

So, that $\dfrac{V_n - V_{n-1}}{U_{n-1}} + \dfrac{1}{n}\dfrac{U_n}{V_n} = -\tan \theta + \dfrac{\tan n\theta}{n}$

33. $\sin\left(\dfrac{3\pi}{2} - \alpha\right) = -\cos \alpha, \sin\left(\dfrac{\pi}{2} + \alpha\right) = \cos \alpha$

$\sin(3\pi + \alpha) = -\sin \alpha$

$\sin(5\pi - \alpha) = -\sin \alpha$

$\therefore \quad 3\left\{\sin^4\left(\dfrac{3\pi}{2} - \alpha\right) + \sin^4(3\pi + \alpha)\right\}$

$-2\left[\sin^6\left(\dfrac{\pi}{2} + \alpha\right) + \sin^6(5\pi - \alpha)\right]$

$= 3\{\cos^4 \alpha + \sin^4 \alpha\} - 2\{\cos^6 \alpha + \sin^6 \alpha\}$

$= 3\{1 - 2\sin^2 \alpha \cos^2 \alpha\} - 2\{1 - 3\sin^2 \alpha \cos^2 \alpha\} = 1$

34. $\sin\left(x + \dfrac{\pi}{6}\right) + \cos\left(x + \dfrac{\pi}{6}\right)$

$= \sqrt{2}\left[\sin\left(x + \dfrac{\pi}{6} + \dfrac{\pi}{4}\right)\right]$

$= \sqrt{2}\sin\left(x + \dfrac{5\pi}{12}\right) \leq \sqrt{2}$

Equality holds when $x + \dfrac{5\pi}{12} = \dfrac{\pi}{2}$ i.e. $x = \dfrac{\pi}{12}$

Therefore, maximum value of given expression is attained at

$x = \dfrac{\pi}{12}$

35. $\cos x - \sin \alpha \cot \beta \sin x = \cos \alpha$

$\Rightarrow \sin \beta \cos x - \sin \alpha \cos \beta \sin x = \cos \alpha \sin \beta$

$\Rightarrow \sin \beta\left(1 - \tan^2 \dfrac{x}{2}\right) - \sin \alpha \cos \beta \cdot 2 \tan \dfrac{x}{2}$

$= \cos \alpha \sin \beta\left(1 + \tan^2 \dfrac{x}{2}\right)$

$\Rightarrow \tan^2 \dfrac{x}{2}(-\sin \beta - \cos \alpha \sin \beta) - \sin \alpha \cos \beta \cdot 2 \tan \dfrac{x}{2}$

$+ \sin \beta(1 - \cos \alpha) = 0$

$\Rightarrow \quad \tan \dfrac{x}{2} = \dfrac{-2\sin \alpha \cos \beta \pm \sqrt{4[\sin^2 \alpha \cos^2 \beta + \sin^2 \beta (1 + \cos \alpha)(1 - \cos \alpha)]}}{2\sin \beta(1 + \cos \alpha)}$

$= \dfrac{-\sin\alpha \cos \beta \pm \sqrt{\sin^2 \alpha(\sin^2 \beta + \cos^2 \beta)}}{\sin \beta(1 + \cos \alpha)}$

$= \dfrac{-\sin \alpha \cos \beta \pm \sin \alpha}{\sin \beta(1 + \cos \alpha)} = \dfrac{\sin \alpha(1 - \cos \beta \pm 1)}{\sin \beta(1 + \cos \alpha)}$

$= \tan \dfrac{\beta}{2} \tan \dfrac{\alpha}{2}$ or $-\tan \dfrac{\alpha}{2} \cot \dfrac{\beta}{2}$

36. Given, $0 < x < \pi \Rightarrow \sin x > 0$

We have, $1 + \sin x + \sin^2 x + \ldots = 4 + 2\sqrt{3}$

$$\Rightarrow \quad \frac{1}{1 - \sin x} = 4 + 2\sqrt{3} \quad \text{[sum of infinite GP]}$$

$$\Rightarrow \quad \sin x = 1 - \frac{1}{4 + 2\sqrt{3}} = \frac{3 + 2\sqrt{3}}{4 + 2\sqrt{3}} = \frac{\sqrt{3}}{2}$$

$$\Rightarrow \quad x = \frac{\pi}{3} \text{ or } \frac{2\pi}{3}$$

37. We know that $-\sqrt{2} \le \sin x + \cos x \le \sqrt{2}$

When $x = -\frac{3\pi}{4}$, we have $\sin x + \cos x = -\sqrt{2}$

When $x = -\frac{3\pi}{4}$, we have $y = -\sqrt{2} + 1 < 0$

which implies that options (a) and (b) are incorrect.

Now, at $x = \frac{\pi}{4}$, we have $\sin x + \cos x = \sqrt{2}$

That is, $(\sin 4x + \cos 4x)^2 \neq 2$.

Therefore, $y \neq \sqrt{2} + 2$ for any $x \in R$.

which implies that option (d) is incorrect.

Note The maximum value of $\sin x + \cos x$ is $\sqrt{2}$, for $x = \frac{\pi}{4}$ and the maximum value of $(\sin 4x + \cos 4x)^2$ is 2, for $x = \frac{\pi}{16}$.

38. We know that $l = r\theta$

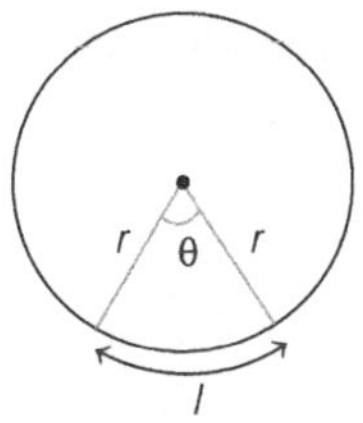

Since, $l(OA) = l(OB) = 1$

$$l(\text{Arc } AB) = 1$$

Using, $l(\text{Arc } AB) = l(OA) \cdot \theta_1$

$$\theta_1 = 1^c = \angle BOA = \angle COA$$

$$\angle COD = \pi - 1$$

$$l(\text{Arc } CD) = (\pi - 1) \cdot 2 = 2(\pi - 1)$$

$$l(\text{Arc } EF) = 3 \times \angle EOF = 3 \times 2 = 6$$

and $l(\text{Arc } CD) + l(\text{Arc } EF) = 2\pi - 2 + 6 = 2\pi + 4$

39. $f(\theta) = 16 \cos^3 2\theta - 32 \sin^3\theta - 12 \cos 2\theta + 24 \sin \theta$

$f(\theta) = (16 \cos^3 2\theta - 12 \cos 2\theta) + (24 \sin \theta - 32 \sin^3\theta)$

$f(\theta) = 4(4 \cos^3 2\theta - 3 \cos 2\theta) + 8(3 \sin \theta - 4 \sin^3\theta)$

$f(\theta) = 4 \cos 6\theta + 8 \sin 3\theta$

$$f\left(\frac{\pi}{30}\right) = 4 \cos \frac{\pi}{5} + 8 \sin \frac{\pi}{10}$$

$$f\left(\frac{\pi}{30}\right) = 4\left(\frac{\sqrt{5} + 1}{4}\right) + 8\left(\frac{\sqrt{5} - 1}{4}\right)$$

$$f\left(\frac{\pi}{30}\right) = \sqrt{5} + 1 + 2\sqrt{5} - 2$$

$$= 3\sqrt{5} - 1 = 3\sqrt{a} - b$$

$$\therefore \quad a = 5, b = 1$$

$$a + b = 5 + 1 = 6$$

40. $2A \in \left(0, \frac{\pi}{2}\right)$ $2A \in \left(\frac{\pi}{2}, \frac{2\pi}{3}\right)$ $2A \in \left(\frac{2\pi}{3}, \pi\right)$ $2A \in \left(0, \frac{\pi}{3}\right)$

$3A \in \left(0, \frac{3\pi}{4}\right)$ $3A \in \left(\frac{3\pi}{4}, \pi\right)$ $3A \in \left(\pi, \frac{3\pi}{2}\right)$ $3A \in \left(0, \frac{\pi}{2}\right)$

In option (a), $\sin 2A > 0$ but $\cos 3A$ may be (+) or (–)ve

Hence, option (a) is not correct.

In option (b), $\sin 2A > 0$ and $\cos 3A < 0$

Hence, option (b) is not correct.

In option (c), $\sin 2A > 0$ but $\cos 3A < 0$

Hence, option (c) is not correct.

In option (d), $\sin 2A > 0$ and $\cos 3A > 0$

Hence, option (d) is correct.

41. Consider, $x = \sin (\alpha - \beta) \sin (\gamma - \delta)$, multiply both sides by 2, we get

$$2x = 2 \sin (\alpha - \beta) \sin (\gamma - \delta)$$

$$2x = \cos (\alpha - \beta - \gamma + \delta) - \cos (\alpha - \beta + \gamma - \delta) \quad \ldots\text{(i)}$$

and similarly,

$$2y = \cos (\beta - \gamma - \alpha + \delta) - \cos (\beta - \gamma + \alpha - \delta) \quad \ldots\text{(ii)}$$

$$2z = \cos (\gamma - \alpha - \beta + \delta) - \cos (\gamma - \alpha + \beta - \delta) \quad \ldots\text{(iii)}$$

Now, adding Eqs. (i), (ii) and (iii), we get

$$2x + 2y + 2z = \cos (\alpha - \beta - \gamma + \delta) - \cos (\alpha - \beta + \gamma - \delta) + \cos (\beta - \gamma - \alpha + \delta) - \cos (\beta - \gamma + \alpha - \delta) + \cos (\gamma - \alpha - \beta + \delta) - \cos (\gamma - \alpha + \beta - \delta)$$

As, $\cos (\alpha - \beta - \gamma + \delta) = \cos (\gamma - \alpha + \beta - \delta)$

$\Rightarrow \cos (\beta - \gamma - \alpha + \delta) = \cos (\alpha - \beta + \gamma - \delta)$

$\Rightarrow \cos (\gamma - \alpha - \beta + \delta) = \cos (\beta - \gamma - \alpha - \delta)$

[as $\cos (-\theta) = \cos \theta$]

$$\Rightarrow \quad 2x + 2y + 2z = 0$$

$$\Rightarrow \quad x + y + z = 0$$

42. $\tan (3\alpha + 3\beta) = \tan [(2\alpha + \beta) + (\alpha + 2\beta)]$

$$= \frac{\tan (2\alpha + \beta) + \tan (\alpha + 2\beta)}{1 - \tan (2\alpha + \beta) \tan (\alpha + 2\beta)}$$

$$= \frac{x + y}{1 - xy}$$

$\Rightarrow \tan (\alpha - \beta) = \tan [(2\alpha + \beta) - (\alpha + 2\beta)]$

$$\Rightarrow \tan (\alpha - \beta) = \frac{\tan (2\alpha + \beta) - \tan (\alpha + 2\beta)}{1 + \tan (2\alpha + \beta) \tan (\alpha + 2\beta)}$$

$$= \frac{x - y}{1 + xy}$$

$$\Rightarrow [\tan 3(\alpha + \beta)] [\tan (\alpha - \beta)] = \left(\frac{x + y}{1 - xy}\right)\left(\frac{x - y}{1 + xy}\right)$$

$$= \frac{x^2 - y^2}{1 - x^2y^2}$$

43. Let $\frac{2\pi}{9}=C$ and $\frac{\pi}{36}=D$

Now, $\frac{\sin C-\sin D}{\cos C-\cos D}=\frac{2\cos\left(\frac{C+D}{2}\right)\sin\left(\frac{C-D}{2}\right)}{-2\sin\left(\frac{C+D}{2}\right)\sin\left(\frac{C-D}{2}\right)}$

$$=-\cot\left(\frac{C+D}{2}\right)=-\cot\left(\frac{\frac{2\pi}{9}+\frac{\pi}{36}}{2}\right)$$

$$=-\cot\left(\frac{9\pi}{36\times 2}\right)=-\cot\frac{\pi}{8}=-(\sqrt{2}+1)$$

44. Let $m=2k, k\in I$.

Then, $\beta=2k\pi+\frac{\pi}{2}-A=\left(2k+\frac{1}{2}\right)\pi-A$ ...(i)

Let $m=2k+1, k\in I$.

Then, $\beta=(2k+1)\pi-\left(\frac{\pi}{2}-A\right)=\left(2k+\frac{1}{2}\right)\pi+A$ ...(ii)

From Eqs. (i) and (ii), it follows that

$$\beta=\left(2k+\frac{1}{2}\right)\pi\pm A, k\in I,$$

which is same as α.

45. $y=(\sin^2 x+\text{cosec}^2 x)+2(\sin x\ \text{cosec}\ x+\cos x\sec x)+(\sec^2 x+\cos^2 x)$

$\Rightarrow y=5+2+\tan^2 x+\cot^2 x$

$\Rightarrow y=7+(\tan x-\cot x)^2+2$

$\therefore\ y_{\min}=9$

46. We have, $f(x)=\sqrt{4-|2-3|\sin x||}$

$0\le 3|\sin x|\le 3$

$\therefore\ -3\le -3|\sin x|\le 0$

$\Rightarrow -1\le 2-3|\sin x|\le 2$

$\Rightarrow 0\le |2-3|\sin x||\le 2$

$\Rightarrow -2\le -|2-3|\sin x||\le 0$

$\Rightarrow 2\le 4-|2-3|\sin x||\le 4$

$\Rightarrow \sqrt{2}\le\sqrt{4-|2-3\sqrt{\sin^2 x}|}\le 2$

Hence, the minimum value is $\sqrt{2}$ and maximum value is 2.

$(\text{Minimum value})^2+(\text{Maximum value})^2=2+4=6$

47. $\sin y=x^2-2x=(x-1)^2-1\ge -1$

But $\sin y\in[-1,1]$

Hence, the infinite values of x are possible.

48. $\sum\frac{\sec A\sec B}{\tan A\tan B\sec C}=\sum\frac{\cos C}{\sin A\cdot\sin B}=\frac{\Sigma\, 2\sin C\cos C}{2\sin A\sin B\sin C}$

$$=\frac{\Sigma\sin 2C}{2\sin A\sin B\sin C}$$

$$=\frac{\sin 2A+\sin 2B+\sin 2C}{2\sin A\sin B\sin C}$$

$$=\frac{4\sin A\sin B\sin C}{2\sin A\sin B\sin C}=2$$

49. $\theta=\pi-\left(C+\frac{A}{2}\right)$

$\Rightarrow \sin\theta=\sin\left(C+\frac{A}{2}\right)$

$\Rightarrow \sin\theta=\sin\left(C+\frac{\pi}{2}-\frac{B+C}{2}\right)\Rightarrow \sin\theta=\cos\left(\frac{B-C}{2}\right)$

50. $S_1:\sin^2\theta_1+\sin^2\theta_2+\ldots+\sin^2\theta_n=0$

$\Rightarrow\ \sin\theta_1=\sin\theta_2=\ldots=\sin\theta_n=0$

$\Rightarrow\ \cos^2\theta_1=\cos^2\theta_2=\ldots=\cos^2\theta_n=1$

$\Rightarrow\ \cos\theta_1=\cos\theta_2=\ldots=\cos\theta_n=\pm 1$

Now, $\cos\theta_1+\cos\theta_2+\ldots+\cos\theta_n=n-2$ means one of $\cos\theta_1,\cos\theta_2,\ldots,\cos\theta_n$ must be -1 and each of the rest must be 1. The one which is -1 can be selected in n ways.

$S_2: f(2A)=f(2B)$

$\Rightarrow\ 2A=2n\pi+2B, n\in Z$

$\Rightarrow\ A-B=n\pi, n\in Z$

51. $\sin(x+3\alpha)=3\sin(\alpha-x)$

$\Rightarrow \sin x\cos 3\alpha+\cos x\sin 3\alpha=3(\sin\alpha\cos x-\cos\alpha\sin x)$

$\Rightarrow\ \sin x(\cos 3\alpha+3\cos\alpha)=\cos x(3\sin\alpha-\sin 3\alpha)$

$\Rightarrow\ \tan x=\frac{4\sin^3\alpha}{4\cos^3\alpha}=\tan^3\alpha$

52. We have, $BD=DC$ and $\angle DAB=90°$

Draw CN perpendicular to BA produced, then in ΔBCN, we have $DA=\frac{1}{2}CN$ and $AB=AN$.

Let $\angle CAN=\alpha$.

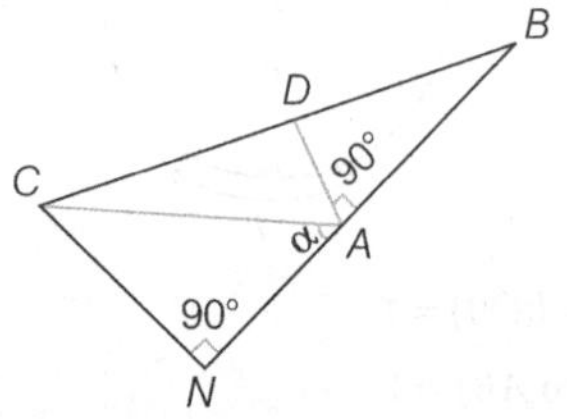

Now, in ΔABC, we have

$$\tan A=\tan(\pi-\alpha)=-\tan\alpha$$

$\Rightarrow\ -\frac{CN}{NA}=-2\frac{AD}{AB}=-2\tan B$

$\Rightarrow \tan A+2\tan B=0$

53. $\frac{1+\sin 2\alpha}{\cos 2\alpha\cdot\tan\left(\frac{\pi}{4}+\alpha\right)}-\frac{\sin 2\alpha}{4}\left[\cot\frac{\alpha}{2}-\tan\frac{\alpha}{2}\right]$

$$=\frac{1+\sin 2\alpha}{\cos 2\alpha\cdot\tan\left(\frac{\pi}{4}+\alpha\right)}-\frac{\sin 2\alpha}{4}\left[\frac{\cos^2\frac{\alpha}{2}-\sin^2\frac{\alpha}{2}}{\cos\frac{\alpha}{2}\sin\frac{\alpha}{2}}\right]$$

$$=\frac{(\sin\alpha+\cos\alpha)^2}{\cos 2\alpha\left(\frac{\sin\alpha+\cos\alpha}{\cos\alpha-\sin\alpha}\right)}-\cos^2\alpha$$

$$=\frac{\cos 2\alpha}{\cos 2\alpha}-\cos^2\alpha=\sin^2\alpha$$

54. From given relation,

$$2\cos^2 B - 1 = 3(1-\cos^2 A)$$

or $$\cos 2B = 3\sin^2 A \quad ...(i)$$

Also, given that $\dfrac{3\sin A}{\sin B} = \dfrac{2\cos B}{\cos A}$

$$\Rightarrow \quad 3\sin 2A = 2\sin 2B \quad ...(ii)$$

Now, $$\cos(A+2B) = \cos A\cos 2B - \sin A \sin 2B$$

$$= \cos A(3\sin^2 A) - \sin A\left(\frac{3}{2}\sin 2A\right)$$

$$= 3\cos A\sin^2 A - 3\sin^2 A\cos A = 0$$

$\therefore A + 2B = 90°$

55. $f(\theta) = \dfrac{1-\sin 2\theta + \cos 2\theta}{2\cos 2\theta}$

$$f(\theta) = \frac{(\cos\theta - \sin\theta)^2 + (\cos^2\theta - \sin^2\theta)}{2(\cos\theta - \sin\theta)(\cos\theta + \sin\theta)}$$

$$f(\theta) = \frac{\cos\theta}{\cos\theta + \sin\theta} = \frac{1}{1+\tan\theta}$$

$$f(11°)\times f(34°) = \frac{1}{1+\tan(11°)} \times \frac{1}{1+\tan(34°)}$$

$$= \frac{1}{1+\tan(11°)} \times \frac{1}{(1+\tan(45°-11°))}$$

$$= \frac{1}{(1+\tan 11°)} \times \frac{1}{\left(1+\dfrac{1-\tan 11°}{1+\tan 11°}\right)}$$

$$= \frac{1}{(1+\tan 11°)} \times \frac{(1+\tan 11°)}{2} = \frac{1}{2}$$

$$\therefore 8f(11°)\cdot f(34°) = 8\times\frac{1}{2} = 4$$

56. $f(x) = 2(7\cos x + 24\sin x)(7\sin x - 24\cos x)$

$$r\cos\theta = 7;\ r\sin\theta = 24$$

$$r^2 = 625;\ \tan\theta = \frac{24}{7}$$

$$f(x) = 2r\cos(x-\theta)\times r\sin(x-\theta)$$

$$f(x) = r^2\sin[2(x-\theta)]$$

$$[f(x)]_{\max} = r^2 = (625) = 5^4$$

$$[[f(x)]_{\max}]^{1/4} = 5$$

57. $$\frac{\sin^2\left(x-\dfrac{\pi}{4}\right)}{\cos 2x} = \frac{\dfrac{1}{2}(\sin x - \cos x)^2}{\cos^2 x - \sin^2 x}$$

$$= \frac{-\dfrac{1}{2}(\sin x - \cos x)}{\cos x + \sin x}$$

$$= -\frac{1}{2}\tan\left(x - \frac{\pi}{4}\right)$$

Given equation reduces to

$$2^{\tan\left(x-\frac{\pi}{4}\right)} - 2\left(\frac{1}{2}\right)^{2\times-\frac{1}{2}\tan\left(x-\frac{\pi}{4}\right)} + 1 = 0$$

$$\Rightarrow \quad 2^{\tan\left(x-\frac{\pi}{4}\right)} - 2(2)^{\tan\left(x-\frac{\pi}{4}\right)} + 1 = 0$$

$$\Rightarrow \quad 2^{\tan\left(x-\frac{\pi}{4}\right)} = 1$$

$\Rightarrow x = \dfrac{\pi}{4}$, which is not possible as $\cos 2x = 0$ for this value of x, which is not defining the original equation.

58. $$\frac{2\sin 4°\cos 3° + 2\sin 4°\cos 1°}{\cos 1°\cdot\cos 2°\cdot\sin 4°}$$

$$= \frac{2\sin 4°[\cos 3° + \cos 1°]}{\cos 1°\cdot\cos 2°\cdot\sin 4°} = \frac{4\cos 2°\cdot\cos 1°}{\cos 1°\cdot\cos 2°} = 4$$

59. $\sin^4\alpha + \cos^4\beta + 2 = 4\sin\alpha\cos\beta$

$$\Rightarrow (\sin^2\alpha - 1)^2 + (\cos^2\beta - 1)^2 + 2(\sin\alpha - \cos\beta)^2 = 0$$

$$\Rightarrow \sin^2\alpha = 1,\ \cos^2\beta = 1 \text{ and } \sin\alpha = \cos\beta$$

Now, $0 \le \alpha, \beta \le \dfrac{\pi}{2}$

$\therefore \sin\alpha = 1$ and $\cos\beta = 1$

Hence, $(\sin\alpha + \cos\beta) = 1 + 1 = 2$

60. From the given equations, we have

$$(2\cos a + 9\cos d)^2 = (6\cos b + 7\cos c)^2$$

and $$(2\sin a - 9\sin d)^2 = (6\sin b - 7\sin c)^2$$

On adding, we get

$$36\cos(a+d) = 84\cos(b+c)$$

or $$3\frac{\cos(a+d)}{\cos(b+c)} = 7$$

61. $$\frac{2\sin x}{\sin 3x} + \frac{\tan x}{\tan 3x} = \frac{2\sin x}{\sin x(3-4\sin^2 x)} + \frac{\tan x}{\dfrac{(3\tan x - \tan^3 x)}{(1-3\tan^2 x)}}$$

$$= \frac{2}{3-4\sin^2 x} + \frac{1-3\tan^2 x}{3-\tan^2 x}$$

$$= \frac{2}{3-4\sin^2 x} + \frac{1-\left(\dfrac{3\sin^2 x}{1-\sin^2 x}\right)}{3-\left(\dfrac{\sin^2 x}{1-\sin^2 x}\right)}$$

$$= \frac{2}{3-4\sin^2 x} + \frac{(1-4\sin^2 x)}{(3-4\sin^2 x)}$$

$$= \frac{(3-4\sin^2 x)}{(3-4\sin^2 x)} = 1$$

62. $$\sin^2\alpha + \sin^2\beta + \sin^2\gamma = \frac{\tan^2\alpha}{1+\tan^2\alpha} + \frac{\tan^2\beta}{1+\tan^2\beta} + \frac{\tan^2\gamma}{1+\tan^2\gamma}$$

$$= \frac{x}{1+x} + \frac{y}{1+y} + \frac{z}{1+z} \quad [\text{take, } x = \tan^2\alpha,\ y = \tan^2\beta,\ z = \tan^2\gamma]$$

$$= \frac{(x+y+z) + (xy+yz+zx+2xyz) + xy+yz+zx+xyz}{(1+x)(1+y)(1+z)}$$

$$= \frac{1+x+y+z+xy+yz+zx+xyz}{(1+x)(1+y)(1+z)} = 1$$

$$[\because xy+yz+zx+2xyz = 1]$$

63. $5 \times \frac{2\tan\beta}{1+\tan^2\beta} = 3 \times \frac{2\tan\alpha}{1+\tan^2\alpha}$

$\Rightarrow \frac{5\tan\beta}{1+\tan^2\beta} = \frac{3\tan\alpha}{1+\tan^2\alpha}$

On substituting $\tan\beta = 3\tan\alpha$, we have

$$\frac{5\times 3\tan\alpha}{1+9\tan^2\alpha} = \frac{3\tan\alpha}{1+\tan^2\alpha}$$

$\Rightarrow \quad 5 + 5\tan^2\alpha = 1 + 9\tan^2\alpha$

$\Rightarrow \quad 4\tan^2\alpha = 4$

$\Rightarrow \quad \tan\alpha = 1$ i.e. $\tan\beta = 3$

$\therefore \quad \tan\alpha + \tan\beta = 4$

64. $\sin^2 12° + \sin^2 21° + \sin^2 39° + \sin^2 48° - \sin^2 9° - \sin^2 18°$

$= \sin^2 12° + \sin^2 21° + (\sin^2 39° - \sin^2 9°) + (\sin^2 48° - \sin^2 18°)$

$= 1 - (\cos^2 12° - \sin^2 21°) + \sin 48° \sin 30° + \sin 66° \sin 30°$

$= 1 - \cos 33° \cos 9° + \frac{1}{2} \times 2\sin 57° \cos 9°$

$= 1 - \cos 33° \cos 9° + \cos 33° \cos 9°$

$= 1$

65. $\cos 290° = \sin 20°$; $\sin 250° = -\sin 70° = -\cos 20°$

$\Rightarrow \frac{1}{\sin 20°} - \frac{1}{\sqrt{3}\cos 20°} = \frac{\sqrt{3}\cos 20° - \sin 20°}{\sqrt{3}\cos 20° \sin 20°}$

$= \frac{2[\sin 60° \cos 20° - \sin 20° \cos 60°]}{\sqrt{3}\sin 20° \cos 20°}$

$= \frac{4\sin 40°}{\sqrt{3}\sin 40°} = \frac{4\sqrt{3}}{3}$

Hence, the greatest integer less than or equal to is 2.

66. We have, $p\,\text{cosec}\,\theta + q\cot\theta = 2$ ...(i)

and $(p\,\text{cosec}\,\theta)^2 - (q\cot\theta)^2 = 5$

$\Rightarrow \quad p\,\text{cosec}\,\theta - q\cot\theta = \frac{5}{2}$ ...(ii)

From Eqs. (i) and (ii), we get

$$p\,\text{cosec}\,\theta = \frac{9}{4} \text{ and } q\cot\theta = -\frac{1}{4}$$

Now, $\quad \text{cosec}^2\theta - \cot^2\theta = 1$

$\Rightarrow \quad \frac{81}{16p^2} - \frac{1}{16q^2} = 1$

$\Rightarrow \quad 81p^{-2} - q^{-2} = 16$

67. $\left(\sin\frac{\pi}{9}\right)\left(4 + \sec\frac{\pi}{9}\right) = \sin 20°\left(4 + \frac{1}{\cos 20°}\right)$

$= \frac{4\sin 20° \cos 20° + \sin 20°}{\cos 20°}$

$= \frac{2\sin 40° + \sin 20°}{\cos 20°}$

$= \frac{\sin 40° + (\sin 40° + \sin 20°)}{\cos 20°}$

$= \frac{\sin 40° + 2\sin 30° \cos 10°}{\cos 20°}$

$= \frac{\sin 40° + \cos 10°}{\cos 20°} = \frac{\cos 50° + \cos 10°}{\cos 20°}$

$= \frac{2\cos 30° \cos 20°}{\cos 20°} = 2\cos 30° = \sqrt{3}$

$\therefore \quad \left[\left(\sin\frac{\pi}{9}\right)\left(4 + \sec\frac{\pi}{9}\right)\right]^2 = 3$

68. Given, $\log_{10}\left(\frac{\sin 2x}{2}\right) = -1$

or $\quad \frac{\sin 2x}{2} = \frac{1}{10}$ or $\sin 2x = \frac{1}{5}$ ...(i)

Also, $\log_{10}(\sin x + \cos x) = \frac{\log_{10}\left(\frac{n}{10}\right)}{2}$

or $\quad \log_{10}(\sin x + \cos x)^2 = \log_{10}\left(\frac{n}{10}\right)$

or $\quad 1 + \sin 2x = \frac{n}{10}$

or $\quad 1 + \frac{1}{5} = \frac{n}{10}$

or $\quad \frac{6}{5} = \frac{n}{10}$

$\therefore \quad n = 12$

69. $\tan x = 2t$, $\tan y = 3t$ and $\tan z = 5t$

Also, $x + y + z = \pi$

$\therefore \quad \tan x + \tan y + \tan z = \tan x \tan y \tan z$

$\Rightarrow \quad t^2 = \frac{1}{3}$

$\Rightarrow \tan^2 x + \tan^2 y + \tan^2 z = t^2(4 + 9 + 25) = 38t^2$

$\therefore \quad k = 3$

70. We have,

$$\frac{2^{10}\sin\left(\frac{5\pi}{2^{11}}\right)\cos\left(\frac{5\pi}{2^{11}}\right)\cos\left(\frac{5\pi}{2^{10}}\right)\cos\left(\frac{5\pi}{2^{9}}\right)\ldots\cos\left(\frac{5\pi}{2^{3}}\right)\cos\left(\frac{5\pi}{2^{2}}\right)}{2^{10}}$$

$= \frac{\sin\left(\frac{5\pi}{2}\right)}{2^{10}} = \frac{\sin 450°}{2^{10}} = \frac{1}{2^{10}}$

Hence, the required answer is $2^{10} = 1024$.

71. Given, $\cot(\theta - \alpha)$, $3\cot\theta$, $\cot(\theta + \alpha)$ are in AP.

$\Rightarrow \quad 6\cot\theta = \cot(\theta - \alpha) + \cot(\theta + \alpha)$

$\Rightarrow \quad \frac{6\cos\theta}{\sin\theta} = \frac{\sin 2\theta}{\sin(\theta + \alpha) + \sin(\theta - \alpha)}$

$\Rightarrow 6\cos\theta[\sin^2\theta - \sin^2\alpha] = 2\sin^2\theta \cos\theta$

$\Rightarrow \quad 3(\sin^2\theta - \sin^2\alpha) = \sin^2\theta$

$\Rightarrow \quad 2\sin^2\theta = 3\sin^2\alpha$

$\therefore \quad \frac{2\sin^2\theta}{3\sin^2\alpha} = 1$

$\Rightarrow \quad \frac{4\sin^2\theta}{3\sin^2\alpha} = 2$

72. Given, $\tan A = \dfrac{1}{\sqrt{x(x^2+x+1)}}$, $\tan B = \dfrac{\sqrt{x}}{\sqrt{x^2+x+1}}$

and $\tan C = \sqrt{\left(\dfrac{1}{x^3}+\dfrac{1}{x^2}+\dfrac{1}{x}\right)} = \sqrt{\dfrac{1+x+x^2}{x^3}} = \dfrac{\sqrt{x^2+x+1}}{x\sqrt{x}}$

Now, $\tan(A+B) = \dfrac{\tan A + \tan B}{1 - \tan A \tan B}$

$$= \left[\frac{\dfrac{1}{\sqrt{x}\sqrt{x^2+x+1}} + \dfrac{\sqrt{x}}{\sqrt{x^2+x+1}}}{1 - \dfrac{1}{\sqrt{x}\sqrt{x^2+x+1}}\dfrac{\sqrt{x}}{\sqrt{x^2+x+1}}}\right]$$

$$= \left(\frac{1+x}{x^2+x+1-1}\right)\frac{\sqrt{x^2+x+1}}{\sqrt{x}}$$

$$= \frac{(1+x)\sqrt{x^2+x+1}}{x(x+1)\sqrt{x}} = \frac{\sqrt{x^2+x+1}}{x\sqrt{x}}$$

$\Rightarrow \quad \tan(A+B) = \tan C$

$\therefore \quad A + B = C$

73. Given, $\quad 3\sin(\alpha+\beta) = 2\sin(\alpha-\beta)$

$\Rightarrow 3\sin\alpha\cos\beta + 3\cos\alpha\sin\beta = 2\sin\alpha\cos\beta - 2\cos\alpha\sin\beta$

$\Rightarrow \quad \sin\alpha\cos\beta = -5\cos\alpha\sin\beta$

$\Rightarrow \quad \tan\alpha = -5\tan\beta$

On comparing, $\tan\alpha = k\tan\beta \Rightarrow k = -5$

74. Given equation is

$$\cos 2x + a\sin x = 2a - 7$$

$\Rightarrow \quad a\sin x - 2a = -7 - \cos 2x$

$= -7 - (1 - 2\sin^2 x)$

$= -8 + 2\sin^2 x = 2(\sin^2 x - 4)$

$\Rightarrow \quad a(\sin x - 2) = 2(\sin x - 2)(\sin x + 2)$

$\Rightarrow \quad (\sin x - 2)[a - 2(\sin x + 2)] = 0$

$\Rightarrow \quad \sin x = 2$ or $a = 2(\sin x + 2)$

But $\sin x = 2$ [not possible]

Also, $\quad -1 \le \sin x \le 1$

$\Rightarrow \quad 1 \le \sin x + 2 \le 3$

$\Rightarrow \quad 2 \le 2(\sin x + 2) \le 6$

$\Rightarrow \quad 2 \le a \le 6$

$\Rightarrow \quad a \in [2, 6]$

On comparing this with $a \in [p, q]$, we get

$$p = 2 \text{ and } q = 6$$

Now, given

$$r = \tan 9° - \tan 27° - \frac{1}{\cot 63°} + \tan 81°$$

$\Rightarrow \quad r = (\tan 9° + \cot 9°) - \tan 27° - \cot 27°$

[$\because \tan 81° = \cot 9°$ and $\cot 63° = \tan 27°$]

$\Rightarrow \quad r = \dfrac{1}{\sin 9° \cdot \cos 9°} - \dfrac{1}{\sin 27° \cdot \cos 27°}$

$\Rightarrow \quad r = 2\left[\dfrac{4}{\sqrt{5}-1} - \dfrac{4}{\sqrt{5}+1}\right] = 4$

Hence, $pqr = 2 \times 6 \times 4 = 48$

75. We have, $S = \left\{x \in \left(-\dfrac{\pi}{2}, \dfrac{\pi}{2}\right) : 9^{1-\tan^2 x} + 9^{\tan^2 x} = 10\right\}$

and $\quad \beta = \sum_{x \in S} \tan^2\left(\dfrac{x}{3}\right)$

$$9^{1-\tan^2 x} + 9^{\tan^2 x} = 10$$

$\Rightarrow \quad \dfrac{9}{9^{\tan^2 x}} + 9^{\tan^2 x} = 10$

Let $\quad 9^{\tan^2 x} = t$

$\Rightarrow \quad \dfrac{9}{t} + t = 10$

$\Rightarrow \quad t^2 - 10t + 9 = 0$

$\Rightarrow \quad t = 9$ or 1

If $t = 9$, $9^{\tan^2 x} = 9 \Rightarrow x = \pm\dfrac{\pi}{4}$

If $t = 1$, $9^{\tan^2 x} = 1 \Rightarrow x = 0$

Also, $\beta = \sum_{x \in S} \tan^2\left(\dfrac{x}{3}\right)$

$$= \tan^2\left(\frac{0}{3}\right) + \tan^2\left(\frac{\pi}{12}\right) + \tan^2\left(-\frac{\pi}{12}\right)$$

$$= 0 + 2\tan^2\frac{\pi}{12} = 2[2 - \sqrt{3}]^2$$

$$= 2[4 + 3 - 4\sqrt{3}] = 14 - 8\sqrt{3}$$

So, $\dfrac{1}{6}(\beta - 14)^2 = \dfrac{1}{6}[14 - 8\sqrt{3} - 14]^2$

$$= \frac{1}{6} \times 64 \times 3 = 32$$

76. Let $\quad A = 96\cos\dfrac{\pi}{33}\cos\dfrac{2\pi}{33}\cos\dfrac{4\pi}{33}\cos\dfrac{8\pi}{33}\cos\dfrac{16\pi}{33}$

$\Rightarrow \quad 2A = 96 \times 2\left(\cos\dfrac{\pi}{33}\cos\dfrac{2\pi}{33}\cos\dfrac{4\pi}{33}\cos\dfrac{8\pi}{33}\cos\dfrac{16\pi}{33}\right)$

$\Rightarrow 2A \times \sin\dfrac{\pi}{33}$

$$= 96 \times \left(2\sin\frac{\pi}{33}\cos\frac{\pi}{33}\cos\frac{2\pi}{33}\cos\frac{4\pi}{33}\cdot\cos\frac{8\pi}{33}\cos\frac{16\pi}{33}\right)$$

$\Rightarrow \quad 2A \times \sin\dfrac{\pi}{33} = 6 \times \sin\dfrac{32\pi}{33} = 6 \times \sin\dfrac{\pi}{33}$

$\Rightarrow \quad 2A = 6 \Rightarrow A = 3$

77. $4\cos^2\theta - 1 = 4 - 4\sin^2\theta$

$$-1 = 3 - 4\sin^2\theta = \frac{3\sin\theta - 4\sin^3\theta}{\sin\theta} = \frac{\sin 3\theta}{\sin\theta}$$

$\therefore$ Given expression,

$$36 \cdot \frac{\sin(3 \times 9°)}{\sin 9°} \times \frac{\sin(3 \times 27°)}{\sin 27°} \times \frac{\sin(3 \times 81°)}{\sin 81°} \times \frac{\sin(3 \times 243°)}{\sin 243°}$$

$$= 36 \cdot \frac{\sin 729°}{\sin 9°} = 36 \times \frac{\sin(2 \times 360° + 9°)}{\sin 9°}$$

$$= 36 \times \frac{\sin 9°}{\sin 9°} = 36$$

78. Given, $\tan 9° - \tan 27° - \tan 63° + \tan 81°$

$= \tan 9° + \tan(90° - 9°) - \tan 27° - \tan(90° - 27°)$

$= \tan 9° + \cot 9° - \tan 27° - \cot 27°$

$= \frac{\sin 9°}{\cos 9°} + \frac{\cos 9°}{\sin 9°} - \left(\frac{\sin 27°}{\cos 27°} + \frac{\cos 27°}{\sin 27°}\right)$

$= \frac{\sin^2 9° + \cos^2 9°}{\sin 9° \cos 9°} - \left(\frac{\sin^2 27° + \cos^2 27°}{\cos 27° \sin 27°}\right)$

$= \frac{2}{\sin 18°} - \frac{2}{\sin 54°}$

$= \frac{2 \times 4}{\sqrt{5} - 1} - \frac{2 \times 4}{\sqrt{5} + 1}$

$= 8\left(\frac{\sqrt{5} + 1 - \sqrt{5} + 1}{5 - 1}\right)$

$= 4$

79. Since, $\sin\left(\frac{\pi}{22}\right) = \cos\left(\frac{\pi}{2} - \frac{\pi}{22}\right) = \cos\frac{5\pi}{11} = -\cos\frac{16\pi}{11}$

Similarly, $\sin\frac{3\pi}{22} = \cos\frac{4\pi}{11}$, $\sin\frac{5\pi}{22} = \cos\frac{3\pi}{11} = -\cos\frac{8\pi}{11}$

$\sin\frac{7\pi}{22} = \cos\frac{2\pi}{11}$, $\sin\frac{9\pi}{11} = \cos\frac{\pi}{11}$

Now, $2\sin\frac{\pi}{22}\cdot\sin\frac{3\pi}{22}\cdot\sin\frac{5\pi}{22}\cdot\sin\frac{7\pi}{22}\cdot\sin\frac{9\pi}{22}$

$= 2\cos\frac{\pi}{11}\cdot\cos\frac{2\pi}{11}\cdot\cos\frac{4\pi}{11}\cdot\cos\frac{8\pi}{11}\cdot\cos\frac{16\pi}{11}$

$= \frac{2 \times \sin 2^5 \frac{\pi}{11}}{2^5 \sin\frac{\pi}{11}} = \frac{1}{16}$ $\left[\because \sin 2^5\frac{\pi}{11} = \sin\frac{\pi}{11}\right]$

80. Given that $\cot\alpha = 1, \sec\beta = \frac{-5}{3}$,

$\Rightarrow \cos\beta = -\frac{3}{5}, \tan\beta = -\frac{4}{3}, \tan\alpha = 1$

$\Rightarrow \tan(\alpha + \beta) = \frac{1 - \frac{4}{3}}{1 + \frac{4}{3} \times 1} = \frac{-1}{7}$

$\left[\because \tan(\alpha + \beta) = \frac{\tan\alpha + \tan\beta}{1 - \tan\alpha \cdot \tan\beta}\right]$

$\Rightarrow \tan(\alpha + \beta) = \frac{-1}{7}$ lies in IVth quadrant.

81. Take $\cos 72° = \frac{\sqrt{5} - 1}{4}$

Let $\sin 36° = \alpha$

Now, $1 - 2\sin^2 36° = \cos 72°$

$\Rightarrow 1 - 2\sin^2 36° = \frac{\sqrt{5} - 1}{4}$

$\Rightarrow 4 - 8\alpha^2 = \sqrt{5} - 1 \Rightarrow 5 - 8\alpha^2 = \sqrt{5}$

On squaring both sides, we get

$(5 - 8\alpha^2)^2 = 5 \Rightarrow 25 + 64\alpha^4 - 80\alpha^2 = 5$

$\Rightarrow 64\alpha^4 - 80\alpha^2 + 20 = 0 \Rightarrow 16\alpha^4 + 20\alpha^2 + 5 = 0$

So, $\alpha = \sin 36°$ is a root of $16x^4 - 20x^2 + 5 = 0$.

82. $\cos 2\pi/7 + \cos 4\pi/7 + \cos 6\pi/7$

Applying sum formula of cos series

$\frac{\cos\left(\frac{\text{1st} + \text{last angle}}{2}\right)\sin\left(n\frac{CD}{2}\right)}{\sin\left(\frac{CD}{2}\right)}$ [CD = common difference]

$= \frac{\cos\left(\frac{\frac{2\pi}{7} + \frac{6\pi}{7}}{2}\right)\sin\left(3 \times \frac{2\pi/7}{2}\right)}{\sin\left(\frac{\frac{2\pi}{7}}{2}\right)} = \frac{\sin\frac{3\pi}{7}\cos\frac{4\pi}{7}}{\sin\frac{\pi}{7}}$

$= \frac{\sin\left(\pi - \frac{4\pi}{7}\right)\cos\frac{4\pi}{7}}{\sin\frac{\pi}{7}} = \frac{2\sin\frac{4\pi}{7}\cos\frac{4\pi}{7}}{2\sin\frac{\pi}{7}} = \frac{\sin\frac{8\pi}{7}}{2\sin\frac{\pi}{7}}$

$= \frac{\sin\left(\pi + \frac{\pi}{7}\right)}{2\sin\frac{\pi}{7}} = \frac{-\sin\frac{\pi}{7}}{2\sin\frac{\pi}{7}} = \frac{-1}{2}$

83. Given trigonometric equation is

$16\sin 20°\sin 40°\sin 80° = 16\sin 40°\sin 20°\sin 80°$

$= 4(4\sin(60 - 20)\sin(20)\sin(60 + 20))$

$= 4 \times \sin(3 \times 20°)$

$[\because \sin 3\theta = 4\sin(60 - \theta) \times \sin\theta \times \sin(60 + \theta)]$

$= 4 \times \sin 60°$

$= 4 \times \frac{\sqrt{3}}{2}$

$= 2\sqrt{3}$

84. Given trigonometric equation is

$\sin 12° + \sin 12° - \sin 72° = \sin 12° - 2\cos 42°\sin 30°$

$\left[\because \sin A - \sin B = 2\sin\frac{(A - B)}{2}\cdot\cos\left(\frac{A + B}{2}\right)\right]$

$= \sin 12° - \sin(90° - 42°)$

$= \sin 12° - \sin 48°$

$= -2\cos 30°\sin 18°$

$= -2 \times \frac{\sqrt{3}}{2} \times \frac{\sqrt{5} - 1}{4}$

$= \frac{\sqrt{3}}{4}(1 - \sqrt{5})$

85. Given, $\sin 10°\left(\frac{1}{2}\cdot 2\sin 20°\ \sin 40°\right)$

$\cdot \sin 10°\sin(60° - 10°)\sin(60° + 10°)$

$= \sin 10°\frac{1}{2}(\cos 20° - \cos 60°)\cdot\frac{1}{4}\sin 30°$

$= \frac{1}{2}\cdot\frac{1}{4}\cdot\frac{1}{2}\cdot\sin 10°\left(\cos 20° - \frac{1}{2}\right)$

$$= \frac{1}{32}(2\sin 10° \cos 20° - \sin 10°)$$
$$= \frac{1}{32}(\sin 30° - \sin 10° - \sin 10°)$$
$$= \frac{1}{32}\left(\frac{1}{2} - 2\sin 10°\right)$$
$$= \frac{1}{64}(1 - 4\sin 10°)$$
$$= \frac{1}{64} - \frac{1}{16}(\sin 10°)$$

On comparing with LHS, we get

$$\alpha = \frac{1}{64}$$
$$\Rightarrow \quad \alpha^{-1} = 64$$

Hence, $16 + \alpha^{-1} = 80$

86. We have,

$$2\sin\left(\frac{\pi}{8}\right)\sin\left(\frac{2\pi}{8}\right)\sin\left(\frac{3\pi}{8}\right)\sin\left(\frac{5\pi}{8}\right)\sin\left(\frac{6\pi}{8}\right)\sin\left(\frac{7\pi}{8}\right)$$
$$= 2\sin^2\frac{\pi}{8}\sin^2\frac{2\pi}{8}\sin^2\frac{3\pi}{8}$$
$$= 2\sin^2\frac{\pi}{8}\sin^2\frac{3\pi}{8}\cdot\frac{1}{2}$$
$$\left[\because \sin\frac{7\pi}{8} = \sin\frac{\pi}{8} \text{ and } \sin\frac{6\pi}{8} = \sin\frac{2\pi}{8}\right]$$
$$= \sin^2\frac{\pi}{8}\sin^2\frac{3\pi}{8} = \sin^2\frac{\pi}{8}\sin^2\left(\frac{\pi}{2} - \frac{\pi}{8}\right)$$
$$= \sin^2\frac{\pi}{8}\cos^2\frac{\pi}{8} = \frac{1}{4}\sin^2\left(\frac{\pi}{4}\right) = \frac{1}{8}$$

87. $\sin\theta + \cos\theta = \frac{1}{2}$

$$\Rightarrow \sin^2\theta + \cos^2\theta + 2\sin\theta\cos\theta = \frac{1}{4}$$
$$\Rightarrow \sin 2\theta = \frac{1}{4} - 1 = -\frac{3}{4} \qquad [\because \sin 2A = 2\sin A\cos A]$$
$$\therefore \cos 2\theta = \sqrt{1 - \sin^2 2\theta} = \sqrt{1 - \frac{9}{16}} = \pm\frac{\sqrt{7}}{4}$$
$$\Rightarrow 1 + \cos 4\theta = 2\cos^2 2\theta \qquad [\because 1 + \cos 2A = 2\cos^2 A]$$
$$\Rightarrow \quad \cos 4\theta = 2\left(\frac{7}{16}\right) - 1 = \frac{-2}{16} = \frac{-1}{8}$$
$$\therefore 16(\sin 2\theta + \cos 4\theta + \sin 6\theta) = 16[(\sin 2\theta + \sin 6\theta) + \cos 4\theta]$$
$$= 16(2\sin 4\theta\cos 2\theta + \cos 4\theta)$$
$$= 16(4\sin 2\theta\cos^2 2\theta + \cos 4\theta)$$
$$= 16\left[4\left(\frac{-3}{4}\right)\left(\frac{7}{16}\right) - \frac{1}{8}\right]$$
$$= -21 - 2 = -23$$

88. We know that $\cot\theta = \frac{1 + \cos 2\theta}{\sin 2\theta}$

When $\theta = \frac{\pi}{24}$,

$$\cot\left(\frac{\pi}{24}\right) = \frac{1 + \cos\left(\frac{\pi}{12}\right)}{\sin\left(\frac{\pi}{12}\right)}$$
$$= \frac{1 + \left(\frac{\sqrt{3}+1}{2\sqrt{2}}\right)}{\frac{\sqrt{3}-1}{2\sqrt{2}}}$$
$$= \frac{2\sqrt{2} + \sqrt{3} + 1}{\sqrt{3} - 1} \times \frac{\sqrt{3}+1}{\sqrt{3}+1}$$
$$= \frac{2\sqrt{6} + 2\sqrt{2} + 3 + \sqrt{3} + \sqrt{3} + 1}{2}$$
$$= \frac{2(\sqrt{6} + \sqrt{2} + \sqrt{3} + 2)}{2}$$
$$= \sqrt{6} + \sqrt{2} + \sqrt{3} + 2$$

89. Given, $\cos x + \cos y - \cos(x+y) = \frac{3}{2}$

$$\Rightarrow 2\cos\left(\frac{x+y}{2}\right)\cos\left(\frac{x-y}{2}\right) - \left[2\cos^2\left(\frac{x+y}{2}\right) - 1\right] = \frac{3}{2}$$

$\left[\text{use formula, } \cos a + \cos b = 2\cos\left(\frac{a+b}{2}\right)\cos\left(\frac{a-b}{2}\right),\ \cos 2x = 2\cos^2 x - 1\right]$

$$\Rightarrow 2\cos\left(\frac{x+y}{2}\right)\cos\left(\frac{x-y}{2}\right) - 2\cos^2\left(\frac{x+y}{2}\right) = \frac{3}{2} - 1 = \frac{1}{2}$$
$$\Rightarrow 4\cos\left(\frac{x+y}{2}\right)\cos\left(\frac{x-y}{2}\right) - 4\cos^2\left(\frac{x+y}{2}\right) = \frac{1}{2}\times 2 = 1$$

and $\quad \cos^2\frac{(x-y)}{2} + \sin^2\frac{(x-y)}{2} = 1$

$$\Rightarrow \left[\cos\left(\frac{x-y}{2}\right) - 2\cos\left(\frac{x+y}{2}\right)\right]^2 + \sin^2\left(\frac{x-y}{2}\right) = 0$$
$$\Rightarrow \quad \sin\left(\frac{x-y}{2}\right) = 0$$

or $\quad \cos\left(\frac{x-y}{2}\right) - 2\cos\left(\frac{x+y}{2}\right) = 0$

$\Rightarrow \quad x = y$ and $\cos 0 - 2\cos x = 0$ [use $x = y$]

Given, $\cos x = \frac{1}{2} = \cos y$

$$\therefore \sin x = \sqrt{1 - \cos^2 x} = \sqrt{1 - \frac{1}{4}} = \frac{\sqrt{3}}{2}$$
$$\therefore \sin x + \cos y = \frac{\sqrt{3}}{2} + \frac{1}{2} = \frac{1+\sqrt{3}}{2}$$

90. Given trigonometric expression

$$\cos^3\left(\frac{\pi}{8}\right)\cos\left(\frac{3\pi}{8}\right) + \sin^3\left(\frac{\pi}{8}\right)\sin\frac{3\pi}{8}$$
$$\Rightarrow \quad \cos^3\left(\frac{\pi}{8}\right)\cos\left(\frac{\pi}{2} - \frac{\pi}{8}\right) + \sin^3\left(\frac{\pi}{8}\right)\sin\left(\frac{\pi}{2} - \frac{\pi}{8}\right)$$
$$\left[\because \frac{\pi}{2} - \frac{\pi}{8} = \frac{3\pi}{8}\right]$$

$$= \cos^3\left(\frac{\pi}{8}\right)\sin\left(\frac{\pi}{8}\right) + \sin^3\left(\frac{\pi}{8}\right)\cos\left(\frac{\pi}{8}\right)$$

$$= \sin\left(\frac{\pi}{8}\right)\cos\left(\frac{\pi}{8}\right)\left[\cos^2\left(\frac{\pi}{8}\right) + \sin^2\left(\frac{\pi}{8}\right)\right]$$

$$= \frac{1}{2}\times 2\sin\left(\frac{\pi}{8}\right)\cos\left(\frac{\pi}{8}\right)$$

$$= \frac{1}{2}\sin\frac{\pi}{4} = \frac{1}{2\sqrt{2}}$$

91. It is given that for $\alpha, \beta \in (0, \pi/2)$

$$\frac{\sqrt{2}\sin\alpha}{\sqrt{1+\cos 2\alpha}} = \frac{1}{7}$$

$$\Rightarrow \quad \frac{\sqrt{2}\sin\alpha}{\sqrt{2}|\cos\alpha|} = \frac{1}{7} \Rightarrow \tan\alpha = \frac{1}{7}$$

$$\because \quad \alpha \in \left(0, \frac{\pi}{2}\right) \quad \text{...(i)}$$

and $$\sqrt{\frac{1-\cos 2\beta}{2}} = \frac{1}{\sqrt{10}}$$

$$\Rightarrow \quad |\sin\beta| = \frac{1}{\sqrt{10}}$$

$$\Rightarrow \quad \sin\beta = \frac{1}{\sqrt{10}} \quad \left[\because \beta \in \left(0, \frac{\pi}{2}\right)\right]$$

$$\therefore \quad \tan\beta = \frac{1}{3} \quad \text{...(ii)}$$

$$\therefore \quad \tan 2\beta = \frac{2\tan\beta}{1-\tan^2\beta}$$

$$= \frac{\frac{2}{3}}{1-\frac{1}{9}} = \frac{6}{8} = \frac{3}{4}$$

Now, $$\tan(\alpha + 2\beta) = \frac{\tan\alpha + \tan 2\beta}{1 - \tan\alpha\tan 2\beta}$$

$$= \frac{\frac{1}{7}+\frac{3}{4}}{1-\left(\frac{1}{7}\times\frac{3}{4}\right)} = \frac{4+21}{28-3} = \frac{25}{25} = 1$$

92. Given expression $3\cos\theta + 5\sin\left(\theta - \frac{\pi}{6}\right)$

$$= 3\cos\theta + 5\left(\sin\theta\cos\frac{\pi}{6} - \sin\frac{\pi}{6}\cos\theta\right)$$

$$= 3\cos\theta + 5\left(\frac{\sqrt{3}}{2}\sin\theta - \frac{1}{2}\cos\theta\right)$$

$$= 3\cos\theta - \frac{5}{2}\cos\theta + \frac{5\sqrt{3}}{2}\sin\theta$$

$$= \frac{1}{2}\cos\theta + \frac{5\sqrt{3}}{2}\sin\theta$$

$\because$ The maximum value of $a\cos\theta + b\sin\theta$ is $\sqrt{a^2+b^2}$.

So, maximum value of $\frac{1}{2}\cos\theta + \frac{5\sqrt{3}}{2}\sin\theta$

$$= \sqrt{\left(\frac{1}{2}\right)^2 + \left(\frac{5\sqrt{3}}{2}\right)^2} = \sqrt{\frac{1}{4}+\frac{75}{4}} = \sqrt{\frac{76}{4}} = \sqrt{19}$$

Exercise 2 - JEE Advanced Pattern

1. $[\tan^2 x] \in Z$ and $a \in N$

$$[\tan^2 x] - \tan x - a = 0$$

$$\tan x = [\tan^2 x] - a \Rightarrow \tan x \in Z$$

Let $\tan x = t$

$$t^2 - t - a = 0$$

$$t = \frac{1 \pm \sqrt{1+4a}}{2}$$

$$t \in Z,$$

if $4a + 1$ becomes perfect square.

$$4a + 1 = m^2$$

or $a = \dfrac{(m-1)(m+1)}{4}$; $m = 3, 5, 7, \ldots, 19$

Hence, the total 9 numbers of elements in S.

2. $$\tan\left(\frac{\pi}{4}+\frac{y}{2}\right) = \tan^3\left(\frac{\pi}{4}+\frac{x}{2}\right)$$

$$\frac{1+\tan\frac{y}{2}}{1-\tan\frac{y}{2}} = \left[\frac{1+\tan\frac{x}{2}}{1-\tan\frac{x}{2}}\right]^3$$

$$\frac{\cos\frac{y}{2}+\sin\frac{y}{2}}{\cos\frac{y}{2}-\sin\frac{y}{2}} = \left[\frac{\cos\frac{x}{2}+\sin\frac{x}{2}}{\cos\frac{x}{2}-\sin\frac{x}{2}}\right]^3$$

On squaring both sides, we get

$$\frac{1+\sin y}{1-\sin y} = \left(\frac{1+\sin x}{1-\sin x}\right)^3 = \frac{(1+\sin x)^3}{(1-\sin x)^3}$$

$$\frac{(1+\sin y)+(1-\sin y)}{(1+\sin y)-(1-\sin y)}$$

$$= \frac{(1+\sin^3 x + 3\sin x + 3\sin^2 x) + (1 - \sin^3 x - 3\sin x + 3\sin^2 x)}{(1+\sin^3 x + 3\sin x + 3\sin^2 x) - (1 - \sin^3 x - 3\sin x + 3\sin^2 x)}$$

$$\frac{2}{2\sin y} = \frac{2+6\sin^2 x}{2\sin^3 x + 6\sin x} = \frac{2(1+3\sin^2 x)}{2\sin x(\sin^2 x + 3)}$$

$$\frac{\sin x(3+\sin^2 x)}{1+3\sin^2 x} = \sin y$$

3. We have, $Q = \sum_{r=0}^{n} \dfrac{\sin(3^r\theta)}{\cos(3^{r+1}\theta)}$

$$= \frac{\sin\theta}{\cos 3\theta} + \frac{\sin 3\theta}{\cos 9\theta} + \frac{\sin 9\theta}{\cos 27\theta} + \ldots\ldots + \frac{\sin(3^n\theta)}{\cos(3^{n+1}\theta)}$$

As, $$\frac{\sin\theta}{\cos 3\theta} = \frac{2\sin\theta\cos\theta}{2\cos\theta\cos 3\theta} = \frac{\sin 2\theta}{2\cos\theta\cos 3\theta}$$

$$= \frac{1}{2}\left[\frac{\sin(3\theta-\theta)}{\cos\theta\cos 3\theta}\right] = \frac{1}{2}(\tan 3\theta - \tan\theta)$$

$$\therefore \quad Q = \frac{1}{2}[(\tan 3\theta - \tan\theta) + (\tan 9\theta - \tan 3\theta) + \ldots + \tan 3^{n+1}\theta - \tan 3^n\theta)]$$

$$\Rightarrow \quad Q = \frac{P}{2} \Rightarrow P = 2Q$$

4. Consider $y = 5\sec^2\theta - \tan^2\theta + 4\text{cosec}^2\theta$

$\therefore \quad y = 5 + 5\tan^2\theta - \tan^2\theta + 4 + 4\cot^2\theta$

$y = 9 + 4(\tan^2 + \cot^2) = 9 + 4[(\tan\theta - \cot\theta)^2 + 2]$

$\therefore \quad y_{\min} = 9 + 8 = 17$

$\Rightarrow$ Maximum value of the expression is $\frac{1}{17} = \frac{p}{q}$

$\Rightarrow \quad p + q = 1 + 17 = 18$

5. $f_n(\alpha) = \tan n\alpha$ and $f_n\left(\frac{\pi}{32}\right) = \tan\frac{\pi}{8} = \sqrt{2} - 1$

6. $BD = x\tan C$ in ΔPDB and $DC = x\tan B$ for ΔPDC.

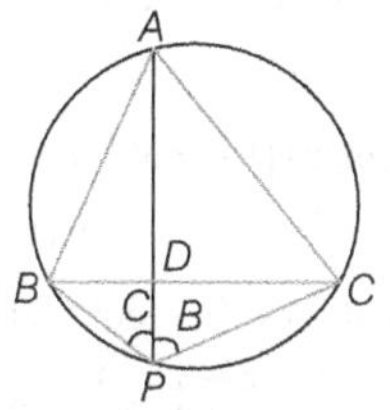

$\therefore \quad BD + DC = a = x(\tan B + \tan C)$

$\frac{a}{x} = \tan B + \tan C$

Similarly, $\frac{b}{y} = \tan A + \tan C$

$\frac{c}{z} = \tan A + \tan B$

$\therefore \quad \frac{a}{2x} + \frac{b}{2y} + \frac{c}{2z} = \frac{1}{2}\left(\frac{a}{x} + \frac{b}{y} + \frac{c}{z}\right) = \tan A + \tan B + \tan C$

7. $\left|\sin x + \cos x + \frac{\cos x + \sin x}{\cos^4 x - \sin^4 x}\right|$

$= \left|\sin x + \cos x + \frac{1}{\cos x - \sin x}\right|$

$= \left|\frac{\cos^2 x - \sin^2 x + 1}{\cos x - \sin x}\right|$

$= \left|\frac{\cos 2x + 1}{\sqrt{2}\left[\sin\frac{\pi}{4}\cos x - \cos\frac{\pi}{4}\sin x\right]}\right|$

$= \left|\frac{\cos 2x + 1}{\sqrt{2}\left(\sin\left(\frac{\pi}{4} - x\right)\right)}\right|$ is minimum ...(i)

So, $\sqrt{2}\left(\sin\left(\frac{\pi}{4} - x\right)\right)$ must be maximum.

$\therefore \quad \sqrt{2}\sin\left(\frac{\pi}{4} - x\right) = 1$

$\Rightarrow \quad \sin\left(\frac{\pi}{4} - x\right) = \frac{1}{\sqrt{2}}$

$\Rightarrow \quad \sin\left(\frac{\pi}{4} - x\right) = \sin\frac{\pi}{4}$

$\Rightarrow \quad x = 0$

On putting $x = 0$ in Eq. (i), we get

$$\left|\frac{\cos 0 + 1}{\sqrt{2}\sin\frac{\pi}{4}}\right| = \left|\frac{1 + 1}{\sqrt{2}\cdot\frac{1}{\sqrt{2}}}\right| = 2$$

8. $\sin\theta = \frac{x}{l}$ ...(i)

Also, $\cos 2\theta = \frac{6 - x}{x}$

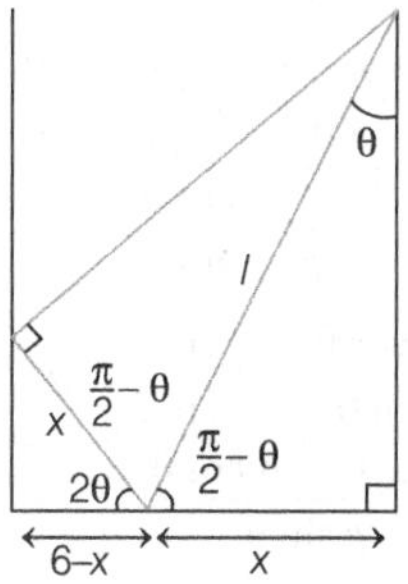

$\Rightarrow \quad 1 + \cos 2\theta = \frac{6}{x} \Rightarrow 2\cos^2\theta = \frac{6}{l\sin\theta}$

[substituting $x = l\sin\theta$ from Eq. (i)]

$\Rightarrow \quad l = \frac{3}{\sin\theta\cos^2\theta}$

9. In 1st case, $r = \cot\frac{\pi}{5}$; $R = \text{cosec}\frac{\pi}{5}$

2nd case, $r_1 = \cot\frac{\pi}{7}$; $R_1 = \text{cosec}\frac{\pi}{7}$

$\therefore \quad A_1 = \pi(R^2 - r^2) = \pi\left(\text{cosec}^2\frac{\pi}{5} - \cot^2\frac{\pi}{5}\right) = \pi$

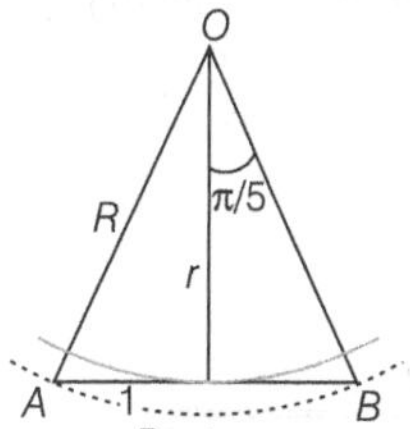

Pentagon

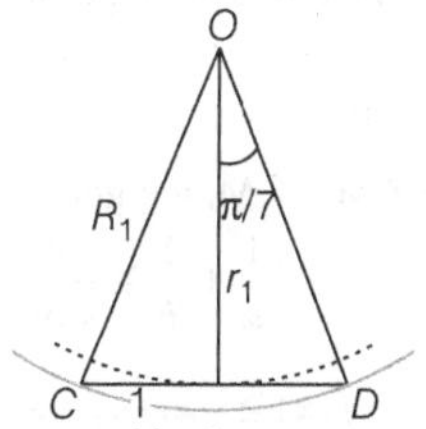

Heptagon

M $\quad A_2 = \pi(R_1^2 - r_1^2) = \pi\left(\text{cosec}^2\frac{\pi}{7} - \cot^2\frac{\pi}{7}\right) = \pi$

$\Rightarrow \quad A_1 = A_2$

10. Let $AB = x$ and $\angle BDC = \alpha$

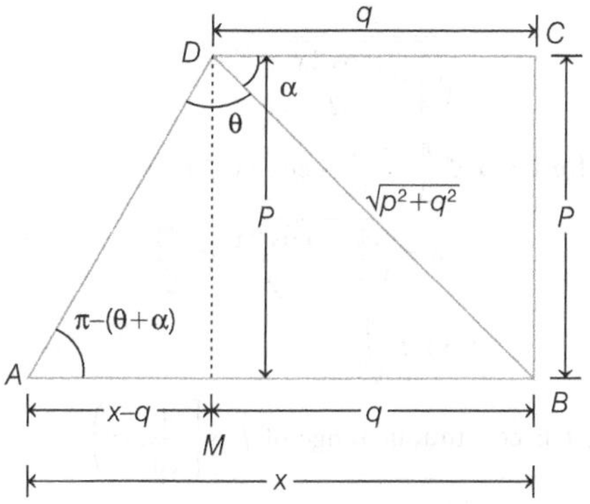

In ΔDAM, $\tan(\pi - \theta - \alpha) = \dfrac{p}{x-q}$

$$\Rightarrow \quad \tan(\theta + \alpha) = \frac{p}{q - x}$$

$$\Rightarrow \quad q - x = p\cot(\theta + \alpha)$$

$$\Rightarrow x = q - p\cot(\theta+\alpha) = q - p\left(\frac{\cot\theta\cot\alpha - 1}{\cot\alpha + \cot\theta}\right)$$

$$= \frac{q(\cot\alpha + \cot\theta) - p(\cot\theta\cot\alpha) + p}{\cot\alpha + \cot\theta}$$

$$= \frac{q\left(\dfrac{q}{p} + \dfrac{\cos\theta}{\sin\theta}\right) - p\left(\dfrac{q}{p}\dfrac{\cos\theta}{\sin\theta}\right) + p}{\dfrac{q}{p} + \dfrac{\cos\theta}{\sin\theta}} \qquad \left[\because \cot\alpha = \frac{q}{p}\right]$$

$$= \frac{\dfrac{q^2}{p} + \dfrac{q\cos\theta}{\sin\theta} - q\dfrac{\cos\theta}{\sin\theta} + p}{\dfrac{q\sin\theta + p\cos\theta}{p\sin\theta}} = \frac{(q^2+p^2)\sin\theta}{q\sin\theta + p\cos\theta}$$

11. Let $y = \cos x\cos(x+2) - \cos^2(x+1)$

$$= \frac{1}{2}[\cos(2x+2) + \cos 2] - \cos^2(x+1)$$

$$= \frac{1}{2}[2\cos^2(x+1) - 1 + \cos 2] - \cos^2(x+1)$$

$$= -\frac{1}{2}(1 - \cos 2)$$

$$= -\frac{1}{2}(2\sin^2 1) = -\sin^2 1$$

This shows that $y = -\sin^2 1$ is a straight line which is parallel to X-axis and clearly passes through the point $\left(\dfrac{\pi}{2}, -\sin^2 1\right)$.

12. If $a, b > 0$

Using AM $\geq$ GM, we get

$$\frac{1}{a} + \frac{1}{b} \geq \frac{2}{\sqrt{ab}}$$

$$\Rightarrow \quad f(x) \geq \frac{2}{\sqrt{\cos\left(\dfrac{\pi}{6} - x\right)\cos\left(\dfrac{\pi}{6} + x\right)}}$$

$$= \frac{2}{\sqrt{\cos^2\dfrac{\pi}{6} - \sin^2 x}} = \frac{2}{\sqrt{\dfrac{3}{4} - \dfrac{1 - \cos 2x}{2}}}$$

$$= \frac{2}{\sqrt{\dfrac{1}{4} + \dfrac{\cos 2x}{2}}}$$

Now, for $0 \leq x \leq \dfrac{\pi}{3}$, $\dfrac{-1}{2} \leq \cos 2x \leq 1$

$$\Rightarrow \quad 0 \leq \sqrt{\frac{1}{4} + \frac{\cos 2x}{2}} \leq \frac{\sqrt{3}}{2}$$

$$\Rightarrow \quad f(x) \geq \frac{4}{\sqrt{3}}$$

Since, f is continuous range of f is $\left[\dfrac{4}{\sqrt{3}}, \infty\right)$.

13. $\because 0 \leq \sin^2\theta \leq 1$ and $0 \leq \cos^2\theta \leq 1$

$$\Rightarrow \quad 0 \leq \sin^8\theta \leq \sin^2\theta \text{ and } 0 \leq \cos^{14}\theta \leq \cos^2\theta$$

$$\therefore \quad 0 < \sin^8\theta + \cos^{14}\theta \leq \sin^2\theta + \cos^2\theta$$

Hence, $0 < A \leq 1$

14. $\cot^2 x = \cot(x - y)\cdot\cot(x - z)$

$$\Rightarrow \cot^2 x = \left(\frac{\cot x\cot y + 1}{\cot y - \cot x}\right)\left(\frac{\cot x\cdot\cot z + 1}{\cot z - \cot x}\right)$$

$$\Rightarrow \cot^2 x\cdot\cot y\cdot\cot z - \cot^3 x\cdot\cot y - \cot^3 x\cot z + \cot^4 x$$

$$= \cot^2 x\cdot\cot y\cdot\cot z + \cot x\cdot\cot y + \cot x\cdot\cot z + 1$$

$$\Rightarrow \cot x\cot y(1 + \cot^2 x) + \cot x\cot z(1 + \cot^2 x) + 1 - \cot^4 x = 0$$

$$\Rightarrow \cot x(\cot y + \cot z)(1 + \cot^2 x) + (1 - \cot^2 x)(1 + \cot^2 x) = 0$$

$$\Rightarrow \cot x(\cot y + \cot z) + (1 - \cot^2 x) = 0$$

$$\Rightarrow \quad \frac{\cot^2 x - 1}{2\cot x} = \frac{1}{2}(\cot y + \cot z)$$

$$\Rightarrow \quad \frac{1}{2}(\cot y + \cot z) = \cot 2x$$

15. Given that, $\alpha + \beta + \gamma = \pi$

Taking $\alpha = -\dfrac{\pi}{2}$; $\beta = -\dfrac{\pi}{2}$ and $\gamma = 2\pi$

$$\therefore \quad \sin\alpha + \sin\beta + \sin\gamma = -1 - 1 + 0 = -2$$

but $\sin\alpha + \sin\beta + \sin\gamma \geq -3$ for any α, β, γ

Hence, minimum value of $\sin\alpha + \sin\beta + \sin\gamma$ is negative.

16. $\because \cos^4\theta\sec^2\alpha, \dfrac{1}{2}$ and $\sin^4\theta\operatorname{cosec}^2\alpha$ are in AP

$$1 = \cos^4\theta\sec^2\alpha + \sin^4\theta\operatorname{cosec}^2\alpha$$

$$\Rightarrow \quad 1 = \frac{\cos^4\theta}{\cos^2\alpha} + \frac{\sin^4\theta}{\sin^2\alpha}$$

$$\Rightarrow \quad (\sin^2\theta + \cos^2\theta)^2 = \frac{\cos^4\theta}{\cos^2\alpha} + \frac{\sin^4\theta}{\sin^2\alpha}$$

$$\Rightarrow \quad \cos^4\theta\left(\frac{1}{\cos^2\alpha} - 1\right) + \sin^4\theta\left(\frac{1}{\sin^2\alpha} - 1\right) - 2\sin^2\theta\cos^2\theta = 0$$

$$\Rightarrow \quad \sin^4\alpha\cos^4\theta + \sin^4\theta\cos^4\alpha - 2\sin^2\theta\cos^2\theta\sin^2\alpha\cos^2\alpha = 0$$

$$\Rightarrow (\sin^2\alpha\cos^2\theta - \cos^2\alpha\sin^2\theta)^2 = 0$$

$$\Rightarrow \quad \tan^2\theta = \tan^2\alpha$$

$$\therefore \quad \theta = n\pi \pm \alpha, n \in I$$

Now, $\cos^8\theta\sec^6\alpha = \cos^8\alpha\sec^6\alpha = \cos^2\alpha$

and $\sin^8\theta\operatorname{cosec}^6\alpha = \sin^8\alpha\cdot\operatorname{cosec}^6\alpha = \sin^2\alpha$

Hence, $\cos^8\theta\sec^6\alpha, \dfrac{1}{2}, \sin^8\theta\operatorname{cosec}^6\alpha$

i.e. $\cos^2\alpha, \dfrac{1}{2}, \sin^2\alpha$ are in AP.

17. Given, $(\cot\alpha_1)\cdot(\cot\alpha_2)\ldots(\cot\alpha_n)=1$

$$\Rightarrow \prod_{i=1}^{n}\cos\alpha_i=\prod_{i=1}^{n}\sin\alpha_i$$

$$\Rightarrow \prod_{i=1}^{n}\cos^2\alpha_i=\prod_{i=1}^{n}\sin\alpha_i\cos\alpha_i=\prod_{i=1}^{n}\frac{\sin 2\alpha_i}{2}\le\frac{1}{2^n}$$

$$\Rightarrow \prod_{i=1}^{n}\cos\alpha_i\le\frac{1}{2^{\frac{n}{2}}}$$

Hence, the maximum value of $\prod_{i=1}^{n}\cos\alpha_i$ is $\frac{1}{2^{\frac{n}{2}}}$.

18. $\sin x\cdot\cos^3 x>\cos x\cdot\sin^3 x$

$$\Rightarrow \sin x\cdot\cos x(\cos^2 x-\sin^2 x)>0$$

$$\Rightarrow \sin x\cdot\cos x\cdot\cos 2x>0$$

$$\Rightarrow \sin 2x\cdot\cos 2x>0$$

$$\Rightarrow \sin 4x>0$$

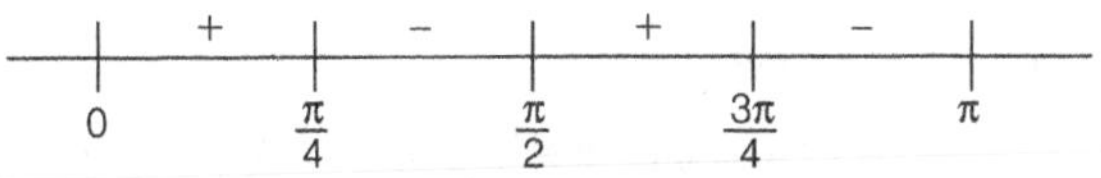

$$\therefore \quad x\in\left(0,\frac{\pi}{4}\right)\cup\left(\frac{\pi}{2},\frac{3\pi}{4}\right)$$

19. $u^2=a^2+b^2+2\sqrt{a^2\cos^2\theta+b^2\sin^2\theta}\times\sqrt{a^2\sin^2\theta+b^2\cos^2\theta}$

$$=a^2+b^2+2\sqrt{\sin^2\theta\cos^2\theta(a^4+b^4)+a^2b^2(\sin^4\theta+\cos^4\theta)}$$

$$=a^2+b^2+2\sqrt{a^2b^2(1-2\sin^2\theta\cos^2\theta)+(a^4+b^4)\sin^2\theta\cos^2\theta}$$

$$=(a^2+b^2)+2\sqrt{a^2b^2+(a^2-b^2)^2\sin^2\theta\cos^2\theta}$$

$$=(a^2+b^2)+2\sqrt{a^2b^2+\frac{(a^2-b^2)^2}{4}\sin^2 2\theta}$$

Max. $u^2=(a^2+b^2)+2\sqrt{a^2b^2+\frac{(a^2-b^2)^2}{4}}$

Min. $u^2=(a^2+b^2)+2ab$

$\Rightarrow$ Difference $2\sqrt{a^2b^2+\frac{(a^2-b^2)^2}{4}}-2ab$

$$=\sqrt{4a^2b^2+a^4+b^4-2a^2b^2}-2ab$$

$$=\sqrt{(a^2+b^2)^2}-2ab=a^2+b^2-2ab=(a-b)^2$$

20. $\cos x=0\Rightarrow x=(2n+1)\frac{\pi}{2}$

$$\Rightarrow \cos\left((2n+1)\frac{\pi}{2}+z\right)=\frac{1}{2}$$

$$\Rightarrow \sin z=\frac{1}{2}\text{ or }\sin z=-\frac{1}{2}$$

$$\Rightarrow z=\frac{\pi}{6},\frac{5\pi}{6},\frac{7\pi}{6},\frac{11\pi}{6}$$

21. $f_n(\theta)=\cos\theta-\cos 2\theta+\cos 2\theta-\cos 3\theta+\ldots+\cos(n)\theta-\cos(n+1)\theta$

$f_n(\theta)=\cos\theta-\cos(n+1)\theta$

Now, put the value of θ and n in the above equation to find the correct option.

22. $P=\sin 25^\circ\sin 35^\circ\sin 60^\circ\sin 85^\circ$

$$=\sin 25^\circ\sin(60^\circ-25^\circ)\sin 60^\circ\sin(60^\circ+25^\circ)$$

$$=\sin 60^\circ\sin 25^\circ\sin(60^\circ-25^\circ)\sin(60^\circ+25^\circ)$$

$$\therefore \quad P=\sin 60^\circ\times\frac{1}{4}\sin 75^\circ \qquad \ldots\text{(i)}$$

$$Q=\sin 20^\circ\sin 40^\circ\sin 75^\circ\sin 80^\circ$$

$$=\sin 20^\circ\sin(60^\circ-20^\circ)\sin 75^\circ\sin(60^\circ+20^\circ)$$

$$=\sin 75^\circ\sin 20^\circ\sin(60^\circ-20^\circ)\sin(60^\circ+20^\circ)$$

$$\therefore \quad Q=\sin 75^\circ\times\frac{1}{4}\times\sin 60^\circ \qquad \ldots\text{(ii)}$$

Hence, $P=Q$

23. $x=\frac{1}{1-\cos^2\theta}=\frac{1}{\sin^2\theta},\ y=\frac{1}{\cos^2\theta},\ z=\frac{1}{1-\sin^2\theta\cos^2\theta}$

$$\Rightarrow \frac{1}{x}+\frac{1}{y}=1\Rightarrow xy=x+y\Rightarrow\frac{1}{z}=1-\frac{1}{xy}$$

$$\Rightarrow xyz=xy+z=x+y+z$$

24. Given, $P(x)=\cot^2 x\left(\frac{1+\tan x+\tan^2 x}{1+\cot x+\cot^2 x}\right)+\left(\frac{\cos x-\cos 3x+\sin 3x-\sin x}{2(\sin 2x+\cos 2x)}\right)^2$

$$=\frac{\cot^2+\cot x+1}{1+\cot x+\cot^2 x}+\left(\frac{2\sin x(\sin 2x+\cos 2x)}{2(\sin 2x+\cos 2x)}\right)^2$$

$$=1+\sin^2 x$$

$$\therefore \quad P(18^\circ)+P(72^\circ)=(1+\sin^2 18^\circ)+(1+\sin^2 72^\circ)$$

$$=1+1+(\sin^2 18^\circ+\cos^2 18^\circ)=3$$

Similarly, $P\left(\frac{4\pi}{3}\right)+P\left(\frac{7\pi}{6}\right)=3$

25. $E=\frac{3\sin(\alpha+\beta)-4\cos(\alpha+\beta)}{\sqrt{3}\sin\alpha}$

$$=\frac{3(\sin\alpha\cos\beta+\cos\alpha\sin\beta)-4(\cos\alpha\cos\beta-\sin\alpha\sin\beta)}{\sqrt{3}\sin\alpha}$$

$$=\frac{5}{\sqrt{3}}\text{ for }0<\beta<\frac{\pi}{2}$$

and $E=\frac{\sqrt{3}(7+24\cot\alpha)}{15}$ for $\frac{\pi}{2}<\beta<\pi$.

26. $\cot A=\frac{3}{4}\Rightarrow\cot C=\frac{-3}{4}$

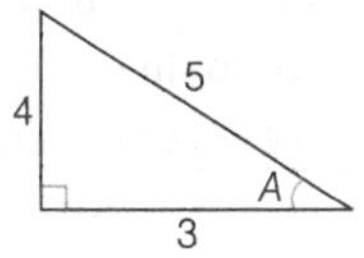

$\Rightarrow$ C is obtuse angle.

$$\therefore \quad \sin C=\frac{4}{5},\ \cos C=-\frac{3}{5}$$

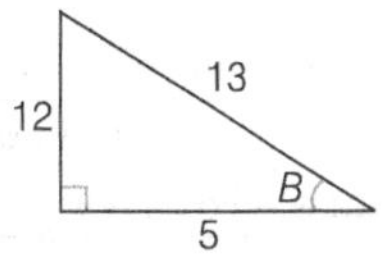

$$\tan B = \frac{-12}{5} \Rightarrow \tan D = \frac{12}{5}$$

$\Rightarrow D$ is an acute angle.

$$\therefore \quad \sin D = \frac{12}{13} \quad \cos D = \frac{5}{13}$$

Hence, $\sin(C + D) = \sin C \cdot \cos D + \cos C \cdot \sin D$

$$= \left(\frac{4}{5}\right)\left(\frac{5}{13}\right) + \left(\frac{-3}{5}\right)\left(\frac{12}{13}\right) = \frac{20 - 36}{65} = \frac{-16}{65}$$

Also, $\sin(A + B) = \sin(2\pi - (C + D))$

$$= -\sin(C + D) = \frac{16}{65}.$$

27. $2\left(\cos^2 x + \frac{1}{2}\cos x\right) = a$

$$2\left(\cos x + \frac{1}{4}\right)^2 = a + \frac{1}{8}$$

$$\therefore \quad \left(\cos x + \frac{1}{4}\right)^2 = \frac{a}{2} + \frac{1}{16}$$

$$\Rightarrow \quad \left(\cos x + \frac{1}{4}\right)^2 \in \left[0, \frac{25}{16}\right]$$

$$\therefore \quad \frac{8a + 1}{16} \in \left[0, \frac{25}{16}\right]$$

$$\Rightarrow \quad 8a + 1 \in [0, 25]$$

$$\Rightarrow \quad a \in \left[\frac{-1}{8}, 3\right]$$

28. $A = \sin 44° + \cos 44°$

$= \cos 46° + \sin 46° = C$

$B = \sin 45° + \cos 45° = \sqrt{2}[\sin 90°]$

$A = \sqrt{2}\left[\frac{1}{\sqrt{2}} \sin 44° + \frac{1}{\sqrt{2}} \cos 44°\right]$

$= \sqrt{2}\,[\sin 44° \cdot \cos 45° + \cos 44° \cdot \sin 45°]$

$= \sqrt{2} \sin 89°$

$\Rightarrow \quad B > A$

29. We have, $x = \frac{1 - \sin\phi}{\cos\phi}, y = \frac{1 + \cos\phi}{\sin\phi}$

On multiplying, we get

$$xy = \frac{(1 - \sin\phi)(1 + \cos\phi)}{\cos\phi \sin\phi}$$

$$\Rightarrow \quad xy + 1 = \frac{1 - \sin\phi + \cos\phi - \sin\phi\cos\phi + \sin\phi\cos\phi}{\cos\phi\sin\phi}$$

$$= \frac{1 - \sin\phi + \cos\phi}{\cos\phi\sin\phi}$$

and
$$x - y = \frac{(1 - \sin\phi)\sin\phi - \cos\phi(1 + \cos\phi)}{\cos\phi\sin\phi}$$

$$= \frac{\sin\phi - \sin^2\phi - \cos\phi - \cos^2\phi}{\cos\phi\sin\phi}$$

$$= \frac{\sin\phi - \cos\phi - 1}{\cos\phi\sin\phi} = -(xy + 1)$$

Thus, $xy + x - y + 1 = 0$.

$$\Rightarrow \quad x = \frac{y - 1}{y + 1} \text{ and } y = \frac{1 + x}{1 - x}.$$

30. The given relation can be written as

$$\tan\left(\frac{x}{2}\right) = \frac{1 - \sin^2 x}{\sin x} = \frac{\cos^2 x}{\sin x}$$

$$\Rightarrow \quad 2\sin^2\left(\frac{x}{2}\right) = \left[\cos^2\left(\frac{x}{2}\right) - \sin^2\left(\frac{x}{2}\right)\right]^2$$

$$\Rightarrow \quad 2\tan^2\left(\frac{x}{2}\right) = \left[1 - \tan^2\left(\frac{x}{2}\right)\right]^2 / \left[1 + \tan^2\left(\frac{x}{2}\right)\right]$$

$$\Rightarrow \quad 2y(1 + y) = (1 - y)^2 \qquad \left[\text{where, } y = \tan^2\frac{x}{2}\right]$$

$$\Rightarrow \quad y^2 + 4y - 1 = 0$$

$$\Rightarrow \quad y = \frac{-4 \pm \sqrt{16 + 4}}{2} = -2 \pm \sqrt{5}$$

Since, $y > 0$, we get

$$y = \sqrt{5} - 2 = \frac{(\sqrt{5} - 2)^2}{\sqrt{5} + 2} \cdot \frac{2 + \sqrt{5}}{2 + \sqrt{5}}$$

$$= (9 - 4\sqrt{5})(2 + \sqrt{5})$$

31. $y = \dfrac{\sqrt{(\cos 2A - \sin 2A)^2} + 1}{\sqrt{(\cos 2A + \sin 2A)^2} - 1}$

$$\Rightarrow \quad y = \frac{\pm(\cos 2A - \sin 2A) + 1}{\pm(\cos 2A + \sin 2A) - 1}$$

which gives us four values of y, say y_1, y_2, y_3 and y_4

We have, $y_1 = \dfrac{\cos 2A - \sin 2A + 1}{\cos 2A + \sin 2A - 1} = \dfrac{(1 + \cos 2A) - \sin 2A}{(\cos 2A - 1) + \sin 2A}$

$$= \frac{2\cos^2 A - 2\sin A\cos A}{-2\sin^2 A + 2\sin A\cos A}$$

$$= \frac{\cos A(\cos A - \sin A)}{\sin A(\cos A - \sin A)} = \cot A$$

$$y_2 = \frac{-(\cos 2A - \sin 2A) + 1}{-(\cos 2A + \sin 2A) - 1}$$

$$= \frac{(1 - \cos 2A) + \sin 2A}{-(1 + \cos 2A) - \sin 2A}$$

$$= \frac{2\sin^2 A + 2\sin A\cos A}{-2\cos^2 A - 2\sin A\cos A} = -\tan A$$

$$y_3 = \frac{(\cos 2A - \sin 2A) + 1}{-(\cos 2A + \sin 2A) - 1}$$

$$= \frac{(1 + \cos 2A) - \sin 2A}{-(1 + \cos 2A) - \sin 2A}$$

$$= \frac{2\cos^2 A - 2\sin A\cos A}{-2\cos^2 A - 2\sin A\cos A}$$

$$= -\frac{\cos A - \sin A}{\cos A + \sin A}$$

$$= -\frac{1 - \tan A}{1 + \tan A} = -\tan\left(\frac{\pi}{4} - A\right) = -\cot\left(\frac{\pi}{4} + A\right)$$

$$y_4 = \frac{-(\cos 2A - \sin 2A) + 1}{(\cos 2A + \sin 2A) - 1}$$
$$= \frac{(1 - \cos 2A) + \sin 2A}{-(1 - \cos 2A) + \sin 2A}$$
$$= \frac{2\sin^2 A + 2\sin A \cos A}{-2\sin 2A + 2\sin A\cos A}$$
$$= \tan\left(\frac{\pi}{4} + A\right)$$

32. $\because 3\sin\beta = \sin(2\alpha + \beta)$

$\Rightarrow \quad 2\sin\beta = \sin(2\alpha+\beta) - \sin\beta = 2\cos(\alpha+\beta)\sin\alpha$

$\therefore \quad \sin\beta = \cos(\alpha+\beta)\sin\alpha$ ...(i)

$\therefore$ **Alternate** (b) is correct

Also, $\sin\beta = \sin(\alpha+\beta) - \alpha)$

$= \sin(\alpha+\beta)\cos\alpha - \cos(\alpha+\beta)\sin\alpha$ ...(ii)

From Eqs. (i) and (ii), we get

$\sin\beta = \sin(\alpha+\beta)\cos\alpha - \sin\beta$

$\therefore \quad 2\sin\beta = \sin(\alpha+\beta)\cos\alpha$

[$\therefore$ Alternate (c) is correct]

Alternate (a)

LHS $= (\cot\alpha + \cot(\alpha+\beta))(\cot\beta - 3\cot(2\alpha+\beta))$

$$= \left(\frac{\sin(2\alpha+\beta)}{\sin\alpha\cdot\sin(\alpha+\beta)}\right)\left(\frac{\cos\beta}{\sin\beta} - \frac{3\cos(2\alpha+\beta)}{\sin(2\alpha+\beta)}\right)$$
$$= \left(\frac{3\sin\beta}{\sin\alpha\cdot\sin(\alpha+\beta)}\right)\left(\frac{\cos\beta}{\sin\beta} - \frac{3\cos(2\alpha+\beta)}{3\sin\beta}\right)$$

[$\because 3\sin\beta = \sin(2\alpha+\beta)$]

$$= \left(\frac{3\sin\beta}{\sin\alpha\cdot\sin(\alpha+\beta)}\right)\left(\frac{\cos\beta - \cos(2\alpha+\beta)}{\sin\beta}\right)$$
$$= \left(\frac{3\sin\beta}{\sin\alpha\cdot\sin(\alpha+\beta)}\right)\left(\frac{2\sin(\alpha+\beta)\sin\alpha}{\sin\beta}\right)$$
$$= 6$$

Alternate (d)

$\because \quad \tan(\alpha+\beta) = 2\tan\alpha$

$\Rightarrow \quad \dfrac{\sin(\alpha+\beta)}{\cos(\alpha+\beta)} = \dfrac{2\sin\alpha}{\cos\alpha}$

$\Rightarrow \quad \sin(\alpha+\beta)\cos\alpha = 2\cos(\alpha+\beta)\sin\alpha$

$\Rightarrow \quad \sin(\alpha+\beta)\cos\alpha - \cos(\alpha+\beta)\sin\alpha = \cos(\alpha+\beta)\sin\alpha$

$\sin\beta = \cos(\alpha+\beta)\sin\alpha$ [Alternate (b)]

33. $P_n(u)$ be a polynomial in u of degree n.

$\therefore \quad \sin 2nx = 2\sin nx\cos nx$

$= \sin x\, P_{2n-1}(\cos x)$ or $\cos x\, P_{2n-1}(\sin x)$

34. $\tan\theta = \dfrac{\sin\alpha - \cos\alpha}{\sin\alpha + \cos\alpha} = \dfrac{\tan\alpha - 1}{\tan\alpha + 1}$

$\Rightarrow \quad \tan\theta = \tan\left(\alpha - \dfrac{\pi}{4}\right)$

$\Rightarrow \quad \theta = n\pi + \alpha - \dfrac{\pi}{4}, n \in I$

or $\quad 2\theta = 2n\pi + 2\alpha - \dfrac{\pi}{2}$

$\sin 2\theta = \sin\left(2\alpha - \dfrac{\pi}{2}\right) = -\cos 2\alpha$

and $\quad \cos 2\theta = \cos\left(2\alpha - \dfrac{\pi}{2}\right) = \sin 2\alpha$

and $\quad \sin\alpha - \cos\alpha = \sqrt{2}\sin\left(\alpha - \dfrac{\pi}{4}\right)$

$= \sqrt{2}\sin\{\theta - n\pi\} = \pm\sqrt{2}\sin\theta$

and $\sin\alpha + \cos\alpha = \sqrt{2}\sin\left(\alpha + \dfrac{\pi}{4}\right) = \sqrt{2}\sin\left\{\dfrac{\pi}{2} + \theta - n\pi\right\}$

$= \sqrt{2}\cos(\theta - n\pi) = \pm\sqrt{2}\cos\theta$

35. $\cos 5\theta = \cos(4\theta + \theta) = \cos 4\theta\cos\theta - \sin 4\theta\sin\theta$

$= (2\cos^2 2\theta - 1)\cos\theta - 2\sin 2\theta\cos 2\theta\sin\theta$

$= [2(2\cos^2\theta - 1)^2 - 1]\cos\theta - 2\cdot 2\cos\theta$

$\sin^2\theta(2\cos^2\theta - 1)$

$= [2(4\cos^4\theta - 4\cos^2\theta + 1) - 1]\cos\theta$

$- 4\cos\theta(2\cos^2\theta - 1)(1 - \cos^2\theta)$

$= \cos\theta(8\cos^4\theta - 8\cos^2\theta + 1)$

$- 4\cos\theta(3\cos^2\theta - 2\cos^4\theta - 1)$

$= \cos\theta(16\cos^4\theta - 20\cos^2\theta + 5)$

36. $x = \sqrt{a^2\cos^2\alpha + b^2\sin^2\alpha} + \sqrt{a^2\sin^2\alpha + b^2\cos^2\alpha}$

$\Rightarrow x^2 = a^2 + b^2 + 2\sqrt{(a^2\cos^2\alpha + b^2\sin^2\alpha)}\cdot\sqrt{(a^2\sin^2\alpha + b^2\cos^2\alpha)}$

$= a^2 + b^2 + 2k$

where $k = \sqrt{(a^2\cos^2\alpha + b^2\sin^2\alpha)\cdot(a^2\sin^2\alpha + b^2\cos^2\alpha)}$

$\therefore \quad x = a^2 + b^2 + 2\sqrt{(a^2+b^2)p - p^2}$

where $p = a^2\sin^2\alpha + b^2\cos^2\alpha$

$= \dfrac{a^2}{2}(1 - \cos 2\alpha) + \dfrac{b^2}{2}(1 + \cos 2\alpha)$

37. $\left(\dfrac{\cos A + \cos B}{\sin A - \sin B}\right)^n + \left(\dfrac{\sin A + \sin B}{\cos A - \cos B}\right)^n$

$= \cot^n\left(\dfrac{A-B}{2}\right) + \cot^n\left(\dfrac{B-A}{2}\right)$

If n even, $2\cot^n\left(\dfrac{A-B}{2}\right)$, if n odd, 0.

38. $P(k) = \left(1 + \cos\dfrac{\pi}{4k}\right)\left(1 + \cos\left(\dfrac{\pi}{2} - \dfrac{\pi}{4k}\right)\right)\left(1 + \cos\left(\dfrac{\pi}{2} + \dfrac{\pi}{4k}\right)\right)$

$\left(1 + \cos\left(\pi - \dfrac{\pi}{4k}\right)\right)$

$= \left(1 + \cos\dfrac{\pi}{4k}\right)\left(1 + \sin\dfrac{\pi}{4k}\right)\left(1 - \sin\dfrac{\pi}{4k}\right)\left(1 - \cos\dfrac{\pi}{4k}\right)$

$= \left(1 - \cos^2\dfrac{\pi}{4k}\right)\left(1 - \sin^2\dfrac{\pi}{4k}\right)$

$= \dfrac{4\sin^2\dfrac{\pi}{4k}\cdot\cos^2\dfrac{\pi}{4k}}{4}$

$$P(k) = \frac{1}{4}\sin^2\left(\frac{\pi}{2k}\right)$$

$$\Rightarrow \quad P(3) = \frac{1}{4}\cdot\frac{1}{4} = \frac{1}{16}$$

$$\Rightarrow \quad P(4) = \frac{\pi}{4}\sin^2\frac{\pi}{2k} = \frac{1}{4}\sin^2\frac{\pi}{8}$$

$$= \frac{1}{8}\left(1 - \cos\frac{\pi}{4}\right) = \frac{2-\sqrt{2}}{16}$$

$$\Rightarrow \quad P(5) = \frac{1}{4}\sin^2\frac{\pi}{10} = \frac{1}{8}\left(2\sin^2\frac{\pi}{10}\right) = \frac{1}{8}(1 - \cos 36°)$$

$$= \frac{1}{8}\left(1 - \frac{\sqrt{5}+1}{4}\right) = \frac{3-\sqrt{5}}{32}$$

$$\Rightarrow \quad P(6) = \frac{1}{4}\sin^2\frac{\pi}{12} = \frac{1}{8}\left(2\sin^2\frac{\pi}{12}\right) = \frac{1}{8}\left(1 - \cos\frac{\pi}{6}\right)$$

$$= \frac{1}{8}\left(1 - \frac{\sqrt{3}}{2}\right) = \frac{2-\sqrt{3}}{16}$$

39. $x^2 + y^2 = a^2 \sin^4\theta \cos^4\theta$

$$xy = a^2 \sin^5\theta \cos^5\theta$$

$$\therefore \quad \frac{(x^2+y^2)^p}{(xy)^q} = \frac{a^{2p}(\sin\theta\cos\theta)^{4p}}{a^{2q}(\sin\theta\cos\theta)^{5q}}$$

which is independent of θ if $4p = 5q$ i.e. $p = 5, q = 4$.

Sol. (Q. Nos. 40 to 41)

40. Let $3^{a^2} = A$ and $3^{b^2+c^2} = B$

$$\Rightarrow \quad A^2 - 2A.B + B^2 = 0 \Rightarrow A = B \Rightarrow a^2 = b^2 + c^2$$

41.

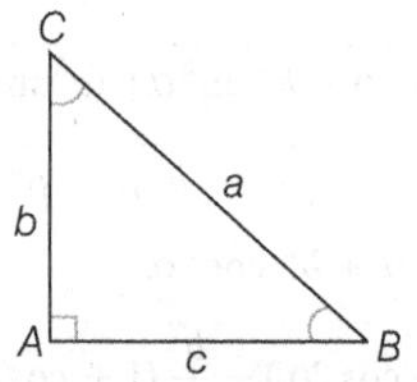

From figure, it is clear that $a = b\sec C = c\,\text{cosec}\,C$

$\Rightarrow$ Equilateral triangle $\Rightarrow$ Area $= \frac{\sqrt{3}}{4}a^2$

Sol. (Q. Nos. 42 to 43)

42. $P_{mn} = m\log_{\cos x}(\sin x) + n\log_{\cos x}(\cot x)$

$$\geq n(\log_{\cos x}(\sin x) + \log_{\cos x}(\cot x))\ \forall\ m \geq n$$

$$= n(\log_{\cos x}(\sin x\cdot\cot x)) = n\log_{\cos x}\cos x = n$$

Thus, $P_{mn} \geq n\ \forall\ m \geq n$

43.

> **Decoding the Question**
>
> We know that mean proportional of three numbers a, b and x is $x^2 = \sqrt{ab}$.

Clearly, $P_{49}\left(\frac{\pi}{4}\right) = 4\log_{\frac{1}{\sqrt{2}}}\left(\frac{1}{\sqrt{2}}\right) + 9\log_{\frac{1}{\sqrt{2}}}(1) = 4$

Similarly, $P_{94} = \left(\frac{\pi}{4}\right) = 9$

Mean proportional of $P_{49}\left(\frac{\pi}{4}\right)$ and $P_{94}\left(\frac{\pi}{4}\right)$ is $\sqrt{9\times 4} = 6$

Sol. (Q. Nos. 44 to 45)

$$7\theta = (2n+1)\pi, n = 0 \text{ to } 6$$

$$4\theta = (2n+1)\pi - 3\theta$$

$$\cos 4\theta = -\cos 3\theta$$

$$\Rightarrow \quad 2\cos^2 2\theta - 1 = -(4\cos^3\theta - 3\cos\theta)$$

$$\Rightarrow 2(2x^2-1)^2 - 1 = -(4x^3 - 3x), \text{ where } x = \cos\theta$$

$$\Rightarrow \quad 8x^4 + 4x^3 - 8x^2 - 3x + 1 = 0$$

$$(x+1)(8x^3 - 4x^2 - 4x - 1) = 0$$

44. The roots are $\cos\frac{\pi}{7}, \cos\frac{2\pi}{7}, \ldots, \cos\frac{13\pi}{7}$

where $\cos\frac{\pi}{7} = \cos\frac{13\pi}{7}$, $\cos\frac{3\pi}{7} = \cos\frac{11\pi}{7}$, $\cos\frac{5\pi}{7} = \cos\frac{9\pi}{7}$

$\therefore$ The roots of $8x^3 - 4x^2 - 4x + 1 = 0$ are $\cos\frac{\pi}{7}, \cos\frac{3\pi}{7}, \cos\frac{5\pi}{7}$.

45. $\sec\frac{\pi}{7}, \sec\frac{3\pi}{7}, \sec\frac{5\pi}{7}$ are roots of $\frac{8}{x^3} - \frac{4}{x^2} - \frac{4}{x} + 1 = 0$

$$\Rightarrow \quad x^3 - 4x^2 - 4x + 8 = 0$$

$$\therefore \quad \sec\frac{\pi}{7} + \sec\frac{3\pi}{7} + \sec\frac{5\pi}{7} = 4$$

Sol. (Q. Nos. 46 to 47)

Let $\quad S = 1 + 2\sin x + 3\sin^2 x + 4\sin^3 x + \ldots$

$$\Rightarrow \sin x.\ S = \sin x + 2\sin^2 x + 3\sin^3 x + \ldots$$

$$\therefore \quad (1-\sin x)\,S = 1 + \sin x + \sin^2 x + \ldots$$

$$\Rightarrow \quad (1-\sin x)\,S = \frac{1}{1-\sin x}$$

$$\therefore \quad S = \frac{1}{(1-\sin x)^2}$$

Given, $S = 4 \Rightarrow \frac{1}{(1-\sin x)^2} = 4 \Rightarrow \sin x = \frac{1}{2}$ or $\frac{3}{2}$ (rejected)

Number of solutions in $\left[\frac{-3\pi}{2}, 4\pi\right]$ is $k = 5$.

46. $k = 5$

47. $\left|\frac{\cos 2x - 1}{\sin 2x}\right| = \left|\frac{2\sin^2 x}{2\cos x\sin x}\right| = |\tan x| = \frac{1}{\sqrt{3}}$

Sol. (Q. Nos. 48 to 49)

48. Now, $\quad (2\sin x - \cos x)(1 + \cos x) = \sin^2 x$

$$\Rightarrow (1+\cos x)[2\sin x - \cos x - 1 + \cos x] = 0$$

$$\Rightarrow \quad (1+\cos x)(2\sin x - 1) = 0$$

$$\Rightarrow \quad \cos x = -1 \text{ or } \sin x = \frac{1}{2}$$

So, $\quad \sin\alpha = \frac{1}{2} \quad \left[\text{as } 0 \leq \alpha \leq \frac{\pi}{2}\right]$

$$\therefore \quad \cos\alpha = \frac{\sqrt{3}}{2}$$

$$\Rightarrow \quad 3\cos^2 x - 10\cos x + 3 = 0$$

$$\Rightarrow \quad \cos x = \frac{1}{3}, \cos x \neq 3$$

$$\Rightarrow \quad \cos\beta = \frac{1}{3}, \sin\beta = \frac{2\sqrt{2}}{3}$$

and $\quad 1-\sin 2x=\cos x-\sin x$

$\Rightarrow \quad \sin^2 x+\cos^2 x-2\sin x\cos x=\cos x-\sin x$

$\Rightarrow (\cos x-\sin x)(\cos x-\sin x-1)=0$

$\Rightarrow \quad \sin x=\cos x=\dfrac{1}{\sqrt{2}}$ or $\cos x-\sin x=1$

$\Rightarrow \quad \cos x=1, \sin x=0$

$\Rightarrow \quad \cos\gamma=1, \sin\gamma=0$

$\therefore \quad \cos\alpha+\cos\beta+\cos\gamma=\dfrac{\sqrt{3}}{2}+\dfrac{1}{3}+1=\dfrac{3\sqrt{3}+8}{6}$

49. $\sin(\alpha-\beta)=\sin\alpha\cos\beta-\cos\alpha\sin\beta$

$$=\frac{1}{2}\times\frac{1}{3}-\frac{\sqrt{3}}{2}\times\frac{2\sqrt{2}}{3}=\frac{1-2\sqrt{6}}{6}$$

Sol. (Q. Nos. 50 to 51)

We have, $f_n(\theta)=\dfrac{\cos\dfrac{\theta}{2}+\cos 2\theta+\cos\dfrac{7\theta}{2}+\ldots+\cos(3n-2)\dfrac{\theta}{2}}{\sin\dfrac{\theta}{2}+\sin 2\theta+\sin\dfrac{7\theta}{2}+\ldots+\sin(3n-2)\dfrac{\theta}{2}}$

$$=\frac{\dfrac{\sin\left(n\cdot\dfrac{3\theta}{4}\right)\cos\left(\dfrac{\theta}{2}+(n-1)\dfrac{3\theta}{4}\right)}{\sin\left(\dfrac{3\theta}{4}\right)}}{\dfrac{\sin\left(n\cdot\dfrac{3\theta}{4}\right)\sin\left(\dfrac{\theta}{2}+(n-1)\dfrac{3\theta}{4}\right)}{\sin\left(\dfrac{3\theta}{4}\right)}}$$

$$=\cot\left(\frac{\theta}{2}+(n-1)\frac{3\theta}{4}\right)=\cot\left((3n-1)\frac{\theta}{4}\right)$$

50. $f_3\left(\dfrac{3\pi}{16}\right)=\cot\left(8\times\dfrac{1}{4}\times\dfrac{3\pi}{16}\right)=\cot\left(\dfrac{3\pi}{8}\right)=\sqrt{2}-1$

$\therefore \quad k=2$

51. $f_5\left(\dfrac{\pi}{28}\right)=\cot\left(14\times\dfrac{1}{4}\times\dfrac{\pi}{28}\right)=\cot\left(\dfrac{\pi}{8}\right)=\sqrt{2}+1$

$\therefore \quad k=2$

Sol. (Q. Nos. 52 to 53)

We have, $\tan\left(\theta+\dfrac{\pi}{4}\right)=3\tan 3\theta$

$\Rightarrow \quad \dfrac{1+\tan\theta}{1-\tan\theta}=3\times\dfrac{3\tan\theta-\tan^3\theta}{1-3\tan^2\theta}$

$\Rightarrow \quad \dfrac{1+\tan\theta}{1-\tan\theta}=3\left(\dfrac{3\tan\theta-\tan^3\theta}{1-3\tan^2\theta}\right)$

$\Rightarrow \quad 3\tan^4\theta-6\tan^2\theta+8\tan\theta-1=0$

52. $S_1=$ Sum of roots $=\tan\alpha+\tan\beta+\tan\gamma+\tan\delta$

$$=-\frac{0}{3}=0$$

$\therefore 3(\tan\alpha+\tan\beta+\tan\gamma+\tan\delta)=0$

53. $S_4=$ Product of all roots $=\tan\alpha\tan\beta\tan\gamma\tan\delta=\dfrac{-1}{3}$

$\therefore \quad -3\tan\alpha\tan\beta\tan\gamma\tan\delta=1$

54. Given, $\sec x+\sec^2 x=1$

$\Rightarrow \quad \sec x=1-\sec^2 x \Rightarrow \sec x=-\tan^2 x$

On squaring both sides, we get

$$\sec^2 x=\tan^4 x \Rightarrow 1+\tan^2 x=\tan^4 x$$

Again, on squaring both sides, we get

$$\tan^8 x=(1+\tan^2 x)^2$$

$\Rightarrow \quad \tan^8 x=1+\tan^4 x+2\tan^2 x$

$\Rightarrow \quad \tan^8 x-\tan^4 x-2\tan^2 x=1$

55. LHS $=\dfrac{1}{1+\tan^2\dfrac{A}{2}}+\dfrac{1}{1+\tan^2\dfrac{B}{2}}+\dfrac{1}{1+\tan^2\dfrac{C}{2}}$

$\Rightarrow \cos^2\dfrac{A}{2}+\cos^2\dfrac{B}{2}+\cos^2\dfrac{C}{2}$

$$=2\left[1+\sin\frac{A}{2}\sin\frac{B}{2}\sin\frac{C}{2}\right] \quad \text{[using identity]}$$

$\therefore \quad k=2$

56. $\dfrac{\sin\alpha}{\sin\beta}=\dfrac{\cos\gamma}{\cos\delta}$

$\Rightarrow \quad \dfrac{\sin\alpha-\sin\beta}{\sin\beta}=\dfrac{\cos\gamma-\cos\delta}{\cos\delta}$ [using dividendo]

$\Rightarrow \dfrac{2\cos\left(\dfrac{\alpha+\beta}{2}\right)\sin\left(\dfrac{\alpha-\beta}{2}\right)}{\sin\beta}=\dfrac{2\sin\left(\dfrac{\gamma+\delta}{2}\right)\sin\left(\dfrac{\delta-\gamma}{2}\right)}{\cos\delta}$

$\therefore \quad \dfrac{\cos\left(\dfrac{\alpha+\beta}{2}\right)\sin\left(\dfrac{\alpha-\beta}{2}\right)\cdot\cos\delta}{\sin\left(\dfrac{\delta-\gamma}{2}\right)\sin\left(\dfrac{\delta+\gamma}{2}\right)\cdot\sin\beta}=1$

57. Let $\dfrac{\pi}{20}=\theta \Rightarrow 10\theta=\dfrac{\pi}{2} \Rightarrow 2\theta=18^\circ$ or $\theta=9^\circ$

Now, $\tan\theta-\tan 3\theta+\tan 5\theta-\tan 7\theta+\tan 9\theta$

$\tan\theta-\tan 3\theta+\tan 5\theta-\cot 3\theta+\cot\theta$

$(\tan\theta+\cot\theta)-(\tan 3\theta+\cot 3\theta)+\tan 45^\circ$

[using $\tan 5\theta=\tan 45^\circ$]

$$E=\frac{2}{\sin 2\theta}-\frac{2}{\sin 6\theta}+1$$

$$E=2\left(\frac{1}{\sin 2\theta}-\frac{1}{\cos 4\theta}\right)+1$$

$$E=2\left(\frac{1}{\sin 18^\circ}-\frac{1}{\cos 36^\circ}\right)+1$$

$$E=2\left(\frac{4}{\sqrt{5}-1}-\frac{4}{\sqrt{5}+1}\right)+1=5$$

Alternate Solution

$$E=1+2\left(\frac{\sin 6\theta-\sin 2\theta}{\sin 2\theta\cdot\sin 6\theta}\right)$$

$$=1+2\left(\frac{2\cos 4\theta\cdot\sin 2\theta}{\sin 2\theta\cdot\cos 4\theta}\right)=1+4=5$$

58. $x = \dfrac{\cos 1^\circ + \cos 2^\circ + \ldots + \cos 44^\circ}{\sin 1^\circ + \sin 2^\circ + \ldots + \sin 44^\circ}$

$$= \dfrac{\dfrac{\sin 22^\circ}{\sin(1/2)^\circ} \cdot \cos 22.5^\circ}{\dfrac{\sin 22^\circ}{\sin(1/2)^\circ} \cdot \sin 22.5^\circ} = \cot 22.5^\circ$$

[using the formula of sum of cos series

$$S = \frac{\sin(n\theta/2)}{\sin(\theta/2)} \cos\frac{(n+1)\theta}{2},$$

For sine series, $S = \dfrac{\sin(n\theta/2)}{\sin(\theta/2)} \sin\dfrac{(n+1)\theta}{2}$]

$$\cot\left(\frac{\pi}{8}\right) = \sqrt{2} + 1 = 2.414\ldots$$

$\therefore \quad x = 2.414\ldots$

Greatest integer = 2.

59. LHS $= \tan 15^\circ \cdot \tan(30^\circ - 5^\circ) \cdot \tan(30^\circ + 5^\circ)$

Let $t = \tan 30^\circ$ and $m = \tan 5^\circ$

$$\therefore \text{LHS} = \tan 15^\circ \cdot \frac{t-m}{1+tm} \cdot \frac{t+m}{1-tm} = \tan(3(5^\circ)) \cdot \frac{t^2 - m^2}{1 - t^2 m^2}$$

$$= \frac{3m - m^3}{1 - 3m^2} \cdot \frac{1 - 3m^2}{3 - m^2}$$

$$= \frac{m(3 - m^2)}{(1 - 3m^2)} \cdot \frac{(1 - 3m^2)}{3 - m^2} = m = \tan 5^\circ$$

Hence, $\tan\theta = \tan 5^\circ \Rightarrow \theta = 5^\circ$

60. We have, $\dfrac{1}{\sin 10^\circ} + \dfrac{1}{\sin 50^\circ} - \dfrac{1}{\sin 70^\circ}$

$$= \frac{1}{\cos 80^\circ} + \frac{1}{\cos 40^\circ} - \frac{1}{\cos 20^\circ}$$

$$= \frac{\cos 40^\circ \cos 20^\circ + \cos 80^\circ \cos 20^\circ - \cos 40^\circ \cos 80^\circ}{\cos 20^\circ \,.\, \cos 40^\circ \,.\, \cos 80^\circ}$$

$$\left[\because \cos\theta \cdot \cos(60^\circ + \theta) \cdot \cos(60^\circ - \theta) = \frac{1}{4}\cos 3\theta\right]$$

$$= 8\,[\cos 20^\circ (\cos 40^\circ + \cos 80^\circ) - \cos 40^\circ \cos 80^\circ]$$

$$= 8[2\cos 20^\circ \cos 60^\circ \cos 20^\circ - \cos 40^\circ \cos 80^\circ]$$

$$= 4[2\cos^2 20^\circ - 2\cos 40^\circ \cos 80^\circ]$$

$$= 4[1 + \cos 40^\circ - (\cos 120^\circ + \cos 40^\circ)] = 4 \cdot \frac{3}{2} = 6$$

61. We have, $\cos 5\alpha = \cos^5 \alpha$

$$\cos 5\alpha = \cos(3\alpha + 2\alpha) = \cos 3\alpha \cos 2\alpha - \sin 3\alpha \sin 2\alpha$$

$$= (4\cos^3\alpha - 3\cos\alpha)(2\cos^2\alpha - 1) - (3\sin\alpha - 4\sin^3\alpha) 2\sin\alpha\cos\alpha$$

$$= (4\cos^3\alpha - 3\cos\alpha)(2\cos^2\alpha - 1) - (1\cos^2\alpha)(3 - 4 + 4\cos^2\alpha)\, 2\cos\alpha$$

$$= (4\cos^3\alpha - 3\cos\alpha)(2\cos^2\alpha - 1) - (2\cos\alpha - 2\cos^3\alpha)(4\cos^2\alpha - 1)$$

$$= 8\cos^5\alpha - 4\cos^3\alpha - 6\cos^3\alpha + 3\cos\alpha - [8\cos^3\alpha - 2\cos\alpha - 8\cos^5\alpha + 2\cos^3\alpha]$$

$$= 16\cos^5\alpha - 20\cos^3\alpha + 5\cos\alpha$$

$\therefore \quad 16\cos^5\alpha - 20\cos^3\alpha + 5\cos\alpha = \cos^5\alpha$

$\Rightarrow \quad 15\cos^5\alpha - 20\cos^3\alpha + 5\cos\alpha = 0$

$\Rightarrow \quad 5\cos\alpha\,[3\cos^4\alpha - 4\cos^2\alpha + 1] = 0$

Also $\cos\alpha = 0$

$\Rightarrow \quad 3\cos^4\alpha - 3\cos^2\alpha - \cos^2\alpha + 1 = 0$

$\Rightarrow \quad 3\cos^2\alpha(\cos^2\alpha - 1) - (\cos^2\alpha - 1) = 0$

$\Rightarrow \quad (3\cos^2\alpha - 1)(1 - \cos^2\alpha) = 0 \Rightarrow 3\cos^2\alpha = 1$

$\Rightarrow \quad \cos^2\alpha = \dfrac{1}{3}$ and $\cos^2\alpha = 1$

$\Rightarrow \quad \sec^2\alpha = 3;\ \operatorname{cosec}^2\alpha = \dfrac{3}{2};\ \cot^2\alpha = \dfrac{1}{2}$

$\therefore \quad (\sec^2\alpha + \operatorname{cosec}^2\alpha + \cot^2\alpha) = 3 + \dfrac{3}{2} + \dfrac{1}{2} = 5$

62. We have,

$$k = \tan^2\frac{\pi}{16} + \tan^2\frac{2\pi}{16} + \tan^2\frac{3\pi}{16} + \ldots + \tan^2\frac{7\pi}{16}$$

$$= \left(\tan^2\frac{\pi}{16} + \cot^2\frac{\pi}{16} + 2\right) + \left(\tan^2\frac{2\pi}{16} + \cot^2\frac{2\pi}{16} + 2\right) + \left(\tan^2\frac{3\pi}{16} + \cot^2\frac{3\pi}{16} + 2\right) + \tan^2\frac{4\pi}{16} - 6$$

$$\left[\begin{array}{l}\text{If } A + B = \dfrac{\pi}{2}, \text{ then } \tan B = \tan\left(\dfrac{\pi}{2} - A\right) = \cot A \\ \text{So, } \tan^2\dfrac{7\pi}{16} = \tan^2\left(\dfrac{8\pi}{16} - \dfrac{\pi}{16}\right) = \cot^2\dfrac{\pi}{16} \text{ etc.}\end{array}\right]$$

$$= \left(\tan\frac{\pi}{16} + \cot\frac{\pi}{16}\right)^2 + \left(\tan\frac{2\pi}{16} + \cot\frac{2\pi}{16}\right)^2 + \left(\tan\frac{3\pi}{16} + \cot\frac{3\pi}{16}\right)^2 - 5$$

$$= \frac{4}{\sin^2\frac{\pi}{8}} + \frac{4}{\sin^2\frac{3\pi}{8}} + \left(\frac{4}{\sin^2\frac{\pi}{4}} - 5\right)$$

$$= \frac{4\left(\sin^2\frac{3\pi}{8} + \sin^2\frac{\pi}{8}\right)}{\sin^2\frac{\pi}{8}\sin^2\frac{3\pi}{8}} + 3 = \frac{16}{\sin^2\frac{\pi}{4}} + 3 = 32 + 3 = 35$$

$$\therefore \frac{k}{7} = \frac{35}{7} = 5$$

63. We have, $\dfrac{4 + \sec 20^\circ}{\operatorname{cosec} 20^\circ} = \dfrac{\sin 20^\circ}{\cos 20^\circ}(4\cos 20^\circ + 1)$

$$= \frac{2\sin 40^\circ + \sin 20^\circ}{\cos 20^\circ}$$

$$= \frac{\sin 40^\circ + (\sin 40^\circ + \sin 20^\circ)}{\cos 20^\circ}$$

$$= \frac{\sin 40^\circ + 2\sin 30^\circ \cos 10^\circ}{\cos 20^\circ}$$

$$= \frac{\sin 40^\circ + \sin 80^\circ}{\cos 20^\circ}$$

$$= \frac{2\sin 60^\circ \cos 20^\circ}{\cos 20^\circ} = 2 \times \frac{\sqrt{3}}{2} = \sqrt{3}$$

Hence, the square of the value of expression = 3

64. $A + B + C = \pi$ ...(i)

$$\frac{\sin A}{3} = \frac{\cos B}{3} = \frac{\tan C}{2}$$ ...(ii)

$\Rightarrow$ $\sin A = \cos B \Rightarrow A + B = \frac{\pi}{2}$ (rejected)

Or $A - B = \frac{\pi}{2}$ ...(iii)

$\Rightarrow$ $2A + C = \frac{3\pi}{2}$ [from Eqs. (i) and (ii)]

Now, $\frac{\sin A}{\tan C} = \frac{3}{2}$ [from Eq. (ii)

$\Rightarrow$ $\frac{\sin A}{\tan\left(\frac{3\pi}{2} - 2A\right)} = \frac{3}{2}$ [from Eq. (iii)]

$\Rightarrow$ $2\sin A = 3\cot 2A$

$\Rightarrow$ $2\sin A = \frac{3\cdot(2\cos^2 A - 1)}{2\sin A\cos A}$

$\Rightarrow 4\cos A(1 - \cos^2 A) = 3(2\cos^2 A - 1)$

$\Rightarrow 4\cos^3 A + 6\cos^2 A - 4\cos A - 3 = 0$

On putting $\cos A = -\frac{1}{2}$, we get

$\Rightarrow$ $(2\cos A + 1)(2\cos^2 A + 2\cos A - 3) = 0$

$\Rightarrow$ $\cos A = -\frac{1}{2}$,

or $\cos A = \frac{-2 \pm \sqrt{4 + 24}}{4} = -1 \pm \sqrt{7}$ (rejected)

$\Rightarrow$ $A = \frac{2\pi}{3}, B = \frac{\pi}{6}, C = \frac{\pi}{6}$

$\therefore$ $\frac{\sin A}{\cot 2A} + \frac{\cos B}{\cot 2B} + \frac{\tan C}{\cot 2C} = \frac{3}{2} + \frac{3}{2} + 1 = 4$

65. $f(\theta) = \frac{1}{1 + g(\theta)}$ ...(i)

Given, $2f(\alpha) - g(\beta) = 1$

$2f(\alpha) = 1 + g(\beta) = \frac{1}{f(\beta)}$ [from Eq. (i)]

$2f(\alpha)f(\beta) = 1$ ...(ii)

Now, $2f(\beta) - g(\alpha) = 2f(\beta) + 1 - (1 + g(\alpha))$

$= 2f(\beta) + 1 - \frac{1}{f(\alpha)}$

$= \frac{2f(\alpha)f(\beta) - 1}{f(\alpha)} + 1 = 1$ [from Eq. (ii)]

66. As we know that $\frac{1 - \sin x}{\cos x} = \frac{\cos x}{1 + \sin x}$

$$\log_{\left|\frac{1 - \sin x}{\cos x}\right|}\left|\frac{1 + \sin x}{\cos x}\right| = -1$$

Now, series is

Let $S = 1 - \frac{x}{2} - \frac{x^2}{4} - \ldots = 1 - \frac{\frac{x}{2}}{1 - \frac{x}{2}}$

$= 1 - \frac{x}{2 - x} = \frac{2 - x - x}{2 - x}$

$= \frac{2(1 - x)}{(2 - x)} = \frac{k(1 - x)}{(2 - x)}$

Thus, $k = 2$

67. From the second relation $9x\sin^3\theta = 5y\cos^3\theta$.

$\Rightarrow$ $\frac{\cos^3\theta}{9x} = \frac{\sin^3\theta}{5y} = k^3$ (say)

$\Rightarrow$ $\cos\theta = k(9x)^{\frac{1}{3}}$ and $\sin\theta = k(5y)^{\frac{1}{3}}$

On squaring and adding, we get

$$1 = \cos^2\theta + \sin^2\theta = k^2\left[(9x)^{\frac{2}{3}} + (5y)^{\frac{2}{3}}\right]$$

and $\frac{9x}{k(9x)^{\frac{1}{3}}} + \frac{5y}{k(5y)^{\frac{1}{3}}} = 56$ (From Ist relation)

$\Rightarrow$ $(9x)^{\frac{2}{3}} + (5y)^{\frac{2}{3}} = 56k$

$\Rightarrow$ $\left[(9x)^{\frac{2}{3}} + (5y)^{\frac{2}{3}}\right]^2 = (56)^2k^2 = \frac{(56)^2}{(9x)^{\frac{2}{3}} + (5y)^{\frac{2}{3}}}$

$\Rightarrow$ $\left[(9x)^{\frac{2}{3}} + (5y)^{\frac{2}{3}}\right]^3 = (56)^2 = 3136$

68. $A > \frac{\pi}{2} \Rightarrow B + C < \frac{\pi}{2}$

$\Rightarrow$ $\tan(B + C) > 0 \Rightarrow \frac{\tan B + \tan C}{1 - \tan B\tan C} > 0$

$\Rightarrow$ $\tan B\tan C < 1$ as $\tan B > 0, \tan C > 0$

$\Rightarrow$ $[x] = 2635 - 1 = 2634$

69. $\because$ $\cot\left(7\frac{1°}{2}\right) = \frac{1 + \cos 15°}{\sin 15°}$

$= \frac{1 + \frac{\sqrt{3} + 1}{2\sqrt{2}}}{\frac{\sqrt{3} - 1}{2\sqrt{2}}} = \frac{2\sqrt{2} + \sqrt{3} + 1}{\sqrt{3} - 1}$

$= \frac{(2\sqrt{2} + \sqrt{3} + 1)(\sqrt{3} + 1)}{2}$

$= \frac{2\sqrt{6} + 2\sqrt{2} + 3 + \sqrt{3} + \sqrt{3} + 1}{2}$

$= \sqrt{6} + \sqrt{2} + 2 + \sqrt{3}$

$= \sqrt{2} + \sqrt{3} + \sqrt{4} + \sqrt{6}$

and $4\cos 36° = 4\left(\frac{\sqrt{5} + 1}{4}\right) = \sqrt{5} + 1 = \sqrt{5} + \sqrt{1}$

Hence, $4\cos 36° + \cot\left(7\frac{1°}{2}\right)$

$= \sqrt{1} + \sqrt{2} + \sqrt{3} + \sqrt{4} + \sqrt{5} + \sqrt{6}$

$\therefore$ $n_1 = 1, n_2 = 2, n_3 = 3, n_4 = 4, n_5 = 5$ and $n_6 = 6$

$\therefore \quad \sum_{i=1}^{6} n_i^2 = n_1^2 + n_2^2 + n_3^2 + n_4^2 + n_5^3 + n_6^2$

$= 1^2 + 2^2 + 3^2 + 4^2 + 5^2 + 6^2 = 91$

70. $\because \prod_{r=1}^{4} \sin(rA) = \sin A \sin 2A \sin 3A \sin 4A$

$= \sin A \cdot 2\sin A\cos A \cdot (3\sin A - 4\sin^3 A \cdot 2\sin 2A\cos 2A)$

$= 2\sin^2 A\cos A \cdot \sin A(3 - 4\sin^2 A)$

$\cdot 4\sin A\cos A \cdot (1 - 2\sin^2 A)$

$= 8x^2(1-x)(3-4x)(1-2x) = 24x^2(-104)x^3 + 144x^4(-64)x^5$

On comparing, we get $a = 24$, $b = -104$, $c = 144$, $d = -64$

$10a - 7b + 15c - 5d$

$= 10 \times 24 - 7 \times (-104) + 15 \times 144 - 5 \times (-64)$

$= 240 + 728 + 2160 + 320 = 3448$

71. Let $x + 5 = 14\cos\theta$ and $y - 12 = 14\sin\theta$

$\therefore \quad x^2 + y^2 = (14\cos\theta - 5)^2 + (14\sin\theta + 12)^2$

$= 196 + 25 + 144 + 28(12\sin\theta - 5\cos\theta)$

$= 365 + 28(12\sin\theta - 5\cos\theta)$

$\therefore \quad 10\sqrt{x^2 + y^2}\Big|_{\min} = 10\sqrt{365 - 28 \times 13} = 10\sqrt{365 - 364} = 10$

72. $\because 12° \times 5 = 60°$

Let $\quad 12° = \theta$

$\therefore \quad 5\theta = 60° \Rightarrow 3\theta + 2\theta = 60°$

$\therefore \quad \cos(3\theta + 2\theta) = \cos 60°$

$\Rightarrow \cos 3\theta\cos 2\theta - \sin 3\theta\sin 2\theta = \frac{1}{2}$

$\Rightarrow (4\cos^3\theta - 3\cos\theta)(2\cos^2\theta - 1) - (3\sin\theta - 4\sin^3\theta)$

$2\sin\theta\cos\theta = \frac{1}{2}$

Let $\quad \cos\theta = x$

$\therefore \quad (4x^3 - 3x)(2x^2 - 1) - 2x(3 - 4(1 - x^2))(1 - x^2) = \frac{1}{2}$

$\Rightarrow \quad (8x^5 - 10x^3 + 3x) - (2x - 2x^3)(4x^2 - 1) = \frac{1}{2}$

$\Rightarrow \quad (16x^5 - 20x^3 + 6x) - (4x - 4x^3)(4x^2 - 1) - 1 = 0$

$\Rightarrow \quad 32x^5 - 40x^3 + 10x - 1 = 0$

$\Rightarrow \quad \left(x - \frac{1}{2}\right)(32x^4 + 16x^3 - 32x^2 - 16x + 2) = 0$

but $x \neq \frac{1}{2}$,

$\therefore \quad 16x^4 + 8x^3 - 16x^2 - 8x + 1 = 0$

$\therefore$ Degree is 4.

Hence, $11k = 11(4) = 44$

73. From conditional identities, we have

$\frac{\sin 2A + \sin 2B + \sin 2C}{\sin A + \sin B + \sin C} = \frac{4\sin A\sin B\sin C}{4\cos\left(\frac{A}{2}\right)\cos\left(\frac{B}{2}\right)\cos\left(\frac{C}{2}\right)}$

$= 8\sin\left(\frac{A}{2}\right)\sin\left(\frac{B}{2}\right)\sin\left(\frac{C}{2}\right)$

$\Rightarrow \quad k = 8$

and $\quad 3k^3 + 2k^2 + k + 1 = 1536 + 128 + 8 + 1 = 1673$

74. $x = \cot\frac{11\pi}{8} = \cot\left(\pi + \frac{3\pi}{8}\right) = \cot\frac{3\pi}{8} = \sqrt{2} - 1$

$\Rightarrow \quad (x + 1)^2 = 2$

$\therefore \quad x^2 + 2x - 1 = 0$

Now, $\quad f(x) = x^4 + 4x^3 + 2x^2 - 4x + 17$

$= x^2(x^2 + 2x - 1) + 2x^3 + 3x^2 - 4x + 17$

$= 0 + 2x^3 + 3x^2 - 4x + 17$

$= 2x(x^2 + 2x - 1) - x^2 - 2x + 17$

$= -x^2 - 2x + 17$

$= -(x^2 + 2x - 1) + 16$

$= 0 + 16 = 16$

75. $\frac{\sqrt{(\sin A)}}{\sqrt{(\sin B)} + \sqrt{(\sin C)} - \sqrt{(\sin A)}} = \frac{\sqrt{a}}{\sqrt{b} + \sqrt{c} - \sqrt{a}}$

Now, $\sqrt{b} + \sqrt{c} - \sqrt{a} = \frac{(\sqrt{b} + \sqrt{c} - \sqrt{a})(\sqrt{b} + \sqrt{c} + \sqrt{a})}{(\sqrt{b} + \sqrt{c} + \sqrt{a})}$

$= \frac{(\sqrt{b} + \sqrt{c})^2 - a}{(\sqrt{b} + \sqrt{c} + \sqrt{a})} = \frac{(b + c - a) + 2\sqrt{bc}}{(\sqrt{b} + \sqrt{c} + \sqrt{a})} > 0$

Hence, $\sqrt{b} + \sqrt{c} - \sqrt{a} > 0$

Now, let $\sqrt{b} + \sqrt{c} - \sqrt{a} = x$, $\sqrt{c} + \sqrt{a} - \sqrt{b} = y$

and $\quad \sqrt{a} + \sqrt{b} - \sqrt{c} = z$

$\therefore \quad \frac{\sqrt{\sin A}}{\sqrt{\sin B} + \sqrt{\sin C} - \sqrt{\sin A}} = \frac{y + z}{2x}$

$\Rightarrow \sum \frac{\sqrt{(\sin A)}}{\sqrt{(\sin B)} + \sqrt{(\sin C)} - \sqrt{(\sin A)}}$

$= \frac{1}{2}\left\{\frac{y}{x} + \frac{z}{x}\right\} + \frac{1}{2}\left\{\frac{z}{y} + \frac{x}{y}\right\} + \frac{1}{2}\left\{\frac{x}{z} + \frac{y}{z}\right\}$

$= \frac{1}{2}\left(\frac{x}{y} + \frac{y}{x}\right) + \frac{1}{2}\left(\frac{y}{z} + \frac{z}{y}\right) + \frac{1}{2}\left(\frac{z}{x} + \frac{x}{z}\right)$

$\geq 1 + 1 + 1$ [$\because$ AM $\geq$ GM]

$2020 \sum \frac{\sqrt{(\sin A)}}{\sqrt{(\sin B)} + \sqrt{(\sin C)} - \sqrt{(\sin A)}} \leq 6060$

$\therefore$ Minimum value is 6060.

76. We have, $\sin\theta(1 + \sin^2\theta) = 1 - \sin^2\theta$

$\Rightarrow \quad \sin\theta(2 - \cos^2\theta) = \cos^2\theta$

On squaring both sides, we get

$\sin^2\theta(2 - \cos^2\theta)^2 = \cos^4\theta$

$\Rightarrow \quad (1 - \cos^2\theta)(4 - 4\cos^2\theta + \cos^4\theta) = \cos^4\theta$

$\Rightarrow \quad -\cos^6\theta + 5\cos^4\theta - 8\cos^2\theta + 4 = \cos^4\theta$

$\therefore \quad 10 + \cos^6\theta - 4\cos^4\theta + 8\cos^2\theta = 14$

77. $80\left(\cos\theta - \cos\frac{\pi}{8}\right)\left(\cos\theta - \cos\frac{3\pi}{8}\right)\left(\cos\theta - \cos\frac{5\pi}{8}\right)$

$\left(\cos\theta - \cos\frac{7\pi}{8}\right)$

$= 80\left(\cos\theta - \cos\frac{\pi}{8}\right)\left(\cos\theta - \cos\frac{7\pi}{8}\right)$

$\times\left(\cos\theta - \cos\frac{3\pi}{8}\right)\left(\cos\theta - \cos\frac{5\pi}{8}\right)$

$$= 80\left(\cos\theta - \cos\frac{\pi}{8}\right)\left(\cos\theta + \cos\frac{\pi}{8}\right) \times \left(\cos\theta - \cos\frac{3\pi}{8}\right)\left(\cos\theta + \cos\frac{3\pi}{8}\right)$$

$$= 80\left(\cos^2\theta - \cos^2\frac{\pi}{8}\right)\left(\cos^2\theta - \cos^2\frac{3\pi}{8}\right)$$

$$= 80\left(\cos^2\theta - \cos^2\frac{\pi}{8}\right)\left(\cos^2\theta - \sin^2\frac{\pi}{8}\right)$$

$$= 80\left(\cos^4\theta - \cos^2\theta + \sin^2\frac{\pi}{8}\cos^2\frac{\pi}{8}\right)$$

$$= 80\left(\cos^4\theta - \cos^2\theta + \frac{1}{8}\right)$$

$$= 80\left(-\cos^2\theta\sin^2\theta + \frac{1}{8}\right) = 80\left(\frac{-\sin^2 2\theta}{4} + \frac{1}{8}\right)$$

$$= 80\left(\frac{1 - 2\sin^2 2\theta}{8}\right) = \frac{80\cos 4\theta}{8} = 10\cos 4\theta$$

$\therefore \quad \lambda = 10$

78. $2k\cos 40° = \dfrac{1}{\sin 20°} + \dfrac{1}{\sqrt{3}\cos 20°}$

$$= \frac{\sqrt{3}\cos 20° + \sin 20°}{\sqrt{3}\sin 20°\cos 20°} = \frac{\frac{\sqrt{3}}{2}\cos 20° + \frac{1}{2}\sin 20°}{\frac{\sqrt{3}}{4}\sin 40°}$$

$$= \frac{\sin 60°\cos 20° + \cos 60°\sin 20°}{\left(\frac{\sqrt{3}}{4}\right)\sin 40°} = \left(\frac{4}{\sqrt{3}}\right) 2\cos 40°$$

$\Rightarrow \quad 3k^2 = 16$

So, $18k^4 + 162k^2 + 369 = 1521$

79. **(A)** If M is mid-point of PQ, then $M = \left(\dfrac{\theta + \phi}{2}, \dfrac{\sin\theta + \sin\phi}{2}\right)$

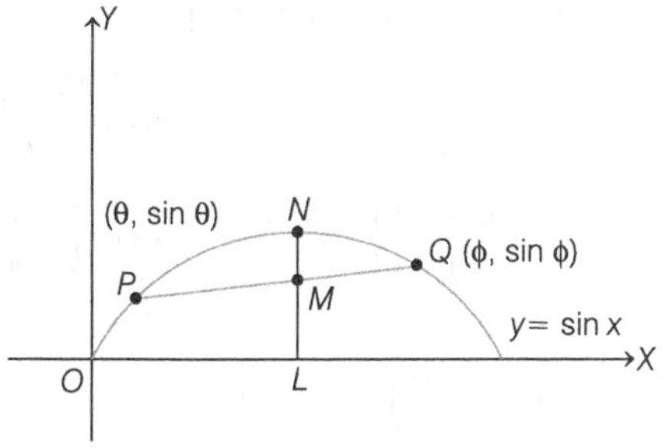

Also, $\quad N \equiv \left(\dfrac{\theta+\phi}{2}, \sin\left(\dfrac{\theta+\phi}{2}\right)\right)$

It is clear from the figure,

$ML \le NL$

$\Rightarrow \quad \dfrac{\sin\theta + \sin\phi}{2} \le \sin\left(\dfrac{\theta+\phi}{2}\right)$

$\Rightarrow \quad \sin\theta + \sin\phi \le 2\sin\left(\dfrac{\theta+\phi}{2}\right) = 2\sin\left(\dfrac{\pi}{4}\right) = \sqrt{2}$

$\therefore \quad \sin\theta + \sin\phi \le \sqrt{2}$

and $\quad (\sin\theta + \sin\phi)\sin\dfrac{\pi}{4} \le 1$ (p, q, r, s, t)

(B) $\because a^2 + b^2 = (\sin\theta - \sin\phi)^2 + (\cos\theta + \cos\phi)^2$

$$= 2 + 2\cos(\theta + \phi) = 4\cos^2\left(\frac{\theta+\phi}{2}\right) \le 4 \text{ (s, t)}$$

(C) $\because 3\sin\theta + 5\cos\theta = 5 \Rightarrow 3\sin\theta = 5(1 - \cos\theta)$

On squaring both sides, we get

$$9\sin^2\theta = 25(1 - \cos\theta)^2$$

$\Rightarrow 9(1 - \cos\theta)(1 + \cos\theta) = 25(1 - \cos\theta)^2$

$\Rightarrow \quad 9(1 + \cos\theta) = 25(1 - \cos\theta),$

where $1 - \cos\theta \ne 0$.

$\therefore \quad 34\cos\theta = 16$

$\cos\theta = \dfrac{8}{17}$, then $\sin\theta = \dfrac{15}{17}$

$\therefore \quad 5\sin\theta - 3\cos\theta = \dfrac{75}{17} - \dfrac{24}{17} = 3$ (r)

Hence, $5\sin\theta - 3\cos\theta = 3$

(D) $-\sqrt{4^2 + 3^2} \le 4\sin\theta - 3\cos\theta \le \sqrt{4^2 + 3^2}$

$\Rightarrow \quad -5 \le 4\sin\theta - 3\cos\theta \le 5$ (t)

80. **(A)** Let $y = \dfrac{7 + 6\tan\theta - \tan^2\theta}{(1 + \tan^2\theta)}$

$$= 7\cos^2\theta + 6\sin\theta\cos\theta - \sin^2\theta$$

$$= 7\left(\frac{1 + \cos 2\theta}{2}\right) + 3\sin 2\theta - \left(\frac{1 - \cos 2\theta}{2}\right)$$

$$= 3\sin 2\theta + 4\cos 2\theta + 3$$

$$= -\sqrt{(3^2 + 4^2)} + 3 \le 3$$

$$= \sin 2\theta + 4\cos 2\theta + 3 \le \sqrt{(3^2 + 4^2)} + 3$$

$\therefore \quad -2 \le y \le 8 \Rightarrow \lambda = 8, \mu = -2$

$\Rightarrow \quad \lambda + \mu = 6, \lambda - \mu = 10$ (r, s)

(B) Let $y = 5\cos\theta + 3\cos\left(\theta + \dfrac{\pi}{3}\right) + 3$

$$= 5\cos\theta + 3\left(\frac{1}{2}\cos\theta - \frac{\sqrt{3}}{2}\sin\theta\right) + 3$$

$$= \frac{13}{2}\cos\theta - \frac{3\sqrt{3}}{2}\sin\theta + 3$$

$$\therefore\ 3 - \sqrt{\left(\frac{13}{2}\right)^2 + \left(\frac{-3\sqrt{3}}{2}\right)^2} \le \frac{13}{2}\cos\theta - \frac{3\sqrt{3}}{2}\sin\theta + 3$$

$$\le 3 + \sqrt{\left(\frac{13}{2}\right)^2 + \left(\frac{-3\sqrt{3}}{2}\right)^2}$$

$\Rightarrow \quad 3 - 7 \le y \le 3 + 7$

$\Rightarrow \quad -4 \le y \le 10$

$\therefore \quad \lambda = 10, \mu = -4$

$\Rightarrow \quad \lambda + \mu = 6, \lambda - \mu = 14$ (r, t)

(C) Let $y = 1 + \sin\left(\dfrac{\pi}{4} + \theta\right) + 2\cos\left(\dfrac{\pi}{4} - \theta\right)$

$$= 1 + \cos\left(\frac{\pi}{2} - \left(\frac{\pi}{2} + \theta\right)\right) + 2\cos\left(\frac{\pi}{4} - \theta\right)$$

$$= 1 + \cos\left(\frac{\pi}{4} - \theta\right) + 2\cos\left(\frac{\pi}{4} - \theta\right)$$

$$= 1 + 3\cos\left(\frac{\pi}{4} - \theta\right)$$

$\therefore \quad -1 \le \cos\left(\frac{\pi}{4} - \theta\right) \le 1$

$\Rightarrow \quad -3 \le 3\cos\left(\frac{\pi}{4} - \theta\right) \le 3$

$\Rightarrow \quad 1 - 3 \le 1 + 3\cos\left(\frac{\pi}{4} - \theta\right) \le 1 + 3$

$\therefore \quad -2 \le y \le 4$

$\Rightarrow \quad \lambda = 4, \mu = -2$

$\therefore \lambda + \mu = 2, \lambda - \mu = 6$ (p, q)

(D) Let $y = 3 + \sin\left(\frac{\pi}{4} + \theta\right) + 2\cos\left(\frac{\pi}{4} + \theta\right)$

$$= 3 + \frac{1}{\sqrt{2}}\cos\theta + \frac{1}{\sqrt{2}}\sin\theta + \sqrt{2}\cos\theta - \sqrt{2}\sin\theta$$

$$= 3 + \left(\frac{1}{\sqrt{2}} + \sqrt{2}\right)\cos\theta + \left(\frac{1}{\sqrt{2}} - \sqrt{2}\right)\sin\theta$$

$\therefore \quad \lambda = 3 + \sqrt{5}$ and $\mu = 3 - \sqrt{5}$

$\therefore \lambda + \mu = 6$ (r)

81. **(A)** $|\cot x| = \cot x + \frac{1}{\sin x}$

If $0 < x < \frac{\pi}{2} \Rightarrow \cot x > 0$

So, $\cot x = \cot x + \frac{1}{\sin x} \Rightarrow \frac{1}{\sin x} = 0$, no solution

If $\frac{\pi}{2} < \cot x < \pi$, $-\cot x = \cot x + \frac{1}{\sin x}$

$\Rightarrow \quad \frac{2\cos x}{\sin x} + \frac{1}{\sin x} = 0$

$\Rightarrow \quad 1 + 2\cos x = 0$ and $\sin x \ne 0 \Rightarrow x = \frac{2\pi}{3}$ (r)

(B) Since, $\sin\phi + \sin\theta = \frac{1}{2}$ ...(i)

and $\quad \cos\theta + \cos\phi = 2$ ...(ii)

Eq. (ii) is true only if $\theta = \phi = 0$ or 2π but $\theta = \phi = 0$ or 2π do not satisfy Eq. (i).

Hence, given system of equation has no solution. (p)

(C) $\sin^2\alpha + \sin\left(\frac{\pi}{3} - \alpha\right) \cdot \sin\left(\frac{\pi}{3} + \alpha\right)$

$$= \sin^2\alpha + \sin^2\frac{\pi}{3} - \sin^2\alpha = \frac{3}{4}.$$

(D) $\tan\theta = 3\tan\phi$

$$\tan(\theta - \phi) = \frac{\tan\theta - \tan\phi}{1 + \tan\theta\tan\phi} = \frac{2\tan\phi}{1 + 3\tan^2\phi}$$

$$= \frac{2}{\cot\phi + 3\tan\phi} \cdot \text{Max if } \tan\phi > 0$$

$\frac{\cot\phi + 3\tan\phi}{2} \ge \sqrt{3}$ [using AM $\ge$ GM]

$\Rightarrow \quad (\cot\phi + 3\tan\phi)^2 \ge 12$

$\Rightarrow \quad \left[\frac{2}{\tan(\theta - \phi)}\right]^2 \ge 12$

$\Rightarrow \quad \tan^2(\theta - \phi) \le \frac{1}{3}$ (q)

82. **(A)** $\sin\left(\frac{A}{2}\right) + \sin\left(\frac{B}{2}\right) + \sin\left(\frac{C}{2}\right)$

$$= 1 + \left(\sin\left(\frac{A}{2}\right) + \sin\left(\frac{B}{2}\right)\right) - \left(\sin\frac{\pi}{2} - \sin\frac{C}{2}\right)$$

$$= 1 + 2\sin\left(\frac{A+B}{4}\right)\cos\left(\frac{A-B}{4}\right) - 2\cos\left(\frac{\pi+C}{4}\right)\sin\left(\frac{\pi-C}{4}\right)$$

$$= 1 + 2\sin\left(\frac{\pi-C}{4}\right)\left\{\cos\left(\frac{A-B}{4}\right) - \cos\left(\frac{\pi+C}{4}\right)\right\}$$

$[\because A + B + C = \pi]$

$$= 1 + 2\sin\left(\frac{\pi-C}{4}\right)\left\{2\sin\left(\frac{\pi+C+A-B}{8}\right)\sin\left(\frac{\pi+C+B-A}{8}\right)\right\}$$

$$= 1 + 4\sin\left(\frac{\pi-C}{4}\right)\sin\left(\frac{\pi-B}{4}\right)\sin\left(\frac{\pi-A}{4}\right)$$

$$= 1 + 4\sin\left(\frac{\pi-A}{4}\right)\sin\left(\frac{\pi-B}{4}\right)\sin\left(\frac{\pi-C}{4}\right)$$

(B) $\sin\left(\frac{A}{2}\right) + \sin\left(\frac{B}{2}\right) - \sin\left(\frac{C}{2}\right)$

$$= -1 + \left(\sin\left(\frac{A}{2}\right) + \sin\left(\frac{B}{2}\right)\right) + \left(\sin\left(\frac{\pi}{2}\right) - \sin\left(\frac{C}{2}\right)\right)$$

$$= -1 + 2\sin\left(\frac{A+B}{4}\right)\cos\left(\frac{A-B}{4}\right) + 2\cos\left(\frac{\pi+C}{4}\right)\sin\left(\frac{\pi-C}{4}\right)$$

$$= -1 + 2\sin\left(\frac{\pi-C}{4}\right)\left\{\cos\left(\frac{A-B}{4}\right) + \cos\left(\frac{\pi+C}{4}\right)\right\}$$

$[\because A + B + C = \pi]$

$$= -1 + 2\sin\left(\frac{\pi-C}{4}\right)\left\{2\cos\left(\frac{\pi+C+A-B}{8}\right)\cos\left(\frac{\pi+C+B-A}{8}\right)\right\}$$

$$= -1 + 4\sin\left(\frac{\pi-C}{4}\right)\cos\left(\frac{\pi-B}{4}\right)\cos\left(\frac{\pi-A}{4}\right)$$

$$= -1 + 4\cos\left(\frac{\pi-A}{4}\right)\cos\left(\frac{\pi-B}{4}\right)\sin\left(\frac{\pi-C}{4}\right)$$

$$= -1 + 4\sin\left(\frac{\pi}{2} - \frac{\pi-A}{4}\right)\sin\left(\frac{\pi}{2} - \frac{\pi-B}{4}\right)\cos\left(\frac{\pi}{2} - \frac{\pi-C}{4}\right)$$

$$= -1 + 4\sin\left(\frac{\pi+A}{4}\right)\sin\left(\frac{\pi+B}{4}\right)\cos\left(\frac{\pi+C}{4}\right)$$

(C) $\cos\left(\frac{A}{2}\right) + \cos\left(\frac{B}{2}\right) - \cos\left(\frac{C}{2}\right)$

$$= \left(\cos\left(\frac{A}{2}\right) + \cos\left(\frac{B}{2}\right)\right) - \left(\cos\left(\frac{C}{2}\right) + \cos\left(\frac{\pi}{2}\right)\right)$$

$$= 2\cos\left(\frac{A+B}{4}\right)\cos\left(\frac{A-B}{4}\right) - \cos\left(\frac{\pi+C}{4}\right)\cos\left(\frac{\pi-C}{4}\right)$$

$$= 2\cos\left(\frac{\pi-C}{4}\right)\left\{\cos\left(\frac{A-B}{4}\right) - \cos\left(\frac{\pi+C}{4}\right)\right\}$$

$$[\because A+B+C=\pi]$$

$$= 2\cos\left(\frac{\pi-C}{4}\right)\left\{2\sin\left(\frac{\pi+C+A-B}{8}\right)\sin\left(\frac{\pi+C+B-A}{8}\right)\right\}$$

$$= 4\cos\left(\frac{\pi-C}{4}\right)\sin\left(\frac{\pi-B}{4}\right)\sin\left(\frac{\pi-A}{4}\right)$$

$$= 4\cos\left(\frac{\pi-C}{4}\right)\cos\left(\frac{\pi}{2}-\frac{\pi-B}{4}\right)\cos\left(\frac{\pi}{2}-\frac{\pi-A}{4}\right)$$

$$= 4\cos\left(\frac{\pi+A}{4}\right)\cos\left(\frac{\pi+B}{4}\right)\cos\left(\frac{\pi-C}{4}\right)$$

(D) $\cos\left(\frac{A}{2}\right) + \cos\left(\frac{B}{2}\right) + \cos\left(\frac{C}{2}\right) + \cos\left(\frac{\pi}{2}\right)$

$$\Rightarrow 2\cos\left(\frac{A+B}{2}\right)\cos\left(\frac{A-B}{4}\right) + \cos\left(\frac{\pi+C}{4}\right)\cos\left(\frac{\pi-C}{4}\right)$$

$$\Rightarrow 2\cos\left(\frac{\pi-C}{4}\right)\left\{\cos\left(\frac{A-B}{4}\right) + \cos\left(\frac{\pi+C}{4}\right)\right\}$$

$$\Rightarrow 2\cos\left(\frac{\pi-C}{4}\right)\left\{2\cos\left(\frac{A-B+\pi+C}{4}\right)\cos\left(\frac{\pi+C+B-A}{4}\right)\right\}$$

$$\Rightarrow 4\cos\left(\frac{\pi-C}{4}\right)\cos\left(\frac{\pi-B}{4}\right)\cos\left(\frac{\pi-A}{4}\right)$$

$$\text{or } 4\cos\left(\frac{\pi-A}{4}\right)\cos\left(\frac{\pi-B}{4}\right)\cos\left(\frac{\pi-C}{4}\right)$$

83. **(A)** $\cos 2A + \cos 2B + \cos 2C = -1$

$\Rightarrow \quad -1 - 4\cos A\cos B\cos C = -1$

$\Rightarrow \quad \cos A\cos B\cos C = 0$

$\Rightarrow \quad \cos A = 0$ or $\cos B = 0$ or $\cos C = 0$

Thus, the triangle is right angled.

(B) $\tan A > 0$, $\tan B > 0$ and $\tan A\tan B < 1$

$\therefore \quad \tan C = \dfrac{\tan A + \tan B}{\tan A\tan B - 1} < 0$

$\Rightarrow \quad \angle C > 90^\circ$

Thus, the triangle is obtuse angled.

(C) $\cos^3 A + \cos^3 B + \cos^3 C = 3\cos A\cos B\cos C$

$\Rightarrow (\cos A + \cos B + \cos C)(\cos^2 A + \cos^2 B + \cos^2 C$

$- \cos A\cos B - \cos B\cos C - \cos A\cos C) = 0$

$\Rightarrow \quad \cos A + \cos B + \cos C = 0$

or $\cos^2 A + \cos^2 B + \cos^2 C$

$= \cos A\cos B + \cos B\cos C + \cos A\cos C$

$$\Rightarrow 1 + 4\sin\left(\frac{A}{2}\right)\sin\left(\frac{B}{2}\right)\sin\left(\frac{C}{2}\right) = 0$$

or $\cos A = \cos B = \cos C$

$$\Rightarrow \sin\left(\frac{A}{2}\right)\sin\left(\frac{B}{2}\right)\sin\left(\frac{C}{2}\right) = -\frac{1}{4}$$

$\left[\text{which is not possible as } \sin\left(\frac{A}{2}\right), \sin\left(\frac{B}{2}\right), \sin\left(\frac{C}{2}\right) > 0\right]$

or $\cos A = \cos B = \cos C$

Thus, the triangle is equilateral.

(D) $\cot A > 0$, $\cot B > 0$ and $\cot A\cot B < 1$

$\therefore \quad \tan A > 0$, $\tan B > 0$ and $\tan A\tan B > 1$

$\therefore \quad \tan C > 0 \Rightarrow \angle C < 90^\circ$

Thus, the triangle is acute.

84. We have, $-\frac{\pi}{4} < \beta < 0 < \alpha < \frac{\pi}{4}\sin(\alpha+\beta) = \frac{1}{3}$

$$\Rightarrow \quad \cos(\alpha+\beta) = \frac{2\sqrt{2}}{3} \text{ and } \cos(\alpha-\beta) = \frac{2}{3}$$

$$\Rightarrow \quad \sin(\alpha-\beta) = \frac{\sqrt{5}}{3}$$

Now, $\dfrac{\sin\alpha}{\cos\beta} + \dfrac{\cos\beta}{\sin\alpha} + \dfrac{\cos\alpha}{\sin\beta} + \dfrac{\sin\beta}{\cos\alpha}$

$$= \frac{\sin^2\alpha + \cos^2\beta}{\sin\alpha\cos\beta} + \frac{\cos^2\alpha + \sin^2\beta}{\cos\alpha\sin\beta}$$

$$= \frac{\sin^2\alpha + \cos^2\beta}{\sin\alpha\cos\beta} + \frac{1 - \sin^2\alpha + 1 - \cos^2\beta}{\cos\alpha\sin\beta}$$

$$= (\sin^2\alpha + \cos^2\beta)\left(\frac{\sin\beta\cos\alpha - \sin\alpha\cos\beta}{\sin\alpha\cos\alpha\sin\beta\cos\beta}\right) + \frac{2}{\sin\beta\cos\alpha}$$

$$= \frac{4(\sin^2\alpha + \cos^2\beta)\sin(\beta-\alpha)}{[\sin(\alpha+\beta) + \sin(\alpha-\beta)][\sin(\alpha+\beta) - \sin(\alpha-\beta)]} + \frac{4}{[\sin(\alpha+\beta) - \sin(\alpha-\beta)]}$$

$$[\because \sin^2\alpha + \cos^2\beta = 1 + \sin^2\alpha - \sin^2\beta$$

$$= 1 + \sin(\alpha+\beta)\sin(\alpha-\beta) = 1 + \frac{\sqrt{5}}{9}]$$

$$= \frac{-4\left(1 + \frac{\sqrt{5}}{9}\right)\left(\frac{\sqrt{5}}{3}\right)}{\left(\frac{1+\sqrt{5}}{3}\right)\left(\frac{1-\sqrt{5}}{3}\right)} + \frac{4}{\left[\frac{1-\sqrt{5}}{3}\right]}$$

$$= (9 + \sqrt{5})\frac{\sqrt{5}}{3} + \frac{12}{1-\sqrt{5}}$$

$$= 3\sqrt{5} + \frac{5}{3} + \frac{12}{-4}(1 + \sqrt{5})$$

$$= 3\sqrt{5} + \frac{5}{3} - 3 - 3\sqrt{5} = -\frac{4}{3}$$

$$\therefore \left(\frac{\sin\alpha}{\cos\beta} + \frac{\cos\beta}{\sin\alpha} + \frac{\cos\alpha}{\sin\beta} + \frac{\sin\beta}{\cos\alpha}\right)^2 = \frac{16}{9}$$

and its greatest integer $= \frac{16}{9} = 1$

85. We have, $2(\cos\beta - \cos\alpha) + \cos\alpha\cos\beta = 1$

or $\quad 4(\cos\beta - \cos\alpha) + 2\cos\alpha\cos\beta = 2$

$\Rightarrow \quad 1 - \cos\alpha + \cos\beta - \cos\alpha\cos\beta$

$= 3 + 3\cos\alpha - 3\cos\beta - 3\cos\alpha\cos\beta$

$\Rightarrow (1-\cos\alpha)(1+\cos\beta) = 3(1+\cos\alpha)(1-\cos\beta)$

$\Rightarrow \dfrac{(1-\cos\alpha)}{(1+\cos\alpha)} = \dfrac{3(1-\cos\beta)}{1+\cos\beta}$

$\Rightarrow \tan^2\dfrac{\alpha}{2} = 3\tan^2\dfrac{\beta}{2}$

$\therefore \tan\dfrac{\alpha}{2} \pm \sqrt{3}\tan\dfrac{\beta}{2} = 0$

86. Here, $x^2 - 2x\sec\theta + 1 = 0$ has roots α_1 and β_1.

$\therefore \alpha_1, \beta_1 = \dfrac{2\sec\theta \pm \sqrt{4\sec^2\theta - 4}}{2\times 1} = \dfrac{2\sec\theta \pm 2|\tan\theta|}{2}$

Since, $\theta \in \left(-\dfrac{\pi}{6}, -\dfrac{\pi}{12}\right)$,

i.e. $\theta \in$ IV quadrant $= \dfrac{2\sec\theta \mp 2\tan\theta}{2}$

$\therefore \alpha_1 = \sec\theta - \tan\theta$ and $\beta_1 = \sec\theta + \tan\theta$ [as $\alpha_1 > \beta_1$]

and $x^2 + 2x\tan\theta - 1 = 0$ has roots α_2 and β_2.

i.e. $\alpha_2, \beta_2 = \dfrac{-2\tan\theta \pm \sqrt{4\tan^2\theta + 4}}{2}$

$\therefore \alpha_2 = -\tan\theta + \sec\theta$

and $\beta_2 = -\tan\theta - \sec\theta$ [as $\alpha_2 > \beta_2$]

Thus, $\alpha_1 + \beta_2 = -2\tan\theta$

87. Here, $\displaystyle\sum_{k=1}^{13} \frac{1}{\sin\left\{\frac{\pi}{4} + \frac{(k-1)\pi}{6}\right\}\sin\left(\frac{\pi}{4} + \frac{k\pi}{6}\right)}$

Converting into differences, by multiplying and dividing by

$\sin\left[\left(\dfrac{\pi}{4} + \dfrac{k\pi}{6}\right) - \left\{\dfrac{\pi}{4} + \dfrac{(k-1)\pi}{6}\right\}\right]$ i.e. $\sin\left(\dfrac{\pi}{6}\right)$.

$$\therefore \sum_{k=1}^{13} \frac{\sin\left[\left(\frac{\pi}{4} + k\frac{\pi}{6}\right) - \left\{\frac{\pi}{4} + (k-1)\frac{\pi}{6}\right\}\right]}{\sin\frac{\pi}{6}\left\{\sin\left\{\frac{\pi}{4} + (k-1)\frac{\pi}{6}\right\}\sin\left(\frac{\pi}{4} + k\frac{\pi}{6}\right)\right\}}$$

$$= 2\sum_{k=1}^{13} \frac{\left[\begin{array}{l}\sin\left(\frac{\pi}{4} + \frac{k\pi}{6}\right)\cos\left\{\frac{\pi}{4} + (k-1)\frac{\pi}{6}\right\} \\ -\sin\left\{\frac{\pi}{4} + (k-1)\frac{\pi}{6}\right\}\cos\left(\frac{\pi}{4} + \frac{k\pi}{6}\right)\end{array}\right]}{\sin\left\{\frac{\pi}{4} + (k-1)\frac{\pi}{6}\right\}\sin\left(\frac{\pi}{4} + k\frac{\pi}{6}\right)}$$

$$= 2\sum_{k=1}^{13}\left[\cot\left\{\frac{\pi}{4} + (k-1)\frac{\pi}{6}\right\} - \cot\left(\frac{\pi}{4} + k\frac{\pi}{6}\right)\right]$$

$$= 2\left[\left\{\cot\left(\frac{\pi}{4}\right) - \cot\left(\frac{\pi}{4} + \frac{\pi}{6}\right)\right\} + \left\{\cot\left(\frac{\pi}{4} + \frac{\pi}{6}\right) - \cot\left(\frac{\pi}{4} + \frac{2\pi}{6}\right)\right\} + \dots + \left\{\cot\left(\frac{\pi}{4} + 12\frac{\pi}{6}\right) - \cot\left(\frac{\pi}{4} + 13\frac{\pi}{6}\right)\right\}\right]$$

$$= 2\left\{\cot\frac{\pi}{4} - \cot\left(\frac{\pi}{4} + 13\frac{\pi}{6}\right)\right\}$$

$$= 2\left[1 - \cot\left(\frac{29\pi}{12}\right)\right]$$

$$= 2\left[1 - \cot\left(2\pi + \frac{5\pi}{12}\right)\right]$$

$$= 2\left[1 - \cot\frac{5\pi}{12}\right] \qquad \left[\because \cot\frac{5\pi}{12} = (2-\sqrt{3})\right]$$

$$= 2(1 - 2 + \sqrt{3}) = 2(\sqrt{3} - 1)$$

Exercise 3 - Challenging Problems

1. We know that

$$\cos\theta + \sin\theta = \sqrt{2}\left[\frac{1}{\sqrt{2}}\cos\theta + \frac{1}{\sqrt{2}}\sin\theta\right]$$

$$= \sqrt{2}\left[\sin\frac{\pi}{4}\cos\theta + \cos\frac{\pi}{4}\sin\theta\right] = \sqrt{2}\sin\left(\frac{\pi}{4} + \theta\right)$$

$\Rightarrow \cos\theta + \sin\theta \le \sqrt{2} < \dfrac{\pi}{2}$ [as $\sqrt{2} = 1.414$]

$\Rightarrow \cos\theta + \sin\theta < \dfrac{\pi}{2}$ [$\pi/2 = 1.57$ approx.]

$\Rightarrow \cos\theta < \dfrac{\pi}{2} - \sin\theta$

On taking sine both sides, we get

$$\sin(\cos\theta) < \sin\left(\frac{\pi}{2} - \sin\theta\right)$$

$\Rightarrow \sin(\cos\theta) < \cos(\sin\theta)$

$\therefore \cos(\sin\theta) > \sin(\cos\theta)$

Alternate Solution

For $0 \le x \le \dfrac{\pi}{2}$

$x \ge \sin x$ ...(i)

Replace x by $\cos\theta$, we get

$\cos\theta \ge \sin(\cos\theta)$ ...(ii)

Also, we know $\cos\theta$ is decreasing for $0 \le \theta \le \dfrac{\pi}{2}$.

As $\theta_1 < \theta_2 \Rightarrow \cos\theta_1 > \cos\theta_2$ when $\theta_1, \theta_2 \in [0, \pi/2]$

On taking cos on both side of Eq. (i) and putting θ for x, we get

$\cos\theta \le \cos(\sin\theta)$ ...(iii)

Using Eqs. (ii) and (iii),

$\cos(\sin\theta) \ge \cos\theta \ge \sin(\cos\theta)$

$\Rightarrow \cos(\sin\theta) > \sin(\cos\theta)$

2. Clearly, $2^{\sin x}$ and $2^{\cos x}$ are positive, so their AM $\ge$ GM

$\therefore \dfrac{2^{\sin x} + 2^{\cos x}}{2} \ge \sqrt{2^{\sin x} . 2^{\cos x}} = \sqrt{2^{\sin x + \cos x}}$ ...(i)

As we know that

$\sin x + \cos x \ge -\sqrt{2}$

[using $-\sqrt{a^2 + b^2} \le a\sin x + b\cos x \le \sqrt{a^2 + b^2}$]

$$2^{\sin x + \cos x} \ge 2^{-\sqrt{2}}$$

or $$\sqrt{2^{\sin x + \cos x}} \ge 2^{-\sqrt{2}/2}$$

or $$\sqrt{2^{\sin x + \cos x}} \ge 2^{-1/\sqrt{2}} \qquad \text{...(ii)}$$

From Eqs. (i) and (ii),

$$\frac{2^{\sin x} + 2^{\cos x}}{2} \ge \sqrt{2^{\sin x+\cos x}} \ge 2^{-1/\sqrt{2}}$$

$$\therefore \quad 2^{\sin x} + 2^{\cos x} \ge 2 \cdot 2^{-1/\sqrt{2}}$$

or $2^{\sin x} + 2^{\cos x} \ge 2^{1 - 1/\sqrt{2}}$ for all values of x.

3. $$\frac{\tan 3A}{\tan A} = \frac{3\tan A - \tan^3 A}{1 - 3\tan^2 A} \cdot \frac{1}{\tan A} = k$$

$$\Rightarrow \quad \frac{3 - \tan^2 A}{1 - 3\tan^2 A} = k$$

$$\Rightarrow \quad (3 - \tan^2 A) = k(1 - 3\tan^2 A)$$

$$\Rightarrow \quad (3k - 1)\tan^2 A = k - 3$$

$$\Rightarrow \quad \tan^2 A = \left(\frac{k-3}{3k-1}\right) \qquad \text{...(i)}$$

Now, $$\frac{\sin 3A}{\sin A} = \frac{3\sin A - 4\sin^3 A}{\sin A} = 3 - 4\sin^2 A$$

$$\Rightarrow \quad 3 - 4\sin^2 A = 3 - \frac{4}{\operatorname{cosec}^2 A} = 3 - \frac{4}{1 + \cot^2 A}$$

$$= 3 - \frac{4}{1 + \dfrac{1}{\tan^2 A}}$$

$$= 3 - \frac{4}{1 + \left(\dfrac{3k-1}{k-3}\right)} \qquad \text{[using Eq. (i)]}$$

$$\Rightarrow \quad 3 - \frac{4(k-3)}{4(k-1)} = \frac{3k - 3 - k + 3}{k-1} = \frac{2k}{k-1} \qquad \text{...(ii)}$$

Again, from Eq. (i), we get

$$\tan^2 A = \frac{k-3}{3k-1} \qquad [\tan A \ne 0 \text{ and } \tan^2 A > 0]$$

$\Rightarrow \quad \dfrac{k-3}{3k-1} > 0$, using number line rule.

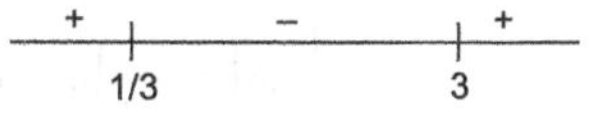

which shows $k < 1/3$ or $k > 3$

4. $A + B + C = \pi$

$$\Rightarrow \quad \frac{A}{2} + \frac{B}{2} = \frac{\pi}{2} - \frac{C}{2}$$

$$\Rightarrow \quad \cot\left(\frac{A}{2} + \frac{B}{2}\right) = \cot\left(\frac{\pi}{2} - \frac{C}{2}\right)$$

$$\Rightarrow \quad \frac{\cot\dfrac{A}{2}\cdot\cot\dfrac{B}{2} - 1}{\cot\dfrac{A}{2} + \cot\dfrac{B}{2}} = \tan\left(\frac{C}{2}\right) = \frac{1}{\cot\left(\dfrac{C}{2}\right)}$$

$$\Rightarrow \quad \cot\frac{A}{2}\cdot\cot\frac{B}{2}\cdot\cot\frac{C}{2} = \cot\frac{A}{2} + \cot\frac{B}{2} + \cot\frac{C}{2} \qquad \text{...(i)}$$

But $\tan\dfrac{A}{2}, \tan\dfrac{B}{2}, \tan\dfrac{C}{2}$ are in HP

$$\Rightarrow \quad \cot\frac{A}{2}, \cot\frac{B}{2}, \cot\frac{C}{2} \text{ are in AP}$$

$$\therefore \quad \cot\frac{A}{2} + \cot\frac{C}{2} = 2\cot\frac{B}{2} \qquad \text{...(ii)}$$

From Eqs. (i) and (ii), we get

$$\cot\frac{A}{2}\cdot\cot\frac{B}{2}\cot\frac{C}{2} = 3\cot\frac{B}{2}$$

$$\Rightarrow \quad \cot\frac{A}{2}\cdot\cot\frac{C}{2} = 3 \qquad \text{...(iii)}$$

As we know that AM $\ge$ GM

$$\Rightarrow \quad \frac{\cot\dfrac{A}{2} + \cot\dfrac{C}{2}}{2} \ge \sqrt{\cot\frac{A}{2}\cdot\cot\frac{C}{2}}$$

$$\Rightarrow \quad \frac{2\cot\dfrac{B}{2}}{2} \ge \sqrt{3} \qquad \text{[using Eq. (iii)]}$$

$$\Rightarrow \quad \cot\frac{B}{2} \ge \sqrt{3}$$

$\therefore$ Minimum value of $\cot\dfrac{B}{2}$ is $\sqrt{3}$.

5. (i) If $\cot B - \cot A = y \Rightarrow \dfrac{\tan A - \tan B}{\tan A \tan B} = y$

$$\therefore \quad \frac{x}{y} = \tan A \tan B$$

Now, $$\cot(A - B) = \frac{1}{\tan(A - B)}$$

$$= \frac{1 + \tan A \tan B}{\tan A - \tan B}$$

$$= \frac{1 + \dfrac{x}{y}}{x} = \frac{1}{x} + \frac{1}{y}$$

$$= \text{RHS}$$

(ii) $2\cos A = x + \dfrac{1}{x}$,

$$\therefore \sin A = \sqrt{1 - \cos^2 A} = \sqrt{1 - \frac{1}{4}\left(x + \frac{1}{x}\right)^2}$$

$$= \sqrt{1 - \frac{1}{4}\left(x^2 + \frac{1}{x^2} + 2\right)}$$

$$\Rightarrow \quad 2\sin A = i\left(x - \frac{1}{x}\right) \qquad \text{...(i)}$$

Similarly, $$2\cos B = y + \frac{1}{y}$$

$$\Rightarrow \quad 2\sin B = i\left(y - \frac{1}{y}\right) \qquad \text{...(ii)}$$

Now, $2\cos(A-B) = 2[\cos A\cos B + \sin A\sin B]$

$$= \frac{2}{4}\left[\left(x+\frac{1}{x}\right)\left(y+\frac{1}{y}\right) + i^2\left(x-\frac{1}{x}\right)\left(y-\frac{1}{y}\right)\right]$$

$$= \frac{1}{2}\left[\left\{xy+\frac{1}{xy}+\frac{y}{x}+\frac{x}{y}\right\}-\left\{xy+\frac{1}{xy}-\frac{y}{x}-\frac{x}{y}\right\}\right]$$

$$= \frac{1}{2}\left[2\frac{y}{x}+2\frac{x}{y}\right]$$

$$= \frac{x}{y}+\frac{y}{x} = \text{RHS}$$

6. We know that

$$\sin 2A \sin 2B = \frac{1}{2}[\cos(2A-2B)-\cos(2A+2B)]$$

$$= \frac{1}{2}[2\cos^2(A-B)-1-2\cos^2(A+B)+1]$$

$$= \cos^2(A-B)-\cos^2(A+B)$$

$\therefore\ \sin 2A\cdot\sin 2B = \cos^2(A-B)-\cos^2(A+B)$ ...(i)

Now, $2x^3-3x^2\cos(A-B)-2x\cos^2(A+B)$

$$+\sin 2A\cdot\sin 2B.\cos(A-B)=0$$

$\Rightarrow 2x^3-3x^2\cos(A-B)-2x\cos^2(A+B)$

$$+\cos^3(A-B)-\cos^2(A+B).\cos(A-B)=0$$

By inspection, we find that $x=-\frac{1}{2}\cos(A-B)$ because

$$\left(-\frac{1}{4}-\frac{3}{4}+1\right)\cos^3(A-B)+\cos^2(A+B)\cos(A-B)$$

$$-\cos^2(A+B)\cos(A-B)=0$$

Hence, $2x+\cos(A-B)$ is factor of the given equation which when divided by it, given the other factor as,

$x^2-2x\cos(A-B)+\cos^2(A-B)-\cos^2(A+B)=0$

So,

$$x=\frac{2\cos(A-B)\pm\sqrt{4\cos^2(A-B)-4\cos^2(A-B)+4\cos^2(A+B)}}{2}$$

$$x=\frac{2\cos(A-B)\pm 2\cos(A+B)}{2}$$

$x=\cos(A-B)+\cos(A+B)$ or $\cos(A-B)-\cos(A+B)$

Hence, the roots are,

$$2\cos A\cos B,\ 2\sin A\sin B \text{ and } -\frac{1}{2}\cos(A-B).$$

7. $m^2+m'^2+2mm'\cos\theta=1$

or $(m^2\cos^2\theta+m^2\sin^2\theta)+m'^2+2mm'\cos\theta=1$

or $m^2\cos^2\theta+2mm'\cos\theta+m'^2=1-m^2\sin^2\theta$

or $(m\cos\theta+m')^2=1-m^2\sin^2\theta$ ...(i)

Similarly, $n^2+n'^2+2nn'\cos\theta=1$

$\Rightarrow (n\cos\theta+n')^2=1-n^2\sin^2\theta$ ...(ii)

Finally, $mn+m'n'+(mn'+m'n)\cos\theta=0$

$\Rightarrow (mn\cos^2\theta+mn\sin^2\theta)+m'n'+mn'\cos\theta+m'n\cos\theta=0$

$\Rightarrow mn\cos^2\theta+m'n\cos\theta+m'n'+mn'\cos\theta=-mn\sin^2\theta$

$\Rightarrow n\cos\theta(m\cos\theta+m')+n'(m'+m\cos\theta)=-mn\sin^2\theta$

$\Rightarrow (m\cos\theta+m')(n\cos\theta+n')=-mn\sin^2\theta$

or $(m\cos\theta+m')^2(n\cos\theta+n')^2=m^2n^2\sin^4\theta$

$\Rightarrow (1-m^2\sin^2\theta)(1-n^2\sin^2\theta)=m^2n^2\sin^4\theta$

[using Eqs. (i) and (ii)]

$\Rightarrow 1-(m^2+n^2)\sin^2\theta+m^2n^2\sin^4\theta=m^2n^2\sin^4\theta$

$\Rightarrow (m^2+n^2)\sin^2\theta=1$

$\Rightarrow m^2+n^2=\operatorname{cosec}^2\theta$

8. Given condition can be rewritten as,

$$b(\sin^2\alpha)^2+a\cos^4\alpha=\frac{ab}{a+b}$$

$$\Rightarrow b(1-\cos^2\alpha)^2+a\cos^4\alpha=\frac{ab}{a+b}$$

$$\Rightarrow b(\cos^4\alpha-2\cos^2\alpha+1)+a\cos^4\alpha=\frac{ab}{a+b}$$

$$\Rightarrow (a+b)^2\cos^4\alpha-2b(a+b)\cos^2\alpha+b(a+b)=ab$$

$$\Rightarrow (a+b)^2\cos^4\alpha-2b(a+b)\cos^2\alpha+b^2=0$$

$$\Rightarrow [(a+b)\cos^2\alpha-b]^2=0$$

$$\Rightarrow \cos^2\alpha=\frac{b}{a+b}$$

$$\Rightarrow \sin^2\alpha=\frac{a}{a+b} \quad \text{...(i)}$$

$$\therefore \frac{\sin^8\alpha}{a^3}+\frac{\cos^8\alpha}{b^3}=\frac{a^4}{a^3(a+b)^4}+\frac{b^4}{b^3(a+b)^4}$$

$$=\frac{a}{(a+b)^4}+\frac{b}{(a+b)^4}=\frac{a+b}{(a+b)^4}=\frac{1}{(a+b)^3}$$

$$\therefore \frac{\sin^8\alpha}{a^3}+\frac{\cos^8\alpha}{b^3}=\frac{1}{(a+b)^3}$$

Now, $\frac{\sin^{4n}x}{a^{2n-1}}+\frac{\cos^{4n}x}{b^{2n-1}}=\frac{a^{2n}}{a^{2n-1}(a+b)^{2n}}+\frac{b^{2n}}{b^{2n-1}(a+b)^{2n}}$

$$=\frac{a+b}{(a+b)^{2n}}=\frac{1}{(a+b)^{2n-1}}$$

9. Let $S=\sum_{r=2}^{n}\sin r\alpha=\sin 2\alpha+\sin 3\alpha+\sin 4\alpha+\ldots+\sin n\alpha$

$\therefore\ 2\sin\frac{\alpha}{2}\cdot S=2\sin\alpha/2\sin 2\alpha+2\sin\frac{\alpha}{2}\cdot\sin 3\alpha+2\sin\frac{\alpha}{2}$

$\cdot\sin 4\alpha+\ldots+2\sin\alpha/2.\sin n\alpha$

$$=\left\{\cos\frac{3\alpha}{2}-\cos\frac{5\alpha}{2}\right\}+\left\{\cos\frac{5\alpha}{2}-\cos\frac{7\alpha}{2}\right\}+\ldots+$$

$$\left\{\cos\left(n-\frac{1}{2}\right)\alpha-\cos\left(n+\frac{1}{2}\right)\alpha\right\}$$

$$=\cos\frac{3\alpha}{2}-\cos\left(n+\frac{1}{2}\right)\alpha$$

$$=2\sin\left(\frac{\frac{3\alpha}{2}+\left(n+\frac{1}{2}\right)\alpha}{2}\right)\sin\left(\frac{\left(n+\frac{1}{2}\right)\alpha-\frac{3\alpha}{2}}{2}\right)$$

$$2\sin\frac{\alpha}{2}\cdot S=2\sin\frac{(n+2)\alpha}{2}\cdot\sin\frac{(n-1)\alpha}{2}$$

$$\Rightarrow S=\frac{\sin\frac{(n-1)\alpha}{2}}{\sin\frac{\alpha}{2}}\cdot\sin\frac{(n+2)\alpha}{2}=\frac{\sin\frac{(n-1)\alpha}{2}}{\sin\frac{\alpha}{2}}\cdot\sin\frac{2\pi}{2}=0$$

10. We have,

$$\sqrt{1+\cos\alpha}+\sqrt{1+\cos 2\alpha}+\sqrt{1+\cos 3\alpha}+\ldots+\sqrt{1+\cos n\alpha}$$

$$=\sqrt{2\cos^2\alpha/2}+\sqrt{2\cos^2\alpha}+\sqrt{2\cos^2\frac{3\alpha}{2}}+\ldots \text{ to } n \text{ terms}$$

$$=\sqrt{2}\left\{\cos\frac{\alpha}{2}+\cos\frac{2\alpha}{2}+\cos\frac{3\alpha}{2}+\ldots+\text{ to } n \text{ terms}\right\}$$

$$=\sqrt{2}\cdot\frac{\sin\frac{n\alpha}{4}}{\sin\frac{\alpha}{4}}\cdot\cos\left\{\frac{\alpha}{2}+(n-1)\frac{\alpha}{4}\right\} \quad \text{[using formula]}$$

$$=\sqrt{2}\frac{\sin\frac{n\alpha}{4}}{\sin\frac{\alpha}{4}}.\cos\left\{(n+1)\frac{\alpha}{4}\right\}$$

11. $$\text{LHS}=\frac{\cos A}{\sin A}+\frac{\cos B}{\sin B}+\frac{\cos C}{\sin C}-\frac{1}{\sin A\cdot\sin B\cdot\sin C}$$

$$=\frac{\cos A\cdot\sin B\sin C+\cos B\sin A\sin C+\cos C\sin A\sin B-1}{\sin A\sin B\sin C}$$

$$=\frac{\sin C(\cos A\sin B+\cos B\sin A)+\cos C\sin A\sin B-1}{\sin A\sin B\sin C}$$

$$=\frac{\sin C\sin(A+B)+\cos C\sin A\sin B-1}{\sin A\sin B\sin C}$$

$$=\frac{\sin^2 C+\cos C\sin A\sin B-1}{\sin A\sin B\sin C}$$

[using $\sin(A+B)=\sin(\pi-C)=\sin C$]

$$=\frac{\cos C.\sin A\sin B-\cos^2 C}{\sin A\sin B\sin C}$$

$$=\frac{\cos C\{\sin A\sin B-\cos C\}}{\sin A\sin B\sin C}$$

[$\because \cos C=\cos(\pi-(A+B))=-\cos(A+B)$]

$$=\frac{\cos C\{\sin A\sin B+\cos(A+B)\}}{\sin A\sin B\sin C}$$

$$=\frac{\cos C\{\sin A\sin B+\cos A\cos B-\sin A\sin B\}}{\sin A\sin B\sin C}$$

$$=\frac{\cos A\cos B\cos C}{\sin A\sin B\sin C}=\cot A\cdot\cot B\cdot\cot C=\text{RHS}$$

12. We have, $\cot\theta=\cot A+\cot B+\cot C$

$$\Rightarrow \cot(\theta)-\cot(A)=\cot B+\cot C$$

$$\Rightarrow \frac{\cos\theta}{\sin\theta}-\frac{\cos A}{\sin A}=\frac{\cos B}{\sin B}+\frac{\cos C}{\sin C}$$

$$\Rightarrow \frac{\cos\theta\sin A-\cos A\sin\theta}{\sin\theta\sin A}=\frac{\cos B\sin C+\sin B\cos C}{\sin B\sin C}$$

$$\Rightarrow \frac{\sin(A-\theta)}{\sin A\sin\theta}=\frac{\sin(B+C)}{\sin B\sin C}$$

$$\Rightarrow \sin(A-\theta)=\frac{\sin^2 A\sin\theta}{\sin B\sin C} \quad \ldots\text{(i)}$$

Similarly, $$\sin(B-\theta)=\frac{\sin^2 B\sin\theta}{\sin A\sin C} \quad \ldots\text{(ii)}$$

and $$\sin(C-\theta)=\frac{\sin^2 C\sin\theta}{\sin A\sin B} \quad \ldots\text{(iii)}$$

On multiplying Eqs. (i), (ii) and (iii), we get

$$\sin(A-\theta)\sin(B-\theta)\sin(C-\theta)=\sin^3\theta.$$

13. We have, $bc\cos\theta\cos\phi=ab-ac\sin\theta\sin\phi.$

$$\Rightarrow b^2c^2\cos^2\theta\cos^2\phi=a^2b^2+a^2c^2\sin^2\theta\sin^2\phi-2a^2bc\sin\theta\sin\phi$$

$$\Rightarrow (a^2c^2\sin^2\phi+b^2c^2\cos^2\phi)\sin^2\theta-2a^2bc\sin\theta\sin\phi+a^2b^2-b^2c^2\cos^2\phi=0$$

$$\Rightarrow \sin\alpha\sin\beta=\frac{a^2b^2-b^2c^2\cos^2\phi}{a^2c^2\sin^2\phi+b^2c^2\cos^2\phi} \quad \ldots\text{(i)}$$

Similarly, $ac\sin\theta\sin\phi=ab-bc\cos\phi\cos\theta$

$$\Rightarrow a^2c^2\sin^2\theta\sin^2\phi=a^2b^2+b^2c^2\cos^2\theta\cos^2\phi-2ab^2c\cos\theta\cos\phi$$

$$\therefore \quad \cos\alpha\cos\beta=\frac{a^2b^2-a^2c^2\sin^2\phi}{a^2c^2\sin^2\phi+b^2c^2\cos^2\phi} \quad \ldots\text{(ii)}$$

On substituting the value from Eqs. (i) and (ii) in $(b^2+c^2-a^2)\cos\alpha\cos\beta+ac\sin\alpha\sin\beta$, we get

$$\Rightarrow \frac{(b^2+c^2-a^2)(a^2b^2-a^2c^2\sin^2\phi)+ac(a^2b^2-b^2c^2\cos^2\phi)}{a^2c^2\sin^2\phi+b^2c^2\cos^2\phi}$$

$$\Rightarrow (a^2+b^2-c^2)=\text{RHS}$$

14. We know, $a^4+b^4\geq 2a^2b^2$

[AM $\geq$ GM]

$$\therefore \quad \tan^4 x+\tan^4 y\geq 2\tan^2 x\tan^2 y \quad \ldots\text{(i)}$$

Equality occurring only when $\tan^2 x=\tan^2 y=1.$

Also, $$\tan^2 x\tan^2 y+\cot^2 x\cot^2 y\geq 2 \quad \ldots\text{(ii)}$$

Since, $a+\frac{1}{a}\geq 2$ and equality occurring only when

$a=1$, i.e. $\tan^2 x\tan^2 y=1$

From Eqs. (i) and (ii),

$$\tan^4 x+\tan^4 y+2\cot^2 x\cot^2 y\geq 4 \quad \ldots\text{(iii)}$$

Also, $$\text{RHS}=3+\sin^2(x+y)\leq 4 \quad \ldots\text{(iv)}$$

From Eqs. (iii) and (iv),

$$\text{LHS}=\text{RHS}=4$$

$$\Rightarrow \tan^2 x=\tan^2 y=\tan^2 x\tan^2 y=1$$

$$\Rightarrow \tan x=\tan y=\pm 1$$

$$\Rightarrow \tan x=\tan y=1 \quad \{\text{as } x, y\in[0,\pi/2]\}$$

$$\therefore \quad x=y=\pi/4$$

Only one solution i.e. $(x=\pi/4, y=\pi/4)$.

15. Let $$y=\tan\frac{3\pi}{11}+4\sin\frac{2\pi}{11}=\frac{1}{\cos\frac{3\pi}{11}}\left(\sin\frac{3\pi}{11}+4\sin\frac{2\pi}{11}\cos\frac{3\pi}{11}\right)$$

$$\Rightarrow y^2.\cos^2\frac{3\pi}{11}=\sin^2\frac{3\pi}{11}+16\sin^2\frac{2\pi}{11}\cdot\cos^2\frac{3\pi}{11}+8\sin\frac{2\pi}{11}\cdot\cos\frac{3\pi}{11}\cdot\sin\frac{3\pi}{11}$$

$$\Rightarrow 2\cos^2\frac{3\pi}{11}y^2=2\sin^2\frac{3\pi}{11}+32\sin^2\frac{2\pi}{11}\cdot\cos^2\frac{3\pi}{11}+8\sin\frac{2\pi}{11}\cdot\sin\frac{6\pi}{11}$$

$$=\left(1-\cos\frac{6\pi}{11}\right)+8\left(1-\cos\frac{4\pi}{11}\right)\cdot\left(1+\cos\frac{6\pi}{11}\right)+4\left(\cos\frac{4\pi}{11}-\cos\frac{8\pi}{11}\right)$$

$$= 9 + 7\cos\frac{6\pi}{11} - 4\cos\frac{4\pi}{11} - 8\cos\frac{4\pi}{11}\cdot\cos\frac{6\pi}{11} - 4\cos\frac{8\pi}{11}$$

$$= 9 + 7\cos\frac{6\pi}{11} - 4\cos\frac{4\pi}{11} - 4\left(\cos\frac{10\pi}{11} + \cos\frac{2\pi}{11}\right) - 4\cos\frac{8\pi}{11}$$

$$= 9 + 11\cos\frac{6\pi}{11} - 4\begin{pmatrix}\cos\frac{2\pi}{11} + \cos\frac{4\pi}{11} + \cos\frac{6\pi}{11} \\ + \cos\frac{8\pi}{11} + \cos\frac{10\pi}{11}\end{pmatrix}$$

$$= 9 + 11\cos\frac{6\pi}{11} - 4\left(\frac{\cos\left(\frac{2\pi}{11} + 2\cdot\frac{2\pi}{11}\right)\cdot\sin\left(\frac{5\pi}{11}\right)}{\sin\pi/11}\right)$$

$$= 9 + 11\cos\frac{6\pi}{11} - \frac{4\cos\frac{6\pi}{11}\cdot\sin\frac{5\pi}{11}}{\sin\frac{\pi}{11}}$$

$$= 9 + 11\cos\frac{6\pi}{11} - \frac{2\sin\frac{12\pi}{11}}{\sin\frac{\pi}{11}}$$

$$= 9 + 11\cos\frac{6\pi}{11} + 2 = 11\left(1 + \cos\frac{6\pi}{11}\right)$$

$$\Rightarrow \quad 2y^2\cdot\left(\cos^2\frac{3\pi}{11}\right) = 22\cos^2\frac{3\pi}{11}$$

$$\Rightarrow \quad y^2 = 11$$

$$\Rightarrow \quad y = \sqrt{11} \qquad [\text{as } y > 0]$$

16. Let $A = B$, then

$2A + C = 180°$

and $\quad 2\tan A + \tan C = k \qquad \ldots(i)$

Now, $\quad 2A + C = 180°$

$\Rightarrow \quad \tan 2A = -\tan C$

Also, $\quad 2\tan A + \tan C = k$

$\Rightarrow \quad 2\tan A + \tan(180 - 2A) = k$

$\Rightarrow \quad 2\tan A - \tan 2A = k$

$$\Rightarrow \quad 2\tan A - \frac{2\tan A}{1 - \tan^2 A} = k$$

$\Rightarrow \quad 2\tan A(1 - \tan^2 A - 1) = k - k\tan^2 A$

$\Rightarrow \quad 2\tan^3 A - k\tan^2 A + k = 0$

Let $\tan A = x$, $x > 0$ (as $A < 90°$)

Then, let $\quad f(x) = 2x^3 - kx^2 + k \qquad \ldots(ii)$

$f'(x) = 6x^2 - 2kx = 0$

$\Rightarrow \quad x = k/3, 0$

Following cases arises

(i) $k < 0$, three graphs of cubic equation (ii) are possible. Clearly, in all these case, only one triangle is possible and the condition for that triangle to be possible is $f(0) < 0 \Rightarrow k < 0$ so for $k < 0$ only one isosceles triangle is possible.

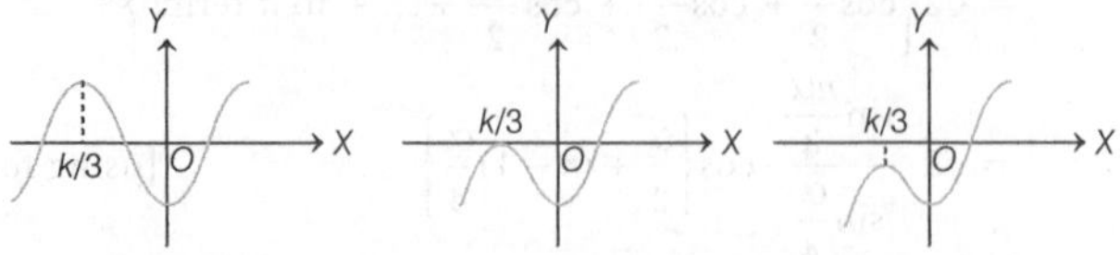

(ii) $k > 0$, three graphs of the cubic equation (ii) are possible. In fig. (i), two such triangle are possible. The condition is $f(k/3) < 0$.

$$\Rightarrow \quad k\left(1 - \frac{k^2}{27}\right) < 0$$

$$\Rightarrow \quad k > 3\sqrt{3}$$

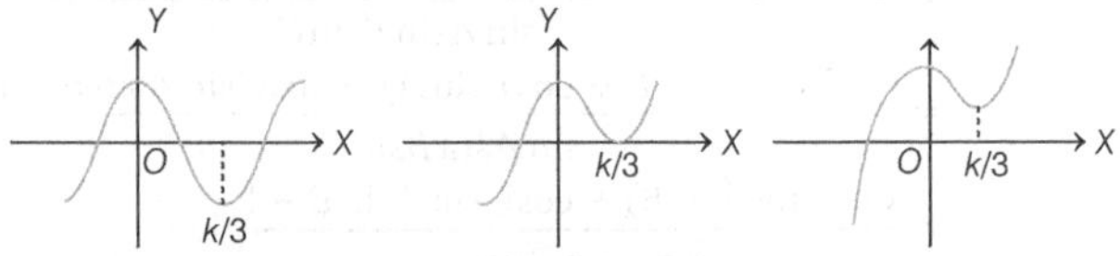

In figure (ii), one such triangle is possible. The condition is $f(k/3) = 0$

$$\Rightarrow \quad k = 3\sqrt{3}.$$

In figure (iii), no such triangle is possible. The condition is $f(k/3) > 0$

$$\Rightarrow \quad k\left(1 - \frac{k^2}{27}\right) > 0$$

$$\Rightarrow \quad k < 3\sqrt{3}.$$

(iii) $k = 0$, graph will be shown as, so no such triangle is possible. Hence, the solution for mentioned conditions;

(A) either $k < 0$

or $\quad k = 3\sqrt{3}$

(B) $k > 3\sqrt{3}$

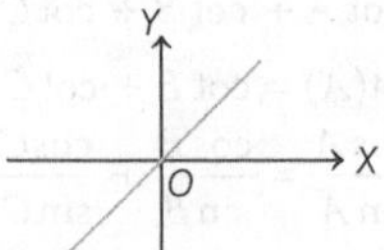

(C) Clearly, there will never exists three or more than three non-similar isosceles triangle for any value of k.

2

> The essence of Maths is not to make simple things complicated, but to make complicated things simple.
>
> **-Stan Gudder**

Trigonometric Equations and Inequations

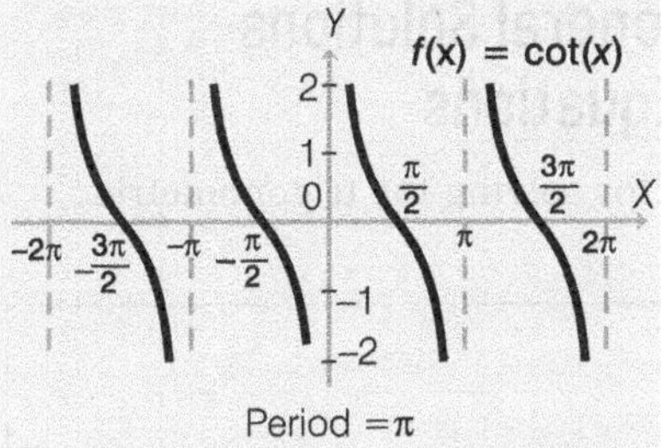

Learning Milestones

Milestone 1 Trigonometric Equations
- Trigonometric Equations
- Solution of Trigonometric Equations

Milestone 2 Method to Solve Trigonometric Equations

Milestone 3 Solution of Simultaneous Trigonometric Equations
- Equation of the Form $a\cos\theta + b\sin\theta = c$
- Solution of Simultaneous Trigonometric Equations

Milestone 4 Solution of Trigonometric Equations Using Graph
- Solution of Trigonometric Equations Using Graph
- Trigonometric Inequality

Practice Milestones

Practice Milestone 1- JEE Main Pattern
Practice Milestone 2 - JEE Advanced Pattern
Practice Milestone 3 - Challenging Problems

Milestone 1 Trigonometric Equations

• Trigonometric Equations • Solution of Trigonometric Equations

2.1 Trigonometric Equations

The equations involving trigonometric functions of unknown angles are known as trigonometric equations.

e.g. $\cos\theta = 0, \cos^2\theta - 4\cos\theta = 1,$

$\sin^2\theta + \sin\theta = 2, \cos^2\theta - 4\sin\theta = 1.$

2.2 Solution of Trigonometric Equations

A solution of a trigonometric equation is the value of the unknown angle that satisfies the equation.

e.g. $\sin\theta = \frac{1}{\sqrt{2}} \Rightarrow \theta = \frac{\pi}{4}$

or $\theta = \frac{\pi}{4}, \frac{3\pi}{4}, \frac{9\pi}{4}, \frac{11\pi}{4}, \ldots$

Thus, the trigonometric equation may have infinite number of solutions and can be classified as

(i) Principal solution (ii) Particular solution

(iii) General solution

(i) Principal Solution

The solution lying in the interval $[0, 2\pi)$ are called principle solution.

Example 1. Find the principal solutions of the following trigonometric equations :

(i) $\sin x = \frac{1}{2}$ (ii) $\cos x = \frac{1}{\sqrt{2}}$

(iii) $\tan x = -\frac{1}{\sqrt{3}}$

Sol. (i) Given, $\sin x = \frac{1}{2}$

As we know that

$$\sin\frac{\pi}{6} = \frac{1}{2}, \sin\frac{5\pi}{6} = \frac{1}{2} \text{ and } \frac{\pi}{6}, \frac{5\pi}{6} \in [0, 2\pi)$$

Hence, principle solution for $\sin x = \frac{1}{2}$ are $\frac{\pi}{6}, \frac{5\pi}{6}$.

(ii) Given, $\cos x = \frac{1}{\sqrt{2}}$

$\because \quad \cos\frac{\pi}{4} = \cos\frac{7\pi}{4} = \frac{1}{\sqrt{2}}$

$\therefore \frac{\pi}{4}, \frac{7\pi}{4} \in [0, 2\pi)$ are the principal solutions.

(iii) Given, $\tan x = -\frac{1}{\sqrt{3}}$

$$= \tan\left(\frac{5\pi}{6}\right) = \tan\left(\frac{11\pi}{6}\right)$$

Hence, $x = \frac{5\pi}{6}, \frac{11\pi}{6} \in [0, 2\pi)$ are its principal solutions.

(ii) Particular Solution

The solutions lying in a particular interval are called particular solutions.

(iii) General Solution

Since, trigonometric functions are periodic, a solution generalised by means of periodicity of the trigonometrical functions. The solution consisting of all possible solutions of a trigonometric equation is called its general solution.

Some Important General Solutions of Trigonometric Equations

We use following results for solving the trigonometric equations.

RESULT 1

$\sin\theta = 0 \Leftrightarrow \theta = n\pi, n \in I.$

Explanation We know that $\sin\theta = 0$ for all integral multiples of π.

$\therefore \quad \sin\theta = 0 \Leftrightarrow \theta = 0, \pm\pi, \pm 2\pi, \pm 3\pi, \ldots$

$\Rightarrow \quad \theta = n\pi, n \in I$

Thus, $\sin\theta = 0 \Leftrightarrow \theta = n\pi, n \in I.$

RESULT 2

$\cos\theta = 0 \Leftrightarrow \theta = (2n+1)\dfrac{\pi}{2}, n \in I$

Explanation We know that $\cos\theta = 0$ for all odd multiples of $\dfrac{\pi}{2}$.

$\therefore \quad \cos\theta = 0 \Leftrightarrow \theta = \pm\dfrac{\pi}{2}, \pm\dfrac{3\pi}{2}, \pm\dfrac{5\pi}{2}, \ldots$

$\Rightarrow \quad \theta = (2n+1)\dfrac{\pi}{2}, n \in I$

Thus, $\quad \cos\theta = 0$

$\Leftrightarrow \quad \theta = (2n+1)\dfrac{\pi}{2}, n \in I$

RESULT 3

$\tan\theta = 0 \Leftrightarrow \theta = n\pi, n \in I$

Explanation We know that $\tan\theta = 0$ for all integral multiple of π.

$\therefore \quad \tan\theta = 0 \Leftrightarrow \theta = 0, \pm\pi, \pm 2\pi, \pm 3\pi, \ldots$

$\Rightarrow \quad \theta = n\pi, n \in I$

Thus, $\quad \tan\theta = 0$

$\Leftrightarrow \quad \theta = n\pi, n \in I$

RESULT 4

$\sin\theta = 1 \Leftrightarrow \theta = (4n+1)\dfrac{\pi}{2}, n \in I$

Explanation We know that

$$\sin\theta = 1 \Leftrightarrow \theta = \ldots, -\frac{3\pi}{2}, \frac{\pi}{2}, \frac{5\pi}{2}, \ldots$$

$\therefore \quad \sin\theta = 1 \Leftrightarrow \theta = 2n\pi + \dfrac{\pi}{2}$

$\Rightarrow \quad \theta = (4n+1)\dfrac{\pi}{2}, n \in I$

Thus, $\sin\theta = 1 \Leftrightarrow \theta = (4n+1)\dfrac{\pi}{2}, n \in I$

RESULT 5

$\sin\theta = -1 \Leftrightarrow \theta = (4n-1)\dfrac{\pi}{2}, n \in I$

Explanation We know that

$$\sin\theta = -1 \Leftrightarrow \theta = \ldots, -\frac{\pi}{2}, \frac{3\pi}{2}, \ldots$$

$\therefore \quad \sin\theta = -1 \Leftrightarrow \theta = -\dfrac{\pi}{2} + 2n\pi \Rightarrow \theta = (4n-1)\dfrac{\pi}{2}, n \in I$

Thus, $\sin\theta = -1 \Leftrightarrow \theta = (4n-1)\dfrac{\pi}{2}, n \in I$

RESULT 6

$\cos\theta = 1 \Leftrightarrow \theta = 2n\pi, n \in I$

RESULT 7

$\cos\theta = -1 \Leftrightarrow \theta = (2n+1)\pi, n \in I$

RESULT 8

$\tan\theta = 1 \Leftrightarrow \theta = (4n+1)\dfrac{\pi}{4}, n \in I$

RESULT 9

$\tan\theta = -1 \Leftrightarrow \theta = n\pi + \dfrac{3\pi}{4}, n \in I$

RESULT 10

$\sin\theta = \sin\alpha \Leftrightarrow \theta = n\pi + (-1)^n \alpha,$

where $n \in I$ and $\alpha \in \left[-\dfrac{\pi}{2}, \dfrac{\pi}{2}\right]$

Explanation We have, $\sin\theta = \sin\alpha$, where $\alpha \in \left[-\dfrac{\pi}{2}, \dfrac{\pi}{2}\right]$

Now, $\quad \sin\theta - \sin\alpha = 0$

$\Leftrightarrow \quad 2\cos\left(\dfrac{\theta+\alpha}{2}\right)\sin\left(\dfrac{\theta-\alpha}{2}\right) = 0$

$\Leftrightarrow \quad \cos\left(\dfrac{\theta+\alpha}{2}\right) = 0 \quad \text{or} \quad \sin\left(\dfrac{\theta-\alpha}{2}\right) = 0$

$\Leftrightarrow \quad \left(\dfrac{\theta+\alpha}{2}\right) = (2m+1)\dfrac{\pi}{2}, m \in I \quad \text{or} \quad \left(\dfrac{\theta-\alpha}{2}\right) = m\pi, m \in I$

$\Leftrightarrow \quad (\theta+\alpha) = (2m+1)\pi, m \in I \quad \text{or} \quad (\theta-\alpha) = 2m\pi, m \in I$

$\Leftrightarrow \quad \theta = (2m+1)\pi - \alpha, m \in I \quad \ldots\text{(i)}$

or $\quad \theta = (2m\pi) + \alpha, m \in I \quad \ldots\text{(ii)}$

$\Leftrightarrow \quad \theta = (\text{any odd multiple of } \pi) - \alpha$

or $\quad \theta = (\text{any even multiple of } \pi) + \alpha$

From Eqs. (i) and (ii), we get

$$\theta = n\pi + (-1)^n \alpha, \text{ where } n \in I$$

Thus, $\sin\theta = \sin\alpha \Leftrightarrow \theta = n\pi + (-1)^n\alpha,$

where $n \in I$ and $\alpha \in \left[-\dfrac{\pi}{2}, \dfrac{\pi}{2}\right]$

Example 2. Find the general and principal solution of trigonometric equation $\sin\theta = \frac{1}{2}$.

Sol. Given, $\sin\theta = \frac{1}{2}$

$$\Rightarrow \quad \sin\theta = \sin\frac{\pi}{6}$$

$$\Rightarrow \quad \theta = n\pi + (-1)^n \frac{\pi}{6}, n \in I \qquad \text{[general solution]}$$

$$\Rightarrow \quad \theta = \left\{\frac{\pi}{6}, \frac{5\pi}{6}\right\} \qquad \text{[principal solution]}$$

Example 3. Find the general solution of trigonometric equation $\sin\left(\theta + \frac{\pi}{6}\right) = -\frac{1}{\sqrt{2}}$.

Sol. Given, $\sin\left(\theta + \frac{\pi}{6}\right) = -\frac{1}{\sqrt{2}}$

$$\Rightarrow \quad \sin\left(\theta + \frac{\pi}{6}\right) = \sin\left(-\frac{\pi}{4}\right)$$

$$\Rightarrow \quad \theta + \frac{\pi}{6} = n\pi + (-1)^n\left(-\frac{\pi}{4}\right)$$

$$\Rightarrow \quad \theta = n\pi + (-1)^n\left(-\frac{\pi}{4}\right) - \frac{\pi}{6}, n \in I$$

RESULT 11

$\cos\theta = \cos\alpha \Leftrightarrow \theta = 2n\pi \pm \alpha, n \in I$ and $\alpha \in [0, \pi]$.

Explanation We have,

$$\cos\theta = \cos\alpha, \text{ where } \alpha \in [0, \pi]$$

Now, $\cos\theta - \cos\alpha = 0$

$$\Leftrightarrow \quad -2\sin\left(\frac{\theta+\alpha}{2}\right)\cdot\sin\left(\frac{\theta-\alpha}{2}\right) = 0$$

$$\Leftrightarrow \quad \sin\left(\frac{\theta+\alpha}{2}\right) = 0 \text{ or } \sin\left(\frac{\theta-\alpha}{2}\right) = 0$$

$$\Leftrightarrow \quad \frac{\theta+\alpha}{2} = n\pi \text{ or } \frac{\theta-\alpha}{2} = n\pi, n \in I$$

$$\Leftrightarrow \quad \theta + \alpha = 2n\pi \text{ or } \theta - \alpha = 2n\pi, n \in I$$

$$\Leftrightarrow \quad \theta = 2n\pi - \alpha \text{ or } \theta = 2n\pi + \alpha, n \in I$$

$$\Leftrightarrow \quad \theta = 2n\pi \pm \alpha, n \in I$$

Thus, $\cos\theta = \cos\alpha$

$$\Leftrightarrow \quad \theta = 2n\pi \pm \alpha, n \in I,$$

where $\alpha \in [0, \pi]$

Example 4. Find the general solution of trigonometric equation $\cos 3\theta = \frac{\sqrt{3}}{2}$.

Sol. Given, $\cos 3\theta = \frac{\sqrt{3}}{2}$

$$\Rightarrow \quad \cos 3\theta = \cos\left(\frac{\pi}{6}\right)$$

$$\Rightarrow \quad 3\theta = 2n\pi \pm \frac{\pi}{6}$$

$$\Rightarrow \quad \theta = \frac{2n\pi}{3} \pm \frac{\pi}{18}, n \in I$$

Example 5. Find the general solution of trigonometric equation $\cos 2\theta = \frac{1}{3}$.

Sol. Given, $\cos 2\theta = \frac{1}{3}$

Let $\cos\alpha = \frac{1}{3}$ or $\alpha = \cos^{-1}\left(\frac{1}{3}\right)$

$$\Rightarrow \quad \cos 2\theta = \cos\alpha$$

$$\Rightarrow \quad 2\theta = 2n\pi \pm \alpha$$

$$\Rightarrow \quad \theta = n\pi \pm \frac{\alpha}{2}$$

or $\theta = n\pi \pm \frac{1}{2}\cos^{-1}\left(\frac{1}{3}\right), n \in I$

Example 6. Find the general solution of trigonometric equation $\sec 2x = -2$.

Sol. Given, $\sec 2x = -2$

$$\Rightarrow \quad \cos 2x = -\frac{1}{2} = \cos\left(\frac{2\pi}{3}\right)$$

$$\Rightarrow \quad 2x = 2n\pi \pm \frac{2\pi}{3}$$

$$\Rightarrow \quad x = n\pi \pm \frac{\pi}{3}, n \in I$$

RESULT 12

$\tan\theta = \tan\alpha \Leftrightarrow \theta = n\pi + \alpha, n \in I$, where $\alpha \in \left(-\frac{\pi}{2}, \frac{\pi}{2}\right)$

Explanation We have,

$$\tan\theta = \tan\alpha, \text{ where } \alpha \in \left(-\frac{\pi}{2}, \frac{\pi}{2}\right)$$

$$\Leftrightarrow \quad \frac{\sin\theta}{\cos\theta} = \frac{\sin\alpha}{\cos\alpha}$$

$$\Leftrightarrow \quad \sin\theta\cos\alpha - \cos\theta\sin\alpha = 0$$

$$\Leftrightarrow \quad \sin(\theta - \alpha) = 0$$

$\Leftrightarrow \quad \theta - \alpha = n\pi, n \in I$

$\Leftrightarrow \quad \theta = n\pi + \alpha, n \in I$

Thus, $\tan\theta = \tan\alpha$

$\Leftrightarrow \quad \theta = n\pi + \alpha$, where $\alpha \in \left(-\frac{\pi}{2}, \frac{\pi}{2}\right)$

Example 7. Find the general solution of trigonometric equation $\tan 3x = -\cot\left(x + \frac{\pi}{6}\right)$.

Sol. Given, $\tan 3x = -\cot\left(x + \frac{\pi}{6}\right)$

$$\Rightarrow \quad \tan 3x = -\cot\left(x + \frac{\pi}{6}\right) = \tan\left(\frac{\pi}{2} + x + \frac{\pi}{6}\right)$$

$$\Rightarrow \quad 3x = n\pi + x + \frac{\pi}{2} + \frac{\pi}{6}$$

$$\Rightarrow \quad 2x = n\pi + \frac{4\pi}{6}$$

$$\text{or} \quad x = \frac{n\pi}{2} + \frac{\pi}{3}, n \in I$$

RESULT 13

$\sin^2\theta = \sin^2\alpha$, $\cos^2\theta = \cos^2\alpha$,
$\tan^2\theta = \tan^2\alpha \Rightarrow \theta = n\pi \pm \alpha$

Explanation

(i) $\sin^2\theta = \sin^2\alpha$

$$\Leftrightarrow \quad \frac{1 - \cos 2\theta}{2} = \frac{1 - \cos 2\alpha}{2}$$

$$\Leftrightarrow \quad \cos 2\theta = \cos 2\alpha \Leftrightarrow 2\theta = 2n\pi \pm 2\alpha, n \in I$$

$$\Leftrightarrow \quad \theta = n\pi \pm \alpha, n \in I$$

(ii) $\cos^2\theta = \cos^2\alpha$

$$\Leftrightarrow \quad \frac{1 + \cos 2\theta}{2} = \frac{1 + \cos 2\alpha}{2}$$

$$\Leftrightarrow \quad \cos 2\theta = \cos 2\alpha$$

$$\Leftrightarrow \quad 2\theta = 2n\pi \pm 2\alpha, n \in I$$

$$\Leftrightarrow \quad \theta = n\pi \pm \alpha, n \in I$$

(iii) $\tan^2\theta = \tan^2\alpha$

$$\Leftrightarrow \quad \frac{1 - \tan^2\theta}{1 + \tan^2\theta} = \frac{1 - \tan^2\alpha}{1 + \tan^2\alpha}$$

[applying componendo and dividendo]

$$\Leftrightarrow \quad \cos 2\theta = \cos 2\alpha \Leftrightarrow 2\theta = 2n\pi \pm 2\alpha, n \in I$$

$$\Leftrightarrow \quad \theta = n\pi \pm \alpha, n \in I$$

JEE Focus Points

Concept Inside Video

- In the above results, α is called principal angle.
- The general solution should be given unless the solution is required in a specified interval or range.
- Union of $(4m+1)\frac{\pi}{2}$ and $(4m-1)\frac{\pi}{2}$ i.e. $\left\{(4m+1)\frac{\pi}{2}\right\} \cup \left\{(4m-1)\frac{\pi}{2}\right\}$ is $(2n+1)\frac{\pi}{2}$, where $m, n \in I$
- Union of $2m\pi$ and $(2m+1)\pi$ is $n\pi$, where $m, n \in I$.

Example 8. Solve the equation $\cos^2\frac{\theta}{2} = \frac{1}{2}$.

Sol. We have, $\cos^2\frac{\theta}{2} = \frac{1}{2} \Rightarrow \cos^2\frac{\theta}{2} = \left(\frac{1}{\sqrt{2}}\right)^2$

$$\Rightarrow \quad \cos^2\frac{\theta}{2} = \cos^2\frac{\pi}{4} \Rightarrow \frac{\theta}{2} = n\pi \pm \frac{\pi}{4}$$

$$\Rightarrow \quad \theta = 2n\pi \pm \frac{\pi}{2}, n \in I$$

Example 9. Solve the equation $7\sin^2\theta + 3\cos^2\theta = 4$.

Sol. We have, $7\sin^2\theta + 3\cos^2\theta = 4$

$$\Rightarrow \quad 7\sin^2\theta + 3(1 - \sin^2\theta) = 4$$

$$\Rightarrow \quad 4\sin^2\theta = 1$$

$$\Rightarrow \quad \sin^2\theta = \frac{1}{4} = \left(\frac{1}{2}\right)^2 = \sin^2\frac{\pi}{6}$$

$$\Rightarrow \quad \sin^2\theta = \sin^2\frac{\pi}{6}$$

$$\Rightarrow \quad \theta = n\pi \pm \frac{\pi}{6}, n \in I$$

Example 10. Solve the equation $\cos^2\left(x + \frac{\pi}{3}\right) = \sin^2\left(\frac{\pi}{3} - x\right)$.

Sol. We have, $\cos^2\left(x + \frac{\pi}{3}\right) = \sin^2\left(\frac{\pi}{3} - x\right)$

$$\Rightarrow \quad \cos^2\left(x + \frac{\pi}{3}\right) = \cos^2\left(\frac{\pi}{2} - \left(\frac{\pi}{3} - x\right)\right)$$

$$\Rightarrow \quad x + \frac{\pi}{3} = n\pi \pm \left[\frac{\pi}{2} - \frac{\pi}{3} + x\right]$$

$$\Rightarrow \quad x + \frac{\pi}{3} = n\pi \pm \frac{\pi}{6} \pm x$$

$$\Rightarrow \quad x + \frac{\pi}{3} = n\pi - \frac{\pi}{6} - x$$

$$\text{or} \quad x + \frac{\pi}{3} = n\pi + \frac{\pi}{6} + x \text{ (ignore)}$$

$$\Rightarrow \quad 2x = n\pi - \frac{\pi}{2} \Rightarrow x = \frac{n\pi}{2} - \frac{\pi}{4}, n \in I$$

Milestone Practice 2.1

1. Find the general and principle solutions of the following equations

(i) $\sin x = \frac{\sqrt{3}}{2}$ (ii) $2\sin x + 1 = 0$ (iii) $\operatorname{cosec} x = 2$

2. Find the general and principle solutions of the following equations

(i) $\cos x = \frac{1}{2}$ (ii) $\cos 3x = -\frac{1}{2}$ (iii) $\sqrt{3}\sec 2x = 2$

3. Solve the following trigonometric equations

(i) $\tan x = \frac{1}{\sqrt{3}}$ (ii) $\tan 2x = \sqrt{3}$ (iii) $\tan 3x = -1$

4. Solve the following trigonometric equations

(i) $\sin\frac{x}{2} = -1$ (ii) $\cos\frac{3x}{2} = \frac{1}{2}$ (iii) $\tan\left(\frac{2}{3}x\right) = \sqrt{3}$

5. The solution of the equation $4\cos^2 x + 6\sin^2 x = 5$ is

(a) $x = n\pi$ (b) $x = n\pi + \frac{\pi}{4}$

(c) $x = n\pi \pm \frac{\pi}{4}$ (d) None of these

6. The solution of the equation $3\sec^2\theta + \tan^2\theta = 5$ is

(a) $\theta = (2n+1)\frac{\pi}{2}$ (b) $\theta = n\pi \pm \frac{\pi}{4}$

(c) $\theta = n\pi \pm \frac{\pi}{6}$ (d) $\theta = n\pi \pm 1$

7. The general solution of the equation $7\cos^2 x + 3\sin^2 x = 4$ is

(a) $x = n\pi \pm \frac{\pi}{4}$ (b) $x = n\pi \pm \frac{\pi}{3}$

(c) $x = n\pi \pm \frac{\pi}{2}$ (d) None of these

8. Solve $2\sin^2 x + \sin^2 2x = 2$.

9. General solution of x for which $\sin 3\alpha = 4\sin\alpha \sin(x+\alpha)\sin(x-\alpha)$, where $\alpha \neq n\pi$, $n \in I$, is

(a) $x = n\pi + (-1)^n\left(\frac{-\pi}{6}\right)$ (b) $x = n\pi \pm \frac{\pi}{2}$

(c) $x = n\pi \pm \frac{\pi}{3}$ (d) None of these

Answer Key

1. (i) $x = n\pi + (-1)^n\frac{\pi}{3}, n \in I$ (ii) $x = n\pi + (-1)^{n+1}\frac{\pi}{6}, n \in I$ (iii) $x = n\pi + (-1)^n\frac{\pi}{6}, n \in I$
2. (i) $x = 2n\pi \pm \frac{\pi}{3}, n \in I$ (ii) $x = \frac{2n\pi}{3} \pm \frac{2\pi}{9}, n \in I$ (iii) $x = n\pi \pm \frac{\pi}{12}, n \in I$
3. (i) $x = n\pi + \frac{\pi}{6}, n \in I$ (ii) $x = \frac{n\pi}{2} + \frac{\pi}{6}, n \in I$ (iii) $x = \frac{n\pi}{3} - \frac{\pi}{12}, n \in I$
4. (i) $x = 2n\pi + (-1)^{n+1}\pi, n \in I$ (ii) $x = \frac{4n\pi}{3} \pm \frac{2\pi}{9}, n \in I$ (iii) $x = \frac{3n\pi}{2} + \frac{\pi}{2}, n \in I$
5. (c) 6. (c) 7. (b) 8. $x = n\pi \pm \frac{\pi}{2}$ or $x = m\pi \pm \frac{\pi}{4}$, where $m, n \in I$ 9. (c)

For Detailed Solution

Milestone 2 Method to Solve Trigonometric Equations

While Solving Equations, Following Points Must be Kept in Mind

(i) Squaring should be avoided as for as possible, if squaring is done check for the extraneous roots.

(ii) Never cancel equal terms containing 'unknown or variable' on two sides which are in product. It may cause root loss.

(iii) The answer should not contain such values of θ which make any of the terms undefined.

(iv) Domain should not change. If it changes, necessary corrections must be made.

(v) Check that denominator is not zero at any stage while solving equations.

TYPE 1

Problems Based on Method of Factorisation.

Working Rule

Step I Take all the terms to LHS i.e. make RHS zero, then factorise LHS.

Step II Equate each factor to zero and solve.

Step III Check for root loss and extraneous roots.

Example 11. Find the principal and general solution of the following equation

$$(2\sin x - \cos x)(1 + \cos x) = \sin^2 x.$$

Sol. We have, $(2\sin x - \cos x)(1+\cos x) = \sin^2 x$

$\Rightarrow (2\sin x - \cos x)(1+\cos x) - \sin^2 x = 0$

$\Rightarrow (2\sin x - \cos x)(1+\cos x) - (1-\cos^2 x) = 0$

$\Rightarrow (1+\cos x)[(2\sin x - \cos x) - (1-\cos x)] = 0$

$\Rightarrow (1+\cos x)[2\sin x - 1] = 0$

$\Rightarrow \cos x + 1 = 0$ or $2\sin x - 1 = 0$

$\Rightarrow \cos x = -1$ or $\sin x = \dfrac{1}{2}$

$\Rightarrow x = (2n+1)\pi, n \in I$ or $x = n\pi + (-1)^n \dfrac{\pi}{6}, n \in I$

Principal Solution

At $n = 0 \Rightarrow x = \pi$

or at $n = 0 \Rightarrow x = \dfrac{\pi}{6}$

At $n = 1 \Rightarrow x = \dfrac{5\pi}{6}$

Principal solutions $= \left\{\dfrac{\pi}{6}, \pi, \dfrac{5\pi}{6}\right\}$.

Example 12. Solve the following equation

$$2\sin^2 2x - 6\cos^2 x + 1 = 0.$$

Sol. We have, $2\sin^2 2x - 6\cos^2 x + 1 = 0$

$\Rightarrow 2[2\sin x \cos x]^2 - 6\cos^2 x + 1 = 0$

$\Rightarrow 8\sin^2 x \cos^2 x - 6\cos^2 x + 1 = 0$

$\Rightarrow 8(1-\cos^2 x)\cos^2 x - 6\cos^2 x + 1 = 0$

$\Rightarrow 8\cos^4 x - 2\cos^2 x - 1 = 0$

Let $\cos^2 x = t \Rightarrow 8t^2 - 2t - 1 = 0 \Rightarrow (4t+1)(2t-1) = 0$

Either $4t + 1 = 0$ or $2t - 1 = 0$

Either $t = -\dfrac{1}{4}$ or $t = \dfrac{1}{2}$

Either $\cos^2 x = -\dfrac{1}{4}$ (not possible)

or $\cos^2 x = \dfrac{1}{2} \Rightarrow \cos^2 x = \left(\dfrac{1}{\sqrt{2}}\right)^2 \Rightarrow \cos^2 x = \cos^2 \dfrac{\pi}{4}$

$$x = n\pi \pm \frac{\pi}{4}, n \in I$$

Example 13. Solve the following equation

$$(1 + \tan\theta)(1 - \sin 2\theta) = (1 - \tan\theta).$$

Sol. We have, $(1+\tan\theta)(1-\sin 2\theta) = (1-\tan\theta)$

$\Rightarrow (1+\tan\theta)\left(1 - \dfrac{2\tan\theta}{1+\tan^2\theta}\right) = (1-\tan\theta)$

$\Rightarrow (1+\tan\theta)\left(\dfrac{\tan^2\theta + 1 - 2\tan\theta}{1+\tan^2\theta}\right) = (1-\tan\theta)$

$\Rightarrow (1+\tan\theta)\dfrac{(1-\tan\theta)^2}{(1+\tan^2\theta)} = (1-\tan\theta)$

$\Rightarrow (1-\tan\theta)\left[\dfrac{(1-\tan^2\theta)}{1+\tan^2\theta} - 1\right] = 0$

$\Rightarrow (1-\tan\theta)(\cos 2\theta - 1) = 0$

Either $\tan\theta = 1$ or $\cos 2\theta = 1$

Either $\theta = n\pi + \frac{\pi}{4}$ or $2\theta = 2n\pi,\ n \in I$

$\Rightarrow \quad \theta = n\pi + \frac{\pi}{4}$ or $\theta = n\pi$ [where, $n \in I$]

Example 14. Find the principal solutions of the following equation

$$16^{\sin^2 x} + 16^{\cos^2 x} = 10.$$

Sol. We have, $16^{\sin^2 x} + 16^{\cos^2 x} = 10$

$\Rightarrow \quad 16^{\sin^2 x} + 16^{(1-\sin^2 x)} = 10$

$\Rightarrow \quad 16^{\sin^2 x} + \frac{16}{16^{\sin^2 x}} = 10$

Let $\quad (16)^{\sin^2 x} = t \Rightarrow t + \frac{16}{t} = 10$

$\Rightarrow \quad t^2 - 10t + 16 = 0 \Rightarrow (t-2)(t-8) = 0$

Either $\quad t = 2$ or $t = 8$

$\Rightarrow \quad (16)^{\sin^2 x} = 2$ or $(16)^{\sin^2 x} = 8$

$\Rightarrow \quad 2^{4\sin^2 x} = 2^1$ or $2^{4\sin^2 x} = 2^3$

$\Rightarrow \quad 4\sin^2 x = 1$ or $4\sin^2 x = 3$

$\Rightarrow \quad \sin^2 x = \left(\frac{1}{2}\right)^2 = \sin^2\frac{\pi}{6}$ or $\sin^2 x = \left(\frac{\sqrt{3}}{2}\right)^2 = \sin^2\frac{\pi}{3}$

$\Rightarrow \quad x = n\pi \pm \frac{\pi}{6},\ n \in I$ or $x = n\pi \pm \frac{\pi}{3},\ n \in I$

Principal solution

$n = 0 \Rightarrow x = \frac{\pi}{6}$ $\qquad n = 0 \Rightarrow x = \frac{\pi}{3}$

$n = 1 \Rightarrow x = \pi \pm \frac{\pi}{6} = \frac{5\pi}{6}, \frac{7\pi}{6}$ $\qquad n = 1 \Rightarrow x = \frac{2\pi}{3}, \frac{4\pi}{3}$

$n = 2 \Rightarrow x = \frac{11\pi}{6}$ $\qquad n = 2 \Rightarrow x = \frac{5\pi}{3}$

$$x = \left\{\frac{\pi}{6}, \frac{\pi}{3}, \frac{2\pi}{3}, \frac{5\pi}{6}, \frac{7\pi}{6}, \frac{4\pi}{3}, \frac{5\pi}{3}, \frac{11\pi}{6}\right\}$$

Example 15. If $x \in (0,1)$, then find the largest root of the equation $\sin(2\pi x) = \sqrt{2}\cos(\pi x)$.

Sol. Given, $\quad \sin(2\pi x) = \sqrt{2}\cos(\pi x)$

$\Rightarrow \quad 2\cdot\sin(\pi x)\cdot\cos(\pi x) = \sqrt{2}\cos(\pi x)$

$\Rightarrow \quad \cos(\pi x)[2\sin(\pi x) - \sqrt{2}] = 0$

$\Rightarrow \quad \cos \pi x = 0$ or $\sin(\pi x) = \frac{1}{\sqrt{2}}$

$\Rightarrow \quad \pi x = \frac{\pi}{2}$ or $\pi x = \frac{\pi}{4}, \frac{3\pi}{4}$ $\quad \begin{bmatrix} \because 0 < x < 1 \\ \therefore 0 < \pi x < \pi \end{bmatrix}$

$\Rightarrow \quad x = \frac{1}{2}, \frac{1}{4}, \frac{3}{4}$

Hence, largest root $= \frac{3}{4}$

JEE SCANNER

Example Similar to PYQ Asked in JEE Main 2017

If $5\operatorname{cosec}^2 x + 6 = -3\sin^2 x - 2$, then the value of $\cos 2x$ is

(a) 3 (b) -3 (c) 2 (d) -1

Sol. (a) Given, $5\operatorname{cosec}^2 x + 6 = -3\sin^2 x - 2$

Let $\quad \sin^2 x = t$

$\Rightarrow \quad \frac{5}{t} + 6 = -3t - 2$

$\Rightarrow \quad \frac{5}{t} = -3t - 8$

$\Rightarrow \quad 5 = -3t^2 - 8t$

$\Rightarrow \quad 3t^2 + 8t + 5 = 0$

$\Rightarrow \quad t = -1$ as $t \neq -\frac{5}{3}$

$\Rightarrow \quad \sin^2 x = -1$

Now, $\quad \cos 2x = 1 - 2\sin^2 x = 1 - 2(-1) = 1 + 2 = 3$

Skill Builder

If $\sin^2\theta - \cos\theta = \frac{1}{4}$ for θ, $0 \le \theta \le 2\pi$, then the value of $\cos 2\theta$ is

(a) $-\frac{1}{2}$ (b) $\frac{1}{2}$

(c) $\frac{1}{4}$ (d) $-\frac{1}{4}$

For Sol.

■ **For more practice** See Q.16 of Milestone Practice 2.

Example 16. If $\sin\alpha$, 1, $\cos 2\alpha$ are in GP, then find the general solution for α.

Sol. Since, $\sin\alpha$, 1, $\cos 2\alpha$ are in GP.

$\therefore \quad 1 = \sin\alpha \cos 2\alpha$

$\Rightarrow \quad 1 = \sin\alpha(1 - 2\sin^2\alpha)$

$\Rightarrow \quad 2\sin^3\alpha - \sin\alpha + 1 = 0$

$\Rightarrow \quad (\sin\alpha + 1)(2\sin^2\alpha - 2\sin\alpha + 1) = 0$

$\Rightarrow \quad \sin\alpha + 1 = 0$ $\quad$ [as $2\sin^2\alpha - 2\sin\alpha + 1 \neq 0$]

$\therefore \quad \sin\alpha = -1$

$\Rightarrow \quad \sin\alpha = \sin\left(-\frac{\pi}{2}\right)$

$\Rightarrow \quad \alpha = n\pi + (-1)^n\left(-\frac{\pi}{2}\right),\ n \in Z$

$\Rightarrow \quad \alpha = n\pi + (-1)^{n+1}\left(\frac{\pi}{2}\right),\ n \in Z$

Example 17. Solve $\sin x = 0$ and $\dfrac{\sin x}{\cos \frac{x}{2} \cos \frac{3x}{2}} = 0$ and show their solutions are different.

Sol. We have, $\sin x = 0 \Rightarrow x = n\pi$

i.e. $\quad x = 0, \pi, 2\pi, 3\pi, \ldots \quad$ ...(i)

whereas,

$$\frac{\sin x}{\cos \frac{x}{2} \cos \frac{3x}{2}} = 0, \text{ where } \cos \frac{x}{2} \neq 0 \text{ and } \cos \frac{3x}{2} \neq 0$$

i.e. $\quad \dfrac{x}{2} \neq \dfrac{\pi}{2}, \dfrac{3\pi}{2}, \dfrac{5\pi}{2}, \ldots$ and $\dfrac{3x}{2} \neq \dfrac{\pi}{2}, \dfrac{3\pi}{2}, \dfrac{5\pi}{2}, \ldots$

i.e. $\quad x \neq \pi, 3\pi, 5\pi, \ldots$ and $\dfrac{\pi}{3}, \pi, \dfrac{5\pi}{3}, \ldots \quad$ ...(ii)

But $\dfrac{\sin x}{\cos \frac{x}{2} \cos \frac{3x}{2}} = 0 \Rightarrow \sin x = 0$

$\Rightarrow \quad x = 0, \pi, 2\pi, 3\pi, 4\pi, \ldots \quad$ ...(iii)

From Eqs. (ii) and (iii),

$x = 0, 2\pi, 4\pi, 6\pi, \ldots \quad$ ...(iv)

From Eqs. (i) and (iv),

The two equations are not equivalent. Since, some solutions of the first do not satisfy the second equation.

Example 18. Find the general solutions of $2^{1 + |\cos x| + |\cos x|^2 + |\cos x|^3 + \ldots \text{ to } \infty} = 4.$

Sol. $2^{1 + |\cos x| + |\cos x|^2 + |\cos x|^3 + \ldots \text{ to } \infty}$

$$\Rightarrow 2^{\left(\frac{1}{1 - |\cos x|}\right)} = 2^2 \Rightarrow \frac{1}{1 - |\cos x|} = 2$$

$$\Rightarrow |\cos x| = \frac{1}{2} \Rightarrow \cos x = \pm \frac{1}{2}$$

$$\therefore x = 2n\pi \pm \frac{\pi}{3}, 2n\pi \pm \left(\pi - \frac{\pi}{3}\right) = 2n\pi \pm \frac{\pi}{3}, (2n \pm 1)\pi \mp \frac{\pi}{3}$$

$$\Rightarrow x = n\pi \pm \frac{\pi}{3}$$

Example 19. Solve the equation $\sin^4 x + \cos^4 x = \dfrac{7}{2} \sin x \cdot \cos x.$

Sol. We have, $\quad \sin^4 x + \cos^4 x = \dfrac{7}{2} \sin x \cdot \cos x$

$$\Rightarrow (\sin^2 x + \cos^2 x)^2 - 2\sin^2 x \cdot \cos^2 x = \frac{7}{2} \sin x \cdot \cos x$$

$$\Rightarrow 1 - \frac{1}{2}(\sin 2x)^2 = \frac{7}{4}(\sin 2x)$$

$$\Rightarrow 2\sin^2 2x + 7\sin 2x - 4 = 0$$

$$\Rightarrow (2\sin 2x - 1)(\sin 2x + 4) = 0$$

$$\Rightarrow \sin 2x = \frac{1}{2} \text{ or } \sin 2x = -4 \text{ (not possible)}$$

$$\Rightarrow 2x = n\pi + (-1)^n \frac{\pi}{6}, n \in I$$

$$\Rightarrow x = \frac{n\pi}{2} + (-1)^n \frac{\pi}{12}, n \in I$$

Example 20. Solve $\dfrac{\sin x + i\cos x}{1 + i}$, $i = \sqrt{-1}$ when it is purely imaginary.

Sol. Here, $\quad \dfrac{\sin x + i\cos x}{1 + i} = \dfrac{(1 - i)(\sin x + i\cos x)}{(1 - i)(1 + i)}$

$$= \frac{\sin x + \cos x + i(\cos x - \sin x)}{2}$$

which will be purely imaginary, if

$\sin x + \cos x = 0$

$$\Rightarrow \tan x = -1 = \tan\left(-\frac{\pi}{4}\right)$$

$$\Rightarrow x = n\pi - \frac{\pi}{4}, \text{ is the general solution.}$$

JEE SCANNER

Example Similar to PYQ Asked in JEE Main 2022

The number of solutions of $|\cos x| = \sin x$, $0 \le x \le 4\pi$ *is*

(a) 4 (b) 6 (c) 10 (d) 8

Sol. (a) **Case I** If $\cos x \ge 0$ i.e. $x \in \left[0, \dfrac{\pi}{2}\right] \cup \left[\dfrac{3\pi}{2}, \dfrac{5\pi}{2}\right] \cup \left[\dfrac{7\pi}{2}, 4\pi\right]$

Then, $\cos x = \sin x$.

$$\Rightarrow \tan x = 1 \Rightarrow x = n\pi + \frac{\pi}{4} = \frac{\pi}{4}, \frac{5\pi}{4}, \frac{9\pi}{4}, \frac{13\pi}{4}$$

$\therefore$ If $\cos x \ge 0$, the possible values of x are $\dfrac{\pi}{4}, \dfrac{9\pi}{4}$.

Case II If $\cos x < 0$ i.e. $x \in \left(\dfrac{\pi}{2}, \dfrac{3\pi}{2}\right) \cup \left(\dfrac{5\pi}{2}, \dfrac{7\pi}{2}\right)$, then

$-\cos x = \sin x$

$$\Rightarrow \tan x = -1 \Rightarrow x = n\pi - \frac{\pi}{4} = \frac{3\pi}{4}, \frac{7\pi}{4}, \frac{11\pi}{4}, \frac{15\pi}{4}$$

$\therefore$ If $\cos x < 0$, the possible values of x are $\dfrac{3\pi}{4}, \dfrac{11\pi}{4}$.

Thus, the possible number of solutions are 4.

Skill Builder

The number of solutions of θ in the interval $[0, 4\pi]$ satisfying the equation $2\sin^2 \theta - \cos 2\theta = 0$ is

(a) 4 (b) 6
(c) 8 (d) 10

For Sol.

■ **For more practice** See Q.3 of Milestone Practice 2.

TYPE 2
Problems Based on Use of Quadratic Formula

Equation in quadratic form can be simplified by using quadratic formula.

Working rule

Step I Take all the terms to LHS i.e. make RHS zero.

Step II Then, use the quadratic formula to solve the given quadratic equation.

Step III Check for root loss and extraneous roots.

Example 21. Solve
$$3\cos^2\theta - 2\sqrt{3}\sin\theta\cos\theta - 3\sin^2\theta = 0.$$

Sol. The given equation can be written as $(\cos\theta \neq 0)$

$$3\tan^2\theta + 2\sqrt{3}\tan\theta - 3 = 0$$

$$\Rightarrow \quad \tan\theta = \frac{-2\sqrt{3} \pm \sqrt{12+36}}{6}$$

$$= \frac{-2\sqrt{3} \pm 4\sqrt{3}}{6} = \frac{1}{\sqrt{3}}, -\sqrt{3}$$

Either $\quad \tan\theta = \frac{1}{\sqrt{3}} = \tan\frac{\pi}{6}$

$$\Rightarrow \quad \theta = n\pi + \frac{\pi}{6}, n \in I$$

or $\quad \tan\theta = -\sqrt{3} = \tan\left(-\frac{\pi}{3}\right) \Rightarrow \theta = n\pi - \frac{\pi}{3}, n \in I$

Example 22. Solve $2\cos^2 x + 4\cos x = 3\sin^2 x$.

Sol. We have, $2\cos^2 x + 4\cos x = 3\sin^2 x$

$$\Rightarrow \quad 2\cos^2 x + 4\cos x = 3(1-\cos^2 x)$$

$$\Rightarrow \quad 5\cos^2 x + 4\cos x - 3 = 0$$

$$\Rightarrow \quad \cos x = \frac{-4 \pm \sqrt{16+60}}{2\times 5}$$

$$= \frac{-4 \pm \sqrt{76}}{10} = \frac{-4 \pm 2\sqrt{19}}{2\times 5}$$

$$\Rightarrow \quad \cos x = \frac{-2 \pm \sqrt{19}}{5}$$

Either $\cos x = \frac{-2-\sqrt{19}}{5} \Rightarrow \cos x < -1$ (not possible)

or $\quad \cos x = \frac{-2+\sqrt{19}}{5} = \frac{\sqrt{19}-2}{5}$

Let $\quad \cos\alpha = \frac{\sqrt{19}-2}{5}$

$$\cos x = \cos\alpha$$

$$x = 2n\pi \pm \alpha,$$

where $n \in I$ and $\alpha = \cos^{-1}\left(\frac{\sqrt{19}-2}{5}\right)$

TYPE 3
Problem Based on Use of Transformation Formula

Working rule

Step I Take all the terms to LHS i.e. make RHS zero.

Step II Then, use the transformation formula and then factorise LHS.

Step III Equate each factor to zero and solve.

Example 23. Solve the equation $\sin x + \sin 3x + \sin 5x = 0$.

Sol. We have, $\sin x + \sin 3x + \sin 5x = 0$

$$\Rightarrow \quad (\sin 5x + \sin x) + \sin 3x = 0$$

$$\Rightarrow \quad 2\sin 3x\cos 2x + \sin 3x = 0$$

$$\Rightarrow \quad \sin 3x(2\cos 2x + 1) = 0$$

$$\Rightarrow \quad \sin 3x = 0 \text{ or } \cos 2x = \frac{-1}{2}$$

Now, $\quad \sin 3x = 0 \Rightarrow 3x = n\pi$

$$\Rightarrow \quad x = \frac{n\pi}{3}, n \in I$$

and $\quad \cos 2x = -\frac{1}{2}$

$$\Rightarrow \quad \cos 2x = \cos\frac{2\pi}{3}$$

$$\Rightarrow \quad 2x = 2m\pi \pm \frac{2\pi}{3}, m \in I$$

$$\Rightarrow \quad x = m\pi \pm \frac{\pi}{3}, m \in I$$

Hence, the general solution of the given equation is

$x = \frac{n\pi}{3}$ or $x = m\pi \pm \frac{\pi}{3}$, where $m, n \in I$.

Example 24. Solve the equation $\cos x + \cos 3x - 2\cos 2x = 0$.

Sol. We have, $\cos x + \cos 3x - 2\cos 2x = 0$

$$\Rightarrow \quad 2\cos 2x\cos x - 2\cos 2x = 0$$

$$\Rightarrow \quad 2\cos 2x(\cos x - 1) = 0$$

$$\Rightarrow \quad \cos 2x = 0 \text{ or } \cos x - 1 = 0$$

Now, $\quad \cos 2x = 0$

$$\Rightarrow \quad 2x = (2n+1)\frac{\pi}{2}, n \in I$$

$$\Rightarrow \quad x = (2n+1)\frac{\pi}{4}, n \in I$$

and $\quad \cos x - 1 = 0$

$$\Rightarrow \quad \cos x = 1 = \cos 0$$

$$\Rightarrow \quad x = 2m\pi \pm 0, m \in I$$

$$\Rightarrow \quad x = 2m\pi, m \in I$$

Hence, $x = (2n+1)\frac{\pi}{4}$ or $x = 2m\pi$, where $m, n \in I$

Example 25. Find the sum of all solutions of $\cos x \cos\left(x+\frac{\pi}{3}\right)\cos\left(\frac{\pi}{3}-x\right)=\frac{1}{4}$, $x \in [0, 6\pi]$

Sol. We have, $\cos x \cos\left(\frac{\pi}{3}+x\right)\cos\left(\frac{\pi}{3}-x\right)=\frac{1}{4}$

$$\Rightarrow \quad \frac{1}{4}\cos 3x = \frac{1}{4}$$

$$\left[\because \cos x \cos\left(\frac{\pi}{3}+x\right)\cos\left(\frac{\pi}{3}-x\right)=\frac{1}{4}\cos 3x\right]$$

$$\Rightarrow \quad \cos 3x = 1 \Rightarrow \cos 3x = \cos 0$$

$$\Rightarrow \quad 3x = 2n\pi,\ n \in I$$

$$\Rightarrow \quad x = \frac{2n\pi}{3}, n \in I$$

But $x \in [0, 6\pi]$.

Therefore, $x = 0, \frac{2\pi}{3}, \frac{4\pi}{3}, \frac{8\pi}{3}, \ldots, \frac{18\pi}{3}$

Sum of all these solutions $= 0 + \frac{2\pi}{3} + \frac{4\pi}{3} + \ldots + \frac{18\pi}{3}$

$$= \frac{2\pi}{3}(1+2+3+\ldots 9)$$

$$= \frac{2\pi}{3} \times \frac{9 \times 10}{2} = 30\pi$$

Hence, required sum $= 30\pi$

JEE SCANNER

Example Similar to PYQ Asked in JEE Main 2022

The number of solutions of $\tan x + \sec x = 2\cos x$ *in* $[0, 2\pi]$ *is*

(a) 2 (b) 4 (c) 6 (d) 10

Sol. Here, $\tan x + \sec x = 2\cos x \Rightarrow \sin x + 1 = 2\cos^2 x$

$$\Rightarrow \quad 2\sin^2 x + \sin x - 1 = 0 \Rightarrow \sin x = \frac{1}{2}, -1$$

But $\sin x = -1 \Rightarrow x = \frac{3\pi}{2}$ which does not satisfy $\tan x + \sec x = 2\cos x$.

Thus, $\sin x = \frac{1}{2} \Rightarrow x = \frac{\pi}{6}, \frac{5\pi}{6}$

Number of solutions of $\tan x + \sec x = 2\cos x$ is 2.

Skill Builder

The number of solutions of the equation $|\cos x - \sin x| = 2\cos x$ in $[0, 2\pi]$ is

(a) 1 (b) 2
(c) 3 (d) 4

For Sol.

▪ **For more practice** See Q.18 of Milestone Practice 2.

Example 26. Find the sum of all values of x in $[0, \pi]$ for which $\sin x + \sin 2x + \sin 3x + \sin 4x = 0$.

Sol. We have, $\sin x + \sin 2x + \sin 3x + \sin 4x = 0$

$$\Rightarrow \quad (\sin x + \sin 3x) + (\sin 2x + \sin 4x) = 0$$

$$\Rightarrow \quad 2\cdot\sin 2x \cdot \cos x + 2\sin 3x \cdot \cos x = 0$$

$$\Rightarrow \quad 2\cos x(\sin 2x + \sin 3x) = 0$$

$$\Rightarrow \quad 2\cdot\cos x \cdot 2\cdot\sin\frac{5x}{2}\cdot\cos\frac{x}{2} = 0$$

When $\cos x = 0 \Rightarrow x = \frac{\pi}{2} \in [0, \pi]$

When $\sin\frac{5x}{2} = 0 \Rightarrow x = 0, \frac{2\pi}{5}, \frac{4\pi}{5} \in [0, \pi]$

When $\cos\frac{x}{2} = 0 \Rightarrow x = \pi \in [0, \pi]$

$\therefore$ Its sum $= \frac{\pi}{2} + 0 + \frac{2\pi}{5} + \frac{4\pi}{5} + \pi$

$$= \frac{5\pi + 4\pi + 8\pi + 10\pi}{10} = \frac{27\pi}{10}$$

Example 27. Solve
$5\sin x + 6\sin 2x + 5\sin 3x + \sin 4x = 0$.

Sol. We have, $5(\sin x + \sin 3x) + 6\sin 2x + \sin 4x = 0$

$$\Rightarrow \quad 5(2\sin 2x \cos x) + 6\sin 2x + \sin 4x = 0$$

$$\Rightarrow \quad 10\sin 2x \cos x + 6\sin 2x + \sin 4x = 0$$

$$\Rightarrow \quad 2\sin 2x[5\cos x + 3 + \cos 2x] = 0$$

$$\Rightarrow \quad 2\sin 2x[5\cos x + 3 + 2\cos^2 x - 1] = 0$$

$$\Rightarrow \quad 2\sin 2x[2\cos^2 x + 5\cos x + 2] = 0$$

$$\Rightarrow \quad 2\sin 2x(2\cos^2 x + 4\cos x + \cos x + 2) = 0$$

$$\Rightarrow \quad 2\sin 2x(2\cos x + 1)(\cos x + 2) = 0$$

Either $\sin 2x = 0 \Rightarrow 2x = n\pi, n \in I \Rightarrow x = \frac{n\pi}{2}, n \in I$

or $\cos x = -\frac{1}{2} \Rightarrow x = 2n\pi \pm \frac{2\pi}{3}; n \in I$

Example 28. Solve
$\cos^2 x + \cos^2 2x + \cos^2 3x + \cos^2 4x = 2$.

Sol. We have, $\cos^2 x + \cos^2 2x + \cos^2 3x + \cos^2 4x = 2$

$$\Rightarrow \quad (\cos^2 x - 1) + (\cos^2 2x - 1) + \cos^2 3x + \cos^2 4x = 0$$

$$\Rightarrow \quad -\sin^2 x - \sin^2 2x + \cos^2 3x + \cos^2 4x = 0$$

$$\Rightarrow \quad (\cos^2 3x - \sin^2 x) + (\cos^2 4x - \sin^2 2x) = 0$$

$$\Rightarrow \quad (\cos 4x \cdot \cos 2x) + (\cos 6x \cdot \cos 2x) = 0$$

$$\Rightarrow \quad \cos 2x(\cos 4x + \cos 6x) = 0$$

$$\Rightarrow \quad \cos 2x \cdot (2\cos(5x)\cos(x)) = 0$$

$$\Rightarrow \quad 2\cos x \cos 2x \cos 5x = 0$$

Either $\cos x = 0 \Rightarrow x = (2n+1)\frac{\pi}{2}, n \in I$

or $\cos 2x = 0 \Rightarrow 2x = (2n+1)\frac{\pi}{2}, n \in I$

$$\Rightarrow \quad x = (2n+1)\frac{\pi}{4}, n \in I$$

or $\cos 5x = 0 \Rightarrow 5x = (2n+1)\frac{\pi}{2}, n \in I$

$$\Rightarrow \quad x = (2n+1)\frac{\pi}{10}, n \in I$$

Example 29. Solve $\sqrt{1+\cos x} = \sin x$.

Sol. We have, $\sqrt{1+\cos x} = \sin x$ ...(i)

On squaring both sides, we get

$$1+\cos x = \sin^2 x = 1-\cos^2 x \Rightarrow \cos x = -\cos^2 x$$

$\Rightarrow \quad \cos x + \cos^2 x = 0 \Rightarrow \cos x(1+\cos x) = 0$

$\Rightarrow \quad \cos x = 0$ or $\cos x = -1$

$\Rightarrow \quad x = (2n+1)\frac{\pi}{2}$ or $x = (2n+1)\pi, n \in I$

Now, when $x = (2n+1)\frac{\pi}{2}, n \in I$

$(4m+1)\frac{\pi}{2}, m \in I$ $\quad$ $(4m-1)\frac{\pi}{2}, m \in I$

(extraneous root)

Let's verify this, when $x = (4m+1)\frac{\pi}{2}, m \in I$, then

$$\sqrt{1+\cos(4m+1)\frac{\pi}{2}} = \sin(4m+1)\frac{\pi}{2}$$

$\Rightarrow \quad \sqrt{1+0} = 1 \Rightarrow 1 = 1$, which is true.

But when $x = (4m-1)\frac{\pi}{2}, m \in I$, then

$$\sqrt{1+\cos(4m-1)\frac{\pi}{2}} = -\sin(4m-1)\frac{\pi}{2}$$

$\Rightarrow \quad \sqrt{1+0} = -1 \Rightarrow 1 = -1$, which is absurd.

TYPE 4

Problem Based on Use of Converting Product to Sum or Difference

Working rule

Step I Take all the terms to LHS i.e. make RHS zero.

Step II Then, convert product to sum or difference and simplify the equation.

Step III Then, take common term outside and make factor.

Step IV Equate each factor equal to zero and check the roots.

Example 30. Solve $\sin 5x \cdot \cos 3x = \sin 6x \cdot \cos 2x$

Sol. We have, $\quad 2\sin 5x \cdot \cos 3x = 2\sin 6x \cdot \cos 2x$

$\Rightarrow \quad \sin 8x + \sin 2x = \sin 8x + \sin 4x$

$\Rightarrow \quad \sin 2x - \sin 4x = 0$

$\Rightarrow \quad \sin 2x - 2\sin 2x \cos 2x = 0 \Rightarrow \sin 2x(1-2\cos 2x) = 0$

Either $\sin 2x = 0 \Rightarrow 2x = n\pi, n \in I$

$\Rightarrow \quad x = \frac{n\pi}{2}, n \in I$ or $\cos 2x = \frac{1}{2}$

$\Rightarrow \quad 2x = 2n\pi \pm \frac{\pi}{3}, n \in I \Rightarrow x = n\pi \pm \frac{\pi}{6}, n \in I$

Example 31. Find the number of solutions for $\sin 5\theta \cdot \cos 3\theta = \sin 9\theta \cdot \cos 7\theta$ in $\left[0, \frac{\pi}{2}\right]$.

Sol. Here, $\quad 2\sin 5\theta \cdot \cos 3\theta = 2\sin 9\theta \cdot \cos 7\theta$

$\Rightarrow \quad \sin 8\theta + \sin 2\theta = \sin 16\theta + \sin 2\theta$

$\Rightarrow \quad \sin 8\theta = \sin 16\theta \Rightarrow \sin 16\theta = \sin 8\theta$

$\therefore \quad 16\theta = n\pi + (-1)^n 8\theta$ ...(i)

when n is even Eq. (i) becomes;

$8\theta = n\pi \Rightarrow \theta = \frac{n\pi}{8}$ ...(ii)

when n is odd Eq. (i) becomes;

$24\theta = n\pi \Rightarrow \theta = \frac{n\pi}{24}$ ...(iii)

$\therefore$ For the given interval $\left[0, \frac{\pi}{2}\right]$ Eqs. (ii) and (iii) gives the solution as,

$$\theta = 0, \frac{\pi}{4}, \frac{\pi}{2} \text{ and } \frac{\pi}{24}, \frac{\pi}{8}, \frac{5\pi}{24}, \frac{7\pi}{24}, \frac{3\pi}{8}, \frac{11\pi}{24}$$

$\therefore$ Number of solutions is 9.

Example 32. Solve $\cos x = \cos^2 x$.

Sol. We have, $\cos x = \cos^2 x$

Incorrect approach $\cos x = \cos x \cdot \cos x$

$\Rightarrow \quad \cos x = 1 \Rightarrow x = 2n\pi, n \in I$

Correct approach $\cos x - \cos^2 x = 0 \Rightarrow \cos x(1-\cos x) = 0$

$\Rightarrow \quad \cos x = 0$ or $\cos x = 1$

$\Rightarrow \quad x = (2n+1)\frac{\pi}{2}, n \in I$ or $x = 2n\pi, n \in I$

Example 33. Solve $\cos x \cdot \tan x = \cos x$.

Sol. We have, $\cos x \cdot \tan x = \cos x \Rightarrow \cos x(\tan x - 1) = 0$

$\Rightarrow \quad \cos x = 0$ or $\tan x = 1 = \tan\frac{\pi}{4}$

$\Rightarrow \quad x = (2n+1)\frac{\pi}{2}, n \in I$ or $x = n\pi + \frac{\pi}{4}, n \in I$

Here, $x = (2n+1)\frac{\pi}{2}, n \in I$ [rejected]

Because $\tan x$ is not defined at $x = (2n+1)\frac{\pi}{2}, n \in I$.

Example 34. Solve $\sqrt{5-2\sin x} = 6\sin x - 1$.

Sol. We have, $\sqrt{5-2\sin x} = 6\sin x - 1$ ...(i)

On squaring both sides, we get

$$5-2\sin x = 36\sin^2 x - 12\sin x + 1$$

$\Rightarrow \quad 18\sin^2 x - 5\sin x - 2 = 0$

$\Rightarrow (9\sin x + 2)(2\sin x - 1) = 0$

$\Rightarrow \quad \sin x = \frac{1}{2}$ or $\sin x = -\frac{2}{9}$ ...(ii)

But we observe that Eq. (i) will be meaningful, if

$$5 - 2\sin x \geq 0$$

$\Rightarrow \quad \sin x \leq \frac{5}{2} \Rightarrow x \in R$

i.e. domain of Eq. (i) is $x \in R$.

But $\sqrt{5-2\sin x} > 0 \; \forall x \in R$.

So, $6\sin x - 1 > 0 \Rightarrow \sin x > \frac{1}{6}$

i.e. Any x for which $\sin x \le \frac{1}{6}$ cannot be solution.

From Eq. (ii), $\sin x = -\frac{2}{9}$ [rejected]

Hence, $\sin x = \frac{1}{2} \Rightarrow x = n\pi + (-1)^n \frac{\pi}{6}, n \in I$

Example 35. If $x \neq \frac{n\pi}{2}$ and $(\cos x)^{\sin^2 x - 3\sin x + 2} = 1$, then find the general solutions of x.

Sol. As $x \neq \frac{n\pi}{2} \Rightarrow \cos x \neq 0, 1, -1$

So, $(\cos x)^{\sin^2 x - 3\sin x + 2} = 1 \Rightarrow \sin^2 x - 3\sin x + 2 = 0$

$\therefore \quad (\sin x - 2)(\sin x - 1) = 0 \Rightarrow \sin x = 1, 2$

where, $\sin x = 2$ is not possible and $\sin x = 1$ does not satisfy the equation.

$\therefore$ No general solution is possible.

Example 36. Find the set of values of x for which $\frac{\tan 3x - \tan 2x}{1 + \tan 3x \cdot \tan 2x} = 1$.

Sol. We have, $\frac{\tan 3x - \tan 2x}{1 + \tan 3x \cdot \tan 2x} = 1 \Rightarrow \tan(3x - 2x) = 1$

$$\Rightarrow \quad \tan x = 1 \Rightarrow \tan x = \tan\frac{\pi}{4}$$

$$\Rightarrow \quad x = n\pi + \frac{\pi}{4}$$

[using $\tan\theta = \tan\alpha \Leftrightarrow \theta = n\pi + \alpha$]

But for this value of x,

$\tan 2x = \tan\left(2n\pi + \frac{\pi}{2}\right) = \infty$, which does not satisfy the given equation as it reduces to indeterminate form.

Hence, the solution set for x is ϕ.

Example 37. Solve $\cot\theta = \sin 2\theta$ by substituting $\sin 2\theta = \frac{2\tan\theta}{1+\tan^2\theta}$ and again by substituting $\sin 2\theta = 2\sin\theta \cdot \cos\theta$ and check whether the two answer are same or not.

Sol. Method I Put $\sin 2\theta = \frac{2\tan\theta}{1+\tan^2\theta}$

$$\therefore \quad \cot\theta = \sin 2\theta$$

$$\Rightarrow \quad \cot\theta = \frac{2\tan\theta}{1+\tan^2\theta} \Rightarrow \frac{1}{\tan\theta} = \frac{2\tan\theta}{1+\tan^2\theta}$$

$$\Rightarrow \quad 2\tan^2\theta = 1 + \tan^2\theta \Rightarrow \tan^2\theta = 1$$

$$\Rightarrow \quad \tan^2\theta = (1)^2 = \tan^2\frac{\pi}{4} \Rightarrow \theta = n\pi \pm \frac{\pi}{4} \quad \text{...(i)}$$

Method II Put $\sin 2\theta = 2\sin\theta\cos\theta$

$$\therefore \quad \cot\theta = \sin 2\theta \Rightarrow \frac{\cos\theta}{\sin\theta} = 2\sin\theta\cos\theta$$

$$\Rightarrow \quad \cos\theta = 2\sin^2\theta\cos\theta \Rightarrow \cos\theta(1 - 2\sin^2\theta) = 0$$

$$\Rightarrow \quad \cos\theta = 0 \text{ or } \sin^2\theta = \frac{1}{2} = \left(\frac{1}{\sqrt{2}}\right)^2 = \sin^2\frac{\pi}{4}$$

$$\Rightarrow \quad \theta = (2n+1)\frac{\pi}{2} \text{ or } \theta = n\pi \pm \frac{\pi}{4} \quad \text{...(ii)}$$

From Eqs. (i) and (ii), it is clear, first method gives less number of roots than the second method.

Caution As far as possible, avoid the use of following formulae

$$\sin 2x = \frac{2\tan x}{1+\tan^2 x}, \cos 2x = \frac{1-\tan^2 x}{1+\tan^2 x},$$

$$\tan 2x = \frac{2\tan x}{1-\tan^2 x} \text{ and } \tan 3x = \frac{3\tan x - \tan^3 x}{1 - 3\tan^2 x}$$

As these formulae are not defined for some real values of x. Hence, in many cases the solution obtained with use of these formulae may not be the complete solutions set of the given equation.

Example 38. If λ is the total number of solutions of the equation $\cos x \cdot \cos 2x \cdot \cos 3x = \frac{1}{4}$ in $[0, \pi]$, then find the value of $\left(\left[\lambda - \frac{3}{2}\right]\right)! + 4$, $[\cdot]$ denotes GIF and (!) denotes factorial.

Sol. Given, $\cos x \cdot \cos 2x \cdot \cos 3x = \frac{1}{4}$

$$\Rightarrow \quad 4\cos 3x \cdot \cos x \cdot \cos 2x = 1$$

$$\Rightarrow \quad 2(\cos 4x + \cos 2x) \cdot \cos 2x = 1$$

$$\Rightarrow \quad 2(2\cos^2 2x - 1 + \cos 2x) \cdot \cos 2x = 1$$

$$\Rightarrow \quad 4\cos^3 2x + 2\cos^2 2x - 2\cos 2x - 1 = 0$$

$$\Rightarrow \quad 2\cos^2 2x(2\cos 2x + 1) - (2\cos 2x + 1) = 0$$

$$\Rightarrow \quad (2\cos 2x + 1)(2\cos^2 2x - 1) = 0$$

$$\Rightarrow \quad \cos 4x(2\cos 2x + 1) = 0$$

$$\Rightarrow \quad \cos 4x = 0 \text{ or } \cos 2x = -\frac{1}{2}$$

$$\Rightarrow \quad 4x = (2K+1)\frac{\pi}{2}, K \in I \text{ or } 2x = 2m\pi \pm \frac{2\pi}{3}, m \in I$$

$$\Rightarrow \quad x = (2K+1)\frac{\pi}{8}, K \in I \text{ or } x = m\pi \pm \frac{\pi}{3}, m \in I$$

$$\Rightarrow \quad x = \frac{\pi}{8}, \frac{3\pi}{8}, \frac{5\pi}{8}, \frac{7\pi}{8} \in [0, \pi] \text{ or } x = \frac{\pi}{3}, \frac{2\pi}{3} \in [0, \pi]$$

Hence, total number of solutions $= 6 = \lambda$ [given]

Now, $\left[6 - \frac{3}{2}\right] = [6 - 1.5] = [4.5] = 4$

Thus, $4 + 4! = (4 \times 3 \times 2 \times 1) + 4 = 24 + 4 = 28$

Milestone Practice 2.2

1. Solve $\tan^2\theta + \cot^2\theta = 2$.
2. Solve $2^{\cos 2x} + 1 = 3 \cdot 2^{-\sin^2 x}$.
3. The number of solutions of the equation $\cot^2(\sin x + 3) = 1$ in $[0, 3\pi]$, is
   (a) 6 (b) 8 (c) 9 (d) 10
4. Solve $\sin^3\theta\cos\theta - \cos^3\theta\sin\theta = \frac{1}{4}$.
5. The solution of the equation $\dfrac{\sin^3\frac{x}{2} - \cos^3\frac{x}{2}}{2 + \sin x} = \dfrac{\cos x}{3}$ is
   (a) $2n\pi - \frac{\pi}{2}$ (b) $2n\pi + \frac{\pi}{4}$ (c) $\frac{2n\pi + \pi}{2}$ (d) $2n\pi + \frac{\pi}{2}$
6. Solve $\dfrac{\sqrt{5} - 1}{\sin x} + \dfrac{\sqrt{10 + 2\sqrt{5}}}{\cos x} = 8,\ x \in \left(0, \frac{\pi}{2}\right)$.
7. Solve $\sin^2 n\theta - \sin^2(n-1)\theta = \sin^2\theta$.
8. Solve $(\sin 10°)^{\tan x + \tan 3x}$
   $= \tan 15° + \tan 30° + \tan 15° \tan 30°,\ x \in (0, \pi]$.
9. The least positive value of θ for which $(\cos\theta + \cos 2\theta)^3 = \cos^3\theta + \cos^3 2\theta$, is
   (a) $\frac{\pi}{6}$ (b) $\frac{\pi}{3}$ (c) $\frac{\pi}{4}$ (d) $\frac{\pi}{2}$
10. Solve the equation $\frac{\sqrt{3}}{2}\sin x - \cos x = \cos^2 x$.
11. Solve $8\sin x = \dfrac{\sqrt{3}}{\cos x} + \dfrac{1}{\sin x}$.
12. If $\cos p\theta + \cos q\theta = 0$, then prove that the different values of θ are in AP with common difference $2\pi/(p \pm q)$.
13. If $\tan a\theta - \tan b\theta = 0$, then prove that the values of θ forms on AP.
14. Solve $\log_{\tan x}(2 + 4\cos^2 x) = 2$.
15. If $2\tan^2 x - 5\sec x$ is equal to 1 for exactly 7 distinct values of $x \in \left[0, \frac{n\pi}{2}\right], n \in N$, then the greatest value of n is
    (a) 10 (b) 15 (c) 20 (d) 25
16. If $\tan\theta + \tan\left(\frac{3\pi}{4} + \theta\right) = 2$, then find the value of $\cos 2\theta$.
17. If the equation $x^2 + 4x\sin\theta + \tan\theta = 0 \left(0 < \theta < \frac{\pi}{2}\right)$ has repeated roots, then the value of θ is
    (a) $\frac{\pi}{6}$ (b) $\frac{\pi}{12}$ (c) $\frac{\pi}{12}$ or $\frac{5\pi}{12}$ (d) $\frac{\pi}{6}$ or $\frac{\pi}{3}$
18. The number of solutions of the equation $2\sin^3 x + 6\sin^2 x - \sin x - 3 = 0$ in $(0, 2\pi)$, is
    (a) 3 (b) 4 (c) 5 (d) 6
19. The number of roots of the equation $16\sec^3\theta - 12\tan^2\theta - 4\sec\theta = 9$ in interval $(-\pi, \pi)$, is
    (a) 0 (b) 1 (c) 2 (d) 3
20. Solve
    $\tan^2 x \tan^2 3x \tan 4x = \tan^2 x - \tan^2 3x + \tan 4x$.
21. Solve $\sin 3\alpha = 4\sin\alpha\sin(x + \alpha)\sin(x - \alpha)$, where $\alpha \neq n\pi, n \in I$.
22. If $x \in [0, 2\pi)$, then find the number of real values of x which satisfy the equation $\cos x + \cos 2x + \cos 3x + \cos 4x = 0$.
23. If $0 \le x \le \frac{\pi}{2}$ and $81^{\sin^2 x} + 81^{\cos^2 x} = 30$, then the values of x is
    (a) $\frac{\pi}{3}$ (b) $\frac{\pi}{6}$ (c) $\frac{\pi}{12}$ (d) Both (a) and (b)

Answer Key

1. $n\pi \pm \frac{\pi}{4}, n \in I$ 2. $n\pi$ or $n\pi \pm \frac{\pi}{2}, n \in I$ 3. (a) 4. $\frac{n\pi}{2} - \frac{\pi}{8}, n \in I$ 5. (d) 6. $\frac{\pi}{10}$ or $\frac{3\pi}{10}$
7. $k\pi, \frac{p\pi}{n-1}, \frac{(2q+1)\pi}{2n}; k, p, q, n \in I$ 8. $\frac{\pi}{4}, \frac{3\pi}{4}, \pi$ 9. (c) 10. $x = (2n+1)\pi$ or $2n\pi \pm \frac{\pi}{3}, n \in I$
11. $n\pi + \frac{\pi}{6}$ or $\frac{n\pi}{2} - \frac{\pi}{12}, n \in I$ 14. $n\pi + \frac{\pi}{3}, n \in I$ 15. (b) 16. $-\frac{1}{2}$ 17. (c)
18. (b) 19. (a) 20. $x = \frac{n\pi}{4}$ or $2x = n\pi + \frac{\pi}{4}$ or $x = \frac{n\pi}{2} + \frac{\pi}{8}, n \in I$
21. $x = n\pi \pm \frac{\pi}{3}, n \in I$ 22. 7 23. (d)

For Detailed Solution

Milestone 3 Solution of Simultaneous Trigonometric Equations

- Equation of the Form $a \cos\theta + b \sin\theta = c$ • Solution of Simultaneous Trigonometric Equations

2.3 Equation of the Form $a\cos\theta + b\sin\theta = c$

TYPE 5

Problem Based on Equation of the Form $a\cos\theta + b\sin\theta = c$

Working rule

To solve the equation $a\cos\theta + b\sin\theta = c$, put $a = r\cos\phi$ and $b = r\sin\phi$, where $r = \sqrt{a^2+b^2}$ and $\phi = \tan^{-1}\dfrac{b}{a}$

Substituting these values in the equation, we get

$r\cos\phi\cos\theta + r\sin\phi\sin\theta = c$

$\Rightarrow \quad \cos(\theta-\phi) = \dfrac{c}{r} \Rightarrow \cos(\theta-\phi) = \dfrac{c}{\sqrt{a^2+b^2}}$

If $|c| > \sqrt{a^2+b^2}$, then the equation $a\cos\theta + b\sin\theta = c$ has no solution.

If $|c| \le \sqrt{a^2+b^2}$, then put $\dfrac{|c|}{\sqrt{a^2+b^2}} = \cos\alpha$, so that

$\cos(\theta-\phi) = \cos\alpha \Rightarrow (\theta-\phi) = 2n\pi \pm \alpha$

$\Rightarrow \quad \theta = 2n\pi \pm \alpha + \phi$, where $n \in I$

How to Solve

Step I Check whether $|c| \le \sqrt{a^2+b^2}$ or not. If it is not satisfied, no real solution exists.

Step II If the above condition is satisfied, divide both sides of the equation by $\sqrt{a^2+b^2}$.

Example 39. Check whether the equation $3\cos x + 4\sin x = 6$ has solution or not .

Sol. Method I Given equation is

$$3\cos x + 4\sin x = 6 \quad \text{...(i)}$$

Here, $|6| \le \sqrt{3^2+4^2}$ does not satisfy.

So, Eq. (i) has no solution.

Method II Given, $3\cos x + 4\sin x = 6$

$$\Rightarrow \quad \frac{3}{5}\cos x + \frac{4}{5}\sin x = \frac{6}{5}$$

$$\Rightarrow \quad \cos(x-\alpha) = \frac{6}{5},$$

where $\alpha = \cos^{-1}\left(\dfrac{3}{5}\right)$

which is not possible because $\dfrac{6}{5} > 1$ and $-1 \le \cos(x-\alpha) \le 1$.

Hence, no solution.

Example 40. Find the range of k for which the equation $k\cos x - 3\sin x = k+1$ is solvable.

Sol. Given, $k\cos x - 3\sin x = k+1$ is solvable, if

$$|k+1| \le \sqrt{k^2+(-3)^2}$$

$$\Rightarrow \quad (k+1)^2 \le k^2+9$$

$$\Rightarrow \quad k^2+2k+1 \le k^2+9 \Rightarrow k \le 4$$

Thus, the interval in which, $k\cos x - 3\sin x = k+1$ admits solution for k is $(-\infty, 4]$.

Example 41. Find the number of distinct solutions of $\sec x + \tan x = \sqrt{3}$, where $0 \le x \le 3\pi$.

Sol. Here, we have $\sec x + \tan x = \sqrt{3}$

$$\Rightarrow \quad 1+\sin x = \sqrt{3}\cos x$$

or $$\sqrt{3}\cos x - \sin x = 1$$

On dividing both sides by $\sqrt{a^2+b^2}$ i.e. $\sqrt{4} = 2$, we get

$$\Rightarrow \quad \frac{\sqrt{3}}{2}\cos x - \frac{1}{2}\sin x = \frac{1}{2}$$

$$\Rightarrow \quad \cos\frac{\pi}{6}\cos x - \sin\frac{\pi}{6}\sin x = \frac{1}{2}$$

$$\Rightarrow \quad \cos\left(x+\frac{\pi}{6}\right) = \cos\left(\frac{\pi}{3}\right)$$

$$\Rightarrow \quad x+\frac{\pi}{6} = 2n\pi \pm \frac{\pi}{3}$$

or $$x = 2n\pi + \frac{\pi}{6}, 2n\pi - \frac{\pi}{2}$$

Now, when $x = 2n\pi + \dfrac{\pi}{6}$, there are solution for $n = 0, 1$ and when $x = 2n\pi - \dfrac{\pi}{2}$, there are solution for $n = 1$.

Thus, total number of solutions are 3.

Example 42. Find the number of solutions of $\cos x = |1 + \sin x|, 0 \le x \le 3\pi$.

Sol. As we know, $1 + \sin x \ge 0$, for all x

So, $\cos x = 1 + \sin x$, for all $x \Rightarrow \cos x - \sin x = 1$

On dividing both sides by $\sqrt{a^2 + b^2}$ i.e. by $\sqrt{2}$, we get

$$\frac{1}{\sqrt{2}} \cos x - \frac{1}{\sqrt{2}} \sin x = \frac{1}{\sqrt{2}}$$

$$\Rightarrow \cos \frac{\pi}{4} \cos x - \sin \frac{\pi}{4} \sin x = \cos \frac{\pi}{4}$$

$$\Rightarrow \cos\left(x + \frac{\pi}{4}\right) = \cos \frac{\pi}{4} \Rightarrow x + \frac{\pi}{4} = 2n\pi \pm \frac{\pi}{4}$$

$$\Rightarrow x = 2n\pi, 2n\pi - \frac{\pi}{2}, \quad \text{where } 0 \le x \le 3\pi$$

$$\Rightarrow x = 0, \frac{3\pi}{2}, 2\pi \text{ are the only solution.}$$

Thus, number of solutions is 3.

Example 43. Let [.] denotes the greatest integer less than or equal to x and $f(x) = \sin x + \cos x$. Then, find the most general solution of $f(x) = \left[f\left(\frac{\pi}{10}\right)\right]$.

Sol. Here, $f\left(\frac{\pi}{10}\right) = \sin 18^\circ + \cos 18^\circ$

$$= \sqrt{2} [\sin (45^\circ + 18^\circ)] = \sqrt{2} \sin 63^\circ$$

As, $\sin 63^\circ > \sin 45^\circ = \frac{1}{\sqrt{2}}$ and $\sin 63^\circ < 1$

$$\therefore \quad 1 < f\left(\frac{\pi}{10}\right) < \sqrt{2} \Rightarrow \left[f\left(\frac{\pi}{10}\right)\right] = 1$$

So, the equation is $\sin x + \cos x = 1$.

$$\therefore \cos\left(x - \frac{\pi}{4}\right) = \frac{1}{\sqrt{2}} \text{ or } x - \frac{\pi}{4} = 2n\pi \pm \frac{\pi}{4} \Rightarrow x = 2n\pi + \frac{\pi}{2}, 2n\pi$$

TYPE 6

Problems Based on Use of Substitution $\sin x \pm \cos x = t$

Working rule

(i) Let $\sin x + \cos x = t$

On squaring both sides, we get

$$(\sin x + \cos x)^2 = t^2$$

$$\Rightarrow 1 + 2\sin x \cos x = t^2 \text{ or } 1 + \sin 2x = t^2$$

$$\Rightarrow \sin x \cos x = \frac{t^2 - 1}{2} \text{ or } \sin 2x = t^2 - 1$$

(ii) Let $\sin x - \cos x = t$

On squaring both sides, we get

$$(\sin x - \cos x)^2 = t^2$$

$$\Rightarrow 1 - 2\sin x \cos x = t^2 \text{ or } 1 - \sin 2x = t^2$$

$$\Rightarrow \sin x \cos x = \frac{1 - t^2}{2} \text{ or } \sin 2x = 1 - t^2$$

Example 44. Solve the equation $3\cos x + 3\sin x + \sin 3x - \cos 3x = 0$.

Sol. $3(\sin x + \cos x) + (3\sin x - 4\sin^3 x) - (4\cos^3 x - 3\cos x) = 0$

$$\Rightarrow 6\sin x + 6\cos x - 4(\sin^3 x + \cos^3 x) = 0$$

$$\Rightarrow 6(\sin x + \cos x) - 4[(\sin x + \cos x)^3 - 3\sin x \cos x(\sin x + \cos x)] = 0$$

$$[\because a^3 + b^3 = (a+b)^3 - 3ab(a+b)]$$

Let $\sin x + \cos x = t \Rightarrow \sin x \cos x = \left(\frac{t^2 - 1}{2}\right)$

$$\Rightarrow 6t - 4\left[t^3 - 3\left(\frac{t^2 - 1}{2}\right)t\right] = 0 \Rightarrow 6t - 4t^3 + 6t^3 - 6t = 0$$

$$\Rightarrow 2t^3 = 0 \Rightarrow t = 0$$

$$\Rightarrow \sin x + \cos x = 0 \Rightarrow \tan x = -1$$

$$\Rightarrow x = n\pi - \frac{\pi}{4}, n \in I$$

Example 45. Solve the equation $\sin x + \cos x - 2\sqrt{2} \sin x \cos x = 0$

Sol. Let $(\sin x + \cos x) = t$ and using the equation

$\sin x \cdot \cos x = \frac{t^2 - 1}{2}$, we get

$$t - 2\sqrt{2}\left(\frac{t^2 - 1}{2}\right) = 0 \Rightarrow \sqrt{2}t^2 - t - \sqrt{2} = 0$$

The numbers $t_1 = \sqrt{2}, t_2 = -\frac{1}{\sqrt{2}}$ are roots of this quadratic equation.

Thus, the solution of the given equation reduces to the solution of two trigonometric equations

$$\sin x + \cos x = \sqrt{2} \text{ and } \sin x + \cos x = -\frac{1}{\sqrt{2}}$$

$$\text{or } \frac{1}{\sqrt{2}} \sin x + \frac{1}{\sqrt{2}} \cos x = 1 \text{ and } \frac{1}{\sqrt{2}} \sin x + \frac{1}{\sqrt{2}} \cos x = -\frac{1}{2}$$

$$\text{or } \sin x \cdot \cos \frac{\pi}{4} + \sin \frac{\pi}{4} \cos x = 1$$

$$\text{and } \sin x \cos \frac{\pi}{4} + \sin \frac{\pi}{4} \cos x = -\frac{1}{2}$$

$$\Rightarrow \sin\left(x + \frac{\pi}{4}\right) = 1 \text{ and } \sin\left(x + \frac{\pi}{4}\right) = -\frac{1}{2}$$

$$\Rightarrow x + \frac{\pi}{4} = (4n + 1)\frac{\pi}{2} \text{ and } x + \frac{\pi}{4} = n\pi + (-1)^n \cdot \left(-\frac{\pi}{6}\right)$$

$$\Rightarrow x = 2n\pi + \frac{\pi}{4} \text{ and } x = n\pi + (-1)^{n+1}\frac{\pi}{6} - \left(\frac{\pi}{4}\right)$$

TYPE 7

Problems Based on Extreme Value of sinx and cos x

Working rule

Step I Factorise the given equation on LHS and equate to RHS.

Step II On RHS, take the range of given trigonometric function.

Step III Then, solve for x and check for root loss and extraneous roots.

Example 46. If $x, y \in [0, 2\pi]$, then total number of ordered pairs (x, y) satisfying the equation $\sin x \cdot \cos y = 1$, is equal to

(a) 1 (b) 3 (c) 5 (d) 7

Sol. (b) We have, $\sin x \cdot \cos y = 1$

Case I $\sin x = 1$ and $\cos y = 1$

$$x = (4n+1)\frac{\pi}{2} \text{ and } y = 2n\pi, n \in I$$

Case II $\sin x = -1$ and $\cos y = -1$

$$x = (4n-1)\frac{\pi}{2} \text{ and } y = (2n+1)\pi, n \in I$$

From Case I, $x = \frac{\pi}{2}$ and $y = 0, 2\pi \Rightarrow \left(\frac{\pi}{2}, 0\right), \left(\frac{\pi}{2}, 2\pi\right)$

From Case II, $x = \frac{3\pi}{2}$ and $y = \pi \Rightarrow \left(\frac{3\pi}{2}, \pi\right)$

Hence, the total number of ordered pairs are 3.

Example 47. The general solution of the equation, $\cos x \cdot \cos 6x = -1$ is

(a) $x = (2n+1)\pi, n \in I$ (b) $x = 2n\pi, n \in I$

(c) $x = (2n-1)\pi, n \in I$ (d) None of these

Sol. (c) $\cos x \cdot \cos 6x = -1$

Case I $\cos x = 1$ and $\cos 6x = -1$

$\Rightarrow \quad x = 2n\pi$ and $6x = (2n+1)\pi, n \in I$

$\Rightarrow \quad x = 2n\pi$ and $x = (2n+1)\frac{\pi}{6}, n \in I$

No common values.

Case II $\cos x = -1$ and $\cos 6x = 1$

$\Rightarrow \quad x = (2n+1)\pi$ and $6x = 2n\pi$

$\Rightarrow \quad x = (2n+1)\pi$ and $x = \frac{n\pi}{3}, n \in I$

When $\quad x = (2n+1)\pi, n \in I$

$\Rightarrow \quad x = \ldots, \pi, 3\pi, 5\pi, \ldots$

and $\quad x = \frac{n\pi}{3}, n \in I$

$\Rightarrow \quad x = \ldots, 0, \frac{\pi}{3}, \frac{2\pi}{3}, \pi, \ldots$

Common values $x = \ldots, \pi, 3\pi, 5\pi, \ldots$

or $\quad x = (2n+1)\pi, n \in I$

or $\quad x = (2n-1)\pi, n \in I$

Example 48. The value of a for which of the equation, $a^2 - 2a + \sec^2 \pi (a + x) = 0$ is

(a) 1

(b) 2

(c) 0 or 1

(d) 1 or 2

Sol. (a) We have, $\quad a^2 - 2a + \sec^2 \pi(a+x) = 0$

$\Rightarrow \quad (a^2 - 2a + 1) + \sec^2 \pi(a+x) - 1 = 0$

$\Rightarrow \quad (a-1)^2 + \tan^2 \pi(a+x) = 0$

Possible only when

$\Rightarrow \quad (a-1)^2 = 0$ and $\tan^2 \pi(a+x) = 0$

$a = 1$ and $\tan^2 \pi(1+x) = 0$ for $a = 1$

Example 49. Solve $\sin^4 x = 1 + \tan^8 x$.

Sol. LHS $= \sin^4 x \le 1$

RHS $= 1 + \tan^8 x \ge 1$

$\Rightarrow$ LHS = RHS only when

$\sin^4 x = 1$ and $1 + \tan^8 x = 1$

$\Rightarrow \quad \sin^2 x = 1$ and $\tan^8 x = 0$

which is never possible, since $\sin x$ and $\tan x$ vanish simultaneously.

Therefore, the given equation has no solution.

Example 50. Solve $\sin^6 x = 1 + \cos^4 3x$.

Sol. LHS $= \sin^6 x \le 1$

RHS $= 1 + \cos^4 3x \ge 1$

Hence, $\sin^6 x = 1 + \cos^4 3x$ is possible only when.

LHS = RHS = 1

$\Rightarrow \quad \sin^6 x = 1$ and $1 + \cos^4 3x = 1$

$\Rightarrow \quad \sin^2 x = 1$ and $\cos^4 3x = 0$

$\Rightarrow \quad \cos^2 x = 0$ and $\cos 3x = 0$

$\Rightarrow \quad \cos x = 0$ and $\cos 3x = 0$

$\Rightarrow \quad x = (2m+1)\frac{\pi}{2}$

and $\quad 3x = (2n+1)\frac{\pi}{2}$, where $m, n \in I$

$\Rightarrow \quad x = (2m+1)\frac{\pi}{2}$ and $x = (2n+1)\frac{\pi}{6}$,

where $m, n \in I$

$\Rightarrow \quad x = (2m+1)\frac{\pi}{2}$ and $x = (2n+1)\frac{\pi}{6}$

Common values of x is $(2n+1)\frac{\pi}{2}$, where $n \in I$.

The required solution, $x = (2n+1)\frac{\pi}{2}, n \in I$

Example 51. Solve

$$2\cos^2\frac{x}{2}\cdot\sin^2 x = x^2 + \frac{1}{x^2},\ 0 < x \le \frac{\pi}{2}.$$

Sol. In this problem, terms on the two sides of the equation are different in nature.

LHS is in trigonometric form, whereas RHS is in algebraic form. Hence, we will used inequality method.

Here, LHS $= 2\cos^2\frac{x}{2}\cdot\sin^2 x = (1+\cos x)\sin^2 x < 2$

$[\because 1+\cos x < 2, \sin^2 x \le 1]$

and RHS $= x^2 + \frac{1}{x^2} \ge 2$ $[\because \text{AM} \ge \text{GM}]$

Hence, LHS is never equal to RHS

$\therefore$ The given equation has no solution.

TYPE 8

Problems Based on Use of Limited Range of Trigonometric Expressions.

$$-\sqrt{a^2+b^2} \le a\cos x \pm b\sin x \le \sqrt{a^2+b^2}$$

Working rule

Step I Simplify the given equation first.

Step II Then, take the minimum and maximum range of given function.

Step III Then, solve for x.

Example 52. $\sin\theta + \sqrt{3}\cos\theta = 6x - x^2 - 11,\ 0 < \theta < 4\pi$, $x \in R$, holds for

(a) No value of x and θ

(b) Two-pair of values of (x, θ)

(c) Two values of x and two values of θ

(d) One values of x and one values of θ

Sol. (b) We have, $\sin\theta + \sqrt{3}\cos\theta = 6x - x^2 - 11; 0 < \theta < 4\pi$

$$-2 \le \sin\theta + \sqrt{3}\cos\theta \le 2$$

$$\Rightarrow \sin\theta + \sqrt{3}\cos\theta = -(x^2 - 6x + 11)$$

$$= -(x^2 - 6x + 9 + 2)$$

$$= -[(x-3)^2 + 2]$$

Hence, LHS and RHS have only one common value (-2).

Range of LHS $= [-2, 2]$

Range of RHS $= (-\infty, -2]$

Only possibility is LHS $= -2$ and RHS $= -2$

For RHS $-(x-3)^2 - 2 = -2 \Rightarrow x = 3$

For LHS $= -2$

$$\Rightarrow \sin\theta + \sqrt{3}\cos\theta = -2$$

$$\Rightarrow \frac{1}{2}\sin\theta + \frac{\sqrt{3}}{2}\cos\theta = -1$$

$$\Rightarrow \cos\left(\theta - \frac{\pi}{6}\right) = -1$$

$$\Rightarrow \theta - \frac{\pi}{6} = (2n+1)\pi, n \in I$$

$$\Rightarrow \theta = (2n+1)\pi + \frac{\pi}{6}, n \in I \text{ and } \theta \in (0, 4\pi)$$

$$\Rightarrow \theta = \left(\pi + \frac{\pi}{6}\right), \left(3\pi + \frac{\pi}{6}\right)$$

$$\Rightarrow (x, \theta) = \left(3, \frac{7\pi}{6}\right) \text{ and } (x, \theta) = \left(3, \frac{19\pi}{6}\right)$$

JEE SCANNER

Example Similar to PYQ Asked in JEE Main 2021

The number of integral values of 'k' for which the equation $7\cos x + 5\sin x = 2k+1$ has a solution is

(a) 4 (b) 8 (c) 10 (d) 12

Sol. (b) We know that, $a\cos\theta + b\sin\theta = C$ has one solution only, that is

$$|C| \le \sqrt{a^2+b^2}$$

Then, for the given equation $7\cos x + 5\sin x = 2k+1$, we have

$$|2k+1| \le \sqrt{49+25} = \sqrt{74}$$

$$\Rightarrow -\sqrt{74} \le 2k+1 \le \sqrt{74}$$

$$\Rightarrow -8.60 \le 2k+1 \le 8.60$$

$$\Rightarrow -9.6 \le 2k \le 7.60$$

$$\Rightarrow -4.8 \le k \le 3.8$$

$$\therefore k = -4, -3, -2, -1, 0, 1, 2, 3$$

Thus, there are 8 values which satisfy the above inequality.

Skill Builder

The number of integral values of k for which the equation $k\cos x - 3\sin x = k+1$ has a solution in the interval [0, 5] is

(a) 1 (b) 2 (c) 4 (d) 5

For Sol.

- **For more practice** See Q.6 of Milestone Practice 3.

Example 53. If x and y are the solutions of the equations, $12\sin x + 5\cos x = 2y^2 - 8y + 21$. Then, find the value of $\frac{24}{5}\cot\left(\frac{xy}{2}\right)$.

Sol. We have, $12\sin x + 5\cos x = 2y^2 - 8y + 21$

$$\Rightarrow -13 \le 12\sin x + 5\cos x \le 13$$

and $2y^2 - 8y + 21 = 2(y^2 - 4y) + 21$

$$= 2[(y-2)^2 - 4] + 21$$

$$= 2(y-2)^2 + 13$$

$$\Rightarrow 13 \le 2(y-2)^2 + 13 < \infty$$

Hence, for solution RHS = 13 $\Rightarrow$ $y = 2$

LHS = 13

$$\Rightarrow \quad 12\sin x + 5\cos x = 13$$

$$\Rightarrow \quad \frac{12}{13}\sin x + \frac{5}{13}\cos x = 1$$

$$\Rightarrow \quad \cos(x - \alpha) = 1$$

$$\left[\text{where, } \sin\alpha = \frac{12}{13} \text{ and } \cos\alpha = \frac{5}{13}\right]$$

$$\Rightarrow \quad x - \alpha = 2n\pi \Rightarrow x = 2n\pi + \alpha$$

$$\frac{24}{5}\cot\left(\frac{xy}{2}\right) = \frac{24}{5}\cot\left[\frac{(2n\pi + \alpha)\cdot 2}{2}\right]$$

$$= \frac{24}{5}\cot(2n\pi + \alpha) = \frac{24}{5}\cot\alpha$$

$$= \frac{24}{5}\frac{\cos\alpha}{\sin\alpha} = \frac{24}{5} \times \frac{5}{12} = 2$$

Example 54. Find the number of solutions of $\sin\theta + 2\sin 2\theta + 3\sin 3\theta + 4\sin 4\theta = 10$ in $(0, \pi)$.

Sol. Given, $\sin\theta + 2\sin 2\theta + 3\sin 3\theta + 4\sin 4\theta = 10$ ...(i)

Eq. (i) will be true only if sine function attains its maximum so that $(1 + 2 + 3 + 4 = 10)$

i.e. $\sin\theta = 1$ and $\sin 2\theta = 1$ and $\sin 3\theta = 1$ and $\sin 4\theta = 1$

$\Rightarrow \theta = 2K\pi + \frac{\pi}{2}$ and $2\theta = 2\lambda\pi + \frac{\pi}{2}$ and $3\theta = 2m\pi + \frac{\pi}{2}$

and $4\theta = 2n\pi + \frac{\pi}{2}$

where, $K, \lambda, m, n \in I$.

So, $\theta = \frac{\pi}{2}$ and $\theta = \frac{\pi}{4}$ and $\theta = \frac{\pi}{6}, \frac{5\pi}{6}$ and $\theta = \frac{\pi}{8}, \frac{5\pi}{8}$

$$\therefore \quad \theta \in \left\{\frac{\pi}{2}\right\} \cap \left\{\frac{\pi}{4}\right\} \cap \left\{\frac{\pi}{6}, \frac{5\pi}{6}\right\} \cap \left\{\frac{\pi}{8}, \frac{5\pi}{8}\right\}$$

$\Rightarrow \theta \in \{\}$ i.e. $\theta \in \phi$

Hence, total number of solutions = 0.

Example 55. Solve the equation $(\sin x + \cos x)^{1 + \sin 2x} = 2$, when $-\pi \le x \le \pi$.

Sol. We know, $-\sqrt{a^2 + b^2} \le a\sin\theta + b\cos\theta \le \sqrt{a^2 + b^2}$ and $-1 \le \sin\theta \le 1$.

$\therefore$ $(\sin x + \cos x)$ admits the maximum value as $\sqrt{2}$ and minimum value as $-\sqrt{2}$, $(1 + \sin 2x)$ admits the maximum value as 2.

Also, $(\pm\sqrt{2})^2 = 2$.

$\therefore$ The equation could hold only when,

$$\sin x + \cos x = \pm\sqrt{2} \text{ and } 1 + \sin 2x = 2$$

Now, $\quad \sin x + \cos x = \sqrt{2}$

$$\Rightarrow \quad \cos\left(x - \frac{\pi}{4}\right) = 1$$

$$\Rightarrow \quad x = 2n\pi + \frac{\pi}{4} \quad \text{...(i)}$$

and $\quad \sin x + \cos x = -\sqrt{2}$

$$\cos\left(x - \frac{\pi}{4}\right) = -1$$

$$x = (2n \pm 1)\pi + \frac{\pi}{4} \quad \text{...(ii)}$$

and $\quad 1 + \sin 2x = 2$

$$\Rightarrow \quad \sin 2x = 1 = \sin\frac{\pi}{2}$$

$$\Rightarrow \quad 2x = n\pi + (-1)^n\frac{\pi}{2}$$

$$\Rightarrow \quad x = \frac{n\pi}{2} + (-1)^n\frac{\pi}{4} \quad \text{...(iii)}$$

The value in $[-\pi, \pi]$ satisfying Eqs. (i), (ii) and (iii) is

$x = \frac{\pi}{4}, \frac{-3\pi}{4}$ (when $n = 0, -1$).

Example 56. Solve $|\sqrt{3}\cos x - \sin x| \ge 2$ for $x \in [0, 4\pi]$.

Sol. We know, $|\sqrt{3}\cos x - \sin x| \le \sqrt{3 + 1} = 2$ ...(i)

and $\quad |\sqrt{3}\cos x - \sin x| \ge 2$ (given) ...(ii)

Thus, from Eqs. (i) and (ii), we must have

$$|\sqrt{3}\cos x - \sin x| = 2$$

$$\Rightarrow \quad \left|\frac{\sqrt{3}}{2}\cos x - \frac{1}{2}\sin x\right| = 1$$

$$\Rightarrow \quad \left|\cos\frac{\pi}{6}\cos x - \sin\frac{\pi}{6}\cdot\sin x\right| = 1$$

$$\Rightarrow \quad \left|\cos\left(x + \frac{\pi}{6}\right)\right| = 1$$

$$\Rightarrow \quad \cos\left(x + \frac{\pi}{6}\right) = 1 \text{ or } \cos\left(x + \frac{\pi}{6}\right) = -1$$

$$\Rightarrow \quad x + \frac{\pi}{6} = 0, 2\pi, 4\pi, \ldots \text{ or } \pi, 3\pi, 5\pi, \ldots$$

$$\Rightarrow \quad x = \frac{11\pi}{6}, \frac{23\pi}{6}, \frac{5\pi}{6}, \frac{17\pi}{6}, \text{ for } x \in [0, 4\pi]$$

Hence, $x \in \left\{\frac{11\pi}{6}, \frac{23\pi}{6}, \frac{5\pi}{6}, \frac{17\pi}{6}\right\}$

Example 57. Find the most general solutions for $2^{\sin x} + 2^{\cos x} = 2^{1 - 1/\sqrt{2}}$.

Sol. As we know, AM $\ge$ GM

$$\therefore \quad \frac{2^{\sin x} + 2^{\cos x}}{2} \ge \sqrt{2^{\sin x}\cdot 2^{\cos x}} \quad \text{...(i)}$$

Now, Eq. (i) admits minimum value when

$\sin x + \cos x$ is $(-\sqrt{2})$

$\{$using $-\sqrt{a^2 + b^2} \le a\cos x + b\sin x \le \sqrt{a^2 + b^2}\}$

$$\therefore \quad 2^{\sin x} + 2^{\cos x} \ge 2\cdot\sqrt{2^{-\sqrt{2}}}$$

or $$2^{\sin x}+2^{\cos x}\geq 2\cdot 2^{-\frac{\sqrt{2}}{2}}$$

or $$2^{\sin x}+2^{\cos x}\geq 2^{1-\frac{1}{\sqrt{2}}}$$

Thus, the equation holds only when,

$$\sin x+\cos x=-\sqrt{2} \Rightarrow \cos\left(x-\frac{\pi}{4}\right)=-1$$

$$\Rightarrow \quad x-\frac{\pi}{4}=2n\pi\pm\pi$$

$$\Rightarrow \quad x=(2n\pm 1)\pi+\frac{\pi}{4}$$

Example 58. Find the ordered pair (x, y) satisfying the equation $\sin x+\cos x=\sqrt{y+\frac{1}{y}}$, where $x\in(0,\pi)$.

Sol. Given, $\sin x+\cos x=\sqrt{y+\frac{1}{y}}$ ...(i)

Here, LHS of Eq. (i) $\in[-\sqrt{2},\sqrt{2}]$ ...(ii)

But RHS of Eq. (i) $\in[\sqrt{2},\infty)$ ...(iii)

From Eqs. (ii) and (iii), we can say that Eq. (i) will holds true if

$$\sin x+\cos x=\sqrt{y+\frac{1}{y}}=\sqrt{2}$$

$$\Rightarrow \frac{1}{\sqrt{2}}\sin x+\frac{1}{\sqrt{2}}\cos x=\frac{\sqrt{2}}{\sqrt{2}} \Rightarrow \sin\left(x+\frac{\pi}{4}\right)=1=\sin\frac{\pi}{2}$$

$$\Rightarrow x+\frac{\pi}{4}=n\pi+(-1)^n\frac{\pi}{2}, n\in I \Rightarrow x=\frac{\pi}{4}\in(0,\pi)$$

and $y+\frac{1}{y}=2 \Rightarrow y=1$

Hence, ordered pair is $(x,y)\equiv\left(\frac{\pi}{4},1\right)$

TYPE 9

Problem Based on Use of Equation of the Form

$$a_0\sin^n x+a_1\sin^{n-1}x\cos x+a_2\sin^{n-2}x\cos^2 x+\ldots+a_n\cos^n x=0,$$

where $a_0, a_1, \ldots, a_n$ are real number and the sum of the exponents of $\sin x$ and $\cos x$ in each term is equal to n, are said to be homogeneous with respect to $\sin x$ and $\cos x$. For $\cos x\neq 0$, above equation can be written as,

$$a_0\tan^n x+a_1\tan^{n-1}x+\ldots+a_n=0$$

Example 59. Solve the equation $5\sin^2 x-7\sin x\cos x+16\cos^2 x=4$.

Sol. To solve this equation, we use the fundamental trigonometric identity, $\sin^2 x+\cos^2 x=1$

Given equation can be written as

$$4(\sin^2 x+\cos^2 x)+\sin^2 x-7\sin x\cos x+12\cos^2 x=4$$

$$\Rightarrow \quad \sin^2 x-7\sin x\cos x+12\cos^2 x=0$$

On dividing by $\cos^2 x$ both sides, we get

$$\tan^2 x-7\tan x+12=0$$

Now, it can be factorised as;

$$(\tan x-3)(\tan x-4)=0 \Rightarrow \tan x=3, 4$$

i.e. $\tan x=\tan(\tan^{-1}3)$ or $\tan x=\tan(\tan^{-1}4)$

$$\Rightarrow \quad x=n\pi+\tan^{-1}3 \text{ or } x=n\pi+\tan^{-1}4$$

TYPE 10

Problem Based on Use of Equation of the Form $R(\sin kx, \cos nx, \tan mx, \cot lx)=0$

Working rule

$$R(\sin kx, \cos nx, \tan mx, \cot lx)=0,$$

where R is a rational function of the indicated arguments and k, l, m, n are natural numbers, can be reduced to a rational equation with respect to the arguments $\sin x$, $\cos x$, $\tan x$ and $\cot x$ by means of the formulae for trigonometric functions of the sum of angles (in particular, the formulas for double and triple angle) and then reduce the obtained equation to a rational equation with respect to the unknown, $t=\tan\frac{x}{2}$, by means of following formulae;

$$\sin x=\frac{2\tan\frac{x}{2}}{1+\tan^2\frac{x}{2}},\ \cos x=\frac{1-\tan^2\frac{x}{2}}{1+\tan^2\frac{x}{2}},$$

$$\tan x=\frac{2\tan\frac{x}{2}}{1-\tan^2\frac{x}{2}},\ \cot x=\frac{1-\tan^2\frac{x}{2}}{2\tan\frac{x}{2}}$$

Example 60. Solve the equation $(\cos x-\sin x)\left(2\tan x+\frac{1}{\cos x}\right)+2=0$

Sol. Using above formulae, we get

$$\left\{\frac{1-\tan^2\frac{x}{2}}{1+\tan^2\frac{x}{2}}-\frac{2\tan\frac{x}{2}}{1+\tan^2\frac{x}{2}}\right\}\left\{\frac{4\tan\frac{x}{2}}{1-\tan^2\frac{x}{2}}+\frac{1+\tan^2\frac{x}{2}}{1-\tan^2\frac{x}{2}}\right\}+2=0$$

$$\Rightarrow \left(\frac{1-t^2}{1+t^2}-\frac{2t}{1+t^2}\right)\left(\frac{4t}{1-t^2}+\frac{1+t^2}{1-t^2}\right)+2=0$$

$$\left[\text{taking } \tan\frac{x}{2}=t\right]$$

$$\Rightarrow \quad \frac{3t^4+6t^3+8t^2-2t-3}{(t^2+1)(1-t^2)}=0$$

Its roots are $t_1=\frac{1}{\sqrt{3}}$ and $t_2=-\frac{1}{\sqrt{3}}$.

Thus, the solution of the equation reduces to that of two elementary euqations,

$$\tan \frac{x}{2} = \frac{1}{\sqrt{3}} \text{ and } \tan \frac{x}{2} = -\frac{1}{\sqrt{3}}$$

$$\Rightarrow \quad \frac{x}{2} = n\pi \pm \frac{\pi}{6} \Rightarrow x = 2n\pi \pm \frac{\pi}{3}, \text{ is required solution.}$$

Example 61. Solve the equation

$$\sin^{10} x + \cos^{10} x = \frac{29}{16} \cos^4 2x$$

Sol. Using half-angle formulae, we can represent the given equation in the form;

$$\left(\frac{1-\cos 2x}{2}\right)^5 + \left(\frac{1+\cos 2x}{2}\right)^5 = \frac{29}{16}\cos^4 2x$$

Put $\cos 2x = t$,

$$\left(\frac{1-t}{2}\right)^5 + \left(\frac{1+t}{2}\right)^5 = \frac{29}{16}t^4 \Rightarrow 24t^4 - 10t^2 - 1 = 0$$

whose only real root is, $t^2 = \frac{1}{2}$.

$$\therefore \quad \cos^2 2x = \frac{1}{2} \Rightarrow 1 + \cos 4x = 1$$

$$\Rightarrow \quad \cos 4x = 0 \Rightarrow 4x = (2n+1)\frac{\pi}{2} \Rightarrow x = \frac{n\pi}{4} + \frac{\pi}{8};\ n \in I$$

Example 62. Find the number of solutions of equation $8[x^2 - x] + 4[x] = 13 + 12[\sin x]$, [.] denotes GIF.

Sol. $8[x^2 - x] + 4[x] = 13 + 12[\sin x]$

LHS is always even and RHS is always odd.

Hence, no solution.

Example 63. If $[\sin x] + [\sqrt{2}\cos x] = -3$, where $x \in [0, 2\pi]$ and $[\cdot]$ denotes GIF, then find x.

Sol. Given, $[\sin x] + [\sqrt{2}\cos x] = -3,\ x \in [0, 2\pi]$

$$\because \quad -1 \le \sin x \le 1$$

$\therefore$ Only possible solution, $[\sin x] = -1$ and $[\sqrt{2}\cos x] = -2$

$[\sin x] = -1$ when $-1 \le \sin x < 0 \Rightarrow x \in (\pi, 2\pi)$ ...(i)

and $[\sqrt{2}\cos x] = -2 \Rightarrow -2 \le \sqrt{2}\cos x < -1$

$$\Rightarrow \quad -\sqrt{2} \le \cos x < \frac{-1}{\sqrt{2}} \Rightarrow x \in \left(\frac{3\pi}{4}, \frac{5\pi}{4}\right) \quad \text{...(ii)}$$

Hence, Eq. (i) $\cap$ Eq. (ii) $\Rightarrow x \in \left(\pi, \frac{5\pi}{4}\right)$.

Example 64. Show that the equation, $\sin x = [1 + \sin x] + [1 - \cos x]$ has no solution for $x \in R$. (where [.] represents greatest integers function).

Sol. As we know that the period of $\sin x$ is 2π, we need to check the solution for $x \in [0, 2\pi]$.

Let us first check at those points on which $\sin x$ and $\cos x$ are integer and then for the values lying between them.

Case I (a) At $x = 0$,

$[1 + \sin x] = 1$ and $[1 - \cos x] = 0$

$\therefore \quad \sin x = 1 + 0 = 1$ or $\sin 0 = 1$ [as $x = 0$]

$\Rightarrow 0 = 1$ [absurd]

(b) At $x = \frac{\pi}{2}$,

$[1 + \sin x] = 2$ and $[1 - \cos x] = 1$

$\therefore \quad \sin x = 2 + 1 = 3$ [absurd]

(c) At $x = \pi$,

$[1 + \sin x] = 1$ and $[1 - \cos x] = 2$

$\therefore \quad \sin x = 1 + 2 = 3$ [absurd]

(d) At $x = \frac{3\pi}{2}$,

$[1 + \sin x] = 0$ and $[1 - \cos x] = 1$

$\therefore \quad \sin x = 0 + 1$ or $\sin \frac{3\pi}{2} = 1$ $\left[\text{as } x = \frac{3\pi}{2}\right]$

$\Rightarrow \quad -1 = 1$ [absurd]

(e) At $x = 2\pi$,

$[1 + \sin x] = 1$ and $[1 - \cos x] = 0$

$\therefore \quad \sin x = 1 + 0$

or $\quad \sin 0 = 1$ (as $x = 0$) $\Rightarrow 0 = 1$ [absurd]

$$\therefore \quad \text{At } x = \left\{0, \frac{\pi}{2}, \pi, \frac{3\pi}{2}, 2\pi\right\}$$

we do not have any solution.

Now, to check for the values lying between them.

Case II (a) When $x \in \left(0, \frac{\pi}{2}\right)$

$[1 + \sin x] = 1$, $[1 - \cos x] = 0 \Rightarrow \sin x = 1 + 0$

But since $x \in \left(0, \frac{\pi}{2}\right)$, $\sin x \ne 1$

$\therefore$ $\sin x = 1$ is absurd when $x \in \left(0, \frac{\pi}{2}\right)$

(b) When $x \in \left(\frac{\pi}{2}, \pi\right)$

$[1 + \sin x] = 1$, $[1 - \cos x] = 1$

$\Rightarrow \quad \sin x = 1 + 1 = 2$ [absurd]

(c) When $x \in \left(\pi, \frac{3\pi}{2}\right)$

$[1 + \sin x] = 0$, $[1 - \cos x] = 1 \Rightarrow \sin x = 0 + 1 = 1$

But $x \in \left(\pi, \frac{3\pi}{2}\right)$ in which $\sin x \ne 1$

$\therefore$ $\sin x = 1$ is absurd, when $x \in \left(\pi, \frac{3\pi}{2}\right)$

(d) When $x \in \left(\frac{3\pi}{2}, 2\pi\right)$

$[1 + \sin x] = 0$, $[1 - \cos x] = 0$

$\therefore \quad \sin x = 0 + 0 = 0$

But $\sin x \ne 0$ when $x \in \left(\frac{3\pi}{2}, 2\pi\right)$

Thus, the given equation does not posses any solution for $x \in [0, 2\pi]$ or in general, $\sin x = [1 + \sin x] + [1 - \cos x]$ does not posses any solution for $x \in R$.

2.4 Solution of Simultaneous Trigonometric Equations

TYPE 11

Problems Based on Solution of Simultaneous Trigonometric Equations

(i) Two Equations in One Variable

Working Rule

(i) If two equations in one unknown (say x) are given, then solve given equations separately for x lying between 0 and 2π.

(ii) Select the value of x for which both the equations are satisfied.

(iii) Add $2n\pi$ to get general solution.

Example 65. Solve $\cos x = \frac{1}{\sqrt{2}}$ and $\tan x = -1$.

Sol. $\cos x = \frac{1}{\sqrt{2}} \Rightarrow x = \frac{\pi}{4}, \frac{7\pi}{4}$ in $(0, 2\pi)$

$\tan x = -1 \Rightarrow x = \frac{3\pi}{4}, \frac{7\pi}{4}$ in $(0, 2\pi)$

$\therefore$ Common value of $x = \frac{7\pi}{4}$.

Now, for general solution add $2n\pi$.

$\therefore$ General solution is $x = 2n\pi + \frac{7\pi}{4}$.

Example 66. Find the most general values of θ which satisfies the equations $\sin\theta = -\frac{1}{2}$ and $\tan\theta = \frac{1}{\sqrt{3}}$.

Sol. First, find the values of θ lying between 0 and 2π and satisfying the two given equations separately.

Select the value of θ which satisfies both the equations, then generalise it.

$$\sin\theta = -\frac{1}{2}$$

$$\Rightarrow \quad \theta = \frac{7\pi}{6} \text{ or } \frac{11\pi}{6}$$

$$\tan\theta = \frac{1}{\sqrt{3}}$$

$$\Rightarrow \quad \theta = \frac{\pi}{6} \text{ or } \frac{7\pi}{6} \quad \text{[value between 0 and } 2\pi]$$

$\therefore$ Common value of $\theta = \frac{7\pi}{6}$.

The required solution is $\theta = 2n\pi + \frac{7\pi}{6}$.

(ii) Two Equations in Two Variables

Working Rule

Step I Find $A + B$ and $A - B$ between 0 and 2π from the two equations. Impose the condition that A and B must be smallest and positive, since A and B are positive angles, $A + B > A - B$.

Find $A + B$ and $A - B$ accordingly.

Step II Solve the two equation to get A and B.

Step III Then, generalised it with the help of common period.

Example 67. If $\tan(A - B) = 1$ and $\sec(A + B) = \frac{2}{\sqrt{3}}$, then find the smallest positive values of A and B and their most general values.

Sol. For the smallest positive values, find $A + B$ and $A - B$ between 0 and 2π from the given equations.

Since, A and B are positive angles, $A + B > A - B$. Solve the two to get A and B.

For the most general values, find the general values of $A - B$ and $A + B$ by solving the given equations separately. Solve two to get A and B

$$\tan(A - B) = 1 \Rightarrow A - B = \frac{\pi}{4} \text{ or } \frac{5\pi}{4} \quad \text{...(i)}$$

Also, $\sec(A + B) = \frac{2}{\sqrt{3}} \Rightarrow A + B = \frac{\pi}{6} \text{ or } \frac{11\pi}{6}$

Since, $A + B > A - B$

$$\therefore \quad A + B = \frac{11\pi}{6} \quad \text{...(ii)}$$

On solving Eqs. (i) and (ii), we get

$$A = \frac{25\pi}{24}, B = \frac{19\pi}{24}$$

or $$A = \frac{37\pi}{24}, B = \frac{7\pi}{24}$$

Solve for the most general values

$$\tan(A - B) = 1 \Rightarrow A - B = n\pi + \frac{\pi}{4} \quad \text{...(iii)}$$

$$\sec(A + B) = \frac{2}{\sqrt{3}} \Rightarrow \cos(A + B) = \frac{\sqrt{3}}{2}$$

$$\Rightarrow \quad A + B = 2m\pi \pm \frac{\pi}{6} \quad \text{...(iv)}$$

On solving Eqs. (iii) and (iv), we get,

$$A = \frac{1}{2}\left[(2m + n)\pi + \frac{\pi}{4} \pm \frac{\pi}{6}\right]$$

and $$B = \frac{1}{2}\left[(2m - n)\pi - \frac{\pi}{4} \pm \frac{\pi}{6}\right],$$

where $m, n \in I$.

Example 68. Find the most general value of θ satisfying the system of equations $\cos(2x+3y)=\frac{1}{2}$ and $\cos(3x+2y)=\frac{\sqrt{3}}{2}$.

Sol. Given equations are

$$\cos(2x+3y)=\frac{1}{2} \text{ and } \cos(3x+2y)=\frac{\sqrt{3}}{2}$$

$$\Rightarrow \quad \cos(2x+3y)=\cos\frac{\pi}{3} \text{ and } \cos(3x+2y)=\cos\frac{\pi}{6}$$

$$\Rightarrow \quad 2x+3y=2n\pi\pm\frac{\pi}{3}, n\in I \quad \text{...(i)}$$

and

$$3x+2y=2m\pi\pm\frac{\pi}{6}, m\in I \quad \text{...(ii)}$$

On solving Eqs. (i) and (ii), we have

$$x=\frac{1}{5}\left[(6m-4n)\pi\pm\frac{\pi}{2}\mp\frac{2\pi}{3}\right],$$

$$y=\frac{1}{5}\left[(6n-4m)\pi\pm\pi\mp\frac{\pi}{3}\right]$$

Example 69. If $r>0, -\pi\le\theta\le\pi$ and r, θ satisfy $r\sin\theta=3$ and $r=4(1+\sin\theta)$, then find the possible solutions of the pair (r,θ).

Sol. Here, $r=4(1+\sin\theta)$ and $r\sin\theta=3$

On eliminating θ from above equations;

$$r=4\left(1+\frac{3}{r}\right)$$

$$\Rightarrow \quad r^2-4r-12=0$$

$$\Rightarrow \quad (r-6)(r+2)=0$$

$$\Rightarrow \quad r=6 \text{ or } r=-2$$

$$\therefore \quad r\sin\theta=3$$

$$\Rightarrow \quad \sin\theta=\frac{1}{2} \text{ or } \sin\theta=-\frac{3}{2}$$

Neglecting $\sin\theta=-\frac{3}{2}$, we get

$$\theta=\frac{\pi}{6},\frac{5\pi}{6}$$

$\therefore \quad (r,\theta)=\left(6,\frac{\pi}{6}\right)$ and $\left(6,\frac{5\pi}{6}\right)$ are the required pairs.

Milestone Practice 2.3

1. Solve the equation $\sin x+\cos x=1$.
2. Solve $\sqrt{3}\cos\theta-3\sin\theta=4\sin2\theta\cos3\theta$.
3. Solve $\cot\theta+\text{cosec}\,\theta=\sqrt{3}$.
4. Solve $\sqrt{2}\sec\theta+\tan\theta=1$.
5. The general solution of the equation $(\sqrt{3}-1)\sin\theta+(\sqrt{3}+1)\cos\theta=2$, is
   (a) $\frac{\pi}{4}+n\pi$ (b) $n\pi-\frac{\pi}{12}$
   (c) $n\pi-\frac{\pi}{4}$ (d) $2n\pi+\frac{\pi}{3}$
6. The number of integral values of k for which equation $7\cos x+5\sin x=2k+1$ has atleast one solution, is
   [**Hint** $a\cos\theta+b\sin\theta=c$ has solution only when $|c|\le\sqrt{a^2+b^2}$].
   (a) 4 (b) 6 (c) 8 (d) 10
7. Solve $2\sin^2x-5\sin x\cos x-8\cos^2x=-2$.
8. Solve the equation $(1-\tan\theta)(1+\sin2\theta)=1+\tan\theta$.
9. Find the most general value of $4^{\sin x}+4^{\cos x}=2^{1-\sqrt{2}}$.
10. The number of solutions of equation $\sin^2x\cos^2x=1+\cos^2x\sin^4x$ in the interval $[0,\pi]$, is
    (a) 0 (b) 1
    (c) 2 (d) 3
11. Solve $1+\sin x\sin^2\frac{x}{2}=0$.
12. Solve $\cos^{50}x-\sin^{50}x=1$.
13. The number of real solutions of the equation $(\cos x)^5+(\sin x)^3=1$ in the interval $[0,2\pi]$, is
    (a) 1 (b) 2
    (c) 3 (d) 4
14. The number of solutions of the equation $1+e^{\cot^2x}=\sqrt{2|\sin x|-1}+\frac{1-\cos2x}{1+\sin^4x}$ for $x\in(0,5\pi)$, is
    (a) 3 (b) 5
    (c) 7 (d) 9
15. Find the number of solutions as ordered pair (x,y) of the equation $2^{\sec^2x}+2^{\text{cosec}^2y}=2\cos^2x(1-\cos^22y)$ in $[0,2\pi]$.

16. The solution of the equation $\cos^2\left[\frac{\pi}{4}(\sin x+\sqrt{2}\cos^2 x)\right]-\tan^2\left[x+\frac{\pi}{4}\tan^2 x\right]=1$, is

(a) $2n\pi+\frac{\pi}{6}$ (b) $2n\pi+\frac{\pi}{3}$

(c) $2n\pi-\frac{\pi}{2}$ (d) $2n\pi-\frac{\pi}{4}$

17. If the equation $\tan(p\cot x)=\cot(p\tan x)$ has a solution in $x\in(0,\pi)-\left\{\frac{\pi}{2}\right\}$, then prove that $p\le\frac{\pi}{4}$.

18. Solve for x and y : $\sqrt{3}\sin x+\cos x=8y-y^2-18$, where $0\le x\le 4\pi$, $y\in R$.

19. Solve
$$\sin x\left(\cos\frac{x}{4}-2\sin x\right)+\left(1+\sin\frac{x}{4}-2\cos x\right)\cos x=0.$$

20. The number of ordered pairs (x, y), where x and y satisfy $x+y=\frac{2\pi}{3}$ and $\cos x+\cos y=\frac{3}{2}$ is

(a) 0 (b) 1 (c) 2 (d) infinite

21. A ΔABC is such that $\sin(2A+B)=\frac{1}{2}$. If A, B and C are in AP, then find the value of A and C.

22. Solve for x and y, if $x+y=\frac{2\pi}{3}$ and $\frac{\sin x}{\sin y}=2$.

23. If $\sin\alpha=\frac{1}{\sqrt{5}}$, $\sin\beta=\frac{3}{5}$, then $\beta-\alpha$ lies in the interval

(a) $\left[0,\frac{\pi}{4}\right]$ (b) $\left[\frac{\pi}{2},\frac{3\pi}{4}\right]$ (c) $\left[\pi,\frac{5\pi}{4}\right]$ (d) $\left[\frac{5\pi}{4},\frac{3\pi}{2}\right]$

24. The total number of ordered pair (x, y), where x and y satisfy $|x|+|y|=3$ and $\sin\left(\frac{\pi x^2}{3}\right)=1$ is ....

Answer Key

1. $2n\pi$ or $(4n+1)\frac{\pi}{2}, n\in I$
2. $\frac{n\pi}{3}+\frac{\pi}{18}$ or $\frac{-n\pi}{2}+\frac{\pi}{6}, n\in I$
3. $2n\pi\pm\frac{\pi}{3}, n\in I$
4. $2n\pi-\frac{\pi}{4}, n\in I$
5. (d)
6. (c)
7. $n\pi+\tan^{-1}2$ or $n\pi+\tan^{-1}\left(-\frac{3}{4}\right), n\in I$
8. $n\pi, n\pi-\frac{\pi}{4}, n\in I$
9. $(2n\pm 1)\pi+\frac{\pi}{4}, n\in I$
10. (a)
11. No solution
12. $n\pi, n\in I$
13. (c)
14. (b)
15. 0
16. (d)
18. $x=\frac{4\pi}{3},\frac{10\pi}{3}$ and $y=4$
19. $x=(8p-6)\pi, p\in I$
20. (a)
21. $\frac{\pi}{4},\frac{5\pi}{12}$
22. $(x, y)=\left(n\pi+\frac{\pi}{2},\frac{\pi}{6}-n\pi\right), n\in I$
23. (a)
24. 8

For Detailed Solution

Milestone 4 Solution of Trigonometric Equations Using Graph

• Solution of Trigonometric Equations Using Graph • Trigonometric Inequality

2.5 Solution of Trigonometric Equation Using Graph

Graphical approach plays very important role in solving trigonometric equation of the form $f(x) = g(x)$ where $f(x)$ is trigonometric function and $g(x)$ is either trigonometric or non-trigonometric (constant, polynomial, logarithmic, exponential , etc). If question demands to find the total number of values of x (not exact value(s) of x), then we may think, one time about graphical approach also.

To find the total number of roots (or values or solutions) of the equation, firstly we must draw the graph of $y = f(x)$ and $y = g(x)$ and then we count total number of points of intersection in the given interval.

Example 70. Find the total number of solutions of the equation $|\cos x| = |x|$.

Sol. We have, $|\cos x| = |x|$

Let $f(x) = |\cos x|$ and $g(x) = |x|$

First we draw the graph of $f(x)$ and $g(x)$ and then find total number of points of intersection.

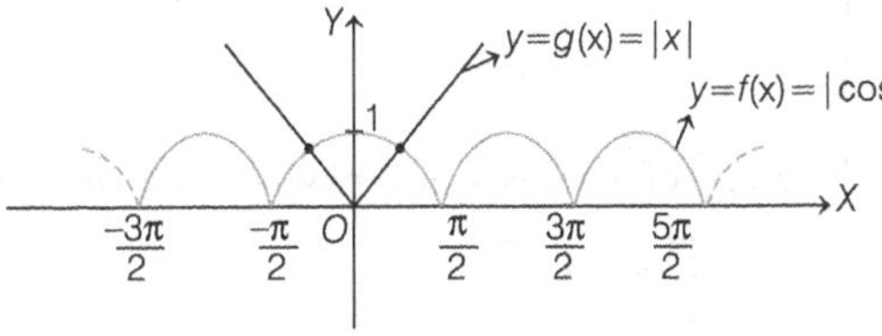

Hence, total number of points of intersection $= 2$.

Example 71. Find the total number of solutions of the equation $2\theta - \cos^2\theta + \sqrt{2} = 0$.

Sol. We have, $2\theta - \cos^2\theta + \sqrt{2} = 0 \Rightarrow \cos^2\theta = 2\theta + \sqrt{2}$

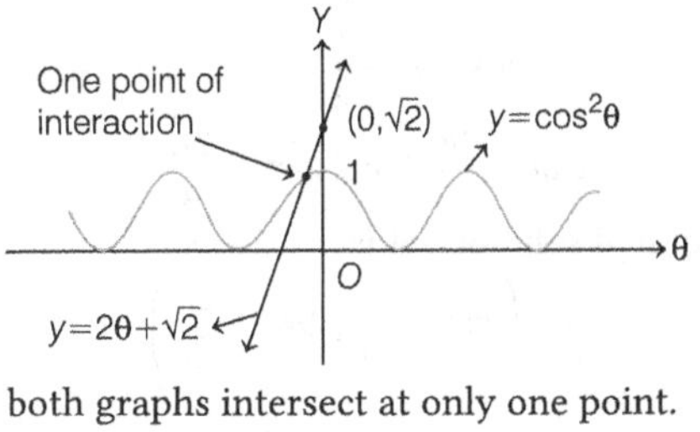

Hence, both graphs intersect at only one point.

So, total number of solutions $= 1$.

Example 72. If $\tan x = x + 1$, then find the interval in which least positive value of x lies.

Sol. Given equation is $\tan x = x + 1$.

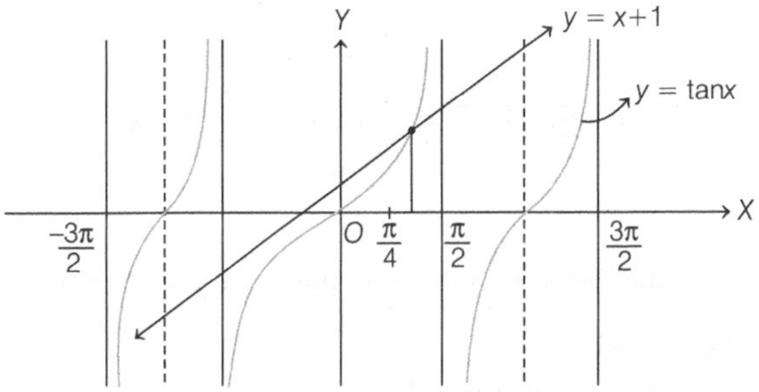

From above figure, it is clear that $y = \tan x$ and $y = x + 1$ intersect each other at infinite number of points.

But the least positive value of $x \in \left(\frac{\pi}{4}, \frac{\pi}{2}\right)$.

JEE SCANNER

Example Similar to PYQ Asked in JEE Main 2022

Let $\phi(x) = \max\{1 - x, 1 + x\}$. Then, the number of solutions in the interval $[0, 2\pi]$ satisfying $\phi(x) = \tan x$ is

Sol.

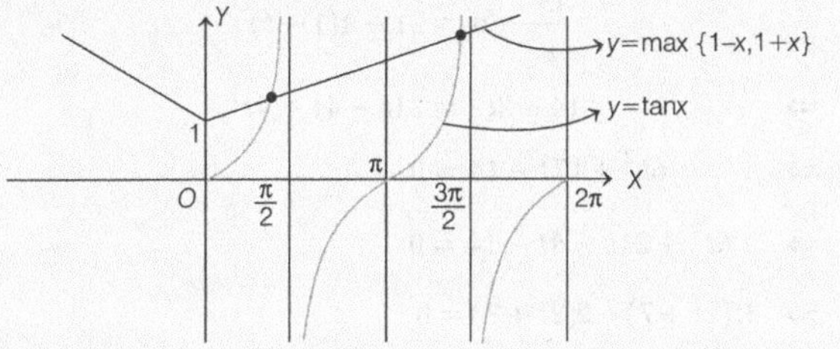

From above graph, we see that $\max\{1 - x, 1 + x\}$ intersects the graph of $\tan x$ at 2 points only in $[0, 2\pi]$.

Hence, total number of solutions $= 2$ in $[0, 2\pi]$.

Skill Builder

Let $\phi(x) = \max(x - 1, -x - 1\}$. Then, the number of solutions in the interval $[-\pi, \pi]$ satisfying $\phi(x) = \sin x$ is

For Sol.

■ **For more practice** See Q.4 of Milestone Practice 5.

Example 73. In $x \in (-2\pi, 2\pi)$, find the total number of solutions of the equation $3\cos^2 x - 10\cos x + 3 = 0$.

Sol. We have, $3\cos^2 x - 10\cos x + 3 = 0$

$$\Rightarrow \quad 3\cos^2 x - 9\cos x - \cos x + 3 = 0$$

$$\Rightarrow 3\cos x(\cos x - 3) - 1(\cos x - 3) = 0$$

$$\Rightarrow \quad (\cos x - 3)(3\cos x - 1) = 0$$

$$\Rightarrow \quad \cos x = 3 \text{ or } \cos x = \frac{1}{3}$$

But we know that $-1 \le \cos x \le 1$

So, $\cos x = 3$ (rejected)

Hence, $\cos x = \dfrac{1}{3}$ only possible.

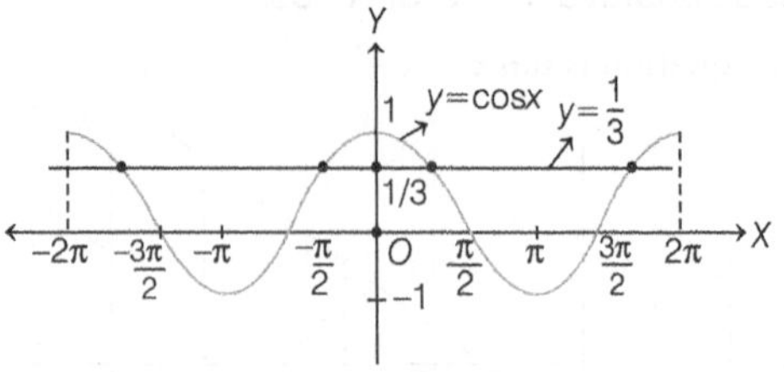

Here, the line $y = \dfrac{1}{3}$ intersects the curve $y = \cos x$ four times in $(-2\pi, 2\pi)$.

Thus, total number of solutions = 4.

Example 74. Find the number of values of x in the interval $\left(\dfrac{\pi}{4}, \dfrac{7\pi}{4}\right)$ for which

$14\operatorname{cosec}^2 x - 2\sin^2 x = 21 - 4\cos^2 x$ holds.

Sol. Given, $14\operatorname{cosec}^2 x - 2\sin^2 x = 21 - 4\cos^2 x$

$$\Rightarrow \quad \frac{14}{\sin^2 x} - 2\sin^2 x = 21 - 4(1 - \sin^2 x) \quad \text{...(i)}$$

Let $\sin^2 x = t$, then Eq. (i) becomes

$$\frac{14}{t} - 2t = 21 - 4(1 - t)$$

$$\Rightarrow \quad 14 - 2t^2 = 21t - 4t + 4t^2$$

$$\Rightarrow \quad 6t^2 + 17t - 14 = 0$$

$$\Rightarrow \quad 6t^2 + 21t - 4t - 14 = 0$$

$$\Rightarrow 3t(2t + 7) - 2(2t + 7) = 0$$

$$\Rightarrow \quad (2t + 7)(3t - 2) = 0$$

$$\Rightarrow \quad t = \frac{2}{3} \text{ or } t = \frac{-7}{2}$$

$$\Rightarrow \quad \sin^2 x = \frac{2}{3} \text{ or } \sin^2 x = \frac{-7}{2} \text{ (not possible)}$$

$$\Rightarrow \quad \sin x = \pm\sqrt{\frac{2}{3}}$$

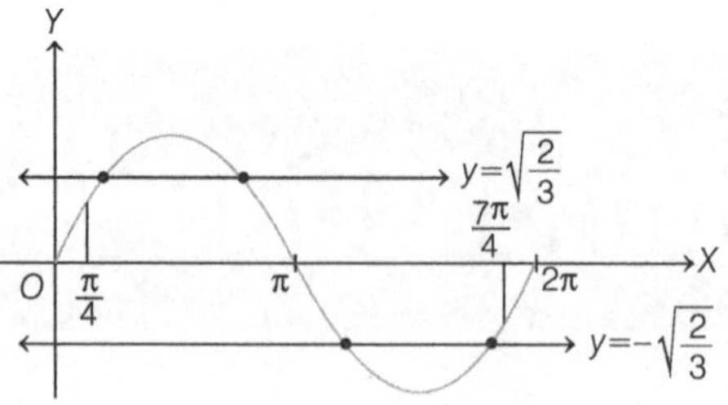

Hence, total number of solutions = 4 in $\left(\dfrac{\pi}{4}, \dfrac{7\pi}{4}\right)$.

2.6 Trigonometric Inequality

An inequality involving trigonometric function of an unknown angle is called a trigonometric inequality.

Method to Find Solution of Trigonometric Inequality

To solve the trigonometric inequation of type $f(x) \le a$, or $f(x) \ge a$ where $f(x)$ is some trigonometric ratio, the following steps should be taken:

1. Draw the graph of $f(x)$ is an interval length equal to the fundamental period of $f(x)$.
2. Draw the line $y = a$.
3. Take the portion of the graph for which the inequalities satisfied.
4. To generalize, add $nT (n \in I)$ and take union over the set of integers, where T, is the fundamental period of $f(x)$.

Example 75. Find the solution set of inequality $\cos x \ge -\dfrac{1}{2}$.

Sol. From the graph of $y = \cos x$, it is obvious that $\cos x \ge -\dfrac{1}{2}$.

For $\quad -\dfrac{2\pi}{3} \le x \le \dfrac{2\pi}{3}$

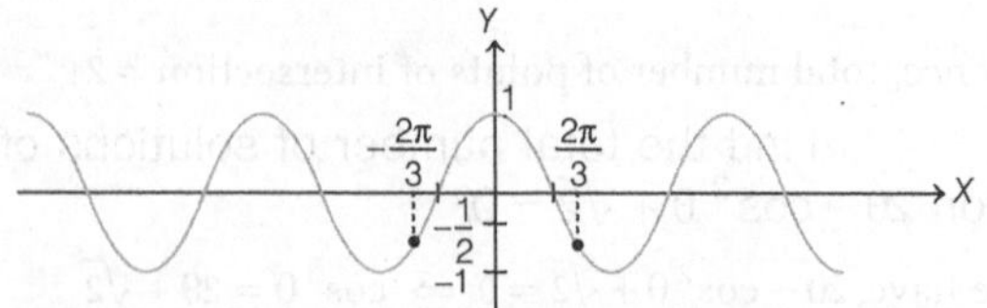

Hence, $\quad \cos x \ge -\dfrac{1}{2}$

$$\Rightarrow \quad 2n\pi - \frac{2\pi}{3} \le x \le 2n\pi + \frac{2\pi}{3}$$

The required solution set is

$$\bigcup_{n \in I} \left(2n\pi - \frac{2\pi}{3}, 2n\pi + \frac{2\pi}{3}\right)$$

Example 76. Find the interval of values of θ in which $2\sin^2\theta - 5\sin\theta + 2 > 0$, where $\theta \in (0, 2\pi)$.

Sol. Given, $2\sin^2\theta - 5\sin\theta + 2 > 0$

$$\Rightarrow \quad (2\sin\theta - 1)(\sin\theta - 2) > 0$$

$$\Rightarrow \quad \sin\theta < \frac{1}{2} \quad \left[\begin{array}{l} \because -1 \le \sin\theta \le 1 \\ \therefore -3 \le \sin\theta - 2 \le -1 \end{array}\right]$$

$$\Rightarrow \quad \theta \in \left(0, \frac{\pi}{6}\right) \cup \left(\frac{5\pi}{6}, 2\pi\right)$$

Example 77. Find the solution set for, $4\sin^2 x - 8\sin x + 3 \le 0$ where $x \in [0, 2\pi]$.

Sol. Here, $4\sin^2 x - 8\sin x + 3 \le 0$

$$\Rightarrow \quad (2\sin x - 1)(2\sin x - 3) \le 0$$

Here, $2\sin x - 3$ is always negative.

$$\therefore \quad 2\sin x - 1 \ge 0 \text{ i.e. } \sin x \ge \frac{1}{2}$$

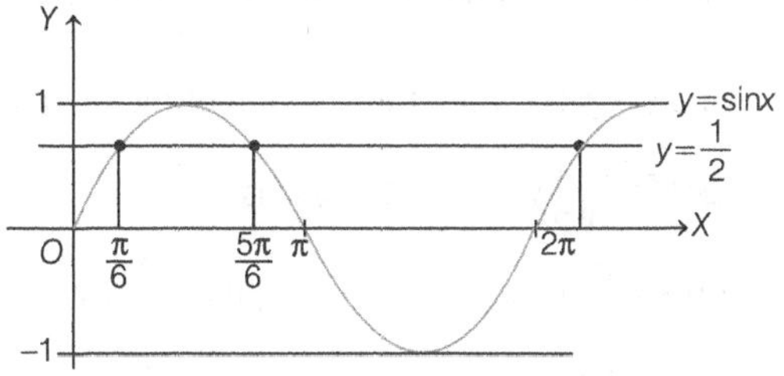

$\therefore$ From the figure, $\frac{\pi}{6} \le x \le \frac{5\pi}{6}$

Example 78. Solve $2\cos^2\theta + \sin\theta \le 2$, where $\frac{\pi}{2} \le \theta \le \frac{3\pi}{2}$.

Sol. $2\cos^2\theta + \sin\theta \le 2$

or $\quad 2(1 - \sin^2\theta) + \sin\theta \le 2$

or $\quad -2\sin^2\theta + \sin\theta \le 0$

or $\quad 2\sin^2\theta - \sin\theta \ge 0$

or $\quad \sin\theta(2\sin\theta - 1) \ge 0$

or $\quad \sin\theta(\sin\theta - 1/2) \ge 0$

which is possible if $\sin\theta \le 0$ or $\sin\theta \ge 1/2$

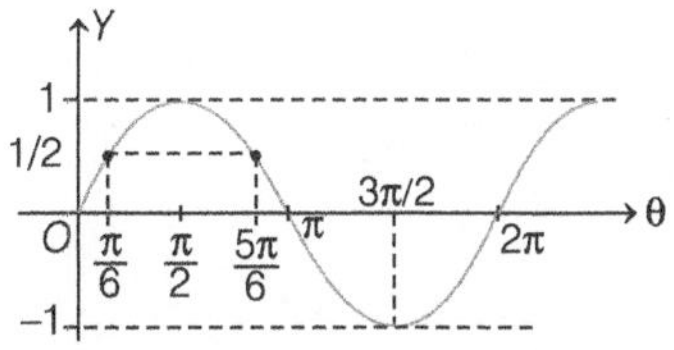

From the graph

$$\sin\theta \ge 1/2 \Rightarrow \pi/2 \le \theta \le 5\pi/6$$

$$\sin\theta \le 0 \Rightarrow \pi \le \theta \le 3\pi/2$$

Hence, the required values of θ are given by

$$\theta \in [\pi/2, 5\pi/6] \cup [\pi, 3\pi/2]$$

Example 79. Solve $\sin^2\theta > \cos^2\theta$

Sol. We have, $\sin^2\theta > \cos^2\theta \Rightarrow \cos 2\theta < 0$

$$\Rightarrow \quad (\pi/2) < 2\theta < (3\pi/2) \text{ or } (\pi/4) < \theta < (3\pi/4)$$

Taking general values i.e. adding $2n\pi$, we get

$$2n\pi + \pi/2 < 2\theta < 2n\pi + 3\pi/2,\ n \in Z$$

or $\quad n\pi + \pi/4 < \theta < n\pi + 3\pi/4$

Example 80. Find the solution set for, $|\tan x| \le 1$ when $x \in [-\pi, \pi]$.

Sol. Here, $|\tan x| \le 1 \Rightarrow -1 \le \tan x \le 1$,
the value scheme for this is shown below.

From the figure, $-\frac{\pi}{4} \le x \le \frac{\pi}{4}$

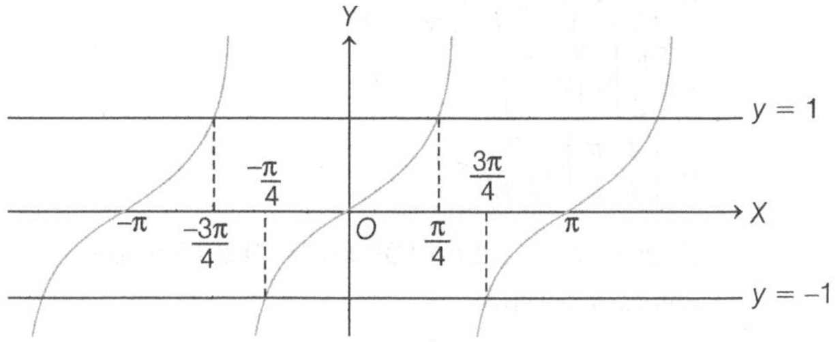

or $\quad -\pi \le x \le -\frac{3\pi}{4}$ or $\frac{3\pi}{4} \le x \le \pi$

$$\therefore \quad x \in \left[-\pi, -\frac{3\pi}{4}\right] \cup \left[-\frac{\pi}{4}, \frac{\pi}{4}\right] \cup \left[\frac{3\pi}{4}, \pi\right]$$

Example 81. Solve $\sin 2x > \sqrt{2}\sin^2 x + (2 - \sqrt{2})\cos^2 x$

Sol. $\sin 2x > \sqrt{2}\sin^2 x + (2 - \sqrt{2})\cos^2 x$

$$\Rightarrow \quad 2\sin x\cos x > \sqrt{2}\sin^2 x + (2 - \sqrt{2})\cos^2 x$$

$$\Rightarrow \quad \tan^2 x - \sqrt{2}\tan x + (\sqrt{2} - 1) < 0$$

$$\Rightarrow \quad (\tan x - 1)(\tan x - (\sqrt{2} - 1)) < 0$$

$$\Rightarrow \quad (\sqrt{2} - 1) < \tan x < 1 \Rightarrow \pi/8 < x < \pi/4$$

$$\therefore \quad x \in \left(n\pi + \frac{\pi}{8},\ n\pi + \frac{\pi}{4}\right), \text{ where } n \in Z.$$

Example 82. Solve $\tan^3 x + 3 > 3\tan x + \tan^2 x$

Sol. $\tan^3 x - \tan^2 x + 3 - 3\tan x > 0$

$$\Rightarrow \quad \tan^2 x(\tan x - 1) - 3(\tan x - 1) > 0$$

$$\Rightarrow \quad (\tan x - 1)(\tan^2 x - 3) > 0$$

$$\Rightarrow \quad (\tan x - 1)(\tan x + \sqrt{3})(\tan x - \sqrt{3}) > 0$$

$$\Rightarrow \quad (y - 1)(y + \sqrt{3})(y - \sqrt{3}) > 0, \text{ where } \tan x = y$$

Sign-scheme of above inequality is as follows:

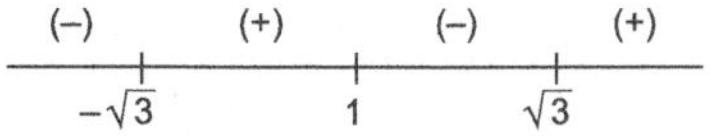

$\therefore -\sqrt{3} < y < 1$ or $y > \sqrt{3} \Rightarrow -\sqrt{3} < \tan x < 1$ or $\tan x > \sqrt{3}$

For $-\pi/2 < x < \pi/2$

$$-\pi/3 < x < x/4 \text{ or } \pi/3 < x < \pi/2$$

$\therefore$ General solution is

$$x \in \left(n\pi + \frac{\pi}{3}, n\pi + \frac{\pi}{2}\right) \cup \left(n\pi - \frac{\pi}{3}, n\pi + \frac{\pi}{4}\right), \text{ where } n \in Z.$$

Milestone Practice 2.4

1. If $2\cos x<\sqrt{3}$ and $x\in[-\pi,\pi]$, then find the solution set for x.

2. The set of all x in the interval $[0,\pi]$ for which $2\sin^2 x-3\sin x+1\geq 0$ is
   (a) $\frac{\pi}{2}\cup\left[-\pi,\frac{-\pi}{6}\right]$
   (b) $\left\{\frac{\pi}{2}\right\}\cup\left[0,\frac{\pi}{6}\right]\cup\left[\frac{5\pi}{6},\pi\right]$
   (c) $\left[\frac{\pi}{2}\right]\cup\left[0,\frac{\pi}{6}\right]$
   (d) $\left[\frac{\pi}{4},\frac{\pi}{6}\right]\cup\left[\frac{5\pi}{6},\pi\right]$

3. If $\cos x-\sin x\geq 1$ and $0\leq x\leq 2\pi$, then find the solution set for x.

4. Let $\phi(x)=\max\{\tan x,\cot x\}$. Then, find the number of solutions in the interval $(0,2\pi)$ satisfying $\phi(x)=\frac{1}{2}$.

5. Find the set of values of x, which satisfy $\sin x\cdot\cos^3 x>\cos x\cdot\sin^3 x,\ 0\leq x\leq 2\pi$.

6. The set of all x in $\left(\frac{-\pi}{2},\frac{\pi}{2}\right)$ which satisfy $|4\sin x-1|<\sqrt{5}$, is
   (a) $\left(\frac{\pi}{2},\frac{\pi}{6}\right)$ (b) $\left(-\pi,\frac{\pi}{6}\right)$
   (c) $\left(-\frac{\pi}{10},\frac{3\pi}{10}\right)$ (d) $\left(\frac{\pi}{4},\frac{3\pi}{2}\right)$

7. Solve $\sin^4\left(\frac{x}{3}\right)+\cos^4\left(\frac{x}{3}\right)>\frac{1}{2}$.

8. Solve $\tan x-\tan^2 x>0$ and $|2\sin x|<1$.

9. Solve the inequality $\frac{5}{4}\sin^2 x+\sin^2 x\cdot\cos^2 x>\cos 2x$.

10. Solve the inequality $\sin x\cos x+\frac{1}{2}\tan x\geq 1$.

11. If $0\leq x\leq 2\pi$, then the solution of the inequality, $2^{\operatorname{cosec}^2 x}\sqrt{\frac{1}{2}y^2-y+1}\leq\sqrt{2}$, is
   (a) $x=\frac{\pi}{2},\ y=1$ (b) $x=\frac{3\pi}{2},\ y=1$
   (c) $x=\left\{\frac{\pi}{2},\frac{3\pi}{2}\right\},\ y=1$ (d) $x=\left\{\frac{-3\pi}{2},\pi\right\},\ y=1$

12. Solve the inequality $5+2\cos 2x\leq 3\,|2\sin x-1|$.

Answer Key

1. $\left[-\pi,-\frac{\pi}{6}\right)\cup\left(\frac{\pi}{6},\pi\right]$
2. (b)
3. $\left[\frac{3\pi}{2},2\pi\right]\cup\{0\}$
4. No solution
5. $\left(0,\frac{\pi}{4}\right)$
6. (c)
7. $R-\left\{x:x=\frac{3n\pi}{2}\pm\frac{3\pi}{4},n\in Z\right\}$
8. $\left(n\pi,n\pi+\frac{\pi}{6}\right),\ n\in Z$
9. $n\pi+\frac{\pi}{6}<x<n\pi+\frac{5\pi}{6},\ n\in Z$
10. $\left[n\pi+\frac{\pi}{4},n\pi+\frac{\pi}{2}\right),\ n\in Z$
11. (c)
12. $2n\pi+\frac{\pi}{2},\left[2n\pi-\frac{5\pi}{6},2n\pi-\frac{\pi}{6}\right],\ n\in Z$

For Detailed Solution

JEE Pattern EXAMPLES

Single Option Correct Type Questions

Example 1 *The general solution of* $\sin^2\theta\sec\theta+\sqrt{3}\tan\theta=0$ *is*

(a) $\theta=n\pi+(-1)^{n+1}\frac{\pi}{3}, \theta=n\pi; n\in I$

(b) $\theta=n\pi, n\in I$

(c) $\theta=\frac{n\pi}{2}, n\in I$

(d) $\theta=n\pi+(-1)^{n+1}\frac{\pi}{3}, n\in I$

Sol. (b) Given, $\sin^2\theta\sec\theta+\sqrt{3}\tan\theta=0$

$\Rightarrow \sin\theta(\sin\theta+\sqrt{3})\sec\theta=0 \Rightarrow \sin\theta=0$

$\Rightarrow \theta=n\pi, n\in I$

$[\because \sin\theta\neq-\sqrt{3}, \sec\theta\neq0]$

Example 2 *The product of common differences of all possible AP which are made from values of 'x' satisfying*

$$\cos^2\left(\frac{1}{2}\lambda x\right)+\cos^2\left(\frac{1}{2}\mu x\right)=1$$

(a) $\frac{4\pi^2}{\lambda^2-\mu^2}$ (b) $\frac{4\pi}{\lambda-\mu}$

(c) $\frac{2\pi^2}{\lambda^2-\mu^2}$ (d) None of these

Sol. (a) Given, $\frac{1+\cos(\lambda x)}{2}+\frac{1+\cos(\mu x)}{2}=1$

$\Rightarrow \cos(\lambda x)+\cos(\mu x)=0$

$\Rightarrow 2\cos\left(\frac{(\lambda+\mu)x}{2}\right)\cdot\cos\left(\frac{(\lambda-\mu)x}{2}\right)=0$

$\Rightarrow \frac{(\lambda+\mu)x}{2}=(2n+1)\frac{\pi}{2}$ or $\frac{(\lambda-\mu)x}{2}=(2n+1)\frac{\pi}{2}$

$x=\frac{(2n+1)\pi}{\lambda+\mu}$ or $x=\frac{(2n+1)\pi}{\lambda-\mu}$

Thus, common difference can be $\frac{2\pi}{\lambda+\mu}$ or $\frac{2\pi}{\lambda-\mu}$.

Now, product $=\frac{4\pi^2}{\lambda^2-\mu^2}$

JEE SCANNER

Example 3 Similar to PYQ Asked in JEE Main 2018

If the sum of all solutions of equations $\sin x+2\cos x=1+\sqrt{3}\cos x$ *in* $[0,\pi]$ *is* $\frac{k\pi}{6}$, *then* $\frac{2k}{3}$ *is*

(a) $\frac{3}{2}$ (b) 1 (c) 2 (d) $\frac{1}{3}$

Sol. (c) Given, $\sin x+2\cos x=1+\sqrt{3}\cos x$ ...(i)

Since, $x\in[0,\pi]$, so let's take $x=0$

$\therefore \sin 0+2\cos 0=1+\sqrt{3}\cos 0 \Rightarrow 0+2\neq1+\sqrt{3}$

$\therefore x=\frac{0+\pi}{2}=\frac{\pi}{2}$

So, $\sin\frac{\pi}{2}+2\cos\frac{\pi}{2}=1+\sqrt{3}\cos\frac{\pi}{2} \Rightarrow 1=1$

$\therefore x=\frac{\pi}{2}$ satisfies the equation $\sin x+2\cos x=1+\sqrt{3}\cos x$.

Now, let $x=\frac{\pi}{4}$

$\therefore \sin\frac{\pi}{4}+2\cos\frac{\pi}{4}=1+\sqrt{3}\cos\frac{\pi}{4}$

$\Rightarrow \frac{1}{\sqrt{2}}+\frac{2}{\sqrt{2}}\neq1+\sqrt{3}\cdot\frac{1}{\sqrt{2}} \Rightarrow \frac{3}{\sqrt{2}}\neq\frac{\sqrt{2}+\sqrt{3}}{2}$

Let $x=\pi$

$\therefore \sin\pi+2\cos\pi=1+\sqrt{3}\cos\pi \Rightarrow -2\neq1-\sqrt{3}$

$\therefore x=\frac{\pi}{2}$ is the only solution which satisfies the above Eq. (i).

Sum of solutions $=\frac{\pi}{2}=\frac{k\pi}{6}\Rightarrow k=3$

$\therefore \frac{2k}{3}=\frac{2}{3}\times3=2$

Skill Builder

If sum of all the solutions of the equation $\sin x+\frac{1}{2}\cos x=\sin^2\left(x+\frac{\pi}{4}\right)$ in $x\in[0,\pi]$ is $\frac{k\pi}{4}$, then the value of k is equal to

(a) 2 (b) 4 (c) 6 (d) 8

For Sol.

Example 4 *Number of solutions of*

$$\cos^2\left[\frac{\pi}{4}(\sin x+\sqrt{2}\cos^2 x)\right]$$
$$-\tan^2\left[x+\frac{\pi}{4}\tan^2 x\right]=1,\ x\in[-2\pi,2\pi] \text{ is } \ldots\ldots\ldots$$

(a) 1 (b) 2
(c) 4 (d) 8

Sol. (b) The solution is only possible, when

$$\cos^2\left(\frac{\pi}{4}(\sin x+\sqrt{2}\cos^2 x)\right)=1 \quad \ldots\text{(i)}$$

and $$\tan^2\left(x+\frac{\pi}{4}\tan^2 x\right)=0 \quad \ldots\text{(ii)}$$

Let's solved Eq. (i),

$$\frac{\pi}{4}(\sin x+\sqrt{2}\cos^2 x)=k\pi$$

$$\Rightarrow \quad \sin x+\sqrt{2}\cos^2 x=4k$$

Now, as $|\sin x+\sqrt{2}\cos^2 x|\le|\sin x|+\sqrt{2}\,|\cos^2 x|\le 1+\sqrt{2}<4$

$\therefore$ $k=0$ is only possible value.

$$\Rightarrow \quad \sin x+\sqrt{2}\cos^2 x=0$$

$$\Rightarrow \quad \sqrt{2}\sin^2 x-\sin x-\sqrt{2}=0$$

$$\Rightarrow \quad \sin x=\frac{-1}{\sqrt{2}},\sqrt{2}$$

$$\Rightarrow \quad \sin x=-\frac{1}{\sqrt{2}} \quad [\because \sin x\ne\sqrt{2}]$$

$$\Rightarrow \quad x=2n\pi-\frac{\pi}{4} \text{ or } 2n\pi+\frac{5\pi}{4}$$

From Eq. (ii) we can say that the only solution possible is $x=2n\pi-\frac{\pi}{4}$.

Hence, for $x\in[-2\pi,2\pi]$ we have 2 solutions.

Example 5 *Find the number of solutions of the equation* $2^{\cos x}=|\sin x|$, *when* $x\in[-2\pi,2\pi]$.

(a) 8 (b) 3
(c) 5 (d) 2

Sol. (a)

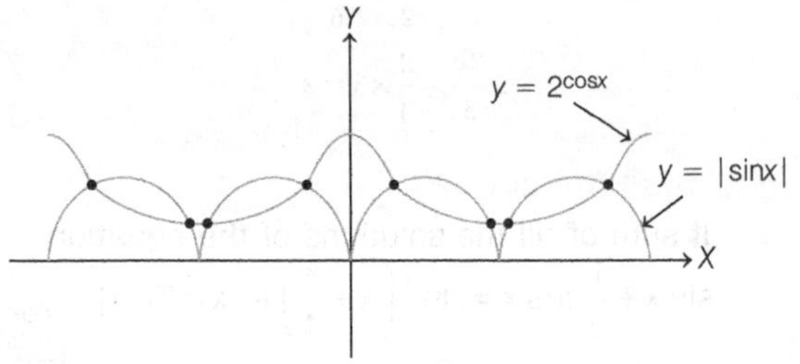

From the graph, we observe that $y=|\sin x|$ intersects the graph of $y=2^{\cos x}$ at 8 points in $[-2\pi,2\pi]$.

Hence, total number of solutions = 8

JEE SCANNER

Example 6 Similar to PYQ Asked in JEE Main 2023

The set of all values of λ *for which the equation* $\frac{1}{2}\cos^2 2x-2\sin^4 x-5\cos^2 x=\lambda$ *has a real solution* x *is*

(a) $\left[-\frac{9}{2},-\frac{3}{2}\right]$ (b) $\left[0,-\frac{3}{2}\right]$
(c) $\left[-\frac{9}{2},0\right]$ (d) $\left[-\frac{9}{2},\frac{3}{2}\right]$

Sol. (a) Given, $$\frac{1}{2}\cos^2 2x-2\sin^4 x-5\cos^2 x=\lambda$$

$$\Rightarrow \quad \frac{1}{2}\cos^2 2x-\frac{(1-2\cos 2x+\cos^2 2x)}{2}-5\cos^2 x=\lambda$$

$$\Rightarrow \quad \frac{1}{2}\cos^2 2x-\frac{\left(\frac{2}{2}-\frac{4\cos 2x}{2}+\frac{\cos 4x+1}{2}\right)-5\cos^2 x}{2}=\lambda$$

$$\Rightarrow \quad \frac{1}{2}\cos^2 2x-\left(\frac{\cos 4x-4\cos 2x+3}{4}\right)-5\left(\frac{\cos 2x+1}{2}\right)=\lambda$$

$$\Rightarrow \quad \frac{1}{2}\frac{(\cos 4x+1)}{2}-\frac{(\cos 4x-4\cos 2x+3)}{4}-\frac{5(\cos 2x+1)}{2}=\lambda$$

$$\Rightarrow \quad \frac{\cos 4x+1-\cos 4x+4\cos 2x-3-10\cos 2x-10}{4}=\lambda$$

$$\Rightarrow \quad \frac{-6\cos 2x-12}{4}=\lambda$$

$$\Rightarrow \quad \frac{-3\cos 2x-6}{2}=\lambda$$

As we know that

$$-1\le\cos 2x\le 1$$

$$\Rightarrow \quad -3\le-3\cos 2x\le+3$$

$$\Rightarrow \quad -9\le-3\cos 2x-6\le+3-6$$

$$\Rightarrow \quad -9\le-3\cos 2x-6\le-3$$

$$\Rightarrow \quad -\frac{9}{2}\le\frac{-3\cos 2x-6}{2}\le-\frac{3}{2}$$

$$\Rightarrow \quad -\frac{9}{2}\le\lambda\le-\frac{3}{2}$$

So, $$\lambda\in\left[-\frac{9}{2},-\frac{3}{2}\right]$$

Skill Builder

The set of all values of λ for which the equation $4\sin^2 x-4\cos^3 x+9+3\cos x=(\lambda-\cos 3x)$ has a real solution x, is

(a) $[-9, 0]$ (b) $[0, 9]$
(c) $[0, 13]$ (d) $[9, 13]$

For Sol.

Example 7 *The number of values of θ in the interval $\left(-\frac{\pi}{2}, \frac{\pi}{2}\right)$ satisfying the equation $(\sqrt{3})^{\sec^2\theta} = \tan^4\theta + 2\tan^2\theta$ is*

(a) 2 (b) 4 (c) 0 (d) 1

Sol. (a) $\tan^4\theta + 2\tan^2\theta = (\tan^2\theta + 1)^2 - 1$

$$= (\sec^2\theta)^2 - 1 = \sec^4\theta - 1$$

Put $\sec^2\theta = t \Rightarrow (\sqrt{3})^t = t^2 - 1$

$\Rightarrow t = 2$ is only solution as $t > 1$

$\therefore$ There will be 2 values of θ in given interval.

Example 8 *The number of ordered pairs (x, y) satisfying $|x| + |y| = 2$ and $\sin\left(\frac{\pi x^2}{3}\right) = 1$ is/are*

(a) 1 (b) 2 (c) 3 (d) 4

Sol. (d) $|x| + |y| = 2 \Rightarrow |x|, |y| \in [0, 2]$

Also, $\sin\left(\frac{\pi x^2}{3}\right) = 1$

$$\Rightarrow \frac{\pi x^2}{3} = (4n+1)\frac{\pi}{2} \Rightarrow x^2 = (4n+1)\frac{3}{2}$$

$\because$ $|x| \in [0, 2]$, then only possible value of x^2 is $\frac{3}{2}$

$$\therefore \quad |x| = \sqrt{\frac{3}{2}}, |y| = 2 - \sqrt{\frac{3}{2}}$$

Hence, total number of ordered pairs is 4.

More than One Correct Option Type Questions

Example 9 *For $0 < \theta < \frac{\pi}{2}$, the solution(s) of $\sum_{m=1}^{6} \operatorname{cosec}\left(\theta + \frac{(m-1)\pi}{4}\right) \operatorname{cosec}\left(\theta + \frac{m\pi}{4}\right) = 4\sqrt{2}$ is (are)*

(a) $\frac{\pi}{4}$ (b) $\frac{\pi}{6}$ (c) $\frac{\pi}{12}$ (d) $\frac{5\pi}{12}$

Sol. (c, d) We have,

$$\sum_{m=1}^{6} \operatorname{cosec}\left[\theta + \frac{(m-1)\pi}{4}\right] \operatorname{cosec}\left[\theta + \frac{m\pi}{4}\right] = 4\sqrt{2}$$

$$\Rightarrow \sum_{m=1}^{6} \frac{\sin\frac{\pi}{4}}{\sin\left[\theta + \frac{(m-1)\pi}{4}\right] \sin\left[\theta + \frac{m\pi}{4}\right]} = 4$$

$$\Rightarrow \sum_{m=1}^{6} \frac{\sin\left[\left(\theta + \frac{m\pi}{4}\right) - \left(\theta + \frac{(m-1)\pi}{4}\right)\right]}{\sin\left(\theta + \frac{(m-1)\pi}{4}\right) \sin\left(\theta + \frac{m\pi}{4}\right)} = 4$$

$$\Rightarrow \sum_{m=1}^{6} \left[\frac{\sin\left(\theta + \frac{m\pi}{4}\right) \cos\left(\theta + \frac{(m-1)\pi}{4}\right) - \cos\left(\theta + \frac{m\pi}{4}\right) \sin\left(\theta + \frac{(m-1)\pi}{4}\right)}{\sin\left(\theta + \frac{(m-1)\pi}{4}\right) \sin\left(\theta + \frac{m\pi}{4}\right)}\right] = 4$$

$$\Rightarrow \sum_{m=1}^{6} \left[\cot\left(\theta + \frac{(m-1)\pi}{4}\right) - \cot\left(\theta + \frac{m\pi}{4}\right)\right] = 4$$

$$\Rightarrow \left[\cot\theta - \cot\left(\theta + \frac{\pi}{4}\right)\right] + \left[\cot\left(\theta + \frac{\pi}{4}\right) - \cot\left(\theta + \frac{2\pi}{4}\right)\right] + \ldots + \left[\cot\left(\theta + \frac{5\pi}{4}\right) - \cot\left(\theta + \frac{6\pi}{4}\right)\right] = 4$$

$$\Rightarrow \quad \cot\theta - \cot\left(\theta + \frac{3\pi}{2}\right) = 4$$

$$\Rightarrow \quad \cot\theta + \tan\theta = 4$$

$$\Rightarrow \quad \cos^2\theta + \sin^2\theta = 4\sin\theta\cos\theta$$

$$\Rightarrow \quad \sin 2\theta = \frac{1}{2}$$

$$\Rightarrow \quad 2\theta = \frac{\pi}{6} \text{ or } \frac{5\pi}{6}$$

$$\Rightarrow \quad \theta = \frac{\pi}{12} \text{ or } \frac{5\pi}{12}$$

Example 10 *The value of x in $\left(0, \frac{\pi}{2}\right)$ satisfying equation $\frac{\sqrt{5}-1}{\sin x} + \frac{\sqrt{10+2\sqrt{5}}}{\cos x} = 8$ is*

(a) $\frac{\pi}{10}$ (b) $\frac{3\pi}{10}$ (c) $\frac{9\pi}{10}$ (d) $\frac{7\pi}{10}$

Sol. (a,b) $\frac{\sqrt{5}-1}{4} \times \frac{1}{\sin x} + \frac{\sqrt{10+2\sqrt{5}}}{4} \times \frac{1}{\cos x} = 2$

$$\frac{\sqrt{5}-1}{4}\cos x + \frac{\sqrt{10+2\sqrt{5}}}{4} \times \sin x = 2\sin x \cdot \cos x$$

$$\Rightarrow \quad \sin\left[x + \frac{\pi}{10}\right] = \sin 2x$$

$$x + \frac{\pi}{10} = 2x \Rightarrow x = \frac{\pi}{10}$$

or

$$\sin\left(x + \frac{\pi}{10}\right) = \sin(\pi - 2x)$$

$$\Rightarrow \quad x + \frac{\pi}{10} = \pi - 2x$$

$$\Rightarrow \quad 3x = \pi - \frac{\pi}{10} = \frac{9\pi}{10} \Rightarrow x = \frac{3\pi}{10}$$

Example 11 *All values between 0 and π which satisfies the equation $\sin^8 x + \cos^8 x = \frac{17}{16}\cos^2 2x$ is/are*

(a) $\frac{\pi}{4}$ (b) $\frac{5\pi}{8}$ (c) $\frac{\pi}{6}$ (d) $\frac{7\pi}{8}$

Sol. (b, d) The given equation can be rewritten as

$$(\sin^4 x + \cos^4 x)^2 - 2\sin^4 x \cos^4 x = \frac{17}{16}(1 - \sin^2 2x)$$

Put $t = \sin x . \cos x$,

$$(1 - 2t^2)^2 - 2t^4 = \frac{17}{16}(1 - 4t^2)$$

$$\Rightarrow \quad 32t^4 + 4t^2 - 1 = 0$$

$$\Rightarrow \quad 32t^4 + 8t^2 - 4t^2 - 1 = 0$$

$$\Rightarrow \quad (4t^2 + 1)(8t^2 - 1) = 0$$

$$\Rightarrow \quad t = \pm \frac{1}{2\sqrt{2}} \qquad [\because 4t^2 + 1 \neq 0]$$

$$\Rightarrow \quad \sin x . \cos x = \pm \frac{1}{2\sqrt{2}} \Rightarrow \sin 2x = \pm \frac{1}{\sqrt{2}}$$

$$\Rightarrow \quad 2x = n\pi \pm (-1)^n \left(\frac{\pi}{4}\right) \Rightarrow x = \frac{n\pi}{2} \pm (-1)^n \frac{\pi}{8}$$

Example 12 *General values of x and y for the trigonometric equation* $|\sin x + \cos x|^{\sin^2 x - \frac{1}{4}} = 1 + |\sin y|$ *and* $\cos^2 y = 1 + \sin^2 y$ *are*

(a) $x = 2m\pi, m \in I$ (b) $y = k\pi, k \in I$

(c) $x = 2m\pi \pm \frac{\pi}{6}, m \in I$ (d) $y = n\pi \pm \frac{\pi}{6}, n \in I$

Sol. (a, b) $|\sin x + \cos x|^{\sin^2 x - 1/4} = 1 + |\sin y|$ ...(i)

and $\cos^2 y = 1 + \sin^2 y$ ...(ii)

$$\Rightarrow \quad 1 - \sin^2 y = 1 + \sin^2 y$$

$$\Rightarrow \quad \sin^2 y = 0, y = k\pi, k \in I$$

$$\Rightarrow \quad |\sin x + \cos x|^{\sin^2 x - 1/4} = 1$$

Then, either $\sin^2 x = \frac{1}{4}$ or $\sin x + \cos x = 1$

$$\Rightarrow x = n\pi \pm \frac{\pi}{6}, n \in I \text{ or } \cos\left(x - \frac{\pi}{4}\right) = \cos\frac{\pi}{4}$$

Now, $\cos\left(x - \frac{\pi}{4}\right) = \cos\frac{\pi}{4} \Rightarrow x - \frac{\pi}{4} = 2m\pi \pm \frac{\pi}{4}, m \in I$

$$\Rightarrow \quad x = 2m\pi + \frac{\pi}{2} \text{ or } x = 2m\pi, m \in I$$

$$\Rightarrow \quad x = 2m\pi \text{ or } 2m\pi + \frac{\pi}{2}, m \in I$$

$$\Rightarrow x = 2m\pi + \frac{\pi}{2}, 2m\pi, n\pi \pm \frac{\pi}{6} \text{ and } y = k\pi; m, n, k \in I.$$

Example 13 *If* $\frac{y+3}{2y+5} = \sin^2 x + 2\cos x + 1$, *then the value of y lie in the interval*

(a) $\left(-\infty, -\frac{8}{3}\right]$ (b) $\left[-\frac{12}{5}, \infty\right)$

(c) $\left[-\frac{8}{3}, -\frac{12}{5}\right]$ (d) $\left(-\infty, -\frac{8}{3}\right] \cup \left[-\frac{12}{5}, \infty\right)$

Sol. (a,b,d) $\cos^2 x - 2\cos x + 1 = 3 - \frac{y+3}{2y+5}$

$$(\cos x - 1)^2 = \frac{5y + 12}{2y + 5}$$

Also, $-1 \le \cos x \le 1 \Rightarrow -2 \le \cos x - 1 \le 0$

$$\Rightarrow \quad 0 \le (\cos x - 1)^2 \le 4 \Rightarrow 0 \le \frac{5y + 12}{2y + 5} \le 4$$

Now, $\frac{5y + 12}{2y + 5} - 4 \le 0 \Rightarrow \frac{-3y - 8}{2y + 5} \le 0$

$$\Rightarrow \quad \frac{3y + 8}{2y + 5} \ge 0 \Rightarrow (3y + 8)(2y + 5) \ge 0$$

and $\frac{5y + 12}{2y + 5} \ge 0 \Rightarrow (5y + 12)(2y + 5) \ge 0$

$$\Rightarrow \quad \left(-\infty, -\frac{8}{3}\right] \cup \left[-\frac{5}{2}, \infty\right) \text{ and } \left(-\infty, -\frac{5}{2}\right) \cup \left[-\frac{12}{5}, \infty\right)$$

$$\therefore \quad y \in \left(-\infty, -\frac{8}{3}\right] \cup \left[-\frac{12}{5}, \infty\right)$$

Example 14 *Given* $2\sin t = \frac{1 - 2x + 5x^2}{3x^2 - 2x - 1}$ *the real values of* $t \in \left[-\frac{\pi}{2}, \frac{\pi}{2}\right]$ *satisfying this lie in the interval*

(a) $\left[-\frac{\pi}{2}, \frac{\pi}{2}\right]$ (b) $\left[\frac{3\pi}{10}, \frac{\pi}{2}\right]$

(c) $\left[-\frac{\pi}{2}, -\frac{\pi}{10}\right] \cup \left[\frac{3\pi}{10}, \frac{\pi}{2}\right]$ (d) All of these

Sol. (b,c) Given, $x^2(6\sin t - 5) + x(2 - 4\sin t) - (1 + 2\sin t) = 0$, since $x \in R, \Delta \ge 0$

$$\Rightarrow \quad \sin t \le \frac{1 - \sqrt{5}}{4} \text{ or } \sin t \ge \frac{1 + \sqrt{5}}{4}$$

$$\therefore \quad t \in \left[-\frac{\pi}{2}, -\frac{\pi}{10}\right] \cup \left[\frac{3\pi}{10}, \frac{\pi}{2}\right]$$

Example 15 $0 < a < 2\pi$, $\sin^{-1}(\sin a) < x^2 - 2x$ *for all* $x \in I$, *then* $a \in$

(a) $(0, \pi + 1)$ (b) $\left(\pi + 1, \frac{3\pi}{2}\right)$

(c) $\left(\frac{3\pi}{2}, 2\pi - 1\right)$ (d) $(2\pi - 1, 2\pi)$

Sol. (b,c) $\sin^{-1}(\sin a) < x^2 - 2x$ for all $x \in I$.

$$\therefore \quad \sin^{-1}(\sin a) < \min(x^2 - 2x) = -1$$

For $a \in \left(0, \frac{\pi}{2}\right), a < -1 \Rightarrow a \in \phi$

For $a \in \left(\frac{\pi}{2}, \frac{3\pi}{2}\right)$, $\sin^{-1}(\sin a) = \pi - a$

$$\pi - a < -1$$

$$a > \pi + 1 \Rightarrow a \in \left(\pi + 1, \frac{3\pi}{2}\right)$$

For $a \in \left(\frac{3\pi}{2}, 2\pi\right)$, $\sin^{-1}(\sin a) = a - 2\pi$

$$a - 2\pi < -1 \Rightarrow a < 2\pi - 1$$

$$\Rightarrow \quad a < 2\pi - 1 \Rightarrow a \in \left(\frac{3\pi}{2}, 2\pi - 1\right).$$

Example 16 *If $a \in (0, 1)$, then the general solution of the equation $\log_{\sin x} 2 \cdot \log_{\sin^2 x} a = -1$ is/are*

(a) $x = n\pi + (-1)^n \sin^{-1}(2^{-\sqrt{(-\log_2 a)/2}})$

(b) $x = n\pi \pm (-1)^n \sin^{-1}(2^{\sqrt{(-\log_2 a)/2}})$

(c) $x = n\pi - (-1)^n \cos^{-1}(2^{-\sqrt{(\log_2 a)/2}})$

(d) None of the above

Sol. (a) We have, $\log_{\sin x} 2 \cdot \log_{\sin^2 x} a = -1$

$$\Rightarrow \quad \log_{\sin x} 2 \cdot \log_{\sin x} a = -2 \quad \begin{pmatrix} \sin x > 0 \\ a > 0 \end{pmatrix} \ldots\text{(i)}$$

$$\Rightarrow \quad \log_{\sin x} 2 \cdot \frac{\log_2 a}{\log_2 \sin x} = -2$$

$$\Rightarrow \quad \log_2 a = -2(\log_2 \sin x)^2$$

$$\Rightarrow \quad \log_2 \sin x = \pm\sqrt{\frac{(-\log_2 a)}{2}}$$

$$\left\{\text{as } \sin x < 1 \Rightarrow \log_2 \sin x < 0, \text{ so reject } \log_2 \sin x = \sqrt{\frac{(-\log_2 a)}{2}}\right\}$$

$$\Rightarrow \quad \log_2 \sin x = -\sqrt{\frac{(-\log_2 a)}{2}} \Rightarrow \sin x = 2^{-\sqrt{(-\log_2 a)/2}}$$

$\Rightarrow x = n\pi + (-1)^n \sin^{-1}\{2^{-\sqrt{(-\log_2 a)/2}}\}$ and the condition is $0 < a < 1$ so that $\log_2 a$ is defined and $\log_2 a < 0$.

Example 17 *The system of equations*

$$\tan x = a \cot x, \ \tan 2x = b \cos y$$

(a) Cannot have a solution if $a = 0$

(b) Cannot have a solution if $a = 1$

(c) Cannot have a solution if $2\sqrt{a} > |b(1 - a)|$

(d) has a solution for all a and b

Sol. (b,c) If $a = 0$, then $\tan x = 0 \Rightarrow x = n\pi$ and then for any value of y such that $\cos y = 0$ the second equation satisfies option (a) is false.

If $a = 1$, then $\tan x = \cot x \Rightarrow \tan^2 x = 1$

$\Rightarrow$ $\tan 2x$ is not defined.

$\Rightarrow$ option (b) is true.

Now, from the first equation $\tan x = \sqrt{a}$

$\Rightarrow$ a must be positive

$$|\cos y| = \left|\frac{2\tan x}{b(1 - \tan^2 x)}\right| = \left|\frac{2\sqrt{a}}{b(1 - a)}\right| \le 1$$

$$\Rightarrow \quad 2\sqrt{a} \le |b(1 - a)|$$

Example 18 *General solution of system of the following equations $4^{\sin x} + 3^{\frac{1}{\cos y}} = 11$ and $5.16^{\sin x} - 2.3^{\frac{1}{\cos y}} = 2$ are*

(a) $y = n\pi \pm \frac{\pi}{3}, n \in I$ (b) $y = 2m\pi \pm \frac{\pi}{3}, m \in I$

(c) $x = n\pi + (-1)^n \frac{\pi}{6}, n \in I$ (d) $x = 2m\pi \pm \frac{\pi}{3}, m \in I$

Sol. (b, c) Let $4^{\sin x} = \lambda$ and $3^{1/\cos y} = \mu$

Then, the equation becomes, $\lambda + \mu = 11$

$5\lambda^2 - 2\mu = 2$, solving these equations we get,

$$2\lambda + 5\lambda^2 = 24$$

or $\quad 5\lambda^2 + 2\lambda - 24 = 0$ or $(5\lambda + 12)(\lambda - 2) = 0$

So, $\quad \lambda = 2, -\frac{12}{5}$

If $\quad \lambda = 2, \ 4^{\sin x} = 2,$

$$\therefore \quad 2^{2\sin x} = 2^1$$

$$\therefore \quad \sin x = \frac{1}{2}$$

If $\lambda = -\frac{12}{5}$, then $4^{\sin x} = -\frac{12}{5}$, which is impossible as $4^{\sin x} > 0$

when $\lambda = 2$, we get

$$\mu = 11 - 2 = 9$$

$$\Rightarrow \quad \frac{1}{3^{\cos y}} = 9 = 3^2$$

$$\Rightarrow \quad \cos y = \frac{1}{2}$$

$$\Rightarrow \quad y = 2m\pi + \frac{\pi}{3}, \ m \in I$$

Thus, $x = n\pi + (-1)^n \frac{\pi}{6}$ and $y = 2m\pi \pm \frac{\pi}{3}$, where $m, n \in I$.

Example 19 *General values of x, y and z for the system of equations $\tan^2 x + \cot^2 x = 2\cos^2 y$ and $\cos^2 y + \sin^2 z = 1$ are*

(a) $y = m\pi, m \in I$ (b) $x = K\pi + \frac{\pi}{4}, K \in I$

(c) $z = n\pi, n \in I$ (d) $x = K\pi - \frac{\pi}{3}, K \in I$

Sol. (a, b, c) As we know, AM $\ge$ GM

$$\therefore \quad \frac{\tan^2 x + \cot^2 x}{2} \ge \sqrt{\tan^2 x \cdot \cot^2 x}$$

$$\Rightarrow \quad \tan^2 x + \cot^2 x \ge 2$$

Now, from the first equation,

$$2\cos^2 y \ge 2$$

$\cos^2 y \ge 1$, which is only possible when,

$$\cos^2 y = 1$$

Putting $\cos^2 y = 1$ in second equation we get,

$$\sin^2 z = 0 \Rightarrow z = n\pi \quad \text{...(ii)}$$

Similarly, $\cos^2 y = 1 \Rightarrow y = m\pi$ ...(iii)

Also, $\tan^2 x + \cot^2 x = 2\cos^2 y$

$\Rightarrow \tan^2 x + \cot^2 x = 2$

$\Rightarrow \tan^2 x = \cot^2 x = 1$

$\Rightarrow x = k\pi \pm \frac{\pi}{4}$ ...(iv)

Hence, the solutions are

$$x = k\pi \pm \frac{\pi}{4}, y = m\pi, z = n\pi,$$

where $k, m, n \in I$.

Example 20 *All number of pairs x, y that satisfy the equation* $\tan^4 x + \tan^4 y + 2\cot^2 x \cdot \cot^2 y = 3 + \sin^2(x+y)$ *are*

(a) $x = p\pi + \frac{\pi}{4}, p \in I$ (b) $y = p\pi - \frac{\pi}{4}, p \in I$

(c) $x = p\pi - \frac{\pi}{4}, p \in I$ (d) $y = p\pi + \frac{\pi}{4}, p \in I$

Sol. (a, b, c, d) We have, $\tan^4 x + \tan^4 y + 2\cot^2 x \cot^2 y = 3 + \sin^2(x+y)$

$\Rightarrow \tan^4 x + \tan^4 y + 2\cot^2 x \cot^2 y - 2 = 1 + \sin^2(x+y)$

$\Rightarrow (\tan^2 x - \tan^2 y) + 2(\tan x \tan y - \cot x \cot y)^2 = -1 + \sin^2(x+y)$

Clearly, LHS ≥ 0 and RHS ≤ 0

$\therefore$ LHS = RHS = 0

$\Rightarrow \tan^2 x = \tan^2 y$, $\tan x \tan y = \cot x \cot y$ and $\sin^2(x+y) = 1$

$\Rightarrow \tan^2 x = \tan^2 y$, $\tan^2 x \tan^2 y = 1$ and $\sin^2(x+y) = 1$

$\Rightarrow \tan^2 x = 1$ and $x + y = n\pi \pm \frac{\pi}{2}$, $n, m, \in I$

$\Rightarrow x = m\pi \pm \frac{\pi}{4}$ and $y = (n-m)\pi \mp \frac{\pi}{4}$, $n, m, \in I$

Thus, $x = y = p\pi \pm \frac{\pi}{4}, p \in I$

Example 21 *All the solutions of x, y in the equation*

$$4\left(3\sqrt{4x - x^2}\sin^2\left(\frac{x+y}{2}\right) + 2\cos(x+y)\right) = 13 + 4\cos^2(x+y) \text{ are}$$

(a) $\left(2, 2n\pi + \frac{2\pi}{3} + 2\right)$ (b) $\left(2, 2n\pi - \frac{2\pi}{3} - 2\right)$

(c) $\left(2, 2n\pi + \frac{2\pi}{3} - 2\right)$ (d) $\left(4, 2n\pi - \frac{2\pi}{3} - 2\right)$, where $n \in I$

Sol. (b, c) We have,

$$4\left[3\sqrt{4x - x^2}\left(\frac{1 - \cos(x+y)}{2}\right) + 2\cos(x+y)\right] = 13 + 4\cos^2(x+y)$$

$$\Rightarrow 6\sqrt{4x - x^2} - 6\sqrt{4x - x^2}\cos(x+y) + 8\cos(x+y) = 13 + 4\cos^2(x+y)$$

$$\Rightarrow 4\cos^2(x+y) + (6\sqrt{4x - x^2} - 8)\cos(x+y) + (13 - 6\sqrt{4x - x^2}) = 0 \quad \text{...(i)}$$

Let $\cos(x+y) = t$

and $6\sqrt{4x - x^2} - 8 = a$

$\Rightarrow 6\sqrt{4x - x^2} = 8 + a$

Clearly, $4x - x^2 \geq 0$ or $x(x-4) \leq 0$ or $0 \leq x \leq 4$ ...(ii)

Now, Eq. (i) reduces to;

$$4t^2 + at + (5 - a) = 0$$

which is quadratic in t.

$\therefore D \geq 0$

$a^2 - 4.4(5 - a) \geq 0$

$a^2 + 16a - 80 \geq 0$

$(a + 20)(a - 4) \geq 0$

$\Rightarrow a \leq -20$ or $a \geq 4$ ...(iii)

However, according to substitution;

$a = 6\sqrt{4x - x^2} - 8 = 6\sqrt{4 - (x-2)^2} - 8$

$-8 \leq a \leq 4$ ...(iv)

$\Rightarrow a = 4$ [from Eqs. (iii) and (iv)]

Hence, $6\sqrt{4x - x^2} - 8 = 4$

$\Rightarrow \sqrt{4x - x^2} = 2$

$\Rightarrow 4x - x^2 = 4 \Rightarrow x^2 - 4x + 4 = 0$

$\Rightarrow (x-2)^2 = 0$ or $x = 2$

Now, Eq. (i) becomes;

$\Rightarrow 4\cos^2(2+y) + 4\cos(2+y) + 1 = 0$

$\Rightarrow (2\cos(2+y) + 1)^2 = 0$

$\Rightarrow 2\cos(2+y) + 1 = 0$

$\Rightarrow \cos(2+y) = -\frac{1}{2} = \cos\left(\pi - \frac{\pi}{3}\right)$

$\Rightarrow 2 + y = 2n\pi \pm \frac{2\pi}{3}$

$\Rightarrow y = 2n\pi \pm \frac{2\pi}{3} - 2, n \in I$

Thus, the solutions are $\left(2, 2n\pi \pm \frac{2\pi}{3} - 2\right)$.

Example 22 *If* $\left(\cos^2 x + \frac{1}{\cos^2 x}\right)(1 + \tan^2 2y)(3 + \sin 3z) = 4$, *then*

(a) x may be a multiple of π

(b) x cannot be an even multiple of π

(c) z can be a multiple of π

(d) y can be a multiple of $\frac{\pi}{2}$

Sol. (a,d) $\left(\cos^2 x + \dfrac{1}{\cos^2 x}\right)(1+\tan^2 2y)(3+\sin 3z) = 4$

Since, $\cos^2 x + \dfrac{1}{\cos^2 x} > 2,\ 1+\tan^2 2y \ge 1,\ 2 \le 3 + \sin 3z \le 4$

so, the only possibility is

$$\cos^2 x + \frac{1}{\cos^2 x} = 2,\ 1+\tan^2 2y = 1,\ 3+\sin 3z = 2$$

$$\Rightarrow \quad \cos x = \pm 1 \Rightarrow x = n\pi$$

$$\tan 2y = 0 \Rightarrow y = \frac{m\pi}{2}$$

$$\sin 3z = -1 \Rightarrow z = (4k-1)\frac{\pi}{6};\ m, n, k \in I$$

Example 23 *For $x \in (-\pi, \pi)$, the value of x for which the given equation $(\sqrt{3}\sin x + \cos x)^{\sqrt{\sqrt{3}\sin 2x - \cos 2x + 2}} = 4$ is satisfied, is/are*

(a) $x = \dfrac{\pi}{2}$ (b) $x = \dfrac{\pi}{4}$ (c) $x = \dfrac{\pi}{6}$ (d) $x = \dfrac{\pi}{3}$

Sol. (d) Here, $\left[2\sin\left(x+\dfrac{\pi}{6}\right)\right]^{\sqrt{2\sin^2 x + 2\sqrt{3}\sin x \,.\, \cos x + 1}} = 4$

$$\Rightarrow \left[2\sin\left(x+\frac{\pi}{6}\right)\right]^{\sqrt{3\sin^2 x + \cos^2 x + 2\sqrt{3}\sin x \,.\, \cos x}} = 4$$

$$\Rightarrow \left[2\sin\left(x+\frac{\pi}{6}\right)\right]^{|\sqrt{3}\sin x + \cos x|} = 4$$

$$\Rightarrow \left[2\sin\left(x+\frac{\pi}{6}\right)\right]^{|2\sin(x+\pi/6)|} = 4$$

$$\Rightarrow \left\{\sin\left(x+\frac{\pi}{6}\right)\right\}^{|\sin(x+\pi/6)|} = 1$$

To make the RHS well defined it is necessary that,

$$\sin\left(x+\frac{\pi}{6}\right) > 0 \Rightarrow x \in \left(-\frac{\pi}{6}, \frac{5\pi}{6}\right)$$

Now, we have $\left\{\sin\left(x+\dfrac{\pi}{6}\right)\right\}^{\sin(x+\pi/6)} = 1$

$$\Rightarrow \quad \sin\left(x+\frac{\pi}{6}\right) = 1 \Rightarrow x = \frac{\pi}{3}$$

Passage Based Questions

Passage I

(Ex. Nos. 24 to 25)

Consider a circle, in which a point P is lying inside the circle such that $(PA)(PB) = (PC)(PD)$ (as shown in figure).

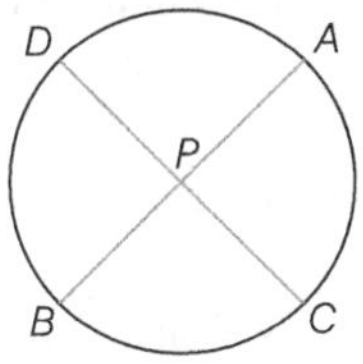

Example 24 *Let $PA = 4$, $PB = 3$ and CD is diameter of the circle having the length 8. If $PC > PD$, then $\dfrac{PC}{PD}$ is equal to*

(a) 3 (b) 4 (c) 5 (d) 6

Sol. (a) $(PA)(PB) = (PC)(PD)$

$$4 \times 3 = x(2r - x) \Rightarrow 12 = x(8 - x)$$

$$\Rightarrow \quad x^2 - 8x + 12 = 0 \Rightarrow x = 6, 2$$

$$\frac{PC}{PD} = \frac{6}{2} = 3$$

Example 25 *If $\log_{PA} x = 2$, $\log_{PB} x = 3$, $\log_x PC = 4$, then $\log_{PD} x$ is equal to*

(a) $\dfrac{7}{12}$ (b) $\dfrac{12}{7}$ (c) $-\dfrac{7}{12}$ (d) $-\dfrac{6}{19}$

Sol. (d) $(PA)(PB) = (PC)(PD)$

$$\log_x((PA)(PB)) = \log_x((PC)(PD))$$

$$\log_x PA + \log_x PB = \log_x PC + \log_x PD$$

$$\frac{1}{2} + \frac{1}{3} = 4 + \log_x PD$$

$$\log_x PD = \frac{5}{6} - 4 = -\frac{19}{6} \Rightarrow \log_{PD} x = -\frac{6}{19}$$

Passage II

(Ex. Nos. 26 to 27)

PA and PB are two tangents drawn from point P to circle of radius 5. A line is drawn from point P which cuts circle at C and D such that $PC = 5$ and $PD = 15$ and $\angle APB = \theta$.

Example 26 *Area of ΔAPB is*

(a) $\dfrac{25\sqrt{3}}{2}$ (b) $25\sqrt{3}$ (c) $\dfrac{75\sqrt{3}}{2}$ (d) $\dfrac{75\sqrt{3}}{4}$

Example 27 *Number of solution(s) of the equation $\log_{\cos\theta}(x+2) = 2 + 3\log_{(x+2)}\sin\left(\dfrac{5\theta}{2}\right)$ is*

(a) 0 (b) 1 (c) 2 (d) 3

Sol. (Ex. Nos. 26 to 27)

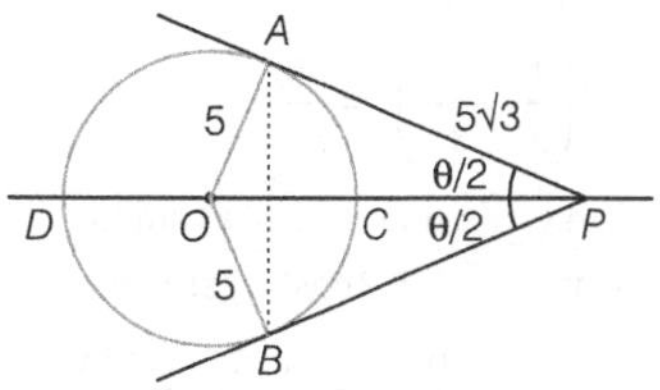

$$OD = OC = 5,\ PD = DC + CP$$

$$\Rightarrow \quad CP = 15 - 10 = 5,\ OP = 10$$

$$\Rightarrow \quad \sin\frac{\theta}{2} = \frac{OA}{OP} = \frac{5}{10} = \frac{1}{2} \Rightarrow \frac{\theta}{2} = 30^\circ \Rightarrow \theta = 60^\circ$$

26. (d) $\therefore$ *APB* is an equilateral triangle.

$$\text{Area} = \frac{\sqrt{3}}{4}(5\sqrt{3})^2 = \frac{75\sqrt{3}}{4}$$

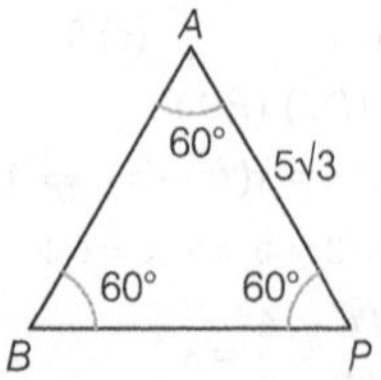

27. (c) Given, $\log_{1/2}(x+2) = 2 + 3\log_{(x+2)}\left(\frac{1}{2}\right)$

Let $\log_{1/2}(x+2) = t \Rightarrow t = 2 + \frac{3}{t}$

$\Rightarrow \quad t^2 - 2t - 3 = 0 \Rightarrow t = 3 \text{ or } -1$

$\Rightarrow \quad \log_{1/2}(x+2) = 3 \text{ or } \log_{1/2}(x+2) = -1$

$\Rightarrow \quad x = -\frac{15}{8} \text{ or } x = 0$

$\Rightarrow$ Two solutions.

Passage III

(Ex. Nos. 28 and 29)

If $3\sin^2 x - 7\sin x + 2 = 0,\ x \in \left[0, \frac{\pi}{2}\right]$ and $f_n(\theta) = \sin^n\theta + \cos^n\theta$.

Example 28 *The value of $f_4(x)$ is*

(a) $\frac{97}{81}$ (b) $\frac{57}{81}$ (c) $\frac{65}{81}$ (d) $\frac{73}{81}$

Example 29 *The value of $\frac{\sin 5x + \sin 4x}{1 + 2\cos 3x}$ is*

(a) $\frac{3+2\sqrt{2}}{9}$ (b) $\frac{3+4\sqrt{2}}{9}$

(c) $\frac{4\sqrt{2}-2}{9}$ (d) $\frac{4\sqrt{2}-3}{9}$

Sol. (Ex. Nos. 28 to 29) $3\sin^2 x - 7\sin x + 2 = 0$

$\Rightarrow \quad \sin x = \frac{1}{3}$ or $\sin x = 2$ (reject)

28. (c) $f_4(x) = \sin^4 x + \cos^4 x = 1 - 2(\sin x \cos x)^2$

$$= 1 - 2\left(\frac{1}{3}\cdot\frac{2\sqrt{2}}{3}\right)^2 = \frac{65}{81}$$

29. (b) $\frac{\sin 5x + \sin 4x}{1 + 2\cos 3x} = \frac{(\sin 5x + \sin 4x)\sin 3x}{(1 + 2\cos 3x)\sin 3x}$

$$= \frac{(\sin 5x + \sin 4x)\sin 3x}{\sin 3x + \sin 6x}$$

$$= \frac{2\sin\frac{9x}{2}\cos\frac{x}{2}\sin 3x}{2\sin\frac{9x}{2}\cos\frac{3x}{2}}$$

$$= \frac{\cos\frac{x}{2}\cdot 2\sin\frac{3x}{2}\cos\frac{3x}{2}}{\cos\frac{3x}{2}} = \sin 2x + \sin x$$

$$= \frac{4\sqrt{2}}{9} + \frac{1}{3} = \frac{4\sqrt{2}+3}{9}$$

Passage IV

(Ex. Nos. 30 and 31)

Equation of the form $\lambda(\sin x \pm \cos x, \sin x \cdot \cos x) = 0$, where $\lambda(y, z)$ is a polynomial can be solved by the change $\cos x \pm \sin x = t$ and $1 \pm 2\sin x \cdot \cos x = t^2$

Reduce the given equation into $\lambda\left(t, \frac{t^2-1}{2}\right) = 0$.

Example 30 *If $(\cos x - \sin x)\left(2\tan x + \frac{1}{\cos x}\right) + 2 = 0$, then x is*

(a) $n\pi \pm \frac{\pi}{3}$ (b) $2n\pi \pm \frac{\pi}{3}$

(c) $n\pi \pm \frac{\pi}{6}$ (d) $2n\pi \pm \frac{\pi}{6}, n \in I$

Sol. (b) $(\cos x - \sin x)(2\sin x + 1) + 2\cos x = 0$

$\Rightarrow \quad \sin x(2\cos x - 1) + 3\cos x - 2(1 - \cos^2 x) = 0$

$\Rightarrow \sin x(2\cos x - 1) + 2\cos x(\cos x + 2) - 1(\cos x + 2) = 0$

$\Rightarrow \quad (\sin x + \cos x + 2)(2\cos x - 1) = 0$

$\therefore \quad \cos x = \frac{1}{2} \Rightarrow x = 2n\pi \pm \frac{\pi}{3}, n \in I$

Example 31 *If $\sin^4 x + \cos^4 x = \sin x \cdot \cos x$, then x is equal to*

(a) $(6n+1)\frac{\pi}{6}$ (b) $n\pi$

(c) $(4n+1)\frac{\pi}{4}$ (d) $n\pi + \frac{\pi}{2}, n \in I$

Sol. (c) Given, $\sin^4 x + \cos^4 x = \sin x \cdot \cos x$

$\Rightarrow \quad 1 - \frac{(t^2-1)^2}{2} = t^2 - 1$

$\Rightarrow \quad t^4 - t^2 - 2 = 0 \quad$ ...(i)

Let $t^2 = u \geq 0$

Eq. (i) becomes,

$u^2 - u - 2 = 0$

$\Rightarrow \quad u = 2$ or $u = -1$ (rejected)

$\therefore \quad t = \pm\sqrt{2}$

$\Rightarrow \quad \sin x + \cos x = \pm\sqrt{2} \Rightarrow \sin\left(x + \frac{\pi}{4}\right) = 1$

$\Rightarrow \quad x = n\pi + \frac{\pi}{4}, n \in I$

Stem Based Questions

Stem I

(Ex. Nos. 32 and 33)

Let $g(\alpha, x) = 2\sin^2\alpha + 4\cos(\alpha + x)\cdot\sin\alpha\cdot\sin x + \cos[2(\alpha + x)]$.

Then,

Example 32 *The value of* $g\left(\frac{\pi}{3}, \frac{\pi}{4}\right)$ *is ....*

Example 33 *The number of solutions for* $g\left(\frac{\pi}{3}, x\right) = 0$ *in the interval* $\left[0, \frac{7\pi}{2}\right)$ *is*

Sol. (Ex. Nos. 32 to 33)

Given,

$$\begin{aligned} g(\alpha, x) &= 2\sin^2\alpha + 4\cos(\alpha + x)\cdot\sin\alpha\cdot\sin x + \cos[2(\alpha + x)] \\ &= 2\sin^2\alpha + 4\cos(\alpha + x)\cdot\sin\alpha\cdot\sin x + 2\cos^2(\alpha + x) - 1 \\ &= 2\sin^2\alpha + 2\cos(\alpha + x)[2\sin\alpha\cdot\sin x + \cos(\alpha + x)] - 1 \\ &= 2\sin^2\alpha + 2\cos(\alpha + x) \\ &\qquad [2\sin\alpha\cdot\sin x + \cos\alpha\cdot\cos x - \sin\alpha\cdot\sin x] - 1 \\ &= 2\sin^2\alpha + 2\cos(\alpha + x)[\sin\alpha\cdot\sin x + \cos\alpha\cdot\cos x] - 1 \\ &= 2\sin^2\alpha + 2\cos(\alpha + x)\cos(\alpha - x) - 1 \\ &= 2\sin^2\alpha + 2\cos^2\alpha - 2\sin^2 x - 1 \\ &= \cos 2x \end{aligned}$$

32. Now, $g\left(\frac{\pi}{3}, \frac{\pi}{4}\right) = \cos\left[2\times\frac{\pi}{4}\right] = \cos\frac{\pi}{2} = 0 \quad \left[\text{put } \alpha = \frac{\pi}{3}, x = \frac{\pi}{4}\right]$

33. Also, $g\left(\frac{\pi}{3}, x\right) = 0$

$\Rightarrow \quad \cos x = 0 \quad \left[\text{put } \alpha = \frac{\pi}{3} \text{ and } x = x\right]$

$\Rightarrow \quad x = \frac{\pi}{2}, \frac{3\pi}{2}, \frac{5\pi}{2} \in \left[0, \frac{7\pi}{2}\right)$

Hence, number of solutions = 3

Stem II

(Ex. Nos. 34 and 35)

Consider the equation

$$\cos(3^x\pi) - 2\cos^2(3^x\pi) + 2\cos(4(3^x)\pi) - \cos(7(3^x)\pi) = \sin(3^x\pi) + 2\sin^2(3^x\pi) - 2\sin(4(3^x)\pi) + 2\sin(3^{x+1}\pi) - \sin(7(3^x)\pi)$$

has the solutions of the form $x = \log_a\left(\frac{bn-1}{c}\right) - d$ or $x = \log_\lambda\left(\frac{n}{\mu} + (-1)^n\frac{\pi}{p} - \frac{\pi}{q}\right)$, $n \in I$ and $a, b, c, d, \lambda, \mu, p, q \in \theta$

Example 34 *The value of* $[\log_q p - d + \lambda\mu]$ *is equal to ....*

Example 35 *The value of* $\sin^{-1}\left[\left(\frac{c}{\sqrt{\lambda}}\right)\cdot\left(\sqrt{\frac{a}{b}}\right)\right]$ *(in degrees) is equal to ......*

Sol. (Ex. Nos. 34 to 35)

We have,

$$\cos(3^x\pi) - 2\cos^2(3^x\pi) + 2\cos(4(3^x)\pi) - \cos(7(3^x)\pi) = \sin(3^x\pi) + 2\sin^2(3^x\pi) - 2\sin(4(3^x)\pi) + 2\sin(3^{x+1}\pi) - \sin(7(3^x)\pi)$$

Putting $3^x\pi = t$ in above equation, we have

$$\cos t - 2\cos^2 t + 2\cos 4t - \cos 7t = \sin t + 2\sin^2 t - 2\sin 4t + 2\sin 3t - \sin 7t$$

$$\begin{aligned} &\Rightarrow \cos t - \cos 7t + \sin 7t - \sin t + 2(\cos 4t + \sin 4t) = 2 + 2\sin 3t \\ &\Rightarrow \sin 4t(\sin 3t + 1) + \cos 4t(\sin 3t + 1) - (1 + \sin 3t) = 0 \\ &\Rightarrow (\sin 3t + 1)(\sin 4t + \cos 4t - 1) = 0 \\ &\Rightarrow \sin 3t = -1 \text{ or } \sin 4t + \cos 4t - 1 = 0 \\ &\Rightarrow 3t = 2n\pi - \frac{\pi}{2}, n \in I \\ &\text{or} \quad \sin\left(4t + \frac{\pi}{4}\right) = \sin\frac{\pi}{4} \\ &\Rightarrow 3(3^x\pi) = 2n\pi - \frac{\pi}{2}, n \in I \\ &\text{or} \quad 4t + \frac{\pi}{4} = n\pi + (-1)^n\frac{\pi}{4}, n \in I \\ &\Rightarrow 3^{x+1} = 2n - \frac{1}{2}, n \in I \\ &\text{or} \quad 4\pi(3^x) = n\pi + (-1)^n\frac{\pi}{4} - \frac{\pi}{4}, n \in I \\ &\Rightarrow x + 1 = \log_3\left(\frac{4n-1}{2}\right), n \in I \\ &\text{or} \quad 3^x = \frac{n}{4} + (-1)^n\frac{\pi}{16} - \frac{\pi}{16}, n \in I \\ &\Rightarrow x = \log_3\left(\frac{4n-1}{2}\right) - 1, n \in I \\ &\text{or} \quad x = \log_3\left(\frac{n}{4} + (-1)^n\frac{\pi}{16} - \frac{\pi}{16}\right), n \in I \end{aligned}$$

On comparing with $x = \log_a\left(\frac{bn-1}{c}\right) - d$

or $x = \log_\lambda\left(\frac{n}{\mu} + (-1)^n\frac{\pi}{p} - \frac{\pi}{q}\right), n \in I$ respectively, we get

$$a = 3, b = 4, c = 2, d = 1, \lambda = 3, \mu = 4, p = q = 16$$

34. $\log_q p - d + \lambda\mu = \log_{16} 16 - 1 + (3\times 4) = 1 - 1 + 12 = 12$

35. $\sin^{-1}\left[\left(\frac{c}{\sqrt{\lambda}}\right)\cdot\left(\sqrt{\frac{a}{b}}\right)\right] = \sin^{-1}\left[\frac{2}{\sqrt{3}}\times\frac{\sqrt{3}}{2}\right] = 90°$

Single Integer Answer Type Questions

Example 36 *If $0 \le x \le 3\pi$, $0 \le y \le 3\pi$ and $\cos x \cdot \sin y = 1$, then the possible number of values of the ordered pair (x, y) is ....*

Sol. (6) Clearly, $\cos x \cdot \sin y = 1$

$\Rightarrow \quad \cos x = 1, \sin y = 1$ or $\cos x = -1, \sin y = -1$

Now, $\cos x = 1;\ \sin y = 1$

$\Rightarrow \quad x = 0,\ 2\pi$ and $y = \frac{\pi}{2}, \frac{5\pi}{2}$ ...(i)

and $\cos x = -1, \sin y = -1$

$\Rightarrow \quad x = \pi, 3\pi$ and $y = \frac{3\pi}{2}$ ...(ii)

$\therefore$ From Eqs. (i) and (ii), the required of ordered pairs are

$$\left(0, \frac{\pi}{2}\right)\left(0, \frac{5\pi}{2}\right)\left(2\pi, \frac{\pi}{2}\right)\left(2\pi, \frac{5\pi}{2}\right)\left(\pi, \frac{3\pi}{2}\right)\left(3\pi, \frac{3\pi}{2}\right)$$

i.e. 6 solutions.

Example 37 *Number of integral solutions of the equation $\log_{\sin x} \sqrt{\sin^2 x} + \log_{\cos x} \sqrt{\cos^2 x} = 2$, where $x \in [0, 6\pi]$ is*

Sol. (4) $\log_{\sin x} \sqrt{\sin^2 x} + \log_{\cos x} \sqrt{\cos^2 x} = 2$

$\therefore \quad \sin x > 0$ and $\sin x \ne 1$

$\cos x > 0$ and $\cos x \ne 1$

Domain $x \in \left(0, \frac{\pi}{2}\right) \cup \left(2\pi, \frac{5\pi}{2}\right) \cup \left(4\pi, \frac{9\pi}{2}\right)$

$\Rightarrow$ Number of integers $= 1 + 1 + 2 = 4$

Example 38 *If $x_k = (\sec\theta)^{\frac{1}{2^k}} + (\tan\theta)^{\frac{1}{2^k}}$ and $y_k = (\sec\theta)^{\frac{1}{2^k}} - (\tan\theta)^{\frac{1}{2^k}}$, then value of $3y_n \prod_{k=0}^{n} (x_k)$ is equal to ....*

Sol. (3) $x_k \cdot y_k = (\sec\theta)^{\frac{1}{2^{k-1}}} - (\tan\theta)^{\frac{1}{2^{k-1}}} \Rightarrow x_k \cdot y_k = y_{k-1}$

Now, $y_n \cdot \prod_{k=0}^{n} x_k = y_n \cdot \prod_{k=0}^{n} \frac{y_{k-1}}{y_k}$

$= y_n \times \frac{y_{-1}}{y_0} \times \frac{y_0}{y_1} \times \ldots\ldots \times \frac{y_{n-1}}{y_n} = y_{-1}$

$= (\sec\theta)^2 - (\tan\theta)^2 = 1$

$\therefore \quad 3y_n \prod_{k=0}^{n} (x_k) = 3$

Example 39 *The number of ordered pairs (α, β), where $\alpha, \beta \in [0, 2\pi]$ satisfying $\log_{2\sec x}(\beta^2 - 6\beta + 10) = \log_3 |\cos\alpha|$ is*

Sol. (2) $\log_{2\sec x}(\beta^2 - 6\beta + 10) = \log_3 |\cos\alpha|$

it is only possible when

$\beta^2 - 6\beta + 10 = 1$ and $\cos\alpha = 1$

$\Rightarrow \quad \beta = 3$ and $\alpha = 0, 2\pi$

$\therefore$ Two ordered pairs $(0, 3)$ and $(2\pi, 3)$.

Example 40 *If $\frac{\cos^3\theta}{(1 - \sin\theta)} + \frac{\sin^3\theta}{(1 + \cos\theta)} = 1 + \cos\theta$, then number of possible values of θ is (where $\theta \in [0, 2\pi]$).*

Sol. (0) $\frac{\cos\theta \cos^2\theta}{(1 - \sin\theta)} + \frac{\sin\theta \sin^2\theta}{(1 + \cos\theta)} = \cos\theta + 1$

$\Rightarrow \quad \cos\theta \frac{(1 - \sin^2\theta)}{(1 - \sin\theta)} + \frac{(1 - \cos^2\theta)\sin\theta}{(1 + \cos\theta)} = \cos\theta + 1$

$\Rightarrow \quad \cos\theta(1 + \sin\theta) + \sin\theta(1 - \cos\theta) = \cos\theta + 1$

$\Rightarrow \quad \sin\theta + \cos\theta = \cos\theta + 1$

$\Rightarrow \quad \sin\theta = 1 \Rightarrow \theta = \frac{\pi}{2},$

which is not possible.

Example 41 *If the sum of all values of x satisfying the system of equations*

$$\tan x + \tan y + \tan x \cdot \tan y = 5$$
$$\sin(x + y) = 4\cos x \cdot \cos y$$

is $\frac{k\pi}{2}$, where $x \in \left(0, \frac{\pi}{2}\right)$, then find the values of k.

Sol. (1) Given, $\tan x + \tan y + \tan x \cdot \tan y = 5$ ...(i)

and $\sin(x + y) = 4\cos x \cdot \cos y$ ...(ii)

Now, from Eq. (ii), we get

$\sin x \cos y + \cos x \sin y = 4\cos x \cos y$

On dividing by $\cos x \cdot \cos y$, we get

$\tan x + \tan y = 4$ ...(iii)

$\therefore$ Eqs. (i) and (iii),

$\tan x(4 - \tan x) = 1$

$\Rightarrow \quad \tan^2 x - 4\tan x + 1 = 0$

$\Rightarrow \quad \tan x = 2 + \sqrt{3}$ or $2 - \sqrt{3}$

$\Rightarrow \quad x = \frac{5\pi}{12}$ or $\frac{\pi}{12}$

$\therefore$ Sum $= \frac{6\pi}{12} = \frac{\pi}{2} = \frac{k\pi}{2} \Rightarrow k = 1$

Example 42 *The total number of ordered pairs of (r, θ) satisfying the equation $2\sin\theta = r^4 - 2r^2 + 3$, where $\theta \in [0, 3\pi]$ is ....*

Sol. (4) Here, $2\sin\theta = r^4 - 2r^2 + 3$

$\Rightarrow \quad 2\sin\theta = (r^2 - 1)^2 + 2$

$\Rightarrow \quad 2\sin\theta = (r^2 - 1)^2 + 2 \ge 2$ ...(i)

But max $(\sin\theta) = 1$

$\Rightarrow \quad$ max $(2\sin\theta) = 2$ ...(ii)

$\therefore$ From Eqs. (i) and (ii),

$\sin\theta = 1$ and $r^2 - 1 = 0$

$\Rightarrow \quad \theta = \frac{\pi}{2}, \frac{5\pi}{2}$ and $r = \pm 1$

$\therefore$ Required ordered pairs are

$$\left(1, \frac{\pi}{2}\right)\left(-1, \frac{\pi}{2}\right)\left(1, \frac{5\pi}{2}\right)\left(-1, \frac{5\pi}{2}\right)$$

i.e. 4 ordered pairs.

Example 43 *Total number of values of θ lying between 0 and 2π, satisfying the equations $r\sin\theta = \sqrt{3}$, $r + 4\sin\theta = 2(\sqrt{3}+1)$ is ....*

Sol. (4) We have to solve for θ,

Here, $r\sin\theta = \sqrt{3}$ ...(i)

$r + 4\sin\theta = 2(\sqrt{3}+1)$ ...(ii)

$\therefore$ We shall eliminate r from Eqs. (i) and (ii),

From Eq. (i), $r = \dfrac{\sqrt{3}}{\sin\theta}$

$\therefore$From Eq. (ii), $\dfrac{\sqrt{3}}{\sin\theta} + 4\sin\theta = 2(\sqrt{3}+1)$

$\Rightarrow$ $\sqrt{3} + 4\sin^2\theta = 2(\sqrt{3}+1)\cdot\sin\theta$

$\Rightarrow$ $4\sin^2\theta - 2\sqrt{3}\sin\theta - 2\sin\theta + \sqrt{3} = 0$

$\Rightarrow$ $2\sin\theta(2\sin\theta - \sqrt{3}) - 1(2\sin\theta - \sqrt{3}) = 0$

$\Rightarrow$ $(2\sin\theta - 1)(2\sin\theta - \sqrt{3}) = 0$

$\Rightarrow$ $\sin\theta = \dfrac{1}{2}$ or $\sin\theta = \dfrac{\sqrt{3}}{2}$

$\Rightarrow$ $\theta = n\pi + (-1)^n\dfrac{\pi}{6}$ or $\theta = n\pi + (-1)^n\dfrac{\pi}{3}$

$\Rightarrow$ General solution set is,

$$\left\{\theta \mid \theta = n\pi + (-1)^n\frac{\pi}{6}\right\} \cup \left\{\theta \mid \theta = n\pi + (-1)^n\frac{\pi}{3}\right\}$$

Put $n = 0, \theta = \dfrac{\pi}{6}$ or $\dfrac{\pi}{3}$

Put $n = 1, \theta = \pi - \dfrac{\pi}{6} = \dfrac{5\pi}{6}$ or $\pi - \dfrac{\pi}{3} = \dfrac{2\pi}{3}$

$\therefore$ Solutions are $\dfrac{\pi}{6}, \dfrac{\pi}{3}, \dfrac{2\pi}{3}$ and $\dfrac{5\pi}{6}$.

Example 44 *Sum of all the values of θ satisfying the equation $\sin 7\theta = \sin\theta + \sin 3\theta$ such that $0 \le \theta \le \pi$ is $k\pi$, then the value of $\dfrac{k}{2}$ is equal to ....*

Sol. (2) Given, $\sin 7\theta = \sin\theta + \sin 3\theta$

$\Rightarrow$ $\sin 7\theta - \sin\theta - \sin 3\theta = 0$

$\therefore$ $2\sin 3\theta\cdot\cos 4\theta - \sin 3\theta = 0$

$\therefore$ $\sin 3\theta(2\cos 4\theta - 1) = 0$

$\Rightarrow$ $\sin 3\theta = 0$ or $\cos 4\theta = \dfrac{1}{2}$

i.e. $3\theta = n\pi, n \in I$ or $4\theta = 2n\pi \pm \dfrac{\pi}{3}, n \in I$

$\Rightarrow$ $\theta = \dfrac{n\pi}{3}$ or $\theta = \dfrac{n\pi}{2} \pm \dfrac{\pi}{12}$

Put $n = 0, \theta = 0$ or $\theta = \pm\dfrac{\pi}{12}, \left(-\dfrac{\pi}{12} \text{ rejected}\right)$

Put $n = 1, \theta = \dfrac{\pi}{3}$ or $\theta = \dfrac{\pi}{2} + \dfrac{\pi}{12}, \dfrac{\pi}{2} - \dfrac{\pi}{12} \Rightarrow \theta = \dfrac{7\pi}{12}, \dfrac{5\pi}{12}$

Put $n = 2, \theta = \dfrac{2\pi}{3}$ or $\theta = \pi \pm \dfrac{\pi}{12}\left(\pi + \dfrac{\pi}{12} \text{ rejected}\right)$

Put $n = 3, \theta = \pi$

$\therefore$ Solutions are $0, \dfrac{\pi}{12}, \dfrac{\pi}{3}, \dfrac{5\pi}{12}, \dfrac{7\pi}{12}, \dfrac{2\pi}{3}, \dfrac{11\pi}{12}$ and π

$\therefore$ Sum $= \dfrac{48\pi}{12} = 4\pi = k\pi$

Hence, $\dfrac{k}{2} = \dfrac{4}{2} = 2$

Example 45 *The number of values of θ in the interval $\left(-\dfrac{\pi}{2}, \dfrac{\pi}{2}\right)$, satisfying the equation,*

$(1-\tan\theta)(1+\tan\theta)\cdot\sec^2\theta + 2^{\tan^2\theta} = 0$ is ....

Sol. (4) Given, $(1-\tan\theta)(1+\tan\theta)\sec^2\theta + 2^{\tan^2\theta} = 0$

$\Rightarrow$ $(1-\tan^2\theta)(1+\tan^2\theta) + 2^{\tan^2\theta} = 0$

$\Rightarrow$ $1 - \tan^4\theta + 2^{\tan^2\theta} = 0$

$\Rightarrow$ $1 + 2^{\tan^2\theta} = \tan^4\theta$

By observation, we have $\tan^2\theta = 3 \Rightarrow \theta = n\pi \pm \left(\dfrac{\pi}{3}\right)$

Moreover there will be values of θ, satisfying, $3 < \tan^2\theta < 4$ and satisfying the given equation as if $f(x) = x^2 - 2^x - 1$, then $f(3^+)\,f(4^-) < 0$.

So the number of values of θ is 4.

Numerical Value Type Questions

Example 46 *The number of distinct real roots of*

$$\begin{vmatrix} \sin x & \cos x & \cos x \\ \cos x & \sin x & \cos x \\ \cos x & \cos x & \sin x \end{vmatrix} = 0 \text{ in } \left[\frac{-\pi}{4}, \frac{\pi}{4}\right] \text{ is ....}$$

Sol. (1) Given, $\begin{vmatrix} \sin x & \cos x & \cos x \\ \cos x & \sin x & \cos x \\ \cos x & \cos x & \sin x \end{vmatrix} = 0$

Applying $C_1 \to C_1 + C_2 + C_3$, we get

$$\begin{vmatrix} \sin x + 2\cos x & \cos x & \cos x \\ \sin x + 2\cos x & \sin x & \cos x \\ \sin x + 2\cos x & \cos x & \sin x \end{vmatrix} = 0$$

$\Rightarrow$ $(\sin x + 2\cos x)\begin{vmatrix} 1 & \cos x & \cos x \\ 1 & \sin x & \cos x \\ 1 & \cos x & \sin x \end{vmatrix} = 0$

$$\Rightarrow (\sin x + 2\cos x)\begin{vmatrix} 1 & \cos x & \cos x \\ 0 & \sin x - \cos x & 0 \\ 0 & 0 & \sin x - \cos x \end{vmatrix} = 0$$

$$\begin{bmatrix} R_2 \to R_2 - R_1 \\ R_3 \to R_3 - R_1 \end{bmatrix}$$

$$\Rightarrow \quad (\sin x + 2\cos x)(\sin x - \cos x)^2 = 0$$

$$\Rightarrow \quad \tan x = 1, -2$$

So, there is only one solution, $x = \frac{\pi}{4}$ in $\left[-\frac{\pi}{4}, \frac{\pi}{4}\right]$.

Example 47 *Maximum value of*

$$f(x) = \begin{vmatrix} 1+\sin^2 x & \cos^2 x & 4\sin 2x \\ \sin^2 x & 1+\cos^2 x & 4\sin 2x \\ \sin^2 x & \cos^2 x & 1+4\sin 2x \end{vmatrix} \text{ is ………}$$

Sol. (6) Given expression is

$$f(x) = \begin{vmatrix} 1+\sin^2 x & \cos^2 x & 4\sin 2x \\ \sin^2 x & 1+\cos^2 x & 4\sin 2x \\ \sin^2 x & \cos^2 x & 1+4\sin 2x \end{vmatrix}$$

Applying $R_2 \to R_2 - R_1$ and $R_3 \to R_3 - R_1$, we get

$$f(x) = \begin{vmatrix} 1+\sin^2 x & \cos^2 x & 4\sin 2x \\ -1 & 1 & 0 \\ -1 & 0 & 1 \end{vmatrix}$$

$$= 4\sin 2x + (1 + \sin^2 x + \cos^2 x)$$

$$= 4\sin 2x + 2$$

$\because -1 \le \sin 2x \le 1$

$\Rightarrow -4 \le 4\sin 2x \le 4$

$\Rightarrow -2 \le 4\sin 2x + 2 \le 6$.

$\therefore$ Maximum value of $f(x) = 6$.

Example 48 *The number of solutions of* $(\sqrt{3}+1)^{2x} + (\sqrt{3}-1)^{2x} = 2^{3x}$ *is ………*

Sol. (1) Given equation is

$$(\sqrt{3}+1)^{2x} + (\sqrt{3}-1)^{2x} = 2^{3x}$$

$$\Rightarrow \quad (\sqrt{3}+1)^{2x} + (\sqrt{3}-1)^{2x} = (2\sqrt{2})^{2x}$$

$$\Rightarrow \quad \left(\frac{\sqrt{3}+1}{2\sqrt{2}}\right)^{2x} + \left(\frac{\sqrt{3}-1}{2\sqrt{2}}\right)^{2x} = 1$$

$$\Rightarrow \quad \left(\sin\left(\frac{5\pi}{12}\right)\right)^{2x} + \left(\cos\left(\frac{5\pi}{12}\right)\right)^{2x} = 1 \quad \text{...(i)}$$

Eq. (i) will be satisfied only when $x = 1$

Hence, the number of solution is 1.

JEE SCANNER

Example 49 Similar to PYQ Asked in JEE Main 2021

If n is the number of solution of the equation $2\sin^2\theta - \cos 2\theta = 0$ and $2\cos^2\theta - 3\sin\theta = 0$, $\theta \in [0, 2\pi]$ and S is the sum of all these solutions, then the ordered pair (n, S) is ………

Sol. Given, $\quad 2\sin^2\theta - \cos 2\theta = 0$

$$\Rightarrow \quad 2\sin^2\theta - (1 - 2\sin^2\theta) = 0$$

$$\Rightarrow \quad 2\sin^2\theta - 1 + 2\sin^2\theta = 0$$

$$\Rightarrow \quad 4\sin^2\theta = 1$$

$$\Rightarrow \quad \sin^2\theta = \frac{1}{4}$$

$$\Rightarrow \quad \sin\theta = \pm\frac{1}{2}$$

and $\quad 2\cos^2\theta - 3\sin\theta = 0$

$$\Rightarrow \quad 2(1 - \sin^2\theta) - 3\sin\theta = 0$$

$$\Rightarrow \quad 2 - 2\sin^2\theta - 3\sin\theta = 0$$

$$\Rightarrow \quad 2\sin^2\theta + 3\sin\theta - 2 = 0$$

$$\Rightarrow \quad (\sin\theta + 2)(2\sin\theta - 1) = 0$$

$$\Rightarrow \quad \sin\theta = \frac{1}{2}, -2$$

$\therefore \theta = \frac{\pi}{6}, \frac{5\pi}{6}$ in the given interval $[0, 2\pi]$

So, $n = 2$

and $S = \frac{\pi}{6} + \frac{5\pi}{6} = \frac{6\pi}{6} = \pi$

So, ordered pair $(n, S) = (2, \pi)$

Skill Builder

If n is the number of solution of the equation $|\sin(2x)| + |\cos(2x)| = |\sin(y)|$; $y \in [-2\pi, 2\pi]$ and S is the sum of all these solutions, then the ordered pair (n, S) is ………

For Sol.

Example 50 *Total number of solution, in $(0, 2\pi)$ of the equation $\log_{\tan x}(2 + 4\cos^2 x) = 2$ is ………*

Sol. (2) Given, $\log_{\tan x}(2 + 4\cos^2 x) = 2$ ...(i)

$$\Rightarrow \quad 2 + 4\cos^2 x = \tan^2 x = \frac{\sin^2 x}{\cos^2 x}$$

$$\Rightarrow \quad 2\cos^2 x + 4\cos^4 x = \sin^2 x = 1 - \cos^2 x$$

$$\Rightarrow \quad 4\cos^4 x + 3\cos^2 x - 1 = 0$$

Put $\cos^2 x = t$, we get

$$4t^2 + 3t - 1 = 0 \Rightarrow t = \frac{1}{4}, -1$$

$$\Rightarrow \quad \cos^2 x = \frac{1}{4}, -1$$

But $\cos^2 x \in [0,1]$

So, $\cos^2 x = -1$ (rejected)

So, $\cos^2 x = \frac{1}{4} \Rightarrow \cos x = \pm\frac{1}{2}$

$$\Rightarrow \quad x = \frac{\pi}{3}, \frac{2\pi}{3}, \frac{4\pi}{3}, \frac{5\pi}{3} \in (0, 2\pi).$$

But for log to be defined

$$2 + 4\cos^2 x > 0 \Rightarrow x \in R \quad \text{...(ii)}$$

$$[\because 0 \le \cos^2 x \le 1 \Rightarrow 0 \le 4\cos^2 x \le 4 \Rightarrow 2 \le 2 + 4\cos^2 x \le 6]$$

and $\tan x > 0$ but $\tan x \ne 1$

$$\Rightarrow \quad x \in \left(0, \frac{\pi}{2}\right) \cup \left(\pi, \frac{3\pi}{2}\right) \quad [\because x \in (0, 2\pi) \text{ given}] \text{ ...(iii)}$$

and $\quad x \ne \frac{\pi}{4}, \frac{5\pi}{4}$ ...(iv)

From Eqs. (ii), (iii) and (iv), we get

$$x \in \left(0, \frac{\pi}{2}\right) \cup \left(\pi, \frac{3\pi}{2}\right) - \left\{\frac{\pi}{4}, \frac{5\pi}{4}\right\} \text{as } x \in (0, 2\pi)$$

Hence, out of $x = \frac{\pi}{3}, \frac{2\pi}{3}, \frac{4\pi}{3}, \frac{5\pi}{3}$, only $x = \frac{\pi}{3}, \frac{2\pi}{3}$ are solutions.

Thus, total number of solutions = 2

Example 51 *If $\cos^2\theta - 2\cos\theta - 1 = 0$ is to be satisfied for exactly 4 distinct values of $\theta \in [0, \alpha\pi]$, then the least value of α where $\alpha \in I^+$ is ....*

Sol. (4) Given,

$$\cos^2\theta - 2\cos\theta - 1 = 0$$

$$\Rightarrow \quad \cos\theta = \frac{2 \pm \sqrt{4 - 4 \times 1 \times (-1)}}{2 \times 1} = \frac{2 \pm 2\sqrt{2}}{2}$$

$$\Rightarrow \quad \cos\theta = 1 \pm \sqrt{2}$$

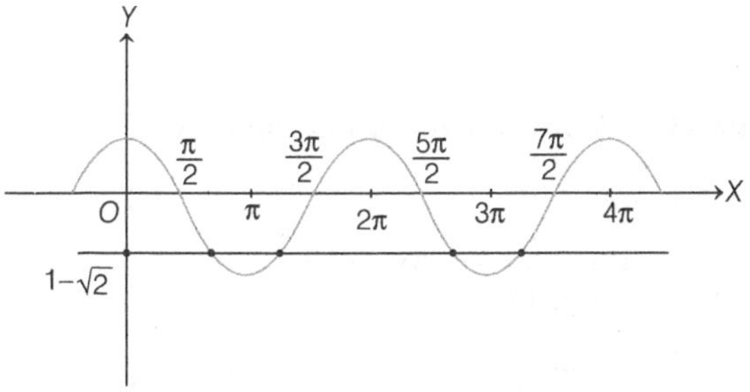

Since, $-1 \le \cos\theta \le 1$

So, $\cos\theta = 1 + \sqrt{2}$ (not possible)

Hence, $\cos\theta = 1 - \sqrt{2}$

It has exactly four solutions in $[0, \alpha\pi]$ for $\alpha = 4$

Example 52 *If the sum of all values of $x, 0 \le x \le 3\pi$ satisfying the equation $(8\cos 4x - 3)(\cot x + \tan x - 2)$ $(\cot x + \tan x + 2) = 12$ is $3K\pi$, then K is equal to ....*

Sol. (6) Given, $(8\cos 4x - 3)(\cot x + \tan x - 2)(\cot x + \tan x + 2) = 12$

$$\Rightarrow \quad (8\cos 4x - 3)(\cot^2 x + \tan^2 x + 2 - 4) = 12$$

$$\Rightarrow \quad (8\cos 4x - 3)(\cot x - \tan x)^2 = 12$$

$$\Rightarrow \quad [8(2\cos^2 2x - 1) - 3]\left(\frac{\cos x}{\sin x} - \frac{\sin x}{\cos x}\right)^2 = 12$$

$$\Rightarrow \quad (16\cos^2 2x - 8 - 3)\left(\frac{\cos^2 x - \sin^2 x}{2\sin x \cos x}\right)^2 \times 4 = 12$$

$$\Rightarrow \quad (16\cos^2 2x - 11)\cos^2 2x = 3\sin^2 2x$$

$$\Rightarrow \quad 16\cos^4 2x - 11\cos^2 2x + 3\cos^2 2x - 3 = 0$$

$$\Rightarrow \quad 16\cos^4 2x - 8\cos^2 2x - 3 = 0$$

$$\Rightarrow \quad (4\cos^2 2x - 3)(4\cos^2 2x + 1) = 0$$

$$\Rightarrow \quad 4\cos^2 2x - 3 = 0 \text{ or } 4\cos^2 2x + 1 = 0$$

$$\Rightarrow \quad \cos^2(2x) = \frac{3}{4} \text{ or } \cos^2 2x = -\frac{1}{4} \text{ (not possible)}$$

$$\Rightarrow \quad \cos(2x) = \pm\frac{\sqrt{3}}{2}$$

Since, $0 \le x \le 3\pi \Rightarrow 0 \le 2x \le 6\pi$

So, $2x = \frac{\pi}{6}, \frac{5\pi}{6}, \frac{7\pi}{6}, \frac{11\pi}{6}, \frac{13\pi}{6}, \frac{17\pi}{6}, \frac{19\pi}{6}, \frac{23\pi}{6}, \frac{25\pi}{6}, \frac{29\pi}{6}, \frac{31\pi}{6}, \frac{35\pi}{6}$

$$\Rightarrow x = \frac{\pi}{12}, \frac{5\pi}{12}, \frac{7\pi}{12}, \frac{11\pi}{12}, \frac{13\pi}{12}, \frac{17\pi}{12}, \frac{19\pi}{12}, \frac{23\pi}{12}, \frac{25\pi}{12}, \frac{29\pi}{12}, \frac{31\pi}{12}, \frac{35\pi}{12}$$

$$\Rightarrow \Sigma x = \frac{216\pi}{12} = 18\pi$$

According to the question,

$$3K\pi = 18\pi \Rightarrow K = 6$$

Example 53 *The number of values of θ satisfying the equation, $2^{\tan(\theta - \pi/4)} - 2 \cdot (0.25)^{\frac{\sin^2(\theta - \pi/4)}{\cos 2\theta}} + 1 = 0, \theta \in [0, 2\pi]$ is ....*

Sol. (0) $\because \sin^2\left(\theta - \frac{\pi}{4}\right) = \frac{(\sin\theta - \cos\theta)^2}{2}$

and $\quad \cos 2\theta = (\cos\theta + \sin\theta)(\cos\theta - \sin\theta)$

$$\text{So,} \quad \frac{\sin^2\left(\theta - \frac{\pi}{4}\right)}{\cos 2\theta} = \frac{1}{2} \times \frac{\cos\theta - \sin\theta}{\cos\theta + \sin\theta}$$

$$= \frac{1}{2} \times \frac{1 - \tan\theta}{1 + \tan\theta} = -\frac{1}{2}\tan\left(\theta - \frac{\pi}{4}\right)$$

Let $\tan\left(\theta - \frac{\pi}{4}\right) = t$

So, given equation becomes

$$2^t - 2 \cdot \left(\frac{1}{4}\right)^{\frac{-t}{2}} + 1 = 0 \Rightarrow 2^t - 2 \cdot 2^t + 1 = 0$$

$$\Rightarrow \quad 2^t = 1 \Rightarrow t = 0 \Rightarrow \theta = \frac{\pi}{4}$$

Hence, no solution.

Example 54 *Solution for the equation*

$5^{\frac{1}{2}}+5^{\frac{1}{2}+\log_5(\sin x)}=15^{\frac{1}{2}+\log_{15}(\cos x)}$ *in* $(0,\pi)$ *is* $\lambda\pi$, *then* $\left[\frac{2}{\lambda}+\cos 6\lambda\pi\right]$ *is equal to ....*

Sol. (11) Given, $5^{\frac{1}{2}}+5^{\frac{1}{2}+\log_5(\sin x)}=(15)^{\frac{1}{2}+\log_{15}(\cos x)}$

$$\Rightarrow \quad 5^{\frac{1}{2}}(1+5^{\log_5(\sin x)})=15^{\frac{1}{2}}\cdot 15^{\log_{15}(\cos x)}$$

$$\Rightarrow \quad 5^{\frac{1}{2}}(1+\sin x)=5^{\frac{1}{2}}\cdot 3^{\frac{1}{2}}\cdot\cos x$$

$$\Rightarrow \quad 5^{\frac{1}{2}}[(1+\sin x)-3^{\frac{1}{2}}\cos x]=0$$

$$\Rightarrow \quad 1+\sin x=3^{\frac{1}{2}}\cdot\cos x \Rightarrow \frac{1+\sin x}{\cos x}=\sqrt{3}$$

$$\Rightarrow \quad \frac{\sin^2\frac{x}{2}+\cos^2\frac{x}{2}+2\sin\frac{x}{2}\cdot\cos\frac{x}{2}}{\cos^2\frac{x}{2}-\sin^2\frac{x}{2}}=\sqrt{3}$$

$$\Rightarrow \quad \frac{\left(\sin\frac{x}{2}+\cos\frac{x}{2}\right)^2}{\left(\cos\frac{x}{2}+\sin\frac{x}{2}\right)\left(\cos\frac{x}{2}-\sin\frac{x}{2}\right)}=\sqrt{3}$$

$$\Rightarrow \quad \frac{\cos\frac{x}{2}+\sin\frac{x}{2}}{\cos\frac{x}{2}-\sin\frac{x}{2}}=\sqrt{3}$$

On dividing both sides by $\cos\frac{x}{2}$, we get

$$\frac{1+\frac{\sin\frac{x}{2}}{\cos\frac{x}{2}}}{1-\frac{\sin\frac{x}{2}}{\cos\frac{x}{2}}}=\sqrt{3} \Rightarrow \frac{\tan\frac{x}{2}+\tan\frac{\pi}{4}}{1-\tan\frac{\pi}{4}\cdot\tan\frac{x}{2}}=\sqrt{3}$$

$$\Rightarrow \quad \tan\left(\frac{x}{2}+\frac{\pi}{4}\right)=\tan\frac{\pi}{3} \Rightarrow \frac{x}{2}+\frac{\pi}{4}=n\pi+\frac{\pi}{3}, n\in I$$

$$\Rightarrow \quad x=2n\pi+\frac{\pi}{6}, n\in I$$

But $x\in(0,\pi)$

$$\therefore \quad x=\frac{\pi}{6}=\lambda\pi \quad \text{[given]}$$

So, $\lambda=\frac{1}{6} \Rightarrow \frac{2}{\lambda}=2\times 6=12$

and $\cos(6\pi\lambda)=\cos\left(6\pi\times\frac{1}{6}\right)=\cos\pi=-1$

Hence, $\frac{2}{\lambda}+\cos(6\pi\lambda)=12-1=11$

JEE SCANNER

Example 55 Similar to PYQ Asked in JEE Main 2023

If m and n respectively are the number of positive and negative values of θ in the interval $[0,2\pi]$ *that satisfy the equation* $\tan(\pi\cos\theta)+\tan(\pi\sin\theta)=0$, *then the value of* $\frac{n}{m}$ *is ....*

Sol. Given, $\tan(\pi\cos\theta)+\tan(\pi\sin\theta)=0$

$$\Rightarrow \quad \tan(\pi\cos\theta)=-\tan(\pi\sin\theta)$$

$$\Rightarrow \quad \tan(\pi\cos\theta)=\tan[-\pi\sin\theta]$$

$$\Rightarrow \quad \pi\cos\theta=n\pi-\pi\sin\theta$$

$$\Rightarrow \quad \pi\cos\theta+\pi\sin\theta=n\pi$$

$$\Rightarrow \quad \cos\theta+\sin\theta=n, \text{ where } n\in I$$

So, possible values of $n=0$, 1 and -1; because

$$-\sqrt{2}\le\sin\theta+\cos\theta\le\sqrt{2}$$

This gives $\theta\in\left\{0,\frac{\pi}{2},\frac{3\pi}{4},\frac{7\pi}{4},\frac{3\pi}{2},\pi\right\}$

$\therefore \quad m=6$ and $n=0$ $\quad$ [$\because$ no negative value of $\theta\in[0,2\pi]$]

Thus, $\frac{n}{m}=\frac{0}{6}=0$

Skill Builder

The complete set of values of x satisfying $\frac{2\sin 6\theta}{\sin\theta-1}<0$ and $\sec^2\theta-2\sqrt{2}\tan\theta\le 0$ in $\left(0,\frac{\pi}{2}\right)$ is $[m,n)\cup(p,q]$, then the value of $\left(\frac{pq}{mn}\right)$ is equal to ....

For Sol.

Matching Type Questions

Example 56 *Match the following columns*

	Column I		Column II
A.	If $\cos 3x\cdot\cos^3 x=-\sin 3x\cdot\sin^3 x$, then x is equal to	p.	$\left(n\pi\pm\frac{\pi}{3}\right), n\in I$
B.	$\sin 3\alpha+2\sin\alpha$ $(\cos 2x-\cos 2\alpha)=0$, then x is ... (where $\alpha\ne n\pi$)	q.	$\left(n\pi+\frac{\pi}{4}\right), n\in I$
C.	If $\lvert 2\tan x-1\rvert+\lvert 2\cot x-1\rvert=2$, then x is	r.	$\left(\frac{n\pi}{4}+\frac{\pi}{8}\right), n\in I$
D.	If $\sin^{10}x+\cos^{10}x=\frac{29}{16}\cos^4(2x)$, then x is	s.	$\left(\frac{n\pi}{2}\pm\frac{\pi}{4}\right), n\in I$

Sol. (A) $\to$(q,s); (B) $\to$ (p); (C) $\to$ (q); (D) $\to$ (r)

(A) $\cos 3x\cdot\cos^3 x+\sin 3x\cdot\sin^3 x=0$

$$\Rightarrow (4\cos^3 x-3\cos x)\cos^3 x+(3\sin x-4\sin^3 x)\sin^3 x=0$$

$$\Rightarrow \quad 4(\cos^6 x - \sin^6 x) - 3(\cos^4 x - \sin^4 x) = 0$$

$$\Rightarrow \quad 4(\cos^6 x - \sin^6 x) - 3(\cos^2 x - \sin^2 x) = 0$$

$$\Rightarrow \quad \cos 2x = 0 \text{ or } \sin^2 2x = 1 = \sin\frac{\pi}{2}$$

$$\Rightarrow \quad 2x = 2n\pi \pm \frac{\pi}{2} \text{ or } 2x = n\pi \pm \frac{\pi}{2}, n \in I$$

$$\Rightarrow \quad x = n\pi \pm \frac{\pi}{4} \text{ or } x = \frac{n\pi}{2} \pm \frac{\pi}{4}, n \in I$$

(B) $\sin 3\alpha = 2\sin\alpha(\cos 2\alpha - \cos 2x)$

$$\Rightarrow \quad 3\sin\alpha - 4\sin^3\alpha = 2\sin\alpha(\cos 2\alpha - \cos 2x)$$

$$\Rightarrow \quad 3 - 4\sin^2\alpha = 2\cos 2\alpha - 2\cos 2x \quad [\because \alpha \neq n\pi \therefore \sin\alpha \neq 0]$$

$$\Rightarrow \quad 3 - 2(1 - \cos 2\alpha) = 2\cos 2\alpha - 2\cos 2x$$

$$\Rightarrow \quad 3 - 2 + 2\cos 2\alpha = 2\cos 2\alpha - 2\cos 2x$$

$$\Rightarrow \quad \cos 2x = -\frac{1}{2}$$

$$\Rightarrow \quad x = n\pi \pm \frac{\pi}{3}, n \in I$$

(C) $|2\tan x - 1| + |2\cot x - 1| = 2$

$\Rightarrow$ Sum of two non-negative quantities $= 2$

$$\Rightarrow \quad 2\tan x - 1 = 1$$

$$\Rightarrow \quad \tan x = 1$$

$$\Rightarrow \quad x = n\pi + \frac{\pi}{4}, n \in I$$

(D) $\sin^{10} x + \cos^{10} x = \frac{29}{16}\cos^4(2x)$

$$\Rightarrow \left(\frac{1 - \cos 2x}{2}\right)^5 + \left(\frac{1 + \cos 2x}{2}\right)^5 = \frac{29}{16}\cos^4(2x)$$

$$\Rightarrow \frac{1}{16}(1 + 10\cos^2 2x + 5\cos^4 2x) = \frac{29}{16}\cos^4(2x)$$

$$\Rightarrow \quad 24\cos^4(2x) - 10\cos^2(2x) - 1 = 0$$

$$\Rightarrow \quad (12\cos^2 2x + 1)(2\cos^2 2x - 1) = 0 \Rightarrow \cos^2 2x = \frac{1}{2}$$

$$\Rightarrow \quad 1 + \cos 4x = 1 \Rightarrow \cos 4x = 0$$

$$\Rightarrow \quad 4x = (2n + 1)\frac{\pi}{2}, n \in I$$

$$\Rightarrow \quad x = \frac{n\pi}{4} + \frac{\pi}{8}, n \in I$$

Example 57 *Match the statement of Column I with the value of Column II.*

	Column I		Column II
A.	The number of solutions of the equation $\lvert\tan 2x\rvert = \sin x$; $x \in [0, \pi]$	p.	1
B.	The value of $4\tan\frac{\pi}{16} - 4\tan^3\frac{\pi}{16} + 6\tan^2\frac{\pi}{16} - \tan^4\frac{\pi}{16} + 1$	q.	4
C.	If the equation $\tan(p\cot x) = \cot p(\tan x)$ has a solution in $(0, x) - \left\{\frac{\pi}{2}\right\}$, then $\frac{4}{\pi}P_{max}$ is	r.	3
D.	The value of $\frac{2x}{\pi}$ in $[0, 2\pi]$, if $5^{\cos^2 2x + 2\sin^2 x} + 5^{2\cos^2 x + \sin^2 2x} = 126$ has a solution	s.	2

Sol. (A) $\to$ (q); (B) $\to$ (s); (C) $\to$ (p); (D) $\to$ (p,r)

(A) Clearly, number of solutions of $|\tan 2x| = \sin x$ in $[0, \pi]$ are 4.

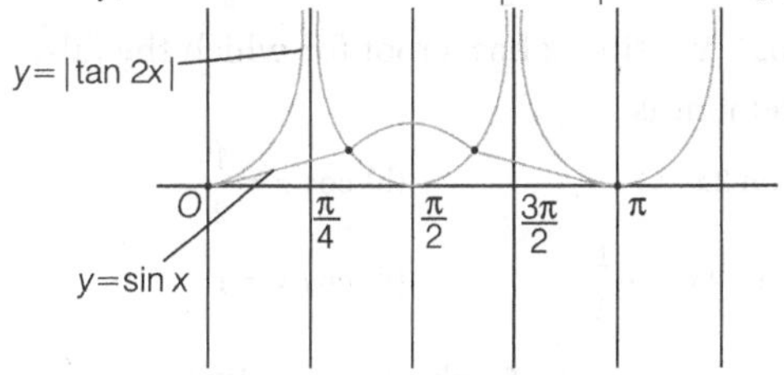

(B) $$\tan 4A = \frac{2\tan 2A}{1 - \tan^2 2A} = \frac{\frac{4\tan A}{1 - \tan^2 A}}{1 - \left(\frac{2\tan A}{1 - \tan^2 A}\right)^2}$$

$$\Rightarrow \tan 4A = \frac{4\tan A(1 - \tan^2 A)}{1 + \tan^4 A - 6\tan^2 A}$$

$$= 4\tan A - 4\tan^3 A + (6\tan^2 A - \tan^4 A - 1)\tan 4A = 0$$

If $A = \frac{\pi}{16} \Rightarrow 4\tan\frac{\pi}{16} - 4\tan^3\frac{\pi}{6} + 6\tan^2\frac{\pi}{16} - \tan^4\frac{\pi}{16} - 1 = 0$

$\therefore$ Required value is 2.

(C) $\tan(p\cot x) = \cot(p\tan x)$

$$\tan(p\cot x) = \tan\left(\frac{\pi}{2} - p\tan x\right)$$

$$p\cot x = n\pi + \frac{\pi}{2} - p\tan x$$

$$p = \frac{n\pi + \frac{\pi}{2}}{\tan x + \cot x} = \frac{\pi}{2}\sin x\cos x \quad [\because x \in [0, \pi]]$$

$$P_{max} = \frac{\pi}{4}; \frac{4P_{max}}{\pi} = 1$$

(D) $5^{\cos^2 2x + 2\sin^2 x} + 5^{2\cos^2 x + \sin^2 2x} = 126$

$$5^{\cos^2 2x + 2\sin^2 x} + 5^{2 - 2\sin^2 x + 1 - \cos^2 2x}$$

$$5^{\cos^2 2x + 2\sin^2 x} + 5^{3 - \cos^2 2x - 2\sin^2 x}$$

Put $\cos^2 2x + 2\sin^2 x = y$, we get

$$5^y + 5^{3-y} = 126$$

$$5^y + \frac{125}{5^y} = 126 \Rightarrow 5^y = 125, 1 \Rightarrow y = 3, 0$$

$$\cos^2 2x + 2\sin^2 x = 3 \Rightarrow x = \frac{\pi}{2}, \frac{3\pi}{2}$$

$$\cos^2 2x + 2\sin^2 x \neq 0; \frac{2x}{\pi} = 1, 3$$

EXERCISE 1

JEE Main Pattern

Single Option Correct Type Questions

1. The equation $2\sin\frac{x}{2}\cos^2 x - 2\sin\frac{x}{2}\sin^2 x$ $= \cos^2 x - \sin^2 x$ has a root for which the false statement is

   (a) $\sin 2x = 1$ (b) $\cos x = \frac{1}{2}$

   (c) $\cos 2x = -\frac{1}{2}$ (d) $\cos x = 1$

2. If $\sec x \cos 5x + 1 = 0$, where $0 < x < 2\pi$, then x is equal to

   (a) $\frac{\pi}{5}, \frac{\pi}{4}$ (b) $\frac{\pi}{5}$

   (c) $\frac{\pi}{4}$ (d) None of these

3. If $\cot(\alpha + \beta) = 0$, then $\sin(\alpha + 2\beta)$ is equal to

   (a) $\sin\alpha$ (b) $\cos\alpha$

   (c) $\sin\beta$ (d) $\cos 2\beta$

4. If $\cot\theta + \cot\left(\frac{\pi}{4} + \theta\right) = 2$, then the general value of θ is

   (a) $2n\pi \pm \frac{\pi}{6}$ (b) $2n\pi \pm \frac{\pi}{3}$

   (c) $n\pi \pm \frac{\pi}{3}$ (d) $n\pi \pm \frac{\pi}{6}$

5. The number of solutions of the equation $16(\sin^5 x + \cos^5 x) = 11(\sin x + \cos x)$ in the interval $[0, 2\pi]$ is

   (a) 6 (b) 7 (c) 8 (d) 9

6. The general solution of $8\tan^2\frac{x}{2} = 1 + \sec x$ is

   (a) $x = 2n\pi \pm \cos^{-1}\left(\frac{-1}{3}\right)$ (b) $x = 2n\pi \pm \frac{\pi}{6}$

   (c) $x = 2n\pi \pm \cos^{-1}\left(\frac{1}{3}\right)$ (d) None of these

7. The solution of the equation $e^{\sin x} - e^{-\sin x} - 4 = 0$ is

   (a) $x = 0$ (b) $x = \sin^{-1}[\log(2 - \sqrt{5})]$

   (c) no real solution (d) None of these

8. If $\sin 3\alpha = 4\sin\alpha\sin(x + \alpha)\sin(x - \alpha)$, then

   (a) $x = n\pi \pm \frac{\pi}{3}, n \in I$ (b) $x = n\pi \pm \frac{\pi}{6}, n \in I$

   (c) $x = n\pi \pm \frac{\pi}{2}, n \in I$ (d) None of these

9. If $x = n\pi + (-1)^n\alpha, n \in I$ and $x = n\pi + (-1)^n\beta$ are the roots of $4\cos x - 3\sec x = \tan x$, then $4(\sin\alpha + \sin\beta)$ is

   (a) -1 (b) 1

   (c) 2 (d) None of these

10. $\cos 2x - 3\cos x + 1 = \frac{1}{(\cot 2x - \cot x)\sin(x - \pi)}$ holds, if

    (a) $\cos x = 0$ (b) $\cos x = 1$

    (c) $\cos x = \frac{5}{2}$ (d) for no value of x

11. If $\cos 2\theta = (\sqrt{2} + 1)\left(\cos\theta - \frac{1}{\sqrt{2}}\right)$, then the value of θ is

    (a) $2n\pi + \frac{\pi}{4}$ (b) $2n\pi \pm \frac{\pi}{4}$

    (c) $2n\pi - \frac{\pi}{4}$ (d) None of these

12. x_1 and x_2 are two positive values of x for which $2\cos x, |\cos x|$ and $3\sin^2 x - 2$ are in GP. The minimum value of $|x_1 - x_2|$ is equal to

    (a) $\frac{4\pi}{3}$ (b) $\frac{\pi}{3}$

    (c) $2\cos^{-1}\left(\frac{2}{3}\right)$ (d) $\cos^{-1}\left(\frac{2}{3}\right)$

13. If $\cos x - \frac{\cot\beta\sin x}{2} = \frac{\sqrt{3}}{2}$, then the value of $\tan\frac{x}{2}$ is

    (a) $\tan\frac{\beta}{2}\tan 15°$ (b) $\tan\frac{\beta}{2}$

    (c) $\tan 15°$ (d) None of these

14. If exp $[(\sin^2 x + \sin^4 x + \sin^6 x + \ldots\infty)$ In 2] satisfies the equation $y^2 - 9y + 8 = 0$, then the value of $\frac{\cos x}{\cos x + \sin x}, 0 < x < \frac{\pi}{2}$, is

    (a) $\sqrt{3} + 1$ (b) $\frac{\sqrt{3} - 1}{2}$

    (c) $\sqrt{3} - 1$ (d) None of these

15. The number of solutions of the equation $\cos 4x + 6 = 7\cos 2x$, when $x \in [315°, 317°]$ is

    (a) 0 (b) 1 (c) 2 (d) 4

16. The least positive value of x satisfying $\frac{\sin^2 2x + 4\sin^4 x - 4\sin^2 x\cos^2 x}{4 - \sin^2 2x - 4\sin^2 x} = \frac{1}{9}$ is

    (a) $\frac{\pi}{3}$ (b) $\frac{\pi}{6}$ (c) $\frac{2\pi}{3}$ (d) $\frac{5\pi}{6}$

17. The general solution of
$\tan\theta+\tan 4\theta+\tan 7\theta=\tan\theta\cdot\tan 4\theta\cdot\tan 7\theta$

(a) $\theta=\frac{n\pi}{4}$
(b) $\theta=\frac{n\pi}{2}$
(c) $\theta=\frac{n\pi}{12}$
(d) None of these

18. ABC is a triangle such that $\sin(2A+B)=\sin(C-A)$ $=-\sin(B+2C)=1/2$. If A, B and C are in AP, then the value of A, B and C are

(a) 45°, 60°, 75°
(b) 30°, 60°, 90°
(c) 20°, 60°, 100°
(d) None of these

19. If $\tan m\theta=\tan n\theta$ and general value of θ are in AP, then common difference is

(a) $\frac{1}{m-n}$
(b) $\frac{\pi}{m+n}$
(c) $\frac{\pi}{m-n}$
(d) None of these

20. If $\sec x\cos 5x=-1$ and $0<x<\frac{\pi}{4}$, then x is equal to

(a) $\frac{\pi}{6}$
(b) $\frac{\pi}{3}$
(c) $\frac{\pi}{4}$
(d) None of these

21. If the equation $\cos 3x\cos^3 x+\sin 3x\sin^3 x=0$, then x is equal to

(a) $(2n+1)\frac{\pi}{4}$
(b) $(2n-1)\frac{\pi}{4}$
(c) $\frac{n\pi}{4}$
(d) None of these

22. The number of the solution of the equation $\cos(\pi\sqrt{x-4})\cdot\cos\pi\sqrt{x}=1$ is

(a) >2 (b) 2 (c) 1 (d) 0

23. In interval $\left[\frac{-\pi}{2},\frac{\pi}{2}\right]$, the equation $\log_{\sin\theta}(\cos^2\theta)=2$ has

(a) no solution
(b) a unique solution
(c) two solution
(d) infinitely many solution

24. $\lambda\cos x-3\sin x=\lambda+1$ is solvable only, if

(a) $\lambda\in[0,5]$
(b) $\lambda\in[4,5]$
(c) $\lambda\in(-\infty,4]$
(d) None of these

25. If $\max\{5\sin\theta+3\sin(\theta-\alpha)\}=7$, then the set of possible value of α is $\theta\in R$

(a) $\left\{x:x=2n\pi\pm\frac{\pi}{3},n\in I\right\}$
(b) $\left\{x:x=2n\pi\pm\frac{2\pi}{3},n\in I\right\}$
(c) $\left[\frac{\pi}{3},\frac{2\pi}{3}\right]$
(d) None of these

26. The number of integral values of 'n' so that $\sin x(\sin x+\cos x)=n$ has atleast one solution, is

(a) 2
(b) 1
(c) 3
(d) zero

27. If $\tan\left(\frac{\pi}{2}\sin\theta\right)=\cot\left(\frac{\pi}{2}\cos\theta\right)$, then $\sin\theta+\cos\theta$ is equal to

(a) 0
(b) 1
(c) −1
(d) 1 or −1

28. If $\sqrt{3}\sin x-\cos x=\min_{\alpha\in R}\{2,e^2,\pi,\alpha^2-4\alpha+7\}$, then

(a) $x=2n\pi, n\in I$
(b) $x=2n\pi+\frac{2\pi}{3}, n\in I$
(c) $x=n\pi+(-1)^n\frac{\pi}{4}+\frac{\pi}{6}, n\in I$
(d) $x=n\pi+(-1)^{n+1}\frac{\pi}{4}-\frac{\pi}{3}, n\in I$

29. The number of solutions of $\cot(5\pi\sin\theta)=\tan(5\pi\cos\theta)$, $\forall\,\theta\in(0,2\pi)$ is

(a) 7 (b) 14 (c) 21 (d) 28

30. If $|k|=5$ and $0°\le\theta\le 360°$, then the number of different solutions of $3\cos\theta+4\sin\theta=k$ is

(a) Zero
(b) Two
(c) One
(d) Infinite

31. $x\sin a+y\sin 2a+z\sin 3a=\sin 4a$
$x\sin b+y\sin 2b+z\sin 3b=\sin 4b$
$x\sin c+y\sin 2c+z\sin 3c=\sin 4c$.
Then, the roots of the equation.

$t^3-\frac{z}{2}t^2-\frac{y+2}{4}t+\frac{z-x}{8}=0\,(a,b,c\ne n\pi)$ are

(a) $\sin a$, $\sin b$, $\sin c$
(b) $\cos a$, $\cos b$, $\cos c$
(c) $\sin 2a$, $\sin 2b$, $\sin 2c$
(d) $\cos 2a$, $\cos 2b$, $\cos 2c$

32. The number of all possible triplets (a_1,a_2,a_3) such that $a_1+a_2\cos 2x+a_3\sin^2 x=0$ for all x is

(a) 0
(b) 1
(c) 3
(d) Infinite

33. The number of all possible 5-tuples (a_1,a_2,a_3,a_4,a_5) such that $a_1+a_2\sin x+a_3\cos x$ $+a_4\sin 2x+a_5\cos 2x=0$ holds for all x is

(a) zero
(b) 1
(c) 2
(d) infinite

34. Value of 'x' and 'y' satisfying the equation
$\sin^7 y=|x^3-x^2-9x+9|+|x^3-4x-x^2+4|$ $+\sec^2 2y+\cos^4 y$ are

(a) $x=1$, $y=n\pi$
(b) $x=1$, $y=2n\pi+\frac{\pi}{2}$
(c) $x=1$, $y=2n\pi$
(d) None of these

35. The equation $\sin x+\sin y+\sin z=-3$ for $0\le x\le 2\pi$, $0\le y\le 2\pi$, $0\le z\le 2\pi$ has

(a) one solution
(b) two sets of solutions
(c) four sets of solutions
(d) no solution

36. If $0 \le x < 2\pi$, then the number of the real values of x, which satisfy the equation
$\cos x + \cos 2x + \cos 3x + \cos 4x = 0$, is
(a) 9 (b) 3 (c) 7 (d) 5

37. If $\sum_{i=1}^{n} \cos \theta_i = n$, then $\sum_{i=1}^{n} \sin \theta_i$ is
(a) $n-1$ (b) 0
(c) n (d) $n+1$

38. Let the smallest positive value of x for which the function $f(x) = \sin \frac{x}{3} + \sin \frac{x}{11}, (x \in R)$ achieves its maximum value be x_0. Express x_0 in degree i.e. $x_0 = \alpha^0$. Then, the sum of the digits in α is
(a) 15 (b) 17
(c) 16 (d) 18

39. The maximum value of the expression $\left|\sqrt{\sin^2 x + 2a^2} - \sqrt{2a^2 - 1 - \cos^2 x}\right|$, where a and x are real number, is
(a) 1 (b) 2
(c) $\sqrt{2}$ (d) $\sqrt{3}$

40. The number of real solution of the equation. $\sin(e^x) = 5^x + 5^{-x}$ is
(a) 0 (b) 1
(c) 2 (d) Infinitely many

41. The number of points of intersection of the two curves $y = 2\sin x$ and $y = 5x^2 + 2x + 3$ is
(a) 0 (b) 1
(c) 2 (d) ∞

42. The equation $\sin^4 x - (k+2)\sin^2 x - (k+3) = 0$ possesses a solution if
(a) $k > -3$ (b) $k < -2$
(c) $-3 \le k \le -2$ (d) k is any (+ve) value

43. If $0 < x < \pi/2$ and $\sin^n x + \cos^n x \ge 1$, then
(a) $n \in [2, \infty)$ (b) $(-\infty, 2]$
(c) $n \in [-1, 1]$ (d) None of these

44. The most general values of 'x' for which $\sin x + \cos x = \min_{a \in R} [1, a^2 - 4a + 6]$ are given by
(a) $2n\pi$ (b) $2n\pi + \frac{\pi}{2}$
(c) $n\pi + (-1)^n \frac{\pi}{4} - \frac{\pi}{4}$ (d) None of these

45. If $a, b \in [0, \pi]$ and the equation $x^2 + 4 + 3\sin(ax + b) - 2x = 0$ has atleast one solution, then the value of $(a+b)$ can be:
(a) $\frac{7\pi}{2}$ (b) $\frac{3\pi}{2}$
(c) $\frac{9\pi}{2}$ (d) None of these

46. The value of a for which the equation $4\operatorname{cosec}^2(\pi(a+x)) + a^2 - 4a = 0$ has a real solution, is
(a) $a=1$ (b) $a=2$
(c) $a=10$ (d) None of these

47. If the equation $2\cos x + \cos 2\lambda x = 3$ has only one solution, then λ is
(a) 1 (b) a rational number
(c) an irrational number (d) None of these

48. Let n be positive integer such that $\sin \frac{\pi}{2n} + \cos \frac{\pi}{2n} = \frac{\sqrt{n}}{2}$. Then
(a) $6 \le n \le 8$ (b) $4 < n \le 8$
(c) $6 < n < 8$ (d) $4 < n < 8$

49. If $\sin^{100} \theta - \cos^{100} \theta = 1$, then θ is
(a) $2n\pi + \frac{\pi}{3}, n \in I$ (b) $n\pi + \frac{\pi}{2}, n \in I$
(c) $n\pi + \frac{\pi}{4}, n \in I$ (d) $2n\pi - \frac{\pi}{3}, n \in I$

50. Total number of solution of $\sin\{x\} = \cos\{x\}$, where {} denotes the fractional part, in $[0, 2\pi]$ is equal to
(a) 5 (b) 6
(c) 7 (d) None of these

51. Total number of solutions of $\sin x = \frac{|x|}{10}$ is equal to
(a) 4 (b) 6
(c) 7 (d) None of these

52. If $\left|1 - \frac{|\sin x|}{1 + \sin x}\right| \ge \frac{2}{3}$, then $\sin x$ lies in
(a) $\left(-\infty, \frac{-1}{2}\right] \cup \left[\frac{1}{2}, \infty\right)$ (b) $\left(-\frac{1}{2}, \frac{1}{2}\right)$
(c) $\left[-\frac{1}{2}, \frac{1}{2}\right]$ (d) None of these

53. Let $2\sin^2 x + 3\sin x - 2 > 0$ and $x^2 - x - 2 < 0$ (x is measured in radian). Then 'x' lies in the internal.
(a) $\left(\frac{\pi}{6}, \frac{5\pi}{6}\right)$ (b) $\left(-1, \frac{5\pi}{6}\right)$ (c) $(-1, 2)$ (d) $\left(\frac{\pi}{6}, 2\right)$

54. The number of solution of equation $x^3 + x^2 + 4x + 2\sin x = 0$ in $0 \le x \le 2\pi$ is
(a) Zero (b) One
(c) Two (d) Four

55. Total number of solutions of $\cos x = \sqrt{1 - \sin 2x}$ in $[0, 2\pi]$, is equal to
(a) 2 (b) 3
(c) 5 (d) None of these

56. $\frac{\sin 3\alpha}{\cos 2\alpha} < 0$ if α lies in
(a) $(13\pi/48, 14\pi/48)$ (b) $(14\pi/48, 18\pi/48)$
(c) $(18\pi/48, 23\pi/48)$ (d) any of these intervals

57. The expression $n\sin^2\theta+2n\cos(\theta+\alpha)\sin\alpha\sin\theta+\cos 2(\alpha+\theta)$ is independent of 'θ', the value of n is
(a) 1
(b) 2
(c) 3
(d) 4

58. The value of the determinant
$$\begin{vmatrix} 1 & a & a^2 \\ \cos(n-1)x & \cos nx & \cos(n+1)x \\ \sin(n-1)x & \sin nx & \sin(n+1)x \end{vmatrix}$$ is zero if
(a) $x=n\pi$
(b) $x=n\pi/2$
(c) $x=(2n+1)\pi/2$
(d) $x=\dfrac{1+a^2}{2a}\; n\in I$

59. If $f(x)=\begin{vmatrix} \sin^2\theta & \cos^2\theta & x \\ \cos^2\theta & x & \sin^2\theta \\ x & \sin^2\theta & \cos^2\theta \end{vmatrix}$, $\theta\in(0,\pi/2)$, then roots of $f(x)=0$ are
(a) $1/2,-1$
(b) $1/2,-1,0$
(c) $-1/2,1,0$
(d) $-1/2,-1,0$

60. For the equation $3^{\sin 2x+2\cos^2 x}+3^{1+2\sin x(\sin x-\cos x)}=28$, then number of solutions lying in the interval $[0,2\pi]$ is
(a) 8
(b) 4
(c) 2
(d) 1

61. Let $f(x)=3\left(\cos^4\dfrac{x}{2}+\sin^4\dfrac{x}{2}\right)-2\cos^2 x$ and $S=\left\{x\in[0,2\pi]: f'(x)=-\dfrac{\sqrt{3}}{4}\right\}$. If $4\beta=\sum_{x\in S} x$, then $f(\beta)$ is equal to
(a) $\dfrac{5}{4}$
(b) $\dfrac{4}{5}$
(c) $\dfrac{7}{5}$
(d) $\dfrac{5}{7}$

Numerical Value Type Questions

62. Find the number of solutions of the equation $|\cot x|=\cot x+\dfrac{1}{\sin x}$, when $x\in[0,\ 2\pi]$.

63. Find the number of solutions of the equation $|\cos x|=[x]$, (where [.] denotes the greatest integer function).

64. If the sum of the roots of the equation $\cos 4x+6=7\cos 2x$ in the interval $[0,314]$ is $k\pi$, $k\in R$ Find $(k-4948)$.

65. If equation $x^2\tan^2\theta-(2\tan\theta)x+1=0$ and $\left(\dfrac{1}{1+\log_b ac}\right)x^2+\left(\dfrac{1}{1+\log_c ab}\right)x+\left(\dfrac{1}{1+\log_a bc}-1\right)=0$ (where $a, b, c, >1$) have a common root and then 2nd equation has equal roots, then number of possible value of θ in $(0,\pi)$ is ....

66. If α be the smallest positive root of the equation $\sqrt{\sin(1-x)}=\sqrt{\cos x}$, then the approximate integral value of α must be ....

67. Number of ordered pairs (x, y) which satisfies the relation $\dfrac{x^4+1}{8x^2}=\sin^2 y\cdot\cos^2 y$, where $y\in[0,2\pi]$.

68. If $\cos A\sin\left(A-\dfrac{\pi}{6}\right)$ is maximum, when the values of A is equal to $\dfrac{\pi}{\lambda}$, then the value of λ is ....

69. If $3\sin x+4\cos x=5$, then the value of $90\tan^2(x/2)-60\tan(x/2)+10$ is equal to ....

70. If $\tan(\pi\cos\theta)=\cot(\pi\sin\theta)$, then $16\cos^2(\theta-\pi/4)$ is equal to ....

71. The number of solutions for,
$$\left.\begin{aligned} &\sin\left(x-\frac{\pi}{4}\right)-\sin\left(x-\frac{3\pi}{4}\right)=1 \\ &\frac{2\cos 7x}{\cos 3+\sin 3}>2^{\cos 2x} \end{aligned}\right\}$$ in $(0,2\pi)$, is ....

72. Let $p,q\in N$ and $q>p$, the number of solutions of the equation $q|\sin\theta|=p|\cos\theta|$ in the interval $[0,2\pi]$ is ....

73. The number of solutions of the equation $(1-\sin x)^3-(\cos x-1)^3-(\sin x)^3=(2-\cos x-2\sin x)^3$ in $[0,2\pi]$ is ....

74. Number of roots of the equation $\cos^2 x+\dfrac{\sqrt{3}+1}{2}\sin x-\dfrac{\sqrt{3}}{4}-1=0$, which lie in the interval $[-\pi,\pi]$ is ....

75. If $\sin^2\theta-2\sin\theta-1=0$ is to be satisfied for exactly 4 distinct values of $\theta\in[0,n\pi]$, $n\in N$, then the least value of n is ....

76. Total number of real solution in $[0,\pi]$ of the equation $|\cos x|^{\sin^2 x-\frac{3}{2}\sin x+\frac{1}{2}}=1$ is ....

77. If $x+\sin y=2024$ and $x+2024\cos y=2023$, $0\le y\le\dfrac{\pi}{2}$, then the value of $[x+y]-1$ is ....

78. Number of ordered pairs (λ, x) satisfying the equation $\sec^2(\lambda+2)x+\lambda^2-1=0$; $-\pi<x<\pi$ is ....

79. If $\tan^2[\pi(x+y)]+\cot^2[\pi(x+y)]=1+\sqrt{\dfrac{2x}{1+x^2}}$, where $x,y\in R$, then [4 (least positive value of y)] is ....

80. If α,β be any two positive values of x for which $2\cos x$, $|\cos x|$ and $(1-3\cos^2 x)$ are in GP, then the minimum value of $\left[\left(\dfrac{168}{\pi}\right)|\alpha-\beta|\right]$ is ....

81. If solution for the inequality $\sin^4\left(\frac{x}{3}\right)+\cos^4\left(\frac{x}{3}\right)>\frac{1}{2}$ is $x\in R-\left\{x: x=\frac{a\cdot(n\pi)}{b}\pm\frac{c\pi}{d}, n\in I \text{ and } a,b,c,d\in Q\right\}$, then $(2ac-bd)$ is equal to ......

82. The number of solutions of $x\in[0,2\pi]$ satisfying the equation $(\log_{\sqrt{3}}\tan x)(\sqrt{\log_{\tan x}3+\log_{\sqrt{3}}3\sqrt{3}})=-1$ is ....

Previous Years Questions

83. If $2\tan^2\theta-5\sec\theta=1$ has exactly 7 solutions in the interval $\left[0,\frac{n\pi}{2}\right]$, for the least value of $n\in N$, then $\sum_{K=1}^{n}\frac{K}{2^k}$ is equal to **[Single Correct Type, 2024 Main]**

(a) $\frac{1}{2^{13}}(2^{14}-15)$ (b) $\frac{1}{2^{15}}(2^{14}-14)$

(c) $\frac{1}{2^{14}}(2^{15}-15)$ (d) $1-\frac{15}{2^{13}}$

84. The number of solutions of the equation $4\sin^2 x-4\cos^3 x+9-4\cos x=0, x\in|-2\pi,2\pi|$ is **[Single Correct Type, 2024 Main]**

(a) 1 (b) 3

(c) 2 (d) 0

85. The number of solution of the equation $e^{\sin x}-2e^{-\sin x}=2$, is **[Single Correct Type, 2024 Main]**

(a) 1 (b) more than 2

(c) 2 (d) 0

86. If $2\sin^3 x+\sin 2x\cos x+4\sin x-4=0$ has exactly 3 solutions in the interval $\left[0,\frac{n\pi}{2}\right]$, $n\in N$, then the roots of the equation $x^2+nx+(n-3)=0$ belong to **[Single Correct Type, 2024 Main]**

(a) $\left(-\frac{\sqrt{17}}{2},\frac{\sqrt{17}}{2}\right)$ (b) z

(c) $(0,\infty)$ (d) $(-\infty,0)$

87. The sum of the solutions $x\in R$ of the equation $\frac{3\cos 2x+\cos^3 2x}{\cos^6 x-\sin^6 x}=x^3-x^2+6$ is **[Single Correct Type, 2024 Main]**

(a) 0 (b) -1

(c) 3 (d) 1

88. If $\alpha, -\frac{\pi}{2}<\alpha<\frac{\pi}{2}$ is the solution of $4\cos\theta+5\sin\theta=1$, then the value of $\tan\alpha$ is **[Single Correct Type, 2024 Main]**

(a) $\frac{10-\sqrt{10}}{12}$ (b) $\frac{\sqrt{10}-10}{6}$

(c) $\frac{\sqrt{10}-10}{12}$ (d) $\frac{10-\sqrt{10}}{6}$

89. The number of elements in the set $S=\{\theta\in[0,2\pi]: 3\cos^4\theta-5\cos^2\theta-2\sin^6\theta+2=0\}$ is **[Single Correct Type, 2023 Main]**

(a) 12 (b) 8

(c) 9 (d) 10

90. If $\tan 15°+\frac{1}{\tan 75°}+\frac{1}{\tan 105°}+\tan 195°=2a$, then the value of $(a+1/a)$ is **[Single Correct Type, 2023 Main]**

(a) $5-\frac{3}{2}\sqrt{3}$ (b) $4-2\sqrt{3}$

(c) 4 (d) 2

91. The set of all values of λ for which the equation $\cos^2 2x-2\sin^4 x-2\cos^2 x=\lambda$ has a real solution x, is **[Single Correct Type, 2023 Main]**

(a) $\left[-\frac{3}{2},-1\right]$ (b) $[-2,-1]$

(c) $\left[-2,-\frac{3}{2}\right]$ (d) $\left[-1,-\frac{1}{2}\right]$

92. Let $f(\theta)=3\left(\sin^4\left(\frac{3\pi}{2}-\theta\right)+\sin^4(3\pi+\theta)\right)-2(1-\sin^2 2\theta)$ and $S=\left\{\theta\in[0,\pi]: f'(\theta)=-\frac{\sqrt{3}}{2}\right\}$.

If $4\beta=\sum_{\theta\in S}\theta$, then $f(\beta)$ is equal to **[Single Correct Type, 2023 Main]**

(a) 5/4 (b) 3/2 (c) 11/8 (d) 9/8

93. If the solution of the equation $\log_{\cos x}\cot x+4\log_{\sin x}\tan x=1, x\in\left(0,\frac{\pi}{2}\right)$, is $\sin^{-1}\left(\frac{\alpha+\sqrt{\beta}}{2}\right)$, where α,β are integers, then $\alpha+\beta$ is equal to **[Single Correct Type, 2023 Main]**

(a) 3 (b) 5 (c) 6 (d) 4

94. If m and n respectively are the numbers of positive and negative values of θ in the interval $[-\pi,\pi]$ that satisfy the equation $\cos 2\theta\cos\frac{\theta}{2}=\cos 3\theta\cos\frac{9\theta}{2}$, then mn is equal to .... **[Numerical Value Type, 2023 Main]**

95. Let $S=\{\theta\in[0,2\pi): \tan(\pi\cos\theta)+\tan(\pi\sin\theta)=0\}$. Then, $\sum_{\theta\in S}\sin^2\left(\theta+\frac{\pi}{4}\right)$ is equal to .... **[Numerical Value Type, 2023 Main]**

96. The number of elements in the set $S=\left\{x\in R: 2\cos\left(\frac{x^2+x}{6}\right)=4^x+4^{-x}\right\}$ is **[Single Correct Type, 2022 Main]**

(a) 1 (b) 3

(c) 0 (d) infinite

97. Let $S=\left\{\theta\in\left(0,\frac{\pi}{2}\right):\sum_{m=1}^{9}\sec\left(\theta+(m-1)\frac{\pi}{6}\right)\sec\left(\theta+\frac{m\pi}{6}\right)=-\frac{8}{\sqrt{3}}\right\}$. Then,

[Single Correct Type, 2022 Main]

(a) $S=\left\{\frac{\pi}{12}\right\}$ (b) $S=\left\{\frac{2\pi}{3}\right\}$

(c) $\sum_{\theta\in S}\theta=\frac{\pi}{2}$ (d) $\sum_{\theta\in S}\theta=\frac{3\pi}{4}$

98. Let $S=\{\theta\in[0,2\pi]:8^{2\cos^2\theta}+8^{2\cos^2\theta}=16\}$. Then,

$n(S)+\sum_{\theta\in S}\left(\sec\left(\frac{\pi}{4}+2\theta\right)\operatorname{cosec}\left(\frac{\pi}{4}+2\theta\right)\right)$ is equal to

[Single Correct Type, 2022 Main]

(a) 0 (b) -2

(c) -4 (d) 12

99. The number of solutions of $|\cos x|=\sin x$, such that $-4\pi\le x\le 4\pi$ is [Single Correct Type, 2022 Main]

(a) 4 (b) 6

(c) 8 (d) 12

100. Let $S=\left\{\theta\in[-\pi,\pi]-\left\{\pm\frac{\pi}{2}\right\}:\sin\theta\tan\theta+\tan\theta=\sin 2\theta\right\}$.

If $T=\sum_{\theta\in S}\cos 2\theta$, then $T+n(S)$ is equal to

[Single Correct Type, 2022 Main]

(a) $7+\sqrt{3}$ (b) 9

(c) $8+\sqrt{3}$ (d) 10

101. The number of solutions of the equation

$\cos\left(x+\frac{\pi}{3}\right)\cos\left(\frac{\pi}{3}-x\right)=\frac{1}{4}\cos^2 2x,\ x\in[-3\pi,3\pi]$ is

[Single Correct Type, 2022 Main]

(a) 8 (b) 5

(c) 6 (d) 7

102. The number of elements in the set

$S=\{\theta\in[-4\pi,4\pi]:3\cos^2 2\theta+6\cos 2\theta-10\cos^2\theta+5=0$ is ....

[Numerical Value Type, 2022 Main]

103. If n is the number of solutions of the equation

$2\cos x\left(4\sin\left(\frac{\pi}{4}+x\right)\sin\left(\frac{\pi}{4}-x\right)-1\right)=1,\ x\in[0,\pi]$ and

S is the sum of all these solutions, then the ordered pair (n,S) is [Single Correct Type, 2021 Main]

(a) $\left(3,\frac{13\pi}{9}\right)$ (b) $\left(2,\frac{2\pi}{3}\right)$

(c) $\left(2,\frac{8\pi}{9}\right)$ (d) $\left(3,\frac{5\pi}{3}\right)$

104. The number of integral values of 'k' for which the equation $3\sin x+4\cos x=k+1$ has a solution, $k\in R$ is ....

[Numerical Value Type, 2021 Main]

105. If the equation $\cos^4\theta+\sin^4\theta+\lambda=0$ has real solutions for θ, then λ lies in the interval

[Single Correct Type, 2020 Main]

(a) $\left(-\frac{5}{4},-1\right)$ (b) $\left[-1,-\frac{1}{2}\right]$

(c) $\left(-\frac{1}{2},-\frac{1}{4}\right]$ (d) $\left[-\frac{3}{2},-\frac{5}{4}\right]$

106. Let S be the set of all $\alpha\in R$ such that the equation, $\cos 2x+\alpha\sin x=2\alpha-7$ has a solution. Then, S is equal to [Single Correct Type, 2019 Main]

(a) R (b) $[1, 4]$

(c) $[3, 7]$ (d) $[2, 6]$

107. Let $S=\{\theta\in[-2\pi,2\pi]:2\cos^2\theta+3\sin\theta=0\}$, then the sum of the elements of S is

[Single Correct Type, 2019 Main]

(a) 2π (b) π

(c) $5\pi/3$ (d) $13\pi/6$

108. If sum of all the solutions of the equation

$8\cos x\cdot\left(\cos\left(\frac{\pi}{6}+x\right)\cdot\cos\left(\frac{\pi}{6}-x\right)-\frac{1}{2}\right)=1$ in $[0,\pi]$ is $k\pi$,

then k is equal to [Single Correct Type, 2018 Main]

(a) 2/3 (b) 13/9

(c) 8/9 (d) 20/9

109. If $5(\tan^2 x-\cos^2 x)=2\cos 2x+9$, then the value of $\cos 4x$ is [Single Correct Type, 2017 Main]

(a) $-3/5$ (b) 1/3 (c) 2/9 (d) $-7/9$

EXERCISE 2
JEE Advanced Pattern

Single Option Correct Type Questions

1. For the equation $3^{2\sec^2 x}+1=10\cdot 3^{\tan^2 x}$, the number of solutions lying in the interval $[0, 2\pi]$ is
(a) 8 (b) 6
(c) 3 (d) 1

2. The general solution of the equation $\dfrac{1-\sin x+\ldots+(-1)^n\sin^n x+\ldots}{1+\sin x+\ldots+\sin^n x+\ldots}=\dfrac{1-\cos 2x}{1+\cos 2x}$ is $(n\in z)$ is
(a) $(-1)^n\left(\frac{\pi}{3}\right)+n\pi$ (b) $(-1)^n\left(\frac{\pi}{6}\right)+n\pi$
(c) $(-1)^n\left(\frac{\pi}{12}\right)+n\pi$ (d) $(-1)^n\left(\frac{\pi}{4}\right)+n\pi$

3. Find the number of pairs of integer (x, y) that satisfy the following two equations $\begin{cases}\cos(xy)=x\\ \tan(xy)=y\end{cases}$
(a) 1 (b) 2
(c) 4 (d) 6

4. The number of solutions of the equation $16(\sin^5 x+\cos^5 x)=11(\sin x+\cos x)$, where $x\in[0, 2\pi]$, is
(a) 6 (b) 7
(c) 8 (d) 9

5. The smallest positive x satisfying the equation $\log_{\cos x}\sin x+\log_{\sin x}\cos x=2$ is
(a) $\frac{\pi}{2}$ (b) $\frac{\pi}{3}$ (c) $\frac{\pi}{4}$ (d) $\frac{\pi}{6}$

6. If $\alpha<\beta<\gamma$ and $\sin\gamma\cdot\cos\alpha=1$, where $\alpha, \gamma\in[\pi, 2\pi]$, then the least integral value of $f(x)=|x-\alpha|+|x-\beta|+|x-\gamma|$ is
(a) 0 (b) 1 (c) 2 (d) 3

7. The number of solutions of the equation $5^{1/2}+5^{\frac{1}{2}+\log_5(\sin x)}=15^{\frac{1}{2}+\log_{15}\cos x}$ for $x\in[0, 100\pi]$ is
(a) 50 (b) 100
(c) 200 (d) 400

8. Let $0<\theta_1<\theta_2<\theta_3<\ldots$ denote the positive solution of the equation $3+3\cos\theta=2\sin^2\theta$. The value of $\theta_3+\theta_7$ is
(a) 6π (b) 7π (c) 8π (d) 4π

9. The smallest positive value of x (in radians) satisfying the equation $\log_{\cos x}\left(\frac{\sqrt{3}}{2}\sin x\right)=2-\log_{\sec x}(\tan x)$, is
(a) $\frac{\pi}{12}$ (b) $\frac{\pi}{6}$ (c) $\frac{\pi}{4}$ (d) $\frac{\pi}{3}$

10. Consider the system of linear equations in x, y and z

$$(\sin 3\theta)x-y+z=0$$
$$(\cos 2\theta)x+4y+3z=0$$
$$2x+7y+7z=0$$

which of the following can be the values of θ for which the system has a non-trivial solution?
(a) $n\pi+(-1)^n\frac{\pi}{6}, \forall\, n\in z$ (b) $n\pi+(-1)^n\frac{\pi}{3}, \forall\, n\in z$
(c) $n\pi+(-1)^n\frac{\pi}{9}, \forall\, n\in z$ (d) None of these

11. If the equation $x^2+12+3\sin(a+bx)+6x=0$ has at least one real solution, where $a, b\in[0, 2\pi]$, then the value of $(a-3b)$ is
(a) $2n\pi$ (b) $(2n+1)\pi$
(c) $(4n-1)\frac{\pi}{2}$ (d) $(4n+1)\frac{\pi}{2}$

12. If $2\sin^2\left(x-\frac{\pi}{3}\right)-5\sin\left(x-\frac{\pi}{3}\right)+2<0$, then x belongs to
(a) $\left(\frac{(12n-5)\pi}{6}, \frac{(4n+1)\pi}{2}\right), n\in z$
(b) $\left(\frac{(6n-7)\pi}{6}, \frac{(2n+1)\pi}{2}\right), n\in z$
(c) $\left(\frac{(4n+1)\pi}{6}, n\pi\right), n\in z$
(d) $\left(\frac{(4n+1)\pi}{2}, \frac{(12n+7)\pi}{6}\right), n\in z$

13. The number of solutions of $[\sin x+\cos x]=3+[-\sin x]+[-\cos x]$, where [.] denotes the greatest integer function), $x\in[0, 2\pi]$, is
(a) 0 (b) 4 (c) infinite (d) 1

14. If no solution of $3\sin y+12\sin^3 x=a$, lies on the line $y=3x$, then
(a) $a\in(-\infty, -9)\cup(9, \infty)$ (b) $a\in[-9, 9]$
(c) $a\in\{-9, 9\}$ (d) None of these

15. Let $S=\left\{x\in(-\pi,\pi): x\neq 0, \pm\frac{\pi}{2}\right\}$. The number of distinct solutions of the equation $2\cos 2x-\sqrt{3}\sin x=\cos x$ in the set S is equal to
(a) 0 (b) 2
(c) 4 (d) 6

More than One Correct Option Type Questions

16. The general solution of $4\sin^4 x+\cos^4 x=1$ is
(a) $(2n+1)\frac{\pi}{2}$ (b) $n\pi$
(c) $n\pi+(-1)^n\sin^{-1}\sqrt{\frac{2}{5}}$ (d) None of these

17. If $\alpha\in[-2\pi,2\pi]$ and $\cos\frac{\alpha}{2}+\sin\frac{\alpha}{2}=\sqrt{2}(\cos 36°-\sin 18°)$, then values of α is/are
(a) $\frac{7\pi}{6}$ (b) $\frac{\pi}{6}$ (c) $-\frac{5\pi}{6}$ (d) $-\frac{\pi}{6}$

18. All values of $x\in\left(0,\frac{\pi}{2}\right)$ such that $\frac{\sqrt{3}-1}{\sin x}+\frac{\sqrt{3}+1}{\cos x}=4\sqrt{2}$ are
(a) $\frac{\pi}{15}$ (b) $\frac{\pi}{12}$ (c) $\frac{11\pi}{36}$ (d) $\frac{3\pi}{10}$

19. Let $f(x)=\cos(a_1+x)+\frac{1}{2}\cos(a_2+x)+\frac{1}{2^2}\cos(a_3+x)$
$+\ldots+\frac{1}{2^{n-1}}\cos(a_n+x)$
where $a_1, a_2, \ldots, a_n\in R$. If $f(x_1)=f(x_2)=0$, then $|x_2-x_1|$ may be equal to
(a) π (b) 2π (c) 3π (d) $\frac{\pi}{2}$

20. The value of θ, lying between $\theta=0$ and $\theta=\frac{\pi}{2}$ and 2satisfying the equation.
$$\begin{vmatrix} 1+\cos^2\theta & \sin^2\theta & 4\sin 4\theta \\ \cos^2\theta & 1+\sin^2\theta & 4\sin 4\theta \\ \cos^2\theta & \sin^2\theta & 1+4\sin 4\theta \end{vmatrix}=0, \text{ is}$$
(a) $\frac{11\pi}{24}$ (b) $\frac{7\pi}{24}$
(c) $\frac{5\pi}{24}$ (d) None of these

21. The number of values of α in the interval $[-\pi,0]$ satisfying $\sin\alpha+\int_{\alpha}^{2\alpha}\cos 2x\,dx=0$, then
(a) $\alpha=0$ (b) $\alpha=0,-\pi,-\frac{\pi}{3}$
(c) $\alpha=\frac{\pi}{6},\frac{5\pi}{6}$ (d) None of these

22. The values of x, $0\le x\le\frac{\pi}{2}$ whcih satisfy the equation $81^{\sin^2 x}+81^{\cos^2 x}=30$ are
(a) $\frac{\pi}{3}$ (b) $\frac{\pi}{4}$ (c) $\frac{\pi}{6}$ (d) $\frac{7\pi}{18}$

23. The solutions of $\theta\in[0,2\pi]$ satisfying the equation $\log_{\sqrt{3}}\tan\theta(\sqrt{\log_{\tan\theta}3+\log_{\sqrt{3}}3\sqrt{3}})=-1$, then
(a) $\theta=\frac{\pi}{6}$ (b) $\frac{\pi}{3},\frac{5\pi}{3}$
(c) has sum $\frac{4\pi}{3}$ (d) >2

24. The value of 't' which satisfies $(t-[|\sin x|])!=3!5!7!$ is/are .... where [.] is GIF
(a) 9 (b) 10 (c) 11 (d) 12

25. If $[\sin x]+[\sqrt{2}\cos x]=-3$, $x\in[0,2\pi]$, (where, [·] denotes the greatest integer function), then
(a) $x\in\left(\pi,\frac{5\pi}{4}\right)$ (b) $x\in\left(\pi,\frac{7\pi}{6}\right)$
(c) $x\in\left[\pi,\frac{5\pi}{4}\right]$ (d) None of these

26. The number of solutions of the equations $y=\frac{1}{3}[\sin\theta+[\sin\theta+[\sin\theta]]]$ and $[y+[y]]=2\cos\theta$ [where, [·] denotes the greatest integer function] is /are
(a) 0 (b) 1
(c) 2 (d) infinite

27. General value of α, if $32\tan^8\theta=2\cos^8\alpha-3\cos\alpha$ and $3\cos 2\theta=1$ is/are
(a) $2n\pi+\frac{\pi}{3}, n\in Z$ (b) $2n\pi-\frac{2\pi}{3}, n\in Z$
(c) $2n\pi+\frac{2\pi}{3}, n\in Z$ (d) $2n\pi-\frac{\pi}{3}, n\in Z$

28. The general solution of the equation $\cot\left(\frac{\theta}{2}\right)-\text{cosec}\left(\frac{\theta}{2}\right)=\cot\theta$ is/are
(a) $4n\pi+\frac{2\pi}{3}, n\in I$ (b) $4n\pi-\frac{2\pi}{3}, n\in I$
(c) $2n\pi, n\in I$ (d) $2n\pi\pm\frac{\pi}{3}, n\in I$

29. The number of integral values of a for which the system of linear equations $x\sin\theta-2y\cos\theta-az=0$, $x+2y+z=0$, $-x+y+z=0$ may have non- trivial solutions, then
(a) at $a=2$ the given system will have finite solutions for $\theta\in R$
(b) number of possible integral values of a is 3
(c) for $a=1$ the system will have infinite solutions
(d) for $a=3$ the system will have unique solution

30. General solution for the trigonometric equation $1+\sin^3 x+\cos^3 x=\frac{3}{2}\sin 2x$ is/are

(a) $2n\pi-\frac{\pi}{2}, n\in I$ (b) $2n\pi+\frac{\pi}{2}, n\in I$

(c) $(2n+1)\pi, n\in I$ (d) $2n\pi\pm\frac{3\pi}{4}, n\in I$

31. The equation $2\sin^3\theta+(2\lambda-3)\sin^2\theta-(3\lambda+2)\sin\theta-2\lambda=0$ has exactly three roots in $(0, 2\pi)$, then λ can be equal to

(a) 0 (b) $\frac{1}{2}$

(c) 1 (d) -1

32. Let x, y, z be elements from interval $[0, 2\pi]$ satisfying the inequality $(4+\sin 4x)(2+\cot^2 y)(1+\sin^4 z)\le 12\sin^2 z$, then

(a) the number of ordered pairs (x, y) is 5

(b) the number of ordered pairs (y, z) is 8

(c) the number of ordered pairs (z, x) is 8

(d) the number of pairs (y, z) such that $z=y$ is 2

33. If $x+y=2\pi/3$ and $\sin x/\sin y=2$, then the

(a) number of values of $x\in[0,4\pi]$ are 4

(b) number of values of $x\in[0,4\pi]$ are 2

(c) number of values of $y\in[0,4\pi]$ are 2

(d) number of values of $y\in[0,4\pi]$ are 8

34. If x and y are positive acute angles such that $(x+y)$ and $(x-y)$ satisfy the equation $\tan^2\theta-4\tan\theta+1=0$, then

(a) $x=\frac{\pi}{6}$ (b) $y=\frac{\pi}{4}$ (c) $y=\frac{\pi}{6}$ (d) $x=\frac{\pi}{4}$

35. If $[x]$ denotes the greatest integer less than or equal to x then the equation $\sin x=[1+\sin x]+[1-\cos x]$ has no solution in

(a) $\left[-\frac{\pi}{2},\frac{\pi}{2}\right]$ (b) $\left[\frac{\pi}{2},\pi\right]$ (c) $\left[\pi,\frac{3\pi}{2}\right]$ (d) R

36. If $x+y=\frac{4\pi}{3}$ and $\sin x=2\sin y$, then

(a) $x=n\pi+\frac{\pi}{2}, n\in I$ (b) $y=\frac{5\pi}{6}-n\pi, n\in I$

(c) Both (a) and (b) (d) None of these

37. For the trigonometric equation

$$\left(\sin^2 x+\frac{1}{\sin^2 x}\right)^2+\left(\cos^2 x+\frac{1}{\cos^2 x}\right)^2=12+\frac{1}{2}\sin y,$$

choose the correct options

(a) $x=(2m+1)\frac{\pi}{2}, m\in I$ (b) $y=2n\pi+\frac{\pi}{4}, n\in I$

(c) $x=(2m\pm 1)\frac{\pi}{4}, m\in I$ (d) $y=2n\pi+\frac{\pi}{2}, n\in I$

38. The value of x and y which satisfy the non-standard equation $1-2x-x^2=\tan^2(x+y)+\cot^2(x+y)$ is/are

(a) $x=1$ (b) $y=n\pi\pm\frac{\pi}{4}+1, n\in I$

(c) $x=-1$ (d) $y=n\pi\pm\frac{\pi}{4}-1, n\in I$

39. All pairs of x, y that satisfy the equation $\cos x+\cos y+\cos(x+y)=\frac{-3}{2}$ is

(a) $x=2m\pi\pm\frac{2\pi}{3}, m\in I$

(b) $x=2m\pi\pm\frac{\pi}{4}, m\in I$

(c) $y=(m-n)\pi\pm\frac{2\pi}{3}, m, n\in I$

(d) $y=2(m-n)\pi\pm\frac{2\pi}{3}, m, n\in I$

40. If $\int_0^x (t^2-8t+13)dt=x\sin\frac{a}{x}$ (where $a\neq 0$) has a solution, then choose the incorrect option(s).

(a) $x=5$ (b) $x=6$

(c) $a=\frac{1}{3}\pi(4n+1), n\in I$ (d) $a=3\pi(4n+1), n\in I$

41. If $\cos^4 x-(a+2)\cos^2 x-(a+3)=0$ possesses solution then choose the correct options

(a) $a\in[2,3]$

(b) $a\in[-3,-2]$

(c) $x=2n\pi\pm\cos^{-1}\sqrt{a-3}, n\in I$

(d) $x=n\pi\pm\cos^{-1}\sqrt{a+3}, n\in I$

42. $\frac{\alpha^2}{1-\tan^2 x}=\frac{\sin^2 x+\alpha^2-2}{\cos 2x}$ has a solution if

(a) $\alpha\le -1$ (b) $\alpha\ge 1$

(c) $\alpha=1/2$ (d) α is any real number

43. The equation $4\sin(x+\pi/3)\cos(x-\pi/6)=a^2+\sqrt{3}\sin 2x-\cos 2x$ has a solution if the value of a is

(a) -2 (b) 0

(c) 2 (d) $a\in[-2,2]$

44. If $0\le x\le 2\pi$ and $|\cos x|\le\sin x$, then

(a) the set of all values of x is $\left[\frac{\pi}{4},\frac{3\pi}{4}\right]$

(b) the number of solutions that are integral multiple of $\frac{\pi}{4}$ is four

(c) the sum of the largest and the smallest solution is π

(d) the set of all values of x is $x\in\left[\frac{\pi}{4},\frac{\pi}{2}\right)\cup\left(\frac{\pi}{2},\frac{3\pi}{4}\right]$

45. Which of the following is/are correct.

(a) $(\tan x)^{\ln(\sin x)}>(\cot x)^{\ln(\sin x)}, \forall x\in(0,\pi/4)$

(b) $4^{\ln(\operatorname{cosec} x)}<5^{\ln(\operatorname{cosec} x)}, \forall x\in(0,\pi/2)$

(c) $(1/2)^{\ln(\cos x)}<(1/3)^{\ln(\cos x)}, \forall x\in(0,\pi/2)$

(d) $2^{\ln(\sin x)}>2^{\ln(\tan x)}, \forall x\in(0,\pi/2)$

Passage Based Questions

Passage I

(Q. Nos. 46 to 47)

- If number of solutions and sum of solutions of the equation $3\sin^2 x - 7\sin x + 2 = 0$, $x \in [0, 2\pi]$ are respectively N and S and $f_n(\theta) = \sin^n \theta + \cos^n \theta$. On the basis of above information, answer the following questions.

46. Value of $N + S$ is

(a) $1+\pi$ (b) $2+\pi$ (c) $3+\pi$ (d) $4+\pi$

47. If α is solution of equation $3\sin^2 x - 7\sin x + 2 = 0$, $x \in [0, 2\pi]$, then the value of $f_4(\alpha)$ is.

(a) $\frac{97}{81}$ (b) $\frac{57}{81}$ (c) $\frac{65}{81}$ (d) 0

Passage II

(Q. Nos. 48 to 49)

- Let $\log_a N = \alpha + \beta$ where α is integer and $\beta = [0, 1)$. Then, On the basis of above information, answer the following questions.

48. The difference of largest and smallest integral value of N satisfying $\alpha = 3$ and $a = 5$, is

(a) 499 (b) 500 (c) 501 (d) 502

49. If N_1 is number of integers when $a = 2$ and $\alpha = 2$ and N_2 is number of integers when $\alpha = 1$ and $a = 3$, then the minimum value of $(N_1 \sec^2\theta + N_2 \operatorname{cosec}^2\theta)$

(a) $10 + 4\sqrt{6}$ (b) $10 + \sqrt{6}$ (c) 10 (d) 100

Passage III

(Q. Nos. 50 to 51)

- If an angle and a side of a right angled triangle is known, then rest of the sides and angles can be found as follows In ΔABC (Figure 1), if $\angle B = 90°$, $\angle C = \theta$ and $BC = x$, then $AB = x\tan\theta$ and $AC = x\sec\theta$.

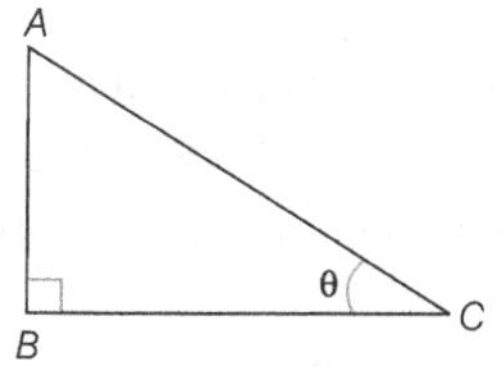

Now, consider an isosceles triangle PQR (Figure 2),

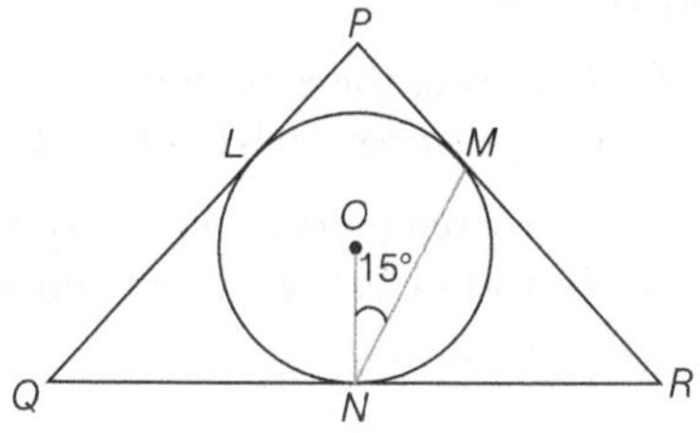

where $PQ = PR$ and $2ON = \sqrt{3}$

On the basis of above information answer the following.

50. If $\frac{AB}{BC} = 1$, then θ is equal to

(a) $\frac{\pi}{6}$ (b) $\frac{\pi}{4}$ (c) $\frac{\pi}{3}$ (d) $\frac{\pi}{2}$

51. The angles of ΔPQR are

(a) 150°, 15°, 15° (b) 60°, 60°, 60°
(c) 120°, 30°, 30° (d) 75°, 52.5°, 52.5°

Passage IV

(Q. Nos. 52 to 53)

- α is a root of equation $(2\sin x - \cos x)(1 + \cos x) = \sin^2 x$, β is a root of the equation $3\cos^2 x - 10\cos x + 3 = 0$ and γ is a root of the equation $1 - \sin 2x = \cos x - \sin x$: $0 \le \alpha, \beta, \gamma \le \pi/2$.

52. $\cos\alpha + \cos\beta + \cos\gamma$ can be equal to

(a) $\frac{3\sqrt{6}+2\sqrt{2}+6}{6\sqrt{2}}$ (b) $\frac{3\sqrt{3}-8}{6}$
(c) $\frac{3\sqrt{3}+2}{6}$ (d) None of these

53. $\sin\alpha + \sin\beta + \sin\gamma$ can be equal to

(a) $\frac{14-3\sqrt{2}}{6\sqrt{2}}$ (b) $\frac{5}{6}$ (c) $\frac{3+4\sqrt{2}}{6}$ (d) $\frac{1+\sqrt{2}}{2}$

Passage V

(Q. Nos. 54 to 55)

- Consider the equations

$$5\sin^2 x + 3\sin x\cos x - 3\cos^2 x = 2 \quad \text{...(i)}$$
$$\sin^2 x - \cos 2x = 2 - \sin 2x \quad \text{...(ii)}$$

54. If α is a root of (i) and β is a root of (ii), then $\tan\alpha + \tan\beta$ can be equal to

(a) $1 + \sqrt{69}/6$ (b) $-1 - \sqrt{69}/6$
(c) $\frac{-3+\sqrt{69}}{6}$ (d) $\frac{3-\sqrt{69}}{3}$

55. If $\tan\alpha$, $\tan\beta$ satisfy (i) and $\cos\gamma$, $\cos\delta$ satisfy (ii), then $\tan\alpha \cdot \tan\beta + \cos\gamma + \cos\delta$ can be equal to

(a) -1 (b) $-\frac{5}{3} + \frac{2}{\sqrt{13}}$
(c) $\frac{5}{3} - \frac{2}{\sqrt{13}}$ (d) $\frac{5}{3} + \frac{2}{\sqrt{13}}$

Passage VI

(Q. Nos. 56 to 57)

- Consider the cubic equation $x^3 - (1 + \cos\theta + \sin\theta)x^2 + (\cos\theta \cdot \sin\theta + \cos\theta + \sin\theta)\, x - \sin\theta \cdot \cos\theta = 0$, where x_1, x_2, x_3 are roots.

56. The value of $x_1^2 + x_2^2 + x_3^2$ is
(a) 1 (b) $2\cos\theta$ (c) $2\sin\theta$ (d) 2

57. Number of values of θ in $[0, 2\pi]$ for which atleast two roots are equal
(a) 3 (b) 4 (c) 5 (d) 6

Stem Based Questions

Stem I
(Q. Nos. 58 to 59)

- Consider the equation $\sin\sqrt{x} = -1$. If sum of all the roots of this trigonometric equation, which are less than $100\pi^2$, is of the form $\frac{m\pi^n}{K}$. Also, sum of the square roots of these roots takes the form $\frac{\lambda\mu}{\Delta}$, where $m, n, k, \lambda, \mu, \Delta \in R$.

Then,

58. The value of $[(5K + m + n) - 1]$, where $(\cdot)$ and $[\cdot]$ represent least and greatest integer function respectively, is..........

59. The value of $(\lambda - 0.8) + [\mu] + 15\{\Delta\} - 30$, where $(\cdot), \{\cdot\}$ and $[\cdot]$ represent least, fractional part and greatest integer function respectively, is.........

Stem II
(Q. Nos. 60 to 61)

- Let $x, y \in [0, 2\pi]$ and satisfying the equation $\sin^3 x + \cos^3 y + 6\sin x \cdot \cos y = 8$. If $\lambda = x + y$ and $\mu = x - y$ and least and greatest value of λ is $\frac{K\pi}{a}$ and $\frac{b\pi}{c}$ respectively as well as least and greatest value of μ is $\frac{l\pi}{m}$ and $\frac{p\pi}{q}$ respectively, where $\lambda, \mu, a, b, c, k, l, m, p, q \in R$, then

60. The value of $(Kbc) - (lmp)$ is equal to ....

61. The value of $\left(\frac{Kq}{p} + l\right)^{mbc}$ is equal to ....

Single Integer Type Questions

62. Number of roots of the equation
$$2^{\tan\left(x - \frac{\pi}{4}\right)} - 2(0.25)^{\frac{\sin^2\left(x - \frac{\pi}{4}\right)}{\cos 2x}} + 1 = 0 \text{ is } \ldots\ldots\ldots$$

63. The number of solutions of the equation $(|\cos x| = \cos x - 2\sin x$, where $x \in [0, 6\pi]$, is ....

64. The number of ordered pairs (x, y) satisfying $x\left(\sin^2 x + \frac{1}{x^2}\right) = 2\sin x \cdot \sin^2 y$, where $x \in (-\pi, 0) \cup (0, \pi)$ and $y \in [0, 2\pi]$ is ....

65. The number of solutions of the equation $\sin x \cdot \sin 2x \cdot \sin 3x = 1$, where $x \in [0, 100\pi]$, is ....

66. Number of values of p for which equation $\sin^3 x + 1 + p^3 - 3p\sin x = 0 (p > 0)$ has a root is ....

67. If $\cos 4x = a_0 + a_1\cos^2 x + a_2\cos^4 x$ is true for all values of $x \in R$, then the value of $5a_0 + a_1 + a_2$ is ....

68. Number of integral value (s) of m for which the equation $\sin x - \sqrt{3}\cos x = \frac{4m - 6}{4 - m}$ has solutions, $x \in [0, 2\pi]$, is ....

69. If $\sin(\sin x + \cos x) = \cos(\cos x - \sin x)$ and largest possible value of $\sin x$ is $\frac{\pi}{K}$, then the value of K is ....

70. Number of solutions of the equation $(\sin 2x + \cos 2x)^{1 + \sin 4x} = 2$, when $x \in [-\pi, \pi]$ is ....

71. If $2\tan^2 x - 5\sec x = 1$ is satisfied by exactly seven distinct values of $x \in \left[0, (2n + 1)\frac{\pi}{2}\right]$, $n \in N$, then the greatest value of n is ....

72. Number of solutions of the equation $\sin^4 x - \cos^2 x \sin x + 2\sin^2 x + \sin x = 0$ in $0 \le x \le 3\pi$ is ....

Numerical Value Type Questions

73. The least value of a for which the equation $2\sqrt{a}\sin^2 x + \sqrt{a - 3}\sin 2x = 5 + \sqrt{a}$ has at least one solution is ....

74. Consider the following inequality $2^{\sin^2 u + 3\cos^2 v} \times 3^{\sin^2 w + \cos^2 x} \times 5^{\cos^2 y} \ge 720$, where $u, v, w, x, y \in [1, 11]$. The number of ordered 5-tuples (u, v, w, x, y) is ....

75. The sum of solution of $\sin\pi x + \cos\pi x = 0$, where $x \in [0, 100]$, is ....

76. Number of solutions of the equation $\cos 5x \times \tan(6|x|) + \sin 5x = 0$ lying in $[-2\pi, \pi)$ is ....

77. The number of ordered pairs (x, y) satisfying the equation $\sin^2(x + y) + \cos^2(x - y) = 1$ which lie on the circle $x^2 + y^2 = \pi^2$ is ....

Matching Type Questions

78.

	Column I		Column II
(A)	$2\sin\theta\lvert\cos\theta\rvert=\frac{1}{\sqrt{2}}$	(p)	$\theta=3\pi/8$
(B)	$2\cos2\theta\cos4\theta+2\cos^2 2\theta-1=0$	(q)	$\theta=7\pi/8$
(C)	$8\cos^2\theta\sin\theta-4\cos^2\theta-2\sin\theta+1=0$	(r)	$\theta=2\pi/3$
(D)	$\sin 4\theta=\pm1$	(s)	$\theta=\pi/6$

79. If $f_n(\theta)=\dfrac{\sin\theta+\sin3\theta+\sin5\theta+\ldots+\sin((2n-1)\theta)}{\cos\theta+\cos3\theta+\cos5\theta+\ldots+\cos((2n-1)\theta)}$

	Column I		Column II
(A)	$f_3\left(\frac{\pi}{12}\right)$	(p)	$\sqrt{2}-1$
(B)	$f_4\left(\frac{\pi}{32}\right)$	(q)	$2-\sqrt{3}$
(C)	$f_6\left(\frac{\pi}{16}\right)$	(r)	$\sqrt{2}+1$
(D)	$f_7\left(\frac{\pi}{84}\right)$	(s)	$2+\sqrt{3}$
		(t)	1

80.

	Column I		Column II
(A)	The general solution of the equation $\sin^2 x+\cos^2(3x)=1$ is equal to	(p)	$n\pi$
(B)	The general solution of the equation $e^{\cot^2\theta}+\sin^2\theta-2\cos^2 2\theta+4=4\sin\theta$ is	(q)	$\frac{n\pi}{4}$
(C)	For all real values of 'λ' the general solutions of the equation $\lambda^2\sin x-\lambda\sin2x+\sin x=0$ is equal to	(r)	$n\pi+\frac{\pi}{4}$
(D)	The general solution of the equation $\sqrt[3]{2\tan\theta-1}+\sqrt[3]{\tan\theta-1}=1$, is	(s)	$(2n+1)\frac{\pi}{2}$

Previous Years Questions

81. Consider the following columns.

[Matching Type, 2022 Adv.]

	Column I		Column II
I.	$\left\{x\in\left[-\frac{2\pi}{3},\frac{2\pi}{3}\right]:\cos x+\sin x=1\right\}$	P.	has two elements
II.	$\left\{x\in\left[-\frac{5\pi}{18},\frac{5\pi}{18}\right]:\sqrt{3}\tan3x=1\right\}$	Q.	has three elements
III.	$\left\{x\in\left[-\frac{6\pi}{5},\frac{6\pi}{5}\right]:2\cos(2x)=\sqrt{3}\right\}$	R.	has four elements
IV.	$\left\{x\in\left[-\frac{7\pi}{4},\frac{7\pi}{4}\right]:\sin x-\cos x=1\right\}$	S.	has five elements
		T.	has six elements

The correct option is

(a) I → (P), II → (S), III → (P), IV → (S)
(b) I → (P), II → (P), III → (T), IV → (R)
(c) I → (Q), II → (P), III → (T), IV → (S)
(d) I → (Q), II → (S), III → (P), IV → (R)

82. Let $f:[0,2]\to R$ be the function defined by

$$f(x)=(3-\sin(2\pi x))\sin\left(\pi x-\frac{\pi}{4}\right)-\sin\left(3\pi x+\frac{\pi}{4}\right).$$

If $\alpha,\beta\in[0,2]$ are such that $\{x\in[0,2]:f(x)\geq0\}=[\alpha,\beta]$, then the value of $\beta-\alpha$ is ....

[Numerical Value Type, 2020 Adv.]

83. Let $f(x)=\sin(\pi\cos x)$ and $g(x)=\cos(2\pi\sin x)$ be two functions defined for $x>0$. Define the following sets whose elements are written in the increasing order :

$$X=\{x:f(x)=0\},\ Y=\{x:f'(x)=0\}$$
$$Z=\{x:g(x)=0\},\ W=\{x:g'(x)=0\}$$

List I contains the sets X, Y, Z and W. List II contains some information regarding these sets.

[Matching Type, 2019 Adv.]

	List I		List II
(I)	X	(P)	$\supseteq\left\{\frac{\pi}{2},\frac{3\pi}{2},4\pi,7\pi\right\}$
(II)	Y	(Q)	an arithmetic progression
(III)	Z	(R)	NOT an arithmetic progression
(IV)	W	(S)	$\supseteq\left\{\frac{\pi}{6},\frac{7\pi}{6},\frac{13\pi}{6}\right\}$
		(T)	$\supseteq\left\{\frac{\pi}{3},\frac{2\pi}{3},\pi\right\}$
		(U)	$\supseteq\left\{\frac{\pi}{6},\frac{3\pi}{4}\right\}$

Which of the following is the only CORRECT combination?

(a) (IV), (P), (R), (S)
(b) (III), (P), (Q), (U)
(c) (III), (R), (U)
(d) (IV), (Q), (T)

84. Let $f(x)=\dfrac{\sin\pi x}{x^2}$, $x>0$

Let $x_1<x_2<x_3<\ldots<x_n<\ldots$ be all the points of local maximum of f and $y_1<y_2<y_3<\ldots<y_n<\ldots$ be all the points of local minimum of f.

Then which of the following options is/are correct?

[More Than One Correct, 2019 Adv.]

(a) $|x_n-y_n|>1$ for every n
(b) $x_{n+1}-x_n>2$ for every n
(c) $x_1<y_1$
(d) $x_n\in(2n, 2n+1/2)$ for every n

85. Let a, b, c be three non-zero real numbers such that the equation $\sqrt{3}\,a\cos x+2b\sin x=c$, $x\in\left[-\frac{\pi}{2},\frac{\pi}{2}\right]$, has two distinct real roots α and β with $\alpha+\beta=\frac{\pi}{3}$. Then, the value of b/a is .... **[Numerical Value Type, 2018 Adv.]**

EXERCISE 3

Challenging Problems

1. Solve $\sin 3x + \cos 2x = -2$.

2. Solve the equation
$$\sin^4 x + \cos^4 x = \frac{7}{2} \sin x \cdot \cos x.$$

3. Find all values of θ which satisfy, $\sin(3\theta + \alpha) + \sin(3\theta - \alpha) + \sin(\alpha - \theta) - \sin(\alpha + \theta) = \cos \alpha$ given $\cos \alpha \neq 0$.

4. Find all the solutions of
$$4 \cos^2 x \sin x - 2 \sin^2 x = 3 \sin x.$$

5. Solve the equation $1 + 2 \operatorname{cosec} x = \dfrac{-\sec^2 \dfrac{x}{2}}{2}$.

6. Find the range of y such that the equation in x, $y + \cos x = \sin x$ has a real solutions. For $y = 1$, find x such that $0 < x < 2\pi$.

7. Find the general solutions of the equation
$$\left(\cos \frac{x}{4} - 2 \sin x\right) \sin x + \left(1 + \sin \frac{x}{4} - 2 \cos x\right) \cos x = 0.$$

8. Solve the following system of equations.
$$\sin x + \cos y = 1, \; \cos 2x - \cos 2y = 1.$$

9. Find the coordinates of the points of intersection of the curves $y = \cos x$, $y = \sin 3x$ if $-\dfrac{\pi}{2} \leq x \leq \dfrac{\pi}{2}$.

10. Find all possible triplets (x, y, z) such that $(x + y) + (y + 2z) \cos 2\theta + (z - x) \sin^2 \theta = 0$, for all θ.

11. Find the values of 'a' which the system of equations $\sin x \cdot \cos y = a^2$ and $\sin y \cdot \cos x = a$ have a solution.

12. For every real number find all the real solutions to equation $\sin x + \cos(a + x) + \cos(a - x) = 2$.

13. Find the solutions of the equation $(\sin x + \cos x) \sin 2x = a(\sin^3 x + \cos^3 x)$ located between $\dfrac{\pi}{2}$ and π and for which values of 'a' does this equation have at most one solution satisfying the condition $\dfrac{\pi}{2} \leq x \leq \pi$.

14. Solve the equation $(\tan x)^{\cos^2 x} = (\cot x)^{\sin x}$.

15. Solve the equation $a \cos x + \cot x + 1 = \operatorname{cosec} x$.

16. Find all the numbers 'a' for which any root of the equation $\sin 3x = a \sin x + (4 - 2|a|) \sin^2 x$ is a root of the equation $\sin 3x + \cos 2x = 1 + 2 \sin x \cos 2x$ and any root of the latter equation is a root of the former.

17. Solve $|\cos x - 2 \sin 2x - \cos 3x| = 1 - 2 \sin x - \cos 2x$.

18. Prove that the equation $2 \sin x = |x| + a$ has no solution for $a \in \left(\dfrac{3\sqrt{3} - \pi}{3}, \infty\right)$.

19. For what values of 'b' does the equation $\dfrac{b \cos x}{2 \cos 2x - 1} = \dfrac{b + \sin x}{(\cos^2 x - 3 \sin^2 x) \tan x}$ possess solutions.

Answer Key

Exercise 1

1. (d) 2. (c) 3. (a) 4. (d) 5. (a) 6. (c) 7. (c) 8. (a) 9. (a) 10. (a)
11. (b) 12. (c) 13. (a) 14. (b) 15. (a) 16. (b) 17. (c) 18. (a) 19. (c) 20. (a)
21. (a) 22. (c) 23. (b) 24. (c) 25. (a) 26. (a) 27. (d) 28. (b) 29. (b) 30. (b)
31. (b) 32. (d) 33. (b) 34. (b) 35. (a) 36. (c) 37. (b) 38. (d) 39. (c) 40. (a)
41. (a) 42. (c) 43. (b) 44. (c) 45. (b) 46. (b) 47. (c) 48. (d) 49. (b) 50. (a)
51. (b) 52. (c) 53. (d) 54. (b) 55. (a) 56. (a) 57. (b) 58. (d) 59. (a) 60. (b)
61. (a) 62. (2) 63. (0) 64. (2) 65. (1) 66. (2) 67. (8) 68. (3) 69. (0) 70. (2)
71. (1) 72. (4) 73. (5) 74. (4) 75. (4) 76. (4) 77. (2023) 78. (3) 79. (1) 80. (28)
81. (10) 82. (2) 83. (a) 84. (d) 85. (d) 86. (d) 87. (d) 88. (c) 89. (c) 90. (c)
91. (a) 92. (a) 93. (d) 94. (25) 95. (2) 96. (a) 97. (c) 98. (c) 99. (c) 100. (b)
101. (d) 102. (32) 103. (a) 104. (11) 105. (b) 106. (d) 107. (a) 108. (b) 109. (d)

Exercise 2

1. (c) 2. (b) 3. (a) 4. (a) 5. (c) 6. (c) 7. (a) 8. (a) 9. (b) 10. (a)
11. (c) 12. (d) 13. (c) 14. (a) 15. (c) 16. (c) 17. (a,d) 18. (b,c) 19. (a,b,c) 20. (a,b)
21. (b) 22. (a,c) 23. (a,c) 24. (b) 25. (a) 26. (a) 27. (b,c) 28. (a,b) 29. (b) 30. (a,c)
31. (a,c,d) 32. (c,d) 33. (a) 34. (c,d) 35. (a,b,c,d) 36. (c) 37. (c) 38. (b,c) 39. (a,d) 40. (d)
41. (d) 42. (a,b) 43. (a,b,c,d) 44. (a) 45. (a,b,c) 46. (b) 47. (c) 48. (a) 49. (a) 50. (b)
51. (c) 52. (a) 53. (c) 54. (a) 55. (b) 56. (d) 57. (c) 58. (786) 59. (28) 60. (16)
61. (1) 62. (0) 63. (7) 64. (8) 65. (0) 66. (1) 67. (5) 68. (4) 69. (4) 70. (4)
71. (15) 72. (4) 73. (14) 74. (432) 75. (5025) 76. (13) 77. (12)
78. (A) → (p,q), (B) → (p,q,r), (C) → (r,s), (D) → (p,q) 79. (A) → (t), (B) → (p), (C) → (r), (D) → (q)
80. (A) → (q), (B) → (s), (C) → (p,s), (D) → (r) 81. (b) 82. (1) 83. (a) 84. (d) 85. (0.5)

Solutions

Exercise 1 - JEE Main Pattern

1. $(\cos^2 x - \sin^2 x)\left(2\sin\frac{x}{2} - 1\right) = 0$

$$\cos 2x = 0 \text{ or } \sin\frac{x}{2} = \frac{1}{2}$$

$2x = (2n+1)\frac{\pi}{2}$ or $\frac{x}{2} = k\pi + (-1)^k\frac{\pi}{6}$, where $n, k \in Z$

If $x = \frac{n\pi}{2} + \frac{\pi}{4}$, then $\sin 2x = \pm 1$

and if $x = 2k\pi + (-1)^k\frac{\pi}{3}$, then $\cos x = \cos\frac{\pi}{3} = \frac{1}{2}$

and $\cos 2x = \cos\frac{2\pi}{3} = -\frac{1}{2}$

2. $\sec x \cos 5x = -1 \Rightarrow \cos 5x = -\cos x$

$\Rightarrow \quad 5x = 2n\pi \pm (\pi - x)$

$\Rightarrow \quad x = \frac{(2n+1)\pi}{6}$ or $\frac{(2n-1)\pi}{4}$

Hence, $x = \frac{\pi}{4}, \frac{\pi}{2}, \frac{3\pi}{4}, \frac{5\pi}{6}, \frac{5\pi}{6}, \frac{7\pi}{6}, \frac{7\pi}{4}, \frac{9\pi}{6}, \frac{11\pi}{6}$

3. Given, $\cot(\alpha+\beta) = 0 \Rightarrow \cos(\alpha+\beta) = 0$

$\Rightarrow \quad \alpha+\beta = (2n+1)\frac{\pi}{2}, n \in I$

$\therefore \quad \sin(a+2\beta) = \sin(2\alpha+2\beta-\alpha) = \sin[(2n+1)\pi - \alpha]$

$= \sin(2n\pi + \pi - \alpha) = \sin(\pi - \alpha) = \sin\alpha$

4. $\cot\theta + \cot\left(\frac{\pi}{4} + \theta\right) = 2$

$\Rightarrow \quad \cot\theta + \frac{\cot\theta - 1}{\cot\theta + 1} = 2$

$\Rightarrow \quad \cot^2\theta - 3 = 0$

$\Rightarrow \quad \tan^2\theta = \frac{1}{3}$

$\Rightarrow \quad \tan\theta = \pm\frac{1}{\sqrt{3}} \Rightarrow \theta = n\pi \pm \frac{\pi}{6}$

5. $16(\sin^5 x + \cos^5 x) - 11(\sin x + \cos x) = 0$

$\Rightarrow (\sin x + \cos x)\{16(\sin^4 x - \sin^3 x \cos x + \sin^2 x \cos^2 x$

$- \sin x \cos^3 x + \cos^4 x) - 11\} = 0$

$\Rightarrow \quad (\sin x + \cos x)\{16(1 - \sin^2 x \cos^2 x - \sin x \cos x) - 11\} = 0$

$\Rightarrow \quad (\sin x + \cos x)(4\sin x \cos x - 1)(4\sin x \cos x + 5) = 0$

As, $4\sin x \cos x + 5 \neq 0$, we have

$$\sin x + \cos x = 0,\ 4\sin x \cos x - 1 = 0$$

The required values are

$$\frac{\pi}{12}, \frac{5\pi}{12}, \frac{9\pi}{12}, \frac{13\pi}{12}, \frac{17\pi}{12}, \frac{21\pi}{12}$$

There are 6 solutions in $[0, 2\pi]$.

6. Consider, $8\tan^2\frac{x}{2} = 1 + \sec x$

$\Rightarrow \quad 8\left(\frac{1-\cos x}{1+\cos x}\right) = 1 + \frac{1}{\cos x}$

$\Rightarrow \quad 8\cos x - 8\cos^2 x = (1+\cos x)^2$

$\Rightarrow \quad 8\cos x - 8\cos^2 x = 1 + \cos^2 x + 2\cos x$

$\Rightarrow \quad 9\cos^2 x - 6\cos x + 1 = 0$

$\Rightarrow \quad (3\cos x - 1)^2 = 0$

$\Rightarrow \quad \cos x = \frac{1}{3} = \cos\alpha$

$\Rightarrow \quad x = 2n\pi \pm \alpha$, where '$\alpha$' $= \cos^{-1}\frac{1}{3}$

[using $\cos\theta = \cos\alpha \Rightarrow \theta = 2n\pi \pm \alpha$]

$\Rightarrow \quad x = 2n\pi \pm \cos^{-1}\left(\frac{1}{3}\right)$

7. Put $e^{\sin x} = t$

Given equation becomes $t^2 - 4t - 1 = 0$

$\Rightarrow \quad t = 2 \pm \sqrt{5} \Rightarrow e^{\sin x} = 2 \pm \sqrt{5}$

Either $\quad \sin x = \log_e(2+\sqrt{5})$

or $\quad \sin x = \log_e(2-\sqrt{5})$

as $2+\sqrt{5} > e$ or as $(2-\sqrt{5})$ is $(-\text{ve})$ and log is not defined for $(-\text{ve})$ values.

$\Rightarrow \sin x > 1 \Rightarrow$ No solution.

8. $\because \sin 3\alpha = 4\sin\alpha \sin(x-\alpha)\sin(x+\alpha)$

$3\sin\alpha - 4\sin^3\alpha = 4\sin\alpha(\sin^2 x - \sin^2\alpha)$

On dividing both sides by $\sin\alpha$, we get

$$3 - 4\sin^2\alpha = 4\sin^2 x - 4\sin^2\alpha$$

$\Rightarrow \quad 4\sin^2 x = 3$

$\Rightarrow \quad \sin^2 x = \frac{3}{4}$

$\Rightarrow \quad \sin^2 x = \left(\frac{\sqrt{3}}{2}\right)^2 = \sin^2\frac{\pi}{3}$

$\therefore \quad x = n\pi \pm \frac{\pi}{3}, \forall n \in I$ [using formula]

9. We have, $4\cos x - 3\sec x = \tan x$

$\left[\cos x \neq 0 \text{ i.e. } x \text{ odd multiplied of } \frac{\pi}{2}\right]$

Then, $4\cos x - \frac{3}{\cos x} = \frac{\sin x}{\cos x}$

$\Rightarrow \quad 4\cos^2 x - 3 = \sin x$

$\Rightarrow \quad 4 - 4\sin^2 x - 3 = \sin x \Rightarrow 4\sin^2 x + \sin x - 1 = 0$

$\therefore \quad \sin x = \frac{-1 \pm \sqrt{5}}{8}$

Either $\sin x = \frac{-1+\sqrt{5}}{8} = \sin\alpha$ (let)

or $\sin x = \frac{-1-\sqrt{5}}{8} = \sin\beta$ (let)

$\therefore \quad x = n\pi + (-1)^n \alpha$ or $x = n\pi + (-1)^n \beta$

$\therefore \quad \sin\alpha = \frac{-1+\sqrt{5}}{8}, \sin\beta = \frac{-1-\sqrt{5}}{8}$

So, $4(\sin\alpha + \sin\beta) = 4\left[\frac{-1+\sqrt{5}}{8} + \frac{-1-\sqrt{5}}{8}\right] = 4\left[\frac{-2}{8}\right] = -1$

10. We have, $\cos 2x - 3\cos x + 1 = \frac{1}{(\cot 2x - \cot x)\sin(x-\pi)}$

$\Rightarrow \quad 2\cos^2 x - 1 - 3\cos x + 1 = \frac{1}{\frac{\sin(x-2x)}{\sin 2x \cdot \sin x} \cdot (-\sin x)}$

$\left[\text{using formula, } \cot A - \cot B = \frac{\sin(B-A)}{\sin A \cdot \sin B}\right]$

$2\cos^2 x - 3\cos x = \frac{2\sin x \cdot \cos x \cdot \sin x}{\sin^2 x}$

$2\cos^2 x - 3\cos x - 2\cos x = 0$

$2\cos^2 x - 5\cos x = 0$

$\cos x(2\cos x - 5) = 0$

Either $2\cos x - 5 = 0$

$\Rightarrow \quad \cos x = \frac{5}{2}$ [which is not possible]

Then, $\cos x = 0$

11. $2\cos^2\theta - (\sqrt{2}+1)\cos\theta - 1 + \frac{(\sqrt{2}+1)}{\sqrt{2}} = 0$

$\Rightarrow \quad \cos\theta = \frac{(\sqrt{2}+1) \pm \sqrt{(\sqrt{2}+1)^2 - \frac{8}{\sqrt{2}}}}{4}$

$\Rightarrow \quad \cos\theta = \cos\left(\frac{\pi}{4}\right)$

$\Rightarrow \quad \theta = 2n\pi \pm \frac{\pi}{4}$

12. $\cos^2 x = 2\cos x(3\sin^2 x - 2)$

$\Rightarrow \quad \cos x[\cos x - 2\{3(1-\cos^2 x) - 2\}] = 0$

$\Rightarrow \quad \cos x(6\cos^2 x - 2 + \cos x) = 0$

$\Rightarrow \quad \cos x = 0$, which is not possible.

or $\quad 6\cos^2 x + \cos x - 2 = 0$

$\Rightarrow \quad \cos x = \frac{1}{2}, -\frac{2}{3}$

$\Rightarrow \quad x = \frac{\pi}{3}, \frac{5\pi}{3}$ or $x = \pi - \cos^{-1}\left(\frac{2}{3}\right), \pi + \cos^{-1}\left(\frac{2}{3}\right)$

$\Rightarrow \quad |x_1 - x_2| = \frac{4\pi}{3}$ or $|x_1 - x_2| = 2\cos^{-1}\left(\frac{2}{3}\right)$

$\Rightarrow \quad |x_1 - x_2|_{\min} = 2\cos^{-1}\left(\frac{2}{3}\right)$

13. $\cos x - \frac{\cot\beta \sin x}{2} = \frac{\sqrt{3}}{2}$

$\Rightarrow \quad \frac{1-\tan^2\frac{x}{2}}{1+\tan^2\frac{x}{2}} - \frac{\cot\beta \tan\frac{x}{2}}{1+\tan^2\frac{x}{2}} = \frac{\sqrt{3}}{2}$

$\Rightarrow \quad 1 - \tan^2\frac{x}{2} - \cot\beta \tan\frac{x}{2} = \frac{\sqrt{3}}{2}\left(1+\tan^2\frac{x}{2}\right)$

$\Rightarrow \quad (2+\sqrt{3})\tan^2\frac{x}{2} + 2\cot\beta \tan\frac{x}{2} + (\sqrt{3}-2) = 0$

$\Rightarrow \quad \tan\frac{x}{2} = \frac{-2\cot\beta \pm \sqrt{4\cot^2\beta + 4}}{2(2+\sqrt{3})} = \frac{-2\cot\beta \pm 2\operatorname{cosec}\beta}{2(2+\sqrt{3})}$

$\Rightarrow \quad \tan\frac{x}{2} = \frac{-\cot\beta + \operatorname{cosec}\beta}{(2+\sqrt{3})}$

or $\quad \tan\frac{x}{2} = \frac{-\cot\beta - \operatorname{cosec}\beta}{(2+\sqrt{3})} \Rightarrow \tan\frac{x}{2} = \tan\frac{\beta}{2}\tan 15°$

14. $\sin^2 x + \sin^4 x + \sin^6 x + \ldots \infty = \frac{\sin^2 x}{1-\sin^2 x} = \tan^2 x$

$\Rightarrow \quad \exp^{[(\sin^2 x + \sin^4 x + \ldots)\ln 2]} = e^{\tan^2 x \ln 2} = e^{\ln 2^{\tan^2 x}}$

The given equation is $y^2 - 9y + 8 \Rightarrow (y-1)(y-8) = 0$

Either $y = 1 \Rightarrow 2^{\tan x} = 1 = 2^0 \Rightarrow \tan^2 x = 0$, but $x \in \left(0, \frac{\pi}{2}\right)$

$\therefore$ Neglecting $x = 0$ or $y = 2^3 \Rightarrow \tan^2 x = 3$

$\Rightarrow \quad \tan x = \pm\sqrt{3} \Rightarrow x = \frac{\pi}{3}$, as $0 < x < \frac{\pi}{2}$

$\Rightarrow \quad \frac{\cos x}{\cos x + \sin x} = \frac{1/2}{1/2 + \sqrt{3}/2} = \frac{1}{\sqrt{3}+1} = \frac{\sqrt{3}-1}{2}$

15. We have, $\cos 4x + 6 = 7\cos 2x$

$2\cos^2 2x - 1 + 6 - 7\cos 2x = 0$

$2\cos^2 2x - 7\cos 2x + 5 = 0$

$(2\cos x - 5)(\cos 2x - 1) = 0$

Thus, $\quad \cos 2x = 1$

and $\quad \cos 2x = \frac{5}{2}$ [which is not possible, $-1 \le \cos\theta \le 1$]

$\therefore \quad \cos 2x = 1$

$2x = 2n\pi, \forall n \in I$ [using formula]

$x = n\pi, \forall n \in I$

$x = \pi, 2\pi, 3\pi, \ldots\ldots$

i.e., $\quad x = 180°, 360°, 540°, \ldots\ldots.$

$x \notin [315°, 317°]$

So, $x = n\pi \notin [315°, 317°], \forall n \in I$

Hence, number of solutions is 0.

16. $\frac{\sin^2 2x + 4\sin^4 x - 4\sin^2 x \cos^2 x}{4 - \sin^2 2x - 4\sin^2 x} = \frac{1}{9}$

$\Rightarrow \quad \frac{4\sin^4 x}{4\cos^2 x - 4\sin^2 x \cos^2 x} = \frac{1}{9}$

$\Rightarrow \quad \frac{\sin^4 x}{\cos^4 x} = \frac{1}{9}$

$\Rightarrow \quad \tan x = \pm\frac{1}{\sqrt{3}} \Rightarrow x = \frac{\pi}{6}$

17. We have, $\tan\theta+\tan 4\theta+\tan 7\theta=\tan\theta\cdot\tan 4\theta\cdot\tan 7\theta$

$\Rightarrow \quad \tan\theta+\tan 4\theta=-\tan 7\theta+\tan\theta\cdot\tan 4\theta\cdot\tan 7\theta$

$\Rightarrow \quad \tan\theta+\tan 4\theta=-\tan 7\theta(1-\tan\theta\cdot\tan 4\theta)$

$\Rightarrow \quad \dfrac{\tan\theta+\tan 4\theta}{1-\tan\theta\cdot\tan 4\theta}=-\tan 7\theta$

$\Rightarrow \quad \tan(\theta+4\theta)=-\tan 7\theta$

$\Rightarrow \quad \tan 5\theta=\tan(-7\theta)$

$\Rightarrow \quad 5\theta=n\pi+(-7\theta)$

$\Rightarrow \quad 12\theta=n\pi$

$\Rightarrow \quad \theta=\dfrac{n\pi}{12}$ [where $n\in I$]

18. We know that in a triangle $A+B+C=180°$

and $2B=A+C$ (as A, B, C are in AP)

$\Rightarrow \quad 3B=180$ or $B=60°$

Now θ be the common difference between A, B and C,

then $C-A=2\theta$ ...(i)

$\Rightarrow \quad \sin(C-A)=\dfrac{1}{2}$ [given]

$\Rightarrow \quad \sin(2\theta)=\dfrac{1}{2}$ [using Eq. (i)]

$\Rightarrow \quad 2\theta=\dfrac{\pi}{6}$ or $\dfrac{5\pi}{6} \Rightarrow \theta=\dfrac{\pi}{12}$ or $\dfrac{5\pi}{12}$

Now, $A=B-\theta \Rightarrow \dfrac{\pi}{3}-\dfrac{\pi}{12}$ or $\dfrac{\pi}{3}-\dfrac{5\pi}{12}$

$\Rightarrow A=\dfrac{\pi}{4}$ as a cannot be less than '0' and $C=\dfrac{\pi}{3}+\dfrac{\pi}{12}=\dfrac{5\pi}{12}$

$\Rightarrow \quad A=45°, B=60°, C=75°$

19. We have, $\tan m\theta=\tan n\theta$

$m\theta=k\pi+n\theta, \forall k\in I$ [using formula]

$m\theta-n\theta=k\pi, \forall k\in I$

$\theta=k\cdot\dfrac{\pi}{m-n}, \forall k\in I$ [$\because$ m and n are constants]

Then, if we put $k=1, 2, 3, \dots$ we get

$\theta=\dfrac{\pi}{m-n}, \dfrac{2\pi}{m-n}, \dfrac{3\pi}{m-n}, \dots$, which is AP.

Thus, common difference $=\dfrac{\pi}{m-n}$

20. $\because \sec x\cdot\cos 5x=-1$ and $0<x<\dfrac{\pi}{4}$

$\dfrac{\cos 5x}{\cos x}=-1 \Rightarrow \cos 5x=-\cos x$

$\Rightarrow \quad \cos 5x+\cos x=0 \Rightarrow 2\cos 3x\cdot\cos 2x=0$

Either $2\cos 3x=0$ or $\cos 2x=0$

$\cos 3x=0$ or $2x=(2n+1)\dfrac{\pi}{2}$

$3x=(2n+1)\dfrac{\pi}{2}$ or $x=(2n+1)\dfrac{\pi}{4}, \forall n\in I$

[not possible]

$\therefore \quad x=(2n+1)\dfrac{\pi}{6}$

Put $n=0$, then $x=\dfrac{\pi}{6}$

21. We have, $\sin 3x=3\sin x-4\sin^3 x \Rightarrow \sin^3 x=\dfrac{1}{4}(3\sin x-\sin 3x)$

and $\cos 3x=4\cos^3 x-3\cos x$

$\Rightarrow \quad \cos^3 x=\dfrac{1}{4}(\cos 3x+3\cos x)$

$\therefore \quad \cos 3x\cos^3 x+\sin 3x\sin^3 x$

$=\dfrac{1}{4}[\cos^2 3x+3\cos x\cos 3x+3\sin x\sin 3x-\sin^2 3x]$

$=\dfrac{1}{4}[3\cos 2x+\cos 6x]=\cos^3 2x$

$\Rightarrow \quad \cos 2x=0$

$\Rightarrow \quad 2x=(2n+1)\dfrac{\pi}{2}$

$\Rightarrow \quad x=(2n+1)\dfrac{\pi}{4}$

22. For $\sqrt{x-4}$ to be real $x\ge 4$, for which $\sqrt{x}$ is also real.

Now, if $\cos(\pi\sqrt{x})<1$, then $\cos(\pi\sqrt{x-4})>1$

and, if $\cos(\pi\sqrt{x})>1$, then $\cos(\pi\sqrt{x-4})<1$

[since their product = 1]

But both of these are not possible as $\cos\theta$ cannot be greater than 1.

$\Rightarrow \quad \cos(\pi\sqrt{x-4})=1$ and $\cos(\pi\sqrt{x})=1$

$\Rightarrow \quad x-4=0$ and $x=0$

$\Rightarrow \quad x=4$ or $x=0$

But $x=0$ is not possible (as $x\ge 4$).

$\Rightarrow x=4$ is only solution.

23. $\theta\in\left[\dfrac{-\pi}{2}, \dfrac{\pi}{2}\right]\Rightarrow -1\le\sin\theta\le 1$

But here $0<\sin\theta<1$ [as $\log_a x$ is define for $a>0$ or $0<a<1$]

Now, $\log_{\sin\theta}\cos^2\theta=2$ [using $\log_a b=c\Rightarrow b=a^c$]

$\Rightarrow \quad \cos^2\theta=\sin^2\theta$

$\Rightarrow \quad \tan^2\theta=1$

$\Rightarrow \quad \theta=n\pi+\dfrac{\pi}{4}\forall\theta\in\left[\dfrac{-\pi}{2}, \dfrac{\pi}{2}\right]$

$\Rightarrow \quad \theta=\dfrac{\pi}{4}, \theta=\dfrac{-\pi}{4}$ [reject as $\sin\left(\dfrac{-\pi}{4}\right)=\dfrac{-1}{\sqrt{2}}<0$]

The given equation has unique solution.

24. We know that

$a\sin\theta\pm b\cos\theta=c$ is solvable, if

$$|c|\le\sqrt{a^2+b^2}$$

Now, $\lambda\cos x-3\sin x=\lambda+1$ is solvable, if

$$|\lambda+1|\le\sqrt{\lambda^2+9}$$

$\Rightarrow \quad (\lambda+1)^2\le\lambda^2+9$

$\Rightarrow \quad \lambda^2+1+2\lambda\le\lambda^2+9$

$\Rightarrow \quad 2\lambda\le 9-1$

$\Rightarrow \quad \lambda\le 4$

$\therefore \quad \lambda\in(-\infty, 4]$

25. As, $\max\{5\sin\theta + 3\sin\theta\cos\alpha - 3\cos\theta\sin\alpha\}$

Now, $-\sqrt{(5+3\cos\alpha)^2+9\sin^2\alpha} \le 5\sin\theta + 3\sin(\theta-\alpha)$

$$\le\sqrt{(5+3\cos\alpha)^2+9\sin^2\alpha}$$

$\Rightarrow \max_{\theta\in R}\{5\sin\theta+3\sin(\theta-\alpha)\} = \sqrt{34+30\cos\alpha}$

$\Rightarrow \sqrt{34+30\cos\alpha} = 7$

$\Rightarrow \cos\alpha = \dfrac{49-34}{30}$

$\Rightarrow \cos\alpha = \dfrac{1}{2} = \cos\dfrac{\pi}{3}$

$\Rightarrow \alpha = 2n\pi \pm \dfrac{\pi}{3}$

26. Consider, $\sin x(\sin x + \cos x) = n$

$\Rightarrow \sin^2 x + \sin x\cdot\cos x = n$

$\Rightarrow \dfrac{1-\cos 2x}{2} + \dfrac{\sin 2x}{2} = n$

$\Rightarrow \sin 2x - \cos 2x = 2n - 1$

$\Rightarrow$ As $-\sqrt{2} \le \sin 2x - \cos 2x \le \sqrt{2}$

$\Rightarrow -\sqrt{2} \le 2n-1 \le \sqrt{2}$

$\Rightarrow \dfrac{1-\sqrt{2}}{2} \le n \le \dfrac{1+\sqrt{2}}{2}$

$\Rightarrow n = 0, 1$

27. If $\tan\left(\dfrac{\pi}{2}\sin\theta\right) = \cot\left(\dfrac{\pi}{2}\cos\theta\right)$

$\Rightarrow \tan\left(\dfrac{\pi}{2}\sin\theta\right) = \tan\left(\dfrac{\pi}{2} - \dfrac{\pi}{2}\cos\theta\right)$

$\Rightarrow \dfrac{\pi}{2}\sin\theta = n\pi + \dfrac{\pi}{2} - \dfrac{\pi}{2}\cos\theta, n\in I$

$\Rightarrow \sin\theta + \cos\theta = 2n+1, n\in I$

but $-\sqrt{2} \le \sin\theta + \cos\theta \le \sqrt{2}$

Therefore, $\sin\theta + \cos\theta = 1$ or -1.

28. $\because \alpha^2 - 4\alpha + 7 = \alpha^2 - 4\alpha + 4 + 3 = (\alpha-2)^2 + 3 \ge 3$

and $2 < e < 3$ and $\pi = 3.14$

$4 < e^2 < 9$

Now, $\sqrt{3}\sin x - \cos x = \min_{\alpha\in R}\{2, e^2, \pi, \alpha^2 - 4\alpha + 7\}$

$\Rightarrow \sqrt{3}\sin x - \cos x = 2$

$\Rightarrow \dfrac{\sqrt{3}}{2}\sin x - \dfrac{1}{2}\cos x = 1$

$\Rightarrow \sin x\cdot\cos\dfrac{\pi}{6} - \cos x\cdot\sin\dfrac{\pi}{6} = 1$

$\Rightarrow \sin\left(x - \dfrac{\pi}{6}\right) = 1$

$\therefore x - \dfrac{\pi}{6} = 2n\pi + \dfrac{\pi}{2}, \forall n\in I$

$\Rightarrow x = 2n\pi + \dfrac{\pi}{2} + \dfrac{\pi}{6}, \forall n \in I$

$\Rightarrow x = 2n\pi + \dfrac{2\pi}{3}, \forall n\in I$

29. Let $A = 5\pi\sin\theta$ and $B = 5\pi\cos\theta$

Then, $\cot A - \tan B = 0$

$\dfrac{\cos A}{\sin A} - \dfrac{\sin B}{\cos B} = 0 \Rightarrow \cos A\cdot\cos B - \sin A\cdot\sin B = 0$

$\therefore \cos(A+B) = 0$

$\Rightarrow A + B = (2n+1)\dfrac{\pi}{2}, \forall n\in I$ ...(i)

Now, $5\pi\sin\theta + 5\pi\cos\theta = (2n+1)\dfrac{\pi}{2}, \forall n \in I$

$\Rightarrow \sin\theta + \cos\theta = \dfrac{2n+1}{10}$

$\Rightarrow \sin\theta\cdot\dfrac{1}{\sqrt{2}} + \cos\theta\cdot\dfrac{1}{\sqrt{2}} = \dfrac{2n+1}{10\sqrt{2}}$

$\Rightarrow \sin\left(\theta + \dfrac{\pi}{4}\right) = \dfrac{2n+1}{10\sqrt{2}}$ ...(ii)

$\because -1 \le \sin\left(\theta + \dfrac{\pi}{4}\right) \le 1$

$\Rightarrow -1 \le \dfrac{2n+1}{10\sqrt{2}} \le 1 \Rightarrow \dfrac{-10\sqrt{2}-1}{2} \le n \le \dfrac{10\sqrt{2}-1}{2}$

$\Rightarrow -7.5 \le n \le 6.5$ [$\because \sqrt{2} = 1.4$ (let)]

$\therefore n = -7, -6, -5, -4, -3, -2, -1, 0, 1, 2, 3, 4, 5, 6$

Hence, number of solutions is 14.

30. $3\cos\theta + 4\sin\theta = 5\left[\dfrac{3}{5}\cos\theta + \dfrac{4}{5}\sin\theta\right] = 5\cos(\theta-\alpha)$

where $\cos\alpha = \dfrac{3}{5}, \sin\alpha = \dfrac{4}{5}$

Now, $3\cos\theta + 4\sin\theta = k$

$\therefore 5\cos(\theta-\alpha) = \pm 5$

$\Rightarrow \cos(\theta-\alpha) = \pm 1$

$\Rightarrow \theta - \alpha = 0°, 180°$

$\Rightarrow \theta = \alpha, 180° + \alpha$

31. a, b, c are roots of equation

$x\sin\theta + y\sin 2\theta + + z\sin 3\theta = \sin 4\theta$

$\Rightarrow x\sin\theta + y(2\sin\theta\cos\theta) + z(3\sin\theta - 4\sin^3\theta)$

$= 4\sin\theta\cos\theta\cos 2\theta$

$\Rightarrow \cos^3\theta - \dfrac{z}{2}\cos^2\theta - \dfrac{y+2}{4}\cos\theta + \dfrac{z-x}{8} = 0$

32. We have, $a_1 + a_2\cos 2x + a_3\sin^2 x = 0$

$\Rightarrow a_1 + a_2\cos 2x + a_3(1-\cos 2x)/2 = 0$

$\Rightarrow$ which is zero for all value of 'x'.

If $a_1 = -\dfrac{a_3}{2} = -a_2$ or $a_1 = \dfrac{-k}{2}, a_2 = \dfrac{k}{2}, a_3 = k$

For any $k\in R$

Hence, the required number of triplets is infinite.

33. Since, the equation $a_1 + a_2\sin x + a_3\cos x + a_4\sin 2x + a_5\cos 2x = 0$ holds for all values of x,

$a_1 + a_3 + a_5 = 0$ [on putting $x = 0$]

$a_1 - a_3 + a_5 = 0$ [on putting $x = \pi$]

$\Rightarrow a_3 = 0$ and $a_1 + a_5 = 0$ ...(i)

Putting $x=\frac{\pi}{2}$ and $\frac{3\pi}{2}$, we get

$$a_1+a_2-a_5=0 \text{ and } a_1-a_2-a_5=0$$

$\Rightarrow$ $a_2=0$ and $a_1-a_5=0$ ...(ii)

Eqs. (i) and (ii) give $a_1=a_2=a_3=a_5=0$

The given equation reduces to $a_4\sin 2x=0$.

This is true for all values of x, therefore $a_4=0$

Hence, $a_1=a_2=a_3=a_4=a_5=0$

Thus, the number of 5-tuples is one.

34. $\sin^7 y=|x^3-x^2-9x+9|+|x^3-4x-x^2+4|+\sec^2 2y+\cos^4 y$

Now, for $x=1$ [according to the choices]

$$\sin^7 y=\sec^2 2y+\cos^4 y$$

$\Rightarrow$ $\sin^7 y\cdot\cos^2 2y=1+\cos^4 y\cdot\cos^2 2y$

Now, RHS ≥ 1 and LHS ≤ 1

$\Rightarrow$ LHS $=1$

$\Rightarrow$ $\sin^7 y\cdot\cos^2 2y=1$

$\Rightarrow$ $\sin^7 y=1$ and $\cos^2 2y=1$

$\Rightarrow$ $y=\frac{\pi}{2}$

General values of 'y' is $2n\pi+\frac{\pi}{2}$

Hence, $x=1$ and $y=2n\pi+\frac{\pi}{2}$

35. We have, $\sin x+\sin y+\sin z=-3$

$$0\leq x\leq 2\pi$$
$$0\leq y\leq 2\pi$$
$$0\leq z\leq 2\pi$$

It is possible only, when $\sin x=\sin y=\sin z=-1$

$\therefore$ $x=y=z=\frac{3\pi}{2}$ for $x,y,z\in[0,2\pi]$

36. We have, $\cos x+\cos 2x+\cos 3x+\cos 4x=0$

$\Rightarrow$ $\cos x+\cos 3x+\cos 2x+\cos 4x=0$

$\Rightarrow$ $2\cos 2x\cos x+2\cos 3x\cos x=0$

$\Rightarrow$ $2\cos x(\cos 2x+\cos 3x)=0$

$\Rightarrow$ $2\cos x\cdot 2\cos\frac{5x}{2}\cos\frac{x}{2}=0$

$\Rightarrow$ $4\cos x\cos\frac{x}{2}\cos\frac{5x}{2}=0$

When $\cos x=0\Rightarrow x=90°, 270°$

When $\cos\frac{5x}{2}=0$

$\Rightarrow$ $\frac{5x}{2}=(2n+1)\frac{\pi}{2}$

$\Rightarrow$ $x=(2n+1)\frac{\pi}{5}=\frac{\pi}{5},\frac{3\pi}{5},\frac{7\pi}{5},\frac{9\pi}{5}$

When $\cos\frac{x}{2}=0\Rightarrow x=(2m+1)\frac{\pi}{2}\Rightarrow x=(2m+1)\pi$

$\therefore$ Total number of solutions is 7.

37. Consider $\sum_{i=1}^{n}\cos\theta_i=n$

$\cos\theta_1+\cos\theta_2+\cos\theta_3+\ldots+\cos\theta_n=\underbrace{1+1+1\ldots+n}_{n \text{ times}}$ is valid only when

$$\cos\theta_1=1, \cos\theta_2=1, \cos\theta_3=1,\ldots, \cos\theta_n=1$$

$\Rightarrow$ $\theta_1=\theta_2=\theta_3=\ldots=\theta_n=0$

$\Rightarrow$ $\sum_{i=1}^{n}\sin\theta_i=0$

38. The maximum possible value is 2.

$\sin\left(\frac{x}{3}\right)$ takes the value 1 when

$$\frac{x}{3}=2m\pi+\frac{\pi}{2} \text{ i.e. } \frac{x}{3}=90+360m$$

$\sin\left(\frac{x}{11}\right)$ takes the value 1

when $\frac{x}{11}=2n\pi+\frac{\pi}{2}$ i.e. $\frac{x}{11}=90+360n$

We are looking for a common solution, we have $3m-11n=2$.

Clearly, the smallest positive solution to this is $m=8$, $n=2$, thus $x_0=8910°$, giving $\alpha=8910$.

$\Rightarrow$ Sum $=8+9+1+0=18$

Sum of the digits in $x=8+9+1+0=18$

39. $|\sqrt{m}-\sqrt{n}|\leq\sqrt{|m-n|}$

$\Rightarrow$ $\left|\sqrt{\sin^2 x+2a^2}-\sqrt{2a^2-1-\cos^2 x}\right|$

$$\leq\sqrt{\sin^2 x+2a^2-2a^2+1+\cos^2 x}\leq\sqrt{2}$$

40. Consider RHS i.e., 5^x+5^{-x}

$\Rightarrow$ $\frac{5^x+5^{-x}}{2}\geq(5^x\cdot 5^{-x})^{1/2}$

$\Rightarrow$ $5^x+5^{-x}\geq 2$ [by using AM $\geq$ GM]

$\Rightarrow$ From the given equation $\sin(e^x)\geq 2$

which is not possible for any real values of 'x'.

Thus, the given equation has no solution.

41. Consider, $y=5x^2+2x+3=5\left[x^2+\frac{2}{5}x+\frac{3}{5}\right]$

$$=5\left[\left(x+\frac{1}{5}\right)^2+\frac{3}{5}-\frac{1}{25}\right]=5\left(x+\frac{1}{5}\right)^2+\frac{14}{5}>2$$

As $y=2\sin x\leq 2$, so there cannot be any point of intersection.

42. We have, $\sin^4 x-(k+2)\sin^2 x-(k+3)=0$

$\Rightarrow$ $\sin^2 x=\frac{(k+2)\pm\sqrt{(k+2)^2+4(k+3)}}{2}=\frac{(k+2)\pm(k+4)}{2}$

$\Rightarrow$ Either $\sin^2 x=k+3$ or $\sin^2 x=-1$

$\Rightarrow$ $0\leq\sin^2 x\leq 1$ or not possible.

$\Rightarrow$ $0\leq k+3\leq 1\Rightarrow -3\leq k\leq -2$

43. **Case I** For $n=2$, $\sin^2 x+\cos^2 x=1$.

Case II If $n>2$, $\sin^n x$ and $\cos^n x$ both decrease then

$\sin^n x+\cos^n x<1$ [as $0<x<\pi/2$]

Case III If $n<2$, $\sin^n x$ and $\cos^n x$ both increases then

$\sin^n x+\cos^n x>1$ [as $0<x<\pi/2$]

Then, $\sin^n x+\cos^n x\geq 1$ for $n\leq 2 \Rightarrow n\in(-\infty,2]$

44. $\sin x+\cos x=\min_{a\in R}\{1,a^2-4a+6\}$ ...(i)

As, $a^2-4a+6=(a-2)^2+2\geq 2$ for all a

Eq. (i) becomes $\sin x+\cos x=1$

$\Rightarrow \sin\left(x+\frac{\pi}{4}\right)=\frac{1}{\sqrt{2}}$

$\Rightarrow x+\frac{\pi}{4}=n\pi+(-1)^n\frac{\pi}{4}$

$\Rightarrow x=n\pi+(-1)^n\frac{\pi}{4}-\frac{\pi}{4}$

45. $x^2+4-2x+3\sin(ax+b)=0$

$\Rightarrow (x-1)^2+3+3\sin(ax+b)=0$

$\Rightarrow x=1$ and $\sin(ax+b)=-1$

$\Rightarrow \sin(a+b)=-1 \Rightarrow a+b=\frac{3\pi}{2}$

46. Here, $4[1+\cot^2\pi(a+x)]+a^2-4a=0$

$\Rightarrow 4\cot^2\pi(a+x)+(a-2)^2=0$

$\Rightarrow a-2=0$ and $\cot^2\pi(a+x)=0$

$\Rightarrow a=2$

47. As max. $\cos\theta=1$, $2\cos x+\cos 2\lambda x=3$ is possible only when $\cos x=1$ and $\cos 2\lambda x=1$

i.e. $\cos x=1$ and $\sin\lambda x=0$

Clearly, if λ is rational, say p/q, then $x=2q\pi$, $q\in I$, satisfies both the equations.

Therefore, for exactly one solution, $x=0$, λ should be irrational.

48. $\sin\frac{\pi}{2n}+\cos\frac{\pi}{2n}=\sqrt{2}\sin\left(\frac{\pi}{2n}+\frac{\pi}{4}\right)$ or $\sin\left(\frac{\pi}{2n}+\frac{\pi}{4}\right)=\frac{\sqrt{n}}{2\sqrt{2}}$

Since, $\frac{\pi}{4}<\frac{\pi}{2n}+\frac{\pi}{4}<\frac{3\pi}{4}$ for $n>1$

or $\frac{1}{\sqrt{2}}<\frac{\sqrt{n}}{2\sqrt{2}}<1$ or $2<\sqrt{n}<2\sqrt{2}$ or $4<n<8$

If $n=1$, LHS $=1$,

RHS $=\frac{1}{2}$

Similarly for $n=8$, $\sin\left(\frac{\pi}{16}+\frac{\pi}{4}\right)\neq 1$

$\therefore 4<n<8$

49. $\because \sin^{100}\theta-\cos^{100}\theta=1$

$\Rightarrow \sin^{100}\theta=1+\cos^{100}\theta$

This equation is valid, if $\cos^{100}\theta=0$ and $\sin^{100}\theta=1$

[$\because 0\leq\cos^2\theta\leq 1$, $0\leq\sin^2\theta\leq 1$]

$\therefore \cos\theta=0$, then $\sin\theta=1$

$\Rightarrow \theta=(2n+1)\frac{\pi}{2}, \forall n\in I \Rightarrow \theta=n\pi+\frac{\pi}{2}, \forall n\in I$

50. $\sin\{x\}=\cos\{x\}$ graph of $y=\sin\{x\}$ and $y\cos\{x\}$ meet exactly 6 times in $[0, 2\pi]$.

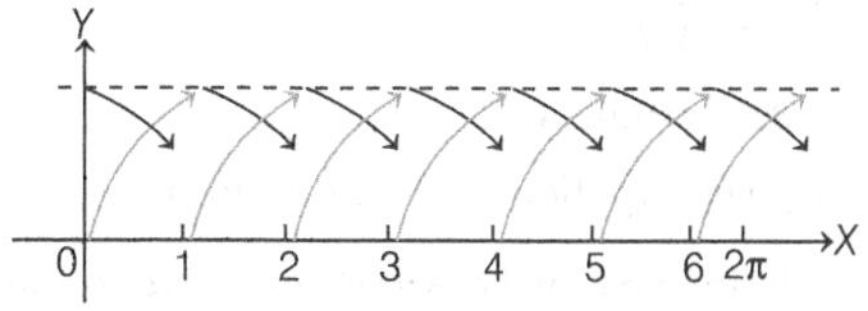

Points of intersection are at

$x=\frac{\pi}{4}, 1+\frac{\pi}{4}, 2+\frac{\pi}{4}, 3+\frac{\pi}{4}, 5+\frac{\pi}{4}$

51. Graphs of $y=\sin x$ and $y=\frac{|x|}{10}$ meet exactly six times. Hence, there are six solutions.

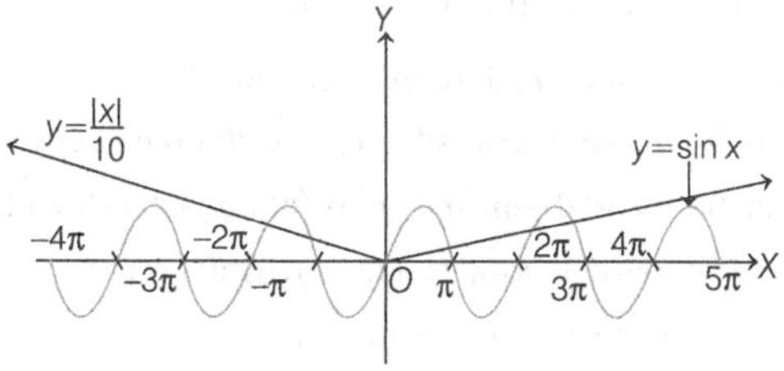

52. $|\sin x|\geq 0 \Rightarrow \frac{|\sin x|}{1+|\sin x|}<1 \Rightarrow 1-\frac{|\sin x|}{1+|\sin x|}>0$

So, the given in equation becomes

$1-\frac{|\sin x|}{1+|\sin x|}\geq\frac{2}{3} \Rightarrow \frac{1}{3}\geq\frac{|\sin x|}{1+|\sin x|} \Rightarrow |\sin x|\leq\frac{1}{2}$

$\Rightarrow -\frac{1}{2}\leq\sin x\leq\frac{1}{2} \Rightarrow \sin x\in\left[-\frac{1}{2},\frac{1}{2}\right]$

53. Consider, Ist equation i.e. $2\sin^2 x+3\sin x-2>0$

$\Rightarrow (2\sin x-1)(\sin x+2)>0$

$\Rightarrow (2\sin x-1)>0$ [as, $\sin x+2>0\,\forall\, x\in R$]

$\Rightarrow \sin x>\frac{1}{2}$

$\Rightarrow x\in\left(\frac{\pi}{6},\frac{5\pi}{6}\right)$ ...(i)

Consider $x^2-x-2<0 \Rightarrow (x-2)(x+1)<0 \Rightarrow -1<x<2$ ...(ii)

From Eqs. (i) and (ii) ,

Now, as, $2<\frac{5\pi}{6}$, we obtain that 'x' must lie in $\left(\frac{\pi}{6}, 2\right)$.

54. Here, $x^3+(x+2)^2+2\sin x=4$.

Clearly, $x=0$ satisfies the equation.

If $0<x\leq\pi$, $x^3+(x+2)^2+2\sin x>4$

If $\pi<x\leq 2\pi$, $x^3+(x+2)^2+2\sin x>27+25-2$

So, $x=0$ is the only solution.

55. $\cos x=\sqrt{1-\sin 2x}=|\sin x-\cos x|$

Eq. (i) $\sin x\leq\cos x$

$\Rightarrow \cos x=\cos x-\sin x \Rightarrow \sin x=0$

where, $x\in\left[0,\frac{\pi}{4}\right)\cup\left(\frac{5\pi}{4},2\pi\right]$

$\therefore \sin x=0$

$\Rightarrow x=2\pi$, neglecting $x=\pi$

Eq. (ii) $\sin x > \cos x \Rightarrow \tan x = 2$

where $x \in \left(\frac{\pi}{4}, \frac{5\pi}{4}\right)$,

$\therefore \tan x = 2 \Rightarrow x = \tan^{-1}(2)$

Thus, the given equation has two solutions.

56. $\frac{\sin 3\alpha}{\cos 2\alpha} < 0$ if $\sin 3\alpha > 0$ and $\cos 2\alpha < 0$ or $\sin 3\alpha < 0$ and $\cos 2\alpha > 0$

i.e. if $3\alpha \in (0, \pi)$ and $2\alpha \in (\pi/2, 3\pi/2)$

or $3\alpha \in (\pi, 2\pi)$ and $2\alpha \in (-\pi/2, \pi/2)$

i.e. if $\alpha \in (0, \pi/3)$ and $\alpha \in (\pi/4, 3\pi/4)$

or $\alpha \in (\pi/3, 2\pi/3)$ and $\alpha \in (-\pi/4, \pi/4)$

i.e. if $\alpha \in (\pi/4, \pi/3)$

since $(13\pi/48, 14\pi/48) \subset (\pi/4, \pi/3)$,

57. $n\sin^2\theta + 2n\cos(\theta+\alpha)\sin\alpha\sin\theta + \cos 2(\alpha+\theta)$

$= n\sin^2\theta + n\cos(\theta+\alpha)\{\cos(\theta-\alpha) - \cos(\theta+\alpha)\} + 2\cos^2(\theta+\alpha) - 1$

$= n\sin^2\theta + n(\cos^2\theta - \sin^2\alpha) - n\cos^2(\theta+\alpha) + 2\cos^2(\alpha+\theta) - 1$

$= n\sin^2\theta + n\cos^2\theta - n\sin^2\alpha + (2-n)\cos^2(\theta+\alpha) - 1$

$= (n-1) - n\sin^2\alpha + (2-n)\cos^2(\theta+\alpha)$

$\Rightarrow n = 2$

58. Applying $C_1 \to C_1 - 2\cos x C_2 + C_3$ to the given determinant, we get

$$\begin{vmatrix} 1-2a\cos x + a^2 & a & a^2 \\ 0 & \cos nx & \cos(n+1)x \\ 0 & \sin nx & \sin(n+1)x \end{vmatrix} = (1-2a\cos x + a^2)\sin x = 0$$

if $\sin x = 0$ or $\cos x = (1+a^2)/2a$ i.e. if $n = n\pi$, $n \in I$

59. $f(x) = (\sin^2\theta + \cos^2\theta + x)\begin{vmatrix} 1 & \cos^2\theta & x \\ 1 & x & \sin^2\theta \\ 1 & \sin^2\theta & \cos^2\theta \end{vmatrix}$

$$= (x+1)\begin{vmatrix} 1 & \cos^2\theta & x \\ 0 & x-\cos^2\theta & \sin^2\theta - x \\ 0 & \sin^2\theta - \cos^2\theta & \cos^2\theta - x \end{vmatrix}$$

$= (x+1)[(x-\cos^2\theta)(\cos^2\theta - x) - (\sin^2\theta - \cos^2\theta)(\sin^2\theta - x)]$

$= (x+1)[-x^2 - \cos^4\theta + 2x\cos^2\theta$

$- x\cos^2\theta + x\sin^2\theta - \sin^4\theta + \sin^2\theta\cos^2\theta]$

$= (-1/2)(x+1)[(x-\sin^2\theta)^2 + (x-\cos^2\theta)^2 + (\sin^2\theta - \cos^2\theta)]^2$

So, $f(x) = 0$, if $x = -1$ or $x = \sin^2\theta = \cos^2\theta$

$\sin^2\theta = \cos^2\theta \Rightarrow \theta = \pi/4 \Rightarrow x = 1/2$

Hence, $x = -1, 1/2$

60. $3^{\sin 2x + 2\cos^2 x} + 3^{1+2(1-\cos^2 x) - \sin 2x} = 28$

$\Rightarrow 3^{\sin 2x + 2\cos^2 x} + \frac{27}{3^{\sin 2x + 2\cos^2 x}} = 28$

Let $\sin 2x + 2\cos^2 x = t$

$\Rightarrow \quad 3^t + \frac{27}{3^t} = 28$

$\Rightarrow (3^t)^2 - 28(3^t) + 27 = 0$

$\Rightarrow \quad 3^t = 27$ or 1

$\Rightarrow \quad \sin 2x + 2\cos^2 x = 0$ or 3

$\Rightarrow \quad \sin x + \cos 2x + 1 = 0$ or 3

$\Rightarrow \quad \sin 2x + \cos 2x = -1$

[as $\sin 2x + \cos 2x = 2$ is not possible]

$\Rightarrow \quad \cos\left(2x - \frac{\pi}{4}\right) = \cos\left(\frac{3\pi}{4}\right) \Rightarrow 2x - \frac{\pi}{4} = 2n\pi \pm \frac{3\pi}{4}$

$\Rightarrow \quad x = n\pi + \frac{\pi}{2}$ or $x = n\pi - \frac{\pi}{4}$

$\Rightarrow \quad x = \frac{3\pi}{4}, \frac{7\pi}{4}, \frac{\pi}{2}, \frac{3\pi}{2}$

61. We have,

$f(x) = 3\left(\cos^4\frac{x}{2} + \sin^4\frac{x}{2}\right) - 2\cos^2 x$

$f(x) = 3\left[\left(\cos^2\frac{x}{2} + \sin^2\frac{x}{2}\right)^2 - 2\sin^2\frac{x}{2}\cos^2\frac{x}{2}\right] - 2(1-\sin^2 x)$

$f(x) = 3\left[1 - \frac{(2\sin x/2\cos x/2)^2}{2}\right] - 2 + 2\sin^2 x$

$f(x) = 3 - \frac{3}{2}\sin^2 x - 2 + 2\sin^2 x = 1 + \frac{\sin^2 x}{2}$

Now, $S = \{x \in [0, 2\pi] : f'(x) = -\frac{\sqrt{3}}{4}\}$

$f'(x) = \frac{2\sin x\cos x}{2} = \frac{\sin 2x}{2}$

$x \in [0, 2\pi] \Rightarrow 2x \in [0, 4\pi]$

Now, $f'(x) = \frac{\sin 2x}{2} = -\frac{\sqrt{3}}{4}$ in $[0, 4\pi]$

$\sin 2x = -\frac{\sqrt{3}}{2}$ in $[0, 4\pi]$

$2x = \frac{4\pi}{3}, \frac{5\pi}{3}, \frac{10\pi}{3}, \frac{11\pi}{3}$

$x = \frac{2\pi}{3}, \frac{5\pi}{6}, \frac{5\pi}{3}, \frac{11\pi}{6}$

Now, $4\beta = \sum_{x \in S} x = \frac{2\pi}{3} + \frac{5\pi}{6} + \frac{5\pi}{3} + \frac{11\pi}{6}$

$= \frac{4\pi + 5\pi + 10\pi + 11\pi}{6} = \frac{30\pi}{6} = 5\pi$

$\Rightarrow \quad \beta = \frac{5\pi}{4}$

$f(\beta) = 1 + \frac{\sin^2\frac{5\pi}{4}}{2} = 1 + \frac{\sin^2\frac{\pi}{4}}{2} = 1 + \frac{1}{4} = \frac{5}{4}$

62. If $\cot x > 0$, then $\frac{1}{\sin x} = 0$ which is not possible.

Now, if $\cot x < 0$,

then $\quad -\cot x = \cot x + \frac{1}{\sin x}$

$\Rightarrow \quad \frac{2\cos x + 1}{\sin x} = 0 \Rightarrow \cos x = -\frac{1}{2}$

$\Rightarrow \quad x = 2n\pi \pm \frac{2\pi}{3}$, $n \in I$ and $0 \le x \le 2\pi$

$\therefore \quad x = \frac{2\pi}{3}, \frac{4\pi}{3}$

63. We have, $|\cos x| = [x] = y$ (say)

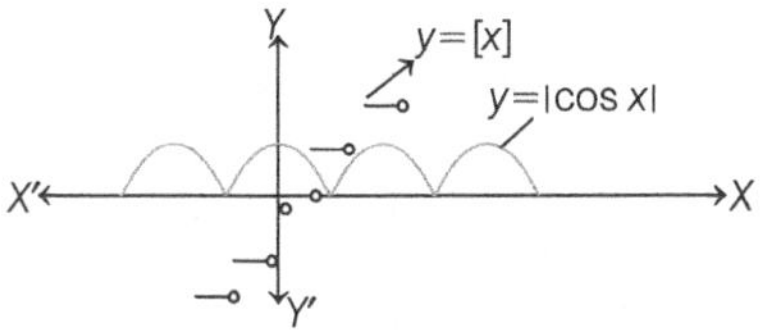

Graph of $|\cos x|$ and $[x]$ don't cut each other for any real value of x.

Hence, number of solutions is zero.

64. $2\cos^2 2x - 7\cos 2x + 5 = 0$

$$\Rightarrow \quad \cos 2x = 1$$

$$\Rightarrow \quad x = n\pi$$

$$k = 1 + 2 + \ldots + 99$$

$$= \frac{99 \times 100}{2} = 4950$$

Now, $k - 4948 \;= 4950 - 4948 = 2$

65. In 2nd equation sum of coefficients is zero, hence its one root is 1 and second root is also 1 as it has equal roots.

Common root of first equation is 1.

$$\Rightarrow \quad \tan^2\theta - 2\tan\theta + 1 = 0$$

$$\Rightarrow \quad (\tan\theta - 1)^2 = 0$$

$\Rightarrow \tan\theta = 1$, hence one solution in $(0, \pi)$.

66. $\sin(1-x) \geq 0$, $\cos x \geq 0$

$$\cos x = \cos\left\{\frac{\pi}{2} - (1-x)\right\}$$

$$\therefore \quad x = 2n\pi - \left(\frac{\pi}{2} - (1-x)\right) \Rightarrow x = n\pi - \frac{\pi}{4} + \frac{1}{2}$$

Put $n=1$, $x = \frac{3\pi}{4} + \frac{1}{2} \Rightarrow [x] = 2$

67. $\dfrac{x^4+1}{8x^2} = \dfrac{(2\sin y\cos y)^2}{4}$

$$\Rightarrow \quad x^2 + \frac{1}{x^2} = 2\sin^2 2y$$

LHS ≥ 2 and RHS ≤ 2

LHS = RHS will hold.

Only if LHS = 2 = RHS

i.e. $x^2 = 1$ and $\sin^2 2y = 1$

$$\Rightarrow \quad x = \pm 1 \text{ and } 2y = \frac{\pi}{2}, \frac{3\pi}{2}, \frac{5\pi}{2}, \frac{7\pi}{2}$$

So, total number of ordered pairs are 8.

68. $\because \cos A \sin\left(A - \frac{\pi}{6}\right) = \frac{1}{2}\left[2\cos A\sin\left(A - \frac{\pi}{6}\right)\right]$

$$= \frac{1}{2}\left[\sin\left(A + A - \frac{\pi}{6}\right) - \sin\left(A - A + \frac{\pi}{6}\right)\right]$$

$$= \frac{1}{2}\left[\sin\left(2A - \frac{\pi}{6}\right) - \sin\frac{\pi}{6}\right]$$

So, it is maximum, when $\sin\left(2A - \frac{\pi}{6}\right)$ is maximum.

i.e. $\quad 2A - \frac{\pi}{6} = \frac{\pi}{2} \Rightarrow 2A = \frac{\pi}{2} + \frac{\pi}{6}$

$$\Rightarrow \quad A = \frac{\pi}{3}$$

but $\quad A = \frac{\pi}{\lambda}$

Hence, $\lambda = 3$

69. From the given equation we have

$$3\frac{2\tan(x/2)}{1+\tan^2(x/2)} + 4\frac{1-\tan^2(x/2)}{1+\tan^2(x/2)} = 5$$

$$\Rightarrow \quad 6\tan(x/2) + 4 - 4\tan^2(x/2) = 5 + 5\tan^2(x/2)$$

$$\Rightarrow \quad 9\tan^2(x/2) - 6\tan(x/2) + 1 = 0$$

$$\Rightarrow \quad 90\tan^2(x/2) - 60\tan(x/2) = -10$$

$$\because \quad 90\tan^2\frac{x}{2} - 60\tan\frac{x}{2} + 10 = -10 + 10 = 0$$

70. $\tan(\pi\cos\theta) = \tan(\pi/2 - \pi\sin\theta)$

$$\Rightarrow \quad \pi\cos\theta = n\pi + \pi/2 - \pi\sin\theta \; (n \in I)$$

$$\Rightarrow \quad \pi(\sin\theta + \cos\theta) = (2n+1)\frac{\pi}{2}$$

$$\Rightarrow \quad \sin\theta + \cos\theta = \frac{2n+1}{2} \Rightarrow \cos(\pi/4 - \theta) = \frac{2n+1}{2\sqrt{2}}$$

Since $\quad -1 \leq \cos(\pi/4 - \theta) \leq 1$

$$\Rightarrow \quad -1 \leq \frac{2n+1}{2\sqrt{2}} \leq 1$$

$\Rightarrow$ $n = 0$ or -1 as n is an integer

$$\Rightarrow \quad \cos(\pi/4 - \theta) = \pm(1/2\sqrt{2})$$

$$\Rightarrow \quad 8\cos^2(\pi/4 - \theta) = 1$$

$$\Rightarrow \quad 16\cos^2\left(\frac{\pi}{4} - \theta\right) = 2$$

71. We have, $\quad \sin\left(x - \frac{\pi}{4}\right) - \sin\left(x - \frac{3\pi}{4}\right) = 1$

$$\sin\left(x - \frac{\pi}{4}\right) + \sin\left(x + \frac{\pi}{4}\right) = 1$$

$$\Rightarrow \quad 2\sin x\cos\frac{\pi}{4} = 1 \quad [\because \sin\theta = \sin(\pi - \theta)]$$

$$\Rightarrow \quad \sin x = \frac{1}{\sqrt{2}} \Rightarrow x = \frac{\pi}{4}, \frac{3\pi}{4}$$

We know that 3 radians $\cong 171°22'$.

Therefore, $\sin 3 > 0$, $\cos 3 < 0$ and $|\cos 3| > \sin 3$

$$\therefore \quad \cos 3 + \sin 3 < 0$$

Now, $\quad \dfrac{2\cos 7x}{\cos 3 + \sin 3} > 2^{\cos 2x}$

$$\Rightarrow \quad 2\cos 7x < 2^{\cos 2x}(\cos 3 + \sin 3) \quad [\because \cos 3 + \sin 3 < 0]$$

$$\Rightarrow \quad 2\cos 7x < 0$$

$$\Rightarrow \quad \cos 7x < 0 \quad [\because 2^{\cos x} > 0]$$

Clearly, $x=\frac{3\pi}{4}$ satisfies this equation.

Hence, $x=\frac{3\pi}{4}$ is the required solution.

Hence, only one solution.

72. Draw the curves $p|\cos\theta|$ and $q|\sin\theta|$ and find the number of intersection points.

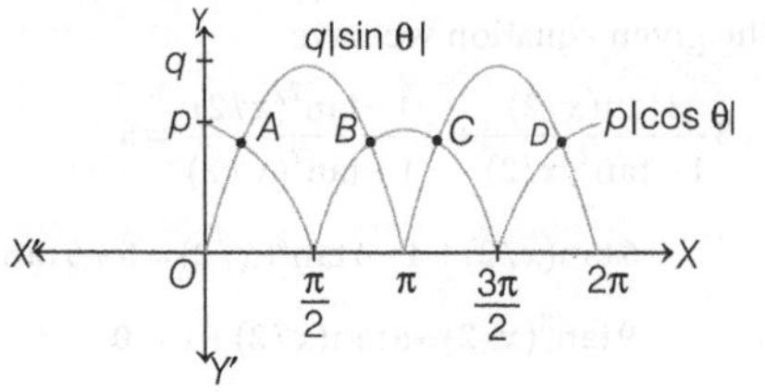

Hence, intersection points are A, B, C, D

$\therefore$ Number of solutions is 4.

73. Given, $(1-\sin x)^3-(\cos x-1)^3-(\sin x)^3=(2-\cos x-2\sin x)^3$

$\Rightarrow (\sin x-1)^3+(\cos x-1)^3+(\sin x)^3=(2\sin x+\cos x-2)^3$ ...(i)

Let $\sin x-1=a$

$\cos x-1=b$

$\sin x=c$

So, Eq. (i) is of the form $a^3+b^3+c^3=(a+b+c)^3$

$\therefore\ \sin x+\cos x=2$

$\Rightarrow x\in\phi$ i.e. no solution

or $\sin x+\cos x=1$

$$\Rightarrow \quad x=0,\frac{\pi}{2},2\pi\in[0,2\pi]$$

$$\text{or} \quad \sin x=\frac{1}{2}\Rightarrow x=\frac{\pi}{6},\frac{5\pi}{6}\in[0,2\pi]$$

Hence, total number of solutions = 5

74. Given, $\cos^2 x+\frac{\sqrt{3}+1}{2}\sin x-\frac{\sqrt{3}}{4}-1=0$

$$\Rightarrow 1-\sin^2 x+\frac{\sqrt{3}+1}{2}\sin x-\frac{\sqrt{3}}{4}-1=0$$

$$\Rightarrow \quad \sin^2 x-\frac{\sqrt{3}+1}{2}\sin x+\frac{\sqrt{3}}{4}=0$$

$$\Rightarrow 4\sin^2 x-2\sqrt{3}\sin x-2\sin x+\sqrt{3}=0$$

$$\Rightarrow \quad \sin x=\frac{1}{2},\frac{\sqrt{3}}{2}$$

$$\Rightarrow \quad x=\frac{\pi}{6},\frac{5\pi}{6},\frac{\pi}{3},\frac{2\pi}{3}$$

75. Here, $\sin^2\theta-2\sin\theta-1=0$

$$\therefore \quad \sin\theta=1\pm\sqrt{2}$$

But $|\sin\theta|\le 1$

$\therefore\ \sin\theta=1-\sqrt{2}=\sin(-\alpha)$ [let say]

$\therefore$ General solution is

$\theta=n\pi+(-1)^n\alpha$ in $[0,n\pi]$

$\therefore\ \theta=\pi+\alpha,\ 2\pi-\alpha,3\pi+\alpha,4\pi-\alpha$

Hence, for 4 distinct solutions, the least value of $n\in N$ is 4.

76. Given, $|\cos x|^{\sin^2 x-\frac{3}{2}\sin x+\frac{1}{2}}=1$

$$\Rightarrow \quad \left(\sin^2 x-\frac{3}{2}\sin x+\frac{1}{2}\right)\cdot\log_e|\cos x|=0$$

$$\Rightarrow \sin^2 x-\frac{3}{2}\sin x+\frac{1}{2}=0 \text{ or } \log_e|\cos x|=0$$

$$\Rightarrow (2\sin x-1)(\sin x-1)=0 \text{ or } |\cos x|=1$$

$$\Rightarrow \sin x=\frac{1}{2} \text{ or } \sin x=1 \text{ or } \cos x=\pm 1$$

$$\Rightarrow \quad x=\frac{\pi}{6},\frac{5\pi}{6}\in[0,\pi] \text{ or } \sin x=1 \text{ (rejected)}$$

because $\cos x=0$ at $x=\frac{\pi}{2}$ or $\cos x=\pm 1$

$$\Rightarrow \quad x=0,\pi$$

Hence, total number of solutions = 4

77. Given, $x+\sin y=2024$ ...(i)

$x+2024\cos y=2023$ ...(ii)

On subtracting Eqs. (i) from Eq. (ii), we get

$$\sin y-2024\cos y=1$$

$$\Rightarrow \quad \sin y=1+2024\cos y \quad \text{...(iii)}$$

$$\because \quad 0\le y\le\frac{\pi}{2}$$

$$\therefore \quad 0\le\cos y\le 1$$

So, Eq. (iii) will be possible only when $\sin y=1$ and $\cos y=0$

$$\Rightarrow \quad y=\frac{\pi}{2}$$

From Eq. (i), $x+1=2024\Rightarrow x=2023$

Hence, $[x+y]-1=[2023+\frac{\pi}{2}]-1$

$$=[2024...]-1=2024-1=2023$$

78. Given equation is

$$\sec^2(\lambda+2)x+\lambda^2-1=0$$

$$\Rightarrow \quad \tan^2(\lambda+2)x+\lambda^2=0$$

$$\Rightarrow \quad \tan^2(\lambda+2)x=0 \text{ or } \lambda=0$$

$$\Rightarrow \quad \tan^2(0+2)x=0\Rightarrow\tan^2 2x=0$$

$$\Rightarrow \quad x=0,\frac{\pi}{2},-\frac{\pi}{2}\in(-\pi,\pi)$$

$\therefore (0,0),\left(0,\frac{\pi}{2}\right),\left(0,-\frac{\pi}{2}\right)$ are ordered pairs satisfying the equation.

79. Given, $\tan^2[\pi(x+y)]+\cot^2[\pi(x+y)]=1+\sqrt{\frac{2x}{1+x^2}}$

Here, minimum value of LHS is $2\left(x+\frac{1}{x}\text{form where } x>0\right)$

and $1+\sqrt{\frac{2}{x+\frac{1}{x}}}\le 2.$

Equality is possible only when both sides are at $x=1$

i.e. $\quad \tan^2[\pi(x+y)]=1$

$$\Rightarrow \quad \pi(x+y)=n\pi\pm\frac{\pi}{4},n\in I$$

$\Rightarrow \quad \pi(x+y) = \dfrac{5\pi}{4}$ (for least value of y)

$\therefore \quad y = \dfrac{1}{4}$

Hence, $4 \times \dfrac{1}{4} = 1$

80. Given, $2\cos x, |\cos x|$ and $1 - 3\cos^2 x$ are in GP.

So, $\quad |\cos x|^2 = (2\cos x)(1 - 3\cos^2 x)$

$\Rightarrow \quad \cos^2 x = 2\cos x - 6\cos^3 x \quad [\because |x|^2 = |x^2| = x^2]$

$\Rightarrow \quad 6\cos^3 x + \cos^2 x - 2\cos x = 0$

$\Rightarrow \quad \cos x(6\cos^2 x + \cos x - 2) = 0$

$\Rightarrow \quad \cos x(2\cos x - 1)(3\cos x + 2) = 0$

$\Rightarrow \quad \cos x = 0, \dfrac{1}{2}, \dfrac{-2}{3}$

$\Rightarrow \quad x = \dfrac{\pi}{2}, \dfrac{\pi}{3}, \cos^{-1}\left(-\dfrac{2}{3}\right)$

So, $\alpha = \dfrac{\pi}{2}$ and $\beta = \dfrac{\pi}{3}$ $\quad [\because \alpha$ and β are positive$]$

Hence, $|\alpha - \beta| = \dfrac{\pi}{6}$

Thus, $\dfrac{168}{\pi}|\alpha - \beta| = \dfrac{168}{\pi} \times \dfrac{\pi}{6} = 28$

81. Given, $\sin^4\left(\dfrac{x}{3}\right) + \cos^4\left(\dfrac{x}{3}\right) > \dfrac{1}{2}$

$\Rightarrow \quad 1 - 2\sin^2\left(\dfrac{x}{3}\right)\cos^2\left(\dfrac{x}{3}\right) > \dfrac{1}{2}$

$\Rightarrow \quad 1 - \dfrac{1}{2}\sin^2\left(\dfrac{2x}{3}\right) > \dfrac{1}{2} \Rightarrow \sin^2\left(\dfrac{2x}{3}\right) < 1$

which is always true except when $\sin^2\left(\dfrac{2x}{3}\right) = 1$

i.e. $\dfrac{2x}{3} = n\pi \pm \dfrac{\pi}{2}, n \in I$

i.e. $\quad x = \dfrac{3n\pi}{2} \pm \dfrac{3\pi}{4}, n \in I$

So, solution of x is $R - \left\{x : x = \dfrac{3n\pi}{2} \pm \dfrac{3\pi}{4}, n \in I\right\}$.

On comparing, we get

$a = 3, b = 2, c = 3, d = 4$

Hence, $2ac - bd = (2 \times 9) - (8) = 10$

82. $(\log_{\sqrt{3}} \tan x)\left(\sqrt{\dfrac{\log_{\sqrt{3}} 3}{\log_{\sqrt{3}} \tan x} + \log_{\sqrt{3}}(\sqrt{3})^3}\right) = -1$

$\Rightarrow \quad (\log_{\sqrt{3}} \tan x)\left(\sqrt{\dfrac{2}{\log_{\sqrt{3}} \tan x} + 3}\right) = -1$

Put $\log_{\sqrt{3}} \tan x = t$, we get

$\Rightarrow \quad t\sqrt{\dfrac{2}{t} + 3} = -1 \Rightarrow \sqrt{\dfrac{2}{t} + 3} = \dfrac{-1}{t}$

$\Rightarrow \quad \dfrac{2}{t} + 3 = \dfrac{1}{t^2} \quad$ [where, $t < 0$]

$\Rightarrow \quad (3t^2 + 2t - 1) = 0$

$\Rightarrow \quad (3t - 1)(t + 1) = 0$

$\Rightarrow \quad t = -1 \quad [\because t$ cannot be positive$]$

$\Rightarrow \quad \log_{\sqrt{3}} \tan x = -1$

$\Rightarrow \quad \tan x = \dfrac{1}{\sqrt{3}} \Rightarrow x = \dfrac{\pi}{6}$ and $\dfrac{7\pi}{6} \in [0, 2\pi]$

Hence, there are total two solutions in $[0, 2\pi]$.

83. Given, $\quad 2\tan^2\theta - 5\sec\theta = 1$

$\Rightarrow \quad 2(\sec^2\theta - 1) - 5\sec\theta - 1 = 0$

$\Rightarrow \quad 2\sec^2\theta - 5\sec\theta - 3 = 0$

$\Rightarrow \quad 2\sec^2\theta - 6\sec\theta + \sec\theta - 3 = 0$

$\Rightarrow \quad (2\sec\theta + 1)(\sec\theta - 3) = 0$

$\because \quad \sec\theta = -\dfrac{1}{2}$ (not possible)

$\therefore \quad \sec\theta = 3 \Rightarrow \cos\theta = \dfrac{1}{3}$

From graph,

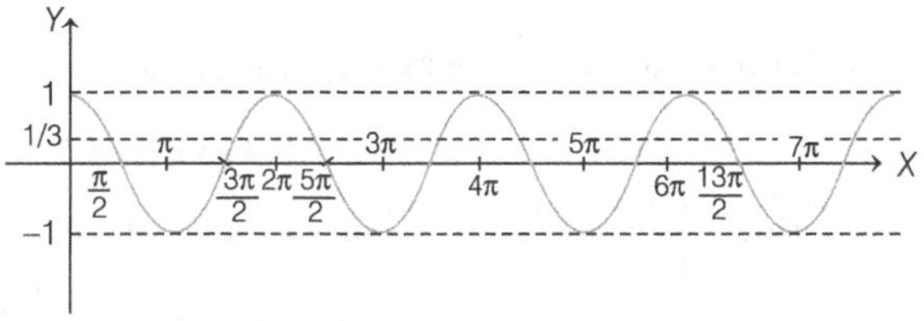

2 solutions in $[0, 2\pi]$

2 solution in $[2\pi, 4\pi]$

2 solution in $[4\pi, 6\pi]$

and 1 solution in $\left[6\pi, \dfrac{13\pi}{2}\right]$

Hence, $n = 13$

Now, $\quad \displaystyle\sum_{K=1}^{13} \dfrac{K}{2^k} = S$ [say]

So, $\quad S = \dfrac{1}{2} + \dfrac{2}{2^2} + \dfrac{3}{2^3} + \ldots + \dfrac{13}{2^{13}}$

$\Rightarrow \quad \dfrac{1}{2}S = \dfrac{1}{2^2} + \dfrac{2}{2^3} + \ldots + \dfrac{13}{2^{14}}$

$\Rightarrow \quad \dfrac{1}{2}S = \dfrac{1}{2} + \dfrac{1}{2^2} + \dfrac{1}{2^3} + \ldots + \dfrac{1}{2^{13}} - \dfrac{13}{2^{14}}$

$\Rightarrow \quad \dfrac{S}{2} = \dfrac{1}{2}\left[\dfrac{\left(1 - \dfrac{1}{2^{13}}\right)}{\left(1 - \dfrac{1}{2}\right)}\right] - \dfrac{13}{2^{14}}$

$\Rightarrow \quad S = 2\left(\dfrac{2^{13} - 1}{2^{13}}\right) - \dfrac{13}{2^{13}} = \dfrac{2^{14} - 15}{2^{13}}$

84. We have,

$4\sin^2 x - 4\cos^3 x + 9 - 4\cos x = 0$

$\Rightarrow \quad 4(1 - \cos^2 x) - 4\cos^3 x + 9 - 4\cos x = 0$

$\Rightarrow \quad 4\cos^3 x + 4\cos^2 x + 4\cos x - 13 = 0$

We know maximum value of $\cos x = 1$

So, $4\cos^3 x + 4\cos^2 x + 4\cos x$ can never be greater than 12, therefore no solution.

85. We have, $e^{\sin x} - \dfrac{2}{e^{\sin x}} = 2$

Let $e^{\sin x} = t (t > 0)$

$\Rightarrow \quad t - \dfrac{2}{t} = 2$

$\Rightarrow \quad t^2 - 2t - 2 = 0$

$\Rightarrow \quad t = \dfrac{2 \pm \sqrt{4+8}}{2} = 1 \pm \sqrt{3}$

$\Rightarrow \quad t = 1 - \sqrt{3}$ (rejected as $t > 0$)

$\therefore \quad t = 1 + \sqrt{3}$

$\Rightarrow \quad e^{\sin x} = 1 + \sqrt{3}$

$\Rightarrow \quad \sin x = \log_e(1+\sqrt{3}) = \log_e 2.73 > 1$

So, no solution.

86. We have, $2\sin^3 x + \sin 2x \cos x + 4\sin x - 4 = 0$

$\Rightarrow \quad 2\left(\dfrac{3\sin x - \sin 3x}{4}\right) + \sin 2x \cos x + 4\sin x - 4 = 0$

$\Rightarrow \quad \dfrac{1}{2}(3\sin x - \sin 3x) + \dfrac{1}{2}\{\sin(2x + x) + \sin(2x - x)\} + 4\sin x - 4 = 0$

$\Rightarrow \quad \dfrac{3}{2}\sin x - \dfrac{1}{2}\sin 3x + \dfrac{1}{2}\sin 3x + \dfrac{1}{2}\sin x + 4\sin x - 4 = 0$

$\Rightarrow \quad \sin x\left(\dfrac{3}{2} + \dfrac{1}{2} + 4\right) - 4 = 0$

$\Rightarrow \quad 6\sin x - 4 = 0$

$\Rightarrow \quad \sin x = \dfrac{2}{3}$

$\Rightarrow \quad \sin x = 0.66,\ x \in \left[0, \dfrac{n\pi}{2}\right]$

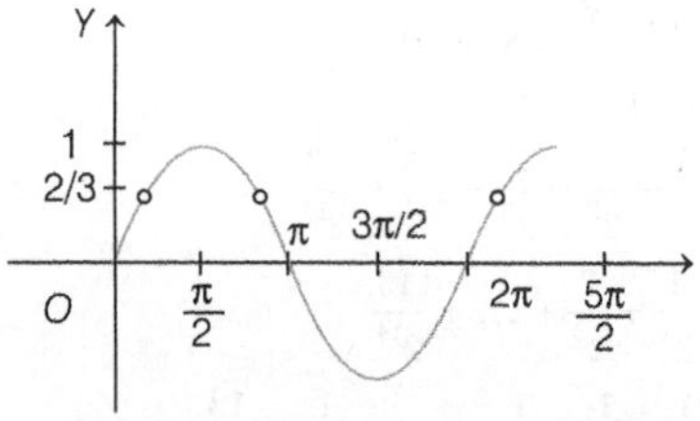

For exact 3 solutions, $n = 5$

$\therefore \quad x^2 + 5x + 2 = 0$

$\Rightarrow \quad x = \dfrac{-5 \pm \sqrt{25-8}}{2} = \dfrac{-5 \pm \sqrt{17}}{2}$

$\Rightarrow \quad x = -0.438, -4.56$

$\Rightarrow \quad x \in (-\infty, 0)$

87. $\dfrac{3\cos 2x + \cos^3 2x}{\cos^6 x - \sin^6 x} = x^3 - x^2 + 6$

$$\text{LHS} = \frac{\cos 2x(3 + \cos^2 2x)}{(\cos^2 x - \sin^2 x)(\cos^4 x + \sin^4 x + \cos^2 x \sin^2 x)}$$

$[\because \cos 2x = \cos^2 x - \sin^2 x]$

$$= \frac{\cos 2x(3 + \cos^2 2x)}{\cos 2x((\cos^2 x + \sin^2 x)^2 - \cos^2 x \sin^2 x)}$$

$$= \frac{3 + \cos^2 2x}{1 - \frac{1}{4}\sin^2 2x} \qquad [\because \sin 2x = 2\sin x \cos x]$$

$$= \frac{4(3 + 1 - \sin^2 2x)}{4 - \sin^2 2x} = \frac{4(4 - \sin^2 2x)}{(4 - \sin^2 2x)} = 4$$

Now, $x^3 - x^2 + 6 = 4$

$x^3 - x^2 + 2 = 0$

$\therefore$ Sum of solution $= -\dfrac{b}{a} = 1$

88. We have, $4\cos\theta + 5\sin\theta = 1$

$\Rightarrow 16\cos^2\theta + 25\sin^2\theta + 40\sin\theta\cos\theta = 1$

$\Rightarrow \quad 16 + 9\sin^2\theta + 20\sin 2\theta = 1$

$\Rightarrow \quad 16 + 9\left(\dfrac{1 - \cos 2\theta}{2}\right) + 20\sin 2\theta = 1$

$\Rightarrow \quad -\dfrac{9}{2}\cos 2\theta + 20\sin 2\theta = -\dfrac{39}{2}$

$\Rightarrow \quad -9\cos 2\theta + 40\sin 2\theta = -39$

$\Rightarrow \quad -9\left(\dfrac{1 - \tan^2\theta}{1 + \tan^2\theta}\right) + 40\left(\dfrac{2\tan\theta}{1 + \tan^2\theta}\right) = -39$

$\Rightarrow \quad 48\tan^2\theta + 80\tan\theta + 30 = 0$

$\Rightarrow \quad 24\tan^2\theta + 40\tan\theta + 15 = 0$

$\Rightarrow \quad \tan\theta = \dfrac{-40 \pm \sqrt{160}}{2 \times 24}$

$\Rightarrow \quad \tan\theta = \dfrac{\sqrt{10} - 10}{12}, \dfrac{-\sqrt{10} - 10}{12}$

Since, $\alpha \in \left(-\dfrac{\pi}{2}, \dfrac{\pi}{2}\right)$

$\therefore \quad \tan\alpha = \dfrac{\sqrt{10} - 10}{12}$

89. We have, $S = \{\theta \in [0, 2\pi] : 3\cos^4\theta - 5\cos^2\theta - 2\sin^6\theta + 2 = 0\}$

$\because \quad 3\cos^4\theta - 5\cos^2\theta - 2\sin^6\theta + 2 = 0$

$\Rightarrow \quad 3\cos^4\theta - 3\cos^2\theta - 2\cos^2\theta - 2\sin^6\theta + 2 = 0$

$\Rightarrow \quad 3\cos^2\theta(\cos^2\theta - 1) - 2(\cos^2\theta - 1) - 2\sin^6\theta = 0$

$\Rightarrow \quad -3\cos^2\theta\sin^2\theta + 2\sin^2\theta - 2\sin^6\theta = 0$

$\Rightarrow \quad -3\cos^2\theta\sin^2\theta + 2\sin^2\theta(1 - \sin^4\theta) = 0$

$\Rightarrow -3\cos^2\theta\sin^2\theta + 2\sin^2\theta(1 - \sin^2\theta)(1 + \sin^2\theta) = 0$

$\Rightarrow \quad -3\cos^2\theta\sin^2\theta + 2\sin^2\theta\cos^2\theta(1 + \sin^2\theta) = 0$

$\Rightarrow \quad \cos^2\theta\sin^2\theta[-3 + 2 + 2\sin^2\theta] = 0$

$\Rightarrow \quad \cos^2\theta\sin^2\theta(2\sin^2\theta - 1) = 0$

Either $\cos^2\theta = 0$ or $\sin^2\theta = 0$ or $2\sin^2\theta - 1 = 0$

If $\sin^2\theta = 0$, then $\theta = \{0, \pi, 2\pi\}$.

If $\cos^2\theta = 0$, then $\theta = \left\{\dfrac{\pi}{2}, \dfrac{3\pi}{2}\right\}$.

If $2\sin^2\theta - 1 = 0$, then $\theta = \left\{\dfrac{\pi}{4}, \dfrac{3\pi}{4}, \dfrac{5\pi}{4}, \dfrac{7\pi}{4}\right\}$.

Hence, there are total 9 solutions of the given set.

90. Given, $\tan 15° + \frac{1}{\tan 75°} + \frac{1}{\tan 105°} + \tan 195° = 2a$ ... (i)

Since, $\tan 15° = 2 - \sqrt{3}$

$$\frac{1}{\tan 75°} = \cot 75° = \tan 15° = 2 - \sqrt{3} \quad [\because \cot\theta = \tan(90° - \theta)]$$

$$\frac{1}{\tan 105°} = \cot(105°) = -\cot 75° = \sqrt{3} - 2$$

and $\tan(195°) = \tan(180° + 15°) = \tan 15° = 2 - \sqrt{3}$

From Eq. (i), $2a = (2 - \sqrt{3}) + (2 - \sqrt{3}) + (\sqrt{3} - 2) + (2 - \sqrt{3})$

$$\Rightarrow \quad 2a = 2(2 - \sqrt{3}) \Rightarrow a = 2 - \sqrt{3}$$

Hence, $a + \frac{1}{a} = (2 - \sqrt{3}) + \frac{1}{(2 - \sqrt{3})}$

$$= (2 - \sqrt{3}) + \frac{2 + \sqrt{3}}{(2 - \sqrt{3})(2 + \sqrt{3})}$$

$$= (2 - \sqrt{3}) + \frac{(2 + \sqrt{3})}{4 - 3} = 2 - \sqrt{3} + 2 + \sqrt{3} = 4$$

91. $\cos^2 2x - 2\sin^4 x - 2\cos^2 x = \lambda$

$$\Rightarrow \quad \cos^2 2x - \frac{1 - 2\cos 2x + \cos^2 2x}{2} - 2\cos^2 x = \lambda$$

$$\Rightarrow \cos^2 2x + \frac{-\left(\frac{2}{2} - \frac{4\cos 2x}{2} + \frac{\cos 4x + 1}{2}\right)}{2} - 2\cos^2 x = \lambda$$

$$\Rightarrow \cos^2 2x + \frac{-\frac{(\cos 4x - 4\cos 2x + (2 + 1))}{2}}{2} - 2\cos^2 x = \lambda$$

$$\Rightarrow \cos^2 2x + \frac{(-3) + 4\cos 2x - \cos 4x}{4} - 2\left(\frac{\cos 2x + 1}{2}\right) = \lambda$$

$$\Rightarrow \quad \frac{\cos 4x + (4\cos 2x - 4\cos 2x) + (2 - 7)}{4} = \lambda$$

$$\Rightarrow \quad \frac{\cos 4x - 5}{4} = \lambda$$

As we know,

$$-1 \le \cos 4x \le 1$$

$$\Rightarrow \quad -6 \le \cos 4x - 5 \le -4$$

$$\Rightarrow \quad \frac{-6}{4} \le \frac{\cos 4x - 5}{4} \le \frac{-4}{4}$$

$$\Rightarrow \quad -\frac{3}{2} \le \lambda \le -1$$

So, $\lambda \in \left[-\frac{3}{2}, -1\right]$

92. We have,

$$f(\theta) = 3\left[\sin^4\left(\frac{3\pi}{2} - \theta\right) + \sin^4(3\pi + \theta)\right] - 2(1 - \sin^2(2\theta))$$

Using $\sin\left(\frac{3\pi}{2} - \theta\right) = -\cos\theta$ and $\sin(3\pi + \theta) = \sin\theta$, we get

$$f(\theta) = 3(\cos^4\theta + \sin^4\theta) - 2(1 - \sin^2(2\theta))$$

$$= 3[(\cos^2\theta + \sin^2\theta)^2 - 2\sin^2\theta\cos^2\theta] - 2[(1 - \sin^2(2\theta)]$$

$$= 3\left[1 - \frac{(2\sin\theta\cos\theta)^2}{2}\right] - 2 + 2\sin^2(2\theta)$$

$$= 3 - \frac{3\sin^2(2\theta)}{2} - 2 + 2\sin^2(2\theta) = 1 + \frac{\sin^2(2\theta)}{2} \quad \text{... (i)}$$

Now, $S = \left\{\theta \in [0, \pi] : f'(\theta) = -\frac{\sqrt{3}}{2}\right\}$

$$f'(\theta) = \left[1 + \frac{\sin^2(2\theta)}{2}\right]' = \frac{1}{2} \times [\sin^2(2\theta)]'$$

$$= \sin(2\theta) \cdot \cos(2\theta) \cdot 2 = \sin(4\theta)$$

$$\theta \in [0, \pi] \Rightarrow 4\theta \in [0, 4\pi]$$

Now, $\sin(4\theta) = -\frac{\sqrt{3}}{2}$ in $[0, 4\pi]$

$$\Rightarrow \quad 4\theta = \frac{4\pi}{3}, \frac{5\pi}{3}, \frac{10\pi}{3}, \frac{11\pi}{3}$$

$$\Rightarrow \quad \theta = \frac{\pi}{3}, \frac{5\pi}{12}, \frac{5\pi}{6}, \frac{11\pi}{12}$$

Now, $4\beta = \sum_{\theta \in S} \theta = \frac{\pi}{3} + \frac{5\pi}{12} + \frac{5\pi}{6} + \frac{11\pi}{12}$

$$= \frac{4\pi + 5\pi + 10\pi + 11\pi}{12} = \frac{5\pi}{2}$$

$$\Rightarrow \quad \beta = \frac{5\pi}{8}$$

$$\therefore \quad f(\beta) = 1 + \frac{\sin^2(2\beta)}{2} = 1 + \frac{\sin^2\left(\frac{5\pi}{4}\right)}{2}$$

$$= 1 + \frac{\sin^2\left(\pi + \frac{\pi}{4}\right)}{2} \quad [\text{using } \sin(\pi + x) = -\sin x]$$

$$= 1 + \frac{\sin^2\left(\frac{\pi}{4}\right)}{2} = 1 + \frac{\left(\frac{1}{\sqrt{2}}\right)^2}{2} = \frac{5}{4}$$

93. Given equation is

$$\log_{\cos x}\cot x + 4\log_{\sin x}\tan x = 1,$$

where $x \in \left(0, \frac{\pi}{2}\right)$

$$\Rightarrow \frac{\log_e \cot x}{\log_e \cos x} + 4\frac{\log_e \tan x}{\log_e \sin x} = 1 \quad [\text{using base change formula}]$$

$$\Rightarrow \frac{\log\cos x - \log\sin x}{\log\cos x} + 4\left(\frac{\log\sin x - \log\cos x}{\log\sin x}\right) = 1$$

$$\Rightarrow (\log\cos x)(\log\sin x) - (\log(\sin x))^2 + 4(\ln\sin x)(\log\cos x) - 4(\log(\cos x))^2 = \log\sin x \cdot \log\cos x$$

$$\Rightarrow (\log\sin x)^2 - 4(\log\sin x)(\log\cos x) + 4(\log\cos x)^2 = 0$$

$$\Rightarrow \quad (\log\sin x - 2\log\cos x)^2 = 0$$

$$\Rightarrow \quad \log\sin x = 2\log\cos x$$

$$\Rightarrow \quad \log\sin x = \log(\cos x)^2$$

$$\Rightarrow \quad \sin x = \cos^2 x$$

$$\Rightarrow \quad 1 - \sin^2 x = \sin x$$

$$\Rightarrow \quad \sin^2 x + \sin x - 1 = 0$$

$$\Rightarrow \quad \sin x = \frac{-1 \pm \sqrt{5}}{2}$$

But, $x \in \left(0, \frac{\pi}{2}\right)$

So, $\sin x > 0$

$\therefore \sin x = \frac{-1-\sqrt{5}}{2} < 0$ [rejected]

Hence, $\sin x = \frac{-1+\sqrt{5}}{2} = \frac{\alpha + \sqrt{\beta}}{2}$ [given]

Therefore, $\alpha + \beta = -1 + 5 = 4$

94. Given, m = Number of positive values of θ in $[-\pi, \pi]$

n = Number of negative values of θ in $[-\pi, \pi]$

$\because \cos 2\theta \cdot \cos\frac{\theta}{2} = \cos 3\theta \cdot \cos\left(\frac{9\theta}{2}\right)$

On multiplying by 2 both the side, we get

$$2\cos 2\theta \cdot \cos\frac{\theta}{2} = 2\cos 3\theta \cdot \cos\left(\frac{9\theta}{2}\right)$$

As we know that

$$2\cos A \cdot \cos B = \cos(A+B) + \cos(A-B)$$

So, $\cos\left(2\theta + \frac{\theta}{2}\right) + \cos\left(2\theta - \frac{\theta}{2}\right) = \cos\left(3\theta + \frac{9\theta}{2}\right) + \cos\left(3\theta - \frac{9\theta}{2}\right)$

$\Rightarrow \cos\frac{5\theta}{2} + \cos\frac{3\theta}{2} = \cos\frac{15\theta}{2} + \cos\left(-\frac{3\theta}{2}\right)$ [$\because \cos(-x) = \cos x$]

So, $\cos\frac{5\theta}{2} + \cos\frac{3\theta}{2} = \cos\frac{15\theta}{2} + \cos\frac{3\theta}{2}$

or $\cos\frac{5\theta}{2} = \cos\frac{15\theta}{2}$

$\because$ We know that, if $\cos\theta = \cos\alpha$,

then $\theta = 2n\pi \pm \alpha, n \in I$

So, $\frac{5\theta}{2} = 2n\pi \pm \frac{15\theta}{2}$

On multiplying by 2 both the sides, we get

$$5\theta = 4n\pi \pm 15\theta$$

Case I Taking (+)

$5\theta = 4n\pi + 15\theta \Rightarrow 10\theta = -4n\pi \Rightarrow \theta = \frac{-2n\pi}{5}$ ...(i)

Case II Taking (−)

$5\theta = 4n\pi - 15\theta \Rightarrow 20\theta = 4n\pi \Rightarrow \theta = \frac{n\pi}{5}$ ...(ii)

From Eqs. (i) and (ii), solution set of Eq. (i) is subset of solution set of Eq. (ii)

So, $\theta = \frac{n\pi}{5}$

For $n = 1, \theta = \frac{\pi}{5}$ $\quad n = -1, \theta = \frac{-\pi}{5}$

$n = 2, \theta = \frac{2\pi}{5}$ $\quad n = -2, \theta = \frac{-2\pi}{5}$

$n = 3, \theta = \frac{3\pi}{5}$ $\quad n = -3, \theta = \frac{-3\pi}{5}$

$n = 4, \theta = \frac{4\pi}{5}$ $\quad n = -4, \theta = \frac{4\pi}{5}$,

$n = 5, \theta = \frac{5\pi}{5}$ $\quad n = -5, \theta = \frac{-5\pi}{5}$

So, $m = 5$ and $n = 5$

Now, $mn = 5 \times 5 = 25$

95. Given, $\tan(\pi\cos\theta) + \tan(\pi\sin\theta) = 0$

$\Rightarrow \tan(\pi\cos\theta) = -\tan(\pi\sin\theta)$

$\Rightarrow \tan(\pi\cos\theta) = \tan(-\pi\sin\theta)$

$\Rightarrow \pi\cos\theta = n\pi - \pi\sin\theta$

$\Rightarrow \pi(\sin\theta + \cos\theta) = n\pi$

$\Rightarrow \sin\theta + \cos\theta = n, n \in I$

Since, $-\sqrt{2} \le \sin\theta + \cos\theta \le \sqrt{2}$

$\therefore$ Possible value of n are −1, 0, 1.

$\therefore \quad \theta \in \left\{0, \frac{\pi}{2}, \frac{3\pi}{4}, \frac{7\pi}{4}, \pi, \frac{3\pi}{2}\right\}$

$\therefore \quad \sum_{\theta \in S} \sin^2\left(\theta + \frac{\pi}{4}\right) = \sin^2\left(\frac{\pi}{4}\right) + \sin^2\left(\frac{\pi}{2} + \frac{\pi}{4}\right)$

$\sin^2\left(\frac{3\pi}{4} + \frac{\pi}{4}\right) + \sin^2\left(\frac{7\pi}{4} + \frac{\pi}{4}\right)$

$+\sin^2\left(\pi + \frac{\pi}{4}\right) + \sin^2\left(\frac{3\pi}{2} + \frac{\pi}{4}\right)$

$= \left(\frac{1}{\sqrt{2}}\right)^2 + \left(\frac{1}{\sqrt{2}}\right)^2 + (0)^2 + (0)^2 + \left(-\frac{1}{\sqrt{2}}\right)^2 + \left(\frac{-1}{\sqrt{2}}\right)^2$

$= \frac{1}{2} + \frac{1}{2} + 0 + 0 + \frac{1}{2} + \frac{1}{2} = 2$

96. Given expression is

$$2\cos\left(\frac{x^2 + x}{6}\right) = 4^x + 4^{-x}$$

LHS ≤ 2 and RHS ≥ 2 (AM $\ge$ GM)

Hence, LHS = 2 and RHS = 2

when $x = 0$, then $2\cos\left(\frac{x^2+x}{6}\right) = 2$ and $4^x + 4^{-x} = 2$

Therefore, $x = 0$ is the only possible solution.

97. Let $\alpha = \theta + (m-1)\frac{\pi}{6}$ and $\beta = \theta + m\frac{\pi}{6}$

So, $\beta - \alpha = \frac{\pi}{6}$ ...(i)

Here, $\sum_{m=1}^{9} \sec\alpha \cdot \sec\beta = \sum_{m=1}^{9} \frac{1}{\cos\alpha \cdot \cos\beta}$

Using Eq. (i),

$$2\sum_{m=1}^{9} \frac{\sin(\beta - \alpha)}{\cos\alpha \cdot \cos\beta} = 2\sum_{m=1}^{9} (\tan\beta - \tan\alpha)$$

$$= 2\sum_{m=1}^{9}\left(\tan\left(\theta + m\frac{\pi}{6}\right) - \tan\left(\theta + (m-1)\frac{\pi}{6}\right)\right)$$

$2\left(\tan\left(\theta + \frac{9\pi}{6}\right) - \tan\theta\right) = 2(-\cot\theta - \tan\theta) = -\frac{8}{\sqrt{3}}$ [given]

Therefore, $\tan\theta + \cot\theta = \frac{4}{\sqrt{3}}$

$\Rightarrow \tan\theta = \frac{1}{\sqrt{3}}$ or $\sqrt{3}$

So, $S = \left\{\frac{\pi}{6}, \frac{\pi}{3}\right\} \Rightarrow \sum_{\theta \in S} \theta = \frac{\pi}{6} + \frac{\pi}{3} = \frac{\pi}{2}$

98. Given equation

$$8^{2\sin^2\theta} + 8^{2-2\sin^2\theta} = 16$$

Let $8^{2\sin^2\theta} = y$

$\Rightarrow\ y + \dfrac{64}{y} = 16;\ y^2 - 16y' + 64 = 0$

Then, $\quad y = 8$

$\therefore\quad \sin^2\theta = \dfrac{1}{2}$

Take $n(S) + \sum_{\theta \in S}\left(\sec\left(\dfrac{\pi}{4} + 2\theta\right)\operatorname{cosec}\left(\dfrac{\pi}{4} + 2\theta\right)\right)$

$$= 4 + (-2) \times 4 = -4$$

99.

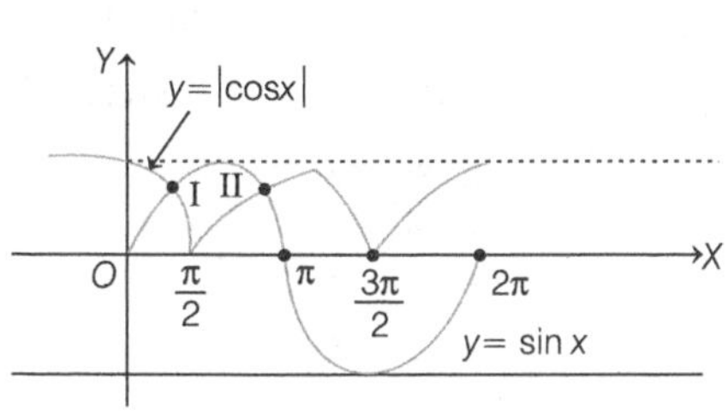

The number of solution of the equation $|\cos x| = \sin x$ $\forall,\ x \in [-4\pi, 4\pi]$ will be equal to 4 times the number of solutions of the same equation $|\cos x| = \sin x$ for $x \in [0, 2\pi]$.

Clearly, from the above graph, two solution of the equation $|\cos x| = \sin x$ in $[0, 2\pi]$.

Thus, total '8' solutions in $[-4\pi, 4\pi]$.

100. Given equation is

$$\sin\theta\tan\theta + \tan\theta = \sin 2\theta$$

$$\tan\theta\,(\sin\theta + 1) = \frac{2\tan\theta}{1 + \tan^2\theta}$$

When $\tan\theta = 0$, then $\theta = \pi, 0, -\pi$

$$(\sin\theta + 1) = 2\cdot\cos^2\theta = 2(1 + \sin\theta)(1 - \sin\theta)$$

Here, $\sin\theta = -1$ is not possible.

$\therefore\quad \sin\theta = \dfrac{1}{2}$ and $\theta = \dfrac{\pi}{6}, \dfrac{5\pi}{6}$

Therefore, total numbers of solutions are 5.

Put all solution in T,

$T = \cos 0 + \cos 2\pi + \cos 2\pi + \cos\dfrac{\pi}{3} + \cos\dfrac{5\pi}{3}$

So, $T = 4$

Required solutions are $T + n(S) = 9$.

101. Given equation is

$\cos\left(\dfrac{\pi}{3} + x\right)\cos\left(\dfrac{\pi}{3} - x\right) = \dfrac{1}{4}\cos^2 2x,\ x \in [-3\pi, 3\pi]$

$\Rightarrow 4\left(\cos^2\left(\dfrac{\pi}{3}\right) - \sin^2 x\right) = \cos^2 2x$

$\Rightarrow\quad 4\left(\dfrac{1}{4} - \sin^2 x\right) = \cos^2 2x \ \Rightarrow\ 1 - 4\sin^2 x = \cos^2 2x$

$\Rightarrow\quad 1 - 2(1 - \cos 2x) = \cos^2 2x \qquad \left[\because \sin^2 x = \dfrac{1 - \cos 2x}{2}\right]$

$\Rightarrow -1 + 2\cos 2x = \cos^2 2x$

Let $\quad \cos 2x = t$

$\Rightarrow t^2 - 2t + 1 = 0 \Rightarrow (t-1)^2 = 0 \Rightarrow t = 1$

Then, $\cos 2x = 1$

$$2x = 2n\pi,\ n \in I$$

$\Rightarrow\quad x = n\pi,\ n \in I$

$\Rightarrow\quad n = -3, -2, -1, 0, 1, 2, 3$

Therefore, there are 7 solutions.

102. Given, $3\cos^2 2\theta + 6\cos 2\theta - 10\cos^2\theta + 5 = 0$

$\Rightarrow 3\cos^2 2\theta + 6\cos 2\theta - \dfrac{10(1 + \cos 2\theta)}{2} + 5 = 0$

$\Rightarrow\quad 3\cos^2 2\theta + \cos 2\theta = 0$

$\Rightarrow\quad \cos 2\theta = 0$ or $\cos 2\theta = -\dfrac{1}{3}$

$\because\quad \theta \in [-4\pi, 4\pi]$

$\Rightarrow\quad 2\theta = (2n+1)\cdot\dfrac{\pi}{2}$

$\therefore\ \theta = \pm\dfrac{\pi}{4}, \pm\dfrac{3\pi}{4} \ldots \pm\dfrac{15\pi}{4}$

Similarly, $\cos 2\theta = -\dfrac{1}{3}$ gives 16 solution for $\theta \in [-4\pi, 4\pi]$.

So, number of elements in the set is 32.

103. Given, that

$2\cos x\left(4\sin\left(\dfrac{\pi}{4} + x\right)\sin\left(\dfrac{\pi}{4} - x\right) - 1\right) = 1$

$[\because \sin(A+B)\cdot\sin(A-B) = \sin^2 A - \sin^2 B]$

$\Rightarrow 2\cos x\left(4\left(\sin^2\dfrac{\pi}{4} - \sin^2 x\right) - 1\right) = 1$

$\Rightarrow\quad 2\cos x\left(4\left(\dfrac{1}{2} - \sin^2 x\right) - 1\right) = 1$

$\Rightarrow\quad 2\cos x\,(2 - 4\sin^2 x - 1) = 1$

$\Rightarrow\quad 2\cos x(1 - 4\sin^2 x) = 1$

$\Rightarrow\quad 2\cos x\,(4\cos^2 x - 3) = 1$

$\Rightarrow\quad 4\cos^3 x - 3\cos x = \dfrac{1}{2}$

$\Rightarrow\quad \cos 3x = \dfrac{1}{2} = \cos\dfrac{\pi}{3}$

$\Rightarrow\quad 3x = 2n\pi \pm \dfrac{\pi}{3},\ n \in I$

$\Rightarrow\quad x = \dfrac{\pi}{9}, \dfrac{5\pi}{9}, \dfrac{7\pi}{9} \qquad [\because x \in [0, \pi]]$

$\therefore\ $ Number of solutions $= n = 3$

and sum of all solutions $= S = \dfrac{\pi}{9} + \dfrac{5\pi}{9} + \dfrac{7\pi}{9} = \dfrac{13\pi}{9}$

104. Given, $3\sin x + 4\cos x = k + 1$ has a solution, then

$$5\left(\frac{3}{5}\sin x + \frac{4}{5}\cos x\right) = k + 1$$

$\Rightarrow\quad 5\sin(x + \alpha) = k + 1,$

where $\alpha = \sin^{-1}\dfrac{4}{5}$

$\because\ -1 \le \sin(x+\alpha) \le 1$

$\Rightarrow -5 \le k+1 \le 5$

$\Rightarrow -6 \le k \le 4$

Therefore, the range of k is $[-6, 4]$

So, there are 11 integers in the given interval.

105. The expression, $\cos^4\theta + \sin^4\theta$

$$= (\cos^2\theta + \sin^2\theta)^2 - 2\sin^2\theta\cos^2\theta$$

$$= 1 - \frac{[\sin^2(2\theta)]}{2}$$

$\because \quad \sin^2(2\theta) \in [0, 1]$

$\Rightarrow \quad -\frac{1}{2}\sin^2(2\theta) \in \left[-\frac{1}{2}, 0\right] \Rightarrow 1 - \frac{1}{2}\sin^2(2\theta) \in \left[\frac{1}{2}, 1\right]$

Now, as $\cos^4\theta + \sin^4\theta + \lambda = 0$

$\Rightarrow \quad \lambda = -(\cos^4\theta + \sin^4\theta)$

$\Rightarrow \lambda \in [-1, -1/2]$ for real solution of the given equation $\cos^4\theta + \sin^4\theta + \lambda = 0$ for θ.

Hence, option (b) is correct.

106. The given trigonometric equation is

$$\cos 2x + \alpha \sin x = 2\alpha - 7$$

$\Rightarrow \quad 1 - 2\sin^2 x + \alpha \sin x = 2\alpha - 7$

$[\because \cos 2x = 1 - 2\sin^2 x]$

$\Rightarrow \quad 2\sin^2 x - \alpha \sin x + 2\alpha - 8 = 0$

$\Rightarrow \quad 2(\sin^2 x - 4) - \alpha(\sin x - 2) = 0$

$\Rightarrow \quad 2(\sin x - 2)(\sin x + 2) - \alpha(\sin x - 2) = 0$

$\Rightarrow \quad (\sin x - 2)(2\sin x + 4 - \alpha) = 0$

$\therefore \quad 2\sin x + 4 - \alpha = 0 \quad [\because \sin x - 2 \ne 0]$

$\Rightarrow \quad \sin x = \frac{\alpha - 4}{2} \quad$ ...(i)

Now, as we know $-1 \le \sin x \le 1$

$\therefore \quad -1 \le \frac{\alpha - 4}{2} \le 1 \quad$ [from Eq. (i)]

$\Rightarrow \quad -2 \le \alpha - 4 \le 2$

$\Rightarrow \quad 2 \le \alpha \le 6$

$\Rightarrow \quad \alpha \in [2, 6]$

107. We have, $\theta \in [-2\pi, 2\pi]$

and $\quad 2\cos^2\theta + 3\sin\theta = 0$

$\Rightarrow \quad 2(1 - \sin^2\theta) + 3\sin\theta = 0$

$\Rightarrow \quad 2\sin^2\theta - 3\sin\theta - 2 = 0$

$\Rightarrow \quad (\sin\theta - 2)(2\sin\theta + 1) = 0$

$\therefore \quad \sin\theta = -\frac{1}{2} \quad [\because (\sin\theta - 2) \ne 0]$

$\therefore \quad \theta = 2\pi - \frac{\pi}{6}, -\pi + \frac{\pi}{6}, -\frac{\pi}{6}, \pi + \frac{\pi}{6} \quad [\because \theta \in [-2\pi, 2\pi]]$

Now, sum of all solutions $= 2\pi - \frac{\pi}{6} - \pi + \frac{\pi}{6} - \frac{\pi}{6} + \pi + \frac{\pi}{6}$

$$= 2\pi$$

108. We have, $8\cos x\left(\cos\left(\frac{\pi}{6} + x\right)\cos\left(\frac{\pi}{6} - x\right) - \frac{1}{2}\right) = 1$

$\Rightarrow \quad 8\cos x\left(\cos^2\frac{\pi}{6} - \sin^2 x - \frac{1}{2}\right) = 1$

$\Rightarrow \quad 8\cos x\left(\frac{3}{4} - \sin^2 x - \frac{1}{2}\right) = 1$

$\Rightarrow \quad 8\cos x\left(\frac{3}{4} - \frac{1}{2} - 1 + \cos^2 x\right) = 1$

$\Rightarrow \quad 8\cos x\left(\frac{-3 + 4\cos^2 x}{4}\right) = 1$

$\Rightarrow \quad 2(4\cos^3 x - 3\cos x) = 1$

$\Rightarrow \quad 2\cos 3x = 1$

$\Rightarrow \quad \cos 3x = \frac{1}{2}$

$\Rightarrow \quad 3x = \frac{\pi}{3}, \frac{5\pi}{3}, \frac{7\pi}{3} \quad [0 \le 3x \le 3\pi]$

$\Rightarrow \quad x = \frac{\pi}{9}, \frac{5\pi}{9}, \frac{7\pi}{9}$

Sum $= \frac{\pi}{9} + \frac{5\pi}{9} + \frac{7\pi}{9} = \frac{13\pi}{9}$

$\Rightarrow \quad k\pi = \frac{13\pi}{9}$

Hence, $\quad k = \frac{13}{9}$

109. Given, $\quad 5(\tan^2 x - \cos^2 x) = 2\cos 2x + 9$

$\Rightarrow \quad 5\left(\frac{2\sin^2 x}{2\cos^2 x} - \cos^2 x\right) = 2\cos 2x + 9$

$\Rightarrow 5\left(\frac{1 - \cos 2x}{1 + \cos 2x} - \frac{1 + \cos 2x}{2}\right) = 2\cos 2x + 9$

Put $\cos 2x = y$, we have

$$5\left(\frac{1-y}{1+y} - \frac{1+y}{2}\right) = 2y + 9$$

$\Rightarrow \quad 5(2 - 2y - 1 - y^2 - 2y) = 2(1+y)(2y+9)$

$\Rightarrow \quad 5(1 - 4y - y^2) = 2(2y + 9 + 2y^2 + 9y)$

$\Rightarrow \quad 5 - 20y - 5y^2 = 22y + 18 + 4y^2$

$\Rightarrow \quad 9y^2 + 42y + 13 = 0$

$\Rightarrow \quad 9y^2 + 3y + 39y + 13 = 0$

$\Rightarrow \quad (3y+1)(3y+13) = 0$

$\Rightarrow \quad y = -\frac{1}{3}, -\frac{13}{3}$

$\therefore \quad \cos 2x = -\frac{1}{3}, -\frac{13}{3}$

$\therefore \quad \cos 2x = -\frac{1}{3} \quad \left[\because \cos 2x \ne -\frac{13}{3}\right]$

Now, $\cos 4x = 2\cos^2 2x - 1$

$$= 2\left(-\frac{1}{3}\right)^2 - 1 = \frac{2}{9} - 1 = -\frac{7}{9}$$

Exercise 2 - JEE Advanced Pattern

1. Given, $3^{2(1+\tan^2 x)} + 1 - 10 \cdot 3^{\tan^2 x} = 0$

$\Rightarrow \quad 3^2 \cdot (3^{\tan^2 x})^2 - 10 \cdot 3^{\tan^2 x} + 1 = 0$

Let $3^{\tan^2 x} = t$.

Then, the equation reduces to $9t^2 - 10t + 1 = 0$.

So, $t = \frac{1}{9}$ and $t = 1$

Hence, $3^{\tan^2 x} = 3^{-2}$ and $3^{\tan^2 x} = 1$

Now, $\tan^2 x = -2$ gives no solution and $\tan^2 x = 0$ gives three solutions in $[0, 2\pi]$.

2. $\frac{1 - \sin x + \ldots + (-1)^n \sin^n x + \ldots}{1 + \sin x + \ldots + \sin^n x + \ldots} = \frac{1 - \cos 2x}{1 + \cos 2x}$

$\Rightarrow \quad \frac{1}{1 + \sin x} \times \frac{1 - \sin x}{1} = \frac{2\sin^2 x}{2\cos^2 x}$

$\Rightarrow \quad \cos^2 x - \cos^2 x \sin x = \sin^2 x + \sin^3 x$

$[\because \sin x + 1 \neq 0]$

$\Rightarrow \quad (1 - \sin^2 x)(1 - \sin x) = \sin^2 x + \sin^3 x$

$\Rightarrow \quad 2\sin^2 x + \sin x - 1 = 0$

$\Rightarrow \quad \sin x = -1 \text{ or } \sin x = \frac{1}{2}$

Since, $\sin x \neq -1$, $\sin x = \frac{1}{2} = \sin \frac{\pi}{6}$

$\Rightarrow \quad x = n\pi + (-1)^n \left(\frac{\pi}{6}\right)$

3. $\frac{\sin(xy)}{\cos(xy)} = y$ or $\sin(xy) = xy$ or $xy = 0$

$\therefore \quad x = 0$ or $y = 0$

But $x = 0$ is not possible.

$\therefore y = 0$ and $x = 1$, i.e. $(1, 0)$

4. $16(\sin^5 x + \cos^5 x) - 11(\sin x + \cos x) = 0$

$\Rightarrow (\sin x + \cos x)\{16(\sin^4 x - \sin^3 x \cos x + \sin^2 x \cos^2 x$

$- \sin x \cos^3 x + \cos^4 x) - 11\} = 0$

$\Rightarrow \quad (\sin x + \cos x)\{16(1 - \sin^2 x \cos^2 x - \sin x \cos x) - 11\} = 0$

$\Rightarrow \quad (\sin x + \cos x)(4\sin x \cos x - 1)(4\sin x \cos x + 5) = 0$

As $4\sin x \cos x + 5 \neq 0$, we have

$\sin x + \cos x = 0$ or $4\sin x \cos x - 1 = 0$

$\therefore \quad \tan x = -1$ or $\sin 2x = \frac{1}{2}$

So, the required values are

$\frac{\pi}{12}, \frac{5\pi}{12}, \frac{9\pi}{12}, \frac{13\pi}{12}, \frac{17\pi}{12}, \frac{21\pi}{12}$

So, there are 6 solutions in $[0, 2\pi]$.

5. Let $\log_{\cos x} \sin x = t$, then the given equation is $t + \frac{1}{t} = 2$

or $\quad (t-1)^2 = 0$ or $t = 1$

or $\quad \log_{\cos x} \sin x = 1$ or $\sin x = \cos x$

$\Rightarrow \quad \tan x = 1$

or $\quad x = \frac{\pi}{4}$

6. The only possibility is $\sin \gamma = \cos \alpha = -1$

$\Rightarrow \quad \gamma = \frac{3\pi}{2}, \alpha = \pi$

$f(x)|_{\min} = f(\beta) = \beta - \alpha + 0 + \gamma - \beta = \gamma - \alpha$

$= \frac{3\pi}{2} - \pi = \frac{\pi}{2}$

$f(x) \geq \frac{\pi}{2}$

Therefore, the least integral value of $f(x)$ is 2.

7. $5^{1/2} + 5^{1/2 + \log_5 (\sin x)} = 15^{1/2 + \log_{15} (\cos x)}$

$\Rightarrow \quad 5^{1/2} + 5^{1/2} \cdot 5^{\log_5 (\sin x)} = 15^{1/2} \cdot 15^{\log_{15} \cos x}$

$\Rightarrow \quad 5^{1/2} + 5^{1/2} \cdot \sin x = 15^{1/2} \cdot \cos x$

$\Rightarrow \quad 1 + \sin x = \sqrt{3} \cos x$

$\Rightarrow \quad \frac{\sqrt{3}}{2} \cos x - \frac{\sin x}{2} = \frac{1}{2} \Rightarrow \cos\left(x + \frac{\pi}{6}\right) = \cos \frac{\pi}{3}$

$\Rightarrow \quad x + \frac{\pi}{6} = 2n\pi \pm \frac{\pi}{3}, n \in z$

$\Rightarrow \quad x = 2n\pi - \frac{\pi}{2}, 2n\pi + \frac{\pi}{6}, n \in z$

But we must have $\sin x, \cos x > 0$

$\therefore \quad x = 2n\pi + \frac{\pi}{6}, n \in z$

8. We have, $\quad 3 + 3\cos\theta = 2 - 2\cos^2\theta$

$\Rightarrow \quad 2\cos^2\theta + 3\cos\theta + 1 = 0$

$\Rightarrow \quad (2\cos\theta + 1)(\cos\theta + 1) = 0$

$\therefore \quad \cos\theta = -1$ or $\cos\theta = -\frac{1}{2}$

If $\cos\theta = -1$, then $\theta = \pi, 3\pi, 5\pi, 7\pi, 9\pi, \ldots$

If $\cos\theta = -\frac{1}{2}$, then $\theta = \frac{2\pi}{3}, \frac{4\pi}{3}, \frac{8\pi}{3}, \frac{10\pi}{3}, \frac{14\pi}{3}, \ldots$

Solutions in increasing order are

$\frac{2\pi}{3} < \pi < \frac{4\pi}{3} < \frac{8\pi}{3} < 3\pi < \frac{10\pi}{3} < \frac{14\pi}{3} < 5\pi, \ldots$

$\therefore \quad \theta_3 + \theta_7 = \frac{4\pi}{3} + \frac{14\pi}{3} = 6\pi$

9. We have, $\log_{\cos x}\left(\frac{\sqrt{3}}{2} \sin x\right) - \log_{\cos x}(\tan x) = 2$

$\Rightarrow \quad \log_{\cos x}\left(\frac{\sqrt{3}}{2} \cos x\right) = 2$

$\Rightarrow \quad \frac{\sqrt{3}}{2} \cos x = \cos^2 x$

$\Rightarrow \quad \cos x\left(\cos x - \frac{\sqrt{3}}{2}\right) = 0$

$\therefore \quad x = \frac{\pi}{6} \quad \left(x = \frac{\pi}{2} \text{ is rejected}\right)$

10. Since, the system has a non-trivial solution, the determinant of coefficients is 0.

Thus, $\quad \begin{vmatrix} \sin 3\theta & -1 & 1 \\ \cos 2\theta & 4 & 3 \\ 2 & 7 & 7 \end{vmatrix} = 0$

or $\sin 3\theta\,(28-21)-\cos 2\theta\,(-7-7)+2(-3-4)=0$

or $\sin 3\theta + 2\cos 2\theta - 2 = 0$

or $(3\sin\theta - 4\sin^3\theta) + 2(1-2\sin^2\theta) - 2 = 0$

or $4\sin^3\theta + 4\sin^2\theta - 3\sin\theta = 0$

or $\sin\theta\,(2\sin\theta - 1)(2\sin\theta + 3) = 0$

or $\sin\theta = 0, \frac{1}{2}$

$\therefore \quad \theta = n\pi$ or $n\pi + (-1)^n \frac{\pi}{6}, \forall\, n \in z$

11. $x^2 + 12 + 3\sin(a+bx) + 6x = 0$

$\Rightarrow (x+3)^2 + 3 + 3\sin(a+bx) = 0$

$\Rightarrow (x+3)^2 + 3 = -3\sin(a+bx)$

LHS ≥ 3 but RHS ≤ 3

So, solution exists only if LHS = RHS = 3

$\therefore \quad x = -3$ and $\sin(a+bx) = -1$

$\Rightarrow \sin(a-3b) = -1$

$\Rightarrow a - 3b = (4n-1)\frac{\pi}{2}, n \in z$

12. $2\sin^2\left(x-\frac{\pi}{3}\right) - 5\sin\left(x-\frac{\pi}{3}\right) + 2 < 0$

$\Rightarrow \left(2\sin\left(x-\frac{\pi}{3}\right)-1\right)\cdot\left(\sin\left(x-\frac{\pi}{3}\right)-2\right) < 0$

$\Rightarrow \frac{1}{2} < \sin\left(x-\frac{\pi}{3}\right) < 2$

$\Rightarrow \frac{1}{2} < \sin\left(x-\frac{\pi}{3}\right) \leq 2$

$\Rightarrow \frac{1}{2} < \sin\left(x-\frac{\pi}{3}\right) \leq 1$

$\therefore \quad x - \frac{\pi}{3} \in \left(2n\pi + \frac{\pi}{6}, 2n\pi + \frac{5\pi}{6}\right)$

$x \in \left(2n\pi + \frac{\pi}{2}, 2n\pi + \frac{7\pi}{6}\right), n \in Z$

13. $[\sin x + \cos x] = 3 + [-\sin x] + [-\cos x]$

The maximum value of the LHS is 1 and the minimum of RHS is also 1. Thus,

$[\sin x + \cos x] = 3 + [-\sin x] + [-\cos x] = 1$

or $[\sin x + \cos x] = 1, [-\sin x] = -1, [-\cos x] = -1$

$[\sin x + \cos x] = 1$

$\therefore \quad 1 \leq \sin x + \cos x \leq \sqrt{2}$

$\therefore \quad x \in \left[0, \frac{\pi}{2}\right]$ ...(i)

$[-\sin x] = -1$

$\therefore \quad -1 \leq -\sin x < 0$

$0 < \sin x \leq 1$ ...(ii)

$[-\cos x] = -1$

$\therefore \quad -1 \leq -\cos x < 0$

$\therefore \quad 0 < \cos x \leq 1$ ...(iii)

From Eqs. (i), (ii), (iii), $x \in \left(0, \frac{\pi}{2}\right)$

14. If solution lies on the line $y = 3x$, then $3\sin 3x + 12\sin^3 x = a$ should have real solution.

$\Rightarrow 3(3\sin x - 4\sin^3 x) + 12\sin^3 x = a$

$\Rightarrow \quad \sin x = \frac{a}{9}$

Hence, for no solution, $a > 9$ or $a < -9$

15. $2\cos 2x - \sqrt{3}\sin x = \cos x, (-\pi < x < \pi) - \left\{0, \pm\frac{\pi}{2}\right\}$

$\Rightarrow \sqrt{3}\sin x + \cos x - 2\cos 2x = 0$

Multiplying and dividing by $\sqrt{a^2+b^2}$, i.e. $\sqrt{3+1} = 2$, we get

$2\left(\frac{\sqrt{3}}{2}\sin x + \frac{1}{2}\cos x\right) - 2\cos 2x = 0$

$\Rightarrow \quad \cos\left(x - \frac{\pi}{3}\right) = \cos 2x$

$\therefore \quad 2x = 2n\pi \pm \left(x - \frac{\pi}{3}\right)$

$\Rightarrow \quad 2x = 2n\pi + x - \frac{\pi}{3}$

or $\quad 2x = 2n\pi - x + \frac{\pi}{3}$

$\Rightarrow \quad x = 2n\pi - \frac{\pi}{3}$

or $\quad 3x = 2n\pi + \frac{\pi}{3}$

or $\quad x = \frac{2n\pi}{3} + \frac{\pi}{9}$

$\therefore \quad x = -\frac{\pi}{3}$ or $x = \frac{\pi}{9}, -\frac{5\pi}{9}, \frac{7\pi}{9}$

Hence, the total number of solutions is 4.

16. We have, $4\sin^4 x + \cos^4 x = 1$

$\Rightarrow \quad 4\sin^4 x = 1 - \cos^4 x$

$\Rightarrow \quad 4\sin^4 x - [(1-\cos^2 x)(1+\cos^2 x)] = 0$

$\Rightarrow \quad 4\sin^4 x - [\sin^2 x(1+\cos^2 x)] = 0$

$\Rightarrow \quad \sin^2 x[4\sin^2 x - (1+\cos^2 x)] = 0$

$\Rightarrow \quad \sin^2 x[4\sin^2 x - (1+1-\sin^2 x)] = 0$

$\Rightarrow \quad \sin^2 x(5\sin^2 x - 2) = 0$

Either $\sin x = 0$ or $\sin x = \pm\sqrt{\frac{2}{5}}$

$\Rightarrow \quad x = n\pi$ or $x = n\pi \pm (-1)^n \alpha$

where $\alpha = \sin^{-1}\sqrt{\frac{2}{5}}$ and $n \in I$

17. Here, $\cos\left(\frac{\alpha}{2} - \frac{\pi}{4}\right) = \frac{\sqrt{5}+1}{4} - \frac{\sqrt{5}-1}{4} = \frac{1}{2}$

$\Rightarrow \quad \frac{\alpha}{2} - \frac{\pi}{4} = 2n\pi \pm \frac{\pi}{3}$

$\therefore \quad \alpha = 4n\pi + \frac{\pi}{2} \pm \frac{2\pi}{3} = 4n\pi + \frac{7\pi}{6}, 4n\pi - \frac{\pi}{6}$

For, $n = 0, \alpha = \frac{7\pi}{6}, -\frac{\pi}{6}$

18. The given equation can be written as

$$\frac{\left(\frac{\sqrt{3}-1}{2\sqrt{2}}\right)}{\sin x}+\frac{\left(\frac{\sqrt{3}+1}{2\sqrt{2}}\right)}{\cos x}=2$$

$$\Rightarrow \quad \frac{\sin\frac{\pi}{12}}{\sin x}+\frac{\cos\frac{\pi}{12}}{\cos x}=2$$

$$\Rightarrow \quad \sin\left(\frac{\pi}{12}+x\right)=\sin 2x$$

$$\therefore \quad \frac{\pi}{12}+x=2x \text{ or } \frac{\pi}{12}+x=\pi-2x$$

$$\Rightarrow \quad x=\frac{\pi}{12} \text{ or } \frac{11\pi}{36}$$

19. $f(x)=\left(\cos a_1+\frac{\cos a_2}{2}+\dots+\frac{\cos a_n}{2^{n-1}}\right)\cos x$

$$-\left(\frac{\sin a_1}{1}+\frac{\sin a_2}{2}+\dots+\frac{\sin a_n}{2^{n-1}}\right)\sin x$$

$$\Rightarrow \quad f(x)=A\cos x-B\sin x$$

Now, $\quad f(x_1)=f(x_2)=0$

$$\Rightarrow \quad \left.\begin{array}{l}A\cos x_1-B\sin x_1=0\\ A\cos x_2-B\sin x_2=0\end{array}\right\}$$

$$\Rightarrow \quad \tan x_1=\tan x_2$$

$$\Rightarrow \quad x_1=n\pi+x_2$$

$$\Rightarrow \quad x_1-x_2=n\pi$$

20. The given equation can be written as

$$\begin{vmatrix}1+\cos^2\theta & \sin^2\theta & 4\sin 4\theta\\ -1 & 1 & 0\\ 0 & -1 & 1\end{vmatrix}=0$$

[applying $R_3\to R_3-R_2$ and $R_2\to R_2-R_1$]

$$\Rightarrow \quad \begin{vmatrix}2 & \sin^2\theta & 4\sin 4\theta\\ 0 & 1 & 0\\ -1 & -1 & 1\end{vmatrix}=0 \quad [\text{applying } C_1\to C_1+C_2]$$

$$\Rightarrow \quad 2+4\sin 4\theta=0$$

$$\Rightarrow \quad \sin 4\theta=-\frac{1}{2}$$

$$\Rightarrow \quad 4\theta=n\pi+(-1)^n\left(-\frac{\pi}{6}\right)$$

$$\Rightarrow \quad \theta=\frac{n\pi}{4}+(-1)^{n+1}\frac{\pi}{24}$$

We have to choose values of θ s.t $0<\theta<\frac{\pi}{2}$

$$\therefore \quad \theta=\frac{7\pi}{24},\frac{11\pi}{24}$$

21. $\sin\alpha+\left[\frac{\sin 2x}{2}\right]_{\alpha}^{2\alpha}=0$

$\Rightarrow \sin\alpha(1+\cos 3\alpha)=0$

$\Rightarrow \quad \alpha=0,\ \cos 3\alpha=-1$

$3\alpha=-\pi,-3\pi \Rightarrow \alpha=-\frac{\pi}{3},-\pi$

22. Let $\quad 81^{\sin^2 x}=y \quad$ ...(i)

then $\quad 81^{\cos^2 x}=81^{(1-\sin^2 x)}$

$$=81.81^{-\sin^2 x}=81\cdot y^{-1} \quad \text{...(ii)}$$

So, the given can be written as

$$y^2-30y+81=0$$

$$\Rightarrow \quad y=3 \text{ or } y=27$$

Using Eqs. (i) and (ii)

$\Rightarrow$ Either $81^{\sin^2 x}=3$ or $81^{\sin^2 x}=27$

$$\Rightarrow \quad 4\sin^2 x=1 \text{ or } 4\sin^2 x=3$$

$$\Rightarrow \quad \sin x=\frac{1}{2} \text{ or } \sin x=\frac{\sqrt{3}}{2} \quad \left[\text{as } 0\le x\le\frac{\pi}{2}\right]$$

$$\Rightarrow \quad x=\frac{\pi}{6} \text{ or } x=\frac{\pi}{3} \text{ are only the solution.}$$

23. $\log_{\sqrt{3}}\tan\theta\left[\sqrt{\frac{\log_{\sqrt{3}}3}{\log_{\sqrt{3}}\tan\theta}+3\log_{\sqrt{3}}\sqrt{3}}\right]=-1$

$$\Rightarrow \quad \log_{\sqrt{3}}\tan\theta\left[\sqrt{\frac{2}{\log_{\sqrt{3}}\tan\theta}+3}\right]=-1$$

Let $\quad \log_{\sqrt{3}}\tan\theta=y$

$$\Rightarrow \quad y\sqrt{\frac{2}{y}+3}=-1$$

$$\Rightarrow \quad \sqrt{\frac{2}{y}+3}=-\frac{1}{y}$$

$$\Rightarrow \quad \frac{2}{y}+3=\frac{1}{y^2}$$

or $\quad y^2(2+3y)=y$

$$\Rightarrow \quad y[3y^2+2y-1]=0$$

$$\because \quad y<0$$

$$\Rightarrow \quad y(3y-1)(y+1)=0$$

$$\Rightarrow \quad y=-1 \quad [\because y \text{ cannot be positive}]$$

$$\Rightarrow \quad \log_{\sqrt{3}}\tan\theta=-1$$

$$\Rightarrow \quad \tan\theta=\frac{1}{\sqrt{3}}$$

$$\therefore \quad \theta=\frac{\pi}{6} \text{ and } \frac{7\pi}{6}$$

$\therefore$ There are two values of θ in $[0,2\pi]$

24. $(t-[|\sin x|])!=3!5!7!$

If $x=n\pi+\frac{\pi}{2}\ (n\in I)$

then $(t-1)!=3!\,5!\,7!$

$$\Rightarrow \quad (t-1)!=10!$$

$$\Rightarrow \quad t-1=10$$

$$\Rightarrow \quad t=11$$

If $x\ne n\pi+\frac{\pi}{2}\ (n\in I)$, then

$$(t-0)!=10!$$

$$\Rightarrow \quad t=10$$

25. $\because [\sin x]+[\sqrt{2}\cos x]=-3,\ x\in[0,2\pi]$

It is possible only when $[\sin x]=-1$ and $[\sqrt{2}\cos x]=-2$

If $[\sin x]=-1 \Rightarrow -1\le \sin x<0$

$\therefore \quad x\in(\pi,2\pi)$

If $[\sqrt{2}\cos x]=-2$

$\Rightarrow \quad -2\le\sqrt{2}\cos x<-1 \Rightarrow -\sqrt{2}\le\cos x<-\frac{1}{\sqrt{2}}$

$\Rightarrow \quad -1\le\cos x<-\frac{1}{\sqrt{2}} \Rightarrow x\in\left[\pi,\frac{5\pi}{4}\right)$

From Eqs. (i) and (ii), we get $x\in\left(\pi,\frac{5\pi}{4}\right)$

26. We know that

$[x+I]=[x]+I$, if I is an integer.

then, $\quad y=\frac{1}{3}[\sin\theta+[\sin\theta+[\sin\theta]]]$

$=\frac{1}{3}[\sin\theta+[\sin\theta]+[\sin\theta]]$

$=\frac{1}{3}([\sin\theta]+[\sin\theta]+[\sin\theta])$

$\Rightarrow \quad y=[\sin\theta]$ ...(i)

$\Rightarrow \quad [y+[y]]=2\cos\theta$

$\Rightarrow \quad [y]+[y]=2\cos\theta$

$\Rightarrow \quad [y]=\cos\theta$ ...(ii)

$\because \quad -1\le\sin\theta\le1$, then three cases arise:

Case I If $-1\le\sin\theta<0$, then $[\sin\theta]=-1$

$y=-1$ put in Eq. (ii), then

$\cos\theta=[-1]=-1$

$\Rightarrow \quad \sin\theta=0$

But $\quad -1\le\sin\theta<0$

Hence, this case is not possible.

Case II If $0\le\sin\theta<1$, then $[\sin\theta]=0$

and $\quad y=0$ [from Eq. (i)]

Put in Eq.(ii), $\cos\theta=0$

$\Rightarrow \quad \sin\theta=1$

But we have $0\le\sin\theta<1$, so this case is not possible.

Case III If $\sin\theta=1$, then $[\sin\theta]=1$

$y=1$ put in Eq. (ii), $\cos\theta=1 \Rightarrow \sin\theta=0$

But, we have $\sin\theta=1$, so this case is not possible.

$\therefore$ Number of solutions is 0.

27. Here, $3\cos2\theta=1 \Rightarrow 3(2\cos^2\theta-1)=1$

$\Rightarrow \quad 6\cos^2\theta=4 \Rightarrow \cos^2\theta=\frac{2}{3}$

Now, $\tan^2\theta=\frac{\sin^2\theta}{\cos^2\theta}=\frac{1-\cos^2\theta}{\frac{2}{3}}=\frac{1-\frac{2}{3}}{\frac{2}{3}}=\frac{1}{2}$

$\therefore \quad 32\tan^8\theta=2\cos^2\alpha-3\cos\alpha$

$\Rightarrow \quad 32\left(\frac{1}{2}\right)^4=2\cos^2\alpha-3\cos\alpha$

$\Rightarrow \quad 2\cos^2\alpha-3\cos\alpha-2=0$

$\Rightarrow \quad (2\cos\alpha+1)(\cos\alpha-2)=0$

$\Rightarrow \quad 2\cos\alpha+1=0$ or $\cos\alpha-2=0$

$\Rightarrow \quad \cos\alpha=-\frac{1}{2}$ or $\cos\alpha=2$ (impossible)

$\Rightarrow \quad \alpha=2n\pi\pm\left(\pi-\frac{\pi}{3}\right)=2n\pi\pm\frac{2\pi}{3}, n\in Z$

28. Here, $\quad \cot\frac{\theta}{2}-\cot\theta=\operatorname{cosec}\frac{\theta}{2}$

$\Rightarrow \quad \frac{\cos\frac{\theta}{2}}{\sin\frac{\theta}{2}}-\frac{\cos\theta}{\sin\theta}=\operatorname{cosec}\left(\frac{\theta}{2}\right)$

$\Rightarrow \quad \frac{2\cos^2\frac{\theta}{2}-\cos\theta}{\sin\theta}=\operatorname{cosec}\frac{\theta}{2}$

$\Rightarrow 2\cos^2\frac{\theta}{2}-\left(\cos^2\frac{\theta}{2}-\sin^2\frac{\theta}{2}\right)=\sin\theta\,.\operatorname{cosec}\frac{\theta}{2}$

$\Rightarrow \quad 1=\operatorname{cosec}\frac{\theta}{2}\,.\sin\theta$

$\Rightarrow \quad \sin\theta=\sin\frac{\theta}{2} \Rightarrow \sin\frac{\theta}{2}\left(2\cos\frac{\theta}{2}-1\right)=0$

$\Rightarrow \quad \sin\frac{\theta}{2}=0$ or $\cos\frac{\theta}{2}=\frac{1}{2}$

$\Rightarrow \quad \theta=2n\pi$ or $\theta=2\left(2n\pi\pm\frac{\pi}{3}\right)$

For $\theta=2n\pi$, $\cot\frac{\theta}{2}$ and $\cot\theta$ are undefined.

Hence, do not satisfy the given equation.

$\therefore$ The only solution is $\theta=4n\pi\pm\frac{2\pi}{3}$

29. For non-trivial solution

$$\begin{vmatrix}\sin\theta & -2\cos\theta & -a\\ -1 & 1 & 1\\ 1 & 2 & 1\end{vmatrix}=0$$

$\Rightarrow \quad \sin\theta+4\cos\theta=3a$

$\Rightarrow \quad -\frac{\sqrt{17}}{3}\le a\le\frac{\sqrt{17}}{3}$

So, 3 integral values.

30. We know, $a+b+c=0, \Leftrightarrow a^3+b^3+c^3=3abc$

Put $a=\sin x$, $b=\cos x$, $c=1$

$1+\sin^3x+\cos^3x=3\sin x\,.\cos x=\frac{3}{2}\sin2x$

$\Rightarrow \quad a+b+c=0$

$\Rightarrow \quad 1+\sin x+\cos x=0$

$\Rightarrow \quad \sqrt{2}\cos\left(x-\frac{\pi}{4}\right)=-1$

$\Rightarrow \quad \cos\left(x-\frac{\pi}{4}\right)=\cos\frac{3\pi}{4}$

$\Rightarrow \quad x=2n\pi\pm\frac{3\pi}{4}+\frac{\pi}{4}$

31. Given, $2\sin^3\theta + (2\lambda - 3)\sin^2\theta - (3\lambda + 2)\sin\theta - 2\lambda = 0$

The equation becomes $(\sin\theta - 2)(\sin\theta + \lambda)(2\sin\theta + 1) = 0$

$\Rightarrow \quad \lambda = \pm 1, 0$

32. $\sin^2 z + \text{cosec}^2 z \ge 2,\ 2 + \cot^2 y \ge 2,\ 4 + \sin 4x \ge 3$

$\Rightarrow \quad \sin^2 z = 1,\ \cot^2 y = 0,\ \sin 4x = -1$

$\Rightarrow \quad z \in \left\{\frac{\pi}{2}, \frac{3\pi}{2}\right\},$

$y \in \left\{\frac{\pi}{2}, \frac{3\pi}{2}\right\},\ x \in \left\{\frac{3\pi}{8}, \frac{7\pi}{8}, \frac{11\pi}{8}, \frac{15\pi}{8}\right\}.$

33. $x + y = 2\pi/3$ or $y = (2\pi/3) - x$

$\therefore \quad \sin x = 2\sin\left(\frac{2\pi}{3} - x\right)$

$= 2\left[\left(\frac{\sqrt{3}}{2}\right)\cos x + \left(\frac{1}{2}\right)\sin x\right]$

$= \sqrt{3}\cos x + \sin x$

$\Rightarrow \quad \cos x = 0$

$\Rightarrow \quad x = n\pi + \frac{\pi}{2}, n \in Z$

$\Rightarrow \quad y = \frac{2\pi}{3} - n\pi - \frac{\pi}{2} = \frac{\pi}{6} - n\pi$

Hence, for $x \in [0, 4\pi]$, $x = \pi/2, 3\pi/2, 5\pi/2, 7\pi/2$

and for $y \in [0, 4\pi]$, $y = \pi/6, 7\pi/6, 13\pi/6, 19\pi/6$

34. $(x+y)$ and $(x-y)$ satisfy the equation $\tan^2\theta - 4\tan\theta + 1 = 0$.

Thus, $\tan(x+y) + \tan(x-y) = 4$

and $\tan(x+y)\tan(x-y) = 1$

or $\tan 2x = \tan((x+y) + (x-y))$

or $\tan 2x = \dfrac{\tan(x+y) + \tan(x-y)}{1 - \tan(x+y)\tan(x-y)}$

$\therefore \quad \tan 2x = \infty$ or $2x = 90°$ or $x = 45° = \frac{\pi}{4}$

Now, $\tan 2y = \tan((x+y) - (x-y))$

$= \dfrac{\tan(x+y) - \tan(x-y)}{1 + \tan(x+y)\tan(x-y)}$

$= \dfrac{\{[\tan(x+y) + \tan(x-y)]^2 - 4\tan(x+y)\tan(x-y)\}^{1/2}}{1 + \tan(x+y)\tan(x-y)}$

$= \dfrac{((4)^2 - 2\times 1)^{1/2}}{1+1} = \dfrac{(16-4)^{1/2}}{2} = \dfrac{(12)^{1/2}}{2} = \dfrac{2\sqrt{3}}{2}$

$\therefore \quad \tan 2y = \sqrt{3} \Rightarrow 2y = \frac{\pi}{3} \Rightarrow y = \frac{\pi}{6}$

35. At $x = -\frac{\pi}{2}, \frac{3\pi}{2}$

$\Rightarrow \quad [1 + \sin x] = 0,\ [1 - \cos x] = 1$

$\therefore \quad \sin x = 0 + 1$

$\Rightarrow \quad -1 = 1$ [absurd]

At $x = 0$,

$[1 + \sin x] = 1,\ [1 - \cos x] = 0$

$\therefore \quad \sin x = 1 + 0 \Rightarrow 0 = 1$ [absurd]

At $x = \frac{\pi}{2}$,

$[1 + \sin x] = 2 \cdot [1 - \cos x] = 1$

$\sin x = 2 + 1 = 3 \Rightarrow 1 = 3$ [absurd]

At $x = \pi$,

$\sin x = 1 + 2 = 3 \Rightarrow 0 = 3$ [absurd]

In $\left(-\frac{\pi}{2}, 0\right)$, $[1 + \sin x] = 0,\ [1 - \cos x] = 0$

$\therefore \quad \sin x = 0 + 0 = 0$ [absurd]

In $\left(0, \frac{\pi}{2}\right)$, $[1 + \sin x] = 1,\ [1 - \cos x] = 0$

$\therefore \quad \sin x = 1 + 0 = 1$ [absurd]

In $\left(\frac{\pi}{2}, \pi\right)$, $[1 + \sin x] = 1,\ [1 - \cos x] = 1$

$\therefore \quad \sin x = 1 + 1 = 2$ [absurd]

In $\left(\pi, \frac{3\pi}{2}\right)$, $[1 + \sin x] = 0,\ [1 - \cos x] = 1$

$\therefore \quad \sin x = 0 + 1 = 1$ [absurd]

$\therefore$ All the four results hold.

36. $\because x + y = \frac{4\pi}{3}$ ...(i)

and $\sin x = 2\sin y$ [given]

$\Rightarrow \quad \sin x = 2\sin\left(\frac{4\pi}{3} - x\right)$ [from Eq. (i)]

$\Rightarrow \quad \sin x = 2\left[\sin\frac{4\pi}{3}\cdot\cos x - \cos\frac{4\pi}{3}\cdot\sin x\right]$

$\Rightarrow \quad \sin x = 2\left[\frac{\sqrt{3}}{2}\cos x + \frac{1}{2}\sin x\right]$

$\Rightarrow \quad \sin x = \sqrt{3}\cos x + \sin x$

$\cos x = 0$

$\Rightarrow \quad x = (2n+1)\frac{\pi}{2}, \forall n \in I$

$\Rightarrow \quad x = n\pi + \frac{\pi}{2}$

Putting the value of x in Eq. (i) we get

$y = \frac{4\pi}{3} - n\pi - \frac{\pi}{2}$

$y = \frac{5\pi}{6} - n\pi, \forall n \in I$

$\therefore \quad (x, y) = \left(n\pi + \frac{\pi}{2}, \frac{5\pi}{6} - n\pi\right), \forall n \in I$

37. The given equation is,

$$\sin y = 2\left(\sin^4 x + \frac{1}{\sin^4 x} + 2\right) + 2\left(\cos^4 x + \frac{1}{\cos^4 x} + 2\right) - 24$$

$$= 2(\sin^4 x + \cos^4 x) + 2\left(\frac{1}{\sin^4 x} + \frac{1}{\cos^4 x}\right) + 8 - 24$$

$$= 2(\sin^4 x + \cos^4 x)\left\{1 + \frac{1}{\sin^4 x \cdot \cos^4 x}\right\} - 16$$

$\Rightarrow \sin y = 2\left(1 - \frac{1}{2}\sin^2 2x\right)\left(1 + \frac{16}{\sin^4 2x}\right) - 16$

$\Rightarrow 16 + \sin y = (2 - \sin^2 2x)\left(1 + \frac{16}{\sin^4 2x}\right)$ ...(i)

Since, $\sin y \le 1$

$\Rightarrow 16 + \sin y \le 17$

$\therefore$ LHS. is not greater than 17, on the other hand

$0 \le \sin^2 2x \le 1$

$\Rightarrow \quad 2 - \sin^2 2x \ge 1$ and $\sin^4 2x \le 1$

$\Rightarrow \quad \frac{16}{\sin^4 2x} \ge 16$

$\therefore \quad 1 + \frac{16}{\sin^4 2x} \ge 17$

$\Rightarrow (2 - \sin^2 2x)\left(1 + \frac{16}{\sin^4 2x}\right) \ge 17$

This shows that right member of equation (i) is not less than 17. Thus, the inequality holds only when

$\sin y = 1$ and $\sin^2 2x = 1$

$\Rightarrow \quad y = (4n+1)\frac{\pi}{2}, n \in I$

Since, $\quad \sin^2 2x = 1 = \sin^2\frac{\pi}{2}$

$\therefore \quad 2x = m\pi \pm \frac{\pi}{2}, m \in I$

$\Rightarrow \quad x = (2m \pm 1)\frac{\pi}{4}$

Thus, the solution are $\left((2m \pm 1)\frac{\pi}{4}, (4n+1)\frac{\pi}{2}\right)$.

38. Rewriting the given equation as,

$\{\tan(x+y) - \cot(x+y)\}^2 = -(1 + 2x + x^2) = -(1+x)^2$

or $\quad \{\tan(x+y) - \cot(x+y)\}^2 + (1+x)^2 = 0$

which is possible only when,

$\tan(x+y) - \cot(x+y) = 0$ and $1 + x = 0$

$\tan^2(x+y) = 1 = \tan^2\frac{\pi}{4}$ and $x = -1$

Now, $\tan^2(x+y) = \tan^2\frac{\pi}{4}$

$\Rightarrow \quad x + y = n\pi \pm \frac{\pi}{4}, n \in I$

$\Rightarrow \quad y = n\pi \pm \frac{\pi}{4} + 1, n \in I$

$\therefore$ The required solutions are $\left(-1, n\pi \pm \frac{\pi}{4} + 1\right), n \in I$.

39. The given equation can be rewrite as

$$2\cos\left(\frac{x+y}{2}\right)\cos\left(\frac{x-y}{2}\right) + 2\cos^2\left(\frac{x+y}{2}\right) - 1 = -\frac{3}{2}$$

or $\quad 4\cos^2\left(\frac{x+y}{2}\right) + 4\cos\left(\frac{x+y}{2}\right)\cos\left(\frac{x-y}{2}\right) + 1 = 0$

or $\quad \left(2\cos\left(\frac{x+y}{2}\right) + \cos\left(\frac{x-y}{2}\right)\right)^2 + \sin^2\left(\frac{x-y}{2}\right) = 0$

which is possible only, when

$2\cos\left(\frac{x+y}{2}\right) = -\cos\left(\frac{x-y}{2}\right)$ ...(i)

and $\quad \sin^2\left(\frac{x-y}{2}\right) = 0$ ...(ii)

$x - y = 2n\pi$, where $n \in I$ [from Eq. (ii)]

or $\quad y = x - 2n\pi$ ...(iii)

Substituting the values of y in Eq. (i), we get

$2\cos(x - n\pi) = -\cos n\pi$

$\Rightarrow \quad 2\cos x \,.\, \cos n\pi = -\cos n\pi$

$\Rightarrow \quad \cos x = -\frac{1}{2} = \cos\left(\pi - \frac{\pi}{3}\right)$

$\Rightarrow \quad x = 2m\pi \pm \frac{2\pi}{3}, m \in I$

Now, $y = 2m\pi \pm \frac{2\pi}{3} - 2n\pi$ [from Eq. (iii)]

If $y = 2(m-n)\pi \pm \frac{2\pi}{3}$; $m, n \in I$

$\therefore$ Solutions are $\left\{\left(2m\pi \pm \frac{2\pi}{3}\right), \left(2(m-n)\pi \pm \frac{2\pi}{3}\right)\right\}$.

40. We have, $\int_0^x (t^2 - 8t + 13)\,dt = x\sin\frac{a}{x}$

$\Rightarrow \quad \left(\frac{t^3}{3} - \frac{8t^2}{2} + 13t\right)_0^x = x\sin\frac{a}{x}$

$\Rightarrow \quad \frac{x^3}{3} - 4x^2 + 13x = x\sin\frac{a}{x}$

$\Rightarrow \quad x^2 - 12x + 39 = 3\sin\frac{a}{x}$ $\quad \{\because x \ne 0\}$

$\Rightarrow \quad (x-6)^2 + 3 = 3\sin\left(\frac{a}{x}\right)$

Minimum LHS = 3 and maximum RHS = 3

$\Rightarrow \quad (x-6)^2 + 3 = 3$ and $3\sin\left(\frac{a}{x}\right) = 3$

$\Rightarrow \quad x = 6$ and $\sin\frac{a}{x} = 1$

$\Rightarrow \quad x = 6$ and $\frac{a}{x} = (4n+1)\frac{\pi}{2}, n \in I$

$\Rightarrow \quad a = 3\pi(4n+1), n \in I$

41. $\cos^2 x = \frac{(a+2) \pm \sqrt{(a+2)^2 + 4(a+3)}}{2}$

$\cos^2 x = \frac{(a+2) \pm (a+4)}{2}$

either, $\quad \cos^2 x = -1$ (not possible)

or $\quad \cos^2 x = a + 3$

Since, $\quad 0 \le \cos^2 x \le 1$

$\therefore \quad 0 \le a + 3 \le 1 \Rightarrow -3 \le a \le -2$

Also, $\cos^2 x = (a+3)$

$\Rightarrow \quad x = n\pi \pm \cos^{-1}\sqrt{a+3}$, where $n \in I$ and $a \in [-3, -2]$

42. $\dfrac{\alpha^2}{1-\tan^2 x}=\dfrac{(\sin^2 x+\alpha^2-2)(1+\tan^2 x)}{1-\tan^2 x}$

$\Rightarrow \quad \alpha^2\cos^2 x=\sin^2 x+\alpha^2-2$

$\Rightarrow \quad \alpha^2(1-\sin^2 x)=\sin^2 x+\alpha^2-2$

$\Rightarrow \quad 2=(1+\alpha^2)\sin^2 x$

$\Rightarrow \quad \sin^2 x=\dfrac{2}{1+\alpha^2}$

Since, $0\le\sin^2 x\le1$

$\therefore \quad 0\le\dfrac{2}{1+\alpha^2}\le1$

$\Rightarrow \quad \alpha^2\ge1 \Rightarrow \alpha\le-1 \text{ or } \alpha\ge1$

43. $4[\sin x\cos(\pi/3)+\cos x\sin(\pi/3)]$
$\times[\cos x\cos(\pi/6)+\sin x\sin(\pi/6)]=a^2+\sqrt{3}\sin2x-\cos2x$

$\Rightarrow 4\left[\dfrac{1}{2}\sin x+\dfrac{\sqrt3}{2}\cos x\right]\left[\dfrac{\sqrt3}{2}\cos x+\dfrac{1}{2}\sin x\right]$
$=a^2+\sqrt3\sin2x-\cos2x$

$\Rightarrow \sqrt3\sin2x+3\cos^2 x+\sin^2 x=a^2+\sqrt3\sin2x-\cos2x$

$\Rightarrow \quad 3\cos^2 x+1-\cos^2 x=a^2-\cos2x$

$\Rightarrow \quad \cos2x+2=a^2-\cos2x$

$\Rightarrow \quad \cos2x=\dfrac{a^2-2}{2}$

$\Rightarrow \quad -1\le\cos2x\le1$

$\Rightarrow \quad -1\le\dfrac{a^2-2}{2}\le1$

$\Rightarrow \quad 0\le a^2\le4$

$\Rightarrow \quad -2\le a\le2$

All values of a given in (a), (b), (c), (d) satisfy this relation.

44. It is easier to solve the inequality using graphical method. The graphs of $y=|\cos x|$ and $y=\sin x$ are shown in the following figure.

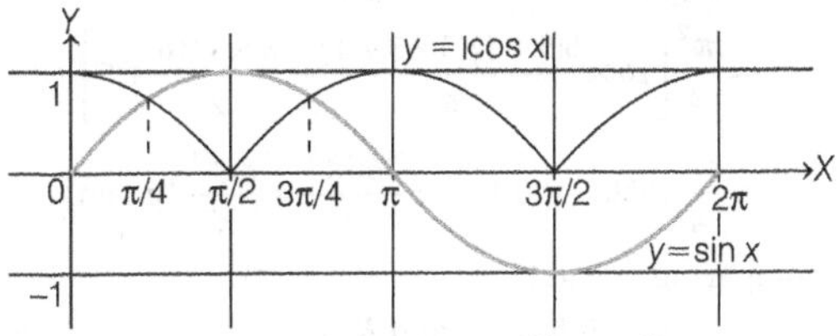

From the figure, $|\cos x|\le\sin x$ for $x\in\left[\dfrac{\pi}{4},\dfrac{3\pi}{4}\right]$

45. (a) For $x\in\left(0,\dfrac{\pi}{4}\right)$, $\tan x<\cot x$

Also, $\ln(\sin x)<0$

$\Rightarrow (\tan x)^{\ln(\sin x)}>(\cot x)^{\ln(\sin x)}$

(b) For $x\in\left(0,\dfrac{\pi}{2}\right)$, $\operatorname{cosec} x\ge1$

$\Rightarrow \ln(\operatorname{cosec} x)\ge0$

$\Rightarrow \quad 4^{\ln\operatorname{cosec} x}<5^{\ln(\operatorname{cosec} x)}$

(c) $x\in\left(0,\dfrac{\pi}{2}\right)\Rightarrow \cos x\in(0,1)\Rightarrow \ln(\cos x)<0$

Also, $\dfrac{1}{2}>\dfrac{1}{3}\Rightarrow \left(\dfrac{1}{2}\right)^{\ln(\cos x)}<\left(\dfrac{1}{3}\right)^{\ln(\cos x)}$

(d) For $x\in\left(0,\dfrac{\pi}{2}\right)$

Since, $\sin x<\tan x$, we get

$\ln(\sin x)<\ln(\tan x)\Rightarrow 2^{\ln(\sin x)}<2^{\ln(\tan x)}$

Sol. (Q. Nos. 46 to 47)

$3\sin^2 x-7\sin x+2=0\Rightarrow \sin x=\dfrac{1}{3}$ or 2(Reject)

46. $N=1$

One value in first quadrant and other lies in second quadrant.

Let $x+\alpha$, then two values α and $\pi-\alpha$.

$\Rightarrow$ Sum is π.

$\therefore \quad N+S=2+\pi$

47. $\because \quad \sin\alpha=\dfrac{1}{3} \Rightarrow \cos\alpha=\pm\dfrac{2\sqrt2}{3}$

$f_4(\alpha)=\sin^4 x+\cos^4\alpha$

$=1-2\sin^2\alpha\cos^2\alpha=\dfrac{65}{81}$

Sol. (Q. Nos. 48 to 49)

48. If $\alpha=3$ and $a=5$, then $N\in[5^3,5^4]$

Largest value of N is $5^4-1=624$

Smallest value of N is $5^3=125$

Difference of largest and smallest integral value of N
$=624-125=499$

49. If $\alpha=2$ and $a=2$, then

N_1 is $(2^3)-(2^2)=4$

If $\alpha=1$ and $a=3$ then N_2 is $3^2-3^1=6$

$y=(N_1\sec^2\theta+N_2\operatorname{cosec}^2\theta)=(4\sec^2\theta+6\operatorname{cosec}^2\theta)$

$\therefore$ The minimum values of y is $(2+\sqrt6)^2=10+4\sqrt6$

Sol. (Q. Nos. 50 to 51)

50. Given, $AB=x\tan\theta$, $BC=x$ and $\dfrac{AB}{BC}=1$

$\therefore \quad \dfrac{x\tan\theta}{x}=1\Rightarrow\theta=45^\circ\Rightarrow\theta=\dfrac{\pi}{4}$

51. $\because \quad \angle OMN=15^\circ=\angle ONM$

[$\because$ ΔONM is an isosceles triangle, $OM=ON$]

$\therefore \quad \angle MON=180^\circ-15^\circ-15^\circ=150^\circ$

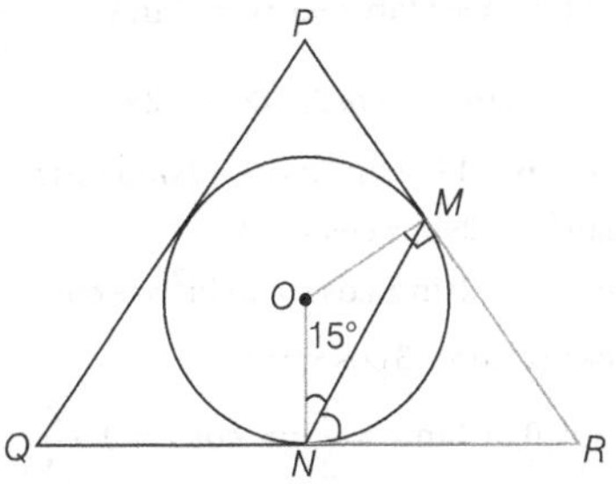

Now, quadrilateral $ONRM$ is cyclic. $[\because \angle OMR = \angle ONR = 90°]$

$\therefore \quad \angle R = 180° - 150° = 30° = \angle Q \quad [\because PR = PQ]$

$\Rightarrow \quad \angle P = 120°$

Sol. (Q. Nos. 52 to 53)

$$(2\sin x - \cos x)(1+\cos x) = \sin^2 x$$

$$\Rightarrow (1+\cos x)[2\sin x - \cos x - 1 + \cos x] = 0$$

$$\Rightarrow (1+\cos x)(2\sin x - 1) = 0$$

$$\Rightarrow \cos x = -1 \text{ or } \sin x = \frac{1}{2}$$

So, $\sin\alpha = \frac{1}{2}$ [as $0 \le \alpha \le \pi/2$]

and $\cos\alpha = \sqrt{3}/2$

Next, $3\cos^2 x - 10\cos x + 3 = 0$ ...(i)

$$\Rightarrow (3\cos x - 1)(\cos x - 3) = 0$$

$$\Rightarrow \cos x = \frac{1}{3} \text{ as } \cos x \ne 3$$

So, $\cos\beta = \frac{1}{3}$ and $\sin\beta = \frac{2\sqrt{2}}{3}$ ...(ii)

and $1 - \sin 2x = \cos x - \sin x$

$$\Rightarrow \cos^2 x + \sin^2 x - 2\sin x\cos x = \cos x - \sin x$$

$$\Rightarrow (\cos x - \sin x)(\cos x - \sin x - 1) = 0$$

Either $\sin x = \cos x \Rightarrow \sin\gamma = \cos\gamma = 1/\sqrt{2}$ ...(iii)

or $\cos x - \sin x = 1 \Rightarrow \cos x = 1, \sin x = 0$

$\Rightarrow \cos\gamma = 1$ and $\sin\gamma = 0$

52. $\cos\alpha + \cos\beta + \cos\gamma$ can be equal to ...(iv)

$$\frac{\sqrt{3}}{2} + \frac{1}{3} + \frac{1}{\sqrt{2}} \text{ or } \frac{\sqrt{3}}{2} + \frac{1}{3} + 1$$

i.e. $$\frac{3\sqrt{6} + 2\sqrt{2} + 6}{6\sqrt{2}} \text{ or } \frac{3\sqrt{3} + 8}{6}$$

53. $\sin\alpha + \sin\beta + \sin\gamma$ can be equal to

$$\frac{1}{2} + \frac{2\sqrt{2}}{3} + \frac{1}{\sqrt{2}} \text{ or } \frac{1}{2} + \frac{2\sqrt{2}}{3} + 0$$

i.e. $$\frac{3\sqrt{2} + 14}{6\sqrt{2}} \text{ or } \frac{3 + 4\sqrt{2}}{6}$$

Sol. (Q. Nos. 54 to 55)

Decoding the Question

First divide Eq. (i) by $\cos x$ and then solve it and convert in $\tan x$. Second, simplify Eq. (ii).

54. $5\sin^2 x + 3\sin x\cos x - 3\cos^2 x = 2(\sin^2 x + \cos^2 x)$

$$\Rightarrow 3\tan^2 x + 3\tan x - 5 = 0 \Rightarrow \tan x = \frac{-3 \pm \sqrt{69}}{6}$$

and $\sin^2 x - \cos 2x = 2 - \sin 2x$

$$\Rightarrow \sin^2 x - 1 + 2\sin^2 x = 2 - 2\sin x\cos x$$

$$\Rightarrow 3\sin^2 x + 2\sin x\cos x = 3$$

$$\Rightarrow 3\sin^2 x + 2\sin x\cos x = 3(\sin^2 x + \cos^2 x)$$

$$\Rightarrow \cos x(2\sin x - 3\cos x) = 0$$

Either $\cos x = 0$ or $\tan x = \frac{3}{2} \Rightarrow \cos x = \pm\frac{2}{\sqrt{13}}$

Taking $\tan\alpha = \frac{-3 \pm \sqrt{69}}{6}$, $\tan\beta = \frac{3}{2}$, we get

$$\tan\alpha + \tan\beta = 1 \pm \frac{\sqrt{69}}{6}$$

55. Taking, $\tan\alpha = \frac{-3+\sqrt{69}}{6}$, $\tan\beta = \frac{-3-\sqrt{69}}{6}$

and $\cos\gamma = 0$, $\cos\delta = \pm\frac{2}{\sqrt{13}}$, we get

$$\tan\alpha\tan\beta + \cos\gamma + \cos\delta = -\frac{5}{3} \pm \frac{2}{\sqrt{13}}$$

Sol. (Q. Nos. 56 to 57)

56. Given, $x^3 - (1 + \cos\theta + \sin\theta)x^2 + (\cos\theta \cdot \sin\theta + \cos\theta + \sin\theta)x - \sin\theta\cos\theta = 0$

$$\Rightarrow (x^3 - 1)(x - \cos\theta)(x - \sin\theta) = 0$$

Thus, $1, \cos\theta, \sin\theta$ are roots of given equation

Hence, $x_1^2 + x_2^2 + x_3^2 = 1 + \sin^2\theta + \cos^2\theta = 2$

57. Now, if $1 = \sin\theta$, we get $\theta = \frac{\pi}{2}$

and $1 = \cos\theta$, then we get $\theta = 0, 2\pi$

and if $\sin\theta = \cos\theta$, then we get

$$\tan\theta = 1$$

$$\Rightarrow \theta = \frac{\pi}{4}, \frac{5\pi}{4}$$

Hence, the number of values of θ in $[0, 2\pi]$ is 5.

Sol. (Q, Nos. 58 to 59)

Given, $\sin\sqrt{x} = -1 = -\sin\frac{\pi}{2} \Rightarrow \sqrt{x} = 2n\pi - \frac{\pi}{2}, n \in I^+$

$$\Rightarrow \sqrt{x} = (4n-1)\frac{\pi}{2}, n \in I^+ \Rightarrow x^2 = (4n-1)^2\frac{\pi^2}{4}, n \in I^+$$

So, roots less than $100\pi^2$ are $9\frac{\pi^2}{4}, 49\frac{\pi^2}{4}, \ldots\ldots\ldots, (19)^2\frac{\pi^2}{4}$.

Its sum $= \sum_{n=1}^{5} (4n-1)^2\frac{\pi^2}{4} = \frac{\pi^2}{4}\sum_{n=1}^{5}(16n^2 - 8n + 1)$

$$= \frac{\pi^2}{4}\left[16 \times \frac{5(5+1)(2\times 5+1)}{6} - \frac{8 \times 5 \times 6}{2} + 5\right]$$

$$= \frac{\pi^2}{4}[880 - 120 + 5] = \frac{765\pi^2}{4} = \frac{m\pi^n}{K} \text{ [given]}$$

On comparing, we get

$$m = 765, n = 2 \text{ and } K = 4$$

Also, sum of square roots of these roots $= \sum_{n=1}^{5}(4n-1)\frac{\pi}{2}$

$$= \frac{\pi}{2}\sum_{n=1}^{5}(4n-1)$$

$$= \frac{\pi}{2}\left[4 \times \frac{5\times 6}{2} - 5\right]$$

$$= \frac{\pi}{2} \times 55$$

$$= \frac{55\pi}{2} = \frac{\lambda\mu}{\Delta} \quad \text{[given]}$$

On comparing, we get

$$\lambda = 55, \mu = \pi \text{ and } \Delta = 2$$

Now, $5K + m + n = 5\times 4 + 765 + 2 = 20 + 765 + 2 = 787$

So, $[(5K + m + n) - 1] = [787 - 1] = [786] = 786$, where $[\cdot]$ is GIF.

$\because \lambda - 0.8 = 55 - 0.8 = 54.2$

$\therefore (\lambda - 0.8) = (54.2) = 55$, where $(\cdot)$ is LIF.

and $[\mu] = [\pi] = [3.14...] = 3$, where $[\cdot]$ is GIF.

and $15\{\Delta\} = 15\times\{2\} = 15\times 0 = 0$, where $\{\}$ is FPF

Hence, $(\lambda - 0.8) + [\mu] + 15\{\Delta\} - 30 = 55 + 3 + 0 - 30 = 28$

58. (786) 59. (28)

Sol. (Q. Nos. 60 to 61)

Given, $\sin^3 x + \cos^3 y + 6\sin x\cdot\cos y = 8$

$$\Rightarrow \sin^3 x + \cos^3 y - 8 = -6\sin x\cos y$$

$$\Rightarrow \sin^3 x + \cos^3 y + (-2)^3 = (3)(\sin x)(\cos y)(-2)$$

which is of the form ($a^3 + b^3 + c^3 = 3abc$ formula).

So, $\sin x + \cos y - 2 = 0$

$\Rightarrow \sin x + \cos y = 2$, which is possible when $\sin x = \cos y = 1$

$$\Rightarrow x = \frac{\pi}{2} \in [0,2\pi] \text{ and } y = 0, 2\pi \in [0,2\pi]$$

So, $\lambda = x + y$

$$\therefore \lambda_{\min} = \frac{\pi}{2} + 0 = \frac{\pi}{2} = \frac{K\pi}{a} \Rightarrow K = 1 \text{ and } a = 2$$

$$\text{and } \lambda_{\max} = \frac{\pi}{2} + 2\pi = \frac{5\pi}{2} = \frac{b\pi}{c}$$

$\Rightarrow b = 5$ and $c = 2$

Also, $\mu = x - y$

$$\therefore \mu_{\min} = \frac{\pi}{2} - 2\pi = \frac{-3\pi}{2} = \frac{l\pi}{m}$$

$\Rightarrow l = -3$ and $m = 2$

$$\text{and } \mu_{\max} = \frac{\pi}{2} - 0 = \frac{\pi}{2} = \frac{p\pi}{q} \Rightarrow p = 1 \text{ and } q = 2$$

60. Now, $(Kbc) - (lmp) = (1\times 5\times 2) - [(-3)\times 2\times 1] = 10 + 6 = 16$

61. $$\left(\frac{Kq}{p} + l\right)^{mbc} = \left(\frac{1\times 2}{1} + (-3)\right)^{2\times5\times2} = (-1)^{20} = 1$$

62. $$\frac{\sin^2\left(x - \frac{\pi}{4}\right)}{\cos 2x} = \frac{\frac{1}{2}(\sin x - \cos x)^2}{\cos^2 x - \sin^2 x} = \frac{-\frac{1}{2}(\sin x - \cos x)}{\cos x + \sin x}$$

$$= -\frac{1}{2}\frac{(\tan x - 1)}{(1 + \tan x)} = -\frac{1}{2}\tan\left(x - \frac{\pi}{4}\right)$$

Given equation reduces to

$$2^{\tan\left(x - \frac{\pi}{4}\right)} - 2(0.25)^{-\frac{1}{2}\tan\left(x - \frac{\pi}{4}\right)} + 1 = 0 \Rightarrow 2^{\tan\left(x - \frac{\pi}{4}\right)} = 1$$

$\Rightarrow x = \frac{\pi}{4}$, which is not possible as $\cos 2x = 0$ for this value of x, which is not defining the original equation.

Hence, number of roots of the equation is zero.

63. **Case I** $\cos x \ge 0$

$$\cos x = \cos x - 2\sin x$$

$$\therefore \sin x = 0$$

$$\therefore x = 0, 2\pi, 4\pi, 6\pi$$

Case II $\cos x < 0$

$$\tan x = 1$$

Thus, x lies in the third quadrant.

$$\therefore x = \frac{5\pi}{4}, \frac{5\pi}{4} + 2\pi, \frac{5\pi}{4} + 4\pi$$

Hence, the number of solutions of the equation is 7.

64. $$x\left(\sin^2 x + \frac{1}{x^2}\right) = 2\sin x\cdot\sin^2 y$$

$$\Rightarrow \sin^2 x + \frac{1}{x^2} = 2\left(\frac{\sin x}{x}\right)\sin^2 y \Rightarrow \sin^2 x + \frac{1}{x^2} \le 2\left(\frac{\sin x}{x}\right)$$

But using AM $\ge$ GM, we have

$$\sin^2 x + \frac{1}{x^2} \ge 2\left(\frac{\sin x}{x}\right) \Rightarrow \sin^2 x = \frac{1}{x^2} \text{ or } |\sin x| = \left|\frac{1}{x}\right|$$

Draw the graph of $y = |\sin x|$ and $y = \left|\frac{1}{x}\right|$ as shown in the following figure

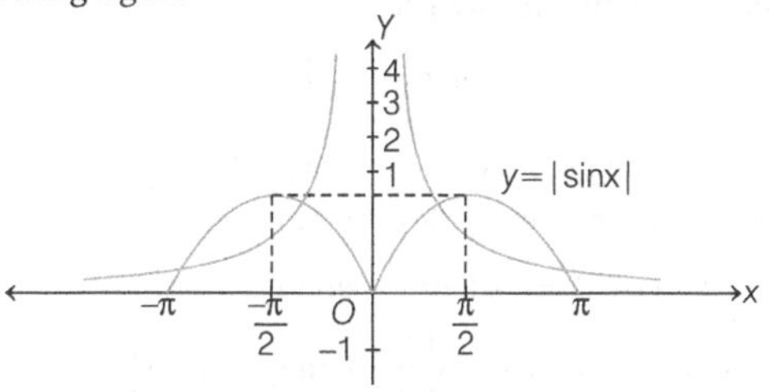

From the figure, we get the four values of x

$$\sin^2 y = 1 \text{ gives } y = \frac{\pi}{2}, \frac{3\pi}{2}$$

So, there will be $4\times 2 = 8$ ordered pairs.

65. $\sin x\cdot\sin 2x\cdot\sin 3x = 1$

Case I $\sin x = 1$ and $\sin 2x = -1$ and $\sin 3x = -1$

This does not hold simultaneously as when $\sin x = 1$, the value of $\cos x = -\frac{1}{2}$

Case II $\sin x = -1$ and $\sin 2x = 1$ and $\sin 3x = -1$

This does not hold simultaneously as when $\sin x = -1$, the value of $\sin 3x = 3\sin x - 4\sin^3 x = 1$.

Case III $\sin x = -1$ and $\sin 2x = -1$ and $\sin 3x = 1$

This is not possible as $\sin x$ and $\sin 2x$ cannot be simultaneously -1.

66. $\sin^3 x + p^3 + 1 - 3p\sin x = 0$

$\Rightarrow (\sin x + p + 1)(\sin^2 x + 1 + p^2 - \sin x - p - p\sin x) = 0$

Therefore, either $\sin x + p + 1 = 0$

$$\Rightarrow p = -(1 + \sin x) \text{ or } \sin x = 1 = p$$

Hence, only one value of $p(p > 0)$ is possible which is given by $p = 1$.

67. $\cos 4x = 2\cos^2 2x - 1$

$\cos 4x = 2(2\cos^2 x - 1)^2 - 1$

$\cos 4x = 2(4\cos^4 x + 1 - 4\cos^2 x) - 1$

$\cos 4x = 8\cos^4 x - 8\cos^2 x + 1$

$\therefore a_0 = 1, a_1 = -8, a_2 = 8$

$$\therefore 5a_0 + a_1 + a_2 = 5$$

68. Since, $-2 \le \sin x - \sqrt{3}\cos x \le 2$, we have

$$-2 \le \frac{4m-6}{4-m} \le 2 \text{ or } -1 \le \frac{2m-3}{4-m} \le 1$$

If $\frac{2m-3}{4-m} \le 1$, we have

$$\frac{(2m-3)-(4-m)}{(4-m)} \le 0$$

or $$\frac{3m-7}{m-4} \ge 0 \quad \text{...(i)}$$

Also, $$-1 \le \frac{2m-3}{4-m}$$

$$\Rightarrow \quad 0 \le \frac{(2m-3)+(4-m)}{(4-m)}$$

$$\Rightarrow \quad \frac{m+1}{m-4} \le 0 \quad \text{...(ii)}$$

From Eqs. (i) and (ii), we get

$$m \in \left[-1, \frac{7}{3}\right]$$

Therefore, the possible integers are – 1, 0, 1, 2.
Hence, number of integral values is 4.

69. $\sin(\sin x + \cos x) = \cos(\cos x - \sin x)$

or $\cos(\cos x - \sin x) = \cos\left[\frac{\pi}{2} - (\sin x + \cos x)\right]$

or $\cos x - \sin x = 2n\pi \pm \left(\frac{\pi}{2} - \sin x - \cos x\right)$

Taking +ve sign, we get

$$\cos x - \sin x = 2n\pi + \frac{\pi}{2} - \sin x - \cos x$$

$$\Rightarrow \quad \cos x = n\pi + \frac{\pi}{4}$$

For $n = 0$, $\cos x = \frac{\pi}{4}$, which is the only possible value

$$\therefore \quad \sin x = \frac{\sqrt{16-\pi^2}}{4} \quad \text{...(i)}$$

Taking –ve sign, we get

$$\sin x = \frac{\pi}{4} \quad \text{...(ii)}$$

From Eqs. (i) and (ii), we get

$\frac{\pi}{4}$ as the largest value

Hence, $K = 4$

70. $(\sin 2x + \cos 2x)^{1+\sin 4x} = 2$

$$\Rightarrow (\sqrt{2})^{1+\sin 4x}\left(\sin\left(2x+\frac{\pi}{4}\right)\right)^{1+\sin 4x} = 2$$

$$\Rightarrow \quad 1 + \sin 4x = 2$$

and $$\sin\left(2x + \frac{\pi}{4}\right) = \pm 1$$

$$\Rightarrow \quad x = -\frac{7\pi}{8}, -\frac{3\pi}{8}, \frac{\pi}{8}, \frac{5\pi}{8}$$

Hence, number of solutions is four.

71. Here, $(2\sec x + 1)(\sec x - 3) = 0$ which gives two values of θ in each of $[0, 2\pi]$, $(2\pi, 4\pi]$, $(4\pi, 6\pi]$ and one value in $\left(6\pi, 6\pi + \frac{3\pi}{2}\right)$.

$$\therefore \quad n = 15$$

72. $\sin^4 x - \cos^2 x \sin x + 2\sin^2 x + \sin x = 0$

or $\sin x[\sin^3 x - \cos^2 x + 2\sin x + 1] = 0$

or $\sin x[\sin^3 x + \sin^2 x + 2\sin x] = 0$

or $\sin^2 x[\sin^2 x + \sin x + 2] = 0$

or $\sin x = 0$,

where $x = 0, \pi, 2\pi, 3\pi$

Hence, there are four solutions.

73. We have, $\sqrt{a-3}\sin 2x - \sqrt{a}(1 - 2\sin^2 x) = 5$

$$\therefore \quad \sqrt{a-3}\sin 2x - \sqrt{a}\cos 2x = 5$$

This equation has at least one solution, if

$$5 \le \sqrt{(\sqrt{a-3})^2 + (\sqrt{a})^2}$$

or $$2a - 3 \ge 25$$

$$a \ge 14$$

So, least value of a is 14.

74. Given, $2^{\sin^2 u + 3\cos^2 v} \times 3^{\sin^2 w + \cos^2 x} \times 5^{\cos^2 y} \ge 2^4 \times 3^2 \times 5^1$

The equality holds when

$\sin^2 u = \sin^2 w = \cos^2 v = \cos^2 x = \cos^2 y = 1$

Therefore, $u, w \in \left\{\frac{\pi}{2}, \frac{3\pi}{2}, \frac{5\pi}{2}, \frac{7\pi}{2}\right\}$ and $x, y, v \in \{\pi, 2\pi, 3\pi\}$

$\therefore$ Number of ordered 5-tuples $= 4^2 \times 3^3 = 432$

75. $\sin \pi x + \cos \pi x = 0$

$$\Rightarrow \quad \tan \pi x = -1 \Rightarrow \pi x = n\pi - \frac{\pi}{4}, n \in z$$

$$\Rightarrow \quad x = n - \frac{1}{4}, \text{ where } n \in z$$

So, sum of roots $= \sum_{n=0}^{100}\left(n - \frac{1}{4}\right) = \frac{100 \times 101}{2} - \frac{100}{4} = 5025$

76. We have, $\cos 5x \times \tan 6|x| + \sin 5x = 0$

Case I $x \ge 0$

$$\cos 5x \tan 6x + \sin 5x = 0$$

$$\Rightarrow \cos 5x \sin 6x + \sin 5x \cos 6x = 0$$

$$\Rightarrow \quad \sin 11x = 0 \Rightarrow 11x = n\pi$$

$$\Rightarrow \quad x = \frac{n\pi}{11}, n \in z^+ \cup \{0\}$$

So, there will be eleven solutions for $n = 0, 1, 2, \ldots, 10$.

Case II $x < 0$

$$-\cos 5x \tan 6x + \sin 5x = 0$$

$$\Rightarrow \quad -\cos 5x \sin 6x + \cos 6x \sin 5x = 0$$

$$\Rightarrow \quad \sin(5x - 6x) = 0$$

$$\Rightarrow \quad \sin(-x) = 0 \Rightarrow \sin x = 0$$

$$\Rightarrow \quad x = n\pi, N \in Z^-$$

$\therefore$ $x = -\pi, -2\pi$

So, total number of solutions is 13.

77. On rewrite the given equation as

$$\sin^2(x+y) = \sin^2(x-y)$$

$$\Rightarrow \quad x + y = n\pi \pm (x - y)$$

$$\Rightarrow \quad x = \frac{n\pi}{2}, y \in R \text{ or } y = \frac{n\pi}{2}, x \in R$$

Thus, for each of $x = 0, \pm \frac{\pi}{2}$, there are two values of y, for each of $y = 0, \pm \frac{\pi}{2}$, there are two values of x.

So, total number of ordered pairs is 12.

78. **(A)** $2\sin\theta\cos\theta = 1/\sqrt{2}$ if $\cos\theta > 0$

$\Rightarrow \quad \sin 2\theta = 1/\sqrt{2} \Rightarrow \theta = \pi/8$ or $3\pi/8$

$\sin 2\theta = -1/\sqrt{2}$ if $\cos\theta < 0$

$\Rightarrow \quad \theta = 5\pi/8$ or $7\pi/8$

$\therefore$ A$\to$ p, q

(B) $2\cos 2\theta \cos 4\theta + \cos 4\theta = 0$

$\Rightarrow (2\cos 2\theta + 1)\cos 4\theta = 0$

Either $\cos 4\theta = 0 \Rightarrow \theta = \frac{\pi}{8}, \frac{3\pi}{8}, \frac{5\pi}{8}, \frac{7\pi}{8}$

or $\quad \cos 2\theta = -\frac{1}{2} \Rightarrow \theta = \pi/3$ or $2\pi/3$

$\therefore$ B$\to$ p, q, r

(C) $(4\cos^2\theta - 1)(2\sin\theta - 1) = 0$

Either $\cos^2\theta = 1/4 \Rightarrow \cos\theta = \pm 1/2 \Rightarrow \theta = \pi/3, 2\pi/3$

or $\sin\theta = 1/2 \Rightarrow \theta = \pi/6$

$\therefore$ C$\to$ r, s

(D) If $\sin 4\theta = \pm 1$, $\theta = \frac{\pi}{8}, \frac{3\pi}{8}, \frac{5\pi}{8}, \frac{7\pi}{8}$

$\therefore$ D$\to$ p, q

79. $$f_n(\theta) = \frac{\sin\theta + \sin 3\theta + \sin 5\theta + \ldots + \sin((2n-1)\theta)}{\cos\theta + \cos 3\theta + \cos 5\theta + \cdots + \cos((2n-1)\theta)}$$

$$= \frac{\dfrac{\sin\left[\theta + \dfrac{(n-1)2\theta}{2}\right]\sin\dfrac{n}{2}(2\theta)}{\sin\dfrac{2\theta}{2}}}{\dfrac{\cos\left[\theta + \dfrac{(n-1)2\theta}{2}\right]\sin\dfrac{n}{2}(2\theta)}{\sin\dfrac{2\theta}{2}}} = \frac{\sin(n\theta)}{\cos(n\theta)} = \tan n\theta$$

(A) $f_3\left(\frac{\pi}{12}\right) = \tan\left(\frac{\pi}{4}\right) = 1$

$\therefore$ A$\to$t

(B) $f_4\left(\frac{\pi}{32}\right) = \tan\left(\frac{\pi}{8}\right) = \sqrt{2} - 1$

$\therefore$ B$\to$p

(C) $f_6\left(\frac{\pi}{16}\right) = \tan\left(\frac{3\pi}{8}\right) = \sqrt{2} + 1$

$\therefore$ C$\to$r

(D) $f_7\left(\frac{\pi}{84}\right) = \tan\left(\frac{\pi}{12}\right) = 2 - \sqrt{3}$

$\therefore$ D$\to$q

80. **(A)** $\sin^2 x + \cos^2 3x = 1$

$\Rightarrow \quad \cos^2 3x = \cos^2 x$

$\Rightarrow \quad 3x = n\pi \pm x, n \in I$

$\Rightarrow \quad x = \frac{n\pi}{2}, \frac{n\pi}{4}, n \in I$

$\therefore$ A$\to$q

(B) $e^{\cot^2\theta} + \sin^2\theta - 2\cos^2 2\theta + 4 = 4\sin\theta$

$$\Rightarrow \quad \underbrace{e^{\cot^2\theta} + (\sin\theta - 2)^2}_{\geq 2} = \underbrace{2\cos^2 2\theta}_{\leq 2}$$

$\Rightarrow \quad \cot\theta = 0, \sin\theta = 1, \cos^2 2\theta = 0$

Now, $\quad \sin\theta = 1$

$\Rightarrow \quad \theta = 2n\pi + \frac{\pi}{2}, n \in I$

$\Rightarrow \quad \theta = (2n+1)\frac{\pi}{2}, n \in I$

$\therefore$ B$\to$s

(C) $\lambda^2 \sin x - \lambda \sin 2x + \sin x = 0$ is true for all values of λ.

$\Rightarrow \sin x = 0$ and $\sin 2x = 0$

$\Rightarrow \sin x = 0$ and $2\sin x \cos x = 0$

Either $\sin x = 0 \Rightarrow x = n\pi, n \in I$

or $\cos x = 0 \Rightarrow x = (2n+1)\frac{\pi}{2}, n \in I$

$\therefore$ C$\to$p, s

(D) $\sqrt[3]{2\tan\theta - 1} + \sqrt[3]{\tan\theta - 1} = 1$

$\Rightarrow \quad \tan\theta = 1 \Rightarrow \theta = n\pi + \frac{\pi}{4}, n \in I$

$\therefore$ D$\to$r

81. **For (I)** $\left\{x \in \left[\frac{-2\pi}{3}, \frac{2\pi}{3}\right], \cos x + \sin x = 1\right\}$

Since, $\cos x + \sin x = 1$

$$\Rightarrow \frac{1}{\sqrt{2}}\cos x + \frac{1}{\sqrt{2}}\sin x = \frac{1}{\sqrt{2}} \Rightarrow \sin\left(x + \frac{\pi}{4}\right) = \frac{1}{\sqrt{2}}$$

$$\Rightarrow \quad x + \frac{\pi}{4} = n\pi + (-1)^n \frac{\pi}{4}, n \in I$$

$$\Rightarrow \quad x = n\pi + (-1)^n \frac{\pi}{4} - \frac{\pi}{4}, n \in I$$

Since, $x \in \left[\frac{-2\pi}{3}, \frac{2\pi}{3}\right]$,

So, only 2 values of x in the set.

Thus, x has 2 elements. $\therefore$ (I) $\to$ (P)

For (II) $\left\{x \in \left[\frac{-5\pi}{18}, \frac{5\pi}{18}\right], \sqrt{3}\tan 3x = 1\right\}$

Since, $\quad \sqrt{3}\tan 3x = 1 \Rightarrow \tan 3x = \frac{1}{\sqrt{3}}$

$$\Rightarrow \quad 3x = n\pi + \frac{\pi}{6}, n \in I \Rightarrow x = \frac{n\pi}{3} + \frac{\pi}{18}, n \in I$$

Since, $x \in \left[\frac{-5\pi}{18}, \frac{5\pi}{18}\right]$.

So, only 2 values of x in the set.

Thus, x has 2 elements.

$\therefore$ (II) $\to$ (P)

For (III) $\left\{x \in \left[\frac{-6\pi}{5}, \frac{6\pi}{5}\right], 2\cos 2x = \sqrt{3}\right\}$

Since, $\quad 2\cos 2x = \sqrt{3} \Rightarrow \cos 2x = \frac{\sqrt{3}}{2}$

$\Rightarrow \quad 2x = 2n\pi \pm \frac{\pi}{6}, n \in I$

$\Rightarrow \quad x = n\pi \pm \frac{\pi}{12}, n \in I$

Thus, x has 6 elements.

$\therefore$ (III) $\rightarrow$ (T)

For (IV) $\left\{x \in \left[-\frac{7\pi}{4}, \frac{7\pi}{4}\right], \sin x - \cos x = 1\right\}$

Since, $\quad \sin x - \cos x = 1$

$\Rightarrow \frac{1}{\sqrt{2}}\sin x - \frac{1}{\sqrt{2}}\cos x = \frac{1}{\sqrt{2}}$

$\Rightarrow \quad \sin\left(x - \frac{\pi}{4}\right) = \frac{1}{\sqrt{2}}$

$\Rightarrow \quad x - \frac{\pi}{4} = n\pi + (-1)^n \frac{\pi}{4}, n \in I$

$\Rightarrow \quad x = n\pi + (-1)^n \frac{\pi}{4} + \frac{\pi}{4}, n \in I$

Thus, since, $x \in \left[-\frac{7\pi}{4}, \frac{7\pi}{4}\right]$.

So, x has 4 elements.

$\therefore$ (IV) $\rightarrow$ (R)

82. The given function $f : [0,2] \rightarrow R$ defined by

$f(x) = (3 - \sin(2\pi x))\sin\left(\pi x - \frac{\pi}{4}\right) - \sin\left(3\pi x + \frac{\pi}{4}\right)$

$= (3 - \sin(2\pi x))\left[\frac{\sin \pi x}{\sqrt{2}} - \frac{\cos \pi x}{\sqrt{2}}\right] - \left\{\frac{\sin(3\pi x)}{\sqrt{2}} + \frac{\cos(3\pi x)}{\sqrt{2}}\right\}$

$= (3 - \sin(2\pi x))\frac{[\sin(\pi x) - \cos(\pi x)]}{\sqrt{2}}$

$\quad - \frac{1}{\sqrt{2}}[3\sin(\pi x) - 4\sin^3(\pi x) + 4\cos^3(\pi x) - 3\cos(\pi x)]$

$= \frac{\sin(\pi x) - \cos(\pi x)}{\sqrt{2}}[3 - \sin(2\pi x) - 3 + 4\{\sin^2(\pi x) + \cos^2(\pi x)$

$\quad + \sin(\pi x)\cos(\pi x)\}]$

$= \frac{\sin(\pi x) - \cos(\pi x)}{\sqrt{2}}[4 + \sin(2\pi x)]$

As, $f(x) \geq 0$, $\forall \in [\alpha, \beta]$, where $\alpha, \beta \in [0, 2]$.

So, $\sin(\pi x) - \cos(\pi x) \geq 0$ as $4 + \sin(2\pi x) > 0 \quad \forall x \in R$.

$\Rightarrow \pi x \in \left[\frac{\pi}{4}, \frac{5\pi}{4}\right] \Rightarrow x \in \left[\frac{1}{4}, \frac{5}{4}\right]$

$\therefore \quad \alpha = \frac{1}{4}$ and $\beta = \frac{5}{4}$

Therefore, the value of $(\beta - \alpha) = 1$

83. For III, $\quad Z = \{x : g(x) = 0\}, x > 0$

$\because \quad g(x) = \cos(2\pi \sin x) = 0$

$\Rightarrow 2\pi \sin x = (2n + 1)\frac{\pi}{2}, n \in I$

$\Rightarrow \quad \sin x = \frac{2n + 1}{4}$

$\Rightarrow \quad \sin x = -\frac{3}{4}, -\frac{1}{4}, \frac{1}{4}, \frac{3}{4} \qquad [\because \sin x \in [-1, 1]]$

Here, values of $\sin x$, $-\frac{3}{4}, -\frac{1}{4}, \frac{1}{4}, \frac{3}{4}$ are in an AP but corresponding values of x are not in an AP so,

(III) $\rightarrow$ R.

For IV, $W = \{x : g'(x) = 0\}, x > 0$

So, $\quad g'(x) = -2\pi \cos x \sin(2\pi \sin x) = 0$

$\Rightarrow$ Either $\cos x = 0$ or $\sin(2\pi \sin x) = 0$

$\Rightarrow$ Either $x = (2n + 1)\frac{\pi}{2}$

or $2\pi \sin x = n\pi$, $n \in I$

$\because \quad 2\pi \sin x = n\pi$

$\Rightarrow \quad \sin x = \frac{n}{2} = -1, -\frac{1}{2}, 0, \frac{1}{2}, 1 \qquad [\because \sin x \in [-1, 1]]$

$\therefore \quad x = n\pi, (2n + 1)\frac{\pi}{2}$

or $\quad n\pi + (-1)^n\left(\pm\frac{\pi}{6}\right)$

(IV) $\rightarrow$ P, R, S

84. Given, $\quad f(x) = \frac{\sin(\pi x)}{x^2}, x > 0$

$\Rightarrow \quad f'(x) = \frac{x^2\pi\cos(\pi x) - 2x\sin(\pi x)}{x^4}$

$= \frac{2\cos(\pi x)\left[\frac{x\pi}{2} - \tan(\pi x)\right]}{x^3}$

Since, for maxima and minima of $f(x)$, $f'(x) = 0$

Either $\cos(\pi x) = 0$ or $\tan(\pi x) = \frac{\pi x}{2}$, (as $x > 0$)

$\because \quad \cos(\pi x) \neq 0$

$\Rightarrow \tan(\pi x) = \frac{\pi x}{2}$

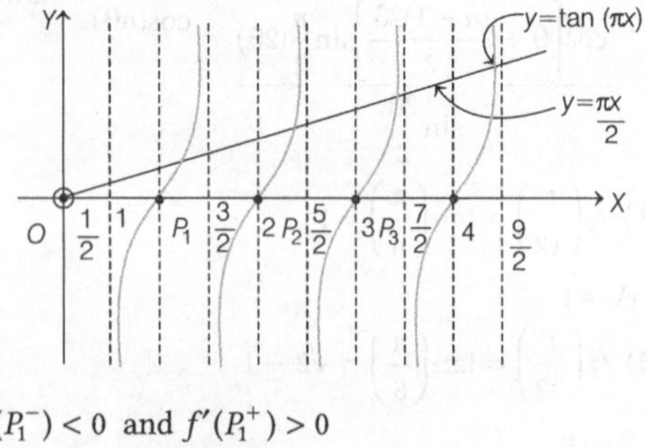

$\because f'(P_1^-) < 0$ and $f'(P_1^+) > 0$

$\Rightarrow x = P_1 \in \left(1, \frac{3}{2}\right)$ is point of local minimum.

$\because f'(P_2^-) > 0$ and $f'(P_2^+) < 0$

$\Rightarrow x = P_2 \in \left(2, \frac{5}{2}\right)$ is point of local maximum.

From the graph, for points of maxima $x_1, x_2, x_3 \ldots$ it is clear that

$\frac{5}{2} - x_1 > \frac{9}{2} - x_2 > \frac{13}{2} - x_3 > \frac{17}{2} - x_4 \ldots\ldots \Rightarrow x_{n+1} - x_n > 2, \forall n.$

From the graph for points of minima $y_1, y_2, y_3 \ldots$, it is clear that

$\frac{3}{2} - y_1 > \frac{5}{2} - x_1 > \frac{7}{2} - y_2 > \frac{9}{2} - x_2 \ldots\ldots |x_n - y_n| > 1, \forall n$ and

$x_1 > (y_1 + 1)$

And $x_1 \in \left(2, \frac{5}{2}\right), x_2 \in \left(4, \frac{9}{2}\right), x_3 \in \left(6, \frac{13}{2}\right) \ldots$

$\Rightarrow \quad x_n \in \left(2n, 2n + \frac{1}{2}\right), \forall n.$

85. We have, α, β are the roots of

$\sqrt{3}\, a \cos x + 2b \sin x = c$

$\therefore \quad \sqrt{3}\, a \cos\alpha + 2b \sin\alpha = c \quad \ldots(i)$

and $\sqrt{3}\, a \cos\beta + 2b \sin\beta = c \quad \ldots(ii)$

On subtracting Eq. (ii) from Eq. (i), we get

$\sqrt{3}a\,(\cos\alpha - \cos\beta) + 2b(\sin\alpha - \sin\beta) = 0$

$$\Rightarrow \sqrt{3}\, a \left(-2\sin\left(\frac{\alpha+\beta}{2}\right)\right) \sin\left(\frac{\alpha-\beta}{2}\right) + 2b\left(2\cos\left(\frac{\alpha+\beta}{2}\right)\right)\sin\left(\frac{\alpha-\beta}{2}\right) = 0$$

$$\Rightarrow \sqrt{3}\, a \sin\left(\frac{\alpha+\beta}{2}\right) = 2b \cos\left(\frac{\alpha+\beta}{2}\right)$$

$$\Rightarrow \quad \tan\left(\frac{\alpha+\beta}{2}\right) = \frac{2b}{\sqrt{3}\, a}$$

$$\Rightarrow \quad \tan\left(\frac{\pi}{6}\right) = \frac{2b}{\sqrt{3}\, a} \quad \left[\because \alpha + \beta = \frac{\pi}{3}, \text{ given}\right]$$

$$\Rightarrow \quad \frac{1}{\sqrt{3}} = \frac{2b}{\sqrt{3}\, a} \Rightarrow \frac{b}{a} = \frac{1}{2} \Rightarrow \frac{b}{a} = 0.5$$

Exercise 3 - Challenging Problems

1. **Decoding the Question**

Here unlike all other problems the solution set consists of the intersection of two solution sets and not the union of the solution sets.

Since, $\sin 3x \geq -1$ and $\cos 2x \geq -1$. we have

$\sin 3x + \cos 2x \geq -2$

Thus, the equality holds true if and only if;

$\sin 3x = -1$ and $\cos 2x = -1$

$$\Rightarrow \quad 3x = n\pi + (-1)^n \left(-\frac{\pi}{2}\right) \text{ and } 2x = 2n\pi \pm \pi.$$

$$\text{i.e.} \quad x = \frac{n\pi}{3} + (-1)^n \left(-\frac{\pi}{6}\right) \text{ and } x = n\pi \pm \frac{\pi}{2}, n \in I$$

$$\therefore \text{ Solution set is } \left\{x \mid x = \frac{n\pi}{3} + (-1)^n\left(-\frac{\pi}{6}\right)\right\} \cap \left\{x \mid x = n\pi \pm \frac{\pi}{2}\right\}.$$

2. Given, $\quad \sin^4 x + \cos^4 x = \frac{7}{2} \sin x \cdot \cos x$

$$\Rightarrow (\sin^2 x + \cos^2 x)^2 - 2\sin^2 x \cos^2 x = \frac{7}{2} \sin x \cdot \cos x$$

$$\Rightarrow \quad 1 - \frac{1}{2}(\sin 2x)^2 = \frac{7}{4}(\sin 2x)$$

$$\Rightarrow \quad 2\sin^2 2x + 7\sin 2x - 4 = 0$$

$$\Rightarrow \quad (2\sin 2x - 1)(\sin 2x + 4) = 0$$

Either $\sin 2x = \frac{1}{2}$

or $\quad \sin 2x = -4 < -1$ [rejected]

$$\therefore \quad 2x = n\pi + (-1)^n \frac{\pi}{6} \text{ i.e. } x = \frac{n\pi}{2} + (-1)^n \frac{\pi}{12}$$

3. Given, $\sin(3\theta + \alpha) + \sin(3\theta - \alpha) + \sin(\alpha - \theta) - \sin(\alpha + \theta) = \cos\alpha$

$$\Rightarrow \quad 2\sin(3\theta)\cdot\cos(\alpha) + 2\sin(-\theta)\cos(\alpha) = \cos\alpha$$

$$\Rightarrow \quad 2(\sin 3\theta - \sin\theta)\cos\alpha = \cos\alpha$$

$$\Rightarrow \quad 2(\sin 3\theta - \sin\theta) = 1$$

[as $\cos\alpha \neq 0$ given]

$$\Rightarrow \quad 2\cdot 2\sin\theta\cdot\cos 2\theta = 1$$

$$\Rightarrow \quad 4\sin\theta(1 - 2\sin^2\theta) = 1$$

$$\Rightarrow \quad 4\sin\theta - 8\sin^3\theta = 1$$

$$\Rightarrow \quad 8\sin^3\theta - 4\sin\theta + 1 = 0$$

$$\Rightarrow \quad (2\sin\theta - 1)(4\sin^2\theta + 2\sin\theta - 1) = 0$$

$$\text{Either } \sin\theta = \frac{1}{2} \text{ or } \sin\theta = \frac{-2 \pm \sqrt{4 + 16}}{8} = \frac{-1 \pm \sqrt{5}}{4}$$

$$\Rightarrow \quad \theta = n\pi + (-1)^n \frac{\pi}{6}, n\pi + (-1)^n \sin^{-1}\left(\frac{\sqrt{5} - 1}{4}\right)$$

$$\text{or} \quad n\pi + (-1)^n \sin^{-1}\left(\frac{-1 - \sqrt{5}}{4}\right)$$

$$\Rightarrow \quad \theta = n\pi + (-1)^n \frac{\pi}{6}, \; n\pi + (-1)^n \frac{\pi}{10}$$

$$\text{or} \quad n\pi + (-1)^n \left(\frac{-3\pi}{10}\right), n \in I$$

$$\left[\because \sin\frac{\pi}{10} = \sin 18° = \frac{\sqrt{5} - 1}{4}, \sin\left(-\frac{3\pi}{10}\right) = \sin(-54°) = \frac{-1 - \sqrt{5}}{4}\right]$$

$\therefore$ General solution set

$$= \left\{\theta \mid \theta = n\pi + (-1)^n \frac{\pi}{6}\right\} \cup \left\{\theta \mid \theta = n\pi + (-1)^n \frac{\pi}{10}\right\} \cup \left\{\theta \mid \theta = n\pi - (-1)^n \frac{3\pi}{10}\right\}$$

4. Given, $\quad 4\cos^2 x \sin x - 2\sin^2 x = 3\sin x$

$$\Rightarrow 4(1 - \sin^2 x)\sin x - 2\sin^2 x - 3\sin x = 0$$

$$\Rightarrow 4\sin x - 4\sin^3 x - 2\sin^2 x - 3\sin x = 0$$

$$\Rightarrow \quad -4\sin^3 x - 2\sin^2 x + \sin x = 0$$

$$\Rightarrow \quad -\sin x(4\sin^2 x + 2\sin x - 1) = 0$$

Either $\sin x = 0$ or $4\sin^2 x + 2\sin x - 1 = 0$

$$\Rightarrow \quad \sin x = \sin 0 \text{ or } \sin x = \frac{-2 \pm \sqrt{4 + 16}}{2(4)}$$

$$\Rightarrow \quad x = n\pi \quad \text{or } \sin x = \frac{-1 \pm \sqrt{5}}{4} = \sin\frac{\pi}{10}, \sin\left(-\frac{3\pi}{10}\right)$$

$$\Rightarrow \quad x = n\pi, x = n\pi + (-1)^n \frac{\pi}{10}, x = n\pi + (-1)^n \left(-\frac{3\pi}{10}\right)$$

$\therefore$ General solution set

$$= \{x | x = n\pi\} \cup \left\{x | x = n\pi + (-1)^n \frac{\pi}{10}\right\} \cup \left\{x | x = n\pi + (-1)^n \left(-\frac{3\pi}{10}\right)\right\}$$

5. Here, $1 + 2 \operatorname{cosec} x = \dfrac{-\sec^2 \frac{x}{2}}{2}$

$$\Rightarrow \quad 1 + \frac{2}{\sin x} = -\frac{\left[1 + \tan^2 \frac{x}{2}\right]}{2}$$

i.e $\quad 2[2 + \sin x] = -\left[1 + \tan^2 \frac{x}{2}\right] \sin x$

$$\therefore 2\left[\frac{2 \tan\left(\frac{x}{2}\right)}{1 + \tan^2\left(\frac{x}{2}\right)} + 2\right] = -\left[1 + \tan^2 \frac{x}{2}\right] \cdot \left[\frac{2 \tan \frac{x}{2}}{1 + \tan^2 \frac{x}{2}}\right]$$

Put $\tan \frac{x}{2} = t$,

$$2\left[\frac{2t}{1+t^2} + 2\right] = -(1+t^2)\left(\frac{2t}{1+t^2}\right)$$

$\therefore \quad 4t^2 + 4t + 4 + 2t(1+t^2) = 0$

$\therefore \quad 2t^3 + 4t^2 + 6t + 4 = 0$

i.e. $\quad t^3 + 2t^2 + 3t + 2 = 0$

$\therefore \quad (t+1)(t^2 + t + 2) = 0$

$\Rightarrow \quad t = -1 \quad [\because t^2 + t + 2 \neq 0]$

or $\quad \tan \frac{x}{2} = -1$

$\Rightarrow \quad \frac{x}{2} = n\pi - \frac{\pi}{4}, n \in I$

Thus, $x = 2n\pi - \frac{\pi}{2}, n \in I$ is the required solution.

6. We have, $y = \sin x - \cos x = \sqrt{2}\left(\frac{1}{\sqrt{2}} \sin x - \frac{1}{\sqrt{2}} \cos x\right)$

$$= \sqrt{2} \sin\left(x - \frac{\pi}{4}\right)$$

$\Rightarrow \quad -\sqrt{2} \leq y \leq \sqrt{2} \quad$ ...(i)

Now, for $y = 1$

$$\sin x - \cos x = 1$$

$\Rightarrow \quad \frac{1}{\sqrt{2}} \sin x - \frac{1}{\sqrt{2}} \cos x = \frac{1}{\sqrt{2}}$

$\Rightarrow \quad \sin\left(x - \frac{\pi}{4}\right) = \sin\left(\frac{\pi}{4}\right)$

$\Rightarrow \quad x - \frac{\pi}{4} = n\pi + (-1)^n \frac{\pi}{4}$

$\Rightarrow \quad x = n\pi + (-1)^n \frac{\pi}{4} + \frac{\pi}{4}$

$\therefore \quad x = \frac{\pi}{2}, \pi$

7. Here, $\left(\cos \frac{x}{4} - 2 \sin x\right) \sin x + \left(1 + \sin \frac{x}{4} - 2 \cos x\right) \cos x = 0$

$$\Rightarrow \cos \frac{x}{4} \cdot \sin x - 2 \sin^2 x + \cos x + \sin \frac{x}{4} \cdot \cos x - 2 \cos^2 x = 0$$

$$\Rightarrow \left(\sin x \cdot \cos\left(\frac{x}{4}\right) + \sin\left(\frac{x}{4}\right) \cdot \cos x\right) + \cos x - 2(\sin^2 x + \cos^2 x) = 0$$

$\Rightarrow \quad \sin\left(x + \frac{x}{4}\right) + \cos x = 2$

Since, the greatest value of $\sin\left(\frac{5x}{4}\right)$ and $\cos(x)$ is 1.

Therefore, their sum is equal to 2 only if,

$$\sin\left(\frac{5x}{4}\right) = 1 \text{ and } \cos(x) = 1.$$

$\Rightarrow \quad \frac{5x}{4} = 2n\pi + \frac{\pi}{2}$ and $x = 2k\pi \ (n, k \in I)$

Since, we have to choose those values of x which satisfy both of these equations, we have

$$2k\pi = \frac{8n\pi}{5} + \frac{2\pi}{5}$$

$\Rightarrow k = \frac{4n+1}{5}$, where both k and n are integers.

We write, $k = n - \frac{(n-1)}{5}$ for $\frac{n-1}{5} = m$, we have

$$n = 1 + 5m \text{ and } k = 1 + 4m \ (m \in I)$$

$\therefore \quad x = 2\pi + 8m\pi, m \in I.$

8. Given, $\quad \sin x + \cos y = 1 \quad$ ...(i)

and $\quad (1 - 2\sin^2 x) - (2\cos^2 y - 1) = 1$

i.e. $\quad \sin^2 x + \cos^2 y = \frac{1}{2} \quad$ ...(ii)

Put $\sin x = u$ and $\cos y = v$ in Eqs. (i) and (ii),

$$u + v = 1 \text{ and } u^2 + v^2 = \frac{1}{2}$$

Solving above equations;

$$u = \frac{1}{2} \text{ and } v = \frac{1}{2}$$

$\therefore \quad \sin x = \frac{1}{2} \Rightarrow x = n\pi + (-1)^n \frac{\pi}{6}, n \in I$

and $\quad \cos y = \frac{1}{2} \Rightarrow y = 2m\pi \pm \frac{\pi}{3}, m \in I$

$\therefore$ The given equations have solutions,

$$x = n\pi + (-1)^n \frac{\pi}{6}, n \in I \text{ and } y = 2m\pi \pm \frac{\pi}{3}, m \in I$$

9. The point of intersection is given by

$$\sin 3x = \cos x = \sin\left(\frac{\pi}{2} - x\right)$$

$\Rightarrow \quad 3x = n\pi + (-1)^n \left(\frac{\pi}{2} - x\right)$

(i) Let n be even i.e. $n = 2m$

$\Rightarrow \quad 3x = 2m\pi + \left(\frac{\pi}{2} - x\right) \Rightarrow x = \frac{m\pi}{2} + \frac{\pi}{8} \quad$ ...(i)

(ii) Let n be odd i.e. $n = 2m + 1$

$$\Rightarrow \quad 3x = (2m+1)\pi - \left(\frac{\pi}{2} - x\right)$$

$$\Rightarrow \quad 3x = 2m\pi + \frac{\pi}{2} + x \Rightarrow 2x = 2m\pi + \frac{\pi}{2}$$

$$\Rightarrow \quad x = m\pi + \frac{\pi}{4} \quad \text{...(ii)}$$

Now, as $-\frac{\pi}{2} \le x \le \frac{\pi}{2}$

$$\therefore \quad x = \frac{\pi}{8}, \frac{\pi}{4}, -\frac{3\pi}{8} \quad \text{[from Eqs. (i) and (ii)]}$$

Thus, point of intersection are

$$\left(\frac{\pi}{8}, \cos\frac{\pi}{8}\right), \left(\frac{\pi}{4}, \cos\frac{\pi}{4}\right), \left(-\frac{3\pi}{8}, \cos\frac{3\pi}{8}\right)$$

10. We have,

$$(x+y) + (y+2z)\cos 2\theta + (z-x)\left(\frac{1-\cos 2\theta}{2}\right) = 0$$

$$\Rightarrow (2x+2y) + (2y+4z)\cos 2\theta + (z-x) - (z-x)\cos 2\theta = 0$$

$$\Rightarrow \quad (2x+2y+z-x) + (2y+4z-z+x)\cos 2\theta = 0$$

$$\Rightarrow \quad (x+2y+z) + (x+2y+3z)\cos 2\theta = 0$$

Which is zero for all values of θ, if

$$x + 2y + z = 0 \text{ and } x + 2y + 3z = 0$$

$$\Rightarrow \quad x + 2y + z = 0$$

and $\quad x + 2y + 3z = 0$

$$\frac{x}{6-2} = \frac{y}{1-3} = \frac{z}{2-2} = k$$

$$\Rightarrow \quad x = 4k, y = -2k, z = 0$$

or $\quad x = 2k, y = -k, z = 0$

i.e. $(2k, -k, 0)$ for any $k \in R$.

Hence, there are infinite number of triplets.

11. We have, $\sin x \cdot \cos y = a^2$ and $\cos x \cdot \sin y = a$

On adding above equations,

$$\sin x \cos y + \cos x \sin y = a^2 + a$$

$$\Rightarrow \quad \sin(x+y) = a^2 + a \quad \text{...(i)}$$

As we know,

$$-1 \le \sin(x+y) \le 1$$

$$\therefore \quad -1 \le a^2 + a \le 1$$

i.e. $\quad -1 \le a^2 + a$ and $a^2 + a \le 1$

$$\Rightarrow \quad a^2 + a + 1 \ge 0 \text{ and } a^2 + a - 1 \le 0$$

$$\Rightarrow \quad \left(a + \frac{1}{2}\right)^2 + \frac{3}{4} \ge 0 \text{ and } \left(a + \frac{1}{2}\right)^2 - \frac{5}{4} \le 0$$

$\Rightarrow$ True for all real 'a' and $-\frac{\sqrt{5}}{2} \le a + \frac{1}{2} \le \frac{\sqrt{5}}{2}$

$$\Rightarrow \quad -\left(\frac{\sqrt{5}+1}{2}\right) \le a \le \frac{\sqrt{5}-1}{2} \quad \text{...(ii)}$$

Again, on subtracting the two given equations,

$$\sin x \cos y - \cos x \sin y = a^2 - a$$

$$\Rightarrow \quad \sin(x-y) = a^2 - a \quad \text{...(iii)}$$

As we know,

$$-1 \le \sin(x-y) \le 1$$

$$\Rightarrow \quad -1 \le a^2 - a \le 1$$

$$\Rightarrow \quad -1 \le a^2 - a \text{ and } a^2 - a \le 1$$

$$\Rightarrow \quad a^2 - a + 1 \ge 0 \text{ and } a^2 - a - 1 \le 0$$

$$\Rightarrow \quad \left(a - \frac{1}{2}\right)^2 + \frac{3}{4} \ge 0 \text{ and } \left(a - \frac{1}{2}\right)^2 \le \frac{5}{4}$$

$\Rightarrow$ True for all real 'a' and $-\frac{\sqrt{5}}{2} \le a - \frac{1}{2} \le \frac{\sqrt{5}}{2}$

$$\Rightarrow \quad \left(\frac{1-\sqrt{5}}{2}\right) \le a \le \frac{1+\sqrt{5}}{2} \quad \text{...(iv)}$$

From Eqs. (ii) and (iv) common solution is

$$\left(\frac{1-\sqrt{5}}{2}\right) \le a \le \left(\frac{\sqrt{5}-1}{2}\right)$$

or $\quad a \in \left[\frac{1-\sqrt{5}}{2}, \frac{\sqrt{5}-1}{2}\right]$

12. Given, $\sin x + \cos(a+x) + \cos(a-x) = 2$

$$\Rightarrow \quad 1 \cdot \sin x + 2 \cdot \cos a \cdot \cos x = 2$$

Let $\quad 1 = r\sin\phi, 2\cos a = r\cos\phi$

$$\Rightarrow \quad r(\cos x \cos\phi + \sin x \cdot \sin\phi) = 2$$

$$\Rightarrow \quad r\cos(x-\phi) = 2, \left\{\begin{array}{l}\text{where } r^2 = 1 + 4\cos^2 a \\ \Rightarrow r = \sqrt{1 + 4\cos^2 a}\end{array}\right.$$

$$\Rightarrow \quad \cos(x-\phi) = \frac{2}{r}$$

$$\Rightarrow \quad \cos(x-\phi) = \frac{2}{\sqrt{1+4\cos^2 a}} \quad \text{...(i)}$$

This equation has real solution if,

$$\frac{2}{\sqrt{1+4\cos^2 a}} \le 1$$

or $\quad 2 \le \sqrt{1+4\cos^2 a}$ or $4\cos^2 a \ge 3$

or $\quad \cos^2 a \ge \frac{3}{4}$

$$-\cos^2 a \le -\frac{3}{4} \Rightarrow 1 - \cos^2 a \le 1 - \frac{3}{4}$$

$$\Rightarrow \quad \sin^2 a \le \frac{1}{4}$$

$$\Rightarrow \quad (\sin a + 1/2)(\sin a - 1/2) \le 0$$

$$\Rightarrow \quad -\frac{1}{2} \le \sin a \le \frac{1}{2}$$

$\therefore \; m\pi - \frac{\pi}{6} \le a \le m\pi + \frac{\pi}{6}$, where $m \in I$

Clearly, $x - \phi = 2n\pi \pm \cos^{-1}\left(\frac{2}{\sqrt{1+4\cos^2 a}}\right)$ [From Eq. (i)]

$$\Rightarrow \quad x = \phi + 2n\pi \pm \cos^{-1}\left(\frac{2}{\sqrt{1+4\cos^2 a}}\right)$$

where $\quad \cos\phi = \frac{2\cos a}{\sqrt{1+4\cos^2 a}}$ or $\phi = \cos^{-1}\left(\frac{2\cos a}{\sqrt{1+4\cos^2 a}}\right)$

13. $(\sin x + \cos x)\sin 2x = a(\sin x + \cos x)$
$[\sin^2 x + \cos^2 x - \sin x \cos x]$

$$\Rightarrow (\sin x + \cos x)\left[\sin 2x - a\left(1 - \frac{1}{2}\sin 2x\right)\right] = 0 \quad \text{...(i)}$$

Now, $\sin x + \cos x = 0 \Rightarrow \tan x = -1 = \tan\frac{3\pi}{4}$

$$\therefore \quad x = \frac{3\pi}{4} \qquad \left[\because \frac{\pi}{2} \le x \le \pi\right]$$

Hence, there is always at least one root lying in $\frac{\pi}{2}$ and π for any value of the parameter a.

Now, $2\sin 2x - 2a + a\sin 2x = 0$ [from Eq. (i)]

$$\Rightarrow \quad \sin 2x = \frac{2a}{2+a} \quad \text{...(ii)}$$

Since, $\frac{\pi}{2} < x < \pi$ or $\pi < 2x < 2\pi$

$$\Rightarrow \quad -1 \le \sin 2x < 0 \quad \text{...(iii)}$$

Now, from Eqs. (ii) and (iii), we have

$$-1 \le \frac{2a}{2+a} < 0, \text{ where } a \ne -2$$

$$\Rightarrow \quad -1 \le \frac{2a}{2+a} \text{ and } \frac{2a}{2+a} < 0$$

$$\Rightarrow \quad 0 \le \frac{2a}{2+a} + 1 \text{ and } a(2+a) < 0$$

Using number line rules, we get

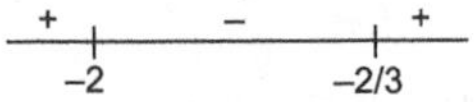

$$a < -2 \text{ or } a \ge -\frac{2}{3} \quad \text{...(A)}$$

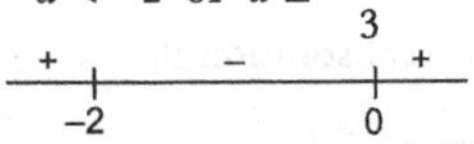

and $-2 < a \le 0$ ...(B)

From (A) and (B) $-\frac{2}{3} \le a \le 0$ ...(iv)

[i.e. common to both (A) and (B)]

Hence, for every value of 'a' satisfying the condition $-\frac{2}{3} \le a \le 0$ the equation, $\sin 2x = \frac{2a}{2+a}$ has the roots lying between $\frac{\pi}{2}$ and π.

Now, we have to find the solution of the equation

$$\sin 2x = \frac{2a}{2+a}, \text{ where } -\frac{2}{3} \le a \le 0 \text{ and } \frac{\pi}{2} < x < \pi$$

Clearly, $\pi < 2x < 2\pi$

Case I $\pi < 2x < \frac{3\pi}{2}$

$$0 < 2x - \pi < \frac{\pi}{2}$$

$$\because \quad \sin(2x) = \frac{2a}{2+a}$$

$$\therefore \quad \sin(2x - \pi) = -\frac{2a}{2+a};\ x = \frac{\pi}{2} - \frac{1}{2}\sin^{-1}\left(\frac{2a}{2+a}\right)$$

Case II $\frac{3\pi}{2} < 2x < 2\pi$

$$-\frac{\pi}{2} < 2x - 2\pi < 0$$

Since, $\sin 2x = \frac{2a}{2+a}$

$$\therefore \quad \sin(2x - 2\pi) = \frac{2a}{2+a}$$

$$2x - 2\pi = \sin^{-1}\left(\frac{2a}{2+a}\right)$$

$$x = \pi + \frac{1}{2}\sin^{-1}\left(\frac{2a}{2+a}\right)$$

$$\text{Thus, } x = \begin{cases} \frac{3\pi}{4}, \text{ for } a \leftarrow (-\infty, \infty) \\ \frac{\pi}{2} - \frac{1}{2}\sin^{-1}\left(\frac{2a}{2+a}\right), \text{ for } \frac{-2}{3} \le a \le 0 \\ \pi + \frac{1}{2}\sin^{-1}\left(\frac{2a}{2+a}\right), \text{ for } \frac{-2}{3} \le a \le 0 \end{cases}$$

14. $(\tan x)^{\cos^2 x} = \left(\frac{1}{\tan x}\right)^{\sin x} \Rightarrow (\tan x)^{\cos^2 x + \sin x} = 1$

Now, here two case arises,

Case I When $\tan x = 1$, the power $(\cos^2 x + \sin x)$ can take any value.

$$\therefore \quad \tan x = 1 \Rightarrow x = n\pi + \frac{\pi}{4}$$

Case II When $\tan x \ne 1$, 0 and $\cos^2 x + \sin x = 0$

or $x \ne n\pi, n\pi + \frac{\pi}{4}$

and $1 - \sin^2 x + \sin x = 0.$

$$\Rightarrow \quad \sin^2 x - \sin x - 1 = 0$$

$$\therefore \quad \sin x = \frac{1 \pm \sqrt{1+4}}{2} = \frac{\sqrt{5}+1}{2}, \frac{1-\sqrt{5}}{2}$$

Here, $\frac{\sqrt{5}+1}{2} > 1$ which is not possible.

$$\sin x = \frac{1-\sqrt{5}}{2} = \sin\alpha$$

$$\therefore \ x = n\pi + (-1)^n\alpha, \text{ where } \alpha = \sin^{-1}\left(\frac{1-\sqrt{5}}{2}\right)$$

Thus, $x = n\pi + \frac{\pi}{4}$ or $x = n\pi + (-1)^n\alpha$,

where $\alpha = \sin^{-1}\left(\frac{1-\sqrt{5}}{2}\right)$

15. $a\cos x + \frac{\cos x}{\sin x} + 1 = \frac{1}{\sin x}$

$$\Rightarrow a\sin x\cos x + \cos x + \sin x = 1 \ (\sin x \ne 0)$$

$$\Rightarrow \quad \sin x + \cos x = 1 - a\sin x\cos x$$

On squaring both sides, we get

$$1 + 2\sin x\cos x = 1 + a^2\sin^2 x\cos^2 x - 2a\sin x\cdot\cos x$$

$$a^2\sin^2 x\cos^2 x - 2(a+1)\sin x\cos x = 0$$

$$\sin x\cos x[a^2\sin x\cos x - 2(a+1)] = 0$$

$$\sin 2x[a^2\sin 2x - 4(a+1)] = 0$$

Either $\sin 2x = 0$ for any value of a.

$$2x = n\pi$$

$$x = \frac{n\pi}{2} \text{ for } a \in (-\infty, \infty)$$

or $\quad a^2\sin 2x - 4(a+1) = 0$

$$\Rightarrow \quad \sin 2x = \frac{4(a+1)}{a^2}$$

$\because -1 \le \sin 2x \le 1$ for all values of x.

$$\therefore \quad -1 \le \frac{4(a+1)}{a^2} \le 1$$

$$-a^2 \le 4(a+1) \le a^2$$

i.e. $\quad -a^2 \le 4a + 4$ or $4a + 4 \le a^2$

$\Rightarrow \quad a^2 + 4a + 4 \ge 0$

or $\quad a^2 - 4a - 4 \ge 0$

$\Rightarrow \quad (a+2)^2 \ge 0$

or $\quad (a-2)^2 - 8 \ge 0$

which is true for all 'a' or $(a-2)^2 \ge 8$

$\Rightarrow \quad a - 2 \ge 2\sqrt{2}$

or $\quad a - 2 \le -2\sqrt{2}$

$\Rightarrow \quad a \le 2 - 2\sqrt{2}$ or $a \ge 2 + 2\sqrt{2}$

or $\quad a \in (-\infty, 2 - 2\sqrt{2}] \cup [2 + 2\sqrt{2}, \infty)$

$$\Rightarrow \quad 2x = n\pi + (-1)^n \sin^{-1}\left(\frac{4(a+1)}{a^2}\right)$$

$$x = \frac{n\pi}{2} + \frac{(-1)^n}{2}\sin^{-1}\left(\frac{4(a+1)}{a^2}\right)$$

$$\Rightarrow \quad x = \begin{cases} \dfrac{n\pi}{2}; \text{ for } a \in (-\infty, \infty) \\ \dfrac{n\pi}{2} + \dfrac{(-1)^n}{2}\sin^{-1}\left(\dfrac{4(a+1)}{2}\right); \\ \text{for } a \in (-\infty, 2 - 2\sqrt{2}] \cup [2 + 2\sqrt{2}, \infty) \end{cases}$$

16. The first equation of the system can be written as;

$$3\sin x - 4\sin^3 x = a\sin x + (4 - 2|a|)\sin^2 x$$

$$\sin x\{4\sin^2 x + (4 - 2|a|)\sin x + (a-3)\} = 0 \quad \text{...(i)}$$

The second equation is,

$$\sin 3x + \cos 2x = 1 + 2\sin x\cos 2x$$

$$\sin 3x + \cos 2x = 1 + \sin 3x - \sin x$$

$$\cos 2x = 1 - \sin x$$

$$1 - 2\sin^2 x = 1 - \sin x$$

$$\sin x(2\sin x - 1) = 0 \quad \text{...(ii)}$$

$\because$ Both equations have a common solution, therefore

$$\sin x = 0$$

Also, second root of Eq. (ii) i.e. $\sin x = \frac{1}{2}$, satisfy Eq. (i).

From Eq. (i), $4\left(\frac{1}{2}\right)^2 + (4 - 2|a|)\frac{1}{2} + (a-3) = 0$

$\Rightarrow \quad 1 + 2 - |a| + (a-3) = 0$

$\Rightarrow \quad |a| = a$ or $a \ge 0$ for $\sin x = \frac{1}{2}$ ...(iii)

Again from Eq. (i);

$$4\sin^2 x + (4 - 2|a|)\sin x + (a-3) = 0$$

For real x, $\quad (4 - 2|a|)^2 - 4\cdot 4\cdot(a-3) \ge 0$

$\Rightarrow \quad (2-a)^2 - 4(a-3) \ge 0$

$\Rightarrow \quad 4 - 4a + a^2 - 4a + 12 \ge 0$

$\Rightarrow \quad a^2 - 8a + 16 \ge 0$

$\Rightarrow \quad (a-4)^2 \ge 0$

$$\therefore \quad \sin x = \frac{-(4 - 2|a|) \pm 2\sqrt{(a-4)^2}}{2\cdot 4}$$

$$\Rightarrow \quad \sin x = \frac{|a| - 2 \pm \sqrt{(a-4)^2}}{4}$$

$$\Rightarrow \quad \sin x = \frac{|a| - 2 + a - 4}{4} \text{ or } \sin x = \frac{|a| - 2 - a + 4}{4}$$

$$\Rightarrow \quad \sin x = \frac{2a - 6}{4} \text{ or } \sin x = \frac{1}{2} \quad [\because |a| = a \text{ from Eq. (iii)}]$$

$$\Rightarrow \sin x = \frac{a-3}{2} \text{ or } \sin x = \frac{1}{2}$$

For real x the values of 'a' will be suitable in the following three cases (also $a \ge 0$).

(i) $\frac{a-3}{2} = 0 \Rightarrow a = 3$

(ii) $\frac{a-3}{2} = \frac{1}{2} \quad \Rightarrow \quad a = 4$

(iii) $\left|\frac{a-3}{2}\right| \le 1$ or $|a-3| \le 2$ or $-2 \le a - 3 \le 2$

$\Rightarrow \quad 1 \le a \le 5$

$\therefore \quad$ Hence, $a \in [1, 5]$.

17. Here, LHS $= |\cos x - 2\sin 2x - \cos 3x|$

$$= |(\cos x - \cos 3x) - 2\sin 2x|$$

$$= |2\sin 2x\cdot\sin x - 2\sin 2x|$$

$$= |2\sin 2x(\sin x - 1)|$$

and $\quad$ RHS $= 1 - 2\sin x - \cos 2x$

$$= 2\sin^2 x - 2\sin x = 2\sin x(\sin x - 1)$$

Thus, $|\cos x - 2\sin 2x - \cos 3x| = 1 - 2\sin x - \cos 2x$ could be rewritten as,

$$|2\sin 2x(\sin x - 1)| = 2\sin x(\sin x - 1)$$

where $1 - \sin x \ge 0$, for all real x

$\therefore \quad |2\sin 2x|(1 - \sin x) = 2\sin x(\sin x - 1)$

$\Rightarrow \quad (|2\sin 2x| + 2\sin x)(1 - \sin x) = 0$

Either $\sin x = 1$

or $4|\sin x||\cos x| + 2\sin x = 0$.

So, two cases arises

Case I $\sin x = 1$

$\Rightarrow \quad x = 2n\pi + \dfrac{\pi}{2}, n \in I$

Case II $2|\sin x||\cos x| + \sin x = 0$

If $\sin x > 0$

$\Rightarrow 2\sin x|\cos x| + \sin x = 0$

or $\quad |\cos x| = -\dfrac{1}{2}$ [not possible]

Thus, no solution for $\sin x > 0$.

Consider $\sin x \le 0$

$\Rightarrow \quad -2\sin x|\cos x| + \sin x = 0$

$\Rightarrow \quad \sin x = 0$ i.e. $x = n\pi, n \in I$.

or $\quad |\cos x| = \dfrac{1}{2} \Rightarrow \cos x = \pm\dfrac{1}{2}$ and $\sin x < 0$

$\Rightarrow$ Those values which lie in III or IV quadrant

$$\therefore \quad x = \begin{cases} k\pi + \dfrac{\pi}{3}, & \text{for } k = (2m+1), m \in I \\ k\pi - \dfrac{\pi}{3}, & \text{for } k = (2m), m \in I \end{cases}$$

$$\text{Hence,} \quad x = \begin{cases} 2n\pi + \dfrac{\pi}{2}, n \in I \\ (2n+1)\pi + \dfrac{\pi}{3}, n \in I \\ 2n\pi - \dfrac{\pi}{3}, n \in I \end{cases}$$

18. We have, $\dfrac{3\sqrt{3} - \pi}{3} > 0$ and hence their arises three cases

Case I When $|x| \ge 2$, we have

$|x| + a > 2$, whereas $2\sin x \le 2$

Hence the equation,

$2\sin x = |x| + a$, possesses no solution for $|x| \ge 2$

Case II When, $-2 \le x \le 0$, we have $0 \le |x| \le 2$

$\Rightarrow \quad 2\sin x \le 0$ and $|x| + a > 0$

$\therefore$ The equation $2\sin x = |x| + a$ has no solution.

Case III When, $0 < x < 2$, we have

In this case the given equation reduces to

$$2\sin x = x + a$$

Let $\quad f(x) = 2\sin x - x$

$\Rightarrow \quad f'(x) = 2\cos x - 1 = 0$

$\Rightarrow \quad x = \dfrac{\pi}{3} \in (0, 2)$ is a critical point.

$f''(x) = -2\sin x < 0$ for $x = \dfrac{\pi}{3}$

$\Rightarrow \quad x = \dfrac{\pi}{3}$ is a point of maxima.

$$(f(x))_{\max} = 2\sin\frac{\pi}{3} - \frac{\pi}{3} = \frac{2\sqrt{3}}{2} - \frac{\pi}{3} = \frac{3\sqrt{3} - \pi}{3}$$

$\therefore a = 2\sin x - x$, cannot be greater $\dfrac{3\sqrt{3} - \pi}{3}$ for the equation to have a solution.

Hence, the result.

Alternate Solution

We have, $\sin x = \dfrac{1}{2}|x| + \dfrac{a}{2}$

Now, consider the graphs of $y_1 = \sin x$ and $y_2 = \dfrac{1}{2}|x|$.

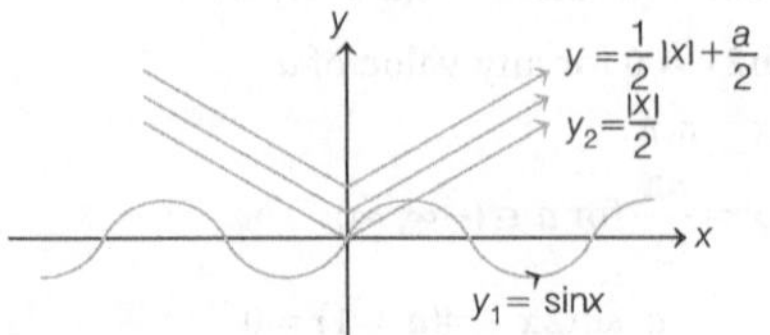

The equation $\sin x = \dfrac{1}{2}|x| + \dfrac{a}{2}$ will have solution, if the line $y = \dfrac{1}{2}|x| + \dfrac{a}{2}$ (parallel to y_2) intersects or touches the curve $y_1 = \sin x$ at least one point.

In this case we must have $\dfrac{dy_1}{dx} = \cos x = \dfrac{1}{2}$ (i.e. the slope of the line)

$\Rightarrow x = \dfrac{\pi}{3}$.

Hence, the solution exists if,

$$\frac{1}{2}\cdot\frac{\pi}{3} + \frac{1}{2}a \le \sin\frac{\pi}{3} \Rightarrow a \le \frac{3\sqrt{3} - \pi}{3}$$

19. The condition for the existence of solution are,

$$\left.\begin{array}{l} \text{I. } 2\cos 2x - 1 \ne 0 \text{ i.e. } \cos 2x \ne \dfrac{1}{2} \text{ i.e. } x \ne \dfrac{\pi}{6} \\ \text{II. } \tan x \ne 0 \text{ i.e. } x \ne 0, \pm\dfrac{\pi}{2} \\ \text{III. } \cos^2 x - 3\sin^2 x \ne 0 \text{ i.e. } \tan^2 x \ne \dfrac{1}{3} \text{ i.e. } x \ne \pm\dfrac{\pi}{6} \end{array}\right\} \quad \text{...(i)}$$

Since, $2\cos 2x - 1 = 2(\cos^2 x - \sin^2 x) - (\cos^2 x + \sin^2 x)$

$= \cos^2 x - 3\sin^2 x$

Subject to the above condition, the equation reduces to

$$b\sin x = b + \sin x \Rightarrow \sin x = \frac{b}{b-1} \quad \text{...(ii)}$$

which is only possible if ; $-1 \le \dfrac{b}{b-1} \le 1$

i.e. $\quad \dfrac{b}{b-1} + 1 \ge 0$ and $\dfrac{b}{b-1} - 1 \le 0$

+ + | − | + +, with points 1/2 and 1

and $\quad \dfrac{1}{b-1} \le 0$

− | +, with point 1

i.e. $\quad b \le \dfrac{1}{2}$ or $b > 1$ and $b \le 1$ ...(iii)

From Eqs. (i), (ii) and (iii),

$$b \le \frac{1}{2} \quad \text{...(iv)}$$

When $b = \dfrac{1}{2}$, $x = \dfrac{-\pi}{2}$ [from Eq. (ii)]

But from Eq. (i) $\quad x \ne \dfrac{-\pi}{2} \Rightarrow b \ne \dfrac{1}{2}$ ...(v)

From (iv) and (v) the equation possess solutions only when $b < \dfrac{1}{2}$.

Mathematics consists in proving the most obvious thing in the least obvious way.

–George Polya

3

Properties and Solutions of Triangles

Learning Milestones

Milestone 1 Basic Relation Between the Sides and Angles of Triangle

- Sine Formulae or Sine Rules
- Cosine Formulae or Cosine Rules
- Projection Formulae
- Tangent Rule or Napier's Analogy

Milestone 2 Auxiliary Formulae

- Trigonometric Ratios of Half-angles
- Area of Triangle

Milestone 3 Circles Connected with Triangle

- Circumcircle of a Triangle
- In-circle or Inscribed Circle of a Triangle
- Escribed Circles of a Triangle

Milestone 4 Solution of Triangles

- Solution of a Right Angled Triangle
- Solution of a Triangle in General

Milestone 5 Height and Distance

- Angle of Elevation
- Angle of Depression
- Bearing

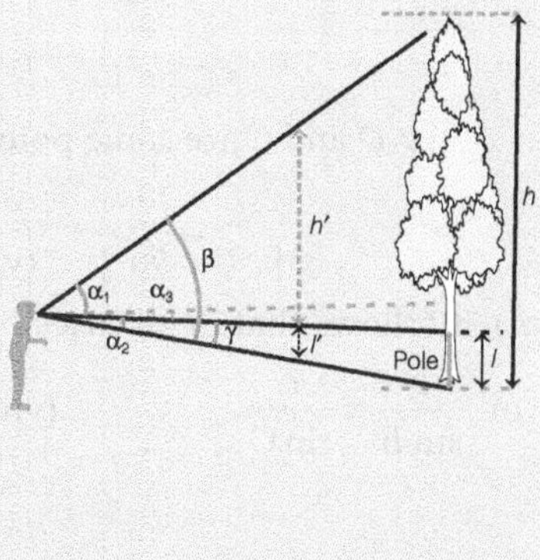

Practice Milestones

Practice Milestone 1 - JEE Advanced Pattern
Practice Milestone 2 - Challenging Problems

Milestone 1 Basic Relation Between the Sides and Angles of Triangle

• Sine Formulae or Sine Rules • Cosine Formulae or Cosine Rules • Projection Formulae
• Tangent Rule or Napier's Analogy

In a ΔABC, the angles are denoted by capital letters A, B and C and the lengths of the sides opposite to these angles are denoted by small letters a, b and c, respectively.

Semi-perimeter of the triangle is written as

$$s = \frac{a+b+c}{2}$$

and its area is denoted by Δ.

Some geometrical properties of A, B, C and a, b, c.

In ΔABC,

(i) $A + B + C = 180°$

(ii) $a + b > c, b + c > a, c + a > b$

(iii) $a > 0, b > 0, c > 0$

3.1 Sine Formulae or Sine Rules

In any ΔABC, the sides are proportional to sines of the opposite angles

i.e. $$\frac{a}{\sin A} = \frac{b}{\sin B} = \frac{c}{\sin C}$$

Proof : ***Case* I. When $\angle C$ is acute**

From A, draw $AD \perp BC$

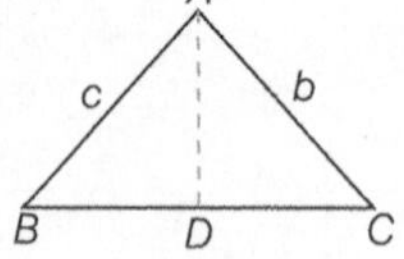

In ΔABD, $$\sin B = \frac{AD}{AB} = \frac{AD}{c}$$

or $$AD = c \sin B \quad \text{...(i)}$$

In ΔACD, $$\sin C = \frac{AD}{AC} = \frac{AD}{b}$$

or $$AD = b \sin C \quad \text{...(ii)}$$

From Eqs. (i) and (ii), we get

$$c \sin B = b \sin C \quad \text{...(iii)}$$

***Case* II. When $\angle C$ is obtuse**

From A, draw $AD \perp BC$

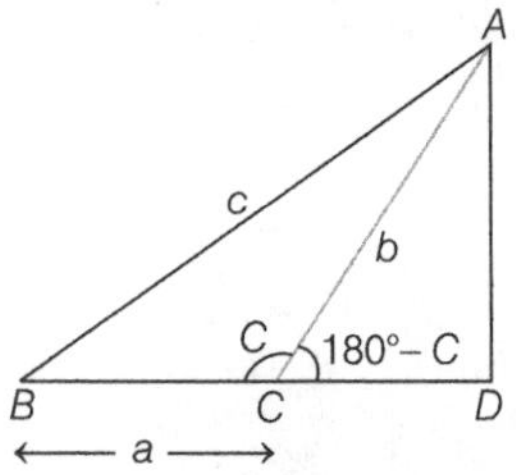

In ΔABD, $$\sin B = \frac{AD}{AB} = \frac{AD}{c}$$

$\therefore$ $$AD = c \sin B \quad \text{...(iv)}$$

From ΔACD, $$\sin(180° - C) = \frac{AD}{AC} = \frac{AD}{b}$$

$\therefore$ $$AD = b \sin(180° - C) = b \sin C \quad \text{...(v)}$$

From Eqs. (iv) and (v), we get

$$c \sin B = b \sin C \quad \text{...(vi)}$$

***Case* III. When $\angle C = 90°$**

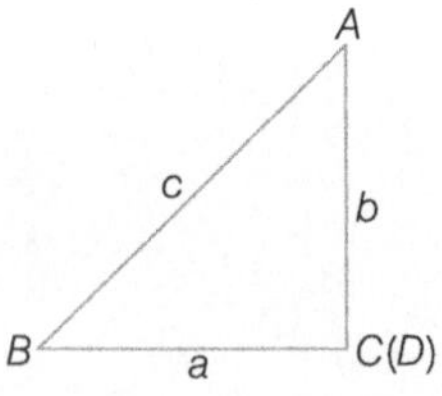

Draw $AD \perp BC$

In ΔABC, $$\sin B = \frac{AD}{AB} = \frac{AD}{c}$$

$\therefore$ $$AD = c \sin B$$

or $$AC = c \sin B \quad [\because D \text{ and } C \text{ are same point}]$$

or $$b = c \sin B$$

or $$b \sin C = c \sin B \quad [\because C = 90°] \quad \text{...(vii)}$$

Thus, from (iii), (vi) and (vii), it follows that in all cases

$$b \sin C = c \sin B \text{ or } \frac{b}{\sin B} = \frac{c}{\sin C} \quad \text{...(viii)}$$

Similarly, by drawing perpendicular from from C to AB, we can prove that

$$\frac{a}{\sin A} = \frac{b}{\sin B} \quad \ldots\text{(ix)}$$

From (viii) and (ix), we get

$$\frac{a}{\sin A} = \frac{b}{\sin B} = \frac{c}{\sin C}$$

Example 1. If in a ΔABC, $b = 3c$ and $C - B = 90°$, then find the value of $\tan B$.

Sol. Since, $\frac{b}{\sin B} = \frac{c}{\sin C}$, we have

$$\frac{\sin B}{\sin C} = \frac{b}{c}$$

$$\Rightarrow \quad \frac{\sin B}{\sin(90° + B)} = \frac{b}{c}$$

$$\Rightarrow \quad \tan B = \frac{b}{c} = 3$$

Example 2. In a ΔABC, if $BC = 1$ and $AC = 2$, then what is the maximum possible value of $\angle A$?

Sol. Using sine rule,

$$\frac{1}{\sin A} = \frac{2}{\sin B}$$

$$\Rightarrow \quad \sin A = \frac{\sin B}{2}$$

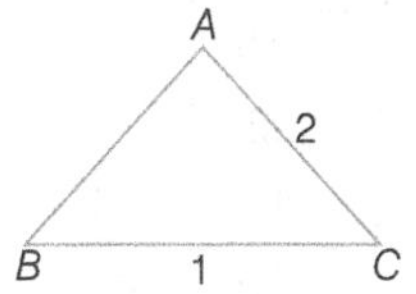

$\Rightarrow$ Maximum value of $\sin A$ is $\frac{1}{2}$.

Hence, $A = \frac{\pi}{6}$

Example 3. The perimeter of a ΔABC is six times the arithmetic mean of the sines of its angles. If the side a is 1, then find $\angle A$.

Sol. Given that

$$a + b + c = 6 \times \frac{\sin A + \sin B + \sin C}{3}$$

$$\Rightarrow 2R(\sin A + \sin B + \sin C) = 2(\sin A + \sin B + \sin C)$$

$$\Rightarrow \quad R = 1$$

Now, $\frac{a}{\sin A} = 2R$

$$\Rightarrow \quad \sin A = \frac{1}{2} \quad [\because a = 1]$$

$$\Rightarrow \quad A = 30°$$

Example 4. If the angles of a triangle are in the ratio $4:1:1$, then the ratio of the longest side to the perimeter is

(a) $\sqrt{3}:(2+\sqrt{3})$ (b) $1:6$
(c) $1:(2+\sqrt{3})$ (d) $2:3$

Sol. (a) $4x + x + x = 180°$

$$\Rightarrow \quad 6x = 180°$$

$$\Rightarrow \quad x = 30°$$

$$\frac{\sin 120°}{a} = \frac{\sin 30°}{b} = \frac{\sin 30°}{c}$$

Therefore, $a:(a+b+c)$

$$= (\sin 120°):(\sin 120° + \sin 30° + \sin 30°)$$

$$= \frac{\sqrt{3}}{2} : \frac{\sqrt{3}+2}{2}$$

$$= \sqrt{3} : (\sqrt{3} + 2)$$

Example 5. If $A = 75°$, $B = 45°$, then prove that $b + c\sqrt{2} = 2a$.

Sol. $A = 75°, B = 45° \Rightarrow C = 60°$

Now, $\frac{a}{\sin A} = \frac{b}{\sin B} = \frac{c}{\sin C} = 2R$

$$\Rightarrow \quad \frac{a}{\sin 75°} = \frac{b}{\sin 45°} = \frac{c}{\sin 60°} = 2R$$

$$\Rightarrow \quad b + c\sqrt{2} = \frac{\sin 45°}{\sin 75°} \cdot a + \sqrt{2}\,\frac{\sin 60°}{\sin 75°} \cdot a$$

$$= \frac{\frac{1}{\sqrt{2}}}{\frac{\sqrt{3}+1}{2\sqrt{2}}} a + \sqrt{2}\,\frac{\frac{\sqrt{3}}{2}}{\frac{\sqrt{3}+1}{2\sqrt{2}}} a$$

$$= \frac{2}{\sqrt{3}+1} a + \frac{2\sqrt{3}a}{\sqrt{3}+1} = 2a$$

Example 6. In a ΔABC, $\angle B = \frac{\pi}{3}$, $\angle C = \frac{\pi}{4}$ and D divides BC internally in the ratio $1:3$. Then, $\frac{\sin \angle BAD}{\sin \angle CAD}$ is equal to

(a) $\frac{1}{3}$ (b) $\frac{1}{\sqrt{3}}$ (c) $\frac{1}{\sqrt{6}}$ (d) $\sqrt{\frac{2}{3}}$

Sol. (c) Let $\angle BAD = \alpha$, $\angle CAD = \beta$

In ΔADB, on applying sine formulae, we get

$$\frac{x}{\sin \alpha} = \frac{AD}{\sin\left(\frac{\pi}{3}\right)} \quad \ldots\text{(i)}$$

In ΔADC, on applying sine formulae, we get

$$\frac{3x}{\sin \beta} = \frac{AD}{\sin\left(\frac{\pi}{4}\right)} \quad \ldots\text{(ii)}$$

Dividing Eq. (i) by Eq. (ii), we get

$$\frac{x}{\sin \alpha} \times \frac{\sin \beta}{3x} = \frac{\frac{AD}{\sin\left(\frac{\pi}{3}\right)}}{} \times \frac{\sin\left(\frac{\pi}{4}\right)}{AD}$$

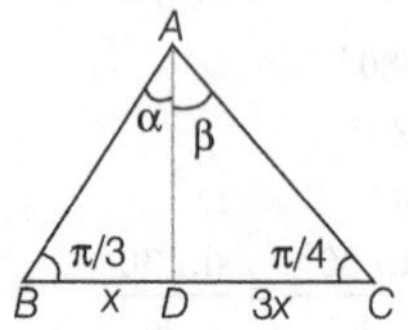

$$\Rightarrow \quad \frac{\sin \beta}{3 \sin \alpha} = \frac{\frac{1}{\sqrt{2}}}{\frac{\sqrt{3}}{2}} = \sqrt{\frac{2}{3}}$$

$$\Rightarrow \quad \frac{\sin \beta}{\sin \alpha} = 3\sqrt{\frac{2}{3}} = \sqrt{6}$$

Therefore, $\dfrac{\sin \angle BAD}{\sin \angle CAD} = \dfrac{\sin \alpha}{\sin \beta} = \dfrac{1}{\sqrt{6}}$

Example 7. Let O be a point inside a ΔABC, such that $\angle OAB = \angle OBC = \angle OCA = w$. Then, show that $\cot w = \cot A + \cot B + \cot C$.

Sol. In ΔOAC, using sine rule,

$$\frac{\sin(A - w)}{OC} = \frac{\sin(180° - A)}{b}$$

$$\Rightarrow \quad \frac{\sin(A - w)}{OC} = \frac{\sin A}{b} \quad \text{...(i)}$$

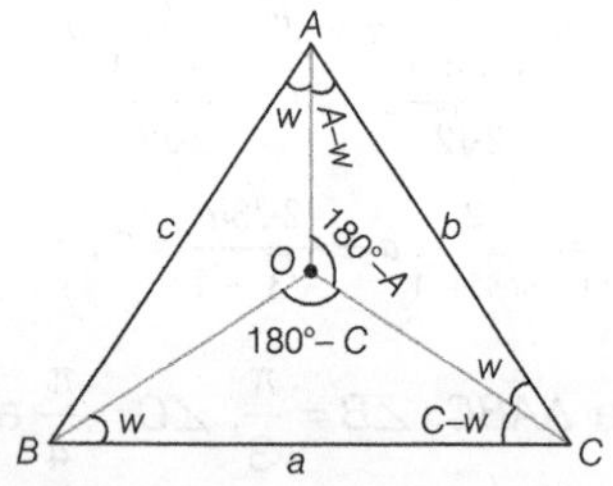

Also, in ΔOBC

$$\frac{\sin w}{OC} = \frac{\sin(180° - C)}{a}$$

$$\Rightarrow \quad \frac{\sin w}{OC} = \frac{\sin C}{a} \quad \text{...(ii)}$$

On dividing Eqs. (i) and (ii), we get

$$\frac{\sin(A - w)}{\sin w} = \frac{a \sin A}{b \sin C}$$

$$\left[\text{as we know, } \frac{a}{\sin A} = \frac{b}{\sin B} = \frac{c}{\sin C} = k\right]$$

$$\Rightarrow \quad \frac{\sin(A - w)}{\sin w} = \frac{k \sin A \cdot \sin A}{k \sin B \cdot \sin C}$$

$$\Rightarrow \quad \frac{\sin A \cos w - \cos A \sin w}{\sin w} = \sin A \frac{\{\sin(\pi - (B + C))\}}{\sin B \sin C}$$

$$\Rightarrow \quad \sin A(\cot w) - \cos A = \sin A\left(\frac{\sin B \cos C + \cos B \sin C}{\sin B \sin C}\right)$$

$$\Rightarrow \quad \sin A(\cot w) - \cos A = \sin A(\cot C + \cot B)$$

$$\Rightarrow \quad \cot w - \cot A = \cot B + \cot C$$

$$\Rightarrow \quad \cot w = \cot A + \cot B + \cot C$$

3.2 Cosine Formulae or Cosine Rules

In any ΔABC, we have

(i) $\cos A = \dfrac{b^2 + c^2 - a^2}{2bc}$ or $a^2 = b^2 + c^2 - 2bc \cos A$

(ii) $\cos B = \dfrac{c^2 + a^2 - b^2}{2ac}$ or $b^2 = c^2 + a^2 - 2ac \cos B$

(iii) $\cos C = \dfrac{a^2 + b^2 - c^2}{2ab}$ or $c^2 = a^2 + b^2 - 2ab \cos C$

Proof : ***Case* I. When $\angle A$ is acute**

Draw $BD \perp AC$.

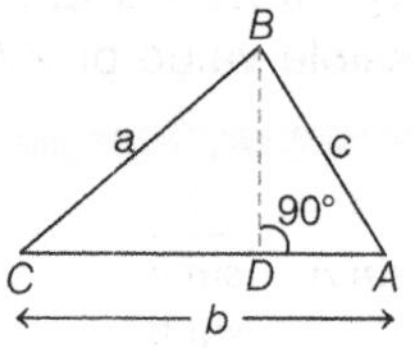

In ΔADB, $\quad \sin A = \dfrac{BD}{AB} = \dfrac{BD}{c}$

$\therefore \quad BD = c \sin A \quad$ ...(i)

and $\quad \cos A = \dfrac{AD}{AB} = \dfrac{AD}{c}$

$\therefore \quad AD = c \cos A \quad$ ...(ii)

Now, $\quad CD = AC - AD$

$\quad = b - c \cos A \quad$ ...(iii)

***Case* II. When $\angle A$ is obtuse**

Draw $BD \perp AC$

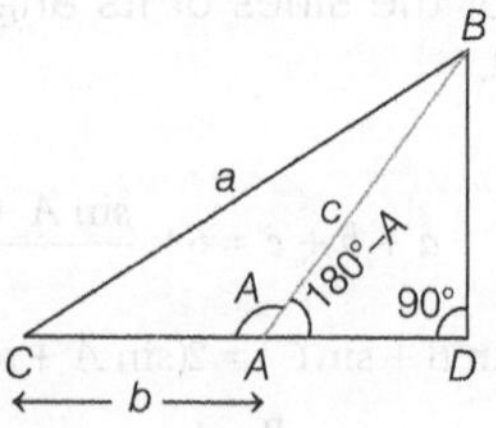

In ΔADB, $\quad \sin(180° - A) = \dfrac{BD}{AB}$

$\therefore \quad \sin A = \dfrac{BD}{c}$

or $\quad BD = c \sin A$

and $\cos(180° - A) = \dfrac{AD}{AB}$

$\therefore$ $-\cos A = \dfrac{AD}{c}$

or $AD = -c\cos A$

Now, $CD = AC + AD$

$= b - c\cos A$

***Case* III. When $\angle A = 90°$**

Here, D and A are same points.

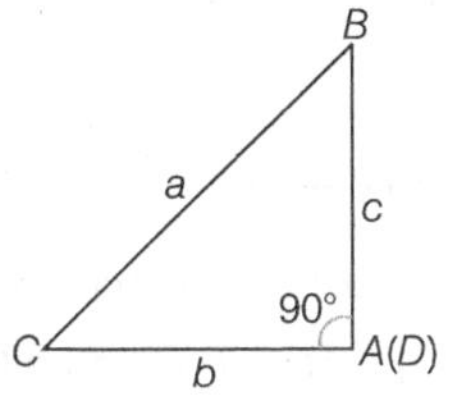

In ΔACB, $BD = BA = c = c\sin A$

$[\because \angle A = 90° \therefore \sin A = \sin 90° = 1]$

and $AD = 0 = c\cos A$ $[\because \cos A = \cos 90° = 0]$

$\therefore$ $CD = AC - AD$

$= b - c\cos A$

Thus, in all cases $BD = c\sin A$ and $CD = b - c\cos A$

Now, in ΔBCD, $BC^2 = CD^2 + BD^2$

$$\therefore \quad a^2 = (b - c\cos A)^2 + c^2\sin^2 A$$

$$= b^2 + c^2\cos^2 A - 2bc\cos A + c^2\sin^2 A$$

$$= b^2 + c^2(\cos^2 A + \sin^2 A) - 2bc\cos A$$

$$= b^2 + c^2 - 2bc\cos A \quad \text{...(iv)}$$

or $2bc\cos A = b^2 + c^2 - a^2$

$$\therefore \quad \cos A = \frac{b^2 + c^2 - a^2}{2bc}$$

Also, from Eq. (iv), we get

$$a^2 = b^2 + c^2 - 2bc\cos A$$

Similarly, we can prove that

$$\cos B = \frac{c^2 + a^2 - b^2}{2ca}$$

or $b^2 = a^2 + c^2 - 2ca\cos B$

and $\cos C = \dfrac{a^2 + b^2 - c^2}{2ab}$

or $c^2 = a^2 + b^2 - 2ab\cos C$

Example 8. Find the angles of the triangles whose sides are $3 + \sqrt{3}$, $2\sqrt{3}$ and $\sqrt{6}$.

Sol. Let $a = 3 + \sqrt{3}$, $b = 2\sqrt{3}$, $c = \sqrt{6}$

$$\Rightarrow \quad \cos A = \frac{b^2 + c^2 - a^2}{2bc}$$

$$= \frac{12 + 6 - (9 + 3 + 6\sqrt{3})}{12\sqrt{2}}$$

$$= \frac{6 - 6\sqrt{3}}{12\sqrt{2}} = \frac{1 - \sqrt{3}}{2\sqrt{2}}$$

$$\Rightarrow \quad \cos A = \cos(60° + 45°)$$

$$\left[\because \cos(60° + 45°) = \frac{1 - \sqrt{3}}{2\sqrt{2}}\right]$$

$$\therefore \quad A = 105°$$

On applying sine formulae, $\dfrac{a}{\sin A} = \dfrac{b}{\sin B}$

$$\Rightarrow \quad \sin B = \frac{b}{a}\sin A$$

$$= \frac{2\sqrt{3}}{3 + \sqrt{3}}\sin(105°)$$

$$= \frac{2\sqrt{3}}{3 + \sqrt{3}}\{\sin 60° . \cos 45° + \cos 60° \cdot \sin 45°\}$$

$$= \frac{2\sqrt{3}}{\sqrt{3}(\sqrt{3} + 1)}\left\{\frac{\sqrt{3} + 1}{2\sqrt{2}}\right\}$$

$$\sin B = \frac{1}{\sqrt{2}} = \sin 45° \quad [\because B \neq 180 - 45° \text{ as } B + A < 180°]$$

$$\Rightarrow \quad B = 45°$$

Here, $A = 105°$, $B = 45°$

$\Rightarrow$ $C = 180° - (A + B) = 180° - (150°) = 30°$

$\therefore$ $\angle A = 105°$, $\angle B = 45°$ and $\angle C = 30°$

Example 9. With usual notations, if in a ΔABC, $\dfrac{b + c}{11} = \dfrac{c + a}{12} = \dfrac{a + b}{13}$, then prove that $\dfrac{\cos A}{7} = \dfrac{\cos B}{19} = \dfrac{\cos C}{25}$.

Sol. Let $\dfrac{b + c}{11} = \dfrac{c + a}{12} = \dfrac{a + b}{13} = k$

$$b + c = 11k \quad \text{...(i)}$$

$$c + a = 12k \quad \text{...(ii)}$$

$$a + b = 13k \quad \text{...(iii)}$$

$$\Rightarrow \quad 2(a + b + c) = 36k \quad \text{...(iv)}$$

On solving Eq. (i) to Eq. (iv), we get

$$a = 7k,\ b = 6k,\ c = 5k$$

Hence, $\cos A = \dfrac{b^2 + c^2 - a^2}{2bc} = \dfrac{36k^2 + 25k^2 - 49k^2}{60k^2}$

$= \dfrac{12}{60} = \dfrac{1}{5} = \dfrac{7}{35}$

$\cos B = \dfrac{a^2 + c^2 - b^2}{2ac} = \dfrac{49k^2 + 25k^2 - 36k^2}{70k^2}$

$= \dfrac{38}{70} = \dfrac{19}{35}$

$\cos C = \dfrac{a^2 + b^2 - c^2}{2ab} = \dfrac{49k^2 + 36k^2 - 25k^2}{84k^2}$

$= \dfrac{60}{84} = \dfrac{5}{7} = \dfrac{25}{35}$

$\Rightarrow \quad \dfrac{\cos A}{7} = \dfrac{\cos B}{19} = \dfrac{\cos C}{25}$

3.3 Projection Formulae

In any ΔABC, we have

(i) $c = a\cos B + b\cos A$

(ii) $b = a\cos C + c\cos A$

(iii) $a = b\cos C + c\cos B$

Proof : ***Case* I. When $\angle B$ is acute**

From ΔCBD, $\cos B = \dfrac{BD}{BC} = \dfrac{BD}{a}$

$\therefore \quad BD = a\cos B \quad$ ...(i)

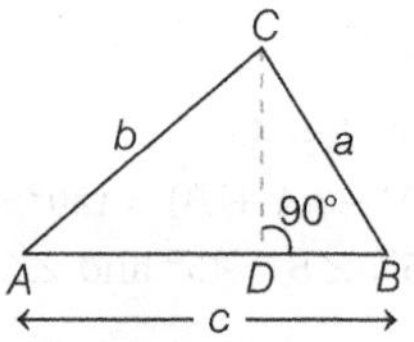

In ΔADC, $\quad \cos A = \dfrac{AD}{AC} = \dfrac{AD}{b}$

$\therefore \quad AD = b\cos A \quad$ ...(ii)

Now, $\quad c = AB = AD + DB = b\cos A + a\cos B$

Thus, $\quad c = b\cos A + a\cos B$

***Case* II. When $\angle B$ is obtuse**

From ΔCBD, $\cos(180° - B) = \dfrac{BD}{BC}$

$\therefore \quad -\cos B = \dfrac{BD}{a}$ or $BD = -a\cos B$

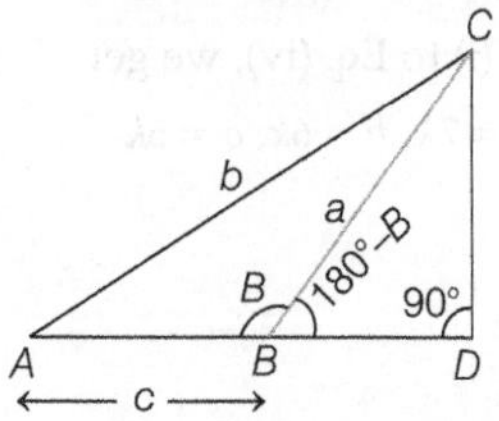

In ΔCAD, $\quad \cos A = \dfrac{AD}{AC} = \dfrac{AD}{b}$ or $AD = b\cos A$

Now, $\quad c = AB = AD - BD = b\cos A + a\cos B \quad$ ...(ii)

Case III. When $\angle B = 90°$

In ΔCAB, $\quad \cos A = \dfrac{AB}{AC} = \dfrac{c}{b}$

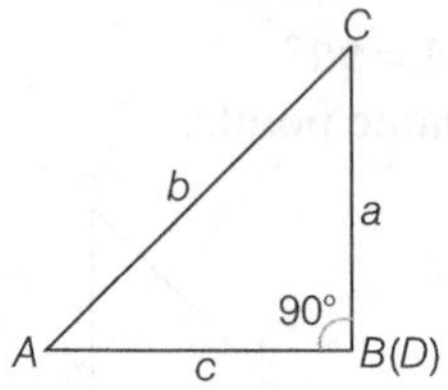

$\therefore \quad c = b\cos A = b\cos A + a\cos B$

$[\because c\cos B = c\cos 90° = 0, \text{ as } \cos 90° = 0]$

Thus, in all cases, $c = b\cos A + a\cos B$

Similarly, we can prove that

$b = c\cos A + a\cos C$

and $\quad a = b\cos C + c\cos B$

Example 10. Solve $b\cos^2\dfrac{C}{2} + c\cos^2\dfrac{B}{2}$ in terms of k, where k is perimeter of the ΔABC.

Sol. We have, $b\cos^2\dfrac{C}{2} + c\cos^2\dfrac{B}{2}$

$= \dfrac{b}{2}(1 + \cos C) + \dfrac{c}{2}(1 + \cos B)$

$= \dfrac{b + c}{2} + \dfrac{1}{2}(b\cos C + c\cos B)$

$= \dfrac{b + c}{2} + \dfrac{1}{2}a \quad$ [using projection formula]

$= \dfrac{a + b + c}{2}$

$\therefore \quad b\cos^2\dfrac{C}{2} + c\cos^2\dfrac{B}{2} = \dfrac{k}{2} \quad$ [where $k = a + b + c$, given]

Example 11. In a ΔABC, $c\cos^2\dfrac{A}{2} + a\cos^2\dfrac{C}{2} = \dfrac{3b}{2}$, then show a, b, c are in AP.

Sol. We have, $\quad c\cos^2\dfrac{A}{2} + a\cos^2\dfrac{C}{2} = \dfrac{3b}{2}$

$\Rightarrow \quad \dfrac{c}{2}(1 + \cos A) + \dfrac{a}{2}(1 + \cos C) = \dfrac{3b}{2}$

$\Rightarrow \quad a + c + (c\cos A + a\cos C) = 3b$

$\Rightarrow \quad a + c + b = 3b$

[using projection formula]

$\Rightarrow \quad a + c = 2b$

which shows a, b, c are in AP.

3.4 Tangent Rule or Napier's Analogy

In any ΔABC, we have

(i) $\tan\left(\dfrac{A-B}{2}\right)=\dfrac{a-b}{a+b}\cot\dfrac{C}{2}$

(ii) $\tan\left(\dfrac{B-C}{2}\right)=\dfrac{b-c}{b+c}\cot\dfrac{A}{2}$

(iii) $\tan\left(\dfrac{C-A}{2}\right)=\dfrac{c-a}{c+a}\cot\dfrac{B}{2}$

Proof In ΔABC, we know

$$\frac{a}{\sin A}=\frac{b}{\sin B}=\frac{c}{\sin C}=k\text{ (say)} \qquad \text{[sine law]}$$

$$\therefore \quad a=k\sin A, b=k\sin B, c=k\sin C \qquad \text{...(i)}$$

Now, RHS of Eq. (i), we get

$$=\left(\frac{a-b}{a+b}\right)\cdot\cot\frac{C}{2}$$

$$=\left(\frac{k\sin A-k\sin B}{k\sin A+k\sin B}\right)\cdot\cot\frac{C}{2} \qquad \text{[using Eq(i)]}$$

$$=\frac{2\cos\left(\frac{A+B}{2}\right)\cdot\sin\left(\frac{A-B}{2}\right)}{2\sin\left(\frac{A+B}{2}\right)\cdot\cos\left(\frac{A-B}{2}\right)}\cdot\frac{\cos\frac{C}{2}}{\sin\frac{C}{2}}$$

$$=\frac{\sin\left(\frac{A-B}{2}\right)}{\cos\left(\frac{A-B}{2}\right)} \qquad \left[\begin{array}{l}\text{as, }\cos\left(\frac{A+B}{2}\right)=\sin\left(\frac{C}{2}\right)\\ \text{and }\sin\left(\frac{A+B}{2}\right)=\cos\left(\frac{C}{2}\right)\end{array}\right]$$

$$=\tan\left(\frac{A-B}{2}\right)=\text{LHS of Eq. (i)}$$

$$\Rightarrow \tan\left(\frac{A-B}{2}\right)=\left(\frac{a-b}{a+b}\right)\cot\frac{C}{2}$$

Similarly, we can prove that

$$\tan\left(\frac{B-C}{2}\right)=\frac{b-c}{b+c}\cot\frac{A}{2}\text{ and }\tan\frac{C-A}{2}=\frac{c-a}{c+a}\cot\frac{B}{2}$$

Example 12. In a ΔABC, $a=2b$ and $|A-B|=\dfrac{\pi}{3}$. Determine the $\angle C$.

Sol. Given, $a=2b$ ...(i)

$\Rightarrow \angle A>\angle B$ [as $a>b$ and we know greater angle is opposite to greater side]

Also, $|A-B|=\dfrac{\pi}{3} \Rightarrow A-B=\dfrac{\pi}{3}$ ...(ii) [as $A>B$]

Using Napier's analogy, we get

$$\tan\left(\frac{A-B}{2}\right)=\frac{a-b}{a+b}\cot\left(\frac{C}{2}\right)$$

$$\Rightarrow \tan\left(\frac{\pi}{6}\right)=\frac{2b-b}{2b+b}\cot\left(\frac{C}{2}\right) \qquad \text{[using Eqs. (i) and (ii)]}$$

$$\Rightarrow \frac{1}{\sqrt{3}}=\frac{1}{3}\cot\left(\frac{C}{2}\right)$$

$$\Rightarrow \cot\left(\frac{C}{2}\right)=\sqrt{3}$$

$$\text{i.e.} \quad \frac{C}{2}=\frac{\pi}{6}\Rightarrow C=\frac{\pi}{3}$$

Example 13. In a ΔABC, the tangent of half the difference of two angles is one-third the tangent of half the sum of the angles. Determine the ratio of the sides opposite to the angles.

Sol. We have, $\tan\left(\dfrac{A-B}{2}\right)=\dfrac{1}{3}\tan\left(\dfrac{A+B}{2}\right)$ ...(i)

Using Napier's analogy, we get

$$\tan\left(\frac{A-B}{2}\right)=\frac{a-b}{a+b}\cdot\cot\left(\frac{C}{2}\right) \qquad \text{...(ii)}$$

From Eqs. (i) and (ii), we get

$$\frac{1}{3}\tan\left(\frac{A+B}{2}\right)=\frac{a-b}{a+b}\cdot\cot\left(\frac{C}{2}\right)$$

$$\Rightarrow \frac{1}{3}\cot\left(\frac{C}{2}\right)=\frac{a-b}{a+b}\cdot\cot\left(\frac{C}{2}\right)$$

$$\left[\text{as } A+B+C=\pi \therefore \tan\left(\frac{A+B}{2}\right)=\tan\left(\frac{\pi}{2}-\frac{C}{2}\right)=\cot\frac{C}{2}\right]$$

$$\Rightarrow \frac{a-b}{a+b}=\frac{1}{3}$$

$$\Rightarrow 3a-3b=a+b$$

$$\Rightarrow 2a=4b \Rightarrow \frac{b}{a}=\frac{1}{2}$$

Thus, the ratio of the sides opposite to the angles is $b:a=1:2$.

m-n Theorem

Let D be a point on the side BC of ΔABC such that

$$DB:CD=m:n \text{ and } \angle CDA=\theta,$$
$$\angle DAB=\alpha \text{ and } \angle CAD=\beta.$$

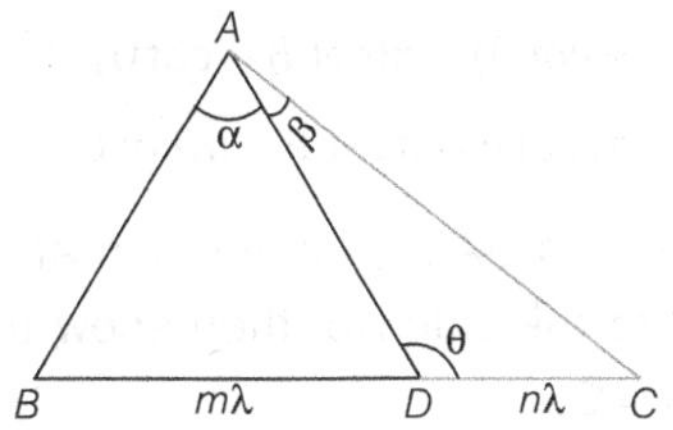

Then,

(i) $(m+n)\cot\theta = m\cot\alpha - n\cot\beta$

(ii) $(m+n)\cot\theta = n\cot B - m\cot C$

Proof (i) Given that $\dfrac{BD}{DC}=\dfrac{m}{n}, \angle ADC=\theta,$

$$\angle BAD=\alpha \text{ and } \angle DAC=\beta$$

Now, $\angle ADB = 180°-\theta$

and $\angle ABD = 180°-(\alpha+180°-\theta)$

$=\theta-\alpha$

Also, $\angle ACD = 180°-(\theta+\beta)$

$\Rightarrow \sin(\angle ACD)=\sin(\theta+\beta)$

In ΔABD, using sine rule, we get

$$\frac{BD}{\sin\alpha}=\frac{AD}{\sin(\theta-\alpha)} \quad \text{...(i)}$$

In ΔADC, using sine rule, we get

$$\frac{DC}{\sin\beta}=\frac{AD}{\sin(\theta+\beta)} \quad \text{...(ii)}$$

Dividing Eq. (i) by Eq. (ii), we get

$$\frac{BD\sin\beta}{DC\sin\alpha}=\frac{\sin(\theta+\beta)}{\sin(\theta-\alpha)} \quad \text{...(iii)}$$

$$\Rightarrow \frac{m}{n}\cdot\frac{\sin\beta}{\sin\alpha}=\frac{\sin\theta\cos\beta+\cos\theta\sin\beta}{\sin\theta\cos\alpha-\cos\theta\sin\alpha}$$

$$\Rightarrow m\sin\beta(\sin\theta\cos\alpha-\cos\theta\sin\alpha) = n\sin\alpha(\sin\theta\cos\beta+\cos\theta\sin\beta)$$

Dividing both sides by $\sin\alpha\sin\beta\sin\theta$, we get

$$m\cot\alpha - m\cot\theta = n\cot\beta + n\cot\theta$$

$$\therefore \quad (m+n)\cot\theta = m\cot\alpha - n\cot\beta$$

(ii) We have,

$$\angle CAD=\beta=180°-(\theta+C)$$

and $\angle BAD=\alpha=\theta-B$

On putting these values in Eq. (iii), we get

$$m\sin(\theta+C)\sin B = n\sin C\sin(\theta-B)$$

$$\Rightarrow m(\sin\theta\cos C+\cos\theta\sin C)\sin B = n\sin C(\sin\theta\cos B-\cos\theta\sin B)$$

On dividing both sides by $\sin\theta\sin B\sin C$, we get

$$m(\cot C+\cot\theta)=n(\cot B-\cot\theta)$$

$$\therefore \quad (m+n)\cot\theta = n\cot B - m\cot C$$

Example 14. If in a ΔABC, the median AD is perpendicular to the side AB, then show that $\tan A + 2\tan B = 0$.

Sol. Let $\angle ADC=\theta$

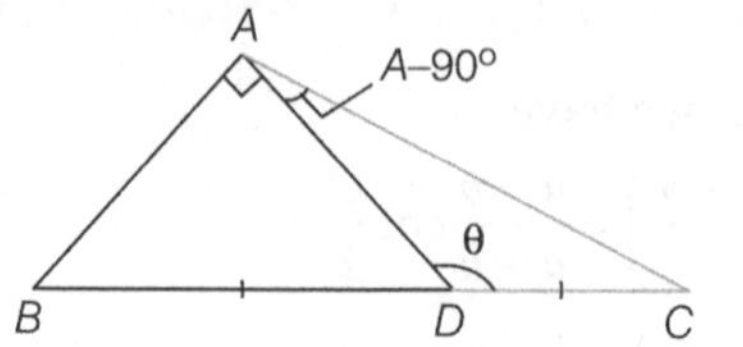

If we apply m-n rule in ΔABC, we get

$$(1+1)\cot\theta = 1\cdot\cot 90° - 1\cdot\cot(A-90°)$$

$$[\because \theta = 90°+B]$$

$$\Rightarrow 2\cot(90°+B) = 0+\cot(90°-A)$$

$$\Rightarrow -2\tan B = \tan A \Rightarrow \tan A + 2\tan B = 0$$

Example 15. The base of a triangle is divided into three equal parts. If the tangents of the angles subtended by these part at opposite vertex are t_1, t_2, t_3, then show that $\dfrac{1}{4}\left(\dfrac{1}{t_1}+\dfrac{1}{t_2}\right)\left(\dfrac{1}{t_2}+\dfrac{1}{t_3}\right)=1+\dfrac{1}{t_2^2}$.

Sol. Let the points P and Q divide the side BC in three equal parts such that $BP=PQ=QC=x$

Also, let $\angle BAP=\alpha$, $\angle PAQ=\beta$, $\angle QAC=\gamma$ and $\angle AQC=\theta$

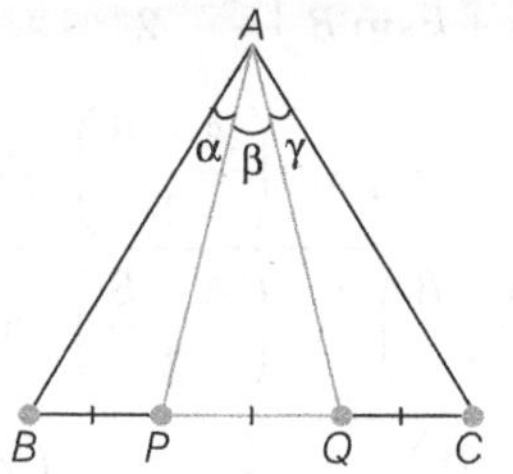

According to the question,

$$\tan\alpha = t_1, \ \tan\beta = t_2 \text{ and } \tan\gamma = t_3$$

On applying m-n rule in ΔABC, we get

$$(2x+x)\cot\theta = 2x\cot(\alpha+\beta) - x\cot\gamma \quad \text{...(i)}$$

From ΔAPC, we get

$$(x+x)\cot\theta = x\cot\beta - x\cot\gamma \quad \text{...(ii)}$$

Dividing Eq (i) by Eq. (ii), we get

$$\frac{3}{2}=\frac{2\cot(\alpha+\beta)-\cot\gamma}{\cot\beta-\cot\gamma}$$

$$\Rightarrow 3\cot\beta - 3\cot\gamma = 4\cot(\alpha+\beta) - 2\cot\gamma$$

$$\Rightarrow 3\cot\beta - \cot\gamma = \frac{4(\cot\alpha\cos\beta-1)}{\cot\beta+\cot\alpha}$$

$$\Rightarrow 3\cot^2\beta - \cot\beta\cot\gamma + 3\cot\alpha\cot\beta - \cot\alpha\cot\gamma = 4\cot\alpha\cot\beta - 4$$

$$\Rightarrow 4+4\cot^2\beta = \cot^2\beta + \cot\alpha\cot\beta + \cot\beta\cot\gamma + \cot\gamma\cot\alpha$$

$$\Rightarrow 4(1+\cot^2\beta) = (\cot\beta+\cot\alpha)(\cot\beta+\cot\gamma)$$

$$\Rightarrow \frac{1}{4}\left(\frac{1}{t_1}+\frac{1}{t_2}\right)\left(\frac{1}{t_2}+\frac{1}{t_3}\right)=1+\frac{1}{t_2^2}$$

Milestone Practice 3.1

1. If the sides of a triangle are in GP and the largest angle is twice the smallest angle, then relation for r is
(a) $r^4 - r - 1 = 0$ (b) $r^4 + r + 1 = 0$
(c) $r^4 - r + 1 = 0$ (d) $r^4 + r - 1 = 0$

2. In ΔABC, $a = 4$, $b = 12$ and $B = 60°$, then the value of $\sin A$ is
(a) $\frac{1}{2\sqrt{3}}$ (b) $\frac{1}{3\sqrt{2}}$ (c) $\frac{2}{\sqrt{3}}$ (d) $\frac{\sqrt{3}}{2}$

3. Let ABC be a triangle such that $\angle A = 45°$, $\angle B = 75°$, then $a + c\sqrt{2}$ is equal to
(a) 0 (b) b (c) $2b$ (d) $-b$

4. Angles A, B and C of a ΔABC are in AP. If $\frac{b}{c} = \frac{\sqrt{3}}{\sqrt{2}}$, then $\angle A$ is equal to
(a) $\frac{\pi}{6}$ (b) $\frac{\pi}{4}$ (c) $\frac{5\pi}{12}$ (d) $\frac{\pi}{2}$

5. If $\cot\frac{A}{2} = \frac{b+c}{a}$, then ΔABC is
(a) isosceles (b) equilateral
(c) right angled (d) None of these

6. If in a ΔABC, $\frac{a^2 - b^2}{a^2 + b^2} = \frac{\sin(A-B)}{\sin(A+B)}$, then the triangle is
(a) right angled or isosceles
(b) right angled and isosceles
(c) equilateral
(d) None of the above

7. In any ΔABC,
$\frac{a^2\sin(B-C)}{\sin B + \sin C} + \frac{b^2\sin(C-A)}{\sin C + \sin A} + \frac{c^2\sin(A-B)}{\sin A + \sin B} =$
(a) $a+b+c$ (b) $a+b-c$ (c) $a-b+c$ (d) 0

8. The equation $ax^2 + bx + c = 0$, where a, b, c are the side of a ΔABC and the equation $x^2 + \sqrt{2}x + 1 = 0$ have a common root. Then, the measure for $\angle C$ is
(a) 90° (b) 60° (c) 45° (d) 30°

9. The expression $\frac{(a+b+c)(b+c-a)(c+a-b)(a+b-c)}{4b^2c^2}$ is equal to
(a) $\cos^2 A$ (b) $\sin^2 A$
(c) $\cos A \cos B \cos C$ (d) None of these

10. In ΔABC, if $a\cos A = b\cos B$, then the triangle is
(a) isosceles (b) right angled
(c) isosceles or right angled (d) right angled isosceles

11. In a ΔABC, $(a+b+c)(b+c-a) = \lambda\, bc$, if
(a) $\lambda < 0$ (b) $\lambda > 0$ (c) $0 < \lambda < 4$ (d) $\lambda < 4$

12. If $a = 9$, $b = 8$ and $c = x$ satisfies $3\cos C = 2$, then
(a) $x = 5$ (b) $x = 6$ (c) $x = 4$ (d) $x = 7$

13. In ΔABC, if $\sin^2 A + \sin^2 B = \sin^2 C$, then the triangle is
(a) equilateral (b) isosceles
(c) right angled (d) None of these

14. The sides of a triangle are $\alpha - \beta, \alpha + \beta$ and $\sqrt{3\alpha^2 + \beta^2}$, $(\alpha > \beta > 0)$. Its largest angle is
(a) $\frac{2\pi}{3}$ (b) $\frac{\pi}{2}$ (c) $\frac{3\pi}{4}$ (d) $\frac{5\pi}{6}$

15. In any triangle, $\frac{1+\cos(A-B)\cos C}{1+\cos(A-C)\cos B} =$
(a) $\frac{a^2+b^2}{a^2+c^2}$ (b) $\frac{b^2+c^2}{b^2-c^2}$
(c) $\frac{c^2-a^2}{a^2+b^2}$ (d) None of these

16. If the sides of a ΔABC are in AP and a is the smallest side, then $\cos A$ equals
(a) $\frac{3c-4b}{2c}$ (b) $\frac{3c-4b}{2b}$
(c) $\frac{4c-3b}{2c}$ (d) None of these

17. In a ΔABC, $a^2\cos 2B + b^2\cos 2A + 2ab\cos(A-B)$ is equal to
(a) a^2 (b) c^2 (c) b^2 (d) $a^2 + b^2$

18. In any ΔABC, $2[bc\cos A + ca\cos B + ab\cos C]$ is equal to
(a) $a^2 + b^2 + c^2$ (b) $a^2 + b^2 - c^2$
(c) $a^2 - b^2 + c^2$ (d) None of these

19. In a ΔABC, $\tan\frac{1}{2}(A+B)\cdot\cot\frac{1}{2}(A-B)$ is equal to
(a) $\frac{a-b}{a+b}$ (b) $\frac{a+b}{c}$ (c) $\frac{a+b}{a-b}$ (d) $\frac{a-b}{2(a+b)}$

20. If in a ΔABC, $b = \sqrt{3}$, $c = 1$ and $B - C = 90°$, then $\angle A$ is
(a) 30° (b) 45° (c) 75° (d) 15°

Answer Key

1. (a)	2. (a)	3. (c)	4. (c)	5. (c)	6. (b)	7. (d)	8. (c)	9. (b)	10. (c)
11. (c)	12. (d)	13. (c)	14. (a)	15. (a)	16. (c)	17. (b)	18. (a)	19. (c)	20. (a)

For Detailed Solution

Milestone 2 Auxiliary Formulae

• Trigonometric Ratios of Half-angles • Area of Triangle

3.5 Trigonometric Ratios of Half-angles

In any ΔABC, we have

$$\cos A = \frac{b^2+c^2-a^2}{2bc} \quad \text{...(i) [using cosine law]}$$

and

$$2\sin^2\frac{A}{2} = 1-\cos A$$

[using half-angle identity]...(ii)

$$= 1-\left(\frac{b^2+c^2-a^2}{2bc}\right) \quad \text{[using Eq. (i)]}$$

$$= \frac{2bc-b^2-c^2+a^2}{2bc}$$

$$= \frac{a^2-(b^2+c^2-2bc)}{2bc} = \frac{a^2-(b-c)^2}{2bc}$$

$$= \frac{(a+b-c)(a-b+c)}{2bc}$$

$$= \frac{(2s-c-c)(2s-b-b)}{2bc}$$

[we know that $a+b+c=2s$

$\therefore a+b=2s-c$ and $a+c=2s-b$]

$$= \frac{4(s-c)(s-b)}{2bc}$$

$$\therefore \quad \sin^2\frac{A}{2} = \frac{(s-b)(s-c)}{bc}$$

$$\Rightarrow \quad \sin\frac{A}{2} = \sqrt{\frac{(s-b)(s-c)}{bc}}$$

[since in a triangle, A is always less than 180°,

$\therefore \sin A/2$ is ('+' ve)]

Similarly, we can prove that

$$\sin\frac{B}{2} = \sqrt{\frac{(s-a)(s-c)}{ac}}$$

$$\sin\frac{C}{2} = \sqrt{\frac{(s-a)(s-b)}{ab}}$$

Again,

$$2\cos^2\frac{A}{2} = 1+\cos A = 1+\frac{b^2+c^2-a^2}{2bc}$$

$$= \frac{2bc+b^2+c^2-a^2}{2bc}$$

$$= \frac{(b+c)^2-a^2}{2bc}$$

$$= \frac{(b+c+a)(b+c-a)}{2bc}$$

$$\therefore \quad 2\cos^2\frac{A}{2} = \frac{2s\times 2(s-a)}{2bc}$$

$$\Rightarrow \quad \cos^2\frac{A}{2} = \frac{s(s-a)}{bc}$$

[where, $a+b+c=2s \Rightarrow b+c=2s-a$]

Since, $A/2$ is less than 90°.

$$\therefore \quad \cos A/2 > 0$$

$$\therefore \quad \cos\frac{A}{2} = \sqrt{\frac{s(s-a)}{bc}}$$

Similarly, we can prove that

$$\cos\frac{B}{2} = \sqrt{\frac{s(s-b)}{ac}}$$

and

$$\cos\frac{C}{2} = \sqrt{\frac{s(s-c)}{ab}}$$

Also,

$$\tan\frac{A}{2} = \frac{\sin A/2}{\cos A/2}$$

$$= \sqrt{\frac{(s-b)(s-c)}{bc}} \times \sqrt{\frac{bc}{s(s-a)}}$$

$$\therefore \quad \tan\frac{A}{2} = \sqrt{\frac{(s-b)(s-c)}{s(s-a)}}$$

Similarly, we can prove that

$$\tan\frac{B}{2} = \sqrt{\frac{(s-a)(s-c)}{s(s-b)}}$$

and

$$\tan\frac{C}{2} = \sqrt{\frac{(s-a)(s-b)}{s(s-c)}}$$

Example 16. In any ΔABC, if $\cos\frac{A}{2}=\sqrt{\frac{b+c}{2c}}$, then prove that $a^2+b^2=c^2$.

Sol. Given, $\cos\frac{A}{2}=\sqrt{\frac{b+c}{2c}}$

$$\Rightarrow \sqrt{\frac{s(s-a)}{bc}}=\sqrt{\frac{b+c}{2c}}$$

$$\Rightarrow \frac{s(s-a)}{bc}=\frac{b+c}{2c}$$

$$\Rightarrow 2s(2s-2a)=2b(b+c)$$

$$\Rightarrow (b+c+a)(b+c-a)=2b^2+2bc$$

$$\Rightarrow (b+c)^2-a^2=2b^2+2bc$$

$$\Rightarrow b^2+c^2+2bc-a^2=2b^2+2bc$$

$$\Rightarrow c^2=a^2+b^2$$

Example 17. In any ΔABC, show that $\left(\cot\frac{A}{2}+\cot\frac{B}{2}\right)\left(a\sin^2\frac{B}{2}+b\sin^2\frac{A}{2}\right)=c\cot\frac{C}{2}$.

Sol. LHS $=\left(\cot\frac{A}{2}+\cot\frac{B}{2}\right)\left(a\sin^2\frac{B}{2}+b\sin^2\frac{A}{2}\right)$

$$=\left[\sqrt{\frac{s(s-a)}{(s-b)(s-c)}}+\sqrt{\frac{s(s-b)}{(s-a)(s-c)}}\right]\left[\frac{a(s-c)(s-a)}{ca}+\frac{b(s-b)(s-c)}{bc}\right]$$

$$=\sqrt{s}\left[\frac{(s-a)+(s-b)}{\sqrt{(s-a)(s-b)(s-c)}}\right]\times\frac{(s-c)}{c}[s-a+s-b]$$

$$=\sqrt{s}\left[\frac{c(s-c)}{\sqrt{(s-a)(s-b)(s-c)}}\right]$$

$$=c\sqrt{\frac{s(s-c)}{(s-a)(s-b)}}=c\cot\frac{C}{2}=\text{RHS}$$

3.6 Area of Triangle

If Δ represents the area of a ΔABC, then

$$\Delta=\frac{1}{2}BC\cdot AD \quad \left[\because \Delta=\frac{1}{2}\times\text{Base}\times\text{Height}\right]$$

$$=\frac{1}{2}a\cdot(c\sin B) \quad \left[\text{as}\sin B=\frac{AD}{c}\right]$$

$$\therefore \quad \Delta=\frac{1}{2}ac\sin B$$

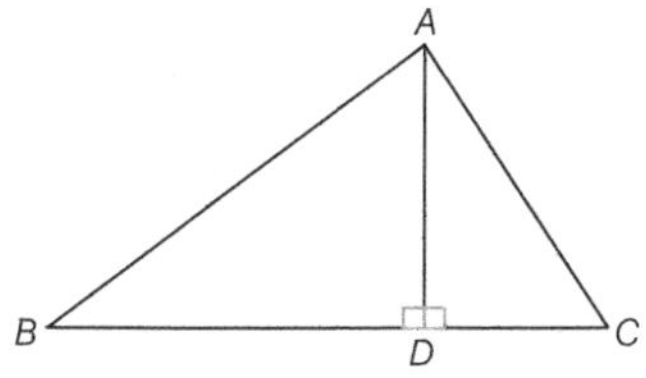

Similarly, $\Delta=\frac{1}{2}bc\sin A$

and $\Delta=\frac{1}{2}ab\sin C$

$$\therefore \quad \boldsymbol{\Delta=\frac{1}{2}ab\sin C=\frac{1}{2}bc\sin A=\frac{1}{2}ca\sin B}$$

JEE SPIKE

(i) Area of a triangle in terms of sides (Heron's formula) :

$$\Delta=\frac{1}{2}bc\sin A=\frac{1}{2}bc\cdot 2\sin\frac{A}{2}\cos\frac{A}{2}$$

$$=bc\sqrt{\frac{(s-b)(s-c)}{bc}}\sqrt{\frac{s(s-a)}{bc}}$$

$$\therefore \quad \Delta=\sqrt{s(s-a)(s-b)(s-c)}.$$

Concept Inside Video

(ii) Area of triangle in terms of one side and sine of three angles:

$$\Delta=\frac{1}{2}bc\sin A=\frac{1}{2}(k\sin B)(k\sin C)\cdot\sin A$$

$$=\frac{1}{2}k^2\sin A\sin B\sin C=\frac{1}{2}\left(\frac{a}{\sin A}\right)^2\sin A\sin B\sin C$$

$$\therefore \quad \Delta=\frac{a^2}{2}\cdot\frac{\sin B\sin C}{\sin A}=\frac{b^2}{2}\cdot\frac{\sin A\sin C}{\sin B}=\frac{c^2}{2}\cdot\frac{\sin A\sin B}{\sin C}$$

Example 18. In any ΔABC, show that

$$\frac{(a+b+c)(b+c-a)(c+a-b)(a+b-c)}{4b^2c^2}=\sin^2 A.$$

Sol. LHS $=\frac{(a+b+c)(b+c-a)(c+a-b)(a+b-c)}{4b^2c^2}$

$$=\frac{(2s)(2(s-a))(2(s-b))(2(s-c))}{4b^2c^2}$$

$$=\frac{16s(s-a)(s-b)(s-c)}{4b^2c^2}$$

$$=\frac{4\Delta^2}{b^2c^2}$$

$$=\frac{4}{b^2c^2}\left(\frac{1}{2}bc\sin A\right)^2$$

$$=\sin^2 A=\text{RHS}$$

Example 19. If the angles of a triangle are 30° and 45°, and the included side is $(\sqrt{3}+1)$ cm, then prove that the area of the triangle is $\frac{1}{2}(\sqrt{3}+1)$.

Sol. We have, $\frac{\sin A}{a}=\frac{\sin B}{b}=\frac{\sin C}{c}$

$$\Rightarrow \frac{\sin 105^\circ}{\sqrt{3}+1}=\frac{\sin 30^\circ}{b}=\frac{\sin 45^\circ}{c}$$

$$\Rightarrow b=\frac{\sqrt{3}+1}{2\sin 105^\circ}\text{ and } c=\frac{\sqrt{3}+1}{\sqrt{2}\sin 105^\circ}$$

So, area of $\Delta ABC = \frac{1}{2} bc \sin A = \frac{1}{2} bc \sin 105°$

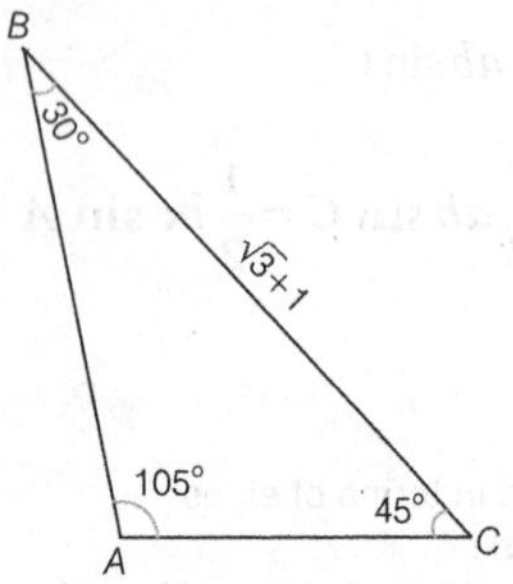

$$= \frac{1}{2} \cdot \frac{(\sqrt{3}+1)^2}{2\sqrt{2}\sin(60° + 45°)}$$

$$= \frac{(\sqrt{3}+1)^2}{4\sqrt{2}\left\{\frac{\sqrt{3}}{2} \cdot \frac{1}{\sqrt{2}} + \frac{1}{2} \cdot \frac{1}{\sqrt{2}}\right\}}$$

$$= \frac{(\sqrt{3}+1)^2}{2(\sqrt{3}+1)}$$

$$= \frac{1}{2}(\sqrt{3}+1)$$

Thus, area of Δ is $\frac{1}{2}(\sqrt{3}+1)$.

Alternate Solution

In above example we have

$\angle A = 105°, \angle B = 30°, \angle C = 45°$ and $a = \sqrt{3} + 1$

Thus, area of $\Delta = \frac{a^2}{2} \frac{\sin B \sin C}{\sin A}$ [using note (ii)]

$$= \frac{(\sqrt{3}+1)^2}{2} \cdot \frac{\sin 30° \sin 45°}{\sin (105°)} = \frac{1}{2}(\sqrt{3}+1)$$

Example 20. Consider the following statements concerning in ΔABC

(i) The sides a, b, c and area Δ are rational.

(ii) $a, \tan\frac{B}{2}, \tan\frac{C}{2}$ are rational.

(iii) $a, \sin A, \sin B, \sin C$ are rational.

Prove that (i) $\Rightarrow$ (ii) $\Rightarrow$ (iii) $\Rightarrow$ (i).

Sol. a, b, c, Δ are rational (given).

$\Rightarrow$ $s, s-a, s-b, s-c$ are rational.

Now, $\tan\frac{B}{2} = \sqrt{\frac{(s-c)(s-a)}{s(s-b)}}$

$$= \sqrt{\frac{s(s-a)(s-b)(s-c)}{s^2(s-b)^2}}$$

$$= \frac{\Delta}{s(s-b)}$$

$\therefore$ $\tan\frac{B}{2}$ = rational [as $\Delta, s, (s-b)$ are rational]

Similarly, $\tan\frac{C}{2}$ is rational.

Hence (i) $\Rightarrow$ (ii).

Now, $\sin B = \dfrac{2\tan\frac{B}{2}}{1+\tan^2\frac{B}{2}}$ is rational by (ii).

Similarly, $\sin C$ is also rational.

$$\tan\frac{A}{2} = \cot\frac{B+C}{2} = \frac{1-\tan\frac{B}{2}\cdot\tan\frac{C}{2}}{\tan\frac{B}{2}+\tan\frac{C}{2}} = \text{rational by (ii)}$$

$\Rightarrow$ $\sin A$ is rational

Hence, (ii) $\Rightarrow$ (iii).

Now, $\frac{a}{\sin A} = \frac{b}{\sin B} = \frac{c}{\sin C} = k$,

which is rational since 'a' and '$\sin A$' are rational.

$\Rightarrow \frac{b}{\sin B}$ and $\frac{c}{\sin C}$ are rational.

But $\sin B$ and $\sin C$ are rational by (iii)

$\Rightarrow$ b and c are rational.

$\Rightarrow$ $\Delta = \frac{1}{2} bc \sin A$ is also rational.

Hence (iii) $\Rightarrow$ (i).

Milestone Practice 3.2

1. If in a ΔABC, $(s-a)(s-b)=s(s-c)$, then angle C is equal to
(a) $90°$ (b) $45°$
(c) $30°$ (d) $60°$

2. In any ΔABC, if $\cot\frac{A}{2}, \cot\frac{B}{2}, \cot\frac{C}{2}$ are in AP, then a, b, c are in
(a) AP
(b) GP
(c) HP
(d) None of the above

3. In any ΔABC, $\dfrac{\tan\frac{A}{2}-\tan\frac{B}{2}}{\tan\frac{A}{2}+\tan\frac{B}{2}}$ equal to
(a) $\frac{a-b}{a+b}$
(b) $\frac{a-b}{c}$
(c) $\frac{a-b}{a+b+c}$
(d) $\frac{c}{a+b}$

4. In a ΔABC, $bc\cos^2\frac{A}{2}+ca\cos^2\frac{B}{2}+ab\cos^2\frac{C}{2}$ is equal to
(a) $(s-a)^2$ (b) $(s-b)^2$
(c) $(s-c)^2$ (d) s^2

5. In a ΔABC, if $\cos A+\cos C=4\sin^2\left(\frac{B}{2}\right)$, then a, b, c are in
(a) AP (b) GP
(c) HP (d) None of these

6. If in a ΔABC, $3a=b+c$, then the value of $\cot\frac{B}{2}\cot\frac{C}{2}$ is
(a) 1 (b) $\sqrt{3}$
(c) 2 (d) None of these

7. If in ΔABC, $\Delta=a^2-(b-c)^2$, then the value of $\tan A$ is
(a) $\frac{8}{15}$ (b) $\frac{7}{15}$
(c) $\frac{15}{8}$ (d) $\frac{15}{7}$

8. If in a triangle, $a\cos^2\frac{C}{2}+c\cos^2\frac{A}{2}=\frac{3b}{2}$, then its sides will be in
(a) AP (b) GP
(c) HP (d) AGP

9. In the adjacent figure 'P' is any interior point of the equilateral ΔABC of side length 2 unit. If x_a, x_b and x_c represent the distance of P from the sides BC, CA and AB respectively then $x_a+x_b+x_c$ is equal to

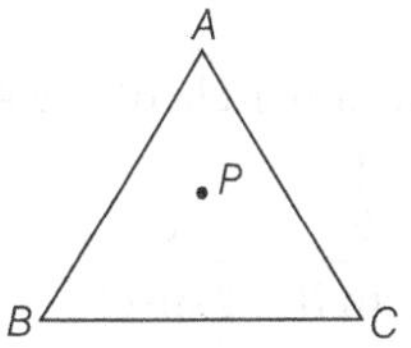

(a) 6 (b) $\sqrt{3}$
(c) $\frac{\sqrt{3}}{2}$ (d) $2\sqrt{3}x$

10. If $c^2=a^2+b^2$, then $4s(s-a)(s-b)(s-c)$ is equal to
(a) s^4 (b) b^2c^2
(c) c^2a^2 (d) a^2b^2

Answer Key

1. (a)	2. (a)	3. (b)	4. (d)	5. (a)
6. (c)	7. (a)	8. (a)	9. (b)	10. (d)

For Detailed Solution

Milestone 3 Circles Connected with Triangle

• Circumcircle of a Triangle • In-circle or Inscribed Circle of a Triangle • Escribed Circles of a Triangle

3.7 Circumcircle of a Triangle

The circle which passes through the angular points of a ΔABC is called its Circumcircle. The centre of this circle is the point of intersection of perpendicular bisectors of the sides and called the Circumcentre. Its radius is always denoted by $\boldsymbol{R}$.

JEE Focus Points

- Circumcentre of an acute angled triangle lies inside the triangle.
- Circumcentre of an obtuse angled triangle lies outside the triangle.
- In a right angled triangle, the circumcentre is the mid-point of hypotenuse.

Circumradius

The radius of the circumcircle of a ΔABC is called the circumradius given by

(i) $R=\dfrac{a}{2\sin A}=\dfrac{b}{2\sin B}=\dfrac{c}{2\sin C}$ (ii) $R=\dfrac{abc}{4\Delta}$

Proof

(i) Here, the perpendicular bisectors of the sides BC, CA and AB intersect at O.

$\therefore$ O is the circumcentre such that,

$$OA=OB=OC=R$$

We have, $\angle BOC=2\angle A$

$\therefore$ $\angle BOD=\angle COD=\angle A$

In ΔOBD, $\sin A=\dfrac{BD}{OB}=\dfrac{a/2}{R}$

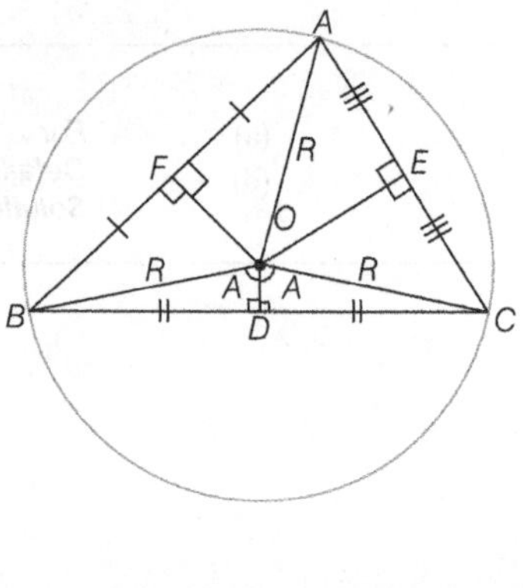

$$\Rightarrow \quad R=\frac{a}{2\sin A}$$

Similarly, $R=\dfrac{b}{2\sin B}$ and $R=\dfrac{c}{2\sin C}$

Hence, $R=\dfrac{a}{2\sin A}=\dfrac{b}{2\sin B}=\dfrac{c}{2\sin C}$

(ii) As discussed,

$$\text{Area of }\Delta=\frac{1}{2}bc\sin A\Rightarrow \sin A=\frac{2\Delta}{bc} \quad \text{...(i)}$$

Also, $$R=\frac{a}{2\sin A} \quad \text{...(ii)}$$

$\therefore$ From Eqs. (i) and (ii), we get

$$R=\frac{a}{2\left(\frac{2\Delta}{bc}\right)}=\frac{abc}{4\Delta} \Rightarrow R=\frac{abc}{4\Delta}$$

Example 21. If in a ΔABC, the value of $\cot A, \cot B, \cot C$ are in AP show a^2, b^2, c^2 are in A.P.

Sol. Here, $\cot A$, $\cot B$, $\cot C$ are in AP.

$$\Rightarrow \frac{b^2+c^2-a^2}{2bc\cdot\frac{a}{2R}}, \frac{c^2+a^2-b^2}{2ac\cdot\frac{b}{2R}}, \frac{a^2+b^2-c^2}{2ab\cdot\frac{c}{2R}} \text{ are in AP.}$$

$\Rightarrow b^2+c^2-a^2, c^2+a^2-b^2, a^2+b^2-c^2$ are in AP.

$\left[\text{multiplying by } \dfrac{abc}{R}\right]$

$\Rightarrow -2a^2, -2b^2, -2c^2$ are in AP.

[subtracting $a^2+b^2+c^2$ from each]

$\Rightarrow$ a^2, b^2, c^2 are in AP.

Alternate Solution

$2\cot B=\cot A+\cot C$

$$\Rightarrow \frac{2(a^2+c^2-b^2)}{2ac\cdot kb}=\frac{b^2+c^2-a^2}{2bc\cdot ka}+\frac{a^2+b^2-c^2}{2ab\cdot kc}$$

[using sine and cosine law]

$\Rightarrow$ $2(a^2+c^2-b^2)=b^2+c^2-a^2+a^2+b^2-c^2$

$\Rightarrow$ $2(a^2+c^2-b^2)=2b^2$

$\Rightarrow$ $a^2+c^2-b^2=b^2$ or $a^2+c^2=2b^2$

i.e. a^2, b^2, c^2 are in AP.

3.8 In-circle or Inscribed Circle of a Triangle

The circle that can be inscribed with in a triangle so as to touch each of its sides is called its inscribed circle or In-circle. The centre of this circle is the points of intersection of bisectors of the angles of the triangle. The radius of the circle is always denoted by r and is equal to the length of perpendicular from its centre to any one of the sides of triangle.

In-radius

The radius of the inscribed circle of a triangle is called the in-radius. It is denoted by 'r' and is given by

(i) $r = \dfrac{\Delta}{s}$

(ii) $r = (s-a)\tan\dfrac{A}{2} = (s-b)\tan\dfrac{B}{2} = (s-c)\tan\dfrac{C}{2}$

(iii) $r = \dfrac{a\sin B/2\cdot\sin C/2}{\cos A/2} = \dfrac{b\sin C/2\cdot\sin A/2}{\cos B/2}$

$= \dfrac{c\sin A/2\cdot\sin B/2}{\cos C/2}$

(iv) $r = 4R\sin A/2\sin B/2\sin C/2$

Proof Let the internal bisectors of the angles of the ΔABC meet at I. Suppose the circle touches the sides BC, CA and AB at D, E and F, respectively.

Then, ID, IE, IF are perpendicular to these sides and $ID = IE = IF = r$.

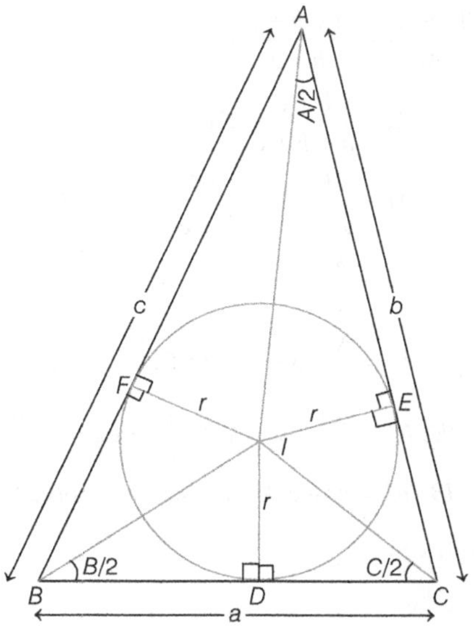

(i) We have,

area of ΔABC = Area of ΔIBC + Area of ΔIAB + Area of ΔICA

$$\Delta = \frac{1}{2}ar + \frac{1}{2}cr + \frac{1}{2}br$$

$$\Rightarrow \quad \Delta = \frac{1}{2}(a+b+c)r = sr \quad \left[\text{as, } s = \frac{a+b+c}{2}\right]$$

$$\Rightarrow \quad \Delta = sr$$

or $$r = \frac{\Delta}{s}$$

(ii) Since, the lengths of the tangents to a circle from given points are equal, therefore

$$AE = AF,\ BD = BF \text{ and } CD = CE.$$

Now, $2s = a+b+c = BC + CA + AB$

$= (BD+DC) + (CE+EA) + (AF+FB)$

$= (BD+BF) + (AE+AF) + (CD+CE)$

$= 2(BD+AE+CD)$

$= 2(BC+AE) = 2(a+AE)$

$\Rightarrow \quad s = a + AE$

$\Rightarrow \quad AE = (s-a)$

Now, in ΔIAE,

$$\tan\frac{A}{2} = \frac{r}{AE}$$

$\Rightarrow \quad r = AE\tan(A/2) = (s-a)\tan A/2$

$\therefore \quad r = (s-a)\tan A/2$

Similarly, $r = (s-b)\tan B/2$

and $r = (s-c)\tan C/2$

Hence, $r = (s-a)\tan A/2$

$= (s-b)\tan B/2 = (s-c)\tan C/2$

(iii) In ΔIBD and ΔICD, we have,

$$\tan B/2 = \frac{r}{BD} \text{ and } \tan\frac{C}{2} = \frac{r}{CD}$$

$$\therefore \quad BD = \frac{r}{\tan B/2} \text{ and } CD = \frac{r}{\tan C/2}$$

Now, $a = BD + CD$

$$\Rightarrow \quad a = \frac{r}{\tan\left(\frac{B}{2}\right)} + \frac{r}{\tan\left(\frac{C}{2}\right)}$$

$$\Rightarrow \quad a = r\left[\frac{\cos B/2}{\sin B/2} + \frac{\cos C/2}{\sin C/2}\right]$$

$$\Rightarrow \quad a = r\left[\frac{\cos B/2\cdot\sin C/2 + \sin B/2\cdot\cos C/2}{\sin B/2\cdot\sin C/2}\right]$$

$$\Rightarrow \quad a = \frac{r\sin(B/2 + C/2)}{\sin B/2\cdot\sin C/2}$$

$$\Rightarrow \quad a = \frac{r\cos A/2}{\sin B/2\cdot\sin C/2} \quad [\because A+B+C=\pi]$$

$$\therefore \quad r = \frac{a \sin B/2 \cdot \sin C/2}{\cos A/2}$$

Similarly, $$r = \frac{b \sin A/2 \cdot \sin C/2}{\cos B/2}$$

and $$r = \frac{c \sin A/2 \cdot \sin B/2}{\cos C/2}$$

(iv) We have, $$r = \frac{a \sin B/2 \cdot \sin C/2}{\cos A/2}$$

and $$R = \frac{a}{2 \sin A}$$

$$\Rightarrow \quad r = \frac{2R \sin A \cdot \sin B/2 \cdot \sin C/2}{\cos A/2}$$

$$\Rightarrow \quad r = \frac{2R \cdot (2 \sin A/2 \cdot \cos A/2) \cdot \sin B/2 \cdot \sin C/2}{\cos A/2}$$

$$\Rightarrow \quad r = 4R \sin A/2 \cdot \sin B/2 \cdot \sin C/2$$

Example 22. In a right angled triangle, prove that $r + 2R = s$.

Sol. In a right angled triangle, the circumcentre lies on the mid-point of the hypotenuse.

Let $\angle A = 90°$

$$\therefore \quad R = \frac{a}{2} \quad \text{...(i)}$$

Also, $$r = (s-a)\tan A/2 = (s-a)\tan 45°$$

$$r = (s-a) \quad \text{...(ii)}$$

From Eqs. (i) and (ii), we get

$$r = s - 2R$$

$$\Rightarrow \quad r + 2R = s$$

Example 23. Find the ratio of the circum-radius and the inradius of ΔABC, whose sides are in the ratio 4 : 5 : 6.

Sol. Here, $a = 4k$, $b = 5k$, $c = 6k$

$$\therefore \quad s = \frac{15k}{2} \quad \text{...(i)}$$

$$\therefore \quad \Delta = \sqrt{s(s-a)(s-b)(s-c)}$$

$$\Rightarrow \quad \Delta = \sqrt{\frac{15k}{2}\left(\frac{15k}{2} - 4k\right)\left(\frac{15k}{2} - 5k\right)\left(\frac{15k}{2} - 6k\right)}$$

$$\Rightarrow \quad \Delta = \frac{15\sqrt{7}}{4}k^2 \quad \text{...(ii)}$$

and $$R = \frac{abc}{4\Delta} = \frac{4k \cdot 5k \cdot 6k}{4 \cdot \frac{15}{4}\sqrt{7}k^2} \quad \text{[using Eq. (ii)]}$$

$$\therefore \quad R = \frac{8}{\sqrt{7}}k \quad \text{...(iii)}$$

and $$r = \frac{\Delta}{s} = \frac{15\sqrt{7}}{4}k^2 \cdot \frac{2}{15k} \quad \text{[using Eqs. (i) and (ii)]}$$

$$\therefore \quad r = \frac{\sqrt{7}}{2}k \quad \text{...(iv)}$$

$$\therefore \quad \frac{R}{r} = \frac{8k/\sqrt{7}}{\sqrt{7}k/2} = \frac{16}{7} \quad \text{[using Eqs. (iii) and (iv)]}$$

$$\Rightarrow R : r = 16 : 7$$

Example 24. Find the ratio of $IA : IB : IC$, where I is the incentre of ΔABC.

Sol. Here, $BD : DC = c : b$

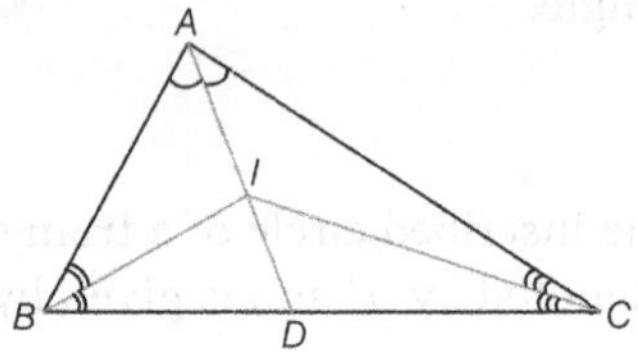

But $BD + DC = a$;

$$\therefore \quad BD = \frac{c}{b+c} \cdot a \quad \text{...(i)}$$

In ΔABD, $$\frac{BD}{\sin A/2} = \frac{AD}{\sin B}$$

$$\therefore \quad AD = \frac{ac}{b+c} \cdot \frac{\sin B}{\sin A/2} = \frac{2\Delta}{b+c} \cdot \operatorname{cosec} A/2 \quad \text{...(ii)}$$

Also, $$\frac{AI}{ID} = \frac{AB}{BD} = \frac{c}{\frac{ac}{b+c}} = \frac{b+c}{a} \quad \text{[using Eq. (i)]}$$

or $$\frac{ID}{AI} = \frac{a}{b+c}$$

On adding '1' both sides, we get

$$\frac{ID}{AI} + 1 = \frac{a}{b+c} + 1$$

$$\Rightarrow \quad \frac{ID + AI}{AI} = \frac{a+b+c}{b+c}$$

$$\Rightarrow \quad AI = \frac{b+c}{a+b+c} \cdot AD$$

$$\therefore \quad AI = \frac{b+c}{a+b+c} \cdot \frac{2\Delta}{b+c} \cdot \operatorname{cosec} A/2$$

$$= \frac{\Delta}{s} \cdot \operatorname{cosec} A/2$$

Similarly, $$BI = \frac{\Delta}{s} \cdot \operatorname{cosec} B/2, \quad CI = \frac{\Delta}{s} \cdot \operatorname{cosec} C/2$$

$$\Rightarrow \quad IA : IB : IC = \frac{\Delta}{s} \cdot \operatorname{cosec} A/2 : \frac{\Delta}{s} \operatorname{cosec} B/2 : \frac{\Delta}{s} \operatorname{cosec} C/2$$

$$\therefore \quad IA : IB : IC = \operatorname{cosec} A/2 : \operatorname{cosec} B/2 : \operatorname{cosec} C/2$$

JEE SPIKE

Student are advised to remember the above result i.e. $IA = r \operatorname{cosec} A/2$, $IB = r \operatorname{cosec} B/2$, $IC = r \operatorname{cosec} C/2$.

3.9 Escribed Circles of a Triangle

The circle which touches the side BC and two sides AB and AC produced of a triangle ABC is called the **escribed circle opposite to the angle A.**

Its radius is denoted by r_1. Similarly, r_2 and r_3 denote the radii of the escribed circles opposite to the angles B and C, respectively. The centres of the escribed circles are called the ex-centres.

The centre of the escribed circles opposite to the angle A is the point of intersection of external bisector of angles B and C. The internal bisector of angle A also passes through the same point. This centre is generally denoted by I_1.

Formulae for r_1, r_2, r_3

In any ΔABC, we have

(i) $r_1 = \dfrac{\Delta}{s-a}, r_2 = \dfrac{\Delta}{s-b}, r_3 = \dfrac{\Delta}{s-c}$

(ii) $r_1 = s\tan A/2, r_2 = s\tan B/2, r_3 = s\tan C/2$

(iii) $r_1 = \dfrac{a\cos B/2\cdot\cos C/2}{\cos A/2}$, $r_2 = \dfrac{b\cos A/2\cdot\cos C/2}{\cos B/2}$,

$r_3 = \dfrac{c\cos A/2\cdot\cos B/2}{\cos C/2}$

(iv) $r_1 = 4R\sin A/2\cos B/2.\cos C/2$,

$r_2 = 4R\cos A/2\sin B/2.\cos C/2$,

$r_3 = 4R\cos A/2\cos B/2.\sin C/2$

Proof (i) Let the ΔABC be as,

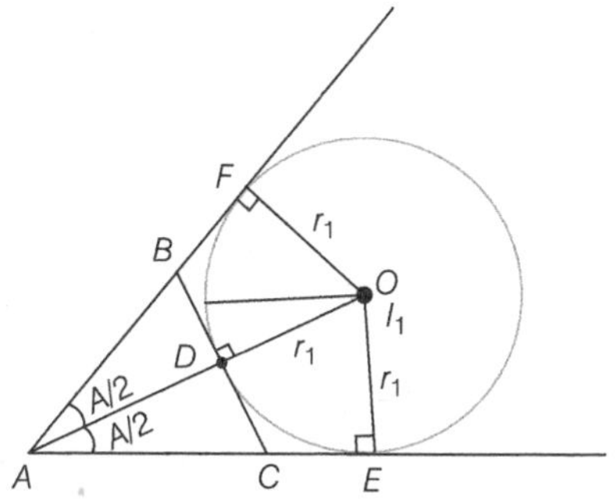

We have, $I_1D = I_1E = I_1F = r_1$

Now, area of ΔABC = Area of ΔI_1AC

+ Area of ΔI_1AB – Area of ΔI_1BC

$\Rightarrow \quad \Delta = \frac{1}{2}I_1E\cdot AC + \frac{1}{2}I_1F\cdot AB - \frac{1}{2}I_1D\cdot BC$

$\Rightarrow \quad \Delta = \frac{1}{2}r_1b + \frac{1}{2}r_1c - \frac{1}{2}r_1a$

$\Rightarrow \quad \Delta = \frac{r_1}{2}(b+c-a)$

$\Rightarrow \quad \Delta = \frac{r_1}{2}(2s-2a)$ [using $a+b+c=2s$]

$\Rightarrow \quad r_1 = \dfrac{\Delta}{s-a}$

Similarly, $r_2 = \dfrac{\Delta}{s-b}$ and $r_3 = \dfrac{\Delta}{s-c}$

(ii) Since, the lengths of tangents to a circle from an external points are equal,

$\therefore \quad AE = AF, BD = BF$ and $CD = CE$

Now, $AE + AF = (AC+CE) + (AB+BF)$

$= (AC+CD) + (AB+BD)$

$= AC + AB + CD + BD$

$= AC + AB + BC$

$= a + b + c = 2s$

$\Rightarrow \quad 2AF = 2s$

$\Rightarrow \quad AE = AF = s$

In ΔI_1AF, $\tan A/2 = \dfrac{I_1F}{AF} = \dfrac{r_1}{AF}$

$\Rightarrow \quad \tan A/2 = \dfrac{r_1}{s}$

$\Rightarrow \quad r_1 = s\tan A/2$

Similarly, $r_2 = s\tan B/2$

and $r_3 = s\tan C/2$

(iii) In ΔI_1BD, we have

$$\tan\left(\frac{B}{2}\right) = \frac{I_1D}{BD} = \frac{r_1}{BD}$$

$\Rightarrow \quad BD = r_1\tan\dfrac{B}{2}$

Similarly, in ΔI_1CD, we have

$$CD = r_1\tan\frac{C}{2}$$

Now, $a = BC = BD + CD = r_1\tan\dfrac{B}{2} + r_1\tan\dfrac{C}{2}$

$$= r_1\left(\tan\frac{B}{2} + \tan\frac{C}{2}\right) = r_1\frac{\cos A/2}{\cos B/2\cos C/2}$$

$\Rightarrow \quad r_1 = \dfrac{a\cos B/2\cos C/2}{\cos A/2}$

Similarly, $r_2 = \dfrac{b\cos A/2\cdot\cos C/2}{\cos B/2}$

and $r_3 = \dfrac{c\cos A/2\cdot\cos B/2}{\cos C/2}$

(iv) We have, $r_1 = \dfrac{a\cos B/2 \cdot \cos C/2}{\cos A/2}$

and $R = \dfrac{a}{2\sin A}$

$\Rightarrow \quad r_1 = \dfrac{2R\sin A \cdot \cos B/2 \cdot \cos C/2}{\cos A/2}$

$\Rightarrow \quad r_1 = \dfrac{4R\sin A/2 \cdot \cos A/2 \cdot \cos B/2 \cdot \cos C/2}{\cos A/2}$

$\therefore \quad r_1 = 4R\sin A/2 \cdot \cos B/2 \cdot \cos C/2$

Similarly, $r_2 = 4R\cos A/2 \cdot \sin B/2 \cdot \cos C/2$

and $r_3 = 4R\cos A/2 \cdot \cos B/2 \cdot \sin C/2$

Example 25. Show that $\dfrac{b-c}{r_1} + \dfrac{c-a}{r_2} + \dfrac{a-b}{r_3} = 0.$

Sol. LHS $= \dfrac{(b-c)}{r_1} + \dfrac{(c-a)}{r_2} + \dfrac{(a-b)}{r_3}$

$= (b-c)\cdot\left(\dfrac{s-a}{\Delta}\right) + (c-a)\cdot\left(\dfrac{s-b}{\Delta}\right) + (a-b)\cdot\left(\dfrac{s-c}{\Delta}\right)$

$= \dfrac{(s-a)(b-c)+(s-b)(c-a)+(s-c)(a-b)}{\Delta}$

$= \dfrac{s(b-c+c-a+a-b)-[ab-ac+bc-ba+ac-bc]}{\Delta}$

$= \dfrac{0}{\Delta} = 0 = \text{RHS}$

Thus, $\dfrac{b-c}{r_1} + \dfrac{c-a}{r_2} + \dfrac{a-b}{r_3} = 0$

Example 26. Prove that $r\cot\dfrac{B}{2}\cdot\cot\dfrac{C}{2} = r_1$.

Sol. LHS $= r\cot B/2 \cdot \cot C/2$

$= 4R\sin A/2 \cdot \sin B/2 \cdot \sin C/2 \cdot \dfrac{\cos B/2}{\sin B/2} \cdot \dfrac{\cos C/2}{\sin C/2}$

[as, $r = 4R\sin A/2 \cdot \sin B/2 \cdot \sin C/2$]

$= 4R\sin A/2 \cdot \cos B/2 \cdot \cos C/2$

$= r_1 = \text{RHS}$ [as, $r_1 = 4R\sin A/2 \cdot \cos B/2 \cdot \cos C/2$]

$\therefore \quad r\cot B/2 \cdot \cot C/2 = r_1$

Example 27. The exradii r_1, r_2, r_3 of a ΔABC are in HP, show that its sides a, b, c are in AP.

Sol. r_1, r_2, r_3 are in HP.

$\Rightarrow \quad \dfrac{2}{r_2} = \dfrac{1}{r_1} + \dfrac{1}{r_3}$

$\Rightarrow \quad \dfrac{2(s-b)}{\Delta} = \dfrac{(s-a)}{\Delta} + \dfrac{(s-c)}{\Delta}$

$\Rightarrow \quad 2s - 2b = 2s - (a+c) \Rightarrow 2b = a + c$

Hence, a, b, c are in AP.

Milestone Practice 3.3

1. The side of a triangle are 22 cm, 28 cm and 36 cm. So, the area of the circumscribed circle is
(a) 1019 cm^2 (b) 1000 cm^2
(c) 1020 cm^2 (d) 1025 cm^2

2. If the lengths of the side of a triangle are 3, 4 and 5 units, then the circumradius R is
(a) $\frac{2}{5}$ (b) $\frac{5}{2}$ (c) $\frac{5}{4}$ (d) $\frac{4}{5}$

3. If $8R^2 = a^2 + b^2 + c^2$, then prove that the Δ is right angled.

4. In a ΔABC, show that $2R^2 \sin A \sin B \sin C = \Delta$.

5. In a ΔABC, show that
$$\frac{a\cos A + b\cos B + c\cos C}{a+b+c} = \frac{r}{R}.$$

6. In an equilateral triangle, show that the in-radius and the circumradius are connected by $r = \frac{R}{2}$.

7. In any ΔABC, show that
$\cos A + \cos B + \cos C = \left(1 + \frac{r}{R}\right)$.

8. If the side be a, b and c, then show that
$\frac{r_1 - r}{a} + \frac{r_2 - r}{b} = \frac{c}{r_3}$.

9. Show that $r_2 r_3 + r_3 r_1 + r_1 r_2 = s^2$.

10. Show that $(r_1 + r_2)(r_2 + r_3)(r_3 + r_1) = 4Rs^2$.

11. If $r_1 = r_2 + r_3 + r$, then Δ is
(a) right angled (b) equilateral
(c) scalene (d) isosceles

12. In an equilateral triangle, show that the in-radius, circumradius and one of the exradii are in the ratio 1 : 2 : 3.

13. Show that $\left(\frac{1}{r} - \frac{1}{r_1}\right)\left(\frac{1}{r} - \frac{1}{r_2}\right)\left(\frac{1}{r} - \frac{1}{r_3}\right) = \frac{16R}{r^2(\Sigma a)^2}$.

14. If r_1, r_2, r_3 in a triangle be in HP, then show that the sides are in AP.

15. In a ΔABC, show that $r \cdot r_1 \cdot r_2 \cdot r_3 = \Delta^2$.

16. If l_1, l_2, l_3 are respectively the perpendicular from the vertices of a triangle on the opposite side, then show that $l_1\, l_2\, l_3 = \frac{a^2b^2c^2}{8R^3}$.

17. If the angle of a triangle are in the ratio 1 : 2 : 3, then show that the sides opposite to the respective angle are in the ratio $1 : \sqrt{3} : 2$.

18. Show that, $4Rr\cos\frac{A}{2}\cos\frac{B}{2}\cos\frac{C}{2} = \Delta$.

19. If $(a-b)(s-c) = (b-c)(s-a)$, then show that r_1, r_2, r_3 are in HP.

20. Show that $\frac{1}{r_1^2} + \frac{1}{r_2^2} + \frac{1}{r_3^2} + \frac{1}{r^2} = \frac{a^2+b^2+c^2}{\Delta^2}$.

21. Show that $(r_1 - r)(r_2 - r)(r_3 - r) = 4Rr^2$.

22. Show that $\left(\frac{1}{r_1} + \frac{1}{r_2}\right)\left(\frac{1}{r_2} + \frac{1}{r_3}\right)\left(\frac{1}{r_3} + \frac{1}{r_1}\right) = \frac{64R^3}{a^2b^2c^2}$.

23. If the sides be a, b and c, then the value of
$$(r + r_1)\tan\frac{B-C}{2} + (r + r_2)\tan\frac{C-A}{2} + (r + r_3)\tan\frac{A-B}{2}$$ is
(a) 0 (b) 1 (c) 2 (d) 3

24. If the sides be a, b, c, then the value of
$\frac{b-c}{r_1} + \frac{c-a}{r_2} + \frac{a-b}{r_3}$ is
(a) 0 (b) 1 (c) 2 (d) 3

25. If the sides be a, b, c, then the value of $(r_1 - r)(r_2 + r_3)$ is
(a) a^2 (b) a^3 (c) a (d) $-a$

26. Show that $\frac{r_1}{bc} + \frac{r_2}{ca} + \frac{r_3}{ab} = \frac{1}{r} - \frac{1}{2R}$.

27. Show that $r_1 + r_2 = c\cot\left(\frac{C}{2}\right)$.

28. Show that $Rr(\sin A + \sin B + \sin C) = \Delta$.

29. Show that $16R^2 r\, r_1\, r_2\, r_3 = a^2b^2c^2$.

30. If $\frac{r}{r_1} = \frac{r_2}{r_3}$, then show that $C = 90°$.

Answer Key

1. (a)	2. (b)	11. (a)
23. (a)	24. (a)	25. (a)

For Detailed Solution

Milestone 4 Solution of Triangles

• Solution of a Right Angled Triangle • Solution of a Triangle in General

In a triangle, there are six variables. Three sides a, b, c and three angles A, B, C when any three of these six variables (except all the three angles) of a triangles are given, the triangle is known completely; that is the other three variables can be expressed in terms of the given variables and can be evaluated. This process is called the solution of triangles.

3.10 Solution of a Right Angled Triangle

***Case* I** When two sides are given.

Let the triangle be right angled at C i.e. $\angle C = 90°$, then we can determine the remaining variables as given in the following table :

	Given	Required
(i)	a, b	$\tan A = \frac{a}{b}, B = 90° - A, c = \frac{a}{\sin A}$
(ii)	a, c	$\sin A = \frac{a}{c}, b = c\cos A, B = 90° - A$

***Case* II** When a side and an acute angle is given. In this case we can determine the remaining variables as given in the following table :

	Given	Required
(i)	a, A	$B = 90° - A, b = a\cot A, c = \frac{a}{\sin A}$
(ii)	c, A	$B = 90° - A, a = c\sin A, b = c\cos A$

3.11 Solution of a Triangle in General

***Case* I** When three sides a, b and c are given.

In this case the remaining variables are determined by using the following table :

Given	Required
a, b, c	(i) Area of $\Delta = \sqrt{s(s-a)(s-b)(s-c)}$, $2s = a + b + c$
	(ii) $\sin A = \frac{2\Delta}{bc}, \sin B = \frac{2\Delta}{ac}, \sin C = \frac{2\Delta}{ab}$

JEE Focus Points

- If $a^2 > b^2 + c^2$, then $\angle A$ is obtuse.
- If $b^2 > a^2 + c^2$, then $\angle B$ is obtuse.
- If $c^2 > a^2 + b^2$, then $\angle C$ is obtuse.

***Case* II** When two sides a, b and included $\angle C$ are given. In this case we use the following table :

Given	Required
a, b and $\angle C$	(i) $c = \sqrt{a^2 + b^2 - 2ab\cos C}$
	(ii) $\sin A = \frac{a\sin C}{c}$ and $\sin B = \frac{b\sin C}{c}$

***Case* III** When one side a and two angles A and B are given. In this case we use the following table :

Given	Required
a and $\angle A, \angle B$	(i) $\angle C = 180° - (\angle A + \angle B)$
	(ii) $b = \frac{a\sin B}{\sin A}$ and $c = \frac{a\sin C}{\sin A}$

***Case* IV** When two sides a, b and $\angle A$ opposite to one side is given then,

$$\sin B = \frac{b}{a}\sin A \qquad \text{...(i)}$$

$$\angle C = 180° - (\angle A + \angle B)\ ;\ c = \frac{a\sin C}{\sin A}$$

From Eq. (i), the following possibilities will arise

(a) **When A is an acute angle and $a < b\sin A$** In this relation $\sin B = \frac{b}{a}\sin A$ gives that $\sin B > 1$ which is impossible.

Hence, no triangle is possible.

(b) **When A is an acute angle and $a = b\sin A$** In this case only one triangle is possible which is right angled at B.

$$\therefore \quad a = b\sin A \Rightarrow \angle B = 90°$$

(c) **When A is an acute angle and $a > b \sin A$** In this case there are two values of B given by $\sin B = \dfrac{b \sin A}{a}$, say B_1 and B_2 such that $B_1 + B_2 = 180°$ side 'c' can be obtained by using $c = \dfrac{a \sin C}{\sin A}$.

$\therefore \quad a > b \sin A \Rightarrow$ Two triangle are possible.

JEE Focus Points

- In any right angled triangle, the orthocentre coincides with the vertex containing the right angled.
- The mid-point of the hypotenuse of a right angled triangle is equidistant from the three vertices of the triangle.
- The mid-point of the hypotenuse of the right angled triangle is the circumcentre of the triangle.

Concept Inside Video

Example 28. In any ΔABC, the sides are 6 cm, 10 cm and 14 cm. Show that the triangle is obtuse-angled with the obtuse angle equal to 120°.

Sol. Let $a = 14$, $b = 10$ and $c = 6$ cm $\Rightarrow s = \dfrac{14 + 10 + 6}{2} = 15$ cm

As we know that largest angle is opposite to the largest side,

$$\therefore \cos A = \frac{b^2 + c^2 - a^2}{2bc} = \frac{100 + 36 - 196}{2(10)(6)} = -\frac{1}{2} \Rightarrow A = 120°$$

Example 29. If $a = 3, b = 4$ and $A = \dfrac{\pi}{3}$, then find the number of triangles that can be constructed.

Sol. Given, $a = 3$, $b = 4$ and $A = \dfrac{\pi}{3}$

So, $\dfrac{\sin(\pi/3)}{3} = \dfrac{\sin B}{4} \Rightarrow \sin B = \dfrac{4}{3} \times \dfrac{\sqrt{3}}{2} = \dfrac{2}{\sqrt{3}} > 1$,

which is not possible. Thus, no triangle is possible.

Example 30. In a ΔABC, the median to the side BC is of length $\dfrac{1}{\sqrt{11 - 6\sqrt{3}}}$ and it divides the $\angle A$ into angles of 30° and 45°. Find the length of the side BC.

Sol. $\angle C = 180° - (75° + B)$

$\angle C = 105° - B$

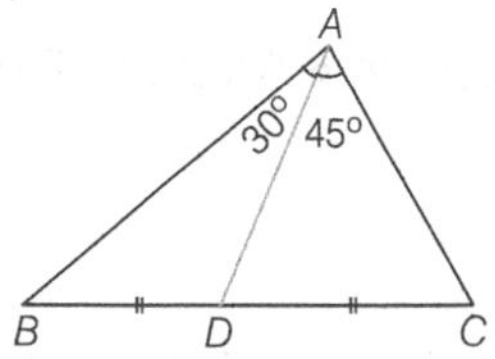

In ΔABD, $\dfrac{BD}{\sin 30°} = \dfrac{AD}{\sin B} \Rightarrow BD = \dfrac{AD}{2 \sin B}$ ...(i)

In ΔADC, $\dfrac{CD}{\sin 45°} = \dfrac{AD}{\sin C} \Rightarrow CD = \dfrac{AD}{\sqrt{2} \sin(105° - B)}$ ...(ii)

Now, $BD = CD$

$$\Rightarrow \frac{AD}{2 \sin B} = \frac{AD}{\sqrt{2}\sin(105° - B)}$$

$$\Rightarrow \sqrt{2} \sin B = \sin(105° - B)$$

$$\Rightarrow \sqrt{2} \sin B = \sin 105° \cdot \cos B - \cos 105° \cdot \sin B$$

$$\Rightarrow \sqrt{2} \sin B = \frac{(\sqrt{3} + 1)}{2\sqrt{2}} \cos B + \frac{(\sqrt{3} - 1)}{2\sqrt{2}} \sin B$$

$$\Rightarrow 4 \sin B = (\sqrt{3} + 1) \cos B + (\sqrt{3} - 1) \sin B$$

$$\Rightarrow \cot B = 3\sqrt{3} - 4 \Rightarrow \sin B = \frac{1}{2\sqrt{11 - 6\sqrt{3}}}$$

Hence, $BC = 2BD = \dfrac{AD}{\sin B} = \dfrac{2\sqrt{11 - 6\sqrt{3}}}{\sqrt{11 - 6\sqrt{3}}} = 2$

Milestone Practice 3.4

1. If $A = 30°$, $a = 7$ and $b = 10$ in ΔABC, then the number of triangles that can be constructed is
   (a) 1 (b) 2 (c) 3 (d) 4

2. In ΔABC, sides b, c and $\angle B$ are given such that a has two values a_1 and a_2. Then, show that $|a_1 - a_2| = 2\sqrt{b^2 - c^2 \sin^2 B}$.

3. In a triangle, the length of two longer sides are 10 and 9, respectively. If the angles are in AP, then the possible length of the third side is
   (a) $\sqrt{6}$ (b) $2 \pm \sqrt{3}$ (c) $5 \pm \sqrt{6}$ (d) $6 \pm \sqrt{3}$

4. If a, b and A are given in a triangle and c_1, c_2 are possible values of the third side, then prove the sum of the areas of two triangles with sides a, b, c_1 and a, b, c_2 is $\dfrac{1}{2} b^2 \sin 2A$.

5. If in ΔABC, $a = (1 + \sqrt{3})$ cm, $b = 2$ cm and $\angle C = 60°$, then the other two angles and the third side is
   (a) 45°, 75°, 3 (b) 45°, 90°, $\sqrt{6}$
   (c) 45°, 75°, $\sqrt{6}$ (d) 75°, 30°, $\sqrt{6}$

Answer Key

1. (b) 3. (c) 5. (c)

For Detailed Solution

Milestone 5 Height and Distance

• Angle of Elevation • Angle of Depression • Bearing

3.12 Angle of Elevation

If 'O' be the observer's eye and OX be the horizontal line and object P is at a higher level than eye, then the $\angle POX$ is called the angle of elevation.

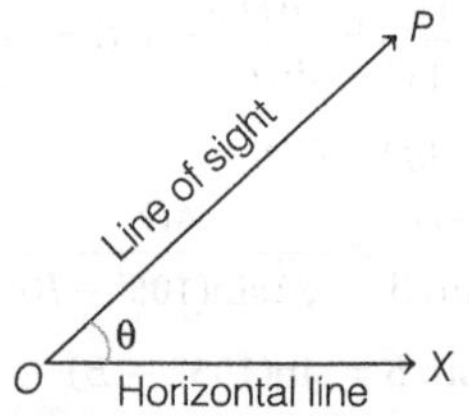

3.13 Angle of Depression

If 'O' be the observer's eye and OX is a horizontal line object P is at a lower level than eye, then the $\angle POX$ is called the angle of depression.

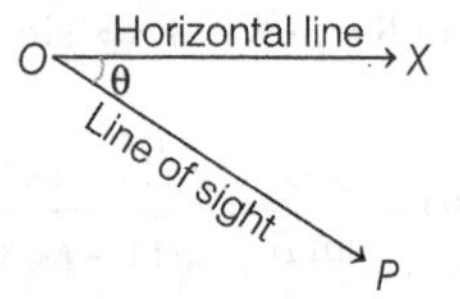

JEE Focus Points

- Angle of elevation and depression are always acute angle.
- Angle of elevation of an object from an observer is same as angle of depression of an observer from the object.

3.14 Bearing

If the observer and the object are O and P be on the same level respectively, then bearings is defined. To measure the bearing the four standard direction East, West, North and South are taken as the cardinal directions. Angle between the line of observation. i.e. OP and any one standard direction is measured.

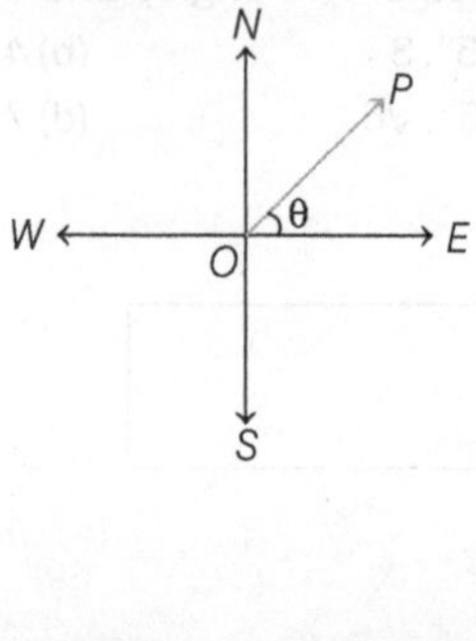

Thus, $\angle POE$ is called the bearing of the point P with respect to O measured from East to North.
In other words the bearing of P as seen from O is the direction in which P is seen from O.

JEE SPIKE

North-East means equally inclined to North and East. ENE means equally inclined to East and North-East.

Example 31. From the top of a tower 50 m high, the angles of depression of the top and bottom of a pole are α and β, respectively. Find the height of the pole.

Sol. Let AE be the tower, CD be the pole and d be the distance between the tower and the pole.
Also, h be the height of the pole.

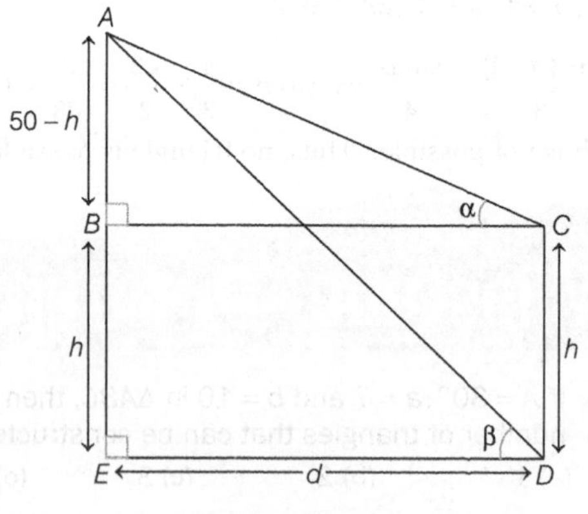

In ΔABC, $\quad d = (50-h)\cot\alpha$

In ΔAED, $\quad d = 50\cot\beta$

$\therefore \quad 50\cot\beta = (50-h)\cot\alpha$

$\Rightarrow \quad 50\cot\beta - 50\cot\alpha = -h\cot\alpha$

$\Rightarrow \quad h\cot\alpha = 50(\cot\alpha - \cot\beta)$

$\Rightarrow \quad h = \dfrac{50(\cot\alpha - \cot\beta)}{\cot\alpha}$

Example 32. An observer on the top of a tree finds the angle of depression of a car moving towards the tree to be 30°. After 6 min this angle becomes 60°. After how much more time the car will reach the tree?

Sol. Let the observer be at point A. Also, let D be initial position of the car and C be the position after 6 min.

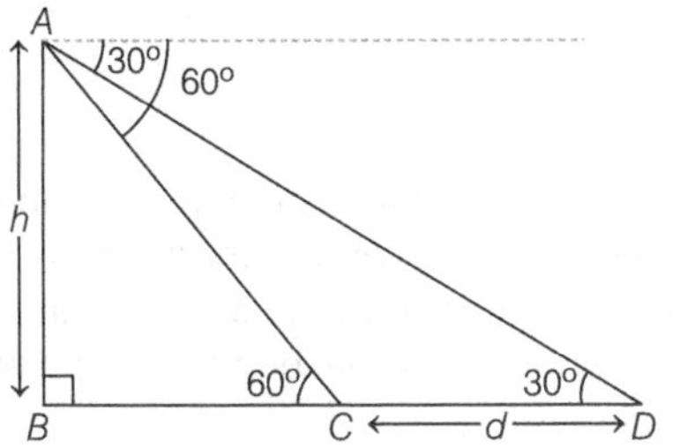

In ΔABD, $\quad BD = h\cot 30°$

In ΔABC, $\quad BC = h\cot 60°$

$\therefore \quad CD = BD - BC \Rightarrow d = h\cot 30° - h\cot 60°$

$\therefore$ Speed of car $= \dfrac{h(\cot 30° - \cot 60°)}{6}$

$\therefore$ Time required to travel distance $BC = \dfrac{(h\cot 60°)\times 6}{h(\cot 30° - \cot 60°)}$

$$= \frac{\frac{6}{\sqrt{3}}}{\sqrt{3} - \frac{1}{\sqrt{3}}} = \frac{6}{2} = 3 \text{ min}$$

Example 33. Two flagstaffs stand on a horizontal plane. A and B are two points on the line joining their feet and between them. The angles of elevation of the tops of the flagstaffs as seen from A are 30° and 60° and as seen from B are 60° and 45°. If AB is 30 m, then find the distance between the flagstaffs in metres.

Sol. Let x and y be the heights of the flagstaffs at P and Q respectively.

Then, $AP = x\cot 60° = \dfrac{x}{\sqrt{3}}$, $AQ = y\cot 30° = y\sqrt{3}$

$$BP = x\cot 45° = x,\ BQ = y\cot 60° = \frac{y}{\sqrt{3}}$$

$$\Rightarrow \quad BP - AP = x - \frac{x}{\sqrt{3}} = AB$$

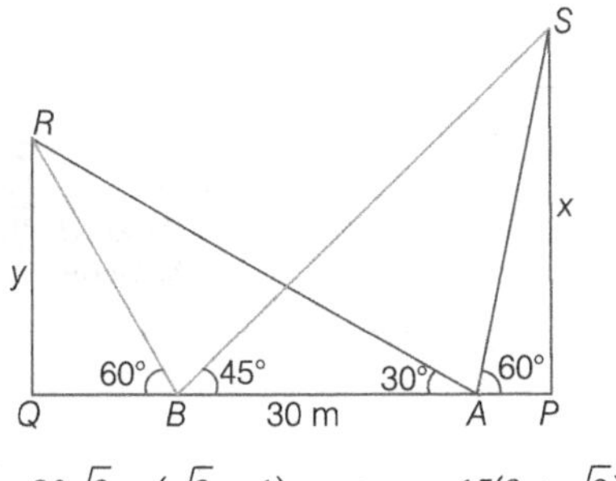

$$\Rightarrow \quad 30\sqrt{3} = (\sqrt{3} - 1)x \Rightarrow x = 15(3 + \sqrt{3})$$

Similarly, $\quad 30 = y\left(\sqrt{3} - \dfrac{1}{\sqrt{3}}\right) \Rightarrow y = 15\sqrt{3}$

So that, $\quad PQ = BP + BQ = x + \dfrac{y}{\sqrt{3}}$

$$= 15(3 + \sqrt{3}) + 15 = (60 + 15\sqrt{3})\text{ m}$$

Example 34. In a cubical hall $ABCD$, $PQRS$ with each side 10 m, G is the centre of the wall $BCRQ$ and T is the mid-point of the side AB. Find the angle of elevation of G at the point T.

Sol.

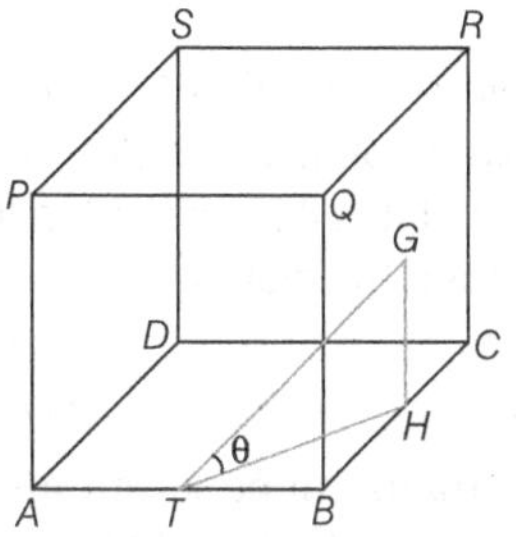

Let H be the mid-point of BC.

Since, $\quad \angle TBH = 90°$,

$\therefore \quad TH^2 = BT^2 + BH^2 = 5^2 + 5^2 = 50$

Also, $\quad \angle THG = 90°$,

$\therefore \quad TG^2 = TH^2 + GH^2 = 50 + 25 = 75$

Let θ be the required angle of elevation of G at T.

Then, $\sin\theta = \dfrac{GH}{TG} = \dfrac{5}{5\sqrt{3}} = \dfrac{1}{\sqrt{3}} \Rightarrow \theta = \sin^{-1}\left(\dfrac{1}{\sqrt{3}}\right)$

Example 35. From a point on a hillside of constant inclination, the angle of elevation of the top of a flagstaff on its summit is observed to be α and a metres nearer the top of the hill, it is β. If h is the height of the flagstaff, then find the inclination of the hill to the horizon.

Sol. Let OP be the flagstaff of height h and θ the inclination of the hill.

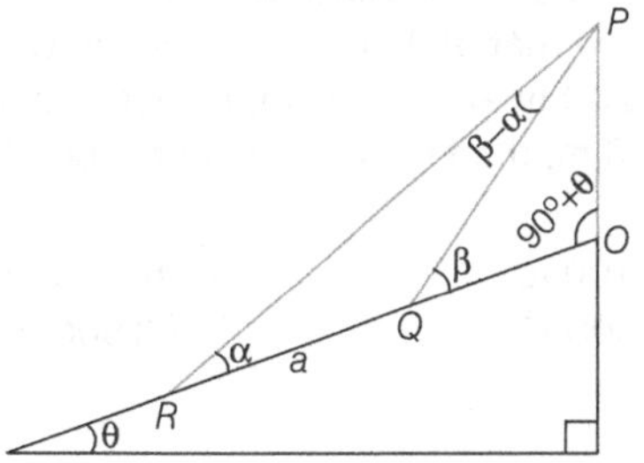

Now, $\angle ORP = \alpha, \angle OQP = \beta$ and $RQ = a$

Also, $\angle RPQ = \beta - \alpha$

Now in ΔPQR, using sine rule, we get

$$\frac{PR}{\sin(180° - \beta)} = \frac{RQ}{\sin(\beta - \alpha)} \Rightarrow PR = \frac{a\sin\beta}{\sin(\beta - \alpha)} \quad \text{...(i)}$$

Also, $\quad \angle POR = \dfrac{\pi}{2} + \theta$

Now in ΔPOR, using sine rule, we get

$$\frac{PO}{\sin\alpha} = \frac{PR}{\sin\left(\frac{\pi}{2} + \theta\right)} \Rightarrow PR = \frac{h\cos\theta}{\sin\alpha} = \frac{a\sin\beta}{\sin(\beta - \alpha)}$$

[using Eq. (i)]

$$\Rightarrow \quad \theta = \cos^{-1}\left[\frac{a\sin\alpha\sin\beta}{h\sin(\beta - \alpha)}\right]$$

Milestone Practice 3.5

1. The angle of elevation of the top of a tower from a point A due South of it is $30°$ and from a point B due West of it is $45°$. If the height of tower is 100 m, then the distance AB is

   (a) 100 m (b) 200 m
   (c) 300 m (d) 400 m

2. ABC is a triangular park with $AB = AC = 100$ m. A clock tower is situated at the mid-point of BC. The angle of elevation α and β of the top of the tower at A and B respectively are such that $\cot\alpha = 3.2$ and $\operatorname{cosec}\beta = 2.6$. Then, the height of the tower is

   (a) 15 m (b) 20 m
   (c) 25 m (d) 30 m

3. Some portion of a 20 m long tree is broken by the wind and its top struck the ground at an angle of $30°$. Then, the height of the point, where the tree is broken, is

   (a) $\frac{20}{3}$ m (b) $\frac{10}{3}$ m
   (c) $\frac{20}{9}$ m (d) $\frac{20}{7}$ m

4. A balloon is observed simultaneously from three points A, B and C on a straight road directly under it. The angular elevation at B is twice and at C is thrice that of A. If the distance between A and B is 200 m and the distance between B and C is 100 m, then the altitude of balloon from the road is

   (a) $100\sqrt{3}$ (b) $400\sqrt{2}$
   (c) $300\sqrt{6}$ (d) $500\sqrt{5}$

5. A balloon of radius r subtends an angle α at the eye of an observer and the elevation of the centre of the balloon from the eye is β. Find the height of the centre of the balloon from the eye of the observer.

6. If a tower subtends angles θ, 2θ and 3θ at three points A, B and C respectively, lying on the same side of a horizontal line through the foot of the tower, show that $\frac{AB}{BC} = \frac{\cot\theta - \cot 2\theta}{\cot 2\theta - \cot 3\theta}$.

7. A person stands at a point A due south of a tower of height h and observes that its elevation is $60°$. He then walks westwards towards B, where the elevation is $45°$. At a point C on AB produced, show that if he find it to be $30°$. OA, OB, OC are in GP.

8. A train travelling on one of two intersecting railway lines, subtends at a certain station on the other line, an angle α when the front of the carriage reaches the junction and an angle β when the end of the carriage reaches it. Then, the two lines are inclined to each other at an angle θ, show that $2\cot\theta = \cot\alpha - \cot\beta$.

9. The angle of elevation of the top of the tower observed from each of the three points A, B, C on the ground, forming a triangle is the same angle α. If R is the circumradius of the ΔABC, then find the height of the tower.

10. The length of the shadow of a pole inclined at $10°$ to the vertical towards the sun is 2.05 metres, when the elevation of the sun is $38°$. Then, find the length of the pole.

Answer Key

1. (b)	2. (c)	3. (a)	4. (a)
5. $r\sin\beta\operatorname{cosec}\frac{\alpha}{2}$	9. $R\tan\alpha$	10. $\frac{2.05\sin 38°}{\sin 42°}$	

For Detailed Solution

JEE Pattern EXAMPLES

Single Option Correct Type Questions

Example 1 *If* $\tan^2 \frac{\pi - A}{4} + \tan^2 \frac{\pi - B}{4} + \tan^2 \frac{\pi - C}{4} = 1$, *then* ΔABC *is*

(a) equilateral (b) isosceles
(c) scalene (d) None of these

Sol. (a) Let $\alpha = \frac{\pi - A}{4}, \beta = \frac{\pi - B}{4}, \gamma = \frac{\pi - C}{4}$ ...(i)

$\Rightarrow \quad \alpha + \beta + \gamma = \frac{\pi}{2}$

$\Rightarrow \quad \Sigma \tan\alpha \cdot \tan\beta = 1$

$\Rightarrow \quad \Sigma \tan^2\alpha = 1 = \Sigma \tan\alpha \tan\beta$

$\Rightarrow \quad \tan\alpha = \tan\beta = \tan\gamma$

$\therefore \quad \alpha = \beta = \gamma$

$\frac{\pi - A}{4} = \frac{\pi - B}{4} = \frac{\pi - C}{4}$ [from Eq. (i)]

$\therefore \quad A = B = C$

Example 2 *In* $\Delta ABC, a^2 + c^2 = 2002b^2$, *then* $\frac{\cot A + \cot C}{\cot B}$ *equals to*

(a) $\frac{1}{2001}$ (b) $\frac{2}{2001}$ (c) $\frac{3}{2001}$ (d) $\frac{4}{2001}$

Sol. (b) $\frac{\cot A + \cot C}{\cot B} = \frac{\sin(A + C) \sin B}{\sin A \sin C \cos B}$

$$= \frac{\sin^2 B}{\sin A \cos B \sin C} = \frac{4R^2 b^2}{4R^2 ac \cos B}$$

$$= \frac{2b^2}{2ac \cos B} = \frac{2b^2}{a^2 + c^2 - b^2}$$

$$= \frac{2b^2}{2002 b^2 - b^2} = \frac{2}{2001}$$

Example 3 *A triangle has vertices A, B and C and the respective opposite sides have lengths a, b and c. This triangle is inscribed in a circle of radius R. If* $b = c = 1$ *and the altitude from A to side BC has length* $\sqrt{\frac{2}{3}}$, *then R equals*

(a) $\frac{1}{\sqrt{3}}$ (b) $\frac{2}{\sqrt{3}}$ (c) $\frac{\sqrt{3}}{2}$ (d) $\frac{\sqrt{3}}{2\sqrt{2}}$

Sol. (d) $a = \frac{2}{\sqrt{3}}$ and $\Delta = \frac{1}{2} ah = \frac{1}{2} \cdot \frac{2}{\sqrt{3}} \cdot \frac{\sqrt{2}}{\sqrt{3}} = \frac{\sqrt{2}}{3}$

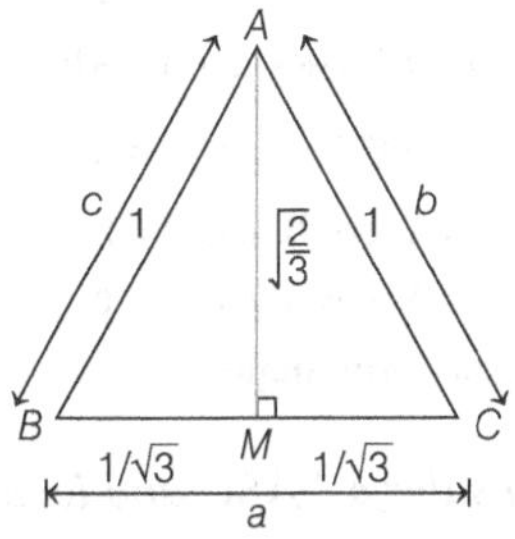

$\therefore \quad R = \frac{abc}{4\Delta} = \frac{(2)(1)(1)(3)}{\sqrt{3}\,(4)\,\sqrt{2}}$

$$= \frac{\sqrt{3}}{2\sqrt{2}}$$

Example 4 *In* ΔABC, *if* $AC = 8$, $BC = 7$ *and D lies between A and B such that* $AD = 2$, $BD = 4$, *then the length CD equals*

(a) $\sqrt{46}$ (b) $\sqrt{48}$ (c) $\sqrt{51}$ (d) $\sqrt{75}$

Sol. (c) $l^2 = 2^2 + 8^2 - 2 \cdot 2 \cdot 8 \cos A = 4 + 64 - 32 \cos A$

and $\cos A = \frac{6^2 + 8^2 - 7^2}{2 \cdot 6 \cdot 8} = \frac{51}{16 \times 6} = \frac{17}{32}$

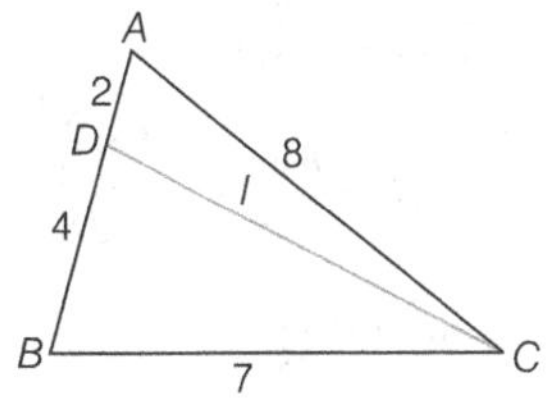

$l^2 = 68 - 32 \times \frac{17}{32} = 51$

$l = \sqrt{51}$

Example 5 *In a triangle, if*

$$(a+b+c)(a+b-c)(b+c-a)(c+a-b) = \frac{8a^2b^2c^2}{a^2+b^2+c^2}, \text{ then the triangle is}$$

(a) isosceles (b) right angled
(c) equilateral (d) obtuse angled

Sol. (b) We have, $s(s-a)(s-b)(s-c) = \dfrac{a^2b^2c^2}{2(a^2+b^2+c^2)}$

$$\Rightarrow \quad a^2+b^2+c^2 = \frac{a^2b^2c^2}{2\Delta^2} \quad \text{...(i)}$$

As, $\Delta = \dfrac{1}{2}bc\sin A = \dfrac{abc}{4R}$

So, Eq. (i) becomes

$$a^2+b^2+c^2 = \frac{(a^2b^2c^2)}{2a^2\cdot b^2\cdot c^2}\times 16R^2$$

$$\Rightarrow 4R^2(\sin^2 A+\sin^2 B+\sin^2 C) = 8R^2$$

$$\Rightarrow \quad \sin^2 A+\sin^2 B+\sin^2 C = 2$$

or $\quad 2+2\cos A\cdot\cos B\cdot\cos C = 2$

$$\Rightarrow \quad \cos A\cdot\cos B\cdot\cos C = 0$$

$\therefore$ ΔABC must be right angled.

Example 6 *Consider a ΔABC and let a, b and c denote the lengths of the sides opposite to vertices A, B and C, respectively. If $a=1$, $b=3$ and $C=60°$, then $\sin^2 B$ is equal to*

(a) $\dfrac{27}{28}$ (b) $\dfrac{3}{28}$ (c) $\dfrac{81}{28}$ (d) $\dfrac{1}{3}$

Sol. (a) By Cosine law, $\cos 60° = \dfrac{1^2+3^2-c^2}{2\cdot 1\cdot 3} \Rightarrow c=\sqrt{7}$

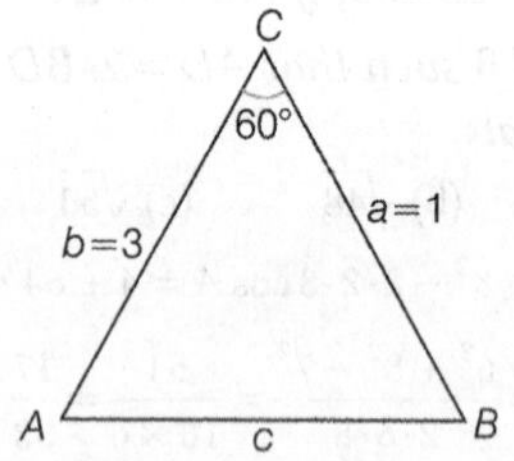

Now, $\dfrac{b}{\sin B} = \dfrac{c}{\sin C}$ [by Sine law]

$$\Rightarrow \quad \sin B = \frac{b\sin C}{c} = \frac{3\times\frac{\sqrt{3}}{2}}{\sqrt{7}} = \frac{3\sqrt{3}}{2\sqrt{7}}$$

Hence, $\quad \sin^2 B = \dfrac{27}{28}$

Example 7 *In ΔABC, if $\cos A+\sin A-\dfrac{2}{\cos B+\sin B}=0$, then $\dfrac{a+b}{c}$ is equal to*

(a) $\sqrt{2}$ (b) 1 (c) $\dfrac{1}{\sqrt{2}}$ (d) $2\sqrt{2}$

Sol. (a) We have,

$$\Rightarrow \cos A\cos B+\sin A\sin B+\cos A\sin B+\sin A\cos B = 2$$

$$\Rightarrow \quad \cos(A-B)+\sin(A+B) = 2$$

$\therefore$ $\quad \cos(A-B)=1$

and $\quad \sin(A+B)=1$

$\Rightarrow$ $\quad A=B$

So, $\quad a=b$

and $\quad \sin 2A = 1$

$\Rightarrow$ $\quad A=45°$

Hence, $\dfrac{a+b}{c} = \dfrac{2a}{a\sqrt{2}} = \sqrt{2}$ $\quad [\because C=90°]$

Example 8 *In ΔABC, if $\angle A=30°$, $b=10$ and $a=x$, then the values of x for which there are 2 possible triangles is given by (All symbol used have usual meaning in a triangle)*

(a) $5<x<10$ (b) $x<\dfrac{5}{2}$

(c) $\dfrac{5}{3}<x<10$ (d) $\dfrac{5}{2}<x<10$

Sol. (a) If c is the third side, then the altitude to c has length $10\sin 30°$ i.e. 5.

There are two triangles if x is greater than this value and less than the length of b.

If $x>10$, point B will come to the left of A and $\angle A$ would be obtuse in the case.

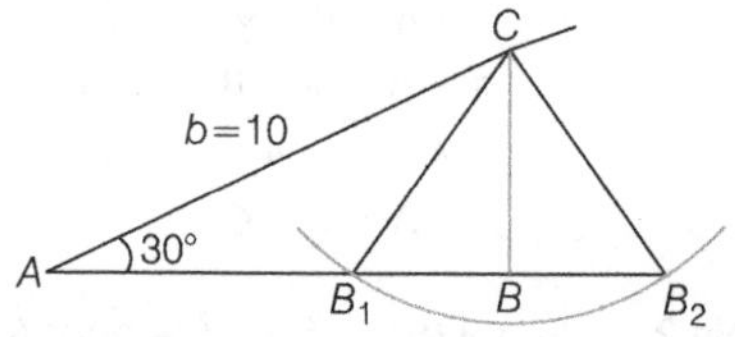

Alternate Solution

We have, $\dfrac{\sqrt{3}}{2} = \cos 30° = \dfrac{100+c^2-x^2}{2(10)(c)}$ [by cosine rule]

$$\Rightarrow \quad c^2-10\sqrt{3}c+(100-x^2)=0$$

$$\Rightarrow \quad c = \frac{10\sqrt{3}\pm\sqrt{4x^2-100}}{2}$$

Now, for 2 distinct positive values of c, we must have

$$10\sqrt{3} > \sqrt{4x^2-100} \text{ and } 4x^2-100>0$$

$$\Rightarrow \quad 300>4x^2-100 \text{ and } x^2>25$$

$$\Rightarrow \quad 25<x^2<100$$

$$\Rightarrow \quad 5<x<10$$

Example 9 *The angle of elevation of tower from a point A due south of it is 30° and from a point B due west of it is 45°. If the height of the tower be 100 m, then AB is equal to*

(a) 150 m (b) 200 m
(c) 173.2 m (d) 141.4 m

Sol. (b) $OB = 100 \cot 45°$

$$OA = 100 \cot 30°$$

$$AB = \sqrt{(OA^2 + OB^2)} = 200 \text{ m}$$

$$AB = 200 \text{ m}$$

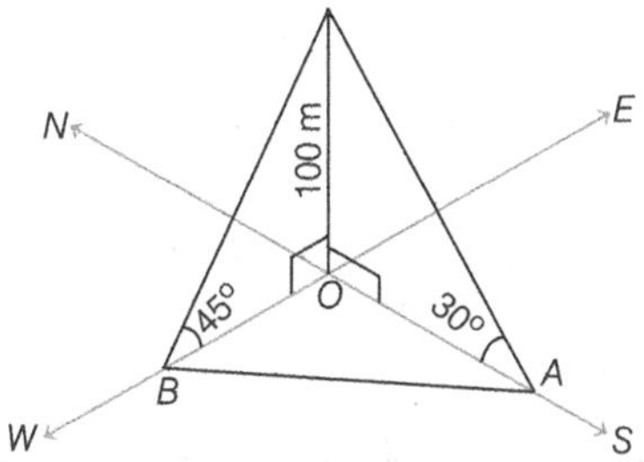

Example 10 *An aeroplane flying horizontally 1 km above the ground is observed at an elevation of 60° and after 10 seconds the elevation is observed to be 30°. The uniform speed of the aeroplane in km/h is*

(a) 240 (b) $240\sqrt{3}$

(c) $60\sqrt{3}$ (d) None of these

Sol. (b) $d = H \cot 30° - H \cot 60°$

Time taken = 10 s

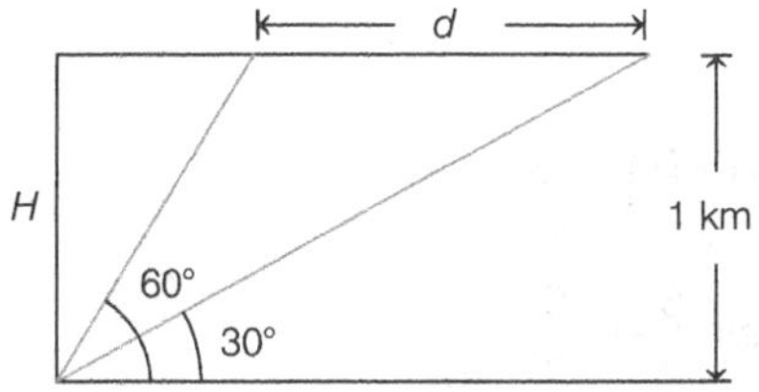

$$\text{Speed} = \frac{\cot 30° - \cot 60°}{10} \times 60 \times 60 = 240\sqrt{3}$$

More than One Correct Option Type Questions

Example 11 *In ΔABC, the ratio $\frac{a}{\sin A} = \frac{b}{\sin B} = \frac{c}{\sin C}$ is always equal to (All symbols used have usual meaning in a triangle.)*

(a) $2R$, where R is the circumradius.

(b) $\frac{abc}{2\Delta}$, where Δ is the area of the triangle.

(c) $\frac{2}{3}(a^2 + b^2 + c^2)^{\frac{1}{2}}$

(d) $\frac{(abc)^{\frac{2}{3}}}{(h_1h_2h_3)^{\frac{1}{3}}}$

Sol. (a,b,d) We know that

$$\frac{a}{\sin A} = \frac{b}{\sin B} = \frac{c}{\sin C} = 2R$$

and $R = \frac{abc}{4\Delta} \Rightarrow 2R = \frac{abc}{2\Delta}$

$\therefore$ Option (a) and (b) are true.

Option (c) will be true iff $a = b = c$.

$\therefore$ Option (c) is incorrect.

Now, for option (d)

We have, $\frac{(abc)^{2/3}}{(h_1h_2h_3)^{1/3}}$

We know that $\frac{1}{2}ah_1 = \frac{1}{2}bh_2 = \frac{1}{2}ch_3 = \Delta$

$$\Rightarrow \quad h_1 = \frac{2\Delta}{a}, h_2 = \frac{2\Delta}{b}, h_3 = \frac{2\Delta}{c}$$

$$\because \quad h_1h_2h_3 = \frac{8\Delta^3}{abc}$$

$$\therefore \quad \frac{(abc)^{2/3}}{(h_1h_2h_3)^{1/3}} = \frac{(abc)^{2/3}}{\left(\frac{8\Delta^3}{abc}\right)^{1/3}} = \frac{(abc)^{2/3}(abc)^{1/3}}{2\Delta} = \frac{abc}{2\Delta} = 2R$$

Example 12 *In a ΔABC, which of the following quantities denote the area of the triangle?*

(a) $\frac{a^2 - b^2}{2}\left(\frac{\sin A \sin B}{\sin(A - B)}\right)$ (b) $\frac{r_1 r_2 r_3}{\sqrt{\Sigma r_1 r_2}}$

(c) $\frac{a^2 + b^2 + c^2}{\cot A + \cot B + \cot C}$ (d) $r^2 \cot\frac{A}{2} \cdot \cot\frac{B}{2} \cdot \cot\frac{C}{2}$

Sol. (a,b,d) (a) $\frac{a^2 - b^2}{2} \times \frac{1}{\sin(A - B)} \times \sin A \sin B$

$$= \frac{4R^2(\sin^2 A - \sin^2 B)}{2} \times \frac{1}{\sin(A - B)} \times \frac{a}{2R} \times \frac{b}{2R}$$

$$= \frac{1}{2}\sin(A + B)\, ab$$

$$= \frac{1}{2}(ab)\sin C = \frac{abc}{4R} = \Delta$$

(b) $r_1 r_2 r_3 = \frac{\Delta^3 \cdot s}{s(s-a)(s-b)(s-c)} = \Delta \cdot s$

$$\sqrt{\Sigma r_1 r_2} = \sqrt{s^2\left(\Sigma \tan\frac{A}{2}\tan\frac{B}{2}\right)} = s \qquad \left[\because \Sigma \tan\frac{A}{2}\tan\frac{B}{2} = 1\right]$$

$$\therefore \quad \frac{r_1 r_2 r_3}{\sqrt{\Sigma r_1 r_2}} = \Delta$$

(c) $\text{Denominator} = \frac{(b^2 + c^2 - a^2)2R}{2bca} + \frac{(a^2 + c^2 - b^2)2R}{2acb} + \frac{(a^2 + b^2 - c^2)2R}{2abc}$

$$= \frac{R}{abc}[b^2 + c^2 - a^2 + c^2 + a^2 - b^2 + a^2 + b^2 - c^2]$$

$$= \frac{(a^2 + b^2 + c^2)R}{abc}$$

$$\therefore \quad \frac{N'}{D'} = \frac{(\Sigma a^2)\, abc}{(\Sigma a^2)\, R} = \frac{abc}{R} = 4\Delta$$

Thus, option (c) is incorrect.

(d) $\dfrac{\Delta^2}{s^2} \cdot \dfrac{s(s-a)}{\Delta} \cdot \dfrac{s(s-b)}{\Delta} \cdot \dfrac{s(s-c)}{\Delta}$

$$= \frac{s(s-a)(s-b)(s-c)}{\Delta} = \frac{\Delta^2}{\Delta} = \Delta$$

JEE SCANNER

Example 13 Similar to PYQ Asked in JEE Adv. 2016

In a ΔABC, Let a, b and c be the lengths of sides opposite to the angles A, B, C respectively and $2s = a + b + c$. If $\dfrac{s-a}{2} = \dfrac{s-b}{3} = \dfrac{s-c}{4}$ and area of incircle of the ΔABC is $\dfrac{32\pi}{3}$, then

(a) area of the ΔABC is $24\sqrt{6}$.

(b) the radius of the circumcircle of the ΔABC is $\dfrac{35\sqrt{6}}{12}$.

(c) $\sin\dfrac{A}{2}\sin\dfrac{B}{2}\sin\dfrac{C}{2} = \dfrac{4}{35}$

(d) $\sin^2\left(\dfrac{A+B}{2}\right) = \dfrac{6}{7}$

Sol. (a,b,c,d) Given ΔABC, where $2s = a + b + c$

and $\dfrac{s-a}{2} = \dfrac{s-b}{3} = \dfrac{s-c}{4}$

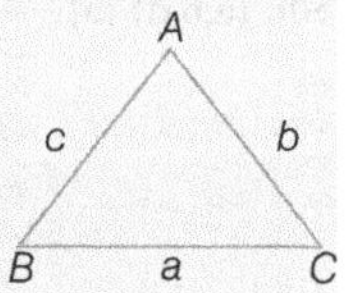

$$\therefore \quad \frac{s-a}{2} = \frac{s-b}{3} = \frac{s-c}{4} = \frac{3s-(a+b+c)}{2+3+4} = \frac{s}{9}$$

or $\dfrac{s-a}{2} = \dfrac{s-b}{3} = \dfrac{s-c}{4} = \dfrac{s}{9} = \lambda$ (let)

$\Rightarrow \quad s = 9\lambda,\ s = 2\lambda + a,\ s = 3\lambda + b,\ s = 4\lambda + c$

$\therefore \quad s = 9\lambda,\ a = 7\lambda,\ b = 6\lambda,\ c = 5\lambda$

Now, $\Delta = \sqrt{s(s-a)(s-b)(s-c)} = 6\sqrt{6}\,\lambda^2$ ...(i)

Also, $\pi r^2 = \dfrac{32\pi}{3} \Rightarrow r^2 = \dfrac{32}{3}$ ...(ii)

and $R = \dfrac{abc}{4\Delta} = \dfrac{(7\lambda)(6\lambda)(5\lambda)}{4\cdot 6\sqrt{6}\,\lambda^2} = \dfrac{35\lambda}{4\sqrt{6}}$ ...(iii)

Now, $r^2 = \dfrac{32}{3} = \dfrac{\Delta^2}{s^2} = \dfrac{216\lambda^4}{81\lambda^2} \Rightarrow \dfrac{8}{3} \times 4 = \dfrac{8}{3}\lambda^2$ [from Eq. (ii)]

$\Rightarrow \quad \lambda = 2$

(a) Area of the $\Delta ABC = 6\sqrt{6}\lambda^2 = 6\sqrt{6} \times 4 = 24\sqrt{6}$

(b) Radius of circumcircle $(R) = \dfrac{35\lambda}{4\sqrt{6}} = \dfrac{35 \times 2}{4\sqrt{6}} = \dfrac{35}{2\sqrt{6}} = \dfrac{35\sqrt{6}}{12}$

(c) Since, $r = 4R\sin\dfrac{A}{2}\sin\dfrac{B}{2}\sin\dfrac{C}{2}$

$$\Rightarrow \frac{4\sqrt{2}}{\sqrt{3}} = 4 \cdot \frac{35}{4\sqrt{6}} \times 2\sin\frac{A}{2}\sin\frac{B}{2}\sin\frac{C}{2}$$

$$\Rightarrow \sin\frac{A}{2}\sin\frac{B}{2}\sin\frac{C}{2} = \frac{4}{35}$$

(d) $\sin^2\left(\dfrac{A+B}{2}\right) = \cos^2\left(\dfrac{C}{2}\right)$ as $\dfrac{A+B}{2} = 90° - \dfrac{C}{2}$

$$= \frac{s(s-c)}{ab}$$

$$= \frac{9\lambda \times 4\lambda}{7\lambda \cdot 6\lambda} = \frac{9 \times 4}{7 \times 6} = \frac{6}{7}$$

Skill Builder

In a ΔABC, Let a, b and c be the lengths of sides opposite to the angles A, B, C respectively and $2s = a + b + c$. If $\dfrac{s-a}{3} = \dfrac{s-b}{4} = \dfrac{s-c}{5}$ and area of incircle of the ΔABC is $\dfrac{24\pi}{5}$, thenwhich of the following option is correct?

(a) area of the ΔABC is $\dfrac{288\sqrt{5}}{25}$.

(b) the radius of the circumcircle of the ΔABC is $\dfrac{21\sqrt{6}}{5}$.

(c) $\sin^2\left(\dfrac{A+B}{2}\right) = \dfrac{5}{12}$

(d) $\sin\dfrac{A}{2}\sin\dfrac{B}{2}\sin\dfrac{C}{2} = \dfrac{5}{42}$

For Sol.

Example 14 *In a Δ PQR, P is the largest angle and $\cos P = \dfrac{1}{3}$. Further incircle of the triangle touches the sides PQ, QR and RP at N, L and M respectively, such that the length of PN, QL and RM are consecutive even integer. Then, the possible length(s) of the side(s) of the triangle is (are)*

(a) 16 (b) 18

(c) 24 (d) 22

Sol. (b,d)

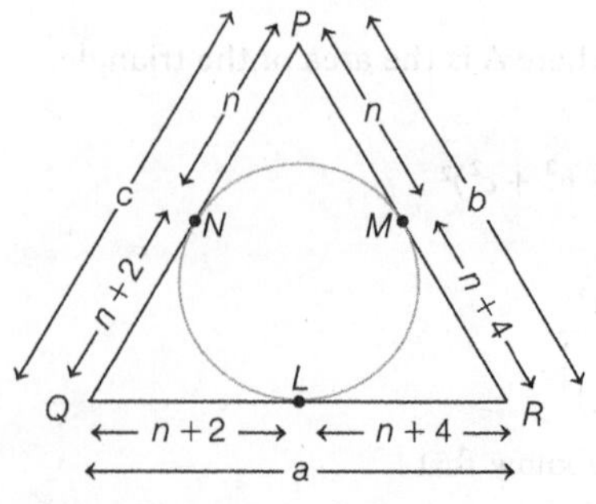

$\therefore \quad \cos P = \dfrac{b^2 + c^2 - a^2}{2bc}$ [using law of cosine]

$$\Rightarrow \quad \frac{1}{3} = \frac{(2n+4)^2 + (2n+2)^2 - (2n+6)^2}{2(2n+4)(2n+2)} \quad \left[\because \cos P = \frac{1}{3}\right]$$

$$\Rightarrow \quad \frac{4n^2 - 16}{8(n+1)(n+2)} = \frac{1}{3}$$

$$\Rightarrow \quad \frac{n^2 - 4}{2(n+1)(n+2)} = \frac{1}{3}$$

$$\Rightarrow \quad \frac{(n-2)(n+2)}{2(n+1)(n+2)} = \frac{1}{3}$$

$$\Rightarrow \quad \frac{n-2}{2(n+1)} = \frac{1}{3}$$

$$\Rightarrow \quad 3n - 6 = 2n + 2$$

$$\Rightarrow \quad n = 8$$

$\therefore$ Sides are $(2n+2), (2n+4), (2n+6)$

i.e. 18, 20, 22.

Example 15 *In a ΔABC, let $2a^2 + 4b^2 + c^2 = 2a(2b + c)$, then which of the following holds good?*

[Note : All symbols used have usual meaning in a triangle]

(a) $\cos B = \frac{-7}{8}$ (b) $\sin(A - C) = 0$

(c) $\frac{r}{r_1} = \frac{1}{5}$ (d) $\sin A : \sin B : \sin C = 1 : 2 : 1$

Sol. (b,c) We have, $2a^2 + 4b^2 + c^2 - 4ab - 2ac = 0$

$$\Rightarrow \quad (a - 2b)^2 + (a - c)^2 = 0$$

$$\Rightarrow \quad a = 2b, a = c$$

$$\Rightarrow \quad b = \frac{a}{2}, c = a$$

$$\therefore \cos A = \frac{b^2 + c^2 - a^2}{2bc} = \frac{\frac{a^2}{4} + a^2 - a^2}{2\left(\frac{a}{2}\right)a} = \frac{1}{4}$$

Similarly, $\cos B = \frac{7}{8}$ and $\cos C = \frac{1}{4}$

Hence, option (a) is not correct.

As $\quad a = c \Rightarrow A = C$

$\Rightarrow \quad A - C = 0$

$\Rightarrow \quad \sin(A - C) = 0$

Hence, option (b) is correct.

$$\text{As, } \frac{r}{r_1} = \frac{(s-a)\tan\frac{A}{2}}{s\tan\frac{A}{2}} = \frac{(s-a)}{s} = 1 - \frac{a}{s} = 1 - \frac{a}{\frac{5a}{4}} = 1 - \frac{4}{5} = \frac{1}{5}$$

Hence, option (c) is correct.

Also, $a : b : c = a : \frac{a}{2} : a = 2 : 1 : 2 = \sin A : \sin B : \sin C$

Hence, option (d) is not correct.

Example 16 *In ΔABC, angles A, B and C are in the ratio 1 : 2 : 3, then which of the following is(are) correct?*

(Note: All symbol used have usual meaning in a triangle).

(a) Circum-radius of $\Delta ABC = c$

(b) $a : b : c = 1 : \sqrt{3} : 2$

(c) Perimeter of $\Delta ABC = 3 + \sqrt{3}$

(d) Area of $\Delta ABC = \frac{\sqrt{3}}{8}c^2$

Sol. (b, d) Given, $A + 2A + 3A = 180°$,

$\Rightarrow A = 30°, B = 60°$ and $C = 90°$

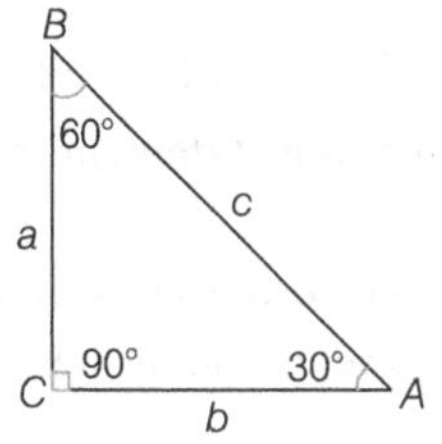

Now, $\quad R = \frac{c}{2}$

$$\frac{a}{\sin A} = \frac{b}{\sin B} = \frac{c}{\sin C} = 2\left(\frac{c}{2}\right)$$

$$a = \frac{c}{2}, b = \frac{\sqrt{3}c}{2}$$

So, $\quad a : b : c = \frac{c}{2} : \frac{\sqrt{3}c}{2} : c = \frac{1}{2} : \frac{\sqrt{3}}{2} : 1 = 1 : \sqrt{3} : 2$

Perimeter $= (3 + \sqrt{3})k$, where $k \in R$

Area of $\Delta ABC = \frac{1}{2}ab$

$$= \frac{1}{2}\left(\frac{c}{2}\right)\left(\frac{\sqrt{3}c}{2}\right) = \frac{\sqrt{3}}{8}c^2$$

Example 17 *If the length of tangents from A, B, C to the incircle of ΔABC are 4, 6, 8, then which of the following is(are) correct? (All symbols used have usual meaning in a triangle.)*

(a) Area of ΔABC is $12\sqrt{6}$ (b) r_1, r_2, r_3 are in HP.

(c) a, b, c are in AP. (d) $r = \frac{4\sqrt{6}}{3}$

Sol. (b, c, d) Given, $s - a = 4$, $s - b = 6$, $s - c = 8$

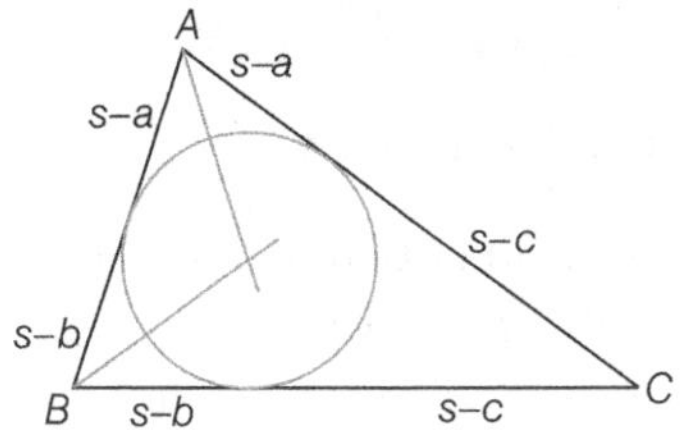

$\therefore \quad s = 18$

$\therefore \quad \Delta = \sqrt{18 \times 4 \times 6 \times 8} = 24\sqrt{6}$

$$a = 14, b = 12 \text{ and } c = 10$$

$s - a, s - b, s - c$ are in AP.

$\therefore$ a, b, c are in AP.

$$\frac{\Delta}{s-a}, \frac{\Delta}{s-b}, \frac{\Delta}{s-c} \text{ are in HP.}$$

$\therefore r_1, r_2, r_3$ are in HP.

$$r = \frac{\Delta}{s} = \frac{4\sqrt{6}}{3}$$

Example 18 *In ΔABC, let $b = 10$, $c = 10\sqrt{2}$ and $R = 5\sqrt{2}$, then which of the following statement (s) is (are) correct?*

(a) Area of ΔABC is 50.

(b) Distance between orthocentre and circumcentre is $5\sqrt{2}$.

(c) Sum of circumradius and in-radius of ΔABC is equal to 10.

(d) Length of internal angle bisector of $\angle ACB$ of ΔABC is $\frac{5}{2\sqrt{2}}$.

Sol. (a,b,c) We know, $\frac{b}{\sin B} = 2R$

$\Rightarrow \quad \sin B = \frac{10}{10\sqrt{2}} = \frac{1}{\sqrt{2}}$

$\Rightarrow \quad B = 45°$

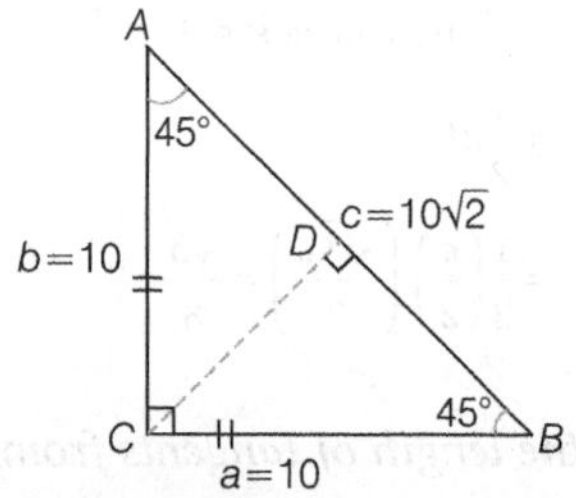

Also, $\frac{c}{\sin C} = 2R$

$\Rightarrow \quad \sin C = \frac{10\sqrt{2}}{10\sqrt{2}} = 1$

$\Rightarrow \quad C = 90°$

$\therefore \quad A = 45°$

$\therefore \Delta ABC$ is isosceles right angled at C.

$\because \quad a = 10, b = 10, c = 10\sqrt{2}$

Area of $\Delta ABC = \frac{1}{2} \times 10 \times 10 = 50$

Distance between orthocentre and circumcentre is

$$BD = DC = 5\sqrt{2}$$

$$R + r = 5\sqrt{2} + 10 - 5\sqrt{2} = 10 \qquad [\because r = 10 - 5\sqrt{2}]$$

JEE SCANNER

Example 19 Similar to PYQ Asked in JEE Adv. 2018

In a ΔABC, let $\angle ABC = 30°$ and the sides AB and BC have lengths $10\sqrt{3}$ and 10 respectively. Then, which of the following statement(s) is (are) TRUE?

(a) $\angle BAC = 30°$

(b) $\angle BCA = 120°$

(c) The area of the ΔABC is $25\sqrt{3}$.

(d) The radius of the incircle of the ΔABC is $10\sqrt{3} - 15$.

Sol. (a,b,c,d) We have, In ΔABC

$$\angle ABC = 30°,$$
$$AB = 10\sqrt{3}$$

and $\quad BC = 10$

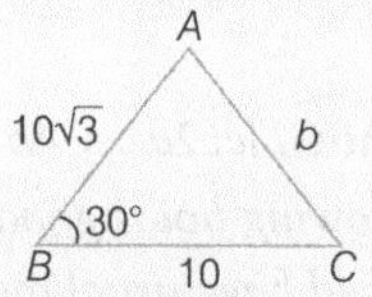

By cosine rule, $\cos 30° = \frac{AB^2 + BC^2 - AC^2}{2AB \cdot BC}$

$\Rightarrow \quad \frac{\sqrt{3}}{2} = \frac{300 + 100 - AC^2}{200\sqrt{3}}$

$\Rightarrow \quad 300 = 300 + 100 - AC^2$

$\Rightarrow \quad AC = 10$

Since, $\quad AC = BC = 10$

$\therefore \quad \angle BAC = 30°$ and $\angle BCA = 120°$

Area of $\Delta ABC = \frac{1}{2} AB \cdot BC \sin 30°$

$$= \frac{1}{2} \times 10\sqrt{3} \times 10 \times \frac{1}{2} = 25\sqrt{3}$$

Radius of incircle, $r = \frac{\Delta}{s}$

$$= \frac{25\sqrt{3}}{\frac{10\sqrt{3} + 10 + 10}{2}}$$

$$= \frac{25\sqrt{3}}{5(\sqrt{3} + 2)} \Rightarrow r = 10\sqrt{3} - 15$$

Skill Builder

In a ΔABC, let $\angle ABC = 30°$ and the sides AB and BC have lengths $20\sqrt{3}$ and 20 respectively. Then, which of the following statement(s) is (are) TRUE?

(a) $\angle BAC = 30°$

(b) $\angle BCA = 90°$

(c) The area of the ΔABC is $100\sqrt{3}$.

(d) The radius of the incircle of the ΔABC is $20\sqrt{3} - 30$.

For Sol.

Example 20 *If a right angled ΔABC of maximum area is inscribed within a circle of radius R, then Δ represents area of ΔABC and r, r_1, r_2, r_3 represent in-radius and ex-radii, and s is the semi-perimeter of ΔABC, then*

(a) $\Delta = R^2$
(b) $\frac{1}{r_1}+\frac{1}{r_2}+\frac{1}{r_3}=\frac{\sqrt{2}+1}{R}$
(c) $r=(\sqrt{2}-1)R$
(d) $s=(1+\sqrt{2})R$

Sol. (a, b, c, d) For a right angled triangle inscribed in a circle of radius R, the length of the hypotenuse is $2R$.

Then, area is maximum when it is isosceles triangle with each side $= \sqrt{2}\ R$

$$\therefore \quad s=\frac{1}{2}(2\sqrt{2}+2)R=(\sqrt{2}+1)R$$

$$\Delta=\frac{1}{2}\sqrt{2}R\cdot\sqrt{2}R=R^2$$

$$r=\frac{\Delta}{s}=\frac{R^2}{(\sqrt{2}+1)R} \Rightarrow r=(\sqrt{2}-1)R$$

$$\therefore \quad \frac{1}{r_1}+\frac{1}{r_2}+\frac{1}{r_3}=\frac{1}{r}=\frac{1}{(\sqrt{2}-1)R}=\frac{\sqrt{2}+1}{R}$$

Passage Based Questions

Passage I

(Ex. Nos. 21 to 22)

Let ABC be an acute triangle with $BC=a, CA=b$ and $AB=c$, where $a \neq b \neq c$. From any point P inside $\Delta\ ABC$ let D, E, F denote foot of perpendicular from P onto the sides BC, CA and AB, respectively.

Example 21 *All positions of point P for which ΔDEF is isosceles lie on*

(a) the incircle of ΔABC
(b) line of internal angle bisectors from A, B and C
(c) arcs of 3 circles
(d) None of the above

Example 22 *Let A(7, 0), B(4, 4) and C(0, 0) and Δ DEF is isosceles with DE = DF. Then, the curve on which P may lie is*

(a) $x=4$ or $x+y=7$ or $4x=3y$
(b) $x=4$ or $x^2+y^2=4x+4y$
(c) $3(x^2+y^2)+196=49(x+y)$
(d) None of the above

Sol. (Ex. Nos. 21 to 22)

21. (c) Let $DE = DF$, then

$BDPF$ is cyclic with BP as diameter.

$$\Rightarrow \quad BP=\frac{DF}{\sin B}$$

$$\Rightarrow \quad DF = BP\sin B$$

$CDPE$ is cyclic with CP as diameter.

$$\Rightarrow \quad CP=\frac{DE}{\sin C}$$

$$\Rightarrow \quad DE = CP\sin C$$

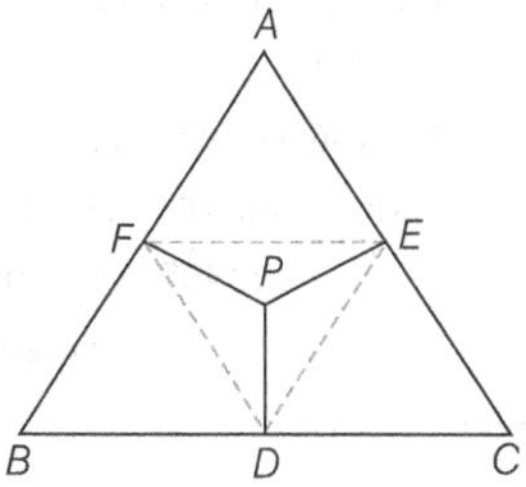

But $\quad DE = DF$

$$\Rightarrow \quad \frac{BP}{CP}=\frac{\sin C}{\sin B}=\frac{c}{b}$$

Hence, the locus of P is arcs of 3 circles.

22. (c) $\frac{PB}{PC}=\frac{c}{b}=\frac{5}{7}$

Hence, P will lie on circle

$$3(x^2+y^2)+196=49(x+y)$$

Passage II

(Ex. Nos. 23 to 24)

Let ABC be any triangle and P be a point inside it such that $\angle PAB=\frac{\pi}{18}$, $\angle PBA=\frac{\pi}{9}$, $\angle PCA=\frac{\pi}{6}$, $\angle PAC=\frac{2\pi}{9}$. Let $\angle PCB = x$

Example 23 *x is equal to*

(a) $\frac{\pi}{9}$
(b) $\frac{2\pi}{9}$
(c) $\frac{\pi}{3}$
(d) None of these

Example 24 *ΔABC is*

(a) Equilateral
(b) Isosceles
(c) Scalene
(d) Right angled

Sol. (Ex. Nos 23 to 24)

23. (a) In ΔPAB, $\frac{PA}{\sin 20^\circ}=\frac{PB}{\sin 10^\circ} \Rightarrow \frac{PA}{PB}=\frac{\sin 20^\circ}{\sin 10^\circ}$

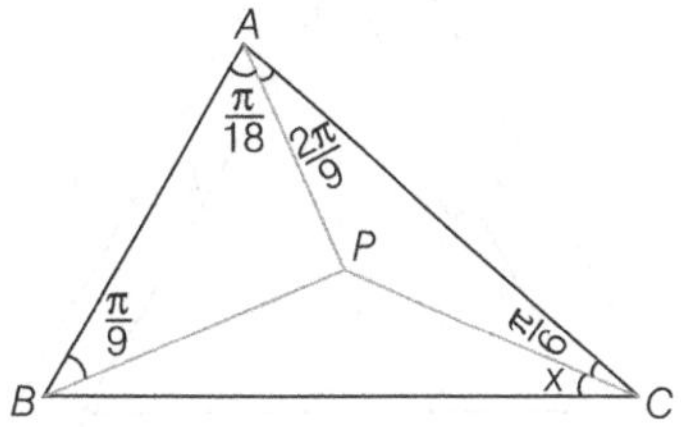

Similarly, In ΔPBC and ΔPAC,

$$\frac{PB}{PC}=\frac{\sin x}{\sin(80^\circ - x)} \text{ and } \frac{PC}{PA}=\frac{\sin 40^\circ}{\sin 30^\circ}$$

$$\Rightarrow \quad \frac{PA}{PB} \times \frac{PB}{PC} \times \frac{PC}{PA} = 1$$

$$\Rightarrow \quad \frac{\sin 20^\circ}{\sin 10^\circ} \times \frac{\sin x}{\sin(80^\circ - x)} \times \frac{\sin 40^\circ}{\sin 30^\circ} = 1$$

$$\Rightarrow \sin(80^\circ - x) = 4\cos 10^\circ \sin 40^\circ \sin x = 2\sin 50^\circ \sin x + \sin x$$

$$\Rightarrow \quad \sin(80^\circ - x) - \sin x = 2\sin 50^\circ \sin x$$

$$\Rightarrow \quad 2\cos 40^\circ \sin(90^\circ - x) = 2\sin 50^\circ \sin x$$

$$\Rightarrow \quad 2\cos 40^\circ \sin(40^\circ - x) = 2\cos 40^\circ \sin x$$

$$\Rightarrow \quad \sin(40^\circ - x) = \sin x$$

$$\Rightarrow \quad x = 20^\circ$$

24. (b) $\angle A = \angle C = 50^\circ$

Stem Based Questions

Stem I

(Ex. Nos. 25 and 26)

Let ΔXYZ be an acute angled triangle with orthocentre O. D, E, F are the feet of perpendicular from X, Y, Z respectively on opposite sides. Also, let R be the circumradius of ΔXYZ.

Given, $XO \cdot YO \cdot ZO = 3$ and $(XO)^2 + (YO)^2 + (ZO)^2 = 7$

Example 25 *If value of* $\dfrac{\cos X \cdot \cos Y \cdot \cos Z}{\cos^2 X + \cos^2 Y + \cos^2 Z}$ *is* $\dfrac{m}{nR}$, *then the value of* $m + n$ *is ....*

Example 26 *If* R *be circumradius of a* ΔXYZ *is* $\dfrac{k}{2}$. *Then, the value of* k *is ....*

Sol. (Ex. Nos 25 and 26)

$$\cos Y = \frac{YD}{XY} = \frac{YD}{z} \Rightarrow YD = z\cos Y$$

Also, $\cos \angle OYD = \dfrac{YD}{OY}$

$$\Rightarrow \quad OY = \frac{YD}{\cos\left(\frac{\pi}{2} - Z\right)} = \frac{YD}{\sin Z} = \frac{z\cos Y}{\sin Z}$$

$$\Rightarrow \quad OY = 2R\cos Y \quad \left[\because \frac{z}{\sin Z} = 2R\right]$$

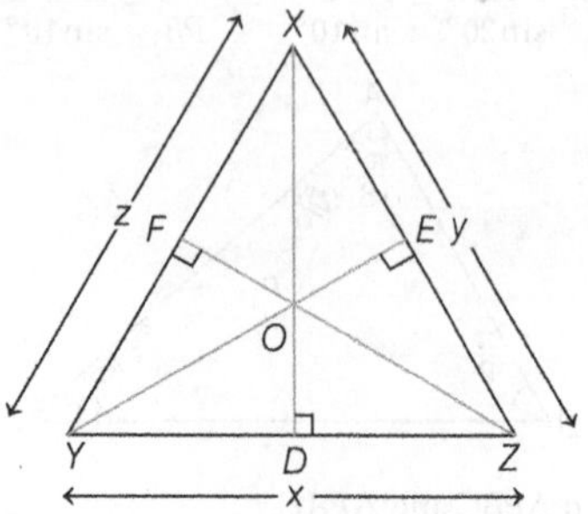

Similarly, $OX = 2R\cos X$ and $OZ = 2R\cos Z$

25. $\because XO \cdot YO \cdot ZO = 3$ [given]

$$\Rightarrow \quad 2R\cos Y \cdot 2R\cos X \cdot 2R\cos Z = 3$$

$$\Rightarrow \quad \cos X \cdot \cos Y \cdot \cos Z = \frac{3}{8R^3} \quad \text{...(i)}$$

and $(XO)^2 + (YO)^2 + (ZO)^2 = 7$ [given]

$$4R^2\cos^2 X + 4R^2\cos^2 Y + 4R^2\cos^2 Z = 7$$

$$\Rightarrow \quad \cos^2 X + \cos^2 Y + \cos^2 Z = \frac{7}{4R^2} \quad \text{...(ii)}$$

$$\therefore \quad \frac{\cos X \cdot \cos Y \cdot \cos Z}{\cos^2 X + \cos^2 Y + \cos^2 Z} = \frac{3}{8R^3} \times \frac{4R^2}{7}$$

[from Eqs. (i) and (ii)]

$$= \frac{3}{14R} = \frac{m}{nR}$$

$\Rightarrow \quad m = 3, n = 14$

$\therefore m + n = 3 + 14 = 17$

26. We know that

$$\cos^2 X + \cos^2 Y + \cos^2 Z = 1 - 2\cos X \cos Y \cos Z$$

$$\Rightarrow \quad \frac{7}{4R^2} = 1 - 2 \times \frac{3}{8R^3} \quad \text{[from Eqs. (i) and (ii)]}$$

$$\Rightarrow \quad 4R^3 - 7R - 3 = 0 \Rightarrow (R+1)(2R+1)(2R-3) = 0$$

$$\Rightarrow \quad R = \frac{3}{2} = \frac{k}{2}$$

$$\therefore \quad k = 3$$

Stem II

(Ex. Nos. 27 and 28)

In a $\Delta\, ABC$, let $\tan A = 1$, $\tan B = 2$, $\tan C = 3$ and $c = 3$.

Example 27 *Area of* ΔABC *is ....*

Example 28 *The radius of the circle circumscribing the* ΔABC *is* $\dfrac{\sqrt{k}}{2}$. *Then, the value of* k *is ....*

Sol. (Ex. Nos 27 and 28)

We have, $\tan A = 1 \Rightarrow \sin A = \dfrac{1}{\sqrt{2}}$ and $\cos A = \dfrac{1}{\sqrt{2}}$

$\tan B = 2 \Rightarrow \sin B = \dfrac{2}{\sqrt{5}}$ and $\cos B = \dfrac{1}{\sqrt{5}}$

$\tan C = 3 \Rightarrow \sin C = \dfrac{3}{\sqrt{10}}$ and $\cos C = \dfrac{1}{\sqrt{10}}$

Using sine law, $a\sqrt{2} = \dfrac{b\sqrt{5}}{2} = \dfrac{c\sqrt{10}}{3}$

$$\therefore \quad a\sqrt{2} = \frac{b\sqrt{5}}{2} = \sqrt{10} \quad \text{[as } c = 3\text{]}$$

$$\Rightarrow \quad a = \sqrt{5},\ b = 2\sqrt{2}$$

27. $\therefore \Delta = \dfrac{1}{2} \cdot \sqrt{5} \cdot 2\sqrt{2} \sin C = \sqrt{10} \cdot \dfrac{3}{\sqrt{10}} = 3$

28. $R = \dfrac{abc}{4\Delta} = \dfrac{\sqrt{5} \cdot 2\sqrt{2} \cdot 3}{4 \cdot 3} = \dfrac{\sqrt{10}}{2}$

$\therefore \quad k = 10$

Single Integer Answer Type Questions

Example 29 *In a ΔABC, if $r_1 + r_3 + r = r_2$, then find the value of $(\sec^2 A + \cos^2 B - \cot^2 C)$.*

[**Note** All symbols used have usual meaning in a triangle.]

Sol. (1) We have, $r_1 + r_3 + r = r_2$

$$\Rightarrow \left(\frac{\Delta}{s-a} + \frac{\Delta}{s-c}\right) = \left(\frac{\Delta}{s-b} - \frac{\Delta}{s}\right)$$

$$\Rightarrow \frac{2s-(a+c)}{(s-a)(s-c)} = \frac{b}{s(s-b)}$$

$$\Rightarrow (s-a)(s-c) = s(s-b)$$

$$\Rightarrow s^2 - (a+c)s + ac = s^2 - bs$$

$$\Rightarrow (a+c-b)s - ac = 0$$

$$\Rightarrow (a+c-b)\frac{(a+b+c)}{2} = ac$$

$$\Rightarrow (a+c)^2 - b^2 = 2ac$$

$$\Rightarrow a^2 + c^2 + 2ac - b^2 = 2ac$$

$$\Rightarrow a^2 + c^2 = b^2$$

So, $\angle B = 90°$ and $\angle A + \angle C = 90°$

Now, $\sec^2 A + \cos^2 B - \cot^2 C = \sec^2(90°-C) + \cos^2 90° - \cot^2 C$

$$= \operatorname{cosec}^2 C + 0 - \cot^2 C$$

$$= 1$$

Hence, $(\sec^2 A + \cos^2 B - \cot^2 C) = 1$

Alternate Solution

We have,

$$(r_1 + r_3) - (r_2 - r) = 0 \quad \ldots(i)$$

As, $r_1 + r_3 = 4R \sin\frac{A}{2}\cos\frac{B}{2}\cos\frac{C}{2} + 4R\cos\frac{A}{2}\cos\frac{B}{2}\sin\frac{C}{2}$

$$= 4R\cos\frac{B}{2}\sin\left(\frac{A+C}{2}\right) = 4R\cos^2\frac{B}{2} \quad \ldots(ii)$$

Also, $r_2 - r = 4R\cos\frac{A}{2}\sin\frac{B}{2}\cos\frac{C}{2} - 4R\sin\frac{A}{2}\sin\frac{B}{2}\sin\frac{C}{2}$

$$= 4R\sin\frac{B}{2}\cos\left(\frac{A+C}{2}\right) = 4R\sin^2\frac{B}{2} \quad \ldots(iii)$$

$\therefore$ Using Eqs. (ii) and (iii) in Eq. (i), we get

$$4R\left(\cos^2\frac{B}{2} - \sin^2\frac{B}{2}\right) = 0$$

$$\Rightarrow 4R\cos B = 0$$

$$\Rightarrow \angle B = 90° \text{ and } \angle A + \angle C = 90°$$

Hence, $(\sec^2 A + \cos^2 B - \cot^2 C) = 1$

Example 30 *Consider an obtuse angled triangles with side 8 cm, 15 cm and x cm (largest side being 15 cm). If x is an integer, then find the number of possible triangles.*

Sol. (5) Since, 15 be the largest side

$$\cos\theta = \frac{x^2 + 8^2 - 15^2}{16x}$$

for obtuse angled $-1 < \cos\theta < 0$

$$-16x < x^2 - 161 < 0$$

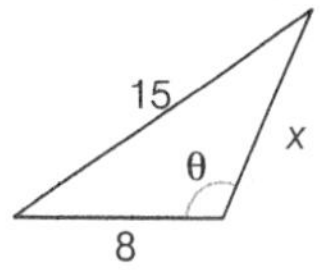

$$\Rightarrow x^2 < 161$$

$$\Rightarrow x < 13 \quad \ldots(i)$$

and $x^2 + 16x - 161 > 0$

$$\Rightarrow (x+23)(x-7) > 0 \text{ or } x > 7 \quad \ldots(ii)$$

$$\therefore 7 < x < 13 \Rightarrow x \in \{8, 9, 10, 11, 12\}$$

Hence, the number of possible values of x is 5.

Example 31 *In a ΔABC, the internal angle bisector of $\angle ABC$ meets AC at K. If $BC = 2$, $CK = 1$ and $BK = \frac{3\sqrt{2}}{2}$, then find the length of side AB.*

Sol. (3) Using cosine law in ΔBKC,

$$\cos\frac{B}{2} = \frac{4 + \frac{18}{4} - 1}{2\cdot\frac{3\sqrt{2}}{2}\cdot 2} = \frac{3 + \frac{9}{2}}{6\sqrt{2}} = \frac{15}{12\sqrt{2}} = \frac{5}{4\sqrt{2}}$$

Now, $\sin\frac{B}{2} = \frac{AK}{AB} = \frac{CK}{BC} = \frac{1}{2} \Rightarrow AB = 2AK$

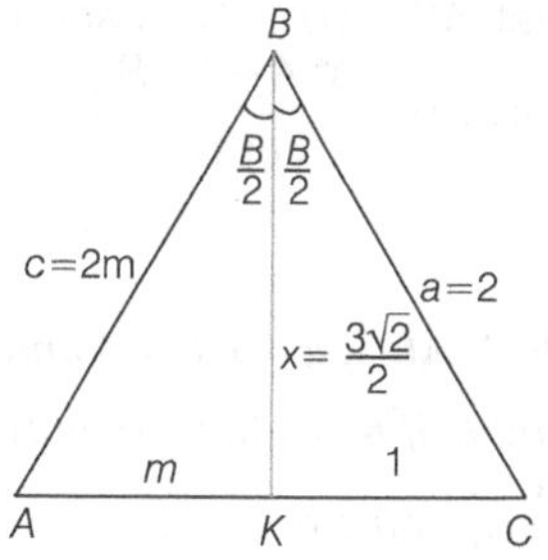

Now, $x = \frac{2ac}{a+c}\cos\frac{B}{2}$

$$= \frac{(2\cdot 2\cdot 2\text{ m})}{2m+2}\cdot\frac{5}{4\sqrt{2}}$$

$$\Rightarrow \frac{3\sqrt{2}}{2} = \frac{4m}{m+1}\cdot\frac{5}{4\sqrt{2}}$$

$$\Rightarrow 3 = \frac{5m}{m+1}$$

$$\Rightarrow 3m + 3 = 5m$$

$$\Rightarrow m = \frac{3}{2}$$

$$\therefore AB = 2m$$

$$\therefore c = 3$$

JEE SCANNER

Example 32 Similar to PYQ Asked in JEE Adv. 2021

In a ΔABC, let $AB=\sqrt{23}$, $BC=4$ and $CA=3$. Then, the value of $\dfrac{\cot B+\cot C}{\cot A}$ is ....

Sol. (2) Given, $AB=\sqrt{23}=c,\ BC=4=a,\ CA=3=b$

Now, $$\frac{\cot B+\cot C}{\cot A}=\frac{\dfrac{\cos B}{\sin B}+\dfrac{\cos C}{\sin C}}{\dfrac{\cos A}{\sin A}}$$

$$=\frac{\dfrac{c^2+a^2-b^2}{2ac(\sin B)}+\dfrac{a^2+b^2-c^2}{2ab(\sin C)}}{\dfrac{b^2+c^2-a^2}{2bc(\sin A)}}$$

$$=\frac{\dfrac{c^2+a^2-b^2}{4\Delta}+\dfrac{a^2+b^2-c^2}{4\Delta}}{\dfrac{b^2+c^2-a^2}{4\Delta}}$$

$$=\frac{c^2+a^2-b^2+a^2+b^2-c^2}{b^2+c^2-a^2}=\frac{2a^2}{b^2+c^2-a^2}$$

$$=\frac{2\times16}{9+23-16}=\frac{32}{16}=2$$

Skill Builder

In a ΔABC, let $AB=10$, $BC=5$ and $CA=8$. Then, the value of $\dfrac{\cot A+\cot B}{\cot C}$ is ....

For Sol.

Example 33 *In ΔABC, $a=5$, $b=4$ and $c=3$. G is the centroid of triangle. If R_1 be the circumradius of ΔGAB, then the value of $\dfrac{144}{65}R_1^2$ must be ....*

Sol. (5) Let A_1, B_1 and C_1 is the mid-point of sides BC, AC and AB respectively.

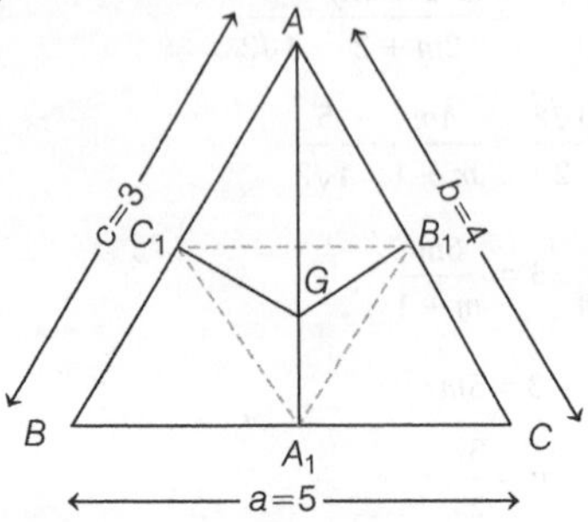

Now, $AG=\dfrac{2}{3}AA_1$ and $BG=\dfrac{2}{3}BB_1$

$$\Rightarrow AG=\frac{2}{3}\times\frac{1}{2}\sqrt{2b^2+2c^2-a^2}\text{ and }BG=\frac{2}{3}\times\frac{1}{2}\sqrt{2a^2+2c^2-b^2}$$

$$\Rightarrow AG=\frac{1}{3}a\text{ and }BG=\frac{1}{3}\sqrt{b^2+4c^2}\text{ as }a^2=b^2+c^2$$

$$\Rightarrow AG=\frac{5}{3}\text{ and }BG=\frac{1}{3}\sqrt{16+36}=\frac{2}{3}\sqrt{13}$$

Also, $AB=c=3$ and $\Delta_{GAB}=\dfrac{1}{3}\Delta_{ABC}=2$

If R_1 be the circumradius of $\Delta\ GAB$, then

$$R_1=\frac{(AG)(BG)(AB)}{4\Delta_{GAB}}=\frac{5}{3}\cdot\frac{2}{3}\sqrt{13}\cdot3\cdot\frac{1}{4\cdot2}=\frac{5\sqrt{13}}{12}$$

$$\therefore\ \frac{144}{65}R_1^2=\frac{144}{65}\times\left(\frac{5\sqrt{13}}{12}\right)^2=5$$

Example 34 *In $\Delta\ ABC$, $a\ge b\ge c$ and if $\dfrac{a^3+b^3+c^3}{\sin^3A+\sin^3B+\sin^3C}=8$, then the maximum value of a is ....*

Sol. (2) According to the sine rule, $a=2R\sin A$, $b=2R\sin B$ and $c=2R\sin C$

$$\therefore\ \frac{(2R\sin A)^3+(2R\sin B)^3+(2R\sin C)^3}{\sin^3A+\sin^3B+\sin^3C}=8$$

$$\Rightarrow\ 8R^3=8\Rightarrow R=1$$

Now, $a=2R\sin A\Rightarrow a=2\sin A\le2$

Hence, the maximum value of a is 2.

Numerical Value Type Questions

Example 35 *In ΔABC, let $b=6$, $c=10$ and $r_1=r_2+r_3+r$, then find area of ΔABC.*

[**Note** All symbols used have usual meaning in a triangle]

Sol. (30) We have, $r_1=r_2+r_3+r$ [given]

$$\Rightarrow\ (r_1-r)=(r_2+r_3)$$

$$\Rightarrow\ \frac{s-(s-a)}{s(s-a)}=\frac{2s-(b+c)}{(s-b)(s-c)}$$

$$\Rightarrow\ \frac{(s-b)(s-c)}{s(s-a)}=1$$

$$\Rightarrow\ \tan^2\frac{A}{2}=1\Rightarrow\frac{A}{2}=45^\circ$$

Hence, $A=90^\circ$

Now, area of $\Delta ABC=\dfrac{1}{2}bc\sin A$

$$=\frac{1}{2}(6)(10)\sin90^\circ$$

$$=30\text{ sq units}$$

Example 36 *Let ABC be a right angled triangle at C. If the inscribed circle touches the side AB to D and (AD) (BD) = 11, then find the area of ΔABC.*

Sol. (11) We have, $(AD)(BD) = 11$

$$\Rightarrow (s-a)(s-b) = 11$$
$$\Rightarrow (2s-2a)(2s-2b) = 44$$
$$\Rightarrow (b+c-a)(a+c-b) = 44$$
$$\Rightarrow c^2 - (b-a)^2 = 44$$
$$\Rightarrow 2ab = 44 \quad [\text{As } c^2 = a^2 + b^2]$$
$$\Rightarrow ab = 22$$

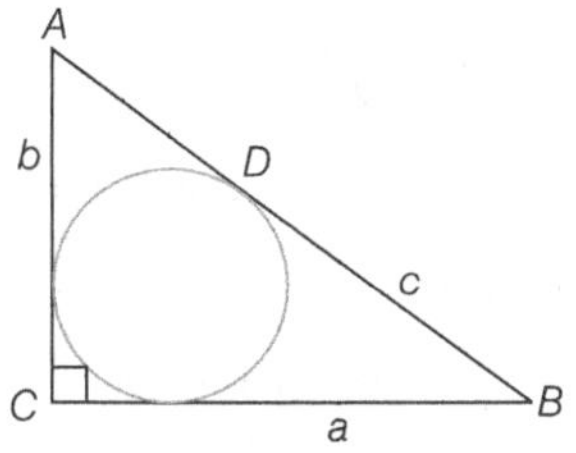

Now, area $(\Delta ABC) = \frac{1}{2}ab = \frac{1}{2}(22) = 11$

Example 37 *Consider a ΔABC and let a, b and c denote the lengths of the sides opposite to vertices A, B and C, respecively. Suppose $a = 2$, $b = 3$, $c = 4$ and H be the orthocentre. Find $15(HA)^2$.*

Sol. (196) We know that $HA = 2R\cos A$, where

$$\cos A = \frac{b^2+c^2-a^2}{2bc} = \frac{9+16-4}{24} = \frac{21}{24} = \frac{7}{8}$$

$$\therefore \sin A = \sqrt{1 - \frac{49}{64}} = \frac{\sqrt{15}}{8}$$

Now, $\frac{a}{\sin A} = 2R$

$$\Rightarrow 2R = \frac{2\times 8}{\sqrt{15}} = \frac{16}{\sqrt{15}}$$

$$\therefore HA = 2R\cos A = \frac{16}{\sqrt{15}} \times \frac{7}{8} = \frac{14}{\sqrt{15}}$$

Hence, $15(HA)^2 = 196$

Example 38 *In ΔABC, $AC = 13$, $AB = 15$ and $BC = 14$. Let O be the circumcentre of the ΔABC. If the length of perpendicular from the point 'O' on BC can be expressed as a rational $\frac{m}{n}$ in the lowest form, then find $(m+n)$.*

Sol. (41) $\Delta = \sqrt{s(s-a)(s-b)(s-c)}$

$$= \sqrt{21\cdot 8\cdot 6\cdot 7} = 84$$

$$R = \frac{abc}{4\Delta} = \frac{(14)(13)(15)}{4\cdot 84} = \frac{2\cdot 13\cdot 15}{4\cdot 12} = \frac{65}{8}$$

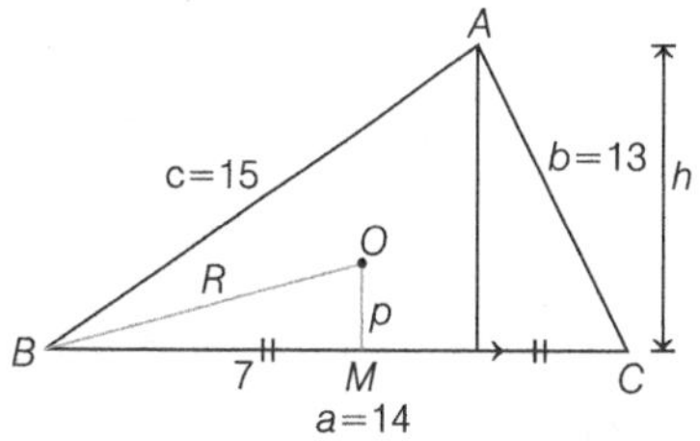

$$\therefore p = \sqrt{R^2 - 7^2} = \sqrt{\left(\frac{65}{8}\right)^2 - 7^2} = \frac{\sqrt{(65)^2-(56)^2}}{8} = \frac{\sqrt{121\cdot 9}}{8} = \frac{33}{8} = \frac{m}{n}$$

$$\Rightarrow m + n = 33 + 8 = 41$$

Matching Type Questions

Example 39 *Match the statement of Column I with value of Column II.*

Column I		Column II
(A)	In a ΔABC, if $a^4 - 2(b^2+c^2)a^2 + b^4 + b^2c^2 + c^4 = 0$, then $\angle A$ is	p. 30°
(B)	In a ΔABC, If $a^4 + b^4 + c^4 = a^2b^2 + 2b^2c^2 + 2c^2a^2$, then $\angle C$ is	q. 60°
(C)	In a ΔABC, If $a^4 + b^4 + c^4 + 2a^2c^2 = 2a^2b^2 + 2b^2c^2$, then $\angle B$ is	r. 90°
(D)	In a ΔABC, if $a^4 + b^4 + c^4 = 2a^2b^2 + 2b^2c^2$, then $\angle B$ is	s. 135°
		t. 150°

Sol. (A) → (q); (B) → (p, t); C → (r); (D) → (s)

(A) $\because$ $a^4 - 2(b^2+c^2)a^2 + b^4 + b^2c^2 + c^4 = 0$

$$\Rightarrow (b^2+c^2-a^2)^2 - (b^2+c^2)^2 + b^4 + b^2c^2 + c^4 = 0$$
$$\Rightarrow (b^2+c^2-a^2)^2 = b^2c^2$$
$$\Rightarrow \left(\frac{b^2+c^2-a^2}{2bc}\right)^2 = \frac{1}{4}$$
$$\Rightarrow \cos^2 A = \frac{1}{4}$$
$$\therefore \cos A = \pm\frac{1}{2}$$

$\therefore$ $A = 60°$ or $120°$

(B) $\because \cos C = \dfrac{a^2+b^2-c^2}{2ab}$ or $a^2+b^2-c^2 = 2ab\cos C$

On squaring both sides, we get

$$a^4+b^4+c^4+2a^2b^2-2a^2c^2-2b^2c^2 = 4a^2b^2\cos^2 C$$

$$\Rightarrow \quad 3a^2b^2 = 4a^2b^2\cos^2 C$$

$$[\because a^4+b^4+c^4 = a^2b^2+2b^2c^2+2c^2a^2]$$

or $$\cos^2 C = \frac{3}{4}$$

$$\Rightarrow \quad \cos C = \pm\frac{\sqrt{3}}{2}$$

$\therefore \quad C = 30^\circ$ or 150°

(C) $\because a^4+b^4+c^4+2a^2c^2 = 2a^2b^2+2b^2c^2$

$$\Rightarrow \quad b^4-2(a^2+c^2)b^2+(a^2+c^2)^2 = 0$$

$$\Rightarrow \quad \{b^2-(a^2+c^2)\}^2 = 0$$

$$\Rightarrow \quad a^2+c^2 = b^2$$

$$\Rightarrow \quad \cos B = 0$$

$\therefore \quad B = 90^\circ$

(D) $\because a^4+b^4+c^4 = 2a^2b^2+2b^2c^2$

$$\Rightarrow a^4+b^4+c^4-2a^2b^2-2b^2c^2+2c^2a^2 = 2c^2a^2$$

$$\Rightarrow \quad (c^2+a^2-b^2)^2 = 2c^2a^2$$

$$\Rightarrow \quad c^2+a^2-b^2 = \pm\sqrt{2}ca$$

Using cosine rule,

$$\cos B = \frac{c^2+a^2-b^2}{2ac} = \frac{\pm\sqrt{2}ca}{2ac} = \pm\frac{1}{\sqrt{2}}$$

$$\Rightarrow \quad \angle B = 45^\circ \text{ or } 135^\circ$$

Example 40 *Match the statement of Column I with the values of Column II.*

Column I	Column II
(A) In a ΔABC, $(c-a)^2 = b^2 - ac$ and $\cos B + \sin C = \dfrac{3}{2}$	(p) $A = 30^\circ$
(B) A, B, C are in AP and $C = 3A$	(q) $B = 60^\circ$
(C) The length of the bisector of $\angle B = \dfrac{\sqrt{3}ca}{(c+a)}$ and $a = b$	(r) $C = 90^\circ$
(D) $\dfrac{1}{a+b} + \dfrac{1}{b+c} = \dfrac{3}{a+b+c}$	(s) $A = B = C = 60^\circ$

Sol. (A) → (p, q, r); (B) → (p, q, r); (C) → (s); (D) → (q)

(A) $c^2+a^2-2ac = b^2-ac$

$$\Rightarrow \quad \frac{c^2+a^2-b^2}{2ac} = \frac{1}{2}$$

$$\Rightarrow \quad \cos B = \frac{1}{2}$$

$$\Rightarrow \quad B = 60^\circ \text{ and } \cos B + \sin C = \frac{3}{2}$$

$$\Rightarrow \quad \sin C = 1$$

$$\Rightarrow \quad C = 90^\circ \text{ and } A = 30^\circ$$

(B) $A+B+C = 180^\circ$, $B = \dfrac{A+C}{2}$

$$\Rightarrow \quad B = 60^\circ, C + A = 120^\circ$$

Now, $\quad C = 3A \Rightarrow A = 30^\circ, C = 90^\circ$

(C) Length of the bisector of $\angle B$ is

$$\frac{2ca}{c+a}\cos(B/2) = \frac{\sqrt{3}ca}{c+a}$$

$$\Rightarrow \quad \cos\left(\frac{B}{2}\right) = \frac{\sqrt{3}}{2} = \cos 30^\circ$$

$$\Rightarrow \quad B = 60^\circ, a = b$$

$$\Rightarrow \quad A = B = 60^\circ = C$$

(D) We have, $(a+b+c)(a+2b+c) = 3(a+b)(b+c)$

$$\Rightarrow \quad (a+c)^2+3b(a+c)+2b^2 = 3(ab+bc+ca+b^2)$$

$$\Rightarrow \quad \frac{a^2+c^2-b^2}{ac} = 1$$

$$\Rightarrow \quad \cos B = \frac{1}{2} \Rightarrow B = 60^\circ$$

EXERCISE 1

JEE Advanced Pattern

Single Option Correct Type Questions

1. In a ΔABC, if $a = 13$, $b = 14$ and $c = 15$, then $\angle A$ is equal to
[**Note** All symbols used have their usual meaning in a triangle]
(a) $\sin^{-1}\frac{4}{5}$ (b) $\sin^{-1}\frac{3}{5}$
(c) $\sin^{-1}\frac{3}{4}$ (d) $\sin^{-1}\frac{2}{3}$

2. In a ΔABC, if $b = (\sqrt{3} - 1)a$ and $\angle C = 30°$, then the value of $(A - B)$ is equal to
[**Note** All symbols used have usual meaning in the triangle]
(a) 30° (b) 45° (c) 60° (d) 75°

3. In ΔABC, if $2b = a + c$ and $A - C = 90°$, then $\sin B$ equals
[**Note** All symbols used have usual meaning in ΔABC.]
(a) $\frac{\sqrt{7}}{5}$ (b) $\frac{\sqrt{5}}{8}$ (c) $\frac{\sqrt{7}}{4}$ (d) $\frac{\sqrt{5}}{3}$

4. Let ABC be a right triangle with length of side $AB = 3$ and hyotenuse $AC = 5$. If D is a point on BC such that $\frac{BD}{DC} = \frac{AB}{AC}$, then AD is equal to
(a) $\frac{4\sqrt{3}}{3}$ (b) $\frac{3\sqrt{5}}{2}$ (c) $\frac{4\sqrt{5}}{3}$ (d) $\frac{5\sqrt{3}}{4}$

5. If in a right angled ΔABC, $4\sin A\cos B - 1 = 0$ and $\tan A$ is finite, then
(a) angles are in AP. (b) angles are in GP.
(c) angles are in HP. (d) None of these

6. In a triangle with one angle $\frac{2\pi}{3}$, the lengths of the sides form an AP. If the length of the greatest side is 7 cm, then the radius of the circumcircle of the triangle is
(a) $\frac{7\sqrt{3}}{3}$ cm (b) $\frac{5\sqrt{3}}{3}$ cm (c) $\frac{2\sqrt{3}}{3}$ cm (d) $\sqrt{3}$ cm

7. Sides of a ΔABC are in AP. If $a < \min\{b, c\}$, then $\cos A$ may be equal to
(a) $\frac{3c - 4b}{2b}$ (b) $\frac{3c - 4b}{2c}$
(c) $\frac{4c - 3b}{2b}$ (d) $\frac{4c - 3b}{2c}$

8. If a ΔABC, a, b, A are given and b_1, b_2 are two values of the third sides b such that $b_2 = 2b_1$. Then, $\sin A$ is equal to
(a) $\sqrt{\frac{9a^2 - c^2}{8a^2}}$ (b) $\sqrt{\frac{9a^2 - c^2}{8c^2}}$
(c) $\sqrt{\frac{9a^2 - c^2}{8b^2}}$ (d) None of these

9. In a ΔABC, if $\cot A = (x^3 + x^2 + x)^{\frac{1}{2}}$, $\cot B = (x + x^{-1} + 1)^{\frac{1}{2}}$ and $\cot C = (x^{-3} + x^{-2} + x^{-1})^{\frac{-1}{2}}$, then the triangle is
(a) equilateral (b) isosceles
(c) right angled (d) obtuse angled

10. In ΔABC, if $a = 10$ and $b\cot B + c\cot C = 2(r + R)$, then the maximum area of ΔABC will be
(a) 50 (b) $\sqrt{50}$
(c) 25 (d) 5

11. Let a, b, c be the sides of a triangle. No two of them are equal and $\lambda \in R$. If the roots of the equation $x^2 + 2(a + b + c)x + 3\lambda(ab + bc + ca) = 0$ are real distinct, then
(a) $\lambda < \frac{4}{3}$ (b) $\lambda > \frac{5}{3}$
(c) $\lambda \in \left(\frac{1}{3}, \frac{5}{3}\right)$ (d) $\lambda \in \left(\frac{4}{3}, \frac{5}{3}\right)$

12. In ΔABC, if P, Q, R divides sides BC, AC and AB, respectively, in the ratio $k : 1$ (in order). If the ratio $\left(\frac{\text{area } \Delta PQR}{\text{area } \Delta ABC}\right)$ is $\frac{1}{3}$, then k is equal to
(a) $\frac{1}{3}$ (b) 2
(c) 3 (d) None of these

13. In an ambiguous case of solving a triangle when $a = \sqrt{5}$, $b = 2$, $\angle A = \frac{\pi}{6}$ and the two possible values of third side are c_1 and c_2, then
(a) $|c_1 - c_2| = 2\sqrt{6}$
(b) $|c_1 - c_2| = 4\sqrt{6}$
(c) $|c_1 - c_2| = 4$
(d) $|c_1 - c_2| = 6$

14. If the median AD of a ΔABC makes an angle θ with side AB, then $\sin(A-\theta)$ is equal to
(a) $\frac{b}{c}\sin\theta$ (b) $\frac{c}{b}\sin\theta$
(c) $\frac{c}{b}\cos\theta$ (d) None of these

15. In a ΔABC, angles A, B, C are in AP, then $\lim_{A\to C}\frac{\sqrt{3-4\sin A\sin C}}{|A-C|}$ is
(a) 1 (b) 2
(c) 3 (d) 4

16. In a ΔABC, $(a+b+c)(b+c-a)=\lambda bc$ if
(a) $\lambda<0$ (b) $\lambda>6$
(c) $0<\lambda<4$ (d) $\lambda>4$

17. In a ΔABC, sides a, b, c are in AP and $\frac{2}{1!9!}+\frac{2}{3!7!}+\frac{1}{5!5!}=\frac{8^a}{(2b)!}$, then the maximum value of $\tan A\tan B$ is equal to
(a) $\frac{1}{2}$ (b) $\frac{1}{3}$ (c) $\frac{1}{4}$ (d) $\frac{1}{5}$

18. If a, b and c be the sides of a ΔABC and if roots of the equation $a(b-c)x^2+b(c-a)x+c(a-b)=0$ are equal, then $\sin^2\left(\frac{A}{2}\right), \sin^2\left(\frac{B}{2}\right), \sin^2\left(\frac{C}{2}\right)$ are in
(a) AP (b) GP
(c) HP (d) AGP

19. In any ΔABC, $\Pi\left(\frac{\sin^2 A+\sin A+1}{\sin A}\right)$ is always greater than
(a) 9 (b) 3
(c) 27 (d) None of these

20. A circle is inscribed in an equilateral triangle of side a. The area of any square inscribed in this circle is
(a) a^2 (b) $\frac{a^2}{4}$ (c) $\frac{a^2}{3}$ (d) $\frac{a^2}{6}$

21. In any ΔABC, if $\sin A, \sin B, \sin C$ are in AP, then the maximum value of $\tan\frac{B}{2}$ is
(a) $-\frac{1}{\sqrt{3}}$ (b) $\frac{1}{\sqrt{3}}$
(c) $\frac{1}{3}$ (d) None of these

22. In ΔABC, AD is an altitude from A on side BC. If $b>c$, $\angle C=23^\circ$ and $AD=\frac{abc}{b^2-c^2}$, then $\angle B$ is
(a) 110° (b) 113° (c) 120° (d) 130°

23. If in a ΔABC, $a=5$, $b=4$ and $\cos(A-B)=\frac{31}{32}$, then the value of $\cos C$ is equal to
(a) $\frac{3}{8}$ (b) $\frac{1}{8}$ (c) $\frac{7}{8}$ (d) $\frac{9}{8}$

24. In ΔABC, if $AB=x$, $BC=x+1$, $\angle C=\frac{\pi}{3}$, then the least integer value of x is
(a) 6 (b) 7
(c) 8 (d) None of these

25. The sides of a triangle are in AP. If the angles A and C are the greatest and smallest angle respectively, then $4(1-\cos A)(1-\cos C)$ is equal to
(a) $\cos A-\cos C$ (b) $\cos A\cos C$
(c) $\cos A+\cos C$ (d) $\cos C-\cos A$

26. If in ΔABC, $c(a+b)\cos\frac{1}{2}B=b(a+c)\cos\frac{1}{2}C$, the triangle is
(a) isosceles
(b) equilateral
(c) right angled but not isosceles
(d) right angled and isosceles

27. A tower of height b subtends an angle at a point O on the level of the foot of the tower and at a distance a from the foot of the tower. If a pole mounted on the tower also subtends an equal angle at O, then the height of the pole is
(a) $b\left(\frac{a^2-b^2}{a^2+b^2}\right)$ (b) $b\left(\frac{a^2+b^2}{a^2-b^2}\right)$
(c) $a\left(\frac{a^2-b^2}{a^2+b^2}\right)$ (d) $a\left(\frac{a^2+b^2}{a^2-b^2}\right)$

28. A balloon is observed simultaneously from three points A, B and C on a straight road directly under it. The angular elevation at B is twice and at C is thrice that of A. If the distance between A and B is 200 m and the distance between B and C is 100 m, then the height of balloon is given by
(a) 50 m (b) $50\sqrt{3}$ m
(c) $50\sqrt{2}$ m (d) None of these

29. A vertical pole (more than 100 m high) consists of two portions, the lower being one third of the whole. If the upper portion subtends an angle $\tan^{-1}\left(\frac{1}{2}\right)$ at a point in a horizontal plane through the foot of the pole and distance 40 ft from it, then the height of the pole is
(a) 100 ft
(b) 120 ft
(c) 150 ft
(d) None of the above

More than One Correct Option Type Questions

30. If area of ΔABC, Δ and $\angle C$, are given and if the side c opposite to given angles is minimum, then

(a) $a = \sqrt{\frac{2\Delta}{\sin C}}$ (b) $b = \sqrt{\frac{2\Delta}{\sin C}}$

(c) $a = \frac{4\Delta}{\sin C}$ (d) $b = \frac{4\Delta}{\sin^2 C}$

31. In ΔABC, if $ac = 3$, $bc = 4$ and $\cos(A - B) = \frac{3}{4}$, then

(a) measure of $\angle A$ is $\frac{\pi}{2}$ (b) measure of $\angle B$ is $\frac{\pi}{2}$

(c) $\cot\frac{C}{2} = \sqrt{7}$ (d) circumradius of ΔABC is $\frac{2}{7^{1/4}}$

32. In ΔABC, let $a = 5$, $b = 4$ and $\cos(A - B) = \frac{31}{32}$, then which of the following statement(s) is (are) correct?

[**Note** All symbols used have usual meaning in a triangle]

(a) The perimeter of ΔABC equals $\frac{15}{2}$.

(b) The radius of circle inscribed in ΔABC equals $\frac{\sqrt{7}}{2}$.

(c) The measure of $\angle C$ equals $\cos^{-1}\frac{1}{8}$.

(d) The value of $R(b^2 \sin 2C + c^2 \sin 2B)$ is 120.

33. In which of the following situations, it is possible to have a ΔABC?

(All symbols used have usual meaning in a triangle)

(a) $(a + c - b)(a - c + b) = 4bc$

(b) $b^2 \sin 2C + c^2 \sin 2B = ab$

(c) $a = 3$, $b = 5$, $c = 7$ and $C = \frac{2\pi}{3}$

(d) $\cos\left(\frac{A - C}{2}\right) = \cos\left(\frac{A + C}{2}\right)$

34. In a ΔABC, let $BC = 1$, $AC = 2$ and measure of $\angle C$ is $30°$. Which of the following statement(s) is(are) correct?

(a) $2\sin A = \sin B$

(b) Length of side AB equals $5 - 2\sqrt{3}$.

(c) Measure of $\angle A$ is less than $30°$.

(d) Circumradius of $\angle ABC$ is equal to length of side AB.

35. Let one angle of a triangle be $60°$, the area of triangle is $10\sqrt{3}$ and perimeter is 20 cm. If $a > b > c$ where a, b and c denote lengths of sides opposite to vertices A, B and C respectively, then which of the following is(are) correct?

(a) Inradius of triangle is $\sqrt{3}$.

(b) Length of longest side of triangle is 7.

(c) Circumradius of triangles is $\frac{7}{\sqrt{3}}$.

(d) Radius of largest escribed circle is $\frac{1}{12}$.

36. In a ΔABC, if $a = 4$, $b = 8$ and $\angle C = 60°$, then which of the following relations is(are) correct?

[**Note** All symbols used have usual meaning in triangles ABC.]

(a) The area of ΔABC is $8\sqrt{3}$.

(b) The value of $\Sigma \sin^2 A = 2$.

(c) Inradius of ΔABC is $\frac{2\sqrt{3}}{3 + \sqrt{3}}$.

(d) The length of internal angle bisector of $\angle C$ is $\frac{4}{\sqrt{3}}$.

37. There exist a ΔABC satisfying

(a) $\tan A + \tan B + \tan C = 0$

(b) $\frac{\sin A}{2} = \frac{\sin B}{3} = \frac{\sin C}{7}$

(c) $(a + b)^2 = c^2 + ab$ and $\sqrt{2}(\sin A + \cos A) = \sqrt{3}$

(d) $\sin A + \sin B = \left(\frac{\sqrt{3} + 1}{2}\right)$ and $\cos A \cos B = \frac{\sqrt{3}}{4} = \sin A \sin B$

38. Let a, b and c be the sides of triangle whose perimeter is P and area is A, then

(a) $P^3 \le 27(b + c - a)(c + a - b)(a + b - c)$

(b) $P^2 \le 3(a^2 + b^2 + c^2)$

(c) $a^2 + b^2 + c^2 \ge 4\sqrt{3}A$

(d) $P^4 \le 25 < A$

39. The sides of ΔABC satisfy the equation $2a^2 + 4b^2 + c^2 = 4ab + 2ac$. Then

(a) the triangle is isosceles (b) the triangle is obtuse

(c) $B = \cos^{-1}\left(\frac{7}{8}\right)$ (d) $A = \cos^{-1}\left(\frac{1}{4}\right)$

40. In ΔABC, if $2a^2b^2 + 2b^2c^2 = a^4 + b^4 + c^4$, then angle B is equal to

(a) $45°$ (b) $135°$ (c) $120°$ (d) $60°$

Passage Based Questions

Passage I

(Q. Nos. 41 to 42)

- R is circumradii of ΔABC, H is orthocentre. R_1, R_2, R_3 are circumradii of $\Delta AHB, \Delta AHC, \Delta BHC$. If AH produced meet the circumradii of ABC at M and intersect BC at L.

$$\angle AHB = 180° - C$$

$$\frac{c}{\sin(180° - C)} = 2R_1$$

$$\frac{c}{\sin C} = 2R_1$$

$$R_1 = R$$

41. $R_1R_2 + R_2R_3 + R_1 R_3$ is equal to
(a) $2R^2$ (b) $3R^2$ (c) $5R^2$ (d) R^2

42. Area of ΔAHB
(a) $2R \cos A \cos B \cos C$ (b) $R^2 \cos A \cos B \cos C$
(c) $2R^2 \cos A \cos B \sin C$ (d) None of these

Passage II

(Q. Nos. 43 to 44)

When any two sides and one of the opposite acute angle are given, under certain additional conditions two triangles are possible. The case when two triangles are possible is called the ambiguous case. In fact when any two sides and the angle opposite to one of them are given either no triangle is possible or only one triangle is possible or two triangles are possible.
In the ambiguous case, let a, b and $\angle A$ are given and c_1, c_2 are two values of the third side c.
On the basis of above information, answer the following questions.

43. Two different triangles are possible when
(a) $b \sin A < a$ (b) $b \sin A < a$ and $b > a$
(c) $b \sin A < a$ and $b < a$ (d) $b \sin A < a$ and $a = b$

44. The value of $c_1^2 - 2c_1c_2 \cos 2A + c_2^2$ is
(a) $4a \cos A$ (b) $4a^2 \cos A$ (c) $4a \cos^2 A$ (d) $4a^2 \cos^2 A$

Passage III

(Q.Nos. 45 to 46)

AL, *BM* and *CN* are perpendicular from angular points of a ΔABC on the opposite sides BC, CA and AB respectively. Δ is the area of ΔABC, (r) and R are the inradius and circumradius.

45. If areas of Δ's AMN, BNL and CLM are Δ_1, Δ_2 and Δ_3 respectively, then the value of $\Delta_1 + \Delta_2 + \Delta_3$ is
(a) $\Delta(2 + 2\cos A \cos B \cos C)$ (b) $\Delta(2 + 2\sin A \sin B \sin C)$
(c) $\Delta(1 - 2\cos A \cos B \cos C)$ (d) $\Delta(1 - 2\sin A \sin B \sin C)$

46. If area of ΔLMN is Δ', then the value of $\dfrac{\Delta'}{\Delta}$ is
(a) $2\sin A \sin B \sin C$ (b) $2\cos A \cos B \cos C$
(c) $\sin A \sin B \sin C$ (d) $\cos A \cos B \cos C$

Stem Based Questions

Stem I

(Q.Nos. 47 to 48)

Let a, b, c are the sides opposite to angles A, B, C respectively in a $\Delta\, ABC$ such that

$$\tan \frac{(A-B)}{2} = \frac{a-b}{a+b} \cot \frac{c}{2} \text{ and } \frac{a}{\sin A} = \frac{b}{\sin B} = \frac{c}{\sin C}.$$

If $a = 6, b = 3$ and $\cos(A - B) = \dfrac{4}{5}$, then answer the following questions.

47. The value of $\dfrac{10}{\pi}$ times of $\angle C$ is ....

48. The area of the triangle is ....

Stem II

(Q.Nos. 49 to 50)

Consider a $\Delta\, ABC$, where x, y and z are the length of perpendicular drawn from the vertices of the triangle to the opposite sides a, b, c, respectively.
Let the letters R, r, S, Δ denote the circumradius, inradius, semi-perimeter and area of the triangle respectively.
Now, answer the following questions.

49. If $\dfrac{bx}{c} + \dfrac{cy}{a} + \dfrac{az}{b} = \dfrac{a^2 + b^2 + c^2}{kR}$, then the value of k is ....

50. If $\cot A + \cot B + \cot C = k\Delta \left(\dfrac{1}{x^2} + \dfrac{1}{y^2} + \dfrac{1}{z^2} \right)$, then the value of k is ....

Single Integer Type Questions

51. If in ΔABC, $\angle C = \dfrac{\pi}{8}$, $a = \sqrt{2}$ and $b = \sqrt{2 + \sqrt{2}}$, then find the sum of digits in the measure of angle A (in degree).

52. In the figure as shown, find the number of digits in the length of AB.

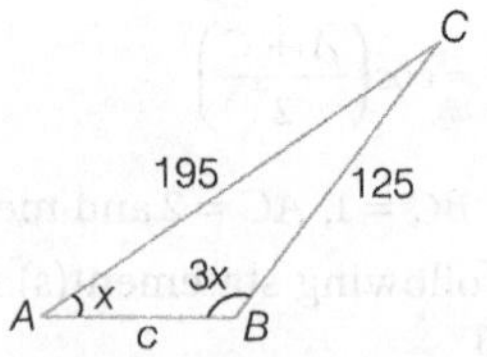

53. If $A = \dfrac{\pi}{7}$, $B = \dfrac{2\pi}{7}$ and $C = \dfrac{4\pi}{7}$, then in ΔABC, $\dfrac{a^2 + b^2 + c^2}{R^2}$ equals to ....

54. If A, B and C the angles of an acute angled ΔABC and

$$D = \begin{vmatrix} (\tan B + \tan C)^2 & \tan^2 A & \tan^2 A \\ \tan^2 B & (\tan A + \tan C)^2 & \tan^2 B \\ \tan^2 C & \tan^2 C & (\tan A + \tan B)^2 \end{vmatrix},$$

then the least integral values of $\dfrac{D}{1000}$ is ....

55. In a ΔABC, P and Q are the mid-point or AB and AC, respectively. If O is the circumcentre of the ΔABC, then the value of $\left(\dfrac{\text{Area of }\Delta ABC}{\text{Area of }\Delta OPQ}\right)\cot B\cot C$ equals to ....

56. With usual notation in ΔABC, the numerical value of $\left(\dfrac{a+b+c}{r_1+r_2+r_3}\right)\left(\dfrac{a}{r_1}+\dfrac{b}{r_2}+\dfrac{c}{r_3}\right)$ is ....

57. In a ΔABC, $\cos A\cdot\cos C=\dfrac{\lambda(c^2-a^2)}{3ca}$, where AD is the median through A and $AD\perp AC$, then the value of λ is ....

58. In a ΔABC, medians AD and CE are drawn. If $AD=5$, $\angle DAC=\dfrac{\pi}{8}$ and $\angle ACE=\dfrac{\pi}{4}$, then the area of the ΔABC is equal to $\dfrac{5a}{b}$, then $a+b$ is equal to ....

59. In ΔABC, $\dfrac{r}{r_1}=\dfrac{1}{2}$, then the value of $16\left[\tan\dfrac{A}{2}\left(\tan\dfrac{B}{2}+\tan\dfrac{C}{2}\right)\right]$ must be ....

Numerical Value Type Questions

60. In a ΔABC, the maximum value of $120\left(\dfrac{\Sigma a\cos^2\left(\dfrac{A}{2}\right)}{a+b+c}\right)$ must be ....

61. The sides of triangle are three consecutive natural numbers and its largest angle is twice the smaller one. Then, two times of the largest side of the triangle must be ....

62. In ΔABC, $\angle C=2\angle A$, and $AC=2BC$, then the value of $\dfrac{a^2+b^2+c^2}{(R/2)^2}$ (where R is circumradius of triangle) is ....

Matching Type Questions

63. Match the statement of Column I with values of Column II.

	Column I		Column II
(A)	In a ΔABC, let $\angle C=\dfrac{\pi}{2}$, $r=$ inradius, $R=$ circumradius, then $2(r+R)$	(p)	$a+b+c$
(B)	If l, m and n are perpendicular drawn from the vertices of triangle having sides a, b and c, then $\sqrt{2R\left(\dfrac{bl}{c}+\dfrac{cm}{a}+\dfrac{an}{b}\right)+2ab+2bc+2ca}$	(q)	$a-b$
(C)	In a ΔABC, $R(b^2\sin 2C+c^2\sin 2B)$ equals	(r)	$a+b$
(D)	In a right angled ΔABC, $\angle C=\dfrac{\pi}{2}$, then $4R\sin\dfrac{A+B}{2}\sin\dfrac{(A-B)}{2}$	(s)	abc

64. Match the statement of Column I with values of Column II.

	Column I		Column II
(A)	In a ΔABC, $(a+b+c)(b+c-a)=\lambda bc$, where $\lambda\in I$, then greatest value of λ is	(p)	3
(B)	In a ΔABC, $\tan A+\tan B+\tan C=9$. If $\tan^2 A+\tan^2 B+\tan^2 C=k$, then least value of k satisfying is	(q)	$9(3)^{1/3}$
(C)	In a ΔABC, then line joining the circumcentre to the incentre is parallel toBC , then value of $\cos B+\cos C$ is	(r)	1
(D)	If in a ΔABC, $a=5$, $b=4$ and $\cos(A-B)=\dfrac{31}{32}$, then the third side c is equal to	(s)	6

Previous Years Questions

■ JEE Main

65. The angle of elevation of the top P of a tower from the feet of one person standing due South of the tower is 45° and from the feet of another person standing due West of the tower is 30°. If the height of the tower is 5 m, then the distance (in meters) between the two persons is equal to **[Single Correct Type, 2023 Main]**

(a) 10 (b) $5\sqrt{5}$ (c) 5 (d) $5/2\sqrt{5}$

66. From the top A of a vertical wall AB of height 30 m, the angles of depression of the top P and bottom Q of a vertical tower PQ are 15° and 60° respectively, B and Q are on the same horizontal level. If C is a point on AB such that $CB=PQ$, then the area (in m^2) of the quadrilateral $BCPQ$ is equal to **[Single Correct Type, 2023 Main]**

(a) $300(\sqrt{3}-1)$ (b) $600(\sqrt{3}-1)$
(c) $200(3-\sqrt{3})$ (d) $300(3-\sqrt{3})$

67. In a $\Delta\ ABC$, if $\cos A+2\cos B+\cos C=2$ and the length of the sides opposite to the angles A and C are 3 and 7 respectively, then $\cos A-\cos C$ is equal to **[Single Correct Type, 2023 Main]**

(a) $\dfrac{5}{7}$ (b) $\dfrac{3}{7}$ (c) $\dfrac{10}{7}$ (d) $\dfrac{9}{7}$

68. If the line $x = y = z$ intersects the line $x \sin A + y \sin B + z \sin C - 18 = 0$ $= x \sin 2A + y \sin 2B + z \sin 2C - 9$, where A, B, C are the angles of a ΔABC, then $80\left(\sin\frac{A}{2}\sin\frac{B}{2}\sin\frac{C}{2}\right)$ is equal to .... **[Numerical Value Type, 2023 Main]**

69. In the figure, $\theta_1 + \theta_2 = \frac{\pi}{2}$ and $\sqrt{3}(BE) = 4(AB)$. If the area of ΔCAB is $2\sqrt{3} - 3$ unit^2, when θ_2/θ_1 is the largest, then the perimeter (in unit) of ΔCED is equal to .... **[Numerical Value Type, 2023 Main]**

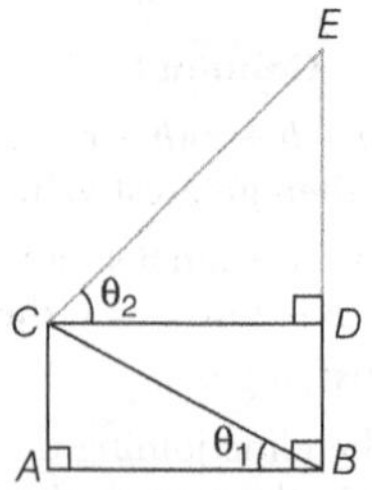

70. The angle of elevation of the top of a tower from a point A due North of it is α and from a point B at a distance of 9 units due West of A is $\cos^{-1}(3/\sqrt{13})$. If the distance of the point B from the tower is 15 units, then $\cot\alpha$ is equal to **[Single Correct Type, 2022 Main]**

(a) 6/5 (b) 9/5 (c) 4/3 (d) 7/3

71. A horizontal park is in the shape of a ΔOAB with $AB = 16$. A vertical lamp post OP is creacted at the point O such that $\angle PAO = \angle PBO = 15°$ and $PCO = 45°$, where C is the mid-point of AB. Then, $(OP)^2$ is equal to **[Single Correct Type, 2022 Main]**

(a) $\frac{32}{\sqrt{3}}(\sqrt{3}-1)$ (b) $\frac{32}{\sqrt{3}}(2-\sqrt{3})$

(c) $\frac{16}{\sqrt{3}}(\sqrt{3}-1)$ (d) $\frac{16}{\sqrt{3}}(2-\sqrt{3})$

72. Let a vertical tower AB of height $2h$ stands on a horizontal ground. Let from a point P on the ground a man can see upto height h of the tower with an angle of elevation 2α. When from P, he moves a distance d in the direction of AP, he can see the top B of the tower with an angle of elevation α. If $d = \sqrt{7}h$, then $\tan\alpha$ is equal to **[Single Correct Type, 2022 Main]**

(a) $\sqrt{5}-2$ (b) $\sqrt{3}-1$

(c) $\sqrt{7}-2$ (d) $\sqrt{7}-\sqrt{3}$

73. A tower PQ stands on a horizontal ground with base Q on the ground. The point R divides the tower in two parts such that $QR = 15$ m. If from a point A on the ground the angle of elevation of R is 60° and the part PR of the tower subtends an angle of 15° at A, then the height of the tower is **[Single Correct Type, 2022 Main]**

(a) $5(2\sqrt{3}+3)$ m (b) $5(\sqrt{3}+3)$ m

(c) $10(\sqrt{3}+1)$ m (d) $10(2\sqrt{3}+1)$ m

74. From the base of a pole of height 20 m, the angle of elevation of the top of a tower is 60°. The pole subtends an angle 30° at the top of the tower. Then, the height of the tower is **[Single Correct Type, 2022 Main]**

(a) $15\sqrt{3}$ (b) $20\sqrt{3}$ (c) $20 + 10\sqrt{3}$ (d) 30

75. Let AB and PQ be two vertical poles, 160 m apart from each other. Let C be the middle point of B and Q, which are feet of these two poles. Let $\frac{\pi}{8}$ and θ be the angles of elevation from C to P and A, respectively. If the height of pole PQ is twice the height of pole AB, then $\tan^2\theta$ is equal to **[Single Correct Type, 2022 Main]**

(a) $\frac{3-2\sqrt{2}}{2}$ (b) $\frac{3+\sqrt{2}}{2}$

(c) $\frac{3-2\sqrt{2}}{4}$ (d) $\frac{3-\sqrt{2}}{4}$

76. Let a, b and c be the length of sides of a ΔABC such that $\frac{a+b}{7} = \frac{b+c}{8} = \frac{c+a}{9}$. If r and R are the radius of in-circle and radius of circumcircle of the ΔABC, respectively, then the value of $\frac{R}{r}$ is equal to .... **[Single Correct Type, 2022 Main]**

(a) $\frac{5}{2}$ (b) 2 (c) $\frac{3}{2}$ (d) 1

77. A vertical pole fixed to the horizontal ground is divided in the ratio 3 : 7 by a mark on it with lower part shorter than the upper part. If the two parts subtend equal angles at a point on the ground 18 m away from the base of the pole, then the height of the pole (in meters) is **[Single Correct Type, 2021 Main]**

(a) $12\sqrt{15}$ (b) $12\sqrt{10}$ (c) $8\sqrt{10}$ (d) $6\sqrt{10}$

78. A spherical gas balloon of radius 16 m subtends an angle 60° at the eye of the observer A while the angle of elevation of its center from the eye of A is 75°. Then, the height (in meter) of the top most point of the balloon from the level of the observer's eye is **[Single Correct Type, 2021 Main]**

(a) $8(2 + 2\sqrt{3} + \sqrt{2})$ (b) $8(\sqrt{6} + \sqrt{2} + 2)$

(c) $8(\sqrt{2} + 2 + \sqrt{3})$ (d) $8(\sqrt{6} - \sqrt{2} + 2)$

79. The angle of elevation of a jet plane from a point A on the ground is 60°. After a flight of 20s at the speed of 432 km/h, the angle of elevation changes to 30°. If the jet plane is flying at a constant height, then its height is **[Single Correct Type, 2021 Main]**

(a) $1800\sqrt{3}$ m (b) $3600\sqrt{3}$ m

(c) $2400\sqrt{3}$ m (d) $1200\sqrt{3}$ m

80. Let $\dfrac{\sin A}{\sin B}=\dfrac{\sin(A-C)}{\sin(C-B)}$, where A, B, C are angles of a ΔABC. If the lengths of the sides opposite these angles are a, b, c respectively, then

[Single Correct Type, 2021 Main]

(a) $b^2-a^2=a^2+c^2$ (b) b^2, c^2, a^2 are in AP.
(c) c^2, a^2, b^2 are in AP. (d) a^2, b^2, c^2 are in AP.

81. A man starts walking from the point $P(-3, 4)$, touches the X-axis at R and then turns to reach at the point $Q(0, 2)$. The man is walking at a constant speed. If the man reaches the point Q in the minimum time, then $50((PR)^2+(RQ)^2)$ is equal is ....

[Numerical Value Type, 2021 Main]

82. Let B be the centre of the circle $x^2+y^2-2x+4y+1=0$. Let the tangents at two points P and Q on the circle intersect at the point $A(3, 1)$. Then, $8\cdot\left(\dfrac{\text{area } \Delta APQ}{\text{area } \Delta BPQ}\right)$ is equal to ....

[Numerical Value Type, 2021 Main]

83. If the minimum area of the triangle formed by a tangent to the ellipse $\dfrac{x^2}{b^2}+\dfrac{y^2}{4a^2}=1$ and the coordinate axis is kab, then k is equal to ....

[Numerical Value Type, 2021 Main]

84. The angle of elevation of the top of a hill from a point on the horizontal plane passing through the foot of the hill is found to be 45°. After walking a distance of 80 m towards the top, the slope inclined at an angle of 30° to the horizontal plane, the angle of elevation of the top of the hill becomes 75°. Then, the height of the hill (in meters) is .... [Numerical Value Type, 2020 Main]

85. A 2 m ladder leans against a vertical wall. If the top of the ladder begins to slide down the wall at the rate 25 cm/s, then the rate (in cm/s) at which the bottom of the ladder slides away from the wall on the horizontal ground when the top of the ladder is 1 m above the ground is

[Single Correct Type, 2019 Main]

(a) $25\sqrt{3}$ (b) $25/\sqrt{3}$
(c) $25/3$ (d) 25

86. Two vertical poles of heights, 20 m and 80 m stand apart on a horizontal plane. The height (in m) of the point of intersection of the lines joining the top of each pole to the foot of the other, from this horizontal plane is

[Single Correct Type, 2019 Main]

(a) 15 (b) 16
(c) 12 (d) 18

87. Consider a triangular plot ABC with sides $AB=7$ m, $BC=5$ m and $CA=6$ m. A vertical lamp-post at the mid-point D of AC subtends an angle 30° at B. The height (in m) of the lamp-post is

[Single Correct Type, 2019 Main]

(a) $\dfrac{2}{3}\sqrt{21}$ (b) $2\sqrt{21}$
(c) $7\sqrt{3}$ (d) $\dfrac{3}{2}\sqrt{21}$

88. The angles A, B and C of a ΔABC are in AP and $a:b=1:\sqrt{3}$. If $c=4$ cm, then the area (in sq cm) of this triangle is [Single Correct Type, 2019 Main]

(a) $\dfrac{2}{\sqrt{3}}$ (b) $4\sqrt{3}$
(c) $2\sqrt{3}$ (d) $\dfrac{4}{\sqrt{3}}$

89. In a triangle, the sum of lengths of two sides is x and the product of the lengths of the same two sides is y. If $x^2-c^2=y$, where c is the length of the third side of the triangle, then the circumradius of the triangle is

[Single Correct Type, 2019 Main]

(a) $\dfrac{c}{3}$ (b) $\dfrac{c}{\sqrt{3}}$
(c) $\dfrac{3}{2}y$ (d) $\dfrac{y}{\sqrt{3}}$

JEE Advanced

90. Let $A_1, A_2, A_3, \ldots, A_8$ be the vertices of a regular octagon that lie on a circle of radius 2. Let P be a point on the circle and let PA_i denote the distance between the points P and A_i for $i=1, 2, \ldots, 8$. If P varies over the circle, then the maximum value of the product $PA_1\cdot PA_2 \ldots PA_8$, is ....

[Numerical Value Type, 2023 Adv.]

Passage

(Q. Nos. 91 and 92)

Consider an obtuse angled ΔABC in which the difference between the largest and the smallest angle is $\dfrac{\pi}{2}$ and whose sides are in arithmetic progression. Suppose that the vertices of this triangle lie on a circle of radius 1.

91. Let a be the area of the ΔABC. Then, the value of $(64a)^2$ is .... [Passage Based Type, 2023 Adv. II]

92. Then, the inradius of the ΔABC is ....

[Passage Based Type, 2023 Adv. II]

93. Let $PQRS$ be a quadrilateral in a plane, where $QR = 1$, $\angle PQR = \angle QRS = 70°$, $\angle PQS = 15°$ and $\angle PRS = 40°$. If $\angle RPS = \theta°$, $PQ = \alpha$ and $PS = \beta$, then the interval(s) that contain(s) the value of $4\alpha\beta \sin\theta$ is/are

[More Than One Correct, 2022 Adv.]

(a) $(0, \sqrt{2})$ (b) $(1, 2)$

(c) $(\sqrt{2}, 3)$ (d) $(2\sqrt{2}, 3\sqrt{2})$

94. Let G be a circle of radius $R > 0$. Let $G_1, G_2, ..., G_n$ be n circles of equal radius $r > 0$. Suppose each of the n circles $G_1, G_2, ..., G_n$ touches the circle G externally. Also, for $i = 1, 2, ..., n-1$, the circle G_i touches G_{i+1} externally, and G_n touches G_1 externally. Then, which of the following statements is/are TRUE ?

[More Than One Correct, 2022 Adv.]

(a) If $n = 4$, then $(\sqrt{2} - 1)r < R$

(b) If $n = 5$, then $r < R$

(c) If $n = 8$, then $(\sqrt{2} - 1)r < R$

(d) If $n = 12$, then $\sqrt{2}(\sqrt{3} + 1)r > R$

95. Consider the hyperbola $\frac{x^2}{100} - \frac{y^2}{64} = 1$ with foci at S and S_1, where S lies on the positive X-axis. Let P be a point on the hyperbola in the first quadrant. Let $\angle SPS_1 = \alpha$, with $\alpha < \pi/2$. The straight line passing through the point S and having the same slope as that of the tangent at P to the hyperbola, intersects the straight line S_1P at P_1. Let δ be the distance of P from the straight line SP_1 and $\beta = S_1P$. Then, the greatest, integer less than or equal to $\frac{\beta\delta}{9} \sin\frac{\alpha}{2}$ is ....

[Numerical Value Type, 2022 Adv.]

96. Consider a $\Delta\, PQR$ having sides of lengths p, q and r opposite to the angles P, Q and R, respectively. Then, which of the following statements is (are) TRUE?

[More Than One Correct, 2021 Adv.]

(a) $\cos P \geq 1 - \frac{p^2}{2qr}$

(b) $\cos R \geq \left(\frac{q-r}{p+q}\right)\cos P + \left(\frac{p-r}{p+q}\right)\cos Q$

(c) $\frac{q+r}{p} < 2\frac{\sqrt{\sin Q \sin R}}{\sin P}$

(d) If $p < q$ and $p < r$, then $\cos Q > \frac{p}{r}$ and $\cos R > \frac{p}{q}$.

97. In a $\Delta\, ABC$, let $AB = \sqrt{23}$, $BC = 3$ and $CA = 4$. Then, the value of $\frac{\cot A + \cot C}{\cot B}$ is ....

[Numerical Value Type, 2021 Adv.]

98. Let x, y and z be positive real numbers. Suppose x, y and z are the lengths of the sides of a triangle opposite to its angles X, Y and Z, respectively.

If $\tan\frac{X}{2} + \tan\frac{Z}{2} = \frac{2y}{x+y+z}$, then which of the following statements is/are TRUE?

[More Than One Correct, 2020 Adv.]

(a) $2Y = X + Z$

(b) $Y = X + Z$

(c) $\tan\frac{X}{2} = \frac{x}{y+z}$

(d) $x^2 + z^2 - y^2 = xz$

EXERCISE 2

Challenging Problems

1. Two sides of a triangle are given by the roots of the equation $x^2 - 2\sqrt{3}x + 2 = 0$. The angle between the sides is $\frac{\pi}{3}$. Find the perimeter of Δ.
2. If A, B and C are angles of a triangle such that $\angle A$ is obtuse, then show $\tan B \tan C < 1$.
3. If A is the area and $2s$ the sum of the sides of a triangle, then show $A \le \frac{s^2}{3\sqrt{3}}$.
4. The internal bisectors of the angles of a ΔABC meet the sides BC, CA, AB in D, E and F, respectively. Show that the area of the ΔDEF is equal to $\frac{2\Delta abc}{(b+c)(c+a)(a+b)}$.
5. In a ΔABC, if $\cot A + \cot B + \cot C = \sqrt{3}$. Prove that the triangle is equilateral.
6. In the ΔABC, if $(a^2 + b^2)\sin(A - B) = (a^2 - b^2)$ $\sin(A + B)$. Prove that the triangle is either isosceles or right angled.
7. Given the base 'a' of a triangle, the opposite angle A, and the product k^2 of the other two sides, show that it is not possible for 'a' to be less than $2k \sin \frac{A}{2}$.
8. In a ΔABC, having sides a, b, c if $C = 60°$, prove that $\frac{1}{a+c} + \frac{1}{b+c} = \frac{3}{a+b+c}$.
9. Let $1 < m < 3$. In a ΔABC, if $2b = (m+1)a$ and $\cos A = \frac{1}{2}\sqrt{\frac{(m-1)(m+3)}{m}}$, prove that there are two values to the third side, one of which is m times the other.
10. $ABCD$ is a trapezium such that AB, DC are parallel and BC is perpendicular to them. If $\angle ADB = \theta$, $BC = p$ and $CD = q$, show that $AB = \frac{(p^2 + q^2)\sin\theta}{p\cos\theta + q\sin\theta}$.
11. If the sides of a triangle are in AP, and its greatest angle exceeds the least angle by α, show that the sides are in the ratio $1 + x : 1 : 1 - x$, where $x = \sqrt{\frac{1-\cos\alpha}{7-\cos\alpha}}$.
12. In a ΔABC, if $\tan A/2$, $\tan B/2$, $\tan C/2$ are in AP. Show that $\cos A$, $\cos B$, $\cos C$ are in AP.
13. If a, b and c are in HP, then prove that $\sin^2\frac{A}{2}$, $\sin^2\frac{B}{2}$, $\sin^2\frac{C}{2}$ are also in HP.
14. Prove that $r_1^2 + r_2^2 + r_3^3 + r^2 = 16R^2 - a^2 - b^2 - c^2$, where r = inradius, R = circumradius, r_1, r_2, r_3 are exradii.
15. In a ΔABC, if $\cos A + 2\cos B + \cos C = 2$. Prove that the sides of the triangle are in AP.

Answer Key

Exercise 1

1. (a)	2. (c)	3. (c)	4. (b)	5. (a)	6. (a)	7. (d)	8. (b)	9. (c)	10. (c)
11. (a)	12. (b)	13. (c)	14. (b)	15. (a)	16. (c)	17. (b)	18. (c)	19. (c)	20. (d)
21. (b)	22. (b)	23. (b)	24. (b)	25. (c)	26. (a)	27. (b)	28. (d)	29. (b)	30. (a,b)
31. (b,c,d)	32. (c,d)	33. (b,c)	34. (a,d)	35. (a,c)	36. (a,b)	37. (c,d)	38. (b,c)	39. (a,c,d)	40. (a,b)
41. (b)	42. (c)	43. (b)	44. (d)	45. (c)	46. (b)	47. (5)	48. (9)	49. (2)	50. (1)
51. (9)	52. (3)	53. (7)	54. (2)	55. (4)	56. (4)	57. (2)	58. (8)	59. (8)	60. (90)
61. (12)	62. (32)	63. (A) → (r), (B) → (p), C → (s), (D) → (q)				64. (A) → (p), (B) → (q), C → (r), (D) → (s)			
65. (a)	66. (b)	67. (c)	68. (5)	69. (6)	70. (a)	71. (b)	72. (c)	73. (a)	74. (d)
75. (c)	76. (a)	77. (b)	78. (b)	79. (d)	80. (b)	81. (1250)	82. (18)	83. (2)	84. (80)
85. (b)	86. (b)	87. (a)	88. (c)	89. (b)	90. (512)	91. (1008)	92. (0.25)	93. (a,b)	94. (c,d)
95. (7)	96. (a,b)	97. (2)	98. (c)						

Solutions

Exercise 1 - JEE Advanced Pattern

1. We have, $s = \dfrac{a+b+c}{2} = 21$

Now, $\sin A = \dfrac{2\Delta}{bc}$

$$= \frac{2}{14\cdot 15}\sqrt{21\cdot 8\cdot 7\cdot 6} = \frac{4}{5}$$

$\Rightarrow \quad A = \sin^{-1}\dfrac{4}{5}$

Alternate Solution

By cosine rule in ΔABC, we get

$$\cos A = \frac{b^2+c^2-a^2}{2bc}$$

$$= \frac{(14)^2 + (15)^2 - (13)^2}{2(14)(15)}$$

$$= \frac{196+225-169}{420}$$

$$= \frac{252}{420} = \frac{3}{5}\left(0 < A < \frac{\pi}{2}\right)$$

Hence, $A = \sin^{-1}\dfrac{4}{5}$

2. Using Napier's Analogy

$$\tan\left(\frac{A-B}{2}\right) = \frac{a-b}{a+b}\cot\frac{C}{2}$$

$$= \frac{1-(\sqrt{3}-1)}{1+(\sqrt{3}-1)}(2+\sqrt{3})$$

$$= \frac{1}{\sqrt{3}}$$

$\therefore \quad \dfrac{A-B}{2} = 30°$

$\Rightarrow \quad A - B = 60°$

3. Given, $2b = a + c$

$\Rightarrow \quad 2\sin B = \sin A + \sin C$

$\Rightarrow \quad 2\left(2\sin\dfrac{B}{2}\cos\dfrac{B}{2}\right) = 2\sin\left(\dfrac{A+C}{2}\right)\cos\left(\dfrac{A-C}{2}\right)$

$\Rightarrow \quad 2\sin\dfrac{B}{2} = \cos\left(\dfrac{90°}{2}\right) = \dfrac{1}{\sqrt{2}}$

$\Rightarrow \quad \sin\dfrac{B}{2} = \dfrac{1}{2\sqrt{2}}$

$\Rightarrow \quad \cos\dfrac{B}{2} = \sqrt{1-\dfrac{1}{8}} = \dfrac{\sqrt{7}}{2\sqrt{2}}$

Hence, $\sin B = 2\sin\dfrac{B}{2}\cos\dfrac{B}{2} = \dfrac{\sqrt{7}}{4}$

4. $\dfrac{BD}{DC} = \dfrac{AB}{AC}$

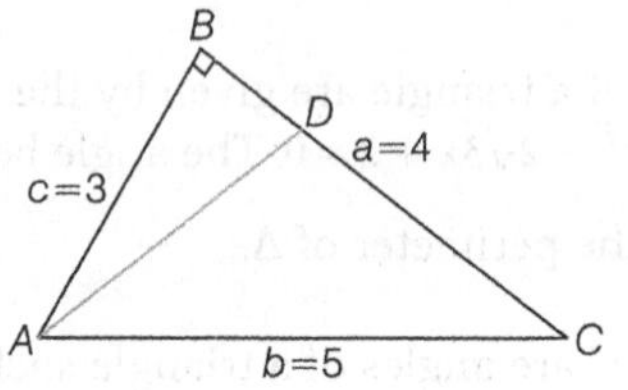

$\Rightarrow$ AD is the angle bisector

$\therefore \quad AD = \dfrac{2bc}{b+c}\cos\dfrac{A}{2}$

$$= \frac{2\times 5\times 3}{8}\sqrt{\frac{1+\cos A}{2}}$$

$$= \frac{15}{4}\sqrt{\frac{1+\frac{3}{5}}{2}} = \frac{15}{4}\times\frac{2}{\sqrt{5}}$$

$$= \frac{3\times\sqrt{5}\times\sqrt{5}}{2\times\sqrt{5}} = \frac{3\sqrt{5}}{2}$$

5. $4\sin A\cos B = 1$, so A and B cannot be $\dfrac{\pi}{2}$

$\left[\text{as if } B = \dfrac{\pi}{2}, \text{ then } \cos B = 0 \text{ and if } A = \dfrac{\pi}{2}, \tan A \text{ is not defined}\right]$

$\Rightarrow \quad C = \dfrac{\pi}{2}, B = \dfrac{\pi}{2} - A$

$\Rightarrow \quad 4\sin A\cos\left(\dfrac{\pi}{2} - A\right) = 1$

$\Rightarrow \quad \sin^2 A = \dfrac{1}{4} \Rightarrow \sin A = \dfrac{1}{2}$

$\Rightarrow \quad A = \dfrac{\pi}{6} \Rightarrow B = \dfrac{\pi}{3}$

So, angles are in AP.

6. Let the sides of the triangle be $7, 7-d, 7-2d$.

Since, the given angle is the greatest (being obtuse) angle of the triangle, it is opposite to the greatest side of the triangle and we have,

$$7^2 = (7-d)^2 + (7-2d)^2 - 2(7-d)(7-2d)\cos\frac{2\pi}{3}$$

$\Rightarrow \quad 7^2 = 2\times 7^2 - 42d + 5d^2 - 2(7^2 - 21d + 2d^2)\left(\dfrac{-1}{2}\right)$

$\Rightarrow \quad d^2 - 9d + 14 = 0$

$\Rightarrow \quad (d-7)(d-2) = 0$

$\Rightarrow \quad d = 2 \quad [d = 7 \text{ is not possible}]$

Therefore, the sides of the triangle are 7 cm, 5 cm, 3 cm.

Area of the triangle, $\Delta = \frac{1}{2} \times 5 \times 3 \times \sin\frac{2\pi}{3} = \frac{15\sqrt{3}}{4}\text{cm}^2$

and the radius of the circumcircle, $R = \dfrac{7 \times 5 \times 3}{4\left(\dfrac{15\sqrt{3}}{4}\right)}$

$$= \frac{7 \times 5 \times 3}{15\sqrt{3}} = \frac{7\sqrt{3}}{3}\text{ cm}$$

7. $\because$ Sides are in AP and $a < \min\{b, c\}$

Case I If $\min(b, c) = b$,

then a, b, c are in AP.

i.e. $2b = a + c$

$$\therefore \quad \cos A = \frac{b^2 + c^2 - a^2}{2bc} = \frac{b^2 + c^2 - (2b - c)^2}{2bc}$$

$$= \frac{4bc - 3b^2}{2bc} = \frac{4c - 3b}{2c}$$

Case II If $\min\{b, c\} = c$,

then a, c, b are in AP.

i.e. $2c = a + b$

$$\therefore \quad \cos A = \frac{b^2 + c^2 - a^2}{2bc}$$

$$= \frac{b^2 + c^2 - (2c - b)^2}{2bc} = \frac{4bc - 3c^2}{2bc} = \frac{4b - 3c}{2b}$$

8. We have, $\cos A = \dfrac{b^2 + c^2 - a^2}{2bc}$

$\Rightarrow \; b^2 - 2bc\cos A + (c^2 - a^2) = 0$

It is given that b_1 and b_2 are roots of this equation. Therefore,

$$b_1 + b_2 = 2c\cos A \text{ and } b_1 b_2 = c^2 - a^2$$

$$\Rightarrow \quad 3b_1 = 2c\cos A \text{ and } 2b_1^2 = c^2 - a^2$$

[since $b_2 = 2b_1$ given]

$$\Rightarrow \quad 2\left(\frac{2c}{3}\cos A\right)^2 = c^2 - a^2$$

$$\Rightarrow \quad 8c^2(1 - \sin^2 A) = 9c^2 - 9a^2$$

$$\Rightarrow \quad \sin A = \sqrt{\frac{9a^2 - c^2}{8c^2}}$$

9. We have, $\cot(A + B) = \dfrac{\cot A \cot B - 1}{\cot B + \cot A}$

$$= \frac{x^{\frac{1}{2}}(x^2 + x + 1)^{\frac{1}{2}} \cdot x^{\frac{-1}{2}}(x^2 + x + 1)^{\frac{1}{2}} - 1}{x^{\frac{-1}{2}}(x^2 + x + 1)^{\frac{1}{2}} + x^{\frac{1}{2}}(x^2 + x + 1)^{\frac{1}{2}}}$$

$$= \frac{x^2 + x + 1 - 1}{(x^2 + x + 1)^{\frac{1}{2}}(x^{\frac{1}{2}} + x^{\frac{-1}{2}})}$$

$$= \frac{x(x + 1)x^{\frac{1}{2}}}{(x^2 + x + 1)^{\frac{1}{2}}(x + 1)}$$

$$= x^{\frac{3}{2}}(x^2 + x + 1)^{\frac{-1}{2}} = \cot C$$

$$\Rightarrow \quad A + B = C \text{ and } A + B + C = \pi$$

$$\therefore \quad C = \frac{\pi}{2}$$

10. $b\cot B + c\cot C = 2(r + R)$

$$\Rightarrow 2R\sin B \cdot \frac{\cos B}{\sin B} + 2R\sin C \cdot \frac{\cos C}{\sin C} = 2(r + R)$$

$$\Rightarrow \quad \cos B + \cos C = 1 + \frac{r}{R}$$

$$\Rightarrow \quad \cos B + \cos C = 1 + 4\sin\frac{A}{2}\sin\frac{B}{2}\sin\frac{C}{2}$$

$$\Rightarrow \quad \cos B + \cos C = \cos A + \cos B + \cos C$$

$$\therefore \quad \cos A = 0$$

$$\Rightarrow \quad A = \frac{\pi}{2}$$

$$\Rightarrow \quad a^2 = b^2 + c^2$$

$$\Rightarrow \quad b^2 + c^2 = 100$$

Using AM $\geq$ GM, we get

$$\frac{b^2 + c^2}{2} \geq \sqrt{b^2c^2} \Rightarrow bc \leq 50$$

Hence, the area of $\Delta ABC = \frac{1}{2}bc \leq 25$

11. $\because$ Roots are real and distinct.

$$\therefore \quad D > 0$$

$$\Rightarrow \quad 4(a + b + c)^2 - 12\lambda(ab + bc + ca) > 0$$

$$\Rightarrow \quad (a^2 + b^2 + c^2 + 2(ab + bc + ca)) - 3\lambda(ab + bc + ca) > 0$$

$$\Rightarrow \quad \frac{\Sigma a^2}{\Sigma ab} > (3\lambda - 2) \qquad \text{...(i)}$$

Now, in a triangle,

Difference of two sides < third side

ie, $\quad |a - b| < c, |b - c| < a \text{ and } |c - a| < b$

$$\Rightarrow \quad (a - b)^2 + (b - c)^2 + (c - a)^2 < a^2 + b^2 + c^2$$

$$\Rightarrow \quad a^2 + b^2 + c^2 < 2(ab + bc + ca)$$

$$\text{or} \quad \frac{\Sigma a^2}{\Sigma ab} < 2 \qquad \text{...(ii)}$$

From Eqs. (i) and (ii), we get

$$3\lambda - 2 < \frac{\Sigma a^2}{\Sigma ab} < 2$$

$$\Rightarrow \quad 3\lambda - 2 < 2 \Rightarrow \lambda < \frac{4}{3}$$

12. Area of $\Delta ARQ = \dfrac{b}{(k + 1)} \times \dfrac{kc}{k + 1} \times \dfrac{1}{2}\sin A = \dfrac{k\Delta}{(k + 1)^2}$

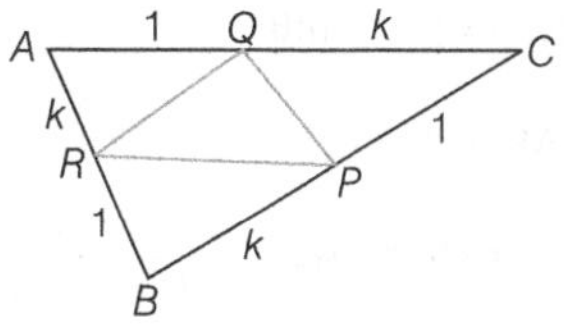

Similarly, area of ΔBPR = Area of $\Delta PCQ = \dfrac{k\Delta}{(k + 1)^2}$

Now, $\dfrac{\Delta PQR}{\Delta ABC} = \dfrac{1}{3}$

$\Rightarrow \dfrac{\Delta - \dfrac{3k}{(k+1)^2}\Delta}{\Delta} = \dfrac{1}{3}$

$\Rightarrow 2k^2 - 5k + 2 = 0$

$\Rightarrow k = \dfrac{1}{2}, 2$

13. $\because \cos A = \dfrac{b^2 + c^2 - a^2}{2bc}$

$\Rightarrow c^2 - 2bc\cos A + b^2 - a^2 = 0$

$\therefore c_1 + c_2 = 2b\cos A = 2 \times 2 \times \dfrac{\sqrt{3}}{2} = 2\sqrt{3}$

and $c_1 c_2 = b^2 - a^2 = 4 - 5 = -1$

$\therefore |c_1 - c_2| = \sqrt{(c_1 + c_2)^2 - 4c_1c_2}$

$= \sqrt{12 + 4} = \sqrt{16} = 4$

14. In ΔABD, $\dfrac{BD}{\sin\theta} = \dfrac{AD}{\sin B}$

$\Rightarrow AD = BD\dfrac{\sin(B)}{\sin\theta}$ ...(i)

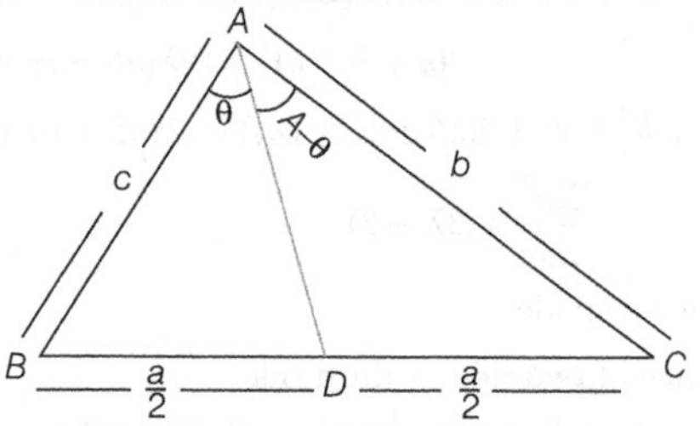

In ΔACD, $\dfrac{CD}{\sin(A-\theta)} = \dfrac{AD}{\sin C}$

$\Rightarrow AD = CD \cdot \dfrac{\sin C}{\sin(A-\theta)}$ ...(ii)

From Eqs. (i) and (ii), we get

$(BD)\dfrac{\sin B}{\sin\theta} = \dfrac{\sin C}{\sin(A-\theta)}(CD)$

$\Rightarrow \dfrac{\sin B}{\sin C} = \dfrac{\sin\theta}{\sin(A-\theta)}$

$\Rightarrow \dfrac{b}{c} = \dfrac{\sin(\theta)}{\sin(A-\theta)}$

$\Rightarrow \sin(A-\theta) = \dfrac{c}{b}\sin\theta$

15. A, B, C are in AP $\Rightarrow B = 60°$

$\Rightarrow \cos B = \cos 60° = \dfrac{1}{2} = \dfrac{c^2 + a^2 - b^2}{2ca}$

$\Rightarrow a^2 + c^2 = b^2 + ac$

$\Rightarrow (a-c)^2 = b^2 - ac$

$\Rightarrow |a - c| = \sqrt{b^2 - ac}$

$\Rightarrow |\sin A - \sin C| = \sqrt{\sin^2 B - \sin A \sin C}$

$\Rightarrow 2\cos\dfrac{A+C}{2}\left|\sin\dfrac{A-C}{2}\right| = \sqrt{\dfrac{3}{4} - \sin A \sin C}$

$\Rightarrow 2\left|\sin\dfrac{A-C}{2}\right| = \sqrt{3 - 4\sin A \sin C}$

So, that $\lim\limits_{A \to C} \dfrac{\sqrt{3 - 4\sin A\sin C}}{|A - C|} = \lim\limits_{A \to C} \dfrac{2\sin\left|\dfrac{A-C}{2}\right|}{|A-C|} = 1$

16. We are given that $(a + b + c)(b + c - a) = \lambda bc$, or $(b + c)^2 - a^2 = \lambda bc$.

That is, $b^2 + c^2 + 2bc - a^2 = \lambda bc$, or $b^2 + c^2 - a^2 = (\lambda - 2)bc$.

Therefore, $\cos A = \dfrac{b^2 + c^2 - a^2}{2bc} = \dfrac{\lambda - 2}{2}$

As A is the angle of a triangle, $-1 < \cos A < 1$.

Therefore, $-1 < \dfrac{(\lambda - 2)}{2} < 1$

$\Rightarrow 0 < \lambda < 4$

17. $\because \dfrac{2}{1!9!} + \dfrac{2}{3!7!} + \dfrac{1}{5!5!} = \dfrac{8^a}{(2b)!}$

$\Rightarrow \dfrac{1}{1!9!} + \dfrac{1}{3!7!} + \dfrac{1}{5!5!} + \dfrac{1}{3!7!} + \dfrac{1}{9!1!} = \dfrac{8^a}{(2b)!}$

$\Rightarrow \dfrac{1}{10!}\left(\dfrac{10!}{1!9!} + \dfrac{10!}{3!7!} + \dfrac{10!}{5!5!} + \dfrac{10!}{7!3!} + \dfrac{10!}{9!1!}\right) = \dfrac{8^a}{(2b)!}$

$\Rightarrow \dfrac{1}{10!}({}^{10}C_1 + {}^{10}C_3 + {}^{10}C_5 + {}^{10}C_7 + {}^{10}C_9) = \dfrac{8^a}{(2b)!}$

$\Rightarrow \dfrac{2^9}{10!} = \dfrac{8^a}{(2b)!} = \dfrac{2^{3a}}{(2b)!} \Rightarrow a = 3, b = 5$

Also, $2b = a + c \Rightarrow 10 = 3 + c$

$\Rightarrow c = 7$

$\therefore a = 3, b = 5, c = 7$

$\because \dfrac{\tan A + \tan B}{2} \geq \sqrt{\tan A \tan B}$ ...(i)

Also, $\cos C = \dfrac{a^2 + b^2 - c^2}{2ab}$

$= \dfrac{9 + 25 - 49}{30}$

$= -\dfrac{1}{2}$

$\therefore C = 120°$ and $A, B < 60°$

$\tan A + \tan B + \tan C = \tan A \tan B \tan C$

$\Rightarrow \tan A + \tan B - \sqrt{3} = -\sqrt{3}\tan A \tan B$

$\Rightarrow \tan A + \tan B - \sqrt{3} = -\sqrt{3}\tan A \tan B$

$\therefore \tan A + \tan B = \sqrt{3}(1 - \tan A \tan B)$ ...(ii)

Also, $\tan A + \tan B > 0$

$\Rightarrow \sqrt{3}(1 - \tan A \tan B) > 0$

$\Rightarrow \tan A \tan B < 1$ ...(iii)

From Eqs. (i) and (ii), we get

$$\frac{\sqrt{3}(1-\tan A\tan B)}{2} \geq \sqrt{(\tan A \tan B)}$$

Let $\tan A \tan B = \lambda$

$\therefore \quad \sqrt{3}(1-\lambda) \geq 2\sqrt{\lambda}$

$\Rightarrow \quad 3\lambda^2 - 10\lambda + 3 \geq 0$

$\Rightarrow \quad (3\lambda - 1)(\lambda - 3) \geq 0$

$\because \quad \lambda - 3 < 0$ [from Eq. (iii)]

$\therefore \quad 3\lambda - 1 \leq 0$

$\Rightarrow \quad \lambda \leq \frac{1}{3}$

$\Rightarrow \quad \tan A \tan B \leq \frac{1}{3}$

18. $\because a(b-c) + b(c-a) + c(a-b) = 0$

$\therefore \quad x = 1$ is a root of the equation

$$a(b-c)x^2 + b(c-a)x + c(a-b) = 0$$

Then, other root = 1 [$\because$ roots are equal]

$\therefore$ Product of roots $= \frac{c(a-b)}{a(b-c)}$

$\Rightarrow \quad 1 = \frac{c(a-b)}{a(b-c)} \Rightarrow ab - ac = ca - bc$

$\therefore \quad b = \frac{2ac}{a+c}$

$\therefore a, b, c$ are in HP.

Then, $\frac{1}{a}, \frac{1}{b}, \frac{1}{c}$ are in AP.

$\Rightarrow \quad \frac{s}{a}, \frac{s}{b}, \frac{s}{c}$ are in AP.

$\Rightarrow \quad \frac{s}{a} - 1, \frac{s}{b} - 1, \frac{s}{c} - 1$ are in AP.

$\Rightarrow \quad \frac{(s-a)}{a}, \frac{(s-b)}{b}, \frac{(s-c)}{c}$ are in AP.

Multiplying in each by $\frac{abc}{(s-a)(s-b)(s-c)}$, then

$\frac{bc}{(s-b)(s-c)}, \frac{ca}{(s-c)(s-a)}, \frac{ab}{(s-a)(s-b)}$ are in AP.

$\Rightarrow \frac{(s-b)(s-c)}{bc}, \frac{(s-c)(s-a)}{ca}, \frac{(s-a)(s-b)}{ab}$ are in HP.

or $\sin^2\left(\frac{A}{2}\right), \sin^2\left(\frac{B}{2}\right), \sin^2\left(\frac{C}{2}\right)$ are in HP.

19. Since, $\quad \sin A + \frac{1}{\sin A} \geq 2$ [if $A = 90°$]

Then, $\sin B + \frac{1}{\sin B} > 2$ and $\sin C + \frac{1}{\sin C} > 2$

$\therefore \left(\sin A + \frac{1}{\sin A} + 1\right)\left(\sin B + \frac{1}{\sin B} + 1\right)\left(\sin C + \frac{1}{\sin C} + 1\right) > 27$

$\therefore \quad \Pi\left(\sin A + \frac{1}{\sin A} + 1\right) > 27$

or $\quad \Pi\left(\frac{\sin A + \sin A + 1}{\sin A}\right) > 27$

20. Let a be the length of each side of the equilateral ΔABC.

Then r, the radius of the in-circle $= \left(\frac{1}{3}\right)AP$ (the altitude, median and the angle bisector of angle A)

$\Rightarrow \quad r = \frac{1}{3}\sqrt{a^2 - \frac{a^2}{4}} = \frac{a}{2\sqrt{3}}$

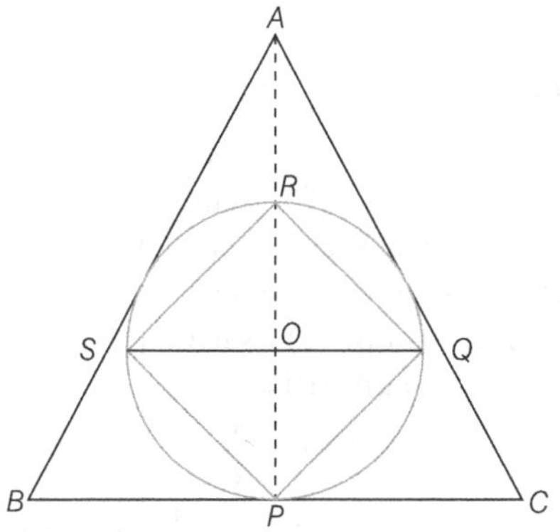

Area of the square $PQRS$ inscribed in this circle

$$= PQ^2 = OP^2 + OQ^2$$

$$= 2r^2 = 2 \times \frac{a^2}{4 \times 3} = \frac{a^2}{6}$$

21. $2\sin B = \sin A + \sin C = \sin A + \sin(A+B)$

$= \sin A + \sin A \cos B + \cos A \sin B$

$\Rightarrow \sin B(2 - \cos A) = \sin A(1 + \cos B)$

$\Rightarrow \quad \frac{\sin B}{1+\cos B} = \frac{\sin A}{2 - \cos A}$

$\Rightarrow \quad \tan\frac{B}{2} = \frac{\sin A}{2-\cos A} = k$ [suppose]

$\Rightarrow \quad \sin A = 2k - k\cos A$

$\Rightarrow \quad \sin A + k\cos A = 2k \Rightarrow \sin(A+\alpha) = \frac{2k}{\sqrt{1+k^2}}$,

where $\tan\alpha = \frac{k}{1}$ $\left[\because \text{we let } \cos\alpha = \frac{1}{\sqrt{1+k^2}}\right]$

$\Rightarrow \quad \frac{2k}{\sqrt{1+k^2}} \leq 1 \Rightarrow 2k \leq \sqrt{1+k^2}$

$\Rightarrow \quad 4k^2 \leq 1 + k^2 \Rightarrow 3k^2 - 1 \leq 0 \Rightarrow |k| \leq \frac{1}{\sqrt{3}}$

$\Rightarrow$ Maximum value of $\tan\frac{B}{2}$ is $\frac{1}{\sqrt{3}}$.

22. $\cos B = \frac{a^2 + c^2 - b^2}{2ac}$

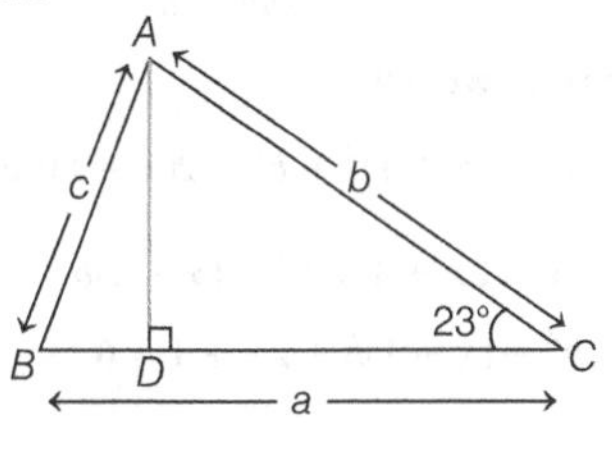

$$= \frac{a}{2c} - \frac{b^2-c^2}{2ac} = \frac{a}{2c} - \frac{b^2-c^2}{abc}\cdot\frac{b}{2}$$

$$= \frac{a}{2c} - \frac{b}{2(AD)}$$

$$= \frac{\sin A}{2\sin C} - \frac{1}{2\sin C}$$

$$\therefore \quad \cos B = \frac{\sin A - 1}{2\sin C}$$

In ΔACD, $\quad \frac{AD}{b} = \sin C$

$$\Rightarrow \quad \frac{b}{AD} = \frac{1}{\sin C}$$

$$\Rightarrow \quad 2\cos B \sin C = \sin A - 1$$

$$\Rightarrow \quad \sin(B+C) - \sin(B-C) = \sin A - 1$$

$$\Rightarrow \quad \sin A - \sin(B-C) = \sin A - 1$$

$$\Rightarrow \quad \sin(B-C) = 1$$

$$\Rightarrow \quad B - C = \frac{\pi}{2}$$

$$\Rightarrow \quad B = C + \frac{\pi}{2} = 23° + 90° = 113°$$

$$\Rightarrow \quad \angle B = 113°$$

23. We have,

$$\frac{31}{32} = \cos(A-B) = \frac{1-\tan^2\frac{A-B}{2}}{1+\tan^2\frac{A-B}{2}}$$

$$\Rightarrow \quad 63\tan^2\frac{A-B}{2} = 1$$

$$\Rightarrow \quad \tan\frac{A-B}{2} = \frac{1}{\sqrt{63}}$$

Now, $\quad \tan\frac{A-B}{2} = \frac{a-b}{a+b}\cot\frac{C}{2}$

$$\Rightarrow \quad \frac{1}{\sqrt{63}} = \frac{5-4}{5+4}\cot\frac{C}{2}$$

$$\Rightarrow \quad \tan\frac{C}{2} = \frac{\sqrt{63}}{9}$$

Also, $\quad \cos C = \frac{1-\tan^2\left(\frac{C}{2}\right)}{1+\tan^2\left(\frac{C}{2}\right)}$

$$= \frac{1-\frac{63}{81}}{1+\frac{63}{81}}$$

$$= \frac{18}{144} = \frac{1}{8}$$

24. Using cosine rule, we get

$$x^2 = (x+1)^2 + b^2 - 2(x+1)b\cos\frac{\pi}{3}$$

$$\Rightarrow \quad 0 = 2x + 1 + b^2 - (x+1)b$$

$$\Rightarrow \quad b^2 - (x+1)b + 2x + 1 = 0$$

Since b is real, we have

$$\Rightarrow \quad (x+1)^2 - 4(2x+1) \ge 0$$

$$\Rightarrow \quad x^2 - 6x - 3 \ge 0 \Rightarrow x \ge 3 + \sqrt{12}$$

The least integral value of x is 7.

25. We have, $\quad 2b = a + c$

$$\therefore \quad 2\sin B = \sin A + \sin C$$

$$4\sin\frac{B}{2}\cos\frac{B}{2} = 2\sin\frac{A+C}{2}\cos\frac{A-C}{2}$$

$$= 2\cos\frac{B}{2}\cos\frac{A-C}{2}$$

$$\therefore \quad 2\sin\frac{B}{2} = \cos\frac{A-C}{2}$$

i.e. $2\cos\frac{A+C}{2} = \cos\frac{A-C}{2}$ ...(i)

Now, $\cos A + \cos C = 2\cos\frac{A+C}{2}\cdot\cos\frac{A-C}{2}$

$$= 2\cos\frac{A+C}{2}\left(2\cos\frac{A+C}{2}\right) \quad \text{[using Eq. (i).]}$$

$$= 4\cos^2\frac{A+C}{2} \qquad \text{...(ii)}$$

$$4(1-\cos A)(1-\cos C) = 4\cdot 2\sin^2\frac{A}{2}\cdot 2\sin^2\frac{C}{2}$$

$$= 4\left(2\sin\frac{A}{2}\sin\frac{C}{2}\right)^2$$

$$= 4\left\{\cos\frac{A-C}{2} - \cos\frac{A+C}{2}\right\}^2$$

$$= 4\left\{2\cos\frac{A+C}{2} - \cos\frac{A+C}{2}\right\}^2$$

$$= 4\cos^2\frac{A+C}{2} \qquad \text{...(iii)}$$

From Eqs. (ii) and (iii), we get

$$\cos A + \cos C = 4(1-\cos A)(1-\cos C)$$

26. We have, $c(a+b)\cos\frac{1}{2}B = b(a+c)\cos\frac{1}{2}C$

$$\therefore \quad c(a+b)\sqrt{\left\{\frac{s(s-b)}{ca}\right\}} = b(a+c)\sqrt{\left\{\frac{s(s-c)}{ab}\right\}}$$

or $\quad (a+b)\sqrt{c(s-b)} = (a+c)\sqrt{b(s-c)}$

Squaring, $(a+b)^2c(s-b) = (a+c)^2b(s-c)$

or $s[c(a+b)^2 - b(a+c)^2] - bc[(a+b)^2 - (a+c)^2] = 0$

or $s\{ca^2 + 2abc + cb^2 - ba^2 - 2abc - bc^2\}$

$$- bc(b-c)(2a+b+c) = 0$$

or $\quad s\{bc(b-c) - a^2(b-c)\} - bc(b-c)(2a+b+c) = 0$

or $\quad (b-c)\{s(bc-a^2) - bc(2a+b+c)\} = 0$

or $\quad (b-c)\{s(bc-a^2) - bc(2s+a\} = 0$

or $\quad -(b-c)\{s(bc+a^2) + abc\} = 0$

Since, a, b, c are all positive and so $s(bc+a^2) + abc \ne 0$

It follows that $b - c = 0$.

Hence, ΔABC is isosceles.

27. $\tan\alpha = \frac{b}{a}, \tan 2\alpha = \frac{2(b/a)}{1-(b/a)^2} = \frac{p+b}{a}$

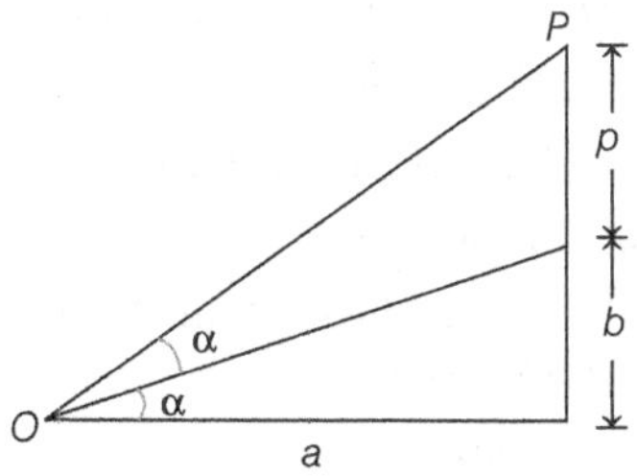

$$\Rightarrow \quad \frac{2ba}{a^2 - b^2} = \frac{p+b}{a}$$

$$\Rightarrow \quad \frac{2ba^2 - a^2b + b^3}{a^2 - b^2} = p$$

$$\Rightarrow \quad p = \frac{b(a^2 + b^2)}{(a^2 - b^2)}$$

28. $x = h\cot 3\alpha$ ...(i)

$(x+100) = h\cot 2\alpha$ ... (ii)

$(x+300) = h\cot\alpha$ ...(iii)

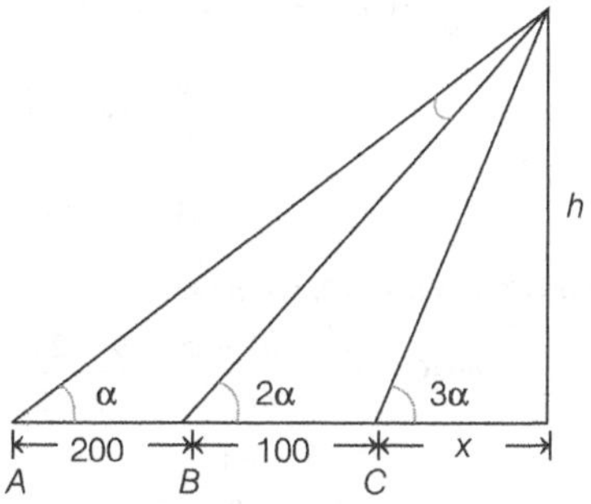

From Eqs. (i) and (ii), we get

$$-100 = h(\cot 3\alpha - \cot 2\alpha)$$

From Eqs. (ii) and (iii), we get

$$-200 = h(\cot 2\alpha - \cot\alpha)$$

$$100 = h\left(\frac{\sin\alpha}{\sin 3\alpha \sin 2\alpha}\right) \text{ and } 200 = h\left(\frac{\sin\alpha}{\sin 2\alpha \sin\alpha}\right)$$

or $$\frac{\sin 3\alpha}{\sin\alpha} = \frac{200}{100}$$

$$\Rightarrow \quad \frac{\sin 3\alpha}{\sin\alpha} = 2$$

$$\Rightarrow \quad 3\sin\alpha - 4\sin^3\alpha - 2\sin\alpha = 0$$

$$\Rightarrow \quad 4\sin^3\alpha - \sin\alpha = 0$$

$$\Rightarrow \quad \sin\alpha = 0$$

or $$\sin^2\alpha = \frac{1}{4} = \sin^2\left(\frac{\pi}{6}\right) \Rightarrow \alpha = \frac{\pi}{6}$$

Hence, $h = 200\sin\frac{\pi}{3} = 200\frac{\sqrt{3}}{2} = 100\sqrt{3}$ [from Eq. (i)]

29. Obviously, from figure

$$\tan\alpha = \frac{h/3}{40} = \frac{h}{120} \quad \text{...(i)}$$

$$\tan\beta = \frac{h}{40} = \frac{3h}{120} \quad \text{...(ii)}$$

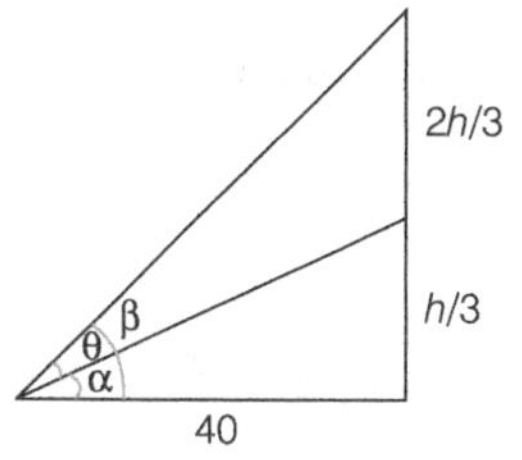

Therefore, $\tan\theta = \tan(\beta - \alpha)$

$$\Rightarrow \quad \frac{1}{2} = \frac{\frac{3h}{120} - \frac{h}{120}}{1 + \frac{3h^2}{14400}} \Rightarrow h = 120, 40$$

But $h = 40$ cannot be taken according to the condition, therefore $h = 120$ ft.

30. $c^2 = a^2 + b^2 - 2ab\cos C = (a-b)^2 + 2ab(1 - \cos C)$

$$= (a-b)^2 + \frac{4\Delta}{\sin C}(1 - \cos C)$$

Hence, for c to be minimum $a = b$

Also, $\Delta = \frac{1}{2}ab\sin C \Rightarrow a^2 = \frac{2\Delta}{\sin C} = b^2$

31. As $ac = 3$ and $bc = 4$

$$\therefore \quad \frac{b}{a} = \frac{4}{3}$$

$$\Rightarrow \quad \frac{b-a}{b+a} = \frac{4-3}{4+3} = \frac{1}{7} \quad [\angle B > \angle A]$$

$$\Rightarrow \quad \tan\left(\frac{B-A}{2}\right) = \frac{b-a}{b+a}\cot\frac{C}{2}$$

$$\Rightarrow \quad \sqrt{\frac{1 - \cos(B-A)}{1 + \cos(B-A)}} = \frac{4-3}{4+3}\cot\frac{C}{2}$$

$$\Rightarrow \quad \sqrt{\frac{1 - \frac{3}{4}}{1 + \frac{3}{4}}} = \frac{1}{7}\cot\frac{C}{2}$$

$$\Rightarrow \quad \sqrt{\frac{1}{7}} = \frac{1}{7}\cot\frac{C}{2}$$

$$\Rightarrow \quad \cot\frac{C}{2} = \sqrt{7}$$

$$\Rightarrow \quad \cos C = \frac{1 - \tan^2\frac{C}{2}}{1 + \tan^2\frac{C}{2}} = \frac{1 - \frac{1}{7}}{1 + \frac{1}{7}}$$

$$= \frac{6}{8} = \frac{3}{4}$$

$$\therefore \quad \cos C = \cos(A - B) \text{ or } \cos C = \cos(B - A)$$

$$\therefore \quad C = A - B \text{ or } C = B - A$$

$$\pi - (A+B) = A - B \text{ or } \pi - (A+B) = B - A$$

$$\therefore \quad 2A = \pi \text{ or } 2B = \pi, \; A = \frac{\pi}{2} \text{ (Rejected) or } B = \frac{\pi}{2}$$

But $\angle B = \dfrac{\pi}{2}$ [As $\angle B > \angle A$]

$\Rightarrow \quad \dfrac{b}{a} = \dfrac{4}{3} = k$ (let)

$\Rightarrow \quad b = 4k, a = 3k$

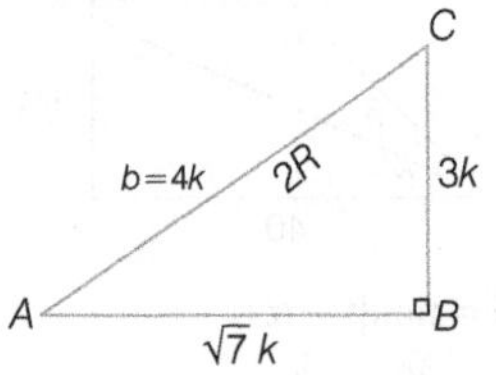

Now, $ac = 3$

$\Rightarrow \quad 3\sqrt{7}\,k^2 = 3$

$\Rightarrow \quad k^2 = \dfrac{1}{\sqrt{7}}$

$\Rightarrow \quad k = \dfrac{1}{7^{1/4}}$

$\therefore \quad R = 2k = \dfrac{2}{7^{1/4}}$

32. We have, $a = 5, b = 4$ and $\cos(A - B) = \dfrac{31}{32}$

As, $\tan\left(\dfrac{A-B}{2}\right) = \left(\dfrac{a-b}{a+b}\right)\cot\dfrac{C}{2} = \dfrac{1}{9}\cot\dfrac{C}{2}$

$\Rightarrow \quad \cos(A-B) = \dfrac{1 - \tan^2\left(\dfrac{A-B}{2}\right)}{1 + \tan^2\left(\dfrac{A-B}{2}\right)}$

$\Rightarrow \quad \dfrac{31}{32} = \dfrac{1 - \dfrac{1}{81}\cot^2\dfrac{C}{2}}{1 + \dfrac{1}{81}\cot^2\dfrac{C}{2}}$

$\Rightarrow \quad 31 + \dfrac{31}{81}\cot^2\dfrac{C}{2} = 32 - \dfrac{32}{81}\cot^2\dfrac{C}{2}$

$\Rightarrow \quad \dfrac{7}{9}\cot^2\dfrac{C}{2} = 1 \Rightarrow \cot^2\dfrac{C}{2} = \dfrac{9}{7}$

As, $\cos C = \dfrac{1 - \tan^2\dfrac{C}{2}}{1 + \tan^2\dfrac{C}{2}} = \dfrac{1 - \dfrac{7}{9}}{1 + \dfrac{7}{9}} = \dfrac{2}{16} = \dfrac{1}{8}$

$\Rightarrow \quad C = \cos^{-1}\left(\dfrac{1}{8}\right)$

Also, $\cos C = \dfrac{a^2 + b^2 - c^2}{2ab}$

$\Rightarrow \quad \dfrac{25 + 16 - c^2}{2(5)(4)} = \dfrac{1}{8} \Rightarrow c = 6$

Perimeter $= a + b + c = 5 + 4 + 6 = 15$

and $r = \dfrac{\Delta}{s} = \dfrac{\dfrac{1}{2} \times a \times b \times \sin C}{\dfrac{15}{2}}$

$= \dfrac{1}{15} \times 5 \times 4 \times \dfrac{\sqrt{63}}{8} = \dfrac{1}{6}\sqrt{63} = \dfrac{\sqrt{7}}{2}$

(d) LHS $= R(b^2 \sin 2C + c^2 \sin 2B)$

$= R(2b^2 \sin C \cos C + 2c^2 \sin B \cos B)$

$= 2R[4R^2 \sin^2 B \sin C \cos C + 4R^2 \sin B \sin^2 C \cos B]$

$= 2R(4R^2)\sin B \sin C[\sin B \cos C + \cos B \sin C]$

$= 8R^3 \sin A \sin B \sin C$

$= (2R\sin A)(2R\sin B)(2R\sin C) = abc$

$= (5)(4)(6) = 120$

33. (a) $a^2 - (c - b)^2 = 4bc$

$\Rightarrow a^2 - (c^2 + b^2 - 2bc) = 4bc$

$\Rightarrow \quad a^2 = b^2 + c^2 + 2bc$

$\Rightarrow \quad \dfrac{-2bc}{2bc} = \dfrac{b^2 + c^2 - a^2}{2bc}$

$\Rightarrow \quad \cos A = -1,$

which is not possible.

(b) $2b^2 \sin C \cos C + 2c^2 \sin B \cos B = ab$

$\Rightarrow \quad \dfrac{(b^2c \cos C + c^2b \cos B)}{R} = ab$

$\Rightarrow \quad \dfrac{bc}{R}(b\cos C + c\cos B) = ab$

$\Rightarrow \quad \dfrac{abc}{R} = ab, \Rightarrow \dfrac{c}{2R} = \dfrac{1}{2}$

$\Rightarrow \quad \sin C = \dfrac{1}{2} \Rightarrow C = \dfrac{\pi}{6}$

(c) For $a = 3, b = 5, c = 7$, we have

$\cos C = \dfrac{a^2 + b^2 - c^2}{2ab} = \dfrac{9 + 25 - 49}{2 \times 3 \times 5}$

$= \dfrac{-15}{30} = \dfrac{-1}{2}$

$\therefore \quad C = \dfrac{2\pi}{3}$

(d) As $\cos\left(\dfrac{A-C}{2}\right) = \cos\left(\dfrac{A+C}{2}\right)$

$\Rightarrow 2\sin\dfrac{A}{2}\sin\dfrac{C}{2} = 0,$

which is not possible in triangle.

34. We have, $\dfrac{1}{\sin A} = \dfrac{2}{\sin B} = \dfrac{c}{\sin 30^\circ}$

So, $2\sin A = \sin B$

Hence, option (a) is correct.

Also, $c^2 = 4 + 1 - 4\cos 30^\circ = 5 - 2\sqrt{3}$

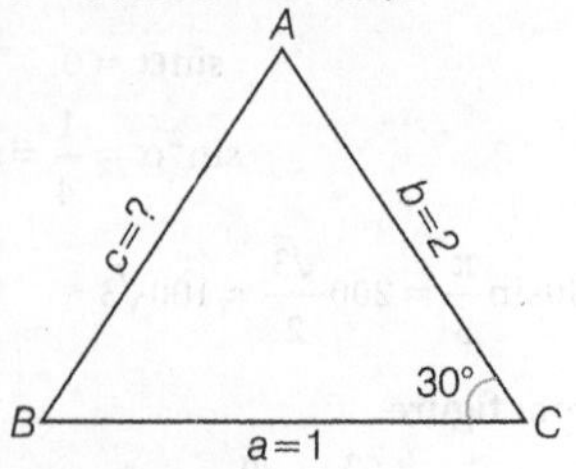

$\Rightarrow \quad c = \sqrt{5 - 2\sqrt{3}}$

As $c > a \Rightarrow \angle A < \angle C$ and $\angle B$ is obtuse.

Also, $\Delta = \frac{1}{2} \times 1 \times 2 \times \frac{1}{2} = \frac{1}{2}$

So, $R = \frac{abc}{4\Delta}$

$= \frac{1 \times 2 \times c}{4\Delta} = c = AB$

35. $\Delta = 10\sqrt{3}, s = 10$

$\Rightarrow r = \frac{\Delta}{s} = \sqrt{3}$ and $r = (s - b) \tan\frac{B}{2}$

$\Rightarrow s - b = 3 \Rightarrow b = 7$

$\Rightarrow a + c = 13$ ...(i)

$\Rightarrow ac = 40$ ...(ii)

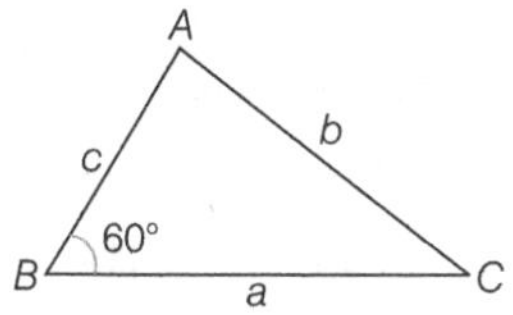

From Eq. (ii), $a^2 - 13a + 40 = 0$

$\Rightarrow a = 5, a = 8$

$\Rightarrow c = 8$ and $c = 5$

Hence, $a = 8, b = 7$ and $c = 5$ (As $a > b > c$)

$\Rightarrow r_1 = \frac{\Delta}{s-a} = \frac{10\sqrt{3}}{2} = 5\sqrt{3}, r_2 = \frac{\Delta}{s-b} = \frac{10\sqrt{3}}{3} = \frac{10}{\sqrt{3}},$

$r_3 = \frac{\Delta}{s-c} = \frac{10\sqrt{3}}{5} = 2\sqrt{3}$

Also, $\frac{b}{\sin B} = 2R \Rightarrow 2R = \frac{7}{\frac{\sqrt{3}}{2}} \Rightarrow R = \frac{7}{\sqrt{3}}$

36. $\cos C = \frac{1}{2} = \frac{16 + 64 - c^2}{64}$

$\Rightarrow c^2 = 48 \Rightarrow c = 4\sqrt{3}$

Also, $\frac{a}{\sin A} = \frac{c}{\sin C} \Rightarrow \frac{4}{\sin A} = \frac{4\sqrt{3}}{\frac{\sqrt{3}}{2}} \Rightarrow A = 30°$

As, $\angle C = 60°, \angle A = 30° \Rightarrow \angle B = 90°$

Now, $r = \frac{\Delta}{s} = \frac{\frac{1}{2}ac}{\frac{a+b+c}{2}} = \frac{ac}{a+b+c}$

$= \frac{4(4\sqrt{3})}{4 + 4\sqrt{3} + 8} = \frac{16\sqrt{3}}{12 + 4\sqrt{3}} = \frac{4\sqrt{3}}{3 + \sqrt{3}}$

Now, verify alternatives.

(a) $\Delta = \frac{1}{2}ab\sin C = \frac{1}{2} \times 4 \times 8 \times \sin 60° = 8\sqrt{3}$

(b) $\Sigma \sin^2 A = \sin^2 A + \sin^2 B + \sin^2 C = 2$

(c) $r = \frac{4\sqrt{3}}{3 + \sqrt{3}}$

(d) The length of internal angle bisector of $\angle C$ is $\frac{8}{\sqrt{3}}$.

37. (a) Since, $\tan A + \tan B + \tan C = \tan A \tan B \tan C$

But here, $\tan A + \tan B + \tan C = 0$, impossible

(b) $\frac{\sin A}{2} = \frac{\sin B}{3} = \frac{\sin C}{7}$ or $\frac{a}{2} = \frac{b}{3} = \frac{c}{7}$

$\Rightarrow \frac{a+b}{5} = \frac{c}{7}$ or $\frac{a+b}{c} = \frac{5}{7} < 1$

$\therefore a + b < c$ impossible.

(c) $(a + b)^2 = c^2 + ab$

$\Rightarrow a^2 + b^2 - c^2 = -ab$

$\Rightarrow \cos C = -\frac{1}{2}$

$\Rightarrow \angle C = 120°$

and $\sqrt{2}(\sin A + \cos A) = \sqrt{3}$

$\Rightarrow \sqrt{2} \cdot \sqrt{2} \sin\left(A + \frac{\pi}{4}\right) = \sqrt{3}$

$\Rightarrow \sin\left(A + \frac{\pi}{4}\right) = \frac{\sqrt{3}}{2}$

$\Rightarrow A + \frac{\pi}{4} = \frac{\pi}{3}$

$\therefore A = \frac{\pi}{12}$ possible

(d) $\because \sin A + \sin B = \frac{\sqrt{3}+1}{2}$ ...(i)

and $\cos A \cos B = \frac{\sqrt{3}}{4} = \sin A \sin B$

$\therefore \cos A \cos B - \sin A \sin B = 0$

$\Rightarrow \cos(A + B) = 0$

$\Rightarrow A + B = \frac{\pi}{2}$

$\therefore B = \frac{\pi}{2} - A$

From Eq. (i),

$\sin A + \cos A = \frac{\sqrt{3}+1}{2}$

$\Rightarrow \sin\left(A + \frac{\pi}{4}\right) = \frac{\sqrt{3}+1}{2\sqrt{2}} = \sin\frac{5\pi}{12}$

$\Rightarrow A + \frac{\pi}{4} = \frac{5\pi}{12} \Rightarrow A = \frac{\pi}{6}$

$\therefore B = \frac{\pi}{3}$

Then, $C = \frac{\pi}{2}$ possible.

38. In ΔABC, $b + c - a > 0, c + a - b > 0, a + b - c > 0$, so

$\frac{(b+c-a)+(c+a-b)+(a+b-c)}{3} \geq \{(b+c-a)(c+a-b)(a+b-c)\}^{1/3}$

$\Rightarrow p^3 \geq 27\,(b+c-a)\,(c+a-b)\,(a+b-c)$

Also, $\frac{(a+b+c)+(b+c-a)+(c+a-b)+(a+b-c)}{4} > \{(a+b+c)(b+c-a)(c+a-b)(a+b-c)\}^{1/4}$

$$\Rightarrow \quad \frac{2P}{4} > (16A)^{1/4}$$

$$\Rightarrow \quad P > 4A^{1/4} \text{ or } P^4 = 256A$$

For a given parameter, equilateral triangle has the largest area, so the area of triangle

$$A \le \frac{\sqrt{3}}{4}\left(\frac{P}{3}\right)^2$$

$$\left[\text{for equilateral triangle, } a = b = c = \frac{P}{3}\right]$$

Now, $P^2 = (a + b + c)^2$

$$= a^2 + b^2 + c^2 + 2(ab + bc + ca)$$

$$= 3(a^2 + b^2 + c^2) - 2(a^2 + b^2 + c^2 - ab - bc - ca \le 3(a^2 + b^2 + c^2)$$

[equality holds iff $a = b = c$]

Thus, $A \le \frac{\sqrt{3}}{4} \frac{a^2 + b^2 + c^2}{3} \Rightarrow a^2 + b^2 + c^2 \ge 4\sqrt{3}A$

39. $(a^2 - 2ac + c^2) + (a^2 - 4ab + 4b^2) = 0$

or $(a - c)^2 + (a - 2b)^2 = 0$

$a = c$ and $a = 2b$

Therefore, the triangle is isosceles.

Also, $\cos B = \frac{a^2 + c^2 - b^2}{2ac} = \frac{7b^2}{8b^2} = \frac{7}{8}$

$\cos A = \frac{b^2 + c^2 - a^2}{2bc} = \frac{1}{4}$

40. $2a^2b^2 + 2b^2c^2 = a^4 + b^4 + c^4$

Also, $(a^2 - b^2 + c^2)^2 = a^4 + b^4 + c^4 - 2(a^2b^2 + b^2c^2 - c^2a^2)$

$\therefore \quad (a^2 - b^2 + c^2)^2 = 2c^2a^2$

$\therefore \quad \frac{a^2 - b^2 + c^2}{2ca} = \pm \frac{1}{\sqrt{2}} = \cos B$

or $B = 45°$ or $135°$

Sol. (Q.Nos 41 to 42)

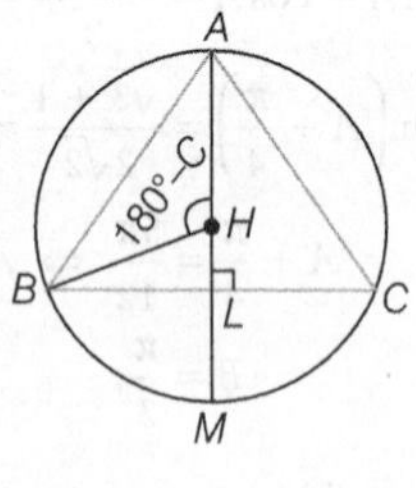

41. $R_1R_2 + R_2R_3 + R_1R_3 = 3R^2$ $\quad [\because R_1 = R_2 = R_3 = R]$

42. $AH = 2R \cos A$

$BH = 2R \cos B$

$\Delta = \frac{1}{2}(AH)(BH)\sin(180° - C)$

$\Delta = 2R^2 \cos A \cos B \sin C$

Sol. (Q.Nos 43 to 44)

43. $\because \cos A = \frac{b^2 + c^2 - a^2}{2bc}$ or $c^2 - 2bc\cos A + b^2 - a^2 = 0$

For real roots, $D > 0$

$$\Rightarrow \quad 4b^2\cos^2 A - 4 \cdot 1 \cdot (b^2 - a^2) > 0$$

$$\Rightarrow \quad a^2 > b^2 \sin^2 A$$

$$\therefore \quad b\sin A < a$$

Also, $c_1 + c_2 = 2b\cos A$ ...(i)

and $c_1c_2 = b^2 - a^2$ ...(ii)

Then, $|c_1 - c_2| = \sqrt{(c_1 + c_2)^2 - 4c_1c_2}$

$= \sqrt{4b^2\cos^2 A - 4(b^2 - a^2)}$

$= 2\sqrt{(a^2 - b^2\sin^2 A)}$ ...(iii)

Consider smaller root, say c_2

Then, $2c_2 = (c_1 + c_2) - (c_1 - c_2)$

$= 2b\cos A - 2\sqrt{(a^2 - b^2\sin^2 A)}$

$\Rightarrow \quad c_2 = b\cos A - \sqrt{(a^2 - b^2\sin^2 A)} > 0$

$\Rightarrow \quad b\cos A > \sqrt{(a^2 - b^2\sin^2 A)}$

$\Rightarrow \quad b^2\cos^2 A > a^2 - b^2\sin^2 A$

$\Rightarrow \quad b^2 > a^2$ or $b > a$

Hence, two different triangle are possible if $b\sin A < a$ and $b > a$

44. $c_1^2 - 2c_1c^2\cos 2A + c_2^2 = (c_1 + c_2)^2 - 2c_1c_2(1 + \cos 2A)$

$= (c_1 + c_2)^2 - 4c_1c_2\cos^2 A$

$= (2b\cos A)^2 - 4(b^2 - a^2)\cos^2 A$

[from Eqs. (i) and (ii)]

$= 4\cos^2 A\{b^2 - (b^2 - a^2)\}$

$= 4a^2\cos^2 A$

Sol. (Q.Nos 45 to 46)

Here, ΔMNL is pedal triangle, then

$MN = a\cos A$

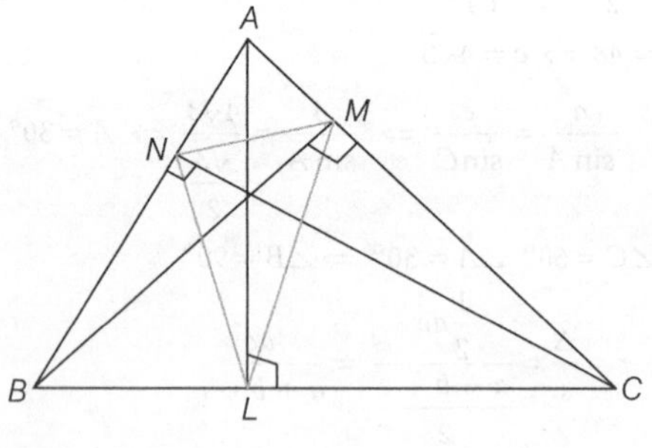

$NL = b\cos B$

and $ML = c\cos C$

and $\angle MLN = \pi - 2A$, $\angle LMN = \pi - 2B$

and $\angle MNL = \pi - 2C$

45. In ΔABM, $\cos A = \frac{AM}{AB} = \frac{AM}{c}$

$\therefore \quad AM = c\cos A$

Similarly, $AN = b\cos A$

$\therefore \quad \Delta_1 = $ Area of ΔAMN

$= \frac{1}{2} \cdot AM \cdot AN \cdot \sin A$

$$= \frac{1}{2}(c\cos A)(b\cos A)(\sin A)$$

$$= \left(\frac{1}{2}bc\sin A\right)\cos^2 A = \Delta\cos^2 A$$

Similarly, $\Delta_2 = \Delta\cos^2 B$ and $\Delta_3 = \Delta\cos^2 C$

$\therefore\ \Delta_1 + \Delta_2 + \Delta_3 = \Delta(\cos^2 A + \cos^2 B + \cos^2 C)$

$= \Delta(1 - 2\cos A\cos B\cos C)$ [from identity]

46. $\Delta' =$ Area of ΔLMN

$$= \frac{1}{2}\cdot ML\cdot NL\cdot\sin(\pi - 2A)$$

$$= \frac{1}{2}\cdot(c\cos C)(b\cos B)(\sin 2A)$$

$$= \frac{1}{2}bc\cos B\cos C(2\sin A\cos A)$$

$$= \left(\frac{1}{2}bc\sin A\right)(2\cos A\cos B\cos C)$$

$\therefore\quad \Delta' = \Delta(2\cos A\cos B\cos C)$

$\Rightarrow\quad \dfrac{\Delta'}{\Delta} = 2\cos A\cos B\cos C$

Sol. (Q.Nos 47 and 48)

Given, $\cos(A - B) = \dfrac{4}{5}$

$$\Rightarrow \frac{1 - \tan^2\frac{A-B}{2}}{1 + \tan^2\frac{A-B}{2}} = \frac{4}{5}$$

$$\Rightarrow \tan^2\frac{A-B}{2} = \frac{1}{9}$$

$$\Rightarrow \tan\frac{A-B}{2} = \frac{1}{3}$$

$$\Rightarrow \frac{1}{3} = \frac{6-3}{6+3}\cot\frac{C}{2}$$

$$\Rightarrow \cot\frac{C}{2} = 1$$

$$\Rightarrow \frac{C}{2} = \frac{\pi}{4}$$

$$\Rightarrow C = \frac{\pi}{2}$$

$\therefore\ \Delta ABC$ is a right angled triangle.

Thus, $c^2 = a^2 + b^2$.

47. The value of $\dfrac{10}{\pi}$ times of $\angle C = \dfrac{10}{\pi}\times\dfrac{\pi}{2} = 5$

48. The area of triangle $= \dfrac{1}{2}ab\sin C = \dfrac{1}{2}\times 6\times 3\times 1 = 9$ sq units

Sol. (Q.Nos 49 and 50)

49. $\dfrac{bx}{c} + \dfrac{cy}{a} + \dfrac{az}{b} = b\sin B + c\sin C + a\sin A$

$$= \frac{b^2}{2R} + \frac{c^2}{2R} + \frac{a^2}{2R}$$

$$= \frac{a^2 + b^2 + c^2}{2R}$$

$\therefore\quad k = 2$

50. $\dfrac{1}{x^2} + \dfrac{1}{y^2} + \dfrac{1}{z^2} = \dfrac{a^2}{4\Delta^2} + \dfrac{b^2}{4\Delta^2} + \dfrac{c^2}{4\Delta^2} = \dfrac{a^2 + b^2 + c^2}{4\Delta^2}$

$\cot A + \cot B + \cot C$

$$= \frac{R}{abc}(b^2 + c^2 - a^2 + c^2 + a^2 - b^2 + a^2 + b^2 - c^2)$$

$$= \frac{R}{abc}(a^2 + b^2 + c^2)$$

$$= \frac{R}{abc}\left(\frac{4\Delta^2}{x^2} + \frac{4\Delta^2}{y^2} + \frac{4\Delta^2}{z^2}\right)$$

$$= \frac{4\Delta^2 R}{abc}\left(\frac{1}{x^2} + \frac{1}{y^2} + \frac{1}{z^2}\right)$$

$$= \frac{4\Delta R}{abc}\Delta\left(\frac{1}{x^2} + \frac{1}{y^2} + \frac{1}{z^2}\right)$$

$$= \Delta\left(\frac{1}{x^2} + \frac{1}{y^2} + \frac{1}{z^2}\right) \quad [\because 4\Delta R = abc]$$

$\therefore\quad k = 1$

51. On applying cosine rule, $2ab\cos C = a^2 + b^2 - c^2$

$$\Rightarrow 2\sqrt{2}\sqrt{2+\sqrt{2}}\cos\frac{\pi}{8} = 2 + 2 + \sqrt{2} - c^2$$

Using $\cos\dfrac{\pi}{8} = \dfrac{\sqrt{2+\sqrt{2}}}{2}$

$$\Rightarrow \frac{2\sqrt{2}(2+\sqrt{2})}{2} = 4 + \sqrt{2} - c^2$$

$$\Rightarrow c^2 = 2 - \sqrt{2} \Rightarrow c = \sqrt{2-\sqrt{2}}$$

On applying sine rule, $\dfrac{\sin C}{c} = \dfrac{\sin A}{a}$

$$\Rightarrow \frac{\sqrt{2-\sqrt{2}}}{2\sqrt{2-\sqrt{2}}} = \frac{\sin A}{\sqrt{2}}$$

$$\Rightarrow \sin A = \frac{1}{\sqrt{2}} \Rightarrow A = 45^\circ$$

[$\because$ b is the longest side

$\therefore\ \angle B$ will be the greatest

$\therefore\ A \neq 135^\circ$]

Sum of the digits is $= 4 + 5 = 9$

52. Using sine law, $\dfrac{125}{\sin x} = \dfrac{195}{\sin 3x} = \dfrac{c}{\sin 4x}$

$$\Rightarrow 3 - 4\sin^2 x = \frac{195}{125} = \frac{39}{25}$$

$$\Rightarrow 4\sin^2 x = 3 - \frac{39}{25} = \frac{75-39}{25} = \frac{36}{25}$$

$$\Rightarrow \sin^2 x = \frac{9}{25} \Rightarrow \sin x = \frac{3}{5}$$

$$\therefore\ c = \frac{125\sin 4x}{\sin x} = 125\frac{2\cos 2x\, 2\sin x\cos x}{\sin x}$$

$$= (125)(4)(\cos x)(1 - 2\sin^2 x) = (500)\left(\frac{4}{5}\right)\left(1 - \frac{18}{25}\right)$$

$$= 400\left(\frac{7}{25}\right) = (16)(7) = 112$$

$\therefore$ Number of digits in the length of side $AB = 3$

53. $a^2 + b^2 + c^2 = 2R^2(1 - \cos 2A + 1 - \cos 2B + 1 - \cos 2C)$

$$= 2R^2\left[3 - \left(\cos\frac{2\pi}{7} + \cos\frac{4\pi}{7} + \cos\frac{8\pi}{7}\right)\right]$$

$$= 2R^2\left(3 - \left(\frac{-1}{2}\right)\right) = 7R^2$$

$$\therefore \quad \frac{a^2 + b^2 + c^2}{R^2} = 7$$

54. $D = 2\tan B \tan B \tan C (\tan A + \tan B + \tan C)^3$

$= 2(\tan A + \tan B + \tan C)^4$

[$\because$ In ΔABC, $\tan A + \tan B + \tan C = \tan A \tan B \tan C$]

$\geq 2(3\sqrt{3})^4 = 1458 \Rightarrow \frac{D}{1000} \geq 1.458$

$\therefore$ Least integer value is 2.

55. Clear $PQ = \frac{a}{2}$, $OA = R$

and $\angle AOQ = B$

In ΔAOQ, $OQ = OA \cos B = R \cos B$

Now, $\angle AQP = C$, since $PQ \parallel BC$

$\Rightarrow \quad \angle PQO = \frac{\pi}{2} - C$

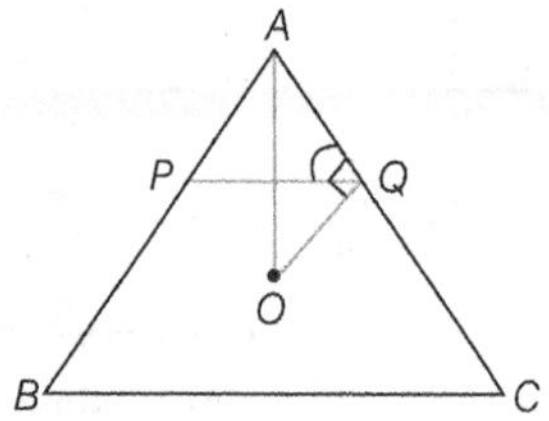

$\Rightarrow$ Area of $\Delta OPQ = \frac{1}{2} PQ \cdot OQ \sin \angle PQO = \frac{aR}{4} \cos B \cos C$

Area of $\Delta ABC = \frac{1}{2} ab \sin c = aR \sin B \sin C$

$$\therefore \quad \frac{\text{Area of } \Delta ABC}{\text{Area of } \Delta OPQ} = \frac{aR \sin B \sin C}{\frac{aR}{4}\cos B \cos C} = 4\tan B \tan C$$

$$\therefore \quad \left(\frac{\text{Area of } \Delta ABC}{\text{Area of } \Delta OPS}\right)\cot B \cdot \cot C = 4$$

56. $$\sum \frac{a}{r_1} = \sum \frac{2R \sin\frac{A}{2} \cdot 2\cos\frac{A}{2}}{4R \sin\frac{A}{2}\cos\frac{B}{2}\cos\frac{C}{2}} = \sum \frac{\sin\left(\frac{B}{2} + \frac{C}{2}\right)}{\cos\frac{B}{2}\cos\frac{C}{2}}$$

$$\sum\left(\tan\frac{B}{2} + \tan\frac{C}{2}\right) = 2\sum\left(\tan\frac{A}{2}\right) = 2\sum\frac{r_1}{s} = 2\left[\frac{r_1 + r_2 + r_3}{s}\right]$$

$$= 2\left[\frac{r_1 + r_2 + r_3}{\frac{a+b+c}{2}}\right]$$

$$= 4\left(\frac{r_1 + r_2 + r_3}{a + b + c}\right)$$

$$\Rightarrow \quad \left(\frac{a+b+c}{r_1 + r_2 + r_3}\right)\left(\frac{a}{r_1} + \frac{b}{r_2} + \frac{c}{r_3}\right) = 4$$

57. From the ΔABC,

$$\cos A = \frac{b^2 + c^2 - a^2}{2bc} \quad \text{...(i)}$$

From the ΔCAD,

$$\cos C = \frac{AC}{CD} = \frac{b}{a/2} = \frac{2b}{a} \quad \text{...(ii)}$$

From the ΔABD,

$$\frac{BD}{\sin(A - 90^\circ)} = \frac{AB}{\sin \angle ADB}$$

or $$\frac{a/2}{-\cos A} = \frac{c}{\sin(90^\circ + C)} \text{ or } \frac{a}{-2\cos A} = \frac{c}{\cos C}$$

$$\therefore \quad \cos A = \frac{a\cos C}{-2c} = \frac{a}{-2c} \cdot \frac{2b}{a} = -\frac{b}{c} \quad \text{[from Eq. (ii)]}$$

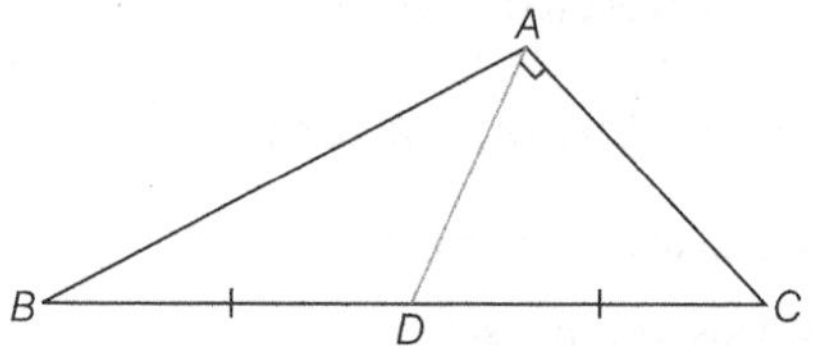

$\therefore$ From Eq. (i), $\frac{b^2 + c^2 - a^2}{2bc} = \frac{-b}{c}$

or $b^2 + c^2 - a^2 = -2b^2$

or $c^2 - a^2 = -3b^2$ ...(iii)

Now, $\cos A \cdot \cos C = \frac{b^2 + c^2 - a^2}{2bc} \cdot \frac{2b}{a} = \frac{b^2 + c^2 - a^2}{ca}$

$$= \frac{3b^2 + 3(c^2 - a^2)}{3ca}$$

$$= \frac{a^2 - c^2 + 3(c^2 - a^2)}{3ca} \quad \text{[from Eq. (iii)]}$$

$$= \frac{2(c^2 - a^2)}{3ca}$$

$\Rightarrow \quad \lambda = 2$

58. Let O be the point of intersection of the medians of ΔABC. Then, the area of ΔABC is three times that of ΔAOC. Now, in ΔAOC, $AO = \frac{2}{3}AD = \frac{10}{3}$.

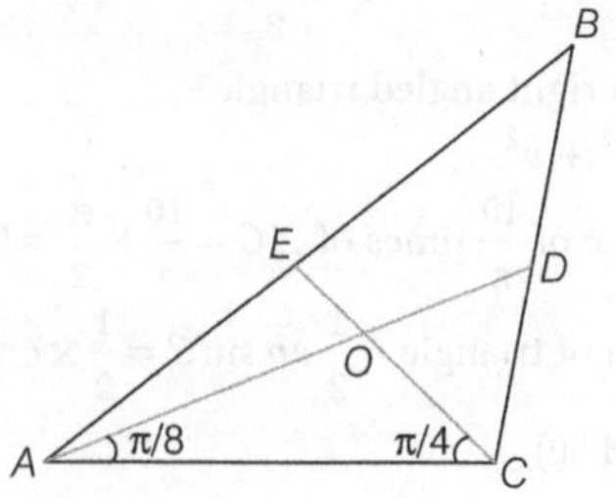

Therefore, applying the sine rule to ΔAOC, we get

$$\frac{OC}{\sin\left(\frac{\pi}{8}\right)} = \frac{AO}{\sin\left(\frac{\pi}{4}\right)} \Rightarrow OC = \frac{10}{3} \cdot \frac{\sin\left(\frac{\pi}{8}\right)}{\sin\left(\frac{\pi}{4}\right)}$$

$$\text{Area of } \Delta AOC = \frac{1}{2} \cdot AO \cdot OC \cdot \sin \angle AOC$$

$$= \frac{1}{2} \cdot \frac{10}{3} \cdot \frac{10}{3} \cdot \frac{\sin\left(\frac{\pi}{8}\right)}{\sin\left(\frac{\pi}{4}\right)} \cdot \sin\left(\frac{\pi}{2} + \frac{\pi}{8}\right)$$

$$= \frac{50}{9} \cdot \frac{\sin\left(\frac{\pi}{8}\right)\cos\left(\frac{\pi}{8}\right)}{\sin\left(\frac{\pi}{4}\right)} = \frac{50}{18} = \frac{25}{9}$$

$\therefore$ Area of $\Delta ABC = 3 \cdot \frac{25}{9} = \frac{25}{3} = \frac{5a}{b}$

$\Rightarrow$ $a = 5$ and $b = 3$

$\therefore$ $a + b = 5 + 3 = 8$

59. $$\frac{r}{r_1} = \frac{4R\sin\frac{A}{2} \cdot \sin\frac{B}{2} \cdot \sin\frac{C}{2}}{4R\sin\frac{A}{2} \cdot \cos\frac{B}{2} \cdot \cos\frac{C}{2}} = \tan\frac{B}{2}\tan\frac{C}{2} = \frac{1}{2}$$

Now, $\tan\frac{A}{2}\left(\tan\frac{B}{2} + \tan\frac{C}{2}\right)$

$$= \tan\frac{A}{2} \cdot \tan\frac{B}{2} + \tan\frac{A}{2} \cdot \tan\frac{C}{2}$$

$$= 1 - \tan\frac{B}{2} \cdot \tan\frac{C}{2}$$

$$= 1 - \frac{1}{2} = \frac{1}{2}$$

$\therefore$ $16\tan\frac{A}{2}\left(\tan\frac{B}{2} + \tan\frac{C}{2}\right) = \frac{1}{2} \times 16 = 8$

60. $$\frac{a\cos^2\frac{A}{2} + b\cos^2\frac{B}{2} + c\cos^2\frac{C}{2}}{a + b + c}$$

$$= \frac{a(1 + \cos A) + b(1 + \cos B) + c(1 + \cos C)}{2(a + b + c)}$$

$$= \frac{(a + b + c) + (a\cos A + b\cos B + c\cos C)}{2(a + b + c)}$$

$$= \frac{1}{2} + \frac{a\cos A + b\cos B + c\cos C}{4s}$$

$$= \frac{1}{2} + \frac{R}{4s}(\sin 2A + \sin 2B + \sin 2C)$$

$$= \frac{1}{2} + \frac{R}{4s}(4\sin A \sin B \sin C)$$

$$= \frac{1}{2} + \frac{R}{4s} \times \left(4 \cdot \frac{a}{2R} \cdot \frac{b}{2R} \cdot \frac{c}{2R}\right) \quad \left[\because \frac{a}{\sin A} = \frac{b}{\sin B} = \frac{c}{\sin C} = 2R\right]$$

$$= \frac{1}{2} + \frac{abc}{8R^2 s}$$

$$= \frac{1}{2} + \frac{4R\Delta}{8R^2 s} \; \frac{1}{2} + \frac{r}{2R}$$

$$= \frac{1}{2}\left(1 + \frac{r}{R}\right) \le \frac{1}{2}\left(1 + \frac{1}{2}\right) = \frac{3}{4} \quad \left[\because \frac{r}{R} \le \frac{1}{2}\right]$$

Hence, $$\frac{a\cos^2\frac{A}{2} + b\cos^2\frac{B}{2} + c\cos^2\frac{C}{2}}{a + b + c} \le \frac{3}{4}$$

$$\therefore \quad 120 \times \frac{\left(a\cos^2\frac{A}{2} + b\cos^2\frac{B}{2} + c\cos^2\frac{C}{2}\right)}{a + b + c} \le 120 \times \frac{3}{4} = 90$$

61. Let $AB = n$, $AC = n + 1$, $BC = n + 2$

Further,

Let $A = 2C$ (since AB is the smallest and BC is largest)

By sine rule, we have

$$\frac{\sin A}{n + 2} = \frac{\sin B}{n + 1} = \frac{\sin C}{n}$$

$\because$ $A = 2C$

and $B = 180° - (A + C)$

$\Rightarrow$ $B = 180° - 3C$

$\therefore$ $$\frac{\sin 2C}{n + 2} = \frac{\sin 3C}{n + 1} = \frac{\sin C}{n}$$

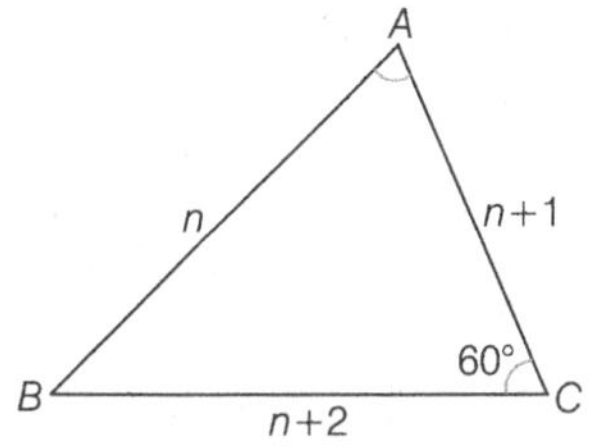

$\Rightarrow$ $$\frac{2\cos C}{n + 2} = \frac{3 - 4\sin^2 C}{n + 1} = \frac{1}{n}$$

$\therefore$ $$\cos C = \frac{n + 2}{2n} \text{ and } \sin^2 C = \frac{2n - 1}{4n}$$

$\therefore$ $$\left(\frac{n + 2}{2n}\right)^2 + \left(\frac{2n - 1}{4n}\right) = 1$$

$\Rightarrow$ $n^2 - 3n - 4 = 0$

$\therefore$ $n = 4, n = -1$

$\Rightarrow$ $n = 4, n \ne -1$

Then, sides are 4, 5, 6.

$\therefore$ Two times of largest side is 12.

62. $A + B + C = \pi$

Given, $C = 2A$

$\Rightarrow$ $B = \pi - 3A$

As $0 < C < \pi \Rightarrow 0 < 2A < \pi \Rightarrow 0 < A < \frac{\pi}{2}$

By sine rule, $$\frac{a}{\sin A} = \frac{b}{\sin B}$$

$\Rightarrow$ $$\frac{a}{\sin A} = \frac{2a}{\sin(\pi - 3A)}$$

$\Rightarrow$ $$\frac{a}{1} = \frac{2a}{3 - 4\sin^2 A} \Rightarrow 3 - 4\sin^2 A = 2$$

$\Rightarrow$ $$\sin^2 A = \frac{1}{4} \text{ or } \sin A = \frac{1}{2} \quad [\because A > 0]$$

$\Rightarrow$ $$A = \frac{\pi}{6} \text{ or } \frac{5\pi}{6}$$

But $\quad 0 < A < \dfrac{\pi}{2}$

$\Rightarrow \quad A = \dfrac{\pi}{6}, \angle B = \dfrac{\pi}{2}$ and $\angle C = \dfrac{\pi}{3}$

$\Rightarrow \quad a^2 + b^2 + c^2 = 4R^2[\sin^2 A + \sin^2 B + \sin^2 C]$

$$= 4R^2\left[\sin^2\frac{\pi}{6} + \sin^2\frac{\pi}{2} + \sin^2\frac{\pi}{3}\right]$$

$$= 4R^2\left[\frac{1}{4} + 1 + \frac{3}{4}\right] = 8R^2$$

$\Rightarrow \quad \dfrac{a^2 + b^2 + c^2}{(R/2)^2} = 32$

63. (A) → (r), (B) → (p), (C) → (s), (D) → (q)

(A) $2(r + R) = 2\left((s - c)\tan\dfrac{C}{2} + \dfrac{c}{2}\right)$

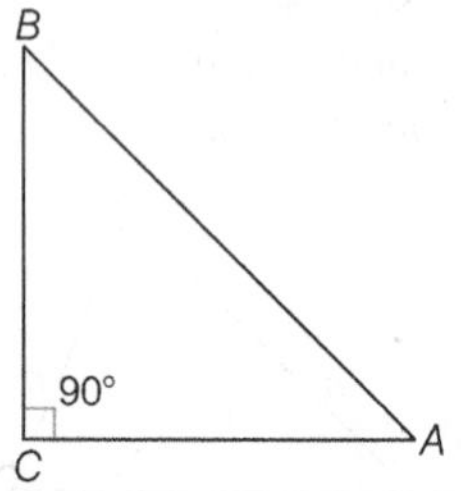

$$= 2\left(s - \frac{c}{2}\right) = a + b$$

(B) $\sin C = \dfrac{l}{b}$ ...(i)

$\sin B = \dfrac{n}{a}$ ...(ii)

$\sin A = \dfrac{m}{c}$ ...(iii)

$$2R\left(\frac{bl}{c}\right) + 2R\left(\frac{cm}{a}\right) + 2R\left(\frac{an}{b}\right) = \frac{c}{\sin C}\frac{bl}{c} + \frac{a}{\sin A}\frac{cm}{a} + \frac{b}{\sin B}\frac{an}{b}$$

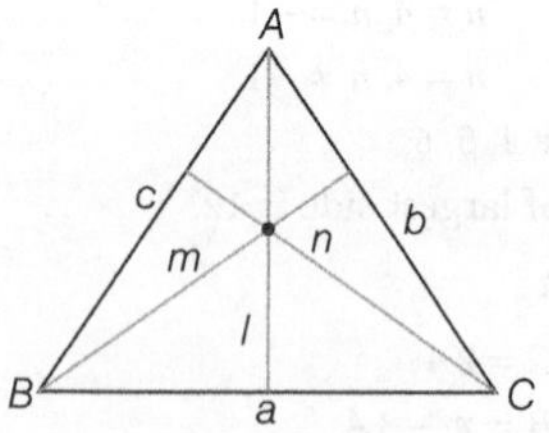

From Eqs. (i), (ii) and (iii), we get

$$2R\left(\frac{bl}{c} + \frac{cm}{a} + \frac{an}{a}\right) = a^2 + b^2 + c^2$$

$$\therefore \quad \sqrt{2R\left(\frac{bl}{c} + \frac{cm}{a} + \frac{an}{b}\right) + 2ab + 2bc + 2ac} = a + b + c$$

(C) $R = \dfrac{b}{2\sin B} = \dfrac{c}{2\sin C}$

Now, $Rb^2\sin 2C + Rc^2\sin 2B$

$$= b^2c\cos C + Rc^2b\cos B$$

$$= bc(b\cos C + c\cos B) = abc$$

(D) We have,

$$4R\sin\left(\frac{A+B}{2}\right)\sin\frac{A-B}{2}$$

$$= 2R\left(2\sin\frac{A+B}{2}\sin\frac{A-B}{2}\right)$$

$$= 2R(\cos B - \cos A)$$

$$= c\left(\frac{a}{c} - \frac{b}{c}\right) \qquad \left[\because R = \frac{c}{2}\right]$$

$$= a - b$$

64. (A) → (p), (B) → (q), (C) → (r), (D) → (s)

(A) $(b + c)^2 - a^2 = \lambda bc$

$\Rightarrow \quad b^2 + c^2 - a^2 = (\lambda - 2)bc$

$\Rightarrow \quad \dfrac{(b^2 + c^2 - a^2)}{2bc} = \dfrac{\lambda - 2}{2}$

$\Rightarrow \quad \cos A = \dfrac{\lambda - 2}{2} < 1$

$\Rightarrow \quad \lambda - 2 < 2$

$\Rightarrow \quad \lambda < 4 \Rightarrow \lambda = 3$

(B) $\tan A + \tan B + \tan C = 9$

In any triangle $\tan A + \tan B + \tan C = \tan A \tan B \tan C$

$$\frac{\tan^2 A + \tan^2 B + \tan^2 C}{3} \geq (\tan A \tan B \tan C)^{2/3}$$

$\Rightarrow \quad k \geq 3(9)^{2/3}$

$\Rightarrow \quad k \geq 9 \cdot 3^{1/3}$

(C) Since, the line joining the circumcentre to the in-centre is parallel to BC

$\therefore \quad r = R\cos A$

$\therefore \quad 4R\sin\dfrac{A}{2}\sin\dfrac{B}{2}\sin\dfrac{C}{2} = R\cos A$

$\therefore \quad -1 + \cos A + \cos B + \cos C = \cos A$

$\therefore \quad \cos B + \cos C = 1$

(D) $a = 5, b = 4$

$$\cos(A - B) = \frac{31}{32}$$

$$\tan\frac{A-B}{2} = \frac{a-b}{a+b}\cot\frac{C}{2}$$

$$= \frac{1}{9}\cot\frac{C}{2}$$

$$\cos(A - B) = \frac{1 - \tan^2\dfrac{A-B}{2}}{1 + \tan^2\dfrac{A-B}{2}}$$

$$\frac{31}{32} = \frac{1 - \dfrac{1}{81}\cot^2\dfrac{C}{2}}{1 + \dfrac{1}{81}\cot^2\dfrac{C}{2}}$$

$$31 + \frac{31}{81}\cot^2\frac{C}{2} = 32 - \frac{32}{81}\cot^2\frac{C}{2}$$

$$\frac{7}{9}\cot^2\frac{C}{2} = 1$$

$$\cot^2\frac{C}{2}=\frac{9}{7}=\tan^2\frac{C}{2}=\frac{7}{9}$$

$$\cos C=\frac{1-\tan^2\frac{C}{2}}{1+\tan^2\frac{C}{2}}=\frac{1-\frac{7}{9}}{1+\frac{7}{9}}=\frac{1}{8}$$

$\because \quad C=\sqrt{a^2+b^2-2ab\cos C}=\sqrt{25+16-5}=6$

65. Consider the following 3D figure.

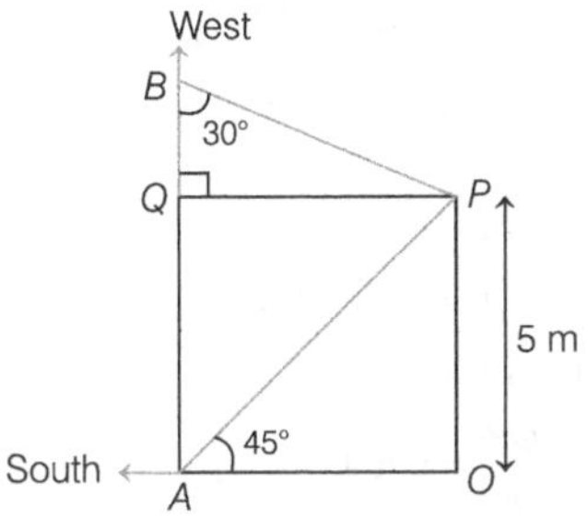

Given, $OP = 5$ m, $\angle OAP = 45°$ and $\angle QBP = 30°$

In ΔOAP, $\tan 45° = \frac{OP}{OA} \Rightarrow OA = \frac{OP}{\tan 45°} = \frac{5}{1} = 5$ m

Similarly, In ΔQBP, $\tan 30° = \frac{QP}{QB}$

$\Rightarrow \quad QB = \frac{QP}{\tan 30°} = \frac{5}{(1/\sqrt{3})} = 5\sqrt{3}$ m

Now, $AB^2 = QB^2 + QA^2 = 25 + 75$

$\Rightarrow \quad AB = \sqrt{100} \Rightarrow AB = 10$ m

66. Given, AB be a vertical wall of height 30 m and PQ be a vertical tower.

Such that $\angle BQA = \angle TAQ = 60°$ [alternate angles]

and $\angle CPA = \angle TAP = 15°$

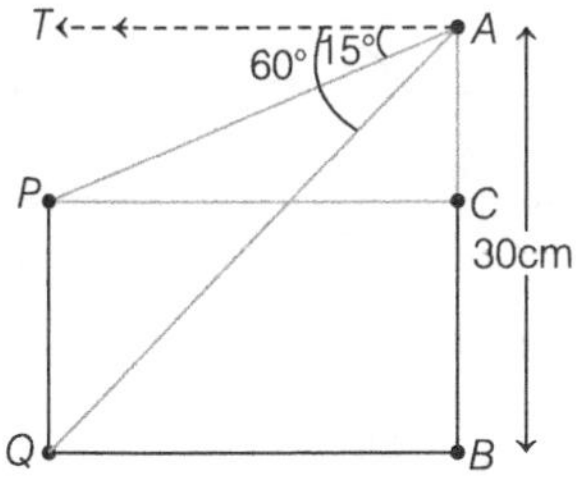

Now, $\tan 60° = \frac{AB}{BQ} = \frac{30}{BQ}$

$\Rightarrow \quad \sqrt{3} = \frac{30}{BQ} \Rightarrow BQ = \frac{30}{\sqrt{3}} = 10\sqrt{3}$

and $\tan 15° = AC/PC$

$\Rightarrow \quad 2-\sqrt{3} = \frac{AC}{10\sqrt{3}}$ $[\because PC = BQ]$

$\Rightarrow \quad AC = 10\sqrt{3}(2-\sqrt{3}) = 20\sqrt{3} - 30$

$\therefore \quad BC = AB - AC = 30 - (20\sqrt{3} - 30) = 60 - 20\sqrt{3}$

$\therefore$ Area of quadrilateal $BCPQ = BQ \times BC$

$= 10\sqrt{3} \times (60 - 20\sqrt{3})$

$= 10(60\sqrt{3} - 60) = 600(\sqrt{3} - 1)\text{ m}^2$

67. $\cos A + 2\cos B + \cos C = 2$

$\Rightarrow \frac{b^2+c^2-a^2}{2bc} + 2\cdot\frac{a^2+c^2-b^2}{2ac} + \frac{a^2+b^2-c^2}{2ab} = 2$

$\Rightarrow \frac{3b^2+120+116b-2b^3+7b^2-280}{42b} = 2$

$\Rightarrow \quad b^3 - 5b^2 - 16b + 80 = 0$

$\Rightarrow \quad (b-5)(b^2-16) = 0$

$\Rightarrow \quad b = \pm 4, 5$

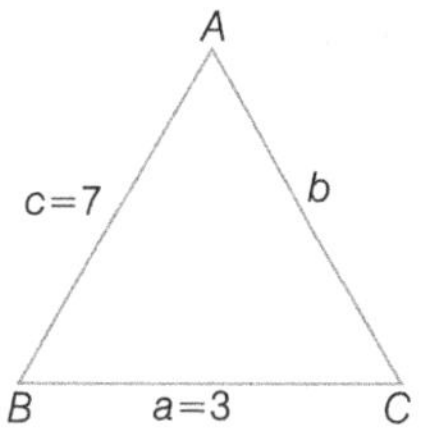

But, $b > 0$.

Also, $a + b > c$

So, $b \neq -4, 4 \Rightarrow b = 5$

$\therefore \cos A - \cos C = \frac{b^2+40}{14b} - \frac{b^2-40}{6b} = \frac{10}{7}$

68. Any point on given line $\frac{x}{1} = \frac{y}{1} = \frac{z}{1} = \lambda$ is $(\lambda, \lambda, \lambda)$

If it intersect the given lines

$\lambda(\sin A + \sin B + \sin C) = 18$ ...(i)

and $\lambda(\sin 2A + \sin 2B + \sin 2C) = 9$ ...(ii)

On dividing Eqs. (ii) by Eq. (i), we get

$$\frac{\sin 2A + \sin 2B + \sin 2C}{\sin A + \sin B + \sin C} = \frac{9}{18} = \frac{1}{2}$$

$\Rightarrow \quad \frac{4\sin A\sin B\sin C}{4\cos\frac{A}{2}\cos\frac{B}{2}\cos\frac{C}{2}} = \frac{1}{2}$

$\Rightarrow \frac{\left(2\sin\frac{A}{2}\cos\frac{A}{2}\,2\sin\frac{B}{2}\cos\frac{B}{2}\,2\sin\frac{C}{2}\cos\frac{C}{2}\right)}{\cos\frac{A}{2}\cos\frac{B}{2}\cos\frac{C}{2}} = \frac{1}{2}$

$\Rightarrow \quad 8\sin\frac{A}{2}\cdot\sin\frac{B}{2}\sin\frac{C}{2} = \frac{1}{2}$

$\Rightarrow \quad \sin\frac{A}{2}\sin\frac{B}{2}\sin\frac{C}{2} = \frac{1}{16}$

$\therefore \quad 80\left(\sin\frac{A}{2}\sin\frac{B}{2}\sin\frac{C}{2}\right) = \frac{1}{16} \times 80 = 5$

69.

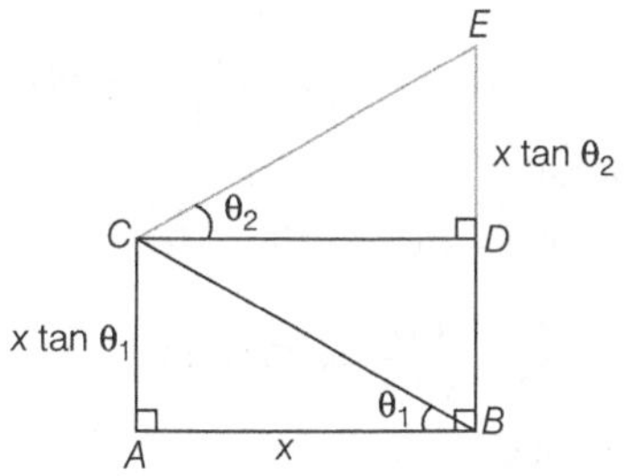

We have, $\theta_1 + \theta_2 = \frac{\pi}{2}$ and $\sqrt{3}(BE) = 4AB$

Let $AB = x$ unit; $AC = x\tan\theta_1$

$ED = x\tan\theta_2$; $BE = BD + DE$

$$\frac{4}{\sqrt{3}}x = x(\tan\theta_1 + \tan\theta_2) \qquad [\because \sqrt{3}BE = 4AB]$$

$$\frac{4}{\sqrt{3}} = \tan\theta_1 + \tan\left(\frac{\pi}{2} - \theta_1\right) \qquad [\because \theta_1 + \theta_2 = \pi/2]$$

$$\tan\theta_1 + \cot\theta_1 = \frac{4}{\sqrt{3}} \Rightarrow \tan\theta_1 = \sqrt{3}, \frac{1}{\sqrt{3}}$$

$\Rightarrow$ If $\theta_1 = \frac{\pi}{6}$, then $\theta_2 = \frac{\pi}{3}$

and if $\theta_2 = \frac{\pi}{3}$, then $\theta_2 = \pi/6$

As, $\frac{\theta_2}{\theta_1}$ is largest, $\theta_1 = \frac{\pi}{6}$ and $\theta_2 = \frac{\pi}{3}$

Area of $\Delta CAB = \frac{1}{2} \times x \times x\tan\theta_1$

$$\Rightarrow \frac{x^2\tan\theta_1}{2} = 2\sqrt{3} - 3 \Rightarrow x^2 = \frac{2(2\sqrt{3}-3)}{\tan\frac{\pi}{6}} = 12 - 6\sqrt{3}$$

$$\Rightarrow x = 3 - \sqrt{3}$$

Also, $CE = \sqrt{x^2 + x^2\tan^2\frac{\pi}{3}} = (3-\sqrt{3}) \times 2 = 6 - 2\sqrt{3}$

Perimeter of $\Delta CED = CD + DE + CE$

$$= (3-\sqrt{3}) + (3-\sqrt{3})\tan\frac{\pi}{3} + 6 - 2\sqrt{3}$$

$$= 3 - \sqrt{3} + 3\sqrt{3} - 3 + 6 - 2\sqrt{3} = 6$$

70. In ΔBAC, $90°$ at A

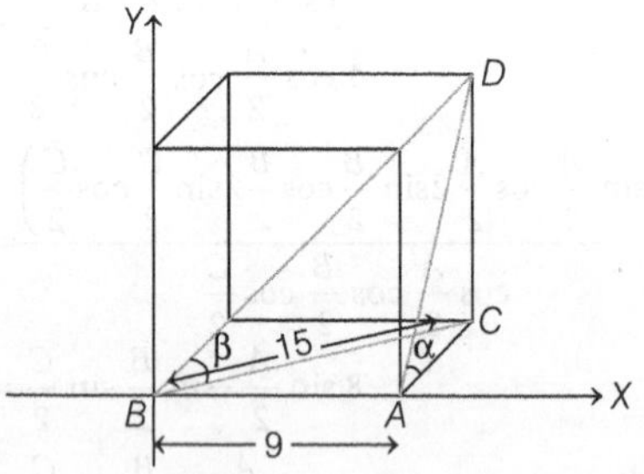

$$\Rightarrow 9^2 + AC^2 = (15)^2$$

$$\Rightarrow AC = 12$$

Also, $\beta = \cos^{-1}\frac{3}{\sqrt{13}}$

$$\cos\beta = \frac{3}{\sqrt{13}} = \frac{15}{5\sqrt{13}} \Rightarrow BD = 5\sqrt{13}$$

In ΔBCD, $90°$ at C

$$\sin\beta = \sqrt{1 - \cos^2\beta} = \frac{2}{\sqrt{13}}$$

$$\Rightarrow \frac{2}{\sqrt{13}} = \frac{CD}{5\sqrt{13}} \Rightarrow CD = 10$$

In ΔACD, $90°$ at C

$$\cot\alpha = \frac{AC}{CD} = \frac{12}{10} = \frac{6}{5}$$

71.

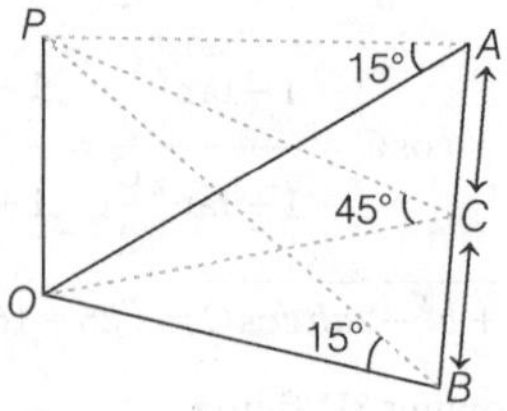

$$AC = \frac{AB}{2} = 8$$

In right angled ΔPOA,

$$\frac{OP}{OA} = \tan 15°$$

$$\Rightarrow OA = OP\cot 15°$$

In right angle ΔPOC,

$$\frac{OP}{OC} = \tan 45°$$

$$\Rightarrow OP = OC$$

Now, $OP = OC = \sqrt{OA^2 - 8^2}$ $[\because AC = 8]$

$$\Rightarrow OP^2 = OP^2\cot^2 15° - 64$$

$$\Rightarrow OP^2 = \frac{32}{\sqrt{3}}(2 - \sqrt{3})$$

72. Here, $AP = \frac{h}{\tan 2\alpha}$, $d = \sqrt{7}\,h$

$AQ = AP + d$

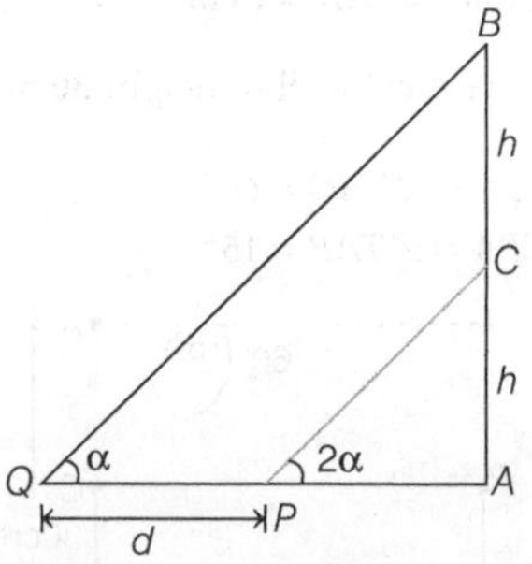

$$AQ = \frac{h}{\tan 2\alpha} + \sqrt{7}h$$

Also, $AQ = \frac{2h}{\tan\alpha}$

$$\therefore \frac{2h}{\tan\alpha} = \frac{h}{\tan 2\alpha} + \sqrt{7}h$$

$$\Rightarrow \frac{2}{\tan\alpha} = \frac{1-\tan^2\alpha}{2\tan\alpha} + \frac{2\sqrt{7}\tan\alpha}{2\tan\alpha}$$

$$\Rightarrow 4 = 1 - \tan^2\alpha + 2\sqrt{7}\tan\alpha$$

$$\Rightarrow \tan^2\alpha - 2\sqrt{7}\tan\alpha + 3 = 0$$

$$\Rightarrow \tan\alpha = \frac{2\sqrt{7} \pm \sqrt{28-12}}{2} = \sqrt{7} \pm 2$$

$$\therefore \tan\alpha = \sqrt{7} - 2$$

[$\because$ for $\tan\alpha = \sqrt{7} + 2$, 2α becomes obtuse]

73.

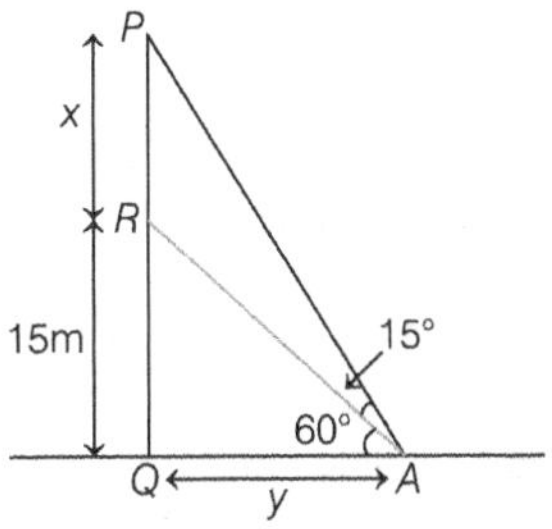

Given, $\angle RAQ = 60°$ and $\angle PAR = 15°$ and $RQ = 15$ m

Let $PR = x$ m and $QA = y$ m

Now, in ΔPQA, $\dfrac{x+15}{y} = \tan 75°$ ... (i)

and ΔRQA, $\dfrac{15}{y} = \tan 60°$ ... (ii)

From Eqs. (i) and (ii), we get

$$\frac{x+15}{15} = \frac{\tan 75°}{\tan 60°} = \frac{\tan(45°+30°)}{\tan 60°}$$

$$= \frac{\dfrac{\tan 45° + \tan 30°}{1 - \tan 45° \tan 30°}}{\tan 60°}$$

$$\Rightarrow \quad \frac{x+15}{15} = \frac{(1+\sqrt{3})}{(-1+\sqrt{3})\sqrt{3}}$$

$$\Rightarrow \quad \frac{x+15}{15} = \frac{(1+\sqrt{3})(1+\sqrt{3})}{\sqrt{3}(-1+\sqrt{3})(1+\sqrt{3})}$$

$$= \frac{4+2\sqrt{3}}{\sqrt{3}(-1+3)} = \frac{(2+\sqrt{3})}{\sqrt{3}} = \frac{(2+\sqrt{3})\sqrt{3}}{3}$$

$$\Rightarrow \quad \frac{x+15}{15} = \frac{2\sqrt{3}+3}{3} \Rightarrow x = 10\sqrt{3} \text{ m}$$

Thus, height of the tower $= (15 + 10\sqrt{3})\text{m} = 5(2\sqrt{3}+3)\text{m}$

74. Let height of the tower be h m.

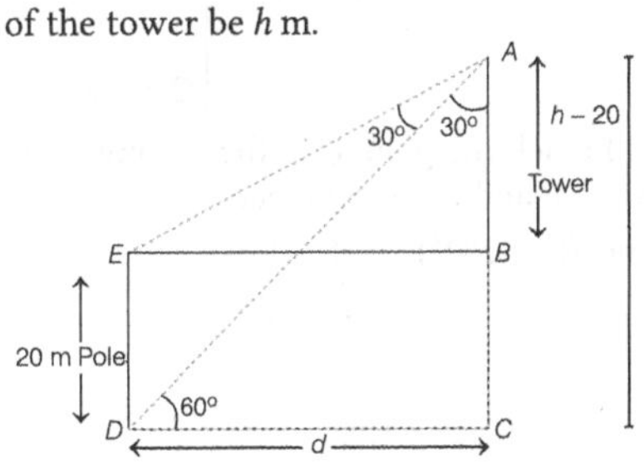

From ΔABE, $\tan 30° = \dfrac{h-20}{d} \Rightarrow \dfrac{1}{\sqrt{3}} = \dfrac{h-20}{d}$

$\Rightarrow \quad d = \sqrt{3}(h-20)$ ...(i)

From ΔACD, $\tan 60° = \dfrac{h}{d} \Rightarrow \sqrt{3} = \dfrac{h}{d}$

$\Rightarrow \quad d = \dfrac{h}{\sqrt{3}}$ ...(ii)

From Eqs. (i) and (ii), we get

$$\sqrt{3}(h-20) = \frac{h}{\sqrt{3}}$$

$\Rightarrow \quad 3(h-20) = h$

$\Rightarrow \quad 3h - h = 60 \Rightarrow h = 30$ m

75.

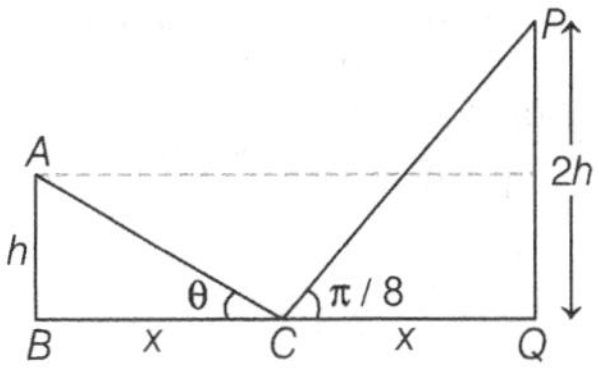

Let $BC = CQ = x$ and $AB = h$ and $PQ = 2h$

In ΔABC, $\tan\theta = \dfrac{h}{x}$ ...(i)

In ΔPQC, $\tan\dfrac{\pi}{8} = \dfrac{2h}{x}$ ...(ii)

Dividing Eq. (i) by Eq. (ii), we get

$$\frac{\tan\theta}{\tan\left(\dfrac{\pi}{8}\right)} = \frac{1}{2}$$

$$\Rightarrow \quad \tan\theta = \frac{1}{2}\tan\left(\frac{\pi}{8}\right) = \frac{1}{2}(\sqrt{2}-1)$$

$$\Rightarrow \quad \tan^2\theta = \frac{1}{4}(3-2\sqrt{2})$$

76. Given relation is

$$\frac{a+b}{7} = \frac{b+c}{8} = \frac{c+a}{9} = k$$

$$a+b = 7k,\ b+c = 8k \text{ and } a+c = 9k$$

Add above three equations

$$a+b+c = 12k$$

After solving all the equations, we get

$$a = 4k,\ b = 3k \text{ and } c = 5k$$

Now, applying Heron's formula to find the area of triangle.

$$s = \frac{a+b+c}{2} = \frac{4k+3k+5k}{2} = 6k$$

$$\Delta = \sqrt{s(s-a)(s-b)(s-c)}$$

$$= \sqrt{6k(6k-4k)(6k-3k)(6k-5k)}$$

$$= \sqrt{6k(2k)(3k)(k)}$$

$$= 6k^2$$

We know that

$$R = \frac{abc}{4\Delta} = \frac{(4k)(5k)(3k)}{4\times 6k^2} = \frac{5k}{2}$$

and $\quad r = \dfrac{\Delta}{s} = \dfrac{6k^2}{6k} = k$

So, $\quad \dfrac{R}{r} = \dfrac{\dfrac{5k}{2}}{k} = \dfrac{5}{2}$

77.

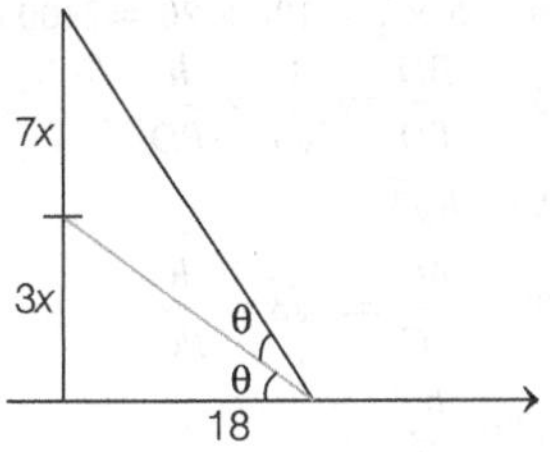

Let height of pole be $10x$.

Now, $\tan\theta = \frac{3x}{18} = \frac{x}{6}$ and $\tan 2\theta = \frac{10x}{18}$

$\Rightarrow \frac{2\tan\theta}{1-\tan^2\theta} = \frac{10x}{18}$ use $\tan\theta = \frac{x}{6}$

$\Rightarrow x = \sqrt{\frac{72}{5}}$

Height of pole $= 10x = 12\sqrt{10}$

78.

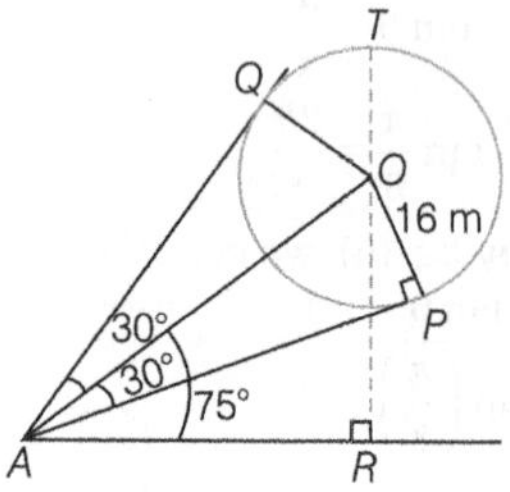

In ΔAOP, $\sin 30° = \frac{16}{OA}$

$\Rightarrow OA = 32$ m

and in ΔAOR, $\sin 75° = \frac{OR}{OA}$

$\Rightarrow \sin(45° + 30°) = \frac{OR}{32}$

$\Rightarrow \sin 45° \cdot \cos 30° + \cos 45° \cdot \sin 30° = \frac{OR}{32}$

$\Rightarrow \frac{1}{\sqrt{2}} \cdot \frac{\sqrt{3}}{2} + \frac{1}{\sqrt{2}} \times \frac{1}{2} = \frac{OR}{32}$

$\Rightarrow 32\frac{(\sqrt{3}+1)}{2\sqrt{2}} = OR$

$\Rightarrow OR = 8(\sqrt{6} + \sqrt{2})$

Hence, the height $TR = 8\sqrt{6} + 8\sqrt{2} + 16 = 8(\sqrt{6} + \sqrt{2} + 2)$ m

79. Given, angle of elevation are 60° and then 30°.

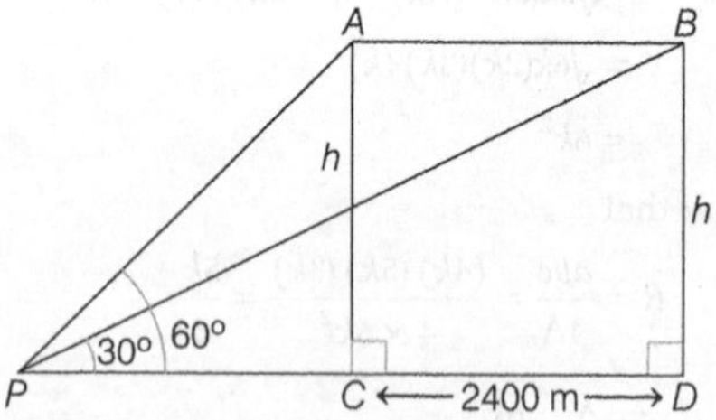

Also, in 20 sec plane covers the distance from A to B with speed 432 km/h.

$\because 432 \times \frac{5}{18}$ m/sec $= 120$ m/sec

$\therefore AB = \text{distance} = S \times T = 120 \times 20 = 2400$ m

In ΔPBD, $\tan 30° = \frac{BD}{PD} \Rightarrow \frac{1}{\sqrt{3}} = \frac{h}{PD}$

$\Rightarrow PD = h\sqrt{3}$

In ΔPAC, $\tan 60° = \frac{AC}{PC} \Rightarrow \sqrt{3} = \frac{h}{PC}$

$\Rightarrow PC = \frac{h}{\sqrt{3}}$

Now, $CD = PD - PC$

$\Rightarrow 2400 = h\sqrt{3} - \frac{h}{\sqrt{3}}$ $[\because AB = CD]$

$\Rightarrow 2400 = h\left(\frac{3-1}{\sqrt{3}}\right)$

$\therefore h = \frac{2400 \times \sqrt{3}}{2} = 1200 \times \sqrt{3}$

$\therefore$ Required height $= 1200\sqrt{3}$ m

80. $\frac{\sin A}{\sin B} = \frac{\sin(A-C)}{\sin(C-B)}$

Since, A, B and C are angles of triangle, then

$A + B + C = \pi \Rightarrow A = \pi - (B + C)$

On taking sine both side, we get

$\sin A = \sin(B + C)$ ...(i)

Similarly, $\sin B = \sin(A + C)$ ...(ii)

From Eqs. (i) and (ii), we get

$\frac{\sin(B+C)}{\sin(A+C)} = \frac{\sin(A-C)}{\sin(C-B)}$

$\Rightarrow \sin(C + B) \cdot \sin(C - B) = \sin(A - C)\sin(A + C)$

$\Rightarrow \sin^2 C - \sin^2 B = \sin^2 A - \sin^2 C$

$\Rightarrow 2\sin^2 C = \sin^2 A + \sin^2 B$

Now, by sine rule, $2c^2 = a^2 + b^2$

$\Rightarrow b^2, c^2$ and a^2 are in AP.

81.

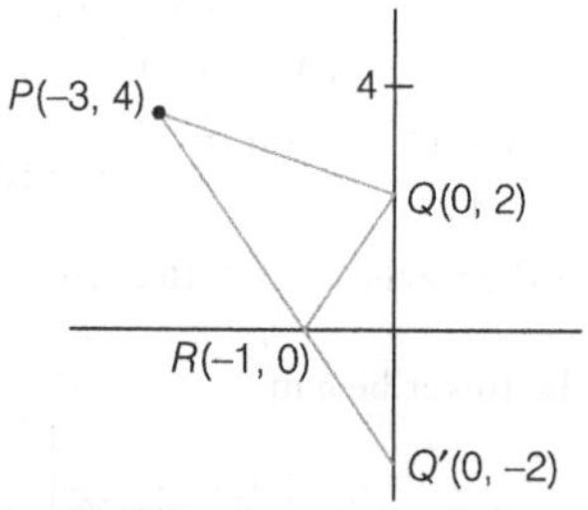

Man will reach the point Q in the minimum time if reflection of Q i.e. Q', P and R are collinear.

$50(PR^2 + RQ^2) = 50(20 + 5)$

$= 50(25) = 1250$

82.

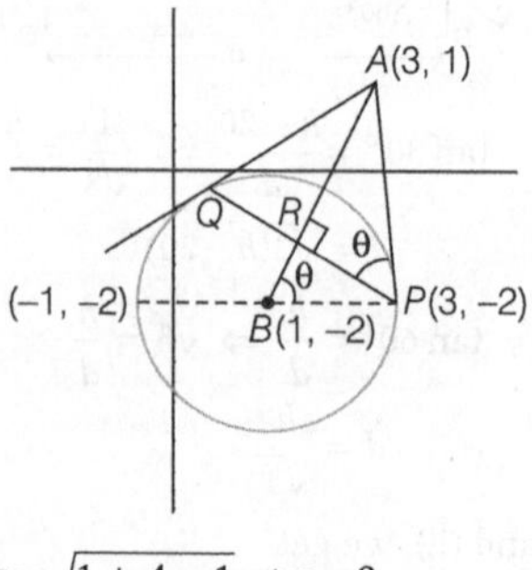

Radius $= \sqrt{1 + 4 - 1} \Rightarrow r = 2$

$AP = \sqrt{(3-3)^2 + (1+2)^2} = 3$

and $BP = r = 2$

$$\tan\theta = \frac{AP}{BP} = \frac{3}{2}$$

$$\frac{\text{Area } \Delta APQ}{\text{Area } \Delta BPQ} = \frac{\frac{1}{2} AR \times PQ}{\frac{1}{2} RB \times PQ} = \frac{AR}{RB} = \frac{3\sin\theta}{2\cos\theta} = \frac{9}{4}$$

$$\Rightarrow 8\left(\frac{\text{Area } \Delta APQ}{\text{Area } \Delta BPQ}\right) = 18$$

83. Let point of contact be $(b\cos\theta, 2a\sin\theta)$.

Equation of tangent to the given ellipse is,

$$\frac{x\cos\theta}{b} + \frac{y\sin\theta}{2a} = 1$$

At $x = 0 \Rightarrow y = \dfrac{2a}{\sin\theta}$

At $y = 0 \Rightarrow x = \dfrac{b}{\cos\theta}$

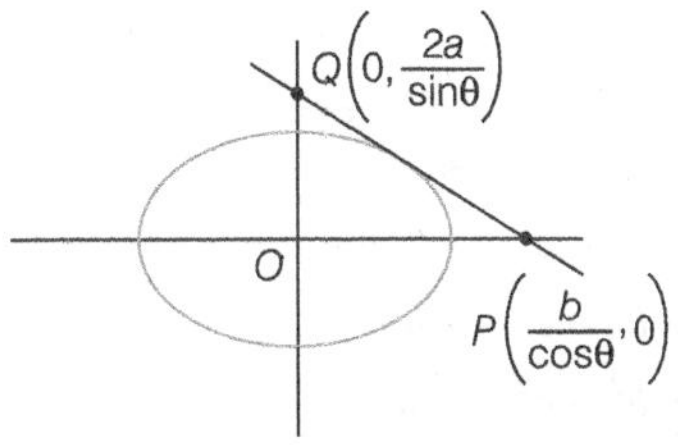

So, area $(\Delta OPQ) = \frac{1}{2} \times \frac{b}{\cos\theta} \times \frac{2a}{\sin\theta} = \frac{2ab}{\sin 2\theta} \geq 2ab$

$\Rightarrow \quad k = 2$

84. Let height $(AB) = h$ m, $CD = x$ m, $ED = y$ m and $CE = 80$ m

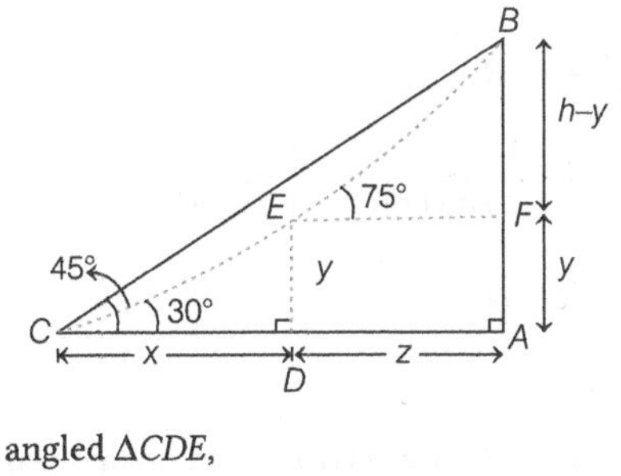

In right angled ΔCDE,

$$\sin 30° = \frac{y}{80} \Rightarrow y = 40 \quad \text{...(i)}$$

$$\cos 30° = \frac{x}{80} \Rightarrow x = 40\sqrt{3} \quad \text{...(ii)}$$

Now, in ΔBEF, $\tan 75° = \dfrac{h-y}{h-x} \Rightarrow (2+\sqrt{3}) = \dfrac{h-40}{h-40\sqrt{3}}$

[putting the value of x and y from Eqs. (i) and (ii)]

$\Rightarrow \quad (2+\sqrt{3})(h - 40\sqrt{3}) = h - 40$

$\Rightarrow \quad 2h - 80\sqrt{3} + \sqrt{3}h - 120 = h - 40$

$\Rightarrow \quad h + \sqrt{3}h = 80 + 80\sqrt{3}$

$\Rightarrow \quad (\sqrt{3}+1)h = 80(\sqrt{3}+1)$

$\therefore \quad h = 80$ m

85. Given, a ladder of length $l = 2$m leans against a vertical wall. Now, the top of ladder begins to slide down the wall at the rate 25 cm/s.

Let the rate at which bottom of the ladder slides away from the wall on the horizontal ground be $\dfrac{dx}{dt}$ cm/s.

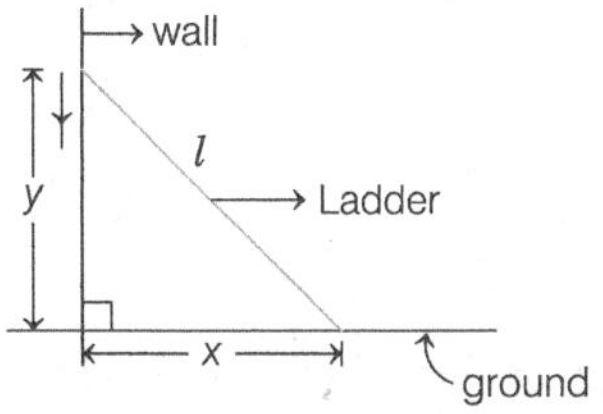

$\because \quad x^2 + y^2 = l^2$ [by Pythagoras theorem]

$\Rightarrow \quad x^2 + y^2 = 4$ [$\because l = 2$ m] ... (i)

On differentiating both sides of Eq. (i) w.r.t. 't', we get

$$2x\frac{dx}{dt} + 2y\frac{dy}{dt} = 0$$

$$\Rightarrow \quad \frac{dx}{dt} = -\left(\frac{y}{x}\right)\frac{dy}{dt} \quad \text{... (ii)}$$

From Eq. (i), when $y = 1$ m, we get

$$x^2 + 1^2 = 4 \Rightarrow x^2 = 3$$

$\Rightarrow \quad x = \sqrt{3}$ m [$\because x > 0$]

On substituting $x = \sqrt{3}$ m and $y = 1$ m in Eq. (ii), we get

$$\frac{dx}{dt} = -\frac{1}{\sqrt{3}}\left(-\frac{25}{100}\right) \text{m/s} \quad \left[\because \frac{dy}{dt} = -25 \text{ cm/sec}\right]$$

$$= \frac{25}{\sqrt{3}} \text{ cm/s}$$

86. Let the first pole AB having height 20 m and second pole PQ having height 80 m and $\angle PBQ = \alpha$, $\angle AQB = \beta$

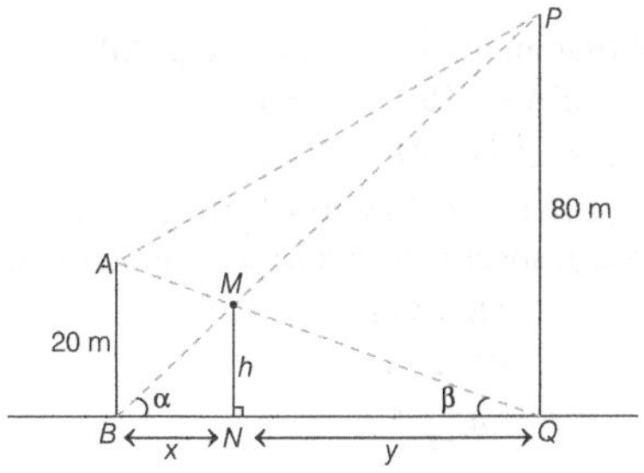

and $MN = h$ m is the height of intersection point from the horizontal plane

$\because \quad \tan\alpha = \dfrac{h}{x} = \dfrac{80}{x+y}$ [In ΔMNB and ΔPQB] ...(i)

and $\quad \tan\beta = \dfrac{h}{y} = \dfrac{20}{x+y}$ [in ΔMNQ and ΔABQ] ...(ii)

From Eqs. (i) and (ii), we get

$$\frac{y}{x} = 4 \Rightarrow y = 4x \quad \text{...(iii)}$$

From Eqs. (i) and (iii), we get

$$\frac{h}{x} = \frac{80}{x+4x} \Rightarrow h = \frac{80}{5} = 16 \text{ m}$$

87. According to given information, we have the following figure

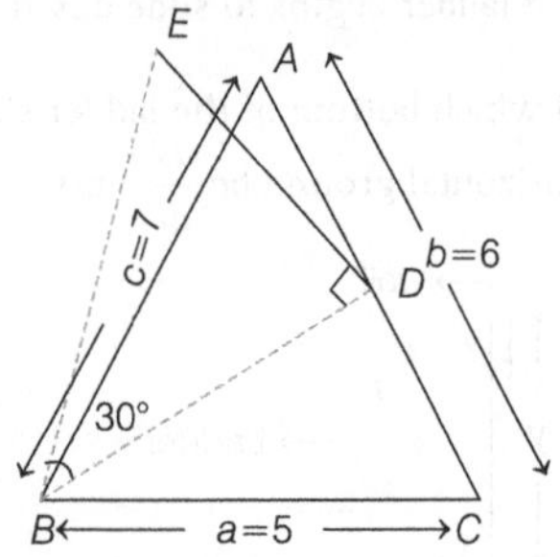

Clearly, length of $BD = \frac{1}{2}\sqrt{2a^2 + 2c^2 - b^2}$,

[using Appollonius theorem]

where, $c = AB = 7$, $a = BC = 5$ and $b = CA = 6$

$\therefore \quad BD = \frac{1}{2}\sqrt{2 \times 25 + 2 \times 49 - 36}$

$= \frac{1}{2}\sqrt{112} = \frac{1}{2}4\sqrt{7} = 2\sqrt{7}$

Now, let $ED = h$ be the height of the lamp post.

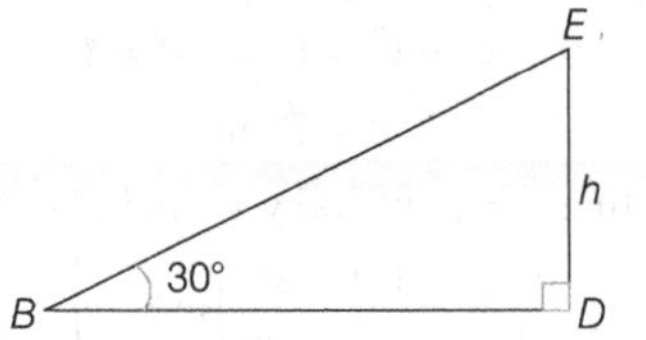

Then, in ΔBDE, $\tan 30° = h / BD$

$\Rightarrow \quad \frac{1}{\sqrt{3}} = \frac{h}{2\sqrt{7}}$

$\Rightarrow \quad h = \frac{2\sqrt{7}}{\sqrt{3}} = \frac{2}{3}\sqrt{21}$

88. It is given that angles of a ΔABC are in AP.

So, $\quad \angle A + \angle B + \angle C = 180°$

$\Rightarrow \quad \angle B - d + \angle B + \angle B + d = 180°$

[if $\angle A$, $\angle B$ and $\angle C$ are in AP, then it taken as $\angle B - d$, $\angle B$, $\angle B + d$ respectively, where d is common difference of AP]

$\Rightarrow \quad 3\angle B = 180°$

$\Rightarrow \quad \angle B = 60° \quad$ ...(i)

and $\quad \frac{a}{b} = \frac{1}{\sqrt{3}} \quad$ [given]

$\Rightarrow \quad \frac{\sin A}{\sin B} = \frac{1}{\sqrt{3}} \quad \left[\text{by sine rule, } \frac{\sin A}{a} = \frac{\sin B}{b} = \frac{\sin C}{c}\right]$

$\Rightarrow \quad \frac{\sin A}{\frac{\sqrt{3}}{2}} = \frac{1}{\sqrt{3}} \quad \left[\because \sin B = \sin 60° = \frac{\sqrt{3}}{2}\right]$

$\Rightarrow \quad \sin A = \frac{1}{2}$

$\Rightarrow \quad \angle A = 30°$

So, $\quad \angle C = 90°$

$\therefore$ From sine rule,

$\frac{a}{\sin A} = \frac{b}{\sin B} = \frac{c}{\sin C}$

$\Rightarrow \quad \frac{a}{\frac{1}{2}} = \frac{b}{\frac{\sqrt{3}}{2}} = \frac{4}{1} \quad [\because c = 4 \text{ cm}]$

$\Rightarrow \quad a = 2 \text{ cm}, b = 2\sqrt{3} \text{ cm}$

$\therefore \quad$ Area of $\Delta ABC = \frac{1}{2} ab\sin C = \frac{1}{2} \times 2 \times 2\sqrt{3} \times 1 = 2\sqrt{3}$ sq cm

89. We know that

$$\frac{a}{\sin A} = \frac{b}{\sin B} = \frac{c}{\sin C} = 2R$$

and given that, $a + b = x$, $ab = y$ and $x^2 - c^2 = y$

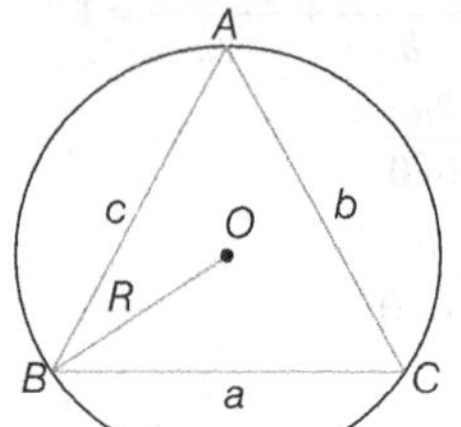

$\therefore \quad (a + b)^2 - c^2 = ab$

$\Rightarrow \quad a^2 + b^2 - c^2 = -2ab + ab$

$\Rightarrow \quad a^2 + b^2 - c^2 = -ab$

$\Rightarrow \quad \frac{a^2 + b^2 - c^2}{2ab} = \frac{-ab}{2ab} = -\frac{1}{2}$

$\therefore \quad \cos C = -\frac{1}{2}$

$\Rightarrow \quad C = 120°$

$\left[\text{using cosine rule, } \cos C = \frac{a^2 + b^2 - c^2}{2ab}\right]$

Now, $\quad \frac{c}{\sin C} = 2R$

$\Rightarrow \quad R = \frac{1}{2} \frac{c}{\sin(120°)} = \frac{c}{2} \frac{2}{\sqrt{3}}$

$\therefore \quad R = \frac{c}{\sqrt{3}}$

90. Here, $\theta + \phi = \frac{\pi}{4}$

Let $A_1, A_2, A_3, \ldots, A_8$ are vertices of a regular octagon lying on a circle of radius = 2

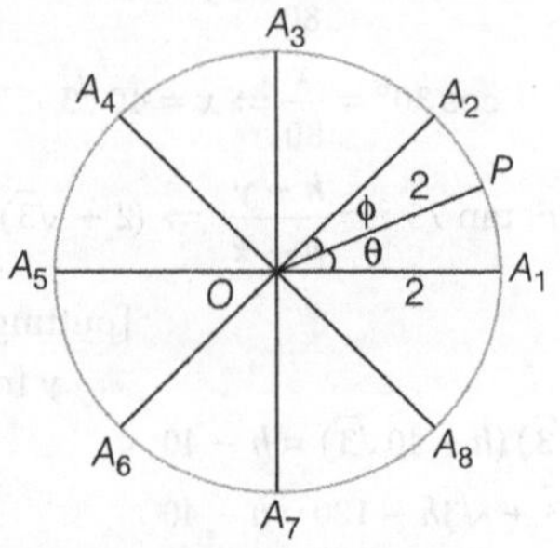

In ΔA_1OP, $\frac{PA_1}{2} = \frac{\sin \theta}{\sin\left(90° - \frac{\theta}{2}\right)} = 2\sin\left(\frac{\theta}{2}\right)$

$$\Rightarrow \quad PA_1 = 4\sin\left(\frac{\theta}{2}\right) = \alpha_1 \text{ (say)}$$

$$PA_8 = 4\sin\left(\frac{\pi}{8}+\frac{\theta}{2}\right) = \alpha_8$$

$$PA_7 = 4\sin\left(\frac{\pi}{4}+\frac{\theta}{2}\right) = \alpha_7$$

$$PA_6 = 4\sin\left(\frac{3\pi}{8}+\frac{\theta}{2}\right) = \alpha_6$$

Similarly, $PA_2 = 4\sin\left(\frac{\phi}{2}\right) = \alpha_2$

$$PA_3 = 4\sin\left(\frac{\pi}{8}+\frac{\phi}{2}\right) = \alpha_3$$

$$PA_4 = 4\sin\left(\frac{\pi}{4}+\frac{\phi}{2}\right) = \alpha_4$$

$$PA_5 = 4\sin\left(\frac{3\pi}{8}+\frac{\phi}{2}\right) = \alpha_5$$

Let $(PA_1)\cdot(PA_2)\ldots(PA_7)(PA_8) = \alpha_1\cdot\alpha_2\cdot\alpha_3\ldots\alpha_7\alpha_8 = M$

$$M = 4^8\cdot\sin\left(\frac{\theta}{2}\right)\cdot\sin\left(\frac{3\pi}{8}+\frac{\phi}{2}\right)$$

$$\cdot\sin\left(\frac{\pi}{8}+\frac{\theta}{2}\right)\cdot\sin\left(\frac{\pi}{4}+\frac{\phi}{2}\right)\cdot\sin\left(\frac{\pi}{4}+\frac{\theta}{2}\right)$$

$$\cdot\sin\left(\frac{\pi}{8}+\frac{\phi}{2}\right)\cdot\sin\left(\frac{3\pi}{8}+\frac{\theta}{2}\right)\cdot\sin\left(\frac{\phi}{2}\right)$$

$$= 4^8\left[\sin\frac{\theta}{2}\cdot\cos\frac{\theta}{2}\cdot\sin\left(\frac{\pi}{8}+\frac{\theta}{2}\right)\right.$$

$$\cdot\cos\left(\frac{\pi}{8}+\frac{\theta}{2}\right)\cdot\sin\left(\frac{\pi}{4}+\frac{\theta}{2}\right)$$

$$\left.\cos\left(\frac{\pi}{4}+\frac{\theta}{2}\right)\cdot\sin\left(\frac{3\pi}{8}+\frac{\theta}{2}\right)\cdot\cos\left(\frac{3\pi}{8}+\frac{\theta}{2}\right)\right]$$

$$= 4^8\left[\frac{\sin\theta\cdot\sin\left(\frac{\pi}{4}+\theta\right)\cdot\sin\left(\frac{\pi}{4}+\theta\right)\cdot\sin\left(\frac{3\pi}{4}+\theta\right)}{2^4}\right]$$

$$= 4^6\left[\sin\theta\cdot\cos\theta\cdot\sin\left(\frac{\pi}{4}+\theta\right)\cdot\cos\left(\frac{\pi}{4}+\theta\right)\right]$$

$$= 4^6\left[\frac{\sin 2\theta\cdot\sin\left(\frac{\pi}{2}+2\theta\right)}{4}\right]$$

$$\Rightarrow \quad M = 4^5\cdot\left[\frac{\sin(4\theta)}{2}\right] = 2^9\cdot\sin 4\theta$$

Now, when $\sin 4\theta = 1 \Rightarrow \theta = \frac{\pi}{8}$, then M will be maximum.

Hence, $(M)_{\max} = 2^9 = 512$

91. **Method I** Let sides be $\alpha - d, \alpha, \alpha + d$ which are in AP.

Since, $(\alpha + d)$ is largest side, so its opposite angle is largest angle 'A'. Similarly, $(\alpha - d)$ is smallest side, then its opposite angle 'C' is smallest angle.

Given, $A - C = \frac{\pi}{2}$

and $\quad R = 1 =$ circumradius

By sine rule,

$$\frac{\alpha+d}{\sin A} = \frac{\alpha}{\sin B} = \frac{\alpha-d}{\sin C} = 2R = 2\times 1 = 2$$

From above, we get

$$\left.\begin{aligned}\sin A &= \frac{\alpha+d}{2}\\ \sin B &= \frac{\alpha}{2}\\ \sin C &= \frac{\alpha-d}{2}\end{aligned}\right\} \quad \ldots\text{(i)}$$

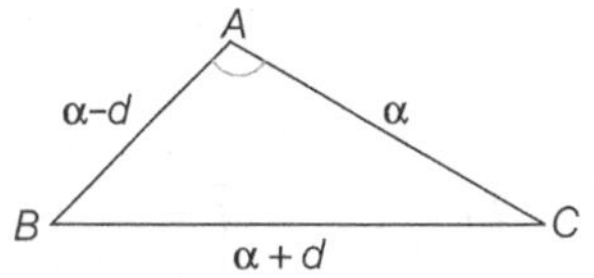

$$\because \quad A = \frac{\pi}{2} + C$$

$$\therefore \quad \sin A = \sin\left(\frac{\pi}{2}+C\right)$$

$$= \cos C = \sqrt{1-\sin^2 C}$$

$$\Rightarrow \quad \frac{\alpha+d}{2} = \sqrt{1-\left(\frac{\alpha-d}{2}\right)^2}$$

$$\Rightarrow \quad \left(\frac{\alpha+d}{2}\right)^2 = 1-\left(\frac{\alpha-d}{2}\right)^2 \quad \text{[using Eq.(i)]}$$

$$\Rightarrow \quad \frac{(\alpha+d)^2+(\alpha-d)^2}{4} = 1$$

$$\Rightarrow \quad \frac{\alpha^2+d^2+2\alpha d+\alpha^2+d^2-2\alpha d}{4} = 1$$

$$\Rightarrow \quad \frac{2(\alpha^2+d^2)}{4} = 1$$

$$\Rightarrow \quad \alpha^2+d^2 = 2 \quad \ldots\text{(ii)}$$

Using cosine rule in ΔABC;

$$\cos B = \frac{(\alpha-d)^2+(\alpha+d)^2-\alpha^2}{2(\alpha-d)(\alpha+d)}$$

$$\Rightarrow \sqrt{1-\sin^2\beta} = \frac{\alpha^2+d^2-2\alpha d+\alpha^2+d^2+2\alpha d-\alpha^2}{2(\alpha^2-d^2)}$$

$$\Rightarrow \sqrt{1-\left(\frac{\alpha}{2}\right)^2} = \frac{2(\alpha^2+d^2)-\alpha^2}{2(\alpha^2-d^2)} \quad \text{[using Eq. (i)]}$$

$$\Rightarrow \quad \frac{\sqrt{4-\alpha^2}}{2} = \frac{(2\times 2)-\alpha^2}{2(\alpha^2-d^2)} \quad \text{[using Eq. (ii)]}$$

$$\Rightarrow \quad \alpha^2-d^2 = \frac{4-\alpha^2}{\sqrt{4-\alpha^2}}$$

$$\Rightarrow \quad \alpha^2-d^2 = \sqrt{4-\alpha^2}$$

$$\Rightarrow \quad (\alpha^2-d^2)^2 = 4-\alpha^2 \quad \ldots\text{(iii)}$$

On solving Eqs. (ii) and (iii), we get

So, $$\left.\begin{aligned} \alpha^2 &= \frac{7}{4}, d^2 = \frac{1}{4} \\ \alpha^2 - d^2 &= \frac{7}{4} - \frac{1}{4} = \frac{6}{4} \end{aligned}\right\} \quad \text{...(i)}$$

Now, area of triangle $= a = \frac{1}{2} \times (\alpha - d) \times (\alpha + d) \sin B$

$$= \frac{1}{2}(\alpha^2 - d^2) \times \frac{\alpha}{2}$$

$$\Rightarrow \quad a = \frac{\alpha(\alpha^2 - d^2)}{4} \Rightarrow a = \frac{\sqrt{7}}{2} \times \frac{6}{4 \times 4} = \frac{3\sqrt{7}}{16}$$

$$\therefore \quad (64a)^2 = 1008$$

Method II

Let side lengths be $\lambda - d, \lambda, \lambda + d$.

By sine rule,

$$\frac{\lambda - d}{\sin\theta} = \frac{\lambda + d}{\sin\left(\frac{\pi}{2} + \theta\right)} = \frac{\lambda}{\sin\left(\frac{\pi}{2} - 2\theta\right)} = 2$$

$$\Rightarrow \lambda - d = 2\sin\theta \quad \text{...(ii)}$$

$$\lambda + d = 2\sin\left(\frac{\pi}{2} + \theta\right) = 2\cos\theta \quad \text{...(iii)}$$

and $$\lambda = 2\sin\left(\frac{\pi}{2} - 2\theta\right) = 2\cos 2\theta \quad \text{...(iv)}$$

$\left[\because B > C > A, \text{ let } \theta = A, \text{ then } B = \frac{\pi}{2} + \theta \right.$

$\left. \text{and } C = \frac{\pi}{2} - 2\theta \text{ according to question} \right]$

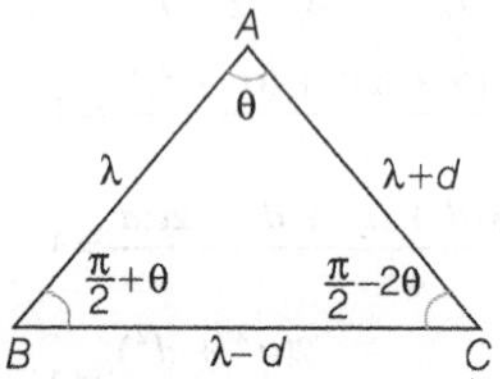

Since, $\lambda - d, \lambda, \lambda + d$ are in AP.

So, $$2\lambda = (\lambda - d) + (\lambda + d)$$

$$\Rightarrow \quad 2 \times 2\cos 2\theta = 2\sin\theta + 2\cos\theta$$

$$\Rightarrow \quad 2\cos 2\theta = \sin\theta + \cos\theta$$

$$\Rightarrow 2[\cos^2\theta - \sin^2\theta] = \cos\theta + \sin\theta$$

$$\Rightarrow 2[(\cos\theta + \sin\theta)(\cos\theta - \sin\theta)] = (\cos\theta + \sin\theta)$$

$$\Rightarrow (\cos\theta + \sin\theta)[2(\cos\theta - \sin\theta) - 1] = 0$$

But $\cos\theta + \sin\theta \neq 0$ so, $2(\cos\theta - \sin\theta) = 1$

$$\Rightarrow \quad \cos\theta - \sin\theta = \frac{1}{2} \Rightarrow \sin 2\theta = \frac{3}{4}$$

Now, area of triangle $= a = \frac{1}{2} \times \lambda \times (\lambda + d)\sin\theta$

$$= \frac{1}{2} \times 2\cos 2\theta \cdot 2\cos\theta\sin\theta$$

$$= \sin 2\theta \cdot \cos 2\theta$$

$$\Rightarrow \quad a = \frac{3}{4} \times \frac{\sqrt{7}}{4} = \frac{3\sqrt{7}}{16}$$

$$\therefore (64a)^2 = \left(64 \times \frac{3\sqrt{7}}{16}\right)^2 = 16 \times 9 \times 7 = 1008$$

92. $\because \quad r = \frac{\Delta}{s} = \frac{a}{s} = \frac{1}{2} \times \frac{\lambda(\lambda + d)\sin\theta}{\left(\frac{3\lambda}{2}\right)}$

$$= \frac{(\lambda + d)\sin\theta}{3} = \frac{2\cos\theta \cdot \sin\theta}{3} \quad \text{[from Eq. (iii)]}$$

$$\Rightarrow r = \frac{\sin 2\theta}{3} = \frac{1}{4} = 0.25$$

93. In ΔPQR,

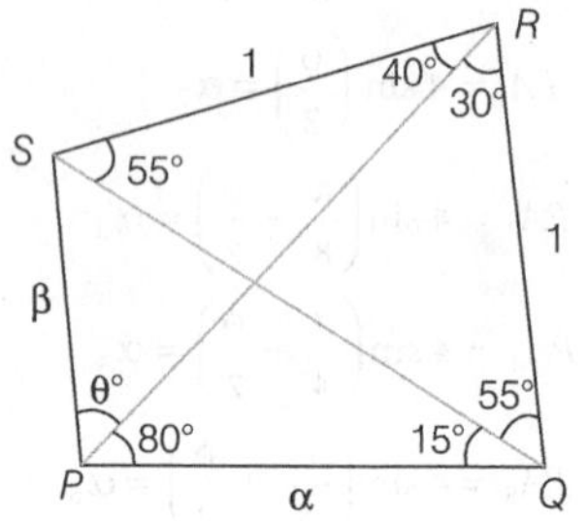

$$\angle RPQ + \angle PQR + \angle QRP = 180°$$

$$\Rightarrow \quad \angle RPQ + 70° + 30° = 180° \Rightarrow \angle RPQ = 80°$$

In ΔSRQ, $\angle QSR + \angle SRQ + \angle RQS = 180°$

$$\Rightarrow \quad \angle QSR + 55° + 70° = 180°$$

$$\therefore \quad \angle QSR = 55°$$

In ΔPQR, on applying sine rule,

$$\frac{\alpha}{\sin 30°} = \frac{1}{\sin 80°}$$

$$\Rightarrow \quad \alpha = \frac{\sin 30°}{\sin 80°} = \frac{1}{2\sin 80°}$$

In ΔPRS, $$\frac{1}{\sin\theta} = \frac{\beta}{\sin 40°} \Rightarrow \beta = \frac{\sin 40°}{\sin\theta}$$

$$\Rightarrow \quad 4\alpha\beta\sin\theta = 4\frac{1}{2\sin 80°} \times \sin 40°$$

$$= \frac{2\sin 40°}{2\sin 40°\cos 40°} = \sec 40°$$

So, $\sec 30° < \sec 40° < \sec 45°$

$$\frac{2}{\sqrt{3}} < \sec 40° < \sqrt{2}$$

Hence, option (a) and (b) is right options.

94.

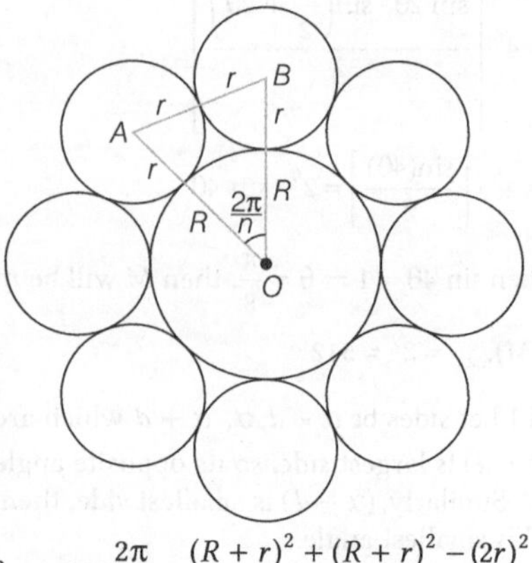

In ΔAOB, $$\cos\frac{2\pi}{n} = \frac{(R + r)^2 + (R + r)^2 - (2r)^2}{2(R + r)(R + r)}$$

$$\Rightarrow 2(R+r)^2 \cos\frac{2\pi}{n} = 2(R+r)^2 - 4r^2$$

$$\Rightarrow 2(R+r)^2\left(\cos\frac{2\pi}{n} - 1\right) = -4r^2$$

$$\Rightarrow \quad 2r^2 = \left(1 - \cos\frac{2\pi}{n}\right)(R+r)^2$$

$$\Rightarrow \quad 2r^2 = 2\sin^2\frac{\pi}{n}(R+r)^2$$

$$\therefore \quad r = (R+r)\sin \pi/n$$

$$\Rightarrow \quad R + r = r \operatorname{cosec} \pi/n$$

$$\Rightarrow \quad R = r\left(\operatorname{cosec}\frac{\pi}{n} - 1\right)$$

For option (a),

If $n = 4$, $\quad R = r\left(\operatorname{cosec}\frac{\pi}{4} - 1\right) = r(\sqrt{2} - 1)$

Option (a) is wrong.

For option (b),

If $n = 5$, $\quad R = r\left(\operatorname{cosec}\frac{\pi}{5} - 1\right)$

$$= r(1.7 - 1) = 0.7r$$

$$R < r$$

Option (b) is wrong.

For option (c),

If $n = 8$, $\quad R = r\left(\operatorname{cosec}\frac{\pi}{8} - 1\right) = r\,(2.63 - 1)$

$$\Rightarrow \quad R = 1.63r$$

$$\Rightarrow \quad (\sqrt{2} - 1)r = 0.414r$$

$$\Rightarrow \quad (\sqrt{2} - 1)\,r < R$$

Option (c) is correct.

For option (d),

If $n = 12$, $\quad R = r\left(\operatorname{cosec}\frac{\pi}{12} - 1\right)$

$$= r\left(\frac{1}{\sin 15^\circ} - 1\right)$$

$$\sqrt{2}(\sqrt{3}+1)\,r > R. \qquad \text{(True)}$$

So, option (d) is correct.

95.

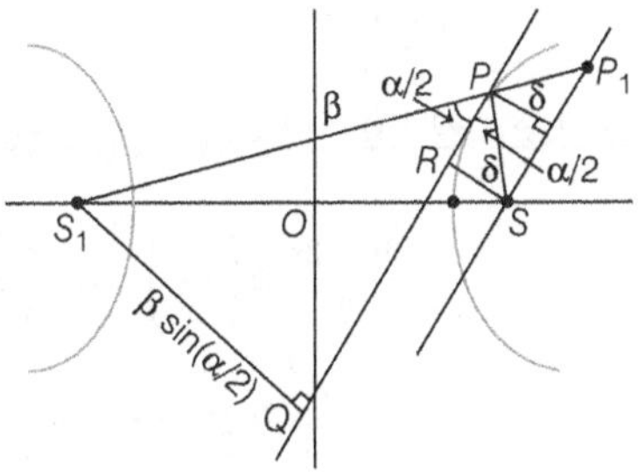

Given, S_1 and S are the foci and $\angle SPS_1 = \alpha$

In ΔS_1QP, $\quad \sin\frac{\alpha}{2} = \frac{S_1Q}{\beta} \Rightarrow S_1Q = \beta\sin\frac{\alpha}{2}$

Product of distances of any tangent from two foci $= b^2$

$$\delta \cdot S_1Q = \delta \times \beta\sin\frac{\alpha}{2} = b^2$$

So, $\quad \dfrac{\beta\delta\sin\frac{\alpha}{2}}{9} = \dfrac{b^2}{9} = \dfrac{64}{9}$

$\therefore \quad \left[\dfrac{64}{9}\right] = 7$

96. **For option (a)**

$$\cos P = \frac{q^2 + r^2 - p^2}{2qr} \qquad \text{...(i)}$$

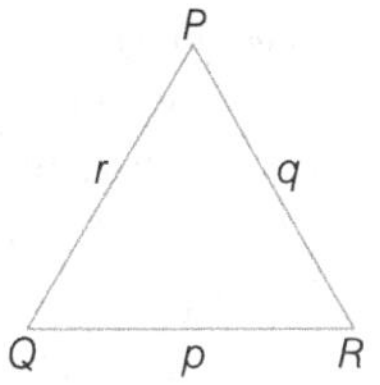

$\because \quad \dfrac{q^2 + r^2}{2} \ge \sqrt{q^2r^2} \qquad$ [AM ≥ GM]

$\Rightarrow \quad q^2 + r^2 \ge 2qr$

From Eq. (i), we get

$$\cos P \ge \frac{2qr - p^2}{2qr} \Rightarrow \cos P \ge 1 - \frac{p^2}{2qr}$$

So, option (a) is correct.

For option (b)

$$\frac{(q-r)\cos P + (p-r)\cos Q}{p+q}$$

$$= \frac{(q\cos P + p\cos Q) - r(\cos P + \cos Q)}{p+q} = \frac{r - r(\cos P + \cos Q)}{p+q}$$

$$= \frac{r - r\cos P - r\cos Q}{p+q}$$

$$= \frac{r - (q - p\cos R) - (p - q\cos R)}{p+q}$$

$$= \frac{(r - p - q) + (p+q)\cos R}{p+q}$$

$$= \cos R + \frac{r - (p+q)}{p+q} \le \cos R \qquad [\because r < p + q]$$

Hence, option (b) is correct.

For option (c)

$$\frac{q+r}{p} = \frac{\sin Q + \sin R}{\sin P} \ge \frac{2\sqrt{\sin Q \cdot \sin R}}{\sin P}$$

So, option (c) is incorrect.

For option (d)

If $p < q$ and $p < r$, then p is the smallest side and hence one of Q or R can be obtuse.

So, one of $\cos Q$ or $\cos R$ can be negative.

Therefore, $\cos Q > \dfrac{p}{r}$ and $\cos R > \dfrac{p}{q}$ cannot hold always.

Option (d) is incorrect.

97. Given, $AB = \sqrt{23} = c,\ BC = 3 = a,\ CA = 4 = b$

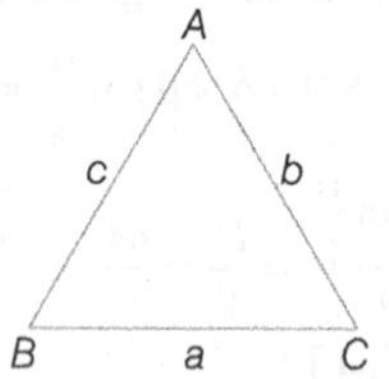

Now, $$\frac{\cot A + \cot C}{\cot B} = \frac{\dfrac{\cos A}{\sin A} + \dfrac{\cos C}{\sin C}}{\dfrac{\cos B}{\sin B}}$$

$$= \frac{\dfrac{b^2 + c^2 - a^2}{2bc(\sin A)} + \dfrac{a^2 + b^2 - c^2}{2ab(\sin C)}}{\dfrac{c^2 + a^2 - b^2}{2ac(\sin B)}}$$

$$= \frac{\dfrac{b^2 + c^2 - a^2}{4\Delta} + \dfrac{a^2 + b^2 - c^2}{4\Delta}}{\dfrac{c^2 + a^2 - b^2}{4\Delta}}$$

$$= \frac{b^2 + c^2 - a^2 + a^2 + b^2 - c^2}{c^2 + a^2 - b^2}$$

$$= \frac{2b^2}{a^2 + c^2 - b^2} = \frac{2 \times 16}{9 + 23 - 16} = \frac{32}{16} = 2$$

98. For a ΔXYZ, it is given that

$$\tan\frac{X}{2} + \tan\frac{Z}{2} = \frac{2y}{x + y + z}$$

$$\Rightarrow \frac{\Delta}{s(s - x)} + \frac{\Delta}{s(s - z)} = \frac{y}{s} \Rightarrow \Delta\frac{(s - z + s - x)}{(s - x)(s - z)} = y$$

$$\Rightarrow \Delta = (s - x)(s - z)$$

$$\Rightarrow s(s - x)(s - y)(s - z) = (s - x)^2 (s - z)^2$$

$$\Rightarrow s^2 - sy = s^2 - (x + z)s + xz$$

$$\Rightarrow s(x + z - y) = xz$$

$$\Rightarrow (x + z)^2 - y^2 = 2xz \Rightarrow x^2 + z^2 = y^2$$

$$\therefore Y = \pi / 2$$

$$\because X + Y + Z = \pi$$

$$\Rightarrow X + Z = \frac{\pi}{2} = Y \Rightarrow X + Z = Y$$

$$\because \tan\frac{X}{2} = \sqrt{\frac{1 - \cos x}{1 + \cos x}} = \sqrt{\frac{1 - \dfrac{z}{y}}{1 + \dfrac{z}{y}}}$$

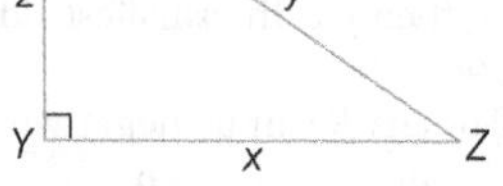

$$= \sqrt{\frac{y - z}{y + z}} = \frac{\sqrt{y^2 - z^2}}{y + z} \Rightarrow \tan\frac{X}{2} = \frac{x}{y + z}$$

$[\because x^2 + z^2 = y^2]$

Exercise 2 - Challenging Problems

1. We have, two sides of a triangle are given by roots of the equation $x^2 - 2\sqrt{3}x + 2 = 0$.

$$\Rightarrow a + b = 2\sqrt{3}$$

and $$ab = 2 \text{ with } \angle C = \frac{\pi}{3} \quad \text{...(i)}$$

Using cosine law, we get

$$\cos C = \frac{a^2 + b^2 - c^2}{2ab}$$

$$\Rightarrow \cos\frac{\pi}{3} = \frac{a^2 + b^2 - c^2}{2ab} \quad \text{[using Eq. (i)]}$$

$$\Rightarrow \frac{1}{2} = \frac{a^2 + b^2 - c^2}{2ab}$$

$$\Rightarrow a^2 + b^2 - c^2 = ab$$

$$\Rightarrow (a + b)^2 - 2ab - c^2 = ab$$

$$\Rightarrow 12 - 4 - c^2 = 2 \quad [\because a + b = 2\sqrt{3} \text{ and } ab = 2]$$

$$\Rightarrow c^2 = 6;\ c = \sqrt{6}$$

$\therefore$ The perimeter of $\Delta = a + b + c = 2\sqrt{3} + \sqrt{6}$

2. Since, A is obtuse angle,

then $$90° < A < 180°$$

$$\Rightarrow 90° < 180 - (B + C) < 180°$$

$$\Rightarrow -90° < -(B + C) < 0$$

$$\Rightarrow 90° > B + C > 0$$

$$\Rightarrow B + C < 90°$$

$$\Rightarrow B < 90° - C$$

$$\therefore \tan B < \tan(90° - C)$$

$$\Rightarrow \tan B < \cot C$$

$$\Rightarrow \tan B \cdot \tan C < 1$$

If A is obtuse, then $\tan B \tan C < 1$.

3. We have, $2s = a + b + c$,

$$A^2 = s(s - a)(s - b)(s - c)$$

Now, AM $\geq$ GM

$$\Rightarrow \frac{s + (s - a) + (s - b) + (s - c)}{4} \geq \{s(s - a)(s - b)(s - c)\}^{1/4}$$

$$\Rightarrow \frac{4s - 2s}{4} \geq (A^2)^{1/4} \Rightarrow \frac{s}{2} \geq A^{1/2}$$

$$\Rightarrow A \leq \frac{s^2}{4} \quad \text{...(i)}$$

Also, $$\frac{(s - a) + (s - b) + (s - c)}{3} \geq \{(s - a)(s - b)(s - c)\}^{1/3}$$

$$\Rightarrow \frac{3s - 2s}{3} \geq \left(\frac{A^2}{s}\right)^{1/3} \Rightarrow \frac{s}{3} \geq \left(\frac{A^2}{s}\right)^{1/3}$$

$$\Rightarrow \frac{A^2}{s} \leq \frac{s^3}{27} \Rightarrow A \leq \frac{s^2}{3\sqrt{3}} \quad \text{...(ii)}$$

Thus, from Eqs. (i) and (ii), we get

$$A \leq \frac{s^2}{3\sqrt{3}}$$

4. AD is the internal bisector of $\angle A$.

$$\Rightarrow \quad \frac{BD}{DC} = \frac{BA}{AC} = \frac{c}{b}$$

$$\Rightarrow \quad \frac{BD}{c} = \frac{DC}{b} = \frac{BD + DC}{c + b} = \frac{a}{b + c}$$

$$\Rightarrow \quad BD = \frac{ac}{b + c}, \; DC = \frac{ab}{b + c}$$

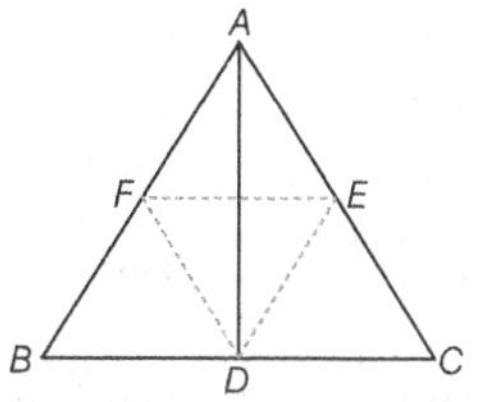

Similarly, $\quad BF = \dfrac{ac}{a + b}$

$$\Rightarrow \quad \text{Area of } \Delta BFD = \frac{1}{2}(BF \cdot BD) \cdot \sin B$$

$$\Rightarrow \quad \frac{\text{Area of } \Delta BFD}{\text{Area of } \Delta ABC} = \frac{(BF \cdot BD) \cdot \sin B}{ac \sin B}$$

$$= \frac{ac}{(a + b)(b + c)}$$

Now, $\quad$ area of $\Delta DEF = \Delta ABC - (\Delta BFD + \Delta DEC + \Delta AFE)$

$$\Rightarrow \quad \frac{\text{Area of } \Delta DEF}{\text{Area of } \Delta ABC} = 1 - \left(\frac{\Delta BFD + \Delta DEC + \Delta AFE}{\Delta ABC}\right)$$

$$= 1 - \left\{\frac{ac}{(a + b)(b + c)} + \frac{cb}{(c + a)(b + a)} + \frac{ab}{(a + c)(b + c)}\right\}$$

$$= \frac{2abc\Delta}{(a + b)(b + c)(c + a)}$$

$$\Rightarrow \text{ Area of } \Delta DEF = \frac{2abc\,\Delta}{(a + b)(b + c)(c + a)}$$

5. $\cot A + \cot B + \cot C = \sqrt{3}$

On squaring both sides, we get

$$\cot^2 A + \cot^2 B + \cot^2 C + 2\cot A \cdot \cot B + 2\cot B \cdot \cot C + 2\cot C \cdot \cot A = 3 \quad \text{...(i)}$$

Also, $\cot A \cot B + \cot B \cot C + \cot C \cot A = 1 \quad$ ...(ii)

From Eqs. (i) and Eqs. (ii), we have

$$\cot^2 A + \cot^2 B + \cot^2 C - \cot A \cot B - \cot C \cot B - \cot C \cot A = 0$$

or $\quad \dfrac{1}{2}\{(\cot A - \cot B)^2 + (\cot B - \cot C)^2 + (\cot C - \cot A)^2\} = 0$

$\Rightarrow \cot A = \cot B = \cot C$

[since, RHS is zero, thus each square must be zero]

$\Rightarrow \quad A = B = C$

i.e. the triangle is equilateral.

6. Let $\quad \dfrac{a}{\sin A} = \dfrac{b}{\sin B} = \dfrac{c}{\sin C} = K$ (say).

$\Rightarrow \quad a = K \sin A, \; b = K \sin B$ and $c = K \sin C$

Now, the given relation is,

$$(a^2 + b^2)\sin(A - B) = (a^2 - b^2)\sin(A - B)$$

$$\Rightarrow \quad K^2(\sin^2 A + \sin^2 B)\sin(A - B) = K^2(\sin^2 A - \sin^2 B)\sin(A - B)$$

$\Rightarrow \; (\sin^2 A + \sin^2 B)\sin(A - B) = \sin^2(A + B) \cdot \sin(A - B)$

or $\; \sin(A - B)\,[\sin^2 A + \sin^2 B - \sin^2 C] = 0$

Hence, either the first factor = 0;

or the second factor = 0

If $\sin(A - B) = 0 \Rightarrow A - B = 0 \Rightarrow A = B$

$\Rightarrow$ triangle is isosceles.

If $\sin^2 A + \sin^2 B - \sin^2 C = 0$

$$\Rightarrow \quad \frac{a^2}{K^2} + \frac{b^2}{K^2} - \frac{c^2}{K^2} = 0 \text{ or } a^2 + b^2 = c^2$$

$\Rightarrow$ The triangle is right angled.

Hence, the result.

7. Given, $b \cdot c = k^2$

Now, $\quad \cos A = \dfrac{b^2 + c^2 - a^2}{2bc}$

or $\quad 2k^2 \cos A = b^2 + \left(\dfrac{k^2}{b}\right)^2 - a^2$

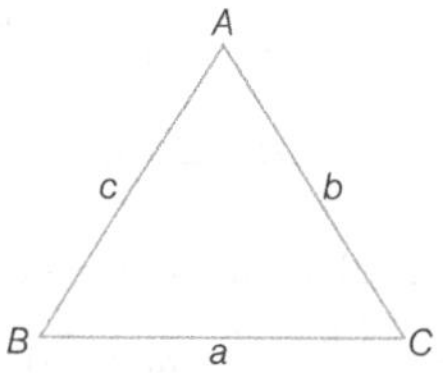

Since b^2 is real,

$$(a^2 + 2k^2 \cos A)^2 - 4k^4 \ge 0$$

$\Rightarrow \; (a^2 + 2k^2 \cos A + 2k^2)(a^2 + 2k^2 \cos A - 2k^2) \ge 0$

$\Rightarrow \; (a^2 + 2k^2 \cdot 2\cos^2 A/2)(a^2 - 2k^2 \cdot 2\sin^2 A/2) \ge 0$

$\Rightarrow \quad (a^2 + 4k^2 \cdot \cos^2 A/2)(a^2 - 4k^2 \sin^2 A/2) \ge 0$

$\Rightarrow \quad a^2 - 4k^2 \sin^2 A/2 \ge 0$

[as, $a^2 + 4k^2 \cos^2 A/2$ is always positive]

$\Rightarrow \quad (a + 2k \sin A/2)(a - 2k \sin A/2) \ge 0$

$\Rightarrow \quad a \le -2k \sin A/2$

or $\quad a \ge 2k \sin A/2$

[since, $2k\sin(A/2)$ is real]

But 'a' must be positive.

$\Rightarrow \quad a \le -2k \sin A/2$ is rejected.

Hence, $a \ge 2k \sin A/2$

i.e. for the triangle to exist,

$$a \ge 2k \sin A/2$$

8. $\cos C = \dfrac{a^2 + b^2 - c^2}{2ab}$ but $C = 60°$

$\therefore \quad \dfrac{1}{2} = \dfrac{a^2 + b^2 - c^2}{2ab}$

$\therefore \quad ab = a^2 + b^2 - c^2$

On adding $2ab$ both sides,

$\therefore \quad 3ab = a^2 + b^2 + 2ab - c^2$

$\Rightarrow \quad 3ab = (a + b)^2 - c^2$

$\Rightarrow \quad 3ab = (a + b + c)(a + b - c) \quad$ ...(i)

Now, $\dfrac{1}{a+c}+\dfrac{1}{b+c}=\dfrac{a+b+2c}{ab+c(a+b+c)}$

On multiplying numerator and denominator by 3,

$$=\frac{3(a+b+2c)}{3ab+3c(a+b+c)}$$

$$=\frac{3(a+b+2c)}{(a+b+c)(a+b-c)+3c(a+b+c)}$$

[using Eq. (i) for $3ab$]

$$=\frac{3(a+b+2c)}{(a+b+c)(a+b+2c)}=\frac{3}{(a+b+c)}$$

$$\therefore\quad \frac{1}{a+c}+\frac{1}{b+c}=\frac{3}{(a+b+c)}$$

9. From the formula for $\cos A$,
we can write $2bc\cos A=b^2+c^2-a^2$

But $\quad b=\left(\dfrac{m+1}{2}\right)a$

$$\therefore\quad (m+1)ac\cos A=\left\{\frac{(m+1)^2}{4}-1\right\}a^2+c^2$$

$$=\left\{\frac{(m+1)^2-4}{4}\right\}a^2+c^2$$

$$=\left\{\frac{(m-1)(m+3)}{4}\right\}a^2+c^2 \qquad \text{...(i)}$$

But from the given values of $\cos A$, we can write

$$\frac{(m-1)(m+3)}{4}=m\cos^2 A,$$

$\therefore$ Eq. (i) gives as

$$(m+1)ac\cos A=ma^2\cos^2 A+c^2$$

or $\quad mac\cos A-c^2=ma^2\cos^2 A-ac\cos A$

$\therefore\quad (ma\cos A-c)=a\cos A(ma\cos A-c)$

$\therefore\quad (c-a\cos A)(c-ma\cos A)=0$

This implies 'c' has two values

$a\cos A$ and $ma\cos A$, and the latter is m times the former.

Hence proved.

10. Let $\angle BDC=\alpha$, then $\angle DAB=180°-(\theta+\alpha)$

On applying sine formula to ΔABD, we get

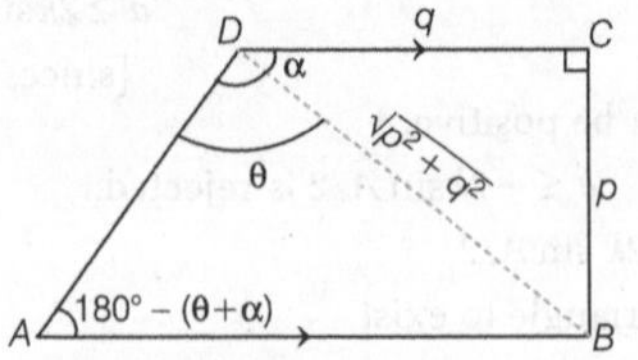

$$\frac{AB}{\sin\theta}=\frac{BD}{\sin(\theta+\alpha)}$$

$$\therefore\quad \frac{AB}{\sin\theta}=\frac{\sqrt{p^2+q^2}}{\sin\theta\cos\alpha+\cos\theta\sin\alpha}$$

$$\left[\begin{array}{l}\text{but in } \Delta BCD,\\ \sin\alpha=\dfrac{p}{\sqrt{p^2+q^2}} \text{ and } \cos\alpha=\dfrac{q}{\sqrt{p^2+q^2}}\end{array}\right]$$

$$\therefore\quad AB=\frac{(p^2+q^2)\sin\theta}{q\sin\theta+p\cos\theta}$$

Hence proved.

11. Let ΔABC be the given Δ in which A is the greatest and C is the least angle.

Then, according to the hypothesis

$$A-C=\alpha \qquad \text{...(i)}$$

But $\quad A+C=\pi-B \qquad$ ...(ii)

$\therefore$ From Eq. (i) and Eq. (ii), we get

$$A=\frac{\pi}{2}+\frac{\alpha-B}{2} \text{ and } C=\frac{\pi}{2}-\frac{\alpha+B}{2} \qquad \text{...(iii)}$$

Again by hypothesis, $\quad a+c=2b$

$$\therefore\quad \sin A+\sin C=2\sin B$$

$$\Rightarrow 2\sin\left(\frac{A+C}{2}\right)\cos\left(\frac{A-C}{2}\right)=4\sin\frac{B}{2}\cdot\cos\frac{B}{2}$$

$$\Rightarrow\quad 2\cos\frac{B}{2}\cos\left(\frac{A-C}{2}\right)=4\sin\frac{B}{2}\cdot\cos\frac{B}{2} \quad \left[\frac{A+C}{2}=\frac{\pi}{2}-\frac{B}{2}\right]$$

$$\Rightarrow\quad \cos\left(\frac{\alpha}{2}\right)=2\sin\frac{B}{2} \qquad \text{[using Eq. (i)]}$$

$$\therefore\quad \sin\frac{B}{2}=\frac{\cos\frac{\alpha}{2}}{2}$$

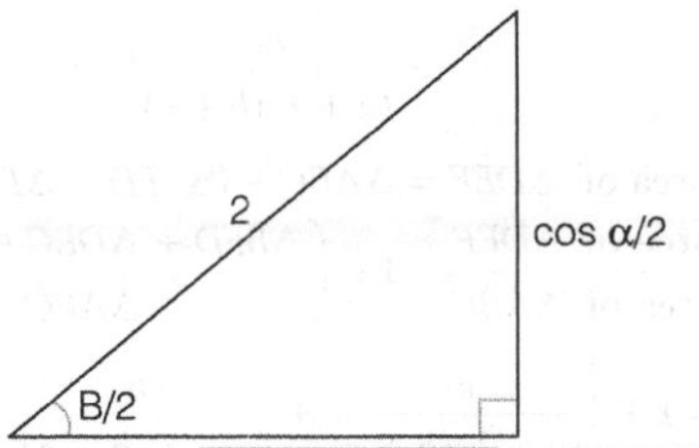

$$\sqrt{4-\cos^2\alpha/2}=\sqrt{4-\left(\frac{1+\cos\alpha}{2}\right)}=\sqrt{\frac{7-\cos\alpha}{2}}$$

But $\quad \dfrac{a}{c}=\dfrac{\sin A}{\sin C}=\dfrac{\cos\left(\dfrac{\alpha-B}{2}\right)}{\cos\left(\dfrac{\alpha+B}{2}\right)} \qquad$ [using Eq. (iii)]

$$=\frac{\cos\alpha/2\cdot\cos B/2+\sin\alpha/2\cdot\sin B/2}{\cos\alpha/2\cdot\cos B/2-\sin\alpha/2\cdot\sin B/2}$$

Dividing numerator and denominator by $\cos\alpha/2.\cos B/2$

$$=\frac{1+\tan\alpha/2\,.\,\tan B/2}{1-\tan\alpha/2\,.\,\tan B/2}$$

Write $\tan\alpha/2\cdot\tan B/2$ from figure;

$$=\frac{1+\sqrt{\dfrac{2\sin^2\alpha/2}{7-\cos\alpha}}}{1-\sqrt{\dfrac{2\sin^2\alpha/2}{7-\cos\alpha}}}=\frac{1+\sqrt{\dfrac{1-\cos\alpha}{7-\cos\alpha}}}{1\sqrt{\dfrac{1-\cos\alpha}{7-\cos\alpha}}}=\frac{1+x}{1-x}$$

$$\left[\text{given } x=\sqrt{\frac{1-\cos\alpha}{7-\cos\alpha}}\right]$$

$$\therefore\quad \frac{a}{1+x}=\frac{c}{1-x}=\frac{a+c}{2}=b$$

$$\therefore\quad \frac{a}{1+x}=\frac{b}{1}=\frac{c}{1-x}$$

Thus, the sides are in the ratio $1+x:1:1-x$.

12. Given $\tan A/2, \tan B/2, \tan C/2$ are in AP.

$\therefore \quad \tan A/2 - \tan B/2 = \tan B/2 - \tan C/2$

$$\therefore \frac{\sin A/2}{\cos A/2} - \frac{\sin B/2}{\cos B/2} = \frac{\sin B/2}{\cos B/2} - \frac{\sin C/2}{\cos C/2}$$

$$\Rightarrow \frac{\sin A/2 \cdot \cos B/2 - \sin B/2 \cdot \cos A/2}{\cos A/2 \cdot \cos B/2} = \frac{\sin B/2 \cdot \cos C/2 - \sin C/2 \cdot \cos B/2}{\cos B/2 \cdot \cos C/2}$$

$$\Rightarrow \frac{\sin\left(\frac{A-B}{2}\right)}{\cos\frac{A}{2}} = \frac{\sin\left(\frac{B-C}{2}\right)}{\cos\frac{C}{2}} \quad \text{...(i)}$$

but $\quad \cos\frac{A}{2} = \sin\frac{B+C}{2}$

and $\quad \cos\frac{C}{2} = \sin\left(\frac{A+B}{2}\right) \quad$ ...(ii)

$$\Rightarrow \sin\left(\frac{A-B}{2}\right) \cdot \sin\left(\frac{A+B}{2}\right) = \sin\left(\frac{B-C}{2}\right) \cdot \sin\left(\frac{B+C}{2}\right)$$

[from Eqs. (i) and (ii)]

$\Rightarrow \quad \cos B - \cos A = \cos C - \cos B$

Hence, $\cos A, \cos B, \cos C$ are in AP.

13. Given that $\frac{2}{b} = \frac{1}{a} + \frac{1}{c}$

i.e. $\quad 2ac = b(a + c) \quad$ ...(i)

We want to prove

$$\frac{2}{\sin^2\frac{B}{2}} = \frac{1}{\sin^2\frac{A}{2}} + \frac{1}{\sin^2\frac{C}{2}}$$

i.e. $$\frac{2ac}{(s-a)(s-c)} = \frac{bc}{(s-b)(s-c)} + \frac{ab}{(s-a)(s-b)}$$

$\left[\text{using } \sin\frac{A}{2} = \sqrt{\frac{(s-b)(s-c)}{bc}}, \sin\frac{B}{2} = \sqrt{\frac{(s-a)(s-c)}{ac}} \text{ and } \sin\frac{C}{2} = \sqrt{\frac{(s-a)(s-b)}{ab}}\right]$

Consider,

$$\text{LHS} = \frac{2ac}{(s-a)(s-c)} = \frac{b(a+c)}{(s-a)(s-c)} \quad \text{[using Eq. (i)]}$$

$$= \frac{b(a+c)(s-b)}{(s-a)(s-b)(s-c)} = \frac{b\,[s(a+c) - b(a+c)]}{(s-a)(s-b)(s-c)}$$

$$= \frac{b\,(sa + sc - 2ac)}{(s-a)(s-b)(s-c)} \quad \text{[using Eq. (i)]}$$

$$= \frac{b\,(sa - ac + sc - ac)}{(s-a)(s-b)(s-c)}$$

$$= \frac{b\,[a(s-c) + c\,(s-a)]}{(s-a)(s-b)(s-c)}$$

$$= \frac{ab}{(s-a)(s-b)} + \frac{bc}{(s-b)(s-c)} = \text{RHS}$$

14. $\text{LHS} = r^2 + r_1^2 + r_2^2 + r_3^2$

$= 16R^2 \sin^2 A/2 \cdot \sin^2 B/2 \sin^2 C/2$
$+ 16R^2 \sin^2 A/2 \cdot \cos^2 B/2 \cdot \cos^2 C/2$
$+ 16R^2 \cos^2 A/2 \sin^2 B/2 . \cos^2 C/2 + 16R^2 \cos^2 A/2 \cdot \cos^2 B/2 \cdot \sin^2 C/2$

$= 16R^2 \sin^2 A/2\,[\sin^2 B/2 \cdot \sin^2 C/2 + \cos^2 B/2 \cdot \cos^2 C/2]$
$+ 16R^2 \cos^2 A/2\,[\sin^2 B/2 \cdot \cos^2 C/2 + \cos^2 B/2 \cdot \sin^2 C/2]$

$= 4R^2 \sin^2 A/2\,[(2\sin^2 B/2)(2\sin^2 C/2) + (2\cos^2 B/2)(2\cos^2 C/2)]$
$+ 4R^2 \cos^2 A/2\,[(2\sin^2 B/2)(2\cos^2 C/2) + (2\cos^2 B/2)(2\cos^2 C/2)]$

$= 4R^2 \sin^2 A/2\,[(1 - \cos B)(1 - \cos C) + (1 + \cos B)(1 + \cos C)] + 4R^2 \cos^2 A/2\,[(1 - \cos B)(1 + \cos C) + (1 + \cos B)(1 - \cos C)]$

$= 4R^2 \sin^2 A/2\,[2 + 2\cos B \cos C] + 4R^2 \cos^2 A/2\,[2 - 2\cos B \cos C]$

$= 8R^2 + 8R^2 \cos B \cos C(\sin^2 A/2 - \cos^2 A/2)$

$= 8R^2 - 8R^2 \cos A . \cos B \cos C$

$= 8R^2 + 4R^2\,[\cos(A+B) + \cos(A-B)] \cdot \cos(A+B)$

$= 8R^2 + 4R^2\,[\cos^2 C + \cos^2 A - \sin^2 B]$

$= 8R^2 + 4R^2\,[1 - \sin^2 C + 1 - \sin^2 A - \sin^2 B]$

$= 16R^2 - 4R^2 \sin^2 A - 4R^2 \sin^2 B - 4R^2 \sin^2 C$

$= 16R^2 - a^2 - b^2 - c^2 = \text{RHS}$

15. $\cos A + 2\cos B + \cos C = 2$

or $\quad \cos A + \cos C = 2(1 - \cos B)$

$$\Rightarrow 2\cos\left(\frac{A+C}{2}\right) \cdot \cos\left(\frac{A-C}{2}\right) = 4\sin^2 B/2$$

$$\Rightarrow \cos\left(\frac{A-C}{2}\right) = 2\sin\frac{B}{2}$$

$$\left[\text{as } \cos\left(\frac{A+C}{2}\right) = \cos\left(\frac{\pi}{2} - \frac{B}{2}\right) = \sin\frac{B}{2}\right]$$

$$\Rightarrow \cos\left(\frac{A-C}{2}\right) = 2\cos\left(\frac{A+C}{2}\right)$$

$$\Rightarrow \cos\frac{A}{2} \cdot \cos\frac{C}{2} + \sin\frac{A}{2} \cdot \sin\frac{C}{2} = 2\cos\frac{A}{2} \cdot \cos\frac{C}{2} - 2\sin\frac{A}{2} \cdot \sin\frac{C}{2}$$

$$\Rightarrow \cot\frac{A}{2} \cdot \cot\frac{C}{2} = 3$$

$$\Rightarrow \sqrt{\frac{s(s-a)}{(s-b)(s-c)}} \cdot \sqrt{\frac{s(s-c)}{(s-a)(s-b)}} = 3$$

$$\Rightarrow \frac{s}{(s-b)} = 3$$

$$\Rightarrow s = 3s - 3b$$

$$\Rightarrow 2s = 3b$$

$$\Rightarrow a + c = 2b$$

$\therefore$ a, b, c are in AP.

> Maths is like going to the gym for your brain. It sharpens your mind.
>
> **–Danika Mckellar**

4

Inverse Trigonometric Functions

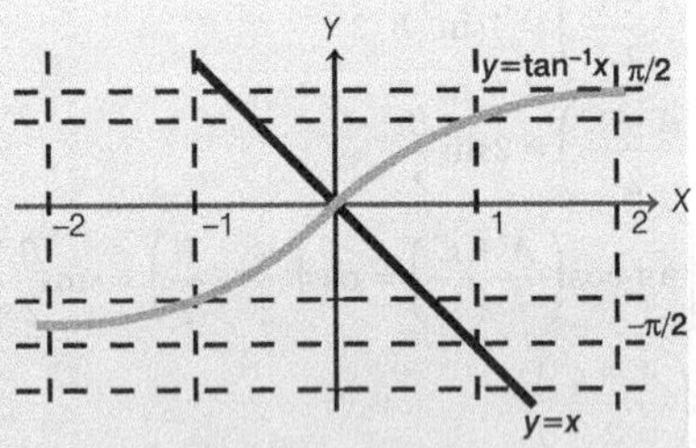

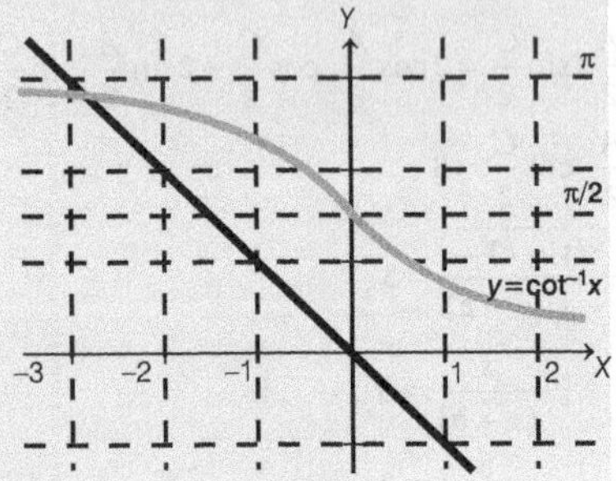

Learning Milestones

Milestone 1 Domain and Range of Inverse Trigonometric Functions
- Introduction
- Inverse Function
- Domain and Range of Inverse Trigonometric Functions
- Monotonic Behaviour of Inverse Trigonometric Functions

Milestone 2 Properties I and II of Inverse Trigonometric Functions

Milestone 3 Properties III, IV and V of Inverse Trigonometric Functions

Milestone 4 Properties VI, VII, VIII and IX of Inverse Trigonometric Functions

Milestone 5 Properties X, XI, XII and XIII of Inverse Trigonometric Functions

Milestone 6 Equations and Inequations Involving Inverse Trigonometric Functions
- Equations and Inequations Involving Inverse Trigonometric Functions
- Summation of Series

Practice Milestones

Practice Milestone 1 - JEE Main Pattern

Practice Milestone 2 - JEE Advanced Pattern

Practice Milestone 3 - Challenging Problems

Milestone 1 Domain and Range of Inverse Trigonometric Functions

• Introduction • Inverse Function • Domain and Range of Inverse Trigonometric Functions
• Monotonic Behaviour of Inverse Trigonometric Functions

4.1 Introduction

We already studied basic trigonometric functions and their table.

e.g. $\sin\frac{\pi}{6}=\frac{1}{2}, \sin\frac{5\pi}{6}=\frac{1}{2}, \sin\frac{13\pi}{6}=\frac{1}{2}, \ldots$ etc.

But if $\sin x=\frac{1}{2}$ is given and we need to find the value of x, then there are infinite answers i.e. there is no unique answer for this.

i.e. $x=\ldots,\frac{-7\pi}{6},\frac{-11\pi}{6},\frac{\pi}{6},\ldots$

For finding the value of angle of any trigonometric function, we use inverse function

i.e. $\sin^{-1}x$, $\cos^{-1}x$, $\tan^{-1}x$, ... etc. which denote an angle or a real number, "whose sine is x", "whose cosine is x", "whose tangent is x^{4}", ... etc. respectively, provided that the answer given are numerically smallest available.

4.2 Inverse Function

Definition If a function, say f is one to one and onto from A to B, then function g which associates each element $y\in B$ to one and only one element $x\in A$, such that $y=f(x)$, then g is called the inverse function of f, denoted by $x=g(y)$.

Usually we denote $g=f^{-1}$ [read as f inverse]

$\therefore$ $x=f^{-1}(y)$

JEE SPIKE

If $y=f(x)$ and $x=g(y)$ are two functions such that $f\{g(y)\}=y$ and $g\{f(x)\}=x$ then f and g are said to be inverse functions of each other. Before we start with the definitions of $\sin^{-1}x$, $\cos^{-1}x$, $\tan^{-1}x$, etc. let us study the following discussion which will help us to define these inverse functions.

4.3 Domain and Range of Inverse Trigonometric Functions

1. If $\sin y=x$, then $y=\sin^{-1}x$, under certain conditions.

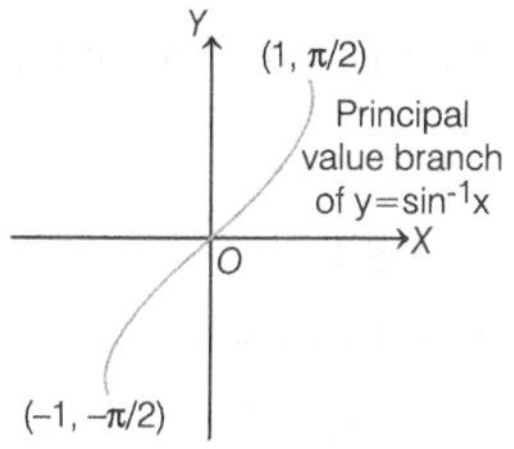

$\because$ $-1\le\sin y\le 1$

But $\sin y=x$,

$\therefore$ $-1\le x\le 1$

Also, $\sin y=-1 \Rightarrow y=-\frac{\pi}{2}$

and $\sin y=1 \Rightarrow y=\frac{\pi}{2}$

Keeping in mind numerically smallest angles or real numbers, we have

$$-\frac{\pi}{2}\le y\le\frac{\pi}{2}$$

These restrictions on the values of x and y make the function $\sin y=x$, one-one and onto so that the inverse function exists i.e. $y=\sin^{-1}x$ is meaningful.

Thus, Domain : $x\in[-1,1]$

Range : $y\in[-\pi/2,\pi/2]$

Example 1. Find the principal values of the following

(i) $\sin^{-1}\left(\frac{1}{2}\right)$ (ii) $\sin^{-1}\left(-\frac{1}{2}\right)$

(iii) $\sin^{-1}\left(-\frac{1}{\sqrt{2}}\right)$

Sol. (i) We know that $\sin^{-1} x$ denotes an angle in the interval $\left[-\frac{\pi}{2}, \frac{\pi}{2}\right]$ whose sine is x for $x \in [-1, 1]$.

$\therefore \sin^{-1}\left(\frac{1}{2}\right)$ = An angle in $\left[-\frac{\pi}{2}, \frac{\pi}{2}\right]$, whose sine is $\frac{1}{2}$.

$\Rightarrow \sin^{-1}\left(\frac{1}{2}\right) = \frac{\pi}{6}$

(ii) $\sin^{-1}\left(-\frac{1}{2}\right)$ = An angle in $\left[-\frac{\pi}{2}, \frac{\pi}{2}\right]$, whose sine is $-\frac{1}{2}$.

$\Rightarrow \sin^{-1}\left(-\frac{1}{2}\right) = -\frac{\pi}{6}$

(iii) $\sin^{-1}\left(\frac{1}{\sqrt{2}}\right)$ = An angle in $\left[-\frac{\pi}{2}, \frac{\pi}{2}\right]$, whose sine is $\frac{1}{\sqrt{2}}$.

$\Rightarrow \sin^{-1}\left(\frac{1}{\sqrt{2}}\right) = \frac{\pi}{4}$.

2. Let $\cos y = x$, then $y = \cos^{-1} x$ under certain conditions

$\because \quad -1 \le \cos y \le 1$

$\therefore \quad -1 \le x \le 1$

Also, $\cos y = -1 \Rightarrow y = \pi$

and $\cos y = 1 \Rightarrow y = 0$

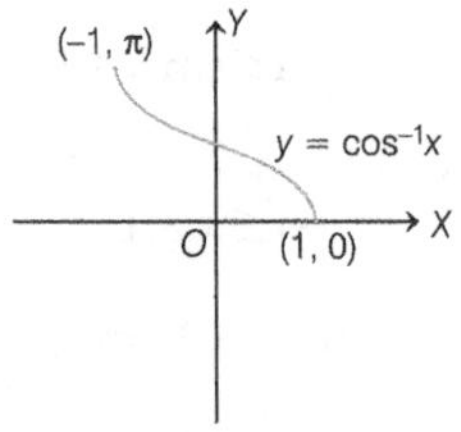

$\therefore \quad 0 \le y \le \pi$

These restrictions on the values of x and y make the function $\cos y = x$ one-one and onto so that the inverse function exists

i.e. $y = \cos^{-1} x$ is meaningful.

Thus, Domain : $x \in [-1, 1]$

Range : $y \in [0, \pi]$

Example 2. Find the principal values of the following.

(i) $\cos^{-1}\left(\frac{1}{2}\right)$ (ii) $\cos^{-1}\left(-\frac{1}{2}\right)$ (iii) $\cos^{-1}\left(\frac{\sqrt{3}}{2}\right)$

Sol. (i) For any $x \in [-1, 1]$, $\cos^{-1} x$ represents an angle in $[0, \pi]$ whose cosine is x.

$\therefore \cos^{-1}\left(\frac{1}{2}\right)$ = An angle in $[0, \pi]$, whose cosine is $\frac{1}{2}$.

$\Rightarrow \cos^{-1}\left(\frac{1}{2}\right) = \frac{\pi}{3}$

(ii) $\cos^{-1}\left(-\frac{1}{2}\right)$ = An angle in $[0, \pi]$, whose cosine is $-\frac{1}{2}$.

$\Rightarrow \cos^{-1}\left(-\frac{1}{2}\right) = \frac{2\pi}{3}$

(iii) $\cos^{-1}\left(\frac{\sqrt{3}}{2}\right)$ = An angle in $[0, \pi]$, whose cosine is $\frac{\sqrt{3}}{2}$.

$\Rightarrow \cos^{-1}\left(\frac{\sqrt{3}}{2}\right) = \frac{\pi}{6}$.

3. If $\tan y = x$, then $y = \tan^{-1} x$, under certain conditions.

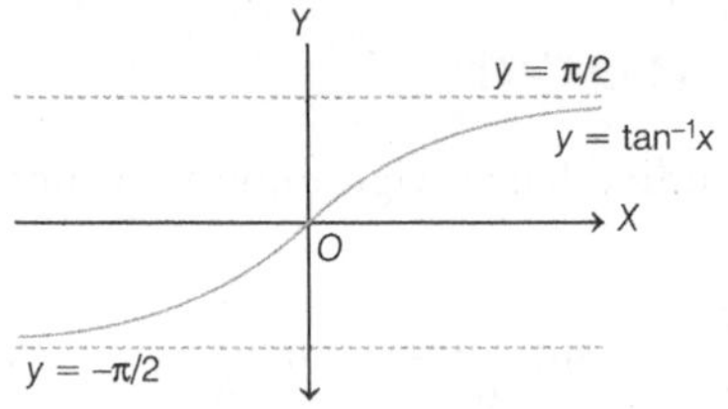

$\because \quad \tan y \in R$

$\therefore \quad x \in R$

Also, $-\infty < \tan y < \infty$

$\Rightarrow \quad -\frac{\pi}{2} < y < \frac{\pi}{2}$

These restrictions on x and y make the function, $\tan y = x$ one-one and onto so that the inverse function exists

i.e. $y = \tan^{-1} x$ is meaningful.

Thus, Domain : $x \in R$,

Range : $y \in (-\pi/2, \pi/2)$

Example 3. Find the principal values of the following.

(i) $\tan^{-1}(1)$ (ii) $\tan^{-1}(-1)$

Sol. (i) We know that $\tan^{-1} x$ denotes an angle in the interval $\left(-\frac{\pi}{2}, \frac{\pi}{2}\right)$ whose tangent is x for $x \in R$.

$\therefore \tan^{-1}(1)$ = An angle in $\left(-\frac{\pi}{2}, \frac{\pi}{2}\right)$, whose tangent is 1.

$\Rightarrow \tan^{-1}(1) = \frac{\pi}{4}$

(ii) $\tan^{-1}(-1)$ = An angle in $\left(-\frac{\pi}{2}, \frac{\pi}{2}\right)$, whose tangent is -1.

$\Rightarrow \tan^{-1}(-1) = -\frac{\pi}{4}$

Example 4. $\tan^{-1} 1 + \cos^{-1}\left(-\frac{1}{2}\right) + \sin^{-1}\left(-\frac{1}{2}\right)$ is equal to

(a) $\frac{5\pi}{12}$ (b) $\frac{\pi}{2}$ (c) $\frac{3\pi}{4}$ (d) $\frac{5\pi}{6}$

Sol. As, $\tan^{-1}(1) = \frac{\pi}{4}$, $\cos^{-1}\left(-\frac{1}{2}\right) = \frac{2\pi}{3}$ and $\sin^{-1}\left(-\frac{1}{2}\right) = -\frac{\pi}{6}$.

$$\Rightarrow \quad \frac{\pi}{4} + \frac{2\pi}{3} - \frac{\pi}{6} = \frac{3\pi}{4}$$

4. If $\cot y = x$, then $y = \cot^{-1} x$, under certain conditions.

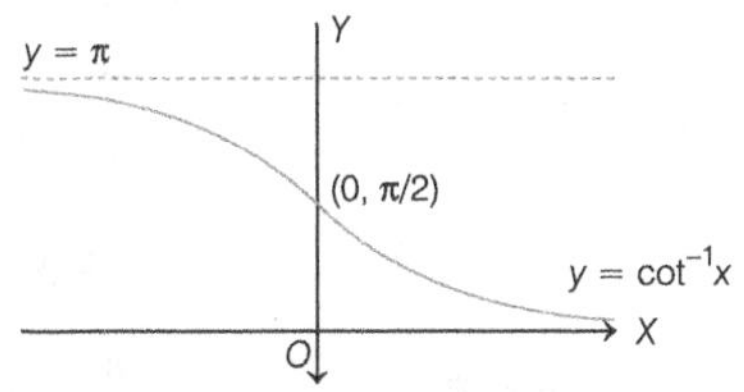

$\because \quad \cot y \in R \qquad \therefore \; x \in R$

Also, $-\infty < \cot y < \infty \Rightarrow 0 < y < \pi$

These restrictions on x and y make the function, $\cot y = x$ one-one and onto so that the inverse function exists

i.e. $y = \cot^{-1} x$ is meaningful.

Thus, Domain : $x \in R$ and Range : $y \in (0, \pi)$

Example 5. Find the principal values of the following

(i) $\cot^{-1}(1)$ (ii) $\cot^{-1}(-1)$

(iii) $\cot^{-1}\sqrt{3}$ (iv) $\cot^{-1}(-\sqrt{3})$

Sol. (i) For any $x \in R$, $\cot^{-1} x$ is an angle $\theta \in (0, \pi)$ such that $\cot\theta = x$.

$\therefore \cot^{-1}(1)$ = An angle $\theta \in (0, \pi)$ such that $\cot\theta = 1$

$= \frac{\pi}{4}$

(ii) $\cot^{-1}(-1)$ = An angle $\theta \in (0, \pi)$ whose cotangent is equal to -1

$= \frac{3\pi}{4}$

(iii) $\cot^{-1}(\sqrt{3})$ = An angle $\theta \in (0, \pi)$ whose cotangent is $\sqrt{3}$

$= \frac{\pi}{6}$

(iv) $\cot^{-1}(-\sqrt{3})$ = An angle $\theta \in (0, \pi)$ whose cotangent is $(-\sqrt{3})$

$= \frac{5\pi}{6}$

5. If $\sec y = x$, then $y = \sec^{-1} x$,

where $|x| \ge 1$ and $0 \le y \le \pi$, $y \ne \frac{\pi}{2}$

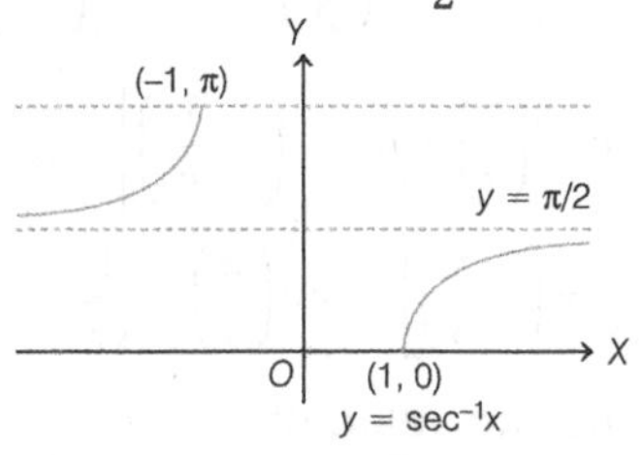

Thus, Domain : $x \in R - (-1, 1)$

Range : $y \in [0, \pi] - \{\pi/2\}$

Example 6. Find the principal values of each of the following.

(i) $\sec^{-1}(2)$ (ii) $\sec^{-1}\left(-\frac{2}{\sqrt{3}}\right)$ (iii) $\sec^{-1}(-2)$

Sol. For any $x \in (-\infty, -1] \cup [1, \infty)$, $\sec^{-1}x$ is an angle.

$\theta \in \left[0, \frac{\pi}{2}\right) \cup \left(\frac{\pi}{2}, \pi\right]$ whose secant is x i.e. $\sec\theta = x$.

Therefore,

(i) $\sec^{-1}(2)$ = (An angle $\theta \in \left[0, \frac{\pi}{2}\right) \cup \left(\frac{\pi}{2}, 1\right]$ such that $\sec\theta = 2$)

$\therefore \quad \theta = \frac{\pi}{3}$

(ii) $\sec^{-1}\left(-\frac{2}{\sqrt{3}}\right)$ = (An angle $\theta \in \left[0, \frac{\pi}{2}\right) \cup \left(\frac{\pi}{2}, \pi\right]$ such that $\sec\theta = \frac{-2}{\sqrt{3}}$)

$\therefore \quad \theta = \frac{5\pi}{6}$

(iii) $\sec^{-1}(-2)$ = (An angle $\theta \in [0, \pi] - \left\{\frac{\pi}{2}\right\}$ such that $\sec\theta = -2$)

$\therefore \quad \theta = \frac{2\pi}{3}$

Example 7. Find the set of values of $\sec^{-1}\left(\frac{\sqrt{3}}{2}\right)$.

Sol. We know that $\sec^{-1}x$ is defined for all $x \le -1$ or $x \ge 1$ and $\frac{\sqrt{3}}{2} < 1$.

$\therefore \sec^{-1}\left(\frac{\sqrt{3}}{2}\right)$ is not meaningful.

Example 8. Find the domain of $\sec^{-1}(2x + 1)$.

Sol. The domain of $\sec^{-1}x$ is $(-\infty, -1] \cup [1, \infty]$.

Therefore, $\sec^{-1}(2x + 1)$ is meaningful, if

$$2x + 1 \ge 1 \text{ or } 2x + 1 \le -1$$

$$\Rightarrow \quad 2x \ge 0 \text{ or } 2x \le -2 \Rightarrow x \ge 0 \text{ or } x \le -1$$

$$\Rightarrow \quad x \in (-\infty, -1] \cup [0, \infty)$$

Hence, the domain of $\sec^{-1}(2x + 1)$ is $(-\infty, -1] \cup [0, \infty)$.

6. If $\operatorname{cosec} y = x$, then $y = \operatorname{cosec}^{-1} x$,

where $|x| \ge 1$ and $-\pi/2 \le y \le \pi/2$, $y \ne 0$

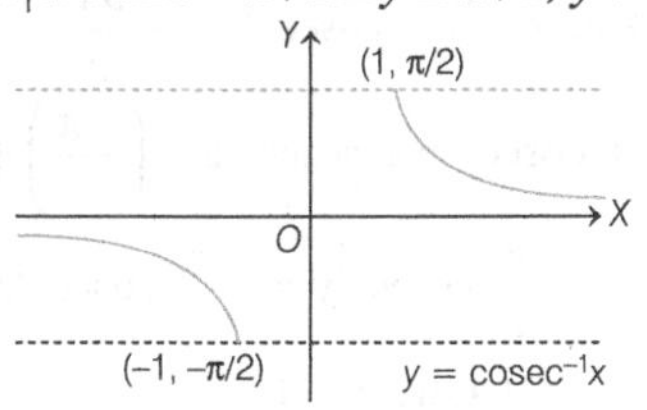

Thus, Domain : $x \in R - (-1, 1)$

Range : $y \in [-\pi/2, \pi/2] - \{0\}$

Example 9. Find the principal values of $\text{cosec}^{-1}(2)$ and $\text{cosec}^{-1}\left(-\frac{2}{\sqrt{3}}\right)$.

Sol. For $x \in (-\infty, -1] \cup [1, \infty)$, $\text{cosec}^{-1}x$ is an angle $\theta \in \left[-\frac{\pi}{2}, 0\right) \cup \left(0, \frac{\pi}{2}\right]$ such that $\text{cosec}\,\theta = x$.

$\therefore$ $\text{cosec}^{-1}(2) = $ (An angle $\theta \in \left[-\frac{\pi}{2}, 0\right) \cup \left(0, \frac{\pi}{2}\right]$ such that $\text{cosec}\,\theta = 2$)

$\therefore \quad \theta = \frac{\pi}{6}$

and $\text{cosec}^{-1}\left(-\frac{2}{\sqrt{3}}\right) = $ (An angle $\theta \in \left[-\frac{\pi}{2}, 0\right) \cup \left(0, \frac{\pi}{2}\right]$ such that $\text{cosec}\,\theta = -\frac{2}{\sqrt{3}}$)

$\therefore \quad \theta = -\frac{\pi}{3}$

Example 10. Find the set of values of $\text{cosec}^{-1}\left(-\frac{1}{2}\right)$.

Sol. We know that $\text{cosec}^{-1}x$ is defined for all $x \le -1$ or $x \ge 1$.

So, $\text{cosec}^{-1}\left(-\frac{1}{2}\right)$ is not meaningful.

Hence, the set of values of $\text{cosec}^{-1}\left(-\frac{1}{2}\right)$ is the null set ϕ.

Example 11. For the principal values, evaluate each of the following.

(i) $\tan^{-1}\sqrt{3} - \sec^{-1}(-2) + \text{cosec}^{-1}\frac{2}{\sqrt{3}}$

(ii) $2\sec^{-1}(2) - 2\,\text{cosec}^{-1}(-2)$

Sol. (i) $\tan^{-1}\sqrt{3} - \sec^{-1}(-2) + \text{cosec}^{-1}\frac{2}{\sqrt{3}} = \frac{\pi}{3} - \frac{2\pi}{3} + \frac{\pi}{3} = 0$

(ii) $2\sec^{-1}2 - 2\,\text{cosec}^{-1}(-2) = 2 \times \frac{\pi}{3} - 2 \times \left(-\frac{\pi}{6}\right) = \pi$

Example 12. If $\text{cosec}^{-1}x + \text{cosec}^{-1}y + \text{cosec}^{-1}z = -\frac{3\pi}{2}$, then find the value of $\frac{x}{y} + \frac{y}{z} + \frac{z}{x}$.

Sol. We know that the minimum value of $\text{cosec}^{-1}x$ is $-\frac{\pi}{2}$ which is attained at $x = -1$.

$\therefore \text{cosec}^{-1}x + \text{cosec}^{-1}y + \text{cosec}^{-1}z = -\frac{3\pi}{2}$

$\Rightarrow \text{cosec}^{-1}x + \text{cosec}^{-1}y + \text{cosec}^{-1}z = \left(-\frac{\pi}{2}\right) + \left(-\frac{\pi}{2}\right) + \left(-\frac{\pi}{2}\right)$

$\Rightarrow \text{cosec}^{-1}x = -\frac{\pi}{2}, \text{cosec}^{-1}y = -\frac{\pi}{2}, \text{cosec}^{-1}z = -\frac{\pi}{2}$

$\Rightarrow x = -1, y = -1$ and $z = -1$

$\therefore \quad \frac{x}{y} + \frac{y}{z} + \frac{z}{x} = \frac{(-1)}{(-1)} + \frac{(-1)}{(-1)} + \frac{(-1)}{(-1)} = 3$

Principal Values and Domains of Inverse Trigonometric/Circular Functions

Function	Domain	Range (Principal Value Branch)
(i) $y = \sin^{-1}x$	$-1 \le x \le 1$	$-\frac{\pi}{2} \le y \le \frac{\pi}{2}$
(ii) $y = \cos^{-1}x$	$-1 \le x \le 1$	$0 \le y \le \pi$
(iii) $y = \tan^{-1}x$	$x \in R$	$-\frac{\pi}{2} < y < \frac{\pi}{2}$
(iv) $y = \text{cosec}^{-1}x$	$x \le -1$ or $x \ge 1$	$-\frac{\pi}{2} \le y \le \frac{\pi}{2}, y \ne 0$
(v) $y = \sec^{-1}x$	$x \le -1$ or $x \ge 1$	$0 \le y \le \pi; y \ne \frac{\pi}{2}$
(vi) $y = \cot^{-1}x$	$x \in R$	$0 < y < \pi$

JEE Focus Points

- 1st quadrant is common to the range of all the inverse trigonometric functions.
- 3rd quadrant is not used in inverse trigonometric functions.
- 4th quadrant is used in the clockwise direction i.e. $-\frac{\pi}{2} \le y \le 0$.
- No inverse function is periodic.
- If no branch of an inverse trigonometric function is mentioned, then it means the principal value branch of the function.

Concept Inside Video

Example 13. Find the value of $\cos\left[\cos^{-1}\left(-\frac{\sqrt{3}}{2}\right) + \frac{\pi}{6}\right]$.

Sol. $\cos\left[\cos^{-1}\left(\frac{-\sqrt{3}}{2}\right) + \frac{\pi}{6}\right] = \cos\left\{\frac{5\pi}{6} + \frac{\pi}{6}\right\} = \cos\pi = -1$

Example 14. Find the value of

$$\tan\left[\cos^{-1}\left(\frac{1}{2}\right) + \tan^{-1}\left(-\frac{1}{\sqrt{3}}\right)\right].$$

Sol. Let $y = \tan\left[\cos^{-1}\left(\frac{1}{2}\right) + \tan^{-1}\left(-\frac{1}{\sqrt{3}}\right)\right]$

$= \tan\left[\frac{\pi}{3} + \left(-\frac{\pi}{6}\right)\right] = \tan\left(\frac{\pi}{6}\right) = \frac{1}{\sqrt{3}}$

Example 15. Find the value of

$$\sin^{-1}\left[\cos\left\{\sin^{-1}\left(-\frac{\sqrt{3}}{2}\right)\right\}\right].$$

Sol. $\sin^{-1}\left[\cos\left\{\sin^{-1}\left(-\frac{\sqrt{3}}{2}\right)\right\}\right]$

$$= \sin^{-1}\left[\cos\left(-\frac{\pi}{3}\right)\right] = \sin^{-1}\left(\cos\frac{\pi}{3}\right)$$

$$= \sin^{-1}\left(\frac{1}{2}\right) = \frac{\pi}{6}$$

4.4 Monotonic Behaviour of Inverse Trigonometric Functions

1. (i) $y = \sin\theta$ and $y = \sin^{-1} x$ are increasing functions on $\theta \in \left[-\frac{\pi}{2}, \frac{\pi}{2}\right]$ and $x \in [-1, 1]$

   i.e. if $\theta_1 < \theta_2$, then

   $$\sin\theta_1 < \sin\theta_2 \forall \theta_1, \theta_2 \in \left[-\frac{\pi}{2}, \frac{\pi}{2}\right]$$

   Also, if $x_1 < x_2$, then

   $$\sin^{-1} x_1 < \sin^{-1} x_2 \forall x_1, x_2 \in [-1,1].$$

   (ii) Minimum value of $\sin^{-1} x$ is $\frac{-\pi}{2}$ at $x = -1$ and the maximum value of $\sin^{-1} x$ is $\frac{\pi}{2}$ at $x = 1$.

Example 16. Solve $\sin^{-1} x > -1$.

Sol. $\sin^{-1} x > -1$

or $-1 < \sin^{-1} x \le \frac{\pi}{2}$

or $\sin(-1) < x \le \sin\left(\frac{\pi}{2}\right)$

$\Rightarrow \quad x \in (-\sin 1, 1]$

2. (i) $y = \cos\theta$ and $y = \cos^{-1} x$ both are decreasing functions on $\theta \in [0, \pi]$ and $x \in [-1, 1]$.

   i.e. if $\theta_1 < \theta_2 \Rightarrow \cos\theta_1 > \cos\theta_2$

   for all $\theta_1, \theta_2 \in [0, \pi]$

   Also, if $x_1 < x_2$

   $\Rightarrow \cos^{-1} x_1 > \cos^{-1} x_2$

   for all $x_1, x_2 \in [-1, 1]$.

   (ii) Minimum value of $\cos^{-1} x$ is zero at $x = 1$ but maximum value of $\cos^{-1} x$ is π at $x = -1$.

Example 17. Solve $\cos^{-1} x > \cos^{-1} x^2$.

Sol. $\cos^{-1} x > \cos^{-1} x^2$ or $x < x^2$ $\quad [\because \cos^{-1}$ is decreasing$]$

or $x^2 - x > 0$

or $x(x-1) > 0$

or $x \in (-1, 0)$

3. (i) $y = \tan\theta$ and $y = \tan^{-1} x$ both are increasing functions in their respective domains

   i.e. if $\theta_1 < \theta_2$, then

   $$\tan\theta_1 < \tan\theta_2 \forall \theta_1, \theta_2 \in \left(\frac{-\pi}{2}, \frac{\pi}{2}\right)$$

   and if $x_1 < x_2$, then

   $$\tan^{-1} x_1 < \tan^{-1} x_2 \forall x_1, x_2 \in R.$$

   (ii) $\tan^{-1} x$ does not attain its minimum value $\left(-\frac{\pi}{2}\right)$ and maximum value $= \frac{\pi}{2}$ at points in R.

Example 18. If $\sin^{-1}(x^2 + 2x + 2) + \tan^{-1}(x^2 - 3x - k^2) > \frac{\pi}{2}$, then find the values of k.

Sol. $\sin^{-1}(x^2 + 2x + 2) + \tan^{-1}(x^2 - 3x - k^2) > \frac{\pi}{2}$

$\Rightarrow \sin^{-1}((x+1)^2 + 1) + \tan^{-1}(x^2 - 3x - k^2) > \frac{\pi}{2}$

Now, $\sin^{-1}((x+1)^2 + 1)$ is defined if $(x+1)^2 = 0$ or $x = -1$.

Putting $x = -1$, we get

$$\frac{\pi}{2} + \tan^{-1}(4 - k^2) > \frac{\pi}{2}$$

$\Rightarrow \quad \tan^{-1}(4 - k^2) > 0$

$\Rightarrow \quad 4 - k^2 > 0$

$\Rightarrow \quad -2 < k < 2$

4. (i) $y = \cot\theta$ and $y = \cot^{-1} x$ are decreasing functions in $(0, \pi)$ and $(-\infty, \infty)$, respectively

   i.e. if $\theta_1 < \theta_2$, then $\cot\theta_1 > \cot\theta_2$ for all $\theta_1, \theta_2 \in (0, \pi)$.

   Also, if $x_1 < x_2$, then $\cot^{-1} x_1 > \cot^{-1} x_2$ for all $x_1, x_2 \in R$.

   (ii) $\cot^{-1} x$ does not attain its maximum value $(= \pi)$ and minimum value $(= 0)$ at points in R.

Example 19. Solve for x if $(\cot^{-1} x)^2 - 3(\cot^{-1} x) + 2 > 0$.

Sol. $(\cot^{-1} x - 1)(\cot^{-1} x - 2) > 0$

$\Rightarrow \quad \cot^{-1} x < 1$ or $\cot^{-1} x > 2$

$\Rightarrow \quad x > \cot 1$ or $x < \cot 2$

$[\because \cot^{-1} x$ is a decreasing function$]$

$\Rightarrow \quad x < \cot 2$ or $x > \cot 1$

Example 20. Solve $[\cot^{-1} x]+[\cos^{-1} x]=0$, where $[\cdot]$ denotes the greatest integer function.

Sol. We have, $[\cot^{-1} x]+[\cos^{-1} x]=0$

Since, $\cos^{-1} x, \cot^{-1} x \geq 0$; we must have

$$[\cot^{-1} x]=[\cos^{-1} x]=0$$

Now, $[\cot^{-1} x]=0$

$\Rightarrow \quad 0<\cot^{-1} x<1$

$\Rightarrow \quad x \in (\cot 1, \infty) \quad$ ...(i)

Also, $[\cos^{-1} x]=0$

$\Rightarrow \quad 0 \leq \cos^{-1} x<1 \quad$ ...(ii)

$\Rightarrow \quad x \in (\cos 1, 1]$

From Eqs. (i) and (ii), we get

$$x \in [\cot 1, 1]$$

5. (i) $y=\sec\theta$ is an increasing function on the interval $\theta \in \left[0, \frac{\pi}{2}\right)$ and $\theta \in \left(\frac{\pi}{2}, \pi\right]$

but $y=\sec\theta$ is neither increasing nor decreasing on $\theta \in \left[0, \frac{\pi}{2}\right) \cup \left(\frac{\pi}{2}, \pi\right]$.

(ii) $y=\sec^{-1} x$ is also an increasing function on the intervals $x \in (-\infty, -1]$ and $x \in [1, \infty)$ but it should be noted that $y=\sec^{-1} x$ is neither increasing nor decreasing on $x \in (-\infty, -1] \cup [1, \infty)$.

(iii) Minimum value of $y=\sec^{-1} x$ is zero at $x=1$ and maximum value of $y=\sec^{-1} x$ is π at $x=-1$.

Example 21. Find the values of x for which the following expressions are defined.

(i) $\sin^{-1}(3x-2)$ (ii) $\cos^{-1}(\log_e x)$

(iii) $\sec^{-1}(x^2-2)$

Sol. (i) $\sin^{-1}(3x-2)$ is defined if

$$-1 \leq 3x-2 \leq 1$$

$\therefore \quad 1 \leq 3x \leq 3$

So, $\frac{1}{3} \leq x \leq 1$

(ii) $\cos^{-1}(\log_e x)$ is defined if

$$-1 \leq \log_e x \leq 1$$

$\therefore \quad e^{-1} \leq x \leq e^{1}$

(iii) $\sec^{-1}(x^2-2)$ is defined if

$$x^2-2 \leq -1 \text{ or } x^2-2 \geq 1$$

$\therefore \quad x^2 \leq 1$ or $x^2 \geq 3$

So, $-1 \leq x \leq 1$ or $x \leq -\sqrt{3}$ or $x \geq \sqrt{3}$

JEE SCANNER

Example Similar to PYQ Asked in JEE Main 2024

If the domain of the function $f(x)=\sin^{-1}\left(\frac{x+1}{3x+2}\right)$ is $R-(\alpha, \beta)$, then $8\alpha\beta$ is equal to

(a) 3 (b) 4 (c) 5 (d) 0

Sol. (a) Given $f(x)=\sin^{-1}\left(\frac{x+1}{3x+2}\right)$

For $f(x)$ to be defined

$$3x+2 \neq 0 \text{ and } -1 \leq \frac{x+1}{3x+2} \leq 1$$

$$\Rightarrow \quad x \neq -\frac{2}{3} \text{ and } \begin{cases} \frac{x+1}{3x+2} \geq -1 \\ \frac{x+1}{3x+2} \leq 1 \end{cases}$$

$$\Rightarrow \quad \begin{cases} \frac{x+1+3x+2}{3x+2} \geq 0 \\ \frac{x+1-3x-2}{3x+2} \leq 0 \end{cases} \Rightarrow \begin{cases} \frac{4x+3}{3x+2} \geq 0 \\ \frac{-2x-1}{3x+2} \leq 0 \end{cases}$$

$$\Rightarrow \quad \begin{cases} x \in \left(-\infty, \frac{-3}{4}\right] \cup \left(\frac{-2}{3}, \infty\right) \\ x \in \left(-\infty, \frac{-2}{3}\right) \cup \left[\frac{-1}{2}, \infty\right) \end{cases}$$

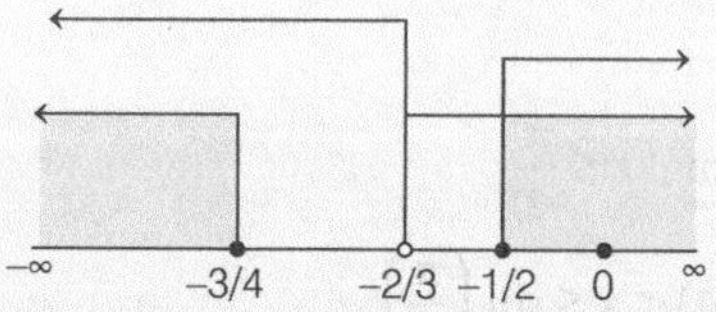

$$x \in \left(-\infty, \frac{-3}{4}\right] \cup \left[\frac{-1}{2}, \infty\right)$$

$$\therefore \quad R-\left(-\frac{3}{4}, \frac{-1}{2}\right)$$

$$\therefore \quad \alpha=\frac{-3}{4}, \beta=\frac{-1}{2}$$

$$\therefore 8\alpha\beta=8\left(\frac{-3}{4}\right)\left(\frac{-1}{2}\right)=3$$

Skill Builder

If the domain of the function $f(x)=\sin^{-1}\left[\frac{x+1}{x+2}\right]$ is $\left(\frac{\alpha}{\beta}, \infty\right)$, then $(\alpha\beta)^2$ is equal to

(a) 42 (b) 36

(c) 0 (d) −36

For Sol.

▪ **For more practice** See Q.5 of Milestone Practice 1.

6. (i) $y = \operatorname{cosec}\theta$ is a decreasing function on $\theta \in \left[-\frac{\pi}{2}, 0\right)$ and $\theta \in \left(0, \frac{\pi}{2}\right]$

but $y = \operatorname{cosec}\theta$ is neither increasing nor decreasing on $\theta \in \left[-\frac{\pi}{2}, 0\right) \cup \left(0, \frac{\pi}{2}\right]$.

(ii) $y = \operatorname{cosec}^{-1} x$ is also a decreasing function on $x \in (-\infty, -1]$ and $[1, \infty)$ but it is neither increasing nor decreasing on $(-\infty, -1] \cup [1, \infty)$.

(iii) Minimum value of $\operatorname{cosec}^{-1} x$ is $\left(-\frac{\pi}{2}\right)$ at $x = -1$

and maximum value of $\operatorname{cosec}^{-1} x$ is $\frac{\pi}{2}$ at $x = 1$.

Example 22. Find the domain of the following functions

(i) $f(x) = \sin^{-1}(x+1)$ (ii) $f(x) = \cos^{-1}(-x^2)$

(iii) $f(x) = \cos^{-1} x + \cos x$ (iv) $f(x) = \sec^{-1} x + \tan^{-1} x$

(v) $f(x) = \operatorname{cosec}^{-1}(x-1)$

Sol. (i) $f(x) = \sin^{-1}(x+1)$

For $f(x)$ to be defined

$-1 < x + 1 < 1 \Rightarrow -2 \le x \le 0 \Rightarrow x \in [-2, 0]$

$\therefore D_f \in [-2, 0]$

(ii) $f(x) = \cos^{-1}(-x^2)$

$f(x)$ will be meaningful if

$-1 \le -x^2 \le 1 \Rightarrow -1 \le x^2 \le 1$ but $x^2 \ge 0$

So, $0 \le x^2 \le 1$

$\Rightarrow x^2 \ge 0$ and $x^2 \le 1 \Rightarrow x \in R$ and $-1 \le x \le 1$

Hence, $x \in [-1, 1]$.

(iii) $f(x) = \cos^{-1} x + \cos x$

D_f will be domain of $\cos^{-1} x \cap$ domain of $\cos x$

$\Rightarrow -1 \le x \le 1 \cap x \in R \Rightarrow -1 \le x \le 1$

(iv) $f(x) = \sec^{-1} x + \tan^{-1} x$

For $f(x)$ to be defined,

$$\begin{cases} |x| \ge 1 \\ x \in R \end{cases} \Rightarrow \begin{cases} x \le -1 \text{ or } x \ge 1 \\ x \in R \end{cases}$$

$\Rightarrow x \in (-\infty, -1] \cup [1, \infty)$

(v) $f(x) = \operatorname{cosec}^{-1}(x-1)$

For $f(x)$ to be defined,

$x - 1 \le -1$ or $x - 1 \ge 1$

$\Rightarrow x \le 0$ or $x \ge 2 \Rightarrow x \in (-\infty, 0] \cup [2, \infty)$

Example 23. Find the domain of $\sin^{-1}(2x^2 - 1)$.

Sol. Let $y = \sin^{-1}(2x^2 - 1)$

For y to be defined $-1 \le (2x^2 - 1) \le 1$

$\Rightarrow 0 \le 2x^2 \le 2 \Rightarrow 0 \le x^2 \le 1 \Rightarrow x \in [-1, 1]$

Example 24. Let $f(x) = \cos^{-1} x$ and $g(x) = \frac{x^2 - x - 2}{2x^2 - x - 6}$.

If $g(2) = \lim_{x \to 2} g(x)$, then the domain of the function fog is [JEE Main 2021]

(a) $(-\infty, -2] \cup \left[\frac{-3}{2}, \infty\right)$ (b) $(-\infty, -2] \cup [-1, \infty)$

(c) $(-\infty, -2] \cup \left[\frac{-4}{3}, \infty\right)$ (d) $(-\infty, -1] \cup [2, \infty)$

Sol. (c) Given, $g(x) = \frac{x^2 - x - 2}{2x^2 - x - 6}$

$f(x) = \cos^{-1} x$

Now, $f(g(x)) = \cos^{-1} g(x) = \cos^{-1}\left(\frac{x^2 - x - 2}{2x^2 - x - 6}\right)$

For domain of $fog(x)$

$|g(x)| \le 1$

$\Rightarrow \left|\frac{x^2 - x - 2}{2x^2 - x - 6}\right| \le 1$

$\Rightarrow \left|\frac{(x+1)(x-2)}{(2x+3)(x-2)}\right| \le 1$

$\Rightarrow \left|\frac{x+1}{2x+3}\right| \le 1$

$\Rightarrow \left(\frac{x+1}{2x+3}\right)^2 \le 1$ [squaring on both sides]

$\Rightarrow (x+1)^2 \le (2x+3)^2$ but $x \ne \frac{-3}{2}$

$\Rightarrow 3x^2 + 10x + 8 \ge 0$

$\Rightarrow (3x+4)(x+2) \ge 0$

$\Rightarrow x \in (-\infty, -2] \cup \left[\frac{-4}{3}, \infty\right)$

Example 25. Find the range of $y = \sin^{-1}\sqrt{x^2 + x + 1}$.

Sol. Let $f(x) = x^2 + x + 1$

$= x^2 + 2 \cdot \frac{1}{2} \cdot x + \frac{1}{4} + 1 - \frac{1}{4} = \left(x + \frac{1}{2}\right)^2 + \frac{3}{4}$

$\Rightarrow f(x) \ge \frac{3}{4}$

So, $\frac{3}{4} \le f(x) \le 1$

[$\because \sin^{-1} x, -1 \le x \le 1$ and $\sqrt{f(x)} \ge 0$]

$\Rightarrow \sin^{-1}\left(\frac{\sqrt{3}}{2}\right) \le \sin^{-1}\sqrt{f(x)} \le \sin^{-1}(1)$

$\Rightarrow$ Range $\equiv \left[\frac{\pi}{3}, \frac{\pi}{2}\right]$

Milestone Practice 4.1

Find the value of the following

1. $\sin\left[\frac{\pi}{3} - \sin^{-1}\left(\frac{1}{2}\right)\right]$

2. $\operatorname{cosec}[\sec^{-1}(-\sqrt{2}) + \cot^{-1}(-1)]$

Find the domain of the following

3. $y = \sec^{-1}(x^2 + 3x + 1)$

4. $y = \cos^{-1}\left(\frac{x^2}{1 + x^2}\right)$

5. $y = \tan^{-1}(\sqrt{x^2 - 1})$

6. $y = \sin^{-1}(\log_e x)$

7. $y = \operatorname{cosec}^{-1}(x^2 - 2)$

8. Find the range of $y = \cos^{-1}\left[\left(\frac{1}{2}\right)^x\right]$.

9. Find the value of $\sec^{-1}\left(x + \frac{1}{x}\right)$.

10. Find the range of $y = \cot^{-1}\left(\frac{x^2}{x^2 + 1}\right)$.

11. Find the range of $\sin^{-1}|x| + \sec^{-1}|x|$.

12. If range of the function $f(x) = \tan^{-1}(3x^2 + bx + 3)$, $x \in R$ is $\left[0, \frac{\pi}{2}\right)$, then find the square of sum of all possible values of b.

Answer Key

1. $\frac{1}{2}$
2. -1
3. $x \in R : x \le -3$ or $-2 \le x \le -1$ or $x \ge 0$
4. R
5. $(-\infty, -1] \cup [1, \infty)$
6. $x \in \left[\frac{1}{e}, e\right]$
7. $x \in (-\infty, -\sqrt{3}]$ or $[-1, -1]$ or $[\sqrt{3}, \infty)$
8. $y \in \left[0, \frac{\pi}{2}\right)$
9. $y \in \left[\frac{\pi}{3}, \frac{\pi}{2}\right) \cup \left(\frac{\pi}{2}, \frac{2\pi}{3}\right]$
10. $y \in \left(\frac{\pi}{4}, \frac{\pi}{2}\right]$
11. $\left\{\frac{\pi}{2}\right\}$
12. 0

For Detailed Solution

Milestone 2 Properties I and II of Inverse Trigonometric Functions

Introduction

There are I to XIII important properties of Inverse trigonometric function in this milestone we will be studied I and II and other properties we will be studied in milestones 3 to 6.

Property I

(i) $y = \sin^{-1}(\sin x), x \in R, y \in \left[-\frac{\pi}{2}, \frac{\pi}{2}\right]$, is periodic with period 2π.

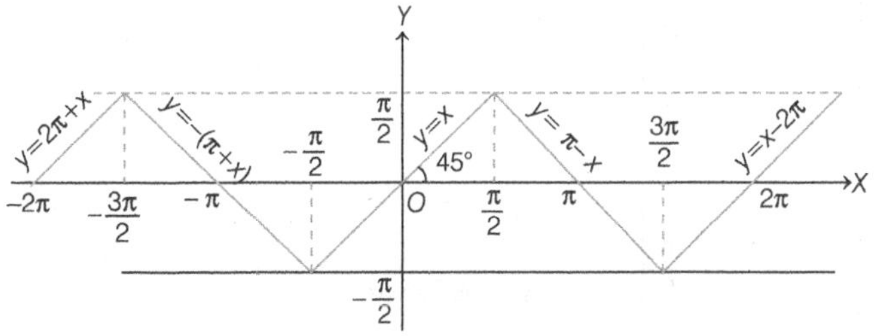

Example 26. Find the principal values of the following.

(i) $\sin^{-1}(\sin 1)$ (ii) $\sin^{-1}(\sin 2)$

(iii) $\sin^{-1}(\sin 10)$ (iv) $\sin^{-1}(\sin 20)$

(v) $\sin^{-1}(\sin 100)$ (vi) $\sin^{-1}\left(\sin \frac{29\pi}{5}\right)$

Sol. (i) Since, $1 \in \left[-\frac{\pi}{2}, \frac{\pi}{2}\right]$, $\sin^{-1}(\sin 1) = 1$

(ii) Since, $2 \notin \left[-\frac{\pi}{2}, \frac{\pi}{2}\right]$, $\sin^{-1}(\sin 2) \neq 2$

$\therefore \sin^{-1}(\sin 2) = \sin^{-1}(\sin(\pi - 2)) = \pi - 2$

as $(\pi - 2) \in \left[-\frac{\pi}{2}, \frac{\pi}{2}\right]$

(iii) $\sin^{-1}(\sin 10) = \sin^{-1}(\sin(3\pi - 10)) = 3\pi - 10$

as $(3\pi - 10) \in \left[-\frac{\pi}{2}, \frac{\pi}{2}\right]$

(iv) $\sin^{-1}(\sin(-20)) = \sin^{-1}(\sin(6\pi - 20)) = 6\pi - 20$

as $(6\pi - 20) \in \left[-\frac{\pi}{2}, \frac{\pi}{2}\right]$

(v) $\sin^{-1}(\sin 100) = \sin^{-1}(\sin(100 - 32\pi))$

$= 100 - 32\pi$ as $(100 - 32\pi) \in \left[-\frac{\pi}{2}, \frac{\pi}{2}\right]$

(vi) $\sin^{-1}\left(\sin \frac{29\pi}{5}\right) = \sin^{-1}\left(\sin\left(6\pi - \frac{\pi}{5}\right)\right)$

$= \sin^{-1}\left(\sin\left(-\frac{\pi}{5}\right)\right) = -\frac{\pi}{5}.$

Example 27. Solve $\sin^{-1}(\sin 6x) = x,\ x \in [0, \pi]$.

Sol. $\sin^{-1}(\sin 6x) = x$

$\Rightarrow \quad \sin 6x = \sin x$

$\Rightarrow \quad \sin 6x - \sin x = 0$

$\Rightarrow \quad 2\sin\frac{5x}{2}\cos\frac{7x}{2} = 0$

$\Rightarrow \quad \frac{5x}{2} = n\pi$ or $\frac{7x}{2} = (2n+1)\frac{\pi}{2}, n \in z$

$\Rightarrow \quad x = \frac{2n\pi}{5}$ or $x = (2n+1)\frac{\pi}{7}$

$\Rightarrow \quad x = \frac{\pi}{7}, \frac{3\pi}{7}, \frac{5\pi}{7}, \pi, 0, \frac{2\pi}{5}, \frac{4\pi}{5}$

But $x = \frac{5\pi}{7}, \pi, \frac{4\pi}{5}$ are not possible as any solution must lie in $\left[-\frac{\pi}{2}, \frac{\pi}{2}\right]$.

Example 28. Solve $\sin^{-1}\left[\sin\left(\frac{2x^2+4}{1+x^2}\right)\right] < \pi - 3$.

Sol. $\sin^{-1}\left[\sin\left(\frac{2x^2+4}{1+x^2}\right)\right] < \pi - 3$ ...(i)

Now, $\frac{2x^2+4}{1+x^2} = \frac{2x^2+2+2}{1+x^2} = 2 + \frac{2}{1+x^2}$

So, $2 + \frac{2}{1+x^2} \in [2, 4]$

Therefore, Eq. (i) reduces to

$$\pi - \left(\frac{2x^2+4}{1+x^2}\right) < \pi - 3 \text{ or } \frac{2x^2+4}{1+x^2} > 3$$

or $\quad 2x^2 + 4 > 3 + 3x^2$ or $x^2 - 1 < 0$ or $-1 < x < 1$

Example 29. Find the area bounded by $y = \sin^{-1}(\sin x)$ and X-axis for $x \in [0, 100\pi]$.

Sol. $y = \sin^{-1}(\sin x)$ is periodic with period 2π.

$\therefore$ Required area $= 50 \times$ (area bounded by $y = \sin^{-1}(\sin x)$ and X-axis for $x \in [0, 2\pi]$).

Graph of $y = \sin^{-1}(\sin x)$ for $x \in [0, 2\pi]$ is as shown in the following figure.

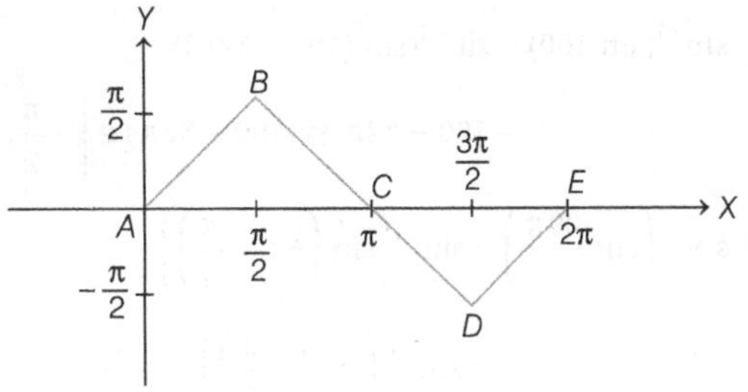

Required area $= 50 \times$ (area of ΔABC + area of ΔCDE)

$= 100 \times$ (area of ΔABC)

[$\because$ area of ΔABC = area of ΔCDE]

$$= 100 \times \left(\frac{1}{2} \times \pi \times \frac{\pi}{2}\right) = 25\pi^2$$

(ii) $y = \cos^{-1}(\cos x)$, $x \in R$, $y \in [0, \pi]$, is periodic with period 2π.

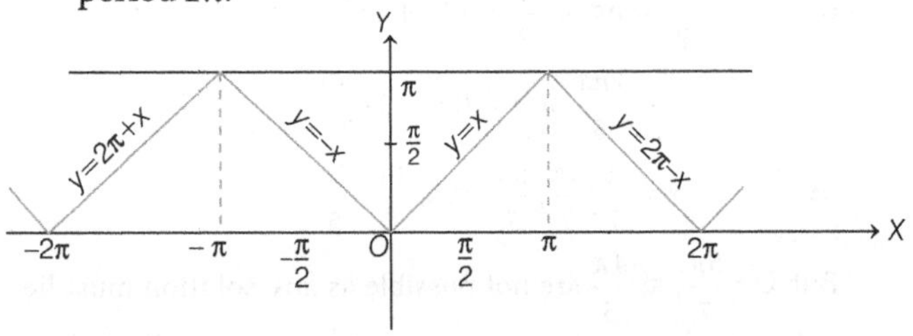

Example 30. Find the principal values of the following.

(i) $\cos^{-1}(\cos 2)$ (ii) $\cos^{-1}(\cos 4)$

(iii) $\cos^{-1}(\cos 15)$ (iv) $\cos^{-1}(\cos 30)$

(v) $\cos^{-1}(\cos 50)$ (vi) $\cos^{-1}\left(\cos \frac{48\pi}{7}\right)$

Sol. (i) Since, $2 \in [0, \pi]$, $\cos^{-1}(\cos 2) = 2$

(ii) Since, $4 \notin [0, \pi]$, $\cos^{-1}(\cos 4) \neq 4$

$\therefore$ $\cos^{-1}(\cos 4) = 2\pi - 4$

(iii) $\cos^{-1}(\cos 15) = 15 - 4\pi$

(iv) $\cos^{-1}(\cos 30) = 10\pi - 30$

(v) $\cos^{-1}(\cos 50) = 16\pi - 50$

(vi) $$\cos^{-1}\left(\cos \frac{48\pi}{7}\right) = \cos^{-1}\left(\cos\left(6\pi + \frac{6\pi}{7}\right)\right)$$

$$= \cos^{-1}\left(\cos \frac{6\pi}{7}\right) = \frac{6\pi}{7}$$

Example 31. Solve $\cos^{-1}(\cos x) > \sin^{-1}(\sin x)$, $x \in [0, 2\pi]$.

Sol. We have, $\cos^{-1}(\cos x) > \sin^{-1}(\sin x)$

To solve this inequality, we draw the graph of $y = \cos^{-1}(\cos x)$ and $y = \sin^{-1}(\sin x)$ for $x \in [0, 2\pi]$.

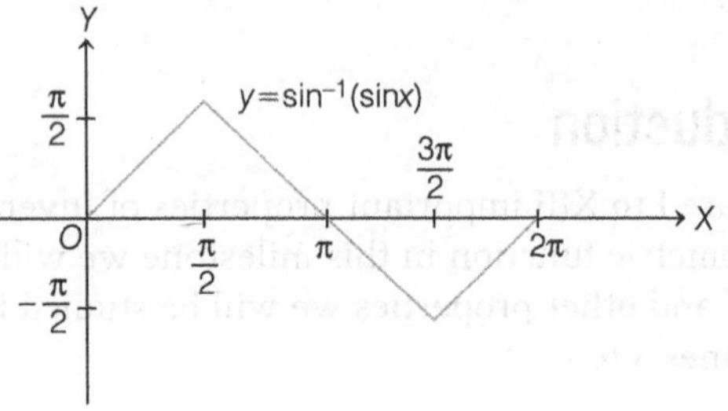

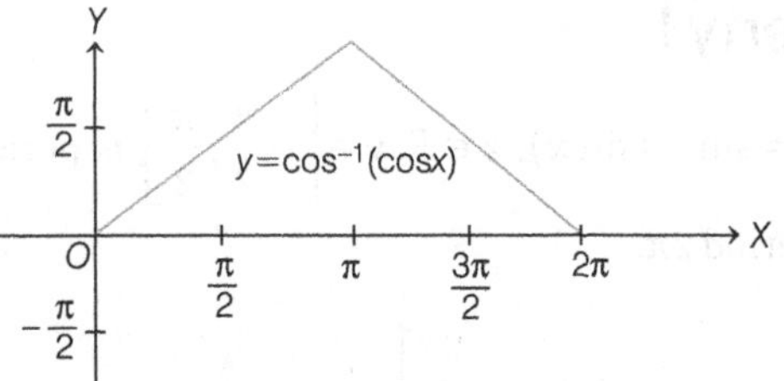

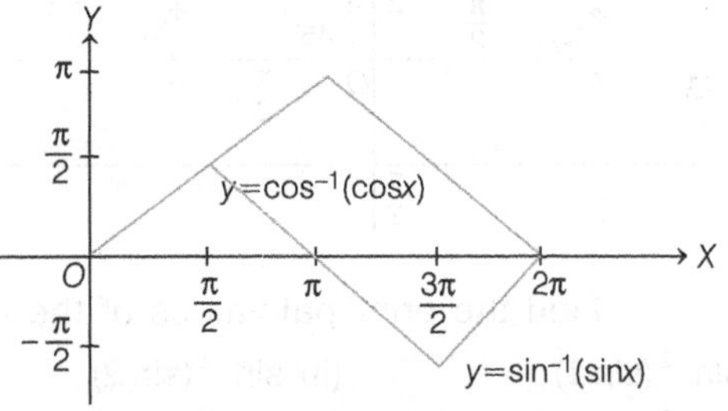

From the figure, we can see that graph of $y = \cos^{-1}(\cos x)$ lies above the graph of $y = \sin^{-1}(\sin x)$ for $x \in \left(\frac{\pi}{2}, 2\pi\right]$.

Thus, the solution of $\cos^{-1}(\cos x) > \sin^{-1}(\sin x)$ is

$$x \in \left(\frac{\pi}{2}, 2\pi\right]$$

(iii) $y = \tan^{-1}(\tan x)$, $x \in R - \left\{(2n-1)\frac{\pi}{2}, n \in I\right\}$,

$y \in \left(-\frac{\pi}{2}, \frac{\pi}{2}\right)$ is periodic with period π.

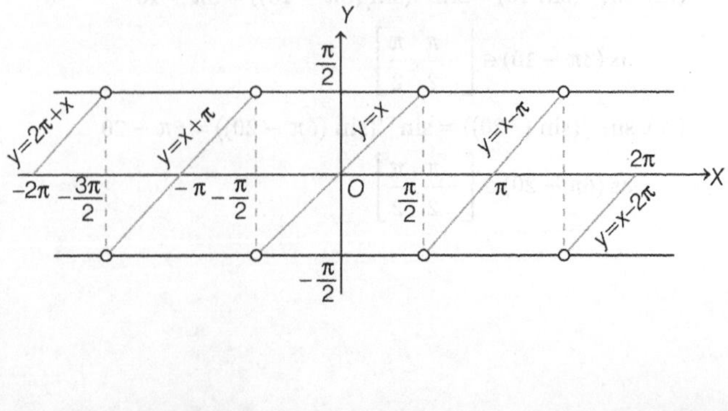

Example 32. Find the principal values of the following :

(i) $\tan^{-1}\left(\tan\dfrac{2\pi}{3}\right)$ (ii) $\tan^{-1}(\tan(-6))$

Sol.

(i) $\tan^{-1}\left(\tan\dfrac{2\pi}{3}\right) \neq \dfrac{2\pi}{3}$, as $\dfrac{2\pi}{3}$ does not lie between $-\dfrac{\pi}{2}$ and $\dfrac{\pi}{2}$.

Now, $\tan^{-1}\left(\tan\dfrac{2\pi}{3}\right) = \tan^{-1}\left(\tan\left(\pi - \dfrac{\pi}{3}\right)\right)$

$$= \tan^{-1}\left(-\tan\frac{\pi}{3}\right) = \tan^{-1}\left(\tan\left(-\frac{\pi}{3}\right)\right) = -\frac{\pi}{3}$$

(ii) $\tan^{-1}(\tan(-6)) = \tan^{-1}(\tan(2\pi - 6)) = 2\pi - 6$

as $(2\pi - 6) \in \left(-\dfrac{\pi}{2}, \dfrac{\pi}{2}\right)$.

(iv) $y = \sec^{-1}(\sec x), x \in R - \left\{(2n-1)\dfrac{\pi}{2}, n \in I\right\}$,

$y \in \left[0, \dfrac{\pi}{2}\right) \cup \left(\dfrac{\pi}{2}, \pi\right]$, is periodic with period 2π.

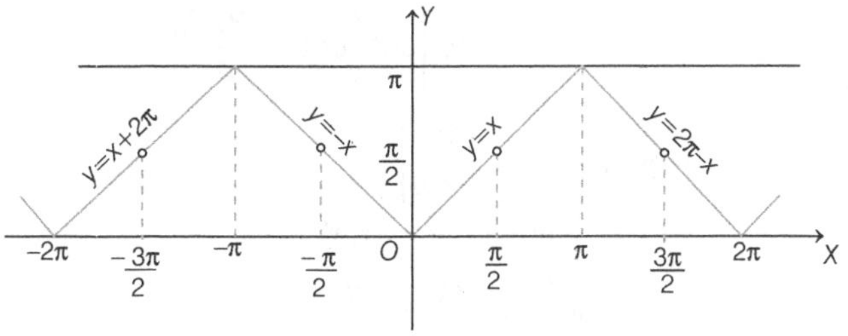

Example 33. Find the following values :

(i) $\sec^{-1}\left(\sec\dfrac{13\pi}{3}\right)$ (ii) $\sec^{-1}(\sec 9)$

Sol. (i) $\sec^{-1}\left(\sec\dfrac{13\pi}{3}\right) = \sec^{-1}\left(\sec\left(4\pi + \dfrac{\pi}{3}\right)\right)$

$$= \sec^{-1}\left(\sec\frac{\pi}{3}\right) = \frac{\pi}{3}$$

(ii) $\sec^{-1}(\sec 9) = \sec^{-1}(\sec(9 - 2\pi)) = 9 - 2\pi$

(v) $y = \cot^{-1}(\cot x), x \in R - \{n\pi, n \in I\}, y \in (0, \pi)$, is periodic with period π.

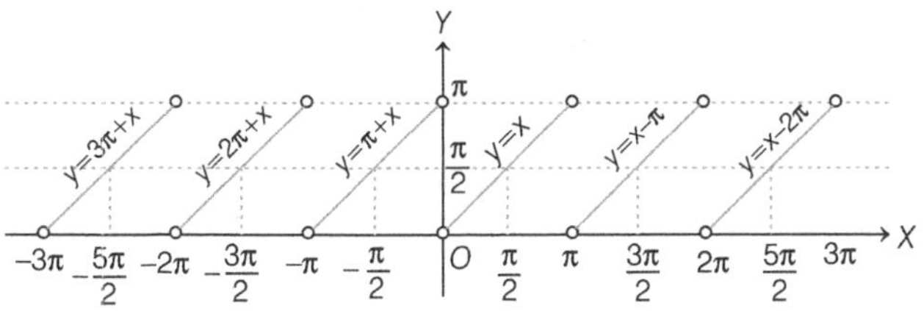

(vi) $y = \operatorname{cosec}^{-1}(\operatorname{cosec} x)$,

$x \in R - \{n\pi, n \in I\}, y \in \left[-\dfrac{\pi}{2}, \dfrac{\pi}{2}\right] - \{0\}$, is periodic with period 2π.

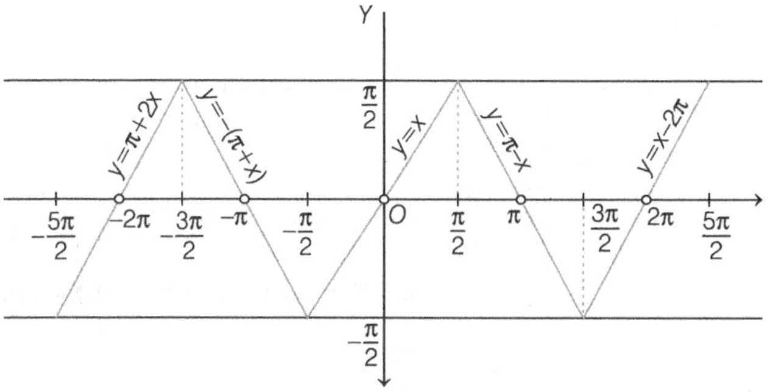

Example 34. Find the following values :

(i) $\cot^{-1}(\cot 6)$ (ii) $\operatorname{cosec}^{-1}(\operatorname{cosec} 7)$

Sol. (i) $\cot^{-1}(\cot 6) = \cot^{-1}(\cot(6 - \pi)) = 6 - \pi$

(ii) $\operatorname{cosec}^{-1}(\operatorname{cosec} 7) = \operatorname{cosec}^{-1}(\operatorname{cosec}(7 - 2\pi)) = 7 - 2\pi$.

JEE SPIKE

It should be noted that, $\sin^{-1}(\sin\theta) \neq \theta$, if $\theta \notin [-\pi/2, \pi/2]$.

Infact, we have

$$\sin^{-1}(\sin\theta) = \begin{cases} -\pi - \theta, \text{ if } \theta \in [-3\pi/2, -\pi/2] \\ \theta, \text{ if } \theta \in [-\pi/2, \pi/2] \\ \pi - \theta, \text{ if } \theta \in [\pi/2, 3\pi/2] \\ -2\pi + \theta, \text{ if } \theta \in [3\pi/2, 5\pi/2] \text{ and so on} \end{cases}$$

Concept Inside Video

Similarly, $\cos^{-1}(\cos\theta) = \begin{cases} -\theta, \text{if } \theta \in [-\pi, 0] \\ \theta, \text{if } \theta \in [0, \pi] \\ 2\pi - \theta, \text{ if } \theta \in [\pi, 2\pi] \\ -2\pi + \theta, \text{ if } \theta \in [2\pi, 3\pi] \text{ and so on} \end{cases}$

$$\tan^{-1}(\tan\theta) = \begin{cases} \theta + \pi, \text{if } \theta \in (-3\pi/2, -\pi/2) \\ \theta, \text{if } \theta \in (-\pi/2, \pi/2) \\ \theta - \pi, \text{if } \theta - \in (\pi/2, 3\pi/2) \\ \theta - 2\pi, \text{if } \theta \in (3\pi/2, 5\pi/2) \text{ and so on} \end{cases}$$

Example 35. Evaluate the following

(i) $\sin^{-1}(\sin\pi/4)$ (ii) $\cos^{-1}\left(\cos\dfrac{2\pi}{3}\right)$

(iii) $\tan^{-1}\left(\tan\dfrac{\pi}{3}\right)$ (iv) $\sin^{-1}\left(\sin\dfrac{2\pi}{3}\right)$

(v) $\cos^{-1}\left(\cos\dfrac{7\pi}{6}\right)$

Sol. Recall that $\sin^{-1}(\sin\theta) = \theta$, if $-\pi/2 \le \theta \le \pi/2$

$\cos^{-1}(\cos\theta) = \theta$, if $0 \le \theta \le \pi$

and $\tan^{-1}(\tan\theta) = \theta$, if $-\pi/2 < \theta < \pi/2$

(i) $\sin^{-1}(\sin\pi/4)=\dfrac{\pi}{4}$

(ii) $\cos^{-1}\left(\cos\dfrac{2\pi}{3}\right)=\dfrac{2\pi}{3}$

(iii) $\tan^{-1}(\tan\pi/3)=\pi/3$

(iv) $\sin^{-1}\left(\sin\dfrac{2\pi}{3}\right)\neq\dfrac{2\pi}{3}$ as $\dfrac{2\pi}{3}$ does not lie between $-\pi/2$ and $\pi/2$.

Now, $\sin^{-1}\left(\sin\dfrac{2\pi}{3}\right)=\sin^{-1}(\sin(\pi-\pi/3))$ $\left[\because \dfrac{2\pi}{3}=\pi-\dfrac{\pi}{3}\right]$

$=\sin^{-1}(\sin\pi/3)$ $[\because \sin(\pi-\theta)=\sin\theta]$

$=\dfrac{\pi}{3}$

(v) $\cos^{-1}\left(\cos\dfrac{7\pi}{6}\right)\neq\dfrac{7\pi}{6}$, because $\dfrac{7\pi}{6}$ does not lie between 0 and π.

Now, $\cos^{-1}\left(\cos\dfrac{7\pi}{6}\right)=\cos^{-1}\left(\cos\left(2\pi-\dfrac{5\pi}{6}\right)\right)$

$\left[\because \dfrac{7\pi}{6}=2\pi-\dfrac{5\pi}{6}\right]$

$=\cos^{-1}\left(\cos\dfrac{5\pi}{6}\right)$

$=\dfrac{5\pi}{6}$ $[\because \cos(2\pi-\theta)=\cos\theta]$

Property II

(i) $y=\sin(\sin^{-1}x)=\cos(\cos^{-1}x)=x$, $x\in[-1,1]$, $y\in[-1,1]$; y is a periodic

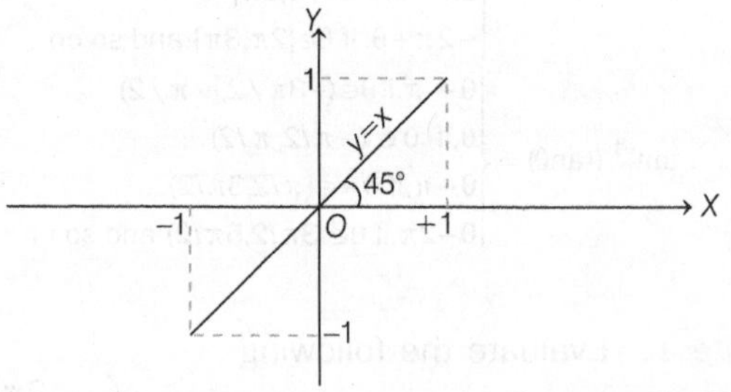

(ii) $y=\tan(\tan^{-1}x)=\cot(\cot^{-1}x)=x$, $x\in R$, $y\in R$; y is aperiodic

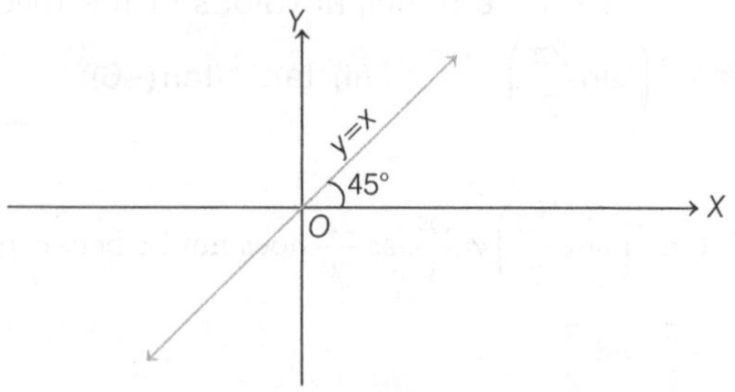

(iii) $y=\operatorname{cosec}(\operatorname{cosec}^{-1}x)=\sec(\sec^{-1}x)=x$, $|x|\geq 1, |y|\geq 1$; y is aperiodic

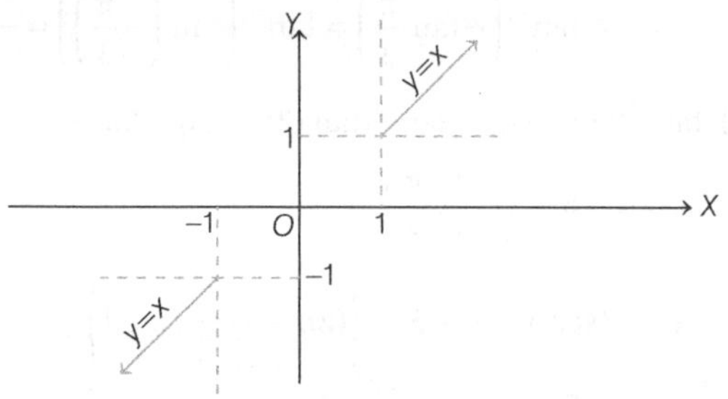

Example 36. Find the value of

$$\operatorname{cosec}\left\{\cot\left(\cot^{-1}\frac{3\pi}{4}\right)\right\}.$$

Sol. Let $y=\operatorname{cosec}\left\{\cot\left(\cot^{-1}\dfrac{3\pi}{4}\right)\right\}$ ...(i)

$\because$ $\cot(\cot^{-1}x)=x, \forall\ x\in R$

$\therefore$ $\cot\left(\cot^{-1}\dfrac{3\pi}{4}\right)=\dfrac{3\pi}{4}$

Now, from Eq. (i), we get

$$y=\operatorname{cosec}\left(\frac{3\pi}{4}\right)=\sqrt{2}$$

Example 37. Prove that

$$\sec^2(\tan^{-1}2)+\operatorname{cosec}^2(\cot^{-1}3)=15$$

Sol. $\sec^2(\tan^{-1}2)+\operatorname{cosec}^2(\cot^{-1}3)$

$=\{1+\tan^2(\tan^{-1}2)\}+\{1+\cot^2(\cot^{-1}3)\}$

$=1+(\tan(\tan^{-1}2))^2+1+(\cot(\cot^{-1}3))^2$

$=2+2^2+3^2=15$

Milestone Practice 4.2

1. Find the value of $\cos^{-1}\left(\cos\frac{2\pi}{3}\right)+\sin^{-1}\left(\sin\frac{2\pi}{3}\right)$.

2. Write the value of $\sin^{-1}\left(\sin\frac{3\pi}{5}\right)$.

3. Find the value of $\sin^{-1}\left(\cos\frac{33\pi}{5}\right)$.

4. Find the value of $\cos^{-1}(\cos 13)$.

5. Find $\sin^{-1}(\sin\theta)$, $\cos^{-1}(\cos\theta)$, $\tan^{-1}(\tan\theta)$, $\cot^{-1}(\cot\theta)$ for $\theta \in \left(\frac{5\pi}{2}, 3\pi\right)$.

Evaluate the following :

6. $\cos\left\{\sin\left(\sin^{-1}\frac{\pi}{6}\right)\right\}$.

7. $\sin\left\{\cos\left(\cos^{-1}\frac{3\pi}{4}\right)\right\}$.

8. $\sin^2\left(\cos^{-1}\frac{1}{2}\right)+\cos^2\left(\sin^{-1}\frac{1}{3}\right)$.

9. $\tan^2(\sec^{-1}2)+\cot^2(\text{cosec}^{-1}3)$.

10. Find the solutions of the equation $\cos(\cos^{-1}x) = \text{cosec}\,(\text{cosec}^{-1}x)$.

Answer Key

1. π
2. $\frac{2\pi}{5}$
3. $-\frac{\pi}{10}$
4. $\frac{13\pi}{180}$
5. $3\pi-\theta,\ \theta-2\pi,\ \theta-3\pi,\ \theta-2\pi$
6. $\frac{\sqrt{3}}{2}$
7. $\frac{1}{\sqrt{2}}$
8. $\frac{59}{36}$
9. 11
10. $x=\pm 1$

For Detailed Solution

Milestone 3 Properties III, IV and V of Inverse Trigonometric Functions

Property III

(i) $\sin^{-1}(-x)=-\sin^{-1} x$, for all $x \in[-1,1]$

(ii) $\cos^{-1}(-x)=\pi-\cos^{-1} x$, for all $x \in[-1,1]$

(iii) $\tan^{-1}(-x)=-\tan^{-1} x$, for all $x \in R$

(iv) $\operatorname{cosec}^{-1}(-x)=-\operatorname{cosec}^{-1} x$, for all $x \in(-\infty,-1] \cup[1, \infty)$

(v) $\sec^{-1}(-x)=\pi-\sec^{-1} x$, for all $x \in(-\infty,-1] \cup[1, \infty)$

(vi) $\cot^{-1}(-x)=\pi-\cot^{-1} x$ for all $x \in R$

Proof (i) Clearly, $-x \in[-1,1]$ for all $x \in[-1,1]$

Let $\quad \sin^{-1}(-x)=\theta \quad$ ...(i)

Then, $\quad -x=\sin \theta$

$\Rightarrow \quad x=-\sin \theta$

$\Rightarrow \quad x=\sin(-\theta)$

$\Rightarrow \quad -\theta=\sin^{-1} x$

$\{\because x \in[-1,1]$ and $-\theta \in[-\pi/2, \pi/2]$ for all $\theta \in[-\pi/2, \pi/2]\}$

$\Rightarrow \quad \theta=-\sin^{-1} x \quad$ ...(ii)

From Eqs. (i) and (ii), we get

$$\sin^{-1}(-x)=-\sin^{-1} x$$

(ii) Clearly, $-x \in[-1,1]$ for all $x \in[-1,1]$

Let $\quad \cos^{-1}(-x)=\theta \quad$ ...(i)

Then, $\quad -x=\cos \theta$

$\Rightarrow \quad x=-\cos \theta$

$\Rightarrow \quad x=\cos(\pi-\theta)$

$\Rightarrow \quad \cos^{-1} x=\pi-\theta$

$\{\because x \in[-1,1]$ and $\pi-\theta \in[0, \pi]$ for all $\theta \in[0, \pi]\}$

$\Rightarrow \quad \theta=\pi-\cos^{-1} x \quad$ ... (ii)

From Eqs. (i) and (ii), we get

$$\cos^{-1}(-x)=\pi-\cos^{-1} x$$

Similarly, we can prove other results.

Example 38. Find the value of $\cos^{-1}\{\sin(-5)\}$

Sol. Let $y=\cos^{-1}\{\sin(-5)\}=\cos^{-1}(-\sin 5)$

$\because \cos^{-1}(-x)=\pi-\cos^{-1} x, |x| \leq 1$

$\therefore \quad y=\pi-\cos^{-1}(\sin 5)$

$$=\pi-\cos^{-1}\left\{\cos\left(\frac{\pi}{2}-5\right)\right\} \quad \text{... (i)}$$

Here, $-2\pi<\left(\frac{\pi}{2}-5\right)<-\pi$

and the graph of $\cos^{-1}(\cos x)$ is as

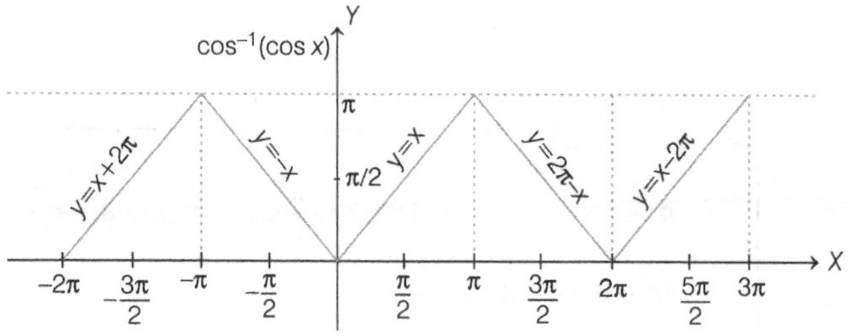

From the graph, we can see that if $-2\pi \leq x \leq -\pi$, then $y=\cos^{-1}(\cos x)$ can be written as $y=x+2\pi$.

$\therefore$ From the graph,

$$\cos^{-1}\left\{\cos\left(\frac{\pi}{2}-5\right)\right\}=\left(\frac{\pi}{2}-5\right)+2\pi=\left(\frac{5\pi}{2}-5\right)$$

Now, from Eq. (i), we get

$$y=\pi-\left(\frac{5\pi}{2}-5\right) \Rightarrow y=5-\frac{3\pi}{2}$$

Example 39. Evaluate the following

(i) $\sin^{-1}\left(\sin\left(\frac{-3\pi}{4}\right)\right)$ (ii) $\cot^{-1}(\cot(-4))$

Sol. (i) $\sin^{-1}\left(\sin\left(\frac{-3\pi}{4}\right)\right)=\sin^{-1}\left(-\sin^{-1}\left(\frac{3\pi}{4}\right)\right)=-\sin^{-1}\left(\sin\frac{3\pi}{4}\right)$

$$=-\sin^{-1}\left(\sin\left(\pi-\frac{\pi}{4}\right)\right)$$

$$=-\sin^{-1}\left(\sin\frac{\pi}{4}\right)=-\frac{\pi}{4}$$

(ii) $\cot^{-1}(\cot(-4))=\cot^{-1}(-\cot 4)=\pi-\cot^{-1}(\cot 4)$

$$=\pi-\cot^{-1}(\cot(\pi+(4-\pi)))$$

$$=\pi-\cot^{-1}(\cot(4-\pi))=2\pi-4$$

Example 40. Evaluate the following

(i) $\sin\left(\frac{\pi}{2}-\sin^{-1}\left(\frac{-1}{2}\right)\right)$ (ii) $\sin\left(\frac{\pi}{2}-\sin^{-1}\left(-\frac{\sqrt{3}}{2}\right)\right)$

Sol. (i) $\sin\left(\frac{\pi}{2}-\sin^{-1}\left(-\frac{1}{2}\right)\right)=\sin\left(\frac{\pi}{2}+\sin^{-1}\left(\frac{1}{2}\right)\right)$

$$=\sin\left(\frac{\pi}{2}+\frac{\pi}{6}\right)=\sin\frac{2\pi}{3}=\frac{\sqrt{3}}{2}$$

(ii) $\sin\left(\frac{\pi}{2}-\sin^{-1}\left(-\frac{\sqrt{3}}{2}\right)\right)=\sin\left(\frac{\pi}{2}+\sin^{-1}\left(\frac{\sqrt{3}}{2}\right)\right)$

$$=\sin\left(\frac{\pi}{2}+\frac{\pi}{3}\right)=\sin\frac{5\pi}{6}=\frac{1}{2}$$

Example 41. Find the values of
$\sin^{-1}(\sin 5)+\cos^{-1}(\cos 10)+\tan^{-1}\{\tan(-6)\}+\cot^{-1}\{\cot(-10)\}$.

Sol. $\sin^{-1}(\sin 5)+\cos^{-1}(\cos 10)+\tan^{-1}\{\tan(-6)\}+\cot^{-1}\{\cot(-10)\}$

$=\sin^{-1}(\sin 5)+\cos^{-1}(\cos 10)-\tan^{-1}\{\tan(6)\}+\pi-\cot^{-1}\{\cot(10)\}$

$=(5-2\pi)+(4\pi-10)-(6-2\pi)+\pi-(10-3\pi)=8\pi-21$

Example 42. Find the minimum value of the function $f(x)=\dfrac{\pi^2}{16\cot^{-1}(-x)}-\cot^{-1}x$.

Sol. $f(x)=\dfrac{\pi^2}{16\cot^{-1}(-x)}-(\pi-\cot^{-1}(-x))$

$f(x)=\cot^{-1}(-x)+\dfrac{\pi^2}{16\cot^{-1}(-x)}-\pi$

$f(x)=\left(\sqrt{\cot^{-1}(-x)}-\dfrac{\pi}{4\sqrt{\cot^{-1}(-x)}}\right)^2+\dfrac{\pi}{2}-\pi\geq-\dfrac{\pi}{2}$

$\therefore f_{\min}=-\dfrac{\pi}{2}$

Example 43. Find the range of $y=(\cot^{-1}x)(\cot^{-1}(-x))$.

Sol. $y=(\cot^{-1}x)(\cot^{-1}(-x))$

$y=\cot^{-1}(x)(\pi-\cot^{-1}(x))$

Now, $\cot^{-1}(x)$ and $(\pi-\cot^{-1}(x))>0$

Using, AM $\geq$ GM, we get

$$\frac{\cot^{-1}x+(\pi-\cot^{-1}x)}{2}\geq\sqrt{(\cot^{-1}x)(\pi-\cot^{-1}x)}$$

$\Rightarrow 0<\cot^{-1}(x)(\pi-\cot^{-1}(x))$

$$\leq\left(\frac{\cot^{-1}x+(\pi-\cot^{-1}x)}{2}\right)^2=\frac{\pi^2}{4}$$

$\Rightarrow \quad 0<y\leq\dfrac{\pi^2}{4}$

Property IV

(i) $\sin^{-1}\left(\frac{1}{x}\right)=\operatorname{cosec}^{-1}x$, for all $x\in(-\infty,-1]\cup[1,\infty)$

(ii) $\cos^{-1}\left(\frac{1}{x}\right)=\sec^{-1}x$, for all $x\in(-\infty,-1]\cup[1,\infty)$

(iii) $\tan^{-1}\left(\frac{1}{x}\right)=\begin{cases}\cot^{-1}x, \text{for } x>0\\ -\pi+\cot^{-1}x, \text{for } x<0\end{cases}$

Proof

(i) Let $\operatorname{cosec}^{-1}x=\theta$ ...(i)

Then, $x=\operatorname{cosec}\theta$

$\Rightarrow \quad \frac{1}{x}=\sin\theta$

$\because \quad x\in(-\infty,-1]\cup[1,\infty)\Rightarrow\frac{1}{x}\in[-1,1]-\{0\}$

$\operatorname{cosec}^{-1}x=\theta\Rightarrow\theta\in[-\pi/2,\pi/2]-\{0\}$

$\Rightarrow \quad \theta=\sin^{-1}\left(\frac{1}{x}\right)$ ...(ii)

From Eqs. (i) and (ii), we get

$$\sin^{-1}\left(\frac{1}{x}\right)=\operatorname{cosec}^{-1}x$$

(ii) Let $\sec^{-1}x=\theta$ ...(i)

Then, $x\in(-\infty,-1]\cup[1,\infty)$ and $\theta\in[0,\pi]-\{\pi/2\}$

Now, $\sec^{-1}x=\theta$

$\Rightarrow \quad x=\sec\theta\Rightarrow\frac{1}{x}=\cos\theta$

$\Rightarrow \quad \theta=\cos^{-1}\left(\frac{1}{x}\right)$ ...(ii)

$$\left\{\begin{array}{l}\because x=(-\infty,-1]\cup[1,\infty)\\ \Rightarrow\frac{1}{x}\in[-1,1]-\{0\}\text{ and }\theta\in[0,\pi]-\left\{\frac{\pi}{2}\right\}\end{array}\right.$$

From Eqs. (i) and (ii), we get

$$\cos^{-1}\left(\frac{1}{x}\right)=\sec^{-1}(x)$$

(iii) Let $\cot^{-1}x=\theta$. Clearly, $x\in R$, $x\neq0$ and $\theta\in(0,\pi)$ ...(i)

Now, two cases arises

Case I When $x>0$

In this case, $\theta\in(0,\pi/2)$

$\therefore \quad \cot^{-1}x=\theta$

$\Rightarrow \quad x=\cot\theta$

$$\Rightarrow \quad \frac{1}{x} = \tan\theta$$

$$\theta = \tan^{-1}\left(\frac{1}{x}\right) \quad \text{...(ii)}$$

$[\because \theta \in (0, \pi/2)]$

From Eqs. (i) and (ii), we get

$$\tan^{-1}\left(\frac{1}{x}\right) = \cot^{-1} x, \text{ for all } x > 0.$$

Case II When $x < 0$

In this case, $\theta \in (\pi/2, \pi)$ $\quad [\because x = \cot\theta < 0]$

Now, $\frac{\pi}{2} < \theta < \pi$

$$\Rightarrow \quad -\frac{\pi}{2} < \theta - \pi < 0$$

$$\Rightarrow \quad \theta - \pi \in (-\pi/2, 0)$$

$$\therefore \quad \cot^{-1} x = \theta$$

$$\Rightarrow \quad x = \cot\theta$$

$$\Rightarrow \quad \frac{1}{x} = \tan\theta$$

$$\Rightarrow \quad \frac{1}{x} = -\tan(\pi - \theta) \quad [\because \tan(\pi - \theta) = -\tan\theta]$$

$$\Rightarrow \quad \frac{1}{x} = \tan(\theta - \pi)$$

$$\Rightarrow \quad \theta - \pi = \tan^{-1}\left(\frac{1}{x}\right) \quad [\because \theta - \pi \in (-\pi/2, 0)]$$

$$\Rightarrow \quad \tan^{-1}\left(\frac{1}{x}\right) = -\pi + \theta \quad \text{...(iii)}$$

From Eqs. (i) and (iii), we get

$$\tan^{-1}\left(\frac{1}{x}\right) = -\pi + \cot^{-1} x, \text{ if } x < 0$$

Hence, $\tan^{-1}\left(\frac{1}{x}\right) = \begin{cases} \cot^{-1} x, \text{for } x > 0 \\ -\pi + \cot^{-1} x, \text{for } x < 0 \end{cases}$

Example 44. Evaluate the following

(i) $\sin\left(\text{cosec}^{-1}\frac{5}{3}\right)$

(ii) $\cot\left(\tan^{-1}\frac{3}{4}\right)$

Sol. (i) $\sin\left(\text{cosec}^{-1}\frac{5}{3}\right) = \sin\left(\sin^{-1}\frac{3}{5}\right) = \frac{3}{5}$

(ii) $\cot\left(\tan^{-1}\frac{3}{4}\right) = \cot\left(\cot^{-1}\frac{4}{3}\right) = \frac{4}{3}$

Example 45. Find the value of $\tan\left\{\cot^{-1}\left(\frac{-2}{3}\right)\right\}$.

Sol. Let $y = \tan\left\{\cot^{-1}\left(\frac{-2}{3}\right)\right\}$ $\quad$ ...(i)

$\because \cot^{-1}(-x) = \pi - \cot^{-1} x, x \in R$

$\therefore$ Eq. (i) can be written as

$$y = \tan\left\{\pi - \cot^{-1}\left(\frac{2}{3}\right)\right\}$$

$$y = -\tan\left(\cot^{-1}\frac{2}{3}\right)$$

$\because \cot^{-1} x = \tan^{-1}\frac{1}{x}$ if $x > 0$

$$\therefore \quad y = -\tan\left(\tan^{-1}\frac{3}{2}\right) \Rightarrow y = -\frac{3}{2}$$

Property V

(i) $\sin^{-1} x + \cos^{-1} x = \pi/2$, for all $x \in [-1, 1]$

(ii) $\tan^{-1} x + \cot^{-1} x = \pi/2$, for all $x \in R$

(iii) $\sec^{-1} x + \text{cosec}^{-1} x = \frac{\pi}{2}$, for all $x \in (-\infty, -1] \cup [1, \infty)$

Proof

(i) Let $\sin^{-1} x = \theta$ $\quad$ ...(i)

Then, $\theta \in [-\pi/2, \pi/2]$ $\quad [\because x \in [-1, 1]]$

$$\Rightarrow \quad -\pi/2 \le \theta \le \pi/2$$

$$\Rightarrow \quad -\pi/2 \le -\theta \le \pi/2$$

$$\Rightarrow \quad 0 \le \frac{\pi}{2} - \theta \le \pi \Rightarrow \frac{\pi}{2} - \theta \in [0, \pi]$$

Now, $\sin^{-1} x = \theta \Rightarrow x = \sin\theta$

$$\Rightarrow \quad x = \cos\left(\frac{\pi}{2} - \theta\right) \Rightarrow \cos^{-1} x = \frac{\pi}{2} - \theta$$

$[\because x \in [-1, 1] \text{ and } (\pi/2 - \theta) \in [0, \pi]]$

$$\Rightarrow \quad \theta + \cos^{-1} x = \pi/2 \quad \text{...(ii)}$$

From Eqs. (i) and (ii), we get

$$\sin^{-1} x + \cos^{-1} x = \frac{\pi}{2}$$

(ii) Let $\tan^{-1} x = \theta$ $\quad$ ...(i)

Then, $\theta \in (-\pi/2, \pi/2)$ $\quad [\because x \in R]$

$$\Rightarrow \quad -\frac{\pi}{2} < \theta < \frac{\pi}{2} \Rightarrow -\frac{\pi}{2} < -\theta < \frac{\pi}{2}$$

$$\Rightarrow \quad 0 < \frac{\pi}{2} - \theta < \pi \Rightarrow \left(\frac{\pi}{2} - \theta\right) \in (0, \pi)$$

Now, $\tan^{-1} x = \theta$

$\Rightarrow \quad x = \tan\theta$

$\Rightarrow \quad x = \cot(\pi/2 - \theta)$

$\Rightarrow \quad \cot^{-1} x = \dfrac{\pi}{2} - \theta \quad [\because \pi/2 - \theta \in (0, \pi)]$

$\Rightarrow \quad \theta + \cot^{-1} x = \dfrac{\pi}{2} \quad \ldots\text{(ii)}$

From Eqs. (i) and (ii), we get

$$\tan^{-1} x + \cot^{-1} x = \frac{\pi}{2}$$

(iii) Let, $\sec^{-1} x = \theta \quad \ldots\text{(i)}$

Then, $\theta \in [0, \pi] - \{\pi/2\} \quad [\because x \in (-\infty, -1] \cup [1, \infty)]$

$\Rightarrow \quad 0 \le \theta \le \pi, \theta \ne \pi/2$

$\Rightarrow \quad -\pi \le -\theta \le 0, \theta \ne \pi/2$

$\Rightarrow \quad -\dfrac{\pi}{2} \le \dfrac{\pi}{2} - \theta \le \dfrac{\pi}{2}, \dfrac{\pi}{2} - \theta \ne 0$

$\Rightarrow \quad \left(\dfrac{\pi}{2} - \theta\right) \in \left[-\dfrac{\pi}{2}, \dfrac{\pi}{2}\right], \dfrac{\pi}{2} - \theta \ne 0$

Now, $\sec^{-1} x = \theta$

$\Rightarrow \quad x = \sec\theta$

$\Rightarrow \quad x = \operatorname{cosec}(\pi/2 - \theta)$

$\Rightarrow \quad \operatorname{cosec}^{-1} x = \pi/2 - \theta$

$$\left[\because \left(\frac{\pi}{2} - \theta\right) \in \left[-\frac{\pi}{2}, \frac{\pi}{2}\right], \frac{\pi}{2} - \theta \ne 0\right]$$

$\Rightarrow \quad \theta + \operatorname{cosec}^{-1} x = \pi/2 \quad \ldots\text{(ii)}$

From Eqs. (i) and (ii), we get

$$\sec^{-1} x + \operatorname{cosec}^{-1} x = \pi/2$$

Example 46. Find the value of of $\sin(2\cos^{-1} x + \sin^{-1} x)$ when $x = \dfrac{1}{5}$.

Sol. Let $y = \sin[2\cos^{-1} x + \sin^{-1} x]$

$\because \quad \sin^{-1} x + \cos^{-1} x = \dfrac{\pi}{2}, |x| \le 1$

$\therefore \quad y = \sin\left[2\cos^{-1} x + \dfrac{\pi}{2} - \cos^{-1} x\right]$

$\quad = \sin\left[\dfrac{\pi}{2} + \cos^{-1} x\right] = \cos(\cos^{-1} x)$

$\because \quad x = \dfrac{1}{5}$

$\therefore \quad y = \cos\left(\cos^{-1}\dfrac{1}{5}\right) \quad \ldots\text{(i)}$

$\because \quad \cos(\cos^{-1} x) = x$ if $x \in [-1, 1]$

and $\quad \dfrac{1}{5} \in [-1, 1]$

$\therefore \quad \cos\left(\cos^{-1}\dfrac{1}{5}\right) = \dfrac{1}{5}$

Now, from Eq. (i), we get

$$y = \frac{1}{5}$$

JEE SCANNER

Example Similar to PYQ Asked in JEE Main 2024

Let the inverse trigonometric function take principal values. The number of real solutions of the equation $\sin^{-1} x + 2\cos^{-1} x = \dfrac{\pi}{3}$ *is ....*

Sol. (1) We have, $\sin^{-1} x + 2\cos^{-1} x = \dfrac{\pi}{3}$

$\Rightarrow \quad \dfrac{\pi}{2} - \cos^{-1} x + 2\cos^{-1} x = \dfrac{\pi}{3}$

$\Rightarrow \quad \dfrac{\pi}{2} + \cos^{-1} x = \dfrac{\pi}{3}$

$\Rightarrow \quad \cos^{-1} x = -\dfrac{\pi}{6}$

$\therefore \quad x = \dfrac{\sqrt{3}}{2}$

Skill Builder

Let the inverse trigonometric function take principal value. The number of real solutions of the equation $\cos^{-1} x + 2\sin^{-1} x = \dfrac{2\pi}{3}$ is ...

For Sol.

■ **For more practice** See Q.9 of Milestone Practice 3.

Example 47. Solve $\sin^{-1} x - \cos^{-1} x = \cos^{-1}\dfrac{\sqrt{3}}{2}$.

Sol. We have, $\sin^{-1} x - \cos^{-1} x = \cos^{-1}\dfrac{\sqrt{3}}{2}$

$\Rightarrow \quad \sin^{-1} x - \cos^{-1} x = \dfrac{\pi}{6} \quad \ldots\text{(i)}$

Also, $\quad \sin^{-1} x + \cos^{-1} x = \dfrac{\pi}{2} \quad \ldots\text{(ii)}$

On solving Eqs. (i) and (ii), we get

$$\sin^{-1} x = \frac{\pi}{3} \text{ and } \cos^{-1} x = \frac{\pi}{6}$$

$\Rightarrow \quad x = \dfrac{\sqrt{3}}{2}$ is the only solution.

Milestone Practice 4.3

Evaluate the following.

1. $\tan^{-1}\left\{\tan\left(-\frac{7\pi}{8}\right)\right\}$.
2. $\tan^{-1}\left\{\cot\left(-\frac{1}{2}\right)\right\}$.
3. $\sec\left(\cos^{-1}\left(\frac{2}{3}\right)\right)$.
4. $\text{cosec}\left(\sin^{-1}\left(-\frac{1}{\sqrt{3}}\right)\right)$.
5. $\cos\left[\cos^{-1}\left(\frac{-1}{3}\right)-\sin^{-1}\left(\frac{1}{3}\right)\right]$.
6. If $\sin^{-1} x=\frac{\pi}{5}$, for some $x \in (-1, 1)$, then find $\cos^{-1} x$.
7. If $\sec^{-1} x = \text{cosec}^{-1} y$, then find the value of $\cos^{-1}\frac{1}{x}+\cos^{-1}\frac{1}{y}$.
8. Prove that $\tan^{-1} x+\tan^{-1}\frac{1}{x}=\begin{cases}\pi/2, & \text{if } x>0\\ -\pi/2, & \text{if } x<0\end{cases}$.

Solve the following

9. $5\tan^{-1} x+3\cot^{-1} x=2\pi$
10. $4\sin^{-1} x=\pi-\cos^{-1} x$

Answer Key

1. $\frac{\pi}{8}$	2. $\frac{1}{2}-\frac{\pi}{2}$	3. $\frac{3}{2}$	4. $-\sqrt{3}$	5. $-\frac{4\sqrt{2}}{9}$
6. $\frac{3\pi}{10}$	7. $\frac{\pi}{2}$	9. $x=-1$ or 1	10. $x=\frac{1}{2}$	

For Detailed Solution

Milestone 4 Properties VI, VII, VIII and IX of Inverse Trigonometric Functions

Property VI

(i) $\tan^{-1} x + \tan^{-1} y$

$$= \begin{cases} \tan^{-1}\left(\dfrac{x+y}{1-xy}\right), \text{if } x>0, y>0 \text{ and } xy<1 \\ \pi + \tan^{-1}\left(\dfrac{x+y}{1-xy}\right), \text{if } x>0, y>0 \text{ and } xy>1 \\ -\pi + \tan^{-1}\left(\dfrac{x+y}{1-xy}\right), \text{if } x<0, y<0 \text{ and } xy>1 \end{cases}$$

(ii) $\tan^{-1} x - \tan^{-1} y$

$$= \begin{cases} \tan^{-1}\left(\dfrac{x-y}{1+xy}\right), \text{if } xy>-1 \\ \pi + \tan^{-1}\left(\dfrac{x-y}{1+xy}\right), \text{if } x>0, y<0 \text{ and } xy<-1 \\ -\pi + \tan^{-1}\left(\dfrac{x-y}{1+xy}\right), \text{if } x<0, y>0 \text{ and } xy<-1 \end{cases}$$

Proof

(i) Let $\tan^{-1} x = A$ and $\tan^{-1} y = B$. Then,

$x = \tan A$ and $y = \tan B$ and $A, B \in (-\pi/2, \pi/2)$

$$\therefore \quad \tan(A+B) = \frac{\tan A + \tan B}{1 - \tan A \tan B} = \frac{x+y}{1-xy} \quad \text{...(i)}$$

Now, the following cases arises.

Case I When $x>0$, $y>0$ and $xy<1$

In this case, $x>0$, $y>0$ and $xy<1 \Rightarrow \dfrac{x+y}{1-xy}>0$

$$\Rightarrow \quad \tan(A+B)>0$$

$\Rightarrow A+B$ lies in I quadrant or in III quadrant.

$$\Rightarrow \quad 0<A+B<\pi/2$$

$$\left[\begin{matrix} \because x>0 \Rightarrow 0<A<\pi/2 \\ y>0 \Rightarrow 0<B<\pi/2 \end{matrix}\right\} \Rightarrow 0<A+B<\pi\right]$$

$$\therefore \quad \tan(A+B) = \frac{x+y}{1-xy} \quad \text{[from Eq. (i)]}$$

$$\Rightarrow \quad A+B = \tan^{-1}\left(\frac{x+y}{1-xy}\right)$$

$$\Rightarrow \tan^{-1} x + \tan^{-1} y = \tan^{-1}\left(\frac{x+y}{1-xy}\right)$$

Case II When $x<0$, $y<0$ and $xy<1$.

In this case,

$$x<0, y<0 \text{ and } xy<1$$

$$\Rightarrow \quad \frac{x+y}{1-xy}<0$$

$$\Rightarrow \quad \tan(A+B)<0 \quad \text{[from Eq. (i)]}$$

$\Rightarrow A+B$ lies in II quadrant or in IV quadrant.

$\Rightarrow A+B$ lies in IV quadrant.

$$\left[\begin{matrix} \because x<0 \Rightarrow -\pi/2<A<0 \\ y<0 \Rightarrow -\pi/2<B<0 \end{matrix}\right\} \Rightarrow -\pi<A+B<0\right]$$

$$\Rightarrow \quad \frac{-\pi}{2}<A+B<0$$

$$\therefore \quad \tan(A+B) = \frac{x+y}{1-xy} \quad \text{[from Eq. (i)]}$$

$$\Rightarrow \quad A+B = \tan^{-1}\left(\frac{x+y}{1-xy}\right)$$

$$\Rightarrow \quad \tan^{-1} x + \tan^{-1} y = \tan^{-1}\left(\frac{x+y}{1-xy}\right)$$

Case III When $x>0$ and $y<0$ or $x<0$ and $y>0$

Consider, $x>0$ and $y<0 \Rightarrow A \in (0, \pi/2)$

and $\quad B \in (-\pi/2, 0) \Rightarrow A+B \in (-\pi/2, \pi/2)$

$$\therefore \quad \tan(A+B) = \frac{x+y}{1-xy} \quad \text{[from Eq. (i)]}$$

$$\Rightarrow \quad A+B = \tan^{-1}\left(\frac{x+y}{1-xy}\right)$$

$$\Rightarrow \quad \tan^{-1} x + \tan^{-1} y = \tan^{-1}\left(\frac{x+y}{1-xy}\right)$$

Similarly, if $x<0$ and $y>0$, we have

$$\tan^{-1} x + \tan^{-1} y = \tan^{-1}\left(\frac{x+y}{1-xy}\right);$$

It follows from above three cases that

$$\tan^{-1} x + \tan^{-1} y = \tan^{-1}\left(\frac{x+y}{1-xy}\right) \text{if } xy<1$$

Case IV $x>0, y>0$ and $xy>1$.

In this case, we have

$$x>0, y>0 \text{ and } xy>1$$

$$\Rightarrow \quad \frac{x+y}{1-xy}<0 \Rightarrow \tan(A+B)<0$$

$$\left[\text{from Eq. (i), } \tan(A+B)=\frac{x+y}{1-xy}\right]$$

$\Rightarrow$ $A+B$ lies in II quadrant or in IV quadrant.

$\Rightarrow$ $A+B$ lies in II quadrant.

$$\left\{\because x>0, y>0 \Rightarrow A, B\in(0,\pi/2) \Rightarrow A+B\in(0,\pi)\right.$$

$$\Rightarrow \quad \pi/2<A+B<\pi$$

$$\Rightarrow \quad \frac{\pi}{2}-\pi<(A+B)-\pi<0$$

$$\Rightarrow \quad -\pi/2<(A+B)-\pi<0$$

$$\therefore \quad \tan(A+B)=\frac{x+y}{1-xy}$$

$$\Rightarrow \quad -\tan\{\pi-(A+B)\}=\frac{x+y}{1-xy}$$

$$[\because \tan(\pi-(A+B))=-\tan(A+B)]$$

$$\Rightarrow \quad \tan((A+B)-\pi)=\frac{x+y}{1-xy}$$

$$\Rightarrow \quad A+B-\pi=\tan^{-1}\left(\frac{x+y}{1-xy}\right)$$

$$\Rightarrow \quad A+B=\pi+\tan^{-1}\left(\frac{x+y}{1-xy}\right)$$

$$\Rightarrow \quad \tan^{-1}x+\tan^{-1}y=\pi+\tan^{-1}\left(\frac{x+y}{1-xy}\right)$$

Case V When $x<0, y<0$ and $xy>1$

In this case, we have

$$x<0, y<0 \text{ and } xy>1$$

$$\Rightarrow \quad \frac{x+y}{1-xy}>0$$

$$\Rightarrow \tan(A+B)>0 \quad \left[\text{from Eq. (i), } \tan(A+B)=\frac{x+y}{1-xy}\right]$$

$\Rightarrow \tan(A+B)$ lies either in I quadrant or III quadrant.

$$[\because x<0, y<0 \Rightarrow A, B\in(-\pi/2,0) \Rightarrow A+B\in(-\pi,0)]$$

$\Rightarrow A+B$ lies in III quadrant.

$$\Rightarrow \quad -\pi<A+B<-\pi/2$$

$$\Rightarrow \quad \pi-\pi<\pi+(A+B)<\pi-\pi/2$$

$$\Rightarrow \quad 0<\pi+(A+B)<\pi/2$$

Now, $\quad \tan(A+B)=\dfrac{x+y}{1-xy}$ [from Eq. (i)]

$$\Rightarrow \quad \tan(\pi+(A+B))=\frac{x+y}{1-xy}$$

$$\Rightarrow \quad \pi+A+B=\tan^{-1}\left(\frac{x+y}{1-xy}\right)$$

$$\Rightarrow \quad A+B=-\pi+\tan^{-1}\left(\frac{x+y}{1-xy}\right)$$

$$\Rightarrow \quad \tan^{-1}x+\tan^{-1}y=-\pi+\tan^{-1}\left(\frac{x+y}{1-xy}\right)$$

(ii) This property can be proved by replacing y by $-y$ in above results.

JEE SPIKE

If $x_1, x_2, x_3, \ldots, x_n \in R$, then

$$\tan^{-1}x_1+\tan^{-1}x_2+\ldots+\tan^{-1}x_n$$

$$=\tan^{-1}\left(\frac{S_1-S_3+S_5\ldots}{1-S_2+S_4-S_6\ldots}\right)$$

where, S_k denotes the sum of the product of $x_1, x_2, \ldots, x_n$ taking k at a time.

Concept Inside Video

Example 48. Prove that

(i) $\tan^{-1}\dfrac{1}{7}+\tan^{-1}\dfrac{1}{13}=\tan^{-1}\dfrac{2}{9}$

(ii) $\tan^{-1}2+\tan^{-1}3=\dfrac{3\pi}{4}$

(iii) $\tan^{-1}\dfrac{1}{2}+\tan^{-1}\dfrac{1}{5}+\tan^{-1}\dfrac{1}{8}=\dfrac{\pi}{4}$

(iv) $\tan^{-1}\dfrac{1}{5}+\tan^{-1}\dfrac{1}{7}+\tan^{-1}\dfrac{1}{3}+\tan^{-1}\dfrac{1}{8}=\dfrac{\pi}{4}$

Sol. (i) LHS $=\tan^{-1}\dfrac{1}{7}+\tan^{-1}\dfrac{1}{13}=\tan^{-1}\left\{\dfrac{\dfrac{1}{7}+\dfrac{1}{13}}{1-\dfrac{1}{7}\times\dfrac{1}{13}}\right\}$

$$\left[\because \tan^{-1}x+\tan^{-1}y=\tan^{-1}\left(\frac{x+y}{1-xy}\right), \text{ if } xy<1\right]$$

$$=\tan^{-1}\left(\frac{20}{90}\right)=\tan^{-1}\left(\frac{2}{9}\right)=\text{RHS}$$

(ii) $\tan^{-1}2+\tan^{-1}3=\pi+\tan^{-1}\left(\dfrac{2+3}{1-2\times3}\right)$

$$\left[\text{using } \tan^{-1}x+\tan^{-1}y=\pi+\tan^{-1}\left(\frac{x+y}{1-xy}\right), \text{ if } xy>1\right]$$

$$=\pi+\tan^{-1}(-1)=\pi-\frac{\pi}{4}=\frac{3\pi}{4}$$

(iii) $\tan^{-1}\frac{1}{2}+\tan^{-1}\frac{1}{5}+\tan^{-1}\frac{1}{8}$

$$=\left(\tan^{-1}\frac{1}{2}+\tan^{-1}\frac{1}{5}\right)+\tan^{-1}\frac{1}{8}$$

$$=\tan^{-1}\left(\frac{\frac{1}{2}+\frac{1}{5}}{1-\frac{1}{2}\times\frac{1}{5}}\right)+\tan^{-1}\left(\frac{1}{8}\right)$$

$$\left[\text{using } \tan^{-1}x+\tan^{-1}y=\tan^{-1}\left(\frac{x+y}{1-xy}\right), \text{ if } xy<1\right]$$

$$=\tan^{-1}\left(\frac{7}{9}\right)+\tan^{-1}\left(\frac{1}{8}\right)$$

$$=\tan^{-1}\left(\frac{\frac{7}{9}+\frac{1}{8}}{1-\frac{7}{9}\times\frac{1}{8}}\right)=\tan^{-1}\left(\frac{65}{65}\right)=\tan^{-1}(1)=\frac{\pi}{4}$$

(iv) $\left(\tan^{-1}\frac{1}{5}+\tan^{-1}\frac{1}{7}\right)+\left(\tan^{-1}\frac{1}{3}+\tan^{-1}\frac{1}{8}\right)$

$$=\tan^{-1}\left(\frac{\frac{1}{5}+\frac{1}{7}}{1-\frac{1}{5}\times\frac{1}{7}}\right)+\tan^{-1}\left(\frac{\frac{1}{3}+\frac{1}{8}}{1-\frac{1}{3}\times\frac{1}{8}}\right)$$

$$=\tan^{-1}\left(\frac{6}{17}\right)+\tan^{-1}\left(\frac{11}{23}\right)$$

$$=\tan^{-1}\left(\frac{\frac{6}{17}+\frac{11}{23}}{1-\frac{6}{17}\times\frac{11}{23}}\right)$$

$$=\tan^{-1}\left(\frac{325}{325}\right)=\tan^{-1}(1)=\frac{\pi}{4}$$

Example 49. Prove that

$$\tan^{-1}\left(\frac{yz}{xr}\right)+\tan^{-1}\left(\frac{zx}{yr}\right)+\tan^{-1}\left(\frac{xy}{zr}\right)=\frac{\pi}{2},$$

where $x^2+y^2+z^2=r^2$

Sol. We know that

$$\tan^{-1}x_1+\tan^{-1}x_2+\tan^{-1}x_3+\ldots+\tan^{-1}x_n$$

$$=\tan^{-1}\left(\frac{S_1-S_3+\ldots}{1-S_2+S_4\ldots}\right)$$

where, S_k denotes the sum of the product of $x_1, x_2, \ldots, x_n$ taking k at a time.

Therefore, LHS $=\tan^{-1}\left(\frac{yz}{xr}\right)+\tan^{-1}\left(\frac{xz}{yr}\right)+\tan^{-1}\left(\frac{xy}{zr}\right)$

$$=\tan^{-1}\left(\frac{\frac{yz}{xr}+\frac{xz}{yr}+\frac{xy}{zr}-\frac{xyz}{r^3}}{1-\left(\frac{x^2+y^2+z^2}{r^2}\right)}\right)$$

$$=\tan^{-1}\left(\frac{r^2\left(\frac{xy}{zr}+\frac{yz}{xr}+\frac{zx}{yr}-\frac{xyz}{r^3}\right)}{(x^2+y^2+z^2)-(x^2+y^2+z^2)}\right)$$

where $r^2=x^2+y^2+z^2$

$$=\tan^{-1}(\infty)=\frac{\pi}{2}=\text{LHS}$$

Example 50. Solve for x

$$\tan^{-1}(x+1)+\tan^{-1}x+\tan^{-1}(x-1)=\tan^{-1}3.$$

Sol. $\tan^{-1}(x+1)+\tan^{-1}(x-1)=\tan^{-1}3-\tan^{-1}x$

$$\Rightarrow \quad \tan^{-1}\left(\frac{x+1+x-1}{1-(x+1)(x-1)}\right)=\tan^{-1}\left(\frac{3-x}{1+3x}\right),$$

When $x^2-1<1$ and $3x<1$

$$\Rightarrow \quad \tan^{-1}\left(\frac{2x}{2-x^2}\right)=\tan^{-1}\left(\frac{3-x}{1+3x}\right),$$

When $-\sqrt{2}<x<\sqrt{2}$ and $x<\frac{1}{3}$

$$\Rightarrow \quad \frac{2x}{2-x^2}=\frac{3-x}{1+3x}, \text{ when } -\sqrt{2}<x<\frac{1}{3}$$

$$\Rightarrow \quad 2x(1+3x)=(2-x^2)(3-x), \text{ when } -\sqrt{2}<x<\frac{1}{3}$$

$$\Rightarrow \quad 2x+6x^2=6-2x-3x^2+x^3$$

$$\Rightarrow \quad x^3-9x^2-4x+6=0$$

$$\Rightarrow \quad (x+1)(x^2-10x+6)=0, \text{ when } -\sqrt{2}<x<\frac{1}{3}$$

$\Rightarrow \quad x=-1$ and neglecting $x^2-10x+6=0$ as its roots does not $\in\left(-\sqrt{2},\frac{1}{3}\right)$

$\therefore \quad x=-1$

Example 51. If $\tan^{-1}2$, $\tan^{-1}3$ are two angles of a triangle. Then, find the third angle.

Sol. Let the angles of Δ be $A=\tan^{-1}2$, $B=\tan^{-1}3$

and $\quad C=\pi-(\tan^{-1}2+\tan^{-1}3)$

$$=\pi-\left\{\pi+\tan^{-1}\left(\frac{2+3}{1-2\cdot3}\right)\right\}$$

$$=\pi-\pi-\tan^{-1}(-1)=-\tan^{-1}(-1) \text{ or } C=\frac{\pi}{4}$$

$\therefore$ Third angle is $\pi/4$

Example 52. Solve $\tan^{-1}\left(\frac{x-1}{x-2}\right)+\tan^{-1}\left(\frac{x+1}{x+2}\right)=\frac{\pi}{4}$

Sol. $\tan^{-1}\left(\frac{x-1}{x-2}\right)+\tan^{-1}\left(\frac{x+1}{x+2}\right)=\frac{\pi}{4}$

$$\Rightarrow \quad \tan^{-1}\left(\frac{x-1}{x-2}\right)=\tan^{-1}(1)-\tan^{-1}\left(\frac{x+1}{x+2}\right)$$

[where, $\tan^{-1}(1)=\pi/4$]

$$\Rightarrow \quad \tan^{-1}\left(\frac{x-1}{x-2}\right)=\tan^{-1}\left(\frac{1-\frac{x+1}{x+2}}{1+\frac{x+1}{x+2}}\right)$$

$$\Rightarrow \quad \tan^{-1}\left(\frac{x-1}{x-2}\right)=\tan^{-1}\left(\frac{x+2-x-1}{x+2+x+1}\right)$$

$$\Rightarrow \quad \tan^{-1}\left(\frac{x-1}{x-2}\right)=\tan^{-1}\left(\frac{1}{2x+3}\right)$$

$$\Rightarrow \quad \frac{x-1}{x-2}=\frac{1}{2x+3}$$

$$\Rightarrow \quad (2x+3)(x-1)=(x-2)$$

$$\Rightarrow \quad 2x^2-2x+3x-3=(x-2)$$

$$\Rightarrow \quad 2x^2+x-3=x-2$$

$$\Rightarrow \quad 2x^2=1$$

$$\Rightarrow \quad x=\pm\frac{1}{\sqrt{2}}$$

Property VII

(1) $\sin^{-1}x+\sin^{-1}y$

$$=\begin{cases}\sin^{-1}\{x\sqrt{1-y^2}+y\sqrt{1-x^2}\}, \text{if } -1\le x,y\le 1 \text{ and } x^2+y^2\le 1 \text{ or if } xy<0 \text{ and } x^2+y^2>1\\ \pi-\sin^{-1}\{x\sqrt{1-y^2}+y\sqrt{1-x^2}\}, \text{if } 0<x,y\le 1 \text{ and } x^2+y^2>1\\ -\pi-\sin^{-1}\{x\sqrt{1-y^2}+y\sqrt{1-x^2}\}, \text{if } -1\le x,y<0 \text{ and } x^2+y^2>1\end{cases}$$

(2) $\sin^{-1}x-\sin^{-1}y$

$$=\begin{cases}\sin^{-1}\{x\sqrt{1-y^2}-y\sqrt{1-x^2}\}, \text{if } -1\le x,y\le 1 \text{ and } x^2+y^2\le 1 \text{ or if } xy>0 \text{ and } x^2+y^2>1\\ \pi-\sin^{-1}\{x\sqrt{1-y^2}-y\sqrt{1-x^2}\}, \text{if } 0<x\le 1, -1\le y<0 \text{ and } x^2+y^2>1\\ -\pi-\sin^{-1}\{x\sqrt{1-y^2}-y\sqrt{1-x^2}\}, \text{if } -1\le x<0, 0<y<1 \text{ and } x^2+y^2>1\end{cases}$$

Proof Let $\sin^{-1}x=A$ and $\sin^{-1}y=B$.

Then, $x=\sin A$, $y=\sin B$ and $A, B\in[-\pi/2,\pi/2]$

$\Rightarrow \cos A=\sqrt{1-x^2}, \cos B=\sqrt{1-y^2}$

[$\because \cos A, \cos B\ge 0$ for $A, B\in[-\pi/2,\pi/2]$]

$\therefore \sin(A+B)=\sin A\cos B+\cos A\sin B$

$$\Rightarrow \sin(A+B)=x\sqrt{1-y^2}+y\sqrt{1-x^2} \quad \text{...(i)}$$

$$\sin(A-B)=x\sqrt{1-y^2}-y\sqrt{1-x^2} \quad \text{...(ii)}$$

$$\cos(A+B)=\sqrt{1-x^2}\sqrt{1-y^2}-xy \quad \text{...(iii)}$$

$$\cos(A-B)=\sqrt{1-x^2}\sqrt{1-y^2}+xy \quad \text{...(iv)}$$

Case I When $-1\le x, y\le 1$ and $x^2+y^2\le 1$

In this case, we have

$$x^2+y^2\le 1 \Rightarrow 1-x^2\ge y^2 \text{ and } 1-y^2\ge x^2$$

$$\Rightarrow \quad (1-x^2)(1-y^2)\ge x^2y^2$$

$$\Rightarrow \quad \sqrt{1-x^2}\sqrt{1-y^2}-xy\ge 0$$

$$\Rightarrow \quad \cos(A+B)\ge 0 \quad \text{[using Eq. (iii)]}$$

$\Rightarrow A+B$ lies either in I quadrant or in IV quadrant.

$$\Rightarrow A+B\in\left[-\frac{\pi}{2},\frac{\pi}{2}\right]$$

$$\left[\because A, B\in\left[-\frac{\pi}{2},\frac{\pi}{2}\right]\Rightarrow -\pi\le A+B\le\pi\right]$$

$$\therefore \quad \sin(A+B)=x\sqrt{1-y^2}+y\sqrt{1-x^2}$$

[from Eq. (i)]

$$\Rightarrow \quad A+B=\sin^{-1}\{x\sqrt{1-y^2}+y\sqrt{1-x^2}\}$$

[$\because -\pi/2\le A+B\le\pi/2$]

$$\Rightarrow \sin^{-1}x+\sin^{-1}y=\sin^{-1}\{x\sqrt{1-y^2}+y\sqrt{1-x^2}\}$$

Case II When $xy<0$ and $x^2+y^2>1$.

In this case, we have

$$xy<0\Rightarrow(x>0 \text{ and } y<0) \text{ or } (x<0 \text{ and } y>0)$$

$$\Rightarrow \left\{A\in\left(0,\frac{\pi}{2}\right] \text{ and } B\in\left[-\frac{\pi}{2},0\right)\right\} \text{ or } \left\{A\in\left[-\frac{\pi}{2},0\right)\right.$$

$$\text{and} \quad \left.B\in\left(0,\frac{\pi}{2}\right]\right\} \Rightarrow -\frac{\pi}{2}\le A+B\le\frac{\pi}{2} \quad \text{...(v)}$$

and $\quad x^2+y^2>1$

$$\Rightarrow \quad 1-x^2<y^2 \text{ and } 1-y^2<x^2$$

$$\Rightarrow \quad (1-x^2)(1-y^2)<x^2y^2$$

$$\Rightarrow \quad (\sqrt{1-x^2}\sqrt{1-y^2})^2<(|xy|)^2 \quad [\because xy<0]$$

$$-|xy|<\sqrt{1-x^2}\sqrt{1-y^2}<|xy|$$

$$\Rightarrow \quad xy<\sqrt{1-x^2}\sqrt{1-y^2}<-xy \quad [\because xy<0]$$

$$\Rightarrow \quad \sqrt{1-x^2}\sqrt{1-y^2}-xy>0 \quad [\therefore |xy|=-xy]$$

$$\Rightarrow \quad \cos(A+B)>0$$

$\Rightarrow A+B$ lies either in I quadrant or in IV quadrant.

$$\Rightarrow \quad A+B \in \left[-\frac{\pi}{2}, \frac{\pi}{2}\right] \quad \text{[using Eq. (v)]}$$

$$\therefore \quad \sin(A+B) = x\sqrt{1-y^2} + y\sqrt{1-x^2}$$

$$\Rightarrow \quad A+B = \sin^{-1}\{x\sqrt{1-y^2} + y\sqrt{1-x^2}\} \quad \left[\because A+B \in \left[-\frac{\pi}{2}, \frac{\pi}{2}\right]\right]$$

$$\Rightarrow \quad \sin^{-1} x + \sin^{-1} y = \sin^{-1}\{x\sqrt{1-y^2} + y\sqrt{1-x^2}\}$$

Case III When $0 < x, y \le 1$ and $x^2 + y^2 > 1$.

In this case, we have

$$0 < x, y \le 1 \Rightarrow A \in \left(0, \frac{\pi}{2}\right] \text{ and } B \in \left(0, \frac{\pi}{2}\right]$$

$$\Rightarrow \quad A+B \in (0, \pi] \quad \text{...(vi)}$$

and, $\quad x^2 + y^2 > 1 \Rightarrow 1 - x^2 < y^2$ and $1 - y^2 < x^2$

$$\Rightarrow \quad (1-x^2)(1-y^2) < x^2y^2$$

$$\Rightarrow \quad \sqrt{1-x^2}\sqrt{1-y^2} < xy \quad [\because xy > 0]$$

$$\Rightarrow \quad \sqrt{1-x^2}\sqrt{1-y^2} - xy < 0$$

$$\Rightarrow \quad \cos(A+B) < 0 \quad \text{[using Eq. (iii)]}$$

$\Rightarrow (A+B)$ lies either in II quadrant or in III quadrant.

$$\Rightarrow \quad \frac{\pi}{2} \le A+B \le \pi \quad [\because A+B \in (0, \pi], \text{ from Eq. (vi)}]$$

$$\Rightarrow \quad -\pi \le -(A+B) \le -\frac{\pi}{2} \Rightarrow 0 \le \pi - (A+B) \le \frac{\pi}{2}$$

$$\therefore \quad \sin(A+B) = x\sqrt{1-y^2} + y\sqrt{1-x^2} \quad \text{[from Eq. (i)]}$$

$$\Rightarrow \quad \sin\{\pi - (A+B)\} = x\sqrt{1-y^2} + y\sqrt{1-x^2} \quad [\because \sin(\pi - \theta) = \sin\theta]$$

$$\Rightarrow \quad \pi - (A+B) = \sin^{-1}\{x\sqrt{1-y^2} + y\sqrt{1-x^2}\}$$

$$\Rightarrow \quad A+B = \pi - \sin^{-1}\{x\sqrt{1-y^2} + y\sqrt{1-x^2}\}$$

$$\Rightarrow \sin^{-1} x + \sin^{-1} y = \pi - \sin^{-1}\{x\sqrt{1-y^2} + y\sqrt{1-x^2}\}$$

Case IV When $-1 \le x, y < 0$ and $x^2 + y^2 > 1$

In this case, we have

$$-1 \le x, y < 0 \Rightarrow A \in \left[-\frac{\pi}{2}, 0\right) \text{ and } B \in \left[-\frac{\pi}{2}, 0\right)$$

$$\Rightarrow \quad A+B \in [-\pi, 0) \quad \text{...(vii)}$$

and $\quad x^2 + y^2 > 1 \Rightarrow 1 - x^2 < y^2$

and $\quad 1 - y^2 < x^2 \Rightarrow (1-x^2)(1-y^2) < x^2y^2$

$$\Rightarrow \quad \sqrt{1-x^2}\sqrt{1-y^2} < xy \quad [\because xy > 0]$$

$$\Rightarrow \quad \sqrt{1-x^2}\sqrt{1-y^2} - xy < 0$$

$$\Rightarrow \quad \cos(A+B) < 0 \quad \text{[using Eq. (iii)]}$$

$\Rightarrow$ $A+B$ lies either in II quadrant or in III quadrant.

$$\Rightarrow \quad -\pi \le A+B \le -\frac{\pi}{2} \quad \text{[using Eq. (vii)]}$$

$$\Rightarrow \quad \frac{\pi}{2} \le -(A+B) \le \pi$$

$$\Rightarrow \quad -\frac{\pi}{2} \le -\pi - (A+B) \le 0$$

$$\therefore \quad \sin(A+B) = x\sqrt{1-y^2} + y\sqrt{1-x^2}$$

$$\Rightarrow \quad -\sin\{\pi + (A+B)\} = x\sqrt{1-y^2} + y\sqrt{1-x^2}$$

$$\Rightarrow \quad \sin\{-\pi - (A+B)\} = x\sqrt{1-y^2} + y\sqrt{1-x^2}$$

$$\Rightarrow \quad -\pi - (A+B) = \sin^{-1}\{x\sqrt{1-y^2} + y\sqrt{1-x^2}\}$$

$$\Rightarrow \quad A+B = -\pi - \sin^{-1}\{x\sqrt{1-y^2} + y\sqrt{1-x^2}\}$$

$$\Rightarrow \quad \sin^{-1} x + \sin^{-1} y = -\pi - \sin^{-1}\{x\sqrt{1-y^2} + y\sqrt{1-x^2}\}$$

(2) Do yourself

Example 53. Solve $\sin^{-1} x + \sin^{-1} 2x = \frac{\pi}{3}$.

Sol. $\sin^{-1} x + \sin^{-1} 2x = \frac{\pi}{3}$

or $\quad \sin^{-1} 2x = \sin^{-1}\frac{\sqrt{3}}{2} - \sin^{-1} x$

$$= \sin^{-1}\left[\frac{\sqrt{3}}{2}\sqrt{1-x^2} - x\sqrt{1-\frac{3}{4}}\right]$$

or $\quad 2x = \frac{\sqrt{3}}{2}\sqrt{1-x^2} - \frac{x}{2}$

or $\quad \left(\frac{5x}{2}\right)^2 = \left(\frac{\sqrt{3}}{2}\sqrt{1-x^2}\right)^2 = \frac{3}{4}(1-x^2)$

or $\quad 28x^2 = 3$

or $\quad x = \sqrt{\frac{3}{28}} = \frac{1}{2}\sqrt{\frac{3}{7}}$

$$\left[x = -\frac{1}{2}\sqrt{\frac{3}{7}} \text{ makes LHS of Eq. (i) negative}\right]$$

Example 54. Solve $\sin^{-1} x + \sin^{-1}(1-x) = \cos^{-1} x$.

Sol. We have, $\sin^{-1} x + \sin^{-1}(1-x) = \cos^{-1} x$

$$\Rightarrow \sin^{-1}[x\sqrt{1-(1-x)^2} + \sqrt{1-x^2}(1-x)] = \sin^{-1}\sqrt{1-x^2}$$

$$\Rightarrow \quad x\sqrt{1-(1-x)^2} + \sqrt{1-x^2}(1-x) = \sqrt{1-x^2}$$

$$\Rightarrow \quad x\sqrt{1-(1-x)^2} = x\sqrt{1-x^2}$$

$$\Rightarrow x = 0 \text{ or } 2x - x^2 = 1 - x^2 \Rightarrow x = 0 \text{ or } x = \frac{1}{2}$$

Example 55. If $\sin^{-1} x + \sin^{-1} y + \sin^{-1} z = \frac{3\pi}{2}$, then find the value of $\sum \frac{(x^{101} + y^{101})(x^{202} + y^{202})}{(x^{303} + y^{303})(x^{404} + y^{404})}$

Sol. We have, $\sin^{-1} x + \sin^{-1} y + \sin^{-1} z = \frac{3\pi}{2}$

As we know that, $\sin^{-1} x \le \frac{\pi}{2}$ for all $x \in [-1, 1]$

Hence, above result is possible only when

$$\sin^{-1} x = \frac{\pi}{2}, \sin^{-1} y = \frac{\pi}{2}, \sin^{-1} z = \frac{\pi}{2}$$

$$\Rightarrow \quad x = 1, y = 1, z = 1 \quad \text{...(i)}$$

$$\therefore \sum \frac{(x^{101} + y^{101})(x^{202} + y^{202})}{(x^{303} + y^{303})(x^{404} + y^{404})}$$

$$= \frac{(x^{101} + y^{101})(x^{202} + y^{202})}{(x^{303} + y^{303})(x^{404} + y^{404})} + \frac{(y^{101} + z^{101})(y^{202} + z^{202})}{(y^{303} + z^{303})(y^{404} + z^{404})} + \frac{(z^{101} + x^{101})(z^{202} + x^{202})}{(z^{303} + x^{303})(z^{404} + x^{404})} \quad \text{[expanding summation]}$$

$$= \frac{(1+1)(1+1)}{(1+1)(1+1)} + \frac{(1+1)(1+1)}{(1+1)(1+1)} + \frac{(1+1)(1+1)}{(1+1)(1+1)} \quad \text{[using Eq. (i)]}$$

$$= 1 + 1 + 1 = 3$$

Property VIII

(1) $\cos^{-1} x + \cos^{-1} y$

$$= \begin{cases} \cos^{-1}\{xy - \sqrt{1-x^2}\sqrt{1-y^2}\}, & \text{if } -1 \le x, y \le 1 \text{ and } x + y \ge 0 \\ 2\pi - \cos^{-1}\{xy - \sqrt{1-x^2}\sqrt{1-y^2}\}, & \text{if } -1 \le x, y \le 1 \text{ and } x + y \le 0 \end{cases}$$

(2) $\cos^{-1} x - \cos^{-1} y$

$$= \begin{cases} \cos^{-1}\{xy + \sqrt{1-x^2}\sqrt{1-y^2}\}, & \text{if } -1 \le x, y \le 1 \text{ and } x \le y \\ -\cos^{-1}\{xy + \sqrt{1-x^2}\sqrt{1-y^2}\}, & \text{if } -1 \le y \le 0, 0 < x \le 1 \text{ and } x \ge y \end{cases}$$

Proof (1) Let $\cos^{-1} x = A$ and $\cos^{-1} y = B$.

Then, $\quad x = \cos A, y = \cos B$ and $A, B \in [0, \pi]$

$$\Rightarrow \quad \sin A = \sqrt{1-x^2} \text{ and } \sin B = \sqrt{1-y^2} \quad [\because \sin A, \sin B \ge 0 \text{ for } A, B \in [0, \pi]]$$

$$\therefore \quad \cos(A+B) = xy - \sqrt{1-x^2}\sqrt{1-y^2} \quad \text{...(i)}$$

$$\cos(A-B) = xy + \sqrt{1-x^2}\sqrt{1-y^2} \quad \text{...(ii)}$$

Case I When $-1 \le x, y \le 1$ and $x + y \ge 0$

In this case,

$$-1 \le x, y \le 1 \Rightarrow A, B \in [0, \pi]$$

$$\Rightarrow \quad 0 \le A + B \le 2\pi \quad \text{...(iii)}$$

and $\quad x + y \ge 0 \Rightarrow \cos A + \cos B \ge 0$

$$\Rightarrow \quad \cos A \ge -\cos B$$

$$\Rightarrow \quad \cos A \ge \cos(\pi - B)$$

$$\Rightarrow \quad A \le \pi - B \quad [\because \cos\theta \text{ is decreasing on } [0, \pi]]$$

$$\Rightarrow \quad A + B \le \pi \quad \text{...(iv)}$$

From Eqs. (iii) and (iv), we get

$$0 \le A + B \le \pi$$

$$\therefore \quad \cos(A+B) = xy - \sqrt{1-x^2}\sqrt{1-y^2}$$

$$\Rightarrow \quad A + B = \cos^{-1}\{xy - \sqrt{1-x^2}\sqrt{1-y^2}\}$$

$$\Rightarrow \quad \cos^{-1} x + \cos^{-1} y = \cos^{-1}\{xy - \sqrt{1-x^2}\sqrt{1-y^2}\}$$

Case II When $-1 \le x, y \le 1$ and $x + y \le 0$

In this case,

$$-1 \le x, y \le 1 \Rightarrow A, B \in [0, \pi]$$

$$\Rightarrow \quad 0 \le A + B \le 2\pi$$

and $\quad x + y \le 0 \Rightarrow \cos A + \cos B \le 0 \quad \text{...(v)}$

$$\Rightarrow \quad \cos A \le -\cos B \Rightarrow \cos A \le \cos(\pi - B)$$

$$\Rightarrow \quad A \ge \pi - B \quad [\because \cos\theta \text{ is decreasing on } [0, \pi]]$$

$$\Rightarrow \quad A + B \ge \pi \quad \text{...(vi)}$$

From Eqs. (v) and (vi), we get $\pi \le A + B \le 2\pi$

$$\Rightarrow \quad -\pi \ge -(A+B) \ge -2\pi$$

$$\Rightarrow \quad \pi \ge 2\pi - (A+B) \ge 0$$

$$\Rightarrow \quad 0 \le 2\pi - (A+B) \le \pi$$

$$\therefore \quad \cos(A+B) = xy - \sqrt{1-x^2}\sqrt{1-y^2}$$

$$\Rightarrow \quad \cos\{2\pi - (A+B)\} = xy - \sqrt{1-x^2}\sqrt{1-y^2}$$

$$\Rightarrow \quad 2\pi - (A+B) = \cos^{-1}\{xy - \sqrt{1-x^2}\sqrt{1-y^2}\}$$

$$\Rightarrow \quad A + B = 2\pi - \cos^{-1}\{xy - \sqrt{1-x^2}\sqrt{1-y^2}\}$$

$$\Rightarrow \cos^{-1} x + \cos^{-1} y = 2\pi - \cos^{-1}\{xy - \sqrt{1-x^2}\sqrt{1-y^2}\}$$

(2) Do yourself.

Example 56. If $\cos^{-1}\frac{x}{a} + \cos^{-1}\frac{y}{b} = \alpha$, then show $\frac{x^2}{a^2} + \frac{y^2}{b^2} - \frac{2xy}{ab}\cos\alpha = \sin^2\alpha$.

Sol. We have, $\quad \cos^{-1}\left(\frac{x}{a}\right) + \cos^{-1}\left(\frac{y}{b}\right) = \alpha$

$$\Rightarrow \quad \cos^{-1}\left(\frac{x}{a}\cdot\frac{y}{b} - \sqrt{1 - \frac{x^2}{a^2}}\sqrt{1 - \frac{y^2}{b^2}}\right) = \alpha$$

$$\Rightarrow \quad \frac{xy}{ab} - \sqrt{\left(1 - \frac{x^2}{a^2}\right)\left(1 - \frac{y^2}{b^2}\right)} = \cos\alpha$$

$$\Rightarrow \quad \left(\frac{xy}{ab}-\cos\alpha\right)^2 = 1-\frac{x^2}{a^2}-\frac{y^2}{b^2}+\frac{x^2y^2}{a^2b^2}$$

$$\Rightarrow \quad \cos^2\alpha+\frac{x^2y^2}{a^2b^2}-\frac{2xy\cos\alpha}{ab} = 1-\frac{x^2}{a^2}-\frac{y^2}{b^2}+\frac{x^2y^2}{a^2b^2}$$

$$\Rightarrow \quad \frac{x^2}{a^2}+\frac{y^2}{b^2}-\frac{2xy}{ab}\cos\alpha = \sin^2\alpha$$

Example 57. If $\cos^{-1}\lambda+\cos^{-1}\mu+\cos^{-1}\gamma=3\pi$, then find the value of $\lambda\mu+\mu\gamma+\gamma\lambda$.

Sol. We know, $0\le\cos^{-1}x\le\pi$

Hence, from the question,

$\cos^{-1}\lambda=\pi$,

$\cos^{-1}\mu=\pi$,

$\cos^{-1}\gamma=\pi$

$\therefore \quad \lambda=\mu=\gamma=-1$

[$\because \cos^{-1}\lambda+\cos^{-1}\mu+\cos^{-1}\gamma=3\pi$ only when each value attains its maximum]

$\Rightarrow \quad \lambda\mu+\mu\gamma+\gamma\lambda=3$

Example 58. If $\sum_{i=1}^{2n}\cos^{-1}x_i=0$, then find the value of $\sum_{i=1}^{2n}x_i$.

Sol. We know, $0\le\cos^{-1}x\le\pi$.

$\therefore \cos^{-1}x_1, \cos^{-1}x_2, \cos^{-1}x_3, \ldots, \cos^{-1}x_{2n}$ are positive and hence their sum is zero only when each value is zero.

i.e. $\quad \cos^{-1}x_i=0$ for all $i \Rightarrow x_i=1$ for all i ...(i)

Now, $\quad \sum_{i=1}^{2n}x_i = x_1+x_2+x_3+\ldots+x_{2n}$

$= \underbrace{\{1+1+1\ldots+1\}}_{2n\text{ times}} = 2n$ [using Eq. (i)]

$\Rightarrow \quad \sum_{1=1}^{2n}x_i=2n$

Example 59. If $\cos^{-1}x+\cos^{-1}y+\cos^{-1}z=\pi$, prove that $x^2+y^2+z^2+2xyz=1$.

Sol. Here, $\cos^{-1}x+\cos^{-1}y+\cos^{-1}z=\pi$

$\Rightarrow \quad \cos^{-1}x+\cos^{-1}y=\pi-\cos^{-1}z$

$\Rightarrow \quad \cos^{-1}x+\cos^{-1}y=\cos^{-1}(-z)$

[$\because \cos^{-1}(-x)=\pi-\cos^{-1}x$]

$\Rightarrow \cos^{-1}\{xy-\sqrt{1-x^2}\sqrt{1-y^2}\}=\cos^{-1}(-z)$

$\Rightarrow \quad xy-\sqrt{1-x^2}\sqrt{1-y^2}=-z$

$\Rightarrow \quad (xy+z)^2=(1-x^2)(1-y^2)$

$\Rightarrow \quad x^2y^2+z^2+2xyz=1-x^2-y^2+x^2y^2$

$\Rightarrow \quad x^2+y^2+z^2+2xyz=1$

Property IX

(i) For $0<x<1$,

$$\sin^{-1}x=\cos^{-1}\sqrt{1-x^2}=\tan^{-1}\left(\frac{x}{\sqrt{1-x^2}}\right)$$
$$=\cot^{-1}\frac{\sqrt{1-x^2}}{x}=\sec^{-1}\left(\frac{1}{\sqrt{1-x^2}}\right)$$
$$=\text{cosec}^{-1}\left(\frac{1}{x}\right)$$

(ii) For $0<x<1$,

$$\cos^{-1}x=\sin^{-1}\sqrt{1-x^2}=\tan^{-1}\left(\frac{\sqrt{1-x^2}}{x}\right)$$
$$=\cot^{-1}\left(\frac{x}{\sqrt{1-x^2}}\right)=\sec^{-1}\left(\frac{1}{x}\right)$$
$$=\text{cosec}^{-1}\left(\frac{1}{\sqrt{1-x^2}}\right)$$

(iii) For $x>0$, $\tan^{-1}x=\sin^{-1}\left(\frac{x}{\sqrt{1+x^2}}\right)=\cos^{-1}\left(\frac{1}{\sqrt{1+x^2}}\right)$

$$=\cot^{-1}\left(\frac{1}{x}\right)=\sec^{-1}(\sqrt{1+x^2})$$
$$=\text{cosec}^{-1}\left(\frac{\sqrt{1+x^2}}{x}\right)$$

Proof

(i) Let $\sin^{-1}x=\theta$. Then, $x=\sin\theta$

Now, $\quad \cos\theta=\sqrt{1-\sin^2\theta}$

$\Rightarrow \quad \cos\theta=\sqrt{1-x^2}$

$\Rightarrow \quad \theta=\cos^{-1}\sqrt{1-x^2}$

$\Rightarrow \quad \sin^{-1}x=\cos^{-1}\sqrt{1-x^2}$

$=\sec^{-1}\left(\frac{1}{\sqrt{1-x^2}}\right)$ [$\because \theta=\sin^{-1}x$]

Again, $\quad \tan\theta=\frac{\sin\theta}{\cos\theta}=\frac{\sin\theta}{\sqrt{1-\sin^2\theta}}$

$\Rightarrow \quad \tan\theta=\frac{x}{\sqrt{1-x^2}}$

$\Rightarrow \quad \theta=\tan^{-1}\left(\frac{x}{\sqrt{1-x^2}}\right)$

$$\Rightarrow \quad \sin^{-1} x = \tan^{-1}\left(\frac{x}{\sqrt{1-x^2}}\right) \qquad [\because \theta = \sin^{-1} x]$$

$$\Rightarrow \quad \sin^{-1} x = \tan^{-1}\left(\frac{x}{\sqrt{1-x^2}}\right) = \cot^{-1}\left(\frac{\sqrt{1-x^2}}{x}\right)$$

$$\left[\because \tan^{-1} x = \cot^{-1}\frac{1}{x} \text{ for } x > 0\right]$$

Hence, $\sin^{-1} x = \cos^{-1}\sqrt{1-x^2} = \sec^{-1}\left(\frac{1}{\sqrt{1-x^2}}\right)$

$$= \tan^{-1}\left(\frac{x}{\sqrt{1-x^2}}\right) = \cot^{-1}\left(\frac{\sqrt{1-x^2}}{x}\right)$$

$$= \operatorname{cosec}^{-1}\left(\frac{1}{x}\right)$$

Similarly, the other results can be proved.

Example 60. Evaluate the following

(i) $\sin\left(\tan^{-1}\frac{3}{4}\right)$ (ii) $\sin\left(\cos^{-1}\frac{3}{5}\right)$

(iii) $\cos\left(\tan^{-1}\frac{3}{4}\right)$ (iv) $\sin(\cot^{-1} x)$

Sol. (i) Let $y = \sin\left(\tan^{-1}\frac{3}{4}\right)$ ...(i)

Note To find y we use $\sin(\sin^{-1} x) = x, -1, \le x \le 1$

For this we convert $\tan^{-1} x$ in $\sin^{-1} x$

Here, $\tan^{-1}\left(\frac{3}{4}\right) = \sin^{-1}\left(\frac{3/4}{\sqrt{1+(3/4)^2}}\right) = \sin^{-1}\left(\frac{3}{5}\right)$

Now, from Eq. (i), we get

or $\quad y = \sin\left(\sin^{-1}\frac{3}{5}\right)$

$\therefore \quad y = \frac{3}{5}$

(ii) $\cos^{-1}\frac{3}{5} = \sin^{-1}\sqrt{1-\left(\frac{3}{5}\right)^2} = \sin^{-1}\frac{4}{5}.$

$\therefore \quad \sin\left(\cos^{-1}\frac{3}{5}\right) = \sin\left(\sin^{-1}\frac{4}{5}\right) = \frac{4}{5}$

(iii) $\tan^{-1}\left(\frac{3}{4}\right) = \cos^{-1}\left(\frac{1}{\sqrt{1-\left(\frac{3}{4}\right)^2}}\right) = \cos^{-1}\frac{4}{5}$

$\therefore \cos\left(\tan^{-1}\frac{3}{4}\right) = \cos\left(\cos^{-1}\frac{4}{5}\right) = \frac{4}{5}$

(iv) Let $\cot^{-1} x = \tan^{-1}\left(\frac{1}{x}\right) = \sin^{-1}\left(\frac{1/x}{\sqrt{1+1/x^2}}\right)$

$$= \sin^{-1}\left(\frac{1}{\sqrt{x^2+1}}\right)$$

$\therefore \quad \sin(\cot^{-1} x) = \sin\left(\sin^{-1}\frac{1}{\sqrt{x^2+1}}\right) = \frac{1}{\sqrt{1+x^2}}$

Example 61. Find the value of $\tan\left(\frac{1}{2}\cos^{-1}\frac{\sqrt{5}}{3}\right)$.

Sol. Let $y = \tan\left(\frac{1}{2}\cos^{-1}\frac{\sqrt{5}}{3}\right)$ ...(i)

Let $\cos^{-1}\frac{\sqrt{5}}{3} = \theta \Rightarrow \theta \in \left(0, \frac{\pi}{2}\right)$ and $\cos\theta = \frac{\sqrt{5}}{3}$

$\therefore$ Eq. (i) becomes

$$y = \tan\left(\frac{\theta}{2}\right) \quad \text{...(ii)}$$

$\because \quad \tan^2\frac{\theta}{2} = \frac{1-\cos\theta}{1+\cos\theta} = \frac{1-\frac{\sqrt{5}}{3}}{1+\frac{\sqrt{5}}{3}}$

$$= \frac{3-\sqrt{5}}{3-\sqrt{5}} = \frac{(3-\sqrt{5})^2}{4}$$

$$\tan\frac{\theta}{2} = \pm\left(\frac{3-\sqrt{5}}{2}\right) \quad \text{... (iii)}$$

$\because \quad \theta \in \left(0, \frac{\pi}{2}\right) \Rightarrow \frac{\theta}{2} \in \left(0, \frac{\pi}{4}\right)$

$\therefore \quad \tan\frac{\theta}{2} > 0$

So, from Eq. (iii), we get

$$\tan\frac{\theta}{2} = \left(\frac{3-\sqrt{5}}{2}\right)$$

Now, from Eq. (ii), we get

$$y = \left(\frac{3-\sqrt{5}}{2}\right)$$

Example 62. Find the value of $\cos(2\cos^{-1} x + \sin^{-1} x)$ when $x = \frac{1}{5}$

Sol. Let $y = \cos[2\cos^{-1} x + \sin^{-1} x]$

$\because \quad \sin^{-1} x + \cos^{1} x = \frac{\pi}{2}, |x| \le 1$

$\therefore \quad y = \cos\left[2\cos^{-1} x + \frac{\pi}{2} - \cos^{-1} x\right]$

$$= \cos\left[\frac{\pi}{2} + \cos^{-1} x\right] = -\sin(\cos^{-1} x)$$

$\because \quad x = \frac{1}{5}$

$\therefore \quad y = -\sin\left(\cos^{-1}\frac{1}{5}\right)$

$\Rightarrow \quad y = -\sin\left(\sin^{-1}\sqrt{1-\left(\frac{1}{5}\right)^2}\right) = -\sin\left(\sin^{-1}\frac{\sqrt{24}}{5}\right) = -\frac{\sqrt{24}}{5}$

Example 63. Find the value of

$$\cos\left[\frac{1}{2}\cos^{-1}\left\{\cos\left(\sin^{-1}\frac{\sqrt{63}}{8}\right)\right\}\right].$$

Sol. We have, $\cos\left[\frac{1}{2}\cos^{-1}\left\{\cos\left(\sin^{-1}\frac{\sqrt{63}}{8}\right)\right\}\right]$

$$= \cos\left[\frac{1}{2}\cos^{-1}\left\{\cos\left(\cos^{-1}\sqrt{1-\frac{63}{64}}\right)\right\}\right]$$

$$= \cos\left(\frac{1}{2}\cos^{-1}\frac{1}{8}\right)$$

Let $\cos^{-1}\frac{1}{8} = \theta \Rightarrow \cos\theta = \frac{1}{8}$

$\therefore \quad 2\cos^2\frac{\theta}{2} - 1 = \frac{1}{8}$

$\Rightarrow \quad 2\cos^2\frac{\theta}{2} = 1 + \frac{1}{8} = \frac{9}{8}$

$\Rightarrow \quad \cos^2\theta = \frac{9}{16}$

$\Rightarrow \quad \cos\theta = \frac{3}{4}$

$\therefore \quad \cos\left(\frac{1}{2}\cos^{-1}\frac{1}{8}\right) = \frac{3}{4}$

Milestone Practice 4.4

1. Show that $\sin^{-1}\frac{3}{5} + \sin^{-1}\frac{15}{17} = \pi - \sin^{-1}\frac{84}{85}$
2. Evaluate $\sin^{-1}\frac{4}{5} + \sin^{-1}\frac{5}{13} + \sin^{-1}\frac{16}{65}$
3. If $\tan^{-1}4 + \tan^{-1}5 = \cot^{-1}\lambda$, then find '$\lambda$'.
4. Prove that
$$\cos^{-1}\left[\frac{7}{2}(1+\cos 2x) + \sqrt{(\sin^2 x - 48\cos^2 x)}\sin x\right] = x - \cos^{-1}(7\cos x),$$
where $x \in \left(0, \frac{\pi}{2}\right)$.

Solve the following

5. $\sin^{-1}\frac{1}{3} + \sin^{-1}\frac{2}{3} = \sin^{-1}x$
6. $\sin^{-1}x + \sin^{-1}2x = \frac{2\pi}{3}$

Evaluate the following.

7. $\tan\left(\operatorname{cosec}^{-1}\frac{\sqrt{41}}{4}\right)$
8. $\sec\left(\cot^{-1}\frac{16}{63}\right)$
9. $\sin^2\left[\tan^{-1}\frac{3}{4}\right]$
10. $\sin\left\{\frac{1}{2}\cot^{-1}\left(\frac{-3}{4}\right)\right\}$
11. Show that $\cot\left[\sin^{-1}\sqrt{\frac{13}{17}}\right] = \sin\left[\tan^{-1}\frac{2}{3}\right]$

Answer Key

2. $\frac{\pi}{2}$ 3. $\lambda = \frac{-19}{9}$ 5. $x = \frac{\sqrt{5}+4\sqrt{2}}{9}$ 6. $x = \pm\frac{1}{2}, \pm\frac{1}{2}\sqrt{\frac{3}{7}}$

7. $\frac{4}{5}$ 8. $\frac{65}{16}$ 9. $\frac{9}{25}$ 10. $\frac{2}{\sqrt{5}}$

For Detailed Solution

Milestone 5 Property X, XI, XII and XIII of Inverse Trigonometric Functions

Property X

(i) $2\sin^{-1}x = \begin{cases} \sin^{-1}(2x\sqrt{1-x^2}), & \text{if } -\frac{1}{\sqrt{2}} \le x \le \frac{1}{\sqrt{2}} \\ \pi - \sin^{-1}(2x\sqrt{1-x^2}), & \text{if } \frac{1}{\sqrt{2}} \le x \le 1 \\ -\pi - \sin^{-1}(2x\sqrt{1-x^2}), & \text{if } -1 \le x \le -\frac{1}{\sqrt{2}} \end{cases}$

(ii) $3\sin^{-1}x = \begin{cases} \sin^{-1}(3x-4x^3), & \text{if } -\frac{1}{2} \le x \le \frac{1}{2} \\ \pi - \sin^{-1}(3x-4x^3), & \text{if } \frac{1}{2} < x \le 1 \\ -\pi - \sin^{-1}(3x-4x^3), & \text{if } -1 \le x < -\frac{1}{2} \end{cases}$

Proof

(i) Let $\sin^{-1}x = \theta$.

Then, $x = \sin\theta$

$\Rightarrow \cos\theta = \sqrt{1-x^2}$ $\left[\because \cos\theta > 0 \text{ for } \theta \in \left[-\frac{\pi}{2}, \frac{\pi}{2}\right]\right]$

$\because \sin 2\theta = 2\sin\theta\cos\theta$

$\therefore \sin 2\theta = 2x\sqrt{1-x^2}$ ...(i)

Case I When $-\frac{1}{\sqrt{2}} \le x \le \frac{1}{\sqrt{2}}$

$-\frac{1}{\sqrt{2}} \le x \le \frac{1}{\sqrt{2}} \Rightarrow -\frac{1}{\sqrt{2}} \le \sin\theta \le \frac{1}{\sqrt{2}}$

$\Rightarrow -\frac{\pi}{4} \le \theta \le \frac{\pi}{4}$

$\Rightarrow -\frac{\pi}{2} \le 2\theta \le \frac{\pi}{2}$

Also, $-\frac{1}{\sqrt{2}} \le x \le \frac{1}{\sqrt{2}}$

$\Rightarrow -1 \le 2x\sqrt{1-x^2} \le 1$

$\therefore \sin 2\theta = 2x\sqrt{1-x^2}$ [from Eq. (i)]

$\Rightarrow 2\theta = \sin^{-1}(2x\sqrt{1-x^2})$

$\Rightarrow 2\sin^{-1}x = \sin^{-1}(2x\sqrt{1-x^2})$

Case II When $\frac{1}{\sqrt{2}} \le x \le 1$

$\frac{1}{\sqrt{2}} \le x \le 1 \Rightarrow \frac{1}{\sqrt{2}} \le \sin\theta \le 1$

$\Rightarrow \frac{\pi}{4} \le \theta \le \frac{\pi}{2}$

$\Rightarrow \frac{\pi}{2} \le 2\theta \le \pi$

$\Rightarrow -\pi \le -2\theta \le -\frac{\pi}{2}$

$\Rightarrow 0 \le \pi - 2\theta \le \frac{\pi}{2}$

Also, $\frac{1}{\sqrt{2}} \le x \le 1 \Rightarrow 0 \le 2x\sqrt{1-x^2} \le 1$

$\therefore \sin 2\theta = 2x\sqrt{1-x^2}$ [from Eq. (i)]

$\Rightarrow \sin(\pi - 2\theta) = 2x\sqrt{1-x^2}$

$\Rightarrow \pi - 2\theta = \sin^{-1}(2x\sqrt{1-x^2})$

$\Rightarrow \pi - 2\sin^{-1}x = \sin^{-1}(2x\sqrt{1-x^2})$

$\Rightarrow 2\sin^{-1}x = \pi - \sin^{-1}(2x\sqrt{1-x^2})$

Case III When $-1 \le x \le -\frac{1}{\sqrt{2}}$

$-1 \le x \le -\frac{1}{\sqrt{2}} \Rightarrow -1 \le \sin\theta \le -\frac{1}{\sqrt{2}}$

$\Rightarrow -\frac{\pi}{2} \le \theta \le -\frac{\pi}{4} \Rightarrow -\pi \le 2\theta \le -\frac{\pi}{2}$

$\Rightarrow 0 \le \pi + 2\theta \le \frac{\pi}{2}$

Also, $-1 \le x \le -\frac{1}{\sqrt{2}} \Rightarrow -1 \le 2x\sqrt{1-x^2} \le 0$

$\therefore \sin 2\theta = 2x\sqrt{1-x^2}$ [from Eq. (i)]

$\Rightarrow -\sin(\pi + 2\theta) = 2x\sqrt{1-x^2}$

$\Rightarrow \sin(-\pi - 2\theta) = 2x\sqrt{1-x^2}$

$$\Rightarrow \quad -\pi - 2\theta = \sin^{-1}(2x\sqrt{1-x^2})$$

$$\Rightarrow \quad -\pi - 2\sin^{-1}x = \sin^{-1}(2x\sqrt{1-x^2})$$

$$\Rightarrow \quad 2\sin^{-1}x = -\pi - \sin^{-1}(2x\sqrt{1-x^2})$$

(ii) Let $\sin^{-1}x = \theta$

Then, $x = \sin\theta$

$$\therefore \quad \sin 3\theta = 3\sin\theta - 4\sin^3\theta$$

$$\Rightarrow \quad \sin 3\theta = 3x - 4x^3$$

Case I When $-\frac{1}{2} \le x \le \frac{1}{2}$

$$-\frac{1}{2} \le x \le \frac{1}{2}$$

$$\Rightarrow \quad -\frac{1}{2} \le \sin\theta \le \frac{1}{2}$$

$$\Rightarrow \quad -\frac{\pi}{6} \le \theta \le \frac{\pi}{6}$$

$$\Rightarrow \quad -\frac{\pi}{2} \le 3\theta \le \frac{\pi}{2}$$

Also, $-\frac{1}{2} \le x \le \frac{1}{2} \Rightarrow -1 \le 3x - 4x^3 \le 1$

$$\therefore \quad \sin 3\theta = 3x - 4x^3$$

$$\Rightarrow \quad 3\theta = \sin^{-1}(3x - 4x^3)$$

$$\Rightarrow \quad 3\sin^{-1}x = \sin^{-1}(3x - 4x^3)$$

Case II When $\frac{1}{2} < x \le 1$

$$\frac{1}{2} < x \le 1 \Rightarrow \frac{1}{2} < \sin\theta \le 1$$

$$\Rightarrow \quad \frac{\pi}{6} < \theta \le \frac{\pi}{2}$$

$$\Rightarrow \quad \frac{\pi}{2} < 3\theta \le \frac{3\pi}{2}$$

$$\Rightarrow \quad -\frac{3\pi}{2} \le -3\theta < -\frac{\pi}{2}$$

$$\Rightarrow \quad -\frac{\pi}{2} \le \pi - 3\theta < \frac{\pi}{2}$$

Also, $\frac{1}{2} < x \le 1 \Rightarrow -1 \le 3x - 4x^3 \le 1$

$$\therefore \quad \sin 3\theta = (3x - 4x^3)$$

$$\Rightarrow \quad \sin(\pi - 3\theta) = (3x - 4x^3)$$

$$\Rightarrow \quad \pi - 3\theta = \sin^{-1}(3x - 4x^3)$$

$$\Rightarrow \quad \pi - 3\sin^{-1}x = \sin^{-1}(3x - 4x^3)$$

$$\Rightarrow \quad 3\sin^{-1}x = \pi - \sin^{-1}(3x - 4x^3)$$

Case III When $-1 \le x < -\frac{1}{2}$

$$-1 \le x < -\frac{1}{2}$$

$$\Rightarrow \quad -1 \le \sin\theta < -\frac{1}{2}$$

$$\Rightarrow \quad -\frac{\pi}{2} \le \theta < -\frac{\pi}{6}$$

$$\Rightarrow \quad -\frac{3\pi}{2} \le 3\theta < -\frac{\pi}{2}$$

$$\Rightarrow \quad -\frac{\pi}{2} \le \pi + 3\theta < \frac{\pi}{2}$$

Also, $-1 \le x < -\frac{1}{2} \Rightarrow -1 \le 3x - 4x^3 \le 1$

$$\therefore \quad \sin 3\theta = 3x - 4x^3$$

$$\Rightarrow \quad -\sin(\pi + 3\theta) = 3x - 4x^3 \quad [\sin(\pi + 3\theta) = -\sin 3\theta]$$

$$\Rightarrow \quad \sin(-\pi - 3\theta) = 3x - 4x^3$$

$$\Rightarrow \quad -\pi - 3\theta = \sin^{-1}(3x - 4x^3)$$

$$\Rightarrow \quad -\pi - 3\sin^{-1}x = \sin^{-1}(3x - 4x^3)$$

$$\Rightarrow \quad 3\sin^{-1}x = -\pi - \sin^{-1}(3x - 4x^3)$$

Example 64. If $f(x) = \sin^{-1}x$, then prove that $\lim_{x \to \frac{1}{2}^+} f(3x - 4x^3) = \pi - 3 \lim_{x \to \frac{1}{2}^+} \sin^{-1}x$.

Sol. $\sin^{-1}(3x - 4x^3) = \pi - 3\sin^{-1}x$ if $\frac{1}{2} < x < 1$

$$\therefore \quad \lim_{x \to \frac{1}{2}^+} f(3x - 4x^3) = \lim_{x \to \frac{1}{2}^+} (\pi - 3\sin^{-1}x)$$

$$= \pi - 3 \lim_{x \to \frac{1}{2}^+} \sin^{-1}x$$

Example 65. Solve $\sin^{-1}x - \cos^{-1}x = \sin^{-1}(3x - 2)$.

Sol. $\sin^{-1}x - \cos^{-1}x = \sin^{-1}(3x - 2)$

This equation is valid if $-1 \le x \le 1$ and $-1 \le 3x - 2 \le 1$

$$\Rightarrow \quad x \in \left[\frac{1}{3}, 1\right]$$

Given equation can be rewritten as

$$\frac{\pi}{2} - \cos^{-1}x - \cos^{-1}x = \frac{\pi}{2} - \cos^{-1}(3x - 2)$$

$$\Rightarrow \quad 2\cos^{-1}x = \cos^{-1}(3x - 2)$$

$$\Rightarrow \quad \cos^{-1}(2x^2 - 1) = \cos^{-1}(3x - 2)$$

$$\Rightarrow \quad 2x^2 - 1 = 3x - 2$$

$$\Rightarrow \quad 2x^2 - 3x + 1 = 0$$

$$\Rightarrow \quad x = 1 \text{ or } \frac{1}{2}$$

Example 66. If $A = 2\tan^{-1}(2\sqrt{2} - 1)$ and $B = 3\sin^{-1}\left(\frac{1}{3}\right) + \sin^{-1}\left(\frac{3}{5}\right)$, then which is greater?

Sol. We have, $A = 2\tan^{-1}(2\sqrt{2} - 1) = 2\tan^{-1}(1.828)$

$\Rightarrow \quad A > 2\tan^{-1}\sqrt{3}$

$\Rightarrow \quad A > \frac{2\pi}{3}$

Now, $\sin^{-1}\left(\frac{1}{3}\right) < \sin^{-1}\left(\frac{1}{2}\right)$

$\Rightarrow \quad \sin^{-1}\left(\frac{1}{3}\right) < \frac{\pi}{6}$

$\Rightarrow \quad 3\sin^{-1}\left(\frac{1}{3}\right) < \frac{\pi}{2}$

Further, $\sin^{-1}\left(\frac{3}{5}\right) = \sin^{-1}(0.6) < \sin^{-1}\left(\frac{\sqrt{3}}{2}\right)$

$\Rightarrow \quad \sin^{-1}\left(\frac{3}{5}\right) < \frac{\pi}{3}$

$\Rightarrow \quad B = 3\sin^{-1}\left(\frac{1}{3}\right) + \sin^{-1}\left(\frac{3}{5}\right) < \frac{\pi}{2} + \frac{\pi}{3}$

$\Rightarrow \quad B < \frac{5\pi}{6}$

From this, we really cannot relate A and B.

Now, $3\sin^{-1}\left(\frac{1}{3}\right) = \sin^{-1}\left[3 \cdot \frac{1}{3} - 4\left(\frac{1}{3}\right)^3\right]$

$= \sin^{-1}\left(\frac{23}{27}\right) = \sin^{-1}(0.852)$

$\Rightarrow \quad 3\sin^{-1}\left(\frac{1}{3}\right) < \sin^{-1}\left(\frac{\sqrt{3}}{2}\right) = \frac{\pi}{3}$

Hence, $B = 3\sin^{-1}\left(\frac{1}{3}\right) + \sin^{-1}\left(\frac{3}{5}\right) < \frac{\pi}{3} + \frac{\pi}{3} = \frac{2\pi}{3}$

$\therefore \quad A > B$

Property XI

(i) $2\cos^{-1}x = \begin{cases} \cos^{-1}(2x^2 - 1), \text{ if } 0 \le x \le 1 \\ 2\pi - \cos^{-1}(2x^2 - 1), \text{ if } -1 \le x \le 0 \end{cases}$

(ii) $3\cos^{-1}x = \begin{cases} \cos^{-1}(4x^3 - 3x), \text{ if } \frac{1}{2} \le x \le 1 \\ 2\pi - \cos^{-1}(4x^3 - 3x), \text{ if } -\frac{1}{2} \le x \le \frac{1}{2} \\ 2\pi + \cos^{-1}(4x^3 - 3x), \text{ if } -1 \le x \le -\frac{1}{2} \end{cases}$

Proof

(i) Let $\cos^{-1}x = \theta$. Then, $x = \cos\theta$

$\therefore \quad \cos 2\theta = 2\cos^2\theta - 1 = 2x^2 - 1$

Case I When $0 \le x \le 1$

$\Rightarrow \quad 0 \le \cos\theta \le 1 \Rightarrow 0 \le \theta \le \frac{\pi}{2}$

$\Rightarrow \quad 0 \le 2\theta \le \pi$

Also, $0 \le x \le 1$

$\Rightarrow \quad -1 \le 2x^2 - 1 \le 1$

$\therefore \quad \cos 2\theta = 2x^2 - 1$

$\Rightarrow \quad 2\theta = \cos^{-1}(2x^2 - 1)$

$\Rightarrow \quad 2\cos^{-1}x = \cos^{-1}(2x^2 - 1)$

Case II When $-1 \le x \le 0$

$-1 \le x \le 0 \Rightarrow -1 \le \cos\theta \le 0$

$\Rightarrow \quad \frac{\pi}{2} \le \theta \le \pi \Rightarrow \pi \le 2\theta \le 2\pi$

$\Rightarrow \quad -2\pi \le -2\theta \le -\pi$

$\Rightarrow \quad 0 \le 2\pi - 2\theta \le \pi$

Also, $-1 \le x \le 0 \Rightarrow -1 \le 2x^2 - 1 \le 1$

$\therefore \quad \cos 2\theta = (2x^2 - 1)$

$\Rightarrow \quad \cos(2\pi - 2\theta) = 2x^2 - 1$

$\Rightarrow \quad 2\pi - 2\theta = \cos^{-1}(2x^2 - 1)$

$\Rightarrow \quad 2\pi - 2\cos^{-1}x = \cos^{-1}(2x^2 - 1)$

$\Rightarrow \quad 2\cos^{-1}x = 2\pi - \cos^{-1}(2x^2 - 1)$

(ii) Let $\cos^{-1}x = \theta$. Then, $x = \cos\theta$

$\therefore \quad \cos 3\theta = 4\cos^3\theta - 3\cos\theta$

$\Rightarrow \quad \cos 3\theta = 4x^3 - 3x$

Case I When $\frac{1}{2} \le x \le 1$

$\frac{1}{2} \le x \le 1 \Rightarrow \frac{1}{2} \le \cos\theta \le 1$

$\Rightarrow \quad 0 \le \theta \le \frac{\pi}{3}$

$\Rightarrow \quad 0 \le 3\theta \le \pi$

Also, $\frac{1}{2} \le x \le 1 \Rightarrow -1 \le 4x^3 - 3x \le 1$

$\therefore \quad \cos 3\theta = 4x^3 - 3x$

$\Rightarrow \quad 3\theta = \cos^{-1}(4x^3 - 3x)$

$\Rightarrow \quad 3\cos^{-1}x = \cos^{-1}(4x^3 - 3x)$

Case II When $-\frac{1}{2} \le x \le \frac{1}{2} \Rightarrow -\frac{1}{2} \le x \le \frac{1}{2}$

$\Rightarrow \quad -\frac{1}{2} \le \cos\theta \le \frac{1}{2}$

$\Rightarrow \quad \frac{\pi}{3} \le \theta \le \frac{2\pi}{3}$

$$\Rightarrow \quad \pi \le 3\theta \le 2\pi$$
$$\Rightarrow \quad -2\pi \le -3\theta \le -\pi$$
$$\Rightarrow \quad 0 \le 2\pi - 3\theta \le \pi$$
$$\therefore \quad \cos 3\theta = 4x^3 - 3x$$
$$\Rightarrow \quad \cos(2\pi - 3\theta) = 4x^3 - 3x$$
$$\Rightarrow \quad 2\pi - 3\theta = \cos^{-1}(4x^3 - 3x)$$
$$\Rightarrow \quad 3\theta = 2\pi - \cos^{-1}(4x^3 - 3x)$$
$$\Rightarrow \quad 3\cos^{-1} x = 2\pi - \cos^{-1}(4x^3 - 3x)$$

Case III When $-1 \le x \le -\frac{1}{2}$

$$-1 \le x \le -\frac{1}{2}$$
$$\Rightarrow \quad -1 \le \cos\theta \le -\frac{1}{2}$$
$$\Rightarrow \quad \frac{2\pi}{3} \le \theta \le \pi$$
$$\Rightarrow \quad 2\pi \le 3\theta \le 3\pi$$
$$\Rightarrow \quad -3\pi \le -3\theta \le -2\pi$$
$$\Rightarrow \quad -\pi \le 2\pi - 3\theta \le 0$$
$$\Rightarrow \quad 0 \le 3\theta - 2\pi \le \pi$$
$$\therefore \quad \cos 3\theta = 4x^3 - 3x$$
$$\Rightarrow \quad \cos(2\pi - 3\theta) = 4x^3 - 3x$$
$$\Rightarrow \quad \cos(3\theta - 2\pi) = 4x^3 - 3x$$
$$\Rightarrow \quad 3\theta - 2\pi = \cos^{-1}(4x^3 - 3x)$$
$$\Rightarrow \quad 3\theta = 2\pi + \cos^{-1}(4x^3 - 3x)$$
$$\Rightarrow \quad 3\cos^{-1} x = 2\pi + \cos^{-1}(4x^3 - 3x)$$

Example 67. Define $y = \cos^{-1}(4x^3 - 3x)$ in terms of $\cos^{-1} x$ and also draw its graph.

Sol. We know,
$$3\cos^{-1} x = \begin{cases} \cos^{-1}(4x^3 - 3x), & \text{if } \frac{1}{2} \le x \le 1 \\ 2\pi - \cos^{-1}(4x^3 - 3x), & \text{if } -\frac{1}{2} \le x < \frac{1}{2} \\ 2\pi + \cos^{-1}(4x^3 - 3x), & \text{if } -1 \le x < -\frac{1}{2} \end{cases}$$

$$\therefore \quad y = \cos^{-1}(4x^3 - 3x)$$
$$= \begin{cases} 3\cos^{-1} x, & \frac{1}{2} \le x \le 1 \\ 2\pi - 3\cos^{-1} x, & -\frac{1}{2} \le x < \frac{1}{2} \\ -2\pi + 3\cos^{-1} x, & -1 \le x < -\frac{1}{2} \end{cases}$$

Graph For $y = \cos^{-1}(4x^3 - 3x)$

Domain : $[-1, 1]$

Range : $[0, \pi]$

(i) If $\frac{1}{2} \le x \le 1$, $y = 3\cos^{-1} x$

$$\Rightarrow \quad \frac{dy}{dx} = \frac{-3}{\sqrt{1 - x^2}} = -3(1 - x^2)^{-1/2} \quad \text{...(i)}$$

$$\Rightarrow \quad \frac{dy}{dx} < 0 \text{ if } x \in \left[\frac{1}{2}, 1\right)$$

$\Rightarrow$ Decreasing if $x \in \left[\frac{1}{2}, 1\right)$

Again, if we differentiate Eq. (i) w.r.t. x, we get

$$\frac{d^2y}{dx^2} = -\frac{3x}{(1 - x^2)^{3/2}}$$

$$\Rightarrow \quad \frac{d^2y}{dx^2} < 0, \text{ if } x \in \left[\frac{1}{2}, 1\right)$$

$\Rightarrow$ concavity downwards if $x \in \left[\frac{1}{2}, 1\right)$

(ii) If $-\frac{1}{2} \le x < \frac{1}{2}$, $y = 2\pi - 3\cos^{-1} x$

$$\therefore \quad \frac{dy}{dx} = \frac{3}{\sqrt{1 - x^2}} \Rightarrow \frac{dy}{dx} > 0 \text{ if } x \in \left[-\frac{1}{2}, \frac{1}{2}\right)$$

$\Rightarrow$ Increasing if $x \in \left[-\frac{1}{2}, \frac{1}{2}\right)$ and $\frac{d^2y}{dx^2} = \frac{3x}{(1 - x^2)^{3/2}}$

(a) If $x \in \left[-\frac{1}{2}, 0\right)$, then $\frac{d^2y}{dx^2} < 0$

$\Rightarrow$ Concavity downwards if $x \in \left[-\frac{1}{2}, 0\right)$

(b) If $x \in \left[0, \frac{1}{2}\right)$, then $\frac{d^2y}{dx^2} > 0$

$\Rightarrow$ Concavity upwards if $x \in \left[0, \frac{1}{2}\right)$

(iii) Similarly, if $-1 \le x < -\frac{1}{2}$, then $\frac{dy}{dx} < 0$ and $\frac{d^2y}{dx^2} > 0$

$\therefore$ The graph of $y = \cos^{-1}(4x^3 - 3x)$ is as

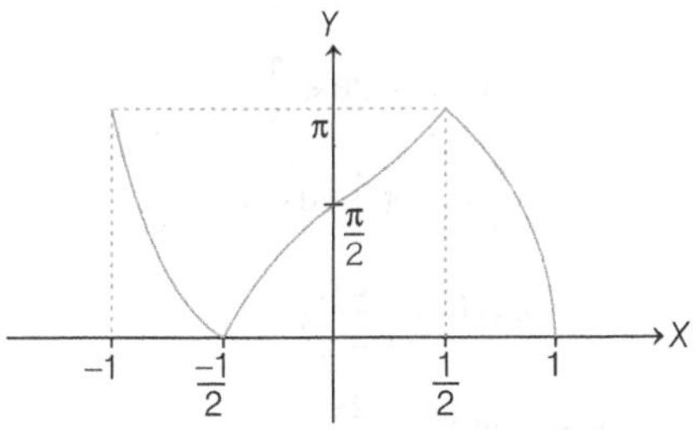

Property XII

(i) $2\tan^{-1} x = \begin{cases} \tan^{-1}\left(\dfrac{2x}{1-x^2}\right), & \text{if } -1 < x < 1 \\ \pi + \tan^{-1}\left(\dfrac{2x}{1-x^2}\right), & \text{if } x > 1 \\ -\pi + \tan^{-1}\left(\dfrac{2x}{1-x^2}\right), & \text{if } x < -1 \end{cases}$

(ii) $3\tan^{-1} x = \begin{cases} \tan^{-1}\left(\dfrac{3x-x^3}{1-3x^2}\right), & \text{if } -\dfrac{1}{\sqrt{3}} < x < \dfrac{1}{\sqrt{3}} \\ \pi + \tan^{-1}\left(\dfrac{3x-x^3}{1-3x^2}\right), & \text{if } x > \dfrac{1}{\sqrt{3}} \\ -\pi + \tan^{-1}\left(\dfrac{3x-x^3}{1-3x^2}\right). & \text{if } x < -\dfrac{1}{\sqrt{3}} \end{cases}$

Proof

(i) Let $\tan^{-1} x = \theta$. Then, $x = \tan\theta$

$\therefore \quad \tan 2\theta = \dfrac{2\tan\theta}{1-\tan^2\theta}$

or $\quad \tan 2\theta = \dfrac{2x}{1-x^2}$

Case I When $-1 < x < 1$

$-1 < x < 1 \Rightarrow -1 < \tan\theta < 1$

$\Rightarrow \quad -\dfrac{\pi}{4} < \theta < \dfrac{\pi}{4} \Rightarrow -\dfrac{\pi}{2} < 2\theta < \dfrac{\pi}{2}$

$\therefore \quad \tan 2\theta = \dfrac{2x}{1-x^2}$

$\Rightarrow \quad 2\theta = \tan^{-1}\left(\dfrac{2x}{1-x^2}\right)$

$\Rightarrow \quad 2\tan^{-1} x = \tan^{-1}\left(\dfrac{2x}{1-x^2}\right)$

Case II When $x > 1$

$x > 1 \Rightarrow \tan\theta > 1$

$\Rightarrow \quad \dfrac{\pi}{2} > \theta > \dfrac{\pi}{4} \Rightarrow \pi > 2\theta > \dfrac{\pi}{2}$

$\Rightarrow \quad -\pi < -2\theta < -\dfrac{\pi}{2}$

$\Rightarrow \quad 0 < \pi - 2\theta < \dfrac{\pi}{2}$

$\Rightarrow \quad -\dfrac{\pi}{2} < -\pi + 2\theta < 0$

$\therefore \quad \tan 2\theta = \dfrac{2x}{1-x^2}$

$\Rightarrow \quad -\tan(\pi - 2\theta) = \dfrac{2x}{1-x^2}$

$\Rightarrow \quad \tan(-\pi + 2\theta) = \dfrac{2x}{1-x^2}$

$\Rightarrow \quad -\pi + 2\theta = \tan^{-1}\left(\dfrac{2x}{1-x^2}\right)$

$\Rightarrow \quad 2\theta = \pi + \tan^{-1}\left(\dfrac{2x}{1-x^2}\right)$

$\Rightarrow \quad 2\tan^{-1} x = \pi + \tan^{-1}\left(\dfrac{2x}{1-x^2}\right)$

Case III When $x < -1$

$x < -1$

$\Rightarrow \quad \tan\theta < -1$

$\Rightarrow \quad -\dfrac{\pi}{2} < \theta < -\dfrac{\pi}{4}$

$\Rightarrow \quad -\pi < 2\theta < -\dfrac{\pi}{2} \Rightarrow 0 < \pi + 2\theta < \dfrac{\pi}{2}$

$\therefore \quad \tan 2\theta = \dfrac{2x}{1-x^2}$

$\Rightarrow \quad \tan(\pi + 2\theta) = \dfrac{2x}{1-x^2} \qquad [\because \tan(\pi + \alpha) = \tan\alpha]$

$\Rightarrow \quad \pi + 2\theta = \tan^{-1}\left(\dfrac{2x}{1-x^2}\right)$

$\Rightarrow \quad 2\theta = -\pi + \tan^{-1}\left(\dfrac{2x}{1-x^2}\right)$

$\Rightarrow \quad 2\tan^{-1} x = -\pi + \tan^{-1}\left(\dfrac{2x}{1-x^2}\right)$

(ii) Let $\tan^{-1} x = \theta$.

Then, $x = \tan\theta$

$\therefore \quad \tan 3\theta = \dfrac{3\tan\theta - \tan^3\theta}{1 - 3\tan^2\theta}$

$\Rightarrow \quad \tan 3\theta = \dfrac{3x - x^3}{1 - 3x^2}$

Case I When $-\dfrac{1}{\sqrt{3}} < x < \dfrac{1}{\sqrt{3}}$

$-\dfrac{1}{\sqrt{3}} < x < \dfrac{1}{\sqrt{3}} \Rightarrow -\dfrac{1}{\sqrt{3}} < \tan\theta < \dfrac{1}{\sqrt{3}}$

$\Rightarrow \quad -\dfrac{\pi}{6} < \theta < \dfrac{\pi}{6} \Rightarrow -\dfrac{\pi}{2} < 3\theta < \dfrac{\pi}{2}$

$\therefore \quad \tan 3\theta = \dfrac{3x - x^3}{1 - 3x^2} \Rightarrow 3\theta = \tan^{-1}\left(\dfrac{3x - x^3}{1 - 3x^2}\right)$

$\Rightarrow \quad 3\tan^{-1} x = \tan^{-1}\left(\dfrac{3x - x^3}{1 - 3x^2}\right)$

Case II When $x > \dfrac{1}{\sqrt{3}}$

$x > \dfrac{1}{\sqrt{3}} \Rightarrow \tan\theta > \dfrac{1}{\sqrt{3}}$

$\Rightarrow \quad \frac{\pi}{2} > \theta > \frac{\pi}{6}$

$\Rightarrow \quad \frac{\pi}{2} < 3\theta < \frac{3\pi}{2}$

$\Rightarrow \quad -\frac{3\pi}{2} < -3\theta < -\frac{\pi}{2}$

$\Rightarrow \quad -\frac{\pi}{2} < \pi - 3\theta < \frac{\pi}{2}$

$\Rightarrow \quad -\frac{\pi}{2} < 3\theta - \pi < \frac{\pi}{2}$

$\therefore \quad \tan 3\theta = \frac{3x - x^3}{1 - 3x^2}$

$\Rightarrow \quad -\tan(\pi - 3\theta) = \frac{3x - x^3}{1 - 3x^2} \quad [\because \tan(\pi - 3\theta) = -\tan 3\theta]$

$\Rightarrow \quad 3\theta - \pi = \tan^{-1}\left(\frac{3x - x^3}{1 - 3x^2}\right)$

$\Rightarrow \quad 3\tan^{-1} x = \pi + \tan^{-1}\left(\frac{3x - x^3}{1 - 3x^2}\right)$

Case III When $x < -\frac{1}{\sqrt{3}}$

$x < -\frac{1}{\sqrt{3}} \Rightarrow \tan\theta < -\frac{1}{\sqrt{3}}$

$\Rightarrow \quad -\frac{\pi}{2} < \theta < -\frac{\pi}{6}$

$\Rightarrow \quad -\frac{3\pi}{2} < 3\theta < -\frac{\pi}{2} \Rightarrow -\frac{\pi}{2} < \pi + 3\theta < \frac{\pi}{2}$

$\therefore \quad \tan 3\theta = \frac{3x - x^3}{1 - 3x^2}$

$\Rightarrow \quad \tan(\pi + 3\theta) = \frac{3x - x^3}{1 - 3x^2} \quad [\because \tan(\pi + x) = \tan x]$

$\Rightarrow \quad \pi + 3\theta = \tan^{-1}\left(\frac{3x - x^3}{1 - 3x^2}\right)$

$\Rightarrow \quad 3\tan^{-1} x = -\pi + \tan^{-1}\left(\frac{3x - x^3}{1 - 3x^2}\right)$

Property XIII

(i) $2\tan^{-1} x = \begin{cases} \sin^{-1}\left(\frac{2x}{1+x^2}\right), & \text{if} -1 \le x \le 1 \\ \pi - \sin^{-1}\left(\frac{2x}{1+x^2}\right), & \text{if } x > 1 \\ -\pi - \sin^{-1}\left(\frac{2x}{1+x^2}\right), & \text{if } x < -1 \end{cases}$

(ii) $2\tan^{-1} x = \begin{cases} \cos^{-1}\left(\frac{1-x^2}{1+x^2}\right), & \text{if } 0 \le x < \infty \\ -\cos^{-1}\left(\frac{1-x^2}{1+x^2}\right), & \text{if } -\infty < x \le 0 \end{cases}$

Proof

(i) Let $\tan^{-1} x = \theta$. Then, $x = \tan\theta$

$\therefore \quad \sin 2\theta = \frac{2\tan\theta}{1 + \tan^2\theta} \Rightarrow \sin 2\theta = \frac{2x}{1+x^2}$

Case I When $-1 \le x \le 1$

$-1 \le x \le 1 \Rightarrow -1 \le \tan\theta \le 1$

$\Rightarrow \quad -\frac{\pi}{4} \le \theta \le \frac{\pi}{4} \Rightarrow -\frac{\pi}{2} \le 2\theta \le \frac{\pi}{2}$

$\therefore \quad \sin 2\theta = \frac{2x}{1+x^2} \Rightarrow 2\theta = \sin^{-1}\left(\frac{2x}{1+x^2}\right)$

$\Rightarrow \quad 2\tan^{-1} x = \sin^{-1}\left(\frac{2x}{1+x^2}\right)$

Case II When $x > 1$

$x > 1$

$\Rightarrow \quad \tan\theta > 1$

$\Rightarrow \quad \frac{\pi}{4} < \theta < \frac{\pi}{2} \Rightarrow \frac{\pi}{2} < 2\theta < \pi$

$\Rightarrow \quad -\pi < -2\theta < -\frac{\pi}{2}$

$\Rightarrow \quad 0 < \pi - 2\theta < \frac{\pi}{2}$

$\therefore \quad \sin 2\theta = \frac{2x}{1+x^2}$

$\Rightarrow \quad \sin(\pi - 2\theta) = \frac{2x}{1+x^2}$

$\Rightarrow \quad \pi - 2\theta = \sin^{-1}\left(\frac{2x}{1+x^2}\right)$

$\Rightarrow \quad \pi - 2\tan^{-1} x = \sin^{-1}\left(\frac{2x}{1+x^2}\right)$

$\Rightarrow \quad 2\tan^{-1} x = \pi - \sin^{-1}\left(\frac{2x}{1+x^2}\right)$

Case III When $x < -1$

$x < -1 \Rightarrow \tan\theta < -1$

$\Rightarrow \quad -\frac{\pi}{2} < \theta < -\frac{\pi}{4} \Rightarrow -\pi < 2\theta < -\frac{\pi}{2}$

$$\Rightarrow \quad 0 < \pi + 2\theta < \frac{\pi}{2}$$

$$\Rightarrow \quad -\frac{\pi}{2} < -\pi - 2\theta < 0$$

$$\therefore \quad \sin 2\theta = \frac{2x}{1+x^2}$$

$$\Rightarrow \quad -\sin(\pi + 2\theta) = \frac{2x}{1+x^2} \Rightarrow \sin(-\pi - 2\theta) = \frac{2x}{1+x^2}$$

$$\Rightarrow \quad -\pi - 2\theta = \sin^{-1}\left(\frac{2x}{1+x^2}\right)$$

$$\Rightarrow \quad -\pi - 2\tan^{-1} x = \sin^{-1}\left(\frac{2x}{1+x^2}\right)$$

$$\Rightarrow \quad 2\tan^{-1} x = -\pi - \sin^{-1}\left(\frac{2x}{1+x^2}\right)$$

(ii) Let $\tan^{-1} x = \theta$

Then, $x = \tan\theta$

$$\therefore \quad \cos 2\theta = \frac{1-\tan^2\theta}{1+\tan^2\theta} \Rightarrow \cos 2\theta = \frac{1-x^2}{1+x^2}$$

Case I When $0 \le x < \infty$

$$0 \le x < \infty$$

$$\Rightarrow \quad 0 \le \theta < \frac{\pi}{2} \Rightarrow 0 \le 2\theta < \pi$$

$$\therefore \quad \cos 2\theta = \frac{1-x^2}{1+x^2} \Rightarrow 2\theta = \cos^{-1}\left(\frac{1-x^2}{1+x^2}\right)$$

$$\Rightarrow \quad 2\tan^{-1} x = \cos^{-1}\left(\frac{1-x^2}{1+x^2}\right)$$

Case II When $-\infty < x \le 0$

$$-\infty < x \le 0$$

$$\Rightarrow \quad -\frac{\pi}{2} < \theta \le 0$$

$$\Rightarrow \quad 0 \le -2\theta < \pi$$

$$\therefore \quad \cos 2\theta = \frac{1-x^2}{1+x^2} \Rightarrow \cos(-2\theta) = \frac{1-x^2}{1+x^2}$$

$$\Rightarrow \quad -2\theta = \cos^{-1}\left(\frac{1-x^2}{1+x^2}\right)$$

$$\Rightarrow \quad -2\tan^{-1} x = \cos^{-1}\left(\frac{1-x^2}{1+x^2}\right)$$

$$\Rightarrow \quad 2\tan^{-1} x = -\cos^{-1}\left(\frac{1-x^2}{1+x^2}\right)$$

Example 68. Prove that

$$4\tan^{-1}\frac{1}{5} - \tan^{-1}\frac{1}{70} + \tan^{-1}\frac{1}{99} = \frac{\pi}{4}$$

Sol. $4\tan^{-1}\frac{1}{5} - \tan^{-1}\frac{1}{70} + \tan^{-1}\frac{1}{99}$

$$= 2\left(2\tan^{-1}\frac{1}{5}\right) - \tan^{-1}\frac{1}{70} + \tan^{-1}\frac{1}{99}$$

$$= 2\left\{\tan^{-1}\frac{2(1/5)}{1-(1/5)^2}\right\} - \tan^{-1}\frac{1}{70} + \tan^{-1}\frac{1}{99}$$

$$\left[\because 2\tan^{-1} x = \tan^{-1}\left(\frac{2x}{1-x^2}\right), \text{ if } |x| < 1\right]$$

$$= 2\tan^{-1}\frac{5}{12} - \left\{\tan^{-1}\frac{1}{70} - \tan^{-1}\frac{1}{99}\right\}$$

$$= \tan^{-1}\left(\frac{2(5/12)}{1-(5/12)^2}\right) - \tan^{-1}\left(\frac{\frac{1}{70} - \frac{1}{99}}{1 + \frac{1}{70} \times \frac{1}{99}}\right)$$

$$\left[\because 2\tan^{-1} x = \tan^{-1}\left(\frac{2x}{1-x^2}\right) \text{ if } |x| < 1 \text{ and } \tan^{-1} x - \tan^{-1} y = \tan^{-1}\left(\frac{x-y}{1+xy}\right)\right]$$

$$= \tan^{-1}\left(\frac{120}{119}\right) - \tan^{-1}\left(\frac{29}{6931}\right)$$

$$= \tan^{-1}\left(\frac{120}{119}\right) - \tan^{-1}\left(\frac{1}{239}\right)$$

$$= \tan^{-1}\left(\frac{\frac{120}{119} - \frac{1}{239}}{1 + \left(\frac{120}{119}\right)\left(\frac{1}{239}\right)}\right)$$

$$= \tan^{-1}(1) = \frac{\pi}{4}$$

Example 69. Solve $\sin[2\cos^{-1}\{\cot(2\tan^{-1} x)\}] = 0$

Sol. We have, $\sin[2\cos^{-1}\{\cot(2\tan^{-1} x)\}] = 0$

$$\Rightarrow \quad \sin\left[2\cos^{-1}\left\{\cot\left(\tan^{-1}\left(\frac{2x}{1-x^2}\right)\right)\right\}\right] = 0$$

$$\left[\because 2\tan^{-1} x = \tan^{-1}\left(\frac{2x}{1-x^2}\right)\right]$$

$$\Rightarrow \quad \sin\left[2\cos^{-1}\left\{\cot\left(\cot^{-1}\left(\frac{1-x^2}{2x}\right)\right)\right\}\right] = 0$$

$$\left[\because \cot^{-1} x = \tan^{-1}\frac{1}{x}\right]$$

$$\Rightarrow \quad \sin\left[2\cos^{-1}\left(\frac{1-x^2}{2x}\right)\right] = 0$$

$$\Rightarrow \sin\left[\sin^{-1}\left\{2\left(\frac{1-x^2}{2x}\right)\sqrt{1-\left(\frac{1-x^2}{2x}\right)^2}\right\}\right]=0$$

$$[\because 2\cos^{-1}x=\sin^{-1}(2x\sqrt{1-x^2})]$$

$$\Rightarrow \left(\frac{1-x^2}{x}\right)\left[\sqrt{1-\left(\frac{1-x^2}{2x}\right)^2}\right]=0$$

$$\Rightarrow \frac{1-x^2}{x}=0 \text{ or } 1-\left(\frac{1-x^2}{2x}\right)^2=0$$

$$\Rightarrow 1-x^2=0 \text{ or } \left(\frac{1-x^2}{2x}\right)^2=1$$

$$\Rightarrow x=\pm 1 \text{ or } (1-x^2)^2=4x^2$$

Now, $(1-x^2)^2=4x^2$

$$\Rightarrow (1-x^2)^2-(2x)^2=0$$

$$\Rightarrow (1-x^2-2x)(1-x^2+2x)=0$$

$$\Rightarrow x^2+2x-1=0$$

or $x^2-2x-1=0$

$$\Rightarrow x=-1\pm\sqrt{2}$$

or $x=1\pm\sqrt{2}$

Hence, $x=\pm 1, -1\pm\sqrt{2}, 1\pm\sqrt{2}$ are the roots of the given equation.

Example 70. Find the value of

$$\tan\left\{\frac{1}{2}\sin^{-1}\left(\frac{2x}{1+x^2}\right)+\frac{1}{2}\cos^{-1}\left(\frac{1-y^2}{1+y^2}\right)\right\}.$$

Sol. Let $x=\tan A$ and $y=\tan B$.

Then, $\tan\left\{\frac{1}{2}\sin^{-1}\left(\frac{2x}{1+x^2}\right)+\frac{1}{2}\cos^{-1}\left(\frac{1-y^2}{1+y^2}\right)\right\}$

$$=\tan\left\{\frac{1}{2}\sin^{-1}\left(\frac{2\tan A}{1+\tan^2 A}\right)+\frac{1}{2}\cos^{-1}\left(\frac{1-\tan^2 B}{1+\tan^2 B}\right)\right\}$$

$$=\tan\left\{\frac{1}{2}\sin^{-1}(\sin 2A)+\frac{1}{2}\cos^{-1}(\cos 2B)\right\}$$

$$=\tan\left(\frac{2A}{2}+\frac{2B}{2}\right)=\tan(A+B)$$

$$=\frac{\tan A+\tan B}{1-\tan A\tan B}=\frac{x+y}{1-xy}$$

Alternate Solution

$$\tan\left[\frac{1}{2}\sin^{-1}\left(\frac{2x}{1+x^2}\right)+\frac{1}{2}\cos^{-1}\left(\frac{1-y^2}{1+y^2}\right)\right]$$

$$=\tan\left[\frac{1}{2}\cdot 2\tan^{-1}x+\frac{1}{2}\cdot 2\tan^{-1}y\right]=\tan(\tan^{-1}x+\tan^{-1}y)$$

$$=\tan\left(\tan^{-1}\left(\frac{x+y}{1-xy}\right)\right)=\frac{x+y}{1-xy}$$

Milestone Practice 4.5

1. Define $y=\sin^{-1}(3x-4x^3)$ in terms of $\sin^{-1}x$ and also draw its graph.
2. Define $y=\tan^{-1}\left(\frac{3x-x^3}{1-3x^2}\right)$ in terms of $\tan^{-1}x$ and also draw its graph.

Draw the graph of the following

3. $y=\cos^{-1}(2x^2-1)$
4. $y=\sin^{-1}(2x\sqrt{1-x^2})$
5. $y=\tan^{-1}\left(\frac{2x}{1-x^2}\right)$
6. $y=\cos^{-1}\left(\frac{1-x^2}{1+x^2}\right)$
7. $50\tan\left(3\tan^{-1}\left(\frac{1}{2}\right)+2\cos^{-1}\left(\frac{1}{\sqrt{5}}\right)\right)$ $+4\sqrt{2}\tan\left(\frac{1}{2}\tan^{-1}(2\sqrt{2})\right)$ is equal to ....
8. If x, y and z are in AP and $\tan^{-1}x$, $\tan^{-1}y$ and $\tan^{-1}z$ are also in AP, then
   (a) $x=y=z$ (b) $2x=3y=6z$
   (c) $6x=3y=2z$ (d) $6x=4y=3z$
9. Let $\tan^{-1}y=\tan^{-1}x+\tan^{-1}\left(\frac{2x}{1-x^2}\right)$, where $|x|<\frac{1}{\sqrt{3}}$. Then, the value of y is
   (a) $\frac{3x-x^3}{1+3x^2}$ (b) $\frac{3x+x^3}{1+3x^2}$ (c) $\frac{3x-x^3}{1-3x^2}$ (d) $\frac{3x+x^3}{1-3x^2}$

Answer Key

7. 29 8. (a) 9. (c)

For Detailed Solution

Milestone 6 Equations and Inequations Involving Inverse Trigonometric Functions

• Equations and Inequations Involving Inverse Trigonometric Functions • Summation of Series

4.5 Equations and Inequations involving Inverse Trigonometric Functions

The equation involving inverse trigonometric functions can be simplify using substitution and trigonometric formula.

Following are solved examples based on this.

Example 71. Solve $\cos^{-1}(\sqrt{3}x)+\cos^{-1}x=\dfrac{\pi}{2}$.

Sol. Given, $\cos^{-1}(\sqrt{3}x)+\cos^{-1}x=\dfrac{\pi}{2}$

$$\Rightarrow \quad \cos^{-1}(\sqrt{3}x)=\frac{\pi}{2}-\cos^{-1}x$$

$$\Rightarrow \quad \cos(\cos^{-1}(\sqrt{3}x))=\cos\left(\frac{\pi}{2}-\cos^{-1}x\right)$$

$$\Rightarrow \quad \sqrt{3}x=\sin(\cos^{-1}x)$$

$$\Rightarrow \quad \sqrt{3}x=\sin(\sin^{-1}\sqrt{1-x^2})$$

$$\Rightarrow \quad \sqrt{3}x=\sqrt{1-x^2} \Rightarrow 3x^2=1-x^2$$

[on squaring both sides]

$$\Rightarrow \quad 4x^2=1 \Rightarrow x=\pm\frac{1}{2}$$

Verification When $x=\dfrac{1}{2}$

LHS of given equation $=\cos^{-1}\left(\dfrac{\sqrt{3}}{2}\right)+\cos^{-1}\left(\dfrac{1}{2}\right)$

$$=\frac{\pi}{6}+\frac{\pi}{3}=\frac{\pi}{2}=\text{RHS}$$

And when $x=-\dfrac{1}{2}$

LHS of equation $=\cos^{-1}\left(-\dfrac{\sqrt{3}}{2}\right)+\cos^{-1}\left(\dfrac{-1}{2}\right)$

$$=\pi-\cos^{-1}\left(\frac{\sqrt{3}}{2}\right)+\pi-\cos^{-1}\left(\frac{1}{2}\right)$$

$$=\pi-\frac{\pi}{6}+\pi-\frac{\pi}{3}=\frac{3\pi}{2}\neq \text{RHS}$$

Hence, $x=\dfrac{1}{2}$ is the only solution.

Example 72. Solve for x, if

$$(\tan^{-1}x)^2+(\cot^{-1}x)^2=\frac{5\pi^2}{8}.$$

Sol. We have, $\quad (\tan^{-1}x)^2+(\cot^{-1}x)^2=\dfrac{5\pi^2}{8}$

$$\Rightarrow (\tan^{-1}x+\cot^{-1}x)^2-2\tan^{-1}x\cdot\cot^{-1}x=\frac{5\pi^2}{8}$$

$$\Rightarrow \quad \left(\frac{\pi}{2}\right)^2-2\tan^{-1}x\cdot\left(\frac{\pi}{2}-\tan^{-1}x\right)=\frac{5\pi^2}{8}$$

$$\Rightarrow \quad \frac{\pi^2}{4}-2\cdot\frac{\pi}{2}\cdot\tan^{-1}x+2(\tan^{-1}x)^2=\frac{5\pi^2}{8}$$

$$\Rightarrow \quad 2(\tan^{-1}x)^2-\pi\tan^{-1}x-\frac{3\pi^2}{8}=0$$

$$\Rightarrow \quad \tan^{-1}x=-\frac{\pi}{4},\frac{3\pi}{4}$$

Here, neglecting $\tan^{-1}x=\dfrac{3\pi}{4}$ as $\tan^{-1}x\in\left(-\dfrac{\pi}{2},\dfrac{\pi}{2}\right)$

So, $\quad \tan^{-1}x=-\dfrac{\pi}{4} \Rightarrow x=-1$

Example 73. If $3\sin^{-1}(\log_2 x)+\cos^{-1}(\log_2 y)=\dfrac{\pi}{2}$ and $\sin^{-1}(\log_2 x)+2\cos^{-1}(\log_2 y)=\dfrac{11\pi}{6}$, then find the value of $\dfrac{1}{x^2}+\dfrac{1}{y^2}$.

Sol. Let $\sin^{-1}(\log_2 x)=u$ ...(i)

and $\cos^{-1}(\log_2 y)=v$ ...(ii)

So, given equation becomes

$$3u+v=\frac{\pi}{2} \qquad \text{...(iii)}$$

and

$$u+2v=\frac{11\pi}{6} \qquad \text{...(iv)}$$

On solving Eqs. (iii) and (iv), we have

$$u=-\frac{\pi}{6} \text{ and } v=\pi$$

Hence, $x=\dfrac{1}{\sqrt{2}}$ and $y=\dfrac{1}{2}$ [from Eqs. (i) and (ii)]

$$\Rightarrow \quad \frac{1}{x^2}+\frac{1}{y^2}=6$$

Example 74. Find the total number of solution of the equation $\sin[2\cos^{-1}\{\cot(2\tan^{-1}x)\}]=0$.

Sol. Given, $\sin[2\cos^{-1}\{\cot(2\tan^{-1}x)\}]=0$

$$\Rightarrow \quad 2\cos^{-1}\{\cot(2\tan^{-1}x)\}=n\pi, n\in I$$

$$\Rightarrow \quad \cos^{-1}(\cot(2\tan^{-1}x))=\frac{n\pi}{2}$$

$$\Rightarrow \quad \cos^{-1}(\cot(2\tan^{-1}x))=\begin{cases}0, & n=0\\ \frac{\pi}{2}, & n=1\\ \pi, & n=2\end{cases}$$

$$\Rightarrow \quad \cot(2\tan^{-1}x)=\begin{cases}1, & n=0\\ 0, & n=1\\ -1, & n=2\end{cases}$$

$$\Rightarrow \quad 2\tan^{-1}x=\begin{cases}k\pi+\frac{\pi}{4}\\ k\pi+\frac{\pi}{2}\\ k\pi-\frac{\pi}{4},\end{cases}$$

$$\Rightarrow \quad \tan^{-1}x=\begin{cases}\frac{k\pi}{2}+\frac{\pi}{8}\\ \frac{k\pi}{2}+\frac{\pi}{4}, \text{ where } k\in I\\ \frac{k\pi}{2}-\frac{\pi}{8},\end{cases}$$

$$\Rightarrow \quad \tan^{-1}x=\begin{cases}\frac{\pi}{8},\frac{-3\pi}{8}\\ \frac{\pi}{4},\frac{-\pi}{4}\\ \frac{-\pi}{8},\frac{3\pi}{8}\end{cases}$$

$$\Rightarrow \quad x=\pm 1, \pm(\sqrt{2}-1), \pm(\sqrt{2}+1)$$

Hence, the total number of solutions is 6.

Example 75. Solve for x, if

$$\cos^{-1}\left(\frac{1+x^2}{2x}\right)-\cos^{-1}x=\frac{\pi}{2}+\sin^{-1}x.$$

Sol. Given, $\cos^{-1}\left(\frac{1+x^2}{2x}\right)-\cos^{-1}x=\frac{\pi}{2}+\sin^{-1}x$

$$\Rightarrow \quad \cos^{-1}\left(\frac{1+x^2}{2x}\right)=\frac{\pi}{2}+\sin^{-1}x+\cos^{-1}x$$

$$\Rightarrow \quad \cos^{-1}\left(\frac{1+x^2}{2x}\right)=\frac{\pi}{2}+\frac{\pi}{2}=\pi$$

$$\Rightarrow \quad \frac{1+x^2}{2x}=\cos\pi=-1$$

$$\Rightarrow \quad x^2+1=-2x \Rightarrow x^2+2x+1=0$$

$$\Rightarrow \quad (x+1)^2=0 \Rightarrow x=-1$$

Example 76. Find the product of all values of x satisfying the equation

$$\sin^{-1}\left[\cos\left(\frac{2x^2+10|x|+4}{x^2+5|x|+3}\right)\right]=\cot\left[\cot^{-1}\left(\frac{2-18|x|}{9|x|}\right)\right]+\frac{\pi}{2}$$

Sol. Given, $\sin^{-1}\left[\cos\left(\frac{2x^2+10|x|+4}{x^2+5|x|+3}\right)\right]=\cot\left[\cot^{-1}\left(\frac{2-18|x|}{9|x|}\right)\right]+\frac{\pi}{2}$

$$\Rightarrow \quad \frac{\pi}{2}-\cos^{-1}\left[\cos\left(\frac{2(x^2+5|x|+3)-2}{x^2+5|x|+3}\right)\right]=\cot\left[\cot^{-1}\left(\frac{2}{9|x|}-2\right)\right]+\frac{\pi}{2}$$

$$\Rightarrow \quad \frac{\pi}{2}-2+\frac{2}{x^2+5|x|+3}=\frac{2}{9|x|}-2+\frac{\pi}{2}$$

$$\Rightarrow \quad |x|^2-4|x|+3=0$$

$$\Rightarrow \quad |x|=1,3$$

$$\Rightarrow \quad x=\pm 1, \pm 3$$

$\therefore$ Product $=(1)(-1)(3)(-3)=9$

Example 77. Find the set of values of parameter λ so that the equation $(\sin^{-1}x)^3+(\cos^{-1}x)^3=\lambda\pi^3$ has a solution.

Sol. Given, $(\sin^{-1}x)^3+(\cos^{-1}x)^3=\lambda\pi^3$

$$\Rightarrow (\sin^{-1}x+\cos^{-1}x)\{(\sin^{-1}x+\cos^{-1}x)^2-3\sin^{-1}x\cdot\cos^{-1}x\}=\lambda\pi^3$$

$$\Rightarrow \quad \frac{\pi^2}{4}-3\sin^{-1}x\cdot\cos^{-1}x=\lambda\pi^3\times\frac{2}{\pi}=2\lambda\pi^2$$

$$\Rightarrow \quad (\sin^{-1}x)\left(\frac{\pi}{2}-\sin^{-1}x\right)=\frac{\pi^2}{12}(1-8\lambda)$$

$$\Rightarrow \quad (\sin^{-1}x)^2-\frac{\pi}{2}\sin^{-1}x=-\frac{\pi^2}{12}(1-8\lambda)$$

$$\Rightarrow \quad \left(\sin^{-1}x-\frac{\pi}{4}\right)^2=\frac{\pi^2}{12}(8\lambda-1)+\frac{\pi^2}{16}$$

$$\Rightarrow \quad \left(\sin^{-1}x-\frac{\pi}{4}\right)^2=\frac{\pi^2}{48}(32\lambda-4+3)=\frac{\pi^2}{16}(32\lambda-1)$$

As we know that

$$\sin^{-1}x\in\left[-\frac{\pi}{2},\frac{\pi}{2}\right]\Rightarrow \sin^{-1}x-\frac{\pi}{4}\in\left[-\frac{3\pi}{4},\frac{\pi}{4}\right]$$

$$\Rightarrow \quad \left(\sin^{-1}x-\frac{\pi}{4}\right)^2\in\left[0,\frac{9\pi^2}{16}\right]$$

$$\Rightarrow \quad \frac{\pi^2}{48}(32\lambda - 1) \in \left[0, \frac{9\pi^2}{16}\right]$$

$$\Rightarrow \quad (32\lambda - 1) \in [0, 27] \Rightarrow \lambda \in \left[\frac{1}{32}, \frac{7}{8}\right]$$

Hence, the required set of values of λ is $\left[\frac{1}{32}, \frac{7}{8}\right]$.

Example 78. Find the number of ordered pairs of (x, y) which satisfy $y = |\sin x|$ and $y = \cos^{-1}(\cos x)$, where $-2\pi \le x \le 2\pi$.

Sol. Given, $y = |\sin x|$

and $\quad y = \cos^{-1}(\cos x)$, where $x \in [-2\pi, 2\pi]$

In $[0, \pi]$, $\quad y = \cos^{-1}(\cos x) = x$

In $[\pi, 2\pi]$, $\quad y = \cos^{-1}\{\cos(2\pi - x)\} = 2\pi - x$

In $[-\pi, 0]$, $\quad y = \cos^{-1}\{\cos(-x)\} = -x$

In $[-2\pi, -\pi]$, $\quad y = \cos^{-1}\{\cos(2\pi + x)\} = 2\pi + x$

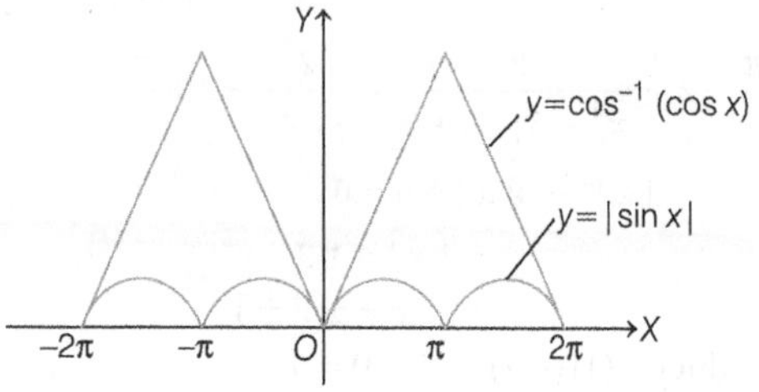

$\therefore$ Required ordered pairs are $(0, 0)$, $(2\pi, 0)$ and $(-2\pi, 0)$.

Hence, required number of ordered pairs = 3.

Example 79. Find the number of ordered pair(s) (x, y) which satisfy $y = \tan^{-1}(\tan x)$ and $16(x^2 + y^2) - 48\pi x + 16\pi y + 31\pi^2 = 0$.

Sol.

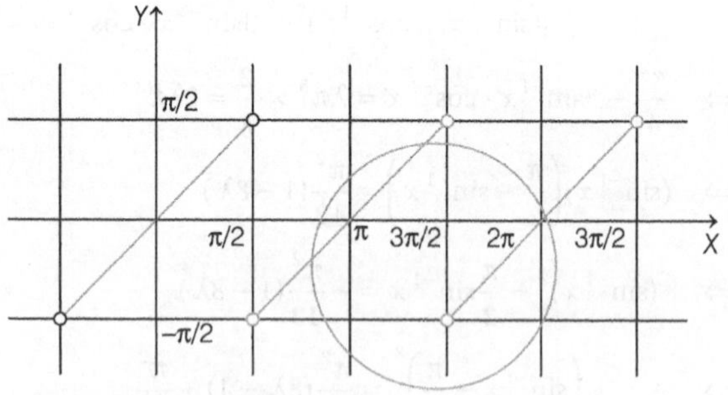

$$16(x^2 + y^2) - 48\pi x + 16\pi y + 31\pi^2 = 0$$

$$\Rightarrow \quad x^2 + y^2 - 3\pi x + \pi y + \frac{31\pi^2}{16} = 0$$

$$\Rightarrow \quad \left(x - \frac{3\pi}{2}\right)^2 + \left(y + \frac{\pi}{2}\right)^2 = \frac{9\pi^2}{16}$$

Centre $\left(\frac{3\pi}{2}, -\frac{\pi}{2}\right)$.

Hence, total 3 ordered pairs are possible.

Example 80. Find the number of solutions of the equation $\cos^{-1}(1 - x) + m\cos^{-1} x = \frac{n\pi}{2}$, (where $m > 0$ and $n \le 0$).

Sol. Given, $\cos^{-1}(1 - x) + m\cos^{-1} x = \frac{n\pi}{2}$ ...(i)

Domain of Eq. (i) is $\begin{cases} -1 \le x \le 1 \\ -1 \le 1 - x \le 1 \end{cases} \Rightarrow \begin{cases} -1 \le x \le 1 \\ 0 \le x \le 2 \end{cases}$

$\Rightarrow \quad x \in [0, 1]$

So, $\cos^{-1}(1 - x) + m\cos^{-1} x > 0$ $\quad [\because m > 0]$

$\Rightarrow$ LHS > 0 but RHS ≤ 0

Hence, number of solutions is 0.

Example 81. Find the number of real solutions of the equation

$$\tan^{-1}\sqrt{x^2 - 3x + 2} + \cos^{-1}\sqrt{4x - x^2 - 3} = \pi.$$

Sol. We have, $\tan^{-1}\sqrt{x^2 - 3x + 2} + \cos^{-1}\sqrt{4x - x^2 - 3} = \pi$

Since, $\quad \sqrt{x^2 - 3x + 2} \ge 0$

$\Rightarrow 0 \le \tan^{-1}\sqrt{x^2 - 3x + 2} < \frac{\pi}{2}$ ...(i) $\left[\because -\frac{\pi}{2} < \tan^{-1} x < \frac{\pi}{2}\right]$

and $\quad \sqrt{4x - x^2 - 3} \ge 0$

$\Rightarrow 0 < \cos^{-1}\sqrt{4x - x^2 - 3} \le \frac{\pi}{2}$ ...(ii)

On adding Eqs. (i) and (ii), we get

$$0 < \tan^{-1}\sqrt{x^2 - 3x + 2} + \cos^{-1}\sqrt{4x - x^2 - 3} < \pi$$

But RHS $= \pi$

Hence, the given equation has no solution.

Example 82. Solve $\cos^{-1} x < 2$.

Sol. Given, $\cos^{-1} x < 2$

$\Rightarrow \quad 0 \le \cos^{-1} x < 2$ $\quad [\because 0 \le \cos^{-1} x \le \pi]$

$\Rightarrow \quad \cos 2 < x \le \cos 0$

$[\because \cos^{-1} x$ is a decreasing function$]$

$\Rightarrow \quad x \in (\cos 2, 1]$

Example 83. Find the real values of x for which the function $g(x) = \cos^{-1}\sqrt{x^2 + 3x + 1} + \cos^{-1}\sqrt{x^2 + 3x}$ is defined.

Sol. Given function is

$$g(x) = \cos^{-1}\sqrt{x^2 + 3x + 1} + \cos^{-1}\sqrt{x^2 + 3x}$$

For $g(x)$ to be defined,

$$0 \le x^2 + 3x + 1 \le 1 \text{ and } 0 \le x^2 + 3x \le 1$$

$\Rightarrow \quad -1 \le x^2 + 3x \le 0$ and $0 \le x^2 + 3x \le 1$

$\Rightarrow \quad x^2 + 3x = 0$

$\Rightarrow \quad x(x + 3) = 0 \Rightarrow x = 0, -3$

Example 84. Find the possible value(s) of $h(x)=\sin^{-1}(1-x)+\cos^{-1}\sqrt{x-2}$.

Sol. Given, $h(x)=\sin^{-1}(1-x)+\cos^{-1}\sqrt{x-2}$

For $h(x)$ to be defined,

$$-1\le 1-x\le 1 \text{ and } x-2\ge 0$$

$$\Rightarrow \quad -2\le -x\le 0 \text{ and } x\ge 2$$

$$\Rightarrow \quad 0\le x\le 2 \text{ and } x\ge 2$$

$$\Rightarrow \quad x=2$$

Thus, $h(x)$ is defined only for $x=2$.

Hence, $h(2)=\sin^{-1}(-1)+\cos^{-1}(0)$

$$=\left(-\frac{\pi}{2}\right)+\left(\frac{\pi}{2}\right)=0$$

Example 85. Find the values of x for which $\sin^{-1}(\cos^{-1}x)<1$ and $\cos^{-1}(\cos^{-1}x)<1$ both are satisfied.

Sol. We have, $\sin^{-1}(\cos^{-1}x)<1$

$$\Rightarrow \quad -\frac{\pi}{2}\le \sin^{-1}(\cos^{-1}x)<1 \quad \left[\because -\frac{\pi}{2}\le \sin^{-1}x\le\frac{\pi}{2}\right]$$

$$\Rightarrow \quad -1\le \cos^{-1}x<\sin 1$$

$$\Rightarrow \quad 0\le \cos^{-1}x<\sin 1 \quad [\because 0\le \cos^{-1}x\le\pi]$$

$$\Rightarrow \quad \cos(\sin 1)<x\le 1 \quad \text{...(i)}$$

[$\because \cos^{-1}x$ is decreasing function]

and $\quad \cos^{-1}(\cos^{-1}x)<1$

$$\Rightarrow \quad 0\le \cos^{-1}(\cos^{-1}x)<1 \quad [\because 0\le \cos^{-1}x\le\pi]$$

$$\cos 1\le \cos^{-1}x\le 1 \quad [\because \cos^{-1}x \text{ is decreasing function}]$$

$$\Rightarrow \quad \cos 1\le x<\cos(\cos 1) \quad \text{...(ii)}$$

Since, we know that $\sin 1<1 \Rightarrow \cos(\sin 1)>\cos 1$

From Eqs. (i) and (ii), we get

$$\cos(\sin 1)<x<\cos(\cos 1)$$

Example 86. Solve for x: $\sin^{-1}x>\tan^{-1}x$.

Sol. Given, $\sin^{-1}x>\tan^{-1}x$ ...(i)

Eq. (i) will be meaningful if $x\in[-1,1]$.

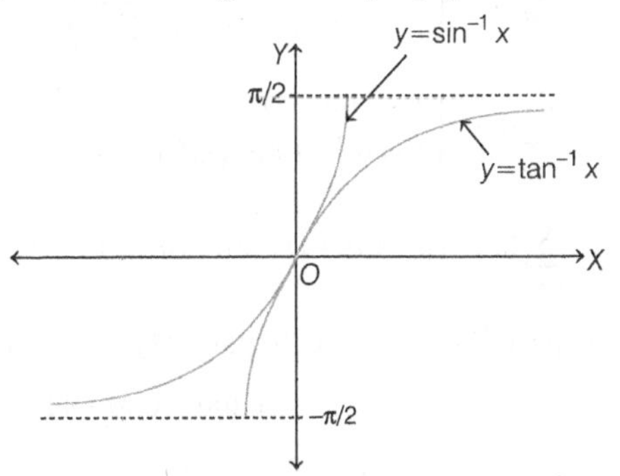

From above graph we can see that Eq. (i) will be true i.e. $\sin^{-1}x>\tan^{-1}x$ for $x\in(0,1]$.

4.6 Summation of Series

To solve these type of series we generally use inverse trigonometric formula like

$$(\tan^{-1}x-\tan^{-1}y), (\cot^{-1}x-\cot^{-1}y) \text{ etc.}$$

Thus, will be more clear by the following solved examples.

Example 87. Find the sum of the series upto n terms, if $\tan^{-1}\left(\frac{2}{4}\right)+\tan^{-1}\left(\frac{2}{9}\right)+\tan^{-1}\left(\frac{2}{16}\right)+\tan^{-1}\left(\frac{2}{25}\right)+\ldots+$ upto 'n' terms. Also, find S_∞.

Sol. Given series is

$$\tan^{-1}\left(\frac{2}{4}\right)+\tan^{-1}\left(\frac{2}{9}\right)+\tan^{-1}\left(\frac{2}{16}\right)+\tan^{-1}\left(\frac{2}{25}\right)+\ldots+n \text{ terms}$$

Let T_n = nth term

$$\text{So, } T_n=\tan^{-1}\left(\frac{2}{n^2+2n+1}\right)$$

$$=\tan^{-1}\left(\frac{2}{n(n+2)+1}\right)$$

$$=\tan^{-1}\left[\frac{(n+2)-n}{1+(n+2)\cdot n}\right]=\tan^{-1}(n+2)-\tan^{-1}(n)$$

Hence, $S_n=\tan^{-1}(n+2)+\tan^{-1}(n+1)-(\tan^{-1}1+\tan^{-1}2)$

$$\text{Also, } S_\infty=\lim_{n\to\infty}S_n=\frac{\pi}{2}+\frac{\pi}{2}-\left(\pi+\tan^{-1}\left(\frac{1+2}{1-2}\right)\right)$$

$$=\tan^{-1}(3)$$

Example 88. Sum the series

$$\tan^{-1}\left(\frac{4}{1+3.4}\right)+\tan^{-1}\left(\frac{6}{1+8.9}\right)+\tan^{-1}\left(\frac{8}{1+15.16}\right)+\ldots+n \text{ terms.}$$

Sol. Let T_n be the nth term of the given series.

$$\text{So, } T_n=\tan^{-1}\left[\frac{2(n+1)}{1+\{(n+1)^2-1\}\{(n+1)\}^2}\right]$$

$$\Rightarrow \quad T_n=\tan^{-1}\left[\frac{2n+2}{1+(n^2+2n)(n+1)^2}\right]$$

$$=\tan^{-1}\left[\frac{2n+2}{1+n(n+2)(n+1)(n+1)}\right]$$

$$=\tan^{-1}\left[\frac{(n+1)(n+2)-(n+1)\cdot n}{1+\{n(n+1)\}\{(n+1)(n+2)\}}\right]$$

$$=\tan^{-1}\{(n+1)(n+2)\}-\tan^{-1}\{n(n+1)\}$$

On putting $n=1,2,3,\ldots,n$ and then adding, we get

$$S_n=\tan^{-1}\{(n+1)(n+2)\}-\tan^{-1}(2)$$

JEE SCANNER

Example Similar to PYQ Asked in JEE Main 2021

If $\cot^{-1}\alpha = \cot^{-1}(3) + \cot^{-1}(7) + \cot^{-1}(13) + \cot^{-1}(21) + \ldots$ *upto 100 terms, then the value of* α *is*

(a) 1.01 (b) 1.02 (c) 1.00 (d) 1.03

Sol. (b) Let T_r denote the rth term of the series 3, 7, 13, 21, ...

and $S = 3 + 7 + 13 + 21 + \ldots + T_n$

Also, $S = 3 + 7 + 13 + 21 + \ldots + T_{n-1} + T_n$

Subtracting $\Rightarrow 0 = 3 + 4 + 6 + \ldots + 2n - T_n$

$\Rightarrow T_n = 3 + 4 + 6 + \ldots + 2n$

$$= 3 + \frac{1}{2}(n-1)(4+2n) = n^2 + n + 1$$

Let $T_r = \cot^{-1}(r^2 + r + 1)$

$$= \tan^{-1}\left(\frac{1}{r^2+r+1}\right) = \tan^{-1}\left(\frac{(r+1)-r}{1+r(r+1)}\right)$$

$$= \tan^{-1}(r+1) - \tan^{-1}(r)$$

Hence, the sum of the first n terms of the given series is

$$\tan^{-1}(n+1) - \tan^{-1}(1) = \tan^{-1}\left[\frac{n+1-1}{1+1(n+1)}\right] = \tan^{-1}\left(\frac{n}{n+2}\right)$$

$$= \cot^{-1}\left(\frac{n+2}{n}\right)$$

Put $n = 100$, we get

$$\cot^{-1}(\alpha) = \cot^{-1}\left(\frac{102}{100}\right)$$

$\therefore \quad \alpha = 1.02$

Skill Builder

If $\tan^{-1}\left(\frac{m}{n}\right)\tan^{-1}\left(\frac{3}{11}\right) + \tan^{-1}\left(\frac{3}{41}\right) + \tan^{-1}\left(\frac{3}{89}\right) + \ldots$ upto 10 terms, then the value of $m+n$ is .... (where m and n are coprime)

(a) 12 (b) 13

(c) 19 (d) 18

For Sol.

▪ **For more practice** See Q.21 of Milestone Practice 7.

Example 89. If the sum $\sum_{n=1}^{10}\sum_{m=1}^{10} \cot^{-1}\left(\frac{m}{n}\right) = \lambda\pi$, then find the value of (2λ).

Sol. Let $S = \sum_{n=1}^{10}\left(\tan^{-1}\left(\frac{1}{n}\right) + \tan^{-1}\left(\frac{2}{n}\right) + \tan^{-1}\left(\frac{3}{n}\right) + \ldots + \tan^{-1}\left(\frac{10}{n}\right)\right)$

Now, consider

$$\sum_{n=1}^{10}\tan^{-1}\left(\frac{1}{n}\right) = \underbrace{\tan^{-1}(1)} + \tan^{-1}\left(\frac{1}{2}\right) + \tan^{-1}\left(\frac{1}{3}\right) + \ldots + \tan^{-1}\left(\frac{1}{9}\right) + \tan^{-1}\left(\frac{1}{10}\right)$$

$$\sum_{n=1}^{10}\tan^{-1}\left(\frac{2}{n}\right) = \tan^{-1}\left(\frac{2}{1}\right) + \underbrace{\tan^{-1}\left(\frac{2}{2}\right)} + \tan^{-1}\left(\frac{2}{3}\right) + \ldots + \tan^{-1}\left(\frac{2}{9}\right) + \tan^{-1}\left(\frac{2}{10}\right)$$

$$\sum_{n=1}^{10}\tan^{-1}\left(\frac{3}{n}\right) = \tan^{-1}\left(\frac{3}{1}\right) + \tan^{-1}\left(\frac{3}{2}\right) + \underbrace{\tan^{-1}\left(\frac{3}{3}\right)} + \tan^{-1}\left(\frac{3}{4}\right) + \tan^{-1}\left(\frac{3}{5}\right) + \ldots + \tan^{-1}\left(\frac{3}{9}\right) + \tan^{-1}\left(\frac{3}{10}\right)$$

and so on

$$\sum_{n=1}^{10}\tan^{-1}\left(\frac{10}{n}\right) = \tan^{-1}\left(\frac{10}{1}\right) + \tan^{-1}\left(\frac{10}{2}\right) + \tan^{-1}\left(\frac{10}{3}\right) + \tan^{-1}\left(\frac{10}{4}\right) + \ldots + \tan^{-1}\left(\frac{10}{9}\right) + \underbrace{\tan^{-1}\left(\frac{10}{10}\right)}$$

Here, 45 such pairs and each pair have value equal to $\frac{\pi}{2}$.

So, $S = 5\left(\frac{\pi}{2}\right) + 45\left(\frac{\pi}{2}\right) = \frac{50\pi}{2} = 25\pi = \lambda\pi$

$\therefore \quad \lambda = 25$

Hence, $2\lambda = 50$

Example 90. Find the sum of the series $\sum_{m=1}^{\infty}\tan^{-1}\left(\frac{2m}{m^4+m^2+2}\right)$.

Sol. We have, $\sum_{m=1}^{\infty}\tan^{-1}\left(\frac{2m}{m^4+m^2+2}\right)$

$$= \sum_{m=1}^{\infty}\tan^{-1}\left(\frac{(m^2+m+1)-(m^2-m+1)}{1+\{(m^2+1)^2-m^2\}}\right)$$

$$= \sum_{m=1}^{\infty}\tan^{-1}\left(\frac{(m^2+m+1)-(m^2-m+1)}{1+(m^2+1+m)(m^2+1-m)}\right)$$

$$= \sum_{m=1}^{\infty}\tan^{-1}(m^2+m+1) - \tan^{-1}(m^2-m+1)$$

$$= \{\tan^{-1}(3) - \tan^{-1}(1)\} + \{\tan^{-1}(7) - \tan^{-1}(3)\} + \{\tan^{-1}(13) - \tan^{-1}(7)\} + \ldots + \infty$$

$$= \tan^{-1}\infty - \tan^{-1}1 = \frac{\pi}{2} - \frac{\pi}{4} = \frac{\pi}{4}$$

Milestone Practice 4.6

1. Find the number of real solutions for the equation $\cos^{-1} x + \cos^{-1} 2x + \pi = 0$.
2. Find the value of K, if
$$\sin^{-1}(x-1) + \cos^{-1}(x-3) + \tan^{-1}\left(\frac{x}{2-x^2}\right) = \cos^{-1}(K) + \pi.$$
3. Find the sum of the solutions of the equation $2\sin^{-1}\sqrt{x^2+x+1} + \cos^{-1}\sqrt{x^2+x} = \frac{3\pi}{2}$.
4. Find the total number of ordered pairs (x, y) satisfying $|y| = \cos x$ and $y = \sin(\sin^{-1} x)$.
5. Find the total number of real solutions of the equation $\sqrt{1+\cos 2x} = \sqrt{2}\sin^{-1}(\sin x)$, where $x \in [-\pi, \pi]$.
6. Consider the function $\phi(x)$ defined on the interval $[0, 1]$. Then, find the number of integers in the domain of $\phi(\sin x)$, if $x \in (0, 2\pi)$.
7. Find the number of ordered pair(s) (x, y) of real numbers satisfying the equation $2x\sin(\cos^{-1} y) + x^2 + 1 = 0$.
8. In which interval x lies so that $|\cos^{-1} x| + |\sin^{-1} x| = \frac{\pi}{2}$.
9. Find the range of m, if $(\sin^{-1} x)^2 - (\cos^{-1} x) = m\pi^2$.
10. If $\sin^{-1}|x-2| + \cos^{-1}(1-|3-x|) = \frac{\pi}{2}$, then find the total number of integers x for which given equation satisfies.
11. Solve for x, $\sin^{-1} x > -1$.
12. Solve $\cos^{-1} x^2 < \cos^{-1} x$.
13. Solve the equation $[\cot^{-1} x] + [\cos^{-1} x] = 0$, where $[\cdot]$ denotes greatest integer function.
14. Find the set of real values of x for which the inequality $\log_{\frac{1}{2}}(\cos^{-1} x) < \log_{\frac{1}{2}}(\sin^{-1} x)$ satisfied.
15. Find the complete solution set of $\tan^2(\sin^{-1} x) > 1$.
16. Find the total number of values of x satisfying $[\cot^{-1} x] + [\tan^{-1} x] = 2$, where $[\cdot]$ denotes the greatest integer function.
17. Solve the inequality $\left|\cos^{-1}\left(\frac{1-x^2}{1+x^2}\right)\right| < \frac{\pi}{3}$.
18. Find the interval in which $1 + \sin^{-1} x < \cos^{-1} x$.
19. Find the solution set of the equation $x^2 - 4x < \sin^{-1}(\sin 5)$.
20. If the solution set of the inequality $(\operatorname{cosec}^{-1} x)^2 - 2\operatorname{cosec}^{-1} x \geq \frac{\pi}{6}(\operatorname{cosec}^{-1} x - 2)$ is $(-\infty, \lambda] \cup [\mu, \infty)$, then find the value of $(\lambda + \mu)$.
21. Find the sum of the series
$$\tan^{-1}\left(\frac{1}{3}\right) + \tan^{-1}\left(\frac{2}{9}\right) + \tan^{-1}\left(\frac{4}{33}\right) + \ldots \infty$$
22. If $a_1, a_2, a_3, a_4, \ldots a_n$ are in AP with common difference k, then find the value of
$$\tan\left[\tan^{-1}\left(\frac{k}{1+a_1 a_2}\right) + \tan^{-1}\left(\frac{k}{1+a_2 a_3}\right) + \ldots + \tan^{-1}\left(\frac{k}{1+a_{n-1}\cdot a_n}\right)\right].$$

Answer Key

1. 0
2. $K = \frac{1}{\sqrt{2}}$
3. -1
4. 5
5. 2
6. 2
7. 1
8. $x \in [0, 1]$
9. $m \in \left[\frac{-3}{4}, \frac{1}{4}\right]$
10. 2
11. $x \in (-\sin 1, 1]$
12. $x \in [-1, 0)$
13. $x \in (\cot 1, 1]$
14. $x \in \left(0, \frac{1}{\sqrt{2}}\right)$
15. $x \in \left(-1, \frac{-1}{\sqrt{2}}\right) \cup \left(\frac{1}{\sqrt{2}}, 1\right)$
16. 0
17. $x \in \left(\frac{-1}{\sqrt{3}}, \frac{1}{\sqrt{3}}\right)$
18. $x \in \left[-1, \sin\left(\frac{\pi}{4} - \frac{1}{2}\right)\right]$
19. $x \in (2 - \sqrt{9-2\pi}, 2 + \sqrt{9-2\pi})$
20. 1
21. $\frac{\pi}{4}$
22. $\left(\frac{(n-1)k}{1+a_1 a_n}\right)$

For Detailed Solution

JEE Pattern EXAMPLES

Single Option Correct Type Questions

Example 1 *Let $f(x) = \sin x + \cos x + \tan x +$ arc $\sin x +$ arc $\cos x +$ arc $\tan x$. If M and m are maximum and minimum values of $f(x)$, then their arithmetic mean is equal to*

(a) $\frac{\pi}{2} + \cos 1$ (b) $\frac{\pi}{2} + \sin 1$

(c) $\frac{\pi}{4} + \tan 1 + \cos 1$ (d) $\frac{\pi}{4} + \tan 1 + \sin 1$

Sol. (a) Domain of f is $[-1,1]$;

$$f(x) = \sin x + \cos x + \tan x + \sin^{-1} x + \cos^{-1} x + \tan^{-1} x$$

$$f'(x) = \cos x - \sin x + \underbrace{\sec^2 x}_{>1} + 0 + \underbrace{\frac{1}{1+x^2}}_{[1/2,1]}$$

Hence, $f'(x) > 0$

$\Rightarrow f$ is increasing.

$\Rightarrow$ Range is $[f(-1), f(1)]$

$$\therefore \quad f(x)|_{\min} = f(-1) = -\sin 1 + \cos 1 - \tan 1$$

$$-\frac{\pi}{2} + \pi - \frac{\pi}{4} = \frac{\pi}{4} + \cos 1 - \sin 1 - \tan 1$$

$$\text{and } f(x)|_{\max} = f(1) = \sin 1 + \cos 1 + \tan 1$$

$$+\frac{\pi}{2} + \frac{\pi}{4} = \frac{3\pi}{4} + \cos 1 + \sin 1 + \tan 1$$

Now, $\frac{M+m}{2} = \frac{\pi}{2} + \cos 1$

Example 2 *The value of $5 \cdot \cot\left(\sum_{k=1}^{5} \cot^{-1}(k^2 + k + 1)\right)$ is equal to*

(a) $\frac{5}{2}$ (b) 7 (c) -7 (d) $\frac{7}{2}$

Sol. (b) Consider

$$\sum_{k=1}^{5}\left(\tan^{-1}\left(\frac{(k+1)-k}{1+k(k+1)}\right)\right) = \sum_{k=1}^{5}(\tan^{-1}(k+1) - \tan^{-1} k)$$

Now, $T_1 = \tan^{-1}(2) - \tan^{-1}(1)$;

$T_2 = \tan^{-1}(3) - \tan^{-1}(2)$ and so on.

Hence, $\sum_{k=1}^{5} \cot^{-1}(k^2 + k + 1) = \tan^{-1}(6) - \tan^{-1}(1)$

$$= \tan^{-1}\left(\frac{5}{7}\right) = \cot^{-1}\left(\frac{7}{5}\right)$$

$$\therefore \quad 5\cot\left(\cot^{-1}\frac{7}{5}\right) = 7$$

JEE SCANNER

Example 3 Similar to PYQ Asked in JEE Main 2024

If the domain of the function $f(x) = \ln\left(\frac{x+1}{x^2-2x-3}\right) + \cos^{-1}\left(\frac{x-1}{x+1}\right)$ is (β, ∞), then the value of 5β is equal to

(a) 0 (b) 2 (c) 51 (d) -4

Sol. (a) We have,

$$f(x) = \ln\left(\frac{x+1}{x^2-2x-3}\right) + \cos^{-1}\left(\frac{x-1}{x+1}\right)$$

Domain of $f(x)$, $\frac{x+1}{x^2-2x-3} > 0$ and $-1 \le \frac{x-1}{x+1} \le 1$

$$\Rightarrow \frac{x+1}{(x-3)(x+1)} > 0 \text{ and } \frac{x-1+x+1}{x+1} \ge 0$$

$$\text{and } \frac{x-1-x-1}{x+1} \le 0$$

$$\Rightarrow \quad \frac{1}{x-3} > 0 \text{ and } \frac{2x}{x+1} \ge 0 \text{ and } \frac{-2}{x+1} \le 0$$

So, $x \in (3, \infty)$, $x \in (-\infty, -1) \cup (0, \infty)$ and $(-1, \infty)$

$\therefore \quad x \in (0, \infty)$

So, $\beta = 0$ and $5\beta = 0$

Skill Builder

If the domain of the function $f(x) = \ln\left(\frac{x+1}{x-1}\right) + \sin^{-1}\left(\frac{x-2}{x+1}\right)$ is $[\alpha, \infty]$, then the value of 4α is equal to

(a) 2 (b) 4 (c) 5 (d) 3

For Sol.

Example 4 *If the equation* $5 \text{ arc } \tan(x^2+x+k)+3$ $\text{arc } \cot(x^2+x+k)=2\pi$, *has two distinct solutions, then the range of k, is*

(a) $\left(0, \frac{5}{4}\right]$ (b) $\left(-\infty, \frac{5}{4}\right)$ (c) $\left(\frac{5}{4}, \infty\right)$ (d) $\left(-\infty, \frac{5}{4}\right]$

Sol. (b) We have, $2\pi = \frac{3\pi}{2} + 2\tan^{-1}(x^2+x+k)$

$$\left[\text{as, } \tan^{-1}\alpha + \cot^{-1}\alpha = \frac{\pi}{2} \forall \alpha \in R\right]$$

$$\Rightarrow \tan^{-1}(x^2+x+k) = \frac{\pi}{4} \Rightarrow x^2+x+k=1$$

$$\Rightarrow x^2+x+(k-1)=0$$

$\therefore$ For required condition, put $D>0$

$$\Rightarrow 1-4(k-1)>0 \Rightarrow 5-4k>0 \Rightarrow k<\frac{5}{4}$$

Example 5 *If* $\sin^{-1}\left(x^2-\frac{x^4}{3}+\frac{x^6}{9}\ldots\ldots\right)+\cos^{-1}\left(x^4-\frac{x^8}{3}+\frac{x^{12}}{9}\ldots\ldots\right)=\frac{\pi}{2}$, *where* $0 \le |x| < \sqrt{3}$, *then number of values of 'x' is equal to*

(a) 1 (b) 2 (c) 3 (d) 4

Sol. (c) $\sin^{-1}\underbrace{\left(x^2-\frac{x^4}{3}+\frac{x^6}{9}\ldots\ldots\right)}_{X}+\cos^{-1}\underbrace{\left(x^4-\frac{x^8}{3}+\frac{x^{12}}{9}\ldots\ldots\right)}_{Y}=\frac{\pi}{2}$

$$\Rightarrow X=Y \Rightarrow \frac{x^2}{1+\frac{x^2}{3}}=\frac{x^4}{1+\frac{x^4}{3}} \Rightarrow \frac{3}{3+x^2}=\frac{3x^2}{3+x^4}$$

$$\Rightarrow 9+3x^4=9x^2+3x^4 \Rightarrow x^2=1$$

Thus, $x=0, 1 \text{ or } -1$

Hence, number of values is equal to 3.

Example 6 *Suppose* $3\sin^{-1}(\log_2 x)+\cos^{-1}(\log_2 y)=\frac{\pi}{2}$ *and* $\sin^{-1}(\log_2 x)+2\cos^{-1}(\log_2 y)=\frac{11\pi}{6}$, *then the value of* $x^{-2}+y^{-2}$ *equals*

(a) 6 (b) 7 (c) 5 (d) $\frac{7}{2}$

Sol. (a) Let $\sin^{-1}(\log_2 x)=a$ and $\cos^{-1}(\log_2 y)=b$

$$\therefore 3a+b=\frac{\pi}{2} \text{ and } a+2b=\frac{11\pi}{6}$$

$$\Rightarrow a=-\frac{\pi}{6} \text{ and } b=\pi$$

Hence, $x=\frac{1}{\sqrt{2}}$ and $y=\frac{1}{2} \Rightarrow \frac{1}{x^2}+\frac{1}{y^2}=6$

Example 7 *Range of* $f(x)=\sin^{-1}\log[x]+\log(\sin^{-1}[x])$, *where [ ] denotes GIF is*

(a) 1 (b) 2 (c) 0 (d) $\left\{\log\frac{\pi}{2}\right\}$

Sol. (d) For log function to defined, $x \ge 1$

$$\Rightarrow 0 \le \log[x] \le 1 \Rightarrow 1 \le [x] \le e \Rightarrow x \in [1, 3) \quad \ldots\text{(i)}$$

and $0 < \sin^{-1}[x] \le \frac{\pi}{2} \Rightarrow 0<[x]\le 1 \Rightarrow x \in [1, 2)$ ...(ii)

Domain of $f(x)$ is $[1, 2)$.

Range $=\sin^{-1}(\log 1)+\log(\sin^{-1}1)=\sin^{-1}(0)+\log\frac{\pi}{2}=\log\frac{\pi}{2}$

$\therefore$ Range is $\left\{\log\frac{\pi}{2}\right\}$.

Example 8 $\sum_{n=1}^{5}\sin^{-1}(\sin(2n-1))$ *is*

(a) 1 (b) 2 (c) 3 (d) 4

Sol. (a) $\sum_{n=1}^{5}\sin^{-1}(\sin(2n-1))$

$$=\sin^{-1}(\sin 1)+\sin^{-1}(\sin 3)+\sin^{-1}(\sin 5)+\sin^{-1}(\sin 7)+\sin^{-1}(\sin 9)$$

$$=1+\pi-3+5-2\pi+7-2\pi+3\pi-9=1$$

Example 9 *If* α *and* $\beta\,(\alpha>\beta)$ *are roots of the equation* $x^2-\sqrt{2}x+\sqrt{3-2\sqrt{2}}=0$, *then the value of* $(\cos^{-1}\alpha+\tan^{-1}\alpha+\tan^{-1}\beta)$ *is equal to*

(a) $\frac{3\pi}{8}$ (b) $\frac{5\pi}{8}$ (c) $\frac{7\pi}{8}$ (d) $\frac{\pi}{3}$

Sol. (a) $x^2-\sqrt{2}x+\sqrt{3-2\sqrt{2}}=0 \Rightarrow x^2-\sqrt{2}x+\sqrt{2}-1=0$

$$\Rightarrow x^2-1-\sqrt{2}(x-1)=0 \Rightarrow (x-1)(x+1-\sqrt{2})=0$$

$$x=1, \sqrt{2}-1$$

$$\therefore \alpha=1 \text{ and } \beta=\sqrt{2}-1$$

Hence, $\cos^{-1}\alpha+\tan^{-1}\alpha+\tan^{-1}\beta=0+\frac{\pi}{4}+\frac{\pi}{8}=\frac{3\pi}{8}$

Example 10 *If the mapping* $f(x)=mx+c$, $m>0$ *maps* $[-1, 1]$ *onto* $[0, 2]$, *then* $\tan\left(\tan^{-1}\frac{1}{7}+\cot^{-1}8+\cot^{-1}18\right)$ *is equal to*

(a) $f\left(\frac{2}{3}\right)$ (b) $f\left(\frac{1}{3}\right)$ (c) $f\left(\frac{-1}{3}\right)$ (d) $f\left(\frac{-2}{3}\right)$

Sol. (d) Clearly, $f(x)=x+1$ (As, $-1 \le x \le 1$, $0 \le x+1 \le 2$) and $f(x)=mx+c$

Now, $\tan\left(\tan^{-1}\frac{1}{7}+\tan^{-1}\frac{1}{8}+\tan^{-1}\frac{1}{18}\right)$

$$=\tan\left(\tan^{-1}\left(\frac{\frac{1}{7}+\frac{1}{8}}{1-\frac{1}{7}\times\frac{1}{8}}\right)+\tan^{-1}\frac{1}{18}\right)$$

$$=\tan\left(\tan^{-1}\left(\frac{15}{55}\right)+\tan^{-1}\left(\frac{1}{18}\right)\right)$$

$$= \tan\left(\tan^{-1}\left(\frac{3}{11}\right) + \tan^{-1}\left(\frac{1}{18}\right)\right)$$

$$= \tan\left(\tan^{-1}\left(\frac{\frac{3}{11}+\frac{1}{18}}{1-\frac{3}{11}\times\frac{1}{18}}\right)\right)$$

$$= \tan\left(\tan^{-1}\frac{1}{3}\right) = \frac{1}{3} = f\left(\frac{-2}{3}\right)$$

Example 11 *If* $(\sin^{-1} a)^2 + (\cos^{-1} b)^2 + (\sec^{-1} c)^2 + (\text{cosec}^{-1} d)^2 = \frac{5\pi^2}{2}$, *then the value of* $(\sin^{-1} a)^2 - (\cos^{-1} b)^2 + (\sec^{-1} c)^2 - (\text{cosec}^{-1} d)^2$ *is*

(a) $-\pi^2$ (b) $-\frac{\pi^2}{2}$

(c) 0 (d) $\frac{\pi^2}{2}$

Sol. (c) As, $0 \le (\sin^{-1} a)^2 \le \frac{\pi^2}{4}$, $0 \le (\cos^{-1} b)^2 \le \pi^2$,

$0 \le (\sec^{-1} c)^2 \le \pi^2 \left(\text{except } \frac{\pi^2}{4}\right)$ and $0 < (\text{cosec}^{-1} d)^2 \le \frac{\pi^2}{4}$

So, $0 < (\sin^{-1} a)^2 + (\cos^{-1} b)^2 + (\sec^{-1} c)^2 + (\text{cosec}^{-1} d)^2 \le \frac{5\pi^2}{2}$

$\therefore (\sin^{-1} a)^2 + (\cos^{-1} b)^2 + (\sec^{-1} c)^2 + (\text{cosec}^{-1} d)^2 = \frac{5\pi^2}{2}$ (Given)

$\Rightarrow \quad (\sin^{-1} a)^2 = \frac{\pi^2}{4}$

$(\cos^{-1} b)^2 = \pi^2$

$(\sec^{-1} c)^2 = \pi^2$

and $(\text{cosec}^{-1} d)^2 = \frac{\pi^2}{4}$

Hence, $(\sin^{-1} a)^2 - (\cos^{-1} b)^2 + (\sec^{-1} b)^2 - (\text{cosec}^{-1} d)^2 = 0$

Example 12 *The range of the function* $f(x) = \sec^{-1}(x) + \tan^{-1}(x)$, *is*

(a) $(0, \pi)$ (b) $\left(\frac{-\pi}{2}, \frac{3\pi}{2}\right)$

(c) $\left(0, \frac{3\pi}{4}\right]$ (d) None of these

Sol. (a) $D_f = (-\infty, -1] \cup [1, \infty)$

Also, f is an increasing function.

For $x \in (-\infty, -1]$, $f(x) \in \left(0, \frac{3\pi}{4}\right]$ ... (i)

and for $x \in [1, \infty)$, $f(x) \in \left[\frac{\pi}{4}, \pi\right)$ ... (ii)

$\therefore$ For range of $f(x)$, (i) $\cup$ (ii) $\Rightarrow (0, \pi)$

JEE SCANNER

Example 13 Similar to PYQ Asked in JEE Main 2024

For $n \in R$, *if* $\tan^{-1} 2 + \tan^{-1} 4 + \tan^{-1} 5 + \tan^{-1} n = \frac{\pi}{4}$, *then* $33n$ *is equal to ....*

Sol. (4) Given, $\tan^{-1} 2 + \tan^{-1} 4 + \tan^{-1} 5 + \tan^{-1} n = \frac{\pi}{4}$

$$\Rightarrow \tan^{-1}\left(\frac{2+4}{1-8}\right) + \tan^{-1}\left(\frac{5+n}{1-5n}\right) = \frac{\pi}{4}$$

$$\Rightarrow \tan^{-1}\left(\frac{6}{-7}\right) + \tan^{-1}\left(\frac{5+n}{1-5n}\right) = \frac{\pi}{4}$$

$$\Rightarrow \tan^{-1}\left(\frac{5+n}{1-5n}\right) - \tan^{-1}\left(\frac{6}{7}\right) = \frac{\pi}{4}$$

$$\Rightarrow \tan^{-1}\left[\frac{\frac{5+n}{1-5n} - \frac{6}{7}}{1 + \frac{(5+n)}{1-5n} \times \frac{6}{7}}\right] = \tan^{-1} 1$$

$$\Rightarrow \frac{\frac{7(5+n) - 6(1-5n)}{7(1-5n)}}{\frac{7(1-5n) + 6(5+n)}{7(1-5n)}} = 1$$

$$\Rightarrow \frac{35 + 7n - 6 + 30n}{7 - 35n + 30 + 6n} = 1$$

$$\Rightarrow \frac{29 + 37n}{37 - 29n} = 1$$

$$\Rightarrow 29 + 37n = 37 - 29n$$

$$\Rightarrow 37n + 29n = 37 - 29$$

$$\Rightarrow 66n = 8$$

$$\Rightarrow n = \frac{8}{66} = \frac{4}{33}$$

$$\therefore 33n = 4$$

Skill Builder

For $n \in R$, if $\cot^{-1}\frac{1}{3} + \cot^{-1}\frac{1}{2} + \cot^{-1}\frac{1}{n} = 0$, then $6n$ is equal to ....

For Sol.

Example 14 *The solution set of inequality* $(\cot^{-1} x)(\tan^{-1} x) + \left(2 - \frac{\pi}{2}\right)\cot^{-1} x - 3\tan^{-1} x - 3\left(2 - \frac{\pi}{2}\right) > 0$, *is*

(a) $x \in (\tan 2, \tan 3)$

(b) $x \in (\cot 3, \cot 2)$

(c) $x \in (-\infty, \tan 2) \cup (\tan 3, \infty)$

(d) $x \in (-\infty, \cot 3) \cup (\cot 2, \infty)$

Sol. (b) Given,

$$(\cot^{-1} x)(\tan^{-1} x) + \left(2 - \frac{\pi}{2}\right) \cot^{-1} x - 3\tan^{-1} x - 3\left(2 - \frac{\pi}{2}\right) > 0$$

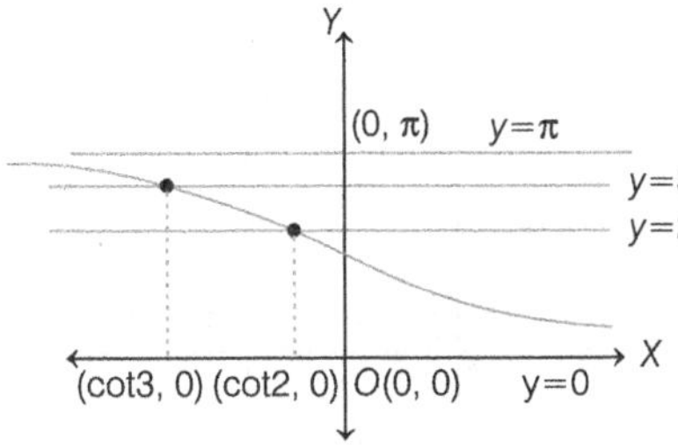

$$\Rightarrow \cot^{-1} x\left(\tan^{-1} x + 2 - \frac{\pi}{2}\right) - 3\left(\tan^{-1} x + 2 - \frac{\pi}{2}\right) > 0$$

$$\Rightarrow (\cot^{-1} x - 3)(2 - \cot^{-1} x) > 0$$

$$\left[\text{as } \tan^{-1} x - \frac{\pi}{2} = -\cot^{-1} x\right]$$

$$\Rightarrow (\cot^{-1} x - 3)(\cot^{-1} x - 2) < 0$$

$$\Rightarrow 2 < \cot^{-1} x < 3$$

$$\Rightarrow \cot 3 < x < \cot 2$$

[as $\cot^{-1} x$ is a decreasing function]

Hence, $x \in (\cot 3, \cot 2)$

Example 15 *Let $f(x) = \sin(\sin^{-1} 2x) + \operatorname{cosec}(\operatorname{cosec}^{-1} 2x) + \tan(\tan^{-1} 2x)$, then which one of the following statement is/are incorrect?*

(a) $f(x)$ is odd function.
(b) $f(x)$ is injective.
(c) Range of $f(x)$ contains only two integers.
(d) The value of $f'\left(\frac{1}{2}\right)$ is equal to 6.

Sol. (d) Clearly, $f(x) = 6x$ and domain $= \left\{\frac{-1}{2}, \frac{1}{2}\right\}$.

Example 16 *Sum to the n terms of the series*

$$\operatorname{cosec}^{-1}\sqrt{10} + \operatorname{cosec}^{-1}\sqrt{50} + \operatorname{cosec}^{-1}\sqrt{170} + \ldots + \operatorname{cosec}^{-1}\sqrt{(n^2+1)(n^2+2n+2)} \text{ is}$$

(a) $\frac{\pi}{4} - \tan^{-1}(n+1)$ (b) $\tan^{-1}(n+1) - \frac{\pi}{4}$
(c) $\frac{\pi}{4} + \tan^{-1}(n-1)$ (d) $\tan^{-1}(n-1) - \frac{\pi}{4}$

Sol. (b) Let $\theta = \operatorname{cosec}^{-1}\sqrt{(n^2+1)(n^2+2n+2)}$

$$\operatorname{cosec}^2\theta = (n^2+1)(n^2+2n+2)$$

$$= (n^2+1)^2 + 2n(n^2+1) + n^2 + 1 = (n^2+n+1)^2 + 1$$

Let $\cot^2\theta = (n^2+n+1)^2$

$$\Rightarrow \tan\theta = \frac{1}{n^2+n+1} = \frac{(n+1)-n}{1+(n+1)n}$$

$$\Rightarrow \theta = \tan^{-1}\left[\frac{(n+1)-n}{1+(n+1)n}\right] = \tan^{-1}(n+1) - \tan^{-1} n$$

Thus, sum of n terms of the given series

$$= (\tan^{-1}2 - \tan^{-1}1) + (\tan^{-1}3 - \tan^{-1}2) + (\tan^{-1}4 - \tan^{-1}3) + \ldots + (\tan^{-1}(n+1) - \tan^{-1}n)$$

$$= \tan^{-1}(n+1) - \frac{\pi}{4}$$

JEE SCANNER

Example 17 Similar to PYQ Asked in JEE Main 2024

Let the inverse trigonometric function take principal value. The number of real solutions of the equation $\tan^{-1} x + 2\cot^{-1} x = \frac{\pi}{4}$ is ....

Sol. (1) We have, $\tan^{-1} x + 2\cot^{-1} x = \frac{\pi}{4}$

$$\Rightarrow \frac{\pi}{2} - \cot^{-1} x + 2\cot^{-1} x = \frac{\pi}{4}$$

$$\Rightarrow \frac{\pi}{2} + \cot^{-1} x = \frac{\pi}{4}$$

$$\Rightarrow \cot^{-1} x = \frac{\pi}{4} - \frac{\pi}{2}$$

$$\Rightarrow \cot^{-1} x = -\frac{\pi}{4}$$

$$\Rightarrow \cot^{-1} x = -\cot^{-1} 1$$

$$\Rightarrow \cot^{-1} x = \cot^{-1}(-1)$$

$$\Rightarrow x = -1$$

Skill Builder

Let the inverse trigonometric function take value. The number of real solutions of the equation $2\sin^{-1} x + \cos^{-1} x = \frac{\pi}{3}$ is ....

For Sol.

Example 18 *The sum of n terms of the series*

$$\tan^{-1}\frac{1}{1+1+1^2} + \tan^{-1}\frac{1}{1+2+2^2} + \tan^{-1}\frac{1}{1+3+3^2} + \ldots \infty \text{ is}$$

(a) $\frac{\pi}{4}$ (b) $\tan^{-1}\left(\frac{n}{n+1}\right)$
(c) $\tan^{-1}\left(\frac{n}{n+2}\right)$ (d) $\tan^{-1}\left(\frac{n+1}{n+2}\right)$

Sol. (c) The nth term of the given series is

$$t_n = \tan^{-1}\frac{1}{1+n+n^2} = \tan^{-1}\left[\frac{(n+1)-n}{1+(n+1)n}\right]$$

$$= \tan^{-1}(n+1) - \tan^{-1} n$$

$$\therefore \quad t_1 = \tan^{-1}2 - \tan^{-1}1$$

$$t_2 = \tan^{-1}3 - \tan^{-1}2 \ldots$$

$$t_n = \tan^{-1}(n+1) - \tan^{-1} n$$

and so, $S_n = t_1 + t_2 + \ldots + t_n$

$$= \tan^{-1}(n+1) - \tan^{-1}1$$

$$= \tan^{-1}\left(\frac{(n+1)-1}{1+(n+1)\cdot 1}\right)$$

$$= \tan^{-1}\left(\frac{n}{n+2}\right)$$

More than One Correct Option Type Questions

Example 19 *If $f(x) = \cos^{-1}(\cos(x+1))$ and $g(x) = \sin^{-1}(\sin(x+2))$, then*

(a) $f(1) + g(1) = (\pi - 1)$ (b) $f(1) > g(1)$

(c) $f(2) > g(2)$ (d) $f(2) < g(2)$

Sol. (a, b, c) $f(1) = \cos^{-1}(\cos 2) = 2$

$$g(1) = \sin^{-1}(\sin 3) = (\pi - 3)$$

$\therefore f(1) + g(1) = (\pi - 1)$

and $f(1) > g(1)$

$$f(2) = \cos^{-1}(\cos 3) = 3$$

$$g(2) = \sin^{-1}(\sin 4) = (\pi - 4)$$

$\therefore$ $f(2) > g(2)$

Example 20 $\sum_{r=1}^{\infty} \tan^{-1}\left(\frac{2}{(r+2)^2}\right)$ *is*

(a) $\pi - (\tan^{-1}2 + \tan^{-1}3)$ (b) $\frac{\pi}{4}$

(c) $\frac{7\pi}{4}$ (d) $\pi + (\tan^{-1}2 + \tan^{-1}3)$

Sol. (a,b) $T_r = \tan^{-1}\left(\frac{2}{(r^2+4r+3)+1}\right) = \tan^{-1}\left(\frac{(r+3)-(r+1)}{1+(r+3)(r+1)}\right)$

$$T_r = \tan^{-1}(r+3) - \tan^{-1}(r+1)$$

$$\text{Sum} = \pi - (\tan^{-1}(2) + \tan^{-1}(3))$$

$$= \pi - (\pi + \tan^{-1}(-1)) = \frac{\pi}{4}$$

Example 21 *If sides AB, BC and CA of a ΔABC are represented by $x + 2 = 0$, $3x + y = 0$ and $x + 3y + 2 = 0$ respectively, then identify the correct statement.*

(a) $\Sigma \tan A = \frac{4}{3}$ (b) $\Pi \tan A = -\frac{4}{3}$

(c) $\Sigma \tan A \tan B = -\frac{41}{9}$ (d) $\sin^2(A+B) + \cos^2 C = \frac{5}{4}$

Sol. (b, c) $\angle A = \frac{\pi}{2} + \tan^{-1}\frac{1}{3}$

$$\angle B = \frac{\pi}{2} - \tan^{-1}3$$

$$\angle C = \pi - (A+B)$$

$$= \tan^{-1}3 - \tan^{-1}\frac{1}{3}$$

$$= 2\tan^{-1}3 - \frac{\pi}{2}$$

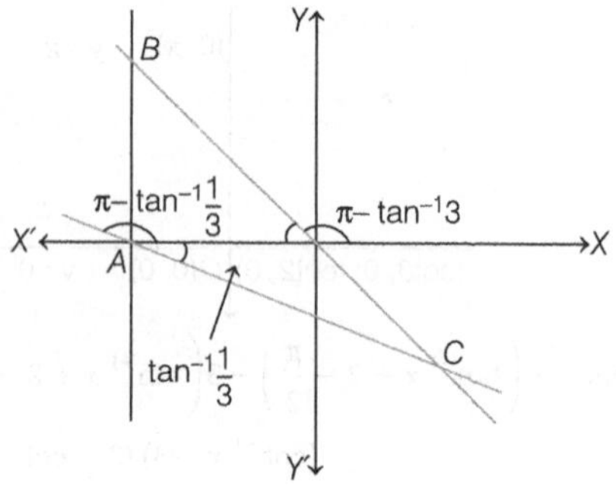

$$\tan A + \tan B + \tan C = \tan\left(\frac{\pi}{2} + \tan^{-1}\frac{1}{3}\right) + \tan\left(\frac{\pi}{2} - \tan^{-1}3\right) + \tan\left(\tan^{-1}3 - \tan^{-1}\frac{1}{3}\right)$$

$$= -\cot\left(\tan^{-1}\frac{1}{3}\right) + \cot(\tan^{-1}3) + \tan\left(\tan^{-1}\left(\frac{3-\frac{1}{3}}{1+3.\frac{1}{3}}\right)\right)$$

$$= -3 + \frac{1}{3} + \frac{4}{3} = -\frac{4}{3}$$

$$\Sigma \tan A = \Pi \tan A = -\frac{4}{3}$$

$$\Sigma \tan A \tan B = -3 . \frac{1}{3} + \frac{1}{3} . \frac{4}{3} + \frac{4}{3}(-3) = -5 + \frac{4}{9} = -\frac{41}{9}$$

$$\sin^2(A+B) + \cos^2 C = \sin^2(\pi - C) + \cos^2 C = 1$$

Example 22 *Which of the following is/are correct?*

(a) $\cos(\cos(\cos^{-1}1)) < \sin(\sin^{-1}(\sin(\pi - 1))) < \sin(\cos^{-1}(\cos(2\pi - 2)))$

(b) $\cos(\cos(\cos^{-1}1)) < \sin(\cos^{-1}(\cos(2\pi - 2))) < \sin(\sin^{-1}(\sin(\pi - 1))) < \tan(\cot^{-1}(\cot 1))$

(c) $\sum_{t=1}^{5000} \cos^{-1}(\cos(2t\pi - 1)) = \sum_{t=1}^{2500} \cot^{-1}(\cot(t\pi + 2))$, where $t \in I$

(d) $\cot^{-1}\cot\operatorname{cosec}^{-1}\operatorname{cosec}\sec^{-1}\sec\tan\tan^{-1}\cos\cos^{-1}\sin^{-1}\sin 4 = 4 - \pi$

Sol. (a,c,d) For (a) and (b)

$$\cos(\cos^{-1}1) = 1 \Rightarrow \cos(\cos(\cos^{-1}1)) = \cos 1$$

$$\sin^{-1}(\sin(\pi - 1)) = \pi - (\pi - 1) = 1$$

$$\Rightarrow \sin(\sin^{-1}(\sin(\pi - 1))) = \sin 1$$

$$\cos^{-1}(\cos(2\pi - 2)) = \cos^{-1}(\cos 2) = 2$$

$$\Rightarrow \sin(\cos^{-1}(\cos(2\pi - 2))) = \sin 2$$

$$\tan(\cot^{-1}(\cot 1)) = \tan 1$$

It is easy to compare cos1, sin1, sin2, tan1

$$\cos 1 < \sin 1 < \sin 2 < \tan 1 \Rightarrow \text{(a) is correct.}$$

For (c)

$\because \cos^{-1}\cos x$ is periodic with period 2π.

$$\therefore \quad \cos^{-1}\cos(2t\pi - 1) = \cos^{-1}(\cos 1) = 1 \ (t \in I)$$

$$\sum_{t=1}^{5000} \cos^{-1}\cos(2t\pi - 1) = 5000$$

Now, $\cot^{-1}\cot(t\pi + 2) = 2$ [$\cot^{-1}\cot x$ is periodic with period π]

$$\therefore \sum_{t=1}^{2500} \cot^{-1}\cot(t\pi + 2) = 5000 \Rightarrow \text{(c) is correct.}$$

For (d)

$$\sin^{-1}\sin 4 = \pi - 4$$

$$\cos\cos^{-1}(\pi - 4) = 4 - \pi$$

$$\tan\tan^{-1}(4 - \pi) = \pi - 4$$

$$\sec^{-1}\sec(\pi - 4) = 4 - \pi$$

$$\text{cosec}^{-1}\text{cosec}(4 - \pi) = 4 - \pi$$

$$\cot^{-1}\cot(4 - \pi) = 4 - \pi$$

$\Rightarrow$ (d) is correct.

Example 23 *If the quadratic equation $4^{\sec^2\alpha} x^2 + 2x + \left(\beta^2 - \beta + \frac{1}{2}\right) = 0$ have real roots, then the possible value(s) of $\cos\alpha + \cos^{-1}\beta$ is/are*

(a) $\frac{\pi}{3} - 1$ (b) $1 - \frac{\pi}{3}$

(c) $\frac{\pi}{3} + 1$ (d) $\frac{\pi}{4} - 1$

Sol. (a,c) The quadratic equation

$4^{\sec^2\alpha} \cdot x^2 + 2x + \left(\beta^2 - \beta + \frac{1}{2}\right) = 0$ have real roots.

$$\Rightarrow \text{Discriminant} = 4 - 4.4^{\sec^2\alpha}\left(\beta^2 - \beta + \frac{1}{2}\right) \ge 0$$

$$\Rightarrow \quad 4^{\sec^2\alpha}\left(\beta^2 - \beta + \frac{1}{2}\right) \le 1 \quad \text{...(i)}$$

But $4^{\sec^2\alpha} \ge 4$, $\beta^2 - \beta + \frac{1}{2} = \left(\beta - \frac{1}{2}\right)^2 + \frac{1}{4} \ge \frac{1}{4}$

i.e. equation will be satisfied only when

$$4^{\sec^2\alpha} = 4 \quad \text{and } \beta^2 - \beta + \frac{1}{2} = \frac{1}{4}$$

$$\Rightarrow \quad \sec^2\alpha = 1 \text{ and } \left(\beta - \frac{1}{2}\right)^2 = 0$$

$$\Rightarrow \quad \cos^2\alpha = 1 \text{ and } \beta = \frac{1}{2}$$

$$\Rightarrow \quad \alpha = n\pi \text{ and } \beta = \frac{1}{2}$$

$$\therefore \quad \cos\alpha + \cos^{-1}\beta = \cos n\pi + \cos^{-1}\frac{1}{2}$$

$$= \begin{cases} 1 + \frac{\pi}{3}, & \text{when } n \text{ is even integer} \\ -1 + \frac{\pi}{3}, & \text{when } n \text{ is odd integer} \end{cases}$$

i.e. the value of $\cos\alpha + \cos^{-1}\beta$ is $\frac{\pi}{3} - 1$ and $\frac{\pi}{3} + 1$.

Example 24 *Let x_1 and x_2 $(x_1 > x_2)$ be roots of the equation $\sin^{-1}(\cos(\tan^{-1}(\text{cosec}(\cot^{-1} x)))) = \frac{\pi}{6}$, then*

(a) $\sin^{-1}\frac{1}{x_1} + \cos^{-1}\frac{1}{x_2} = \pi$

(b) $\sin^{-1}\left(\frac{1}{x_1}\right) + \cos^{-1}\left(\frac{1}{x_2}\right) = 0$

(c) $\sin^{-1}\frac{1}{x_1} + \sin^{-1}\left(\frac{1}{x_2}\right) = 0$

(d) $\cos^{-1}\left(\frac{1}{x_1}\right) + \cos^{-1}\left(\frac{1}{x_2}\right) = \pi$

Sol. (a,c,d) Given, $\sin^{-1}(\cos(\tan^{-1}(\text{cosec}(\cot^{-1} x)))) = \frac{\pi}{6}$

$$\Rightarrow \quad \sin^{-1}(\cos(\tan^{-1}\sqrt{1 + x^2})) = \frac{\pi}{6}$$

$$\Rightarrow \quad \sin^{-1}\left(\frac{1}{\sqrt{x^2 + 2}}\right) = \frac{\pi}{6}$$

$$\Rightarrow \quad \sqrt{x^2 + 2} = 2$$

$$\Rightarrow \quad x^2 = 2$$

$$\Rightarrow \quad x = \pm\sqrt{2}$$

So, $x_1 = \sqrt{2}$

and $x_2 = -\sqrt{2}$

Now, verify alternatives.

Passage Based Questions

Passage I

(Ex. Nos. 25 and 26)

Suppose f, g and h be three real valued function defined on R. Let $f(x) = 2x + |x|$, $g(x) = \frac{1}{3}(2x - |x|)$ and $h(x) = f(g(x))$

Example 25 *The range of the function $k(x) = 1 + \frac{1}{\pi}(\cos^{-1}(h(x)) + \cot^{-1}(h(x)))$ is equal to*

(a) $\left[\frac{1}{4}, \frac{7}{4}\right]$ (b) $\left[\frac{5}{4}, \frac{11}{4}\right]$ (c) $\left[\frac{1}{4}, \frac{5}{4}\right]$ (d) $\left[\frac{7}{4}, \frac{11}{4}\right]$

Example 26 *The domain of definition of the function $l(x) = \sin^{-1}(f(x) - g(x))$ is equal to*

(a) $\left(\frac{3}{8}, \infty\right]$ (b) $(-\infty, 1]$

(c) $[-1, 1]$ (d) $\left(-\infty, \frac{3}{8}\right]$

Sol. (Ex. Nos. 25 to 26)

We have, $f(x) = \begin{cases} 3x, & x \geq 0 \\ x, & x < 0 \end{cases}$ and $g(x) \begin{cases} \frac{x}{3}, & x \geq 0 \\ x, & x < 0 \end{cases}$

Clearly, f and g are inverse of each other.

Now, $h(x) = f(g(x)) = \begin{cases} 3\left(\frac{x}{3}\right) = x, & x \geq 0 \\ x, & x < 0 \end{cases}$

25. (b) As $h(x) = x, \forall\ x \in R$

$$\Rightarrow \quad k(x) = 1 + \frac{1}{\pi}(\cos^{-1} x + \cot^{-1} x)$$

Domain of $k(x) = [-1, 1]$ and $k(x)$ is decreasing function on $[-1, 1]$.

As $k(x)$ is continuous function on $[-1, 1]$.

Now, $k_{min.}(x = 1) = 1 + \frac{1}{\pi}(\cos^{-1} 1 + \cot^{-1} 1)$

$$= 1 + \frac{1}{\pi}\left(0 + \frac{\pi}{4}\right) = 1 + \frac{1}{4} = \frac{5}{4}$$

$$k_{max.}(x = -1) = 1 + \frac{1}{\pi}(\cos^{-1}(-1) + \cot^{-1}(-1))$$

$$= 1 + \frac{1}{\pi}\left[\pi + \frac{3\pi}{4}\right]$$

$$= 1 + \frac{7}{4} = \frac{11}{4}$$

$\Rightarrow$ Range of $k(x) = \left[\frac{5}{4}, \frac{11}{4}\right]$

26. (d) We have, $f(x) - g(x) = (2x + |x|) - \frac{1}{3}(2x - |x|)$

$$= \frac{4x}{3} + \frac{4}{3}|x|$$

$$= \begin{cases} \frac{8}{3}x; & x \geq 0 \\ 0\ ; & x < 0 \end{cases}$$

$\therefore$ For domain of function

$$0 \leq \frac{8x}{3} \leq 1$$

$$\Rightarrow \quad 0 \leq x \leq \frac{3}{8}$$

$\Rightarrow$ Domain of $l(x) = \left(-\infty, \frac{3}{8}\right]$

Note Range of function $l(x) = \left[0, \frac{\pi}{2}\right]$

Passage II

(Ex. Nos. 27 and 28)

In ΔABC, if $\angle B = \sec^{-1}\left(\frac{5}{4}\right) + \text{cosec}^{-1}\sqrt{5}$,

$\angle C = \text{cosec}^{-1}\left(\frac{25}{7}\right) + \cot^{-1}\left(\frac{9}{13}\right)$ and $c = 3$

(All symbols used have their usual meaning in a triangle.) On the basis of above information, answer the following questions.

Example 27 $\tan A$, $\tan B$, $\tan C$ *are in*

(a) AP (b) GP

(c) HP (d) neither AP, GP nor HP

Example 28 *The distance between orthocentre and centroid of triangle with sides a^2, $b^{\frac{4}{3}}$ and c is equal to*

(a) $\frac{5}{2}$ (b) $\frac{5}{3}$ (c) $\frac{10}{3}$ (d) $\frac{7}{2}$

Sol. (Ex. Nos. 27 to 28)

$$\angle B = \sec^{-1}\left(\frac{5}{4}\right) + \text{cosec}^{-1}\sqrt{5} = \tan^{-1}\left(\frac{3}{4}\right) + \tan^{-1}\left(\frac{1}{2}\right)$$

$$= \tan^{-1}\frac{\frac{3}{4} + \frac{1}{2}}{1 - \frac{3}{4}\cdot\frac{1}{2}} = \tan^{-1} 2$$

$$\angle C = \text{cosec}^{-1}\left(\frac{25}{7}\right) + \cot^{-1}\left(\frac{9}{13}\right) = \tan^{-1}\left(\frac{7}{24}\right) + \tan^{-1}\left(\frac{13}{9}\right)$$

$$= \tan^{-1}\left(\frac{\frac{7}{24} + \frac{13}{9}}{1 - \frac{7}{24}\cdot\frac{13}{9}}\right) = \tan^{-1} 3$$

$\tan B = 2$ and $\tan C = 3$

$\Rightarrow \quad \tan A = 1$

$\because \quad \Sigma \tan A = \Pi \tan A$

$\therefore \quad \sin A = \frac{1}{\sqrt{2}}, \sin B = \frac{2}{\sqrt{5}}$ and $\sin C = \frac{3}{\sqrt{10}}$

$\therefore \quad \frac{a}{\sin A} = \frac{b}{\sin B} = \frac{c}{\sin C}$

$\Rightarrow \quad \sqrt{2}a = \frac{\sqrt{5}b}{2} = \frac{3\sqrt{10}}{3}$

Hence, $a = \sqrt{5}$, $b = 2\sqrt{2}$ and $c = 3$.

27. (a) $\tan A = 1$, $\tan B = 2$, $\tan C = 3$ are in AP.

28. (b) The triangle sides a^2, $b^{\frac{4}{3}}$ and c will have side-length 5, 4 and 3 respectively.

$\therefore$ Distance between orthocentre and centroid

$$= \frac{2}{3}(\text{circumradius}) = \frac{\text{hypotenuse}}{3} = \frac{5}{3}$$

Stem Based Questions

Stem I

(Ex. Nos. 29 and 30)

Let F be a real valued function defined on R (the set of real numbers) such that

$$f(x) = \sin^{-1}(\sin x) + \cos^{-1}(\cos x)$$

Example 29 *The area bounded by the curve $y = f(x)$ and X-axis from $\frac{\pi}{2} \le x \le \pi$ is $\frac{\pi^2}{a}$, then a is equal to ....*

Example 30 *Number of value of x in interval (0, 3) so that $f(x)$ is an integer is equal to ....*

Sol. (Ex. Nos. 29 to 30)

29. (2) $f(x) = (\pi - x) + x = \pi \ \forall \ x \in \left[\frac{\pi}{2}, \pi\right]$

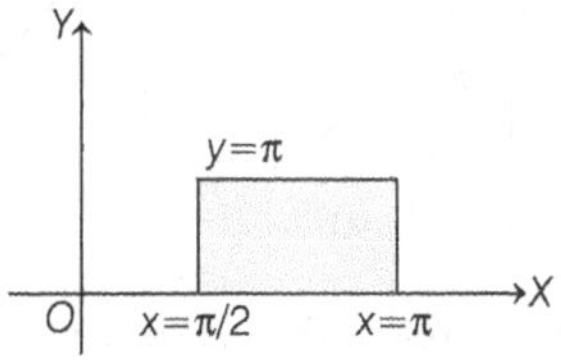

$$\text{Area} = \frac{\pi}{2} \times \pi = \frac{\pi^2}{2} = \frac{\pi^2}{a}$$

$\therefore \ a = 2$

30. (3) As $\sin^{-1}(\sin x) = \begin{cases} x, \ x \in \left(0, \frac{\pi}{2}\right) \\ \pi - x, \ x \in \left[\frac{\pi}{2}, \frac{3\pi}{2}\right] \end{cases}$

$f(x) \in I$ in $x \in (0, 3)$.

$\Rightarrow \qquad x = \frac{1}{2}, 1, \frac{3}{2}$

$\because$ Number of values of x are 3.

Single Integer Answer Type Questions

Example 31 *Let $f(x) = x^2 - 2ax + a - 2$ and $g(x) = \left[2 + \sin^{-1}\frac{2x}{1+x^2}\right]$. If the set of real values of a for which $f(g(x)) < 0, \forall \ x \in R$ is (k_1, k_2), then find the value of $(10k_1 - 3k_2)$.*

[Note : [k] denotes greatest integer less than or equal to k.]

Sol. (8) We have, $g(x) = \left[2 + \sin^{-1}\frac{2x}{1+x^2}\right] = 2 + \left[\sin^{-1}\frac{2x}{1+x^2}\right]$

As, $\quad \sin^{1}\frac{2x}{1+x^2} \in \left[\frac{-\pi}{2}, \frac{\pi}{2}\right]$

$\therefore \quad \left[\sin^{-1}\frac{2x}{1+x^2}\right] = -2, -1, 0, 1$

Range of $g(x) = \{0,1,2,3\}$ for $f(g(x)) < 0 \ \forall \ x \in R$

$\Rightarrow \qquad f(0) < 0$ and $f(3) < 0$

Now, $\qquad f(0) < 0 \Rightarrow a - 2 < 0 \Rightarrow a < 2$

and $\qquad f(3) < 0 \Rightarrow 9 - 6a + a - 2 < 0$

$$a > \frac{7}{5}$$

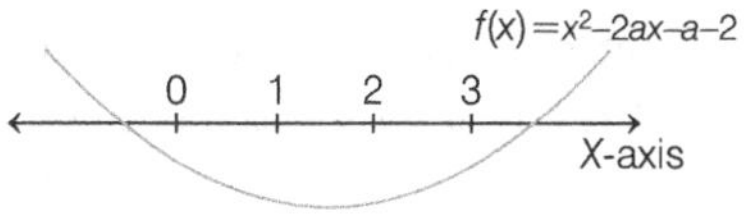

$\therefore \qquad a \in \left(\frac{7}{5}, 2\right)$

Hence, $\qquad k_1 = \frac{7}{5}, k_2 = 2$

$\therefore \qquad (10k_1 - 3k_2) = 14 - 6 = 8$

Example 32 *Let x_1, x_2, x_3 be the solution of $\tan^{-1}\left(\frac{2x+1}{x+1}\right) + \tan^{-1}\left(\frac{2x-1}{x-1}\right) = 2\tan^{-1}(x+1)$, where $x_1 < x_2 < x_3$, then $2x_1 + x_2 + x_3^2$ is equal to*

Sol. (1) Let $\qquad \alpha + \beta = 2\gamma \qquad$ ...(i)

where $\qquad \tan\alpha = \frac{2x+1}{x+1}, \tan\beta = \frac{2x-1}{x-1}$ and

$$\tan\gamma = x + 1$$

Taking tan in Eq. (i), we get

$$\frac{\tan\alpha + \tan\beta}{1 - \tan\alpha\tan\beta} = \frac{2\tan\gamma}{1 - \tan^2\gamma}$$

$$\Rightarrow \qquad \frac{\frac{2x+1}{x+1} + \frac{2x-1}{x-1}}{1 - \frac{4x^2-1}{x^2-1}} = \frac{2(x+1)}{1-(x+1)^2}$$

$$\Rightarrow \qquad \frac{2x^2 - x - 1 + 2x^2 + x - 1}{x^2 - 1 - 4x^2 + 1} = \frac{2(x+1)}{-x^2 - 2x}$$

$$\Rightarrow \qquad \frac{2(2x^2-1)}{-3x^2} = \frac{2(x+1)}{-(x^2+2x)}$$

$$\Rightarrow \qquad x = 0$$

$$\Rightarrow \qquad 2x^3 + 4x^2 - x - 2 = 3x^2 + 3x$$

$$\Rightarrow \qquad 2x^3 + x^2 - 4x - 2 = 0$$

$$\Rightarrow \qquad x^2(2x+1) - 2(2x+1) = 0$$

$$\Rightarrow \qquad (x^2 - 2)(2x+1) = 0$$

$$\Rightarrow \qquad x = \sqrt{2}, -\sqrt{2} \text{ or } x = -\frac{1}{2}$$

$$\Rightarrow \qquad x = -\sqrt{2} \text{ is rejected}$$

$\because$ It does not satisfy (i)

$\Rightarrow \ x_1 = -\frac{1}{2}, x_2 = 0$ and $x_3 = \sqrt{2} \Rightarrow 2x_1 + x_2 + x_3^2 = 1$

Example 33 *If the range of function* $f(x) = (\pi\sqrt{2} + \cos^{-1}\alpha)\,x^2 + 2(\cos^{-1}\beta)\,x + \pi\sqrt{2} - \cos^{-1}\alpha$ *is* $[0, \infty)$, *then find the value of* $|\alpha - \beta| + 2\alpha\beta + 1$.

Sol. (3) Given, $f(x) = (\pi\sqrt{2} + \cos^{-1}\alpha)\,x^2$

$$+ 2(\cos^{-1}\beta)x + \pi\sqrt{2} - \cos^{-1}\alpha$$

Clearly, graph of $f(x)$ is parabola opening upward.

As, range of $f(x)$ is $[0, \infty)$, so discriminant $= 0$

$\Rightarrow \quad b^2 - 4ac = 0$

$\Rightarrow 4(\cos^{-1}\beta)^2 - 4(\pi\sqrt{2} + \cos^{-1}\alpha)(\pi\sqrt{2} - \cos^{-1}\alpha) = 0$

$\Rightarrow \quad 4(\cos^{-1}\beta)^2 - 4(2\pi^2 - (\cos^{-1}\alpha)^2) = 0$

$\Rightarrow \quad (\cos^{-1}\alpha)^2 + (\cos^{-1}\beta)^2 = 2\pi^2$

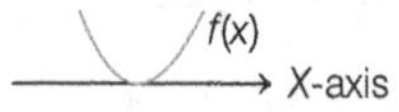

$\Rightarrow \quad \cos^{-1}\alpha = \pi = \cos^{-1}\beta \Rightarrow \alpha = \beta = -1$

Hence, $|\alpha - \beta| + 2\alpha\beta + 1 = 0 + 2 + 1 = 3$

Example 34 *Consider* $f(x) = \sin^{-1}[2x] + \cos^{-1}([x] - 1)$ *(where [.] denotes greatest integer function.) If domain of* $f(x)$ *is* $[a, b)$ *and the range of* $f(x)$ *is* $\{c, d\}$, *then* $a + b + \frac{2d}{c}$ *is equal to (where* $c < d$*)*

Sol. (4) $f(x) = \sin^{-1}[2x] + \cos^{-1}([x] - 1)$

$-1 \le [2x] \le 1$ and $-1 \le [x] - 1 \le 1$

$\Rightarrow \quad -1 \le 2x < 2$ and $0 \le [x] \le 2$

$\Rightarrow \quad -\frac{1}{2} < x < 1$ and $0 \le x < 3$

$\Rightarrow \quad 0 \le x < 1$ (Domain)

$\Rightarrow \quad [x] = 0$

$\Rightarrow \quad 0 \le 2x < 2 \Rightarrow [2x] = 0$ or 1

Now, $\quad f(x) = \sin^{-1}[2x] + \cos^{-1}(-1)$

$$= \left(0 \text{ or } \frac{\pi}{2}\right) + \pi = \pi \text{ or } \frac{3\pi}{2}$$

$\Rightarrow \quad a + b + \frac{2d}{c} = 1 + 3 = 4$

Example 35 *Let* $f(x) = \min(\tan^{-1}x, \cot^{-1}x)$ *and* $h(x) = f(x + 2) - \pi/3$. *Let* x_1, x_2 *(where* $x_1 < x_2$*) be the integers in the range of* $h(x)$, *then the value of* $(\cos^{-1}(\cos x_1) + \sin^{-1}(\sin x_2))$ *is equal to*

Sol. (1) $\quad f(x) = \begin{cases} \tan^{-1}x; & x \le 1 \\ \cot^{-1}x; & x > 1 \end{cases}$

$\Rightarrow f(x + 2) = \begin{cases} \tan^{-1}(x + 2) \;; & x \le -1 \\ \cot^{-1}(x + 2) \;; & x > -1 \end{cases}$

$\therefore$ Range of $h(x)$ is $\left(-\frac{5\pi}{6}, -\frac{\pi}{12}\right]$

$\therefore \quad \cos^{-1}(\cos(-2)) + \sin^{-1}(\sin(-1)) = 1$

Example 36 *If the area enclosed by the curves* $f(x) = \cos^{-1}(\cos x)$ *and* $g(x) = \sin^{-1}(\cos x)$ *in* $x \in \left[\frac{9\pi}{4}, \frac{15\pi}{4}\right]$ *is* $\frac{a\pi^2}{b}$ *(where, a and b coprime), then find* $(a - b)$.

Sol. (1) We have $g(x) = \sin^{-1}(\cos x) = \frac{\pi}{2} - \cos^{-1}(\cos x)$

Both the curves bound the regions of same area in $\left[\frac{\pi}{4}, \frac{7\pi}{4}\right], \left[\frac{9\pi}{4}, \frac{15\pi}{4}\right]$ and so on.

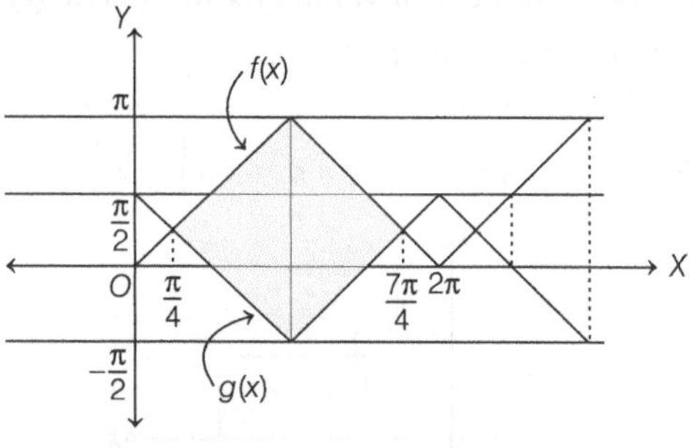

$\therefore$ Required area = Area of shaded square

$$= \frac{9\pi^2}{8} = \frac{a\pi^2}{b}$$

$\therefore \quad a = 9$ and $b = 8$

Hence, $\quad a - b = 1$

Example 37 *Consider the curve* $y = \tan^{-1}x$ *and a point* $A\left(1, \frac{\pi}{4}\right)$ *on it. If the variable point* $P_i\,(x_i, y_i)$ *moves on the curve for* $i = 1, 2, 3, \ldots n\,(n \in N)$ *such that* $y_r = \sum_{m=1}^{r} \tan^{-1}\left(\frac{1}{2m^2}\right)$ *and* $B(x, y)$ *be the limiting position of variable point* P_n *as* $n \to \infty$, *then the value of reciprocal of the slope of AB will be*

Sol. (2) $y = \lim_{n \to \infty} y_n = \lim_{n \to \infty} \sum_{m=1}^{n} \tan^{-1}\left(\frac{1}{2m^2}\right)$

$$= \lim_{n \to \infty} \sum_{m=1}^{n} \tan^{-1}\left\{\frac{2}{1 + (2m + 1)(2m - 1)}\right\}$$

$$= \lim_{n \to \infty} \sum_{m=1}^{n} \{\tan^{-1}(2m + 1) - \tan^{-1}(2m - 1)\}$$

$$= \lim_{n \to \infty} \{(\tan^{-1}3 - \tan^{-1}1) + (\tan^{-1}5 - \tan^{-1}3)$$

$$+ (\tan^{-1}7 - \tan^{-1}5) \ldots. + \tan^{-1}(2n + 1) - \tan^{-1}(2n - 1)\}$$

$$= \lim_{n \to \infty} \{\tan^{-1}(2n + 1) - \tan^{-1}1\} \to \frac{\pi}{4}$$

$\because B \to \left(1, \frac{\pi}{4}\right)$ i.e. coordinates of B approach, towards those of 'A'.

$\therefore$ Chord AB approches to be the tangent to $y = f(x)$ at A

$\therefore$ (slope of $AB)^{-1} = \left[\frac{d}{dx}\tan^{-1} x\right]^{-1}_{\text{at } x=1} = (1 + x^2)_{x=1} = 2$

Example 38 *If* $\tan^{-1} x + \tan^{-1}\frac{\sqrt{1-y^2}}{y} = \frac{\pi}{3}$ *and* $\sin^{-1} y - \cos^{-1}\left(\frac{x}{\sqrt{1+x^2}}\right) = \frac{\pi}{6}$, *then* $\frac{5\sin^{-1} x}{\sin^{-1} y}$ *is*

Sol. (6) $\tan^{-1} x + \cos^{-1} y = \frac{\pi}{3}$ and $\sin^{-1} y - \cot^{-1} x = \frac{\pi}{6}$

$\Rightarrow \tan^{-1} x + \cos^{-1} y + \sin^{-1} y - \cot^{-1} x = \frac{\pi}{2}$

or $\tan^{-1} x = \cot^{-1} x \Rightarrow x = 1$

Also, $\tan^{-1} x + \cos^{-1} y - \sin^{-1} y + \cot^{-1} x = \frac{\pi}{6}$

$\Rightarrow \pi - 2\sin^{-1} y = \frac{\pi}{6} \Rightarrow \sin^{-1} y = \frac{5\pi}{12}$

$\therefore \frac{5\sin^{-1} x}{\sin^{-1} y} = 6$

Example 39 *If* $A = \frac{1}{1}\cot^{-1}\left(\frac{1}{1}\right) + \frac{1}{2}\cot^{-1}\left(\frac{1}{2}\right) + \frac{1}{3}\cot^{-1}\left(\frac{1}{3}\right)$ *and* $B = 1\cot^{-1}(1) + 2\cot^{-1}(2) + 3\cot^{-1}(3)$, *then* $|B - A|$ *is equal to* $\frac{a\pi}{b} + \frac{c}{d}\cot^{-1}(3)$, *where* $a, b, c, d \in N$ *are in their lowest form, find* $(b - a - c - d)$

Sol. (8) $B - A = (2\cot^{-1}(2) + 3\cot^{-1}(3)) - \left(\frac{1}{2}\cot^{-1}\left(\frac{1}{2}\right) + \frac{1}{3}\cot^{-1}\left(\frac{1}{3}\right)\right)$

$= 2(\cot^{-1} 2 + \cot^{-1} 3) + \cot^{-1} 3$

$-\left(\frac{1}{3}\left(\cot^{-1}\frac{1}{2} + \cot^{-1}\frac{1}{3}\right) + \frac{1}{6}\cot^{-1}\frac{1}{2}\right)$

$= \frac{\pi}{2} + \cot^{-1} 3 - \left[\frac{\pi}{4} + \frac{1}{6}\tan^{-1} 2\right]$

$= \frac{\pi}{4} + \cot^{-1} 3 - \frac{1}{6}\left[\frac{3\pi}{4} - \tan^{-1} 3\right]$

$= \frac{\pi}{8} + \cot^{-1} 3 + \frac{1}{6}\tan^{-1} 3$

$= \frac{\pi}{8} + \cot^{-1} 3 = \frac{1}{6}\left(\frac{\pi}{2} - \cot^{-1} 3\right)$

$= \frac{\pi}{8} + \frac{\pi}{12} + \cot^{-1} 3 - \frac{1}{6}\cot^{-1} 3 = \frac{5\pi}{24} + \frac{5}{6}\cot^{-1} 3$

Hence, $a = 5; b = 24; c = 5; d = 6$

$\therefore b - a - c - d = 8$

Numerical Value Type Questions

Example 40 *The number of positive integral solutions of the equation* $\tan^{-1} x + \cos^{-1}\frac{y}{\sqrt{1-y^2}} = \sin^{-1}\frac{3}{\sqrt{10}}$ *is ....*

Sol. (2) Here, $\tan^{-1} x + \cos^{-1}\frac{y}{\sqrt{1-y^2}} = \sin^{-1}\frac{3}{\sqrt{10}}$

$\Rightarrow \tan^{-1} x + \tan^{-1}\left(\frac{1}{y}\right) = \tan^{-1}(3)$

or $\tan^{-1}\left(\frac{1}{y}\right) = \tan^{-1} 3 - \tan^{-1}(x)$

or $\tan^{-1}\left(\frac{1}{y}\right) = \tan^{-1}\left(\frac{3-x}{1+3x}\right)$

$\Rightarrow y = \frac{1+3x}{3-x}$

As x, y are positive integers, $x = 1, 2$ and correspondingly $y = 2, 7$.

$\therefore$Solutions are $(x, y) = (1, 2), (2, 7)$

i.e. two solution.

Example 41 *If* $\cot^{-1}\frac{n}{\pi} > \frac{\pi}{6}$, $n \in N$, *then the maximum value of* n *is ....*

Sol. (5) Here, $\cot^{-1}\frac{n}{\pi} > \frac{\pi}{6}$

$\Rightarrow \cot\left(\cot^{-1}\frac{n}{\pi}\right) < \cot\frac{\pi}{6}$ [as $\cot x$ is decreasing in $[0, \pi/2]$]

$\Rightarrow \frac{n}{\pi} < \sqrt{3}$

$\Rightarrow n < \sqrt{3}\pi = 5.5$ [approximately]

So, the maximum value of n is 5, as $n \in N$.

Example 42 *If* $\cot^{-1}\left(\frac{n^2 - 10n + 21.6}{\pi}\right) > \frac{\pi}{6}$, $n \in N$, *then the minimum value of* n *is ....*

Sol. (3) We have, $\cot^{-1}\left(\frac{n^2 - 10n + 21.6}{\pi}\right) > \frac{\pi}{6}$

$\Rightarrow \frac{n^2 - 10n + 21.6}{\pi} < \cot\frac{\pi}{6}$

[as $\cot x$ is decreasing for $0 < x < \pi$]

$\Rightarrow n^2 - 10n + 21.6 < \pi\sqrt{3}$

$\Rightarrow n^2 - 10n + 25 + 21.6 - 25 < \pi\sqrt{3}$

$\Rightarrow (n-5)^2 < \pi\sqrt{3} + 3.4$

$\Rightarrow -\sqrt{\sqrt{3}\pi + 3.4} < n - 5 < \sqrt{\sqrt{3}\pi + 3.4}$ ...(i)

Since, $\sqrt{3}\pi = 5.5$ nearly

$\therefore \quad \sqrt{\sqrt{3}\pi + 3.4} \sim \sqrt{8.9} \sim 2.9 \Rightarrow 2.1 < n < 7.9$

$\therefore \quad n = 3, 4, 5, 6, 7 \quad$ [as $n \in N$]

or minimum value of $n = 3$.

Example 43 *The sum of greatest and least value of $(\sin^{-1} x)^3 + (\cos^{-1} x)^3$ is $\frac{a\pi^3}{b}$, then $a + b$ is ....*

Sol. (61) We have, $(\sin^{-1} x)^3 + (\cos^{-1} x)^3$

$$= (\sin^{-1} x + \cos^{-1} x)[(\sin^{-1} x + \cos^{-1} x)^2 - 3\sin^{-1} x.\cos^{-1} x]$$

$$= \frac{\pi}{2}\left[\frac{\pi^2}{4} - 3\sin^{-1} x\left(\frac{\pi}{2} - \sin^{-1} x\right)\right]$$

$$= \frac{3\pi}{2}\left[(\sin^{-1} x)^2 - \frac{\pi}{2}\sin^{-1} x + \frac{\pi^2}{12}\right]$$

$$= \frac{3\pi}{2}\left[\left(\sin^{-1} x - \frac{\pi}{4}\right)^2 + \frac{\pi^2}{12} - \frac{\pi^2}{16}\right]$$

$$= \frac{3\pi}{2}\left[\left(\sin^{-1} x - \frac{\pi}{4}\right)^2 + \frac{\pi^2}{48}\right]$$

So, the least value is $\frac{3\pi}{2} \cdot \frac{\pi^2}{48} = \frac{\pi^3}{32} \left\{\text{when}\left(\sin^{-1} x - \frac{\pi}{4}\right) = 0\right\}$

Also, $\left(\sin^{-1} x - \frac{\pi}{4}\right)^2 \le \left(\frac{3\pi}{4}\right)^2$

$\therefore$ The greatest value $= \frac{3\pi}{2}\left[\frac{9\pi^2}{16} + \frac{\pi^2}{48}\right] = \frac{7\pi^3}{8}$

$\therefore$ Sum $= \frac{\pi^3}{32} + \frac{7\pi^3}{8} = \frac{29\pi^3}{32} = \frac{a\pi^3}{b}$

$\Rightarrow \quad a = 29, b = 32$

$\therefore \quad a + b = 29 + 32 = 61$

Matching Type Questions

Example 44 *Match the principal values of $\cos^{-1}(8x^4 - 8x^2 + 1)$ given in column I with the corresponding intervals of x given in column II, for which it holds.*

	Column I		Column II
A.	$4\cos^{-1} x$	p.	$0 \le x \le \frac{1}{\sqrt{2}}$
B.	$4\cos^{-1} x - 2\pi$	q.	$\frac{1}{\sqrt{2}} \le x \le 1$
C.	$2\pi - 4\cos^{-1} x$	r.	$-1 \le x \le -\frac{1}{\sqrt{2}}$
D.	$4\pi - 4\cos^{-1} x$	s.	$-\frac{1}{\sqrt{2}} \le x \le 0$

Sol. A $\rightarrow$ q, B $\rightarrow$ s, C $\rightarrow$ p, D $\rightarrow$ r

(A) $0 \le \cos^{-1}(8x^4 - 8x^2 + 1) \le \pi$

$\Rightarrow \quad 0 \le 4\cos^{-1} x \le \pi$

$\Rightarrow \quad 0 \le \cos^{-1} x \le \frac{\pi}{4}$

$\Rightarrow \quad \frac{1}{\sqrt{2}} \le x \le 1$

(B) $0 \le \cos^{-1}(8x^4 - 8x^2 + 1) \le \pi$

$\Rightarrow \quad 0 \le 4\cos^{-1} x - 2\pi \le \pi$

$\Rightarrow \quad 2\pi \le 4\cos^{-1} x \le 3\pi$

$\Rightarrow \quad \frac{\pi}{2} \le \cos^{-1} x \le \frac{3\pi}{4}$

$\Rightarrow \quad -\frac{1}{\sqrt{2}} \le x \le 0$

(C) $0 \le 2\pi - 4\cos^{-1} x \le \pi$

$\Rightarrow \quad -2\pi \le -4\cos^{-1} x \le -\pi$

$\Rightarrow \quad 2\pi \ge 4\cos^{-1} x \ge \pi$

$\Rightarrow \quad \frac{\pi}{2} \ge \cos^{-1} x \ge \frac{\pi}{4}$

$\Rightarrow \quad 0 \le x \le \frac{1}{\sqrt{2}}$

(D) $0 \le 4\pi - 4\cos^{-1} x \le \pi$

$\Rightarrow \quad -4\pi \le -4\cos^{-1} x \le -3\pi$

$\Rightarrow \quad 4\pi \ge 4\cos^{-1} x \ge 3\pi$

$\Rightarrow \quad \pi \ge \cos^{-1} x \ge \frac{3\pi}{4}$

$\Rightarrow \quad -1 \le x \le -\frac{1}{\sqrt{2}}$

EXERCISE 1

JEE Main Pattern

Single Option Correct Type Questions

1. The value of the angle $\tan^{-1}(\tan 65^\circ - 2\tan 40^\circ)$ in degrees is equal to
(a) -20° (b) 20° (c) 25° (d) 40°

2. Which one of the following statement is meaningless?
(a) $\cos^{-1}\left(\ln\left(\frac{2e+4}{3}\right)\right)$ (b) $\text{cosec}^{-1}\left(\frac{\pi}{3}\right)$
(c) $\cot^{-1}\left(\frac{\pi}{2}\right)$ (d) $\sec^{-1}(\pi)$

3. The value of $\lim_{|x|\to\infty} \cos(\tan^{-1}(\sin(\tan^{-1} x)))$ is equal to
(a) -1 (b) $\sqrt{2}$ (c) $-\frac{1}{\sqrt{2}}$ (d) $\frac{1}{\sqrt{2}}$

4. If $x + \frac{1}{x} = 2$, the principal value of $\sin^{-1} x$ is
(a) $\frac{\pi}{4}$ (b) $\frac{\pi}{2}$ (c) π (d) $\frac{3\pi}{2}$

5. If $\tan^{-1}\frac{\sqrt{(1+x^2)}-\sqrt{(1-x^2)}}{\sqrt{(1+x^2)}+\sqrt{(1-x^2)}} = \alpha$, then x^2 is
(a) $\cos 2\alpha$ (b) $\sin 2\alpha$
(c) $\tan 2\alpha$ (d) $\cot 2\alpha$

6. The value of $\cos\left(\frac{1}{2}\cos^{-1}\frac{1}{8}\right)$ is equal to
(a) $\frac{3}{4}$ (b) $-\frac{3}{4}$ (c) $\frac{1}{16}$ (d) $\frac{1}{4}$

7. $\cot^{-1}\left(\sqrt{\frac{1-x^2}{1+x^2}}\right)$ is equal to
(a) $\cos^{-1}(x^2)$ (b) $\frac{\pi}{2} - \frac{1}{2}\cos^{-1}(x^2)$
(c) $\frac{\pi}{3} - \frac{1}{2}\cos^{-1}(x^2)$ (d) None of these

8. $\sin\left[\tan^{-1}\frac{1-x^2}{2x} + \cos^{-1}\frac{1-x^2}{1+x^2}\right]$ is
(a) 1 (b) 0
(c) -1 (d) None of these

9. Let $u = \cot^{-1}\sqrt{\cos 2\theta} - \tan^{-1}\sqrt{\cos 2\theta}$, then the value of $\sin u$ is
(a) $\cos 2\theta$ (b) $\sin 2\theta$ (c) $\tan^2\theta$ (d) $\cot^2\theta$

10. $\cos^{-1}(\cos(2\cot^{-1}(\sqrt{2}-1)))$ is equal to
(a) $\sqrt{2}-1$ (b) $\frac{\pi}{4}$
(c) $\frac{3\pi}{4}$ (d) None of these

11. If $a \le \tan^{-1}\left(\frac{1-x}{1+x}\right) \le b$, where $0 \le x \le 1$, then (a, b) is equal to
(a) $\left(0, \frac{\pi}{4}\right)$ (b) $\left(0, \frac{\pi}{2}\right)$ (c) $\left(-\frac{\pi}{4}, \frac{\pi}{4}\right)$ (d) $\left(\frac{\pi}{4}, \frac{\pi}{2}\right)$

12. If $\sin^{-1} : [-1, 1] \to \left[\frac{\pi}{2}, \frac{3\pi}{2}\right]$ and $\cos^{-1} : [-1, 1] \to [0, \pi]$ be two bijective function, respectively inverses of bijective functions $\sin : \left[\frac{\pi}{2}, \frac{3\pi}{2}\right] \to [-1, 1]$ and $\cos : [0, \pi] \to [-1, 1]$, then $\sin^{-1} x + \cos^{-1} x$ is
(a) $\frac{\pi}{2}$ (b) π
(c) $\frac{3\pi}{2}$ (d) not a constant

13. The range of values of p for which the equation $\sin \cos^{-1}(\cos(\tan^{-1} x)) = p$ has a solution is
(a) $\left(-\frac{1}{\sqrt{2}}, \frac{1}{\sqrt{2}}\right]$ (b) $[0, 1)$
(c) $\left[\frac{1}{\sqrt{2}}, 1\right)$ (d) $(-1, 1)$

14. Number of solution(s) of the equations $\cos^{-1}(1-x) - 2\cos^{-1} x = \frac{\pi}{2}$ is
(a) 3 (b) 2 (c) 1 (d) 0

15. Which one of the following function contains only one integer in its range?
[**Note** sgn (k) denotes the signum function of k.]
(a) $f(x) = \frac{1}{2}\cos^{-1}\left(\frac{1-x^2}{1+x^2}\right)$
(b) $g(x) = \text{sgn}\left(x + \frac{1}{x}\right)$
(c) $h(x) = \sin^2 x + 2\sin x + 2$
(d) $k(x) = \cos^{-1}(x^2 - 2x + 2)$

16. If range of the function $f(x)=\tan^{-1}(3x^2+bx+3)$, $x\in R$ is $\left[0,\frac{\pi}{2}\right)$, then square of sum of all possible values of b will be

(a) 0 (b) 18
(c) 72 (d) None of these

17. Let $f(x)=1+2\sin\left(\frac{e^x}{e^x+1}\right)$, $x\geq 0$, then $f^{-1}(x)$ is equal to (assuming f is bijective)

(a) $\log\left(\frac{\sin^{-1}\left(\frac{x-1}{2}\right)}{1-\sin^{-1}\left(\frac{x-1}{2}\right)}\right)$ (b) $\log\left(\frac{\sin\left(\frac{x-1}{2}\right)}{1-\sin\left(\frac{x-1}{2}\right)}\right)$

(c) $e^{\frac{\sin^{-1}\left(\frac{x-1}{2}\right)}{1-\sin^{-1}\left(\frac{x-1}{2}\right)}}$ (d) $e^{\frac{\sin\left(\frac{x-1}{2}\right)}{1-\sin\left(\frac{x-1}{2}\right)}}$

18. If $\operatorname{cosec}^{-1}(\operatorname{cosec} x)$ and $\operatorname{cosec}(\operatorname{cosec}^{-1}x)$ are equal functions, then the maximum range of value of x is

(a) $\left[-\frac{\pi}{2},-1\right]\cup\left[1,\frac{\pi}{2}\right]$ (b) $\left[-\frac{\pi}{2},0\right)\cup\left(0,\frac{\pi}{2}\right]$
(c) $(-\infty,-1]\cup[1,\infty)$ (d) $[-1,0)\cup(0,1]$

19. For any real number $x\geq 1$, the expression $\sec^2(\tan^{-1}x)-\tan^2(\sec^{-1}x)$ is equal to

(a) 1 (b) 2
(c) $2x^2$ (d) $2\sqrt{2}$

20. The value of $\sec\left[\sin^{-1}\left(-\sin\frac{50\pi}{9}\right)+\cos^{-1}\cos\left(-\frac{31\pi}{9}\right)\right]$ is equal to

(a) $\sec\frac{10\pi}{9}$ (b) $\sec\frac{\pi}{9}$
(c) 1 (d) -1

21. Solution of equation $\cot^{-1}x+\sin^{-1}\frac{1}{\sqrt{5}}=\frac{\pi}{4}$ is

(a) $x=3$ (b) $x=\frac{1}{\sqrt{5}}$
(c) $x=0$ (d) None of these

22. If $\sin^{-1}x+\sin^{-1}y=\frac{2\pi}{3}$, then $\cos^{-1}x+\cos^{-1}y$

(a) $\frac{2\pi}{3}$ (b) $\frac{\pi}{3}$ (c) $\frac{\pi}{6}$ (d) π

23. The value of $\sin^{-1}\left\{\left(\sin\frac{\pi}{3}\right)\frac{x}{\sqrt{(x^2+k^2-kx)}}\right\}-\cos^{-1}\left\{\left(\cos\frac{\pi}{6}\right)\frac{x}{\sqrt{(x^2+k^2-kx)}}\right\}$, where $\left(\frac{k}{2}<x<2k, k>0\right)$ is

(a) $\tan^{-1}\left(\frac{2x^2+xk-k^2}{x^2-2xk+k^2}\right)$ (b) $\tan^{-1}\left(\frac{x^2+2xk-2k^2}{x^2-2xk+k^2}\right)$

(c) $\tan^{-1}\left(\frac{x^2+2xk-2k^2}{2x^2-2xk+2k^2}\right)$ (d) None of these

24. If $a\sin^{-1}x-b\cos^{-1}x=c$, then $a\sin^{-1}x+b\cos^{-1}x$ is equal to

(a) 0 (b) $\frac{\pi ab+c(b-a)}{a+b}$

(c) $\frac{\pi}{2}$ (d) $\frac{\pi ab+c(a-b)}{a+b}$

25. If the equation $x^3+bx^2+cx+1=0$, $(b<c)$, has only one real root α, then the value of $2\tan^{-1}(\operatorname{cosec}\alpha)+\tan^{-1}(2\sin\alpha\sec^2\alpha)$ is

(a) $-\pi$ (b) $-\frac{\pi}{2}$ (c) $\frac{\pi}{2}$ (d) π

26. Let $f(x)=\sin^{-1}2x+\cos^{-1}2x+\sec^{-1}2x$. Then, the sum of the maximum and minimum values of $f(x)$ is

(a) π (b) 2π
(c) 3π (d) $\frac{\pi}{2}$

27. The range of the function,
$f(x)=\tan^{-1}\left(\frac{1+x}{1-x}\right)-\tan^{-1}x$ is

(a) $\{\pi/4\}$ (b) $\{-(\pi/4), 3\pi/4\}$
(c) $\{\pi/4, -(3\pi/4)\}$ (d) $\{3\pi/4\}$

28. The number of positive integral solutions of $\tan^{-1}x+\cot^{-1}y=\tan^{-1}3$ is

(a) one (b) two (c) three (d) four

29. If $x\in\left(-\frac{\pi}{2},\frac{\pi}{2}\right)$, then the value of $\tan^{-1}\left(\frac{\tan x}{4}\right)+\tan^{-1}\left(\frac{3\sin 2x}{5+3\cos 2x}\right)$ is

(a) $\frac{x}{2}$ (b) $2x$ (c) $3x$ (d) x

30. The value of expression
$\tan^{-1}\left(\frac{\sqrt{2}}{2}\right)+\sin^{-1}\left(\frac{\sqrt{5}}{5}\right)-\cos^{-1}\left(\frac{\sqrt{10}}{10}\right)$ is

(a) $\cot^{-1}\left(\frac{1+\sqrt{2}}{1-\sqrt{2}}\right)$ (b) $\cot^{-1}\left(\frac{\sqrt{2}+1}{\sqrt{2}-1}\right)$

(c) $-\pi+\cot^{-1}\left(\frac{1+\sqrt{2}}{1-\sqrt{2}}\right)$ (d) $\pi-\cot^{-1}\left(\frac{1-\sqrt{2}}{1+\sqrt{2}}\right)$

31. If $\tan^{-1}\frac{b}{c+a}+\tan^{-1}\frac{c}{a+b}=\frac{\pi}{4}$, where a, b, c are the sides of ΔABC, then ΔABC is

(a) Acute angled triangle (b) Obtuse angled triangle
(c) Right angled triangle (d) Equilateral triangle

32. The value of
$$\tan^{-1}\left(\frac{1}{2}\tan 2A\right)+\tan^{-1}(\cot A)+\tan^{-1}(\cot^3 A)\text{ for}$$
$0<A<(\pi/4)$ is

(a) $4\tan^{-1}(1)$ (b) $2\tan^{-1}(2)$
(c) 0 (d) None of these

33. The value of
$$\cos^{-1}\left[\cot\left(\sin^{-1}\sqrt{\frac{2-\sqrt{3}}{4}}+\cos^{-1}\left(\frac{\sqrt{12}}{4}\right)+\sec^{-1}\sqrt{2}\right)\right]\text{ is}$$

(a) 0 (b) $\frac{\pi}{4}$ (c) $\frac{\pi}{6}$ (d) $\frac{\pi}{2}$

34. If $\cos^{-1}\frac{x}{a}-\sin^{-1}\frac{y}{b}=\theta\,(a,b,\neq 0)$, then the maximum value of $b^2x^2+a^2y^2+2ab\,xy\sin\theta$ equals

(a) ab (b) $(a+b)^2$
(c) $2(a+b)^2$ (d) a^2b^2

35. The solution set of the equation
$$\sin^{-1}\sqrt{1-x^2}+\cos^{-1}x=\cot^{-1}\left(\frac{\sqrt{1-x^2}}{x}\right)-\sin^{-1}x$$

(a) $[-1,1]-\{0\}$ (b) $(0,1]\cup\{-1\}$
(c) $[-1,0)\cup\{1\}$ (d) $[-1,1]$

36. There exists a positive real number x satisfying $\cos(\tan^{-1}x)=x$. The number value of $\cos^{-1}\left(\frac{x^2}{2}\right)$ is

(a) $\frac{\pi}{10}$ (b) $\frac{\pi}{5}$ (c) $\frac{2\pi}{5}$ (d) $\frac{4\pi}{5}$

37. The value of α such that $\sin^{-1}\frac{2}{\sqrt{5}}$, $\sin^{-1}\frac{3}{\sqrt{10}}$, $\sin^{-1}\alpha$ are the angles of a triangle is

(a) $\frac{-1}{\sqrt{2}}$ (b) $\frac{1}{2}$ (c) $\frac{1}{\sqrt{3}}$ (d) $\frac{1}{\sqrt{2}}$

38. Let $f(x)=\sin^{-1}\left(\frac{2x}{1+x^2}\right)\forall\, x\in R$. The function $f(x)$ is continuous everywhere but not differentiable at x is/are

(a) 0, 1 (b) – 1, 1
(c) – 1, 0 (d) 0, 2

39. Let
$$f(x)=2\tan^{-1}x=\begin{cases}\cos^{-1}\left(\dfrac{1-x^2}{1+x^2}\right), & x\geq 0\\ -\cos^{-1}\left(\dfrac{1-x^2}{1+x^2}\right), & x<0\end{cases}$$

The function $f(x)$ is continuous everywhere but not differentiable at x equals to

(a) 1 (b) – 1 (c) 0 (d) $\frac{1}{\sqrt{2}}$

40. $\cot\left(\frac{\pi}{4}-2\cot^{-1}3\right)$ is

(a) 1 (b) 7
(c) – 1 (d) None of these

41. If $\cos^{-1}\left(\frac{1-a^2}{1+a^2}\right)-\cos^{-1}\left(\frac{1-b^2}{1+b^2}\right)=2\tan^{-1}x$, then x is

(a) $\frac{a-b}{1+ab}$ (b) $\frac{b-a}{1+ab}$
(c) $\frac{a+b}{1-ab}$ (d) None of these

42. The value of $\sec\left(2\cot^{-1}2+\cos^{-1}\frac{3}{5}\right)$ is equal to

(a) $\frac{25}{24}$ (b) $-\frac{24}{7}$
(c) $\frac{25}{7}$ (d) $-\frac{25}{7}$

Numerical Value Type Questions

43. Let $f(x)=\tan^{-1}\left(\frac{(x-2)}{x^2+2x+2}\right)$, then $26f'(1)$ is ....

44. Let $f(x)=(\text{arc}\tan x)^3+(\text{arc}\cot x)^3$. If the range of $f(x)$ is $[a,b)$, then find the value of $\frac{b}{7a}$.

45. If $\sum_{n=0}^{\infty}2\,\text{arc}\cot\left(\frac{n^2+n+4}{2}\right)=k\pi$, then find the value of k.

46. Find the number of solutions of the equation
$$\tan\left(\sum_{r=1}^{5}\cot^{-1}(2r^2)\right)=\frac{5x+6}{6x+5}.$$

47. $\lim_{z\to 0}\left[\{\max((\sin^{-1}x+\cos^{-1}x)^2,\ \min(x^2+4x+7))\}.\frac{\sin^{-1}z}{z}\right]$ is equal to (where [.] denotes greatest integer function)

48. If $\sin(30°+\text{arc}\tan x)=\frac{13}{14}$ and $0<x<1$, the value of x is $\frac{a\sqrt{3}}{b}$, where a and b are positive integers with no common factors. Find the value of $\left(\frac{a+b}{2}\right)$.

49. Let $f:R\to\left(0,\frac{2\pi}{3}\right]$ defined as $f(x)=\cot^{-1}(x^2-4x+\alpha)$. Find the smallest integral value of α such that $f(x)$ is into function.

50. Let L denotes the number of subjective functions $f: A \to B$, where set A contains 4 elements and set B contains 3 elements, M denotes number of elements in the range of the function $f(x) = \sec^{-1}(\text{sgn } x) + \text{cosec}^{-1}(\text{sgn } x)$, where sgn x denotes signum function of x and N denotes coefficient of t^5 in $(1+t^2)^5 (1+t^3)^8$. Find the value of $(N - LM)$

51. Number of solution(s) of the equations $\cos^{-1}(\cos x) = x^2$ is ....

52. If $\cos^{-1}(x) + \cos^{-1}(y) + \cos^{-1}(z) = \pi(\sec^2(u) + \sec^4(v) + \sec^6(w))$, where u, v, w are least non-negative angles such that $u < v < w$, then the value of $x^{2000} + y^{2002} + z^{2004} + \dfrac{36\pi}{u+v+w}$ is ....

Previous Year Questions

53. If the domain of the function $f(x) = \sin^{-1}\left(\dfrac{x-1}{2x+3}\right)$ is $R - (\alpha, \beta)$, then $12\alpha\beta$ is equal to

[Single Correct Type, 2024 Main]

(a) 36 (b) 32 (c) 40 (d) 24

54. Given that the inverse trigonometric function assumes principal values only. Let x, y be any two real numbers in $[-1, 1]$ such that $\cos^{-1} x - \sin^{-1} y = \alpha, \dfrac{-\pi}{2} \le \alpha \le \pi$.

Then, the minimum value of $x^2 + y^2 + 2xy \sin\alpha$ is

(a) 0 (b) $\dfrac{-1}{2}$ (c) $\dfrac{1}{2}$ (d) -1

[Single Correct Type, 2024 Main]

55. Let the inverse trigonometric function take principal values. The number of real solutions of the equation $2\sin^{-1} x + 3\cos^{-1} x = \dfrac{2\pi}{5}$, is ....

[Numerical Value Type, 2023 Main]

56. For $n \in N$, if $\cot^{-1} 3 + \cot^{-1} 4 + \cot^{-1} 5 + \cot^{-1} n = \dfrac{\pi}{4}$, then n is equal to .... **[Numerical Value Type, 2023 Main]**

57. For $\alpha, \beta, \gamma = \theta$, if $\sin^{-1}\alpha + \sin^{-1}\beta + \sin^{-1}\gamma = \pi$ and $(\alpha+\beta+\gamma)(\alpha-\gamma+\beta) = 3\alpha\beta$, then γ equals

[Single Correct Type, 2024 Main]

(a) $\dfrac{\sqrt{3}-1}{2\sqrt{2}}$ (b) $\sqrt{3}$ (c) $\dfrac{\sqrt{3}}{2}$ (d) $\dfrac{1}{\sqrt{2}}$

58. If the domain of the function

$f(x) = \log_e\left(\dfrac{2x+3}{4x^2+x-3}\right) + \cos^{-1}\left(\dfrac{2x-1}{x+2}\right)$ is $(\alpha, \beta]$, then the value of $5\beta - 4\alpha$ is equal to

[Single Correct Type, 2024 Main]

(a) 11 (b) 9 (c) 12 (d) 10

59. Considering only the principal values of inverse trigonometric functions, the number of positive real values of x satisfying $\tan^{-1}(x) + \tan^{-1}(2x) = \dfrac{\pi}{4}$ is

[Single Correct Type, 2024 Main]

(a) 2 (b) 0
(c) more than 2 (d) 1

60. The range of $f(x) = 4\sin^{-1}\left(\dfrac{x^2}{x^2+1}\right)$ is

[Single Correct Type, 2023 Main]

(a) $[0, \pi)$ (b) $[0, \pi]$ (c) $[0, 2\pi)$ (d) $[0, 2\pi]$

61. Let $S = \left\{ x \in R : 0 < x < 1 \text{ and } 2\tan^{-1}\left(\dfrac{1-x}{1+x}\right) = \cos^{-1}\left(\dfrac{1-x^2}{1+x^2}\right) \right\}$. If $n(S)$ denotes the number of elements in S, then

[Single Correct Type, 2023 Main]

(a) $n(S) = 1$ and the element in S is less than $\dfrac{1}{2}$

(b) $n(S) = 2$ and only one element in S is less than $\dfrac{1}{2}$

(c) $n(S) = 0$

(d) $n(S) = 1$ and the elements in S is more than $\dfrac{1}{2}$

62. Let S be the set of all solutions of the equation $\cos^{-1}(2x) - 2\cos^{-1}(\sqrt{1-x^2}) = \pi, x \in \left[-\dfrac{1}{2}, \dfrac{1}{2}\right]$. Then, $\sum_{x \in S} 2\sin^{-1}(x^2 - 1)$ is equal to

[Single Correct Type, 2023 Main]

(a) $\pi - 2\sin^{-1}\left(\dfrac{\sqrt{3}}{4}\right)$ (b) $\dfrac{-2\pi}{3}$

(c) 0 (d) $\pi - \sin^{-1}\left(\dfrac{\sqrt{3}}{4}\right)$

63. Let $a_1 = 1, a_2, a_3, a_4, \ldots\ldots$ be consecutive natural numbers. Then, $\tan^{-1}\left(\dfrac{1}{1+a_1a_2}\right) + \tan^{-1}\left(\dfrac{1}{1+a_2a_3}\right) + \ldots + \tan^{-1}\left(\dfrac{1}{1+a_{2021}a_{2022}}\right)$ is equal to

[Single Correct Type, 2023 Main]

(a) $\dfrac{\pi}{4} - \cot^{-1}(2022)$ (b) $\tan^{-1}(2022) - \dfrac{\pi}{4}$

(c) $\dfrac{\pi}{4} - \tan^{-1}(2022)$ (d) $\cot^{-1}(2022) - \dfrac{\pi}{4}$

64. If $\sin^{-1}\dfrac{\alpha}{17} + \cos^{-1}\dfrac{4}{5} - \tan^{-1}\dfrac{77}{36} = 0, 0 < \alpha < 13$, then $\sin^{-1}(\sin\alpha) + \cos^{-1}(\cos\alpha)$ is equal to

[Single Correct Type, 2023 Main]

(a) 0 (b) π (c) 16 (d) $16 - 5\pi$

65. $\tan^{-1}\left(\frac{1+\sqrt{3}}{3+\sqrt{3}}\right)+\sec^{-1}\left(\sqrt{\frac{8+4\sqrt{3}}{6+3\sqrt{3}}}\right)$ is equal to

[Single Correct Type, 2023 Main]

(a) $\frac{\pi}{4}$ (b) $\frac{\pi}{6}$
(c) $\frac{\pi}{2}$ (d) $\frac{\pi}{3}$

66. If the domain of the function $f(x)=\sec^{-1}\left(\frac{2x}{5x+3}\right)$ is $[\alpha, \beta) \cup (\gamma, \delta]$, then $|3\alpha+10(\beta+\gamma)+21\delta|$ is equal to ....

[Numerical Value Type, 2023 Main]

67. If $S=\left\{x \in R : \sin^{-1}\left(\frac{x+1}{\sqrt{x^2+2x+2}}\right)-\sin^{-1}\left(\frac{x}{\sqrt{x^2+1}}\right)=\frac{\pi}{4}\right\}$, then $\sum_{x \in S}\left(\sin\left((x^2+x+5)\frac{\pi}{2}\right)-\cos((x^2+x+5)\pi)\right)$ is equal to ....

[Numerical Value Type, 2023 Main]

68. For $x \in (-1, 1]$, the number of solutions of the equation $\sin^{-1} x = 2\tan^{-1} x$ is equal to ....

[Numerical Value Type, 2023 Main]

69. If the sum of all the solutions of $\tan^{-1}\left(\frac{2x}{1-x^2}\right)+\cot^{-1}\left(\frac{1-x^2}{2x}\right)=\frac{\pi}{3}, -1<x<1, x \neq 0$, is $\alpha-\frac{4}{\sqrt{3}}$, then α is equal to ....

[Numerical Value Type, 2023 Main]

70. The domain of the function $f(x)=\sin^{-1}\left(\frac{x^2-3x+2}{x^2+2x+7}\right)$ is

[Single Correct Type, 2022 Main]

(a) $[1, \infty)$ (b) $(-1, 2]$
(c) $[-1, \infty)$ (d) $(-\infty, 2]$

71. The domain of the function $\cos^{-1}\left(\frac{2\sin^{-1}\left(\frac{1}{4x^2-1}\right)}{\pi}\right)$ is

[Single Correct Type, 2022 Main]

(a) $R-\left\{-\frac{1}{2}, \frac{1}{2}\right\}$
(b) $(-\infty, -1] \cup [1, \infty) \cup \{0\}$
(c) $\left(-\infty, \frac{-1}{2}\right) \cup \left(\frac{1}{2}, \infty\right) \cup \{0\}$
(d) $\left(-\infty, \frac{-1}{\sqrt{2}}\right] \cup \left[\frac{1}{\sqrt{2}}, \infty\right) \cup \{0\}$

72. Considering only the principal values of the inverse trigonometric functions, the domain of the function $f(x)=\cos^{-1}\left(\frac{x^2-4x+2}{x^2+3}\right)$ is

[Single Correct Type, 2022 Main]

(a) $\left(-\infty, \frac{1}{4}\right]$ (b) $\left[-\frac{1}{4}, \infty\right)$ (c) $\left(\frac{-1}{3}, \infty\right)$ (d) $\left(-\infty, \frac{1}{3}\right]$

73. The domain of the function $f(x)=\sin^{-1}[2x^2-3]+\log_2\left(\log_{\frac{1}{2}}(x^2-5x+5)\right)$, where $[t]$ is the greatest integer function, is

[Single Correct Type, 2022 Main]

(a) $\left(-\sqrt{\frac{5}{2}}, \frac{5-\sqrt{5}}{2}\right)$ (b) $\left(\frac{5-\sqrt{5}}{2}, \frac{5+\sqrt{5}}{2}\right)$
(c) $\left(1, \frac{5-\sqrt{5}}{2}\right)$ (d) $\left[1, \frac{5+\sqrt{5}}{2}\right)$

74. The domain of the function $f(x)=\frac{\cos^{-1}\left(\frac{x^2-5x+6}{x^2-9}\right)}{\log_e(x^2-3x+2)}$ is

[Single Correct Type, 2022 Main]

(a) $(-\infty, 1) \cup (2, \infty)$
(b) $(2, \infty)$
(c) $\left[-\frac{1}{2}, 1\right) \cup (2, \infty)$
(d) $\left[-\frac{1}{2}, 1\right) \cup (2, \infty)-\left\{\frac{3+\sqrt{5}}{2}, \frac{3-\sqrt{5}}{2}\right\}$

75. If the domain of the function $f(x)=\frac{\cos^{-1}\sqrt{x^2-x+1}}{\sqrt{\sin^{-1}\left(\frac{2x-1}{2}\right)}}$ is the interval $(\alpha, \beta]$, then $\alpha+\beta$ is equal to

[Single Correct Type, 2022 Main]

(a) $\frac{3}{2}$ (b) 2 (c) $\frac{1}{2}$ (d) 1

76. If $0<x<\frac{1}{\sqrt{2}}$ and $\frac{\sin^{-1} x}{\alpha}=\frac{\cos^{-1} x}{\beta}$, then the value of $\sin\left(\frac{2\pi\alpha}{\alpha+\beta}\right)$ is

[Single Correct Type, 2022 Main]

(a) $4\sqrt{(1-x^2)}\,(1-2x^2)$ (b) $4x\sqrt{(1-x^2)}\,(1-2x^2)$
(c) $2x\sqrt{(1-x^2)}\,(1-4x^2)$ (d) $4\sqrt{(1-x^2)}\,(1-4x^2)$

77. $\tan\left(2\tan^{-1}\frac{1}{5}+\sec^{-1}\frac{\sqrt{5}}{2}+2\tan^{-1}\frac{1}{8}\right)$ is equal to

[Single Correct Type, 2022 Main]

(a) 1 (b) 2 (c) 1/4 (d) 5/4

78. Let m and M respectively be the minimum and the maximum values of $f(x) = \sin^{-1} 2x + \sin 2x$

$$+ \cos^{-1} 2x + \cos 2x,\ x \in \left[0, \frac{\pi}{8}\right].$$

Then, $m + M$ is equal to **[Single Correct Type, 2022 Main]**

(a) $1 + \sqrt{2} + \pi$ (b) $(1 + \sqrt{2})\pi$
(c) $\pi + \sqrt{2}$ (d) $1 + \pi$

79. $\sin^{-1}\left(\sin \frac{2\pi}{3}\right) + \cos^{-1}\left(\cos \frac{7\pi}{6}\right) + \tan^{-1}\left(\tan \frac{3\pi}{4}\right)$ is equal to **[Single Correct Type, 2022 Main]**

(a) $\frac{11\pi}{12}$ (b) $\frac{17\pi}{12}$ (c) $\frac{31\pi}{12}$ (d) $-\frac{3\pi}{4}$

80. The value of $\cot\left(\sum_{n=1}^{50} \tan^{-1}\left(\frac{1}{1+n+n^2}\right)\right)$ is

[Single Correct Type, 2022 Main]

(a) $\frac{26}{25}$ (b) $\frac{25}{26}$ (c) $\frac{50}{51}$ (d) $\frac{52}{51}$

81. The value of $\tan^{-1}\left(\frac{\cos\left(\frac{15\pi}{4}\right) - 1}{\sin\left(\frac{\pi}{4}\right)}\right)$ is equal to

[Single Correct Type, 2022 Main]

(a) $-\frac{\pi}{4}$ (b) $-\frac{\pi}{8}$ (c) $-\frac{5\pi}{12}$ (d) $-\frac{4\pi}{9}$

82. Let $x = \sin(2\tan^{-1}\alpha)$ and $y = \sin\left(\frac{1}{2}\tan^{-1}\frac{4}{3}\right)$.

If $S = [a \in R : y^2 = 1 - x]$, then $\sum_{\alpha \in S} 16\alpha^3$ is equal to ....

[Numerical Value Type, 2022 Main]

83. $50 \tan\left(3\tan^{-1}\left(\frac{1}{2}\right) + 2\cos^{-1}\left(\frac{1}{\sqrt{5}}\right)\right) +$

$4\sqrt{2}\tan\left(\frac{1}{2}\tan^{-1}(2\sqrt{2})\right)$ is equal to ....

[Numerical Value Type, 2022 Main]

84. The domain of the function

$f(x) = \sin^{-1}\left(\frac{3x^2 + x - 1}{(x-1)^2}\right) + \cos^{-1}\left(\frac{x-1}{x+1}\right)$ is

[Single Correct Type, 2021 Main]

(a) $\left[0, \frac{1}{4}\right]$ (b) $[-2, 0] \cup \left[\frac{1}{4}, \frac{1}{2}\right]$
(c) $\left[\frac{1}{4}, \frac{1}{2}\right] \cup \{0\}$ (d) $\left[0, \frac{1}{2}\right]$

85. The value of $\tan\left(2\tan^{-1}\left(\frac{3}{5}\right) + \sin^{-1}\left(\frac{5}{13}\right)\right)$ is equal to

[Single Correct Type, 2021 Main]

(a) $\frac{-181}{69}$ (b) $\frac{220}{21}$ (c) $\frac{-291}{76}$ (d) $\frac{151}{63}$

86. If $0 < a, b < 1$ and $\tan^{-1} a + \tan^{-1} b = \pi/4$, then the value of

$(a+b) - \left(\frac{a^2+b^2}{2}\right) + \left(\frac{a^3+b^3}{3}\right) - \left(\frac{a^4+b^4}{4}\right) + \ldots$ is

[Single Correct Type, 2021 Main]

(a) $\log_e 2$ (b) $e^2 - 1$ (c) e (d) $\log_e (e/2)$

87. $2\pi - \left(\sin^{-1}\frac{4}{5} + \sin^{-1}\frac{5}{13} + \sin^{-1}\frac{16}{65}\right)$ is equal to

[Single Correct Type, 2020 Main]

(a) $\frac{\pi}{2}$ (b) $\frac{5\pi}{4}$ (c) $\frac{3\pi}{2}$ (d) $\frac{7\pi}{4}$

88. The domain of the function

$f(x) = \sin^{-1}\left(\frac{|x|+5}{x^2+1}\right)$ is $(-\infty, -a] \cup [a, \infty)$. Then, a is equal to **[Single Correct Type, 2020 Main]**

(a) $\frac{\sqrt{17}}{2} + 1$ (b) $\frac{\sqrt{17} - 1}{2}$ (c) $\frac{1 + \sqrt{17}}{2}$ (d) $\frac{\sqrt{17}}{2}$

89. The value of $\sin^{-1}\left(\frac{12}{13}\right) - \sin^{-1}\left(\frac{3}{5}\right)$ is equal to

[Single Correct Type, 2019 Main]

(a) $\pi - \sin^{-1}\left(\frac{63}{65}\right)$ (b) $\frac{\pi}{2} - \sin^{-1}\left(\frac{56}{65}\right)$
(c) $\frac{\pi}{2} - \cos^{-1}\left(\frac{9}{65}\right)$ (d) $\pi - \cos^{-1}\left(\frac{33}{65}\right)$

90. The value of $\cot\left(\sum_{n=1}^{19} \cot^{-1}\left(1 + \sum_{p=1}^{n} 2p\right)\right)$ is

[Single Correct Type, 2019 Main]

(a) 23/22 (b) 21/19 (c) 19/21 (d) 22/23

91. If $x = \sin^{-1}(\sin 10)$ and $y = \cos^{-1}(\cos 10)$, then $y - x$ is equal to **[Single Correct Type, 2019 Main]**

(a) 0 (b) 10 (c) 7π (d) π

92. If $\cos^{-1} x - \cos^{-1}\frac{y}{2} = \alpha$, where $-1 \le x \le 1$, $-2 \le y \le 2$, $x \le \frac{y}{2}$, then for all x, y, $4x^2 - 4xy\cos\alpha + y^2$ is equal to

[Single Correct Type, 2019 Main]

(a) $2\sin^2\alpha$ (b) $4\cos^2\alpha + 2x^2y^2$
(c) $4\sin^2\alpha$ (d) $4\sin^2\alpha - 2x^2y^2$

93. Let $f(x) = \log_e(\sin x)$, $(0 < x < \pi)$ and $g(x) = \sin^{-1}(e^{-x})$, $(x \ge 0)$. If α is a positive real number such that $a = (fog)'(\alpha)$ and $b = (fog)(\alpha)$, then

[Single Correct Type, 2019 Main]

(a) $a\alpha^2 - b\alpha - a = 0$ (b) $a\alpha^2 - b\alpha - a = 1$
(c) $a\alpha^2 + b\alpha - a = -2\alpha^2$ (d) $a\alpha^2 + b\alpha + a = 0$

94. If $\alpha = \cos^{-1}\left(\frac{3}{5}\right), \beta = \tan^{-1}\left(\frac{1}{3}\right)$, where $0 < \alpha, \beta < \frac{\pi}{2}$, then $\alpha - \beta$ is equal to **[Single Correct Type, 2019 Main]**

(a) $\tan^{-1}\left(\frac{9}{5\sqrt{10}}\right)$

(b) $\cos^{-1}\left(\frac{9}{5\sqrt{10}}\right)$

(c) $\tan^{-1}\left(\frac{9}{14}\right)$

(d) $\sin^{-1}\left(\frac{9}{5\sqrt{10}}\right)$

95. Considering only the principal values of inverse functions, the set $A = \left\{x \geq 0: \tan^{-1}(2x) + \tan^{-1}(3x) = \frac{\pi}{4}\right\}$ **[Single Correct Type, 2019 Main]**

(a) is an empty set
(b) is a singleton
(c) contains more than two elements
(d) contains two elements

96. The value of $\tan^{-1}\left[\frac{\sqrt{1+x^2}+\sqrt{1-x^2}}{\sqrt{1+x^2}-\sqrt{1-x^2}}\right], |x| < \frac{1}{2}, x \neq 0,$ is equal to **[Single Correct Type, 2017 Main]**

(a) $\frac{\pi}{4} + \frac{1}{2}\cos^{-1} x^2$ (b) $\frac{\pi}{4} + \cos^{-1} x^2$

(c) $\frac{\pi}{4} - \frac{1}{2}\cos^{-1} x^2$ (d) $\frac{\pi}{4} - \cos^{-1} x^2$

97. Let $\tan^{-1} y = \tan^{-1} x + \tan^{-1}\left(\frac{2x}{1-x^2}\right)$, where $|x| < \frac{1}{\sqrt{3}}$. Then, a value of y is **[Single Correct Type, 2015 Main]**

(a) $\frac{3x - x^3}{1+3x^2}$ (b) $\frac{3x + x^3}{1+3x^2}$ (c) $\frac{3x - x^3}{1-3x^2}$ (d) $\frac{3x + x^3}{1-3x^2}$

98. The principal value of $\tan^{-1}\left(\cot\frac{43\pi}{4}\right)$ is **[Single Correct Type, 2014 Main]**

(a) $-\frac{3\pi}{4}$ (b) $\frac{3\pi}{4}$ (c) $-\frac{\pi}{4}$ (d) $\frac{\pi}{4}$

EXERCISE 2

JEE Advanced Pattern

Single Option Correct Type Questions

1. Number of values of x satisfying the equation $\cos(3\,\text{arc}\cos(x-1)) = 0$ is equal to
(a) 0 (b) 1
(c) 2 (d) 3

2. The number k is such that $\tan\{\text{arc}\tan(2) + \text{arc}\tan(20k)\} = k$. The sum of all possible values of k is
(a) $-\frac{19}{40}$ (b) $-\frac{21}{40}$ (c) 0 (d) $\frac{1}{5}$

3. Let $f : R \to \left[0, \frac{\pi}{2}\right)$ be defined by $f(x) = \tan^{-1}(3x^2 + 6x + a)$. If $f(x)$ is an onto function, then the value of a is
(a) 1 (b) 2 (c) 3 (d) 4

4. The number of integer x satisfying $\sin^{-1}|x-2| + \cos^{-1}(1 - |3-x|) = \frac{\pi}{2}$ is
(a) 1 (b) 2 (c) 3 (d) 4

5. Let $\begin{vmatrix} \tan^{-1} x & \tan^{-1} 2x & \tan^{-1} 3x \\ \tan^{-1} 3x & \tan^{-1} x & \tan^{-1} 2x \\ \tan^{-1} 2x & \tan^{-1} 3x & \tan^{-1} x \end{vmatrix} = 0$, then the number of values of x satisfying the equation is
(a) 1 (b) 2 (c) 3 (d) 4

6. Complete solution set of $[\cot^{-1} x] + 2[\tan^{-1} x] = 0$, where [.] denotes the greatest integer function, is equal to
(a) $(0, \cot 1)$ (b) $(0, \tan 1)$
(c) $(\tan 1, \infty)$ (d) $(\cot 1, \tan 1)$

7. If $\tan^{-1}\frac{\sqrt{1+x^2}-1}{x} = 4°$, then
(a) $x = \tan 2°$ (b) $x = \tan 4°$
(c) $x = \tan(1/4)°$ (d) $x = \tan 8°$

8. The equation $e^{\frac{2\sin^{-1} x}{\pi}} = \frac{y}{\log y}$, has
(a) Unique solution (b) Infinite many solution
(c) $x = 1$ (d) $y = e$

9. If $x = \tan^{-1} 1 - \cos^{-1}\left(-\frac{1}{2}\right) + \sin^{-1}\frac{1}{2}$; $y = \cos\left(\frac{1}{2}\cos^{-1}\left(\frac{1}{8}\right)\right)$, then
(a) $x = \pi y$ (b) $y = \pi x$
(c) $\tan x = -(4/3)y$ (d) $\tan x = (4/3)y$

10. The number of solutions of the equation $|\tan^{-1}|x|| = \sqrt{(x^2+1)^2 - 4x^2}$ is
(a) 1 (b) 2 (c) 3 (d) 4

11. Solutions of $\sin^{-1}(\sin x) = \sin x$ are, if $x \in (0, 2\pi)$
(a) 1 real root (b) 2 positive real roots
(c) 2 negative real roots (d) 5 real roots

12. Number of solutions of the equation $\log_{10}(\sqrt{5\cos^{-1} x - 1}) + \frac{1}{2}\log_{10}(2\cos^{-1} x + 3) + \log_{10}\sqrt{5} = 1$ is
(a) 0
(b) 1
(c) more than one but finite
(d) infinite

13. Which of the following is the solution set of the equations $\sin^{-1} x = \cos^{-1} x + \sin^{-1}(3x-2)$?
(a) $\left\{\frac{1}{2}, 1\right\}$ (b) $\left[\frac{1}{2}, 1\right]$ (c) $\left[\frac{1}{3}, 1\right]$ (d) $\left\{\frac{1}{3}, 1\right\}$

14. Let $g : R \to \left(0, \frac{\pi}{3}\right]$ is defined by $g(x) = \cos^{-1}\left(\frac{x^2 - k}{1 + x^2}\right)$
Then, the possible values of 'k' for which g is surjective function, is
(a) $\left\{\frac{1}{2}\right\}$ (b) $\left(-1, -\frac{1}{2}\right]$
(c) $\left\{-\frac{1}{2}\right\}$ (d) $\left[-\frac{1}{2}, 1\right)$

15. Number of values of x satisfying simultaneously $\sin^{-1} x = 2\tan^{-1} x$ and $\tan^{-1}\sqrt{x(x-1)} + \text{cosec}^{-1}\sqrt{1 + x - x^2} = \frac{\pi}{2}$, is
(a) 0 (b) 1
(c) 2 (d) 3

16. The inequality $\sin^{-1}(\sin 5) > x^2 - 4x$ holds if

(a) $x = 2 - \sqrt{9 - 2\pi}$
(b) $x = 2 + \sqrt{9 - 2\pi}$
(c) $x \in (2 - \sqrt{9 - 2\pi}, 2 + \sqrt{9 - 2\pi})$
(d) $x > 2 + \sqrt{9 - 2\pi}$

17. Solution set of the inequality $(\cot^{-1} x)^2 - (5\cot^{-1} x) + 6 > 0$ is

(a) $(\cot 3, \cot 2)$
(b) $(-\infty, \cot 3) \cup (\cot 2, \infty)$
(c) $(\cot 2, \infty)$
(d) None of these

18. If $\left|\cos^{-1}\left(\frac{1 - x^2}{1 + x^2}\right)\right| < \frac{\pi}{3}$, then

(a) $x \in \left[-\frac{1}{\sqrt{3}}, \frac{1}{\sqrt{3}}\right]$
(b) $x \in \left(-\frac{1}{\sqrt{3}}, \frac{1}{\sqrt{3}}\right)$
(c) $x \in \left[0, \frac{1}{\sqrt{3}}\right]$
(d) None of these

19. The set of values of x, satisfying the equation $\tan^2(\sin^{-1} x) > 1$ is

(a) $[-1,1]$
(b) $\left[-\frac{\sqrt{2}}{2}, \frac{\sqrt{2}}{2}\right]$
(c) $(-1, 1) - \left[-\frac{\sqrt{2}}{2}, \frac{\sqrt{2}}{2}\right]$
(d) $[-1,1] - \left(-\frac{\sqrt{2}}{2}, \frac{\sqrt{2}}{2}\right)$

20. If $\tan^{-1}\frac{x}{\pi} < \frac{\pi}{3}$, $x \in N$, then the maximum value of x is

(a) 2
(b) 5
(c) 7
(d) None of these

21. Let $f(x) = \tan^{-1}(x^2 - 18x + a) > 0 \ \forall \ x \in R$. Then, the value of a lies in

(a) $(81, \infty)$
(b) $[81, \infty)$
(c) $(-\infty, 81)$
(d) $(-\infty, 81]$

22. If $\tan^{-1}(\sin^2\theta - 2\sin\theta + 3) + \cot^{-1}(5^{\sec^2 y} + 1) = \frac{\pi}{2}$, then the value of $\cos^2\theta - \sin\theta$ is equal to

(a) 0
(b) -1
(c) 1
(d) None of these

23. The maximum value of $f(x) = \tan^{-1}\left(\frac{(\sqrt{12} - 2)x^2}{x^4 + 2x^2 + 3}\right)$ is

(a) 18°
(b) 36°
(c) 22.5°
(d) 15°

24. Sum of infinite terms of the series $\cot^{-1}\left(1^2 + \frac{3}{4}\right) + \cot^{-1}\left(2^2 + \frac{3}{4}\right) + \cot^{-1}\left(3^2 + \frac{3}{4}\right) + \ldots$ is

(a) $\frac{\pi}{4}$
(b) $\tan^{-1} 2$
(c) $\tan^{-1} 3$
(d) $\tan^{-1} 4$

25. Sum to infinite terms of the series $\tan^{-1}\left(\frac{1}{3}\right) + \tan^{-1}\left(\frac{2}{9}\right) + \tan^{-1}\left(\frac{4}{33}\right) + \ldots + \tan^{-1}\left(\frac{2^{n-1}}{1 + 2^{2n-1}}\right) + \ldots$

(a) $\frac{\pi}{4}$
(b) $\frac{\pi}{2}$
(c) π
(d) None of these

26. The value of $\sum_{r=2}^{\infty} \tan^{-1}\left(\frac{1}{r^2 - 5r + 7}\right)$ is

(a) $\frac{\pi}{4}$
(b) $\frac{\pi}{2}$
(c) $\frac{3\pi}{4}$
(d) $\frac{5\pi}{4}$

27. The sum $\sum_{n=1}^{\infty} \tan^{-1}\left(\frac{4n}{n^4 - 2n^2 + 2}\right)$ is equal to

(a) $\tan^{-1}\frac{1}{2} + \tan^{-1}\frac{2}{3}$
(b) $4\tan^{-1} 1$
(c) $\frac{\pi}{2}$
(d) $\sec^{-1}(-\sqrt{2})$

28. The value of $\sum_{r=1}^{\infty} \tan^{-1}\left(\frac{1}{r^2 + 5r + 7}\right)$ is equal to

(a) $\tan^{-1} 3$
(b) $\frac{\pi}{4}$
(c) $\sin^{-1}\frac{1}{\sqrt{10}}$
(d) $\cot^{-1} 2$

29. The sum of infinite terms of the series $\cot^{-1}\left(1^2 + \frac{3}{4}\right) + \cot\left(2^2 + \frac{3}{4}\right) + \cot^{-1}\left(3^2 + \frac{3}{4}\right) + \ldots$ is

(a) $\frac{\pi}{4}$
(b) $\tan^{-1} 2$
(c) $\tan^{-1} 3$
(d) None of these

30. The value of $\tan^{-1}\left(\frac{1}{3}\right) + \tan^{-1}\left(\frac{1}{7}\right) + \tan^{-1}\left(\frac{1}{13}\right) + \ldots + \tan^{-1}\left(\frac{1}{n^2 + n + 1}\right)$ is

(a) $\frac{\pi}{2}$
(b) $\frac{\pi}{4}$
(c) $\frac{2\pi}{3}$
(d) 0

More than One Correct Option Type Questions

31. Let $\theta = \tan^{-1}\left(\tan\frac{5\pi}{4}\right)$ and $\phi = \tan^{-1}\left(-\tan\frac{2\pi}{3}\right)$, then

(a) $\theta > \phi$
(b) $4\theta - 3\phi = 0$
(c) $\theta + \phi = \frac{7\pi}{12}$
(d) None of these

32. Let $f(x) = e^{\cos^{-1}\sin(x + \pi/3)}$, then

(a) $f\left(\frac{8\pi}{9}\right) = e^{5\pi/18}$
(b) $f\left(\frac{8\pi}{9}\right) = e^{13\pi/18}$
(c) $f\left(-\frac{7\pi}{4}\right) = e^{\pi/12}$
(d) $f\left(-\frac{7\pi}{4}\right) = e^{11\pi/12}$

33. If the numerical value of $\tan\left\{\cos^{-1}\left(\frac{4}{5}\right)+\tan^{-1}\left(\frac{2}{3}\right)\right\}$ is $\frac{a}{b}$, HCF $(a, b) = 1$, then

(a) $a + b = 23$ (b) $a - b = 11$
(c) $3b = a + 1$ (d) $2a = 3b$

34. Let $f(x) = \sin^{-1} x + \cos^{-1} x$. Then, $\frac{\pi}{2}$ is equal to

(a) $f\left(-\frac{1}{2}\right)$ (b) $f(k^2 - 2k + 3), k \in R$
(c) $f\left(\frac{1}{1+k^2}\right), k \in R$ (d) $f(-2)$

35. $\cos^{-1} x = \tan^{-1} x$, then

(a) $x^2 = \frac{\sqrt{5}-1}{2}$
(b) $x^2 = \frac{\sqrt{5}+1}{2}$
(c) $\sin(\cos^{-1} x) = \frac{\sqrt{5}-1}{2}$
(d) $\tan(\cos^{-1} x) = \frac{\sqrt{5}-1}{2}$

36. The value(s) of x satisfying the equation $\sin^{-1}|\sin x| = \sqrt{\sin^{-1}|\sin x|}$ is/are given by (n is any integer)

(a) $n\pi - 1$ (b) $n\pi$
(c) $n\pi + 1$ (d) $2n\pi + 1$

37. If $(\sin^{-1} x + \sin^{-1} w)(\sin^{-1} y + \sin^{-1} z) = \pi^2$, then

$$D = \begin{vmatrix} x^{N_1} & y^{N_2} \\ z^{N_3} & w^{N_4} \end{vmatrix} (N_1, N_2, N_3, N_4 \in N)$$

(a) has a maximum value of 2
(b) has a minimum value of 0
(c) 16 different D are possible
(d) has a minimum value of -2

38. Indicate the relation which can hold in their respective domain for infinite values of x.

(a) $\tan|\tan^{-1} x| = |x|$ (b) $\cot|\cot^{-1} x| = |x|$
(c) $\tan^{-1}|\tan x| = |x|$ (d) $\sin|\sin^{-1} x| = |x|$

39. To the equation $2^{2\pi/\cos^{-1} x} - \left(a + \frac{1}{2}\right) \cdot 2^{\pi/\cos^{-1} x} - a^2 = 0$ has only one real root, then

(a) $1 \le a \le 3$ (b) $a \ge 1$
(c) $a \le -3$ (d) $a \ge 3$

40. $\sin^{-1}(\sin 3) + \sin^{-1}(\sin 4) + \sin^{-1}(\sin 5)$ when simplified reduces to

(a) an irrational number (b) a rational number
(c) an even prime (d) a negative integer

41. If $\cos^{-1} x + \cos^{-1} y + \cos^{-1} z = \pi$, then

(a) $x^2 + y^2 + z^2 + 2xyz = 1$
(b) $2(\sin^{-1} x + \sin^{-1} y + \sin^{-1} z) = \cos^{-1} x + \cos^{-1} y + \cos^{-1} z$
(c) $xy + yz + zx = x + y + z - 1$
(d) $\left(x + \frac{1}{x}\right) + \left(y + \frac{1}{y}\right) + \left(z + \frac{1}{z}\right) \ge 6$

42. $2\tan(\tan^{-1}(x) + \tan^{-1}(x^3))$ where $x \in R - \{-1, 1\}$ is equal to

(a) $\frac{2x}{1-x^2}$
(b) $\tan(2\tan^{-1} x)$
(c) $\tan(\cot^{-1}(-x) - \cot^{-1}(x))$
(d) $\tan(2\cot^{-1} x)$

43. Let $f(x) = \sin^{-1}|\sin x| + \cos^{-1}(\cos x)$. Which of the following statement(s) is/are TRUE?

(a) $f(f(3)) = \pi$
(b) $f(x)$ is periodic with fundamental period 2π
(c) $f(x)$ is neither even nor odd
(d) Range of $f(x)$ is $[0, 2\pi]$

44. If $f(x) = \sin^{-1} x \cdot \cos^{-1} x \cdot \tan^{-1} x \cdot \cot^{-1} x \cdot \sec^{-1} x \cdot \operatorname{cosec}^{-1} x$, then which of the following statement(s) hold(s) good?

(a) The graph of $y = f(x)$ does not lie above X-axis
(b) The non-negative difference between maximum minimum value of the function $y = f(x)$ is $\frac{3\pi^6}{64}$
(c) The function $y = f(x)$ is not injective.
(d) Number of non-negative integers in the domain of $f(x)$ is two.

45. Let $\alpha = 3\cos^{-1}\left(\frac{5}{\sqrt{28}}\right) + 3\tan^{-1}\left(\frac{\sqrt{3}}{2}\right)$ and $\beta = 4\sin^{-1}\left(\frac{7\sqrt{2}}{10}\right) - 4\tan^{-1}\left(\frac{3}{4}\right)$, then which of the following does not hold(s) good?

(a) $\alpha < \pi$ but $\beta > \pi$
(b) $\alpha > \pi$ but $\beta < \pi$
(c) Both α and β are equal
(d) $\cos(\alpha + \beta) = 0$

46. Let function $f(x)$ be defined as $f(x) = |\sin^{-1} x| + \cos^{-1}\left(\frac{1}{x}\right)$. Then, which of the following is/are TRUE?

(a) $f(x)$ is injective in its domain.
(b) $f(x)$ is many-one in its domain.
(c) Range of f is singleton set.
(d) $\operatorname{sgn}(f(x)) = 1$, where sgn x denotes signum function of x.

47. Which of the following pairs(s) of function is(are) identical?

(a) $f(x)=\sin(\tan^{-1}x),\ g(x)=\dfrac{x}{\sqrt{1+x^2}}$

(b) $f(x)=\operatorname{sgn}(\cot^{-1}x),\ g(x)=\sec^2 x-\tan^2 x$, where sgn x denotes signum function of x.

(c) $f(x)=e^{\ln\left(\cos^{-1}\left(\frac{x^2-1}{x^2+1}\right)\right)},\ g(x)=\cos^{-1}\left(\dfrac{x^2-1}{x^2+1}\right)$

(d) $f(x)=\sin^{-1}\left(\dfrac{2x}{1+x^2}\right),\ g(x)=2\tan^{-1}x$

48. The value of $\sum_{n=1}^{\infty}\cot^{-1}(n^2+n+1)$ is also equal to

(a) $\cot^{-1}(-1)+\sec^{-1}(1)-\operatorname{cosec}^{-1}(1)$

(b) $\cot^{-1}(2)+\cot^{-1}(3)$

(c) minimum value of the function $f(x)=\tan^{-1}\left(\dfrac{1-x^2}{1+x^2}\right)$

(d) $\cos^{-1}\left(\cos 41\dfrac{\pi}{4}\right)$

49. Let $f:I-\{-1,0,1\}\to[-\pi,\pi]$ be defined as

$f(x)=2\tan^{-1}x-\tan^{-1}\left(\dfrac{2x}{1-x^2}\right)$, then which of the following statements(s) is (are) correct?

(a) $f(x)$ is bijective

(b) $f(x)$ is injective but not surjective

(c) $f(x)$ is neither injective nor surjective

(d) $f(x)$ is an odd function

[**Note** : I denotes the set of integers]

50. If $\log x=\dfrac{-1}{3}$, $\log y=\dfrac{2}{5}$ and

$$P=\log\ (\sin(\text{arc}\cos\sqrt{1-x^2})),$$

$$Q=\log\left(\cos\left(\text{arc}\tan\frac{\sqrt{1-x^2y^2}}{xy}\right)\right),\text{ then}$$

(a) $P=\dfrac{-1}{9}$

(b) $P+Q=\dfrac{-4}{15}$

(c) $P-Q=\dfrac{-2}{5}$

(d) $\dfrac{P}{Q}=-5$

Passage Based Questions

Passage I

(Q. Nos. 51 to 52)

- Let S denotes the set consisting of four functions and $S=\{[x],\sin^{-1}x,|x|,\{x\}\}$ where, $\{x\}$ denotes fractional part and $[x]$ denotes greatest integer function. Let A,B,C are subsets of S.

Suppose, A : consists of odd function(s)

B : consists of discontinuous function(s)

and C : consists of non-decreasing function(s) or increasing function(s).

If $f(x)\in A\cap C$; $g(x)\in B\cap C$; $h(x)\in B$ but not C and $l(x)\in$ neither A nor B nor C. Then, answer the following.

51. The function $l(x)$ is

(a) periodic

(b) even

(c) odd

(d) neither odd nor even

52. The range of $g(f(x))$ is

(a) $\{-1,0,1\}$

(b) $\{-1,0\}$

(c) $\{0,1\}$

(d) $\{-2,-1,0,1\}$

Passage II

(Q. Nos. 53 to 54)

- Let f be a real-valued function defined on R (the set of real numbers) such that $f(x)=\sin^{-1}(\sin x)+\cos^{-1}(\cos x)$

53. The value of $f(10)$ is equal to

(a) $6\pi-20$

(b) $7\pi-20$

(c) $20-7\pi$

(d) $20-6\pi$

54. The area bounded by curve $y=f(x)$ and X-axis from $\dfrac{\pi}{2}\le x\le\pi$ is equal to

(a) $\dfrac{\pi^2}{4}$

(b) $\dfrac{\pi^2}{2}$

(c) π^2

(d) $\dfrac{\pi^2}{8}$

Passage III

(Q. Nos. 55 and 56)

- Consider a real-valued function

$$f(x)=\sqrt{\sin^{-1}x+2}+\sqrt{1-\sin^{-1}x}$$

55. The domain of definition of $f(x)$ is

(a) $[-1,1]$

(b) $[\sin 1,1]$

(c) $[-1,\sin 1]$

(d) $[-1,0]$

56. The range of $f(x)$ is

(a) $[0,\sqrt{3}]$

(b) $[1,\sqrt{3}]$

(c) $[1,\sqrt{6}]$

(d) $[\sqrt{3},\sqrt{6}]$

Passage IV
(Q. Nos. 57 to 58)

- Given that,

$$\tan^{-1}\left(\frac{2x}{1-x^2}\right)=\begin{cases}2\tan^{-1}x, |x|\le 1\\ -\pi+2\tan^{-1}x, x>1\\ \pi+2\tan^{-1}x, x<-1\end{cases}$$

$$\sin^{-1}\left(\frac{2x}{1+x^2}\right)=\begin{cases}2\tan^{-1}x, |x|\le 1\\ \pi-2\tan^{-1}x,\ x>1 \text{ and}\\ -(\pi+2\tan^{-1}x), x<-1\end{cases}$$

$\sin^{-1}x+\cos^{-1}x=\pi/2$ for $-1\le x\le 1$

57. $\sin^{-1}\left(\frac{4x}{x^2+4}\right)+2\tan^{-1}\left(-\frac{x}{2}\right)$ is independent of x, then

(a) $x\in[-3, 4]$
(b) $x\in[-2, 2]$
(c) $x\in[-1, 1]$
(d) $x\in[1, \infty)$

58. If $\cos^{-1}\frac{6x}{1+9x^2}=-\frac{\pi}{2}+2\tan^{-1}3x$, then $x\in$

(a) $\left(\frac{1}{3}, \infty\right)$
(b) $(-1, \infty)$
(c) $(-\infty, m-1)$
(d) None of the above

Passage V
(Q. Nos. 59 to 60)

- For $x, y, z, t\in R$, $\sin^{-1}x+\cos^{-1}y+\sec^{-1}z \ge t^2-\sqrt{2\pi}t+3\pi$

59. The value of $x+y+z$ is equal to

(a) 1
(b) 0
(c) 2
(d) -1

60. The principal value of $\cos^{-1}(\cos 5t^2)$ is

(a) $\frac{3\pi}{2}$
(b) $\frac{\pi}{2}$
(c) $\frac{\pi}{3}$
(d) $\frac{2\pi}{3}$

Stem Based Questions

Passage IV
(Q. Nos. 61 to 62)

- Let $\alpha=2\tan^{-1}\frac{1}{2}+\sin^{-1}\frac{3}{5}$ and $\beta=\sin^{-1}\frac{12}{13}+\cos^{-1}\frac{4}{5}+\cot^{-1}\frac{16}{63}$ be such that $2\sin\alpha$ and $\cos\beta$ are roots of the equation $x^2-ax+b=0$, where $a, b\in R$.

61. The value of $\tan^{-1}\left(\sec\left(\cos^{-1}\left(\sin\frac{\alpha}{2}\right)\right)-1\right)$ is equal to ....

62. The number of solution(s) of the equation $|b|\sin^{-1}x=(a-b)x$, is equal to ....

Single Integer Type Questions

63. Let $f(x)=\cos(\tan^{-1}(\sin(\cot^{-1}x)))$. The simplest form of $f(x)$ can be written as $\left(\frac{x^2+A}{x^2+B}\right)^{1/2}$. Then, the value of $(A+B)$ is ....

64. Find the value of λ for which
$$\tan^{-1}\left\{\frac{\cos 2\alpha\sec 2\beta+\cos 2\beta\sec 2\alpha}{\lambda}\right\}$$
$$=\tan^{-1}\{\tan^2\alpha+\beta)\tan^2(\alpha-\beta)\}+\tan^{-1}1$$

65. The least value of n for which $(n-2)x^2+8x+n+4>\sin^{-1}(\sin 12)+\cos^{-1}(\cos 12)$, $\forall x\in R$, where $n\in N$, is ....

66. If $0<\cos^{-1}x<1$ and $1+\sin(\cos^{-1}x)+\sin^2(\cos^{-1}x)+\sin^3(\cos^{-1}x)+\dots\infty=2$, then the value of $12x^2$ is ....

67. The number of real solutions of the equation $\sqrt{1+\cos 2x}=\sqrt{2}\sin^{-1}(\sin x)$, $-\pi\le x\le\pi$, is ....

Numerical Value Type Questions

68. The value of x for which $\sin^{-1}\left(\frac{5}{x}\right)+\sin^{-1}\left(\frac{12}{x}\right)=\frac{\pi}{2}$ satisfied, is ....

69. Solution for the equation
$$\tan^{-1}\left(\frac{x+1}{x-1}\right)+\tan^{-1}\left(\frac{x-1}{x}\right)=\tan^{-1}(-7)$$ is ....

70. If $a, b, c > 0$ and

$$\tan^{-1}\sqrt{\frac{a(a+b+c)}{bc}}+\tan^{-1}\sqrt{\frac{b(a+b+c)}{ac}}+\tan^{-1}\sqrt{\frac{c(a+b+c)}{ab}}=\lambda,$$ then the value of $\frac{[\lambda]}{2}$, where $[\cdot]$ denotes greatest integer function, is ....

71. If the maximum value of

$$\sqrt{\sin^{-1}x_1}\sqrt{\cos^{-1}x_2}+\sqrt{\sin^{-1}x_2}\sqrt{\cos^{-1}x_3}+\sqrt{\sin^{-1}x_3}\sqrt{\cos^{-1}x_4}+\ldots+\sqrt{\sin^{-1}x_{28}}\sqrt{\cos^{-1}x_1},$$

where $x_1 \in [0,1]\ \forall i = 1, 2, 3, \ldots, 28$ is $M\pi$, then the value of $\frac{(M+1)}{2}$ is ....

72. The value of $\sum_{r=1}^{10}\sum_{s=1}^{10}\tan^{-1}\left(\frac{r}{s}\right)$ is K, then $\frac{2K}{\pi}$ is equal to ....

73. If $\lim_{n\to\infty}\sum_{k=2}^{n}\cos^{-1}\left(\frac{1+\sqrt{(k-1)(k)(k+1)(k+2)}}{k(k+1)}\right)=\lambda$, then the value of $[4\lambda]$, where $[\cdot]$ denotes least integer function is ....

Matching Type Questions

74. Let $t_1 = (\sin^{-1}x)^{\sin^{-1}x}$, $t_2 = (\sin^{-1}x)^{\cos^{-1}x}$, $t_3 = (\cos^{-1}x)^{\sin^{-1}x}$, $t_4 = (\cos^{-1}x)^{\cos^{-1}x}$,

Match the following items of **Column I** with **Column II**

Column I	Column II
A. $x \in (0, \cos 1)$	(p) $t_1 > t_2 > t_4 > t_3$
B. $x \in \left(\cos 1, \frac{1}{\sqrt{2}}\right)$	(q) $t_4 > t_3 > t_1 > t_2$
C. $x \in \left(\frac{1}{\sqrt{2}}, \sin 1\right)$	(r) $t_2 > t_1 > t_4 > t_3$
D. $x \in (\sin 1, 1)$	(s) $t_3 > t_4 > t_1 > t_2$

75. Match the following items of **Column I** with **Column II**

Column I	Column II
A. $\sin^{-1}x + x > 0$, for	(p) $x < 0$
B. $\cos^{-1}x - x \ge 0$, for	(q) $x \in (0, 1]$
C. $\tan^{-1}x + x < 0$, for	(r) $x \in [-1, 0)$
D. $\cot^{-1}x + x > 0$, for	(s) $x > 0$

Previous Years Questions

76. For any $y \in R$, let $\cot^{-1}(y) \in (0, \pi)$ and $\tan^{-1}(y) \in \left(-\frac{\pi}{2}, \frac{\pi}{2}\right)$. Then, the sum of all solutions of the equation $\tan^{-1}\frac{6y}{9-y^2}+\cot^{-1}\frac{9-y^2}{6y}=\frac{2\pi}{3}$ for $0 < |y| < 3$, is equal to **[Single Correct Type, 2023 Adv.]**

(a) $2\sqrt{3}-3$

(b) $3-2\sqrt{3}$

(c) $4\sqrt{3}-6$

(d) $6-4\sqrt{3}$

77. Let $\tan^{-1}(x) \in \left(-\frac{\pi}{2}, \frac{\pi}{2}\right)$, for $x \in R$. Then, the number of real solutions of the equation $\sqrt{1+\cos(2x)} = \sqrt{2}\tan^{-1}(\tan x)$ in the set $\left(\frac{-3\pi}{2}, \frac{-\pi}{2}\right) \cup \left(-\frac{\pi}{2}, \frac{\pi}{2}\right) \cup \left(\frac{\pi}{2}, \frac{3\pi}{2}\right)$ is equal to

[Numerical Value Type, 2023 Adv.]

78. Considering only the principal values of the inverse trigonometric functions, the value of

$$\frac{3}{2}\cos^{-1}\sqrt{\frac{2}{2+\pi^2}}+\frac{1}{4}\sin^{-1}\frac{2\sqrt{2}\pi}{2+\pi^2}+\tan^{-1}\sqrt{2}/\pi \text{ is ......}$$

[Numerical Value Type, 2022 Adv.]

79. For any positive integer n, let $S_n : (0, \infty) \to R$ be defined by $S_n(x) = \sum_{k=1}^{n}\cot^{-1}\left(\frac{1+k(k+1)x^2}{x}\right)$, where for any $x \in R$, $\cot^{-1}(x) \in (0, \pi)$ and $\tan^{-1}(x) \in \left(-\frac{\pi}{2}, \frac{\pi}{2}\right)$.

Then, which of the following statements is (are) TRUE?

[More Than One Correct, 2021 Adv.]

(a) $S_{10}(x) = \frac{\pi}{2} - \tan^{-1}\left(\frac{1+11x^2}{10x}\right)$, for all $x > 0$

(b) $\lim_{n\to\infty}\cot(S_n(x)) = x$, for all $x > 0$

(c) The equation $S_3(x) = \frac{\pi}{4}$ has a root in $(0, \infty)$

(d) $\tan(S_n(x)) \le \frac{1}{2}$, for all $n \ge 1$ and $x > 0$

80. Match List I with List II and select the correct answer using the code given below the lists.

	List I		List II
P.	$\left[\frac{1}{y^2}\left\{\frac{\cos(\tan^{-1}y)+y\sin(\tan^{-1}y)}{\cot(\sin^{-1}y)+\tan(\sin^{-1}y)}\right\}^2+y^4\right]^{1/2}$ takes value	1.	$\frac{1}{2}\sqrt{\frac{5}{3}}$
Q.	If $\cos x+\cos y+\cos z=0=\sin x+\sin y+\sin z$, then possible value of $\cos\frac{x-y}{2}$ is	2.	$\sqrt{2}$
R.	If $\cos\left(\frac{\pi}{4}-x\right)\cos 2x+\sin x\sin 2x\sec x$ $=\cos x\sin 2x\sec x+\cos\left(\frac{\pi}{4}+x\right)\cos 2x$, then possible value of $\sec x$ is	3.	$\frac{1}{2}$
S.	If $\cot(\sin^{-1}\sqrt{1-x^2})=\sin[\tan^{-1}(x\sqrt{6})]$, $x=0$. Then, possible value of x is	4.	1

[Matching Type, 2020 Adv.]

81. The value of

$$\sec^{-1}\left(\frac{1}{4}\sum_{k=0}^{10}\sec\left(\frac{7\pi}{12}+\frac{k\pi}{2}\right)\sec\left(\frac{7\pi}{12}+\frac{(k+1)\pi}{2}\right)\right)$$

in the interval $\left[-\frac{\pi}{4},\frac{3\pi}{4}\right]$ equals ....

[Numerical Value Type, 2019 Adv.]

82. For non-negative integers n, let

$$f(n)=\frac{\sum_{k=0}^{n}\sin\left(\frac{k+1}{n+2}\pi\right)\sin\left(\frac{k+2}{n+2}\pi\right)}{\sum_{k=0}^{n}\sin^2\left(\frac{k+1}{n+2}\pi\right)}$$

Assuming $\cos^{-1}x$ takes values in $[0,\pi]$, which of the following options is/are correct?

[More Than One Correct, 2019 Adv.]

(a) If $\alpha=\tan(\cos^{-1}f(6))$, then $\alpha^2+2\alpha-1=0$

(b) $f(4)=\frac{\sqrt{3}}{2}$

(c) $\sin(7\cos^{-1}f(5))=0$

(d) $\lim_{n\to\infty}f(n)=\frac{1}{2}$

83. The number of real solutions of the equation

$$\sin^{-1}\left(\sum_{i=1}^{\infty}x^{i+1}-x\sum_{i=1}^{\infty}\left(\frac{x}{2}\right)^i\right)=\frac{\pi}{2}-\cos^{-1}\left(\sum_{i=1}^{\infty}\left(-\frac{x}{2}\right)^i-\sum_{i=1}^{\infty}(-x)^i\right)$$ lying in the

interval $\left(-\frac{1}{2},\frac{1}{2}\right)$ is ....

(Here, the inverse trigonometric functions $\sin^{-1}x$ and $\cos^{-1}x$ assume values in $\left[-\frac{\pi}{2},\frac{\pi}{2}\right]$ and $[0,\pi]$, respectively.)

[Numerical Value Type, 2018 Adv.]

84. Let $E_1=\{x\in R: x\neq 1$ and $\frac{x}{x-1}>0\}$ and

$$E_2=\left\{x\in E_1:\sin^{-1}\left(\log_e\left(\frac{x}{x-1}\right)\right)\text{ is a real number}\right\}$$

(Here, the inverse trigonometric function $\sin^{-1}x$ assumes values in $\left[-\frac{\pi}{2},\frac{\pi}{2}\right]$).

	List I		List II
P.	The range of f is	1.	$\left(-\infty,\frac{1}{1-e}\right]\cup\left[\frac{e}{e-1},\infty\right)$
Q.	The range of g contains	2.	$(0,1)$
R.	The domain of f contains	3.	$\left[-\frac{1}{2},\frac{1}{2}\right]$
S.	The domain of g is	4.	$(-\infty,0)\cup(0,\infty)$
		5.	$(-\infty,e/e-1]$
		6.	$(-\infty,0)\cup\left(\frac{1}{2},\frac{e}{e-1}\right]$

Let $f:E_1\to R$ be the function defined by $f(x)=\log_e\left(\frac{x}{x-1}\right)$ and $g:E_2\to R$ be the function defined by $g(x)=\sin^{-1}\left(\log_e\left(\frac{x}{x-1}\right)\right)$.

[Matching Type, 2018 Adv.]

85. If $\alpha=3\sin^{-1}\left(\frac{6}{11}\right)$ and $\beta=3\cos^{-1}\left(\frac{4}{9}\right)$, where the inverse trigonometric functions take only the principal values, then the correct option(s) is (are)

[More Than One Correct, 2015 Adv.]

(a) $\cos\beta>0$

(b) $\sin\beta<0$

(c) $\cos(\alpha+\beta)>0$

(d) $\cos\alpha<0$

86. If $f:[0,4\pi]\to[0,\pi]$ be defined by $f(x)=\cos^{-1}(\cos x)$. Then, the number of points $x\in[0,4\pi]$ satisfying the equation $f(x)=\frac{10-x}{10}$, is

[Numerical Value Type, 2014 Adv.]

EXERCISE 3

Challenging Problems

1. If $A = 2\tan^{-1}(2\sqrt{2} - 1)$ and $B = 3\sin^{-1}\left(\frac{1}{3}\right) + \sin^{-1}\left(\frac{3}{5}\right)$, then show $A > B$.

2. Solve for $x : (\tan^{-1} x)^2 + (\cot^{-1} x)^2 = \frac{5\pi^2}{8}$.

3. Solve for x, if $[\sin^{-1}\cos^{-1}\sin^{-1}\tan^{-1} x] = 1$, where [.] denotes the greatest integer function.

4. If $\tan^{-1} y = 4\tan^{-1} x\left(|x| < \tan\frac{\pi}{8}\right)$, find y as an algebraic function of x and hence prove that $\tan\frac{\pi}{8}$ is a root of the equation $x^4 - 6x^2 + 1 = 0$.

5. Find the set of values of k for which $x^2 - kx + \sin^{-1}(\sin 4) > 0$ for all real x.

6. Express the equation,
$$\cot^{-1}\frac{y}{\sqrt{1 - x^2 - y^2}} = 2\tan^{-1}\sqrt{\frac{3 - 4x^2}{4x^2}} - \tan^{-1}\sqrt{\frac{3 - 4x^2}{x^2}}$$
as a rational integral equation in x and y.

7. Prove that
$$\cos^{-1}\left(\frac{\cos x + \cos y}{1 + \cos x \cdot \cos y}\right) = 2\tan^{-1}\left(\tan\frac{x}{2}\tan\frac{y}{2}\right).$$

8. If $x = \operatorname{cosec}(\tan^{-1}(\cos(\cot^{-1}(\sec(\sin^{-1} a)))))$ and $y = \sec(\cot^{-1}(\sin(\tan^{-1}(\operatorname{cosec}(\cos^{-1} a)))))$, where $a \in [0, 1]$. Find the relationship between x and y in terms of a.

9. Show that $\tan^{-1}\left\{\tan\frac{\alpha}{2}\tan\left(\frac{\pi}{4} - \frac{\beta}{2}\right)\right\}$
$$= \tan^{-1}\left(\frac{\sin\alpha\cos\beta}{\cos\alpha + \sin\beta}\right) \text{ where } \alpha, \beta \in \left(0, \frac{\pi}{2}\right).$$

10. Solve : $3\sin^{-1}\frac{2x}{1 + x^2} - 4\cos^{-1}\frac{1 - x^2}{1 + x^2} + 2\tan^{-1}\frac{2x}{1 - x^2} = \frac{\pi}{3}$.

11. Obtain the integral values of p for which the following system of equations possesses real solutions :
$$\cos^{-1} x + (\sin^{-1} y)^2 = \frac{p\pi^2}{4} \text{ and } (\cos^{-1} x)(\sin^{-1} y)^2 = \frac{\pi^4}{16}$$
Also, find these solution.

12. Solve the equation $2(\sin^{-1} x)^2 - (\sin^{-1} x) - 6 = 0$.

13. Solve the equation $\sin^{-1} 6x + \sin^{-1} 6\sqrt{3}x = -\frac{\pi}{2}$.

Answer Key

■ Exercise 1

1. (c)	2. (a)	3. (d)	4. (b)	5. (b)	6. (a)	7. (b)	8. (a)	9. (c)	10. (c)
11. (a)	12. (d)	13. (b)	14. (c)	15. (d)	16. (a)	17. (a)	18. (a)	19. (b)	20. (d)
21. (a)	22. (b)	23. (d)	24. (d)	25. (a)	26. (b)	27. (c)	28. (b)	29. (d)	30. (c)
31. (c)	32. (a)	33. (d)	34. (d)	35. (c)	36. (c)	37. (d)	38. (b)	39. (c)	40. (b)
41. (a)	42. (d)	43. (9)	44. (4)	45. (1)	46. (0)	47. (3)	48. (8)	49. (4)	50. (4)
51. (3)	52. (9)	53. (b)	54. (a)	55. (0)	56. (47)	57. (c)	58. (c)	59. (d)	60. (c)
61. (a)	62. (b)	63. (b)	64. (b)	65. (d)	66. (24)	67. (4)	68. (2)	69. (2)	70. (c)
71. (d)	72. (b)	73. (c)	74. (d)	75. (a)	76. (b)	77. (b)	78. (a)	79. (a)	80. (a)
81. (b)	82. (130)	83. (29)	84. (c)	85. (b)	86. (a)	87. (c)	88. (c)	89. (b)	90. (b)
91. (d)	92. (c)	93. (b)	94. (d)	95. (b)	96. (a)	97. (c)	98. (c)		

■ Exercise 2

1. (d)	2. (a)	3. (c)	4. (b)	5. (a)	6. (d)	7. (d)	8. (b)	9. (c)	10. (d)
11. (a)	12. (b)	13. (a)	14. (b)	15. (c)	16. (c)	17. (b)	18. (b)	19. (c)	20. (b)
21. (a)	22. (c)	23. (d)	24. (b)	25. (a)	26. (c)	27. (d)	28. (c)	29. (b)	30. (b)
31. (b,c)	32. (b,c)	33. (a,b,c)	34. (a,c)	35. (a,c)	36. (a,b,c)	37. (a,c,d)	38. (a,b,c,d)	39. (b,c)	40. (b,d)
41. (a,b)	42. (a,b,c)	43. (a,b)	44. (a,b)	45. (a,b,d)	46. (a,d)	47. (a,c)	48. (a,b,d)	49. (c,d)	50. (b,c,d)
51. (b)	52. (d)	53. (b)	54. (b)	55. (c)	56. (d)	57. (b)	58. (a)	59. (d)	60. (b)
61. ($\alpha/4$)	62. (3)	63. (3)	64. (2)	65. (5)	66. (9)	67. (2)	68. (13)	69. (0)	70. (1.5)

71. (4) 72. (50) 73. (2) 74. (A $\to$ q; B $\to$ s; C $\to$ r; D $\to$ p) 75. (A $\to$ q,s; B $\to$ p,r; C $\to$ p,r; D $\to$ q,r,s)

76. (c) 77. (3) 78. (2.36) 79. (a,b) 80. (P $\to$ 4; Q $\to$ 3; R $\to$ 2, 4; S $\to$ 1) 81. (0) 82. (a,b,c) 83. (2)

84. (P $\to$ 4; Q $\to$ 2; R $\to$ 1; S $\to$ 1) 85. (b,c,d) 86. (3)

Solutions

Exercise 1 - JEE Main Pattern

1. Consider $\tan 65° - 2\tan 40°$

$$= \tan(45° + 20°) - 2\tan 40°$$

$$= \frac{1+\tan 20°}{1-\tan 20°} - \frac{4\tan 20°}{1-\tan^2 20°}$$

$$= \frac{(1+\tan 20°)^2 - 4\tan 20°}{(1-\tan 20°)(1+\tan 20°)} = \frac{(1-\tan 20°)(1-\tan 20°)}{(1-\tan 20°)(1+\tan 20°)}$$

$$= \frac{(1-\tan 20°)}{(1+\tan 20°)} = \tan(45° - 20°) = \tan 25°$$

$\therefore \quad \tan^{-1}(\tan 25°) = 25°$

2. $\frac{2e+4}{3} > e \Rightarrow \ln\left(\frac{2e+4}{3}\right) > 1$

3. $\lim_{|x|\to\infty} \cos(\tan^{-1}(\sin(\tan^{-1} x)))$

$$= \cos(\tan^{-1}(\sin(\tan^{-1}\infty))) = \cos\left(\tan^{-1}\left(\sin\left(\frac{\pi}{2}\right)\right)\right)$$

$$= \cos(\tan^{-1}(1)) = \cos\left(\frac{\pi}{4}\right) = \frac{1}{\sqrt{2}}$$

4. $x + \frac{1}{x} = 2$

$\Rightarrow \quad \left(\sqrt{x} - \frac{1}{\sqrt{x}}\right) = 0$

$\Rightarrow \quad \frac{x-1}{\sqrt{x}} = 0 \Rightarrow x = 1$

$\therefore \quad \sin^{-1} x = \frac{\pi}{2}$

5. $\frac{\sqrt{(1+x^2)} - \sqrt{(1-x^2)}}{\sqrt{(1+x^2)} + \sqrt{(1-x^2)}} = \frac{\tan\alpha}{1}$

Now, use C and $D \Rightarrow \frac{1+x^2}{1-x^2} = \frac{\tan^2\left(\frac{\pi}{4}+\alpha\right)}{1}$

Again, use C and $D = x^2 = -\cos\left(\frac{\pi}{2} + 2\alpha\right) = \sin 2\alpha$

6. Let $\cos^{-1}\frac{1}{8} = \theta$, where $0 < \theta < \frac{\pi}{2}$.

Then, $\quad \frac{1}{2}\cos^{-1}\frac{1}{8} = \frac{1}{2}\theta$

$\Rightarrow \quad \cos\left(\frac{1}{2}\cos^{-1}\frac{1}{8}\right) = \cos\frac{1}{2}\theta$

Now, $\quad \cos^{-1}\frac{1}{8} = \theta$

$\Rightarrow \quad \cos\theta = \frac{1}{8}$

$\Rightarrow \quad 2\cos^2\frac{\theta}{2} - 1 = \frac{1}{8}$

$\Rightarrow \quad \cos^2\frac{\theta}{2} = \frac{9}{16}$

$\Rightarrow \quad \cos\frac{\theta}{2} = \frac{3}{4} \quad \left[\because 0 < \frac{\theta}{2} < \frac{\pi}{2}, \text{ so } \cos\frac{\theta}{2} \neq -\frac{3}{4}\right]$

7. Substituting $x^2 = \cos 2\theta$, we obtain

$$\cot^{-1}\left(\sqrt{\frac{1-x^2}{1+x^2}}\right) = \cot^{-1}\left(\sqrt{\frac{1-\cos 2\theta}{1+\cos 2\theta}}\right) = \cot^{-1}(\tan\theta)$$

$$= \cot^{-1}\left(\cot\left(\frac{\pi}{2} - \theta\right)\right)$$

$$= \frac{\pi}{2} - \theta$$

8. $\sin\left[\tan^{-1}\frac{1-\tan^2\theta}{2\tan\theta} + \cos^{-1}\frac{1-\tan^2\theta}{1+\tan^2\theta}\right] \quad$ [put $x = \tan\theta$]

$\Rightarrow \quad \sin[\tan^{-1}(\cot 2\theta) + \cos^{-1}(\cos 2\theta)]$

$$= \sin\left[\tan^{-1}\left(\tan\left(\frac{\pi}{2} - 2\theta\right)\right) + 2\theta\right]$$

$$= \sin\left(\frac{\pi}{2} - 2\theta + 2\theta\right) = 1$$

9. Given, $u = \cot^{-1}\sqrt{\cos 2\theta} - \tan^{-1}\sqrt{\cos 2\theta}$,

Put $\quad \cos 2\theta = \tan^2\theta$

$\Rightarrow \quad u = \cot^{-1}(\tan\theta) - \tan^{-1}(\tan\theta)$

$$= \frac{\pi}{2} - \theta - \theta = \frac{\pi}{2} - 2\theta$$

$\Rightarrow \quad \sin u = \sin\left(\frac{\pi}{2} - 2\theta\right) = \cos 2\theta = \tan^2\theta$

10. $\cos^{-1}(\cos(2\cot^{-1}(\sqrt{2} - 1)))$

$$= \cos^{-1}(\cos(2(67\cdot 5°)))$$

$$= \cos^{-1}(\cos(135°)) = 135° = \frac{3\pi}{4}$$

11. $0 \le x \le 1 \Rightarrow 0 \le \tan^{-1} x \le \frac{\pi}{4}$

$\Rightarrow \quad \frac{-\pi}{4} \le -\tan^{-1} x \le 0$

$\Rightarrow \quad 0 \le \frac{\pi}{4} - \tan^{-1} x \le \frac{\pi}{4}$

12. Let $\sin^{-1} x = \theta \Rightarrow x = \sin\theta$, $\frac{\pi}{2} \le \theta \le \frac{3\pi}{2}$

Now, $\cos^{-1} x = \cos^{-1}(\sin\theta) = \cos^{-1}\left(-\cos\left(\frac{3\pi}{2} - \theta\right)\right)$

$$= \pi - \cos^{-1}\left(\cos\left(\frac{3\pi}{2} - \theta\right)\right)$$

$$= \pi - \left(\frac{3\pi}{2} - \theta\right), \text{ as } 0 \le \frac{3\pi}{2} - \theta \le \pi$$

$$= \theta - \frac{\pi}{2} = \sin^{-1} x - \frac{\pi}{2}$$

Hence, $\sin^{-1} x + \cos^{-1} x = 2\sin^{-1} x - \frac{\pi}{2}$

13. $\sin\cos^{-1}(\cos(\tan^{-1} x)) = p$

For $x \in R$, $\tan^{-1} x \in (-\pi/2, \pi/2)$

$$\cos(\tan^{-1} x) \in (0,1]$$

$$\cos^{-1}\cos(\tan^{-1} x) \in [0, \pi/2)$$

$$\sin(\cos^{-1}(\cos(\tan^{-1} x))) \in [0,1)$$

14. $\frac{\pi}{2} - \cos^{-1}(1-x) + 2\cos^{-1} x = 0$

$$\sin^{-1}(1-x) + 2\cos^{-1} x = 0$$

Domain is [0, 1].

Now, in [0, 1], $\sin^{-1}(1-x) \in \left[0, \frac{\pi}{2}\right]$ and $2\cos^{-1} x \in [0, \pi]$

Hence, $\left.\begin{array}{l}\sin^{-1}(1-x) = 0 \\ \text{and } \cos^{-1} x = 0\end{array}\right] \Rightarrow x = 1$

15. (a) $f(x) = \frac{1}{2}\cos^{-1}\left(\frac{1-x^2}{1+x^2}\right)$

$D_f = R$

As, $0 \le \cos^{-1}\left(\frac{1-x^2}{1+x^2}\right) < \pi$

$\therefore R_f = \left[0, \frac{\pi}{2}\right)$

(b) $g(x) = \text{sgn}\left(x + \frac{1}{x}\right)$

$D_g = (-\infty, 0) \cup (0, \infty)$

$R_g = \{-1, 1\}$

(c) $h(x) = \sin^2 x + 2\sin x + 2$

$D_h = R$

Also, $h(x) = (\sin x + 1)^2 + 1$

$\therefore \quad R_h = [1, 5]$

(d) $k(x) = \cos^{-1}(x^2 - 2x + 2) = \cos^{-1}((x-1)^2 + 1)$

$\therefore \quad D_k = \{1\}$

$R_k = \{0\}$

16. $\therefore \quad 0 \le \tan^{-1}(3x^2 + bx + 3) < \frac{\pi}{2}$

$\Rightarrow \quad 0 \le 3x^2 + bx + 3 < \infty$

Thus, range of $3x^2 + bx + 3$ is $[0, \infty)$

Now, $D = b^2 - 4 \cdot 3 \cdot 3 = 0$

$\Rightarrow \quad b^2 = 36 \Rightarrow b = \pm 6$

Sum of values of $b = 0$

$\therefore$ Square of sum of values of $b = 0$

17. $y = 1 + 2\sin\left(\frac{e^x}{e^x + 1}\right), x \ge 0$

$$\Rightarrow \quad y - 1 = 2\sin\left(\frac{e^x}{e^x + 1}\right)$$

$$\Rightarrow \quad \frac{e^x}{e^x + 1} = \sin^{-1}\left(\frac{y-1}{2}\right)$$

$$\Rightarrow \quad e^x\left(\sin^{-1}\left(\frac{y-1}{2}\right) - 1\right) = -\sin^{-1}\left(\frac{y-1}{2}\right)$$

$$\Rightarrow \quad e^x = \frac{\sin^{-1}\left(\frac{y-1}{2}\right)}{1 - \sin^{-1}\left(\frac{y-1}{2}\right)}$$

$$\Rightarrow \quad x = \log\left(\frac{\sin^{-1}\left(\frac{y-1}{2}\right)}{1 - \sin^{-1}\left(\frac{y-1}{2}\right)}\right)$$

$$\Rightarrow \quad f^{-1}(x) = \log\left(\frac{\sin^{-1}\left(\frac{x-1}{2}\right)}{1 - \sin^{-1}\left(\frac{x-1}{2}\right)}\right)$$

18. $\text{cosec}^{-1}(\text{cosec } x) = x \ \forall \ x \in R$ is $-(-1, 1)$.

Also, range of $\text{cosec}^{-1}(\text{cosec } x)$ is $\left[-\frac{\pi}{2}, 0\right) \cup \left(0, \frac{\pi}{2}\right]$.

and the range of $\text{cosec}(\text{cosec}^{-1} x)$ is $(-\infty, -1] \cup [1, \infty)$.

So, combining these two, we get

$$x \in \left[-\frac{\pi}{2}, -1\right] \cup \left[1, \frac{\pi}{2}\right]$$

19. $1 + \tan^2(\tan^{-1} x) - (\sec^2(\sec^{-1} x) - 1)$

$$= 1 + (\tan(\tan^{-1} x))^2 - (\sec(\sec^{-1} x))^2 + 1$$

$$= 1 + x^2 - x^2 + 1 = 2$$

20. $\sin^{-1}\left(-\sin\frac{50\pi}{9}\right) = -\sin^{-1}\sin\left(\frac{50\pi}{9}\right) = -\sin^{-1}\sin\left(\frac{14\pi}{9}\right)$

$$= -\sin^{-1}\sin\left(2\pi - \frac{4\pi}{9}\right)$$

$$= -\sin^{-1}\left(-\sin\left(\frac{4\pi}{9}\right)\right) = \frac{4\pi}{9}$$

$$\cos^{-1}\cos\left(-\frac{31\pi}{9}\right) = \cos^{-1}\cos\left(\frac{31\pi}{9}\right)$$

$$= \cos^{-1}\cos\left(4\pi - \frac{5\pi}{9}\right) = \cos^{-1}\cos\frac{5\pi}{9} = \frac{5\pi}{9}$$

Hence, $\sec\left(\frac{4\pi}{9} + \frac{5\pi}{9}\right) = \sec\pi = -1$

21. We have, $\cot^{-1} x + \sin^{-1}\frac{1}{\sqrt{5}} = \frac{\pi}{4}$

$$\Rightarrow \quad \tan^{-1}\frac{1}{x} + \tan^{-1}\frac{1/\sqrt{5}}{\sqrt{1 - \frac{1}{5}}} = \frac{\pi}{4}$$

$$\Rightarrow \quad \tan^{-1}\frac{1}{x} + \tan^{-1}\frac{1}{2} = \tan^{-1}1$$

$$\Rightarrow \quad \tan^{-1}\frac{1}{x} = \tan^{-1}1 - \tan^{-1}\frac{1}{2}$$

$$\Rightarrow \quad \tan^{-1}\frac{1}{x} = \tan^{-1}\left(\frac{1-\frac{1}{2}}{1+1\cdot\frac{1}{2}}\right)$$

$$\Rightarrow \quad \tan^{-1}\frac{1}{x} = \tan^{-1}\left(\frac{1}{3}\right) \Rightarrow x = 3$$

22. $\left(\frac{\pi}{2} - \cos^{-1}x\right) + \left(\frac{\pi}{2} - \cos^{-1}y\right) = \frac{2\pi}{3}$

$$\Rightarrow \quad \cos^{-1}x + \cos^{-1}y = \frac{\pi}{3}$$

23. We have, $\sin^{-1}\left\{\left(\sin\frac{\pi}{3}\right)\frac{x}{\sqrt{(x^2+k^2-kx)}}\right\}$

$$- \cos^{-1}\left\{\left(\cos\frac{\pi}{6}\right)\frac{x}{\sqrt{(x^2+k^2-kx)}}\right\}$$

$$= \sin^{-1}\left\{\frac{\sqrt{3}x}{2\sqrt{x^2+k^2-kx}}\right\} - \cos^{-1}\left\{\frac{\sqrt{3}x}{2\sqrt{x^2+k^2-kx}}\right\}$$

$$= \frac{\pi}{2} - 2\cos^{-1}\left\{\frac{\sqrt{3}x}{\sqrt{4x^2-4kx+4k^2}}\right\}$$

$$= \frac{\pi}{2} - \cos^{-1}\left\{\frac{6x^2}{4x^2-4kx+4k^2} - 1\right\}$$

$$= \sin^{-1}\left\{\frac{2x^2+4xk-4k^2}{4x^2-4xk+4k^2}\right\}$$

$$= \sin^{-1}\left\{\frac{x^2+2xk-2k^2}{2x^2-2xk+2k^2}\right\}$$

24. $a\sin^{-1}x - b\cos^{-1}x = c$

We have, $b\sin^{-1}x + b\cos^{-1}x = \frac{b\pi}{2}$

Adding $(a+b)\sin^{-1}x = \frac{b\pi}{2} + c$

or $\quad \sin^{-1}x = \dfrac{\left(\frac{b\pi}{2}\right)+c}{a+b} = \dfrac{b\pi+2c}{2(a+b)}$

$\therefore \quad \cos^{-1}x = \dfrac{\pi}{2} - \dfrac{b\pi+2c}{2(a+b)} = \dfrac{\pi a - 2c}{2(a+b)}$

$$\Rightarrow a\sin^{-1}x + b\cos^{-1}x = \frac{\pi ab + c(a-b)}{a+b}$$

25. Let $f(x) = x^3 + bx^2 + cx + 1$

$f(0) = 1 > 0,\ f(-1) = b - c < 0$

So, $\quad \alpha \in (-1, 0)$

So, $2\tan^{-1}(\operatorname{cosec}\alpha) + \tan^{-1}(2\sin\alpha\sec^2\alpha)$

$$= 2\tan^{-1}\left(\frac{1}{\sin\alpha}\right) + \tan^{-1}\left(\frac{2\sin\alpha}{1-\sin^2\alpha}\right)$$

$$= 2\left[\tan^{-1}\left(\frac{1}{\sin\alpha}\right) + \tan^{-1}(\sin\alpha)\right]$$

$$= 2\left(-\frac{\pi}{2}\right) = -\pi \qquad [\text{as } \sin\alpha < 0]$$

26. $f(x) = \sin^{-1}2x + \cos^{-1}2x + \sec^{-1}2x$

$$f(x) = \frac{\pi}{2} + \sec^{-1}2x$$

Graph of $\sec^{-1}2x$ is as following

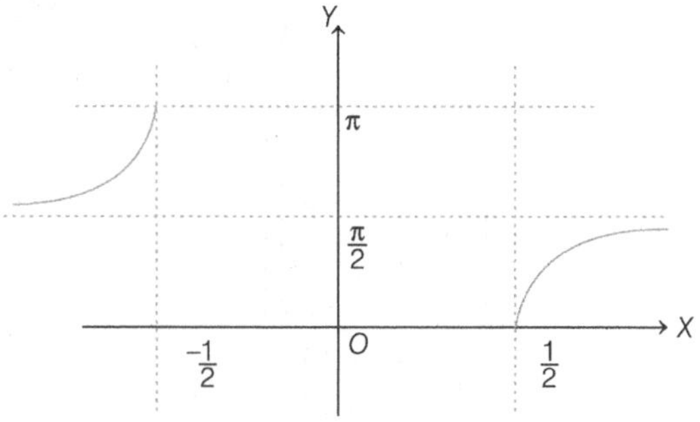

$$(f(x))_{\text{minimum}} = \frac{\pi}{2} + 0 = \frac{\pi}{2}$$

$$(f(x))_{\text{maximum}} = \frac{\pi}{2} + \pi = \frac{3\pi}{2}$$

$$\text{Sum} = \frac{\pi}{2} + \frac{3\pi}{2} = 2\pi$$

27. $\because \tan^{-1}\left(\frac{1+x}{1-x}\right) = \begin{cases} \tan^{-1}(1) + \tan^{-1}x, \text{ if } x < 1 \\ -\pi + \tan^{-1}(1) + \tan^{-1}x, \text{ if } x > 1 \end{cases}$

Now, $\quad f(x) = \begin{cases} \tan^{-1}(1), \text{ if } x < 1 \\ -\pi + \tan^{-1}(1), \text{ if } x > 1 \end{cases}$

$\therefore$ Range $f = \left\{\frac{\pi}{4}, \frac{-3\pi}{4}\right\}$

28. $\tan^{-1}x + \cot^{-1}y = \tan^{-1}3$

$$\Rightarrow \quad \cot^{-1}y = \tan^{-1}3 - \tan^{-1}x$$

$$\Rightarrow \quad \tan^{-1}\left(\frac{1}{y}\right) = \tan^{-1}\left(\frac{3-x}{1+3x}\right) \Rightarrow y = \frac{1+3x}{3-x}$$

Hence $x = 1, 2$ and $y = 2, 7$

29. $\tan^{-1}\left(\frac{\tan x}{4}\right) + \tan^{-1}\left(\dfrac{\frac{6\tan x}{1+\tan^2 x}}{5 + \frac{3(1-\tan^2 x)}{1+\tan^2 x}}\right)$

$$\Rightarrow \tan^{-1}\left(\frac{\tan x}{4}\right) + \tan^{-1}\left(\frac{3\tan x}{4+\tan^2 x}\right)$$

$$= \tan^{-1}\left(\frac{\frac{\tan x}{4} + \frac{3\tan x}{4+\tan^2 x}}{1 - \frac{3\tan^2 x}{4(4+\tan^2 x)}}\right)$$

$$= \tan^{-1}\left(\frac{16\tan x + \tan^3 x}{16+\tan^2 x}\right) = \tan^{-1}(\tan x) = x$$

30. $\tan^{-1}\dfrac{1}{\sqrt{2}}+\sin^{-1}\dfrac{1}{\sqrt{5}}-\cos^{-1}\dfrac{1}{\sqrt{10}}$

$$=\tan^{-1}\frac{1}{\sqrt{2}}+\tan^{-1}\frac{1}{2}-\tan^{-1}3$$

$$=\tan^{-1}\frac{1}{\sqrt{2}}-\left[\tan^{-1}3-\tan^{-1}\frac{1}{2}\right]$$

$$=\tan^{-1}\frac{1}{\sqrt{2}}-\left[\tan^{-1}\left(\frac{3-\frac{1}{2}}{1+\frac{3}{2}}\right)\right]=\tan^{-1}\frac{1}{\sqrt{2}}-\tan^{-1}1$$

$$=-\left[\tan^{-1}1-\tan^{-1}\frac{1}{\sqrt{2}}\right]$$

$$=-\left[\tan^{-1}\left(\frac{1-\frac{1}{\sqrt{2}}}{1+\frac{1}{\sqrt{2}}}\right)\right]$$

$$=-\tan^{-1}\left(\frac{\sqrt{2}-1}{\sqrt{2}+1}\right)$$

$$=-\cot^{-1}\left(\frac{\sqrt{2}+1}{\sqrt{2}-1}\right)$$

$$=-\left[\cot^{-1}-\left(\frac{1+\sqrt{2}}{1-\sqrt{2}}\right)\right]$$

$$=-\left[\pi-\cot^{-1}\left(\frac{1+\sqrt{2}}{1-\sqrt{2}}\right)\right]$$

$$=-\pi+\cot^{-1}\left(\frac{1+\sqrt{2}}{1-\sqrt{2}}\right)$$

31. Given, $\tan^{-1}\dfrac{\left[\dfrac{b}{c+a}+\dfrac{c}{a+b}\right]}{1-\dfrac{b}{c+a}\cdot\dfrac{c}{a+b}}=\dfrac{\pi}{4}$

$$\Rightarrow\quad \frac{ab+b^2+c^2+ac}{ac+bc+a^2+ab-bc}=1$$

$$\Rightarrow\quad ab+b^2+c^2+ac=ac+a^2+ab$$

$$b^2+c^2=a^2$$

$\therefore$ ΔABC is right angled at A.

32. $\tan^{-1}\left(\dfrac{1}{2}\tan 2A\right)+\tan^{-1}(\cot A)+\tan^{-1}(\cot^3 A)$

$$=\tan^{-1}\left(\frac{1}{2}\tan 2A\right)+\tan^{-1}\left(\frac{\cot A+\cot^3 A}{1-\cot^4 A}\right)+\pi$$

$$\left[0<A<\frac{\pi}{4}\Rightarrow\cot A>1\right]$$

$$=\tan^{-1}\left(\frac{\tan A}{1-\tan^2 A}\right)+\pi+\tan^{-1}\frac{\cot A(1+\cot^2 A)}{(1-\cot^2 A)(1+\cot^2 A)}$$

$$=\pi+\tan^{-1}\left(\frac{\tan A}{1-\tan^2 A}\right)+\tan^{-1}\left(\frac{\cot A}{1-\cot^2 A}\right)$$

$$=\pi=4\tan^{-1}(1)$$

33. $\cos^{-1}\left[\cot\left(\sin^{-1}\sqrt{\dfrac{2-\sqrt{3}}{4}}+\cos^{-1}\dfrac{\sqrt{3}}{2}+\cos^{-1}\dfrac{1}{\sqrt{2}}\right)\right]$

$$\Rightarrow\quad \cos^{-1}\left[\cot\left(\sin^{-1}\sqrt{\frac{2-\sqrt{3}}{4}}+\cos^{-1}\sqrt{\frac{2-\sqrt{3}}{4}}\right)\right]$$

$$=\cos^{-1}\left(\cot\frac{\pi}{2}\right)=\frac{\pi}{2}$$

34. We have, $\cos^{-1}\dfrac{x}{a}+\cos^{-1}\dfrac{y}{b}=\dfrac{\pi}{2}+\theta$

$$\Rightarrow\quad \frac{xy}{ab}-\sqrt{1-\frac{x^2}{a^2}}\sqrt{1-\frac{y^2}{b^2}}=-\sin\theta$$

$$\Rightarrow\quad \frac{xy}{ab}+\sin\theta=\sqrt{1-\frac{x^2}{a^2}}\sqrt{1-\frac{y^2}{b^2}}$$

On squaring both sides, we get

$$\frac{x^2y^2}{a^2b^2}+\sin^2\theta+\frac{2xy}{ab}\sin\theta=1-\frac{x^2}{a^2}-\frac{y^2}{b^2}+\frac{x^2y^2}{a^2b^2}$$

$$\Rightarrow\quad b^2x^2+a^2y^2+2ab\;xy\sin\theta=a^2b^2\cos^2\theta\le a^2b^2$$

35. $\sin^{-1}\sqrt{1-x^2}+\cos^{-1}x=\cot^{-1}\left(\dfrac{\sqrt{1-x^2}}{x}\right)-\sin^{-1}x$

or $$\frac{\pi}{2}+\sin^{-1}\sqrt{1-x^2}=\cot^{-1}\left(\frac{\sqrt{1-x^2}}{x}\right)$$

$$\Rightarrow\quad \tan^{-1}\left(\frac{\sqrt{1-x^2}}{x}\right)+\sin^{-1}\sqrt{1-x^2}=0$$

$$\Rightarrow\quad -1\le x<0\cup\{1\}$$

36. Let $\tan^{-1}(x)=\theta\Rightarrow x=\tan\theta$

$$\cos\theta=x \qquad \text{[given]}$$

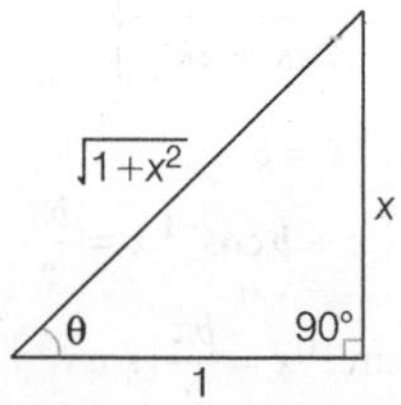

$$\Rightarrow\quad \frac{1}{\sqrt{1+x^2}}=x$$

$$\Rightarrow\quad x^2(1+x^2)=1$$

$$\Rightarrow\quad x^2=\frac{-1\pm\sqrt{5}}{2}$$

$$\Rightarrow\quad x^2=\frac{\sqrt{5}-1}{2} \qquad [x^2 \text{ cannot be} -\text{ve}]$$

$$\Rightarrow\quad \frac{x^2}{2}=\frac{\sqrt{5}-1}{4}$$

$$\Rightarrow\quad \cos^{-1}\left(\frac{\sqrt{5}-1}{4}\right)=\cos^{-1}\left(\sin\frac{\pi}{10}\right)$$

$$=\cos^{-1}\left(\cos\frac{2\pi}{5}\right)=\frac{2\pi}{5}$$

37. According to the question,

$$\sin^{-1}\frac{2}{\sqrt{5}} + \sin^{-1}\frac{3}{\sqrt{10}} + \sin^{-1}\alpha = \pi$$

$$\Rightarrow \quad \tan^{-1}2 + \tan^{-1}3 + \tan^{-1}\left(\frac{\alpha}{\sqrt{1-\alpha^2}}\right) = \pi$$

$$\Rightarrow \quad \pi + \tan^{-1}\frac{2+3}{1-(2)(3)} + \tan^{-1}\left(\frac{\alpha}{\sqrt{1-\alpha^2}}\right) = \pi$$

$$\Rightarrow \quad \tan^{-1}\left(\frac{\alpha}{\sqrt{1-\alpha^2}}\right) = \frac{\pi}{4}$$

$$\Rightarrow \quad \frac{\alpha}{\sqrt{1-\alpha^2}} = 1$$

$$\Rightarrow \quad \alpha = \frac{1}{\sqrt{2}}$$

38.

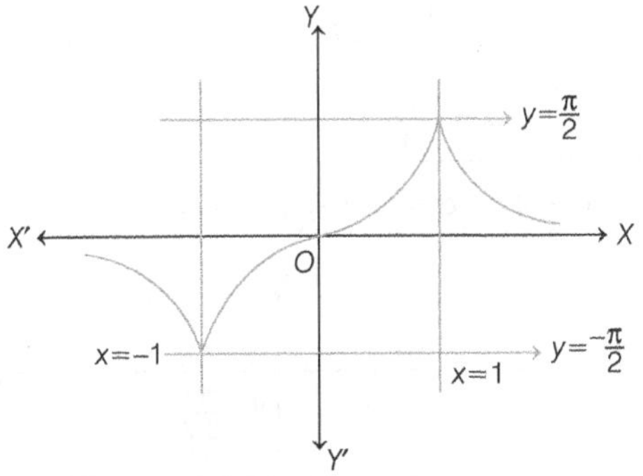

From the graph, it is clear that, $f(x)$ is not differentiable at $x = 1, -1$

39.

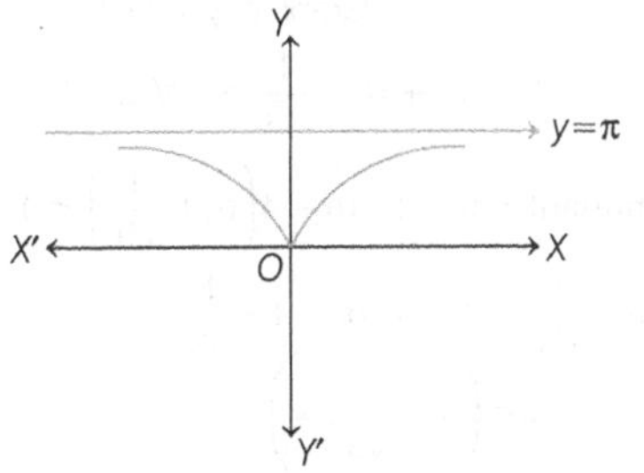

Thus, $f(x)$ is not differentiable at $x = 0$

40. $$\cot\left[\frac{\pi}{4} - \cot^{-1}\frac{3^2-1}{2\times 3}\right] = \cot\left[\frac{\pi}{4} - \cot^{-1}\frac{4}{3}\right]$$

$$= \frac{\cot\frac{\pi}{4}\cdot\frac{4}{3} + 1}{\frac{4}{3} - \cot\frac{\pi}{4}} = \frac{\frac{4}{3}+1}{\frac{4}{3}-1} = 7$$

41. $$2\tan^{-1}x = \cos^{-1}\left(\frac{1-x^2}{1+x^2}\right)$$

$$\Rightarrow 2\tan^{-1}a - 2\tan^{-1}b = 2\tan^{-1}x$$

$$\Rightarrow \quad \frac{a-b}{1+ab} = x$$

42. $$\alpha = 2\tan^{-1}\frac{1}{2} + \tan^{-1}\frac{4}{3}$$

$$= \tan^{-1}\frac{1}{1-\frac{1}{4}} + \tan^{-1}\frac{4}{3} = 2\tan^{-1}\frac{4}{3}$$

$$\left[\text{using } 2\tan^{-1}x = \tan^{-1}\frac{2x}{1-x^2}\right]$$

Let $\theta = \tan^{-1}\frac{4}{3} \Rightarrow \tan\theta = \frac{4}{3}$.

Now, $\sec\alpha = \sec 2\theta = \frac{1+\tan^2\theta}{1-\tan^2\theta} = \frac{1+(16/9)}{1-(16/9)} = \frac{25}{-7}$

Hence, $\sec\alpha = -\frac{25}{7}$

43. $$f(x) = \tan^{-1}\left(\frac{\left(\frac{x}{2}-1\right)}{1+x\left(\frac{x}{2}+1\right)}\right) = \tan^{-1}(x) - \tan^{-1}\left(\frac{x}{2}+1\right)$$

$$\Rightarrow f'(x) = \frac{1}{(1+x^2)} - \frac{1}{\left(1+\left(\frac{x}{2}+1\right)^2\right)} \times \frac{1}{2}$$

$$\Rightarrow f'(1) = \frac{1}{2} - \frac{1}{2\left(1+\frac{9}{4}\right)} = \frac{1}{2} - \frac{2}{13} = \frac{9}{26} \Rightarrow 26f'(1) = 9$$

44. We have, $f(x) = (\tan^{-1}x)^3 + (\cot^{-1}x)^3$

$$= (\tan^{-1}x + \cot^{-1}x)((\tan^{-1}x)^2 - (\tan^{-1}x)(\cot^{-1}x) + (\cot^{-1}x)^2)$$

$$= \frac{\pi}{2}\left((\tan^{-1}x)^2 - (\tan^{-1}x)\left(\frac{\pi}{2} - \tan^{-1}x\right) + \left(\frac{\pi}{2} - \tan^{-1}1x\right)^2\right)$$

$$\left[\text{using } \cot^{-1}x = \frac{\pi}{2} - \tan^{-1}x\right]$$

$$= \frac{3\pi}{2}\left(\left(\tan^{-1}x - \frac{\pi}{4}\right)^2 + \frac{\pi^2}{48}\right)$$

Clearly, $f(x)$ will be minimum when $\left(\tan^{-1}x - \frac{\pi}{4}\right)^2 = 0$

and $f(x)$ will be maximum when $\left(\tan^{-1}x - \frac{\pi}{4}\right)^2 = \left(-\frac{\pi}{2} - \frac{\pi}{4}\right)^2$

$$\therefore \quad a = f(x)_{\min} = \frac{3\pi}{2}\left(0 + \frac{\pi^2}{48}\right) = \frac{\pi^3}{32}$$

and $$b = f(x)_{\max} = \frac{3\pi}{2}\left(\left(\frac{-3\pi}{4}\right)^2 + \frac{\pi^2}{48}\right) = \frac{7\pi^3}{8}$$

Hence, $$\frac{b}{7a} = \frac{\frac{7\pi^3}{8}}{\frac{7\pi^3}{32}} = 4$$

45. We have, $T_n = 2\,\text{arc}\cot\left(\frac{n^2+n+4}{2}\right) = 2\tan^{-1}\left(\frac{2}{n^2+n+4}\right)$

$$T_n = 2\tan^{-1}\left(\frac{\frac{1}{2}}{1+\frac{n(n+1)}{2.2}}\right) = 2\left(\tan^{-1}\left(\frac{n+1}{2}\right) - \tan^{-1}\left(\frac{n}{2}\right)\right)$$

Hence, $S_n = \sum_{n=0}^{n} T_n = 2\sum_{n=0}^{n}\left(\tan^{-1}\left(\frac{n+1}{2}\right) - \tan^{-1}\left(\frac{n}{2}\right)\right)$

$$S_n = \tan^{-1}\left(\frac{1}{2}\right) - \tan^{-1}(0) + \tan^{-1}(1) - \tan^{-1}\left(\frac{1}{2}\right) + \tan^{-1}\left(\frac{n+1}{2}\right) - \tan^{-1}\left(\frac{n}{2}\right)$$

$$\Rightarrow \quad S_n = 2\tan^{-1}\left(\frac{n+1}{2}\right)$$

$$\therefore \lim_{n\to\infty} S_n = 2.\left(\frac{\pi}{2}\right) = \pi = k\pi \qquad \text{(given)}$$

$$\Rightarrow \quad k = 1$$

46. As, $\sum_{r=1}^{5}\cot^{-1}(2r^2) = \sum_{r=1}^{5}\tan^{-1}\left(\frac{2}{4r^2}\right)$

$$= \sum_{r=1}^{5}\tan^{-1}\left(\frac{(2r+1)-(2r-1)}{1+(2r+1)(2r-1)}\right)$$

$$= \sum_{r=1}^{5}(\tan^{-1}(2r+1) - \tan^{-1}(2r-1))$$

$$= \tan^{-1}11 - \tan^{-1}1 = \tan^{-1}\left(\frac{11-1}{1+11\times 1}\right)$$

$$= \tan^{-1}\left(\frac{10}{12}\right) = \tan^{-1}\left(\frac{5}{6}\right)$$

$$\therefore \tan\left(\sum_{r=1}^{5}\cot^{-1}(2r^2)\right) = \tan\left(\tan^{-1}\frac{5}{6}\right) = \frac{5}{6}$$

Now, $\tan\left(\sum_{r=1}^{5}\cot^{-1}(2r^2)\right) = \frac{5x+6}{6x+5}$

$$\Rightarrow \quad \frac{5}{6} = \frac{5x+6}{6x+5}$$

$\Rightarrow$ The given equations has no real solution.

47. $\min(x^2 + 4x + 7) = 3$

$$\max\left\{\frac{\pi^2}{4}, 3\right\} = 3$$

$$\lim_{z\to 0}\left[3.\frac{\sin^{-1}z}{z}\right] = 3$$

48. $\sin\left(\frac{\pi}{6} + \tan^{-1}x\right) = \frac{13}{14}$

$$\frac{\pi}{6} + \tan^{-1}x = \sin^{-1}\left(\frac{13}{14}\right) = \tan^{-1}\left(\frac{13}{3\sqrt{3}}\right)$$

$$\tan^{-1}x = \tan^{-1}\left(\frac{13}{3\sqrt{3}}\right) - \tan^{-1}\left(\frac{1}{\sqrt{3}}\right)$$

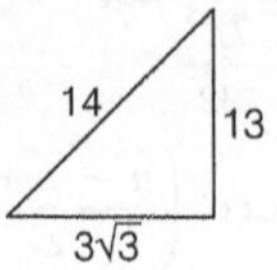

$$= \tan^{-1}\left[\frac{\frac{13}{3\sqrt{3}} - \frac{1}{\sqrt{3}}}{1+\frac{13}{9}}\right] = \tan^{-1}\left[\frac{10}{3\sqrt{3}}\left(\frac{9}{22}\right)\right]$$

$$\tan^{-1}x = \tan^{-1}\left[\frac{5\sqrt{3}}{11}\right]$$

$$\therefore \quad x = \frac{5\sqrt{3}}{11} \Rightarrow \frac{a\sqrt{3}}{b}$$

$$\Rightarrow \quad a+b = 16 \Rightarrow \left(\frac{a+b}{2}\right) = 8$$

Alternate Solution

$$\sin(30^\circ + \tan^{-1}x) = \frac{13}{14}$$

$$\Rightarrow \quad \frac{1}{2}\cos(\tan^{-1}x) + \frac{\sqrt{3}}{2}\sin(\tan^{-1}x) = \frac{13}{14}$$

$$\Rightarrow \quad 7(1+\sqrt{3}x) = 13\sqrt{1+x^2}$$

$$\Rightarrow \quad 11x^2 - 49\sqrt{3}x + 60 = 0 \qquad \text{[on squaring]}$$

$$\therefore \quad x = \frac{49\sqrt{3} \pm 39\sqrt{3}}{22}$$

$$= \frac{5\sqrt{3}}{11}, 4\sqrt{3} \qquad \text{[reject]}$$

$$\therefore \quad x = \frac{5\sqrt{3}}{11}$$

49. Clearly $x^2 - 4x + \alpha >$ or $\geq \frac{-1}{\sqrt{3}}, \forall\ x \in R$

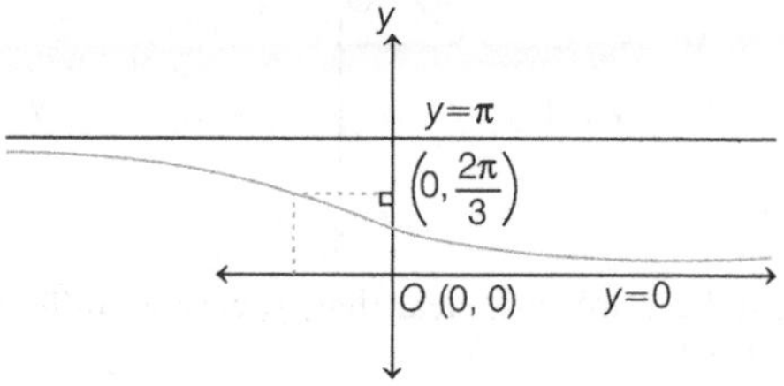

Graph of $y=\cot^{-1}x$

$$\Rightarrow \quad x^2 - 4x + \alpha + \frac{1}{\sqrt{3}} > 0, \forall\ x \in R$$

So, discriminant $< 0 \Rightarrow 16 - 4\left(\alpha + \frac{1}{\sqrt{3}}\right) < 0$

$$4 - \alpha - \frac{1}{\sqrt{3}} < 0 \Rightarrow \alpha > 4 - \frac{1}{\sqrt{3}}$$

$$\therefore \quad \alpha \in \left(4 - \frac{1}{\sqrt{3}}, \infty\right)$$

Hence, minimum integral $\alpha = 4$

50. **L** : $3^4 - [{}^3C_1(2^4 - 2) + {}^3C_2] = 36$

M : If $x > 0$, Sgn $(x) = 1$

$$f(x) = 0 + \frac{\pi}{2} = \frac{\pi}{2}$$

For $x = 0$ $f(x)$ is not defined

$$\therefore \quad \text{for } x < 0,\ f(x) = \pi - \frac{\pi}{2} = \frac{\pi}{2}$$

$$\therefore \quad M = 1$$

N : Coefficient of t^5 = coefficient of t^2 in$(1+t^2)^5$ × coefficient of t^3 in $(1+t^3)^8$

$$= 5 \times 8 = 40$$

Hence, $L = 36$; $M = 1$ and $N = 40$

$$\Rightarrow \quad N - LM = 40 - 36 = 4$$

51.

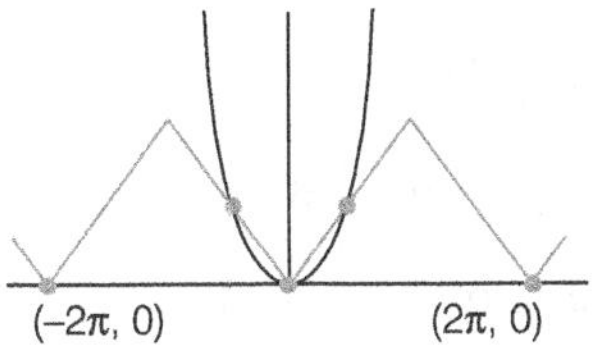

Number of solutions are three.

52. $\sec^2 u, \sec^4 v, \sec^6 w \in [1, \infty)$

$\therefore \quad \sec^2(u) + \sec^4(v) + \sec^6(w) \in [3, \infty)$

$\therefore \quad \pi(\sec^2 u + \sec^4 v + \sec^6 w) \in [3\pi, \infty)$

But $\quad \cos^{-1} x + \cos^{-1} y + \cos^{-1} z \in [0, 3\pi]$

So equation is possible if LHS = RHS = 3π

$\therefore \quad \cos^{-1} x = \cos^{-1} y = \cos^{-1} z = \pi$

$\therefore \quad x = y = z = -1$

and $\quad \sec^2 u = \sec^4 v = \sec^6 w = 1$

$\therefore \quad u = \pi, v = 2\pi, w = 3\pi$

$\therefore \quad x^{2000} + y^{2002} + z^{2004} + \dfrac{36\pi}{u + v + w} = 1 + 1 + 1 + \dfrac{36\pi}{6\pi} = 9$

53. Given, $f(x) = \sin^{-1}\left(\dfrac{x-1}{2x+3}\right)$

For $f(x)$ to be defined

$$2x + 3 \neq 0 \text{ and } \left|\frac{x-1}{2x+3}\right| \leq 1$$

$$\Rightarrow \quad x \neq -\frac{3}{2} \text{ and } |x - 1| \leq |2x + 3|$$

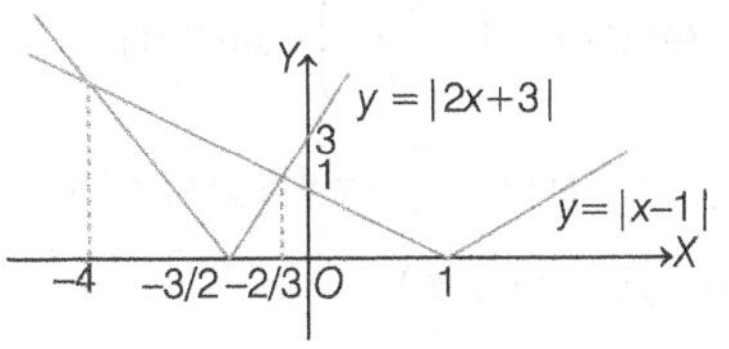

From above graph i.e. graph of $y = |2x + 3|$ and $y = |x - 1|$, we observe that, for $|2x + 3| \geq |x - 1|$

$\Rightarrow x \in (-\infty, -4] \cup \left[-\dfrac{2}{3}, \infty\right)$ i.e. $R - \left(-4, -\dfrac{2}{3}\right)$

So, $\alpha = -4$ and $\beta = -\dfrac{2}{3}$

Hence, $12\alpha\beta = 32$

Alternate Solution

Given, $f(x) = \sin^{-1}\left(\dfrac{x-1}{2x+3}\right)$

For $f(x)$ to be defined

$2x + 3 \neq 0$ and $-1 \leq \dfrac{x-1}{2x+3} \leq 1 \Rightarrow x \neq -\dfrac{3}{2}$

and $\begin{cases} \dfrac{x-1}{2x+3} \geq -1 \\ \dfrac{x-1}{2x+3} \leq 1 \end{cases} \Rightarrow \begin{cases} \dfrac{x-1+2x+3}{2x+3} \geq 0 \\ \dfrac{x-1-2x-3}{2x+3} \leq 0 \end{cases}$

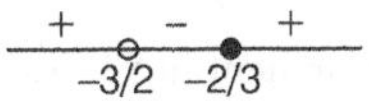

$\Rightarrow \begin{cases} \dfrac{3x+2}{2x+3} \geq 0 \\ \dfrac{-x-4}{2x+3} \leq 0 \end{cases} \Rightarrow \begin{cases} \dfrac{3x+2}{2x+3} \geq 0 \\ \dfrac{x+4}{2x+3} \geq 0 \end{cases}$

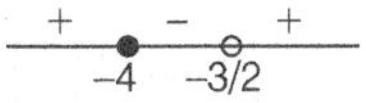

$\Rightarrow \begin{cases} x \in \left(-\infty, -\dfrac{3}{2}\right) \cup \left[-\dfrac{2}{3}, \infty\right) \\ x \in (-\infty, -4] \cup \left(-\dfrac{3}{2}, \infty\right) \end{cases}$

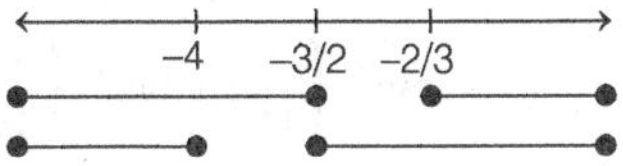

$\Rightarrow x \in (-\infty, -4] \cup \left[-\dfrac{2}{3}, \infty\right)$ i.e. $x \in R - \left(-4, -\dfrac{2}{3}\right)$

So, $\alpha = -4$ and $\beta = \dfrac{-2}{3}$

and hence, $12\alpha\beta = 12 \times (-4) \times \left(\dfrac{-2}{3}\right) = 32$

54. $\cos^{-1} x - \sin^{-1} y = \alpha; -\dfrac{\pi}{2} \leq \alpha \leq \pi$

$\Rightarrow \quad \cos^{-1} x - \dfrac{\pi}{2} + \cos^{-1} y = \alpha$

$\Rightarrow \quad \cos^{-1} x + \cos^{-1} y = \dfrac{\pi}{2} + \alpha$

$\Rightarrow \quad \cos^{-1}(xy - \sqrt{1-x^2}\sqrt{1-y^2}) = \dfrac{\pi}{2} + \alpha$

$\Rightarrow \quad xy - \sqrt{1-x^2}\sqrt{1-y^2} = -\sin \alpha$

$(xy + \sin \alpha)^2 = (1 - x^2)(1 - y^2)$

$x^2y^2 + \sin^2\alpha + 2xy \sin \alpha = 1 + x^2y^2 - x^2 - y^2$

$x^2 + y^2 + 2xy \sin \alpha = 1 - \sin^2\alpha = \cos^2\alpha$

$\therefore$ Minimum value of $x^2 + y^2 + 2xy \sin \alpha = 0$

55. $2\sin^{-1} x + 3\cos^{-1} x = \dfrac{2\pi}{5}$

$\pi + \cos^{-1} x = \dfrac{2\pi}{5}$

$\cos^{-1} x = \dfrac{-3\pi}{5}$

Not possible.

Thus, there are zero solution.

56. **Decoding the Question**

Firstly convert the given equation in the terms of $\tan^{-1} x$, then use the formula,

$$\tan^{-1} x + \tan^{-1} y = \tan^{-1}\left(\frac{x+y}{1-xy}\right)$$

According to the question,

$$\cot^{-1} 3 + \cot^{-1} 4 + \cot^{-1} 5 + \cot^{-1} n = \frac{\pi}{4}$$

By using $\cot^{-1} x = \tan^{-1}\left(\frac{1}{x}\right)$

and $\tan^{-1} x + \tan^{-1} y = \tan^{-1}\left(\frac{x+y}{1-xy}\right)$

$$\Rightarrow \tan^{-1}\left(\frac{1}{3}\right) + \tan^{-1}\left(\frac{1}{4}\right) + \tan^{-1}\left(\frac{1}{5}\right) + \tan^{-1}\left(\frac{1}{n}\right) = \frac{\pi}{4}$$

$$\Rightarrow \tan^{-1}\left(\frac{\frac{1}{3}+\frac{1}{4}}{1-\frac{1}{3}\times\frac{1}{4}}\right) + \tan^{-1}\left(\frac{\frac{1}{5}+\frac{1}{n}}{1-\frac{1}{5}\times\frac{1}{n}}\right) = \frac{\pi}{4}$$

$$\Rightarrow \tan^{-1}\left(\frac{7}{11}\right) + \tan^{-1}\left(\frac{n+5}{5n-1}\right) = \frac{\pi}{4}$$

$$\Rightarrow \tan^{-1}\left(\frac{\frac{7}{11}+\frac{(n+5)}{5n-1}}{1-\left(\frac{7}{11}\right)\left(\frac{n+5}{5n-1}\right)}\right) = \frac{\pi}{4}$$

$$\Rightarrow \frac{35n-7+11n+55}{11(5n-1)-7(n+5)} = 1$$

$$\Rightarrow n = 47$$

57. Let $\sin^{-1}\alpha = A$, $\sin^{-1}\beta = B$ and $\sin^{-1}\gamma = C$

$$\because \sin^{-1}\alpha + \sin^{-1}\beta + \sin^{-1}\gamma = \pi$$

$$\Rightarrow A + B + C = \pi$$

Given, $(\alpha+\beta+\gamma)(\alpha-\gamma+\beta) = 3\alpha\beta$

$$(\alpha+\beta)^2 - \gamma^2 = 3\alpha\beta$$

$$\alpha^2+\beta^2-\gamma^2 = \alpha\beta$$

$$\frac{\alpha^2+\beta^2-\gamma^2}{2\alpha\beta} = \frac{1}{2}$$

$$\therefore \cos C = \frac{1}{2}$$

$$\Rightarrow \sqrt{1-\sin^2 C} = \frac{1}{2}$$

$$\Rightarrow \sqrt{1-\gamma^2} = \frac{1}{2}$$

$$\Rightarrow \gamma = \frac{\sqrt{3}}{2}$$

58. $f(x) = \log_e\left(\frac{2x+3}{4x^2+x-3}\right) + \cos^{-1}\left(\frac{2x-1}{x+2}\right)$

Domain of $f(x)$

$$\frac{2x+3}{4x^2+x-3} > 0 \text{ and } -1 \le \frac{2x-1}{x+2} \le 1$$

$$\frac{2x+3}{(4x-3)(x+1)} > 0 \text{ and } \frac{2x-1}{x+2} + 1 \ge 0 \text{ and } \frac{2x-1}{x+2} - 1 \le 0$$

$\frac{2x+3}{(4x-3)(x+1)} > 0$	$\frac{3x+1}{x+2} \ge 0$	$\frac{x-3}{x+2} \le 0$
− + − + ; −3/2, −1, 3/4	+ − + ; −2, −1/3	+ − + ; −2, 3

common of all solutions.

We get $x \in \left(\frac{3}{4}, 3\right]$

$$\therefore \alpha = \frac{3}{4}, \beta = 3$$

$$\therefore 5\beta - 4\alpha \Rightarrow 15 - 3 = 12$$

59. Given, $\tan^{-1} x + \tan^{-1}(2x) = \frac{\pi}{4}$

$$\Rightarrow \tan^{-1}\left(\frac{3x}{1-2x^2}\right) = \frac{\pi}{4} \Rightarrow \frac{3x}{1-2x^2} = 1$$

$$\Rightarrow 3x = 1-2x^2 \Rightarrow 2x^2+3x-1 = 0$$

$$\Rightarrow x = \frac{-3 \pm \sqrt{9+8}}{4}$$

$$\Rightarrow x = \frac{-3 \pm \sqrt{17}}{4}$$

$$\Rightarrow x = \frac{-3-\sqrt{17}}{4} < 0$$

or
$$x = \frac{-3+\sqrt{17}}{4} > 0$$

Hence, total number of positive real values of $x = 1$.

60. Given that $f(x) = 4\sin^{-1}\left(\frac{x^2}{x^2+1}\right)$

$$\Rightarrow \frac{x^2}{x^2+1} = \frac{x^2+1-1}{x^2+1} = 1 - \frac{1}{x^2+1}$$

So, $0 \le \frac{x^2}{x^2+1} < 1$

Thus, $\sin^{-1}(0) \le \sin^{-1}\left(\frac{x^2}{x^2+1}\right) < \sin^{-1}(1)$

$$\Rightarrow 0 \le f(x) < \frac{4\pi}{2} \Rightarrow 0 \le f(x) < 2\pi$$

Thus, Range $f(x) = [0, 2\pi)$

61. We have, $2\tan^{-1}\left(\frac{1-x}{1+x}\right) = \cos^{-1}\left(\frac{1-x^2}{1+x^2}\right)$

Puting $x = \tan\theta$.

Also, $0 < x < 1 \Rightarrow 0 < \theta < \frac{\pi}{4}$

Now, $2\tan^{-1}\left(\frac{1-\tan\theta}{1+\tan\theta}\right) = \cos^{-1}\left(\frac{1-\tan^2\theta}{1+\tan^2\theta}\right)$

$$\Rightarrow 2\tan^{-1}\tan\left(\frac{\pi}{4}-\theta\right) = \cos^{-1}\cos 2\theta$$

$$\Rightarrow 2\left(\frac{\pi}{4}-\theta\right) = 2\theta \Rightarrow \frac{\pi}{4}-\theta = \theta$$

$$\Rightarrow \theta = \frac{\pi}{8} \Rightarrow \tan^{-1} x = \frac{\pi}{8}$$

$$\Rightarrow x = \tan\frac{\pi}{8} = \sqrt{2}-1 \approx 0.414$$

$$\therefore x < \frac{1}{2}$$

So, $n(S) = 1$ and the element in S is less than $\frac{1}{2}$.

62. Given, $\cos^{-1}2x - 2\cos^{-1}(\sqrt{1-x^2}) = \pi$

$\Rightarrow \quad \cos^{-1}2x = \pi + 2\cos^{-1}(\sqrt{1-x^2})$

$\Rightarrow \quad 2x = \cos(\pi + 2\cos^{-1}(\sqrt{1-x^2}))$

$\Rightarrow \quad 2x = -\cos(2\cos^{-1}(\sqrt{1-x^2}))$

$\Rightarrow \quad 2x = -\cos[\cos^{-1}(2(\sqrt{1-x^2})^2 - 1)]$

$[\because 2\cos^{-1}x = \cos^{-1}(2x^2 - 1)]$

$\Rightarrow \quad 2x = -\cos[\cos^{-1}(2 - 2x^2 - 1)]$

$\Rightarrow \quad 2x = -(1 - 2x^2)$

$\Rightarrow \quad 2x = -1 + 2x^2$

$\Rightarrow \quad 2x^2 - 2x - 1 = 0$

$$\Rightarrow \quad x = \frac{-(-2) \pm \sqrt{(-2)^2 - 4(2)(-1)}}{2 \times 2}$$

$$= \frac{2 \pm 2\sqrt{3}}{4} = \frac{1}{2} \pm \frac{\sqrt{3}}{2}$$

$$\therefore \quad x = \frac{1}{2} - \frac{\sqrt{3}}{2} \in \left[\frac{-1}{2}, \frac{1}{2}\right]$$

$$\therefore S = \left\{x : x = \frac{1-\sqrt{3}}{2}\right\}$$

Now, $\sum_{x \in S} 2\sin^{-1}(x^2 - 1)$

$$= 2\sin^{-1}\left(\left(\frac{1-\sqrt{3}}{2}\right)^2 - 1\right) = 2\sin^{-1}\left(-\frac{\sqrt{3}}{2}\right)$$

$$= -2\sin^{-1}\frac{\sqrt{3}}{2} = -2 \times \frac{\pi}{3} = -\frac{2\pi}{3}$$

63. Given that $a_1 = 1, a_2 = 2, \ldots, a_{2022} = 2022$,

$$\text{Now, } \tan^{-1}\left(\frac{1}{1+a_1a_2}\right) + \tan^{-1}\left(\frac{1}{1+a_2a_3}\right) + \ldots + \tan^{-1}\left(\frac{1}{1+a_{2021}a_{2022}}\right)$$

On putting $a_1 = 1, a_2 = 2, \ldots\ldots, a_{2021} = 2021, a_{2022} = 2022$, we get

$$\tan^{-1}\left[\frac{1}{1+1\cdot 2}\right] + \tan^{-1}\left[\frac{1}{1+2\cdot 3}\right] + \ldots + \tan^{-1}\left[\frac{1}{1+2021\cdot 2022}\right]$$

$$= \tan^{-1}\left[\frac{2-1}{1+2\cdot 1}\right] + \tan^{-1}\left[\frac{3-2}{1+3\cdot 2}\right] + \ldots + \tan^{-1}\left[\frac{2022-2021}{1+2022\cdot 2021}\right]$$

$$= \tan^{-1}(2) - \tan^{-1}(1) + \tan^{-1}(3) - \tan^{-1}(2) + \ldots + \tan^{-1}(2022) - \tan^{-1}(2021) = \tan^{-1}(2022) - \tan^{-1}(1)$$

$$\left[\because \tan^{-1}x - \tan^{-1}y = \tan^{-1}\left(\frac{x-y}{1+x\cdot y}\right)\right]$$

$$= \tan^{-1}(2022) - \frac{\pi}{4}$$

64. We have, $\sin^{-1}\frac{\alpha}{17} + \cos^{-1}\frac{4}{5} - \tan^{-1}\frac{77}{36} = 0$

$$\Rightarrow \quad \sin^{-1}\frac{\alpha}{17} = \tan^{-1}\frac{77}{36} - \cos^{-1}\frac{4}{5}$$

$$= \sin^{-1}\frac{77}{85} - \sin^{-1}\frac{3}{5}$$

$$= \sin^{-1}\left[\frac{77}{85}\sqrt{1-\left(\frac{3}{5}\right)^2} - \frac{3}{5}\sqrt{1-\left(\frac{77}{85}\right)^2}\right]$$

$$= \sin^{-1}\left(\frac{200}{425}\right)$$

$$\therefore \quad \sin^{-1}\frac{\alpha}{17} = \sin^{-1}\frac{8}{17} \Rightarrow \frac{\alpha}{17} = \frac{8}{17}$$

$\Rightarrow \quad \alpha = 8$

Now, $\sin^{-1}(\sin\alpha) + \cos^{-1}(\cos\alpha)$

$= \sin^{-1}(\sin 8) + \cos^{-1}(\cos 8)$

$= \sin^{-1}\sin(3\pi - 8) + \cos^{-1}\cos(8 - 2\pi)$

$= 3\pi - 8 + 8 - 2\pi = \pi$

65. Given, $\tan^{-1}\left(\frac{1+\sqrt{3}}{3+\sqrt{3}}\right) + \sec^{-1}\left(\sqrt{\frac{8+4\sqrt{3}}{6+3\sqrt{3}}}\right)$

$$= \tan^{-1}\left(\frac{(1+\sqrt{3})}{\sqrt{3}(\sqrt{3}+1)}\right) + \sec^{-1}\left(\sqrt{\frac{4(2+\sqrt{3})}{3(2+\sqrt{3})}}\right)$$

$$= \tan^{-1}(1/\sqrt{3}) + \sec^{-1}(2/\sqrt{3})$$

$$= \frac{\pi}{6} + \frac{\pi}{6} = \frac{2\pi}{6} = \frac{\pi}{3}$$

66. We have, $f(x) = \sec^{-1}\left(\frac{2x}{5x+3}\right)$

$$\frac{2x}{5x+3} \le -1 \text{ or } \frac{2x}{5x+3} \ge 1$$

$$\frac{2x+5x+3}{5x+3} \le 0 \text{ or } \frac{2x-5x-3}{5x+3} \ge 0$$

$$\frac{7x+3}{5x+3} \le 0 \text{ or } \frac{-3(x+1)}{5x+3} \ge 0$$

Case I $7x + 3 \le 0$ and $5x + 3 > 0$

$$x \le -\frac{3}{7} \text{ or } x > -\frac{3}{5} \Rightarrow -\frac{3}{5} < x \le -\frac{3}{7}$$

Case II $7x + 3 \ge 0$ and $5x + 3 < 0$

$$x \ge -\frac{3}{7} \text{ and } x < -\frac{3}{5}$$

which is not possible.

Case III $x + 1 \ge 0$ and $5x + 3 < 0$

$$x \ge -1 \text{ and } x < -\frac{3}{5} \Rightarrow -1 \le x < -\frac{3}{5}$$

Case IV $x + 1 \le 0$ and $5x + 3 \ge 0$

$$x \le -1 \text{ and } x \ge -\frac{3}{5}$$

which is not possible.

$\therefore$ Domain is $\left[-1, -\frac{3}{5}\right) \cup \left(-\frac{3}{5}, -\frac{3}{7}\right]$

$\therefore \alpha = -1, \beta = -\frac{3}{5}, \gamma = -\frac{3}{5}, \delta = -\frac{3}{7}$

$$|3\alpha + 10(\beta + \gamma) + 21\delta| = \left|-3 + 10\left(-\frac{3}{5} - \frac{3}{5}\right) + 21\left(-\frac{3}{7}\right)\right| = 24$$

67. Given, $\sin^{-1}\left(\frac{x+1}{\sqrt{x^2+2x+2}}\right) - \sin^{-1}\left(\frac{x}{\sqrt{x^2+1}}\right) = \frac{\pi}{4}$

$\Rightarrow \tan^{-1}(x+1) - \tan^{-1} x = \frac{\pi}{4}$

$\Rightarrow \tan^{-1}\left(\frac{(x+1) - x}{1 + (x+1)x}\right) = \frac{\pi}{4}$

$\Rightarrow \tan^{-1}\left(\frac{1}{1 + x^2 + x}\right) = \frac{\pi}{4}$

$\Rightarrow \tan^{-1}\left(\frac{1}{1 + x^2 + x}\right) = \frac{\pi}{4}$

$\Rightarrow \frac{1}{1 + x + x^2} = \tan\left(\frac{\pi}{4}\right) = 1$

$\Rightarrow \frac{1}{1 + x + x^2} = 1$

$\Rightarrow 1 + x + x^2 = 1 \Rightarrow x(x+1) = 0$

$\Rightarrow x = 0$ or $x = -1$

$\therefore S = \{-1, 0\}$

Now, $\sum_{x \in S}\left(\sin(x^2 + x + 5)\frac{\pi}{2}\right) - \cos((x^2 + x + 5)\pi)$

$= \left[\sin\left(\frac{5\pi}{2}\right) - \cos 5\pi\right] + \left[\sin\left(\frac{5\pi}{2}\right) - \cos 5\pi\right]$

$= 2\left[\sin\left(2\pi + \frac{\pi}{2}\right) - (-1)\right] = 2[1 + 1] = 4$

68. Given equation is $\sin^{-1} x = 2\tan^{-1} x$

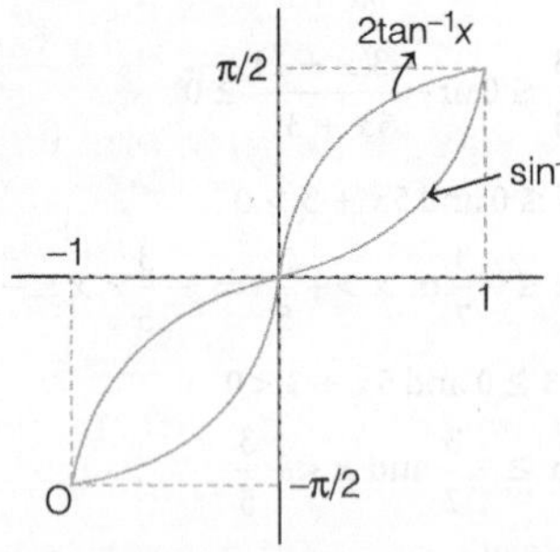

Clearly, from the above figure, the two graphs cut at two points in $-1 < x \leq 1$.

So, required number of solution is 2.

69. $\tan^{-1}\left(\frac{2x}{1-x^2}\right) + \cot^{-1}\left(\frac{1-x^2}{2x}\right) = \frac{\pi}{3}, -1 < x < 1, x \neq 0$

We know that

$\cot^{-1} x = \tan^{-1}\frac{1}{x} : x > 0$

or $\cot^{-1} x = \pi + \tan^{-1}\frac{1}{x} : x < 0$

Now, **Case I** $x > 0$

$\tan^{-1}\frac{2x}{1-x^2} + \tan^{-1}\frac{2x}{1-x^2} = \frac{\pi}{3}$

$\Rightarrow 2\tan^{-1}\left(\frac{2x}{1-x^2}\right) = \frac{\pi}{3}$

$\Rightarrow \tan^{-1}\frac{2x}{1-x^2} = \frac{\pi}{6}$

$\Rightarrow \frac{2x}{1-x^2} = \frac{1}{\sqrt{3}}$

$\Rightarrow x^2 + 2\sqrt{3}x - 1 = 0$

$\Rightarrow x = \frac{-2\sqrt{3} \pm \sqrt{12+4}}{2} = -\sqrt{3} \pm 2$

But $x > 0 \Rightarrow x = 2 - \sqrt{3}$

Case II $x < 0$

$\tan^{-1}\frac{2x}{1-x^2} + \tan^{-1}\frac{2x}{1-x^2} + \pi = \frac{\pi}{3}$

$\Rightarrow \tan^{-1}\left(\frac{2x}{1-x^2}\right) = -\frac{\pi}{3}$

$\Rightarrow \frac{2x}{1-x^2} = -\sqrt{3}$

$\Rightarrow \sqrt{3}x^2 - 2x - \sqrt{3} = 0$

$\Rightarrow x = \frac{2 \pm \sqrt{4+12}}{2\sqrt{3}} = \frac{2 \pm 4}{2\sqrt{3}} = \frac{-1}{\sqrt{3}}, \sqrt{3}$

But $x < 0 \Rightarrow x = \frac{-1}{\sqrt{3}}$

Given, sum of all solutions $= \alpha - \frac{4}{\sqrt{3}}$

$$2 - \sqrt{3} - \frac{1}{\sqrt{3}} = \alpha - \frac{4}{\sqrt{3}} \Rightarrow \alpha = 2$$

70. $f(x) = \sin^{-1}\left(\frac{x^2 - 3x + 2}{x^2 + 2x + 7}\right)$

Now, take domain of $\sin^{-1}x$ as $x \in [-1, 1]$

$\frac{x^2 - 3x + 2}{x^2 + 2x + 7} \geq -1$ and $\frac{x^2 - 3x + 2}{x^2 + 2x + 7} \leq 1,$

$2x^2 - x + 9 \geq 0$ and $5x \geq -5$

$\Rightarrow x \geq -1$ where, $x \in R$.

Hence, Domain $x \in [-1, \infty)$.

71. We know, $-1 \leq \frac{2\sin^{-1}\left(\frac{1}{4x^2 - 1}\right)}{\pi} \leq 1$

$$-\frac{\pi}{2} \leq \sin^{-1}\left(\frac{1}{4x^2-1}\right) \leq \frac{\pi}{2}$$

On solving inequalities, we get

Always $-1 \leq \frac{1}{4x^2 - 1} \leq 1$

$$x \in \left(-\infty, \frac{-1}{\sqrt{2}}\right] \cup \left[\frac{1}{\sqrt{2}}, \infty\right) \cup \{0\}$$

72. **Method I** Given, $f(x) = \cos^{-1}\left(\dfrac{x^2 - 4x + 2}{x^2 + 3}\right)$

For $f(x)$ to be defined, $\left|\dfrac{x^2 - 4x + 2}{x^2 + 3}\right| \le 1$

$$\Rightarrow \quad (x^2 - 4x + 2)^2 \le (x^2 + 3)^2$$

$$\Rightarrow \quad (x^2 - 4x + 2)^2 - (x^2 + 3)^2 \le 0$$

$$\Rightarrow \quad [(x^2 - 4x + 2) + (x^2 + 3)][(x^2 - 4x + 2) - (x^2 + 3)] \le 0$$

$$\Rightarrow \quad (2x^2 - 4x + 5)(-4x - 1) \le 0$$

$$\Rightarrow \quad -4x - 1 \le 0$$

[$\because 2x^2 - 4x + 5 > 0 \ \forall \ x \in R$, because its $a = 2 > 0$ and $D < 0$]

$$\Rightarrow \quad -4x \le 1$$

$$\Rightarrow \quad x \ge \frac{-1}{4}$$

Method II Given, $f(x) = \cos^{-1}\left(\dfrac{x^2 - 4x + 2}{x^2 + 3}\right)$

For $f(x)$ to be defined,

$$-1 \le \frac{x^2 - 4x + 2}{x^2 + 3} \le 1 \qquad [\because |t| \le 1 \Rightarrow -1 \le t \le 1]$$

$$\Rightarrow -(x^2 + 3) \le x^2 - 4x + 2 \le (x^2 + 3)$$

[$\because (x^2 + 3)$ is strictly (+ ve) and inequality remains same]

$$\Rightarrow \begin{cases} x^2 - 4x + 2 \ge -x^2 - 3 \\ x^2 - 4x + 2 \le x^2 + 3 \end{cases}$$

$$\Rightarrow \begin{cases} 2x^2 - 4x + 5 \ge 0 \\ -4x - 1 \le 0 \end{cases} \Rightarrow \begin{cases} x \in R \\ x \ge -\dfrac{1}{4} \end{cases}$$

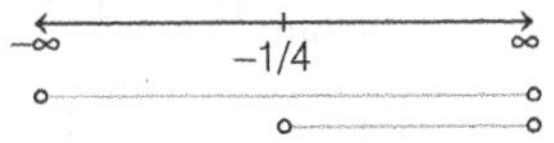

$$\Rightarrow \quad x \ge \frac{-1}{4}$$

73. $f(x) = \sin^{-1}[2x^2 - 3] + \log_2\left[\log_{\frac{1}{2}}(x^2 - 5x + 5)\right]$

Take angle of $\sin^{-1}$ as T_1, which lies between -1 and 1.

$$T_1 : -1 \le [2x^2 - 3] < 1$$

$$\Rightarrow \quad -1 \le [2x^2 - 3] < 2 \Rightarrow 2 < 2x^2 < 5 \Rightarrow 1 < x^2 < \frac{5}{2}$$

$$\Rightarrow \quad T_1 : x \in \left(-\sqrt{\frac{5}{2}}, -1\right) \cup \left(1, \sqrt{\frac{5}{2}}\right)$$

Similarly, $T_2 : x^2 - 5x + 5 > 0$

$$\Rightarrow \left(x - \left(\frac{5 - \sqrt{5}}{2}\right)\right)\left(x - \left(\frac{5 + \sqrt{5}}{2}\right)\right) > 0$$

$$T_3 : \log_{\frac{1}{2}}(x^2 - 5x + 5) > 0$$

$$\Rightarrow \quad x^2 - 5x + 5 < 1 \Rightarrow x^2 - 5x + 4 < 0$$

$$\Rightarrow \quad T_3 : x \in (1, 4)$$

Now, take intersection of T_1, T_2 and T_3.

$$T_1 \cap T_2 \cap T_3 = \left(1, \frac{5 - \sqrt{5}}{2}\right)$$

74. Domain of given function is $[-1, 1]$.

$$-1 \le \frac{x^2 - 5x + 6}{x^2 - 9} \le 1$$

Take maximum value and subtract 1 both sides,

$$\frac{x^2 - 5x + 6}{x^2 - 9} - 1 \le 0, \ \frac{1}{x + 3} \ge 0$$

$$x \in (-3, \infty) \qquad \text{...(i)}$$

Take minimum value and add 1 both sides,

$$\frac{x^2 - 5x + 6}{x^2 - 9} + 1 \ge 0, \ \frac{2x + 1}{x + 3} \ge 0$$

$$x \in (-\infty, -3) \cup \left[-\frac{1}{2}, \infty\right) \qquad \text{...(ii)}$$

Now, take the intersection of two

Eqs. (i) and (ii), $x \in \left[-\dfrac{1}{2}, \infty\right)$

Now, take $x^2 - 3x + 2 > 0$,

$$x \in (-\infty, 1) \cup (2, \infty),$$

$$x^2 - 3x + 2 \ne 1, \ x \ne \frac{3 \pm \sqrt{5}}{2}$$

Take intersection of all the solutions.

$$\left[-\frac{1}{2}, 1\right) \cup (2, \infty) - \left\{\frac{3 + \sqrt{5}}{2}, \frac{3 - \sqrt{5}}{2}\right\}$$

75. $0 \le x^2 - x + 1 \le 1$

$$\Rightarrow \quad x^2 - x \le 0 \Rightarrow x \in [0, 1]$$

Also, $\quad 0 < \sin^{-1}\left(\dfrac{2x - 1}{2}\right) \le \dfrac{\pi}{2}$

$$\Rightarrow \quad 0 < \frac{2x - 1}{2} \le 1$$

$$\Rightarrow \quad 0 < 2x - 1 \le 2$$

$$\Rightarrow \quad 1 < 2x \le 3 \Rightarrow \frac{1}{2} < x \le \frac{3}{2}$$

From Eqs. (i) and (ii), we get

$$x \in \left(\frac{1}{2}, 1\right]$$

$$\Rightarrow \quad \alpha = \frac{1}{2}, \beta = 1$$

So, $\alpha + \beta = \dfrac{3}{2}$

76. Given line is $\dfrac{\sin^{-1} x}{\alpha} = \dfrac{\cos^{-1} x}{\beta} = k$

$$\therefore \quad \sin^{-1} x = k\alpha, \ \cos^{-1} x = k\beta$$

$$k = \frac{\pi}{2(\alpha + \beta)}$$

$$\sin\left(\frac{2\pi\alpha}{\alpha + \beta}\right) = \sin(4 \sin^{-1} x)$$

$$= 2 \sin(2 \sin^{-1} x) \cos(2 \sin^{-1} x)$$

$$= 4x\sqrt{1 - x^2}\,(1 - 2x^2)$$

77. Given, $\tan\left(2\tan^{-1}\frac{1}{5}+\sec^{-1}\frac{\sqrt{5}}{2}+2\tan^{-1}\frac{1}{8}\right)$

$$=\tan\left[2\tan^{-1}\frac{1}{5}+2\tan^{-1}\frac{1}{8}+\sec^{-1}\left(\frac{\sqrt{5}}{2}\right)\right]$$

$$=\tan\left[2\tan^{-1}\left[\frac{\frac{1}{5}+\frac{1}{8}}{1-\frac{1}{5}\times\frac{1}{8}}\right]+\sec^{-1}\frac{\sqrt{5}}{2}\right]$$

$$=\tan\left[2\tan^{-1}\left[\frac{8+5}{40-1}\right]+\sec^{-1}\frac{\sqrt{5}}{2}\right]$$

$$=\tan\left[2\tan^{-1}\left(\frac{1}{3}\right)+\tan^{-1}\frac{1}{2}\right] \quad \left[\because \sec^{-1}\frac{\sqrt{5}}{2}=\tan^{-1}\frac{1}{2}\right]$$

$$=\tan\left[\tan^{-1}\left[\frac{2\times\frac{1}{3}}{1-\left(\frac{1}{3}\right)^2}\right]+\tan^{-1}\frac{1}{2}\right]$$

$$=\tan\left[\tan^{-1}\left(\frac{6}{9-1}\right)+\tan^{-1}\frac{1}{2}\right]$$

$$=\tan\left[\tan^{-1}\frac{3}{4}+\tan^{-1}\frac{1}{2}\right]$$

$$=\tan\left[\tan^{-1}\left(\frac{\frac{3}{4}+\frac{1}{2}}{1-\frac{3}{4}\times\frac{1}{2}}\right)\right]=\tan\left[\tan^{-1}\left(\frac{\frac{3+2}{4}}{\frac{8-3}{8}}\right)\right]$$

$$=\tan\left[\tan^{-1}\frac{5\times 2}{5}\right]=\tan[\tan^{-1}(2)]=2$$

78. We have, $f(x)=\sin^{-1}2x+\sin 2x+\cos^{-1}2x+\cos 2x$

$$=\sin(2x)+\cos(2x)+\frac{\pi}{2}$$

Minimum and maximum values of $f(x)$ will get at $x=0$ and $x=\frac{\pi}{8}$ respectively.

Now, $f(0)=1+\frac{\pi}{2}=(m)$

and $f\left(\frac{\pi}{8}\right)=\sqrt{2}+\frac{\pi}{2}=(M)$

$\therefore$ $m+M=1+\sqrt{2}+\pi$

79. $\sin^{-1}\left(\sin\frac{2\pi}{3}\right)+\cos^{-1}\left(\cos\frac{7\pi}{6}\right)+\tan^{-1}\left(\tan\frac{3\pi}{4}\right)$

$\therefore$ $\sin^{-1}\left(\sin\frac{2\pi}{3}\right)=\sin^{-1}\left(\sin\left(\pi-\frac{\pi}{3}\right)\right)=\frac{\pi}{3}$

and $\cos^{-1}\left(\cos\frac{7\pi}{6}\right)=\cos^{-1}\left(-\cos\frac{\pi}{6}\right)$

$$=\pi-\cos^{-1}\left(\cos\frac{\pi}{6}\right)=\pi-\frac{\pi}{6}=\frac{5\pi}{6}$$

and $\tan^{-1}\left(\tan\frac{3\pi}{4}\right)=\tan^{-1}\left(\tan\left(\pi-\frac{\pi}{4}\right)\right)$

$$=\tan^{-1}\left(-\tan\frac{\pi}{4}\right)=-\frac{\pi}{4}$$

Now, $\sin^{-1}\left(\sin\frac{2\pi}{3}\right)+\cos^{-1}\left(\cos\frac{7\pi}{6}\right)+\tan^{-1}\left(\tan\frac{3\pi}{4}\right)$

$$=\frac{\pi}{3}+\frac{5\pi}{6}-\frac{\pi}{4}=\frac{4\pi+10\pi-3\pi}{12}=\frac{11\pi}{12}$$

80. Take function $\tan^{-1}\left(\frac{1}{1+n+n^2}\right)=\tan^{-1}\left(\frac{(n+1)-n}{1+n(n+1)}\right)$

$$=\tan^{-1}(n+1)-\tan^{-1}n$$

So, $\sum_{n=1}^{50}(\tan^{-1}(n+1)-\tan^{-1}n)=\tan^{-1}51-\tan^{-1}1$

Take cot on both sides,

$$\cot\left(\sum_{n=1}^{50}\tan^{-1}\left(\frac{1}{1+n+n^2}\right)\right)=\cot(\tan^{-1}51+\tan^{-1}1)$$

$$=\frac{1}{\tan(\tan^{-1}51-\tan^{-1}1)}$$

$$=\frac{1+51\times 1}{51-1}=\frac{52}{50}=\frac{26}{25}$$

81. Given equation is $\tan^{-1}\left(\frac{\cos\left(\frac{15\pi}{4}\right)-1}{\sin\frac{\pi}{4}}\right)$

$$=\tan^{-1}\left[\frac{\cos\left(4\pi-\frac{\pi}{4}\right)-1}{\sin\frac{\pi}{4}}\right]$$

$$=\tan^{-1}\left(\frac{\cos\frac{\pi}{4}-1}{\sin\frac{\pi}{4}}\right)$$

$$=\tan^{-1}\left(\frac{1-\sqrt{2}}{1}\right)=-\frac{\pi}{8}$$

82. Given curves are $x=\sin(2\tan^{-1}\alpha)=\frac{2\alpha}{1+\alpha^2}$

and $y=\sin\left(\frac{1}{2}\tan^{-1}\frac{4}{3}\right)=\sin\left(\sin^{-1}\frac{1}{\sqrt{5}}\right)=\frac{1}{\sqrt{5}}$

We have set with relation $y^2=1-x$

$$\frac{1}{5}=1-\frac{2\alpha}{1+\alpha^2} \quad \text{[from values of } x \text{ and } y\text{]}$$

$\Rightarrow$ $1+\alpha^2=5+5\alpha^2-10\alpha$

$\Rightarrow 2\alpha^2-5\alpha+2=0$

Take, $\sum_{\alpha\in S}16\alpha^3=16\times 2^3+16\times\frac{1}{2^3}=130$

83. $50\tan\left(3\tan^{-1}\left(\frac{1}{2}\right)+2\cos^{-1}\left(\frac{1}{\sqrt{5}}\right)\right)+4\sqrt{2}\tan\left(\frac{1}{2}\tan^{-1}(2\sqrt{2})\right)$

$$=50\tan\left(\tan^{-1}\left(\frac{1}{2}\right)+2\left(\tan^{-1}\left(\frac{1}{2}\right)+\tan^{-1}(2)\right)\right)$$

$$+4\sqrt{2}\tan\left(\frac{1}{2}\tan^{-1}(2\sqrt{2})\right)$$

$$= 50 \tan\left(\tan^{-1}\left(\frac{1}{2}\right) + 2\cdot\frac{\pi}{2}\right) + 4\sqrt{2} \times \frac{1}{\sqrt{2}}$$

$$= 50\left(\tan\left(\tan^{-1}\left(\frac{1}{2}\right)\right)\right) + 4$$

$$= 25 + 4 = 29$$

84. $f(x) = \sin^{-1}\left(\frac{3x^2 + x - 1}{(x-1)^2}\right) + \cos^{-1}\left(\frac{x-1}{x+1}\right)$

$$-1 \le \frac{x-1}{x+1} \le 1$$

$$\Rightarrow \quad -1 - 1 \le \frac{x-1}{x+1} - 1 \le 1 - 1$$

$$\Rightarrow \quad -2 \le \frac{-2}{x+1} \le 0$$

$$\Rightarrow \quad 0 \le \frac{1}{x+1} \le 1$$

$$\Rightarrow \quad 1 \le x + 1 < \infty \Rightarrow 0 \le x < \infty$$

$$\Rightarrow \quad x \in [0, \infty) \quad \text{...(i)}$$

and $\quad -1 \le \dfrac{3x^2 + x - 1}{(x-1)^2} \le 1$

$$\Rightarrow -(x-1)^2 \le 3x^2 + x - 1 \le (x-1)^2,\ x \ne 1$$

$$\Rightarrow \quad -(x^2 - 2x + 1) \le 3x^2 + x - 1$$

and $\quad 3x^2 + x - 1 \le x^2 - 2x + 1$

$$\Rightarrow \quad 4x^2 - x \ge 0 \text{ and } 2x^2 + 3x - 2 \le 0$$

$$\Rightarrow \quad x(4x - 1) \ge 0$$

and $\quad (x+2)(2x-1) \le 0$

$$\Rightarrow \quad x \in (-\infty, 0] \cup \left[\frac{1}{4}, \infty\right) \text{ and } x \in \left[-2, \frac{1}{2}\right]$$

$$\Rightarrow \quad x \in (-2, 0] \cup \left[\frac{1}{4}, \frac{1}{2}\right] \quad \text{...(ii)}$$

Domain of f in Eq. (i) $\cap$ Eq. (ii)

$$\therefore \quad x \in \{0\} \cup \left[\frac{1}{4}, \frac{1}{2}\right]$$

85. Let $A = \tan\left(2\tan^{-1}\left(\frac{3}{5}\right) + \sin^{-1}\left(\frac{5}{13}\right)\right)$ ...(i)

Now, using $2\tan^{-1} x = \tan^{-1}\dfrac{2x}{1 - x^2}$

$$\Rightarrow \quad 2\tan^{-1}\left(\frac{3}{5}\right) = \tan^{-1}\left(\frac{2\left(\frac{3}{5}\right)}{1 - \left(\frac{3}{5}\right)^2}\right)$$

$$= \tan^{-1}\left(\frac{\frac{6}{5}}{1 - \frac{9}{25}}\right)$$

$$= \tan^{-1}\left(\frac{30}{16}\right) = \tan^{-1}\left(\frac{15}{8}\right)$$

Let $\sin^{-1}\left(\frac{5}{13}\right) = \theta$, then $\sin\theta = \dfrac{5}{13}$

$$\therefore \tan\theta = \frac{\sin\theta}{\sqrt{1 - \sin^2\theta}} = \frac{\frac{5}{13}}{\sqrt{1 - \left(\frac{5}{13}\right)^2}} = \frac{\frac{5}{13}}{\frac{12}{13}}$$

$$\Rightarrow \quad \theta = \tan^{-1}\left(\frac{5}{12}\right) = \sin^{-1}\left(\frac{5}{13}\right)$$

From Eq. (i),

$$A = \tan\left(\tan^{-1}\left(\frac{15}{8}\right) + \tan^{-1}\left(\frac{5}{12}\right)\right)$$

$$= \tan\left[\tan^{-1}\left(\frac{\frac{15}{8} + \frac{5}{12}}{1 - \left(\frac{15}{8}\right)\left(\frac{5}{12}\right)}\right)\right]$$

$$= \tan\left[\tan^{-1}\left(\frac{\frac{55}{24}}{\frac{21}{96}}\right)\right] = \tan\left[\tan^{-1}\frac{55 \times 4}{21}\right]$$

$$= \tan\left(\tan^{-1}\frac{220}{21}\right) = \frac{220}{21}$$

86. Given, $\tan^{-1} a + \tan^{-1} b = \dfrac{\pi}{4}$

$$\Rightarrow \quad \tan^{-1}\left[\frac{a+b}{1-ab}\right] = \frac{\pi}{4}$$

$$\Rightarrow \quad a + b = 1 - ab \Rightarrow (1+a)(1+b) = 2 \quad \text{...(i)}$$

Now, $(a+b) - \left(\dfrac{a^2+b^2}{2}\right) + \left(\dfrac{a^3+b^3}{3}\right) - \left(\dfrac{a^4+b^4}{4}\right) + \ldots$

$$= \left[a - \frac{a^2}{2} + \frac{a^3}{3} - \frac{a^4}{4} + \ldots\right] + \left[b - \frac{b^2}{2} + \frac{b^3}{3} - \frac{b^4}{4} + \ldots\right]$$

$= \log_e(1+a) + \log_e(1+b)$ [using expansion of $\log_e(1+x)$]

$= \log_e(1+a)(1+b)$ [$\because \log a + \log b = \log ab$]

$= \log_e 2$ [use Eq. (i)]

87. We have, $2\pi - \left(\sin^{-1}\dfrac{4}{5} + \sin^{-1}\dfrac{5}{13} + \sin^{-1}\dfrac{16}{65}\right)$

$$= 2\pi - \left(\tan^{-1}\frac{4}{3} + \tan^{-1}\frac{5}{12} + \tan^{-1}\frac{16}{63}\right)$$

$$= 2\pi - \left(\tan^{-1}\frac{\frac{4}{3} + \frac{5}{12}}{1 - \frac{5}{9}} + \tan^{-1}\frac{16}{63}\right)$$

$$= 2\pi - \left(\tan^{-1}\left(\frac{21 \times 3}{4 \times 4}\right) + \tan^{-1}\frac{16}{63}\right)$$

$$= 2\pi - \left(\tan^{-1}\frac{63}{16} + \tan^{-1}\frac{16}{63}\right)$$

$$= 2\pi - \left(\cot^{-1}\frac{16}{63} + \tan^{-1}\frac{16}{63}\right)$$

$$= 2\pi - \frac{\pi}{2} = \frac{3\pi}{2}$$

88. Given function, $f(x) = \sin^{-1}\left(\frac{|x| + 5}{x^2 + 1}\right)$

For domain of 'f'

$$\frac{|x| + 5}{x^2 + 1} \le 1, \text{ as } \frac{|x| + 5}{x^2 + 1} > 0, \forall\ x \in R$$

$$\Rightarrow \quad |x| + 5 \le x^2 + 1$$

$$\Rightarrow \quad x^2 - |x| - 4 \ge 0$$

$$\Rightarrow \quad |x|^2 - |x| - 4 \ge 0 \quad [\because \forall\ x \in R, x^2 = |x|^2] \ldots\text{(i)}$$

$\because$ For $|x|^2 - |x| - 4 = 0$

$$\Rightarrow \quad |x| = \frac{1 \pm \sqrt{1 + 16}}{2}$$

$$\Rightarrow \quad |x| = \frac{1 \pm \sqrt{17}}{2}$$

$$\Rightarrow \quad |x| = \frac{1 + \sqrt{17}}{2} \text{ as } |x| \ge 0$$

$$\therefore \quad |x| \ge \frac{\sqrt{17} + 1}{2}$$

$$\Rightarrow \quad x \in \left(-\infty, -\frac{\sqrt{17} + 1}{2}\right] \cup \left[\frac{\sqrt{17} + 1}{2}, \infty\right)$$

$$\therefore \quad a = \frac{\sqrt{17} + 1}{2}$$

89. We have, $\sin^{-1}\left(\frac{12}{13}\right) - \sin^{-1}\left(\frac{3}{5}\right)$

$$= \sin^{-1}\left(\frac{12}{13}\sqrt{1 - \left(\frac{3}{5}\right)^2} - \frac{3}{5}\sqrt{1 - \left(\frac{12}{13}\right)^2}\right)$$

$[\because \sin^{-1} x - \sin^{-1} y = \sin^{-1}(x\sqrt{1 - y^2} - y\sqrt{1 - x^2})$, If $x^2 + y^2 \le 1$ or if $xy > 0$ and $x^2 + y^2 > 1\ \forall x, y \in [-1, 1]]$

$$= \sin^{-1}\left(\frac{12}{13} \times \frac{4}{5} - \frac{3}{5} \times \frac{5}{13}\right) = \sin^{-1}\left(\frac{48 - 15}{65}\right)$$

$$= \sin^{-1}\left(\frac{33}{65}\right) = \cos^{-1}\sqrt{1 - \left(\frac{33}{65}\right)^2}$$

$$= \cos^{-1}\sqrt{\frac{3136}{4225}} \quad [\because \sin^{-1} x = \cos^{-1}\sqrt{1 - x^2}]$$

$$= \cos^{-1}\left(\frac{56}{65}\right) = \frac{\pi}{2} - \sin^{-1}\left(\frac{56}{65}\right)$$

$$\left[\because \sin^{-1}\theta + \cot^{-1}\theta = \frac{\pi}{2}\right]$$

90. Consider, $\cot\left(\sum_{n=1}^{19} \cot^{-1}\left(1 + \sum_{p=1}^{n} 2p\right)\right)$

$$= \cot\left(\sum_{n=1}^{19} \cot^{-1}(1 + n(n + 1))\right) \quad \left[\because \sum_{n=1}^{19} p = \frac{n(n + 1)}{2}\right]$$

$$= \cot\left(\sum_{n=1}^{19} \cot^{-1}(1 + n + n^2)\right)$$

$$= \cot\left(\sum_{n=1}^{19} \tan^{-1}\frac{1}{1 + n(n + 1)}\right)$$

$$\left[\because \cot^{-1} x = \tan^{-1}\frac{1}{x}, \text{if } x > 0\right]$$

$$= \cot\left(\sum_{n=1}^{19} \tan^{-1}\left(\frac{(n + 1) - n}{1 + n\,(n + 1)}\right)\right) \quad [\text{put, } 1 = (n + 1) - n]$$

$$= \cot \sum_{n=1}^{19} (\tan^{-1}(n + 1) - \tan^{-1} n)$$

$$\left[\because \tan^{-1}\frac{x - y}{1 + xy} = \tan^{-1} x - \tan^{-1} y\right]$$

$$= \cot\,[(\tan^{-1} 2 - \tan^{-1} 1) + (\tan^{-1} 3 - \tan^{-1} 2) + \ldots\ldots + (\tan^{-1} 20 - \tan^{-1} 19)]$$

$$= \cot\,(\tan^{-1} 20 - \tan^{-1} 1)$$

$$= \cot\left[\left(\frac{\pi}{2} - \cot^{-1} 20\right) - \left(\frac{\pi}{2} - \cot^{-1} 1\right)\right]$$

$$[\because \tan^{-1} x + \cot^{-1} x = \pi / 2]$$

$$= \cot\,(\cot^{-1} 1 - \cot^{-1} 20)$$

$$\left[\because \cot\,(A - B) = \frac{\cot A \cot B + 1}{\cot B - \cot A}\right]$$

$$= \frac{(1 \times 20) + 1}{20 - 1} = \frac{21}{19} \quad [\because \cot\,(\cot^{-1} x) = x]$$

91. The graph of $y = \sin^{-1}(\sin x)$ is

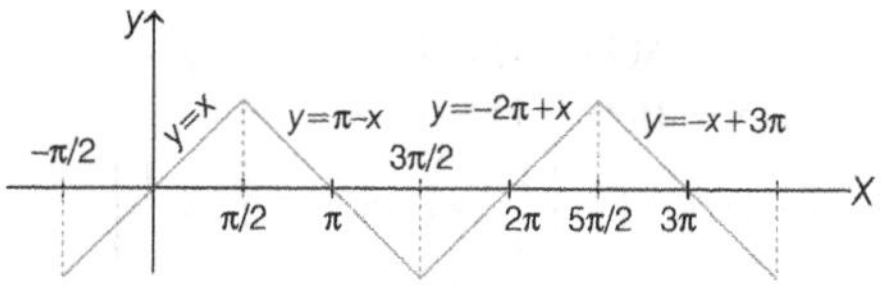

$$\therefore\ x = \sin^{-1}(\sin 10) = -10 + 3\pi \quad [\because 3\pi < 10 < 4\pi] \ldots\text{(i)}$$

and the graph of $y = \cos^{-1}(\cos x)$ is

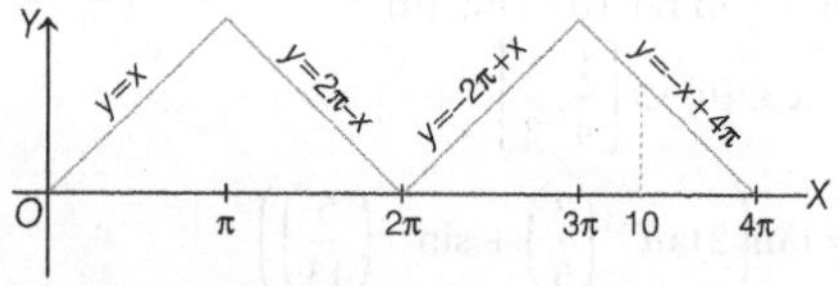

$$\therefore \quad y = \cos^{-1}(\cos 10) = -10 + 4\pi \quad \ldots\text{(ii)}$$

Now, from Eqs. (i) and (ii),

$$y - x = (-10 + 4\pi) - (-10 + 3\pi) = \pi$$

92. Given equation is $\cos^{-1} x - \cos^{-1}\frac{y}{2} = \alpha$,

where $-1 \le x \le 1, -2 \le y \le 2$ and $x \le \frac{y}{2}$

$$\therefore\ \cos^{-1}\left(x\frac{y}{2} + \sqrt{1 - x^2}\,\sqrt{1 - (y/2)^2}\right) = \alpha$$

$[\because \cos^{-1} x - \cos^{-1} y = \cos^{-1}(xy + \sqrt{1 - x^2}\,\sqrt{1 - y^2}),$
$|x|, |y| \le 1$ and $x + y \ge 0]$

$$\Rightarrow \quad \frac{xy}{2} + \sqrt{1 - x^2}\,\sqrt{1 - (y/2)^2} = \cos\alpha$$

$$\Rightarrow \quad \sqrt{1 - x^2}\,\sqrt{1 - (y/2)^2} = \cos\alpha - \frac{xy}{2}$$

On squaring both sides, we get

$$(1-x^2)\left(1-\frac{y^2}{4}\right)=\cos^2\alpha+\frac{x^2y^2}{4}-2\frac{xy}{2}\cos\alpha$$

$$\Rightarrow \quad 1-x^2-\frac{y^2}{4}+\frac{x^2y^2}{4}=\cos^2\alpha+\frac{x^2y^2}{4}-xy\cos\alpha$$

$$\Rightarrow \quad x^2+\frac{y^2}{4}-xy\cos\alpha=1-\cos^2\alpha$$

$$\Rightarrow \quad 4x^2-4xy\cos\alpha+y^2=4\sin^2\alpha$$

93. Given functions, $f(x)=\log_e(\sin x), (0<x<\pi)$ and $g(x)=\sin^{-1}(e^{-x}), x\geq 0.$

Now, $fog(x)=f(g(x))=f(\sin^{-1}(e^{-x}))$

$$=\log_e(\sin(\sin^{-1}(e^{-x})))=\log_e(e^{-x})$$

$$[\because \sin(\sin^{-1}x)=x, \text{ if } x\in[-1,1]]$$

$$=-x \quad \text{...(i)}$$

and $(fog)'(x)=\dfrac{d}{dx}(-x)=-1$ ...(ii)

According to the question,

$\because \quad a=(fog)'(\alpha)=-1$ [from Eq. (ii)]

and $b=(fog)(\alpha)=-(\alpha)$ [from Eq. (i)]

for a positive real value 'α'.

Since, the value of $a=-1$ and $b=-\alpha$, satisfy the quadratic equation (from the given options) $a\alpha^2-b\alpha-a=1$.

94. Given, $\alpha=\cos^{-1}\left(\dfrac{3}{5}\right)$ and $\beta=\tan^{-1}\left(\dfrac{1}{3}\right)$

where, $0<\alpha, \beta<\dfrac{\pi}{2}$

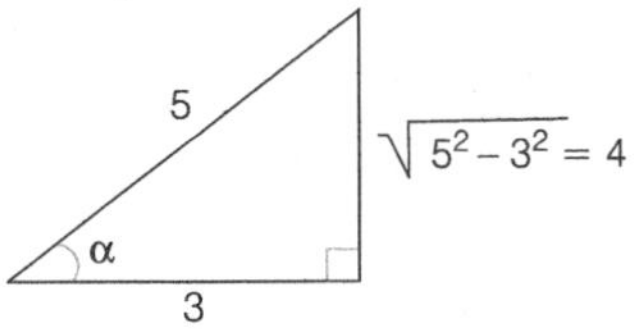

Clearly, $\alpha=\tan^{-1}\dfrac{4}{3}$

$$\text{So, } \alpha-\beta=\tan^{-1}\frac{4}{3}-\tan^{-1}\frac{1}{3}=\tan^{-1}\left(\frac{\frac{4}{3}-\frac{1}{3}}{1+\left(\frac{4}{3}\times\frac{1}{3}\right)}\right)$$

$$\left[\because \tan^{-1}x-\tan^{-1}y=\tan^{-1}\frac{x-y}{1+xy}, \text{if } xy>-1\right]$$

$$=\tan^{-1}\frac{1}{1+\frac{4}{9}}=\tan^{-1}\frac{9}{13}$$

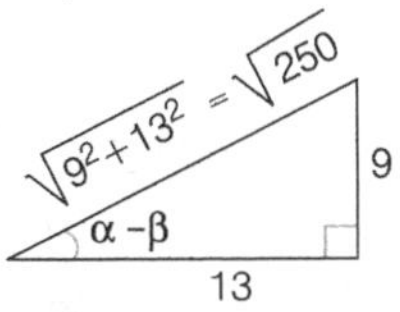

$$=\sin^{-1}\frac{9}{\sqrt{9^2+13^2}}$$

$$=\sin^{-1}\frac{9}{\sqrt{250}}=\sin^{-1}\left(\frac{9}{5\sqrt{10}}\right)$$

95. Given equation is

$$\tan^{-1}(2x)+\tan^{-1}(3x)=\frac{\pi}{4}, x\geq 0$$

$$\Rightarrow \quad \tan^{-1}\frac{5x}{1-6x^2}=\frac{\pi}{4}, 6x^2<1$$

$$\Rightarrow \quad \frac{5x}{1-6x^2}=1, x^2<\frac{1}{6}$$

$$\Rightarrow \quad 6x^2+5x-1=0, 0\leq x<\frac{1}{\sqrt{6}} \quad [\because x\geq 0]$$

$$\Rightarrow \quad 6x^2+6x-x-1=0, \ 0\leq x<\frac{1}{\sqrt{6}}$$

$$\Rightarrow 6x(x+1)-1(x+1)=0, \ 0\leq x<\frac{1}{\sqrt{6}}$$

$$\Rightarrow \quad (6x-1)(x+1)=0, \ 0\leq x<\frac{1}{\sqrt{6}}$$

$$\Rightarrow \quad x=\frac{1}{6}, -1, 0\leq x<\frac{1}{\sqrt{6}}$$

$$\Rightarrow \quad x=\frac{1}{6} \quad \left[\because 0\leq x<\frac{1}{\sqrt{6}}\right]$$

So A is a singleton set.

96. Let $x^2=\cos 2\theta \Rightarrow \theta=\dfrac{1}{2}\cos^{-1}x^2$

$$\Rightarrow \tan^{-1}\left[\frac{\sqrt{1+x^2}+\sqrt{1-x^2}}{\sqrt{1+x^2}-\sqrt{1-x^2}}\right]=\left[\frac{\sqrt{1+\cos 2\theta}+\sqrt{1-\cos 2\theta}}{\sqrt{1+\cos 2\theta}-\sqrt{1-\cos 2\theta}}\right]$$

$$\Rightarrow \quad \tan^{-1}\left[\frac{1+\tan\theta}{1-\tan\theta}\right]=\tan^{-1}\left[\tan\left(\frac{\pi}{4}+\theta\right)\right]$$

$$=\frac{\pi}{4}+\frac{1}{2}\cos^{-1}(x^2)$$

97. Given, $\tan^{-1}y=\tan^{-1}x+\tan^{-1}\left(\dfrac{2x}{1-x^2}\right)$,

where $|x|<\dfrac{1}{\sqrt{3}}$

$$\Rightarrow \quad \tan^{-1}y=\tan^{-1}\left\{\frac{x+\frac{2x}{1-x^2}}{1-x\left(\frac{2x}{1-x^2}\right)}\right\}$$

$$\left[\because \tan^{-1}x+\tan^{-1}y=\tan^{-1}\left(\frac{x+y}{1-xy}\right), \text{ where } x>0, y>0 \text{ and } xy<1\right]$$

$$=\tan^{-1}\left(\frac{x-x^3+2x}{1-x^2-2x^2}\right)$$

$$\Rightarrow \quad \tan^{-1}y=\tan^{-1}\left(\frac{3x-x^3}{1-3x^2}\right)$$

$$\Rightarrow \quad y=\frac{3x-x^3}{1-3x^2}; \ |x|<\frac{1}{\sqrt{3}}$$

98. Consider

$$\tan^{-1}\left[\cot\frac{43\pi}{4}\right]=\tan^{-1}\left[\cot\left(10\pi+\frac{3\pi}{4}\right)\right]$$
$$=\tan^{-1}\left[\cot\frac{3\pi}{4}\right]$$
$$=\tan^{-1}\left[\tan\left(\frac{\pi}{2}-\frac{3\pi}{4}\right)\right]=\frac{\pi}{2}-\frac{3\pi}{4}=-\frac{\pi}{4}$$

Exercise 2 - JEE Advanced Pattern

1. Let $\theta = \text{arc}\cos(x-1)$

Now, $\cos 3\theta = 4\cos^3\theta - 3\cos\theta$

So, $4y^3 - 3y = 0$, where $y = x-1$

$\therefore \quad y = \pm\frac{\sqrt{3}}{2}, 0 \Rightarrow x = 1 \pm \frac{\sqrt{3}}{2}, 1$

Hence, three values of x.

Alternate Solution

$$\cos(3\cos^{-1}(x-1)) = 0$$
$$\Rightarrow 3\cos^{-1}(x-1) = (2n+1)\frac{\pi}{2}, n\in Z$$
$$\Rightarrow \cos^{-1}(x-1) = (2n+1)\frac{\pi}{6}, n\in Z$$
$$\Rightarrow \cos^{-1}(x-1) = \frac{\pi}{6}, \frac{\pi}{2}, \frac{5\pi}{6}$$
$$\Rightarrow x-1 = \frac{\sqrt{3}}{2}, 0, \frac{-\sqrt{3}}{2}$$
$$\therefore x = 1+\frac{\sqrt{3}}{2}, 1, 1-\frac{\sqrt{3}}{2}$$

2. $\tan\left\{\underbrace{\text{arc}\tan(2)}_{A} + \underbrace{\text{arc}\tan(20k)}_{B}\right\} = k;$

$$\Rightarrow \frac{\tan A + \tan B}{1-\tan A\tan B} = k \Rightarrow \frac{2+20k}{1-(2)(20k)} = k$$

or $\quad 40k^2 + 19k + 2 = 0$

Now, sum of solutions, $k_1 + k_2 = -\frac{19}{40}$

3. The equation $3x^2 + 6x + a = 0$ must have equal roots

So, $D = 0$

$\Rightarrow \quad 36 - 12a = 0$

$\Rightarrow \quad a = 3$

4. $\sin^{-1}|x-2| + \cos^{-1}(1-|3-x|) = \frac{\pi}{2}$ or $|x-2| = 1-|3-x|$

$$|x-2| + |3-x| = 1$$

or $\quad |x-2| + |3-x| = |(x-2)+(3-x)|$

or $\quad (x-2)(3-x) \ge 0$ or $2 \le x \le 3$

5. Expanding, we have

$$(\tan^{-1}x)^3 + (\tan^{-1}2x)^3 + (\tan^{-1}3x)^3 = 3\tan^{-1}x\tan^{-1}2x\tan^{-1}3x$$

$\Rightarrow \quad x = 0$

6. $[\cot^{-1}x] + 2[\tan^{-1}x] = 0$

$\Rightarrow \quad [\cot^{-1}x] = 0, [\tan^{-1}x] = 0$

or $\quad [\cot^{-1}x] = 2, [\tan^{-1}x] = -1$

Now, $\quad [\cot^{-1}x] = 0 \Rightarrow x \in (\cot 1, \infty)$

$\quad [\tan^{-1}x] = 0 \Rightarrow x \in (0, \tan 1)$

Therefore, $\quad [\cot^{-1}x] = [\tan^{-1}x] = 0, x \in (\cot 1, \tan 1)$

$\quad [\cot^{-1}x] = 2 \Rightarrow x \in (\cot 3, \cot 2]$

$\quad [\tan^{-1}x] = -1$

$\Rightarrow \quad x \in [-\tan 1, 0)$

Hence, no such x exists.

Thus, the solution set is $(\cot 1, \tan 1)$

7. $\tan^{-1}\left(\frac{\sqrt{1+x^2}-1}{x}\right) = 4° \qquad [x \ne 0]$

$$\Rightarrow \frac{\sqrt{1+x^2}-1}{x} = \tan 4°$$
$$\Rightarrow \sqrt{1+x^2} = 1 + x\tan 4°$$
$$\Rightarrow 1 + x^2 = 2x\tan 4° + 1 + x^2\tan^2 4°$$
$$\Rightarrow x = 0 \text{ or } x = \frac{2\tan 4°}{1-\tan^2 4°} = \tan 8°$$

Since, $x \ne 0$, we have

$$x = \tan 8°$$

8. $-1 \le x \le 1, y > 0$

Both will be equated for infinite values of x and y. Therefore, infinite many solutions.

9. $x = -\pi/4;\ y = \cos\frac{\theta}{2}$; where $\cos\theta = \frac{1}{8}$

and $\quad \cos\frac{\theta}{2} = \sqrt{\frac{1+\cos\theta}{2}} = \frac{3}{4}$

10. $y = |x^2-1| = |\tan^{-1}|x||$

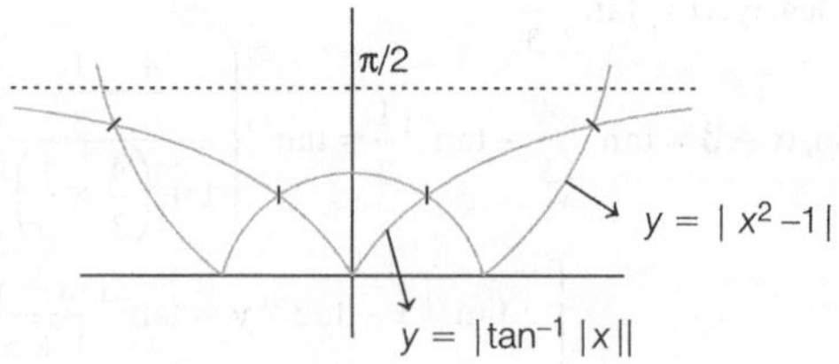

From graph, clearly it has 4 solutions.

11. By graph, clearly it has one real root.

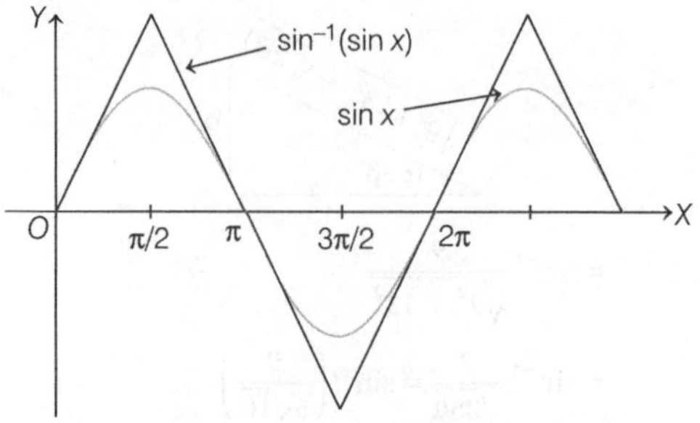

12. $\cos^{-1} x = t \Rightarrow x \in [-1,1]$ and $t \in [0, \pi]$

Now, we have $\log_{10} \sqrt{5t-1} + \frac{1}{2}\log_{10}(2t+3) + \frac{1}{2}\log_{10} 5 = 1;$

$$\left(t > \frac{1}{5} \text{ and } t > -\frac{3}{2}\right)$$

$\Rightarrow \quad \log_{10}((5t-1)(2t+3) \,.\, 5) = 2$

$\Rightarrow \quad (5t-1)(2t+3) \,.\, 5 = 100$

$\Rightarrow \quad (5t-1)(2t+3) = 20$

$\Rightarrow \quad 10t^2 + 13t - 3 = 20$

$\Rightarrow \quad 10t^2 + 23t - 10t - 23 = 0$

$\Rightarrow \quad t(10t+23) - (10t+23) = 0$

$\Rightarrow \quad (t-1)(10t+23) = 0$

$\Rightarrow \quad t = 1 \text{ or } t = -\frac{23}{10}$ (rejected)

$\Rightarrow \quad \cos^{-1} x = 1 \Rightarrow x = \cos 1$

13. $\sin^{-1} x + \cos^{-1} x = \frac{\pi}{2}$ ...(i)

and $\sin^{-1} x - \cos^{-1} x = \sin^{-1}(3x-2)$ ...(ii)

From Eqs. (i) and (ii), we get

$$2\cos^{-1} x = \cos^{-1}(3x-2)$$

Note that $(3x-2) \in [-1,1]$ i.e. $-1 \le 3x - 2 \le 1$

$\Rightarrow \quad x \in \left[\frac{1}{3}, 1\right]$

Now, $\quad 2\cos^{-1} x = \cos^{-1}(3x-2)$

$\Rightarrow \quad \cos^{-1}(2x^2-1) = \cos^{-1}(3x-2)$

$\Rightarrow \quad 2x^2 - 3x + 1 = 0 \Rightarrow x = 1 \text{ or } \frac{1}{2}$

Hence, $x = 1$ or $\frac{1}{2}$

14. We have, $\frac{1}{2} \le \frac{x^2-k}{1+x^2} < 1 \Rightarrow \frac{1}{2} \le 1 - \frac{(k+1)}{x^2+1} < 1, \forall x \in R$

$\Rightarrow \quad k+1 > 0$ and $\frac{k+1}{x^2+1} \le \frac{1}{2}$

So, $\quad k > -1$ and $x^2 + 1 \ge 2k + 2$

$\Rightarrow \quad x^2 - (2k+1) \ge 0, \forall x \in R \Rightarrow 4(2k+1) \le 0$

$\therefore \quad k \le -\frac{1}{2}$

Hence, $k \in \left(-1, \frac{-1}{2}\right]$

15. Domain is $x \in [-1,1]$

Given, $\sin^{-1} x = 2\tan^{-1} x$

$\Rightarrow \quad \tan^{-1}\left(\frac{x}{\sqrt{1-x^2}}\right) = \tan^{-1}\left(\frac{2x}{1-x^2}\right)$

$\Rightarrow \quad \frac{x}{\sqrt{1-x^2}} = \frac{2x}{1-x^2}$

$\therefore \quad x = 0 \text{ or } (1-x^2)^2 = 4(1-x^2)$

$\Rightarrow \quad (1-x^2)(3+x^2) = 0$

$\Rightarrow \quad x = -1, 0, 1$ ... (i)

$$\tan^{-1}\sqrt{x(x-1)} + \operatorname{cosec}^{-1}\sqrt{1+x-x^2} = \frac{\pi}{2}$$

$$x(x-1) \ge 0 \cap x - x^2 \ge 0 \Rightarrow x(x-1) = 0$$

$\Rightarrow \quad x = 0, 1$ ... (ii)

Now, Eqs. (i) $\cap$ (ii) gives $x = 0,1$

Hence, number of common solution are 2.

16. $\sin^{-1}(\sin 5) > x^2 - 4x$

$\Rightarrow \quad \sin^{-1}(\sin(5-2\pi)) > x^2 - 4x$

$\Rightarrow \quad 5 - 2\pi > x^2 - 4x$

$\Rightarrow \quad 9 - 2\pi > (x-2)^2$

$\Rightarrow \quad (x-2)^2 < 9 - 2\pi$

$\Rightarrow \quad -\sqrt{9-2\pi} < x - 2 < \sqrt{9-2\pi}$

$\Rightarrow \quad 2 - \sqrt{9-2\pi} < x < 2 + \sqrt{9-2\pi}$

17. $(\cot^{-1} x)^2 - (5\cot^{-1} x) + 6 > 0$

$$(\cot^{-1} x - 3)(\cot^{-1} x - 2) > 0$$

$$x > \cot 2 \text{ and } x < \cot 3$$

$\therefore \quad x \in (-\infty, \cot 3) \cup (\cot 2, \infty)$

18. $\frac{-\pi}{3} < \cos^{-1}\left(\frac{1-x^2}{1+x^2}\right) < \frac{\pi}{3}$

$\Rightarrow \quad 0 \le \cos^{-1}\left(\frac{1-x^2}{1+x^2}\right) < \frac{\pi}{3}$

$\Rightarrow \quad \frac{1}{2} < \frac{1-x^2}{1+x^2} \le 1$

$\Rightarrow \quad 0 \le x^2 < \frac{1}{3}$

$\Rightarrow \quad x \in \left(\frac{-1}{\sqrt{3}}, \frac{1}{\sqrt{3}}\right)$

19. $\tan^2(\sin^{-1} x) > 1 \Rightarrow \tan(\sin^{-1} x) > 1$ or $\tan(\sin^{-1} x) < -1$

$$\sin^{-1} x > \frac{\pi}{4} \text{ or } \sin^{-1} x < \frac{\pi}{4}; x \in (-1,1) - \left[-\frac{1}{\sqrt{2}}, \frac{1}{\sqrt{2}}\right]$$

Note that domain is $(-1,1)$.

20. $\tan\left(\tan^{-1}\frac{x}{\pi}\right) < \tan\frac{\pi}{3}$

$\Rightarrow \quad \frac{x}{\pi} < \sqrt{3}$

$\Rightarrow \quad x < \sqrt{3}\pi = 5.5.$

Maximum value is 5.

21. Given, $f(x) = \tan^{-1}(x^2 - 18x + a) > 0$

$\Rightarrow \quad \tan^{-1}(x^2 - 18x + a) > 0$

$\Rightarrow \quad x^2 - 18x + a > 0 \Rightarrow 18^2 - 4a < 0$

$\Rightarrow \quad a > \frac{18^2}{4} = \frac{18 \times 18}{4} = 81$

$\Rightarrow \quad a > 81 \Rightarrow a \in (81, \infty)$

22. From the given equation $\sin^2\theta - 2\sin\theta + 3 = 5^{\sec^2 y} + 1$, we get

$$(\sin\theta - 1)^2 + 2 = 5^{\sec^2 y} + 1$$

LHS ≤ 6, RHS ≥ 6

Possible solution is $\sin\theta = -1$ when LHS = RHS

$$\Rightarrow \cos^2\theta = 0$$

$$\Rightarrow \cos^2\theta - \sin\theta = 1$$

23. $f(x) = \tan^{-1}\left(\dfrac{(\sqrt{12}-2)x^2}{x^4 + 2x^2 + 3}\right) = \tan^{-1}\left(\dfrac{2(\sqrt{3}-1)}{x^2 + \dfrac{3}{x^2} + 2}\right)$

As, $x^2 + \dfrac{3}{x^2} \geq 2\sqrt{3}$ [using AM $\geq$ GM]

$$\Rightarrow x^2 + \frac{3}{x^2} + 2 \geq 2 + 2\sqrt{3}$$

$$\therefore \quad (f(x))_{\max} = \tan^{-1}\left(\frac{2(\sqrt{3}-1)}{2(\sqrt{3}+1)}\right) = \frac{\pi}{12} \text{ or } 15^\circ$$

24. $T_n = \cot^{-1}\left(n^2 + \dfrac{3}{4}\right) = \tan^{-1}\left(\dfrac{1}{n^2 + \dfrac{3}{4}}\right)$

$$= \tan^{-1}\left(n + \frac{1}{2}\right) - \tan^{-1}\left(n - \frac{1}{2}\right)$$

$$S_n = \sum_{n=1}^{n} t_n = \tan^{-1}\left(n + \frac{1}{2}\right) - \tan^{-1}\frac{1}{2}$$

$$S_\infty = \tan^{-1}(\infty) - \tan^{-1}\frac{1}{2} = \frac{\pi}{2} - \tan^{-1}\frac{1}{2} = \cot^{-1}\frac{1}{2} = \tan^{-1}2$$

25. $\displaystyle\lim_{n\to\infty}\sum_{r=1}^{n}\tan^{-1}\left(\frac{2^{r-1}}{1 + 2^{2r-1}}\right)$

$$= \lim_{n\to\infty}\sum_{r=1}^{n}\tan^{-1}\left(\frac{2^r - 2^{r-1}}{1 + 2^r \cdot 2^{r-1}}\right)$$

$$= \lim_{n\to\infty}\sum_{r=1}^{n}\{\tan^{-1}(2^r) - \tan^{-1}(2^{r-1})\}$$

$$= \lim_{n\to\infty}(\tan^{-1}2^n - \tan^{-1}2^0)$$

$$= \tan^{-1}2^\infty - \tan^{-1}1$$

$$= \frac{\pi}{2} - \frac{\pi}{4} = \frac{\pi}{4}$$

26. $\displaystyle\sum_{r=2}^{\infty}\tan^{-1}\left(\frac{(r-2)-(r-3)}{1+(r-3)(r-2)}\right) = \sum_{r=2}^{\infty}(\tan^{-1}(r-2) - \tan^{-1}(r-3))$

Now, $T_2 = \tan^{-1}0 - \tan^{-1}(-1)$

$T_3 = \tan^{1}1 - \tan^{-1}0$

$T_4 = \tan^{-1}2 - \tan^{-1}1$

$\vdots \qquad \vdots$

$T_n = \tan^{-1}(n-2) - \tan^{-1}(n-3)$

$$\Rightarrow \quad S_n = \tan^{-1}(n-2) + \frac{\pi}{4}$$

$$\therefore \quad S_\infty = \frac{\pi}{2} + \frac{\pi}{4} = \frac{3\pi}{4}$$

27. $T_n = \tan^{-1}\left(\dfrac{(n+1)^2 - (n-1)^2}{1 + (n^2-1)^2}\right) = \tan^{-1}(n+1)^2 - \tan^{-1}(n-1)^2$

$$S_n = \tan^{-1}(n+1)^2 + \tan^{-1}n^2 - \tan^{-1}1^2$$

$$\Rightarrow S_\infty = \frac{\pi}{2} + \frac{\pi}{2} - \frac{\pi}{4} = \pi - \frac{\pi}{4}$$

$$= \pi - \sec^{-1}(\sqrt{2})$$

$$= \sec^{-1}(-\sqrt{2})$$

28. $a_n = \tan^{-1}\left(\dfrac{1}{1 + (n+3)(n+2)}\right) = \tan^{-1}\left(\dfrac{(n+3)-(n+2)}{1+(n+3)(n+2)}\right)$

$$= \tan^{-1}(n+3) - \tan^{-1}(n+2)$$

$$\therefore \quad S_n = f(n) - f(1) = \tan^{-1}(n+3) - \tan^{-1}3$$

$$\Rightarrow \quad S_\infty = \frac{\pi}{2} - \tan^{-1}3 = \cot^{-1}3 = \sin^{-1}\frac{1}{\sqrt{10}}$$

29. Let $T_n = \cot^{-1}\left(n^2 + \dfrac{3}{4}\right)$

$$\Rightarrow \quad T_n = \cot^{-1}\left(\frac{4n^2+3}{4}\right)$$

$$\Rightarrow \quad T_n = \tan^{-1}\left(\frac{4}{4n^2+3}\right) = \tan^{-1}\left[\frac{1}{n^2 + \frac{3}{4}}\right]$$

$$\Rightarrow \quad T_n = \tan^{-1}\left\{\frac{1}{1 + \left(n^2 - \frac{1}{4}\right)}\right\}$$

$$\Rightarrow \quad T_n = \tan^{-1}\left\{\frac{1}{1 + \left[n - \left(\frac{1}{2}\right)\right]\cdot\left[n + \left(\frac{1}{2}\right)\right]}\right\}$$

$$\Rightarrow \quad T_n = \tan^{-1}\left(n + \frac{1}{2}\right) - \tan^{-1}\left(n - \frac{1}{2}\right)$$

Now, $S_n = T_1 + T_2 + T_3 + \ldots + T_n$

$$\Rightarrow \quad S_n = \tan^{-1}\left(\frac{3}{2}\right) - \tan^{-1}\left(\frac{1}{2}\right) + \tan^{-1}\left(\frac{5}{2}\right) - \tan^{-1}\left(\frac{3}{2}\right) + \tan^{-1}\left(\frac{7}{2}\right) - \tan^{-1}\left(\frac{5}{2}\right) + \ldots + \tan^{-1}\left(n + \frac{1}{2}\right) - \tan^{-1}\left(n - \frac{1}{2}\right)$$

$$\therefore \quad S_\infty = \tan^{-1}\infty - \tan^{-1}\left(\frac{1}{2}\right)$$

$$\Rightarrow \quad S_\infty = \frac{\pi}{2} - \tan^{-1}\left(\frac{1}{2}\right)$$

$$\Rightarrow \quad S_\infty = \cot^{-1}\left(\frac{1}{2}\right)$$

$$\therefore \quad S_\infty = \tan^{-1}(2)$$

30. Series is $\tan^{-1}\left(\dfrac{1}{3}\right) + \tan^{-1}\left(\dfrac{1}{7}\right) + \tan^{-1}\left(\dfrac{1}{13}\right) + \ldots + \tan^{-1}\left(\dfrac{1}{n^2+n+1}\right)$

We know that the n th term of the series

$$T_n = \tan^{-1}\left(\frac{1}{1+n+n^2}\right)$$

$$= \tan^{-1}\left[\frac{(n+1)-n}{1+n(n+1)}\right]$$

$$= \tan^{-1}(n+1) - \tan^{-1} n$$

Substituting $n = 1, 2, 3, \ldots n$ and adding, we get the sum of the series.

$$S_n = \tan^{-1}(n+1) - \tan^{-1}(1)$$

Substituting $n = \infty$, we get

$$S_\infty = \tan^{-1}\infty - \frac{\pi}{4} = \frac{\pi}{2} - \frac{\pi}{4} = \frac{\pi}{4}$$

31. $\theta = \tan^{-1}\left(\tan\frac{5\pi}{4}\right)$ and $\phi = \tan^{-1}\left(-\tan\frac{2\pi}{3}\right)$

$= \tan^{-1}\tan\left(\pi + \frac{\pi}{4}\right)$ and $\phi = \tan^{-1}\left(-\tan\left(\pi - \frac{\pi}{3}\right)\right)$

$= \tan^{-1}\tan\frac{\pi}{4}$ and $\phi = \tan^{-1}\tan\frac{\pi}{3}$

$= \frac{\pi}{4}$ and $\phi = \frac{\pi}{3}$

$\therefore\ 4\theta - 3\phi = 0$ and $\theta + \phi = \frac{7\pi}{12}$

32. $f\left(\frac{8\pi}{9}\right) = e^{\cos^{-1}\left[\sin\left(\frac{8\pi}{9}+\frac{\pi}{3}\right)\right]} = e^{\cos^{-1}\left(\sin\frac{11\pi}{9}\right)}$

$= e^{\cos^{-1}\left(\cos\frac{13\pi}{18}\right)} = e^{13\pi/18}$

and $f\left(-\frac{7\pi}{4}\right) = e^{\cos^{-1}\left[\sin\left(\frac{-7\pi}{4}+\frac{\pi}{3}\right)\right]}$

$= e^{\cos^{-1}\left[\sin\left(\frac{-17\pi}{12}\right)\right]}$

$= e^{\cos^{-1}\left[\cos\left(\frac{\pi}{12}\right)\right]}$

$= e^{\pi/12}$

33. Let $\cos^{-1}\left(\frac{4}{5}\right) = \alpha$, that is $\cos\alpha = \frac{4}{5}$, so that

$$\tan\alpha = \sqrt{\left\{\left(\frac{5}{4}\right)^2 - 1\right\}} = \frac{3}{4}$$

and $\tan\left(\cos^{-1}\frac{4}{5} + \tan^{-1}\frac{2}{3}\right) = \dfrac{\tan\alpha + \frac{2}{3}}{1 - \tan\alpha\cdot\frac{2}{3}}$

$$= \frac{\frac{3}{4}+\frac{2}{3}}{1-\frac{2}{3}\cdot\frac{3}{4}}$$

$$= \frac{17}{6} = \frac{a}{b} \qquad \text{[given]}$$

so, $a = 17, b = 6, a + b = 23$

$a - b = 11$ and $3b = a + 1$

34. $\sin^{-1}x + \cos^{-1}x = \frac{\pi}{2}, \forall\ x \in [-1, 1]$

35. Given, $\cos^{-1}x = \tan^{-1}x$

$\Rightarrow\ x = \cos\theta = \tan\theta$

$\Rightarrow\ \cos^2\theta = \sin\theta$

$\Rightarrow\ \sin^2\theta + \sin\theta - 1 = 0$

$\Rightarrow\ \sin\theta = \dfrac{-1 \pm \sqrt{1+4}}{2}$

$\Rightarrow\ \sin\theta = \dfrac{\sqrt{5}-1}{2}$

$\Rightarrow\ x^2 = \cos^2\theta = \dfrac{\sqrt{5}-1}{2}$

$\therefore$ Option (a) is correct.

and $\sin(\cos^{-1}x) = \sin\theta = \frac{1}{2}(\sqrt{5}-1)$

Also, option (c) is correct

and $\tan(\cos^{-1}x) = \tan\theta = \frac{1}{2}(\sqrt{5}-1)$

$\therefore$ Option (d) is not correct.

36. The solution of $y = \sqrt{y}$ is $y = 0$ or $y = 1$

If $\sin^{-1}|\sin x| = 1 \Rightarrow x = 1$ or $x = \pi - 1$

But $y = \sin^{-1}|\sin x|$ is periodic with period π,

so $x = n\pi + 1$ or $n\pi - 1$.

Again, if $\sin^{-1}|\sin x| = 0$, $x = n\pi$

37. $(\sin^{-1}x + \sin^{-1}w)(\sin^{-1}y + \sin^{-1}z) = \pi^2$

$\therefore\ \sin^{-1}x + \sin^{-1}w = \sin^{-1}y + \sin^{-1}z = \pi$

or $\sin^{-1}x + \sin^{-1}w = \sin^{-1}y + \sin^{-1}z = -\pi$

$\therefore\ x = y = z = w = 1$ or $x = y = z = w = -1$

Hence, the maximum value of $\begin{vmatrix} x^{N_1} & y^{N_2} \\ z^{N_3} & w^{N_4} \end{vmatrix} = \begin{vmatrix} 1 & -1 \\ 1 & 1 \end{vmatrix} = 2$ and

minimum value $\begin{vmatrix} -1 & 1 \\ 1 & 1 \end{vmatrix} = -2$

Also, there are 16 different determinants as each place value is either 1 or -1.

38. Since, $|\tan^{-1}x| = \begin{cases} \tan^{-1}x, & \text{if } x \ge 0 \\ -\tan^{-1}x, & \text{if } x < 0 \end{cases}$

$\Rightarrow\ |\tan^{-1}x| = \tan^{-1}|x|\ \forall\ x \in R$

$\Rightarrow\ \tan|\tan^{-1}x| = \tan\tan^{-1}|x| = |x|$

Also, $|\cot^{-1}x| = \cot^{-1}x;\ \forall\ x \in R$

$\Rightarrow\ \cot|\cot^{-1}x| = x,\ \forall\ x \in R$

$$\tan^{-1}|\tan x| = \begin{cases} x, & \text{if } 0 < x < \frac{\pi}{2} \\ -x, & \text{if } -\frac{\pi}{2} < x < 0 \end{cases}$$

$$\sin|\sin^{-1}x| = \begin{cases} x, & x \in [0, 1] \\ -x, & x \in [-1, 0) \end{cases}$$

39. $1 \le \frac{\pi}{\cos^{-1} x} < \infty \Rightarrow 2 \le 2^{\left(\frac{\pi}{\cos^{-1} x}\right)} < \infty$

Hence, 2 should lie between or on the roots of

$$t^2 - \left(a + \frac{1}{2}\right)t - a^2 = 0, \text{ where } t = 2^{\pi / \cos^{-1} x}$$

$\Rightarrow \quad f(2) \le 0 \Rightarrow a^2 + 2a - 3 \ge 0$

$\Rightarrow \quad a \in (-\infty, -3] \cup [1, \infty)$

40. $E = \pi - 3 + \pi - 4 + 5 - 2\pi = -2$

41. $\cos^{-1} x + \cos^{-1} y + \cos^{-1} z = \pi$

$\Rightarrow \quad \sin^{-1} x + \sin^{-1} y + \sin^{-1} z = \frac{\pi}{2}$

Also, $\quad \cos^{-1} x + \cos^{-1} y + \cos^{-1} z = \pi$

$\Rightarrow \quad \cos^{-1} x + \cos^{-1} y = \cos^{-1}(-z)$

$\Rightarrow \quad xy - \sqrt{1 - x^2}\sqrt{1 - y^2} = -z$

$\Rightarrow \quad x^2 + y^2 + z^2 + 2xyz = 1$

Option (d) can be true only if $x, y, z > 0$; for (c) put

$$x = y = z = 1/2$$

42. Let $\tan^{-1} x = \alpha$ and $\tan^{-1} x^3 = \beta$

$\tan\alpha = x$ and $\tan\beta = x^3$

$\therefore 2\tan(\alpha + \beta) = \frac{2(\tan\alpha + \tan\beta)}{1 - \tan\alpha\tan\beta} = 2\left[\frac{x + x^3}{1 - x^4}\right] = \frac{2x}{1 - x^2}$

Also, $\frac{2x}{1 - x^2} = \frac{2\tan\alpha}{1 - \tan^2\alpha} = \tan 2\alpha = \tan(2\tan^{-1} x)$

$= \tan\left(2\left(\frac{\pi}{2} - \cot^{-1} x\right)\right)$

$= \tan(\pi - \cot^{-1} x - \cot^{-1} x)$

$= \tan(\cot^{-1}(-x) - \cot^{-1}(x))$

43. $f(x) = \begin{cases} 2x & ; \quad 0 \le x \le \frac{\pi}{2} \\ \pi & ; \quad \frac{\pi}{2} < x \le \frac{3\pi}{2} \\ 4\pi - 2x & ; \quad \frac{3\pi}{2} < x \le 2\pi \end{cases}$

Clearly, $f(x)$ is periodic function with period 2π. The graph of $f(x)$ is shown below.

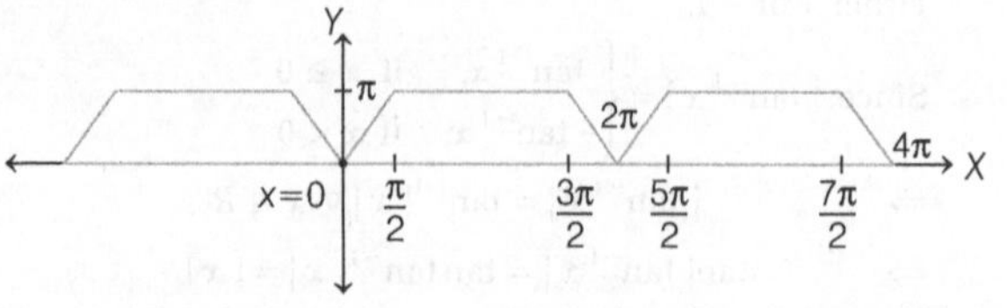

44. Domain of $\sin^{-1} x$ and $\cos^{-1} x$, each is $[-1,1]$ and that of $\sec^{-1} x$ and $\text{cosec}^{-1} x$, each is $(-\infty, -1] \cup [1, \infty)$

$\therefore$ Domain of $f(x)$ must be $\{-1,1\}$

$\therefore$ Range of $f(x)$ will be $\{f(-1), f(1)\}$

where, $f(-1) = \sin^{-1}(-1) \cdot \cos^{-1}(-1) \cdot \tan^{-1}(-1)\cot^{-1}(-1) \cdot \sec^{-1}(-1) \cdot \text{cosec}^{-1}(-1)$

$$= \left(\frac{-\pi}{2}\right) \cdot (\pi) \cdot \left(\frac{-\pi}{4}\right) \cdot \left(\frac{3\pi}{4}\right) \cdot (\pi) \cdot \left(\frac{-\pi}{2}\right) = \frac{-3\pi^6}{64}$$

and $f(1) = 0$ {as $\cos^{-1} 1 = 0$}

(i) Thus, the graph of $f(x)$ is a two point graph which doesn't lies above X-axis.

(ii) $f(x)_{max} = 0$ and $f(x)_{min} = \frac{-3\pi^6}{64}$

Hence, $|f(x)_{max} - f(x)_{min}| = \frac{3\pi^6}{64}$

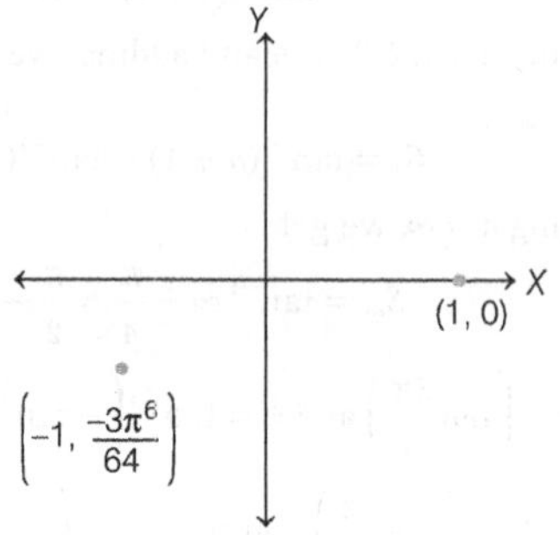

(iii) $f(x)$ is one-one. Hence, injective.

(iv) Domain is $\{-1,1\}$

$\therefore$ Number of non-negative integers in the domain of $f(x)$ is one.

45. $\alpha = 3\tan^{-1}\left(\frac{\sqrt{3}}{5}\right) + 3\tan^{-1}\left(\frac{\sqrt{3}}{2}\right)$

$$= 3\left[\tan^{-1}\left(\frac{\frac{\sqrt{3}}{5} + \frac{\sqrt{3}}{2}}{1 - \frac{3}{10}}\right)\right] = 3\tan^{-1}\left(\frac{7\sqrt{3}}{7}\right) = \pi$$

$$\beta = 4\left[\tan^{-1} 7 - \tan^{-1}\frac{3}{4}\right] = 4\left[\tan^{-1}\left(\frac{7 - \frac{3}{4}}{1 + \frac{21}{4}}\right)\right]$$

$$= 4\tan^{-1}\left(\frac{25}{25}\right) = \pi$$

46. $f(x) = |\sin^{-1} x| + \cos^{-1}\left(\frac{1}{x}\right)$

Domain of $f(x)$ is $\{-1,1\}$

$$f(1) = \frac{\pi}{2}, f(-1) = \frac{3\pi}{2}$$

So, function $f(x)$ is injective.

$$\text{sgn}(f(x)) = 1\ (f(x) > 0)$$

Range of $f(x) = \left\{\frac{\pi}{2}, \frac{3\pi}{2}\right\}$

47. (a) $f(x) = \sin(\tan^{-1} x)$

Put $\tan^{-1} x = \theta \Rightarrow x = \tan\theta$

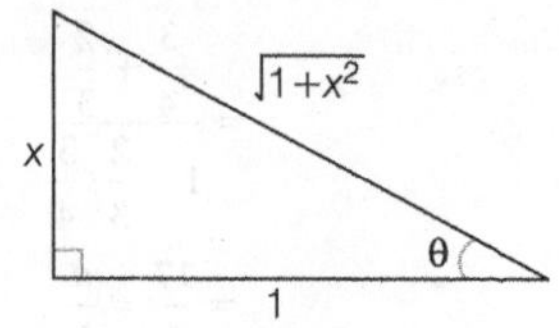

$\Rightarrow f(x) = \frac{x}{\sqrt{1 + x^2}} = g(x) \Rightarrow$ Identical functions

(b) $f(x) = \text{sgn}(\cot^{-1} x) = 1, \forall \in R$

But $g(x) = \sec^2 x - \tan^{-1} x = 1, \forall\ x \in R.$

(Think ? Domain of $g(x)$)

(c) As $\dfrac{x^2 - 1}{x^2 + 1} = \dfrac{x^2 + 1 - 2}{x^2 + 1} = 1 - \dfrac{2}{x^2 + 1} \in [-1, 1)$

So, $\cos^{-1}\left(\dfrac{x^2 - 1}{x^2 + 1}\right) \in (0, \pi]$

So, $f(x)$ and $g(x)$ are identical functions.

(d) $f(x) = \sin^{-1}\left(\dfrac{2x}{1 + x^2}\right) = \begin{cases} -(\pi + 2\tan^{-1} x) & , & x \le -1 \\ 2\tan^{-1} x & , & -1 < x < 1 \\ \pi - 2\tan^{-1} x & , & x \ge 1 \end{cases}$

So, $f(x)$ and $g(x)$ are not identical functions.

48. $T_n = \cot^{-1}(n^2 + n + 1) = \tan^{-1}\left(\dfrac{(n+1) - n}{1 + n(n+1)}\right)$

$= (\tan^{-1}(n+1) - \tan^{-1} n)$

So, $\displaystyle\sum_{n=1}^{n} T_n = (\tan^{-1} 2 - \tan^{-1} 1)$

$+ (\tan^{-1} 3 - \tan^{-1} 2) + \ldots\ldots + (\tan^{-1}(n+1) - \tan^{-1} n)$

$= \tan^{-1}(n+1) - \tan^{-1} 1$

$= \tan^{-1}\left[\dfrac{n + 1 - 1}{1 + (n+1)\cdot 1}\right]$

$= \tan^{-1}\left(\dfrac{n}{n+2}\right)$

$\Rightarrow \displaystyle\sum_{n=1}^{\infty} T_n = \tan^{-1} 1 = \frac{\pi}{4}$

(a) $\cot^{-1}(-1) + \sec^{-1} 1 - \text{cosec}^{-1} 1 = \dfrac{3\pi}{4} + 0 - \dfrac{\pi}{2}$

$= \dfrac{3\pi - 2\pi}{4}$

$= \dfrac{\pi}{4}$

(b) $\cot^{-1} 2 + \cot^{-1} 3 = \tan^{-1}\left(\dfrac{1}{2}\right) + \tan^{1}\left(\dfrac{1}{3}\right)$

$= \dfrac{\pi}{4}$

(c) $\because \quad -1 < \dfrac{1 - x^2}{1 + x^2} \le 1$

$\therefore \quad \dfrac{-\pi}{4} < \tan^{-1}\left(\dfrac{1 - x^2}{1 + x^2}\right) \le \dfrac{\pi}{4}$

Hence, minimum value of $f(x)$ does not exist and maximum value of $f(x)$ is $\dfrac{\pi}{4}$.

(d) As, $\dfrac{41\pi}{4} = \left(10\pi + \dfrac{\pi}{4}\right)$

So, $\cos^{-1}\left(\cos\dfrac{41\pi}{4}\right) = \cos^{-1}\left(\cos\dfrac{\pi}{4}\right) = \dfrac{\pi}{4}$

49. We know that $\tan^{-1}\left(\dfrac{2x}{1 - x^2}\right)$

$= \begin{cases} \pi + 2\tan^{-1} x & , & x < -1 \\ 2\tan^{-1} x & , & -1 < x \le 1 \\ -(\pi - 2\tan^{-1} x) & , & x > 1 \end{cases}$

$\therefore \quad f(x) = \begin{cases} -\pi, & x < -1 \\ \pi, & x > 1 \end{cases}$

So, $\quad R_f = \{-\pi, \pi\}$

50. $P = \dfrac{-5}{15}$ and $Q = \dfrac{1}{15}$

Sol. (Q.Nos. 51-52)

$A = \{\sin^{-1} x\};\ B = \{[x], \{x\}\};\ C = \{[x], \sin^{-1} x\}$

$f(x) = A \cap C = \sin^{-1} x$

$g(x) = B \cap C = [x]$

$h(x) = \{x\}$

$|x|$ is a function which is neither odd, nor discontinuous, nor non-decreasing.

$\therefore \quad l(x)$ is $|x|$

51. $l(x) = |x|$ is an even function

52. $g(f(x)) = [\sin^{-1} x]$

$\because$ Range of $\sin^{-1} x$ is $\left[-\dfrac{\pi}{2}, \dfrac{\pi}{2}\right]$

$\therefore$ Range of $g(f(x)) = \{-2, -1, 0, 1\}$

53. We have, $f(10) = \sin^{-1}(\sin 10) + \cos^{-1}(\cos 10)$

$= (3\pi - 10) + (4\pi - 10)$

$= (7\pi - 20)$

54. Clearly, $f(x) = (\pi - x) + x = \pi, \forall\ x \in \left[\dfrac{\pi}{2}, \pi\right]$

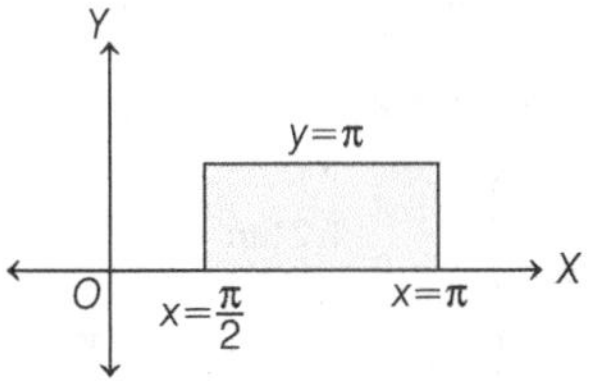

So, area $= \dfrac{\pi}{2} \times \pi$

$= \dfrac{\pi^2}{2}$

55. Given, $f(x) = \sqrt{\sin^{-1} x + 2} + \sqrt{1 - \sin^{-1} x}$

Clearly, for domain of $f(x)$, $1 - \sin^{-1} x \ge 0$

[as, $\sin^{-1} x + 2 > 0, \forall\ x \in [-1, 1]$]

$\Rightarrow \quad \sin^{-1} x \le 1$

$\Rightarrow \quad x \le \sin 1$

$\therefore \quad D_f = [-1, \sin 1]$

56. Given, $f(x)=\sqrt{\sin^{-1}x+2}+\sqrt{1-\sin^{-1}x}$, where $x\in[-1,\sin 1]$

Let $y=\sqrt{\sin^{-1}x+2}+\sqrt{1-\sin^{-1}x}$

Then, $y>0, \forall x\in[-1, \sin 1]$

Now, $y^2=(\sin^{-1}x+2)+(1-\sin^{-1}x)+2\sqrt{(\sin^{-1}x+2)(1-\sin^{-1}x)}$

$\Rightarrow \quad y^2=3+2\sqrt{\frac{9}{4}-\left(\sin^{-1}x+\frac{1}{2}\right)^2}$

Clearly, $y^2_{\max}\left(\sin^{-1}x=\frac{-1}{2}\right)=3+2\sqrt{\frac{9}{4}-0}=3+3=6$

$\Rightarrow \quad y_{\max}\left(x=-\sin\frac{1}{2}\right)=\sqrt{6}$

Also, $\quad y^2_{\min}(\sin^{-1}x=1)=3+2\sqrt{\frac{9}{4}-\frac{9}{4}}=3$

$\Rightarrow \quad y_{\min}(x=\sin 1)=\sqrt{3}$

Hence, range of $f=[\sqrt{3},\sqrt{6}]$

57. $\sin^{-1}\left(\frac{4x}{x^2+4}\right)+2\tan^{-1}\left(-\frac{x}{2}\right)$

$=\sin^{-1}\left(\frac{2\cdot\frac{x}{2}}{\left(\frac{x}{2}\right)^2+1}\right)-2\tan^{-1}\frac{x}{2}$

$=2\tan^{-1}\frac{x}{2}-2\tan^{-1}\frac{x}{2}=0$

Here, $\quad \left|\frac{x}{2}\right|\le 1$

$|x|\le 2$

$\Rightarrow \quad -2\le x\le 2$

58. $\cos^{-1}\left(\frac{6x}{1+9x^2}\right)=-\frac{\pi}{2}+2\tan^{-1}3x$

$\Rightarrow \quad \frac{\pi}{2}-\sin^{-1}\frac{6x}{1-9x^2}=\frac{-\pi}{2}+2\tan^{-1}3x$

$\Rightarrow \quad \sin^{-1}\frac{6x}{1+9x^2}=\pi-2\tan^{-1}3x$

$\Rightarrow \quad \sin^{-1}\frac{2\cdot 3x}{1+(3x)^2}=\pi-2\tan^{-1}3x$

Above is true when $3x>1$

$\Rightarrow \quad x>\frac{1}{3}$

$\Rightarrow \quad x\in\left(\frac{1}{3},\infty\right)$

Sol. (Q. Nos. 59 to 60)

$\sin^{-1}x\in\left[-\frac{\pi}{2},\frac{\pi}{2}\right]$

$\cos^{-1}y\in[0,\pi]$

$\sec^{-1}z\in\left[0,\frac{\pi}{2}\right)\cup\left(\frac{\pi}{2},\pi\right]$

$\Rightarrow \sin^{-1}x+\cos^{-1}y+\sec^{-1}z\le\frac{\pi}{2}+\pi+\pi=\frac{5\pi}{2}$

Also, $t^2-\sqrt{2\pi}t+3\pi=t^2-2\sqrt{\frac{\pi}{2}}t+\frac{\pi}{2}-\frac{\pi}{2}+3\pi$

$=\left(t-\sqrt{\frac{\pi}{2}}\right)^2+\frac{5\pi}{2}\ge\frac{5\pi}{2}$

The given inequation exists if equality holds

i.e. LHS = RHS $=\frac{5\pi}{2}$

$\Rightarrow \quad x=1, y=-1, z=-1$ and $t=\sqrt{\frac{\pi}{2}}$

$\Rightarrow \quad \cos^{-1}(\cos 5t^2)=\cos^{-1}\left(\cos\left(\frac{5\pi}{2}\right)\right)=\frac{\pi}{2}$

Sol. (Q. Nos. 61 to 62)

$\alpha=\tan^{-1}\left(\frac{4}{3}\right)+\tan^{-1}\left(\frac{3}{4}\right)=\frac{\pi}{2}$

$\beta=\left(\tan^{-1}\left(\frac{12}{5}\right)+\tan^{-1}\frac{3}{4}\right)+\tan^{-1}\left(\frac{63}{16}\right)=\pi$

$\therefore$ 2, -1 are roots of equation $x^2-ax+b=0$

So, $a=1$ and $b=-2$

61. $\tan^{-1}\left(\sec\left(\cos^{-1}\left(\sin\frac{\alpha}{2}\right)\right)-1\right)=\tan^{-1}(\sqrt{2}-1)$

$=\frac{\pi}{8}=\frac{\alpha}{4}$

62. We have, $\sin^{-1}x=\frac{3x}{2}$

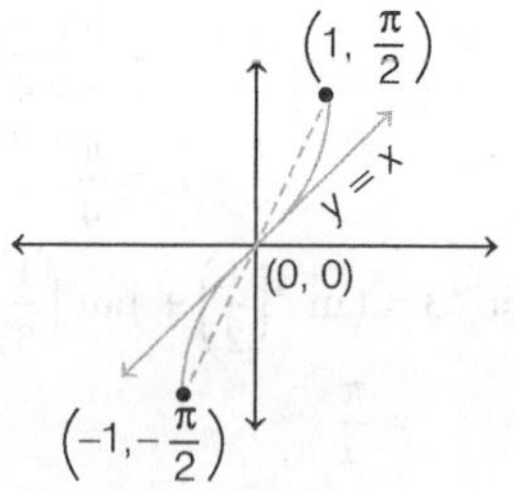

So, number of solution = 3

63. Given, $f(x)=\cos(\tan^{-1}(\sin(\cot^{-1}x)))$

$=\cos\left(\tan^{-1}\left(\sin\left(\sin^{-1}\frac{1}{\sqrt{1+x^2}}\right)\right)\right)$

$=\cos\left(\tan^{-1}\left(\frac{1}{\sqrt{1+x^2}}\right)\right)$

$=\cos\left(\cos^{-1}\left(\frac{\sqrt{1+x^2}}{\sqrt{2+x^2}}\right)\right)=\frac{\sqrt{1+x^2}}{\sqrt{2+x^2}}=\left(\frac{x^2+1}{x^2+2}\right)^{1/2}$

$\Rightarrow \quad A=1, B=2$

$\Rightarrow \quad A+B=1+2=3$

64. We have,

$$\text{RHS} = \tan^{-1}\{\tan^2(\alpha+\beta)\cdot\tan^2(\alpha-\beta)\} + \tan^{-1}1$$

$$= \tan^{-1}\left\{\frac{\tan^2(\alpha+\beta)\tan^2(\alpha-\beta)+1}{1-\tan^2(\alpha+\beta)\tan^2(\alpha-\beta)}\right\}$$

$$= \tan^{-1}\left\{\frac{\sin^2(\alpha+\beta)\sin^2(\alpha-\beta)+\cos^2(\alpha+\beta)\cos^2(\alpha-\beta)}{\cos^2(\alpha+\beta)\cos^2(\alpha-\beta)-\sin^2(\alpha+\beta)\sin^2(\alpha-\beta)}\right\}$$

$$= \tan^{-1}\left\{\frac{\{2\sin(\alpha+\beta)\sin(\alpha-\beta)\}^2}{\{2\cos(\alpha+\beta)\cos(\alpha-\beta)\}^2}\right.$$

$$\left.\frac{+\{2\cos(\alpha+\beta)\cos(\alpha-\beta)\}^2}{-\{2\sin(\alpha+\beta)\sin(\alpha-\beta)\}^2}\right\}$$

$$= \tan^{-1}\left\{\frac{(\cos2\beta-\cos2\alpha)^2+(\cos2\alpha+\cos2\beta)^2}{(\cos2\alpha+\cos2\beta)^2-(\cos2\beta-\cos2\alpha)^2}\right\}$$

$$= \tan^{-1}\left\{\frac{\cos^2 2\alpha+\cos^2 2\beta}{2\cos2\alpha\cos2\beta}\right\}$$

$$= \tan^{-1}\left\{\frac{\cos2\alpha\sec2\beta+\cos2\beta\sec2\alpha)}{2}\right\}$$

Hence, the value of λ is equal to 2.

65. We have, $\sin^{-1}(\sin 12) + \cos^{-1}(\cos 12)$

$$= \sin^{-1}(\sin(4\pi-(4\pi-12))) + \cos^{-1}(\cos(4\pi-(4\pi-12)))$$

$$= -(4\pi-12) + (4\pi-12) = 0$$

So that, $(n-2)x^2 + 8x + n + 4 > 0, \forall\, x \in R$

$\Rightarrow \quad n-2>0 \Rightarrow n \geq 3$

and $\quad 8^2 - 4(n-2)(n+4) < 0$

or $\quad n^2 + 2n - 24 > 0 \Rightarrow n = 4$

$\Rightarrow \quad n \geq 5 \Rightarrow n = 5$

66. $1 + \sin(\cos^{-1}x) + \sin^2(\cos^{-1}x) + \ldots \infty = 2$

$$\Rightarrow \quad \frac{1}{1-\sin(\cos^{-1}x)} = 2$$

$$\Rightarrow \quad \frac{1}{2} = 1 - \sin(\cos^{-1}x)$$

$$\Rightarrow \sin(\cos^{-1}x) = \frac{1}{2} \text{ or } \cos^{-1}x = \frac{\pi}{6} \Rightarrow x = \frac{\sqrt{3}}{2} \text{ or } 12x^2 = 9$$

67. Here $|\cos x| = \sin^{-1}(\sin x)$

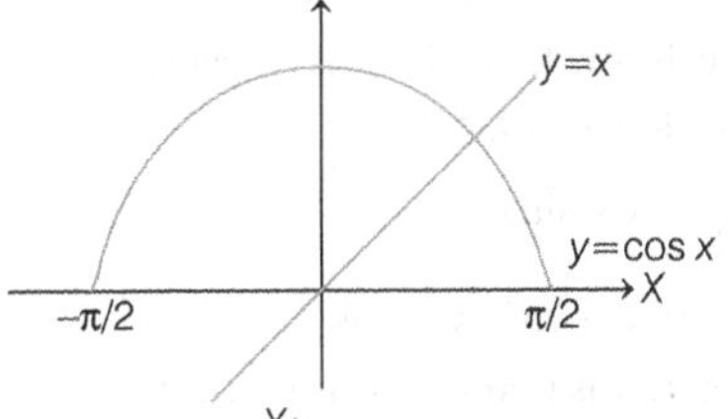

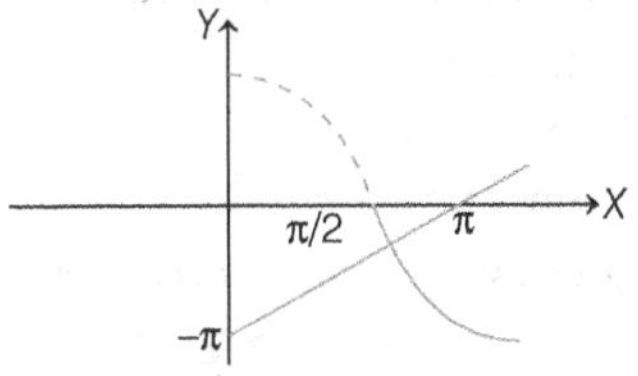

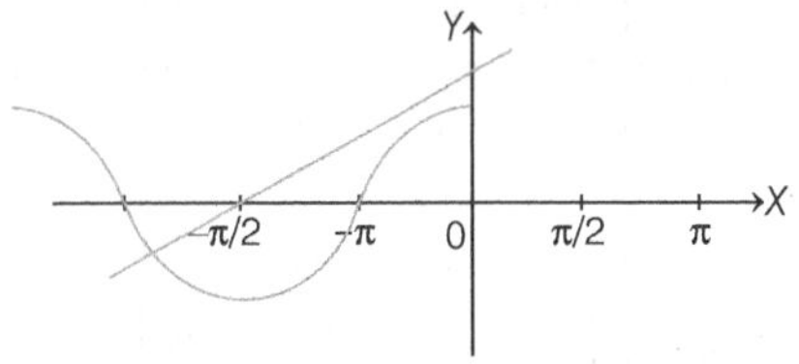

If $-\frac{\pi}{2} \leq x \leq \frac{\pi}{2}$ then $\cos x = x$

In this case, there is one solution obtained graphically.

If $\frac{\pi}{2} < x \leq \pi$ then $-\cos x = \sin^{-1}\{\sin(\pi - x)\} = \pi - x$

$\therefore \quad \cos x = x - \pi$

In this case, there is one solution obtained graphically.

If $-\pi \leq x < -\frac{\pi}{2}$ then

$$-\cos x = \sin^{-1}\{\sin(-\pi-x)\} = -x-\pi$$

i.e. $\quad \cos x = x + \pi$

This gives no solution as can be seen from the graphs.

68. $\sin^{-1}\left(\frac{5}{x}\right) + \sin^{-1}\left(\frac{12}{x}\right) = \frac{\pi}{2}$

$$\Leftrightarrow \quad x > 12 \text{ and } \cos^{-1}\left(\frac{\sqrt{x^2-25}}{x}\right) + \sin^{-1}\left(\frac{12}{x}\right) = \frac{\pi}{2}$$

$$\Leftrightarrow \quad x > 12 \text{ and } \cos^{-1}\left(\frac{\sqrt{x^2-25}}{x}\right) = \cos^{-1}\left(\frac{12}{x}\right)$$

$$\Leftrightarrow \quad x > 12 \text{ and } \frac{\sqrt{x^2-25}}{x} = \frac{12}{x}$$

$$\Leftrightarrow \quad x > 12 \text{ and } x^2 - 25 = 12^2$$

$$\Leftrightarrow \quad x > 12 \text{ and } x^2 = 169$$

$$\Leftrightarrow \quad x > 12 \text{ and } x = \pm 13$$

$\therefore x = 13$ is only solution.

69. Taking tan on both sides

$$\frac{\frac{x+1}{x-1}+\frac{x-1}{x}}{1-\frac{x+1}{x-1}\cdot\frac{x-1}{x}} = -7 \text{ on simplification, we get } x = 2$$

Substituting, we get

$$\tan^{-1}3 + \tan^{-1}\frac{1}{2} = \tan^{-1}(-7) \text{ but LHS is } \pi + \tan^{-1}(-7).$$

Hence, no solution.

70. Let $X = \sqrt{\frac{a(a+b+c)}{bc}}, Y = \sqrt{\frac{b(a+b+c)}{ac}}, Z = \sqrt{\frac{c(a+b+c)}{ab}}$

$$XY = \sqrt{\frac{a(a+b+c)}{bc}\cdot\frac{b(a+b+c)}{ac}} = \frac{a+b+c}{c}$$

$$= \left(1+\frac{a+b}{c}\right) > 1\ (a, b, c > 0)$$

$$\therefore \quad \tan^{-1}X + \tan^{-1}Y = \pi + \tan^{-1}\left[\frac{X+Y}{1-XY}\right]$$

$$= \pi + \tan^{-1}\left(\frac{\sqrt{\frac{a(a+b+c)}{bc}} + \sqrt{\frac{b(a+b+c)}{ac}}}{1 - \frac{a+b+c}{c}}\right)$$

$$= \pi + \tan^{-1}\left(\frac{\sqrt{\frac{a+b+c}{c}}\left(\frac{\sqrt{a}}{\sqrt{b}} + \frac{\sqrt{b}}{\sqrt{a}}\right)}{-\frac{(a+b)}{c}}\right)$$

$$= \pi + \tan^{-1}\left(-\sqrt{\frac{a+b+c}{c}}\left(\frac{a+b}{\sqrt{ab}}\right)\left(\frac{c}{a+c}\right)\right)$$

$$= \pi - \tan^{-1}\frac{\sqrt{c(a+b+c)}}{ab} = \pi - \tan^{-1} Z$$

$\therefore \quad \tan^{-1} X + \tan^{-1} Y + \tan^{-1} Z = \pi$

$\therefore \quad \lambda = \pi \Rightarrow [\lambda] = [\pi] = 3$

Hence, $\frac{[\lambda]}{2} = 1.5$

71. We have,

$$E = \sqrt{\sin^{-1} x_1}\sqrt{\cos^{-1} x_2} + \sqrt{\sin^{-1} x_2}\sqrt{\cos^{-1} x_3} + \sqrt{\sin^{-1} x_3}\sqrt{\cos^{-1} x_4} + \ldots + \sqrt{\sin^{-1} x_{28}}\sqrt{\cos^{-1} x_1}$$

$x_1 \in [0, 1] \ \forall i = 1, 2, 3, \ldots, 28$

$\therefore \sin^{-1} x_1 > 0$

Now, using AM $\geq$ GM we have $\frac{a^2 + b^2}{2} \geq ab$, where $a, b > 0$

$$\therefore \quad \sqrt{\sin^{-1} x_1}\sqrt{\cos^{-1} x_2} \leq \left(\frac{\sin^{-1} x_1 + \cos^{-1} x_2}{2}\right)$$

$$\sqrt{\sin^{-1} x_2}\sqrt{\cos^{-1} x_3} \leq \left(\frac{\sin^{-1} x_2 + \cos^{-1} x_3}{2}\right)$$

$$\sqrt{\sin^{-1} x_{28}}\sqrt{\cos^{-1} x_1} \leq \left(\frac{\sin^{-1} x_{28} + \sin^{-1} x_1}{2}\right)$$

On adding all, we get

$$E \leq \sum_{i=1}^{28} \frac{\sin^{-1} x_i + \cos^{-1} x_i}{2}$$

$$\therefore \quad E \leq \frac{28\left(\frac{\pi}{2}\right)}{2}$$

$$\therefore \quad E_{\max} = 7\pi = M\pi \Rightarrow M = 7$$

Hence, $\frac{M+1}{2} = 4$

72. $S = \sum_{r=1}^{10}\sum_{s=1}^{10} \tan^{-1}\left(\frac{r}{s}\right)$

$$\therefore \quad S = \sum_{r=1}^{10}\sum_{s=1}^{10} \cot^{-1}\left(\frac{s}{r}\right) \text{ (As } r \text{ and } s \text{ are independent)}$$

On adding, we get

$$2S = \sum_{r=1}^{10}\sum_{s=1}^{10}\left(\tan^{-1}\left(\frac{r}{s}\right) + \cot^{-1}\left(\frac{s}{r}\right)\right)$$

$$\Rightarrow \quad 2S = \sum_{r=1}^{10}\sum_{s=1}^{10}\frac{\pi}{2} = \frac{\pi}{2}\sum_{r=1}^{10} 10 = \frac{100\pi}{2}$$

$$\Rightarrow \quad S = 25\pi = K \quad \text{[given]}$$

$$\therefore \quad \frac{2K}{5} = \frac{2 \times 25\pi}{\pi} = 50$$

73. $S_{n-1} = \sum_{k=2}^{n} \cos^{-1}\left(\frac{1 + \sqrt{(k-1)k(k+1)(k+2)}}{k(k+1)}\right)$

$$= \cos^{-1}\left(\frac{1}{k}\cdot\frac{1}{(k+1)} + \frac{\sqrt{(k-1)k(k+1)(k+2)}}{k(k+1)}\right)$$

$$= \cos^{-1}\left(\frac{1}{k}\cdot\frac{1}{k+1} + \sqrt{1 - \frac{1}{k^2}}\sqrt{1 - \frac{1}{(k+1)^2}}\right)$$

$$= \cos^{-1}\frac{1}{k+1} - \cos^{-1}\frac{1}{k}$$

Substituting $k = 2, 3, 4\ldots$, we get

$$t_2 = \cos^{-1}\left(\frac{1}{3}\right) - \cos^{-1}\left(\frac{1}{2}\right)$$

$$t_3 = \cos^{-1}\left(\frac{1}{4}\right) - \cos^{-1}\left(\frac{1}{3}\right)$$

$$t_n = \cos^{-1}\left(\frac{1}{n+1}\right) - \cos^{-1}\left(\frac{1}{n}\right)$$

$$S_{n-1} = \cos^{-1}\left(\frac{1}{n+1}\right) - \cos^{-1}\left(\frac{1}{2}\right)$$

$$\therefore \quad S = \lim_{n\to\infty}\left[\cos^{-1}\left(\frac{1}{n+1}\right) - \cos^{-1}\left(\frac{1}{2}\right)\right]$$

$$= \cos^{-1}(0) - \cos^{-1}\left(\frac{1}{2}\right) = \frac{\pi}{2} - \frac{\pi}{3} = \frac{\pi}{6} = \lambda \quad \text{[given]}$$

$$\therefore \quad [4\lambda] = \left(\frac{2\pi}{3}\right) = 2$$

74. (A) In $(0, \cos 1)$, we have $\cos^{-1} x > \sin^{-1} x$

Also, $\cos^{-1} x > 1$ and $\sin^{-1} x < 1$

The greatest is $(\cos^{-1} x)^{\cos^{-1} x} = t_4$ and the least is

$(\sin^{-1} x)^{\cos^{-1} x} = t_2$

and $(\sin^{-1} x)^{\sin^{-1} x} < (\cos^{-1} x)^{\sin^{-1} x} \Rightarrow t_1 < t_3$

So, $t_4 > t_3 > t_1 > t_2$

(B) Similarly, in $\cos 1 < x < \frac{1}{\sqrt{2}}$

$\cos^{-1} x > \sin^{-1} x$ and both are less than 1.

So, greatest is t_3 and least is t_2 and $t_4 > t_1$.

Hence, $t_3 > t_4 > t_1 > t_2$

(C) For $\frac{1}{\sqrt{2}} < x < \sin 1$

We have, $1 > \sin^{-1} x > \cos^{-1} x$

So, greatest is t_2 and least is t_3 also $t_1 > t_4$

Hence, $t_2 > t_1 > t_4 > t_3$

(D) For $\sin 1 < x < 1$, we have

$\sin^{-1} x > 1 > \cos^{-1} x$

So, the greatest is t_1 and least is t_3 and $t_2 > t_4$

Hence, $t_1 > t_2 > t_4 > t_3$

75. Follow the following graph for solution

(A)

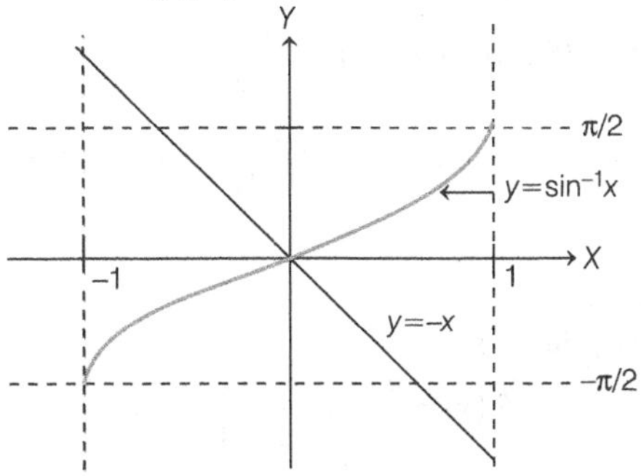

(B)

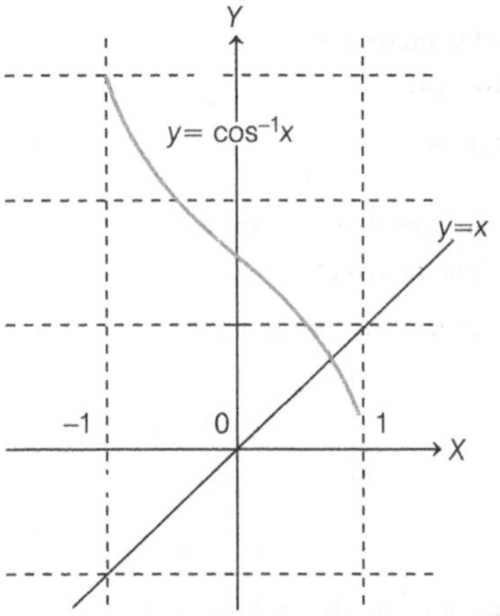

(C)

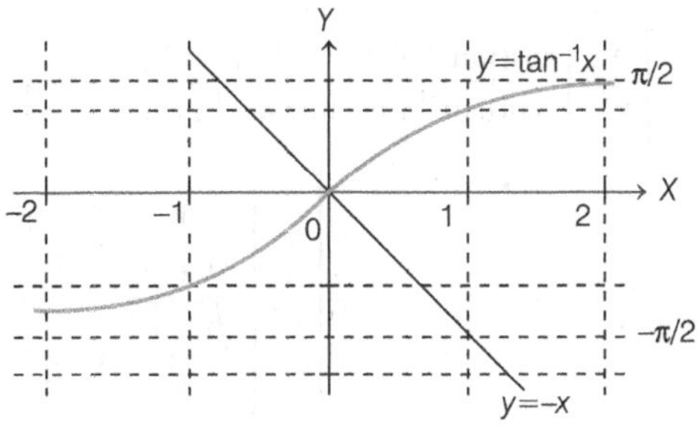

(D)

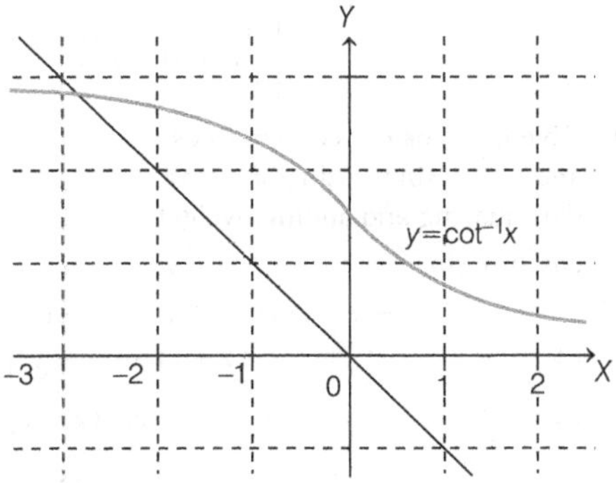

76. Given, $\tan^{-1}\left(\dfrac{6y}{9-y^2}\right)+\cot^{-1}\left(\dfrac{9-y^2}{6y}\right)=\dfrac{2\pi}{3}$ ...(i)

and $0<|y|<3$

$\Rightarrow -3<y<0$ or $0<y<3$

So, there is two cases arise to solve Eq. (i).

Case I When $y\in(-3,0)$, i.e. $-3<y<0$

$$\Rightarrow \tan^{-1}\left(\frac{6y}{9-y^2}\right)+\left\{\pi+\tan^{-1}\left(\frac{6y}{9-y^2}\right)\right\}=\frac{2\pi}{3}$$

$$\Rightarrow \quad 2\tan^{-1}\left(\frac{6y}{9-y^2}\right)=-\frac{\pi}{3}$$

$$\Rightarrow \quad \tan^{-1}\left(\frac{6y}{9-y^2}\right)=-\frac{\pi}{6}$$

$$\Rightarrow \quad \frac{6y}{9-y^2}=-\frac{1}{\sqrt{3}}$$

$$\Rightarrow \quad 6\sqrt{3}y=-9+y^2$$

$$\Rightarrow \quad y^2-6\sqrt{3}y-9=0$$

$\Rightarrow y=3\sqrt{3}\pm 6$ but $y\in(-3,0)$ i.e. y is negative.

So, $\quad y=3\sqrt{3}-6$ ...(i)

Case II When $y\in(0,3)$, i.e. $0<y<3$

$$\Rightarrow \quad \tan^{-1}\left(\frac{6y}{9-y^2}\right)+\tan^{-1}\left(\frac{6y}{9-y^2}\right)=\frac{2\pi}{3}$$

$$\Rightarrow \quad 2\tan^{-1}\left(\frac{6y}{9-y^2}\right)=\frac{2\pi}{3}$$

$$\Rightarrow \quad \frac{6y}{9-y^2}=\tan\left(\frac{\pi}{3}\right)=\sqrt{3}$$

$$\Rightarrow \quad 6y=9\sqrt{3}-\sqrt{3}y^2$$

$$\Rightarrow \quad \sqrt{3}y^2+6y-9\sqrt{3}=0$$

$\Rightarrow \quad y=\sqrt{3},-3\sqrt{3}$ but $y\in(0,3)$

i.e. y is positive.

So, $\quad y=\sqrt{3}$ ...(ii)

Hence, sum of Eqs. (i) and (ii) gives us

$$(\sqrt{3})+(3\sqrt{3}-6)=4\sqrt{3}-6$$

77. Given, $\sqrt{1+\cos 2x}=\sqrt{2}\tan^{-1}(\tan x)$

$$\Rightarrow \quad \sqrt{2\cos^2 x}=\sqrt{2}\tan^{-1}(\tan x)$$

$$\Rightarrow \quad |\cos x|=\tan^{-1}(\tan x) \quad \text{...(i)}$$

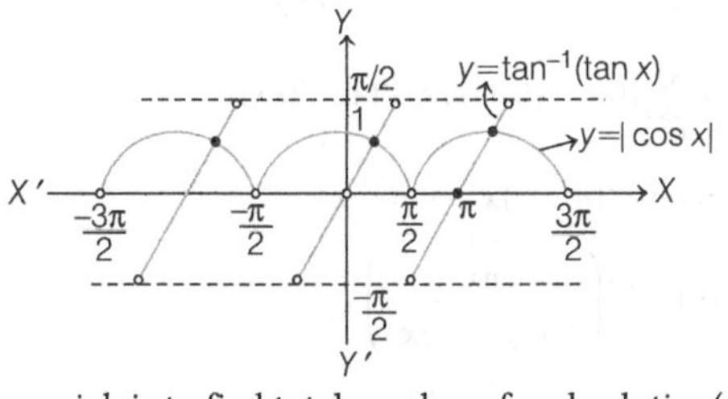

Now, our job is to find total number of real solution(s) of Eq. (i).

For this graphical approach is much more convinent

So, we draw the graph of $y=|\cos x|$ and $y=\tan^{-1}(\tan x)$ in the given domain and hence we count total number of points of intersection.

Hence, total number of real solutions = 3

78. Let $I = \frac{3}{2}\cos^{-1}\sqrt{\frac{2}{2+\pi^2}} + \frac{1}{4}\sin^{-1}\frac{2\sqrt{2}\pi}{2+\pi^2} + \tan^{-1}\frac{\sqrt{2}}{\pi}$

$$= \frac{3}{2}\cos^{-1}\sqrt{\frac{1}{1+\frac{\pi^2}{2}}} + \frac{1}{4}\sin^{-1}\left(\frac{\sqrt{2}\pi}{1+\frac{\pi^2}{2}}\right) + \tan^{-1}\frac{\sqrt{2}}{\pi}$$

Let $\frac{\pi}{\sqrt{2}} = \tan\theta \Rightarrow \pi = \sqrt{2}\tan\theta$

Thus, $\theta \in \left(\frac{\pi}{4}, \frac{\pi}{2}\right)$

$$= \frac{3}{2}\cos^{-1}\sqrt{\frac{1}{1+\tan^2\theta}} + \frac{1}{4}\sin^{-1}\left(\frac{2\tan\theta}{1+\tan^2\theta}\right) + \tan^{-1}(\cot\theta)$$

$$= \frac{3}{2}\cos^{-1}(\cos\theta) + \frac{1}{4}\sin^{-1}(\sin 2\theta) + \tan^{-1}(\cot\theta)$$

$$= \frac{3\theta}{2} + \frac{1}{4}\sin^{-1}(\sin 2\theta) + \frac{\pi}{2} - \cot^{-1}(\cot\theta)$$

Since, $\theta \in \left(\frac{\pi}{4}, \frac{\pi}{2}\right) \Rightarrow 2\theta \in \left(\frac{\pi}{2}, \pi\right)$.

and we also know that,

$$\sin^{-1}(\sin\theta) = \begin{cases} \theta, & -\frac{\pi}{2} \le \theta \le \frac{\pi}{2} \\ \pi - \theta, & \frac{\pi}{2} \le \theta \le \frac{3\pi}{2} \end{cases}$$

$$= \frac{3\theta}{2} + \frac{1}{4}(\pi - 2\theta) + \frac{\pi}{2} - \theta$$

$$= \frac{3\theta}{2} + \frac{\pi}{4} - \frac{\theta}{2} + \frac{\pi}{2} - \theta$$

$$= \frac{\pi}{4} + \frac{\pi}{2} = \frac{3\pi}{4} = 2.356 \approx 2.36$$

79. For option (a)

$$S_n(x) = \sum_{k=1}^{n} \cot^{-1}\left[\frac{1+k(k+1)x^2}{x}\right]$$

can be written as

$$S_n(x) = \sum_{k=1}^{n} \tan^{-1}\left[\frac{(k+1)x - kx}{1 + kx\cdot(k+1)x}\right]$$

$$= \sum_{k=1}^{n} [\tan^{-1}(k+1)x - \tan^{-1}(kx)]$$

$$= \tan^{-1}(n+1)x - \tan^{-1}x$$

$$= \tan^{-1}\left(\frac{nx}{1+(n+1)x^2}\right)$$

Now, $S_{10}(x) = \tan^{-1}\left(\frac{10x}{1+11x^2}\right)$

$$= \frac{\pi}{2} - \cot^{-1}\left(\frac{10x}{1+11x^2}\right)$$

$$= \frac{\pi}{2} - \tan^{-1}\left(\frac{1+11x^2}{10x}\right)$$

Option (a) is correct.

For option (b)

$$\lim_{n\to\infty} \cot(S_n(x)) = \cot\left(\tan^{-1}\left(\frac{x}{x^2}\right)\right)$$

$$= \cot\left(\tan^{-1}\left(\frac{1}{x}\right)\right) = \cot(\cot^{-1}x)$$

$$= x, x > 0$$

Option (b) is correct.

For option (c)

$$S_3(x) = \frac{\pi}{4} \Rightarrow \frac{3x}{1+4x^2} = 1$$

$\Rightarrow$ $4x^2 - 3x + 1 = 0$ has no real root.

Option (c) is incorrect.

For option (d)

For $x = 1$, $\tan(S_n(x)) = \frac{n}{n+2}$,

which is greater than $1/2$ for $n \ge 3$.

Option (d) is incorrect.

80. P. Here, innermost function is inverse.

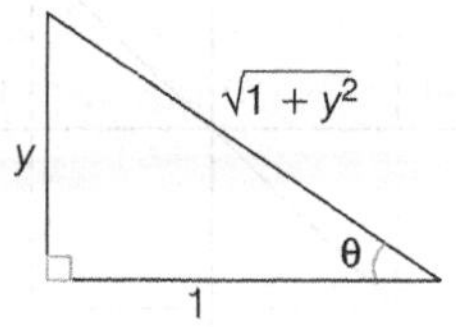

$\therefore$ Put $\tan^{-1}y = \theta \Rightarrow \tan\theta = y$

$$\left[\frac{1}{y^2}\cdot\left\{\frac{\cos(\tan^{-1}y) + y\sin(\tan^{-1}y)}{\cot(\sin^{-1}y) + \tan(\sin^{-1}y)}\right\}^2 + y^4\right]^{1/2}$$

$$= \left[\frac{1}{y^2}\left\{\frac{\frac{1}{\sqrt{1+y^2}} + \frac{y^2}{\sqrt{1+y^2}}}{\frac{\sqrt{1-y^2}}{y} + \frac{y}{\sqrt{1-y^2}}}\right\}^2 + y^4\right]^{1/2}$$

$$= \left[\frac{1}{y^2}\cdot y^2(1-y^4) + y^4\right]^{1/2} = 1$$

Q. Given, $\cos x + \cos y = -\cos z$

and $\sin x + \sin y = -\sin z$

On squaring and adding, we get

$$\cos^2 x + \sin^2 x + \cos^2 y + \sin^2 y + 2\cos x\cos y + 2\sin x\sin y = 1$$

$$\Rightarrow 2 + 2[\cos(x-y)] = 1$$

$$\Rightarrow \cos(x-y) = -\frac{1}{2}$$

$$\Rightarrow 2\cos^2\left(\frac{x-y}{2}\right) - 1 = -\frac{1}{2}$$

$$\Rightarrow 2\cos^2\left(\frac{x-y}{2}\right) = \frac{1}{2}$$

$$\Rightarrow \cos\left(\frac{x-y}{2}\right) = \frac{1}{2}$$

R. $\cos 2x\cdot\left(\cos\left(\frac{\pi}{4}-x\right)-\cos\left(\frac{\pi}{4}+x\right)\right)+2\sin^2 x$
$= 2\sin x\cdot\cos x$

$\Rightarrow \cos 2x\cdot(\sqrt{2}\sin x)+2\sin^2 x = 2\sin x\cdot\cos x$

$\Rightarrow \sqrt{2}\sin x[\cos 2x+\sqrt{2}\sin x-\sqrt{2}\cos x]=0$

$\Rightarrow \sin x = 0, (\cos x-\sin x)(\cos x+\sin x-\sqrt{2})=0$

$\Rightarrow \sec x = 1$ or $\tan x = 1$

$\Rightarrow \sec x = 1$ or $\sqrt{2}$

S. $\cot(\sin^{-1}\sqrt{1-x^2})=\sin(\tan^{-1}(x\sqrt{6}))$

$$\Rightarrow \frac{x}{\sqrt{1-x^2}}=\frac{x\sqrt{6}}{\sqrt{1+6x^2}}$$

$$\Rightarrow 1+6x^2=6-6x^2$$

$$\Rightarrow 12x^2=5$$

$$\Rightarrow x=\sqrt{\frac{5}{12}}=\frac{\sqrt{5}}{2\sqrt{3}}$$

81. $\because \sec^{-1}\left[\frac{1}{4}\sum_{k=0}^{10}\sec\left(\frac{7\pi}{12}+\frac{k\pi}{2}\right)\sec\left(\frac{7\pi}{12}+\frac{(k+1)\pi}{2}\right)\right]$

$$=\sec^{-1}\left[\sum_{k=0}^{10}\frac{1}{\cos\left(\frac{7\pi}{12}+\frac{k\pi}{2}\right)\cos\left(\frac{7\pi}{12}+\frac{(k+1)\pi}{2}\right)}\right]$$

$$=\sec^{-1}\left[\frac{1}{2}\sum_{k=0}^{10}\frac{-1}{\sin\left(\frac{7\pi}{6}+k\pi\right)}\right]$$

$$=\sec^{-1}\left[\frac{1}{2}\sum_{k=0}^{10}\frac{-1}{\sin\left((k+1)\pi+\frac{\pi}{6}\right)}\right]$$

If k is an even integer, then

$$\sin\left((k+1)\pi+\frac{\pi}{6}\right)=-\sin\frac{\pi}{6}=\frac{-1}{2}$$

If k is an odd integer, then

$$\sin\left((k+1)\pi+\frac{\pi}{6}\right)=\sin\frac{\pi}{6}=\frac{1}{2}$$

$$\therefore \sum_{k=0}^{9}\frac{1}{\sin\left((k+1)\pi+\frac{\pi}{6}\right)}=0$$

Hence, $\sec^{-1}\left[\frac{1}{2}\sum_{k=0}^{10}\frac{-1}{\sin\left((k+1)\pi+\frac{\pi}{6}\right)}\right]$

$$=\sec^{-1}\left[\frac{1}{2}\left(\frac{-1}{-1/2}\right)\right]$$

$$=\sec^{-1}(1)=0$$

82. It is given that for non-negative integers 'n',

$$f(n)=\frac{\sum_{k=0}^{n}\sin\left(\frac{k+1}{n+2}\pi\right)\sin\left(\frac{k+2}{n+2}\pi\right)}{\sum_{k=0}^{n}\sin^2\left(\frac{k+1}{n+2}\pi\right)}$$

$$=\frac{\sum_{k=0}^{n}\left(\cos\frac{\pi}{n+2}-\cos\left(\frac{2k+3}{n+2}\pi\right)\right)}{\sum_{k=0}^{n}\left(1-\cos\left(\frac{2k+2}{n+2}\pi\right)\right)}$$

[$\because 2\sin A\sin B=\cos(A-B)-\cos(A+B)$
and $2\sin^2 A = 1-\cos 2A$]

$$=\frac{\left(\cos\left(\frac{\pi}{n+2}\right)\right)\sum_{k=0}^{n}1-\left\{\cos\frac{3\pi}{n+2}+\cos\frac{5\pi}{n+2}+\cos\frac{7\pi}{n+2}+\ldots+\cos\left(\frac{2n+3}{n+2}\pi\right)\right\}}{\sum_{k=0}^{n}1-\left\{\cos\frac{2\pi}{n+2}+\cos\frac{4\pi}{n+2}+\cos\frac{6\pi}{n+2}+\ldots+\cos\left(\frac{2n+2}{n+2}\pi\right)\right\}}$$

$$=\frac{(n+1)\cos\left(\frac{\pi}{n+2}\right)-\frac{\sin\left(\frac{n\pi}{n+2}\right)}{\sin\left(\frac{\pi}{n+2}\right)}\cos\left(\frac{n+3}{n+2}\pi\right)}{(n+1)-\frac{\sin\left(\frac{n\pi}{n+2}\right)}{\sin\left(\frac{\pi}{n+2}\right)}\cos\left(\frac{n+2}{n+2}\pi\right)}$$

[$\because \cos(\alpha)+\cos(\alpha+\beta)+\cos(\alpha+2\beta)$
$+\ldots\ldots+\cos(\alpha+(n-1)\beta)$
$=\frac{\sin(n\beta/2)}{\sin(\beta/2)}\cos\left(\frac{2\alpha+(n-1)\beta}{2}\right)$]

$$=\frac{(n+1)\cos\left(\frac{\pi}{n+2}\right)-\frac{\sin\left(\pi-\frac{\pi}{n+2}\right)}{\sin\left(\frac{\pi}{n+2}\right)}\cos\left(\pi+\frac{\pi}{n+2}\right)}{(n+1)-\frac{\sin\left(\pi-\frac{\pi}{n+2}\right)}{\sin\left(\frac{\pi}{n+2}\right)}\cos(\pi)}$$

$$=\frac{(n+1)\cos\left(\frac{\pi}{n+2}\right)+\frac{\sin\left(\frac{\pi}{n+2}\right)}{\sin\left(\frac{\pi}{n+2}\right)}\cos\left(\frac{\pi}{n+2}\right)}{(n+1)+\frac{\sin\left(\frac{\pi}{n+2}\right)}{\sin\left(\frac{\pi}{n+2}\right)}}$$

$$= \frac{(n+2)\cos\left(\frac{\pi}{n+2}\right)}{(n+2)} = \cos\left(\frac{\pi}{n+2}\right)$$

$$\Rightarrow \quad f(n) = \cos\left(\frac{\pi}{n+2}\right)$$

Now, $f(6) = \cos\left(\frac{\pi}{8}\right)$

$$\because \alpha = \tan(\cos^{-1} f((6))) = \tan\left(\frac{\pi}{8}\right) \qquad \left[\because \cos^{-1}\cos x = x \text{ if } x \in \left(0, \frac{\pi}{2}\right)\right]$$

$$= \sqrt{2} - 1$$

$$\Rightarrow \quad (\alpha + 1) = \sqrt{2}$$

$$\Rightarrow \quad (\alpha + 1)^2 = 2$$

$$\Rightarrow \quad \alpha^2 + 2\alpha + 1 = 2$$

$$\Rightarrow \quad \alpha^2 + 2\alpha - 1 = 0$$

Now, $f(4) = \cos\left(\frac{\pi}{4+2}\right)$

$$= \cos\left(\frac{\pi}{6}\right) = \frac{\sqrt{3}}{2}$$

Now, $\sin(7\cos^{-1} f(5)) = \sin\left(7\cos^{-1}\left(\cos\left(\frac{\pi}{5+2}\right)\right)\right)$

$$= \sin\left(7\left(\frac{\pi}{7}\right)\right) = \sin \pi = 0$$

and Now, $\lim_{n\to\infty} f(x) = \lim_{n\to\infty} \cos\frac{\pi}{n+2} = \cos 0 = 1$

Hence, options (a), (b) and (c) are correct.

83. We have, $\sin^{-1}\left(\sum_{i=1}^{\infty} x^{i+1} - x\sum_{i=1}^{\infty}\left(\frac{x}{2}\right)^i\right)$

$$= \frac{\pi}{2} - \cos^{-1}\left(\sum_{i=1}^{\infty}\left(\frac{-x}{2}\right)^i - \sum_{i=1}^{\infty}(-x)^i\right)$$

$$\Rightarrow \sin^{-1}\left[\frac{x^2}{1-x} - \frac{x\cdot\frac{x}{2}}{1-\frac{x}{2}}\right] = \frac{\pi}{2} - \cos^{-1}\left[\frac{\frac{-x}{2}}{1+\frac{x}{2}} - \frac{(-x)}{1+x}\right]$$

$$\left[\because \sum_{i=1}^{\infty} x^{i+1} = x^2 + x^3 + x^4 + \ldots = \frac{x^2}{1-x} \text{ using sum of infinite terms of GP}\right]$$

$$\Rightarrow \sin^{-1}\left[\frac{x^2}{1-x} - \frac{x^2}{2-x}\right] = \frac{\pi}{2} - \cos^{-1}\left[\frac{x}{1+x} - \frac{x}{2+x}\right]$$

$$\Rightarrow \sin^{-1}\left[\frac{x^2}{1-x} - \frac{x^2}{2-x}\right] = \sin^{-1}\left(\frac{x}{1+x} - \frac{x}{2+x}\right)$$

$$\left[\because \sin^{-1} x = \frac{\pi}{2} - \cos^{-1} x\right]$$

$$\Rightarrow \quad \frac{x^2}{1-x} - \frac{x^2}{2-x} = \frac{x}{1+x} - \frac{x}{2+x}$$

$$\Rightarrow \quad x^2\left(\frac{2-x-1+x}{(1-x)(2-x)}\right) = x\frac{(2+x-1-x)}{(1+x)(2+x)}$$

$$\Rightarrow \quad \frac{x}{2-3x+x^2} = \frac{1}{2+3x+x^2} \quad \text{or } x = 0$$

$$\Rightarrow \quad x^3 + 3x^2 + 2x = x^2 - 3x + 2$$

$$\Rightarrow \quad x^3 + 2x^2 + 5x - 2 = 0 \text{ or } x = 0$$

Let $f(x) = x^3 + 2x^2 + 5x - 2$

$$f'(x) = 3x^2 + 4x + 5$$

$$f'(x) > 0, \forall x \in R$$

$\therefore$ $x^3 + 2x^2 + 5x - 2$ has only one real roots.

Therefore, total number of real solution is 2.

84. We have,

$$E_1 = \left\{x \in R : x \neq 1 \text{ and } \frac{x}{x-1} > 0\right\}$$

$$\therefore \quad E_1 = \frac{x}{x-1} > 0$$

$E_1 = x \in (-\infty, 0) \cup (1, \infty)$ and

$$E_2 = \left\{x \in E_1 : \sin^{-1}\left(\log_e\left(\frac{x}{x-1}\right)\right) \text{ is a real number}\right\}$$

$$E_2 = -1 \le \log_e \frac{x}{x-1} \le 1 \Rightarrow e^{-1} \le \frac{x}{x-1} \le e$$

Now, $\frac{x}{x-1} \ge e^{-1} \Rightarrow \frac{x}{x-1} - \frac{1}{e} \ge 0$

$$\Rightarrow \quad \frac{ex - x + 1}{e(x-1)} \ge 0 \Rightarrow \frac{x(e-1)+1}{(x-1)e} \ge 0$$

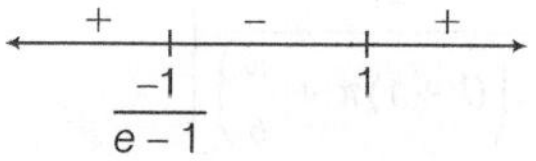

$$\Rightarrow \quad x \in \left(-\infty, \frac{1}{1-e}\right] \cup (1, \infty)$$

Also, $\frac{x}{x-1} \le e \Rightarrow \frac{(e-1)x - e}{x-1} \ge 0$

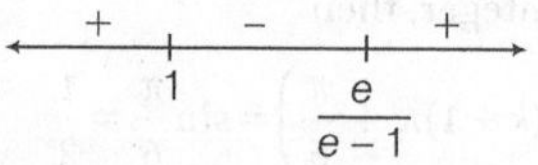

$$\Rightarrow \quad x \in (-\infty, 1) \cup \left[\frac{e}{e-1}, \infty\right)$$

So, $E_2 = \left(-\infty, \frac{1}{1-e}\right] \cup \left[\frac{e}{e-1}, \infty\right)$

$\therefore$ The domain of f and g are $\left(-\infty, \frac{1}{1-e}\right] \cup \left[\frac{e}{e-1}, \infty\right)$.

and Range of $\frac{x}{x-1}$ is $R^+ - \{1\}$

$\Rightarrow$ Range of f is $R - \{0\}$ or $(-\infty, 0) \cup (0, \infty)$.

Range of g is $\left[-\frac{\pi}{2}, \frac{\pi}{2}\right] - \{0\}$ or $\left[-\frac{\pi}{2}, 0\right) \cup \left(0, \frac{\pi}{2}\right]$.

85. $\alpha = 3\sin^{-1}\dfrac{6}{11} > 3\sin^{-1}\dfrac{1}{2}$

$$\Rightarrow \quad \alpha > \frac{\pi}{2} \qquad \left[\because 3\sin^{-1}\left(\frac{1}{2}\right) = \frac{\pi}{2}\right]$$

$\therefore \quad \cos\alpha < 0$

$$\beta = 3\cos^{-1}\frac{4}{9} > 3\cos^{-1}\frac{1}{2}$$

$$\Rightarrow \quad \beta > \pi \qquad \left[\because 3\cos^{-1}\left(\frac{1}{2}\right) = \pi\right]$$

$\cos\beta < 0$ and $\sin\beta < 0$

Now, $\quad \alpha + \beta > \dfrac{3\pi}{2}$

$\therefore \quad \cos(\alpha + \beta) > 0$

86. We know that,

$$\cos^{-1}(\cos x) = \begin{cases} x, & \text{if } x \in [0, \pi] \\ 2\pi - x, & \text{if } x \in [\pi, 2\pi] \\ -2\pi + x, & \text{if } x \in [2\pi, 3\pi] \\ 4\pi - x, & \text{if } x \in [3\pi, 4\pi] \end{cases}$$

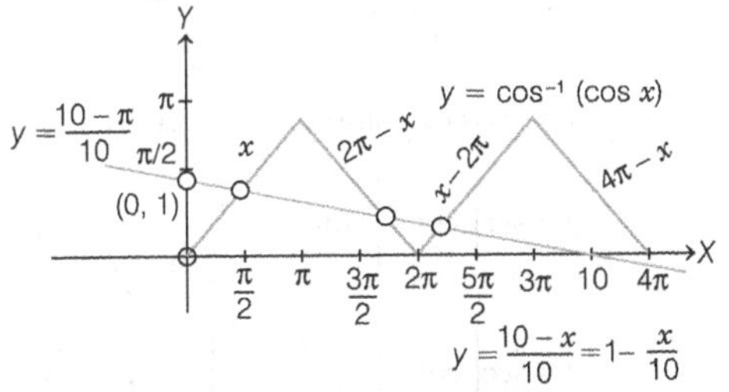

From above graph, it is clear that $y = \dfrac{10 - x}{10}$ and $y = \cos^{-1}(\cos x)$ intersect at three distinct points, so number of solutions is 3.

Exercise 3 - Challenging Problems

1. We have, $\quad A = 2\tan^{-1}(2\sqrt{2} - 1) = 2\tan^{-1}(1.828)$

$$\Rightarrow \quad A > 2\tan^{-1}(\sqrt{3})$$

$$\Rightarrow \quad A > \frac{2\pi}{3} \qquad \text{...(i)}$$

Also we have,

$$\sin^{-1}\left(\frac{1}{3}\right) < \sin^{-1}\left(\frac{1}{2}\right) \Rightarrow \sin^{-1}\left(\frac{1}{3}\right) < \frac{\pi}{6}$$

$$\Rightarrow \quad 3\sin^{-1}\left(\frac{1}{3}\right) < \frac{\pi}{2}$$

Also, $\quad 3\sin^{-1}\left(\dfrac{1}{3}\right) = \sin^{-1}\left(3\cdot\dfrac{1}{3} - 4\left(\dfrac{1}{3}\right)^3\right)$

$$= \sin^{-1}\left(\frac{23}{27}\right) = \sin^{-1}(0.852)$$

$$\Rightarrow \quad 3\sin^{-1}\left(\frac{1}{3}\right) < \sin^{-1}\left(\frac{\sqrt{3}}{2}\right) \Rightarrow 3\sin^{-1}\left(\frac{1}{3}\right) < \frac{\pi}{3}$$

Also, $\quad \sin^{-1}\left(\dfrac{3}{5}\right) = \sin^{-1}(0.6) < \sin^{-1}\left(\dfrac{\sqrt{3}}{2}\right)$

$$\Rightarrow \quad \sin^{-1}\left(\frac{3}{5}\right) < \frac{\pi}{3}$$

Hence, $B = 3\sin^{-1}\left(\dfrac{1}{3}\right) + \sin^{-1}\left(\dfrac{3}{5}\right) < \dfrac{2\pi}{3}$ ...(ii)

From (i) and (ii), we have

$$A > B$$

2. We have, $(\tan^{-1} x)^2 + (\cot^{-1} x)^2 = \dfrac{5\pi^2}{8}$

$$\Rightarrow \quad (\tan^{-1} x + \cot^{-1} x)^2 - 2\tan^{-1} x.\cot^{-1} x = \frac{5\pi^2}{8}$$

$$\Rightarrow \quad \left(\frac{\pi}{2}\right)^2 - 2\tan^{-1} x.\left(\frac{\pi}{2} - \tan^{-1} x\right) = \frac{5\pi^2}{8}$$

$$\left[\because \tan^{-1} x + \cot^{-1} x = \frac{\pi}{2} \Rightarrow \cot^{-1} x = \frac{\pi}{2} - \tan^{-1} x\right]$$

$$\Rightarrow \quad \frac{\pi^2}{4} - 2\cdot\frac{\pi}{2}\cdot\tan^{-1} x + 2(\tan^{-1} x)^2 = \frac{5\pi^2}{8}$$

$$\Rightarrow \quad 2(\tan^{-1} x)^2 - \pi\tan^{-1} x - \frac{3\pi^2}{8} = 0$$

$$\Rightarrow \quad \tan^{-1} x = -\frac{\pi}{4}, \frac{3\pi}{4}$$

$$\Rightarrow \quad \tan^{-1} x = -\frac{\pi}{4}$$

$$\Rightarrow \quad x = -1$$

$$\left[\text{neglecting } \tan^{-1} x = \frac{3\pi}{4} \text{ as } \tan^{-1} x \in \left]-\frac{\pi}{2}, \frac{\pi}{2}\right[\right]$$

3. We have, $[\sin^{-1}\cos^{-1}\sin^{-1}\tan^{-1} x] = 1$

$$\Rightarrow \quad 1 \le \sin^{-1}\cdot\cos^{-1}\cdot\sin^{-1}\cdot\tan^{-1} x \le \frac{\pi}{2}$$

$$\Rightarrow \quad \sin 1 \le \cos^{-1}\cdot\sin^{-1}\cdot\tan^{-1} x \le 1$$

$$\Rightarrow \quad \cos\sin 1 \ge \sin^{-1}\cdot\tan^{-1} x \ge \cos 1$$

$$\Rightarrow \quad \sin\cos\sin 1 \ge \tan^{-1} x \ge \sin\cos 1$$

$$\Rightarrow \quad \tan\sin\cos\sin 1 \ge x \ge \tan\sin\cos 1$$

Hence, $x \in [\tan\sin\cos 1, \tan\sin\cos\sin 1]$

4. We have, $\quad \tan^{-1} y = 4\tan^{-1} x$

$$\Rightarrow \quad \tan^{-1} y = 2\tan^{-1}\frac{2x}{1 - x^2} \qquad [\text{as } |x| < 1]$$

$$= \tan^{-1}\frac{\dfrac{4x}{1 - x^2}}{1 - \dfrac{4x^2}{(1 - x^2)^2}}$$

$$= \tan^{-1}\frac{4x(1 - x^2)}{x^4 - 6x^2 + 1} \qquad \left[\text{as } \left|\frac{2x}{1 - x^2}\right| < 1\right]$$

$$\Rightarrow \quad y = \frac{4x(1 - x^2)}{x^4 - 6x^2 + 1}$$

If $\quad x = \tan\frac{\pi}{8}$

$\Rightarrow \quad \tan^{-1} y = 4\tan^{-1} x = \frac{\pi}{2}$

$\Rightarrow \quad y = \infty \Rightarrow x^4 - 6x^2 + 1 = 0$

5. We know, $\sin^{-1}(\sin 4) = \sin^{-1}(\sin(\pi - 4)) = \pi - 4$

$$\left[\because -\frac{\pi}{2} < \pi - 4 < \frac{\pi}{2}\right]$$

$\therefore$ We have, $x^2 - kx + \pi - 4 > 0$ for all $x \in R$

$\therefore \quad D < 0$ i.e. $k^2 - 4(\pi - 4) < 0$ or $k^2 + 4(4 - \pi) < 0$

which is not true for any real k. {as $k^2 + 4(4 - \pi) > 0$}

6. $\cot^{-1}\left(\frac{y}{\sqrt{1 - x^2 - y^2}}\right) = \tan^{-1}\left(\frac{\sqrt{1 - x^2 - y^2}}{y}\right)$

Also, $\quad 2\tan^{-1}\sqrt{\frac{3 - 4x^2}{4x^2}} = \tan^{-1}\frac{2\cdot\sqrt{\frac{3 - 4x^2}{4x^2}}}{1 - \left(\frac{3 - 4x^2}{4x^2}\right)}$

$$= \tan^{-1}\left(\frac{4x\sqrt{3 - 4x^2}}{8x^2 - 3}\right)$$

Hence, the given equation is

$$\tan^{-1}\frac{\sqrt{1 - x^2 - y^2}}{y} = \tan^{-1}\left(\frac{4x\sqrt{3 - 4x^2}}{8x^2 - 3}\right) - \tan^{-1}\sqrt{\frac{3 - 4x^2}{x^2}}$$

$$= \tan^{-1}\left[\frac{\frac{4x\sqrt{3 - 4x^2}}{8x^2 - 3} - \sqrt{\frac{3 - 4x^2}{x^2}}}{1 + \frac{4x\sqrt{3 - 4x^2}}{8x^2 - 3}\cdot\sqrt{\frac{3 - 4x^2}{x^2}}}\right]$$

$$= \tan^{-1}\left[\frac{(3 - 4x^2)^{3/2}}{9x - 8x^3}\right]$$

$$\therefore \quad \frac{\sqrt{1 - x^2 - y^2}}{y} = \frac{(3 - 4x^2)^{3/2}}{9x - 8x^3}$$

Squaring and simplifying

$$\frac{1 - x^2}{y^2} = 1 + \frac{(3 - 4x^2)^3}{(9x - 8x^3)^2}$$

$$= \frac{(9x - 8x^3)^2 + (3 - 4x^2)^3}{(9x - 8x^3)^2} = \frac{27 - 27x^2}{(9x - 8x^3)^2}$$

$$\therefore \quad y^2 = \frac{x^2(9 - 8x^2)^2}{27}$$

7. Let $\tan\frac{x}{2}\cdot\tan\frac{y}{2} = \tan\theta \qquad$ ...(i)

Consider $\quad \frac{\cos x + \cos y}{1 + \cos x\cdot\cos y} = \frac{\frac{1 - \tan^2 x/2}{1 + \tan^2 x/2} + \frac{1 - \tan^2 y/2}{1 + \tan^2 y/2}}{1 + \frac{(1 - \tan^2 x/2)}{(1 + \tan^2 x/2)}\cdot\frac{(1 - \tan^2 y/2)}{(1 + \tan^2 y/2)}}$

$$= \frac{(1 - \tan^2 x/2)(1 + \tan^2 y/2) + (1 + \tan^2 x/2)(1 - \tan^2 y/2)}{(1 + \tan^2 x/2)(1 + \tan^2 y/2) + (1 - \tan^2 x/2)\cdot(1 - \tan^2 y/2)}$$

$$= \frac{1 - \tan^2 x/2 + \tan^2 y/2 - \tan^2 x/2\tan^2 y/2 + 1 - \tan^2 y/2 + \tan^2 x/2 - \tan^2 x/2\tan^2 y/2}{1 + \tan^2 x/2 + \tan^2 y/2 + \tan^2 x/2\tan^2 y/2 + 1 - \tan^2 x/2 - \tan^2 y/2 + \tan^2 x/2\cdot\tan^2 y/2}$$

$$= \frac{2 - 2\tan^2 x/2\tan^2 y/2}{2 + 2\tan^2 x/2\tan^2 y/2} = \frac{1 - \tan^2\theta}{1 + \tan^2\theta} \qquad \text{[from Eq. (i)]}$$

$$= \cos 2\theta$$

$\therefore \quad \text{LHS} = \cos^{-1}(\cos 2\theta) = 2\theta$

$$= 2\left\{\tan^{-1}\left(\tan\frac{x}{2}\cdot\tan\frac{y}{2}\right)\right\}$$

8. Here, $\quad x = \text{cosec}\,(\tan^{-1}(\cos(\cot^{-1}(\sec(\sin^{-1} a)))))$

$\Rightarrow \quad x = \text{cosec}\left(\tan^{-1}\left(\cos\left(\cot^{-1}\left(\frac{1}{\sqrt{1 - a^2}}\right)\right)\right)\right)$

$\Rightarrow \quad x = \text{cosec}\left(\tan^{-1}\left(\frac{1}{\sqrt{2 - a^2}}\right)\right) \Rightarrow x = \sqrt{3 - a^2}$

and $\quad y = \sec(\cot^{-1}\sin(\tan^{-1}(\text{cosec}(\cos^{-1} a))))$

$\Rightarrow \quad y = \sec\left(\cot^{-1}\left(\sin\left(\tan^{-1}\left(\frac{1}{\sqrt{1 - a^2}}\right)\right)\right)\right)$

$\Rightarrow \quad y = \sec\left(\cot^{-1}\left(\frac{1}{\sqrt{2 - a^2}}\right)\right) \Rightarrow y = \sqrt{3 - a^2} \qquad$ ...(ii)

From Eqs. (i) and (ii),

$$x = y = \sqrt{3 - a^2}$$

9. Since, $0 < \alpha < \frac{\pi}{2}$

$\therefore \quad 0 < \frac{\alpha}{2} < \frac{\pi}{4} \Rightarrow 0 < \tan\frac{\alpha}{2} < 1 \qquad$ ...(i)

Similarly, $\quad 0 < \beta < \frac{\pi}{2}$

$\Rightarrow \quad 0 < \frac{\beta}{2} < \frac{\pi}{4} \Rightarrow -\frac{\pi}{4} < -\frac{\beta}{2} < 0$

$\Rightarrow \quad 0 < \frac{\pi}{4} - \frac{\beta}{2} < \frac{\pi}{4} \Rightarrow 0 < \tan\left(\frac{\pi}{4} - \frac{\beta}{2}\right) < 1 \qquad$ ...(ii)

From Eqs. (i) and (ii), we get

$$0 < \tan\frac{\alpha}{2}\tan\left(\frac{\pi}{4} - \frac{\beta}{2}\right) < 1.$$

Since, $2\tan^{-1} x = \tan^{-1}\frac{2x}{1 - x^2}$, when $x \in (0, 1)$

$\therefore \quad 2\tan^{-1}\left\{\tan\frac{\alpha}{2}\tan\left(\frac{\pi}{4} - \frac{\beta}{2}\right)\right\}$

$$= \tan^{-1}\frac{2\tan\frac{\alpha}{2}\tan\left(\frac{\pi}{4} - \frac{\beta}{2}\right)}{1 - \tan^2\frac{\alpha}{2}.\tan^2\left(\frac{\pi}{4} - \frac{\beta}{2}\right)}$$

$$= \tan^{-1}\frac{2\tan\frac{\alpha}{2}\cdot\dfrac{1-\tan\left(\frac{\beta}{2}\right)}{1+\tan\left(\frac{\beta}{2}\right)}}{1-\tan^2\frac{\alpha}{2}\left[\dfrac{1-\tan\frac{\beta}{2}}{1+\tan\frac{\beta}{2}}\right]^2}$$

$$= \tan^{-1}\frac{2\tan\frac{\alpha}{2}\left(1-\tan^2\frac{\beta}{2}\right)}{\left(1+\tan\frac{\beta}{2}\right)^2-\tan^2\frac{\alpha}{2}\left(1-\tan\frac{\beta}{2}\right)^2}$$

$$= \tan^{-1}\frac{2\tan\frac{\alpha}{2}\left(1-\tan^2\frac{\beta}{2}\right)}{\left(1+\tan^2\frac{\beta}{2}\right)\left(1-\tan^2\frac{\alpha}{2}\right)+2\tan\frac{\beta}{2}\left(1+\tan^2\frac{\alpha}{2}\right)}$$

$$= \tan^{-1}\frac{\dfrac{2\tan\frac{\alpha}{2}}{1+\tan^2\frac{\alpha}{2}}\cdot\dfrac{1-\tan^2\frac{\beta}{2}}{1+\tan^2\frac{\beta}{2}}}{\dfrac{1-\tan^2\frac{\alpha}{2}}{1+\tan^2\frac{\alpha}{2}}+\dfrac{2\tan\frac{\beta}{2}}{1+\tan^2\frac{\beta}{2}}}$$

$$= \tan^{-1}\left(\frac{\sin\alpha\cdot\cos\beta}{\cos\alpha+\sin\beta}\right)$$

10. Let $\tan^{-1}x = \theta$ for $x \geq 0$

Case I When $0 \leq x < 1$, then $0 \leq \theta < \frac{\pi}{4}$ and so $0 \leq 2\theta < \frac{\pi}{2}$

$\therefore$ $$\sin^{-1}\frac{2x}{1+x^2} = \sin^{-1}(\sin 2\theta) = 2\theta = 2\tan^{-1}x$$

$$\cos^{-1}\frac{1-x^2}{1+x^2} = \cos^{-1}(\cos 2\theta) = 2\theta = 2\tan^{-1}x$$

$$\tan^{-1}\frac{2x}{1-x^2} = \tan^{-1}(\tan 2\theta) = 2\theta = 2\tan^{-1}x$$

Thus, $3\left(\sin^{-1}\frac{2x}{1+x^2}\right) - 4\left(\cos^{-1}\frac{1-x^2}{1+x^2}\right) + 2\left(\tan^{-1}\frac{2x}{1-x^2}\right) = \frac{\pi}{3}$

$\Rightarrow$ $3(2\tan^{-1}x) - 4(2\tan^{-1}x) + 2(2\tan^{-1}x) = \frac{\pi}{3}$.

$\Rightarrow$ $2\tan^{-1}x = \frac{\pi}{3}$

$\Rightarrow$ $\tan^{-1}x = \frac{\pi}{6} \Rightarrow x = \frac{1}{\sqrt{3}}$

as $0 \leq \frac{1}{\sqrt{3}} < 1$, $x = \frac{1}{\sqrt{3}}$ is a solution

Case II When $x = 1$, $\tan^{-1}\frac{2x}{1-x^2}$ is not defined.

$\therefore$ $x = 1$, cannot be a solution.

Case III If $x > 1$, then $\frac{\pi}{4} < \theta < \frac{\pi}{2}$ and so $\frac{\pi}{2} < 2\theta < \pi$

$\therefore$ $$\sin^{-1}\left(\frac{2x}{1+x^2}\right) = \sin^{-1}(\sin 2\theta) = \pi - 2\theta = \pi - 2\tan^{-1}x.$$

$$\cos^{-1}\left(\frac{2x}{1+x^2}\right) = \cos^{-1}(\cos 2\theta) = 2\theta = 2\tan^{-1}x$$

and $$\tan^{-1}\left(\frac{2x}{1-x^2}\right) = \tan^{-1}(\tan 2\theta) = 2\theta - \pi = 2\tan^{-1}x - \pi$$

Thus, the given equation becomes

$$3(\pi - 2\tan^{-1}x) - 4(2\tan^{-1}x) + 2(2\tan^{-1}x - \pi) = \frac{\pi}{3}$$

$\Rightarrow$ $\pi - 10\tan^{-1}x = \frac{\pi}{3}$

or $\tan^{-1}x = \frac{\pi}{15}$

i.e. $x = \tan\frac{\pi}{15} < \tan\frac{\pi}{4} < 1$

$\therefore$ $x = \tan\frac{\pi}{15}$ is not a solution.

Thus, $x = \frac{1}{\sqrt{3}}$ is the only solution for the given equation for $x \geq 0$.

11. Let $\cos^{-1}x = a \Rightarrow a \in [0, \pi]$

and $\sin^{-1}y = b \Rightarrow b \in \left[-\frac{\pi}{2}, \frac{\pi}{2}\right]$

We have $a + b^2 = \frac{p\pi^2}{4}$ ...(i)

and $ab^2 = \frac{\pi^4}{16}$ ...(ii)

Since $b^2 \in \left[0, \frac{\pi^2}{4}\right] \Rightarrow a + b^2 \in \left[0, \pi + \frac{\pi^2}{4}\right]$

So, Eq. (i) $\Rightarrow$ $0 \leq \frac{p\pi^2}{4} \leq \pi + \frac{\pi^2}{4}$

i.e. $0 \leq p \leq \frac{4}{\pi} + 1$

Since $p \in Z$, so $p = 0, 1$ or 2

But, if $p = 0$, then $a = b = 0$.

$\Rightarrow$ Equation (ii) will not be satisfied.

Now, substituting the value of b^2 from Eq. (i) in the Eq. (ii), we get

$$a\left(\frac{p\pi^2}{4} - a\right) = \frac{\pi^4}{16} \Rightarrow 16a^2 - 4p\pi^2 a + \pi^4 = 0 \quad \text{...(iii)}$$

Since, $a \in R \Rightarrow D \geq 0$

i.e. $16p^2\pi^4 - 64\pi^4 \geq 0 \Rightarrow p^2 \geq 4 \Rightarrow p \geq 2$

Thus, we conclude that the only value of p that satisfies all conditions is $p = 2$. Substituting $p = 2$ in Eq. (iii), we get

$$16a^2 - 8\pi^2 a + \pi^4 = 0$$

$\Rightarrow$ $(4a - \pi^2)^2 = 0$

$\Rightarrow$ $a = \frac{\pi^2}{4} = \cos^{-1}x \Rightarrow x = \cos\frac{\pi^2}{4}$

From Eq. (ii), we get

$$\frac{\pi^2}{4}\cdot b^2=\frac{\pi^4}{16}\Rightarrow b=\pm\frac{\pi}{2}=\sin^{-1}y$$

$$\Rightarrow \qquad y=\pm 1$$

12. Let $\sin^{-1}x=y$, we get

$$2y^2-y-6=0$$

$$2y^2-4y+3y-6=0$$

$$y=2 \text{ and } y=-1.5$$

$$\therefore \quad \sin^{-1}x=2 \text{ and } \sin^{-1}x=-1.5$$

Since, $2>\frac{\pi}{2}$ and $|-1.5|<\frac{\pi}{2}$, the only solution is $x=\sin(-1.5)$.

13. Let us transfer $\sin^{-1}6\sqrt{3}x$ into the right hand side of the equation and calculate the sine of the both sides of the resulting equation

$$\sin(\sin^{-1}6x)=\sin\left(-\sin^{-1}6\sqrt{3}x-\frac{\pi}{2}\right)$$

$$\Rightarrow \qquad 6x=-\sin(\sin^{-1}6\sqrt{3}x+\sin^{-1}1)$$

[using $\sin(-\theta)=-\sin(\theta)$]

$$\Rightarrow \qquad 6x=-\sin(\sin^{-1}\sqrt{1-108x^2})$$

[using $\sin^{-1}x+\sin^{-1}y=\sin^{-1}\{x\sqrt{1-y^2}+y\sqrt{1-x^2}\}$]

$$\Rightarrow \qquad 6x=-\sqrt{1-108x^2} \qquad \text{...(i)}$$

Squaring both sides, we get

$$36x^2=1-108x^2 \Rightarrow 144x^2=1$$

whose roots are $x=\frac{1}{12}$ and $x=-\frac{1}{12}$.

Let us verify

Substituting $x=\frac{-1}{12}$ in the given equation, we get

$$\sin^{-1}\left(-\frac{1}{2}\right)+\sin^{-1}\left(-\frac{\sqrt{3}}{2}\right)=-\frac{\pi}{6}-\frac{\pi}{3}=-\frac{\pi}{2}$$

Thus, $x=\frac{-1}{12}$ is the root of given equation. But, when substituting $x=\frac{1}{12}$ in Eq. (i), we get

$$\text{LHS}=6x=\frac{1}{2}$$

$$\text{RHS}=-\sqrt{1-108x^2}=-\frac{1}{2}$$

i.e. LHS $\neq$ RHS of Eq. (i).

Hence, $x=-\frac{1}{12}$ is a root of the given equation as it satisfy both given and Eq. (i).